HISTORY *of* POLITICAL THOUGHT

Books by the Same Author

1. Antarjatik Samparka (Bengali)
2. Rashtrachintar Itibritta (Bengali)
3. Adhunik Rashtratatwa (Bengali)
4. Samakalin Shasan Byabastha O Rajniti (Bengali)
5. Janaprashasan (Bengali)
6. Paschatya Rashtrachinta O Bharatiya Rashtradarshan (Bengali)
7. Modern Political Theory (English)
8. Introduction to Higher Secondary Political Science (English)
9. Janaprashasan (Bengali) [only for B.U.]
10. Fundamentals of Public Administration (In Press)

This book is intended for the undergraduate and post-graduate students of various Indian universities and candidates appearing in different competitive examinations

---

HISTORY *of* POLITICAL THOUGHT

[A lucid and in-depth analysis of the History of Political Ideas from Ancient Greece to Mao Zedong]

Prangobinda Das

Ex-Professor, Department of Political Science

S. B. College, Bagati, Hooghly, West Bengal

New Central Book Agency (P) Ltd

Co-Published by

Bijay Publications

E-mail : bijaypublications@gmail.com

Exclusively Distributed by

Bijay Pustak Bhandar (P) Ltd

90/6A M. G. Road, Bhawani Dutta Lane, Kolkata-700007

✆ : (033) 4605-7856, 8777898576, 8274916104

E-mail : bijaypustakbhandar@gmail.com

NCBA

REGD OFFICE
8/1 Chintamoni Das Lane, Kolkata 700 009, India
email: ncbakolkata@gmail.com

OVERSEAS
NCBA (UK) Ltd, 149 Park Avenue North, Northampton, NN3 2HY, UK
email: ncbauk@yahoo.com

CORPORATE OFFICE
212 Shahpur Jat, New Delhi 110 049
email: ncbaexports@ncbapvtltd.com

BIJAY PUBLICATIONS
90/6A M. G. Road, Bhawani Dutta Lane, Kolkata-7
E-mail : bijaypublications@gmail.com

BIJAY PUSTAK BHANDAR (P) LTD
90/6A M. G. Road, Bhawani Dutta Lane, Kolkata-7
E-mail : bijaypustakbhandar@gmail.com

HISTORY OF POLITICAL THOUGHT • Prangobinda Das

First Published: 1995
Second Edition: 1998
Third Revised and Enlarged Edition: 2001
Reprinted: 2002, 2006, 2009, 2015, 2019, **2023**

PUBLISHER • TYPESETTER • PRINTER
New Central Book Agency (P) Ltd
8/1 Chintamoni Das Lane, Kolkata 700 009

CO-PUBLISHED BY
Bijay Publications
90/6A M G Road, Bhawani Dutta Lane, Kolkata 700007

PROJECT SUPERVISOR
Usha Ranjan Bhowmik

PROJECT TEAM
Tarun Dey, Pradyot Majumder, Kushaldev Bhattacharya, Subas Maitra and Prabhat Jas

ISBN: 81-7381-067-2

Price ₹ 750.00

Dedicated to

Anusrita Deb

My beloved granddaughter

CONTENTS

PREFACE TO THE FOURTH EDITION

By the grace of God I have been able to revise **History of Political Thought**, the thoroughly revised edition of which was last published in 2001. In this revised edition some chapters have been thoroughly revised, some partially. The important characteristic feature of this revised edition is that Marxism has been given additional importance on the ground that Marx's philosophy is still being studied by renowned intellectuals of various fields on both sides of the Atlantic. This is a clear indication of the fact that interest in Marxism did not end with the fall of the Soviet Union in 1991. The intellectual aspects of Marxism still create enthusiasm in the minds of thinkers of all shades of thought and idea. In my opinion there is a lot of substance in the ideas of Gramsci, Rosa Luxemburg and Kautsky. The ideas of the Frankfurt School kindle our thoughts, ideas and outlooks, and I think my readers will peruse all these with added interest and enthusiasm.

Plato, Aristotle, Bodin, Machiavelli, Reformation, and Renaissance have been elaborately discussed herein. Specially, political ideas of Machiavelli are still relevant. In the 1980s and 1990s de-Stalinisation was a much discussed topic in both political and academic circles. I have briefly discussed it to quench the thirst for further knowledge of many enthusiasts in this field.

I do not claim any originality and novelty in writing this book. I have simply collected materials from various sources and placed them in my own way before my readers. I have felt that presenting the materials within a few pages of two covers is really a difficult task. It is because of God's grace I have been able to do it. But I do not know whether I have achieved any success.

Finally, I am indebted to many who are directly or indirectly connected with the publication of this edition. However, special mention must be made of Shri Amitabha Sen, Director of New Central Book Agency (P) Ltd, and Shri Prabhat Jas who have ungrudgingly shouldered the burden of publication.

If this edition benefits the readers I will think that my labour has been amply rewarded. I would also like to request my readers to point out the mistakes, if any, and offer their valuable suggestions which will enable me to make the book less imperfect and more reader-friendly in the subsequent editions.

15th August 2012 **Author**
Kolkata

PREFACE TO THE FIRST EDITION

The purpose of writing this book on History of Political Thought is to help the Undergraduate and Postgraduate students of Political Science studying in various colleges and universities of this country to be acquainted with the development of political thought from ancient Greece to Marx. Some people may say that there are serveral books on history of political thought written by renowned foreign authors and also by some Indian authors. Professional ethics prevents me from passing any judgement against the books of Indian authors. But so far as the books of foreign authors are concerned it is quite known to all that standard textbooks are not easily available. Beside this, it is not possible for a student to purchase all the books in order to build up comprehensive and coordinate views about the philosophers and their thought-systems. The present volume, therefore, makes an humble attempt to present the views of the critics and scholars in a precise form.

The author has collected materials from the original works of the philosophers which have been translated into English and the interpretations made by the renowned critics. In relevant places the author has noted the references to these works. He is indebted to all the authors and the publishers of the books.

The indebtedness of the author may also be recorded to Sri J. N. Sen, the Managing Director of New Central Book Agency (P) Ltd, who has shouldered the onerous trouble ungrudgingly in publishing this book. His gratitude is also extended to all the workers of the printing division of Central Educational Enterprises.

The author has left no stone unturned to make the present publication free from printing and other mistakes. The apprehension of the author is that there are still several mistakes and the earliest opportunity will be properly utilised to remove these mistakes. Here the pious hope is that the readers with a touch of liberality will definitely forgive.

Last but not the least, the writer of the present book wants to make it clear that he claims no originality. He has simply gathered matters from various sources and has presented them in a concise and coordinated form.

Comments and suggestions from all readers will be gratefully accepted and implemented.

25th December 1994 **Author**
Kolkata

1 ANCIENT GREEK POLITICAL THOUGHT

Importance of Ancient Greek Political Thought

The students of Western political thought generally, with great interest, study the ancient political thought of ancient Greece and it is believed that there are reasons behind this.

Some reasons may briefly be stated here. In the first place the Greek philosophers in their search for knowledge in general and political philosophy in particular pointed out some basic concepts such as nature of state, its origin, administration, relation between state and individual in their analysis. Though the contents of these concepts have undergone sea-changes during the past two millennia, we still study them because they evoke our interests.

In the second place, the ancient Greek thinkers, it is said, drew a difference between legitimate use of power and indiscriminate use of power or application of force. The Greek thinkers believed that application of force for the realisation of objective is uncalled for. The persons in authority should avoid the use of force. Again, they also thought that power should be legitimate that's authority or power. This confirms their support for democracy. Their argument runs as follows : Since the entire cosmos is governed by law human society cannot be an exception. In today's world we see that everyone gives importance to the sovereignty of law.

In the third place, it appears from the political ideas of the ancient Greek thinkers that in their analysis there was great importance of the rule of law, that is law, must govern both the rulers and the ruled. This conception of rule of law practically governs a major part of Western political thought. One of the central ideas of American constitutional system is the supremacy of the constitution which is treated as basic law of land. Even in UK and some other countries the rule of law and equality before law constitutes the central part of state administration. At least J. S. Mcclelland (*History of Western Political Thought*) thinks in this way (pp. 11-12). He observes modern constitutional theory is in part based on a particular reading of ancient constitutional thought and practice (p. 12).

In the fourth place there is a very good reason for studying ancient Greek political thought. We know that there is an importance of dialectics is the political philosophy of Hegel and Marx. But the dialectics was discovered and abundantly applied by Plato and few other Greek philosophers. Later on, Hegel and Marx borrowed the concept from the Greek philosophers.

There is still another reason why we study ancient political thought of Greek. The Greek thinkers and philosophers had great faith on people's sovereignty and for that reason they made arrangement for periodical open assembly the attendance in which was compulsory—the people will assemble at a particular place in order to frame laws for the administration of the City-state. This is called direct democracy. The Swiss constitutional system borrowed this and it holds till now. Contract thinker Rousseau in his famous work *Social Contract*, revived it. The Greek city-state was small in size and population and this facilitated the functioning of direct democracy.

Another very important reason for studying Greek political thought is "Greek philosophers were the first to raise the most fundamental problems of state, law and politics. The solutions they offered have foreshadowed in many respects the future development of political thought and their echoes have not yet completely died down in our times" (*Political Thought of Ancient Greece*, V.S. Nersesyants. p. 5). Today we are seriously thinking about sovereignty, virtue and politics and many other related ideas. But it is not surprising that the Greek thinkers discussed all these though in embryo form.

There is still another reason. We are at the threshold of the twenty first century. Both the rulers and the ruled are seriously thinking about good government, good state and welfare state. It means that the state is not a helpless spectator in the manifold affairs which occur within the state. It must guide or regulate the affairs for the attainment of general welfare. Plato believed that it is the specific duty of the state to make its citizens good or ideal so that they will be suitable for an ideal state. His—*The Republic* deals with the various aspects of an ideal state. Today we do not definitely think in terms of ideal state because we are sure that ideals are unattainable. But we think about welfare state. Yes, there are lots of difference between ideal state and welfare state. But in ultimate analysis both ideal state and welfare state coincide. Plato thought of an ideal state in the light of general good or welfare of people. He believed that only in an ideal state people could witness the realisation of their general good or well-being. The ancient Greek philosophers repeatedly thought of welfare of people in terms of virtue. We think that the term welfare cannot be detached from virtue is an ethical or to some moral term or concept. Naturally a state is never a helpless onlooker of the events that occur. It must interfere if the happenings interfere negatively with the general good of citizens.

Our point is that the concept of virtue, morality etc. were the key concepts of Greek political philosophy. Today they have reappeared in our political ideas in the form of general welfare. Our conclusion is that there is no basic departure of the present—day politics from the basic ideas of Greek political thought. All these reasons enthuse us to study ancient Greek political thought and these reasons, we firmly believe, will remain valid even in the coming decades.

VIRTUE, MORALITY IN GREEK THOUGHT

Politics is primarily concerned with the political affairs and administrative system of the state. Its association with virtue, morality or ethics is not rated highly because many people do not regard politics or political science as a normative science. But the place of virtue or morality in the vast domain of politics is termed by many as of crucial importance. The Greek thinkers treated politics, virtue and morality as the subjects of same domain because they believed that politics without virtue or morality is barren and not helpful for good and fruitful life of citizens. The relationship between politics and virtue received maximum treatment in the hands of Greek philosophers and specially Plato and Aristotle. John Morrow (*History of Political Thought*, p. 51) writes : Identification of a direct relationship between politics and virtue is one of the central themes of the Western tradition of political thought. This tradition originated in the writings of Plato and Aristotle the foremost political philosophers of the ancient world.

Plato, a piquant observer of various political incidents that took place around him, believed that they were full of corruption and devoid of virtue and morality. So, to attain short term gains and other benefits the political persons and administrators did not hesitate to adopt most heinous and corrupt means and practices. This led to the deterioration of the entire body politic or polis. In Plato's opinion, divorcing politics from virtue and morality practically led the polis to dissolution. The life of the common people ultimately became miserable. The polis was converted into a hell. The entire politics was disfigured. If we go through the *'The Republic'* we shall find that Plato gave maximum importance to the miserable and corrupt condition of the polis. The society was unhealthy and unfit for human habitation. In the *The Republic* he said the polis was bloated and unhealthy. He thought that the foundation of politics must be morality and virtue. After analysing the function of his contemporary states he comes to the conclusion that politics must be based on virtue and morality and corruption must be banished from the domain of politics.

According to Plato, a virtuous and moral state is one that gives utmost importance to justice. That is, a state must make all efforts to achieve justice for its citizens. Therefore morality, virtue and justice are the terms he treated with same importance. Plato finally thought that in an ordinary state or polis virtue cannot be attained. The states of his time were generally corrupt and the rulers of those states neglected virtue in all possible ways. This pained him considerably and for that reason he made an elaborate plan to build up an ideal state whose primary purpose would be to make citizens moral and virtuous. Such a state was called by him an ideal state—ideal in all respects. He chalked out an elaborate programme of his ideal state. He thought that the structure and administration of the contemporary states were such that virtue and morality could never be the foundation of state. Even they could not guide the functioning of the state. Naturally, Plato ardently felt that for the attainment of virtue and morality a new state was required. For that reason he planned for an ideal state. Though Plato believed that the state of his imagination could never see the light of day, yet such a state was required for the sake of virtue and morality. Plato's ideal state was not only a state of virtue and morality but also a just state. That is—an ideal state must be based on justice.

According to Plato "virtue is a kind of mental health or beauty or fitness and vice a kind of illness or deformity or weakness. He treated virtue in this light. It needs to be noted here that for a better and enlightened polis Plato combined psychology with politics. The contents of *The Republic* are based on the dialogues that took place among the various participants. He, along with other participants emphatically said that a good polis and virtue are not different from each other. Virtue anal good qualities—especially morality must occupy most important place in the state and must guide the political affairs of state. It, in other words, must play central role in politics. Plato and other Greek philosophers cherished the idea that politics is an all-embracing concept which virtually means that all the universal values including virtue and morality fall within the purview of politics. Naturally, any attempt to divorce politics from morality and virtue will shorten the ambit of politics. Hence, in Plato's opinion, a state must strive in all possible ways to give utmost importance to the attainment of virtue and morality in its discharge of all normal functions.

Aristotle, the great disciple of Plato, actively and seriously thought of associating virtue and morality with politics. But the method of treatment of the subject in the case of Aristotle is different. In *Politics*, he writes : Every state is a community of some kind and every community is established with a view to some good. If all communities aim at some good, the state or political community, which is the highest of all, and which embraces all the rest, aims at same good in a greater degree than any other, and at the highest good. Aristotle, we think, is very logical. Every community or a family is created for the attainment of some good. Since the state is the highest or greatest community or association, naturally it will aim at the highest good.

Aristotle's idea about the relationship between polis and virtue is quite fascinating and in this respect he differs from his teacher Plato. Plato thought that the state must pursue virtue and morality. This process can make citizens to be moral and virtuous. But Aristotle believed that politics or political science must pursue and preach virtue and morality because political science is the science of polis. The main concern of political science is the realisation of "human good" which includes virtue and morality. Human good does not mean the attainment of material satisfaction—fulfillment of material needs.

Now let us try to follow Aristotle's argument. Political science is an analysis of polis and polis is the supreme association—supreme not simply in structure but in purposes and in realisation of purposes. A supreme association must also take note of the fact that general welfare, virtue, and morality all are attained within the sphere of the polis. It cannot neglect the moral, virtuous and material aspects of the citizens. Polis is all embracing, So we find that in Aristotle's view the polis is both supreme and virtuous organisation or association. Explaining Aristotle's stand in this regard John Morrow observes (p. 59) "polis is natural and man is by nature a political animal. For Aristotle the state comprises a co-operative order through which its members practice virtue and thus enjoy the good life."

When Aristotle says that man is by nature a political animal he specifically means that he is reasonable. Keeping himself within the boundary of polis, man will always sincerely and seriously follows virtue and morality and thus he will act as an active member of the polis. By practising virtue man can lead a good life. A further point is that Aristotle's virtue is never a state sponsored virtue. Virtue, morality or precepts of good life are all known to everybody and, since man is reasonable, he will spontaneously and enthusiastically follow the principles of virtue and morality. Then what is the exact role of the state in this regard? Aristotle does not directly deal with this matter. But from his analysis it is quite manifest that the state cannot impose virtue and morality upon its citizen. But the state will create a congenial atmosphere in which people will pursue virtue. Morrow says (p. 59) "For Aristotle, the state comprises a cooperative order through which its members practice virtue and thus enjoy good life."

Talking about the relationship between attainment of virtue and the role of the state Aristotle has drawn our attention to a very practical issue. He says that people realise virtue and morality through their participation in the affairs of the state. This view of Aristotle opens the door to the citadel of democracy. He believes that by remaining detached from the affairs of the polis, people cannot be virtuous. It means they must participate in the day-to-day affairs of the state and, in this way, they can be virtuous and be called good citizens. He also draws our attention to another important issue which may be stated in the following way. In a polis there are different types of people whose socio-economic position, intellectual capacity and moral perceptions are different. All these people cannot be treated equally. The supreme objective of the polis will be to create a favorable atmosphere in which all will be able to find a suitable atmosphere for the realisation of their moral and virtuous ends. It means that Aristotle was quite democratic minded and he had no intention to brush everyone's shoes with the same colour. Even an association and not a polis can pursue virtue and morality. It further emphasises that Aristotle was never a conservative—minded philosopher.

CONCEPTION OF STATE IN ANCIENT GREECE

It would be a fruitless adventure if we attempt to find in ancient time a state in modern sense. But in ancient Greece there was state which will not corroborate the modern idea of state. In ancient Greece there were small states or political organisations which were called city-states. Why were they called city-states? There is no clear or definite answer. It is believed that in ancient Greece people lived and earned their livelihood through various professions. They lived in small areas which they called city. It is to be remembered that the term city was quite different from the modern conception. Now these small areas or cities were surrounded by areas and were called city-states. The city-states were frequently involved into war or battle among themselves which led to the reorganisation of boundaries of the city-states. The city-states were, however, small in size and population. Because of the change in the boundaries of the city-states there was no fixed territorial boundary. The city-states or polis were various in size and power. The powerful city-states were eager to gobble the weak and small city-states. The result was that in ancient Greece there was no political peace.

Since the city-states were small in size and population there was ample scope for all adult citizens to participate in the affair of the state. But from the history of

Greece we come to know that all the inhabitants of city-states were not treated as citizens. Particularly the slaves—who constituted a major part of population—were debarred from political and other functions. The slaves were not given the status of citizenship. This system was a black spot in the system of city-states. However, so far as the composition and functioning of the city-states are concerned it is claimed by many that in the city-states of ancient Greece there was direct democracy. It means that all adult citizens could shoulder the responsibility of state administration. Today we cannot imagine of such a situation. On face value we can say that the city-state or polis was ideal and it is to be followed as a model.

The state or polis or city-state was regarded by many as an embodiment of virtue, morality, ideal etc. At least Plato believed in this perspective. Plato imagined of an ideal state and he was so much fascinated that he prepared an elaborate blue-print of an ideal state. Aristotle thought of an ideal state in a different way. However, in ancient Greece state, politics and administration were all closely related with virtue and morality. Even Plato believed that state (or ideal state) was the embodiment of highest virtue and morality. The people of city-states were also accustomed to drawing distinction between the civilisation of cities and non-cities. Let us quote few words from Barker's *Greek Political Theory : Plato and his Predecessors.* "The Greek could draw a distinction between his own civilisation, which was that of city, and the civilisation of the Celts or the Germans who lived in the country-side and whose civilisation was that of the tribe". The clear implication is that the Greeks believed that their civilisation was superior to that of other sects or tribe. Sometimes this led to the conflict between two or more communities.

The city-state included both urban and rural areas. But the urban area was the centre of attention and activities. The people of the rural areas visited the urban areas very frequently for business purposes and for free discussion. People of all classes and groups had free access to the cities and they participated in discussions. The cities were thus full of various activities. The free discussion among people brought them together and Barker says that there was good relationship among the people. Some people, however, question the cordiality among the people.

It is said that the city-states were simply small enclaves which denotes that there was no uniformity in the constitution of the city-states. Many city-states were physically separated from each other by seas or mountains. Even different parts of a city-state were separated from each other. This created problems in administration. But the inhabitants of the city-states overcame this physical "inaccessibility". The credit should go to their zeal for free discussion and participation in democracy. Barker says that people of city-states loved democracy so much that they could challenge any and all hurdles. We think that this is correct and because of this direct democracy got the opportunity to thrive.

Chris Harman in his noted work *A People's History of the World* observes that the Greek civilisation was the third great civilisation in the world. This civilisation is great no doubt and the Greek city-state was famous for democracy. It is also true that the city-states were all well administered (Harman pp. 63 to 67). But there were several black spots in the body politic and one such black spot is the class-character of the city-states. Harman says (p. 66) that in most of the city-states there were chiefly two main classes—one is rich landowners. They cultivated their land with the help of slaves and in this sense they were slave owners. On the other hand, there were large number of small farmers who cultivated the land. The big land owners exploited the slaves and other weaker sections of the city-states. The small farmers were also exploited by the big landowners. Harman is of opinion that in ancient Greek city-states the struggle between two classes of farmers was a very common affair. The struggle was due to the fact that the interests of two classes of landowners and farmers were opposite and irreconcilable.

In ancient Greece there was also another type of class struggle. In Greek society, besides big farmers, there were some old families or oligarchs who had strong influence over society. Practically these families ruled city-states. Common people participated in the open general assembly. This was again manipulated by the powerful families. But when the big farmers amassed wealth they tried to exert power over the state administration and this finally created an opportunity for direct clash between powerful families and big farmers. It is also a type of class struggle. Harman says : "The outcome in many states was the overthrow of the kings and the establishment of oligarchies—republics ruled by wealthy" (p. 66). The rich and wealthy people controlled the administration for their personal benefits. This created animosity between classes.

In many areas of the Greek city-states resentment was simmering among many or several sections of community. In Athens at the time of Solon (594 BC) debt-slavery was banned and this was strongly opposed by the owners of the slaves because slavery was a great source of wealth to them. The owners raised their voice who opposed slavery. Again, in several city-states common men cherished to have a legitimate share in power and the fact that only democracy could give them an opportunity. In several parts democracy was set up which enabled poor men to participate in various affairs of state. But rich farmers and owners of wealth strongly opposed this on the ground that democracy was simply a mob rule and naturally unsuitable for efficient administration.

The class struggle in ancient Greece sometimes assumed violent forms of armed conflict. Many upper classes staged counter-revolution with the help of arms and ammunition. In this way the city-states were converted into stage of armed revolution—'The history of many Greek cities was one of continual struggles, often successful' by the richer land owners against democracy. The partial exception was Athens where democracy survived for some 200 years (p. 68). It is believed that dissatisfaction or resentment in one form or the other was the chief cause of class struggle. The poorer section of the city-state or the farmers firmly believed that they were deprived of their legitimate share in politics and economics and that created a lot of apathy against state administration or the richer section of the community. This is an indication of the fact that the city-states of ancient Greece was not an abode of peace and tranquility. There was democracy no doubt but that was meant for wealthier and powerful sections of the city-states.

Barker points out that the city-states of ancient Greece were hardly cities in our sense. They looked perhaps more like districts than towns. The city-states were also called *polis*. Berki says, that why the city-states were so called is not properly known. He says, "The name polis originally signified a military fortress which provided protection for surrounding village" (*History of Political Thought: An Introduction*, p. 49). An important aspect of Greek city-state is in many city-states there were hills which were rich in iron ore. This helped the city-states to manufacture weapons and the rulers of the city-states were encouraged to declare war against other city-states. So in ancient city-states political peace was a misnomer. The war led to the disintegration of many city-states, particularly the large monarchical states. Because of this, life in the ancient Greek city-states was harsh and uncertain. But this was not the case for the people who had ample wealth. They had the power and financial capacity to travel against the tides.

Institutions of Ancient Greece

In ancient Greece not only city-states flourished, but various types of institutions also developed and all of them combinedly strongly cemented the foundation of a democratic system. Before analysing the different institutions we shall make a very short survey of how democratic and other forms of government found their place in Greece.

In different city-states of Greece before 700 B.C. not one form of government prevailed. There were aristocratic, oligarchic and tyrannical forms of governments. Last of all, democracy was established. How did this happen? Dunning[1] says that in many city-states few powerful and wealthy persons or groups formed the government and this was called aristocracy. But, subsequently, because of dissension among groups and persons, aristocracy was faced with crisis and the vacuum created by it was filled up by oligarchy. Oligarchy met the same fate and it was succeeded by tyranny. But the growth of trade and commerce and intellectual development heavily eroded the old values and ideas. Simultaneously, dissension among different persons of tyrannical government led to its disintegration. Consciousness spread among the common people and many of them became aspirants of power. This gave rise to democracy. But regeneration of democracy did not mean the end of conflict between aristocracy or oligarchy. However, democracy advanced. And, with it also grew many institutions.

On the same issue Barker makes the following observation. "The city was not devoid of representative institution, nor unacquainted with political machinery which is connected with those institutions." Here Barker wants to say that the Greek city-state was neither city nor state in modern sense, but it had several institutions and these made Greek democracy very important. Greek people exercised their democratic rights through these institutions. In other words, the institution laid the very foundation of direct democracy. These institutions were mainly political.

The first political and very important institution of ancient Greece was **Assembly.** It was an open gathering. All the Athenians and other citizens of city-state above twenty were entitled to attend the open meeting of Assembly. This was also called **Ecclesia.** The Assembly met ten times in a year and its sessions were regular. There was also the provision of extraordinary session. But only the council had the power to convene the extraordinary session of Assembly.

It would be a mistake to assume that the open session of Assembly was the architect and determiner of everything in ancient Greece. Although the city-state was very small and the people assembled together could easily discharge the duties,

---

1. Dunning : *A History of Political Theories : Ancient and Medieval*, p. 3.

in practice the situation was quite different. The decision-taking and the implementation were entrusted to a small body of persons called the **Council.** There were five hundred members in the council and that is why it was called the Council of Five Hundred. The purpose of making the council so big was to make it more representative. Almost all sections of the Athenian community found their berths in the Council of Five Hundred.

Theoretically, the fate of the **Council** was to be decided by the Assembly, in practice the former was more powerful. The Assembly could take decisions only on issues or proposals raised by **Council.** In the opinion of Aristotle, the **Council** was supreme in all affairs. In other words, the **Council** was vested with sovereign power. It had also the right of presiding in the Assembly. Interpreting Aristotle's view, Barker says—The power of framing the issue and deciding the questions to be put is no small power. We can compare the **Council of Five Hundred** with the cabinet of modern parliamentary system. The main difference is that the cabinet is small in size. It will not be wrong to say that the modern cabinet system is derived from the **Council** of ancient Greece. But so far as composition is concerned the **Council** was the representative of all sections, whereas the modern cabinet is not.

The enormous power enjoyed by the Council of Five Hundred had converted the direct democracy of ancient Greece into a myth. It had also made the Assembly a perfunctory institution. In Sabine's comment we find "Direct democracy conducted by the whole people assembled is rather a political myth than a form of Government... All forms of Greek Government whether aristocratic or democratic, included some sort of assembly of the people, even though its share in the Government might actually be small".[1]

The political institutions of ancient Greece were not confined within Assembly and Council of Five Hundred. Greek people were highly interested in the system of local government. This implies that they wanted to expand democracy to the grassroot level. *Deme* was an institution forming a unit of local government. There were about one hundred demes in Athens. The demes were also called wards or parishes or townships. What was the function of demes? Let us put it in the words of Sabine—But their (demes) really important function was the presentation of candidates to fill the various bodies by which the Central Government was carried on. In other words the demes were authorised to send representative to the Assembly and the Council of Five Hundred.

What was the method of sending representatives? Either the representatives were elected or chosen by lot. Representatives were sent in proportion to their sizes. Barker says that demes adopted the system of proportional representation. The qualifications of prospective candidates were decided by the demes. No Athenian could bypass the deme. The system of proportional representation made the election to Assembly or Council scientific and fool-proof. To choose a candidate by lot was also favourite. Greek people thought that to choose by lot opened the door of chances to hold high offices.

Besides Assembly and Council there was a **body of ten generals.** The generals were not chosen by lot but by election. It is improper to think that the generals were

1. Sabine : A History of Political Theory, Indian edition 1968, p. 6.

entrusted only with the military activities. They looked after military and foreign affairs. They also exercised considerable influence upon the decisions of the Council and Assembly. The political decisions were taken by the generals, although these did not fall within their jurisdiction. This, of course, depended upon the personality of the generals. History says that sometimes one of the ten generals became very important and ultimately he got the leadership. The leader carried with him the body of generals, Assembly and Council. Neither the Council nor the Assembly could nullify the decision of the leader. He might be compared with the Prime Minister of modern parliamentary governments. Pericles was a general and he played a very dominant role.

Few words may be said on the relationship between the Assembly and Council. The functions of legislation and administration were jointly performed by the Assembly and Council. The cooperation between the two makes us think that they were the two houses of a single body. Laws were enacted by Assembly and Council jointly. The Assembly had not the power to introduce any bill. The Assembly was the sovereign body, but without the cooperation and assistance of the Council it could not exercise those sovereign powers. All the major decisions relating to war, peace, agreement, treaty and forming of alliances were taken by the Assembly. But in all these cases the Council was not a helpless spectator. Every matter was first raised in the meeting of the Council and, after its approval, it went to the floor of the Assembly. The extent of the cooperation between these two bodies depended upon mutual goodwill.

Another institution of ancient Greece was the **courts.** The court was both democratic and also a peculiar organisation. The members of the court were called jurymen. They were elected by the people directly. What was the number of the members of the court? It was as high as six thousand. The tenure was only one year. Each court could deal with particular cases. By lot it was decided who would sit in particular court. The number of jurymen in each court was never less than 201. The normal number was 501 and above.

In the legal system of ancient Greece there was no provision of appeal. Naturally the decision of each court was always final. The absence of appeal was in full conformity with the democratic tradition of Greece. Since members of the court were elected by people, they were responsible to them. No authority could challenge the wishes of the electorate.

The courts performed judicial, legislative and executive functions. They settled all legal disputes. The verdict of the courts was carried out by the party concerned. Different types of court functioned independently. There was a very close relation between courts on the one hand and the Assembly and Council on the other. This enabled the courts to perform executive and legislative duties. The courts had also the power to control magistrates. Three different ways were adopted by the courts to exert control. First of all, courts had the power to judge the qualifications of a person. If in the opinion of the court the person was underqualified, the court could disqualify him. To put it in other words, the court was the final authority as regards the appointment of magistrates. Secondly, the court had the power to judge the performance of the magistrates. This was done at the end of tenure. Needless so say that the court review could prevent the magistrates from doing unlawful activitics. Finally, the magistrates had some financial functions. The courts had the authority to look into the accounts of financial matters. As a result of it, the magistrates refrained themselves from misusing public money. The courts had also controlling power over other matters.

The composition and functions of the courts are really unique and surprising. About two thousand and five-hundred years ago, the Greeks showed considerable ingenuity in adopting this judicial system. In modern world it has no parallel. We are at the beginning of the twenty first century, and today we cannot imagine of people's control over the entire judicial system. Now, in many countries, there is a system of judicial review and we highly eulogise it. But, in ancient Greece, courts could review the law or decision of the Assembly or Council. By controlling the magistrates the court exerted its influence over the administration. It may be observed that no organ or part of the Greek administration was outside the control of court, and since members of the courts were elected by the people the system ensured people's authority. Democracy, in ancient Greece, found its wide and varied ramifications. In the background of all these we can say democracy in ancient Greece was not only direct, but also ideal, though, in some cases, the process was not fully democratic.

Political Ideas of Solon

We have so far discussed the nature of Greek city-state and the political institutions of ancient Greece. But all these do not throw sufficient light on the nature and shape of political ideas and theory. Historians and scholars are of opinion that towards the end of the seventh century and beginning of sixth century B. C. in Greece there were Seven Sages who were famous for their philosophical and political ideas. These Seven Sages at different times worked hard to preserve unity and integrity of the polis. Because the entire polis faced disintegration. Some of the Sages tried to enact good laws. Law was the only way to banish anarchy from society. Among the Seven Sages, Most prominent among the Sages was Solon. He was highly respected by the Athenians.

Solon was born in 638 B.C. and died in 559 B.C. He came from a middle-class family. He was a trader and toured extensively different parts of Greece from which he gathered vast and valuable knowledge about law and customs of different countries. In Solon's time, various classes of Athens were engaged in bitter political strife. Solon thought that the Athenian society must be saved from this struggle. The contending classes and parties reposed their faith upon Solon and he decided to be the ruler of Athens. He was elected the first ruler.

Assuming power he first enacted number of laws and introduced many changes of far-reaching consequences. Coming to power Solon found that wealth and property were concentrated in the hands of few persons and in his opinion this was the prime cause of dissension among the citizens. So he decided to remove this inequality by taking away property. He annulled the debts of the poor people, and cancelled private and state debts and also released the slaves.

Solon was a legal reformer and also a constitution maker—Barker. **Solon was the first man to introduce rule of law.** He thought that without rule of law prosperity of society would be a far cry. To Solon, rule of law was most important.

Only law could free the society from lawlessness and fight among the different classes and groups. He took initiative to enact a set of rules which would guide the officials in the day-to-day administration of the state. He treated the officers of state as servants of law. In Solon's time laws were not available in written form. These laws were vague and indistinct. That is why he decided to write laws. Solon established the supremacy or sovereignty of law. It is said that although Solon was not the maker of any constitution in any strict sense he founded a constitutional scheme. His conception of sovereignty of law was highly appreciated and accepted by Aristotle.

Pythagoras and Pythagoreans

Pythagoras was an outstanding Hellenic philosopher. He was born in Samos, an Ionian island. He belonged to a wealthy merchant family. He extensively toured Egypt and Babylonia. When a tyrant came to power in Samos, Pythagoras left his birth place for ever and settled at Croton, an important Greek colony. Croton was in south Italy. There Pythagoras founded a school and taught only a few disciples. Pythagoras and his followers collectively propagated philosophical, political and ethical ideas. The followers of Pythagoras led an ascetic and restricted life. There was strict discipline. The Pythagoreans maintained a good relation among themselves. They were also loyal to their master. No disciple could challenge the authority of Pythagoras. "He was considered the author of all the basic principles of Pythagoreanism as a doctrine, movement and organisation."[1]

Number-doctrine was the central idea of Pythagoreanism. Pythagoras thought that number was the central thing of the whole universe. Pythagoras discovered a unique harmony between mathematical numbers and things of material world. Phythagoreans "observed numerical attributes and ratios in the objects of harmonics; since, then, all other things appeared in their nature to be likeness of numbers and numbers to be first in the whole of nature, they came to the belief that the elements of numbers are the elements of all things and the whole heaven is a harmony and a number." Pythagoras expressed his political ideas and principles in terms of numbers. This is the most outstanding feature of his political philosophy.

He explained the concept of justice with the help of numbers. According to Pythagoras a square number is perfect. All its parts are harmonious. The first such number is 4. It is divided into two equal parts. If the number is not square there will arise disparity among its several parts. Pythagoras explained justice in terms of square number. Justice is a concept like square number. To him justice was a due measure and it contained an idea of equality. He thought that all the sections and groups of society must get their due share and should be treated equally. Analysing Pythagoras's political ideas, particularly his concept of justice, Prof. Barker makes the following observation : "A number is square so long as the equality of parts remains. A state is just, so long as it is distinguished by the equality of its parts, and justice is the preservation of such equality."[2] To Pythagoras, harmony or equilibrium between different parts of society was justice.

---

1. V. S. Nersesvants : *Political Thought of Ancient Greece.* Progrerss Publishers, Moscow, p. 25.
2. Barker : Op. cit., p. 54.

Pythagoras and Pythagoreans also spoke a lot about the law, nature of man and administration of society. Human nature, Pythagoras thought, was very complex, emotional and moody. To bring them together was a very difficult task. For the administration of such a society a competent ruler was necessary. The ruler must also be sympathetic. He must study the mind and nature of the people. The subjects must display utmost obedience to the ruler. Pythagoras thought that docility would be the chief feature of subjects' character. Discord between the ruler and the ruled would invite chaos and that would be the cause of instability. Pythagoras, that is why, emphasised upon the enactment of good laws. Allegiance to laws and traditional customs were essential for any society. He thought that the laws and customs might be defective but that was immaterial. Resentment against law was dangerous.

We have already pointed out that Pythagoras belonged to a wealthy family and this helped build up his proclivity towards aristocratic form of government. He advocated an aristocratic form of government on the ground that aristocrats were competent in running administration and honest in behaviour. Common people had not the sufficient amount of intellectual capacity and they were not fit for administration. "The Pythagoreans held that was unreasonable to heed the opinions of the mob as only few were endowed with the gift of clear thinking and a sense of harmony."

Estimating the influence of Pythagoreans, Barker says—"The Pythagoreans of the fifth century helped the growth of political science by their application of the principles of natural philosophy to the state. Some of them went beyond the application of number to the conception of justice, and taught a definite theory of politics" (p. 55). Pythagoras's Theory of the Wisdom of the Ruler was subsequently accepted by Plato. There is a close relationship between Wisdom of Ruler and Philosopher—King of Plato. Barker has discovered another aspect of Pythagoras's influence upon Plato. There was a Pythagorean principle that "goods of friends are common property." This led Plato to advocate the doctrine of communism. Pythagoras's teaching and ideas were so simple that it created a tremendous impact upon the mind of succeeding generations. Particularly Plato could not escape from his influence, although he never received his teaching directly. Greek politics of Plato's time came under the influence of Pythagoras. Traces of Pythagorean principle were to be found in the constitution of some city-states.

Heraclitus and Democritus

Heraclitus and Democritus are two philosophers of pre-Plato ancient Greece who made remarkable contribution to the political thought. First of all we shall discuss, in brief, the political ideas of Heraclitus. He was born in 530 B.C. and died in 470 B.C. We know Heraclitus as a famous dialectician of ancient Greece. He belonged to a highly aristocratic family. Historians are of opinion that some members of his clan became kings. His family also exerted influence on the politics of city-state.

Heraclitus did not depart from the contemporary or traditional outlook and ideas of other philosophers. Like other philosophers Heraclitus held a world outlook. The city-state or human society is the part of the cosmos. No individual, whatever he may be, can go against the nature and cosmic dictum. In his opinion, all the things of the world are in constant change. They are also in motion. There is also a perennial struggle between different parts of everything and these parts, Heraclitus thought, are opposites. That is, without conflict the opposites cannot co-exist. Unity passes through long and continuous struggle between opposites or various parts of a thing. There are two sides of a thing—good and bad, right and wrong, crooked and straight. In nature there are also opposites such as day and night. He thought that the struggle between the opposites ultimately led to perfection and development. If there were no struggle, there cannot be any progress. The conflict was again not without any orderliness. The struggle traversed along a harmonious and orderly way.

In the cosmic world there is reason and justice and since human society is part of the cosmos, this cannot deny justice nor can neglect it. That is, all efforts must be made to achieve justice. Again, the failure of the authority to ensure justice in its true form is quite unethical. To him, justice was a divine concept. It would be unjust on the part of the human being to violate it. Law was also a divine idea. The primary function of law is to ensure justice.

Heraclitus was a great critic of democracy and this was due to his family background. Democracy, according to Heraclitus, was a mob rule and hence it was bad and unreasonable. He also applied the principle of dialectics to the idea of government. Like the struggle between the opposites, Heraclitus thought, there was a conflict between democracy and aristocracy. In the final stage, democracy was bound to be defeated by aristocracy. Because of its badness and mismanagement democracy failed to draw any sympathy from any quarters. Only the best had the right to rule, and the best could never be many, it was only a few. Heraclitus observed that all cannot have the ability to rule or manage the administration only a few have that ability and naturally majority must carryout the decision of the few.

Although Heraclitus was a great advocate of aristocracy, it should be pointed out here that he was against hereditary aristocracy and nobility. He always favoured aristocracy of wisdom, intellect and merit. Nobility by birth was very harmful for the state. This idea of Heraclitus makes us believe that he was a strong supporter of elitism in politics. The advocacy for elitism, best and wise does not imply that Heraclitus was a reactionary thinker. He was simply saying that only the best few had the capacity to rule.

"The teaching of Heraclitus was far-famed in Hellas and exerted a profound influence on the subsequent philosophical, political and legal thought of Greece. Thus Socrates and Plato advocating respectively the government of the knowing and the rule of the philosophers were obviously under no small debt to Heraclitean idea of the rule of 'the best' capable of understanding the universal logos".[1] His concept of dialectics created a great impact upon the thought-system of Plato. German philosopher Hegel had admitted that he had followed very sincerely Heraclitean system of dialectics in his *logic*.

Democritus, the encyclopaedic scholar and philosopher, was born in 460 B.C. and died in 370 B.C. He, like Heraclitus, came of a very wealthy and aristocratic family. He had an insatiable thirst for knowledge. After his father's death he went out in search for knowledge and widely travelled different countries which included Egypt, Ethiopia, Athens. He wrote several books on philosophy, ethics and also

1. V. S. Nersesyants : *Political Thought of Ancient Greece*, p. 49.

politics. His fame as a scholar spread far and wide. Citizens of Abdera, his birthplace, showed highest regards Democritus. They made him the ruler or archon of Abdera. He was not simply a formal ruler, he was found to take active part in political affairs.

The most important thing about Democritus was that he was the greatest exponent of materialism. Summarising his view of materialism one critic says—"Democritus held that reality was essentially a combination of two primary causes or elements : atmos or indivisible material particles and void. In their eternal motion in void immutable particles impinge on one another and come together to form physical objects."[1] Democritus did not think that the atoms were moving because of the force released by God or divine spirit. They were moving out of necessity and also spontaneously.

Democritus's view on the origin of state or society constitutes another aspect of his thought system. He did not believe in the sudden or accidental appearance of human society. His opinion was that society was the result of long and continuous process of evolution. He believed that there was a state of nature and people were savage. The primitive men had to fight against the vagaries of nature to keep intact their physical existence. Sociability and gregariousness of their nature impelled primitive people to live together and form society. Sociable nature, strong determination to fight against odds and sheer necessity were the weapons which primitive men used to control nature. Necessity and consciousness made men civilise and in this respect God had no part to play. Human society, according to Democritus, was absolutely an artefact of man. The institutions were also shaped and made by man. Democritus's view on the origin of society shows his strong conviction of materialism. It also shows that he was far ahead of his own age and thought. Greek tradition developed around the wishes of providence. Democritus, with his materialist outlook, refused to give any special niche to God or to any of his representatives. In a word, the artificiality of society, law and institution makes his thought system remarkable.

Like many other Greek philosophers Democritus held that there was a harmony and conformity between nature and justice. If something conforms to nature that must be regarded as justice and any deviation from nature was, without doubt, injustice. It implies that in his view nature was the highest manifestation of justice. Democritus believed that there was disparity between artificial laws, customs on the one hand and institutions of natural laws on the other. This disparity was the main cause of discord among various sections of society. But, he thought, there must be a harmony. "On the whole, Democritus observes reconciliation between what exists by nature and by convention giving priority to natural principle of 'truth' over 'opinion'."

Democritus's view of state is also worth mentioning. According to him the state is a community of freemen assembled and united together to serve the common purposes and interests. It is not something imposed by an external force. It is the result of conscious human efforts. A proper scanning of Democritus's conception of state reveals that his idea about state is not only a city-state but a community state. That is, the state exists not for the purposes of any particular individual or section but for the entire community, common cause and interests must always get

1. V. S. Nersesyants, op. cit., p. 53.

priority. Democritus viewed state both from legal and from moral perspectives. This is definitely new. The state, in his opinion, must look after the overall moral upliftment of its citizens and must not involve itself in the materialisation of the sectional interests of few. Democritus analysed the state mainly from ethical standpoint. The relation between the individual and the state is not legal, but moral and ethical. The state must help the individual to achieve the moral goals, and its failure in this sector would nullify its existence.

Few words may be said about his idea on political obligation. Democritus had a great fascination for the best ruler. Almost all the renowned philosophers of ancient Greece expressed their view in favour of a best ruler. He thought that only wise people with clear aristocratic background were fit to rule the city-state, because only these persons were endowed with intellect and virtues. So far as political obligation is concerned, it is the first and foremost duty of the citizens to show unconditional obligation to the state and the ruler and any violation would throw the polis into turmoil. The citizens also must be obedient to law, because law was in conformity with justice and nature. The purpose of law is to upgrade the behaviour and character of individual. But before law fulfils this purpose the citizens must learn how to obey it. Both law and city-state were designed to improve the life of people.

Democritus also had clear conception about punishment, which is regarded as an important part of his political theory. Most of the people, in his view, are of bad mentality and ulterior motives and their purpose is to inflict injury upon others. He suggested that the notorious people must be brought under strict and examplary punishment scheme in order to stop repetition of harmful activities and crimes and any failure on the part of the authority to restrain or punish the culprit would contaminate the entire society, and make normal administration problematic. The laws must be impartial and strict. No misdemeanour should escape the strong vigilance of law. None should be allowed to violate justice and only punishment is offender must be killed. But the law has no right to punish the innocent persons.

We have made a very brief survey about what Democritus thought about politics and politcal problems. It is needless to say that he was a man of versatile genius. No aspect of politics escaped his attention. For his views on different subjects Democritus gained vast popularity and high respect. He was able to mould considerably the nature and idea of subsequent political thought. During his lifetime a number of thinkers were greatly influenced by his philosophy. This shows how popular Democritus was. Socretes, Plato and Aristotle borrowed many of his ideas. Even today Democritus does not appear to us irrelevant. We still hold the view that the state is the product of evolution and it is not for the interests of few.

THE SOPHISTS

Meaning of the Word Sophist

According to *Encyclopedia Britannica*—"Sophists, name given by the Greeks about the middle of the 5th century B.C. to certain teachers of superior grade who distinguishing themselves from philosophers on the one hand and from artists and craftsmen on the other, claimed to prepare their pupils not for any particular study or profession but for civic life." In other words, the term Sophists implies a group of highly qualified teachers specialised not in any particular field of knowledge. Sophists in ancient Greece were different from philosophers and craftsmen.

From etymological point of view the word "sophist" is derived from Greek word "*sophos*" which means wise. Subsequently the word stood for "man of wisdom". Naturally the Sophists came to be regarded as men of knowledge. Because of the disliking of common people for the phrase man of knowledge the Sophists of early periods refrained from using the particular phrase. In popular parlance the word carried derogatory meaning. Ordinary people of ancient Greece were not interested in hair-splitting and subtle analysis of everything which the Sophists did. The Sophists were regarded by them as cunning people. A large number of Sophists were fond of jugglery of words and by this method they wanted to defeat the opponents. They also applied logical fallacies. All these were not approved by the general public.

Nature of Sophists

"The Sophists were the brave and profound innovators in philosophy, logic, epistemology, ethics, politics, rhetoric and many other fields of knowledge." In a word the Sophists had a free movement in all branches of knowledge. Barker says—The Sophists are versatile. Because of this versatility the age of enlightenment dawned in Greece. It is said that the teaching of the Sophists did not go in vain. Greeks were able to rationalise their behaviour coming under the influence of Sophists. They completely changed the traditional relationship between polis and individual.

The philosophers of ancient Greece looked at everything in term of cosmos and as a result of it the role and importance of the individual were plunged into utter negligence and disrespect. On the contrary, the Sophists awarded due regard and importance to the individual. This changed the very nature of society, politics, ethics and many other things. Protagoras, a famous Sophist, said "Man is the measure of all things." The special emphasis given by the Sophists to the individual radically changed the nature of society. The people were placed at the centre of society and they took leading part in social change.

The Sophists were professional teachers. The purpose of their teaching was to give practical training to fellow countrymen in politics. Barker observes that the Sophists represented the university. That is, they performed the function of university. The function of the university was to prepare the after-life and the after-life was politics. To put it in other words, the Sophists prepared the life of Greeks suitable for politics. In this connection it is to be pointed out that the purpose of education portrayed in *The Republic* was to prepare the guardians. Although the Sophists were teachers, at the same time they were journalists and disseminators of things new and strange (Barker, p. 66). Critics are of opinion the Sohpists were in a sense all-rounder.

Another feature of the Sophists is that they never formed any clear-cut school. They did not profess a single set of ideologies or tenets. Different Sophists adhered to different philosophical, political and legal theories. Even on political conceptions they differed among themselves. Such as, earlier Sophists advocated democracy and they were really democratic—minded. But the Sophists of the later ages were supporters of aristocracy and oligarchy.

As regards the taking of payment there was no uniformity among all the Sophists. It is said that the Sophists of the 5th century B.C. received payment. But they did not take it directly. Their pupils took it on their behalf and the amount was also fixed by them.

Although it is true that the Sophists were encyclopedic thinkers they were not radical thinkers. "Like all Greek thinkers they aimed at communicating something of practical aid to right living. They offered instruction in goodness or practical wisdom" (Barker, p. 67). In fact, the Sophists were practical thinkers and they disseminated the knowledge of how to manage affairs of the state and the family properly.

Another characteristic feature of the Sophists was that by origin they were not Athenians. Most of the famous Sophists came to Athens from different city-states and resided in Athens. But their pupils were Athenians and very rich. The Sophists taught these rich students. They learnt practical art of politics and other techniques to control election and manipulate politics in their favour. Since the students of the Sophists were rich people they had no feelings and sympathy for democracy and they were extremely eager to set up or restore oligarchic form of government. We can, therefore, say that the teaching of Sophists were considerably responsible for establishing oligarchy in Athens. It is really an unfortunate aspect of the Sophists' teachings. Some critics say that because of the faulty teachings of Sophists the class rivalry in ancient Greece arose.

Political Ideas of Few Sophists

We have already noted that the Sophists of ancient Greece did not form any school of thought. Not only this, there was no coordination among the Sophists. Different Sophists held different views and they lacked coherence or uniformity. For a clear understanding of their views on politics it is necessary to discuss the political views of some leading Sophists. **Protagoras** of Addera (500 to 430 B.C.) was a prominent Sophist.

It is said that Protagoras was a conservative thinker. He said, "Man is the measure of all things, of the existence of things that are, and of the non-existence of things that are not." Its implication is the existence or non-existence of anything is determined by the common sense of the individual. In other words, individual is the determiner of everything. This comment of Protagoras is the expression of extreme individualism. He had a good deal of faith on the common sense of man. If a man possesses sufficient amount of good common sense he will be able to understand the nature of things. Barker says that this outlook of Protagoras is the indicator of the fact that he was both a great individualist and empiricist. The man-measure doctrine of Protagoras has glorified man and has placed him in the centre of universe. This notion of Protagoras is quite different from that of his predecessors who thought that man was the part of cosmos and devoid of self-reasoning and consciousness.

Barker says that Protagoras's writings throw some light on the origin of human society. He pointed out few stages of the evolution of society. The first stage according to Protagoras was the state of nature. People of state of nature were to some extent acquainted with the arts of industry and agriculture, but they could not build up political organisation. That is, they were far away from civic-life. The second stage of evolution consisted of founding cities and their preservation or maintenance. People of the second stage did not have the political art which they acquired in the final stage. Although Protagoras spoke of state of nature, he was not a believer of social contract theory of origin of state. One critic says—The progress of human society described by Protagoras in the myth shows that he regards the state and the laws as artificial institutions resulting from the spread of political virtues and man's increasing skill in the art of government."[1]

It has been observed that Protagoras has great love for democracy and he wholeheartedly desired its progress. He thought that if justice were fully under the authority of only few persons there could be no state. Every man has certain amount of skill. Naturally, none is negligible. Each individual of the state must be allowed to have a say in the affairs of the state. But he thought that every man could not have an equal measure of skill and intelligence. To make them competent the state must take initiative in propagating and spreading education among the citizens. Proper education also helps the citizens to understand law. He thought that the state was the perfect educator.

Prodicus was another important Sophist. He devoted a good deal of labour to the study of the origin of state and emergence of commonwealth. Prodicus never thought that the state was created by God or by any other supernatural element. Men built up human society or state being driven by sheer necessity and for this purpose they had to do hard labour and invest a lot of ingenuity. Although Prodicus did not clearly say anything about the state of nature in which people lived before laying the foundation of state or political organisation, his analysis shows that men had to fight against the nature. Therefore, it was human labour which banished conflict and brought peace in society and it became possible when an organised polis emerged.

Prodicus also thought that progress of human society and development of consciousness implanted language in the mind of men which helped them to exchange ideas among themselves. Religion, in Prodicus's view, was also the result of the progress of society. People created religion to meet their demands. We can say Prodicus looked at religion simply from utilitarian point of view. They defined only those natural objects such as sun and other natural phenomena. Religion had no connection with elements or phenomena having no utility. It is true that according to Prodicus human endeavour was solely responsible for the creation of society, but he never made individual the central figure. He was not an individualist. However, we can call him the precursor to 19th century utilitarianism.

Thrasymachus was a renowned Sophist of later 5th century B.C. It is observed that he held unambiguous political views cloaked with realism. He drew a distinction between religion and politics. He did not believe that the gods were the creator of civil society and all other things coming to the benefit of human being. The human society, in his opinion, is full of injustice and malpractices. If God were the creator of society, injustice would not get any scope to flourish to its fullest form. Men's behaviour, function attitude etc. are the root causes of injustice. He firmly believed that in actual society there was no justice. What was going on in the name

1. V. S. Nersesyants : Op. cit., p. 76.

of justice was nothing but the self-interests of powerful and wealthy persons holding power over the rest of the society. They declared law to suit their own personal interests and justice was interpreted in their own favour. In a nutshell, in every sphere of society there was flagrant violation of law and justice.

Thrasymachus held that the nature of law differed according to the nature of government. In democracy, there were democratic laws and, in tyranny, tyrannical laws. In a tyrannical form of government common people were forced to show unconditional obligation to law. They were not in possession of any opportunity to judge law or justice. He had no fascination for any particular type of government. He treated all forms of government with equal view. The sole purpose of every type of government, Thrasymachus thought, was to enhance and simultaneously to protect its own interests. He had no doubt that force was the basis of state. The authority ruled the state and demanded unconditional obligation simply with the help of force. The use of force ultimately created a congenial atmosphere for the development of authoritarianism. As regards Thrasymachus's concept of right, Barker makes the following observation : "In view of Thrasymachus there is no such thing at all as natural right. Right is simply whatever is enforced by the strongest power in the state in accordance with its own view of its own interests". The authority never considers people's problems. If we view Thrasymachus's concept of politics deeply we shall find that he considered politics in terms of power. There was no place of ethics or religion in his political ideas.

SOCRATES

Life and Teachings of Socrates

Socrates was the most celebrated philosopher and intellectual giant of pre-Plato Greece. He saw the light of this world on 469 B.C. and left this mortal world on 399 B.C. His philosophical, political and legal thoughts earned him a great fame. Even Karl Marx highly spoke of him. He came from a family of Athenian sculptors or stone masons. Since his father was a sculptor, he devoted to the craft. But in his later life he seriously studied philosophy. His devotion to philosophy, historians say, was not abrupt. Socrates first studied, with all seriousness, physical sciences and this could not satisfy his urge for knowledge, because the physical sciences, in his opinion, contained only mechanical explanation about matter and phenomena. He ardently desired to enter into the deep of everything and this urge led him to study philosophy. He found that physical sciences, says Barker, only gave a mechanical explanation of how things were made, and what he wanted was a teleological explanation, showing why they are and what is their *raison d' etre*.

Socrates spent his entire life in the study of philosophical and political problems and related issues. He discussed these problems with the ordinary members of society and tried to convince them of the inner meaning of various social and philosophical issues. Socrates was chiefly a philosopher. But at the same time he showed keen interest in the affairs of state, politics and law. He was a man of great courage and never hesitated to defy the order of the tyrannical ruler. The then rulers of Athens thought his lessons harmful and he was prevented from preaching further and his lessons were banned. Socrates was against the acceptance of financial remuneration in exchange for giving lessons. We know that the Sophists introduced this system. He thought that taking of fees for lessons was tantamount to prostitution. This indicates how selfless a man Socrates was. Socrates scrupulously adhered to this principle though his family was in great financial crisis.

Socrates was severely penalised for preaching and upholding progressive ideas. He was charged of "corrupting the youth" and impious. The indictment against him was "Socrates is guilty of refusing to recognise the gods recognised by the state, and of introducing the other, new divinities. He is also guilty of corrupting the youth. The penalty demanded his death. The Athenian Court of 501 judges sentenced him to death penalty by a majority of 80 votes."[1]

Like many other Greek philosophers the views of Socrates are not available in written form. He talked with his pupils, friends and opponents. Which were later on noted by them in the form of notes. The best source of Socrates's ideas are Plato, Xenophon and Aristotle.

Political Ideas of Socrates

Socrates, in his analysis of political and philosophical problems and issues, applied the **method of dialectic,** and in this respect he departed from the Sophists who arranged the different topics in a systematic way and then discussed them. Socrates, on the other hand, adopted the question-answer method. Needless to say, his disciple Plato also followed him.

In the view of Socrates ethics and politics are closely connected with each other. Without politics ethics carries no value, and without ethics politics becomes harmful. "The highest of all virtues is the political art which includes statecraft and makes men good politicians and public officials." Almost similar opinion was made by Aristotle. In other words, Socrates thought that the purpose of politics was not to capture power, nor it was an art how to remain in power. Political ethics make good and proper citizens. Both public and private persons must learn the art of political ethics.

Socrates also discussed the concept of law. He divided law into unwritten divine law and written human law. He cautioned us by pointing out that there was no discrepancy between these two sets of laws. Justice was the root of all the laws. If a law is not justified by justice, it is useless. If anything is not approved by justice it cannot be legal. To be precise, Socrates gave priority to justice in his thought system and in this respect Socrates followed his predecessors.

Socrates dealt with a popular and at the same time important concept of politics popularly known as allegiance to law. He devised the theory of concord which means the citizens must show allegiance and obedience to law. Interpreting Socrates's allegiance to law, Xenophon, the most reliable interpreter of Socrates's view, says—"A Republic that is obedient to laws is happy in peace and invincible in war. Moreover, you know that concord is a great happiness in a state." Socrates admitted the diversities among the citizens and differences of opinion. But notwithstanding they must unanimously obey the laws. He thought that without unqualified obedience to law there could not be unity and integrity in the Republic. His

1. V. S. Nersesyants. p. 95.

exaltation of law-abidingness did not rule out the importance and necessity of criticism. Laws, not in conformity with justice, might invite criticism.

Socrates was a great supporter of philosopher-king. He did not like democracy, oligarchy, hereditary aristocracy and tyranny. Only a philosopher-king, he thought, could serve the purpose of the polis. Socrates gave a brief classification of government which runs as follows. Rule of men over the unwilling mass was to him a tyranny. Property qualification for office was for him a plutocracy. It was democracy when all people were allowed to participate in the government. Socrates recommended only the rule of the wise. All other forms of government, in his opinion, were unsuitable.

Socrates had viewed the concept of rule from a different angle. The purpose of the ruler should not be to acquire pleasure or to satisfy personal whims and wishes, but to ensure the welfare of the common people. The ruler must keep a watch upon the needs of the people and he should never try to fulfil his own needs. If a ruler pays more attention to the furtherance of his own interests he should be punished. Ascendency to power, in the opinion of Socrates, is not automatic at all. The above noted qualifications must be satisfied.

Related with the concept of justice is equality and Socrates greatly emphasised it. Equality is a political virtue and it is the utmost duty of the wise ruler to ensure it. A polis must be based on equality. Violation of equality would result in disorder, chaos and disruption of normal activities of the polis. Socrates's equality is geometrical equality. "By geometrical equality Socrates means political justice and equity or right judgment in terms of political virtue as distinct from simple numerical or arithmetical equality".

Socrates, Plato and Aristotle

It is generally observed that the political thought of ancient Greece and particularly of Socrates created a positive and far-reaching impact upon the philosophy of Plato and Aristotle. It is, therefore, necessary, to throw light on how Socrates influenced Plato and Aristotle in forming and propagating their philosophical and political concepts. Socrates (469-399 B.C.) "is one of the most remarkable far-famed characters in the intellectual history of mankind. For over two and a half millennia there has been a ring of glory about his name and aura of enigma surrounding his personality" (V. S. Nersesyants—*Political Thought of Ancient Greece*, p. 93). This was Socrates. Even Karl Marx highly eulogised him.

Though Socrates was not chiefly a political thinker or politician he dealt with a number of subjects, which may conveniently be included into the subject-matter of politics or political philosophy. His main concerns were law, justice and polis. His method of analysis was dialectic. Dialectic is question and answer form. The discussion about any subject could proceed until a final opinion was arrived at he held discussions with his disciples.

If we study the political ideas of Socrates, Plato and Aristotle we shall find that Socrates created a tremendous impact upon the latter two giants of Greek philosophy. Maxey says 'In Plato Socrates lived again. Not in the sense that the pupil was an unvarying facsimile of the master, not even in the sense that Plato was the literary and philosophic executor of the great querist, but rather in the sense that the mind and soul of Plato so completely absorbed in the thought and spirit of his teacher as to inspire his own soaring genius to create a sublimer Socrates than ever trod the bustling streets of Athens' (p. 39). The writings, intellect, logic and above all the thought of Socrates created a great influence upon Plato. What we call the thought system of Plato is of "genuine Socratic origin". Maxey also says that how much of Plato's philosophy is original cannot be said assertively.

V. S. Nersesyants has written : "The ideas of Socrates, particularly his emphasis on the law as the criterion for classification of the forms of government, the contrast between monarchy and tyranny, and others exerted a considerable influence on the subsequent political theories of ancient thinkers, above all Plato, Aristotle and Polibius and through them various politicolegal doctrines of the Middle Ages and modern times (p. 99).

Socrates's views on democracy influenced both Plato and Aristotle. He did not consider democracy as a desirable form of government on the grounds that incompetent officials are appointed to run the administration of democratic state. Another reason is common people have no ability to participate in the state affairs. Socrates also advocated the concept of Philosopher-King. Both these views of Socrates were accepted by Plato.

Socrates's classification of government or constitution influenced Aristotle. Though Aristotle followed Socrates in classifying constitution his criteria were different from those of Socrates.

Socrates introduced a new concept which may be called ethical politics. We find its reappearance in Plato and Aristotle. Without ethics politics is bound to contaminate the whole society. For an ideal or good and well-ordered state both ethics and politics must travel hand in hand. It may be ethical politics or political ethics. However, both Plato and Aristotle took this idea from Socrates. The very foundation of their ideal state was ethics. Socrates and Plato both believed that officials of public services must be moral and ethical persons. Aristotle also held the same view. These three persons were unanimous about that, without good and ideal politicians, citizens cannot be good and moral. "Socrates is traditionally regarded as the founder of theoretical ethics which paved the way for Plato's and Aristotle's logical and political conceptions" (Nersesyants, p. 91).

Though Socrates's thought and philosophy had a direct and positive influence upon Plato and Aristotle, it cannot be said that they were the carbon copies of Socrates. There is no doubt that both Plato and Aristotle were great and original thinkers. These three great Greek philosophers built up the fabric of political philosophy with the help of the experience of Greek city-state, but the thought systems of Plato and Aristotle are really comprehensive. Plato's ideal state's main concern is justice, but it deals with many other aspects which are not available in Socrates. Aristotle borrowed his classification of government or constitution from Socrates. But there is a difference. His classification deals with the comparative aspect of politics which is still remembered by students of political science. Aristotle's views on revolution and polity still deserve special mention. Socrates, Plato and Aristotle were no doubt the great apostles of Greek philosophy. Socrates laid the foundation of many concepts especially dialectic and pitfalls of democracy. Even today these constitute important parts of political thought.

2 PLATO

Life and Major Works

There is a controversy about the date of birth and the majority opinion is he was born in 427 B.C. and died in 347 B.C. in Athens which was involved in the Peloponnesian war (430-404). The war was between Athens and Sparta.

Pericles was a great apostle of Athenian democracy which flourished between 500 B.C. and 321 B.C. From history we come to know that Athenian democracy was direct democracy and Pericles supported and worked for its development. Plato had good connection with the family which was intimately associated with both democracy and aristocracy. This connection put a clear imprint about these two political forms in his mind. Because of this connection Plato had a natural inquisitiveness about politics and political career which finally made him interested about politics.

After the death of Pericles Athenian democracy fell in disgrace because there was severe infighting among various political parties which ultimately put a very bad name on the body of democracy. Again, Plato had the misfortune to witness the squabbles among democracy, oligarchy and other forms of government. This we may call struggle among the classes which was between oligarchy and democracy. Moreover, there were several groups in oligarchy which were involved in infighting among themselves. It was the misfortune that Plato had to gather bad experience about the contemporary political condition. The noted interpreters of Western political thought are of opinion that his contemporary incidents encouraged him to form opinion about politics. J. S. Mcclelland rightly says "political experience of the Athens of his youth and early manhood appears to have sickened Plato" (p. 18). Plato thought that the political turmoil was generally responsible for the general degradation of justice, morality and other universal values. But Plato's mind was imbued with these universally accepted values (justice, morality, virtue etc.) and he wanted to find out a way which could ensure the revival of all these universal values.

The contemporary politics was practically shorn of all accepted values and moral concepts and this miserable situation pained Plato in a considerable way. He was largely convinced that politics, in order to be worthy, ought to be associated with the good qualities such as virtue, morality, justice etc. Diagnosing the degrading political condition of his time Plato arrived at the conclusion that politics must be associated with virtue, morality and its supreme goal shall be to establish justice in society. Plato believed that politics must aim at establishing virtue and justice and in this regerd it must not make any compromise. We have earlier noted that Plato's chief concern was how to make politics the chief way of establishing morality, justice and virtue in society. We are of opinion that keeping this noble objective in mind he planned to set up an ideal state whose main concern shall be to ensure justice and virtue.

At the age of forty Plato bought a grove of trees in a green suburb just outside the city walls and founded there his famous academy called after Athenian hero Academous. He began to teach various subjects in his Academy and we may say the intellectual life of Plato started with the setting up of the Academy. It is said that he had a definite philosophy and clear conception about politics and other related subjects. Though Plato was not the master of all subjects he guided the teaching of subjects. Plato spent the rest forty years of his life in teaching various subjects. Though various subjects were taught in the Academy special emphasis was given to moral teaching. The teachers of the Academy were directed by Plato to streamline their method of teaching which would be able to change the mind of people. Plato had no intention to impart formal or business-like education. His conviction was that moral teaching could make a man suitable for an ideal or moral or good polis. He thought that for a good and ideal state or society the citizens must be made good, moral and virtuous. The entire education system should be made or formed in that perspective. In other words Plato's objective was to set up an education-system for the sole purpose of establishing an ideal state. The scholars of Western political thought have arrived at the conclusion that the influence of Plato's Academy was quite widespread and its good name reached various parts of East and touched Alexander.

Plato authored several books such as *The Statesman*, The *Laws* and *Republic*. Of all these books the most important is the *Republic*. We read Plato for his good ideas and the *Republic* contains the best part of his philosophical ideas. Besides the *Republic* The *Laws* is regarded by many as his second best book. In the *Republic* Plato has given us an elaborate plan of an ideal state. But he had considerable doubt about the setting up of an ideal state. The concept of ideal state was so much favourite to him that he could not jettison the entire scheme of the ideal state. In *The Laws* he gave an alternative plan about a state or polis which would bring about the revival of universal values. He believed that if an ideal state was not feasible a mixed form of government could well be set up. He wrote another book *The Symposium*, which deals with homosexuality. Some people think that, this book unearths the bad aspect of Plato's life and character.

Plato's Method

It is generally observed that Plato is indebted to his teacher and mentor Socrates for many of his ideas and primarily for the method he adopted in his analysis. Socrates, we know, was the originator of dialectic which means the art of investigating or discussing the truth of opinions. It also implies enquiry into metaphysical contradictions and their solutions. Socrates wrote nothing. He had several companions or disciples with whom he discussed contemporary social political and other issues and also philosophical problems and after a thorough discussion a final opinion was formed. If we go through his *The Republic* we shall find that Plato, along with his disciples, raised issues of great importance in the form of questions—and answers were collected from them. *The Republic* also shows that Plato gave answers to questions his disciples raised. In many cases Plato was the final "arbitrator" of many controversial issues or problems. The persons who participated in the discussion enjoyed complete academic freedom and this quite enriched the analysis. The academic freedom and the dialectics both constituted the body of Plato's analysis and the entire thought system. Writing about Plato's method and related matters Prof. Barker, a renowned authority on Greek Political Thought, writes : "Socrates desired to awaken thought. He was the gadfly who stung men into a sense of truth, he gave the shock of the torpedo fish, he practised the art of midwifery and brought through to birth. He appealed to what was in man's mind....he called to the intelligence of man and so it was with Plato."

Plato was a teacher and, in fact, he was a great teacher. He had an idea and a philosophy which he imparted to the students of the Academy. The other teachers of the Academy had the freedom of teaching but no freedom to depart from Plato's method and technique. Plato set up the norm of teaching which was to inculcate the feeling to know more and more. In other words, Plato and all other teachers endeavoured sincerely to stimulate the urge to know more and more. Both Plato and other teachers were averse to spoon-feeding method of teaching. This intention led him to adopt the method of dialectics. The dialectics was used to proceed step by step and after a good deal of debate a final stage was arrived at. Plato also used analogy. In order to make the point clear Plato liberally used analogy. This method he borrowed from Socrates. The analogies used by Plato were generally collected from nature—particularly from the animal world.

The administration of the state, according to Plato, is run by the politician and the quality of the administration depends upon the ability of the politician. But a politician or administrator runs the administration with the help of law. It is, therefore, obvious that administration, politician, and law all are closely connected. One cannot expect good administration from a bad politician. While making such observations, Plato compared a politician with a physician. The physicians need not take any help of law, whereas a politician must follow law while running the administration. To him administration was an art and naturally a politician must possess administrative ability. If a polis is not properly administered the state will never be able to reach its goal. So the politician must possess all the good qualities of an administrator. Plato formed such opinion in the background of experience he gathered from the activities of his contemporary states. Also, to Plato, politics was the supreme art and all politicians cannot have such an art. Plato thought that only philosopher kings can have such art and for that reason he wanted to make a philosopher the supreme administrator of state. Needless to say that, even today, learned people believe that the management of state administration is no doubt a good art.

Socrates and Plato

Before entering into the details about the relationship between Plato and Socrates I like to refer the most cogent remark of Maxey. He says, "In Plato Socrates lived again" (p. 39). The implication of this short remark is that many of the meaningful ideas of Socrates found their reverberation and elaboration in Plato. Of course, this does not mean that Plato was the "unvarying facsimile" of his master. He, in many ways, followed his master. But, like his master, Plato was a great genius. The fact is that the mind and soul of Plato completely absorbed the thought and spirit of Socrates. We can say the method and ideas of Socrates found their resuscitation in Plato. Both Socrates and Plato were influenced by the contemporary political incidents. Both had great belief in democracy but the functioning of contemporary democratic governments created a lot of frustration in their mind and, ultimately, they lost faith in democracy. Many of the good ideas that we call Platonic had their origin in Socrates.

Maxey further observes : it is certain that the genius of Plato deserves no less credit than the influence of Socrates. Plato borrowed the basic concept of dialectics from Socrates and he adopted it in the analysis of various ideas. In his early years Plato came under the great influence of Socrates and their relation was not only teacher and student but also a relation between two friends. Socrates was compelled to the maximum price to open his mind and thought in academic matters and it was not possible for Plato to tolerate the inhuman treatment which Socrates was forced to swallow. Like Socrates, Plato believed that everyone must enjoy the freedom of speech and thought and in *The Republic* he—times without number—emphasised this. In the Academy Plato taught and advised his students to adopt freedom of thought and speech—this he inherited from Socrates.

THEORY OF STATE

Bases of State

It is observed by many that it is not possible for any thinker worthy of name to go against the tide of his time and to ignore the events which happen around him. Needless to say, Plato was no exception. The functioning of the contemporary states created an impact on his mind. Though Plato was a great believer and supporter of democracy, the working of democratic states of his time frustrated him and he lost his faith in democracy as a viable form of government. The states of his time were full of corruptions, inefficiency, instability. The self-interest seeking persons, corrupt politicians and demagogues ruled the state to satisfy their personal interests and, at the same time, manipulated the administration to favour them. It was practically impossible for Plato, a great idealist, and moralist to tolerate this. His conviction was that the foundation of every state, big or small, must havae morality, virtue and ideal. He believed that the instability and moral degradation of the comtemporary states must be traced to the apathy of the rulers to virtue and all the universal values. So he arrived at the conclusion that, in order to make the foundation of state strong and its existence worthy of its name, virtue and morality must be strictly adhered to and the state must make all efforts to establish justice. The state must make all efforts to realise the divine ideas in earthly socio-political life. In other words, the earthly state shall be the highest embodiment of moral values and virtue. Any disregard to it will lead the state to degradation.

Plato also thought of the economic basis of the state. We come to know from his analysis that he had no faith on the historical origin of state. He believed in the historical development of the state. None took the initative to build up the foundation of a state. Nettleship, a renowned interpreter of Plato's philosophy, makes the following observation : "He pursues not the historical order of development but the logical order. That is to say, he takes society roughly as it is and begins at what seems its lowest point (*Lectures on Republic of Plato*, Macmillan 1968, p. 69).

In his opinion the economic necessities drove people to live together and form an association which could meet their day-to-day necessities. In other words, people formed associations to meet the economic needs which pressed them in their daily life. We find the repetition of this view in Barker's analysis. He says : The state first finds its binding force in human needs. Man cannot dispense with his fellows : each while able to confer something upon the rest which they need, needs in turn something which they can confer." The society is guided or controlled by the process of give and take which means that no man can be self-sufficient. He gives what he has and gets from others which he does not possess. This is called exchange. The exchange of goods that took place among the early people had the potentiality to provide the basis of state or association. This exchange of commodities was chiefly economic in nature and formed the cause of association.

In *The Republic* Plato observes that nature has endowed men with certain ability but this ability is limited. A man produces some commodities. He keeps a portion of it for his personal consumption or use and if there is any excess he gives it to others. Other people follow the same. In this way two people exchange the articles among themselves and by doing this they meet their requirements and this, in turn, constitutes the foundation of association. Plato calls the basis of justice because one gets from another man which he has not. So we find that behind the formation of association economic factor was active. His student Aristotle also thought that economic needs were behind the formation of associations and subsequently several associations formed the state. Plato's emphasis on economic factor proves that he was a practical-minded man.

Plato's Ideal State

The ideas and philosophy of Socrates created a tremendous impact on the mind and the thought system of Plato. Therefore while Plato was discussing political and other subjects Socrates's influence is quite discernible. Plato's ideal state is not an exception. It is maintained that while Plato was planning to construct the foundation of an ideal state Socraters's teaching and philosophy were quite in his mind. Throughout his life Socrates preached the ideas of virtue and morality. When he found that the states of his time were neglecting the values and virtue he could not accept it.

After Socrates, Plato thought seriously about constructing a state which would be able to meet both ideals and practical needs. But it is to be remembered that the basic purpose of his state of imagination must be to realise the universal values. V. S. Nersesyants (*Political Thought of Ancient Greece*) writes : "In Plato's eyes the phenomenal world is not absolutely divorced and isolated from the world of ideas as the former is nothing else but the latter's distorted image and bleak shadow" (p. 112). Nersesyants farther maintains that the ideal state imagined by Plato is simply the realisation of divine ideas. We, therefore, hold the view that the contemporary incidents inspired him to think of new or alternative ideas and Plato did so. He inherited from the earlier Greek philosophers the idea that in the state there shall prevail certain noble ideas or concepts and both ruler and ruled must make efforts to realise them.

Plato in *The Republic* prepared a blueprint of an ideal state and he did not give sufficient consideration about the realisation of those ideals in actual situation. We are of opinion that Plato paid very scant consideration to the actual situation. He was chiefly concerned about his ideal. He wanted to build the foundation of a state which would be free from the ills of the present state. The foremost idea that occupied his mind is that in the state of his imagination there must be justice. At the same time he thought that the entire structure of state must be remodelled. So we are of opinion that the central idea of Plato's ideal state is justice.

At the top of the administrative structure of the ideal state there shall be a ruler who invariably will be a king and this king must be a philosopher. The idea of philosopher-king was propounded by Socrates and Plato took it from his teacher. The central idea of philosopher-king is that he will administer the state without giving any consideration to pecuniary gains or benefits. It is said that philosophers generally do not run after money or wealth. The rulers of his contemporary states were greedy and this nature of the kings or rulers was the primary cause of the downfall of the state. Plato also felt that in order to be a good administrator a ruler must have abundant capacity to study the mind of people and only a philosopher has that capacity. Naturally the king must be philosopher. His candid view was "until the philosophers are king or kings and princes of this world have the spirit and power of philosopher, and political greatness and wisdom meet in one, and those commoner natures who pursue either to the exclusion of the other are compelled to stand aside, cities will never have rest from their evils. ...and then only will this our state have a possibility of life and behold the light of the day" (*The Republic* Jowett's translation 473, p. 203).

We are of opinion that there is no ambiguity in Plato's prescription for philosopher-king. In his judgment philosophers are not greedy and unmoved by earthly losses and benefits. They can study the minds of the people and in Plato's opinion this quality is essential because a ruler must know what the subjects want. Greatness, wisdom, self-sacrifice must be considered as the essential qualities of an able ruler. The philosopher-king is supposed to possess all these qualities. For an ideal state, philosopher-king is the most suitable suggestion. It is the view of many that Plato's philosopher-king is a god in the garb of human being.

The philosopher-king is not the only element of the ideal state. If we go through Plato's analyses we shall find that he envisaged of a state which will have several classes and for this reason some critics hold the view that his state is a class-state. But the term class-state is not to be interpreted here in the Marxian sense. According to Plato, in an ideal state there shall be an economic class which is farmers' class. It is an economic class because of the fact that farmers are engaged in productive activities. They produce commodities which go to the consumption of the people. The functions of the farmers are economic in nature. Plato envisaged of a guardian class too. This is called guardian because members of the guardian class are engaged in safeguarding the territorial integrity. This class also protects other interests of the people. Military section is under the jurisdiction of the guardian class. Plato further talked about governmental class whose chief function was to look after the administration of the state. The interesting point is Plato had a deep concern about the general administration of the ideal state. He had great respect for guardian and governmental class because the wisdom and reason of the members of these classes can make the state ideal. Philosopher-king is honest and efficient no doubt but he alone cannot shoulder the onerous burden of maintaining the ideal state. In the light of the above analysis we hold the view that Plato's is a class state.

Though miserable condition of the states of his time led him to build up the foundation of an ideal state, he had also other considerations. We find him make the following observation in *The Republic* : "Our aim in founding the state was not the disproportionate happiness of any one class, but the greatest happiness of the whole; we thought that in a state which is ordered with a view to the good of the whole we should be most likely to find justice and in the ill-ordered state injustice's. Plato made this observation while analysing the concept of justice. His valued opinion is justice must be achieved with the sole aim of achieving happiness. If any man or class is deprived of his due share in general wealth and well-being that will be injustice. Naturally, the structure and administration of the ideal state are to be so arranged that no one will have any grievance. Plato had a special consideration about women. He was of opinion that women in the ideal state will have equal rights and privileges with men. This is really a progressive idea.

Plato disliked the unequal distribution of wealth and he opposed it. So far as the distribution of wealth is concerned he strongly favoured moderation and temperance. If there are gross inequalities among the citizens of the ideal state, the whole state will be deprived of unity. It means that the state will be divided into rich and poor and, finally, ill-feelings among the members of the ideal state will crop up. In the ideal state there shall exist a section of the rich and another section for the poor The division of the ideal state between rich and poor will jeopardise the good relation and halt the progress. Antagonism between wealth and poverty is not a good sign of an ideal state. Plato believes that private interest must be suppressed and general interests shall be given priority.

Ideal State and Reality

Let us now shed light on the practicality of Plato's ideal state. In this respect there are two clear opinions—the Russian thinker V. S. Nersesyants believes that Plato was firmly convinced that the project of an ideal state can be translated into reality (p. 117). While preparing the plan for an ideal state he had firm hopes that sometime in future his project of an ideal state would be able to see the sun. If he had any doubt he could not make an elaborate plan of such a state. The major part of discussion centred around the ideal state. But the other opinion in this regard is that Plato never thought that such a state would ever be able to see the light. The formation of an ideal state was simply his wishful thinking or it may be that he was not interested in the practical aspect of the ideal state. He perhaps thought that if any state was to be set up at all in a planned way then its structure would be in the model suggested by him. We think that it was the intention of Plato. "I understand" says Plato. "You mean that he will be a ruler in the city of which we are the founders, and which exists in idea only; for I do not believe that there is such an one anywhere in earth?" "In heaven, I replied, there is laid up a pattern of it, methinks, which he who desires may behold, and beholding, may set his own house in order. But whether such an one exits, or even will exist in fact, is no matter" (p. 360).

From the standpoint of reality an assessment of Plato's ideal state requires to be made. The Russian scholar observes that "even if an ideal becomes a reality, its existence cannot be eternal. Conceiving the change and succession of various forms of governments, as rotation within a definite circle, Plato proceeds from a certain analogy between the five forms of government (aristocracy, timocracy, oligarchy, democracy and tyranny" (p. 117). It is obvious that in reality Plato's ideal state is unrealisable.

Plato's ideal state can be viewed still from another perspective. Ideally it may be correct that the ruling class will give priority to the general interests and will ignore the interests of private persons or any particular class. But in practice there is hardly any such possibility. If that be the case the whole concept of ideal state will remain as an imagination. A critic says : "perfect unselfishness, complete subordination of the particular to the general interest are nowhere found" (Foster *: Masters of Political Thought*, Vol. I, p. 83). Barker also holds the view that Plato's ideal state is simply an imaginary one. More than this, it tends to produce excessive separation in the state. The guardian class is separate from other classes. This separation will ultimately invite non-coordination among the various classes. This can never be a healthy indicator of a good state. We are not aware whether Plato thought of this aspect at all.

In reality, Plato's ideal state might have faced another problem. For example, in Plato's time, there were several states. It was not possible to make all the states ideal or to convert them into Plato's model. That is, one state might be ideal and other state would remain non-ideal. This will jeopardise the very existence of the ideal state. We are sure Plato did not consider this possibility. However, this criticism can be refuted by pointing out that he did not view his theory or concept considering all the practical aspects. He just wanted to set up a model and he hoped that his model will be scrupulously followed by other states or statesmen. Sabine says that his model of ideal state may not be achieved but the point to be considered is whether the model and ideal state is relevant or irrelevant. In Plato's time, the idea of ideal state was quite relevant but today it may not be so.

Second Best State and Democracy

We know that Plato explained his views in the form of dialogue and *The Republic* is written in that form. He continued the method even in *The Laws*. The scholars of Western political thought believe that *Republic* is the best book of Plato and the second best is *The Laws*. *The Laws* contains the unfinished ideas which he had in mind. This book was written by him in a fairly ripe old age and naturally there are mature ideas and conceptions in this book. In *The Laws* Plato has given a realistic picture of states. In this book he has drawn a picture of the "second best state" while his ideal state is the best one. He prescribed certain criteria of the second best state. In the "second best state" the population shall be 5,040. Each citizen will have separate allotment of land. Landholdings and dwellings will be distributed among the citizens by lot. They cannot transfer or handover the land to other persons. The citizens will have the right to use the land for their private purposes and they shall have no right to sell the land. The state is the sole owner or authority of the entire land. The citizens shall have the right to earn property and to amass wealth but how much they will earn or amass—the law of the state will determine. An interesting aspect of Plato's second best state as stated in *The Laws* is individuals will have no right to possess gold or any other valuable metal. He has prescribed the prohibition of usury.

An interesting aspect of Plato's second best state is each citizen will be provided with sufficient number of slaves. In ancient Greece, slavery was part and parcel of life. Again, slavery was an institution and legal aspect of social life. Plato also advocated equality in the sphere of consumption. He prescribed that all necessary goods fit for consumption would be divided into three parts. Two parts shall be reserved for the consumption of the free members of the society and the slaves. The third part shall be reserved for exchange. In the scheme of the ideal state Plato did not prescribe for individual wife and children as well as private property. In the second best state he meticulously avioded that prescription. Each individual shall have own property and have right to form family. This departure is really interesting. We think that in his ripe old age he arrived at the conclusion that communism in wife, child and property is practically an impractical concept.

In the second best state, Plato said, that the citizens will be guided by the idea of promoting the conformity of opinion and fostering the spirit of collectivism. He did not allow the division of opinion among the citizens of the second best state. It was his belief that division of opinion will lead to dissension and rivalry among the people. He allowed the citizens of the second best state to have private property and family, but in many other respects he prescribed the supreme authority of the state. For example, education shall be controlled by the state. The individuals shall have no freedom to a separate system of education. Again in Plato's second best state, women will be allowed to enjoy equal right and status with men.

As to the nature of the state in *The Laws* the Russian scholar observes : "The state prescribed by Plato in *The Laws* is a hybrid of two forms of government, monarchy and democracy. In his opinion, the Persians and the Athenians respectively carried the two principles to the extreme, whereas a good state partaking of both ought to be moderate regarding the questions of freedom and obedience" (p. 124). Plato preferred a mixed type of government. In the second best state, law will be the supreme authority which means both the ruler and the ruled will be governed by law. This is quite obvious in the following lines which is found in *The Laws*. "For that state in which law is the subject and had no authority, I perceive to be on the highway to ruin; but I see that the state in which the law is above the rulers, and the rulers are the inferiors of the law, is preserved, and has every blessing which the Gods can confer (Quoted by V. S. Nersesyants. *Political Thought of Ancient Greece*, p. 125). The best state must be founded on justice, morality and virtue. In this regard he was extremely strict. Whereas in the second best state he made law the supreme authority. The states of his time were involved in war among themselves and this hindered not only progress but also peaceful life. This created a lot of anger in the mind of Plato. Law alone can ensure the good governance of state and that is why he prescribed an efficient judiciary. A comparison between the ideal state of *The Republic* and the second best state of *The Laws* reveals that in the second case Plato appears to us more practical and mature. Perhaps he realised that ideal state is simply an impossibility and thinking in that light he prescribed an alternative to ideal state which is found in *The Laws*.

Let us now turn to Plato's idea on democracy. Plato admits that democracy as a form of government is attractive both to its leaders and to the people. In such a form of government everyone can expect to rise to power. Common people generally think that it is their own government because they have elected its personnel, and the government is serious about implementing the opinions or wishes of the people. But the attractiveness of democracy withers away when it becomes unstable. In most of the democratic regimes of his time Plato saw that governments did not last. J. S. Mcclelland says (p. 45), "what democracy gains by its attractiveness it loses by its instability. Plato's treatment of democracy is different from his treatment of other forms of rule because he has a very clear grasp of the stages of its political development." Plato closely observed the working of all forms of government—especially democratic system—because he had special interest in this type. It has been found that a democratic government passes through a number of stages or phases and, finally, it sinks into the mire of demagogic tyranny. Why? Diagnosing the causes of the fall of democracy Plato discovered that instability was the primary reason. People in a democracy expect too much from such a government and when they find that their expectations remain unfulfilled they turn their eyes from the existing government. The demagogues in a democracy generally rule the roost and the common people are simply the helpless onlookers.

Plato has said that in democracy the demagogues are all powerful and they in various ways control the various aspects including functions and management for their own benefit. By dint of their speech and maneuvering capacity they control people and all social, political and various other institutions. Democracy is infested with internal conflicts and the self-interest seeking persons utilise this in their favour. Commenting on Plato's observation on democracy J. S. Mcclelland says : "Plato's account of the internal conflicts of the demagogic character in the process of corruption is a brilliant image of what happens in the first stage of democratic politics" (p. 45). Plato further observes that such a form of government is the ideal breeding ground of money-makers, corruption and self-interest seeking persons. It may be noted here that Plato's account of democracy is really unique. Nature of democracy has not even changed today.

This instability and chaotic condition finally leads democratic regimes to fall, and Plato believed that this was inevitable. In such a form of government everyone was leader. Powerful persons always are in search of opportunity to make money. The powerful utilise the situation in their favour and when the most opportune moment arrives they capture power. The collapse of democracy finally creates opportunity for the autocrats to capture power and finally tyrannical rule is established. Almost all the leading philosophers of ancient Greece held the same view. Idealogically they supported democracy but the functioning of democracy disheartened them. They could not wholeheartedly support democracy. Though tyrannical form of government was found in many Greek city-states, there were also oligarchical form of goverment in many city-states. Plato says that political turmoil and other chaotic situations were the chief factors of this political degeneration.

Some people have raised a pertinent question. They say that if "political degeneration" were the prime cause of the fall of democracy then why and how did democracy last in some city-states, and especially Athens? Plato did not investigate the reasons. But some people believe that Athens was fortunate in having some kind of working democracy. Athens had a peculiar constitution which she got from earlier years and that constitution helped her to build a strong foundation of democratic government. It is, however, a mere speculation. Our opinion is Athens had certain favourable circumstances which helped her democracy to face very odd situations. Her people also wanted a democratic form of government. J. S. Mcclelland and many others think that Plato is found to be neutral in assessing democracy. He has said that democracy is no doubt an attractive form of government. But so far its stability is concerned it is full of frustration. J. S. Mcclelland further says that we cannot form a definite opinion about Plato's conception of democracy. He is really a balanced thinker.

THEORY OF JUSTICE

Justice the Most Important Part of Republic

The concept of justice occupies the most important part of Plato's *The Republic*. Sabine says : "The theory of the state in *The Republic* culminates in the conception of justice." He has treated justice as the bond which holds a society together. Hence it is the true principle of social life. *The Republic* deals with the bond and true principle of social life. The purpose of *The Republic* is to ensure justice. The failure will invariably disintegrate the whole society. The philosopher king will take every care to establish justice. That is why *The Republic* is called a "treatise concerning justice." By elaborating the doctrine of justice Plato wanted to combat the false notions which the Sophists spread. Ideal state is the highest manifestation of morality, goodness and idealism and, naturally, in such a state justice cannot be relegated to an inferior position. Rather, it holds the highest position in the state. Different social classes are combined by the bond of justice and this makes the ideal state a perfect one. The purpose of his *Republic* is not simply to provide peace and order and, at the same time, protection, but all the opportunities for social interchange which make up the necessaries and the amenities of civilised existence.

Four Virtues of Good Community

Plato has analysed the virtues or nature of a good community. In his view a community will be called good if it possesses the four cardinal virtues of the Greeks. Plato says that every nation has its own virtues and the Greeks consider that wisdom, courage, temperance or self-control and justice are the four virtues. He proceeds to enquire into the different virtues. Among these four virtues justice is the most important.

The essence of wisdom is good cause or deliberation. Wisdom resides in those persons who perform the deliberative functions of government. Deliberative faculty is not to be found in men of large number. Naturally this quality is treated as rare. Plato says that very small number of men have the capability to participate in the deliberative function of the state. He thinks that only the guardians can exercise the deliberative functions and, hence, wisdom is their virtue.

After wisdom comes courage. Plato has defined courage as the power of resisting fear. Although bravery is not confined to army, it is a fact that battle-ground is the proper place where it is tested. That is, bravery is proved only in war. If we want to know whether a state is brave, we must look at its army. Generally the soldiers through their courageous activities can protect the integrity and unity of a state. Elaborating Plato's view on courage, Nettleship says that bravery is not in the battlefield alone, but the preservation under all circumstances of a right opinion. By courage Plato also means firm belief and conviction. The conviction encourages individual to fight against injustice and irrationality. In this way, courage establishes justice.

The next virtue of a good community is self-control. Plato has clarified the concept of self-control in a peculiar way. He has said that there are two parts of the human soul—inferior and superior part, Self-control implies that the inferior part should be submissive to the superior part. In the same way, in a state, there are also superior and inferior classes and the latter should surrender to the former. The submission of the inferior to the superior is not sufficient for materialisation of self-control in the state. The agreement between the classes is essential. The central idea of the agreement is who will rule the state and who will obey. That is, Plato wants to emphasise that rule and subordination both must be based on agreement so that there cannot be any grievance. Plato's self-control, whether it is in the case of state or individual, is a sort of harmony or symphony.

Definition and Nature of Justice

In Plato's theory to perform the nature-ordained duty is justice. Each class and each individual will do their duty and none will interfere with other's activities. In *The Republic*, Plato has made the following observation....."in the case of citizens generally each individual should be put to the use for which nature intended him, one to one work, and then every man would do his own business and be one and not many; and the whole city would be one and not many". Plato wants to say that nature has made some men physically strong and other men intelligent and wise. It has also made some men brave. Naturally, one man will be unfit for another man's job. If we accept this natural phenomenon it is expected that man will cooperate with nature in all respects. This constitutes the central idea of justice. When this is achieved, Plato says, justice in the society will start to reside.

Plato has analysed the concept of justice in wider perspective and for that reason he has said that justice has full relevance in the state. In *The Republic* we find "And a state was thought by us to be just when the three classes in the state severally did their own business and also thought to be temperate, valiant and wise". Like individuals, classes will also not interfere with each other. This is justice. Plato has assertively said that in the good state this must be found. Plato's theory of justice is another name of specialisation.

Interpreting Plato's theory of justice from the background of specialisation Barker says—"Justice is simply the specialisation ...it is simply the will to fulfil the duties of one's station and not to meddle with the duties of another station and its habitation is therefore in the mind of every citizen who does his duty in his appointed place."[1] Plato in his *The Republic* has said that justice demands that each man shall do his own business and to that business only to which he is best adapted. Meddlesomeness and interference, according to Plato, breed great injustice. Again, he says, just actions cause justice and unjust actions cause injustice. All these observations about justice prove one thing—specialisation is the central idea of justice.

We have already noted that Plato strongly advocated justice to prevent any civil dissension and discord among the several classes and individuals. He thought that if each class were engaged in performing its own duty ordained by nature, then there should not arise any be no ground for dissatisfaction. It was his belief that absence of specialisation was the prime cause of disunity among the citizens—with the advent of specialisation selfish aspiration for government office and meddling with others' functions would disappear.

1. Barker : *Op. cit.*, p. 205.

Justice is Quality of Both Individual and State

Plato did not use the word justice in any legal sense. Nor did he attach any legal significance to the term. Like courage, self-control, and wisdom, justice is a virtue. All these four virtues constitute the moral goodness of the ideal state. Again, this moral goodness is the virtue of both the individual and the state. The logical form, therefore, of justice is moral goodness. Individual and the state are not separate entities. Both require justice. Individual and the state are connected by justice or moral goodness and not by any legal act. Plato's theory of justice rules out the possibility of interference of law.

Plato has further said that there are three elements of soul—reason, spirit and appetite. Goodness is identified with justice in relation to these three elements of soul. In the same way we can say that the goodness of the community is identified with the justice in relation to the members of the state.

Architectonic Nature of Justice

"The architectonic nature of justice accounts for that element of restraint which is the first thing apparent in it. Just as the authority of the architect touches the subordinate craftsmen as a restrictive force, curbing the exuberance of their production, confining their scope and limiting their freedom in the interest of the design as a whole, so justice operates as a restraint upon a man's particular capacity, withholding him from many things which he has both the desire and the ability to do."[1]

In Plato's theory of ideal state there are several virtues or excellences and justice is one of them. But it plays the role of an architect. That is, it is architectonic in relation to other excellences. Michael Foster has illustrated the point in the following way. A carpenter with a high degree of finesse manufactures a door. But the excellence of the door is not to be judged in isolation. The other parts of the building are to be duly considered while analysing and estimating the design and beauty of the building. The design and dimension of the door must be in harmony with other features of the building. The carpenter cannot do this job, it is the architect's job. Architect's skill has not special department, but it is present in all departments. Justice, in Plato's opinion, plays the role of an architect. It acts as a control office upon the capacities of the individual.

Justice in Political Arena

Justice is not simply a moral goodness of human virtue, it has also political value. It is a quality that enables man to enter into relation with other fellow citizens, and this relation forms human society which is the subject-matter of political science. Justice teaches every individual to practise self-control. It prevents many from doing those acts which are harmful to other members of the society. Self-restraint is, therefore, essential for any political society.

While analysing justice the following observation has been made by a critic. "Justice is, for Plato, at once a part of human virtue and the bond which joins men together in state. It is an identical quality which makes man good and which makes him social. This identification is the first and fundamental principle of Plato's political philosophy."

---

1. Foster : *Masters of Political Thought,* Vol. 1, p. 42.

Sophists admitted the political value of justice, but they denied its human value, that is, it is a moral goodness. It was a great drawback on the part of the Sophists. Justice or morality to the Sophists was essential for the formation of political society. Sophists' refusal to accept it as a human value has not been approved by Plato. Analysing from this angle we can say that Plato's theory of justice is a comprehensive and perfect concept.

Criticism

Critics have criticised Plato's famous theory of justice from various angler. He enunciated the doctrine of specialisation as a vital precondition of justice and harmony of society. But it is unfortunate that he has not uttered a single word about the conflict or disagreement among the members of the same class or among the different classes. Only among the gods there may not be any disagreement, but it is unthinkable to assume that people will never enter into conflict. If conflict arises who will resolve it—Plato maintains silence on this issue. Plato was a philosopher of outstanding stature. He might have made provision for the settlement of disputes.

There can be harmony in the body politic if all the categories of persons and classes can practise self-control and adhere to their own appointed business. Without self-control justice can never be achieved. But self-control is a moral principle and not a legal one. If people fail to practise it, that will create problem. Legal provisions are necessary. Barker says—"...the justice of which Plato speaks is not really justice at all. It is an indwelling spirit; but it does not issue in a concrete *jus* and still less in any law. Law is one thing and morality is another. The one is concerned with the external rules...the other with the ideas which lie behind rules and the ideals which lie behind order... Plato has blurred the distinction and confused the boundary which lies between the moral duty and legal obligations."[1] It may be emphasised that, without legal force, moral duty may not always find fruition.

Plato's concept of justice has another drawback. The guardian class endowed with wisdom will predominate over the entire society. It is a very common experience that the persons or class controlling the administrative affairs of the state will ultimately establish hegemony over the entire society. In Plato's view, subordination of one class to another is the cause of unity and integrity. But our idea is quite different. Equal share in the affairs of the state is the potent factor for removing grievances and, hence, materialises unity.

In Plato's theory of justice there is no special or separate importance of the individual. He is not an isolated self, but part of the whole order and the order is the ideal state. The individual is not a whole and even he cannot claim that the whole is the state. Plato has given no scope to the individual of thinking in his own way. In the vast order of the state the individual cannot have separate identity. Individual is completely merged with the state.

THEORY OF EDUCATION

Importance of Education

If we imagine that the whole structure of ideal state is supported by three great pillars, then we should say that education is one such pillar. The other two are justice

1. Barker : *Op. cit.*, p. 206.

and communism. But it has been held by some renowned critics of Plato's philosophy that, to Plato, education was more important than communism. "For education", says Sabine, "is the positive means by which the ruler can shape human nature in the right direction to produce a harmonious state." Communism is regarded as a negative way. It simply hinders the hindrance which the ideal state faces. But the purpose of education is to build up the character, behaviour and outlook of the individuals highly suitable for the ideal state. Rousseau has said that Plato's *Republic* is the greatest book on education that has ever been written.

Plato's theory or idea of education is regarded by many as a mental medicine. Its purpose is to remove the evil and malady from mind. It reforms the mind and broadens the whole outlook. Wrong ways of life are arrested by education. That is why education has been given priority over communism. Education helps man and, more particularly, his soul to be fully and properly acquainted with the environment. Plato has never treated the individual as an isolated entity. He is part of the state or environment. How to adjust with the environment is imparted by education.

From the just-mentioned point we can draw an inference. In the entire Greek thought-system, including Plato's, education is regarded as a social process. With the help of education units of society learn to think of social consciousness and fulfil social obligation. Justice demands that every man must discharge his appointed function. But how he will do it, justice cannot enlighten. Education teaches man how and in what manner an individual will perform his function. Naturally, as Platonic ideal state can never be complete with justice, so also the case of education.

Plato on Education

Plato sees education from the teleological point of view. He says that whenever human mind acts, it acts purposely. Its activities are, again, based on reason. Plato is not prepared to accept that mind or soul acts without any purpose. Rational action can never be purposeless. To what extent mind will act rationally and purposefully that considerably depends upon education. Education teaches man and his mind to act with a definite purpose. So education can be considered teleologically.

Plato thought of a state-controlled education. Education controlled by private persons could not serve real purpose. We have already seen that the chief aim of education is to materialise the well-being and harmony of the state and, to fulfil this mission, education must be controlled by the state. In Plato's mind there was an idea of compulsory education system which we today see in many modern states. Sabine says that state-directed education scheme of Plato is perhaps the most important innovation.

The primary object of education, Plato says, is to turn the eye, which the soul already possesses, to the light. The message which Plato conveys in this metaphor is that the whole function of education is not to put knowledge into the soul, but to bring out the best things that are latent in the soul. Plato thinks that human soul is responsive to its environments. But how it will respond, education teaches that, soul is sometimes ill-nurtured and ill-trained and education places it on a proper footing.

If the purpose of education is the development of soul, Plato proceeds to say that the growth of the soul can be divided into two stages—early stage and later stage. The system of education for young people has been described by him in Books II and III of *The Republic.* According to Plato, education of the young is important. In *The Republic* he says—"the beginning is the most important part of any work, especially in the case of a young and tender thing; for that is the time at which the character is being formed and the desired impression is more readily taken." In Books VI and VII, Plato discusses the education for later stages.

Younger people should be taught mythological stories treating of the divine nature whose very essence is to be good and true. God is the manifestation of good and truth and mythology containing the stories of God should be taught. From the very childhood young people should be well-acquainted with good and truth. Education for the young will present heroic nature in its true and good form. The reason will be presented in the guise of beauty and rhythm. The young will learn art, literature and rudiments of science and figures. The attainment of eighteen years will qualify them to learn gymnastics whose purpose is to fit the young citizens for military and other duties which require a strong and healthy physique.

Let us now discuss the education of the second stage. When people will be mature, they will be taught science and philosophy. In Plato's belief only a mature brain is capable of understanding these two subjects. The purpose of learning science and philosophy is to produce a guardian class or, more particularly, statesmen and rulers.

If we go through the Platonic system of education, we shall find that both the stages are chiefly meant for the guardian class. The purpose of the first stage is to train the young people for military services. Emotions, spirit and courage all will develop in the mind of the young people. Grown up people, Plato believed, were capable of military services efficiently. But for the ruler and statesman a different training is necessary. The grown up people of guardian class will receive the education of science and philosophy.

Importance of Gymnastics and Music

In Platonic model of politics justice, education, and communism all correspond to the concept of ideal state. The absence of one of these will make the state incomplete. Similarly, the character and mind of the individual will be so built up as to suit the state. Remembering this fundamental idea Plato has sketched the scheme of education. His emphasis on music and gymnastics has been highly appreciated by many. Plato has said that gymnastics will train the body, and music the mind. "Both modes of training are really intended to serve a moral purpose, both are means to the formation of character."[1] Plato proceeds to note that although gymnastics aims at improving the body, it also helps healthy development of mind. It is, of course, in an indirect way. The impact of music upon mind is direct. The implication is for an ideal state that type of individual is required whose mind and body are fully and in a balance way developed.

Good and robust health of a people builds up a strong foundation of ambitious military services, as well as it is an asset of the nation. In *The Republic,* Plato has disapproved of making doctors, because they would only encourage diseases. Proper gymnastics make people sound and healthy and stop appearance of all sorts of ailments. Plato believed that music created an artistic appeal and rhythm in the mind of the young men. This makes advent of righteousness easier. By music Plato

1. Barker : *Op. cit.,* p. 221.

meant particularly the study and interpretation of masterpieces of poetry, as well as singing and playing the lyre. The rhythm and diction of poetry, the sounds of musical instruments, the shapes and colours of plastic arts appeal to youth themselves.

Higher Education

"Undoubtedly the most original as well as the most characteristic proposal in *The Republic* is the system of higher education"—says Sabine. The purpose of higher education is to train the guardians and this will be given to a selected number of students between the ages of twenty and thirty-five. In Plato's scheme of higher education the study of mathematics occupies a very vital place. The mathematical studies were serious. In his curriculum of higher education Plato gave almost highest position to mathematics. That is why Greece produced a large number of geniuses in mathematics. Plato believed that the mathematical studies were connected with philosophy. In his opinion the units of arithmetic are not concrete counters presented by the senses, they are abstractions of the intelligence. Only with the help of the study of arithmetic the intelligence can be sharpened and this helps attainment of pure truth.

Besides mathematics Plato recommended the study of geometry, astronomy and logic. The study of geometry "makes more easy the Idea of the Good" (*Republic*). Plato speaks of studying everything philosophically. When student is studying a subject he must remember the concept "The idea of the Good". If any student fails to grasp the idea of philosophy, he will be eliminated. The interest in philosophy is the first and foremost qualification of the higher education. Plato believed that this interest would not arise in early age and that is why he recommended higher education for mature age only. The students must spend a part of their time in the study of pure philosophy. The study of philosophy was essential for a person to be king.

Evaluation

Plato's theory of education is "fascinatingly modern in many respects". His scheme of higher education is really innovating. Today, at the beginning of the 21st century, we fully realise the importance of science. But about twenty four centuries ago Plato prescribed the study of science for grown up people. The study of science which includes mathematics and astronomy makes mind scientific and exact and it prepares a field for an introduction to the study of philosophy and the study of philosophy is essential for the philosopher-king.

Today, in many countries, education has become a state controlled subject. But it is surprising that Plato thought the same thing. He did not want to leave education to private management. An important subject like education should never remain in the hands of private persons. In Plato's realisation these persons will utilise education for furtherance of narrow and parochial interest and the greater objectives of state will be neglected.

Plato realised that the purpose of education is the balanced growth of both mind and body—*mens sana in corpore sano*—healthy mind in healthy body. Only adequate emphasis on both gymnastics and music can ascertain the balanced growth of both mind and body. Even today there is no scope to dispute with Plato in this regard. If one is neglected the other is likely to be affected.

COMMUNISM

Psychological and Historical Basis of Communism of Property

It is said that Plato's theory of communism is based on psychology. Let us see how Plato established his view. We know that Plato has divided the soul into three parts—reason, spirit and appetite. In his opinion if reason and spirit are to discharge their functions and to attain justice, then they must keep themselves away from appetite. Domination of appetite is a great hindrance to the purification and goodness of the soul. Similarly, in the ideal state, there are three classes—the ruling class, military class and farmers. If the former two classes are guided by economic motive, then there will be gross negligence of duty on the part of these two classes and that will erode justice. Plato, for this reason, had prescribed the introduction of communism for these two classes. Only communism could enable the rulers and soldiers to devote their entire energy and enthusiasm to the cause of the state and in this way justice could be achieved. "A communistic life, in the sense of a life divested of economic motive, is thus necessarily connected with and necessarily issues from, the proper position in the state of the two-higher elements of mind" (Barker, p. 243). Plato believed that the absence of communism would invite appetite. But justice demands that these three will discharge functions separately.

To Plato justice was not external, but internal. It was the result of habit. Mind must acquire true habit. But habit depends upon the material conditions. That is how mind will act and react that will be decided by the material conditions of society. Communism in property will make men's mind fully suitable for the attainment of justice.

Many of the political ideas of Plato can be traced to his predecessors and the theory of communism is not an exception. In ancient Greek society which existed before Plato there was a form of communism in land. Land was held in common in many tribal societies. But subsequently land came to be divided among individuals and the authority of the state manipulated and supervised this division. At the time of Pythagoras and Pythagoreans there were traces of communism. "Friends' goods were common goods"—this was the motto at the time of Pythagoras.

Communism as Stated in *Republic*

In *The Republic* Plato says—True education will have the greatest tendency to civilise and humanise the rulers and the soldiers in their relation to one another and to those who are under their protection. Not only their education but their habitations, and all that belongs to them, should be such as will neither impair their virtue as guardians nor tempt them to prey upon the other citizens. None of them should have any property of his own beyond what is absolutely necessary, neither should they have a private house. Their provisions should be only such as are required by trained warriors. They should agree to receive from the citizens a fixed rate of pay—enough to meet the expenses of the year and no more—and they will go to mess and live together like soldiers in a camp. But should they ever acquire homes or lands or moneys of their own, they will become housekeepers and husbandmen instead of guardians, enemies and tyrants instead of allies of other citizens, hating and being hated, plotting and being plotted against, they will pass their whole life in much greater terror of internal than of external enemies. For all which reasons may we not say that thus shall our state be ordered, and that these shall be the regulations appointed by us for our guardians concerning their houses and all other matters?[1]

Interpretation of Plato's Idea

We have quoted above what Plato has said of communism of property in *The Republic*. It requires clarification. Barker says (p. 242) that his arguments of communism in property are ethical. We know that Plato has always adhered to the organic concept which means that the individual is an inseparable part of the state. Similarly, the self is an integral part of the whole order. Individual has no scope to satisfy his personal and selfish desires by remaining away from the whole social order. If he is engaged in satisfying personal ambition or desires that would be quite unethical on his part. Fulfilment of selfish desires does not find place in Plato's thought-system. Plato believed that personal property was a potent instrument to satisfy desires and it clears the way for the appearance of negligence of duty and also of corruption in all its manifestations.

By advocating communism in property Plato wanted to materialise the divorce between economic power and political power. Plato apprehended that the combination of two powers in a single hand would lead to corruption in the ideal state, and this apprehension had factual basis. Plato saw that in the contemporary states the union of these two powers was the source of corruption and mis-management. If a ruler exercises two powers simultaneously he will forget wisdom. This idea urged Plato to recommend the introduction of communism for the guardian class.

Advocating communism of property for the ruling class Plato wanted to set up an example which would be unique in all respects. To shoulder the responsibility of government is not an ordinary function, rather, it is an extraordinary duty. Persons carrying out this extraordinary duty are also not ordinary persons. They belong to guardian class and the king is philosopher. A philosopher is an exceptional person. Hence he should be guided by certain exceptional or unique regulations. Communism of property is one such unique regulation.

Barker has emphasised another interpretation of Plato's communism. It is better to put the matter in his own words : "Platonic communism is ascetic; and just for that reason it is also aristocratic. It is the way of surrender; and it is a surrender imposed upon the best, and only on the best" (p. 247). The rulers will have to forego the personal comfort emanating from the ownership of private property. They will have to forget the attraction for private property. Only very few persons will embrace communism and in that sense it is aristocratic. Since it is aristocratic it is also political. Only the governing class comes under the purview of communism. Its purpose is to make suitable certain people for governmental job.

Communism in Wives

If the purpose of Plato's community of property is to create a congenial atmosphere for the rulers which will enable them to devote their time and energy completely to the administration and progress of the state, then we will say half of the purpose is achieved. Because temptation or distraction will still remain. If property is abolished and family remains as before, people will be encouraged to acquire it,

1. Plato : *Republic*, pp. 127-128 (417-418).

since without property family cannot be maintained. Plato understood it fully and he strongly recommended the community of wives as well as children and his discussion on this subject in *The Republic* occupies much larger space.

In ancient Greek society the family life was private. Women were confined to home. Men met at market-places and assembled at other areas. The functions of women were to look after the domestic chores and to procreate children. They had no freedom and led a very secluded life. Women were not allowed to meet men other than their husbands and to participate in the affairs of the state. This seclusion of women from social life, Plato thought, was absolutely inimical to the unity of state.

In prescribing the community of wives Plato wanted to serve two purposes. To emancipate the women from the bonds of family life and to reform the time-old system of marriage. In Plato's view it was an urgent task to free the women so that they could invest their energy to the all-round progress of the state. In other words, he wanted to bring the family within the ambit of the ideal state by reforming and transforming it in accordance with the ideals of the body-politic. Confinement of the women within the four walls of the family deprived the state of their valuable services.

In order to import the services of women into the state Plato prescribed the community of wives. His theory is based on eugenic and moral grounds. The implication of the first is both men and women guardians will live in barracks like soldiers and discharge their duties in common. Best and healthy men and women guardians will cohabit and their children will naturally be healthy. Plato thought that healthy children would be the best assets for the ideal state. Again, for the benefit of the state, the sexual life of both men and women guardians would be regulated. Plato assumes that as a result of the community of wives, the parentage of the children will remain unknown not only to their parents but also to the society. All the boys and girls will be brothers and sisters. In such a situation a deeper sense of unity and patriotism will grow in their minds. In *The Republic* Plato has said—"There cannot be any greater evil than discord or distraction and plurality. Again, there cannot be any greater good than the bond of unity". There is unity where there is community of pleasures and pains. In Plato's view to think separately and do separately and not to think of the interests of the ideal state is immoral. So, for the sake of the ideal state, feeling of unity must be encouraged and it should be nurtured from the very childhood.

Evaluation

We have briefly stated Plato's theory of Communism and also its various aspects. Now it is high time to throw light upon its dark and bright sides.

Plato's communism has been criticised as "half Communism" due to the fact that it is not the Communism of the whole society, but of the half society. He has prescribed communistic way of life only for rulers and soldiers and not for other classes or sections of society. He believed that non-communistic way of life (i.e., ownership of private property and accumulation of wealth) by guardians and soldiers would invite corruption among the members of these two classes. But the prescription of communism for about half of the society will divide it into two parts—one half will be deprived of the benefits of private property and accumulation of wealth, and the other half will enjoy the benefits. Such a division of society, the critics observe, will frustrate the noble and lofty purpose of communism.

Plato believed that ownership of private property would create dissension among the members of society which might not be ideal for an ideal state. If this argument is accepted (for the sake of argument of course) we are of opinion that any sort of private property is always harmful. It is not true that it is harmful for any particular class and harmless for another class.

It is said that Plato gave top priority to the idea of unity of state and he believed that there could be no greater good than unity. Ernest Barker does not agree with Plato. He says—"He pushed the organic conception too far." Plato laid excessive faith on the organic concept of state. But the experience teaches us that there cannot be solid state of unity among all the sections of society. Various sections of society will try to mould their lives in their own ways and for greater welfare and benefit of society that variety must be accepted. For the sake of artificial unity diversity cannot be sacrificed. Every section of society has its own will and this demands that only through the institution of private property each section will be able to translate its will into reality. But by prescribing the abolition of private property Plato wanted to abolish the will of a part of society.

Another criticism which has been levelled against the concept of communism enunciated in *The Republic* is that the state is composed of various parts, and family is an important part of the state. But by suggesting that no family for guardian and soldier classes Plato had practically inflicted injustice upon these two classes and it is irony that this prescription is in the name of justice.

The state is no doubt the supreme political organisation and aims at supreme good. But this cannot cover all aspects of human life. Even a state cannot fulfil all the objectives of an individual. Family has a definite and purposeful role in society and this should be allowed to play the race. If it is forced to discontinue, human life will be barren. Man can develop the finer and artistic objectives through the institutions of family and private property and, if these are abolished, the development of these qualities will be in critical position.

It is unfortunate that a genius like Plato dismally failed to realise the good effects of family and private property. Unlimited property is no doubt harmful, but a limited amount of private property is always admissible. Even the 1982 Constitution of China recognises private property.

We shall now turn to the brighter aspects of Plato's theory of Communism. Maxey, the renowned interpreter of Western political thought, makes the following observation about Plato's theory of Communism : "Virtually all socialistic and communistic thought has its roots in Plato. Were he alive today Plato would be the reddest of Reds and would no doubt hasten to Russia with the same expectant enthusiasm he displayed in answering the call of the ancient tyrant of Syracuse".

Another critic has said—"The ideal state of Plato and that of Russian communists have many elements in common, both regard private property as the sole source of evil, both would eliminate wealth and poverty, both favour a collective education of children, exempted from paternal care, both regard art and literature only as a means of state education, both would control science and ideology in the interests of the state" (Quotation from Maxey's Book, p. 56).

It is interesting to note that more than two thousand three hundred years ago Plato realised that private property and accumulation of wealth were the chief sources of discord and corruption in society. The right to property as a fundamental right of Indian Constitution was abolished by the 44th amendment.

For proper evaluation and judgment of Plato's concept of communism we are to go back to Plato's time and to understand Plato's political philosophy in the real perspective. There is no doubt that he wanted to establish a corruption-free and discord-free society which is called the ideal state. He believed that if the guardians and soldiers were engaged in the management of private property the whole interest of the body-politic will be adversely affected. For this reason he prescribed that these two classes of people would receive from the general store of the society what is absolutely required. We think that there may be some sort of utopianism in such conception but it is absolutely in consonance with his whole political philosophy.

As to the communism of wife and children it may naively be observed that he always wanted the emancipation of women from the obligation of day to day life. He thought that it is the duty of the state to assume the responsibility of rearing and educating the children and for that reason he recommended communism in wives and children.

We have said that Plato's theory of communism should not be separated from his whole philosophy and this centres around the lofty concept of the ideal state. In *Republic* he has said—our aim in founding the state was not disproportionate happiness of any one class, but the greatest happiness of the whole. He thought that through the establishment of communism the greatest happiness of the whole state would be achieved. We may not agree with the view of Plato but we must say that there are certain clear and definite reasons in his concept of communism. He was not in a position to grant coexistence of opulence and poverty because in his judgment this is harmful for the state as a whole. We conclude that there is ample logic in his theory of Communism.

Place of Plato in History of Political Thought

The place of Plato in the history of political thought is really inestimable. His intellectual heritage, observes one critic, has been exercising the minds of philosophers, political thinkers, jurists and sociologists for about twenty-four centuries. The unique longevity and topicality, continues the same critic, of his conceptions are mainly traceable to a remarkable combination of creative genius and imagination of Plato the poet with the profound insight into the most fundamental and ever new problems of human existence; of Plato the philosopher and investigator. The combination of this creative genius and imagination dominated all Western thought and not simply its political thought. The thinkers and philosophers of all sorts received tremendous impetus from Plato. Berki says that Plato may not be everybody's saint, but undoubtedly he is everybody's teacher.

The reasons of the greatness of Plato, according to Berki, may be the following. His intellectual greatness, his almost incredible richness and refinement of thought have been highly acclaimed by all sections of people. In the most precise way and in the form of dialogue he had entered into the depth of every subject. This implies his vast experience and knowledge.

Plato's political philosophy is explosive and revolutionary. His concept of philosopher-king, his ideas of the classification of governments and the origin of different types of government are regarded as original and, to some extent, explosive. Community of property and wives is his most revolutionary thought. So far as his communism is concerned many people call him the precursor of Marxian socialism. Maxey's comment in this connection may be remembered. He says : "virtually all socialistic and communistic thought has its roots in Plato. Were he alive today Plato would be the reddest of Reds and would no doubt hasten to Russia with the same expectant enthusiasm he displayed in answering the call of the ancient tyrant of Syracuse."[1] Another commentator has said 'the ideal state of Plato and that of the Russian Communists have many elements in common; both regard private property as the sole source of all evil; both would eliminate wealth and poverty; both favour a collective education of the children exempted from paternal care; both regard art and literature only as a means of state education; both would control all science and ideology in the interest of the state; both have a rigid central dogma; a kind of state religion to which all individual and social activity must be subordinated."[2]

In the light of the above observation it has further been observed that there is very little incompatibility between Plato on the one hand and Marx and Lenin on the other hand. Marx's historical materialism is not very much different from Plato's idealism. There was nothing abstruse and otherwordly about Plato's idealism; it rested on truly materialistic foundations. Plato announced his ideal by listing it with reason and experience. Plato was very much a materialist. He had clear conception and sound knowledge about the material world. The dismal functioning of several Greek city states created a lot of frustration in his mind and, in the background of it, he desired to set up a state which would be the guiding star of all practical states. He had a close relationship with the real world. So he cannot be regarded as an impractical man and dream-walker.

Plato's influence upon other thinkers and philosophers must be taken into account. German philosopher Hegel borrowed his dialectics and then Marx applied it to the analysis of historical materialism. Foundation of Rousseau's body-politic is Plato's idealism. Social idealism of Locke, Milton and Goethe has drawn inspiration from Plato. St. Augustine was also indebted to Plato. He transformed the secular conception of Platonic justice into a religious one. There is a striking similarity between Plato's doctrine of ideal state and the Utopia enunciated by Thomas More and Companella. One Marxist thinker has said "founders of utopian socialism borrowed from Plato not only the conception of perfect state, but also the faith in its practicability and a number of theoretical propositions."[3] This Marxist thinker has further observed : "This influence is traceable even in the utopian projects of social restructuring put forward by Saint-Simon, Fourier, and Robert Owen who owe to Plato some of their schemes and propositions (e.g., social stratification due to the division of labour, the harmony of passions and harmonious society, the place of education, the position of women etc.)."

Plato has praised the legitimate monarchy which is another name of limited monarchy. His curse of tyrannical rule and advocacy of mixed government had

1. Maxey : *Political Philosophies*, p. 55.
2. Quoted by Maxey, p. 55.
3. V. S. Nersesyants : *Political Thought of Ancient Greece*, p. 131.

influenced many thinkers of the 16th century. They were dissatisfied with the functioning of the absolute monarchy. The supporters of the limited monarchy were called monarchomachs. They raised their arms against the authoritarian activities of the absolute monarch. Scholars are of opinion that this general discontent had its root in Plato's thought. Plato was not an apostle of democracy, nor was he an advocate of absolutism.

We know that Spinoza and Hobbes applied geometrical method in their analysis of politics and society. But this method can be traced to Plato. Plato treated politics as royal whose purpose was to weave together the different virtues. Hobbes applied it to his analysis of state. His state was a complex mechanism knocked together by different human passions. Plato advocated one civic religion for his ideal state. Spinoza, Rousseau and Pufendorf also recommended a compulsory state religion. Upon the political ideas of Voltaire, Diderot, Holbach and Helvetius we find the influence of Plato's philosopher-king and wise-laws.

Hegel has said that Plato's ideal state is not an empty and abstract ideal, it is the epitome of Greek morality. Kant's notions of state and politics resemble those of Plato. The structure of German bourgeois society is based on Platonic model of ideal state. This structure was sketched by Fichte. Kant has said that it is not possible that the philosophers will be kings. But the ideals and philosophy of philosophers must guide the administratiors.

Several writers such as Bertrand Russell, Karl Popper and Ernst Topitsch have severally criticised Plato. In their opinion, Plato is the father of authoritarian state and modern totalitarianism. To Plato the state was absolute and the individual had no special or separate identity. He had to sacrifice his interests at the altar of the state. In order to arrest the discord among the classes and individuals Plato denied the freedom of the individual. Even he went to the extent of recommending community of property and wives for his citizens. His great disciple Aristotle did not approve his doctrine of communism. Popper says that modern communist totalitarianism has been derived from Platonic communism. Bertrand Russell, has said that Plato introduced authoritarianism in politics.

Plato was suspicious about the practicability of the ideal state. "In heaven there is laid up a pattern of it"—says Plato. In real world the ideal state will never come into existence. On the basis of Plato's suspicion Berki has said that although the Platonic ideal has earned an overwhelming appeal, in reality no state has ever been set up in Platonic model. Even no state of the real world resembles Plato's ideal state. Here lies the failure of Plato.

Conclusion

In the light of present day situation it is very easy to criticise Plato, but if we resort to that technique we shall, without any fail, do great injustice to him. On several occasions we have said that Plato did not build up his political and other philosophies in vacuum. The experience of the city-state was the chief plank of his thought system. Today the whole political and social atmosphere has undergone sea changes. The concept of city-state and other related matters and issues are irrelevant today. Naturally his philosophy has lost relevance in the present day situation. But in spite of this some of his ideas still hold good. One such idea is concept of justice. Since Plato the concept of justice has been emphasised time without number. In the

Preamble to the Constitution of India justice has been declared as one of the principles.

Plato's ideal state will never be realised in the real world. But we must not forget that the central theme of ideal state is still valid. The authority of the state has certain amount of positive role in making citizens good and moral. If the state and its government are corrupt the citizens cannot be honest. The black aspects of democracy pointed and emphasised by Plato have not lost relevance today. R. N. Berki concludes : "Plato's impact on political philosophy may have been unsurpassed or even unequalled by anybody else, but Platonism as a way of life or a viable principle of government has not caught on the real, practical world." Plato emphasised that power should never be the sole aim of any state, establishment of morality, idealism and ethics should be the ultimate goal.

3 ARISTOTLE

Life and Works

After Plato, Aristotle was the doyen of Greek philosophy and perhaps the greatest philosopher of the ancient world. He was the most renowned disciple of Plato but not the copy-cat of the master. It is generally said that Plato found the corrective to his thinking in his own student. He was born in 384 B. C. at Stagira which was a colony of Macedon. In early life he was well acquainted with the problems of colony and colonial life. All these created a lasting imprint on his mind and character. He earned the experience of practical life. Aristotle belonged to an upper middle class family. His father was a physician and attended the family of King Amyntas. Philip the king of Macedon occupied the throne.

In 367 B. C., at the age of seventeen, he left Stagira and migrated to Athens to study philosophy at the Academy of Plato. There he studied for twenty years under the guidance of Plato. After the death of Plato (347 B. C.) he left Plato's Academy. At the time of death Plato nominated his nephew Speusippus to take the charge of the Academy. Most probably this displeased Aristotle because of which he left Academy. Some scholars are of opinion that Plato's Academy could not satisfy his ever-growing zeal for knowledge.

With a few companions he went out for a tour and extensively travelled different countries and returned to his native land. Then he was invited by the Macedonian King Philip to teach his son Alexander and the duration was just two years. During his travel of foreign countries he vigorously studied different science subjects and particularly marine biology. From his father he inherited the practical training of medical science. He also studied physics and natural sciences. Aristotle acquired a good command over both theoretical and practical sides of different science subjects.

In 335 B. C. Aristotle informed Alexandar that he wanted to establish a study centre at Athens. Since he was not a citizen of Athens it was difficult for him to acquire land. Alexandar favoured him. Moreover he had many friends in Athenian and Macedonian highups. All these helped him to set up a school. In 335 B. C. his school, Lyceum, was established. But the death of Alexandar in 323 B. C. revived the anti-Macedonian feeling in Athens and his Lyceum incurred the wrath of Athenians. He left Athens and went to Euboea where he died in 322 B. C.

Aristotle appointed several lecturers to teach various subjects—theology, mathematics, metaphysics, astronomy, biology, botany and meteorology. Aristotle himself lectured on all these subjects and also on Ethics, Politics, Rhetoric and Poetics. To teach different subjects Aristotle generally collected data and materials. He also wrote extensively on Ethics, Politics, Rhetoric and Poetics. He was a prolific writer. But most of his writings have been lost. His politico-legal doctrine as a whole is expounded in *Politics.* It is a classic work. The book contains not only his own views but also a criticism of Plato's views. His other famous books are Ethics, The Athenian Constitution and Rhetoric. His *Politics* is not only a book of Political Science, but also a book on Ethics. It is a scientific book on the combination of politics and ethics as well as human good and morals.

Human Good and Politics

Aristotle has said that Political Science is the architectonic or master discipline and naturally it controls all other disciplines. Under its authority all the subjects including sciences are taught. It also directs the citizens what they will learn and also how much. Since political science is the supreme authority. Aristotle has said, its purpose with also be supreme, that is all-embracing. In his own words—"Now since political science uses the rest of the sciences and since again it legislates as to what we are to do and what we are to abstain from the end of the science must include those of other sciences, so that its end must be the good of man." Political science thus aims at the whole of human good, and not at the good of isolated individuals.

What is human good? In defining it he has followed the standard Greek usage. It means "happiness" or "the good life". Again good life includes the exercise of ethical virtues and intellectual virtues. He thought that the possession of wealth, health and friend would enable a man to be happy and at the same time exercise the ethical virtues. Aristotle called health, wealth etc. as external goods. But he has warned us by saying that their excessive amount is not necessary for the attainment of happiness and exercise of ethical virtues.

Good life also includes the exercise of intellectual virtues. It means wisdom and philosophical contemplation. On this subject we find a great influence of Plato upon Aristotle. "As a young man he had been influenced by Plato's arguments in favour of the philosophical life and in all his ethical writings we find him arguing that philosophical contemplation is the highest and best human activity."[1] But philosophical contemplation is a rare ability. It is not to be found in all the citizens of the Polis. However, for good life, it has necessity. Moreover, he thought that for the exercise of intellectual and ethical virtues a certain amount of leisure and material prosperity was necessary. He did not exclude the material possession from the domain of good life. That is why we find him advocating slavery.

Nature of Political Science

Following Aristotle we can devote a few words to the analysis of the nature of political science. He has said that every reader of science expects certain amount of certainty or accuracy. This he can get from mathematics and astronomy. But hundred percent accuracy cannot be obtained from any science. So far as political

1. R.G. Mulgan : *Aristotle's Political Theory*, p. 5.

science is concerned there is no guarantee of perfect accuracy. It is due to the nature of political science. Human behaviour is the subject-matter of political science and it is impossible to make correct predictions. But degree of accuracy is greater in physical and biological sciences. However, this does not lower the value of political science.

Aristotle has called mathematics, physics etc. "theoretical" subjects because they are engaged in disinterested scientific enquiry. These sciences do not make any analysis of "ought to be". They are rather interested in "what is". On the contrary, political science is a practical science whose aim is to determine how one ought to act. The end of political science is not knowledge but action. The subject deals with human behaviour as well as that of the group. It analyses human behaviour and on the basis of it draws conclusions. These conclusions guide the future course of action relating to political affairs. The aim is to establish the standard of social behaviour. Aristotle's *Politics* is a handbook or guide for the intending statesman. It is not an academically dispassionate account of political phenomena.

STATE

Nature of Polis or State

Chapter One of Book One begins with the analysis of the nature of Polis or State. It is better to put the matter in Aristotle's own words :

"Our own observation tells us that every polis is a community (or association)[1] of persons formed with a view to some good purpose. I say 'good' because in their actions all men do in fact aim at what they think good. Clearly then all communities aim at some good, that one which is the supreme and embraces all others will have also as its aim the supreme good. That is the community which we call polis (or State) and that type of community we call political."

Let us now see what the definition wants to emphasise. According to Aristotle, the state is a community of persons. Every community has certain purpose and that purpose is good. As a community the state has a purpose, and that purpose is also good. But the state is not an ordinary community. It is the highest of all communities and naturally its purpose shall be the highest or supreme. It is thus evident that like all associations the state is an association. But its purpose is different from that of other associations. Again, it is not an ordinary association. It enjoys the highest rank or position in the society or social structure.

As a typical biologist, Aristotle has analysed the nature of state by dividing it into several components. He has said that we are accustomed to analyse other composite things till they can be subdivided no further, let us in the same way examine the state and its component parts. The application of natural method reveals that the state is natural or exists by nature. In the analysis of the natural method we find the application of *physis* and *nomos. Physis* implies growth, nature and fundamental reality. The meaning of *nomos* is man-made, convention and custom. Aristotle says that the state is characterised by natural growth. But, during its different stages of progress, man-made laws and conventions have intervened.

---

1. The Greek word Koinonia means both community and association. Although, according to sociologists, there is a subtle difference between community and association we shall use the words here in the same sense and also interchangeably.

It is true that man is, by nature, a self-interest seeking animal and he does not hesitate to oppose the fulfilment of others' interests. So the law, justice, institutions and conventions which are made by man may be evil. But Aristotle does not accept it. He is of opinion that laws and conventions are basically good and man has made them to serve their beneficial objectives. To sum up, the state has developed naturally. It must not be treated as a result on contract or human contrivance. Men have made laws, institutions and conventions for their own benefit and these have facilitated and enriched the functioning of the state.

If the state is a natural development there are definitely several stages. What are the stages? Aristotle begins his argument by saying that the first stage of the state is the household. The union between male and female constitutes the basis of family. Again, the union between male and female is essential for reproduction, since each is powerless without the other. This is not a matter of choice, but the result of desire implanted by nature and this desire is to be found in all animals. Family includes other components such as slave, ox, plough. Without these components a family cannot maintain its own physical existence. In Aristotle's definition : "This association of persons, established according to the law of nature and continuing day after day, is the household."

The household is the simplest form of association and meets the simplest necessities. But man's necessities are various and naturally it is beyond the capacity of the family to meet those demands. Several families have formed a village to fulfil the greater demands and necessities. It generally comes into being through the processes of nature. The village, although higher than the family, cannot cope with the growing demands of its members.

When several villages are conglomerated that gives rise to a Polis or State : "The final association formed of several villages is the city or state. For all practical purposes the process is now complete., self-sufficiency has been reached and so, while it started as a means of securing life itself, it is now in position to secure the good life"—(Aristotle). Aristotle observes that besides securing life itself, it has also a greater purpose, i.e., to secure a good life. Elsewhere he has said that common interest is a factor in bringing men together, since the interest of all contributes to the good life of each. The good life is indeed the chief end of the state—both corporately and individually.

For Aristotle the nature of everything is not its first but its final condition. And the process of growth towards it is also described as nature. The city-state is a perfectly natural form of association, as the earlier associations from which it sprang were natural. This association is the end of those others and its nature is itself an end. The state is natural not simply because it is the final stage of historical evolution, but because it alone meets all the needs of man, it is alone self-sufficient. Neither household nor village is self-sufficient. They could meet only a part of man's necessities. In his *Politics* we find two types of self-sufficiency—self-sufficiency in the necessities of day-to-day life and self-sufficiency in the need for good life.

Aristotle's idea of the fulfilment of necessities of life is not to be detached from the conception of the attainment of ethical values. We have already noted that, according to Aristotle, for the sake of good life the exercise of both ethical and intellectual virtues is very much essential and the former requires the easy availability of sufficient amount of external goods. Only the state with an adequate size and sufficient population can ensure the smooth supply of external goods. In

Book Seven he has elaborately discussed the proper size of the ideal state. So to meet the necessities of life is not an end in itself. In Aristotle's view, man seeks to satisfy his physical or material demands to attain good life. Any institution or community other than polis is insufficient. Therefore, the membership of polis is essential.

Man is by Nature a Political Animal

It is now clear that the state is a natural form of organisation and by nature man has become the member of the state. Therefore, both state and individuals as its members are natural. Aristotle does not stop here. Continuing his logic he has said that man is by nature a political animal. The term political animal means an animal that lives in polis or state or polis. Nature has inspired and eneouraged man to be a part of the state. Aristotle believed that it was not possible for man to live outside the state. It is the state that fulfills all his requirements. If out of ill luck no man can get the membership of polis he will come down to the level of sub-man. On the other hand, if anybody refuses to live in a state he may be regarded as a superman.

It is the nature of man to live in a state. Aristotle says that nature does nothing without purpose, and for the purpose of making man a political animal she has endowed him alone among the animals with the power of reasoned speech and other good qualities. The implication of the term political animal is man is reasonable and with the power of reason he can distinguish between good and bad; right and wrong; just and unjust. Reasonability is the basis, according to Aristotle, of sharing a common view in the matters that makes a household or city.

The meaning of the term 'as a member of the polis' or 'state' is to be abundantly found in different ethical and political writings of Aristotle. He was also, record shows, interested in life sciences and extensively studied them. In his zoological works, he also used the term political animal. Aristotle has said that gregariousness is to be found both in man and other animals. But the fundamental difference is man possesses consciousness and reasonability while other animals do not have these features. Politicality of man enables him to form organisation and also pursue a good life. Aristotle's analysis of state and individuals as its members is based on stark logic. This is possible due to the fact that Aristotle had sufficient knowledge on various branches of science. He was a man of great reason.

Organic Character of State

A mere glance over Aristotle's theory of state drives home an important point that it is organic in nature—which means that the state is a compounded whole. He has made distinction between "aggregate" and "whole". The former means that different parts of a thing are juxtaposed together to make a unit. By their juxtaposition the parts make a unity. But the whole means a different thing. The polis or state is a whole. The state has several parts. But when they are put together the unity will mean a different matter. The state is not an aggregate of individuals. Its members are not atomised individuals related to one another only by the fact that they inhabit the same territory. When the individuals form a whole they share a joint activity, and, at the same time, lose their separateness. Again, if the parts are separated from the whole, they will be useless. This is the organic theory of state.

Aristotle has said—the city or state has priority over the household and over any individual. For the whole must be prior to the parts. Separate hand or foot from the whole body and they will no longer be hand or foot. An individual is not fully self-sufficient after separation. To put it in other words, only the membership of state makes him self-sufficient and helps him fulfil his ambition and also to be moral and virtuous. The morality and virtuousness are the characteristics of man only. When man reaches the stage of full development he automatically becomes a member of a polis and a separation between man and polis will degenerate the former to the level of beast.

If man is an integral part of the state, can it be said that he is completely blended with it? Aristotle's answer is a categorical no. He never thinks of a mixture. Although man is a part of the whole, he will stand in the same relationship to the whole as other parts. It implies that the individual will be able to keep his separate identity intact. His state is a compound in which original parts are still discernible. In the state the individuals will perform different functions, but these functions are complementary. That is, each person is dependent upon the other. By advocating that the membership of the polis does not obliterate the separate identity of man and group, Aristotle has acknowledged the plurality of parts composing the state. On this point he has criticised Plato who advocated communism to do away with all sorts of differences. Aristotle does not think that by obliterating the differences the state will be a concrete and complete whole.

Individual and State

The city or state has priority over the household and over any individual among us. This observation of Aristotle has encouraged the critics to frame a charge that he has deliberately subordinated the individual to the all-powerful wishes of the state. Although he acknowledged the separate existence of the individual, he did not think that the individual would not have separate ideal, morality and goodness from those of the state. The individual, according to Aristotle, can achieve these qualities only through the membership of and subordination to the state. He cannot have rights and liberties apart from the state or against the state. The individual, althought not merged with the state, is completely dependent upon the state for pursuit of his moral and ethical objectives. Aristotle holds that without the membership of the state the lofty ideals of individuals will remain unrealised.

But the individual's dependence upon or subordination to the state is an issue of great controversy. Now let us analyse the matter from a different angle. If the objective of the state is to help the individual to pursue his own personal interest and objectives, then the state is subordinate to the individual. For example, if the individual thinks that his personal protection must get priority and it is the duty of the state to help him, then the opinion of the individual will get priority over that of the state. No question of compromise can arise in respect of personal protection. But if the purpose of the individual is to help the polis in achieving the common good, then the opinion of the state will always dominate and the individual must submit to the state. Attainment of common good may or may not include private benefit. Whatever may be the case, the individual's interest cannot claim special treatment. He must sacrifice himself for the sake of the common good embodied in the state.

The state imagined by Aristotle is the highest manifestation of morality, ideal, ethics and values, and all these are beyond all sorts of fragmentation. Since the individual is rational and his interest does not exhaust in performing certain political activities, he wants to attain the above-mentioned values and ideals and only the membership of the state can help him. Aristotle is nurtured in Greek philosophy which always thinks of the community as a whole. Like all ancient Greeks, he has never thought actively about the rights and obligations of man. To all Greek philosophers, the attainment of the common good was the sole purpose of any polis. The view of the individual cannot get precedence over that of the state. In this respect we may say that Aristotle subordinates individuals to the state, if we mean that, in balancing the claims of the individuals and the state, he favours the state more and individuals less. Although this was the view of Greek philosophers, the same thing is to be found in the democratic institutions of modern times. The democratic institution of ostracism by which individuals could be banished without being convicted of any formal charge provides a good example of the general Greek view of the legitimate power of the group over the individual.

A Totalitarian State

From the conception—the individual is subordinate to the state—another aspect of Aristotelian theory of state is derived, it is : his state is totalitarian or authoritarian. The very simple meaning of totalitarianism is that the state assumes the full responsibility of the all-round development of the individual. It does not recognise the initiative to be adopted by the individual considering his own advantages and disadvantages, and also the role of various social and political institutions in moulding the character of the individual. Determination of goals and the methods of their attainment will also be decided by the state. In a word, in the authoritarian view, the state is all-powerful.

Critics have called Aristotle's theory of state simply totalitarian. Why? A modicum of democratic value suggests that the individual should have full freedom to pursue his goals independently. As member of different social organisations he can take their help. At best he can expect that, as the supreme organisation, the state can hinder the hindrances which stand on his way to the attainment of success. But under no circumstances the state will assume the whole responsibility. If we look at the Aristotelian theory of state, we shall find that there is hardly any scope for the individual to think in his own way and to do something independently.

The state, according to Aristotle, is all-embracing and it leaves no room for the individual's freedom. The morality of the state and that of the individual do not stand apart. So also ethics and idealism. Since the state is the highest association, it is quite capable of shouldering the responsibility of expounding and enriching the moral and ideal values to which the individual aspires. So the individual must be subordinate to the state and not the reverse. If the reverse is accepted then the authority of the state as the supreme organisation will be thrown in the air, and the non-existence of the state will imply the non-fulfilment of the goals. Again, this is unacceptable. Hence, the subordination of the individual to the state is a *fait accompli.*

This type of subordination of individual to the state—which may also be described as totalitarian, authoritarian or paternalistic—is certainly endorsed by Aristotle. He thinks that people want to be happy and their happiness is required to be maximum. This is possible only if the state takes initiative in making legislation and controlling the entire educational system. That is, the state-controlled education and state-sponsored laws are the only weapons of attaining happiness. The state is the only authority of all the enterprises and the individual has no choice. There is no alternative but subordination.

His concept of organic theory of state is also a powerful hint of totalitarianism. In an animal body the parts have no importance away from the whole. Although this is true, yet the same cannot hold good for the relationship between the individual and the state. The state is essential for the individual no doubt, but it cannot claim to embrace all the aspects of his life. Only in totalitarianism the state is for the individuals and not *vice versa*. The state can fulfil a part of human demands but not all the demands. For complete satisfaction and happiness, the individual seeks the membership of different organisations. Aristotelian state cannot tolerate this. It is absolutely unintelligible how a political association can make all its inhabitants moral, ethical and ideal single-handedly. It is both physically impossible and morally unjustifiable. No person or organisation can take the absolute guardianship of all individuals.

Aristotle's polis is a community and not an association, because men value it for its own sake and not just as a means to the fulfilment of separate individual ends. If this is the nature of Aristotle's polis, the individual finds no honourable position in the state. He is simply a machine to help the state. Again, individual cannot claim any special treatment. All are treated identically. Totalitarianism does not recognise differences. Individual is rational if he unconditionally surrenders to the state. Defiance is tantamount to irrationality. We, therefore, observe that his theory is totalitarian.

Functions of State

Aristotle has not elaborately analysed the different functions of the state. The reason is unknown to us. However, in Book III, Chapter 9, he has said something which may be regarded as his views of the state's functions. He has not viewed the state from an ordinary point of view. The state is not simply a pact of mutual protection or an agreement to exchange goods and services. If certain people assemble together and enter into a pact to materialise commercial interests and mutual protection and for that purpose form an association, that cannot be called a state. In ancient Greece there were many such associations but they were not worthy of being called a state. The state is more than a contractual society and its function is not to help its members to gain few commercial and economic benefits. Its purpose is to attain virtue. If it fails in this sphere it will be an alliance.

The state is intended to enable all, in their households and their kingships, to live well, meaning by that a full and satisfying life. The citizens and inhabitants will not have a satisfying life if they have not established a relationship among themselves through marriages and brotherhoods. So, mere formation of associations does not make a state. In the words of Aristotle "the political association which we call a state exists not simply for the purpose of living together, but for the sake of noble actions. Those who do noble deeds are therefore contributing to the quality of the political association." What Aristotle wants to say is that the objective of the state is to make the life of the individual noble and happy. This is the most important function. But the state must also look after the security and general welfare of its citizens. It, of course, comes under secondary functions.

His theory of the function of the state is quite different from that of Locke. The purpose of Locke's contract is to establish a civil society and the primary function of the civil society is the preservation of rights of its members against the infringement by others. Every individual has a right to his life, liberty and property which he could not exercise and enjoy in the state of nature. The state will ensure rights through the use of force. Any violation of rights and misappropriation of property shall be prevented by the state alone. The state, in Locke's view, is the manifestation of combined strength and force. It is the legal right of the individual to claim that their rights, liberties and property are to be protected and, at the same time, it is the legal as well as moral duty of the state to fulfil this demand. But nowhere has Locke written of ennoblement of the citizens' life. Here lies the fundamental difference between Locke and Aristotle. A real state is concerned with both outward and inward actions of man. If the state makes itself busy only with the outward actions, it will do only half of its functions.

Aristotle has emphasised upon education. Education is the most powerful weapon of making men good or of training them to virtue. Education can be imparted by the institutions set up by the state. On this point Aristotle follows Plato very strictly. The object of institutions should be to train men to goodness, not only to intellectual, but to moral and physical, excellence. The state should be the school of citizens. The state in Aristotle's theory is a reformatory. Why the state is entrusted with this task he has not vividly discussed. Our opinion is, since the state is the supreme organisation it is entitled to look after the interests of all men in a balanced way which no other association or institution can do. The outlook of church or any other religious institution is highly biased. These organisations or institutions cannot maintain discipline in education.

Criticism of Aristotle's Theory of State

Aristotle's theory of state has been variously criticised. The first criticism against his theory of state is it is totalitarian in character. His concept of the state is all-embracing. The individuals in his state have no separate status. They are completely merged with the state. Its organic nature reveals the totalitarian feature. If the individuals are separated from the state they will lose their importance as the separated parts of human or animal body lose their activity. Critics are of view that this contention of Aristotle about the relationship between the state and individuals is unacceptable.

Secondly, in Aristotle's theory of state, associations or communities have no separate importance or position. The state or *polis* embraces all other communities. They owe their existence to the state. It means that all the communities are merged in the body of the state. It implies that the polis has absolute control over all communities. He observes—"all forms of community are like parts of political community". It is now quite obvious that both the individuals and the community are integral parts of the polis. This view of state is anti-democratic. We do not regard individuals or associations as mere appendix parts of the state. In modern times, the community plays the important part in the field of developing the personality of individuals.

Thirdly, it is not true that the state or *polis is* the greatest manifestation of supreme good. It aims at some good no doubt but not the supreme good. By supreme good he means complete human good, the good life of all members of the *polis* as distinct from the lesser goods or partial welfare of the individuals. In real life, the state in no capacity can mould or determine the character of individuals in an absolute way. The state has a role, but it shares with numerous other communities. By denying to give importance to the community he has done injustice to it.

When he says that the *polis* is the manifestation of supreme good he wants to assert that it is an institution of supreme authority. The state, in practical life, is never the holder of supreme authority. Although Aristotle does not talk about sovereignty in its absolute sense, his analysis indicates that he had developed a fascination about absolute nature of sovereignty. The absolutist character of a state is always inimical to the balanced development of human personality.

In spite of these criticisms something need to be said in support of his concept. According to Aristotle the state is not the product of any contract. It is natural. This does not mean that man has no role behind the creation of the state. The evolution of man's consciousness and intelligence has helped the creation of state. It has not been made by certain individuals all on a sudden. Efforts of centuries lie behind the creation of a state. This is the evolutionary theory of state. It is also called the scientific theory. Family, community and state—all are perfectly natural. We all agree with this contention of Aristotle. Even modern thinkers are of opinion that the state is the final form as a political organisation.

Theory of Sovereignty

In Book III Chapter 10 Aristotle discusses the concept of sovereignty. He has pointed out several alternatives. First of all, sovereign power may be vested in the people as a whole. But this possibility has not been approved by him on the ground that numerical majority may create injustice in the state. Majority people will be inclined to distribute the property of the rich among themselves. Although this act is justified by law it is unjust. A tyrant may use force against the interest and wishes of the majority. But force cannot be the permanent feature of the state. Nor has it any moral basis. The third alternative suggested by Aristotle is that few wealthy persons may be allowed to exercise the sovereign power. Here again the greedy wealthy persons with the help of absolute power will plunder the property and wealth of many. This is unjust. In the fourth place, the good should rule. In that case, only the good will dominate the majority and the latter will be deprived of access to state authority. The fifth alternative, that one man, the best, should rule, is no better, by making the number of rulers fewer we still leave larger numbers without official standing.

The Greek philosopher has solved the problem by saying that the sovereign power shall be vested in the hands of the people in general and not in the hands of few men. It may be that everyone of the many is wise and capable of ruling. But when all people assemble together and take decision collectively, their decision is much better and wiser than the decision of a single wise man. For where there are many people, each has some share of goodness and intelligence. That is why the general public is better judge of works of music and poetry.

But Aristotle is not satisfied with this solution. Although the collective judgment is wiser than the individual judgment, the fact remains that the inferior will rule the superior. Aristotle apprehended such a possibility and there was reason behind such apprehension. In many city-states there was popular sovereignty which could not function properly. That is why in the last section of chapter eleven he has said that the law rightly framed ought to be sovereign. In ultimate analysis, laws must govern the society and guide the behaviour of all men and officers. But where the laws are not rightly framed, people individually and collectively will rule. Laws, framed according to the constitution, are right and just. Therefore, first of all, the constitution must be of the right type and any deviation will be unjust. Aristotle was aware of the consequences of the rigidity of law. It may result in injustice. But more injustice will appear from other methods.

CONSTITUTION

Citizenship

Book III of *Politics* is regarded by many as Aristotle's best work on politics. The major part of this book is devoted to the analysis of constitutions and citizenship. These two discussions constitute the kernel of Greek political thought. It begins with the observation of polis or state. He asks what is state? Polis or citizen and politeia or constitution are the two constituent parts of state.

As regards the definition of state he observes that there is no unanimity of definition. Many people define it in their own way. The state, we have already pointed out, is a composite whole. Therefore, it has many parts and the citizen is one such part. Let us see how Aristotle has defined citizenship. He who has the power to take part in the deliberative or judicial administration of any state is said by us to be a citizen of that state; and, speaking generally, a state is a body of citizens sufficing for the purposes of life. Mere participation in the offices of the state is not a criterion of citizenship. The constitutions of the states differ and also their nature and functions. Naturally, the citizenship is also bound to differ. According to Aristotle, the polis or state is not a mere assembly of persons at a certain place. The state is a self-sufficient unit and this self-sufficiency is not for the purposes of life alone, but for good and noble life. Noble and good life is happy life.

Any analysis of Aristotle's conception of citizenship reveals that the definition of citizenship centres around the *exercise of political rights.* That is, the citizens are a group of persons exercising the political rights. No part of the community not possessing such rights comes within the purview of politics proper. But he raises a further question : Who ought to be citizens? Especially mechanics or labourers? His answer is negative. The prime qualification for citizenship is the *capacity both to rule and to be ruled and the cultivation of this two-fold capacity is indispensable. Freedom from concern about the necessities of life is indispensable to the proper performances of political duties. The working classes are, indeed, essential to the state's existence, but this does not constitute them as citizens.*

In his discussion of citizenship, Aristotle has drawn a distinction between good man and good citizen. The excellence of a citizen is relative to the constitution. That is, the excellence must be judged in the background of a constitution. So, if there are several kinds of constitution, there can be several kinds of good citizen. It means one excellence may not be found in every constitution. But in every constitution there is an absolute standard of goodness and when a man possesses it he will be regarded as a good man. It is thus clear that it is possible to be a good citizen without possessing the excellence which is the quality of a good man.

Aristotle's theory of citizenship is not free from certain limitations. Working class, labourers and other ordinary people do not fall within the category of citizenship. This is unjust. It is a fact that the ability to take part in the deliberative, judicial and administrative affairs will qualify a man to be citizen. But we fail to understand why the working class will not have that ability. Today we do not relate citizenship to the constitution. In modern times, there are various types of constitution. But analysis of citizenship does not consider it. The modern criterion is allegiance to the constitution. That is, mere contribution to state affairs is not enough, he must show allegiance to the state or constitution.

Definition and Nature of Constitution

Aristotle's analysis of citizenship is directly related to the concept of the constitution. Constitution is the only factor which will adequately account for the identity of a state. Citizens share in the political functions of citizenship and these functions are determined by the constitution. Hence it is the constitution which determines the identity of a state, and when the constitution changes, the state also changes. We, therefore, see that in Aristotle's view polis, citizenship and constitution are closely connected with each other. The state is the supreme association and has certain purpose. He has defined constitution in the following words :

By the constitution we mean the organisation of the various authorities and in particular the sovereign authority that is above all the others (Politics, p. 113).

To put it in other words, according to Aristotle the constitution is nothing but the organisation of the sovereign authority. In democracy the *demos*, that is people, is sovereign. In oligarchy the sovereign power is vested in the hands of a few. Therefore, a constitutions of different states are not supposed to be identical. In Book IV Chapter One Aristotle has given an elaborate definition of constitution. *Constitution* is the arrangement which states adopt for the distribution of offices of power, and for the determination of sovereignty and of the end which the whole social complex in each case aims at realising. He has distinguished laws from constitution. Laws prescribe the rules by which the rulers shall rule and shall restrain those that transgress the laws. Constitution is original and prime law for the distribution of offices and determination of sovereignty. Whereas laws regulate the day-to-day affairs of the administrators.

Aristotle has analysed the constitution in the background of ethics. But, at the same time, he has not made any attempt to bypass the descriptive aspect. Every community has its own values, ideals objective and, in the light of these, a constitution is framed. Therefore, the aims and values of particular constitution are not to be judged in any absolute sense but in the background of the membership of the constitution. If the constitutions of different polities differ then it is a fact that the values and goodness will also differ. Again the goodness and values which the citizens uphold will also be of different kind. In this way, Aristotle has described the nature of a constitution.

Classification of Constitution

Aristotle has classified the constitutions into two broad categories—right or ideal constitution or government, and wrong or perverted form of government. The constitutions which aim at the common interest or good are called the ideal or right constitutions. But there are many constitutions in which the holders of power give priority to private interests and want to hold office continuously. These constitutions are called perverted or wrong constitutions. The purpose of classifying the constitution in this way is that the principle of political rule is the maximisation of the benefit of the ruled—the people. A man should not desire to hold power with an eye to his personal gain. This was the view not of Aristotle alone but of all leading Greek philosophers.

In Book III Chapter 7 Aristotle has further subdivided each category of constitution into three forms. Thus the normal or right or ideal form of government or constitution has three subdivisions. When a single man is at the helm of the government and looks to the common interest of the society, it is called **kingship.** If few persons run the government with the same objective it is to be called **aristocracy.** Sometimes it is found that people at large govern the state and the purpose is common interest—it comes to be called **polity.** When the administration is conducted for the sole benefit of the ruler the government is perverted. The corresponding forms are one-man rule—**tyranny,** rule of few—**oligarchy,** and the rule of many is **democracy.**

The basis of classification is not simply the common good criterion. There is another criterion which is called number. If a single man rules it may be tyranny or kingship and here there is no confusion. But what about the exact meaning of few and many? How many persons will constitute the few? The term 'many' lacks exactness. These are relative terms and, unfortunately, *Politics* does not throw light on it. In a developed or well-to-do society few will be rich. This contention is unacceptable. A large number of persons may be rich. There is another difficulty. How shall we define common good or interest? Some critics think that Aristotle has identified common interest with absolute justice which means complete social virtue. But the problem remains that how can the common interest of the many in polity or democracy be distinguished from that of the people at large? The concept of common interest is full of ambiguities and its interpretation differs from person to person and changes from time to time. If a dispute arises regarding the interpretation of common interest who will settle it? Aristotle is silent on this matter.

Kingship and Tyranny

According to Aristotle, both kingship and tyranny are rule of one and in spite of this basic similarity there is difference between the two. The oft-repeated difference is : a king looks after the interest of his subjects and the tyrant considers his personal gain. But other differences are : a tyrant captures power by force, but the power of the king is based on law. Tyrant's power is exercised over the unwilling subjects. But people of the king are willing subjects. Even absolute power may be acquired either by heredity or by election.

In Book 3 Chapter 14 Aristotle has distinguished five different types of kingships. The first variety is Spartan kingship. This is not absolute monarchy. King's power is limited. They are vested with the power to command in war. They have the right of dealing with matters of religious observance. They can be called constitutional kings with limited sovereignty.

The second type of kingship is common among the barbarians and is a mixture of kingship and tyranny. The kings have complete power equal to that of tyrannies but they are legally established and hereditary. The relationship between the ruler and the ruled is that of master and slave. The non-Greek kingships derive their stability from hereditary succession.

The third type is elected tyrant. It used to exist among the ancient Greeks and goes by the name of dictatorship (or aesymnetes). This is an elective form of tyranny. It differs from barbarian kingship. The rulers held office sometimes for life, sometimes for a fixed period. They had to discharge fixed duty.

The fourth type of kingship existed in heroic ages. It was both hereditary and legal and willingly accepted by subjects. These kings started their rule by launching welfare programmes and also making discoveries in arts and peace. These activities made the king popular among his subjects. Originally these kings enjoyed unlimited power but gradually their power eroded and ultimately their power was confined in discharging certain religious functions.

Aristotle speaks of a fifth type of monarchy and, in his opinion, it is different from other forms. The king is absolute and controls everything. Aristotle compares his rule to that of the head of a household. He wants to mean that the absolute king has total and unfettered control over his community in the same way as the head of the household is the complete master of all the members. The absolute king claims to be superior to law.

Aristocracy

Aristocracy as defined by Aristotle is the rule of the few best men. These few best men rule for the common interest of the people. They are generally virtuous and the virtues of good men and good citizens are indentical. In Book 4, Chapter 7 Aristotle has described three forms of aristocracy on the basis of practical experience. The first species combines both wealth and numbers. The second species is of Spartan type. It is the combination of virtue and democratic principle of freedom. The third includes those varieties of polity which incline more to oligarchy. Some species combine oligarchic principle and democratic principle of wealth and freedom. But ultimately it gives weight to wealth.

His description of aristocracy suffers from certain problems. The ideal aristocracy and ideal kingship may be indistinguishable. Because, in both cases, virtue is the supreme quality. The only difference will be in number. But if in aristocracy one man takes the leading part and in kingship the king is advised by few virtuous persons, then what is aristocracy and what is kingship will be a problem. He is not clear about the true nature of ideal aristocracy. In several places he has discussed aristocracy. What is the ideal form we do not know.

Oligarchy

Oligarchy is one of the perverted forms of government. The rulers of oligarchy always give priority to private interest and, as a result of it, common good is neglected. Another feature of oligarchy stated by him is that only the wealthy persons dominate the politics as well as administration of the state. Sometimes noble birth and education are regarded as features of oligarchy. But it is on rare occasions.

In Book 4 Chapter 5 Aristotle has described four different types of oligarchy. The first type of oligarchy is based on property qualification. But this is not restrictive. Participation in the affairs of the government is open to persons who acquire property. This property qualification is not very high. The first type of oligarchy is nearer to polity. For second type of oligarchy a high property qualification has been recommended. In a sense, the rulers of the second form of oligarchy are richer and, naturally, fewer. When persons of high property qualification are not available, the deficiency is met by the process of co-option. The third type is narrower still and includes the further restriction that membership of the governing class is hereditary.

Finally, officials and not law exercise the sovereign power. An oligarchy of this type is sometimes called a "power group."

Democracy

In the perverted form of government there are three types and democracy is one of them. Both Plato and Aristotle did not see this form of government with favour. Both of them saw the degrading and pernicious features of this form of constitution. However, democracy prevailed in Athens for over a century and Aristotle got the opportunity to see this form of government from a very close distance. So his observation of democracy is based on practical experience.

According to Aristotle, the foundation of democratic constitution is liberty. Everyone will have the freedom to rule and is legally entitled to all privileges. There is another principle. Democratic principle is based on numerical justice. That is, the decision of the majority is final and to accept it is justice and its denial is injustice. To put it in other words, in democracy, people are sovereign.

Aristotle's analysis reveals certain features and some are stated below : (1) All citizens are eligible for all offices. (2) Property shall not be a qualification for holding office. (3) One person shall not be allowed to hold office very frequently. (4) Tenure of the offices shall be very short so that all or large number of men can get opportunity to hold office. (5) Jury courts shall be introduced. (6) Assembly, whose members are elected by the people, shall be the sovereign authority. (7) Birth, culture and wealth are not to be counted as qualification.

He also discusses four different types of democracy. The first is moderate democracy which will involve certain amount of property qualification. Secondly, all citizens, if not disqualified by birth, are eligible to hold office. Here, no property qualification is recommended. Third form of democracy is, all citizens are eligible. But law is supreme. Finally, we find an extreme form of democracy. Here no restriction has been suggested. Law is not sovereign, but people will exercise sovereign authority.

If we look at Aristotle's classification we shall find that one type of government is not clearly different from another. Dunning says, "clearly *The Politics,* as we have it, is very far from clear in distinguishing each from all the rest. Polity and mixed aristocracy are difficult to disentangle." Different forms of democracy and kingship are no doubt perplexing. In spite of this defect it is to be admitted that in classifying the government, he has actively considered the economic, social, historical and cultural influences. In the classification he has also remembered the three elements of government—the deliberative organ, the system of magistracies, and judicial department. Today what we call the separation of powers, Aristotle is the harbinger of that doctrine.

Polity : The Best Practicable State

Aristotle has analysed in detail the different aspects of oligarchy and democracy and this has enabled him to construct a state which would be both ideal and practicable. This type of state is free from the extremes of oligarchy and democracy, because experience has shown that extreme form of government always breeds chaos and dangers. In Book 3 Aristotle mentions the possibility of such a form of government. This is polity.

In Book 4 Chapter 8 Aristotle has described the nature of polity. It is a mixture of oligarchy and democracy. In common usage the name is confined to those mixtures which incline to democracy, and those which incline to oligarchy are called aristocracy. When the polity is a combination of oligarchy and democracy it has certain advantages. The main advantage is that both common interest and virtue get priority. Because of this characteristic Aristotle has called it an ideal or right type of constitution. In his opinion every polity will have a popular assembly, but its powers will be limited. The appointment of officers will be based on both oligarchic and democratic methods, judicial functions are to be performed by juries.

Polity is also identified with the middle class. Chapter 11 of Book 4 throws ample light on this aspect of polity. Polity as a form of government has both ethical and social foundations. Virtue is a mean, the middle of the two extremes. Happiness of life is possible only if the mean is achieved. Best life must always be the middle way. The same principle is also applicable to practical or political life. The social foundation of polity is the existence of a large number of people constituting the middle class. These men are neither poor nor rich. The city or polis possessing the largest number of middle class people is the best administered polis.

The glaring disparity between the rich and the poor is the root cause of dissension among classes. Both these classes resort to violence as the most effective weapon to gratify personal desires and to achieve material gain. Poor people want to capture power of office to become financially solvent like the rich, and the rich people's greediness and inordinate love for wealth lead them to come into conflict with the poor people. The state is thus converted into a perennial battle-ground. As far as practicable a state should consist of like and equal men who constitute the middle class. The best government is certainly to be found in a polis which is dominated by the middle class. Euripides had said years before that only the middle class could save states. The Middle class is not poor enough to be degraded or rich enough to be factions.

Interpreting Aristotle's views on importance of middle class as a stability factor of administration, Sabine[1] makes the following observation—The principle of middle class state is a balance between two factors—quality and quantity. The first includes the political influences which arise from the prestige of wealth, birth, position and education; the second is the sheer weight of number. If the first predominates, the government becomes an oligarchy; if the second—a democracy. A combination of two factors is the only guarantee of stability. Only a polity can effectuate a balance and, hence, stability. A state ruled by the middle class can be most secure and can be the most law-abiding of practicable constitutions. He thinks that for the stability of a state both quality and quantity count very much. Aristotle believes in the collective wisdom of a sober public opinion and there is less possibility of being corrupted. At the same time men of position, experience and education are required for good administration. A state that can combine these two factors can solve the chief problems of stable and orderly government. But it is not to be understood that the polity is necessarily the best for every people and under every set of conditions. Circumstances may make a government the best.

---

1. *A History of Political Theory*, p. 113.

REVOLUTION

General Causes of Revolution

Aristotle is a piquant thinker who tirelessly investigates all the aspects of any issue. His support for polity is undoubtedly based on his zeal for achieving stability in the political system. But he does not stop here. Although stability should be the sole aim of any constitution, in practice it is found that governments rise and fall; and many factors work behind this. Book 5, Chapter 1 starts with the following observation :

We have still to discuss what are the causes of change in constitutions, their nature and number, what are the destructive agencies that affect each constitution, and from what kinds into what kinds they generally change. We must likewise consider what factors make for the preservation of constitutions, both in general and of each king separately, and also by what means each of the types of constitution could best be preserved.

The above comment made by him clearly reveals his intention as regards the change of constitution or government. He has discussed at first the general causes of revolution or change of constitutions. The synonym of the Greek word *stasis* is chaos or disorder or confusion. Interpreters of Aristotelian political thought have called it revolution.

Aristotle has stated a number of causes which are generally held responsible for constitutional change or what is generally called revolution. Differing conceptions of justice and equality are regarded as one of the basic causes of revolution. He has said that in both oligarchy and democracy, the people differ about the ideas of justice and equality. They agree that justice is proportionate and privileges, opportunities and, above all, political power, should be distributed equally. But to what extent they are equal, that creates a difference of opinion among them. All people think that by birth they are all free and have merit and desert. When some people are deprived of power, they hastily come to the conclusion that justice has not been done to them. The existing system of distribution of power is the prime cause of injustice and inequality and, therefore, in order to bring about justice and equality the constitution should be changed. Aristotle further observes that the notion of abstract justice and equality is a great enemy of stability. "Inequality is generally at the bottom of internal warfare in states."

The nefarious mentality of certain people to harvest benefit or profit and dignity leads them to revolt against the establishment. Profit means economic profit. Dignity or honour is connected with political power. The desire to get these two things determines the course of action people adopt. It is also found that the loss of profit and status infuriates men and to compensate the loss they launch revolutionary movement.

The third cause of sedition is a peculiar one. Aristotle discusses the point in the following way. Some owners of property and holders of honour instigate revolution by misusing their possession. Sometimes it is also found that the owners and holders become aggrieved on the ground that others are getting more and this is injustice. This feeling—right or wrong—provokes them. These people very often do not take part in revolution directly, they instigate other men by supplying men and material.

According to Aristotle the fourth cause of revolution is—when one or more men exercise excessive power out of all proportion to the state or to the power of the citizen body, revolution becomes inevitable. Some rulers or powerful persons give too much importance to dignity and honour. When they see others honoured and themselves degraded, soon they become revolution-minded. Aristotle says that monarchy or oligarchy emerges out of the revolution.

Fear and contempt are the fifth and sixth causes of revolution. According to Aristotle fear operates in two ways—those who have committed a crime look for overthrow of government, because they fear punishment. Fear of punishment leads people to revolution in the hope that they can escape punishment. Contemptuous attitudes also lead to revolution and civil war. In oligarchies, when those who have no share in the constitution is the largest class, they deem themselves greater than the oligarchs and look down upon them. This attitude is also found in democracies, when the upper classes show their contempt of the disorder and inefficiency.

Disproportionate increase has been termed by Aristotle as the seventh factor of sedition. He has described it with the help of a biological analogy. Animal body consists of many parts and their growth is proportionate to each other. But if any part expands disproportionately, that upsets the whole body. That is, the balance of the body is lost and becomes a cause of concern. A state consists of many parts any one of which may start growing bigger. In democracies and polities there is possibility of an increase in the number of citizens who are not well-off. In that case the newly emerged class starts an agitation against the establishment to get privileges, profit and status which the existing class is enjoying. This cause of revolution or constitutional change is similar to the fourth cause—*pre-eminence*. The difference is partly one of degree. Pre-eminence refers to the relative superiority of an individual or a small group of persons, disproportionate increase refers to a whole class.

The above is a complete list of seven causes of revolution analysed by Aristotle. To these, as he said, at least four can be added, not quite parallel since they operate differently, three of them leading to revolution without violence. These causes may be described as "incidental" occasions of change. The first is the effect of election intrigues which may lead to constitutional change without sedition. Aristotle has given an illustration to this point. In some Greek city-states the results of the elections were determined by intrigues. This led to constitutional change. Secondly, wilful negligence, again, may be an occasion of change. Persons who are not loyal to the constitution may be allowed to find their way into the highest position of the state. Sometimes neglect of small matters leads to great changes. This is the third reason. Finally, dissimilarity of elements in the composition of the state may be regarded as another cause of change. This is a broad category including a number of different dissimilarities which can produce friction and disorder within a community. The main one is difference in tribe or stock. The existence of groups of dissimilar origins within a community provides a focus for political strife. He is not thinking of racial differences, but is referring to the differences that can exist between Greeks of different cities.

Causes in Particular Constitutions

After making an in-depth analysis of different causes of revolution which are general in nature, Aristotle discusses why particular constitutions change. This shows his great acumen and vast amount of practical experience. He first takes up democracy for analysis. In democracies, changes take place mainly due to wanton licence of demagogues. They attack the rich people individually by bringing false accusations. This bitter and false attack force the rich men to combine together which results in a change in constitution. The demagogues also attack the rich as a class. In this case also the result repeats. The democratic government is overthrown by the combined power of all rich and notable persons.

In oligarchies, revolutions are caused chiefly by two factors. One is unjust treatment, and the other is dissension. The government treats the mass in unjust way and when they are aggrieved discontent comes to surface or revolution appears. Dissension among the oligarchs is also another powerful factor of constitutional change in oligarchy. Dissension appears when some members of oligarchy—for one reason or other—are impoverished, they turn to the revolution as remedy. Sometimes an inner ring is formed inside the government and this precipitates the fall of oligarchy.

The following reason may be advanced as a cause of revolution in aristocracy. We know that both aristocracy and oligarchy limit the entry of persons to government and this limitation is so stringent that large number of persons who are equally qualified remain away from office and discontent simmers in their mind. Defective distribution of power or defective balance is the main factor of change. It may happen that one section of oligarchs captures power or that power may go to the mass of men which is democracy.

Tyranny is particularly susceptible to external attack from hostile neighbours. Those tyrants who have not won their position for themselves but have inherited it from someone else are likely to be overthrown because they have been brought up in softness and luxury. Because the tyranny combines the evils of both extreme democracy and extreme oligarchy, it is liable to be dislodged from power by the same causes as each to these types.

Kingship is not susceptible to external attack. But its fall is accentuated by the conflict within the royal family and illegal action by the king himself. The dissension among the several members of royal family is not uncommon.

Evaluation

Aristotle's theory of revolution is treated by the interpreters of his thought as very important and of immense value. Many causes of American Revolution have been put forward by historians and textbook writers. Maxey (p. 74) says that all these causes are superficial. The real cause is the failure of the British government to perceive that the American colonists were the victims of inferiority complex. This has made them extraordinarily sensitive about their rights. It is not surprising that this cause has been elaborately stated by Aristotle. Again, as regards the American Civil War, it may be added here that it is not the crusade of the Abolitionists, it is the disproportionate increase of any part of state. This undoubtedly reveals the insight and farsightedness of Aristotle on the functioning and stability of any political system.

His theory of revolution has another importance. In his opinion injustice and inequality are the prime causes of revolution. The gross economic inequality between the rich and the poor ultimately forces the latter to revolt against the former. This idea is hundred percent valid even today. Aristotle has said "poverty is the parent of revolution". That is why we find him saying that for the stability of polis the rule of the middle class is to be established. Marx has analysed class struggle and revolution from the standpoint of historical materialism. But the concept of injustice and inequality is still the central idea of Marxian philosophy. Everywhere inequality breeds discontent and when it assumes an aggressive form, revolution becomes inevitable.

The reasons stated by Aristotle are not *a priori* at all, they are based on facts and experience of contemporary events. His theory of revolution can be used by serious students of history for further research work. From his observations of revolution we come to know that he had a deep acquaintance with Greek political life, and his power of observation is very subtle. He had deeply studied the working of the constitutions of various Greek city-states. On the basis of his experience and study he had framed the reasons of revolutions. In Aristotle's theory of revolutions economics, politics and sociology have met together. Of course his analysis of revolution is not free from shortcomings. The frequent use of phrases such as "especially", "for the most part" reminds us that his generalisations are not meant to be universal. Moreover, he has cited only one or two examples in support of his contention. But critics are of opinion that only from one or two examples no generalisations can be framed. His general causes and particular causes are also confusing. In most of the cases no line of demarcation can be drawn.

Methods of Prevention

We have briefly analysed Aristotle's views on causes of revolution. To know the causes which destroy constitutions is also to know the causes which ensure their preservation. He was considerably interested in the stability of constitutional system, because he knew that without stability of the political system good life and progrerss could never be achieved. As a general rule of stability, Aristotle recommended the establishment of polity, that is the rule of the middle class. The predominance of middle class will be able to remove the gross inequality among different classes, and this recommendation corresponds to the basic cause of revolution—inequality and injustice. Besides this, he has suggested other methods of preserving the constitutions.

There are some constitutions in which several heterogeneous elements are mixed together and in such constitutions lawlessness might surface and lawlessness is the greatest enemy of stability. It is the primary duty of the authority to keep a vigilant watch upon whether laws are scrupulously observed. The government must be sincere and honest towards its citizens. No hide and seek technique can help us any more. It is not proper for the government to adopt devices intended to hoodwink the masses. When the people will come to know the actual position they will revolt. Attempts should be made to establish good relations between the rulers and the ruled. None should be treated unjustly. Proper care must be taken on the sharing of governmental offices among the several qualified aspirants. Rank and file are not to be maltreated in the matters of money and profit. In a word, discontent should never be allowed to grow and—if it at all surfaces—that shall be destroyed without delay.

Aristotle was well aware of the bitter rivalry among the different city-states which sometimes led to aggression. Aggression dismantles structure and destroys stability. That is why he has suggested that it is the duty of the magistrates to inform the public of any aggression or alarm. This may prevent disruption or destruction of constitution. It has been found that the nobles and aristocrats are very often involved in quarrel and this sometimes leads to sedition. Aristotle says that legislation should be enacted to prevent such conflict. Some people with the help of wealth and high connections get superior positions in the state and this is the way for animosity. It should be prevented. One of the important ways of stabilising the constitution is to create a harmony between the subjects and ideals of the state. To put it in other words, the citizens should be taught to inculcate loyalty towards the constitution and principles of the state.

Of all the means that can be used for securing the stability of constitutions, the most effective, according to Aristotle, is a system of education suited to the existing order. In his opinion, as the end of the whole state is one it is imperative that the education also must necessarily be one and the same for all and that its superintendence must be public and not on private lines in the way in which each man superintends the education of his own children. "Neither must we suppose" says Aristotle "that any one of the citizens belongs to himself, for they all belong to the state, and are each of them a part of the state" (Book 8, Chapter 1). He has emphasised the value of education in the following words : "It is useless to have the most beneficial rules of society fully agreed upon by all members of the constitution, if individuals are not going to be trained and have their habits formed for that constitution."[1] It implies that people of democracy must learn the principles and values of democracy. So also of other types of constitutions. Aristotle's emphasis on education is worthy to be remembered. The spread of proper education is a vital factor of stability. It prevents disorder and chaos. Consciousness arises only through education.

Place of Aristotle

The political ideas and philosophy of Aristotle have tremendously influenced the thinkers and philosophers of subsequent periods. Polybius and Cicero may be mentioned in this connection. Polybius's teaching of the forms of government and their successive change originated from the theory of Plato and Aristotle and was instrumental in their popularisation of their views. Cicero held high regards for Aristotle and he shared most of his views on the advantages of mixed form of government. Cicero subscribed to Aristotle's teaching of the correspondence between the laws on the one hand and natural rights and rational principles on the other.

Influence of Aristotle is also to be found on Christian political thought. Church Fathers modified some of the doctrines of Aristotle. St. Augustine placed himself upon the footstep of Aristotle and made a difference between monarch and tyrant and insisted that the government would be limited by law. In the 13th century, *Politics* was translated into Latin and exercised the minds of many persons and Thomas Aquinas was one of them. Aristotle's conception of law, justice and form of government found place in the political ideas of Thomas Aquinas. He reproduces much of the six-fold classification of constitutions. Aristotle was highly respected by Aquinas.

1. Book V, Chapter 9.

Dante has very little respect for Aristotle. In spite of this, in his *De Monarchia* he used a number of Aristotelian arguments in support of his ideal of world monarchy. According to Dante, all the elements of state (family, association) as well as statehood in general come about in a natural way. On the whole, De Monarchia is greatly influenced by Politics. Marsiglio of Padua borrowed a number of Aristotle's political ideas for writing his *Defensor Pacis* (1324). Here the influence of *Politics* is unmistakable. The conception developed by Aristotle in *Politics* were thus used by Marsiglio under very different historical conditions as means for substantiating the doctrine of people's sovereignty anticipating in fact the social contract theory of Rousseau.

Politics continued to be the essential background of political philosophers such as Machiavelli, Jean Bodin and Richard Hooker. Influence of *Politics* upon Hobbes's *Leviathan* cannot be denied. In the thirties of the 19th century *Politics* was published by the Prussian Academy of Berlin and a serious study commenced. A great many thinkers of this century were considerably influenced by the ideas of Aristotle. *Politics* was translated in different European languages.

Machiavelli rejected Aristotle's conception of combination between ethics and politics, but accepted his secular idea of politics. Like Aristotle, he has laboriously investigated the causes of social unrest and revolution, changes of constitutions, sources and causes of strife and impact of all these upon the dynamic political life. The practical aspect of politics was not unknown to Aristotle. Needless to say, Machiavelli has followed the footsteps of the Greek philosopher. The difference is Machiavelli confined himself within Italy, whereas Aristotle's interest crossed the boundary of his own city-state.

The influence of Aristotle upon Jean Bodin is prominent. Bodin largely follows Aristotle in his analysis of natural and geographic factors, the specificity of state power as compared with other kinds of authority and the difference between monarchy and tyranny. Montesquieu also in this respect does not lag behind Bodin. He is indebted to Aristotle in respect of his analysis of the role of geographic and climatic factors, the forms of government and their principles. Following Aristotle, Montesquieu has also developed the concept of law.

So far as the origin of state is concerned, Aristotle and Rousseau are not similar. But the state on both occasions has become the manifestation of idealism and morality. Despotism has been severely castigated by both philosophers. The problem of relationship between the state as a whole (political organism) and its parts (individuals) has been treated by both almost in the same manner. The argument of Rousseau is not very much different from that of Aristotle so far as the relationship between the state and the individual is concerned. Like the Greek philosopher, Rousseau has not assigned any special status to the individual. Rousseau's general will is an indicator of the fact that the individual must surrender to the collective decision. There is a surprising similarity between the common good of Aristotle and that of Rousseau.

To Plato and Aristotle the state was an absolute end, ethically a complete whole. This concept has been borrowed by the German philosopher Hegel. The state, according to Hegel, is the highest embodiment of ethics and morality and these two of the individual cannot be separated. Plato, Aristotle, Rousseau and Hegel all have thought that for the attainment and enrichment of morality the individual must surrender to the state. None of them has recognised the separate existence of association within the ambit of state. Thus Rousseau and Hegel, following different paths and pursuing different aims, have revived and re-emphasised the ethical aspect of the political teachings of Plato and Aristotle which has been rejected by Machiavelli.

Even in the 20th century the interest in Aristotle has not declined at all. His *Politics* is still read by the serious students of all disciplines. The reason is the problems raised by Aristotle are of ethical and political and these problems still haunt us. In order to solve the problems he made certain recommendations. We are studying the problems because these are also our problems and also his recommendations. The world has progressed during the last twenty three centuries. But we have not yet been able to discover what is the best form of government. How can the stability of a constitution be achieved? We are not definitely thinking in setting up a ideal state, but we are aspiring for a well-administered state. We are on the threshhold of the twenty first century. Science and technology have placed enormous power at the disposal of man. But still there are different classes, class-antagonisms, bitter rivalry among the elites and competition among the political brokers.

By criticising Plato's theory of communism in family and property Aristotle has displayed a good deal of pragmatism. It is practically impossible to deny man's attachment to property and family. He is also perfectly correct when he says that by destroying private property and family life the unity of the state cannot be achieved. Today we fully understand the worth of his argument. The causes of revolution and particularly its remedies are really unique in many respects. Maxey asks—can modern political science prescribe any surer remedies than these to counteract the virus of revolution.

Plato and Aristotle Compared

Both Plato and Aristotle are the two great giants of Greek philosophy in general and Greek political thought in particular. For about twenty years he was the student of Plato's Academy which was deemed in those days as university. There is no doubt that he received first lessons about philosophy and other subjects from Plato. But Plato failed to make his disciple as his "shadow creature". Aristotle accepted many of the views of Plato, particularly Plato's concept of an ideal state. But he disagreed with Plato's theory of communism. Aristotle believed that unity of the state is necessary, but not at the cost of identity of individuals. It means that Aristotle approved private property, wife and children. By expressing this view Aristotle displayed a good deal of reality.

In a brief passage R. N. Berki has beautifully compared the two philosophers. He says "......the political philosophies of Plato and Aristotle are the original twin pillars of the whole subsequent edifice of western political thought. ......Plato is the literary genius, the impassioned advocate, the brilliant dialectician, his vision is clear. ......He is the archetype of the political idealist. Aristotle is the scientific genius, the patient debater and the undisputed master of logic, his philosophy is like a vast, unruffled pond compared to Plato's turbulent river. He is the father of political wisdom and political realism". (*The History of Political Thought* : A Short Introduction, pp. 57-59).

Plato has dealt with a number of concepts such as justice, ideal state, laws etc. But his main interest concentrated on the ideal state. We know Plato primarily as a philosopher and secondarily as a political thinker. But Aristotle's contribution to political philosophy is immense. He ranked politics as a master science. He is also regarded as the father of political science. Unfortunately we cannot attribute these adjectives to Plato.

Aristotle's contribution to western political thought is pervasive. While it is not the case of Plato. We remember Plato for his ideas on ideal state, justice and education. But we study Aristotle for his ideas on the origin and nature of state, revolution, classification of constitution, comparative politics, polity etc. Aristotle's *Politics* was textbook for undergraduate and post-graduate students of numerous English speaking universities. But Plato's *Republic* cannot claim this status.

R. N. Berki writes : "He and not Plato is regarded as the real founder of political philosophy by those—possibly the majority of thinkers and academics in our tradition—who accept the state, with the existing warts and blemishes" (p. 58). Aristotle has dealt with the most important aspects of political science. He is regarded as the founder of comparative politics. His theory of revolution is still regarded as unique. We study, with a good deal of interest, his classification of constitution.

Plato was a great philosopher no doubt, but his interest was very limited. On the other hand, there is hardly anything that failed to interest Aristotle. In fact, Aristotle's interest was pervasive. He dealt with all subjects beginning from poetry to midwifery. His interest about Zoology and Botany still surprises us.

Let us conclude that in political thought Aristotle is still very much alive in the 21st century, but Plato is not. Aristotle's influence is all the more remarkable as opposed to Plato.

4 POLITICAL IDEAS OF LATER GREECE AND ROME

Political Extinction of City-state

The great tradition of political ideas and philosophy built up by Plato and his predecessors and partially enriched by Aristotle ended with the death of Aristotle. This tradition centred around the city-state. The political idealism and institutions of which these two thinkers imagined and also thought to apply in practice were possible only in city-state. Although their ideals and philosophy had a universal appeal, because of the narrowness they could not survive. In Sabine's words the political philosophy of Plato and Aristotle could only be described as a *magnificent failure*. They thought that it might not be possible for the city-state to realise the ideals and on the basis of this suspicion they sometimes criticised the functioning of the city-state. Aristotle even went a setp further. The city-state to Aristotle was the haven of common good and higher form of civilisation. The recurrence of sedition or revolution made him very much anxious and that is why he had devoted a lot of pages to the analysis of the causes and preventives of revolution. The successors of Aristotle could not save the city-state as well as its ideals and philosophy.

Frankly speaking, the city-state meant something only for few persons who were at the helm of administration. The city-state was, by and large, elitist. Few persons were awarded citizenship. Handful of persons had the access to administration. Teeming masses were debarred form state authority. The city-state was meaningless to artisans, farmers and wage earners. So after the death of Aristotle the common people began to think something other than the city-state. They thought that it was not for their upliftment. So there was no necessity to make attempts for its improvements, it should be superseded. That is, a large number of people were determined to get rid of the tentacles of the city-state. Aristotle's death brought for them that opportunity. When the city-state had been relegated to history, the political values and idealism held and nurtured by Plato and Aristotle began to recede.

Common people refused to subscribe to the values, ideas, culture, ethics and morality of the city-state. Under changed circumstances they began to think everything differently. Plato and Aristotle thought a lot to make the city-state self-sufficient politically, militarily and economically. But in practice it never achieved that coveted position. There was no self-sufficiency in economics and politics. The policy of isolation stood on the way of attaining self-sufficiency. Political necessity of the new environment forced the people to establish relationship with other cities and nations. Federations with other cities and states were formed. The schools of Plato and Aristotle sank into insignificance.

Through the conquest of Alexander and the partition of his dominion among his successors, the constitutional city-state was entirely overwhelmed by the absolute military empire as the type of political organisation. Different races and cultures were amalgamated together. The city-states of Plato and Aristotle were completely eclipsed by the large empire. The old politics began to disappear swiftly. The conception of citizenship also changed. Individual was more than a citizen. Exchange of ideas and culture between different people emerged, individualism and cosmopalitanism began to live together.

The death (323 B. C.) of Alexander brought about chaos and turmoil in the political field. No change was stable. In the midst of the various and frequent changes as well as the instability in the arena of politics the military force came to control politics and administration of state. The expansion of empire and not the adherence to philosophy was the prime objective of the military rulers. The two centuries followed by the death of Alexander saw this disorder only. The old values and ideas had already disappeared, but nothing new grew. The military administration was not a congenial atmosphere for the emergence of new ideals. Nor was there any systematic political speculation. Military government also did not recognise any philosophy or idealism.

Epicurus and Epicureanism

We have briefly noted how after the death of Aristotle the midday sun of Greek philosophy declined and it has been termed by the scholars as the *twilight of city-state.* People began to show negative attitude towards the philosophy of Plato and Aristotle. The city-state was somehow able to maintain its physical existence, but its past glory no longer existed. It was busy with its own internal affairs. City-state and its philosophy were no longer the determining factors of people's behaviour attitude and morality. Some thinkers and scholars directed their thoughts and ideas to different channels. This may be regarded as a protest against the grand old philosophy of Plato and Aristotle. This is the characteristic feature of all the scholars in the later Greek period. Under the leadership of Epicurus a school was formed. There were other schools such as Cynics and Stoics.

Epicurus (341-270 BC) was born in the period of political disintigration of Greece. Almost all the city-states lost their political freedom and came under the tutelage of Macedon. In the middle of the second century B. C. Macedon itself fell a prey to Rome and became a part of the vast Roman empire. Rise of Epicurus is the characteristic feature of this period. He was born in a well-to-do family. He left his native island and visited several Hellenic cities and finally settled in Athens. The philosophy of Epicurus is to be found in his famous work *De Rerum Natura (On the Nature of Things).*

The purpose of Epicureanism, observes Sabine, was, in general terms, the same as that of all the ethical philosophy of the period after Aristotle, namely, to produce in its students a state of individual self-sufficiency. To this end it taught that a good life consists in the enjoyment of pleasure, but it interpreted this negatively. Happiness consists actually in the avoidance of all pain, worry and anxiety. Epicureanism is thus a strong denial of common good philosophy enunciated by Plato and Aristotle. Man's desire for pleasure and avoidance of pain is his primary aim. Epicurus has said that every individual first thinks of himself and then of others. He believed in the gods, but did not think that they interfered with the day to day activities of man. Epicureanism has vehemently criticised all superstitions. In a word, materialism is the foundation of Epicureanism.

Political Ideas of Epicurus

Epicurus has said that the chief aim of the state administration and political community is to provide safety and security to all its citizens and also to create an atmosphere where there shall be no fear. According to Epicurus, man is by nature selfish and this selfishness drives him to be involved in conflict with others. This creates insecurity and, therefore, any political organisation must first of all ensure security. Trouble-makers shall be removed from society.

The individuals of Epicurus have entered into agreement among themselves in order to make the society trouble-free. In other words, the aims and purposes as well as the essence of the political community arise out of the agreement. The laws of the state are the result of the agreement. The agreement is about their mutual advantage to restrain men from harming one another and save them from being harmed. As a result of the contract the rights and privileges of the citizens are established and justice is achieved. Intolerance is restrained by invoking law and safety ensured by the authority with the help of law.

In order to attain freedom a man must be conscious of his own needs and necessity. Man should never be slave of necessity. An essential nature of freedom is man's ability to control passions and the desire to get unnatural things. Man should try to be satisfied. The desire to get unnecessary commodities and requirements makes him unhappy and ultimately this creates chaos in society. Acquisitive nature is the chief source of disorder. Everyone should try to be self-sufficient and this is the precondition of freedom. Another aspect of Epicurean concept of freedom is man's independence from society. In any society there are political controversies, intrigues and rivalries. All these curtail man's freedom. Man must keep himself away from these.

Epicurus has analysed the political and legal problems in the background of materialism. To him the notions of justice are secondary and practical needs of people's dealings with one another and the bases of social intercourse are primary. The origin and development of social and political institutions have been viewed by Epicurus from materialist standpoint. All these institutions as well as arts, culture and sciences are human creations, other worldly intervention has been ruled out by Epicurus. The behaviour and activities of all living beings are the consequences of physical causes. Man's urge to adapt to the physical environment led him to form social organisation and to develop civilization. Inability of primitive people to solve the natural phenomena led them to discover the existence of God and influence of supernatural elements. But dawn of consciousness resulting from the change of physical environment lessened the superstitious mentality and behaviour. According to Epicurus the notion of justice as well as their change are the products of changing social needs of mankind.

Berki[1] makes the following observation, "In truth, Epicureanism was apolitical or non-political but not anti-political; it did not, in other words, contain anything resembling modern democratic values, let alone socialism and anarchism. Democratic political philosophy was wholly absent from classical political thought". Epicurus always held negative view about democracy and he dissociated himself from the common people or mob. He once said—"I was never anxious to please the mob. For what pleased them I did not know and what I did know was far removed from their comprehension."

STOICS

Origin and Meaning of Stoics

The most representative and influential philosophical school of the five centuries from about 300 B. C. to A. D. 200 was Stoicism, and the founder of this school was Zeno (336-264 BC). Zeno settled in Athens and opened a school to deliver lectures on philosophy and related subjects. The term Stoics is derived from *Stoa poikile* the meaning of which is "painted porch" adorned with frescoes. Zeno was a native of Cyprus and most of the members of the Stoic School were non-Greeks and two of the reprersentative figures were slaves.

The history of Stoicism is divided into three periods. Early Stoicism, Middle Stoicism and Late or Roman Stoicism. Zeno was the leader of early Stoicism. Middle Stoicism was represented by Panaetius. The most important figurers of the Roman Stoicism were Epictetus and Aurelius. The Stoic philosophers did not discuss the political matters directly and they never tried to build up consistent theories of state or political science like Plato and Aristotle. The philosophy propagated by the Stoics can be divided into Logic, Physics and Ethics. Analysis of political issues contained all these three subjects. In this connection it may also be noted that Stoicism cannot be regarded as a theory of state. In spite of this the Stoic philosophers exercised considerable influence upon the functioning of the government, because many kings and officials of Hellenistic and Roman periods were professing Stoics. However, they were not interested in the application of Stoic philosophy.

The Stoic philosophers in their physical theory posited two principles in the universe—the active and the passive principles. The passive principle is a substance without quality that is matter, whereas the active is the reason inherent in this substance, that is God. In the ethical and political philosophy of Stoics we find the notion of cosmos. The cosmos is god who is the creater of the whole universe or nature. So both heaven and earth are assimilated or combined in the cosmos. Hence the cosmos is a totality and gods and men are the integral parts of the cosmos.

Political Philosophy of Stoics

The nature, that is the whole cosmos, constitutes the central theme of Stoic philosophy including political philosophy. Nature is pervaded by goal and purpose and to live according to nature means to work with it towards the harmony and orderliness that is inherent in it. Only one principle governs all things. Everything is with nature and nothing happens against nature. Nature determines all happen-

1. *The History of Political Thought*, p. 71.

ings in the world. Like nature, human beings are also subject to an all-pervading harmonious and rational ordering. Man and nature are not opposites. Both are parts of reason and harmony. Stoic view of morality presents the following notion. Man must act according to reason, that is, according to the principle of nature. The conduct and behaviour of man are determined by the law of the universe and all other creatures are subject to the same law.

If man learns to guide his life by reason or rationality and everyone follows the same principle a harmonious relationship among all men is established. Reason dictates that man should pursue virtue and should not be guided by narrow self-interests. In this way, a unity is set up in the civil society. Civil society, according to the Stoics, is based on the natural bonds of men, their natural attraction to one another. The state is a natural coalescence and not an artificial formation based upon contract. Gregarious nature of man led to the foundation of human society.

In the Stoic form of political ideas we find a peculiar position of man. He is regarded by the Stoic thinkers as a part of single group or "herd". That is, one man is indistinguishable from another. Property, race or rank cannot make any distinction among different individuals. Since all men are same, there cannot be separate law or principle. This is no doubt a utopian thought. But in the utopian way the Stoics have built up a theory of concord. By abolishing all distinctions, the stoics wanted to set up a united and unified human society.

At the head of the civil society or state there is a king who possesses absolute power and his absolute authority is bestowed by God. The king is not only the head of the state, he is practically identical with it. The Stoics further have held that the kingship is the only cohesive force in the state. A true king is divine and he brings harmony in his kingdom. The order of the king is law and to defy his law is to defy God and to go against nature and disturb the harmony. The Stoics further held that the defiance of king is tantamount to immorality. The king as representative of God reprersents morality, ethics and religion. Thus, a king is the spokesman of earthly and heavenly matters.

The idealisation and deification of kingship created a notion of world city and some of the Stoic philosophers propagated it. This comes from the fact that the Stoic philosophers did not give any importance to the various differences between the nations or cities. All were the parts of the universe and were subject to the same laws of nature. The main feature of the world state is it is ruled or guided by the dictum of God and there cannot be any scope of separate opinion or conduct. Gods and men are the denizens of the world-state. The right reason prevails upon them all. The right reason is just and standard and one cannot change it whimsically. A Stoic philósopher has made the following comment :

"Law is the ruler over all acts both of gods and men. It must be the director and governor and the guide in respect to what is honourable and base and hence the standard of what is just and unjust. For all beings that are social by nature the law directs what must be done and forbids what must not be done"[1]

On the one hand Stoicism abolished the differences among the individuals and on the other hand established the harmony between the states. Let us quote Sabine—"If Stoicism diminished the importance of social distinctions between individuals, it tended also to promote harmony between states. *There are for everyman two sets*

1. Quoted by Sabine, p. 150.

law—the law of his city and the law of the world-city; the law of custom and the law of reason. Of the two the second must have the authority and must provide a form to which the statutes and customs of the cities should conform. Customs are various but reason is one...Stoicism tended to conceive a worldwide system of law having endless local branches." Stoic philosophers admitted that there might be differences, but all these must be ignored. Reason and principle of nature must always be given priority. If differences were recognised, fissiparous tendencies would develop which would be harmful for a harmonious society.

By laying great emphasis upon natural law, reason, and world-state the Stoic philosophers threw individuals into most insignificance and obscurity. The universality and all-embracing character of natural law rules out the possibility of all disputes. People are dumb creatures and they obey the law ungrudgingly. If this is reason of nature, we must say that it is absolutely unreasonable. Men cannot be beasts. Nature may have a reason, but people have their own reason. To follow reason and nature blindly is not ethics and justice. But to force a man to follow this or do that is, in our view, unethical and unjust.

The Stoic thinkers contemplated of community of property, wives and other things in order to ensure harmony. Plato thought in this line and he was vehemently criticised by Aristotle. The Stoic criticism of political, social and cultural institutions is also unjustfied. The various institutions play very important role in the development of human personality. The individual cannot be asked to sacrifice himself at the altar of the state. The Stoics also imagined of the world-city where the separate states would not have any importance at all. A recent critic has made the following comment—

"This cynic fervour of Stoicism, directed against cultural progress, enlightenment and being essentially conservative and even reactionary was graphic evidence of the crisis of contemporary slave-owning society and its values."[1]

Stoic philosophers' advocacy of absolute monarchy and world-state is precursor to dictatorship and imperialism. The Stoic philosophy is the most important root of Divine Right Theory. The church in the Middle Ages received inspiration from the Stoic ideas of the divinity of kingship. The idea of divinity made the emperors of various European states not only autocrat but also cruel and heartless rulers. Roman emperors were also inspired by the doctrine of one world, one reason and one law. This left behind many a pernicious effect. Democratic values and principles found no place in the lexicography of Stoic philosophers. Plato and Aristotle were not worshippers of democracy. But the worth of the individual was recognised by their philosophy.

It is not correct to hold that every aspect of Stoic philosophy is to be condemned. Ebenstein observes that the Stoic philosophy of secular law is the foundation of modern legal system both national and international. This Stoics conceived of a world-city. To day the protagonists of internationalism are thinking of a world government, although it is yet to be achieved. The philosophy of French Revolution—liberty, equality and fraternity is the truncated form of universal brotherhood propagated by Stoics. The Stoic idea of a "law above law" has become the fundamental principle of the American constitutional system.

---

1. V. S. Nersesyants—*Political Thought of Ancient Greece*, p. 187.

Transition from Stoicism to Roman Political Ideas

Notwithstanding the fact that *Greece was the birthplace of Stoicism, it found Rome as a fertile field for its development.* The 19th century historian, Mommsen, has said that Stoic philosophy perfectly filled the Roman character. The same view has been shared by many other historians and political scientists. Berki says "Success of Stoicism was due to its being an appropriate kind of philosophy for an expanding and ambitious imperial power which Rome became in the last century before the demise of the Republic."[1] Records of history reveal that Romans were practical-minded people. They had very little respect for philosophy, idealism and ethics etc. But the Stoic doctrine of *one world* had enamoured them and they accepted it without any hesitation.

Guided by the philosophy of one world, and by applying it to practice, Rome became the most powerful imperial state in Europe and for the administration of the vast empire the Romans built up a comprehensive legal system based on stoic concept of law. Stoic concepts of international law, national law and natural law found its application in the Roman philosophical idea.

Sabine[2] has said that *Stoicism in its original form has lost much of its rigour and enchantment,* but the central idea appealed to the educated people. They were not concerned with the technicalities and subtleties of Stoic philosophy. Here lay the success of Stoic philosophy. *The educated Romans were heavily inclined to some of the aspects of Stoicism.* No other Greek system was so well-qualified as Stoicism to appeal to the native virtues of self-control, devotion to duty and public spirit in which the Romans took special pride, and no political conception was so well-qualified as the Stoic world-state to introduce some measures of idealism into to too sordid business of Roman conquest.'[3]

From the above analysis it is now obvious that *three aspects of Stoic philosophy created a lasting impact upon the Romans. Theory of law with its three branches, devotion to duty and unconditional allegiance to the state sovereignty and, finally, the idea of world-state. In fact these three things constitute the kernel of Roman political thought.* The conception of the unity of mankind imbued the Roman rulers so much that by conquering the states and kingdoms they wanted to set up a unified empire and to remove all sorts of barriers such as race, sex and nationality. The Roman emperors with the help of military power translated the Stoic doctrines into reality. It is to be mentioned that only the practical necessity and love for expansionism drove them to action. Dunning (p. 106) has observed that in the constructive work of *Republic* Stoicism played no part. Its doctrine found home only in the spirit of men like Cato the Younger, Cicero and Brutus, whose ideas were as impotent in the presence of Caesar as Aristotle's had been in the presence of Alexander. But in the social adjustment during the stable days of the principle, Stoic doctrines exercised a positive and far-reaching influence.[4]

Expansion of Roman empire needed an intellectual justification and this was provided by Stoic cosmopolitanism and the belief in the basic human equality. To put it in other words, Roman conquerers wanted to conceal their real motive that

---

1. Berki—op. cit., p. 73.
2. Sabine—op. cit., p. 152.
3. Sabine—op. cit., p. 153.
4. Dunning—*History of Political Theories : Ancient and Mediaeval,* p. 106.

is expansionism by propagating the philosophy of cosmopolitanism and unity of mankind. The imperialist powers have always resorted to the same technique. Hitler used the philosophy of Hegel. British imperialism preached the doctrine of white man's burden. In fine, Stoic philosophy found a home in Rome and Roman empire and Roman political thought may be regarded as its direct descendant.

POLYBIUS (204-122 B.C.)

Introduction

For several centuries the civilisation and intellectual development of Greek city-state dominated the entire Greece and other territories surrounding it. But the tempo of this could not be maintained when Greece was occupied by Macedon. Political domination eclipsed the intellectual progress. Then came another phase of political upheaval. Macedon was subjugated by Rome. The scholars and philosophers of Greece got panicky and in the face of new political domination of Rome they wanted to maintain utmost neutrality, but with no success. Many distinguished scholars and statesmen were captured by the Roman soldiers and were deported to Rome as political prisoners.

Among the deported was Polybius, a prominent Greek historian and statesman. He was born in Megalopolis which was a member of Achaean League and when League was subjugated by Rome Megalopolis was reduced to a Roman colony. Although Polybius, when deported to Rome, was a youngman, he attracted many top ranking officials and persons of Rome and the cause of attraction was his vast knowledge in various fields. Personal friendship with top political figures was established and this was utilised by Polybius for the independence of Greek polises.

Polybius on Classification of Constitution

The political theory of Polybius is to be found in *The Histories* (or *The History of Rome)* consisting of forty books, especially Book No 6. Of the forty books, only five are intact and the other thirty-five books are found in fragments. He has classified the constitutions or governments on the line set forty by Plato and Aristotle. Polybius has said that normally governments are divided into kingship, aristocracy and democracy. Buy these three forms, in Polybius's opinion, are not final and satisfactory. Other varieties are also found in it some states.

Polybius observes : "We should therefore assert that there are six kinds of governments, the three above-mentioned and the three which are naturally allied to them. I mean monarchy, oligarchy and mob rule." Therefore three sets and six kinds of government of Polybius are kingship and monarchy; aristocracy and oligarchy; finally democracy and mob rule. The growth of monarchy is natural and unaided. Kingship is a derivative of monarchy. So according to Polybius the primary form of government is monarchy. It is based on force. Several people assembling at a particular place expressed their will in favour of a strong man to rule them and they established monarchy.

Tyranny is the offshoot of monarchy. When the king defies justice and morality he becomes a tyrant. The abolition of both monarchy and tyranny clears the way for the emergency of aristocracy. This, by its very nature, degenerates into oligarchy. When the commons inflamed by anger take vengeance on this government for its unjust rule, democracy comes into being. In due course the license and lawlessness of this form of government produces mob rule.

Polybius, on the basis of his personal experience, observes that a particular form of government is not permanent or stable. For example, when democracy exceeds its limits through violence and excesses, it gives birth to a new despot who rules the community by force. The cycle of the series starts here. Each of the three primary forms of government thus contains within itself the germs of its decay and ruin.

Causes of Political Change

We have just now pointed out that one form of government is changed into other. It is now our task to investigate the causes of change. Polybius is of opinion that the original and in fact the natural form of government is kingship. Kingship is hereditary. Rivalry among the members of the royal family is a general feature of many city-states. Hatred and resentment lead one to revolt against the king and ultimately he captures power. Polybius has said that mode of living, luxury, unscrupulous behaviour and deprivation of power on the part of some members of royal family are the important causes of rivalry. However, the kingship is changed into tyranny. When there were several aspirants of the throne, competition among them was a reality which finally led to fighting among the aspirants. But it is to be remembered that the conspirators are not ordinary persons of the royal family, they are members of royal family or holders of high position.

Polybius has drawn our attention to the several causes of political change. Some rulers aggravate the situation through their unscrupulous behaviour, money-making mentality, extravagance and indulgence in wine. When power is confined in the hands of few persons, common people express resentment on the ground that freedom and equality are abused. Everyone must have free access to power and authority. Democratic right should not be limited only to few persons. This is the demand of the mob. Gross economic inequality, exclusion from honour and office, resort to violence on flimsy grounds and injustice perpetrated upon the people are the causes of the change of government. Needless to say, these are the causes of revolution which Aristotle stated long before Polybius. In the words of Polybius—such is the cycle of political revolution, the course appointed by nature in which constitutions change, disappear and finally return to the point from which they started.

Advantages of Mixed Constitution

To get rid of the changes or transformations of governments Polybius has suggested that a combination of all various forms of governments is needed. It is essential that the best elements of all governments are to be combined together and that is why in Polybius we find an elaborate arrangement of combination which was also introduced for checks and balances. By combination Polybius has said that three different forms of government will cooperate as well as they will counteract.

First of all let us consider consuls. The consul is vested with absolute authority necessary for carrying out his purpose but in fact he requires the support of the people and senate and is not able to bring his operations to a conclusion without them. The senate also controls the supply of food, clothing, other necessary materials and money. So the consul must depend on the senate for the fulfilment of his military objectives and ambitions. The senate also determines whether or not he shall retain command at the expiration of his term of office. In fact, theoretically, consul has absolute power like absolute monarch, but in practice senate checks him.

The senate is like an aristocracy and two forms of governments are combined together. Again, men are indispensable for the consuls to conciliate them. There must be consent of the people behind the activities and celebration of the consul.

The senate, it now appears, has vast administrative, financial and supervisory powers. But the popular assemblies through the acts can restrict the powers and activities of the senate. It cannot carry out enquiries into the most grave and important offences against the state unless the *senatus consultum* is confirmed by the people. So, the people's assemblies exercise ultimate authority. Again, whether the power of the senate can be curtailed or expanded does not depend upon itself. Only the popular assemblies can do it. In this form of mixed constitution we find a combination of aristocracy and democracy.

Finally, assemblies are subject to a restraint on their activity. The assemblies must respect the members of the senate. In Italy, all the contracts and repairing works of public buildings are fully controlled by senate. But people's financial interests are related with these. In all these matters the senate is supreme. It can grant extension of time, it can relieve the contractor if any accident occurs. There are, in fact, many ways in which the senate can either benefit or injure those who manage public property. From the senators are drawn the juries in most lawsuits. As a result, the citizens are at the mercy of senate. Similarly, everyone is reluctant to oppose the projects of the consuls as all are generally and individually under the authority when in the field.

Evaluation

Polybius had initiated an elaborate system of the famous doctrine of checks and balances which was later on adopted by the great architects of American constitution. "While the writings of Plato and Aristotle contained some conception of the value of this principle (checks and balances), the Greek writers preferred a simple form of government, somewhat modified by traces of the other types. Polybius was the first writer to make a clear statement of the advantages of a mixed form of government and of the principles of checks and balances in constitutional organisation. These conceptions were recognised in theory and practice in later periods, and in a slightly changed form remain valid in modern political thought."[1] Whether a mixed form of government is the guarantor of the political stability or not is a separate issue. But stability of any political system is essential and that was conceived by Polybius with great farsightedness and acumen more than two thousand years ago. Again, only checks and balances can ensure stability—this we can easily take for granted. This we find in the writings of Polybius.

CICERO (106-43 B.C.)

Introduction

During the last century of Roman Republic there was severe political agitation and tension. The Roman empire was vast and although the emperors brought the empire under strict administration, dissatisfaction among all people belonging to all sections of society increased beyond all proportions and that this went out of the control of Roman emperors was mainly due to the fact that there were no economic

[1] *History of Political Thought*, Gettell, p. 84.

reforms and this created a clear division of society into two great classes—wealthy nobles and pauperised commons which resembled the patricians and plebians of the old days. These two antagonistic classes were at loggerheads. The senate and assemblies were not free from conflicts. Both the organs somehow managed in sending their representatives. Under such turbulent situation any political speculation was not possible. During this time an enduring political influence was exercised by Cicero. Characteristically, Cicero was not a philosopher of the stature of Plato and Aristotle, nor was he a leader or any philosophical school.

He studied law in Rome and philosophy in Athens. He also visited other Greek centres of learning. He owed his philosophical learning and outlook to Plato and Aristotle and these two philosophers exerted profound influence upon Cicero's thought system. Two main works of Cicero are worthy to be noted—*Republic* and *Laws*. Needless to say, these titles were borrowed by Cicero from Plato. But the superficial resemblance is misleading. The inner meaning of Cicero's work creates a difference. While Plato and Aristotle roamed in the imaginary world, Cicero came down to the real world. Cicero contemplated of a world-city and of Roman empire, Plato and Aristotle limited their thought within the four walls of city-state. Although he thought of a world-city he did not rule out self-governemt and liberty. All the constituent parts of the empire would be given the right to govern themselves so that they could develop their own culture and exercise freedom.

Justice and common good are the *summum bonum* of the ideal state. Only the philosopher king, according to Plato, could ensure these two objectives through his sacrifice. Cicero, on the other hand, does not touch these philosophic concepts. He was a practising lawyer, an experienced administrator and the fighting statesman. He had conceived of state only in terms of law, The "state is a community of law"—the briefest definition given by Cicero. The rule of law was very important to him. Cicero has thought that law is the basis of civilised life. Cicero emphasises love as the mighty social bond and he regards God as the fountain of love and affection. Cicero's idea about christianity has exercised profound influence upon the Church Fathers.

Cicero and Natural Law

The body of Cicero's political philosophy is composed of three related elements—a belief in natural law, natural equality and the state as natural to man. "Cicero's true importance in the history of political thought lies in the fact that he gave to the Stoic doctrine of natural law a statement in which it was universally known throughout Western Europe from his own day down to the nineteenth century."[1] He has combined the Platonic principles of right and justice as eternal and Stoic principle supremacy and universality of law as it exists in nature. The universal law of nature binds all men together. The natural law is unchangeable and it is to be found in all peoples and in all nations. This universality of natural law constitutes the foundation of world-city. Since law of nature is supreme, none can violate it.

In Cicero's words—True law is right reason in agreement with nature. In his opinion nature is the highest manifestation of right reason. It is universal application, unchanging and everlasting; it summons to duty by its commands and averts from wrong doing by its prohibitions. Its commands and prohibitions always

1. Sabine—op. cit., p. 163.

influence good men, but are without effect upon the bad. It is a sin to try to alter this law, nor is it allowable to attempt to repeal any part of it, and it is impossible to abolish it entirely. We cannot be free from its obligations by senate or people. There will not be different laws at Rome and at Athens, or different laws now and in the future, and unchangeable law will be valid for all nations and all times."

Cicero has brought the concept of abstract reason and natural law into immediate relation with the activity of human reason and legislation of the state. If human legislation is in conformity with reason it cannot be in inconformity with nature. It implies that, according to Cicero, human legislation violating law of nature must be declared invalid. When everyone shows obligation to the law of nature, there is to be justice in the state. That is, violation of natural law is violation of justice. Commenting on Cicero's idea of natural law, Gettell has said that his commentary on natural law has become a classic because of the clarity with which he was able to express himself.

Concept of Natural Equality

Cicero's concept of equality is another aspect of his political philosophy. Men are born for justice and that right is based not upon man's opinion but upon nature. There is no difference between man and man in kind in the eye of natural law, all men are equal. So far as the learning and holding of property are concerned there is, no doubt, difference between man and man. But in the possession of reason, in their psychological make-up and in their attitude towards good and bad, men are all equal. Man is born to get justice and in this regard no difference between men should be drawn. All men and races of men possess the same capacity for experience and for the same kinds of experience, and all are equally capable of discriminating between right and wrong.

Commenting on Cicero's view on natural equality, Carlyle has said that no change in political theory is so startling in its completeness as the change from Aristotle to the notion of natural equality. Aristotle also thought of equality among the citizens. But he was not prepared to award citizenship to all people. It was confined only to selected number of persons. So Aristotle's idea of equality was not all-embracing. Only few were equal among themselves. *Cicero has viewed equality in moral perspective.* All men are created by God and they are born for justice. So man-made discrimination is not only unjust but also immoral. It is the duty of every political society to ensure certain amount of dignity to every individual. Cicero has refused the time-old idea of slavery. Slaves are neither tool nor property, they are human beings. So they have the right to just treatment and independent personality.

Idea of State

The purpose of Cicero in *Republic* is to set forth a conception of an ideal state as Plato had done in his *Republic*. He has not made any attempt to conceal his indebtedness to Plato. He has adopted the same technique of dialogue. But Cicero's state is not an imaginary organisation. It is confined to Roman state and he has cited illustrations from the history of Rome.

A Commonwealth is the property of a people.[1] But a people is not any collection of human beings brought together in any sort of way, but an assemblage of people

1. *Res publica* or public thing or property is the same as *res populi* or thing of a people.

in large numbers associated in an agreement with respect to justice and a partnership for the common good. The first cause of such and association is not so much the weakness of the individual as a certain social spirit which nature has implanted in him. For man is not a solitary or unsocial creature, but born with such a nature that not even under conditions of great prosperity of every sort is he willing to be isolated from his fellowmen.

The above observation reveals certain features of Cicero's idea of state. Cicero has designated the nature of the state as the affair or thing or property of the people. This term is quite equivalent to Commonwealth and Cicero has used this. In Cicero's view, the state as Commonwealth is for ethical purposes and if it fails to achieve this mission it is nothing. The state is based on agreement to share common good. Another feature of Cicero's state is people have assembled together not guided by their weakness but by their sociable nature. Man is not a solitary animal. He loves and likes to habit with man. This is the inborn nature of man. It is the rational behaviour of men which is responsible for the foundation of state. Hence we may call it a necessary association. It is useful for achieving common good. Cicero has said there is nothing in which human excellence can more nearly approximate the divine than in the foundation of new states or in the preservation of states already founded. The desire to share common good is so much ardent that people have overcome all enticements to pleasure and comfort. "Cicero thus formulates a vision which is thoroughly political at the same time." His idea of state and citizenship is in striking resemblance with that of Plato and Aristotle.

Sabine has called Cicero's state a *corporate body*. Naturally, all its members will look after the advantages and disadvantages of each other. Since the state is a corporate body its authority is collective and it is derived from the people. When the political power is properly and legally executed it will be regarded as the power of the people. That is, it is corporate power. Finally, the state and its law both are subject to God. In Cicero's theory of state force does not occupy a very important place. Only for the sake of justice and right force can be used.

Like Polybius, Cicero has suggested three types of government—royalty, aristocracy and democracy. But in each form of government there is the germ of corruption and instability and this leads to the fall of government. Only a mixed form of government is the proper guarantee of stability and corruption-free society. Cicero preferred a republican form of government as the perfect example of checks and balances for the stability and good of the political system. In the opinion of Dunning, although Cicero followed Polybius in the theory of checks and balances, it would be wrong to assume that he did not possess any originality of thought. Cicero's mixed form of government is less mechanical. "There can be no doubt that in the border region where ethics, jurisprudence and politics meet, Cicero performed a work which gives him an important place in the history of political theory."[1]

NATURE OF ROMAN POLITICAL THOUGHT

There is a controversy about the contribution of Romans to political theory. Most of the scholars on this field generally agree that the Romans cannot be credited with any spectacular contribution to political thought. For example, Dunning says—the

1. Dunning. Vol. 1, p. 122.

contribution of Rome to the literature of political theory was very slight. Other thinkers say that the Romans were so much busy with building up a strong and powerful empire and with its administration that they got little time for building up theoretical analysis. But this is not the view of all thinkers. Ebenstein is of opinion that it is wrong to say that Roman political thought does not exist at all. It is true that the professional thinkers and publicists have not systematically analysed various aspects of political theory and expressed them in formal treatises as Plato and Aristotle had done.

It is true that we do not find a single philosopher in Rome in the rank of Plato or Aristotle. Naturally, Rome cannot boast of any clear and systematic political theory. But the absence of any systematic political theory does not imply the absence of political thought, and it is not surprising that Rome was really fortunate in having very rich sources of political thought. Legal, administrative and governmental system of Rome can be regarded as fertile sources of political thought.

Romans cannot be singularly blamed for their failure to contribute liberally and scholarly to the development of political thought. Only Britain and France can claim substantial credit in this field. The American political thought has been enriched not by philosophers or first grade theoreticians, but by renowned judges of the Supreme Court. Besides Plato and Aristotle, only Hobbes, Locke, Rousseau, Hegel and Marx have built up independent theoretical works. Even Rousseau and Hegel are to a considerable extent indebted to Plato for their idealism and dialectic. Marx expresses his indebtedness to Hegel and his other predecessors including Utopian socialists. This does not imply that the intellectual world of the West during the last twenty centuries was quite barren. Political thought of each country keeps conformity with the socio-economic-political milieu. This individualist progress sometimes has made slight aberrations from the main stream, but this does not mean an absence of contribution.

In the light of above analysis we can state *some salient features of Roman political thought*. Plato and Aristotle thought of an ideal state which was far away from real world. Polybius and Cicero, two Roman thinkers, although thought of the world-state, analysed the nature of state in the light of the extant Roman state. They did not try to idealise the state. The Romans had no intention to deify the state. State, to them, was a political organisation and its purpose was to fulfil certain definite purpose. The state to them was not an object of heaven, but an institution of the mortal world. This idea of Romans about the state is unique. In fact the Romans completely changed the Greek conception of state and introduced a new one which is modern.

The credit of completing the separation between ethics and politics should definitely to go the Roman thinkers. The Greek philosophers had put a garb of ethics and morality upon politics and made it an abstract concept. To them, the state was the highest manifestation of ethics and its purpose was to enrich the ethical and moral values of individuals. As a result of this, politics, in the hands of the Greek philosophers, failed to establish its separate identity. On ethical and moral consideration the Greek philosophers demanded unconditional allegiance from the citizens. Roman thinkers supported the allegiance to the universality of law of nature and this was based on practical ground. Law and legal system to them were of primary importance. Wisdom and goodness were private affairs. This is no doubt a realistic approach to politics.

Greek philosophy made no attempt to draw a distinction between individual and the state. This has been reversed by the Roman thinkers. The Romans have separated the individuals from the state and have also expounded the eternal democratic principle that they have certain rights and duties. The state is a legal institution and the individuals are its legal units. Their rights are to be protected from illegal encroachments. The citizens also discharge their duties towards the state. Romans have enacted laws to implement this idea. Once the rights are recognised the powers of the state automatically come to be limited. Insertion of duties along with rights is a clear indication of the fact that rights are not absolute. So far as the exercise of rights and enjoyment or privileges are concerned. Romans have made spectacular advance over their predecessors. For two centuries Rome was divided into two great classes—Patricians and Plebians—and there was continuous conflict between these two classes. Ultimately, these two classes combined together and they made a composite body of citizens. The Plebians began to enjoy civil rights.

Theory of checks and balances is another contribution of Roman political thought. The consul, the senate and the popular assemblies were placed against each other, and there was no scope for any organ to go the autocratic way. Polybius thought that in every form of government there was the germ of disentegration and corruption. Roman thinkers were very much obssessed with the expansion and retention of their empire and that is why the question of stability occupied their mind.

Law and administration are the two great contributions of Rome to the conceptions and practices of government and politics of the western world. The Roman law constantly adapting itself to changing environments, is still the law of a goodly portion of the globe.[1] For the administration of a vast empire a clear and well defined legal system was necessary and they devised that. Again, they did not neglect the implementation of law. The building up of the legal system and the attempt to make it responsive to the needs of the empire reveal the Roman people's love for realism.

Roman political thought is characterised by the conglomerate of absolutism, divine right theory and people's authority. Sometimes kings declared themselves as the representatives of God and resorted to absolute power. But because of the predominance and universality of the land of nature the divinity of the kingship could not get any opportunity to last long. Moreover, people had also power to exercise checks upon the authority. The state to the Romans was a corporate body and affairs of the people. Emperors were said to receive their authority from the citizens and were considered to be responsible to them.

The Romans did not believe in the contract as an instrument of establishing civil society. But they accepted another form of contract. Ulpian was a famous jurist of Rome. He said—The will of the emperor has the force of law, because by the passage of the *lex regia* the people transfers to him and vests in him all its own power and authority. This is a beautiful mixture of people's power and king's power. Carlyle observes "few phrases are more remarkable than this almost paradoxical description of an unlimited personal authority founded upon a purely democratic basis. The emperor's will is law, but only because people choose to have it so."[2] This transfer

1. Ebenstein—*Great Political Thinkers*, p. 121.
2. Quoted by Gettell, p. 79.

of power was in the form of contract. Romans delegated their power to the officials and the latter had full freedom to exercise power within the legal system. This was nothing but a contract with the government.

Not only in the delegation of power, but also in other fields, Romans followed the principle of contract. Contract in Rome was a potential source of law. New laws were the result of contract between the magistrates and the popular assemblies. Law was never the command of sovereign power upon his subjects. Religious functions and faiths were also the results of agreement. The worshipper agreed to perform certain ceremonial duties to gods in exchange of certain expected benefits from them. In Rome there were various private laws dealing with the private affairs. The Romans entered into understanding among themselves as regards their own private affairs.

We have already noted that the Romans were practical-minded people. Roman citizens were bound to obey the law not because of its ethical or moral content, but because of the fact that is was the command of the supreme political authority. Similarly, Roman theory of rights had a practical basis. Rights were not the Gifts of God or not based on religion and ethics. Every aspect of Roman political idea had a practical foundation. Hence secularisation and practicalisation of politics may be regarded as chief feature of Roman political thought.

Although in many respects Roman political thought differs from the Greek political thought, yet the influence of the latter upon the former does escape our attention. Polybius's classification of government and his formula of mixed form of government as an instrument of stability are drawn from Plato and Aristotle. Cicero's two works—*Republic* and *Laws*—are the obvious references to Plato's works. Neither Greek philosophers nor Roman thinkers had any preference for revolution. Common good and attainment of general welfare had important bearing upon Roman political thought. Needless to say that these are important aspects of Greek political thought. There is a fine continuity between the ralitical thought of Greek city-state and Roman political ideas.

ROMAN POLITICAL IDEAS

It is a fact that Rome failed to produce a philosopher in the rank of Plato and Aristotle, but this should not be taken as the single criterion of judging whether the Romans had any articulated political theory. Sabine aptly observes—"The fact that their interest in political theory was desultory and unsystematic does not mean that what they had to say was unimportant" (p. 168). The chief contribution of Romans lies in their articulated and systematic treatment of law and from this emerges various other concepts which are treated as important aspects of political science in general and political theory in particular. Let us again quote Sabine : "In the end the Roman law became one of the greatest intellectual forces in the history of European civilisation, because it provided principles and categories in terms of which men thought about all sorts of subjects and not least about politics" (p. 168).

Roman Theory of Law

The earliest Roman legal system was based on religious regulations, customs and conventions about justice. In those days the divine authority was also recognised.

Offenders were punished in the name of religion and by religious laws. The early Romans had very little concept about manmade or positive laws.

But this approach to law could not fulfil the requirements of society and rulers, because religious laws could not serve the purposes which arose out of new situtation. In 450 B. C. modest attempts were made for the codification of religious and customary rules and regulations and the Twelve Tables were the most spectacular result. Twelve Tables were the beginning of new legal system.

But the laws contained in the Twelve Tables proved their incompetence and inadequacy to tackle the new situations arising out of the expansion of Roman empire. Moreover, the importance of religion declined and politics came to dominate the affairs or state and society and this needed the reformulation of ancient laws. Fortunately the jurists and lawyers of Rome released their best efforts to reformulate and codify the laws so that they could meet the new situations. In this way the Romans took a leading part in codifying the laws.

When Rome became the most powerful imperialist power of Europe and its empire expanded far and wide the laws of the Twelve Tables and other newly formulated and codified laws could not meet the social, political, cultural and other challenges. In the opinion of Gettell "The body of civil law growing out of the Twelve Tables was narrow and formal. It contained many survivals of early religious ideas and of conditions peculiar to Rome and involved many technicalities that were destructive of justice. This exclusiveness and rigidity was gradually broken down by the edicts of the proctors, the responses of the juris consults and constitutions of emperors" (p. 80).

The most spectacular aspect of Roman legal system is its useful and practical classification. In Rome there were two great law books—*Digest* and *Institutes.* These two law books contain three types of law—(a) *jus civile,* (b) *jus gentium,* and (c) *jus naturale.* The first was the municipal or civil law. A part of the municipal law contained the customary law. However, the manmade laws constituted the major part of municipal law.

The municipal laws were characterised by particularity. The municipal laws were enacted to meet the requirements of particular regions or states. The Roman rulers made these civil laws for the administration of particular states. Into the civil or municipal laws were included right to property and other individual rights and also the rights of family. Thus the Roman jurists accepted positive steps to protect individual's rights.

But the municipal laws had very little applicability and relevance for the administration of foreign lands and for this reason the judicial magistrates (or as they were called praetors) were asked by the rulers to formulate new laws to deal with the problems of foreigners. This is known as *jus gentium* or law of nations. Today we call it international law. The *jus gentium* was not manmade law and naturally in some cases there were inconsistencies and loopholes. The praetors with the help of their acumen and freedom interpreted the *jus gentium.* It included the customs, conventions of foreign countries and their subjects. But the interpretations were always guided by justice and reason.

The final form of law enunciated and developed by Roman jurists is law of nature. The central theme of such law is natural reason and idea of justice. Roman lawyers believed that nature was not made poorer by law. Moreover, there is maximum reason and rationality in nature. Nature never betrays to anybody. Hence the law of nature should be the guiding force of human and state affairs. Roman jurists also believed principles and reasons of certains basic laws were implanted by nature in the minds of every individual. Talking about the law of nature Maxey makes the following observation : "The chief characteristics of the law of nature were its inherent reasonableness, its universal application, its freedom from technicalities and its intrinsic fairness and justice ... it was simply taken for granted and allowed to remain in the abstract" (p. 83).

Other Political Ideas

The Roman political thought is famous not simply for the formulation and codification of law but also for the enunciation of several other political ideas. It is interesting to note that these political ideas have emerged from the concepts of law. Sabine says that the interpretation of the law of nature by the Roman lawyers aimed at the conceptions such as equality before law, fair dealing or equity, faithfulness to contract, rights of the individual to be protected by the authority. The natural law also emphasised that freedom is a birth-right of every individual. In other words, every individual has the right to freedom, life, and property. Contractualist Locke also said that people of the state of nature abandoned that atmosphere for the protection of life, liberty and property because these natural rights were in-danger in the state of nature. He also said that the state of nature was ruled by the law of nature. However, Roman's emphasis upon natural law created a number of political concepts. Natural law is also the source of another important political concept—equal protection of law. Since every person has the right to life by virtue of natural law like others he will be protected by law.

From the Roman theory of law we come to know that people are the ultimate source of authority. Sabine writes "the Roman law crystallised the theory that the authority of the ruler is derived from the people". A Roman lawyer once said "The will of the emperor has the force of law, because by the passage of the *lex regia* the people transfers to him and vests in him all its own power and authority" (quoted by Sabine, p. 171). This may be interpreted variously. It means that the sovereignty is vested in the people. When people are the final source of authority we may say that the authority cannot be autocratic. The Romans, though imperialists, were also democratic minded. That is, there was a prevailing form of democracy in Rome.

Interpreting the political ideas emanating from the Roman legal system, Sabine says (p. 172) that behind the enactment of law or the administration of state there must be the consent of the people. The authority could promulgate ordinance or issue a decree but all these must be subject to the endorsement of the people. In Rome there was system of open assembly like Greek city-states. It has been stated by scholars that Romans assembled in open place to take decisions about the law and administration. From this we may conclude that Roman legal system gave birth to representative or direct democratic system.

To the Romans liberty consisted in expressing free will about the affairs of the state. Romans treated individuals as legal agents and the state as a legal institution. This indicates that in the Roman political thought individuals had special status, they were not absolutely subordinate to the whims and authority of the state. They were neither vague nor abstract. To speak the truth, compared with the Platonic or Aristotelian concept of individual, the Roman idea was far better and more articulate. The State owned the responsibility to protect the rights of the citizens. The Greek political philosophy thought of an organic concept of state which obliterated all sorts of separateness between the individual and the state. In Roman political ideas we do not find the corroboration of such thought. Individuals in Roman political thought were not mere passive units of certain social classes, but active members of a legal institution. In a very brief passage Ebenstein (*Great Political Thinkers*, p. 125) makes an interesting comparison between Greek and Roman thought. He says—"Plato and Aristotle knew of the *Polis*, the city-state and of social classes, but not of *people*. The conception of the people in western thinking is a contribution, not of Roman philosophy, but to Roman public law".

The Roman legal system also established the norms for the relations among the nations. In those days the relations among the nations were viewed in legal terms and not in political and economic terms. However, it laid the foundations of relations among nations or what we call today international relations. Even today the relations among nations—though they emphasise political and economic issues—do not rule out legal issues.

Contribution of Roman Political Thought

We are well-acquainted with the imperialist designs of Rome. Roman emperors were mainly preoccupied with the expansion of empire through their aggressive activities. Hence Roman civilisation had hardly anything to do with political thought or political philosophy. It is practically impossible to discover an academic of the stature of Plato and Aristotle. In spite of these minus points we very often use the term 'Roman political thought' and the use of the term is the source of a lot of confusion. The reason of confusion is if a civilisation fails to produce a coherent and glorious thought on political science how can we call Roman political thought? Even if we call so, is it justified? All these questions are pertinent. But in order to understand the nature of Roman political thought we shall have to throw light on Roman concept of law and related subjects.

Maxey has rightly observed—"What Rome gave the world was not political theory, but the materials for political theory. In the secularisation of law she laid foundations on which many of the salient doctrines of European and American political thought have been built" (*Political Philosophies*, p. 81). Romans did not directly contribute anything to the domain of political thought. Their main preoccupation was with law and jurisprudence. In fact, their contribution to these fields was original. The Romans evolved the most complete and minutely perfected system of law known to the ancient world. Even the legal system of the subsequent periods almost of all the countries of the world was based on the Roman legal system built up by the renowned lawyers of Rome.

The Romans secularised the legal system and Machiavelli (1469-1527) secularised politics. The Greeks viewed law in term of religion and ethics. This tendency very often clouded the real aspect of law and affected its functioning. The Romans secularised law. They viewed law in a positive and realistic way. They emancipated law from the shackles of religion and ethics. In doing this they considerably enhanced the practical importance of law. Romans did this to establish a wel-ordered empire. This attempt and attitude of Romans laid the foundation of a number of political ideas of Western Europe and America.

The concept of sovereignty emerged out of the Roman concept of law. People obeyed law not because it is ethical or religious, but because it is the command of the supreme political authority and it is the manifestation of the will of body-politic. Only the sovereign authority can sanction such a law and to disobey such a law implies to disobey the sovereign authority which is bound to be followed by punishment.

The theory of political obligation is another offshoot of Roman theory of law. People learnt to show obligation to law duly sanctioned by the highest authority of political organisation. The subsequent thinkers drew their inspiration for building up a coherent theory of political obligation.

The idea of legal rights was also derived from the Roman theory of law and jurisprudence. Religious and ethical view of law cannot be the real source of legal rights. By freeing law from the clutches of religion and ethics the Romans built up a concrete theory of legal rights. Subsequently this view founded a strong basis of an elaborate system of various rights.

Another aspect of Roman contribution to political thought is the separation between state and individual. Gettell writes "The Romans separated state and individual each having definite rights and duties. The state was a necessary and natural framework for social existence; but the individuals rather than the state, was made the centre of legal thought, and protection of rights of the individual was the main purpose for which the state existed. The state was thus viewed as a legal person, exercising its authority within definite limits, but the citizen was viewed as a legal person having rights which were to be safeguarded against other persons and against illegal encroachment by the government itself." The Roman political thought made this important distinction between the individual and the state as well as the relationship between them. It is no doubt a very important contribution. Maxey says that this contention of Roman political thought created a positive impact upon the later day political thought of Western Europe and America. The individuals came to know that they had certain rights and the state authority was legally bound to protect them.

The Romans had developed a legal system applicable for several nations. This is called law of nations or international law. The *jus gentium* of Romans constitutes the basis of modern day's international law. The Romans developed certain basic principles of *jus gentium* in order to establish legal authority upon the foreigners. The Romans also gave special importance to the natural law because of its reasonableness. Even today we hold the view that we obey law because it is reasonable.

5 MEDIEVAL POLITICAL THOUGHT

Introduction

Plato and Aristotle viewed the state from idealist and organic point of view, and this reduced the individual to the status of dependence and insignificance. He was mere appendage to the state. Independent thinking and action were unimaginable for him. The state, to him, was friend, philosopher and guide and, in a word, all in all. Beyond the state and without the state the individual was almost nothing.

The Romans elevated the individual to a higher position by recognising certain rights and making arrangements for their protection. The absolutism of the emperor and the individualism of citizens were made to exist side by side. Whether it was possible or not that is a different issue. The fundamental point is that the importance of the individual was seriously considered and accepted by the Romans. Absolutism of the emperor was the product of political circumstances. However, the Romans had a political thought although not political theory or political philosophy. During the heyday of Roman imperialism, Christianity was not the vital aspect of society. In its declining periods Christianity was recognised as a state religion. With the fall of the Roman empire the medieval period started. The rise of the medieval period coincided with the rise of Christianity and church and it ended with the fall of the church.

In the Middle Ages religion, particularly Christianity, played the most dominant part almost in all affairs of state and it embraced all the aspects of human life. Even the kings and emperors could not escape the overwhelming importance of the church. As a result of it the individuals once again were made insignificant elements of state. The worshipping of trancendental and omnipotent God became the only thing and the church fathers constantly advised the individuals to ignore earthly life. People had nothing to do with the worldly affairs, everything was decided and determined by the Almighty God. The chief function of the individual lay in carrying out the order to God. Church fathers were the gods incarnate. Hence, it was the bounden duty of the individuals to carry out the order of the church fathers. These sermons of the church made a tremendous assault upon the separate identity and existence of the individual.

But some critics observe that the rise of Christianity elevated the position of the individuals by announcing the immortality of soul and all men as parts of God. The church fathers also convinced the people that they were the images of God. This established the belief of the sanctity of life. The church fathers also succeeded in instilling faith on God in people's mind and from subsequent analysis it will be found that the people's faith was fully exploited by the church fathers for the furtherance of their personal interests.

Rise of Christianity

The rise of Christianity and its overall importance characterised the Middle Ages. This ascendency of Christianity was accelerated by Roman philosophy, institutions and, above all, by the Roman emperors, particularly Constantine. The establishment of Christian religion and Christian church in a unified form became so important that it began to control the medieval political thought. Towards the declining periods of Roman empire Christian religion spread rapidly and this received a further impetus when the Roman emperor Constantine declared Christianity as the official religion of the state.

Declaration of Christianity as state religion brought about several far-reaching consequences. First of all, it cornered the pagan beliefs. Towards the end of the Roman imperialism pagan beliefs were almost in a dying condition. At that opportune moment Christianity attacked paganism and clipped its wings. Christian beliefs made heavy inroads into Teutonic barbarians. The Christian religion spread so rapidly that soon it became the legal or official religion of the Roman empire. This elevation of Christianity was really surprising. The emperor, in collaboration with the church, exercised supreme authority and this helped the latter to be involved in active politics. This involvement became the characteristic feature of medieval political thought and supplied the fuel of conflict between the church and the state.

The declining condition of the Roman empire also signalled the weakness of the emperor. This happened during the last century of the empire. Erosion of the imperial power encouraged the ecclesiastical authorities to enter into active politics. The church fathers began to accumulate more and more power and their involvement in political affairs began to increase in astronomical proportions. The weakness of the Roman emperors failed to stop this growth of power. With the fall of the Roman empire, the political tradition and institutions also faced crisis. This again facilitated the growth of the influence of the church. It appeared as the representative of Roman tradition and emphasised the unity and integrity of the empire.

We have noted how political changes brought the church into limelight. These and other changes hastened a central organisation and made it more powerful. Rome was the political capital of the empire and naturally it became the capital of the religious world. As a result of the disintegration of the Roman empire and gradual decline of the imperial power, authority and power were transferred from palace to the church, and, in course of time, the church became a hot-bed of politics. Pope and clergymen threw their weight in favour of intense political propaganda. The church was the real authority and decisions of all affairs would come from the church. "In the absence of emperor from Rome, the bishop became the most important official in the city, and considerable power of local political administration passed into his hands. In this way there was added to the large ecclesiastical power of the Roman bishop the practically independent political government of a little state."[1]

1. Gettell, *op. cit.*, p. 80.

Originally it was the duty of the Pope to look after religious affairs. But circumstances led the Pope and the church fathers to play the role of the potential actor in the political fields. This role reached the zenith towards the beginning of the seventh century. At this time, in fact, there was no political authority in real sense. Every decision on political matters emanated from the church and the emperor had not the courage to alter or defy the decision. The unified church established almost a parallel government or administration to Rome. It created a vast network of religious institutions through which politics was controlled. It has been claimed that the church also controlled the intellectual world of Europe. Rise of church or Christianity eclipsed the importance of state and politics in the Middle Ages.

Political Ideas of Christianity

Christianity or church, *per se,* did not propagate any political doctrine or ideas and it was not the purpose. But its sermons—preached among the people belonging to all sections of society—contained the germs of certain political concepts which were treated by the great academics as remarkable political doctrines. These may be designated as natural law, human equality, necessity of justice in the state and the nature of government. Particularly, the concept of natural law, which the Christian fathers preached, was in agreement with Cicero.

Referring to the Gentiles, St. Paul said—for when the Gentiles, which have not the law, do by nature the things contained in the law, these, having not the law, are a law unto themselves. This is law of nature. It is the embodiment of reason and it lives in the hearts and minds of people. There is a difference between law of nature and law of state. The Stoic philosophers emphasised upon the law of nature and the church fathers accepted it. In the medieval political thought the law of nature played a very crucial role. There are several passages in the *New Testament* which have advocated the law of nature.

The church fathers and other persons closely associated with Christianity propagated the law of nature and the concept of equality. These were prominent ideas in Middle Ages. All men are created by God. So, all men are brothers. There is no difference in respect of caste, sex, high and low. "There is neither Jew nor Greek, there is neither bond nor free, there is neither male nor female, for ye are all one in Jesus Christ." To Jesus, all men are equal. The equality of all men led the church to lay faith on the identity of human nature in all parts of the globe. It may be noted in this connection that although the church acknowledged the equality of all men, the same was not applicable to the institution of slavery. The slaves were not free and the Christian fathers did not make any attempt to abolish or even denounce slavery, on the contrary they advised the slaves to carry out the order of their masters. They did not consider slavery as unlawful. The argument of the church father was that slaves were not endowed with the power to control their own spirit. This is, the spirit or soul of all persons, including that of slaves, was equal.

In the *New Testament* we find a wonderful description of obligation. Everyone must show utmost obligation to higher authority. Few relevant lines from the *New Testament* may be quoted here. "Let every soul be subject unto higher powers. For there is no power but of God : the powers that be are ordained of God. Whoever therefore resisteth the power, resisteth the ordinance of God; and that resist shall receive to themselves damnation." The implication is, every power is ordained by

God and no man can defy the order of God. The church fathers declared that any defiance will be treated as a sacrilegious act. In other words, it is the duty of everyone to show obligation to the power or authority and this constitutes the very foundation of the modern concept of political obligations. Persons showing no obligation will be punished. In support of the theory of obligation another famous passage may be quoted : 'Render unto Caesar the things which are Caesar's, and unto God the things which are God's.' The obedience to civil authority is a must for every citizen. Church fathers believed that God created the rulers to punish the people involved in sinful works and to encourage the honest men. Naturally, no question of disobedience to magistrates could arise.

The concept of obligation, in early Christian political thought, was closely connected with the idea of civil government. The civil government was viewed as a divine institution. The state was created to maintain justice. It was the primary duty of the ruler to do this job. He received authority only from God. So disobedience to civil authority was doubly unjustified. The disobedient person was acting against the justice and acting against the wishes of God. The Christian fathers strongly emphasised the obligation to fight the anarchism which was the characteristic feature of early Christian communities.

The ascendency of the church to great power and importance resulted in some tangible consequences of political tenor. The church fathers became highly conscious of their so-called authority. They also thought that they must keep their separateness and independence. Ultimately, the church was able to establish a parallel authority which was in a sense a "state within a state". The church indulged in an irresistible desire to control not only the religious world but also the political world. People were advised to divide their loyalty, that is, they would show obligation both to the emperor and to the Pope. But in case of conflict they would withdraw their loyalty from the king and must be unconditionally obedient to the church. Summarising the political ideas of church, Gettell says—"As Christianity became the official religion of the Roman empire, it gradually developed its semi-political organisation, acquired property and power, and built up its system of theology, a new attitude began to appear in its political ideas." This attitude was self-consciousness which drove it to be independent of the state authority. The church was determined to assume political power peremptorily. This created an atmosphere of inevitable conflict between the church and the state.

Features of Medieval Political Thought

From the standpoint of political thought, the medieval period has certain special features about political thought which need specific consideration. It is said that *this period was unpolitical. Neither political theory nor any ideology developed in the Middle Ages.* Of course, various institutions and organisations were set up. But all these centred around religious dogmas and beliefs. The church was the most dominating institution. All other institutions remained under its control. As a result, independent thinking in the political arena could not flourish at all.

Hearnshaw holds different view so far as the unproductiveness in political thought of the Middle Ages. He says that although in this period there was no political theory, worthy of its name there was political thought. What is the difference between the two? In the words of Hearnshaw "Political theory is the speculation of particular thinkers which may be remote from the actual facts of the time. Political thought is the immanent philosophy of a whole age which determines its actions and shapes its life."[1] There was abundant political thought in the Middle Ages. The conflict between the church and the state; the relation of church to common people, learned persons, feudal landlords and students of educational institutions provided sufficient live materials for political thought. Moreover, in the Middle Ages, feudalism became one of the dominant forces and this was treated as part of political thought. So it cannot be said that the medieval period was barren or dead. Rather, it was live and fresh. It was full of events and numerous institutions grew. All these moulded the nature of political thought.

Universalism is another feature of medieval political thought. Both in political and spiritual fields universalism was strongly emphasised. The Romans inherited the Stoic philosophy of cosmopolitanism and the medieval period again inherited it from the Romans. The medieval thought assumed of a universal society in political matters and a universal ecclesiastical system. The society was universal and one. On the one side there was the emperor for things temporal, and on the other side there was the Pope for things spiritual. The emperor was supposed to deal with the political issues. Ultimately, he came under the full control of the church. Charlemagne worked hard to revive universalism in the temporal side and Hildebrand worked hard for the sake of universalism in ecclesiastical matters.

In the Middle Ages there was no organised state, not even a state in any loose sense. Hildebrand and his followers advocated an ecclesiastical authority with supreme power. It meant that the emperor would act under the authority of the church. "The state is subordinated to the church as an instrument under the control of the church for the governance of the temporal things and for bringing of temporal relations and values under the absolute spiritual purpose of which the hierarchy is guardian." In place of organised and sovereign state there were feudal communities ruled by feudal lords. Most of the feudal lords were powerful and some possessed sovereign power. The conflict between the church and the state motivated the feudal lords to capture power. Thus the Middle Ages were deprived of the facility of a well-organised state system.

In the medieval period politics, economics, religion all were mingled together. The decision of the church on all issues of politics, economics and religion was final. Politics and economics came to be subordinated to religion or ethics and ethics was theology. The church fathers were supposed to lead a spiritual and austere life, but in practice they led a luxurious life. They received wealth from the public in the form of donations. Towards the end of the Middle Ages the churches were converted into great citadels of wealth. The feudal lords also had enough power to change the direction of politics and economics. The emperor had to depend on them for money which they collected from the farmers and common people in the form of tax or revenue. In order to strengthen their financial position and political power, the church fathers frequently adopted various means which had no connection with ethics and religion. They did not antagonise the feudal lords, because they were also important sources of the church's wealth. Therefore, in the medieval period, both politics and economics failed to establish separate identity.

Hearnshaw has pointed out a parallelism between Platonism and medievalism. Plato subordinated politics and economics to the idealism, ethics and, above all,

1. F. J. C. Hearnshaw : *The Social and Political Ideas of Some Medieval Thinkers*, p. 10.

common good, and he placed the philosopher-king at the apex of society for the administration of ideal state and realisation of idealism, common good etc. In the medieval period, church fathers subjected politics and economics to religion and morality as well as ethics and the church would be in overall charge of the state. "What can be more medieval than the system of persecution which Plato advocates in the *Laws* against all who deny the articles of his creed of natural religion?"[1]

Another important feature of medieval political thought is the predominance of the law of nature. The fathers of church and medieval thinkers accepted the law of nature as sovereign in the society. But they did not adopt the law of nature in its original or Stoic form. Law of nature in its original form did not approve slavery or private property, but in the Middle Ages all these existed. That is why the church modified it to suit its purposes and conditions of society. Law of nature to the Christian fathers was the revelation and commandment of God and the church was the only custodian and exponent. Thus, law of nature was made identical with the law of God. The church thought that the law of nature or, as it was called, the law of God, had authorised it to supervise all the activities of parliament and king to regulate the terms and conditions of international treaties and the working of the royal administration. "For all these are under the law and the church has the knowledge of the law."

The medieval thinkers propagated at stentorian voice the divinity of kingship. King was the representative of God on earth to rule men. His main function was to translate the spiritual aims of God into reality and church was the guardian of those aims. Failure of the king to perform the divine duty would invite excommunication. Church would adopt all steps to excommunicate the king from the Christian society. Divine right theory was very popular in the Middle Ages and it placed the monarchy at the mercy of the church. It converted many kings into autocrat rulers. The kings used divinity as an instrument for demanding obedience from the people.

But the divine right theory was made to co-exist with the social contract theory. Although the power of the king came forth from God, people's power over how he would rule was also accepted. People's power was implied in the oath at his coronation. King's function did not end in implementing the spiritual aims of God, he must also fulfil the objectives of the people. The co-existence between the divine right theory and social contract theory was very popular in the Middle Ages. Hearnshaw says,[2] "The *Old Testament* speaks of David making a covenant with his people; Roman law by the voice of Ulpian, ascribes the force of law to the will of the prince, because the people confers on him all its sovereignty and power" (p. 22). The monarchy in the Middle Ages was limited by two forces—divine right theory and the social contract theory. But, in practice, most of the kings resorted to autocratic tactics and ultimately made them dictator. In the opinion of Hearnshaw, the reconciliation between these two theories was a paradox. It was impossible that divinity and people's will would co-exist. However, the medieval thinkers adopted it.

But this paradox will lose its potency if we enter into the depth of the medieval political thought and this is another feature. The medieval thinkers were imbued with the concept of liberalism. Three powerful limitations were placed upon the authority of the

1. Hearnshaw, *op. cit.*, p. 17.
2. Ibid.

monarch. One is divine right, second is social contract and the third is people's will. People of Middle Ages spoke little about the sovereignty of the state, but they were vociferous about the limitations of the king's power.

The gist of modern liberalism is the expansion of people's power and limitation upon the state authority. We can unhesitatingly add that the medieval scholars expressed the liberal thought in the same line.

Slavery and property had special importance in the realm of political thought in the Middle Ages. There was a contradiction between slavery and property on the one hand and the law of nature on the other. In the eye of the law of nature, all were equal and, naturally, the institution of slavery was required to be abolished and the ownership of private property should not be granted. But the medieval thinkers interpreted the law of nature in relative terms and not in absolute terms. Slavery was the consequence of sin and the persons involved in sinful activities were penalised by God for their sin. The real reason was that the medieval people could not raise themselves above the prevailing socio-economic conditions of society. Industry in the Middle Ages had no scope to flourish and since there was abundance of cheap labour, agriculture developed fully and this was the main source of income or livelihood of all sections of people. Serfdom was universal and personal slavery existed. Church fathers had no intention to go against the prevailing social system. In the Middle Ages, property was not common, although, according to law of nature, it would have been common. The church allowed private property on the ground that it was an instrument for the realisation of goodwill and for the common good of the society. Church also declared that no man would be allowed to possess more than what he needed to meet his day-to-day requirements. Accumulation of property in the medieval period was prohibited. "By such principles private property was at once recognised, as under the conditions of the age was necessary, and yet accommodated to Christian principles, as was equally necessary, if the church was to be true to its mission of christianising human life."[1] But subsequently this compromise formula of church on the distribution of property was severly criticised by the true adherents of Christianity.

According to Gettel the political thought in the Middle Ages was "unhistorical, unscientific and uncritical". We have several times noted that the church controlled the ideas and wisdom of this period with its uncritical, orthodox and theological outlook. Church fathers opposed scientific analysis and rational outlook. Conclusions and dogmas were never tested by observations and experiences. People were forced to accept everything as wishes of God or emanating from invisible authority. Dissenting voice was either controlled or discouraged. In the Middle Ages, church controlled the entire thought system and there was no scope for the development and free play of different thought and ideas. "The whole body of faith developed and handed down by the organised church was the basis of all knowledge, and this material was turned over and over by the narrow intellectual processes of scholasticism or accepted without rational demonstration by the contemplative introspection of mysticism. Thought was enchained by a rigid orthodoxy and dissenting ideas were considered heresies to be ruthlessly hunted down."[2] Church did not want development of independent political and other ideas, because it apprehended that

1. Hearnshaw, *Ibid.*, p. 25.
2. Gettell, *op. cit.*, p. 111.

it would enlighten the minds of common people and would create hindrance on the way of exploitation by the church.

The doctrine of two swords characterised the medieval political thought. It was assumed by the medieval thinkers that it was the wish of God that power and authority would be divided between Pope and emperor. This conception was based on an authoritative statement of Pope Gelasius I who once said "The true and perfect king and priest was Christ Himself... But Christ knowing the weakness of human nature and careful for the welfare of His people, separated the two offices, giving to each its peculiar functions and duties. Thus the Christian emperor needs the ecclesiastic for the attainment of eternal life and ecclesiastic depends upon the government of the emperor in temporal things." This observation of Gelasius I was very frequently quoted by church fathers in support of the two swords theory. But in practice it was never the intention of the church to let it operate. In medieval conditions, the doctrine proved its unworkability. Both the church and the emperor were suspicious of each other and each brought charge of encroachment against the other. In this way, the concept of dual authority surcharged the political atmosphere of the Middle Ages. Originally, the doctrine of two swords was floated in order to attain common good through the fulfilment of spiritual and temporal interests. But in medieval period it remained unfulfilled.

Political Thought in 14th and 15th Centuries

Fourteenth and fifteenth centuries are regarded as the last phases of the Middle Ages. Historians and scholars have noticed that during these two centuries political thought underwent spectacular changes. In the opinion of Hearnshaw—"To the period of an assured institutional church, sitting in calm sovereignty, and regulating human life by a careful accommodation between ideal principle and actual tendency, there succeeds a period of sects and of revolution, a period of Spirituals and Lollards and Hussites, a period marked by a conciliar movement against papal sovereignty. To the period of an assured and static society, in which nobility rose high and proud above dependents and serfs, there succeeded a period of villains risings in the country, and turbulent movements of artisans in the towns."

Radical changes in various aspects of political thought became prominent. Slavery and private property were challenged. Many liberal minded Christians during these two centuries openly revolted against the institution of slavery and private property. Some of them even went further by saying "private property is a mortal sin". Rebels refused to accept any compromise on these two institutions. They attacked the church as the initiator of compromise. They said that true Christianity was above any compromise. The genius of Christianity was much wider than the church.

In the fourteenth and fifteenth centuries the state, which was an emasculated one in the previous centuries, began to gather more and more power. The authority of the church was in the declining condition because of people's loss of faith on church fathers and their activities and emergence of the state as a new force. Loss of church's power changed the entire political scenaro of these two centuries. The theory of the fourteenth century was anti-clerical and pro-state. The impressive rise in the power of the state was particularly discernible in France, where the monarch was the undisputed and unchallenged authority in the Christian world and, since he had no intention to be an imperial power, he was the sovereign in the real sense within his own kingdom. The gradual increase in the power of French kings was strongly supported by all classes and sections of French society. In France a strong and centralised government under the sovereign authority of a powerful king was established auguring the advent of a new age of absolute monarchy. Power of the state far exceeded that of the church. Nation-state assumed a particular shape.

The storm which gathered in the past over the right to impose taxes considerably subsided in the last two centuries of the Middle Ages. The king announced that the power to impose taxes fell within the jurisdiction of secular authority and the church had nothing to do with it. Royal supporters began to increase day-by-day and this strengthened the position of the king. Even a belief which arose was that the Pope could not be regarded as the owner of the church property but simply a steward. This drastically eroded both the prestige and power of the Pope. He remained no longer an unassailable authority in both the temporal and spiritual words.

In the fourteenth century, the church itself was raged by a controversy. Many church people attacked the Pope and other top clergymen for their unreligious activities and attitudes. The ecclesiastical writers also did not hesitate to attack the church authorities. Moreover, the luxurious living standard and accumulation of wealth were strongly resented by people and ultimately the church was alienated from the rest of the society. This caused the alleviation of the influence which the church exercised in earlier centuries. People's apathy towards the church became most spectacular towards the end of the fifteenth century and this betokened the advent of a new era and attitude.

Conflict between the Church and State

The most important feature of the medieval political thought is the long-standing conflict between the church and the state. Before the centralisation of the church system and the advent of the ecclesiastical primacy the emperor was the head of both the secular and spiritual worlds and the church did not hesitate to show obligations to the secular power. But when the supremacy of the spiritual organisation was established beyond doubt, the church fathers proceeded to bring the political world under their full control and then commenced the conflict between the two.

With the recognition of Christianity as state religion and rise of papacy a unified Christian world was established and the boundaries of the Roman Empire and the Christian world ultimately coincided. The powers of the two authorities were never clearly demarcated. This resulted in the overlapping of the powers. Again the field of implementation of the powers of both the spiritual and temporal authorities were poised for conflict. Any compromised formula was unacceptable to both of them. Relations became strained and the conflict appeared inevitable.

The accumulation of wealth in the hands of the church fathers may be regarded as another cause of conflict between the two. There was a gulf of difference between what the church preached and what it practised. While the church advised the people to adopt plain living and high thinking, it itself led a very luxurious and comfortable life and for that purpose it received monetary donations from the people. Gradually wealth began to be accumulated in the fund of the church and before long it became the owner of fabulous amount of wealth which inspired the church fathers to participate actively in politics and in other non-spiritual functions. Involvement in politics considerably curtailed the emperor's sphere of action and freedom which ultimately led to antagonistic relations.

The power of the Pope to excommunicate any temporal person—particularly a person of the royal family—provided a source of conflict between the king and the church. The power of excommunication was coupled with dangerous consequences. If a member of the royal family or prince came under excommunication he was deprived of throne and he could not claim any allegiance from his subjects. Pope was not content with interfering with politics only, he ventured to interfere with the personal matters of the king. For example, king Lothaire of Lorraine once decided to divorce his wife and marry his mistress. Pope Nicholas I strongly objected to it on the ground of immorality. A long-drawn struggle could not settle the dispute between the king and the Pope and finally the king was forced by the Pope to take back his wife. The attitude and interference of the Pope was accepted by weak emperors. But emperors with strong personality resisted the church and this facilitated the struggle between the two.

Consolidation of the royal power may be regarded as another cause of conflict between the church and the state. Historians proceed to state that by the fourteenth century the emperors were able to consolidate their strength. The feudal lords and nobles in the past took the side of the church. Towards the end of the thirteenth century their power was reduced and the Pope's influence over them also tended to decline. This enhanced the authority of the king and he refused to declare himself a subordinate agent of the church. The Church thought it an audacity on the part of the king and it became infuriated and declared crusade against temporal power. Over the question of investiture, a fierce controversy arose between Pope Gregory VII and Emperor Henry IV. Being afraid of excommunication the emperor kneeled before the Pope. But when the political situation changed Henry IV captured Rome and sent Gregory into exile. The Church faced the challenge posed by the king. National monarchs also became adamant. Enhanced strength encouraged them to risk the excommunication, interdict and other papal weapons.

Economic factors also fuelled the bitterness between church and monarch. Church had amassed a vast amount of property and wealth over which the temporal authority wanted to impose tax. The church, through its powerful organisation, exerted tremendous influence upon the masses and threats of excommunication resisted all the moves of taxation. The king as head of the state and in charge of all political and civil functions proceeded to coin money and collect taxes. Here again, the church stood in the way of the temporal authority. The argument of the king was that the imposition and collection of taxes fell within his jurisdiction and the church had nothing to do with it. But the church refused to oblige the monarch and a cold war became inevitable.

The interpretation of and emphasis on the divine right theory served another cause of conflict. Kings in the Middle Ages claimed that the source of power and authority of both the king and the church was God and naturally the final responsibility for all the activities was to God alone and under no circumstances to the church. For any failures or misdeeds he was accountable to God alone and the Pope had no right to interfere with the functions of the king. But this claim was challenged by the church. In no case the power of the Pope could be limited and his decision be contradicted. "The decrees of the princes do not take precedence over, but follow, the decrees of the church." To this argument of the Pope, the emperor's reply was that his jurisdiction extended to the entire Roman world and not to any particular region. The claims and counterclaims however failed to solve the conflict and ultimately both stood face to face.

FEUDALISM

Factors Leading to the Growth of Feudalism

The conflict between the church and the state cannot be called the only characteristic of the Middle Ages. Its another and very important feature is the growth and predominance of feudalism. Taking the opportunity of long-drawn controversy between the church and the state the feudal landlords strengthened their power and position. In other words, feudalism thrived surpassing all the previous records. It would not be irrelevant to investigate the causes of its growth.

The medieval economy was mainly buttressed by agriculture. Village communities and large agricultural holdings were formed. Absence of industrial development facilitated agriculture to play the vital role in the economy. Agricultural land came to be concentrated in the hands of few persons and they became landlords who ultimately dominated both economy and politics. Agricultural labourers were closely tied with land and, as they had no alternative source of livelihood, they were forced to offer maximum loyalty to the landlords. The medieval society was divided into two great classes—landlords and serfs or agricultural labourers. But the lack of well-knit organisation and political consciousness helped the subjugation of serfs to landlords which ultimately resulted in the enhancement of the powers and position of the landlords. The agricultural workers were scattered throughout the country which made coordination among them difficult and the landlords utilised this.

The medieval period was full of disorders short of anarchy. The reality of the nation-state was a far cry. Even large political and economic units did not develop. This enabled the feudal lords to accumulate power and to be sovereign in their own fields. Their activities went unchallenged. The incessant fighting between the church and the state also encouraged them to go ahead in fulfilling their political ambition. The emperor had neither the man-power nor the resources to cut them to size. Again, many priests were also owners of large amounts of land. An unholy alliance developed between the church's priests and the feudal lords. This curtailed the power of the king and augmented that of the feudal lords.

Lack of transport and communication facilities may be regarded as another cause responsible for the growth of feudalism. In the Middle Ages people used the primitive types of transport and communication. It was not possible for the Central Government to come to the aid of the common people, particularly small landholders and property owners when they were in great need. For obvious reasons these persons were inclined to seek help of some other stronger persons having property, arms and other facilities. A type of property and other relations grew in this way. Ultimately, the small property owners surrendered their property to big owners. Landlordism was the natural result. Side by side there emerged tenant system. Originally there was some sort of good relation, afterwards it assumed the shape of tenant and landlord. With the rise of amount of property the power, wealth and influence of landlords began to increase.

Gettel and Sabine have pointed out another factor. The Teutonic invaders had two important characteristics which helped feudalism. They at first formed large organisations and later on they were decentralised. Every organisation had leaders and they owned large amounts of land. The leaders were also locally independent. In this way feudalism developed. Again, the Teutonic invaders were not interested in trade and commerce. And that is why they focussed their attention on agriculture. Naturally, their attachment to land was high. Disintegration of Western Empire and decline in power inspired the local leaders to be independent and exercise political and other influences. Local officials and great landowners became law unto themselves, and, in the anarchy that followed, bonds other than political had to be found to hold the society together and to maintain order and protection.

In the medieval period, the kings were the owners of almost the entire amount of land. The nobles and other members of the royal families were also owners. The lands were leased to their followers and relatives. This created landlordism. In exchange of it, the landlords committed to provide military services and, when required, lump-sum amount of money. The original owners had no connection with the peasants who cultivated the land. The intermediaries became ultimately independent and exerted tremendous coercive influence upon the peasants. Economically and politically, they were the sovereigns. Since the kings were involved in the struggle with the church, they had no time to control the landlords.

Features of Feudalism

Almost all the scholars of history of Western political thought share the view that it is difficult to define feudalism. Berki says that the term "feudalism" is quite often used to denote two distinct phenomena. One is, it is a system of "vassalage", the allegiance and military assistance that semi-independent chieftains, owners of land, power and prestige themselves, owed to their respective kings or ruling princes. The other is the system of servitude or serfdom, the obligation of common people to serve their masters. It is to be noted here that feudalism in the Middle Ages was the combination of these two phenomena. It was not simply a system of vassalage nor a system of serfdom. Landowners appointed cultivators and they were subsequently called serfs.

J. W. Thompson and E. N. Johnson[1] have said that feudalism was primarily the typical medieval system of government. The large landowners exercised political sovereign power over the people. This power was formerly exercised by the monarch. In other words, feudalism and political power were inextricably connected. It was not possible for the medieval monarch to exercise political authority and establish an efficient administration. These were entrusted to large landowners. But the transfer of power was not always legal. Being forced by local circumstances and problems and sometimes driven by the inordinate zeal to exercise power, the landlords resorted to illegal means.

Monarchy as a type of centralised royal government was replaced by innumerable local governments. In many cases, the new lords were persons who formerly governed their localities. The government, thus, became a private affair. It also became personal and non-political. Non-political in the sense that the ruler (i.e., landlords) did not come to power through the political process. Theoretically and politically the king was the sovereign. In other words, landlords were the *de facto* sovereigns. As private property was owned and inherited so the prerogatives were owned and inherited. The landlords waged war, coined money and held court of justice. Thompson and Johnson have rightly said—Feudalism as a system of government may accordingly be defined as private assumption of public authority.

---

1. *An Introduction to Medieval Period*, p. 290.

Another feature of feudalism is that it was more than a system of private government. It was also the system of land tenure upon which that government was based. We have already succinctly pointed it out. For the sake of clarity it may be added that a man held and used land which belonged to another man. This was done in the form of a contract which was again a perpetual lease. The holder of the land was required as a part of his contract to assist the lord in various capacities. For example, to assist the lord in his police function for the maintenance of law and order, to serve him as a soldier. These were the military and police functions. Feudalism in this sense was a military system.

Feudalism was a personal bond that governed the relationship between the lord who granted and the vassal who received the land. The governing landowners of feudal society entered into a network of mutual relationship with one another based upon definite agreement. As a result of the agreement a man surrendered to the service of his powerful neighbour and in doing this he lost nothing of his social prestige. In the system of vassalage, both the persons belonged to the same class. A personal relationship developed between the lord and vassal. Feudal government and feudal tenure thus came to rest, at least in theory, upon loyalty, not to the state, but to an individual.

Feudalism was a combination of private governments, a particular system of land holding and personal dependence. Feudalism in the medieval period embodied the aristocratic manner of life. Feudalism is, says Thompson and Johnson, one more embodiment of the truth that has been repeatedly emphasised in regard to Western European civilization as a whole. It was a compound of Roman, Christian and German elements, moulded into a new form by contemporary conditions of life.

Thompson and Johnson have pointed out the diversity of feudalism. It first developed in France, then it spread in other West European countries, particularly Germany and Italy. But feudalism of these two countries was not uniform. Again, French feudalism also was different from those of Germany and Italy. This was due to the fact that feudalism was conditioned and guided by local elements and conditions. Feudalism of a different form was found, not where it was the outgrowth of centuries of slow change, but in those regions to which it was later transplanted outright from Western Europe.

Feudalism affected the power of monarchy, administration and revenue. The king could not exercise his royal power over his subjects. The subjects, mostly peasants, were under the control of vassals or landlords. They were exploited financially. But the lion's share of the revenue was grabbed by the landlords. We have already noted that disorder short of anarchy prevailed in the medieval period. Rampant corruption, exploitation, and all sorts of irreligious activities in the name of religion were at their heyday. The general administration was in disarray. The king could not assert his power, because he had two powerful rivals—feudal lords and church. Gettell concludes—By its very nature, feudalism prevented the idea of an absolute authority ruling within a definite area. The modern conceptions of sovereignty and law were entirely foreign to the Middle Ages. Law was primarily custom and existed as a part of local or national life, it was not the command of the lawmaker, nor the will of the community. Legislation was merely the promulgation of what was already recognised on finding upon men (p. 100).

Feudalism was characterised by the existence of three estates. The first estate was the clergy which was related to the spiritual affairs. The second estate was the nobility whose function was government, including the defence of society. The third estate consisted of the rest of society, whose duty was to labour and to serve the other two classes. Feudalism was the system that regulated relationship among members of the second estate. Feudal government rested on the coercive power and in this respect it was not different from any other government. There were religious sanctions, loyalty and others. But the feudal government did not hesitate to apply force on the slightest pretext.

War among the feudal lords was also another characteristic feature. It was a curse to feudal society. The feudal society was largely governed by private interests. The common ambition of feudal lords was to increase the bounds of their authority by increasing the extent of their holdings. Sometimes they also attempted to make holdings a big compact territory. This could be easily done by peaceful methods. But they never adopted peaceful means for the unification of discrete holdings. Moreover, when the ambitions ran high, clashes became inevitable. Ultimate consequence was war. The medieval feudal lords were guided by a peculiar idea that since they had every right to safeguard their private interests, *ipso facto*, they had the right to wage war. In the Middle Ages to make private war for proper cause was a feudal right. Medieval wars were wars of rights. It has been observed by a critic that the wars waged by feudal lords were seldom unprovoked wars.

In the period of feudal supremacy, social and political rights were not clearly defined and different social and political institutions did not develop. The chief interest of the feudal lords lay in extracting more and more money from common people. They did very little for the development of society. From Marxian angle we can say that the emergence of feudalism divided the society into two new and major classes—feudal lords and serfs. The production relation of feudal period was also quite different from that of the earlier period. The feudal lords and the church exploited the common people. Because of these two powerful forces, self-sufficient economy could not develop at all.

Disintegration of Feudalism

The last one hundred and fifty years of the medieval period saw several important political, economic and social changes and the most important of them was the disintegration or decline of feudalism. Throughout the medieval period the monarchy was in insignificant position. It could not ensure its power and authority either on public or feudal lords. Feudal nobles and the clergy were the determining factors of everything that counted. But towards the closing decades of this period these two institutions were relegated to insignificance.

The most important factor that contributed to the decline of feudalism was the gradual and steady rise of monarchy. Gettel* says, "The Hundred Years' War, the War of Roses, the use of gunpowder and the rise of national taxation and of standing armies strengthened the royal power at the expense of the great nobles, especially in England, France and Spain" (p. 132). In big wars the feudal lords, in fact, had no part to play. The kings were the main actors. Victory or defeat, whatever might be the result, the power of the king ultimately proliferated. This happened towards the end of the Middle Ages. Previously the kings had to depend upon the feudal lords for the supply of armies. But when they came to realise the difficulties of this

* Op. cit.

system they started to build up personal armies for security purposes. This considerably enhanced their power. The status and power of the nobles declined remarkably.

The development of transport, communication, trade, commerce and, above all, the rise of the bourgeoisie contributed much to the disintegration of feudalism. Towards the end of the medieval period kings, lords and even the church took active interest in building up roads and bridges which were completely neglected in the earlier centuries. The cities and urban areas were connected by road and other means of communication. The thirteenth and fourteenth centuries saw old trade routes changed and new ones opened, old monopolies broken and new ones secured. This great revival of commerce and industry spread throughout the length and breadth of different countries. This again stimulated all Central and Western Europe with new life even down to local manorial and monastic markets. Development of industry, commerce and transport took place simultaneously. With these arose a new class—bourgeoisie—composed of manufacturers, merchants and small traders. For the furtherance of trade and commerce and the progress of economy as a whole this new class wanted a strong and centralised government, which the feudal lords did not want. The importance and influence of landlords as the most dominating class in the society came down considerably. Now the bourgeoisie occupied that coveted position.

The economy of the Middle Ages was agriculture-based and, in such an economy, the feudal lords had an important part to play. The entire economy with the sources of production and production relation was under the strong grip of the feudal lords. But the advent of commerce and growth of manufacturing industry completely changed the infrastructure. The agriculture-based economy was turned to an industry-based economy and its control went to the hands of the new class. Capitalist or bourgeois class became the primary class and the landlords the secondary class. Besides the bourgeoisie, the proletariat class also emerged. Proletarians were also in opposition to the capitalist class.

In the earlier centuries of the medieval period the privileged classes joined the feudal lords. At the close of this period they were found to support the monarchy and also its enhancement of power. Feudalism no longer remained as a rival of monarchy, its position declined. The smaller feudal states were combined to form a larger one. Previously people sought the help of feudal lords for safety and protection, now they sought it from the king. This again cut feudalism to size.

Contribution of Feudalism

Feudalism was not without beneficences. Arising spontaneously to meet the need of law and order in disorderly age, it served the purposes of that rough age. As a kind of stopgap system of government, it served likewise the purposes of the future, until such time as Western society could be recognised again by its kings and princes. Under the authority of feudalism, or more particularly landlords, certain order came out of disorder, justice was produced by force, custom was subsequently converted into law. It produced an atmosphere for the nourishment of colourful life and intellectual progress. It prepared the field for a future and prosperous civilisation. It sowed the seeds of liberty, rights and other democratic principles. Although freedom was confined only to the aristocracy, the dignity and the worth of the individual were recognised.

The feudal courts of kings and nobles developed the system of trial by jury. Historians think that in this process the feudal period acted as a harbinger to the concept of common law. Through a continuous struggle the people of the thirteenth century were able to establish the right to life and property. These rights were not to be abrogated without the due process of law. Subsequently the American Constitution and Supreme Court accepted the concept of due process of law.

It seems strange, indeed, to speak of the later birth of individualism in view of the immoderate individualism of feudal times. Feudal decentralisation and localism brought forth a mervellous variety of Western European civilisation and a good deal of colour that Europe still retains. The emergence of decentralisation and localism, it is said, was the chief source of individualism.

From feudalism two discrete lines of development could emerge. On the one hand, it could result in the formation of numerous autonomous sovereign states. There was very likelihood of this possibility and this possibility actually worked in Germany. It was divided into small sovereign territories. The other possibility was it could lead to absolute monarchy. In most of the European countries the absolute monarchy was the result of feudalism. The self-styled feudal sovereigns were involved in internecine warfare which resulted in anarchy and instability. This opened the opportunity for the king to interfere with the internal affairs of the feudal landlords. Given enough time, enough strength, and enough intelligence a succession of kings could create out of the feudal welter a national state belonging to and governed by the king.

Feudalism directly did not produce any political theory. But its indirect contribution cannot be denied. Modern concept of sovereignty may be traced to the feudalism of medieval period. The feudal lords were independent and they exercised sovereign power in their own area. Many historians observe that modern theory of sovereignty comes from it. The doctrine of political obligation also originated in feudal period. Common people showed allegiance to the lords who were their immediate masters. But their ultimate obligation was to the king. Either out of fear or respect, whatever may be the cause, people never hesitated to show allegiance to the authority. Lord and vassal were equally obliged to obey and maintain law. This obligation to law created mutual rights and duties. Both the ruler and the ruled were bound by the law. It was undoubtedly a healthy development. It was established in the feudal period that the peace and security must be the concern of the authority. Even today this idea persists. In Hobbesian concept of social contract we find that the people of the state of nature left it in search of peace and security and for this purpose they set up a civil society. The obligation to law and the commitment to peace and security of the feudal period were the elements of limited government.

Conclusion

In conclusion we want to make clear some points and aspects of feudalism. Though the power of the feudal lords was very limited, it is a fact that they were not at all democratic-minded. From history we come to know that people were deprived, in the Middle Ages, from the rights, liberty and some minimum privileges. The feudal lords were not exclusively responsible for this. But they had a major share in this deprivation. Their main concern was to collect revenue from the peasants and cultivators. They were not concerned about the improvement of the economic condition of the peasants. This no doubt reveals their heartlessness. They did not display even a scant amount of sympathy to the common people. People were the victims of exploitation.

During the period of feudalism the society was almost divided into two great classes—feudal landlords and serfs or peasants. Though the former were to some extent organised, the latter were not organised and this ensured their exploitation.

An unholy alliance was formed between kings and feudal landlords which cleared the way of victimisation and exploitation of peasants. Whenever any crisis arose the landlords always took the side of kings. This was no good for the common men.

In spite of the above drawbacks the feudalism did something for common people. Powerful feudal lords maintained their own armies which provided security to the peasants. In few cases good relationship developed between the feudal landlords and peasants. Feudalism also initiated a sort of constitutionalism. There were agreements and all sides agreed to abide by them.

Concept of State in Medieval Period

At the outset of this analysis we must make it clear that in the Middle Ages there was no state in the modern sense, but still there was a state when considered by the basic characteristics such as territory, government, sovereignty and population. The main fulcrum of our brief analysis is what type of state there was in the Middle Ages.

There is no doubt that the people of the Medieval Ages failed to witness a nation-state which emerged after the peace treaty of Westphalia in 1648. The medieval states had no clearcut geographical boundary. The frequent armed conflicts among the kings or rulers obliterated the boundary lines and this was a great factor of the absence of nation-state in this period.

Another element of a nation-state is the established political authority. In the Middle Ages the church was perhaps the most powerful institution which succeeded in establishing its authority over the ruler and other political institutions. In fact, in all matters, the final word always came from the head of the church and this ultimately undermined the authority of the king. The state in the Middle Ages had government but, in real terms, it was guided by the *diktat* of the Pope. Naturally the king had no authority to take any decision.

The state in the medieval period was a religious state. It was believed—or the people were made to believe—that both the state and its rulers were the creation of God. God was the ultimate source of all authority. The rulers had to obey the orders of the Pope who was accountable only to God. The king must receive all instructions from the church and particularly from the Pope. He had no authority to rule the state according to his own reason and judgment. God sends advices and instructions to the king through the Pope. The divinity concept lingered even after the fall of the church. The king declared himself as the representative of God on earth and he is accountable only to God. Wishes of God are translated into reality only through the instrumentality of the king. The state of the medieval period was thus the state of God and not the state of people. In real life the religious principles and sermons dominated practically all the aspects of social and political life of people. E. J. C. Hearnshaw in his *Theoretical and Political Ideas of Some Great Medieval Thinkers* writes—"Divine right is in medieval theory compatible and coexistent with popular institution. All power proceeds from God and is an emanation of His sovereignty" (p. 21).

The medieval state was a disintegrated one. Because of the dominance of the Pope over the king the latter failed to exert his authority over the landlords. The feudal lords—being inspired by the continuous conflicts between the king and the church—established their suzerainty over their own areas. The powerful feudal lords maintained separate army to protect their own interests and collected taxes from peasants and cultivators. The king was helpless in the face of the rising authority of the feudal lords.

The medieval state was a class-state in a sense. There were three main classes in the medieval period. These were clergy, baronage and commons. There were other small groups but they were not important. In Plato's *Republic* there were also three main classes. Hearnshaw observes that the development of British Parliament was mainly based on this three-class system and even the representative character of the British government could not do away with this three class system. Hence we may say that the class structure of Western European society may be termed as a legacy of the medieval class system.

It has been observed by some scholars of medieval political thought that the medieval state was federal in nature. In this period many social and local groups emerged and they altogether composed the state. It is said that in the medieval state these groups came into existence of themselves and the state had no control over these groups. "Guilds grew into life; and once they lived, they acted—they legislated and they did justice—as if it were a matter of inherent right" (Hearnshaw, p. 28). The medieval administration was weak and the groups took its full advantage. The guilds established their own authority. In most of the time the central administration made compromises with the groups and their administration.

The medieval state cannot be called a democratic one because of the fact that the people had no voice. Neither the church nor the king had any accountability to the people. The responsibility of the church or the feudal lords ended in collecting taxes from the people and the people had no right to know how that money was being spent. In other words, the medieval state was in a sense an autocratic state which was ruled in the name of God.

6 SOME MEDIEVAL THINKERS

Ambrose of Milan

In the fourth century, Christianity was made the state religion of the Roman Empire and after it the church became supreme, first in the spiritual affairs and then in the temporal matters. But the supremacy of the church could not solve the problem of loyalty. A true Christian must show obligation to the church. But his obligation was not treated as absolute. The orthodox adherents of the church demanded unconditional loyalty from the citizens. On the other hand, supporters of the temporal power argued that citizens' first and foremost obligation would be to the emperor. In the background of this controversy we shall discuss the views of three churchmen—St. Ambrose of Milan, St. Gregory and St. Augustine.

So far as the Christian questions are concerned, St. Ambrose of Milan said nothing new. But he expressed his view in unambiguous terms. He advocates the autonomy of the church in spiritual matters. He said, "In a matter of faith, bishops are wont to judge emperors, not emperors bishops." The emperor has no right to interfere with the religious of spiritual affairs. His business was only with the political affairs. That was the line of action pleaded by Ambrose. In one of his comments we find "palaces belong to the Emperor, churches to the priest. That which is divine is not subject to the imperial power." We thus find that Ambrose drew a clear line between religion and politics.

Ambrose asserted that in spiritual and religious affairs the supreme authority of the church must be accepted by all. Even the king had no right to question the legality or anything of religious decisions. Again, as a Christian, the king must accept the decision of the church. The king was the son of the church and for this reason he should not regard himself above the church. Ambrose was always against the application of force or execution of order. He advised the church not to incite the people against the true principles of Christianity.

St. Gregory

St. Gregory is another Church Father who sought to establish the predominance and autonomy of the church. At the same time he admitted the independence of the king in the temporal field. He thought that the temporai ruler might be weak or inefficient, but that could not be the cause of showing disloyalty to the ruler.

He talked about passive obedience. That is, a wicked on inefficient ruler was entitled to passive obedience. It is interesting to note that no other Church Fathers spoke of obedience to the temporal authority with so much emphasis. He asserted in no uncertain terms the sanctity of the secular government. Gregory supported the view that the emperor should act independently in his own field, but he expected that he would act according to his own conscience. Violation of divine rules or disobedience to God were undoubtedly unbecoming on the part of the emperor. He must remember the basic idea that he was the servant of God.

In his opinion since this universe has been created by God the secular authority must perform his duties remembering this fundamental point. All the rulers must be well-acquainted with the divine rules. Being contrary to it would bring about great harm or disaster. He said "the peace of the state depends on the peace of the universal church."

Although several Church fathers and Christian writers strongly supported the doctrine of two swords, the Pope and his adherents did not apply it and as a result of it, the bitterness between the church and the state heavily stormed the peace and tranquility of the medieval period. The intransigent attitude of the church was singularly responsible for this. Though Ambrose and Gregory were orthodox Christians they openly declared that the secular authority that is king or emperor must have full freedom in the discharge of duties.

ST. AUGUSTINE (354–430)

Life and Time

When St. Augustine was born in 354 A. D. at Tagaste, a town in North Africa, the Roman Empire was at the zenith of its power and glory but showed signs of disintegration. Augustine was pagan in his youth, but was not satisfied with paganism. His ardent desire to search for truth led him finally to adopt Christianity and this he did at the age of thirty-three. In 391 he was ordained a priest and in 395 he became of Bishop. In 429 the Vandals invaded Africa, in the following year he died. St. Augustine was pupil of St. Ambrose. It was the credit of Ambrose to convert him to Christianity. The most famous work of St. Augustine is *City of God (De Civitate Dei)* which he started to write in 413 and finished in 426 A. D. It is a voluminous work of twenty-two books.

In order to understand the political thought of St. Augustine it is necessary to know the background with which he was faced. Christianity achieved the status of state religion in 313 A. D. and after eighty years of this the Roman empire collapsed. When Christianity was declared state religion, paganism was proscribed and prohibited. However, many orthodox Christians and other persons have tried to find out the relation of the fall of the Roman Empire and attainment of Christianity's new status. Christian qualities of other-worldliness, pacific attitude to every affair and contempt for revered national deities were not favourable for a powerful Roman Empire. Moreover, Christianity did not recognise the loyalty to Rome as the first and foremost loyalty.

But the declaration of Christianity as a state religion created resentment in the minds of many, particularly the strong adherents of paganism. The purpose of Christianity was to establish one religion and one faith. On the contrary, paganism was for many faiths and many attitudes to religion. It wanted pluralism in the field of religion. Seeing the disintegration of the Roman Empire the pagans pointed the needle of suspicion to the betrayal to the old Roman deities under which Rome had risen to the position of world power. The Christian fathers failed to understand the disintegration of the empire even after its conversion. The Christians were still more perturbed to realise that the imperial power on which they laid their hope for temporal security and worldwide domination was unable to save even itself from destruction.

The destruction of Roman Empire and the attack of paganism upon Christianity perplexed and perturbed St. Augustine whose father was a pagan and mother was a Christian. He heard both the cry of the pagans and the plaint of the Christians. Augustine started a thorough investigation about the destruction of the Roman Empire and his celebrated work the *City of God* was a reply of pagan challenge to the Christianity. Pagan challenge was that Christianity was solely responsible for its own downfall. His *City of God* combines Plato and Cicero. In Plato's ideal state dogma or idealism was the dominant element. To Cicero love for God was vital and it was a mighty social bond. Augustine treated Christianity as a dogma and he thought that it would be the controlling force of the state. Law, politics, administration and relations among all men are determined by the wish of God.

The Story of Two Cities

In the *City of God* Augustine has imagined of two cities—heavenly city or *Civitas Dei* and earthly city or *Civitas terrena*. Two cities have been formed by two *loves*. The earthly city is the creation of self-love and to the contempt of God and the heavenly city is the creation of love to God, even to the contempt of self. The earthly city glorifies the self and the heavenly city glorifies God. The people of the earthly city run after their personal interests and they are making all sorts of efforts immoral and unethical for the perpetuation of benefits which they have cropped. Feuds and animosity are very common among the princes, administrators and common people. Augustine has lamented that goodliness honesty virtue and other universal values are not to be found in the people of earthly city.

The heavenly city is diametrically opposite to the earthly city. It is inhabited by angels or holy persons. They do not look after their personal benefits or interests. The goodliness and sacrifice dominate the behaviour and attitude of the inhabitants of heavenly city. This city is not raged by feuds and conflicts. Peace, good relation and holiness are the permanent features. People do not lust for power. Since personal interests and lust for power are not motive forces, quarrels and animosity are not found.

People of the earthly city are primarily engaged in quarrels, wars and litigation. In this city, peace is a far-cry. Use of arms against each other is a very common affair. People are victims of vice and all sorts of misdeeds. Pride and glory dominate the entire society. Love for victory sometimes becomes life-destroying. The cost of achievement of victory far exceeds the benefit. People are fools and devoid of good sense. They make arms to make wars and they make war to get peace. But their foolishness knows no bounds. Peace is never achieved.

Augustine has made a clear distinction between the two cities. The foundation of one is appetite and possessive impulses which are found in the lower categories of animal. Heavenly peace and salvation of mankind, according to Augustine, are the foundation of the *Civitas Dei* or heavenly city. The Satans with wicked thought and activities and seeking self-interest, have made the earthly city a den. They have no respect for good qualities which Jesus Christ possessed. The predominance of the pagans is the sole cause of the fall of Rome. There is no possibility of the disintegration of the kingdom of Christ because pagans have no existence there.

There is possibility of survival of the city of Satans. Because profligacy and debauchery cannot lay the foundation of a stable and enduring city. It is evident from the fall of the Roman Empire. The alienation of the people from Christianity is the primary cause of the fall. Augustine has assumed that there is a continuous conflict between these two kingdoms and, finally, the kingdom where only the angels live will survive. The source of Augustine's *City of God,* it is said, is the Stoic conception of cosmopolis,.the true universal home of the righteous and wise human beings. Borrowing the central idea of heavenly city from the Stoic philosophy he has mixed it with biblical and apostolic conceptions and here lies the ingenuity of Augustine's thought.

Political Ideas of Augustine

Augustine was not a political philosopher and, to speak the truth, he had not the intention to build up a well-reasoned political theory. In his elaborate investigation of the causes of the fall of the Roman Empire and all other related matters he has pointed out certain ideas about state, society, human nature etc. which are parts of political thought. According to Augustine, God created man and endowed him with liberty and free will. In the original state of goodliness and justice men exercised this liberty very cautiously and only for the attainment of holiness and worship of God. When wickedness dawned in the minds of men, they fell into the hands of Satans and began to commit sin after sin which precipitated their sufferings and misery.

How did they become prey of sin? He says—"what is man's misery other than his own disobedience to himself : that seeing he would not what he might, how he cannot what he would?, his mind is troubled, his flesh painted, age and death approach, and a thousand other emotions seize on us against our wills which they could not do if our nature were wholly obedient unto our will?"—Berki, 85. Here Augustine wants to emphasise that man's disobedience to himself causes disobedience to God. When man becomes the slave of his own desires to get more pleasure and satisfaction he forgets the wills and wishes of God and also to worship Him. Man comes to be involved in sinful activities. Augustine here speaks of self-control which is the royal path to get the blessings of God. Berki (p. 86)[1] points out that the significant innovation of Augustine is that according to him "the corruption of human body, its inclination to worldly pleasure, is a consequence and not the cause of sin. While Plato, Aristotle as well as the Stoics looked upon the body as the source of baseness and uncleanness and an encumbrance to soaring human intellect, Augustine affords dignity to the fleshy substance of man."

Both society and state[2] were created by God. They were partly punitive and partly remedial institutions. Before the reaction of the state and society the original

1. Ibid.
2. According to St. Augustine the state is an association of a multitude of rational beings united by a common agreement on the objects of their love.

men were innocents and they were shepherds. Sin instigated men to be disobedient and ultimately brought them under servitude. If God did not come out to save men then entire mankind would have been destroyed. That is why out of mercy God created two kingdoms—one for men seeking self-interest and the other for angels sacrificing self-interest and worshipping God only. The purpose of the heavenly city is to save mankind from sin and sufferings. We thus see that Augustine believes in the divine origin of the state and he has opposed the Donatists, who claimed freedom from civil obligations and considered the state as a diabolical institution.

It is surprising to note that although St. Augustine held a very key position in the realm of the church he did not deal with the most vexed question of his time—the relationship between the church and the state. He discussed at length the distinction between the two cities. His *City of God* was neither a state nor a church—but in the words of a critic a "christianised church-state—from which unbelievers are excluded and claimed the supreme power in that state for the leaders of the ecclesiastical hierarchy"[1] Critics are of opinion that Augustine had no sympathy for the earthiy city and that is why in his conception this city could not be a competitor of the kingdom of Jesus. Only a christianised church-state could be a saviour of degraded mankind.

The concept of justice holds a very important place in the thought-system of Augustine. Cicero conceived of the state as an association of people assembled together for the purpose of fulfilling certain common objectives. The natural law was the basis of the state and every individual must obey the law. But Augustine has not accepted this view. To him justice is the most important thing or aspect of any state and if it is removed from the state, then it will be an association of robbers. In a word, a state devoid of justice is not state at all. He, moreover, says that without justice laws are arbitary decrees.

How does he define it? "Justice is a virtue distributing unto everyone his due. What justice is that, then, that takes man from the true God, and given him unto the condemned fiends?" In a godless state individuals are deprived of their due shares and this is quite unjust. Here Augustine is not so much concerned with God. In the state of God, man will get his proper share and that is enough. Whether God is getting his worship that is immaterial.

Justice again conforms to order. Every society or organisation has certain orders and it is the duty of the members of that organisation to show obedience to those orders. Family is the smallest organisation and its members display obedience to it. Similarly, the citizens of the state show obligation to it. But Augustine observes that the state is not the widest society and naturally its order cannot be universal. The widest society is the society of all man under the kingship of God. God is the only authority in the universe who can issue and prescribe order. The individuals are bound to obey only the universal order of God. The state may have its own justice, but that cannot be regarded as absolute. The order of the state must be in conformity with the universal order. The obligation to state order which violates the universal order of God may be just, but, in truth, it is not just at all. Therefore, justice implies conformity with the order of God.

There is a difference between justice of Plato and that of Augustine. The former was confined only within the boundary of the ideal state. Universal morality and

1. J. K. Figgis, Political Aspects of St. Augustine, quoted by Gettell, p. 101.

order were not problems for Plato. He did not make any scheme for the conciliation between the state order and the universal order. On the contrary, Augustine differs from Plato in his approach to justice. An individual is not only a member of the state, he is also a part of the universal order created by God. Augustine has admitted that true justice must conform to law. In his opinion this law is the same for all times and for all men. So justice in Augustinian sense is always absolute.

Augustinian theory of slavery runs as follows. The prime cause of slavery is sin which brings man under the domination of his fellow. This is why the word slave is not found in the Scriptures. Slavery is a name introduced by sin and not by nature. The origin of the Latin word *slave* is supposed to be found in the circumstances that those who by law of war were liable to be killed were sometimes preserved by their victors and were hence called servants. And these circumstances could never have arisen save through sin. Every man who commits sin is the servant of sin. The servitude is penal and is appointed by that law which enjoins the preservation of the natural order and forbids its disturbance.

There is a difference between Aristotle and Augustine so far as the concept of slavery is concerned. According to the former, nature has made some men physically strong and mentally weak and some men the opposite. So the physically strong persons will be slaves of mentally strong persons. Thus slavery is ordained by nature and not manmade. But in Augustine it is the punishment for sin and ordained by God. "His theory is that the institution of slavery as a whole is a collective retribution upon the human race for the fall of harmony in Adam. Such a theory might be employed to explain the reduction of the whole human race to slavery, but it seems powerless to account for a condition of things in which some particular individuals are condemned to serve, while others are elevated to mastery at their expense."[1]

Significance of *City of God*

Augustine's *City of God* contains an analysis and comparison of two cities—one earthly and the other heavenly. But to view the *City of God* simply as a comparison of two imaginary cities is not proper. It has greater and deeper significance and we want to explore it. Let us quote the pertinent observation of Gettell : "The work of Augustine gave to the church at a critical period of its history a crystallized body of thought and put into definite statement the ideal which gave its distinctive existence and self-conscious purpose (p. 101)." When Augustine wrote *City of God* (413–426 A. D.) the whole Roman Empire was completely plunged into fierce controversy and although the united church was able to establish its authority or predominance in certain fields, it was faced with crisis. Strong emperors could easily ignore the authority of the church. Paganism also posed a challenge to Christianity. In such a critical period, Augustine gave the church a definite direction and a clear meaning to Christianity. In unambiguous terms he has suggested that all the ecclesiastical powers shall be vested in the church and, through the allegiance to it, can the salvation of individual be made a matter of reality.

The conception of two cities does not mean the existence of two independent geographical areas completely separate from each other and having no relation between them. Rather, they are closely connected with each other. Maxey says :

1. Michael Foster, *Masters of Political Thought,* Vol. 1, p. 222.

"These two may exist side by side and frequently intermingle and overlap. Because it deals with spiritual things, the church serves as a concrete embodiment of heavenly commonwealth and the state, because it deals with material things, bodies forth the earthly commonwealth. Ideally the two should be so completely fused that the distinction between the secular and spiritual would disappear." The people of the earthly city must break the shackles of bondage to impulses and impiety to achieve God-like character. Unconditional allegiance to God is the only way to penance. This is the central idea of the celebrated work *City of God*.

The *City of God* has another significance. This book emphasises that the state is not an end in itself but a means to an end—and the end is good life. People will atone for their sins through the state. Following Plato and Aristotle, Augustine has proceeded to stress that the state is a reformatory organisation. In the *City of God* he has exhorted the Christians to show obedience to God. Corruption and unfaithfulness were so much prevalent in his time that he was impelled to write this book.

Commenting on the importance of *City of God*, Ebenstein makes the following observation : "The rebuttal of the paganism is only the more negative part of the *City of God*. Having demonstrated the hollowness and inconsistency of paganism, materialism and worldly success, Augustine proceeds to his more constructive task, the vision of the heavenly city. Augustine's use of the word *civitas* should not be interpreted in a political sense... He was interested in God, Faith and Salvation and not so much in the organisation of the state" (p. 169).

The *City of God* is an allegory. It has a special message and this has relevance even today. Rampant corruption, degradation and lack of loyalty are the primary causes of instability of political system. The *City of God* tells us of allegiance to the united church, we speak of allegiance to the political authority. Needless to say that absence of allegiance to an organised authority is the harbinger of anarchism. No sensible person can deny the importance of loyalty. He donned allegiance with the apparel of religion. It was not possible for him to raise himself above religion.

The *City of God* combines Plato's concept of justice with Cicero's law of nature. Law without justice is valueless. The *City of God* asserts that, for the kingdom of earth, both law and justice are essential. We want to make it a point here that Augustine had no intention to banish the earthly city, rather, he wanted to reform it and law and justice could attain this objective.

Sabine says that *City of God* was written to defend Christianity, to refute the pagan charge that it was responsible for the decline of the Roman Empire. But in practice, Augustine developed his philosophy in this book. The *City of God* contains an interesting point. The fundamental fact of human life is that the human interests are divided into two parts—earthly and heavenly. This is the central theme of Christian politics, ethics and theology. The *City of God* says that there is a constant conflict between bad and good, right and wrong and, finally, between body and soul. When soul will dominate over body and wisdom over ignorance, there will be an end of the struggle.

Augustine's *City of God* dominated Christian thought for centuries. It "set over against the declining world of ancient Rome the eternal common wealth of God's elect and sketched in fervid rhetoric the ideals and interests of that church here on earth which striven towards the kingdom of heaven." Several latter-day philosophers, for example Thomas Aquinas, Grotius etc., were considerably influenced by the thought of *City of God.* It is also said that the Holy Roman Empire was built upon the foundation of the *City of God.* Therefore it is quite correct to opine that, after Plato's *Republic* and Aristotle's *Politics,* St. Augustine's *City of God* was the most famous and influential book. It may be called a compendium of Christian ideas and philosophy of the Middle Ages. The *City of God* acted as a radar to the directionless and aberrant Christians. Here lies the significance of the *City of God.*

A recent author makes the following observation regarding the importance of *City of God* : The *City of God* is timeless, does not correspond with any earthly realm and provides a positive framework for the realisation of the supreme end for humanity (John Morrow—*History of Political Thought,* p. 26).

St. Bernard of Clairvaux

St. Bernard of Clairvaux (1091–1153) was an important churchman of the 12th century. He was an orthodox Christian, but he indulged an indifferent attitude towards holding any post and position. The most significant aspect of Bernard's thought is that *he strongly advocated the famous doctrine of two swords.* In a letter addressed to Pope Eugenisus III he unequivocally condemned the interference of the Pope into the secular affairs and, in fact, this single aspect has made him famous. He observed that the church's involvement in politics, intrigue, ambition and avarice had degraded its position and prestige in the public eye. Though he defended the supremacy of the church he did not like that the church would own property and would be interested in the loss and gain of wealth. Bernard scathingly rebuked the mode of living and activities of the church fathers.

Why did he object to the church's interference in secular affairs? He asked *"what is more slavish and unworthy, especially in the chief pontiff, than to sweat everyday and almost every hour over such things?"* His another question was *"why do you rush into another's field?* Why do you set your sickle to another's crop?" According to Bernard the dignity of ecclesiastical authority was much higher than that of the secular authority. The secular duties were to be performed by the prince, and it was beneath the prestige of the church to interfere with the affairs of state.

Bernard said that the church had the authority to possess two swords—the sword of spirit and the sword of flesh or body. But the sword of spirit should be used by the priest, that is, church. The sword of flesh should be handed over to the emperor and in this regard he did not recognise any compromise. While using the sword of flesh the prince would receive suggestion from the church. This contention of Bernard convinces us that although he supported the two swords' theory, he was not prepared to make any compromise so far as the supremacy of the church was concerned. Dunning[1] says *"The venality of the court never received a more direct and cutting rebuke than from Bernard, and the same is true of ostentation, frivolity and extravagance that ruled there"* (p. 184).

It is interesting to note that the church-state conflict assumed a new dimension at the hands of Bernard. Raising church to a very exalted position he narrowed down the scope of the conflict. The Emperor would deal with the secular problems and affairs, but his position was much lower than that of the Pope. The King would discharge his duties remaining under the authority of the church. He had no intention to investigate the causes of corruption and degradation with which the

1. Ibid.

society was faced. We find the influence of Aristotelian logic upon the thought of St. Bernard. Like Augustine, he did not adopt any imaginary city.

John of Salisbury (1120–1180)

The presentation of the supremacy of the church is to be found in the writing of John of Salisbury who is considered by many as the most typical Medieval writer. His famous political book is *Policraticus.* John had gathered wide experience about politics and in this respect he can be compared with Locke, Burke and John Stuart Mill. He came in close contact with politics and government which enabled him to acquire firsthand knowledge about the affairs of the state. In fact, this became his intellectual asset. Being a church-man he earned the reputation of a political writer. But it is to be noted here that John was not the innovator or originator of any political doctrine. His political ideas are mixture of politics and religion and this is due to the fact that he could not keep himself above the influence of the church and religion. He viewed and analysed everything in the background of religious outlook. Again, he did not make any relaxation about the supremacy of the church and in this respect we do not find any difference between St. Bernard and John of Salisbury.

John was the champion of the supremacy of the ecclesiastical authority. The struggle between the church and the state started in the ninth century and in the 12th century, when John started his writing, it had not ceased. In order to find out a solution to this he suggested the supremacy of the church over the secular power. He wanted to destroy the equal status of the state and the church. He was the supporter of the doctrine of two swords but he said that both the swords belonged to the church. The prince would take the sword of flesh from the church and use it under the guidance of the church. *He denied any autonomy to the emperor.* Let us put the matter in John's own words : This sword the prince receives from the hand of the church, although she herself has no sword of blood. Nevertheless she has this sword, but she uses it by the hands of the prince, upon whom she confers the power of bodily coercion, retaining to herself authority over spiritual things in the person of the pontiffs. Since the church was the original and real owner of sword, it had the full authority to dismiss the king if he were found violating the law of God.

In *Policraticus* we find a repetition of the organic theory of the state. Here he has compared the state with the human body. According to John the farmers and the workers of the state are like the feet of the human body. Because, as without feet human beings cannot move at all, so, without farmers and workers, a state cannot exist. The financial officers of the state correspond to the stomach and intestine. The officials and soldiers are like the hands. The senate can be compared with the heart. The prince can duly be compared with the head. Finally, the church of the state is the soul of the body. As the soul is the most vital organ of the body so also the church is the most important part of the state.

John's another contribution to political thought consists in drawing a difference between a tyrant and a prince. A tyrant is one who oppresses the people by rulership based upon force. When a man rules the nation in accordance with law, he deserves to be called a prince. Law is the gift of God, the model of equity, a standard of justice, a likeness of the divine will, the guardian of wellbeing, a bond of union and solidarity among people. The prince defines the duties and creates hindrances on the spread of violence and wrong-doings. The prince fights for the liberty and laws of the people. A tyrant is exactly opposite to the prince. John further observes that tyranny originates from inequity and poisonous root. It is a tree which grows and sprouts into a baleful pestilent growth and to which axe must by all means be laid. John's estimate of tyranny is highly provocative. In this respect he is indebted to Aristotle. His analysis of tyranny holds good even today.

John has ruthlessly attacked the vices and abuses of the ecclesiastical authority and, because of this, it is being underestimated by the public. It is not befitting on the part of the church to be engaged in the struggle for power. The prestige of the church is much higher. But it has deliberately degraded its own position and prestige. His criticism of the church influenced contemporary thought.

ST. THOMAS AQUINAS (1227–1274)

Introduction

Infertility in the intellectual field was the characteristic feature of the Middle Ages. The availability of information in philosophy, science and in other academic fields was very meagre. Only part of Aristotle's logic was known to the Middle Ages. But other parts of Aristotle's philosophy and politics were unknown to the medieval thinkers. The advent of the thirteenth century brought about a new flow in the intellectual field of Europe and this was possible due to the revival of Aristotelian philosophy. Door to knowledge was unlocked and people came in contact with Aristotle's thought system. The bad name of medieval period as Dark Age began to recede.

How was it possible? During the latter half of the 12th century and beginning of the 13th century scholars, historians and philosophers of Western Europe came to be acquainted with the works of Aristotle. Before this the scholars of Western Europe knew only the commentaries on Greek philosophy and politics made by Arabs. Now they got access to the original texts and this opened the windows to knowledge and it was a great academic gain for them. Arrival of Greek texts of Aristotle's politics, philosophy and logic helped the emergence of intellectualism in the middle of the 13th century. Scholars started to analyse different subjects in the light of Aristotelian logic. Several tendencies developed due to this new phenomenon. For example, the church and the Christian scholars who once dominated the intellectual world were pushed to the background and a new thought system emerged. The humanistic studies rapidly spread. Centres of higher education, particularly universities, were established in different parts of Europe such as Paris, Oxford and Bologna. Publicists and philosophers began to publish scholarly works on philosophy, theology and other subjects. Knowledge was systematised and different streams were unified. This attempt of unification threw new light on the intellectual progress. Faculties of arts, theology, law and medicine received priority everywhere—specifically at the University of Paris which was the premier academic institution. Ebenstein says "Henceforth the ideal of unity of knowledge remained the driving force of European universities. The application of the ideal changed with the outlook of times" (p. 211).

This new development of intellect gave rise and shape to scholasticism. Doctrines of the church fathers and dogmas of the church were compiled and commented. This was again mixed up with Aristotelian logic and philosophy. A compact and unified system of knowledge was produced by the scholars. The philosophical expression of this activity was embodied in the doctrines of soholasticism. This is no doubt a new direction of intellectual progress of the thirteenth century.

Let us see what is scholasticism. Dunning defines it in the following words : "In its most general aspects, scholasticism was a system of thought in which philosophy, in the purely rational sense, was so subordinated to established theological doctrines that where philosophy and theology trod on common ground, the latter was received as the absolute norm and criterion of truth" (p. 189). Scholasticism effected a reconciliation between the philosophy and the theological elements of the church fathers.

In the medieval period scholasticism was the embodiment of intellectual system and feudalism was the manifestation of economic and social system. From the ninth to the thirteenth century scholasticism was the predominant pattern of thought. Although scholasticism was the combination of Greek philosophy and ecclesiastical thought, yet it did not possess the dynamic character of the former. Greek philosophy never took anything for granted. In intellectual field Greek philosophy was always against imposition of any idea or conception. It always resorted to reason and argument to arrive at any conclusion. Whereas, the foundation of theological thought was faith and not reason. However, a connection was established by scholasticism between reason and faith. This blending reached its apex at the hands of St. Thomas Aquinas, the greatest of the later scholastics.

Life and Work of Thomas Aquinas

St. Thomas Aquinas, the chief spokesman of medieval scholasticism, was born at Aquino, a tiny place near Naples and from the name of the place he received the title Aquinas. But he is better known as Thomas and his thought is known to us as Thomism. He belonged to an aristocratic Italian family which had connections with European kings and emperors. In order to be a church father and to devote his life to the cause of Christianity and study he surrendered his title "Count." He joined the Dominican Order at the age of nineteen and for this purpose he had to fight his family. He studied in Naples, Cologne and Paris and in the last mentioned place he delivered several lectures on philosophy and theology. At the age of forty-eight he died.

Thomas Aquinas was a voracious reader and voluminous writer. He wrote about seventy books on various subjects and sizes. He was called in his time an encyclopedia. In his literary works Thomas has, with an astute mind, summarised the scholastic philosophy. The most spectacular contribution of Thomas to scholasticism is "the incorporation of Aristotelianism into Christian thought. Both Augustine and Thomas helped the development of the church doctrine. *Augustinianism* is the fusion of Plato and Christianity, *Thomism* is the synthesis of Aristotle and Christianity."[1]

On Kingship and *The Sum of Theology* are treated as important books of Thomas Aquinas on politics. Thomas has discussed the several aspects of scholasticism in The Sum of Theology. The Sum of Theology has been written in the question-answer

---

1. Ebenstein, p. 213.

form. Special attention has been paid to the political and legal questions and problems. Aquinas also wrote many other books on politics and theology. Historians are of opinion that he could not finish all the books. His pupils completed those works. Few more words may be said about *Thomism*. Augustine followed the path of Plato and made a synthesis between Platonism and Christianity. But the social, political and theological scene of Europe considerably changed and Augustinianism proved itself inadequate to cope with the change. To Augustine Christianity was simply a faith. He did not believe that it could have any logic or philosophy or anything about law. In the 13th century people began to view Christianity with a new outlook. They investigated its logic and philosophy. Thomas gave the leadership through his devotional analysis of scholasticism. And thus Thomism earned priority and predominance over Augustinianism.

On Nature of State

Before St. Thomas the church fathers and other medieval thinkers held that the state was ordained by God and the government was the instrument devised by God to punish the evildoers. This view was the product of the unfamiliarity with Aristotelian thought. Since Thomas was the spokesman of Aristotelianism he revived Aristotle's ideas on politics through his writings. In *Summa Theologica* St. Thomas has said that, in the state of nature, there was no slavery. In the state of innocence, man had no dominion over man. Following Aristotle, Thomas says that man is by nature a social animal. Therefore, men must have lived in society in the state of innocence. But there could not be a social life for many members unless there was the common good and members of the society must aim at that common good. Different men assembled together to single out a common end. The assembly of men gave rise to social organisation which was another name of civil society. Thus it is the sociability of man which has originated the civil society. Thomas Aquinas has further said that it is a fact that of all men there may be one man who is superior in excellence. It is quite natural that the superior man should be vested with the power of administration. The aim of the government is common welfare and the city (*civitas)* is a self-sufficing and perfect association.

So far there is a striking similarity between Thomas and Aristotle. But Thomas feels that Aristotle confined himself within the boundary of the city-state and he thought of the good life and welfare of its inhabitants. The other-worldly concern of St. Thomas Aquinas leads him to think that man cannot remain satisfied with the goodness and virtuousness of this mortal world. He tries to enjoy the company with God. In a word, Aristotle was concerned with man-centred values and we find Thomas to be concerned with God-centred values.

Commenting on Thomas's concept of state Berki says "with Aquinas we might say that political conservatism has a better foundation, but by the same token it is also a more moderate, cheerful and discerning king of conservatism, Augustine's Christianity enjoins us to accept, not enthusiastically, but with good grace a strange and hostile world; the Christian vision of Aquinas is a plea that we wholeheartedly accept a world which has in the mean time become friendly and Christian" (p. 107). Summarising Thomas's ideas about state a recent critic writes—The state is the human community which is most fully formed. It must follow from this that God wills the state to exist. J. S. McClelland–*History of Western Political Thought* (p. 115).

Forms of Political Authority

So far as the classification of government is concerned we find a clear influence of Aristotle on the thought of Thomas. Following Aristotle he says that broadly there are two types of government—one aims at the welfare of the ruler and the other seeks the welfare of all men. The latter type of government is just and ideal. In the perverted form of government there are tyranny, oligarchy and democracy. In ideal type we find kingship, polity and aristocracy.

If an unjust government is carried on by one man alone, who seeks his own benefit from his rule and not the good of the multitude, such a ruler is called *tyrant*. If an unjust government is carried on not by one but by several and particularly by the few, it is called an *oligarchy*. The objective of *oligarchy* is the welfare of the few. Finally, if the bad government is carried on by the multitude, it is called a *democracy*. Here the plebian people oppress the rich by force. In this case the whole people will be like a *tyrant*.

In the same manner the ideal or just government is divided into *polity, aristocracy* and *kingship*. Here the authority subjects its interest to the interest of the multitude. Welfare of the entire society is the only aim of the government. St. Thomas is found to be fluctuating between kingship and democracy. But ultimately he supports the kingship. On this issue he departs from Aristotle, because the latter lent his support to democracy. Thomas's argument is based on the consideration that the unity of the state is the main thing and this can be achieved if power is concentrated in the hands of a single man. The characteristic feature of democratic cities and provinces is the dissension. So monarchy is the best form of government. While discussing that kingship is the best form of government he makes several identical statements. Such as—the rule of one man is more useful than the rule of many, every natural governance is governance by one and it is best for human multitude to be ruled by one person.

Functions of Government

Thomas's concept of the functions of government has two aspects—regarding the first type the influence of Aristotle on him is very clear, on the second one he is influenced by the Bible. Aristotle had laboriously established that the true function of the government was to maintain and promote right and moral living of all subjects. The moral purpose of the government is, therefore, of paramount importance. It must also ensure the general welfare. Thomas agrees with this contention. He says that the duty of every ruler is to direct his activities to the happy and virtuous life. Like Aristotle he also emphasises the unity of the state and the government must attain it. According to Thomas the government must provide security to all its citizens and defend its people from any external aggression. Failure in this field will jeopardise the moral and right living of citizens to which it is committed.

But the contemporary conditions suggest, and the Bible is made to confirm, a number of other functions on which the Greeks did not dwell. It is the duty of the prince to keep the roads safe and free. The government shall keep an eye on number, weight and measure. It is the intention of God that all things shall be in order. That is why number, weight and measure are necessary. He has imposed another duty on the ruler by suggesting that the government will carefully look after the poor.

In this respect the Christian dictum is that—Nature is never wanting in necessaries. Christianity has always demonstrated sympathy towards the weak and suffering people. Thomas's emphasis upon the responsibility of the prince in respect of the alleviation of people's sorrows and sufferings is an important aspect of his political doctrine. His view on law and justice constitutes the most important part of his political thought and we shall now turn to that.

Law, Reason and Common Good

"St. Thomas's theory of law and justice is the channel through which the doctrines of Aristotle, the Stoics, Cicero, the Roman Imperial Jurists and St. Augustine blended into a rounded whole, were transmitted to modern times".[1] Thomas's definition and concept of law and its relation to reason and common good are very clear and in this respect he is superior to many medieval thinkers. "Law", according to St. Thomas, "is nothing else than an ordinance of reason for common good, made by him who has care for the community, and promulgated."

The above definition of law has several features which need special mention. Law is a rule and measure of acts whereby man is induced to act or is restrained from acting. Now the rule or measure of human acts is the reason. So law is something pertaining to reason. Besides reason another foundation of law is the common good. Law is ordained to the common good. Although law sometimes aims at the interest of private individuals, its chief purpose is the attainment of the general welfare. Law is imposed on others by way of rule or measure. The notification of law is made by pormulgation. Thomas has suggested a limitation upon the promulgator. He is of opinion that the promulgator must be acquainted with common good of the community.

Fourfold Classification of Law

The fourfold classification of law is a characteristic feature of St. Thomas's political philosophy. His four kinds of law are in fact four forms of reason and all the laws aim at common good of the community. Four different laws are eternal law, natural law, divine law and human law. If we look at different forms a cursory analysis of Thomas's classification reveals that in his philosophy there is no place of arbitrary will or action. Behind every action there must be reason and it is manifested in law. Both the nature and the society are governed by reason that is law.

The eternal law is the reason existing in the mind of God by which the whole universe is governed. The eternal law is identical with the divine reason that governs the universe and St. Thomas calls it eternal because God's rule of the world is not subject to time but is eternal. The eternal law is above the physical nature of man and it is beyond his comprehension. Man acts according to the wishes of God and he participates in His goodness and wisdom. He has no contribution to the making and changing of eternal law. Again, man cannot keep himself away from the operation of this law.

According to Thomas "natural law" belongs those things to which a man is inclined naturally and among these it is proper to man to be inclined to act according to reason. Nature implants the inclination in all animals. But man with his superior intelligence and capability is able to find out the distinction between good and bad

1. Dunning, p. 192.

and he acts according to reason. St. Thomas has distinguished three different species of natural law. There is the good that man pursues in accordance with the nature he has in common with all substances, such as self-preservation. Second, there is the inclination he has towards certain forms of conduct that he shares with all animals, such as sexual activities and education of offspring etc. Finally there is the inclination in him that is specifically human such as the desire to know God and avoid offending those with whom one lives.

Divine law is substantially revelation. It is related by St. Thomas to the fact that man's reason is neither the sole nor the most reliable guide to his apprehension of truth and justice. It is communicated to man through revelation. Thomas treats the divine law as the gift of God's grace rather than a discovery of natural reason. Thomas says that there is no conflict between natural law and divine law. There may be certain imperfections and loopholes in the natural law. The divine law corrects and removes them. "The divine law in the special sense is that through which the limitations and imperfections of human reason are supplemented, and man is infallibly directed to his supramundane end—eternal blessedness, it is the law of Revelation."[1]

The final and the lowest form of law is human law. Human law is the ordinance of reason aiming at common good. It is promulgated by man who cares for welfare of the community. St. Thomas states that it is not always possible for human beings to apprehend perfectly the inner meaning and objective of the divine law. To fill the gap another law is required. That is why man makes the law for himself. St. Thomas further states that the natural law cannot always be applied to specific problems. For this reason man makes law. So far as human law is concerned it has been asserted by Thomas that it introduces no new principles. A law is enacted by man remembering the divine law and natural law. But these laws are accommodated into the human law. Thomas has further admitted that there is hardly any arbitrariness in the human law because it always aims at the common good. Reason must also be embodied in it.

St. Thomas's conception of law is highly significant. The Greek philosophers regarded law as impersonal in origin—as a manifestation of reason, and not an expression of human will. That is, human factor had no role to play in enactment of law. Roman lawyers mainly emphasised upon the personal factor. St. Thomas Aquinas has combined both in his concept of law. In Thomas's definition law is both a reason and an expression of will. Even today we hold the view that reason must be embodied in every law, otherwise it cannot command allegiance from citizens. His attempt to relate common good to law is also noteworthy. "In his vision," observes Berki, "the concept of law is made to play the most prominent role" (p. 107). St. Thomas's concept of law has again combined theology, philosophy and modernism. In eternal and divine law philosophy and theology play the important part. On the contrary, the natural and human law are regarded as crucial parts of political theory.

The idea of justice is also related with his concept of law. In his view justice is the fixed and perpetual will to give to everyone his own rights. The fundamental principle of justice is equality. In defining justice St. Thomas Aquinas has adopted the principle of both Roman jurists and Aristotle. Thomas has based his idea either upon nature or upon decrees promulgated by human authority. He says that if a

1. Dunning, p. 193.

man gives something and in exchange of that he gets back the same then it will be said that there is equality. Similarly, decrees may be pressed into service to achieve equality. Thomas wants to say that nature may not always be conducive to the fostering of justice. It may not be deficiency of nature but the peculiarity of human society. However, human law has a positive part to play in implementing rights and justice. Again, it is to be noted here that the purpose of written law is to supplement the natural justice and not to create new justice. St. Thomas has not placed human law above nature.

St. Thomas's concept of law and justice may be called a confluence of Aristotelian, Roman, Stoic and Christian ideas as to the basis of social order. "The most original contribution that he makes to the subject is that definition and analysis of law through which he displaces at the ultimate source of authority the impersonal forces of nature and reason, and subordinates them to the personal Christian God. It is in accomplishing this that he emphasises the importance of volition in comparison with mere ratiocination, as an element in the definition of law."[1]

The Church and the State

St. Thomas was an orthodox Christian and naturally it is obvious that he will give priority to religion and the church over state affairs in general and politics in particular. But he recognised the importance of secular authority. Under such circumstances it is found that he took a moderate stand on the controversy between the church and the state. Sabine observes "His position may be described as that of a moderate papalist."[2] In fact, he did not scrupulously follow the doctrine of two swords. He said that the secular authority could claim allegiance from individuals, but the hegemony of the church over all matters must be accepted.

In determining the relation between the church and the state, St. Thomas has followed the Aristotelian principle. It shall be the supreme purpose of the government to help the realisation of the true end of the governed. But what is the true end of men? It is not to live according to virtue. But to live through a virtuous life to achieve the eternal enjoyment of the blessings of God. There is another Aristotelian principle which finds place in Thomism. The principle is—"the one to whom it pertains to achieve the final end commands those who execute the things that are ordained to that end" (Quoted by Ebenstein, p. 217).

Thomas's scheme of church-state relation is couched with hierarchical terms. The purpose of the secular authority is to achieve certain legitimate ends. But these ends are not final. "They transcend mundane life. The government through which it is reached must be a higher, that is, the sacerdotal, kind."[3] The temporal government holds the intermediate position. It is concerned only with the temporal matters. These must act as instruments to achieve higher ends. Hence the secular government is and must be subject to the church.

In the treatment of heretics St. Thomas's suggestion also speaks of another aspect of church-state relation. Thomas says that in respect of heretics the church should practise toleration. The church is always against taking drastic action against the heretics. Generally it admonishes them. But if the heretics are incorrigible and if

---

1. Dunning, p. 197.
2. Sabine, p. 256.
3. Dunning, p. 206.

their crime is serious and liable to create bad repercussion upon society, the church excommunicates them and delivers them to the hands of the temporal power for taking drastic action which may be death penalty. Thomas states that when spiritual weapons are exhausted, then, and then only, temporal weapons are resorted to. The Church abhors the shedding of blood and only the government can do it. Ebenstein remarks "yet this separation of ecclesiastical and secular authorities is not final, because the church and state cooperate in the highest task of all—the salvation of the souls" (p. 217).

The king will conduct the temporal affairs in his own way, but under no circumstances will he try to ignore the authority and supremacy of the church. Even his officials are bound to obey the church. Any defiance will be followed by excommunication. St. Thomas was interested in the unity and integrity of the nation and in his view this could be attained only through the church. Any person disobeying the church would surely jeopardise the unity of the nation. Thomas thought is to be a serious crime. He recommended the abridgement of secular authority in the greater interest of the state, and the church was the embodiment of this greater interest.

Although St. Thomas was a pioneer thinker of scholasticism and a great lover of reason, he held the view that the greatest truths would be obtained only through faith. The church was the final authority in faith and nobody could challenge the church. By holding this view, St. Thomas Aquinas allowed inconsistency to creep into his thought system. He did not allow the king to interfere with the spiritual affairs, but allowed the priest to interfere with the temporal matters. This did not solve the polemics between the church and the state which was the characteristic feature of the Middle Ages.

DANTE ALIGHIERI (1265–1321)

Decline of Papacy and Rise of a New Class

Roman civilisation flourished in the cities. All the amenities of urban and civilised life were available in the cities. The rural area was the supplier of agricultural commodities and other raw materials. The foreign invasions and the appearance of feudalism destroyed the city-centred civilisation of Europe. In the countryside, the feudal landlords became all-powerful. Many priests and church fathers were also great feudal lords. The feudal lords—both secular and spiritual—controlled the economy of Western Europe. St. Thomas was mainly concerned with the establishment of hegemony of the church. He was not interested in the broader political and economic aspects of the state. During the heyday of feudalism, the ownership of land was the source of power and influence. Church—by virtue of the ownership of land—exercised power and influence as well as control over the economy. Unfortunately, St. Thomas did not explore this side of the church. In fact, the civilisation and economy of Western Europe developed in the rural area.

But from the twelfth century the economic and political panorama began to change. Feudalism disintegrated. New cities and towns came into existence and then became the new centres of economy and civilisation. The influence of the church over the economy naturally declined. In the past, the church was the centre of intellectual life of Western Europe. Towards the end of the thirteenth century this position of the church was also faced with a challenge and this came from a new class. This erosion in the influence and power of the church threw it into good deal of anxiety. In a word, in economic, political and intellectual fields the decline of the church was the characteristic feature of the late thirteenth century thought, and the church treated it as a serious menace to its predominance. The newly emerged urban population looked askance at the division of power between the church and the aristocracy. People's loyalty to the church did not remain as it was before.

In the late thirteenth and the beginning of the fourteenth century, a new tendency developed. Phenomenal progress of transport and communication considerably facilitated the travelling people and all these collectively changed the economic and commercial picture of many countries of Europe. The feudal economic structure failed to cope with the new tides of economy and commerce and, ultimately, it was on the verge of collapse. A new class called the bourgeoisie surfaced and, displacing the feudal landlords, it became the primary class. In the feudal system there was also the bourgeoisie but it was the secondary class. At the beginning of the 14th century the entire economy came into the fold of this rising class. The bourgeoisie challenged the privileges and domination enjoyed by the church. The bourgeois class thus brought under its fold two forces simultaneously—the monopoly of the church in learning and technical knowledge in arts and crafts, and the predominance of feudal lords over the economy and politics.

With the help of financial power the bourgeois class asserted its full control over the base—the economy. The sources of production and the method of distribution both came to be controlled by the bourgeoisie. After this, the bourgeois remodelled the superstructure, that is arts, literature, history, law and everything after its own image.[1] The accumulation of wealth impelled it to think about its security. The bourgeois class proceeded to strengthen the hands of the state. Only the state—with the help of police and military—could give it maximum protection to its wealth from being taken away by those who did not own it. The rise of the bourgeois class rejuvenated the emasculated state power and helped it to rise from despondency. The state gradually appeared to be powerful and an alliance was established between the state and the bourgeois class. This was the starting point of the new role of the state—the state as an instrument of exploitation. That is why the alliance has been termed by the Marxists as unholy.

In the thirteenth and fourteenth centuries, urban life revived in Italy. Also did arise the capitalist system. The international trade, banking system and financial institutions, all were the products of Italy. Modern historians and political scientists have said that the capitalist system did not start with the Industrial Revolution of the 18th century England, but with the commercial and financial enterprises of Italy. The emergence of the nation state, anti-papacy and the bourgeois class was almost simultaneous.

Life and Thought of Dante

Dante Alighieri was born in Florence in 1265 and died in 1321. He was a man of two centuries and the most vocal antipapal. He was the great supporter of anti-

1. In nearly every respect the traditional civilisation based on church dogma and landed power was challenged, altered and replaced by a new way of life that was more productive in economics, more equalitarian in government and more secular in general outlook. Ebenstein, p. 239.

papacy and imperial power. He defended the imperial authority in its absolute form and ruthlessly criticised the hegemony of the church. In this respect, Dante stood diametrically opposite to St. Thomas and John of Salisbury. Dante wrote a book *De Monarchia* (On Monarchy) by about 1310. He was also the author of *Divine Comedy. De Monarchia* was the most influential anti-papalist and imperialist tract in the fourteenth century.

Dante was a Florentine and he had gathered considerable experience in practical politics. During his exile he wandered from court to court and this enabled him to gain valuable knowledge on judicial and administrative affairs. The anarchic condition of Italy pained him very much. Following Aristotle, he said that man could achieve his purposes only in a united and peaceful state. This could be done by a unified and powerful monarch. A powerful monarch could claim the capacity to decide all the controversies and meet the demands of his citizens. He had no faith in the hegemony of the church. Justice was to be found in an imperial administration. He said that the state should exist for the sake of the individuals. They must have this liberty and rights and he found the dismal condition of the church in this respect. People must have a say in the management of the state. Analysing from this angle we call Dante a democrat and also a modern thinker. But in his approach to history, canon law and theological dogma he was a medieval thinker.

Dante was a great patriot. He realised that the papal authority was mainly responsible for never-ending dissension among the people of Italy. The church never made any sincere attempt to unite the people nor to bring about peace. Building up of a powerful nation-state under the authority of a monarch, according to Dante, was the only remedy to the prevailing ills from which Italy was suffering.

Like other thinkers of imperial power, Dante thought that the power of the emperor was derived from God, and hence it was independent of the church. In all spiritual matters he admitted the authority of the church. But the two powers were united only in God. In order to make the emperor powerful, and to bring about peace and unity in the state, study of law and jurisprudence was necessary and he emphasised this. Dante was responsible for the renewed emphasis in the study of Roman law. He enveloped his thought with a theological garment. We can say Dante had reconciled theology, law, jurisprudence, imperial power and, above all, Aristotelian principles. In the words of Sabine "Like Thomas, he placed his theory of the universal community within a framework of principles derived from Aristotle" (p. 258).

In his celebrated work *De Monarchia* Dante has raised three questions—one is, whether a world government ruled by a monarch is necessary for the welfare of the human race. Secondly, whether the Roman people acquired world domination by right. Thirdly, whether the authority of the emperor derives directly from God or some minister of God.

Whether Temporal Monarchy is Necesary for Welfare of the World

The first question raised by Dante in *De Monarchia* is whether the temporal monarchy is necessary for the welfare of the world. He answers the question from three different angles. The first is the philosophical point of view. The unity of the state is of primary importance. He says "where the unity is greatest, the good is also greatest". Lack of unity affects the good. In his opinion, only the temporal monarchy can ensure unity. The development of the rational qualities of man is possible only in a peaceful atmosphere and this is to be achieved by the temporal monarchy.

Dante has argued that for the settlement of disputes between the states no war is necessary. He says, "wherever there is a controversy, there ought to be a judgment." This judgment is to be delivered only by the temporal monarchy. His decisions are binding on all. If there is a world government, and if all the states act according to the directives of that government, the possibility of war among the states will be much less. It is surprising to note that more than six centuries ago this son of Florence imagined of a world government, world peace and international understanding. In the middle of the 20th century we established United Nations and in the last decade of the century we saw the crises with which the world organisation was faced.

Dante finally has adopted Aristotelian argument. He says that where a number of things are arranged to attain an end it behoves one of them to govern the others, and the others to submit. Take the case of an individual. His objective is to pursue happiness and he subordinates all other objectives to it. He is guided by reason and not by impulses. In a household there is a head of the family and all the members are subordinate to the head who is normally the father. The independence of all members will invite chaos. The same thing happens in the case of city or kingdom. When a kingdom is divided itself it is brought to desolation. The purpose of the whole human race is happiness and peace. Naturally there shall be only one guide to govern. The proper title of this office is Monarchy of Empire. He is necessary for the welfare of the world.

Dante's world government is not an indication of uniformity. In the world government there shall be uniformity of law and government, but ethnic, cultural and linguistic differences should be accepted. Local issues should be settled locally. The monarchy should not be burdened with these matters. Common problems and issues of wider importance needs be vested in the monarchy. In this way, Dante has attempted a reconciliation between regionalism and universalism.

Whether the Roman People were Justified in Assuming the Dignity of Empire

In answering this question Dante has again adopted Aristotelian principle which states that all men are not capable of governing others. Nature makes some men suitable for the purpose. Similarly, all nations do not possess the capacity to govern other nations. Certain races or nations are born to govern, and certain others are to be governed. Here subjection is expedient and for the fulfilment of greater interest this is to be accepted. He further observes it cannot be doubted that nature ordained in the world a country and a nation for universal sovereignty. This nation must perform the nature-ordained duty. In this view, Rome is the nature-ordained state to govern the entire world. He notices that record of Roman achievement is full of miracles. Roman people was by nature ordained to empire and, therefore, it was of right that they gained empire. Dante categorically says that Romans sought empire not from greed, but for the sake of common good of the conquered as well as the conquerors.

Critics are of opinion that it is very difficult to understand what Dante exactly means by Roman people. In the thirteenth century various races lived in Rome. It is also obvious from his observation that he had no animosity against pagans who constituted a major part of Rome. Although Dante was an Italian he advocated Roman supremacy.

Whether the Authority Derives Directly from God or Some Vicar or Minister of God

This is the last question of *De Monarchia.* Dante's anti-papalist idea is quite clear here. His predecessors, including St. Thomas, held that the authority of the emperor was derived from the Heaven, that is God. Dante says that the Roman emperor possessed power even before the church. Therefore, church or any priest cannot be the source of emperor's power and authority. In Dante's own words—the authority of the temporal monarchy comes down, with no intermediate will, from the fountain of universal authority; and this fountain, one in its unity, flows through many channels out of the abundance of goodness of God.

Dante's antipapalist idea is also evident in his analysis of human nature and the objective at which the individual aims. Following Aristotle, Dante says that every man has dual aims—one is the blessedness of the *earthly life* and the other is the blessedness of *heavenly paradise.* The means of attaining these two objectives are quite different, since they are quite apart. To achieve the first aim, man resorts to reason and philosophy. Philosophers and wise men write treatises and people read these books, perfect their knowledge and earthly life. In this respect no supernatural power comes to their assistance. We can get the blessing of heavenly paradise through the spiritual lessons. Revelations of scriptures are the only source of eternal and supernatural truths. The church is not the source at all. Therefore, the claim of the church as the source of spiritual revelations is unfounded and unacceptable.

It is, therefore, obvious that since man has two aims, he wants two guides. The emperor is the guide for earthly blessings. He can guide him to happiness in this world, in accordance with the teaching of philosophy. Only the Supreme Pontiff leads mankind to eternal life...one cannot interfere with the other.

Before Dante two medieval philosophers—St. Augustine and St. Thomas—discussed the origin of the state. According to Augustine, the state is created by divine Providence to punish the frailty and sinfulness of man. Naturally, he has nothing to object. St. Thomas, following Aristotle, says that the state is a natural association embodying man's social character. Ebenstein concludes—"Dante is the first writer in the Middle Ages who ingeniously combines Augustinian and Thomistic elements" (p. 244). The central idea of Dante's political philosophy is that man needs the help of temporal authority for the fulfilment of his earthly requirements and for this he need not run after the church or the Pope.

MARSILIUS OF PADUA (1270–1340)

Boniface Philip Episode

In order to understand the full implications of the political ideas of Marsilius of Padua, it is necessary to go through the events that took place at the beginning of the fourteenth century. Although Dante was an outspoken thinker of antipapalism, he failed to appreciate the importance of the nascent nation-state which was engulfing the political scene of Western Europe. The rise of the nation-state and people's increasing sympathy towards it ultimately made possible the enhancement in the power of the emperor and cornered the papacy. This was particularly discernible in France—towards the fag end of the 13th century. The most remarkable event of this period (end of 13th century and beginning of the 14th century) was the conflict between Pope Boniface VIII (1294–1303) and Philip the Fair, king of France. The conflict was both interesting and complicated and had far-reaching repercussions. Let us now see the nature of the conflict.

The main cause of the controversy was the power to impose taxation. As a result of the disintegration of feudalism, the administrative responsibility of both the English and French emperors increased considerably, and this needed a large amount of money. Since the church was the owner of fabulous amount of property and was not paying any tax, the French king proceeded to impose new taxes upon the property of the church. This infuriated the Pope. On the other hand, the ambitious church wanted to get more and more money by adopting various means. Pope Boniface declared that the mundane authority had no right to levy taxes upon the church and, if at all levied, he was not bound to pay it. He also directed the clergy not to pay any taxes. On the opposite side stood the king of France—Philip the Fair. He said that the church had no power to collect any revenue or money in any form from the public without his permission. His argument was that the French king was the undisputed authority over all temporal matters. He could not recognise a financial state within a state. He further said that political sovereignty was meaningless without tax sovereignty.

In 1302, Pope Boniface issued the Bull **Unam Sanctum.** In this, Pope Boniface admitted the existence of two swords—one would remain at the hands of the king and the other at the hands of the Pope. But both would be fully controlled by the Pope. That is, the temporal authority would not be allowed to use the sword according to its necessity. He further declared that the temporal authority, because of its errors, would be judged by the spiritual authority. But in case of any mistake on the part of the spiritual authority, the temporal power had no right to judge. The declaration of Boniface raised the conflict to the apex point. The French king Philip the Fair accepted the challenge and proceeded to take action.

Philip the Fair brought twenty-nine charges against Boniface and he received overwhelming support from all sections of French society. This encouraged him and he launched a coup against Boniface. The Pope suffered the severest humiliation at the hands of the king and after a few weeks he died. The victory of Philip the Fair over Boniface undoubtedly established the supremacy of the monarch over his own domain and the Pope had nothing to do. Again, the church's unlimited lust for money was halted by the king and this was not temporary. The controversy made the moral position of the French monarch stronger.

The death of Boniface, however, failed to satisfy Philip the Fair and other anti-papalists. They moved to condemn his *post mortem*. This move embarrassed Pope Clement, who succeeded Boniface. In order to appease the anti-papalist sentiment and to save the church from scandal, Pope Clement instituted a commission for investigation and simultaneously annulled all the announcements of Boniface. Philip the Fair was highly praised by Pope Clement for his bold stand against Boniface. A very long chapter of controversy between the church and the state came to an end.

Life and Work of Marsilius of Padua

The defeat of Boniface brought about three definite tendencies towards the end of the medieval period—the secularisation of life, particularly politics, the rise of the bourgeoisie and the formation of the nation-state. Marsilius of Padua was the representative philosopher of these tendencies. He was born in 1275 and died in 1343. There is a gap of one hundred years between the death of St. Thomas and birth of Marsilius. Marsilius or Marsilio is better known in the name of his birth-place Padua which was a city of Ezzelino da Romano. He was a physician and a student of philosophy, theology and law. Marsilio led a wandering life. At one time he was canon of Padua. Study of medicine and to some extent of law made his mind scientific, secular and critical. He was very much hesitant to accept anything on its face-value.

Marsilio went to Paris and studied there different subjects. Later on he became a teacher of Paris University. His stay at Paris contributed to the formation of his ideas and philosophy. He was an energetic and adventurous person. His anti-papacy feeling reached the highest point while he was at Paris and historians say that here he planned to write a book on anti-papacy. His famous book *Defensor Pacis* or *The Defender of Peace* was published in 1324. The book contains fierce hatred against the Pope. It is said that John of Gandun was the co-author of *The Defender of Peace. The Defender of Peace* is a remarkable book. Its approach is quite bold and uncompromising. Critics maintain that Marsilius cannot be regarded as an original thinker, because he collected his ideas from the publicists and pamphleteers. Paris University, at his time, was a congregation of top-ranking philosophers and thinkers. Marsilio's connection with them enriched his outlook and thought.

Marsilius, Dante and Aristotle

Fourteen years after *De Monarchia, The Defender of Peace* was published. Both Dante and Marsilio were contemporaries.[1] They appeared on the transition from the medieval to the modern period. But in outlook and ideas Dante remained a medieval thinker whereas historians and scholars treat Marsilius as a modern thinker. But Marsilio's forms of thought and argument are essentially medieval. In *De Monarchia* and *Peace* both the authors have refuted the claims of the Pope, but the arguments of Marsilio are more decisive and aggressive. The weakness or sympathy to Christianity of both is almost same. None of them is found to finalise the separation of politics from religion. But the attempt of Marsilius in this field is more progressive. Compared with Dante, Marsilio "is regarded by some as the most original medieval political writer, precisely because he seeks so consciously to break the fetters of his age and because he rejects vigorously and unequivocally any clerical control of thought or government."[2] Both are anti-papalists and have placed the state above the church.

However, the link between Marsilio and Aristotle is very clear. In fact, he is called another Aristotelian thinker of the medieval period. Marsilio's use of Aristotle's technique and adoption of Aristotelianism are more decisive than other medieval scholars. His indebtedness to the Greek philosopher is not simply verbal. The minds of both the philosophers are practical, critical and scientific. Like Aristotle he tries

1. Dante (1256-1321); Marsilius (1275-1343).
2. Ebenstein, p. 261.

to use common sense and empirical verification rather than abstract speculation and authoritative dogma. Marsilio's analysis of the origin of the state and self-sufficiency of the community is derived from Aristotle. He also follows Aristotelian classification of government. But he differs from Aristotle when he says that, that government is good which aims at the common good in accordance with the will of the people. The bad government aims at its own benefit and neglects the welfare of the people.

Conception of the State

Marsilio's *The Defender of Peace* has three parts. The first part is a repetition of Aristotelian principles of classification of government, origin of society and state. The second part deals with the church, functions of priests and their relation to the temporal authority. The volume of the third part is very short. It comprises forty-two conclusions from the theories developed in the previous two parts.

The starting point of his analysis is the political society. What we call state or political society originates in a general recognition of common needs. To meet the common necessities, people have built up the foundation of the state. Following Aristotle Marsillius has said that family is the primary or first stage of state. The family arose to meet certain limited demands which were short of common needs. So the evolution of society did not stop there. The association of several families gave birth to a bigger organisation. Again, the bigger organisation or association failed to meet all the common needs. Moreover, it suffered from coordination or cooperation among all the members. The state came into existence to fulfil the common needs and to materialise the cooperation among the members. Marsilio's view of the origin of the state is simply the repetition of Aristotle's views. He frequently quotes Aristotle.

Again in his analysis of various forms of state and its other aspects we find clear influence of Aristotle. He classifies government into two broad types—good and diseased forms. In the first type there are three forms—monarchy, aristocracy and constitutionalism. The second type consists of tyranny, oligarchy and dictatorship. The criterion of this classification it based on whether the ruler serves his own interest or the interests of the subjects. But he departs from Aristotle by adding that the common good at which the good government aims must be based on the consent of the people. What is common benefit and what is not needs to be decided by the people and not by the ruler. Summarising Marsilio's view of state Gettell says "The state was conceived as a living organism, intended to secure to men guarantees of order and free development of capacity, leading to a general welfare. The right of the state to a life of its own independent of any outside control was the basic principle in Marsilius's thought" (p. 128). Another critic observes "Like Aristotle, Marsilis treats the state as a natural organism, and it exists so that men can live sufficient life. The parts of the state are parts making different contributions to the life of the whole. The parts of the state are functionally identified as contributors to the sufficient life". —J. S. McClelland—*History of Political Thought*, p. 138.

Functions of Government

Man, according to Marsilio, is a perverse creature. He is self-seeking, violent and aggressive. He is disposed to regard other men as his rivals and this creates an atmosphere of animosity among all men. Marsilius feels the necessity of the termination of this condition. That is why he suggests that the first duty of the government is the repression of the perverse will of man. Its primary business is to force men to do their own work and not to meddle with others' affairs. This perverse nature of man is injurious to society. The government checks it and creates a congenial atmosphere of development.

There is another necessity of government and it is the realisation of *tranquillitas.* Tranquillitas means peace and security which are preconditions of progress and prosperity. It further means that, without cooperation and adjustment, general welfare of the community is not possible at all. "Government is required not only for the repression of the perversity but for the organisation of cooperation"[1] Marsilio has enumerated the different functions performed by different classes of people—judge, soldier, farmer, artificer, capitalists, priests etc. All these are to be coordinated and organised for the common benefit of the political society. It is the business of the government to allot to each man his proper work and keep him at it. Hearnshaw comments—"The conception is quite what we call socialistic."

Law, Legislator and Popular Sovereignty

Marsilius of Padua speaks of two main types of law—divine law and human law. According to Marsilio the divine law is a direct command of God, without human deliberations, about voluntary acts of human beings to be done or avoided in this world, but for the sake of attaining the best end or some conditions desirable for man, in the world to come.[2]

Human law is a command to the whole body of citizens or of its prevailing party arising directly from the deliberation of those empowered to make law, about voluntary acts of human beings to be done or avoided in this world, for the sake of attaining the best end or some condition desirable for man.[3]

The divine law is the will of God and it has no relation to the man-made law. The punishments and rewards are awarded according to this law, but they are not in this world. Both will be available in heaven. On the contrary, man makes laws to facilitate the performance of something or avoidance of something. Punishments and rewards are the subjects of this world and God is not connected with it at all. Human law is the imperative expression of the common need, formulated by reason, promulgated by recognised authority, and sanctioned by force. Law is also a judgment on what is advantageous or disadvantageous for the community as a whole.

Marsilius then embarks upon the analysis of the source of law and process of enactment. In his opinion, the legislator is the cause of law. The legislator, or the primary and proper efficient cause of the law, is the people or whole body of citizens, or the weightier part thereof, through its election or will expressed by the general assembly of the citizens. It implies that the law is the result of the corporate action of people or the whole body of citizens or its weightier part. When all the citizens assemble together and enact law, it is obvious that Marsilius speaks of direct democracy. But his term 'weightier part' is really confusing. He, however, defines it in the following way. It means the quantity and the quality of persons in that community over which the law is made. It may not always be possible that all the citizens at a particular time will be able to meet together to make a law. In that situation, only the weightier part (to some it is the prevailing part) will participate

1. Hearnshaw, p. 179.
2. & 3. Quoted by Sabine, p. 295.

in the enactment of law. This is the working solution of Marsilius of any probable deadlock.

The subsequent analysis of Marsilius makes it amply clear that for a better law it is necessary that all the citizens should participate in its enactment. The authority to make the law, says Marsilius, belongs only to those men whose making of it will cause the law to be better observed. Only the whole body of citizens are such men. Since the whole body of citizens, by giving consent, makes a law valid, it also creates a legal authority.

Marsilio's conception of law and government lays the foundation of popular sovereignty. Law will be valid when it receives the consent of the people. His emphasis on weightier part of the state does not negate the idea of popular sovereignty. The will of the whole body of citizens will, under all circumstances, get priority and this makes the popular sovereignty complete. Marsilio's idea of popular or democratic sovereignty has good deal of impact upon the thought system of the nineteenth and twentieth centuries.

His theory of the *accountability of the ruler* to the general public also highlights the idea of popular sovereignty. The ruler is susceptible to mistakes and misdeeds and these must be corrected, otherwise he will be a despot. But the question is who will rectify the authority? Here Marsilio's suggestion is the legislator, that is, the whole body of citizens will bring the ruler to order. The legislator will have the power to correct the government or to change it completely. It may so happen that the whole body of citizens may not be in a position to exercise its power and, in that situation, this body will delegate its authority to some other persons. Whatever may be the situation the legislator reserves the right to call for explanation from the authority to correct it. Here we find that, in Marsilius's thought system, the legislator plays a vital role. In fact, the legislator's activities and alertness make the sovereignty popular.

The purpose of enunciating the doctrine of popular sovereignty was to cut the wings of church. It had also another purpose—to destroy the possibility of class rule. He had declared quite explicitly against any class government. Marsilius wrote *Defensor Pacis* in the fourteenth century and in his time there were gross economic and other forms of inequalities. Apprehending class rule he made a strong brief for the sovereignty of all people or at least for the weightier part. He thought that the weightier part would be the numerically majority.

Church and State

In the realisation of tranquillitas the role of the government is to coordinate the activities of different classes of society and particularly the functions of the church with those of the rest of the society. Marsilio is not sure of the functions of the church or the priest. There is no evident necessity of the priest. Yet in all societies religion and ecclesiastical organisations are to be found. Although law checks the nefarious activities of man, yet its uniform application is not possible. Even law cannot reach everywhere. In this situation the true function of the priest, according to Marsilius, is to supplement the action of the police and the judge by the fear of hell. The fear of hell prevents men from doing unlawful and perverse activities harmful for society. The Christian revelation assertively says that there is a future life, and the wellbeing of that life depends on the scrupulous adherence to those principles and revelations propagated by the church. The priests are, therefore, necessary parts of human salvation. There is, therefore, a necessity of the church.

Regarding the church the most important function of temporal power is to recognise and maintain it. Beyond this the temporal authority has nothing to do with the church. It means that the emperor cannot interfere with the ecclesiastical activities of the church. On the contrary, the activities of the priest will have reference to the welfare of the other world. The priest has no possible claim to interfere with the cooperative effort to secure earthly ends. His function is, simply, to give instruction in the requisites of salvation, to exhort and to warn and to administer sacraments. The ecclesiastical organisation has no reason to interfere with the activities of the state. Marsilius does not recognise the special status of the Pope. He simply mentions the priest.

In Marsilio's opinion the church, as such, has no rightful or rational claim to any kind of coercive jurisdiction. The clergy have no rightful claim to any kind of immunity from or independence of secular jurisdiction. Neither Pope nor clergy have any right to govern or even to speak for the church. The clergy have no rightful title to property. As to the coercive jurisdiction, Marsilio's view is very bold and simple. He has deprived the church the power to pass judgment on heresy. The heretics will be punished by the proper authority in the other world on the day of judgment. Again, if the heretics violate the civil law they are to be first of all punished by the civil authority according to the prevailing civil law. On the next stage, his judgment will be conducted by God.

Marsilio's courageous assertion provides the greatest assault upon the church and its authority in the so-called religious atmosphere of the Middle Ages. He treats the church as part of the civil authority and, naturally, it comes within the jurisdiction of civil laws. It cannot claim any special treatment. Any violation of secular law by the priest is to be judged by the judicial department of the government. In this way Marsilio has reduced the church as a simple department of the secular government. Marsilius painfully observed that instead of devoting to spiritual functions, the church was engaged in amassing property and wealth for the attainment of material and earthly comforts—and this was anti-Christianity. The amount of church property is required to be decided by the necessities of the priests. Naturally, there is no scope of accumulating property.

Marsilius also takes away from the hands of the priests, to teach and discipline the public. For this purpose the church should set up organisations and institutions as well as religious organisations. He is of opinion that this function is to be performed by the secular government. The civil authority will decide who will be given this function. In support of his contention Marsilius has recalled the scriptures. Christ himself was against any property and secular rule.

Marsilio did not recognise the hierarchical structure of the church. He observes that the Pope, bishop and all other church personnel are of the same rank. So the spiritual quality and qualification of any Pope or priest is not different from that of an ordinary churchman. The priestly character of the Pope or the priest which authorises him to perform certain rites of religion is purely a mystical stigma. By advocating spiritual equality he has denied the special status of the priests and the Pope.

As to religious faith and doctrine, Marsilius believes that the divine scriptures are to be followed sincerely. Nobody has given the Pope the right of interpretation.

People will judge scriptures according to their own belief, faith and wisdom. If any inconsistency arises in interpretations of scriptures a general council of believers is to be formed for this purpose and this council will be authorised to settle all disputes. Ebenstein says (p. 267) Marsilio's insistence on the return to the scriptures as the sole source of religious faith and divine law, his ruthless demolition of the edifice of dogma and the power which built up the church over centuries of institutional growth, is one of the winds that finally gathers in the hurricane of the Protestant Reformation. Commenting on Marsilio's tirade against the church, Sabine observes—"His theory is a root and branch attack upon the ecclesiastical hierarchy and especially upon a papal *plentitudo potestatis,* but he recognised that, even for spiritual purposes and to resolve spiritual questions, the church requires some organisation distinct from the civil community" (p. 300).

Although Marsilius was against the supremacy of the church, it cannot be said that he was against any organisation or authority of the church as such. On the polemical spiritual issues and other ecclesiastical matters and faith the church will have the authority to deal with them. The Church cannot be allowed to exercise uncalled authority and absolute power. However, by suggesting the establishment of a council, he cut the wings of church.

His General Council may rightly be compared with the executive organ of a government. He transfers to the church and, more particularly, to the General Council, an element of his political theory. Analysing from this angle, Marsilio's whole idea of church-state relation may be called a patchwork, a compromise. Being a scholar and philosopher of the Middle Ages he did not try to keep himself above all sorts of religious beliefs, faiths and dogmas. He wanted to cut the church to size. Marsilio's citizens possessed two capacities—as citizens of the state and members of the church.

Today we are accustomed to treat the state as essentially a secular association. Marsilio's state did not fall in that category. Sabine says that he did not effect a complete divorce between the state and the church. The state was mixed with certain religious elements and the church with certain political elements. It was a patch-work. "It is true that his theory as a whole is something of a compromise. His citizens still appear as members of two corporations, the state and the church."[1] But he has divested the church of its overwhelming authority over the secular organ of the state. This is really a bold step of Marsilio and no other medieval thinker ventured to adopt such a step. His secular authority is not empowered to perform religious duties, but the church will discharge its functions simply as a department of the state. It implies that the civil matters of the church will come under the jurisdiction of the state. In this sense his state may aptly be compared with city-state. It is competent, says Sabine, to regulate every branch of its civilisation.

Church and State in Medieval Thought

In the medieval period there were society, state and church. The former two were non-religious organisations while the latter was purely a religious organisation. In the Middle Ages there developed a close relationship among these three. But this relation was never cordial or cooperative. Before the decline of the medieval period there was intense conflict between the state and the church. However, all the

1. Sabine, pp. 303-304.

thinkers of this age did not view the relation between the two in the same light and perspective. So there is a necessity to survey the relationship between the state and the church.

First we shall consider how St. Augustine (354–430) viewed the state and its relationship with the church. He believed that both the society and the state were created by God as a punitive and remedial institution. Originally men lived in the state of nature. They were innocent and pure-hearted. Sin did not overpower them. But personal greediness and self-aggrandisement ultimately overpowered them to defy the will of God and, finally, they disobeyed their own noble and good sense. God, out of mercy, created an institution, namely, the state to bring these persons in order and to force them to deviate from the path of sin and ungodliness. God also sent a man to rule and punish them. This, Augustine called, is the City of Earth. He also created another institution which was City of Heaven. In the City of Earth there were self-interest seeking persons and, in the latter, there were angels who always sacrificed their personal interests. So in Augustine's view the earthly state was purely a reformative political organisation.

According to Augustine the church was the representative of God on earth and the only spokesman so far as the sermons or orders of God were concerned. Since the Augustine's state was a religious one the king had no authority to defy the order or advice of the church. Moreover, the king was sent by God to punish the sinners. He was accountable only to God. This view of Augustine indicates that the state had no separate existence outside the church.

John of Salisbury (1120–1180) was another medieval thinker who said that the authority of the state must accept the supremacy of the church. He denied the supremacy of the emperor. Though he was the supporter of the doctrine of two swords he believed that the king would receive the temporal sword from the Pope or church and will rule the state in accordance with the advice of the church. Ownership of the sword could not be entrusted to the king.

St. Thomas Aquinas (1227–1274) was another renowned medieval thinker. In his writings, especially *On Kingship*, he had elaborated the controversial issue of the relationship between the church and the state. St. Thomas Aquinas was an orthodox Christian and, naturally, it could not be expected that he would support the supremacy of the secular authority. He, however, believed that the secular authority must have certain amount of autonomy without which he could not administer the state. The emperor could claim allegiance from the individuals but he must recognise the hegemony of the church. Estimating his position between the church and the state, Sabine states that his position may be described as that of a moderate populist. He did not take any extreme stand as to the conflict between the two institutions. Thomas adopted the Aristotelian technique of middle-way. He said that it would be the duty of the government to see that the true end is achieved and, according to Thomas, this true end is the realisation of honesty, goodness, virtue and, to attain the blessings of God. From this it is obvious that Thomas Aquinas had softened the earlier stands of medieval thinkers. He intended to give autonomy to the secular authority.

We now come to Dante Alighieri (1268–1321). He was a thinker of late 13th and early 14th century. We know that in these two centuries the importance of the church declined considerably. The kings began to exert their authority over the society step by step and the church was compelled to accept this new phenomenon. In the early

14th century, because of several reasons, a new class—the bourgeois class—emerged and it started to dominate the economic affairs of the state. Before long it established an entente with the state authority for the realisation of its own pecuniary benefits. All these factors finally strengthened the position of the state's secular authority and enhanced its image. Dante also categorically said that the unity of the state is of primary importance and, for this purpose, the king must have a final say in temporal matters. Again, there might arise controversy and it is the duty of the king to settle this. This requires the supremacy of the king over all other authorities. Dante thus did not recognise the absolute authority of the church.

We shall now focus our attention to Marsilius of Padua (1270–1340) who, according to Berki, was a renowned figure of medieval political thought. He invested his thought and energy for a fruitful separation between the church and the state. His famous book *Defensor of Pacis* (published in 1324) was written to refute the claims of the Pope over the state. This book was written 50 years after the death of Aquinas. Marsilius's stand is quite different from that of St. Augustine or of Aquinas : He strongly emphasised the idea that the secular authority, that is, the state, should not interfere with the ecclesiastical affairs of the church and, on the other hand, the church should not have any business with the secular or political activities of the state. It is the primary duty of the church to give instructions to individuals so far as salvation is concerned.

Marsilius (or it is also spelt as Marsilio) also believed that the church had no rightful claim to any kind of immunity from or independence of secular authority. It implies that the authority of the church must remain under the authority of the king—which is secular in nature. It cannot claim any special status. The Church is simply an ordinary organisation. He also denied any special status to the Pope. In this way Marsilio reduced the lofty position of the church. It must abide by the rules of the secular authority like other citizens.

Marsilius has also said that the church had no right to teach the public or to preach sermons. Who will preach sermons to common people that will be decided by the state. The secular authority shall set up temples and churches and bishops will perform only the religious functions.

Though Marsilius was against the supremacy of the church he recognised the church's authority to settle the polemical or religious conflicts or issues. Sabine says "His theory is a root and branch attack upon the ecclesiastical hierarchy and especially upon a papal *plentitudo potestatis*, but he recognised that, even for spiritual purposes and to resolve spiritual questions, the church requires some organisation distinct from the civil community" (p. 300).

Though Marsilio of Padua vehemently opposed the supremacy of the church over all secular affairs, it cannot be said that he effected a final divorce between the church and the state or he was in strong favour of secularisation of politics. However, considering his background and the religico-political affairs of his contemporary society it may be observed that Marsilio's opinion regarding the position of church *vis-a-vis* state was undoubtedly revolutionary.

Towards the declining years of the medieval period the importance of the church ebbed remarkably which encouraged the secular authority to exert its authority. Marsilio's opinion about the relationship between the church and the state was merely a compromise. But at the hands of Machiavelli the church was practically reduced to an ordinary religious institution. Today we believe that the separation between the two is necessary and several thinkers of the later medieval period realised this. It is true that if there were no conflict between the church and the state the nature of political science and that of the state would assume different colour.

In the concluding phase of the analysis of the church and the state in medieval period we may take note of William of Ockam (1280–1347). William was not a renowned thinker and his work is not worth mentioning. Following Marsilius of Padua, William said that though the chief function of the state is to legislate, the more important function is to maintain justice and moral standard among the citizens. A very important duty of the state is to punish the offenders.

William said that the church cannot claim absolute power over the subjects. They would be allowed to follow their own faith and to act accordingly. He was also not in favour of the state's absolute authority. He has said that the church has no power to punish the religious offenders. This function falls within the jurisdiction of state.

Though William refused to grant supreme power to the church and the emperor it is not very clear what was his exact stand on the location of sovereignty. Gettell observes "For a century the ideas of Marsilius and William of Ockam concerning the location of authority and the system of representation in the church was subject to violent debate in the ecclesiastical world. They were incorporated by the jurists into the civil and canon law and their application to issues of purely political significance gained great importance" (p. 129).

7 RENAISSANCE AND REFORMATION

Renaissance : Definition, Rise and Development

To define Renaissance in a brief and meaningful way is not an easy task and in spite of the problem we shall make an attempt to define it. Literally the term means the revival of art and literature under the influence of classical models in the 14th to 16th centuries. In these centuries there was great and unprecedented revival in various fields of art, literature and other intellectual fields. This overall or combined revival can be called Renaissance. In the fourteenth to sixteenth centuries several countries of Europe witnessed the recovery of intelligence. But the renowned historian H. G. Wells thinks the Renaissance actually emerged in the twelfth century and "there were many signs that the European intelligence was recovering courage and leisure" (*A Short History of the World*, p. 211). Wells further maintains that the Middle Ages are generally called Dark Ages because during this period there was practically no progress in numerous fields of art, literature and science. The last progress in such fields was found in ancient Greece.

The Renaissance may be also called revival and rediscovery of rational, this worldly secular and scientific spirit and mentality. The Renaissance was thus a general revival in all fields of knowledge and enquiry. We say that Renaissance is the general revival in various fields but Ebenstein (*Great Political Thinkers*, p. 278) says that Renaissance took place not only in the intellectual fields but also in all the fields of social life and looking at it from that perspective, Ebenstein says that Renaissance is not the consequence of any single work of art or any one genius—it was the *discovery of man*. "Renaissance is not confined to any particular intellectual field, but in all fields of human knowledge and enquiry. So Renaissance can properly be called an overall revival that man's intelligence can imagine." In a beautiful way Ebenstein says (p. 278) Renaissance goes beyond the moral selfhood of Stoicism, the spiritual uniqueness of Christianity, the aesthetic individuality of the ancient Greeks and views man in his totality, in his flesh and blood as well as in his mind and spirit—man in relation to himself, to society, the world. Displacing God, man becomes the *centre of the universe*".

Numerous fields of human enquiry and intelligence met at a single point and we may call it the confluence of man's multifarious enquiries. There were many tributaries and streams of human knowledge and they maintained their identity. But few people took interest for their development because the mentality of developing them did not activate the mind of the people. It is the Renaissance that inspired people to go through the numerous fields of human knowledge. Renaissance is, therefore, a revival of man's urge to know. Its only message is rise and wake and go forward. It wants to emphasise that there is unlimited latent capacity in man and that must be discovered or revived. In the Middle Ages common people were preoccupied with the feelings of religious thought and the church plays the most vital role in this field. But they were never told that man's preoccupation with religion was doing maximum harm to the progress of intelligence. In fact, man was extremely intoxicated with religion. Finally there emerged a new feeling—the feeling to rise above the present mentality. It is undesirable to be confined within the polis. Man must start his journey to the cosmopolis. It is the spirit of Renaissance.

The message of Renaissance is that man has immense potentialities in himself. That is not all. Those potentialities must be revived. In the Middle Ages the religion and the Pope of the church in various ways suppressed the feelings and urge of man. The restlessness of man could not find avenues to come out. It is the Renaissance that performed the job. Ebenstein, that is why, says : the Renaissance was itself the effect of man's growing restlessness as well as of changing social and technological conditions (p. 278). Man's indomitable urge to know the unknown, to cross the sea and to land on an unknown land worked effectively for the cause of Renaissance. H. G. Wells says (p. 212) Trade was reviving, cities were recovering ease and safety, the standard of education was rising in the church and spreading among laymen. All these helped, in a considerable way, the revival and development of Renaissance. There was a very close relationship between Renaissance and enlightenment in the fields of thoughts and ideas. Man was led by the urge to know the unknown, to sail in an uncharted sea and in this way he started his journey to conquer the world. This feeling of man was practically unknown in the dark atmosphere of the Middle Ages. The bad and unscientific outlook of the church dominated religion, blocked all sorts of progress. Man's urge to know the unknown ultimately obliterated all sorts of geographical barriers and social, cultural, and political differences. The differences remained as before but all these did not stand on the way of free mixing and unhindered progress of ideas and thought. The narrowness of mind and outlook that was the characteristic feature of the Middle Ages and the advent of Renaissance feeling destroyed that obnoxious situation. Renaissance helped man to march forward.

It has reasonably been asserted that there is a close relationship between Renaissance and the development of capitalism and this requires explanation. The Industrial Revolution of the eighteenth century caused the enormous production of commodities and along with it there emerged a flood of commodities. The producers and merchants started to export the excess commodities to several parts of the globe. The relations between different parts developed unprecedentedly. The export and import of commodities brought about a radical change in foreign trade and along with it the academic and intellectual world underwent change which was unimaginable before the advent of Industrial Revolution and merchant capital which grew along with the growth of capitalism. Both Marxist and non-Marxist thinkers say that if Industrial Revolution and international trade did not take place Renaissance could not get the opportunity to emerge. This does not mean that Industrial Revolution is the solitary reason of the rise of Renaissance. The fact is that

Industrial Revolution is an important reason of Renaissance. The chief objective of the capitalists was to earn profit by selling their commodities in different countries and their activities gave birth to a new era—an era of relationship among various nations. It is to be maintained that the capitalists started their business not for the progress of Renaissance but for their economic gains. But Renaissance was indirectly benefited. Marx and Engels have said in their *Manifesto* of the Communist Party : Bourgeoisie creates a new world after its own images. In this way capitalism helped the Renaissance to progress. Due to the tremendous impact of capitalism all the underdeveloped regions of the world came closer. The merchants and capitalists not only exported their goods and commodities but also their ideas and outlook. The cultures of Asia and Africa came in touch with the culture of the developed nations. This added new wings to the body of Renaissance.

Political Theory of Renaissance

It would be highly misleading to say that Renaissance was the originator of unprecedented expansion of worldwide communication network and spread of scientific knowledge and education. In the field of political concepts its contribution is not to be ignored. In an indirect way Renaissance gave birth to the idea of nation-state. Throughout the Middle Ages the church and the Pope fully controlled the political affairs of the state. Kings and rulers had no freedom to decide anything related to politics. The Renaissance successfully diverted the mind of the people from orthodox religion and numerous superstitions. People began to think about religion with a free mind and they discovered that church and the Pope had misguided them for centuries. This change in mind and outlook diverted their attention from religion and simultaneously they changed their loyalty from church to the political authority, especially king. There appeared radical political changes in the sphere of politics. The geographical boundaries of many political units were redrawn or redetermined. This gave birth to a new system which may be called the nation-state. A particular nation or a group of people having a separate identity claimed a separate political entity and this came to be called the nation-state. In 1648 a famous treaty was ratified—the Peace Treaty of Westphalia. From this Treaty the concept of nation-state received maximum encouragement. Many people of Western political thought believe that the rise of the nation-state is a factor of new international relations. In other words, the nation-state was the beginning of international politics.

Renaissance may rightly be called a cause of separation between politics and religion. Many people propagated that, the things that are Caesar's unto Caesar, the things that are Gods unto God. That is, the domain of God and Caesar are separated from each other. The simple implication is there is a clear separation between politics and religion. Church has nothing to do with politics and politics cannot interfere with the religious affairs of the church. The Renaissance indirectly ensured secularism in politics which received its final status and form in the hands of Machiavelli.

Renaissance, to a considerable extent, enlightened the mind of the people and this made them conscious of their rights and obligations. In the new socio-economic political atmosphere people thought of getting more rights and opportunities from the state. Not only this, they began to think about the protection of their rights. They believed that it was the primary duty of the political authority to protect rights. In the Middle Ages the church demanded more and more money and property from common people. People were also made to believe that donation of wealth or property to the church would enable them to get blessings of God and this would save them to be free from sins. Renaissance removed superstition and kindled the idea of rights. People demanded more rights and, simultaneously, their protection. This, we believe, a great contribution of Renaissance.

Quentine Skinner in his extensive research work (*The foundations of modern political thought*, in two volumes) has drawn our attention to another aspect of Renaissance. In Volume I (pp. 3-5) he says that Renaissance, to a considerable extent, gave rise to republicanism. Skinner chiefly refers to the importance of Renaissance in Italy. Rise of consciousness is the primary reason of republicanism. In many parts of Italy and in other places of Europe the rulers were not elected. They were nominated. But in the second half of the twelfth century the system of elective government was introduced which means the members of the government were to be elected by the people. This is republicanism. Skinner says (Vol. I, p. 3) "During the second half of the 12th century a further development took place. The rules of consuls came to be superseded by a stables form of elective government centred on an official known as the *podesta*. He was invested with supreme power or *potestas* over the city." The *podesta* was generally a citizen of another. Naturally he had no local obligation or feeling. *Podesta* was popularly elected and was accountable to people who elected him. This constitutes the central idea of republican form of government. The *Podesta* enjoyed enormous powers. He was supposed to be the supreme administrative and judicial authority. But the comprehensive power did not make him a dictator. Skinner further observes that though the republican type of government was originally set up in selected areas of Italy and other parts gradually this type of government was adopted universally by the leading cities.

A new meaning of liberty was brought about by the Renaissance. It taught people in general that every nation or state had the right to be free from foreign rule and that must be recognised by all nations. Before Renaissance very few nations enjoyed freedom. But this taught nations that the yoke of foreign rule and servitude must be thrown off. We call it national liberty or the liberty of the nation. Skinner says (p. 7) "By liberty they meant first of all their independence from Emperor. ...By liberty they also meant their right to maintain their existing forms of government". The mere implication is every nation has right to live in its own way. The simple fact is that two forms of liberty were emphasised—one personal liberty, and the other liberty of the nation. Skinner is of opinion that Italians thought of the two forms of liberty.

Italy and several parts of Europe were plagued by conflicts and internecine war. This stalled the progress and hindered the attainment of peace. Many people seriously thought of restoring peace and Dante (1265–1321) was the foremost of them. Dante's fundamental plea was for restoration and tranquility. His firm opinion was that the Emperor was the most suitable person for this crucial task. Dante thought that only an Emperor could achieve this mission. Skinner writes (p. 17) "Dante's tract on monarchy asks for total trust to be placed in the figure of Emperor as the only unifying force capable of overcoming the factions of Italy and bringing peace." In other words, Dante's idea of monarchical form of government was circumscribed by a particular thought. Since he wanted unity and progress of Italy he favoured a powerful monarchy or emperor. We think that Dante's is purely a political view and he emphasised it mainly in the background of contemporary circumstances. He thought that the conflicts and chaos in his time were creating numerous problems and hindering progress. All these stood on the way of the attainment of justice. So, in order to maximise justice, overlordship of an emperor was badly needed. Again, by arresting the sources or causes of internal conflicts and chaos, the king would be able to create a peaceful atmosphere in which peace and tranquility could thrive. This would in turn maximise liberty. Skinner is of opinion that all these concepts of politics were brought about by the Renaissance. We, today, seriously think about republicanism, freedom, justice, unity, peace etc. But several centuries ago it introduced them.

The contribution of Renaissance also relates to, other great aspects of political thought, and these are individualism and liberalism. Renaissance enabled man to know what he is. Self-consciousness was brought about by Renaissance. Under the the great influence of Renaissance man *discovered himself* and this was the root of his self-consciousness. Everywhere rise of consciousness plays important and constructive role and political sphere is no exception. Once Ernest Barker said : Political consciousness postulates liberty, liberty involves rights, rights demand the state. The development of self-consciousness led people to demand liberty and rights. Along with it they demanded the protection of rights and liberty. In this field the state must play the key role. We know the expansion of rights and liberties also means the limitation of the power of the state. In the Middle Ages the state had very little opportunity to play crucial role in the fields of guaranting and protecting rights and liberties of individuals Renaissance changed this situation. In real terms the role of the state increased. But at the same time men's consciousness did not allow it to cross limit. In this way individualism became a key-word in society and political discussion. Liberalism also came to be regarded as a product of Renaissance. People became highly conscious of the protection of rights. In earlier epochs church controlled the political and related affairs of state which created inconvenience in the political sphere. After Renaissance, conscious people started to assert themselves everywhere. Which led to limit the sphere and role of the state. In this way the concept of liberalism began to appear slowly but steadily. Renaissance enabled man to think about religion with an open mind. This outlook was also a cause of liberal thought and attitude. To sum up, the emergence of Renaissance is the prime factor of rise of self-consciousness and this ultimately created a series of political issues.

The Renaissance also created some opposite concepts which are political in nature. Under the influence of Renaissance, there was an uprecedented growth in the fields of international trade, transport and communication. Some people took up trade as a profession and began to export commodities to foreign countries. Simultaneously they imported articles from foreign lands to home. Before Renaissance there was international trade in limited scale. The Renaissance enhanced it considerably. Scholars are of opinion that foreign trade enabled people to earn huge profit which was practically unthinkable before the rise of Renaissance. But it is to be remembered that only a microscopic section of people got the opportunity to earn huge profit from trade. The larger section remained in the darkness of poverty. The society in this way was divided into two broad classes—rich and poor. This division brought along with the inevitable consequence—the class struggle. Though class struggle was the inevitable consequence of Industrial Revolution but in a remote sense it arose after Renaissance.

It has been argued by Skinner that scholasticism is the product of Renaissance. What is scholasticism? It is a system of theology and philosophy taught in medieval European Universities, based on Aristotelian logic and the writings of the early Christian Fathers and having a strong emphasis on tradition and dogma. Before the emergence of Renaissance people in general and scholars in particular had little inclination to philosophical knowledge and scholastic ideas. But the discovery of man led people to think about everything philosophically as well as seriously. This was the source of scholasticism. Skinner maintains : The foundations of scholasticism were first laid with the gradual rediscovery of the main corpus of Aristotle's philosophical works (*The Foundations of Modern Political Thought,* Vol. I, p. 49). Aristotle's philosophical work practically remained untouched in Europe. Some scholars of Arab began to translate them for their use. In the twelfth century they were smuggled into European states. The scholars began to study Aristotle's works and started their research on the philosophy of Aristotle. In the thirteenth century Aristotle's philosophy and works were popularised by non-greek scholars and his political works were translated into various European languages. Aristotle's political works, particularly his *Politics,* was popularised by European scholars. Skinner maintains that the impact of Renaissance was quite prominent in many parts of Europe, but it was more prominent in Italy. Concepts and methods of Aristotelian political theory were incorporated in various branches of knowledge. Particularly, the Roman scholars did this job. In the universities of Italy and Paris Aristotle's political and other concepts as well as theories were taught. The origin of state, polis, individual's role, revolution, nature of politics, classification of government etc. were the main aspects of Aristotle's political theories. The scholars and students of European Universities began to study these enthusiastically. From Greek philosophers the scholars of Italy and France borrowed the concept of justice and they began to think to apply it in their political system. It is a fact that Renaissance could not give or provide any origin of new political ideas or views, but it is undeniable that old ideas were seriously discussed and attempts were made in some cases to remodel politics and institutions in the light of Greek political ideas. It can indirectly be called the political concept of Renaissance. Many people of Italy and France, after studying Aristotle's *Politics,* started to think about direct democracy or various forms of government. We finally observe that though Renaissance did not create any new political theory the old theories were viewed in new light.

REFORMATION

Definition, Origin. Development Etc.

No clear and precise definition of the term Reformation is available in books dealing with the subject. However, let us start with a definition provided by C. O. D. According to this definition the Reformation is a sixteenth century movement for the reform of abuses in the Roman Church, ending in the establishment of the Reformed and Protestant Churches. The religion and religious practices were misused and abused for pretty long time and people's grievances were simmering in many parts of the Christian world. It was felt by the conscious section of society that the abuses of Christianity and corruption of church and Pope could not be allowed to continue. But the problem was how to do it. That is, how to reform the church and its activities.

The Reformation of the church started with Martin Luther and for this reason it is also called Lutheranism or Lutheran movement. It is so called because Reformation is closely associated with Martin Luther's name. Skinner says (*The Foundations of Modern Political Thought,* Vol. II, p. 3) Luther's famous act of nailing up the Ninety-Five Theses on the door, of the Castle Church at Wittenberg on the eve of All Saints in 1517 merely marks the culmination of a long spiritual journey. In the Middle Ages the church controlled the religious world and interpreted the principles of Christianity to facilitate its own designs. The church also controlled the political sphere as a result of which politics lost its identity. King, state and important political concepts became a tutelage of church. The church demanded the sole authority to explain and interpret religion and it ordered everyone to accept it. Nobody had any to show courage to criticise the functions and policies of the church. This ultimately came to be the breeding ground of various types of corruption. Many people grumbled but nobody had the courage to raise voice against the Pope or church. Hence Reformation means to reform the activities of church in the light of what the Bible has actually said, what Christianity actually means. Luther gave maximum emphasis on **faith.** Skinner said (Vol. 2, p. 8) : The core of Luther's theology is constituted by his doctrine of justification of *solafide,* by faith alone. He continues to stress that no one can ever hope to be justified—that is granted salvation—by virtue of his own works. But he now argues that it must be open to anyone to perceive God's *gratia*—the "saving grace" which He must already have granted as a totally unmerited favour to those whom He has predestined to be saved." Luther did not accept the special status and importance of priest and priesthood (p. 11). Everybody is entitled to priesthood if he can prove his unadulterated faith in God. This he called "the priesthood of all believers". He further maintained that all believers and not just the priestly class have an equal duty and capacity to help their brethren and assume responsibility for their spiritual welfare (p. 11). The central idea of Luther's attitude to theology or Christianity can be stated in the words of Skinner in the following way : "throughout his ecclesiology, as in his theology as a whole we are continually led back to the central figure of the individual Christian and his faith in God's redeeming grace" (pp. 11-12).

Luther's main attack is to be found in a major work—*The Judgment of Martin Luther on Monastic Vows* published in 1521. In this book it has been maintained that church and priests have all violated evangelical freedom and all of them have acted against the "Christian faith". Luther also did not recognise the special status and power of church, and priests are just like ordinary citizens and they have not been empowered to interpret the ideas of precepts of religious books. He also declared that the church and priests have no authority to exercise any power over the non-religious or political affairs of the state. The political affairs fall within the domain of state or government. Luther has also said that all Christians live simultaneously in two kingdoms—the kingdom of Christ and the kingdom of world. The first world is associated with the Christ and the second with the temporal authority. Naturally the authority of the church is confined within Christianity. Luther in this way drew a clear distinction between spiritual and non-spiritual worlds. Luther's further assertion relates to an important matter. This is "The realm of temporal authority is equally claimed to be ordained by God, but is seen as wholly separate, since the sword is granted to secular rulers simply in order to ensure that civil peace is maintained among sinful men" (p. 14).

Not only Martin Luther, many other persons were annoyed with the functioning and behaviour of the church. These persons came in touch with the church and closely observed the behaviour of priests and other persons related with the church. One such person was Dean Cotel. There was no doubt about his loyalty to the church and faith in Christianity. Once he said : "All the corruption, all the decay of the church, all the offences in the world come of the covetousness of the priests." In other words, the church and the priests were absolutely responsible for the decaying condition of the society. This was the condition of church and papacy and it was believed that church could not be amended by normal procedure. A movement in a bigger way was to be launched. Also a great upheaval was required. Reformation was of that type.

Renaissance and Reformation

The scholars of western political thought have confidently asserted that both Renaissance and Reformation are inextricably connected. If there were no Renaissance, Reformation could not get the opportunity to find its proper progress. Renaissance considerably broadened the mind and outlook of man. Being enlightened by reason and rationality, man came out of the darkness of the Middle Ages. The development of reason and rationality put man on a different stage. He came to believe that the practices and behaviour of the church and the Pope were absolutely responsible for the decaying condition of the religious world. As a result of Renaissance people came to believe that religion was a personal affair and they have the right to lead their religious life in accordance with their own reason and belief and the church or the Pope have no power to dictate them. By asserting this, people started to go according to their own reason. This condition helped the leaders of Reformation to rise against the enormous power and influence of the church. Martin Luther and Calvin properly utilised the situation to challenge the authority of the church. It is true that Renaissance prepared the field, and the leaders of the Reformation, especially Martin Luther and Calvin sowed the seeds of reforming the church. Under such situation we have actually very little scope to separate Renaissance from Reformation. Again we hold the view that Reformation would never be possible without Renaissance. The whole issue is a continuous process. The issue is to enlighten the mind of the people, to free their mind from all sorts of superstition and unreasonable ideas and concepts. A relevant comment of Ebenstein is : In the field of religious thought and experience, the Renaissance opened the gates to a new religious world through the Protestant Reformation (*The Great Political Thinkers*, p. 298).

Renaissance helped Reformation in other ways also. The international relations and trade increased as a result of Renaissance. People of different parts of the globe came in close contact which broadened their mind and outlook. Renaissance prepared the field for the rise and development of nationality and reasonability in their mind. They refused to be guided by orthodox religion and dictates of church. Simultaneously, the Reformation Movement removed the unreligious stigma (at least partially) from the body of Christianity. The liberal aspects of Christianity received wide support from the people of other countries. Renaissance encouraged people to sail to other countries for trading purposes and these people carried with them the reformed Christianity. The world civilisation, liberation, economic progress and development in trade all advanced forward simultaneously. Man was released from darkness and unreasonability by the Renaissance. He was again freed from religious orthodoxy of Reformation. The two—pronged attack launched by Renaissance and Reformation created a new world—a world of liberalism, a world of free thought and free trade. In his *Rise of European Liberalism* Harold Laski says : "The contrast between the eager merchant and the avaricious landlord of the Tudor Age, on the one hand, and the priest and the monk on the other, left no doubt of the result of the struggle for the wealth of the church. When, at the Council of Trent, the papacy awakened to the need for reform, it was already too late. For by that time, it had lost the half of its empire. The new men were in the saddle. The new terms of exploitation had been laid down. It was no longer for the new spirit to make its term with the church. It was now the business of the church to make its terms with the new spirit." Both Renaissance and Reformation radically changed the economic and religious scene of the world.

Political Ideas of Reformation

The Protestant Movement or Reformation was launched not with the purpose of propagating any specific political theory and, naturally, it did not produce any political theory. In spite of this, the thinkers of western political theory have made attempts to build up certain concepts of major political ideas on the basis of what Martin Luther and Calvin said in respect of Reformation. It was not the purpose of the leaders to propagate any political idea. Sabine rightly observes "Everywhere political theories were defended with the theological arguments and political alliances were made in the name of religious truth" (p. 354). In fact, in the Movement, religion was the important factor and political concepts were relegated to secondary position. Sabine further says (p. 355) : "A classification of political theories would never correspond with a classification of religious denomination, though it is true that religious groups did form typical bodies of theory." So it is interesting to note that throughout the Reformation Movement Luther and Calvin made several comments and announced certain ideas about political matters and these provided important clues about important political concepts.

An important aspect of political idea of Reformation is the emergence of **absolute monarch** and monarchy was well articulated—that monarch or king got the opportunity to exercise his power in a clear way. In the Middle Ages the kings were practically forced to work under the authority of the church. The Reformation Movement drew a curtain over it. Luther and Calvin challenged the authority of the church to interfere in the political affairs of the state. In this respect we find a categorical opinion of Sabine. He says (p. 356) : on the whole the Reformation, together with the sectarian controversies to which it gave rise, accelerated the tendency, already in existences, to increase and consolidate the power of the monarchies. We can call it an interesting aspect of Reformation. Because due to the Reformation Movement the church was forced to give up its authority over monarchy and political sphere and this finally encourage and enabled kings or monarchs to gain power. Hence the loss of church was the gain of monarchs. The absolute monarchy, says Sabine, was, in the first instance, the chief political beneficiary.

Martin Luther and his aids were quite aware that without the active cooperation of kings it would not be possible for them to defeat the ill-designs and irreligious activities of the church and for that reason they were quite eager to get all sorts of help from the kings, and the kings were also very eager to extend their helping hand to consolidate their power and position. Both secular and non-secular forces or religious and political sections came under a single umbrella and this supplied new blood to political ideas and views. In the Middle Ages, politics did not enjoy any special status. During the Reformation Movement, though the kings were able to consolidate their power considerably, they were compelled to make alliance with religious forces. In other words there was clear collaboration between kings and religious leaders. This ensured benefit for both, because the king was anxious to come out of the clutch of the church. Luther was not anxious about the rise of absolute monarchy because it was not his concern. He wanted the help of kings in his *jehad* or uncompromising fight against the church. It is the opinion of Skinner that neither Luther nor Calvin wanted the consolidation of kings' power. But the Reformation movement and other circumstances created a favourable atmosphere which enabled the kings to consolidate power and position. This we call absolute monarchy.

An alliance between politics and virtue may aptly be treated as an after-effect of Reformation. Luther is treated as "Father of Reformation". Following Augustine, Luther conceived of two worlds—one is "Kingdom of God" and the other is "Kingdom of the World". The first world is the embodiment of virtue and honesty and the second world is the embodiment of sin and depravity. But the world of sin and immorality, Luther believed, could not be allowed to exist permanently. God wishes the world of sin to be converted into world of virtue and, keeping this in mind, God appoints kings and makes laws. Through the instrumentality of human kings God rules the mortal world with the sole purpose of making it virtuous. Not Luther alone, his German contemporary Philip Melanchthon in his *Philosophical* and *Moral Epistle* has said that the mortal world must be administered in the light of morality and virtue, good life and eternal good. Calvin also thought more or less in the same line. In his *Institutes* he has discussed the moral and virtuous side of state. He believed that kingdom of God could not be achieved easily, but this should not dishearten us. Human kings are representatives of God and they rule the mortal world to translate the wishes of God into reality. All men are children of God and kings rule the state keeping this in mind. Interpreting Calvin's views John Morrow in his *A History of Political Thought* (1998) writes "Thus while government presents "tumults", it also establishes and maintains conditions in which humans may live "holily, honourably and temperately". For Calvin politics is directly connected to the pursuit of virtue. All political authority comes from God, because it is necessary to train humanity in these parts of an all-embracing system of virtue that relate to life on earth. Government exists for the sake of Christian virtue" (p. 66).

It is wrong to assume that Reformation created a favourable environment in which absolute monarchy developed. Along with it there flourished democracy and individual freedom. This is the opinion of Gettell and H. G. Wells. Gettell maintains : while the immediate effect of the Reformation was to strengthen the authority of the state, the ultimate effect was to further individual liberty and democracy. How? Luther, Calvin and other leaders strongly emphasised people's freedom to interpret the Bible and religious sermons in their own way which indicates and establishes people's democratic right to view everything according to their own judgment. The Reformation leaders through the Movement encouraged people to exercise the freedom of thought, speech and action. This, we believe, constitutes the very foundation of democracy and individual liberty. Luther and Calvin encouraged the common people to interpret religion by applying their own intelligence and judgment. To acquire this power of judgment the common people started to be literate. R. N. Berki rightly observes : The great impact of Reformation was on the spread of literacy and thus indirectly also on modern political development. At the initial stages people desired to know what has been written in the Bible and other religious books and this urge and mentality led them to read other books. This habit also expanded the periphery of knowledge. Luther brought about a change in the field of religion. Common people were not confined within the Bible. They acquired political consciousness and at the same time demanded democratic government, self-government. Earlier people could not think of political matters and issues. Reformation diverted people's mind from religion and encouraged them to think about non-religious matters—particularly politics.

Idea of constitutionalism emerged from Reformation. Here I quote a part of the observation of Skinner. He says : "The sixteenth century not only witnessed the beginning of the absolutist ideology, but also the emergence of its greatest theoretical rival, the theory that all political authority inheres in the body of the people and thus that all rulers must be subject to the censures and deprivations of their subjects" (Skinner, Vol. 2, pp. 113-114). In other words, people or subjects are always the ultimate source of governmental authority or power. Luther at first enthusiastically propagated that God was always the source of king's powers. Subsequently he and his lieutenants went few steps further and said that king's authority or power is subject to the ratification of the people. We thus see that Reformation was not only the source of absolutist political ideology but also of democracy or constitutionalism and it is quite known that both these ideologies are quite different from each other. Some commentators say that Reformation is "the arsenal of ideological weapons" (Skinner, p. 114).

There is another aspect of political ideas. It has been pointed out by Skinner (p. 127) that each Emperor at his election signed a contract with the electors and other inferior magistrates swearing to uphold the good of the Empire and to protect the liberties of his subjects. This finally established the concept that the Emperor is not *legibus solutus*, but is bound by the terms of his coronation oath, and depends for the continuation of his authority on the proper discharge of his duties (Skinner, p. 128). At the time of assuming office the Emperor swore that he would perform his duties and any failure would lead to the removal from office.

Another important contribution of Reformation political theory to the concept of nation-state. Before Reformation, church and papacy were the sole authority in all religious and political affairs. Even the kings had no power to utter a single word against the Pope. Naturally politics was subservient to the church. In this situation people were absolutely in the dark about any idea of the nation-state. The Reformation successfully cut the church to size and it was forced to remain satisfied with the religious matters only. The world of Caesar and the world of God were separate. The monarch got ample freedom in discharging his political duties and, at the same time, demanded obligation from his subjects and, simultaneously, claimed that it must be unconditional. All these prepared the ground for a nation-state. With lot of power (political in nature) in the arsenal the kings advanced to settle all geographical disputes with neighbouring areas or states which ultimately led to the creation of the nation-state. It is observed that the Reformation Movement and the Thirty Years' War (1618-1648) settled several political issues and one of them is the political conflicts among the states. Sometimes there was conflict between Protestant and Catholic sects and this conflict very often assumed political colour. The Thirty Years' War drew a curtain over many of the brain-storming conflicts. The creation of nation-states brought about an end of these disputes. One critic has said : It marked the inauguration of the era of absolute monarchy and the birth of the modern nation-state. The birth of the nation-state, to speak the truth, revolutionised the concept to international relations as well as various aspects of national politics. It is known to the students of international relations that nation-states are very important actors.

The concepts such as constitutionalism, right to resist, obligation all are closely related. In our analysis of constitutionalism we have pointed out that the kings or magistrates are accountable to God or common people. They have been empowered or authorised to perform certain duties and, in case of any failure, they must furnish explanation. Both Renaissance and Reformation removed darkness from the mind of people and helped in a considerable way to enlighten people's mind with reason and rationality. People came to believe that it is better to show political obligation to king rather than the Pope or church, because it is the king who has the power and authority to meet their demands. Luther and Calvin inculcated the idea that people have every right to resist un-Biblical ideas propagated by the Pope or any person of the church. An important contribution of Reformation is it enabled people to claim rights and as a result of it when people felt that they were deprived of legitimate rights the resistance to authority followed. In every sphere of public life the right to resist gradually gathered momentum and, finally, resistance and obligation came to be regarded as important political concepts. Critics are of opinion that during Renaissance and Reformation obligation, right to resist and related concepts appeared in embryonic form and gradually but steadily they assumed bigger forms. After the fifteenth century, political obligation or obligation in any other form assumed significance and today they constitute important elements of political theory. We feel that without right to resist a very important part of democracy or democratic government is supposed to remain incomplete. Because in democracy people's will is the final determiner of every issue of importance.

Huguenot Movement and Related Concepts

The central idea of the Reformation movement is—people have the right to resist the irreligious or un-Biblical functions or behaviour of the Pope and the church. Calvin and Calvinists believed that it was a religious duty to resist and immediately it became a part of Protestant theories and, after that, it constituted an important section of political theory of resistance. Thus today what we call the right to resist had its humble origin in the Calvinist idea of religious right to resist. From the Calvinist concept the Huguenots further borrowed it and used it to protest the activities of kings. In the second half of the sixteenth century the Huguenots of France strongly protested the intoleration in religion. It means that, in respect of religion, everyman or group of men have the right to pursue his own religious practices or principles. This is called religious freedom and nobody can prevent anyone from practising his own religious practices. In this concept there lies a number of ideas such as religious toleration, right to religious freedom etc. Huguenots for the first time demanded that everyone must be allowed to practise religious principles in his own way and for this practice there shall exist an atmosphere of religious toleration. This again formed an important part of political thought. It was also demanded that it is the duty of state authority to ensure the atmosphere.

Who are Huguenots? According to COD, Huguenot is a French Protestant of 16-17th centuries. Question is when the concept of religious duty to resist became transformed among Protestant theorists into a modern and strictly concept of a moral right of resistance. ,...The modern theory was first fully articulated by the Huguenots during the French religious wars in the second half of the 16th century (Skinner, Vol. II, p. 240). Let us recapitulate : Calvin and his followers propagated that every citizen has the right to protest any un-religious view or practice and it must be accepted or recognised. It was the central idea of the Reformation Movement. Skinner says (p. 240) that the French Protestants first gave vent to it and subsequently it found support from people of the Netherlands. The claim of the Huguenots was subsequently accepted by the English revolutionaries of 1640s.

Calvin and Calvinists propagated that it is the religious right to protest or resist any religious principle if it is not acceptable. Huguenots borrowed this basic idea from the Calvinists and made it a main part of their protest. It is called "radical theory of resistance". Though Calvinists propagated the right to resist in the first half of the sixteenth century the Huguenots adopted it after the most heinous and cruel massacre of St. Bartholomew in 1572. The St. Bartholomew Massacre was the consequence of religious intoleration. One section of Christianity could not tolerate the other section and behind this intoleration there was no valid reason. The main argument of the Huguenots was that in religious matter there is no guarantee that everyone will have the same opinion, there may be differences and these differences must be accepted or tolerated. But another section could not accept this stand on many issues. Some people may hold different opinion and Huguenots claimed that it must be accepted. They also said that opposite opinion must constitute the main body of thought. It is called the political concept of Huguenots. They further said that nobody can be deprived of the right to express his opinion. So, we find that though the origin of right to resist is religion it spread its wings in other spheres.

The religious war was intense in many parts of Europe and the royal authority in almost all the countries was directly or indirectly involved in the war. The interesting matter is that the kings and queens were anti-Protestant which meant that they were against the Huguenots (Ebenstein, pp. 299-301). The involvement of the kings and queens in the war of religion aggravated the situation. A large number of people took part in the war of religion. The greater parts of Europe were converted into battlefields of religion. In this connection Ebenstein writes (p. 301) : The anti-Protestant frenzy, carefully nursed, with the blessing of Rome, by the Royalist Catholic party, came to a climax in the Massacre of St. Bartholomew (August 24, 1572) in which thirty thousand Huguenots lost their lives. It is believed that there was strong support of Catherine behind the massacre because she was panicked at the meteoric rise of the Huguenots and clandestinely she ordered the elimation of the Huguenots. The Bartholomew Massacre created an unprecedented panic in entire Europe and the consequence was people of all sections of community began to feel the toleration in religion. After the massacre Catherine urged all sides of society to iron out all sorts of differences particularly religious differences.

The great Bartholomew Massacre failed the religious frenzy among a section of people. Rather, many of them were encouraged to propagate the uniformity in religion. In the seventies and eighties of the sixteenth century a new idea was floated and it is : one faith, one law, one king (*une foi, une loi, une roi*). This slogan rejected the Huguenots' stand on religious toleration. There was a dangerous pronouncement of a well-known person in this respect : "It is folly to hope for peace, repose and amity between peoples of different religions".

The religious strife led to the absolutism. Amidst the religious controversy that created great tension in France and other countries of Europe Jean Bodin published his *Six Books of a Commonwealth* in 1576, four years after the notorious Bartholomew Massacre. In this book he enthusiastically argued for religious uniformity and dismissed the variety of religion. He apprehended that variety of religion would destroy the unity of nation and jeopardise the maintenance of law and order. Bodin was an eyewitness of Bartholomew Massacre that occurred on 1572 and for this he blamed the Huguenots. He said that the government must forbid the existence and practice of different religions. Only supreme power and strict law can do this. Bodin's reason was that it was the primary duty of the king or monarch to uphold the unity of nation and advance progress. But at the same time he should also look after the health and welfare of the commonwealth. For all these a prince must have enormous powers at his disposal. Bodin further argued that a prince must ignore the arguments in favour of multiplicity of religions. Bodin claimed that variety of religious faith would lead to tensions and discord among people and this would endanger the security and unity of the nation. He further argued that all religions are based not so much upon demonstrations of reason as upon the assurance of faith and belief. The summary of Bodin's argument is that only a strong monarch can save a commonwealth from disunity and collapse. In his book Bodin favoured religious toleration. But his point was—the Huguenots must accept main argument of Christianity. Some people say that Bodin strongly condemned the Bartholomew Massacre and, at the same time, intransigence of the Huguenots (Skinner).

Even after the Bartholomew Massacre of 1572 the enthusiasm of the Huguenots did not die down. They started their agitation in new form and added spirit because they were determined to establish their conception of religious toleration. The Huguenots were of firm opinion that every individual has the right to follow religion in his own way and faith. They began to publish pamphlets and short literature and *Vindiciae contra tyrannos* is one such pamphlet which was published in 1579 and immediately it drew wide public attention. Sabine says (p. 377) *Vindiciae* became one of the landmarks of revolutionary literature. It was republished again and again and was translated in several European languages. Its English translation is *A Defence of Liberty Against Tyrants*. The very title indicates that its author or authors (some people say that it was written by many) wanted to protest the tyrannical acts or behaviour of the rulers. The authors wanted to emphasise that no belief or faith could be imposed upon the general public in the name of religious unity. Sabine calls it the Protestant attack on absolutism. The concept of absolutism was propagated in a clandestine way by several persons among which Bodin was frontrunner.

There are several parts of the *Vindiciae* and four among them are important. In the first place, are subjects obliged to obey the princes if they command anything against the law of God! Secondly, is it lawful to resist a prince who desires to nullify the law of God? Thirdly, how far is it lawful to resist a prince who is oppressing or destroying the state and to whom, by what means and with what right is such resistance allowable? Finally, can neighbouring princes lawfully aid the subjects of other princes? These are the four important question which *Vindicae* raised.

It has been asserted that *Vindiciae* offered a theory of accountability in the name of contract. In this pamphlet it has been said that there are two forms of contract inherent in this pamphlet. The first type of contract was done between God, king and people. In this type of contract God was one party and king and people were another party. The second was jointly a single party. There was another contract in which the king was one party and people formed the other party. The contract enshrined in the *Vindiciae* clearly states that the kings had no power or reason to claim that he was the representative of God on earth and God was the source of all the power which he would exercise. By declaring this the king wanted to establish that for all his acts he was solely responsible to God alone. But the *Vindiciae* did not recognise the Divine Right Theory. But the author of the *Vindiciae* did not deny the existence of God and His role in the earthly affairs.

We may now look at the importance of *Vindiciae*. It is a fact that this pamphlet did not succeed in establishing the secular politics. It recognised the importance of God in political affairs. But *Vindiciae* succeeded in curtailing the powers of the king in a considerable extent. In the second contract the king was a party to the contract with the people. This condition was designed to curb the power of the king. Ebenstein has said that the idea of *Vindiciae* is a trusteeship. Speaking in terms of the Bible and Roman law, the *Vindiciae* refers to the king as a guardian or tutor. The king must look after the general welfare of the people and any failure on his part will invite people's protest. In other words, *Vindiciae* established that the king had no unlimited power. Ebenstein says "The most powerful impact of the *Vindiciae* has been on Dutch and English thought. What the Huguenots wanted for France the Bloodless Revolution achieved for England in 1688 (p. 304). Ebenstein further observes that vindicial may not be regarded as a book of enormous importance but it is a rare book. The impact of this small book is felt by many.

Talking about the importance of Reformation in the vast arena of political science R. N. Berki (*The History of Political Thought*) says (p. 127) "Reformation comprised diverse schools of thought, the impact of which went in various directions." This opinion of Berki carries sufficient weight. In the previous analysis we have made a modest attempt to show that Reformation laid the foundation stone of major concepts of political science such as democracy, absolutism, secularism in politics, constitutionalism, accountability of the ruler to the people, the contract theory whose central idea is both the ruler and the ruled are bound by contract. Reformation has also thrown light on the nation-state. But this reference is not direct. Decline in the power of the church and rise of monarchical authority provided strong impetus to the nation-state. All these are issues of great importance. Reformation talks of people's right to judge religious issues in their own way by applying their own views. Berki thinks that (p. 126) this is a form of popular sovereignty. Berki further maintains "Reformation acted as an agency of liberation and a spur to innovations in thought and to new forms of knowledge" (p. 126). Reformation, to sum up, had created a new chapter in political science.

MARTIN LUTHER (1483–1536)

Introduction

Martin Luther was mainly a reformer and political agitator and not a political philosopher or thinker in the conventional sense. It is not known to us if he had any clear conception about the various aspects as well as the end of the state or nature and working of society. He was primarily a theologian and his approach to politics was secondary; and it was wrapped with theology. Luther may not have been a political philosopher like Hobbes or Rousseau, he was undoubtedly a political theologian. He was also a great agitator and reformer. Luther revolted against Papalism and vehemently opposed the usury and was against the mechanisms of finance. The revolution against Papalism commenced in October 1517 when Martin Luther pasted his ninety-five theses on the church door at Wittenberg. This move of Luther created, for obvious reason, a good deal of commotion in the church circles.

The medieval church claimed that it was the ultimate arbiter of all temporal questions and this claim was based on the sacramental conception of the church. The church also occupied a special position between man and God. Only through the sacraments of churchmen could people find salvation. The church claimed that it was authorised by God to perform the miracles. It could offer the body and blood of Christ as a sacrifice for the sins of mankind. Luther challenged the claim of the church and rejected the sacramental claims. Luther enthusiastically propagated that people had the right to follow scriptures and take decision on the basis of knowledge they could follow and adopt faith. He declared that priests had no right and power to forgive the people for their sins. Forgiveness of sins was dependent upon the repentance and not on priestly absolutions. He put forward the doctrine of Priesthood of All Believers—the belief that there was no essential distinction between priests and laymen. All the true believers were entitled to mercy of God. Church had nothing to do with mercy. Martin Luther also challenged the papal doctrine of the two swords, with its claim that Pope was the ultimate source of all authority, temporal as well as spiritual. The temporal authority derived its power from God and its functions were purely spiritual. It is evident from his works and ideas that Luther was essentially a medieval thinker. Renaissance had very little influence upon his thought. He belonged to the late medieval German piety.

His conception of theology is the origin of the political ideas. His leading ideas of politics are to be found in the *Sermons on Good Works* and the *Address to the Christian Nobility.* His political treatise is *Of Temporal Government*. It is to be noted here that the scripture is the basis of his theology and politics. Treatise on Christian Liberty, Secular Authority, To What Extent It Should be Obeyed etc. contain Luther's other aspects of political ideas. But all are based on religion. Luther's politics is not separate from religion.

Doctrine of Two Regiments or Kingdoms

Luther's doctrine of Two Regiments or Kingdoms is highly significant not simply because it is central to his theology, but because it is related to his thought about politics and society. In a word, the doctrine of Two Regiments is central to his entire philosophy.

At the centre of the doctrine there is the idea that God has created two kingdoms or regiments in the world and through these two kingdoms He governs the world. One is the spiritual world and the other is the temporal world or regiment. The spiritual kingdom is governed through *word* and without any *sword* and in this kingdom men become righteous and godly only through the *word*. In the spiritual world there is no need of *sword* or law and only *word* is enough. All the habitants of the spiritual kingdom are true Christians or believers of Christianity. The activities of the true Christians are fully governed by the spirit of godliness and spirituality. They are above law and princes. The spiritual Regiment is essentially an inward government of the soul whose purpose is to lead men to everlasting life. God rules through Holy spirit and *word*. The Government of the spiritual kingdom is invisible. Men act and lead their spiritual life only through the sermons preached by human ministers. In the spiritual world there is no place of the use of force and the whole system is based on simply voluntary rule.

The nature of temporal Regiment is quite different. People of this kingdom are not true Christians or ardent believers of Christianity. Their main concern is worldly enjoyment and pleasure as well as possessions. People of this Regiment cannot be governed only by *word* because word carries very little significance and, in most of the cases, its impact upon the people of temporal Regiment is not worthy to mention. Sword and law are essential instruments by which God governs this kingdom. For the maintenance of peace and order God has awarded the government of the temporal kingdom with manifold sources of enjoyment and luxury. So God is himself the founder, lord, master, promoter and rewarder of both forms of righteousness, temporal as well as spiritual.

There is a very close similarity between Luther's doctrine of Two Regiments and St. Augustine's *City of God*. Both offer us interesting narratives of world of God and world of Devil. All are children of Adam. But they are divided into two classes. One lives in the kingdom of God and the other in the kingdom of world or Devil. Luther says that God has created the Regiment of Devil to punish its inhabitants for their sins. The two kingdoms are loosely connected. In between these two worlds there is God who keeps a close watch over them all. The temporal kingdom is dominated by conflict, quarrel and strife and human nature is vicious. Self-interest stands in the way of attaining the mercy and blessings of God. The two Regiments are the weapons which God employs in the struggle against the Devil's kingdom. The first Regiment is at first God appeals through words to the hearts of men in order to ensure obedience to him and if it fails he uses sword against the obdurates and punishes them. Luther drew a distinction in order to emphasise that in the temporal world God created the post of a king or governor to maintain law and order and punish the wrongdoer. The simple implication is a political system was created by God. In this idea religion and politics are mixed.

State and its Relation to Church

W. D. J. Cargill Thompson in his essay *Martin Luther and the Two Kingdoms* published in *Political Ideas* makes the following remark : "Luther's theory of the state or to be more precise his theory of government, followed naturally from these theological assumptions. Like Augustine, Luther held that government was both a consequence of the sinfulness or human nature and a divine institution. It exists because vast majority of men are evil. If all men are Christians the sword would be superfluous, since the true Christian is ruled by word" (p. 43). So we can say that the state according to Luther is a mechanism devised by God to punish the evil-minded people. From theological point of view the state has a necessity. It is the primary duty of the temporal government, with help of sword, to force his people to lead a spiritual life. Otherwise it will have no utility at all. It was the firm belief of Luther that the king or temporal power performs all duties or actions in according to the directives sent through the church. In this process the king himself has no personal liking or disliking, God's wishes are final. This ultimately led to the autocratic rule.

We have already noted that Luther's political views are couched with theological considerations. His state is sacred and ordained by God. The ruler is responsible to God alone. God is the source of all monarchical authority and power. By this doctrine Martin Luther has permanently substituted the authority of the state for that of the church. This is no doubt a great contribution of Reformation. Luther's state is not only an instrument to punish the people for their sinful activities, but also a way which will save them from inevitable destruction. Luther has said that princes, magistrates and other officials of the state apparently act according to their own initiative. But this is not so. God directs them and they simply carry out the order of God. They are merely the instruments of God.

For high-handed usurpation of temporal power and perversion of Christian belief, faith and principles Luther held the church responsible. He demanded a radical reform of the whole system of the church and for this he proposed the institution of a general council. He looked to the secular power for the reform of the church. Luther formulated twenty-seven points of reforms and he said that these reforms would be effected by the secular power or general council. One of these points was all the revenues and all the jurisdiction of the Pope in the regions outside the estate of the Roman Church would be abolished. All the matters of money or material interests would be left to the secular authority. It would be absolutely unbecoming on the part of the church if it involves itself in the acquisition of earthly wealth and possessions. It should try to satisfy itself with religious or spiritual considerations. Pope, priests and bishops are merely officers for the regulation and promotion of Christian principles. Under no circumstances they are to be related to secular affairs. Commenting on the reform initiated by Luther Dunning says "the practical outcome of the distinctively Lutherean reform was the appropriation by the secular authorities of much of that paramount influence in ecclesiastical affairs which was taken away from the papacy." The purpose of his agitation was to dislodge the universal church from its coveted position and to suppress the monastic institutions. The ultimate result was that the checks upon the secular authority were removed and the church started to function as an institution under the secular authority. This is not an ordinary gain. Through his movement he succeeded in establishing absoluteness of political power. We can say Luther was an originator of absolutism in politics.

Luther apprehended that his writings might be misinterpreted by the secular rulers. They would be inclined to encroach upon the spiritual affairs. To remove this possibility he clearly stated that the princes and magistrates had nothing to interfere in spiritual matters. They were concerned with life and goods and also everything external on earth. God cannot and will not allow anyone to rule the soul except Himself alone. He was strongly opposed in theory to any attempt to promote spiritual ends by temporal means. This implies that Luther was in favour of the division of duty. The secular authority was designed for earthly affairs. The spiritual problems would go to the church. But the objective of both the kingdoms would be to bring about peace and salvation. The prince would punish the sin after which people would be fit for receiving the blessings of God. In Luther's conception the state and the church are not completely separated from each other.

Obedience to Secular Authority

In his analysis of obedience to the secular authority, Luther has again taken the help of scripture. He says that the Christians among themselves need no law or sword, because it is neither necessary nor admissible for them. But this does not imply that they will disobey the secular authority or violate the man-made laws. According to Luther a true Christian lives not for himself alone, but for his neighbours. It is the primary duty of a true Christian is to obey the laws of the secular authority and act in accordance with the law made by such authority. The obligation to the authority as well as its law is the duty of a Christian. This idea later on has given the birth of an important political theory—political obligation. He has also said people must pay tax and perform other duties.

A true Christian should serve the state as well as society spontaneously and with undiluted love. That is, his obedience to secular authority must come out of love. While obeying the state he should not bring the question of material gain under his consideration. A true Christian cannot prevent a man from obeying the law of state and if he does, it would be his unchristian act. Luther has emphasised that a secular government is ordained by God and the subjects, therefore, it must obey the rules and orders. To disobey government is to disobey God. It may be that the rules and decisions are unjust and behaviour is cruel. But that should not be the lookout of the subjects and cannot be a reason of withdrawing obligation.

The divinity of the secular government unfolds his conception of non-resistance and horror of rebellion. Rebellion against authority, even against a tyrant, could not get the support of Luther. Because, in his opinion, the tyrant came to power to fulfil the wishes of God. Luther once said in a famous passage "I will always hold by that party which suffers rebellion, however unjust its cause, and be opposed to that party which makes rebellion, however just its cause may be, for there can never be rebellion without the spilling of innocent blood and other atrocities." Luther propagated that rebellion was the worst type of sin and on that ground he did not approve it. He thought that rebellion threatened the very foundations of civil society. The net consequence of rebellion is anarchy. His idea about rebellion is to be found in the following passage :

> Rebellion is not just plain murder; but it is like a great fire which sets a land ablaze and lays it waste; therefore, rebellion brings with it a land full of murder and bloodshed; it creates widows and orphans and destroys everything, like the greatest of all disasters.

Luther got an opportunity to witness a great rebellion of peasants on economic and social reasons and it spread in many parts of Europe. Being frightened by horror and anarchy of rebellion he strongly opposed it and supported the king's attempt to suppress it ruthlessly. He was not unsympathetic to their grievances, but he thought that rebellion was not the proper way of remedy. Luther's attitude to rebellion unfolds the idea that he did not recognise people's right to protest against injustice and all sorts of wrong-doing. This is a reactionary attitude and later on paved the way for capitalist exploitation. Of course his apathy to democratic rights does not surprise us. He was not democratic minded and had no feeling for democracy.

MELANCHTHON (1497–1560)

Luther and Melanchthon

Philip Melanchthon was one of the trusted and beloved disciples of Luther. But intellectually and temperamentally he was opposite to his master. Luther was rough, aggressive and fearless. On the contrary, Melanchthon was refined, conciliatory and timid. He had developed a deep sense of humanistic spirit. Melanchthon had a great devotion and respect for classical learning, antiquity and, finally, Aristotelian ethics and politics. Aristotelian Philosophy could not create any positive impact on Luther. In spite of these differences the two reformers had certain similarities. Both suffered from inconsistency of thought. Melanchthon and Luther started their agitation on the basis of teachings of the Bible as the starting point. That is, agitation was based on scriptures. Both attacked papacy vehemently and held the church responsible for the evils of society. Melanchthon, like Luther, believed that without continuous agitation and other forceful means the papacy—the chief source of evils—could not be changed or amended. Luther wanted to cut the wings of the church and his disciple followed him. Melanchthon, like Luther, opposed the monastic ideals as incompatible with the unity and equality of believers in a Christian Commonwealth. Melanchthon denied political power to the Pope. Both Luther and Melanchthon were nationalist leaders. Unity of the nation and peace were of prime considerations to both. Melanchthon once said "deliberate disobedience against the worldly authority, and against true or reasonable laws, is deadly sin, sin which God punishes with eternal damnation if we obstinately continue in it" (Quoted by Skinner in The Foundation of Modern Political Thought, Vol. 2, pp. 67-68).

Natural Right and Natural Law

Melanchthon's theological and political system is based on his conception of natural law as well as natural right. But there is hardly any fundamental difference between the two. According to Melanchthon natural law has two sources—one is God and the other is man himself.

Natural law is perception which God has implanted in the mind of human beings of the practical principles. These principles relate to the existence of God and to the institutions which promote his glory. The precepts of natural law relating to God and institutions are to be found in the *Decalogue*. The precepts say what determines man's duty towards God and towards his fellowmen. People form different civil institutions. Although these institutions conduct the relations among men, they ultimately glorify God. It is thus obvious that man's obedience to God and his relations with his fellowmen both are based on natural law and this is nothing but the revelation of God.

But according to Melanchthon there is another source of natural law and this is the nature or end of man himself. This furnishes certain universal principles. For example, man is a social being and he adapts himself with the social life. He forms a relation with other men and in this way social intercourse develops which also changes with the change of time and circumstances. From the social life, man forms certain rules or principles for the smooth and comfortable running of social living. This—Melanchthon has called—right or natural living. Both the institutions and the laws, although derived from the revelations of God and nature or end of man, are natural and right. Naturally, man, with his united knowledge and experience, cannot challenge the natural law. Not only Melanchthon, a large number of thinkers of the sixteenth and seventeenth century laid their undiluted faith on the immense importance of natural law and natural right. Even after the seventeenth century this faith continued.

Melanchthon's concept of property is based on his idea of natural law or right. Man has the right to own property and enjoy it. But he has no right to steal the possessions of others. Nor has he the right to misuse the property. On the basis of this principle the fabulous amount of property owned by monasteries was confiscated which had far-reaching repercussions upon social, political and economic affairs.

Melanchthon has defined liberty in the following words : "that condition in which each is permitted to have his own and citizens are not compelled to act contrary to what is lawful and proper." From this definition it is clear that the citizens will not be forced to do improper and unlawful acts. It is to be remembered that liberty conforms to the natural law in both senses. Slavery is not also incompatible with the law of nature.

Concept of State and State-Church Relation

Melanchthon's concept of state is not different from what other thinkers of the period said. Though the state is a civil and political organisation it is covered with religious beliefs and ideals. The rulers of the state must always scrupulously follow the wills of God and scriptures. None has any right to disobey the will of God. In all matters the will of God is final. He repeatedly said it. Melanchthon's political ideas are completely mixed with religious beliefs. But this is not new.

Since the state is the creation of God it discharges the God-ordained functions. Its duty is to promote true religion and prohibit the false worship and prevent unchristian or irreligious activities. To materialise all these objectives the state shall introduce corporal punishments for the offenders. If the state fails to achieve this objective, it will not be able to ensure peace and tranquility in society. It shall promote morality and proper discipline. The magistrate on behalf of the state shall extirpate false worship and heresies.

Melanchthon has said that what is heresy and what is blasphemous shall be decided by a specially constituted council. The secular ruler under normal circumstances cannot interfere with the activities of the council. But in complicated cases the intervention of the secular authority becomes inevitable and in those cases the magistrate will adopt adequate measures against the offenders including the prescription of punishment.

Like Luther, Melanchthon thought that the aberration and accumulation of property on the part of the church were the root causes of corruption and moral degradation. So he suggested that the church property would be confiscated in the name of religious activities. Church misused this property. It could keep that amount which was absolutely necessary for its maintenance.

Melanchthon denied coercive power to ecclesiastic authority. He believed that the making of law and its execution fell within the jurisdiction of the secular ruler. Popes and bishops cannot claim separate treatment from ordinary citizens. They are subordinate to political power.

Melanchthon was a nationalist and, because of his nationalist feeling, he rejected the theory of universal empire. He favoured national governments ruled by kings. World should be divided into separate independent territories. From the scriptures he draws the conclusion that the independent kingdoms are helpful in many respects. There is always tendency for the kings to be tyrants. Rulers of small kingdoms are subject to various limitations and the possibility of being tyrant becomes less. In different kingdoms there are different rules, laws and ecclesiastical institutions and all these limit the power of monarchs.

Doctrine of Obedience

Melanchthon declares "deliberate disobedience against the worldly authority, and against true or reasonable laws, is deadly sin, sin which God punishes with eternal damnation if we obstinately continue in it." Like Luther, Melanchthon did not approve any disobedience. It is the duty of the religious-minded citizens to obey the law of the prince even though the laws are unjust or unreasonable. It is beyond the competence of individuals to judge the reasonability or unreasonability of any law. They should not forget that the rulers of the kingdoms are sent by God and they are simply translating the wishes of God and executing his laws. They are not doing anything deliberately. Naturally, there is hardly any scope on the part of the people to express their discontent against the rulers. Melanchthon has compared the disobedience to sacrilege. By showing disrespect to the authority, citizens will gain nothing. Disobedience is sin and for sin they will again be severely penalised and their salvation will be delayed. He has recognised that tyrants are the worst kinds of rulers. Even then people should not try to disobey them because they are also representing God. He mentions the caveat that we should obey God rather than men, but he insists on the continuing duty of every subject to be patient with reasonable rulers, even if mistakes and defects occur in their government. On this plea, he did not support the peasant revolt. It was the belief of Melanchthon and many other thinkers that since all rulers are given by God to fulfil his own purposes, it follows that they have a duty to rule the people not as they themselves want but rather as God wants. God is the real ruler and there is none above God. The law is God's but not of king's. The king rules in accordance with the wishes and law of God. In short, God is the supreme authority and all are His servants. Hence to disobey a king will mean to disobey God. Melanchthon has given a very beautiful account about the nature of obedience and duty. He, however, did not think about obedience in our sense.

ZWINGLI (1484–1531)

The all-pervasive corruption and the political ambition of church spread to Switzerland. During the 15th century, Swiss reformers started agitation against the church and the leadership was given by Ulrich Zwingli. He claimed that his reform was independent of Luther's, that he had been teaching reforming doctrines even before he had heard of Luther. But historians do not agree with this lofty claim of Zwingli.

His humanism and radical ideas are more advanced than those of Luther. Zwingli's writings reveal that he was more interested in politics than in theology. He started the Reformation movement for the furtherance of welfare objectives of state.

He thought that the church was an invisible organisation of saints and for this reason it could not remove indiscipline and irreligious activities. This could be done only by the secular authority. The church should be concerned only with the inward affairs of Christians and external matters should be dealt with by the civil government. The Zwinglian system, observes Dunning, thus blended state and church in a single organisation (p. 25).

Zwingli was out and out a nationalist and democrat. Zwingli's democratic and patriotic feeling injected aggressiveness into the Reformation movement. Because of his movements, democratic government was established in Zurich and many other cantons of Switzerland. The political and social atmosphere of Switzerland were different from those of other European countries and this difference led Zwingli to launch a different movement. He advised the Christians to cooperate with the secular authority to strengthen the tradition of Switzerland. Gettell commenting on Zwingli's political ideas, writes "A democratic state imbued with social spirit of primitive Christianity was Zwingli's political ideal" (p. 160).

Like Luther and Melanchthon he propagated the doctrine of passive obedience on the part of the subjects and the toleration of difference in belief only so far as the teachings of the scriptures were not contravened. To disobey the secular ruler is to disobey God.

"Zwingli sympathised with the quest for reform by cool ridicule. He had more wit, more philosophy, more learning, less profundity, less religious sense than Luther. His desire to reform the church was a little more like the desire of the humanist who hated inefficiency and obscurantism."[1]

Zwingli lost his life in an attempt to prevent the Catholic cantons from enforcing their views of the scriptures upon adherents of the reformed faith.

CALVIN (1509–1564)

Introduction

Reformation movement under the leadership of Luther could not make any remarkable headway. The French leader John Calvin injected a new lease of life into Reformation and made the movement more vigorous and widespread. He gave it a logical character and the political doctrine of the Reformation is more discernible. John Calvin was a lawyer by profession. He was a generation later than Luther. Luther married an ex-nun, Calvin the widow of an Anabaptist; and the difference is symbolic. The problem was not the overthrow of a papacy, but the construction of new modes of power. Luther rested much upon the doctrine of priesthood of the laity and derived part of his practical programme from the doctrine. Calvin recognised that the doctrine was in scriptures and emphasised the theoretical consequences. There was little that was democratic in Calvin's ideal.[2] He did not recognise the individual interpretation of the scriptuers.

1. Owen Chadwick—*The Reformation*, p. 77.
2. Owen Chadwick—*The Reformation*, p. 83.

The purpose of Calvin was to give a comprehensive exposition of Christian faith. He wanted to bring church, papacy and all Christian people under the umbrella of law. The crucial fact was that Calvinism, especially in France and Scotland, was in opposition to governments which it had practically no chance to convert or capture. Calvinism in its initial form lacked all leaning towards liberalism, constitutionalism and representative principles.

State and State-Church Relation

The principal work of John Calvin is *Institutes of Christian Religion* and this contains his political ideas. The interesting aspect of Calvin's political thought is that he did not discuss political ideas in a methodical way. His main interest was religion and in the course of analysing religion and its relation with the state and other political organisation he mentioned some political concepts—particularly state and its rulers—and this invited some political concepts. From this approach of Calvin scholars have suggested few ideas about his political philosophy. In the *Institutes* he makes the following observation :

Man is under two kinds of government, one spiritual, by which the conscience is formed to piety and the service of God; the other political by which a man is instructed in the duties of humanity and civility, which are to be observed in an intercourse with mankind...the former species of government pertains to the life of the soul, and that the latter relates to the concerns of the present state, not only to the provision of food and clothing, but to the enactment of laws to regulate man's life among his neighbours, by the rules of holiness, integrity and sobriety. The former has its seat in the interior of the mind whilst latter only directs the external conduct : one may be termed spiritual kingdom, the other a political kingdom.

Calvin admits that the spiritual and political kingdom—though different from each other—exist side by side. The functions of the two kingdoms are different and there is justification behind each function. This may be called separation of power and functions. The spiritual kingdom will not interfere with the secular world, but the latter has something of the spiritual world to do. The spiritual government deals with the inward activities of individuals. The functions of the civil government include the assurance of physical existence of men through the preservation of law, order, property and liberty. The primary concern of the civil or political government is to ensure the realisation of physical needs and life of the common people.

It is the duty of the civil government to support and encourage the worship of God, to preserve the pure doctrine of religion, to defend the constitution of the church, to regulate the lives of people in a manner requisite for the society of men, form our manner of civil justice, to promote our concord with each other, and to establish general peace and tranquility. The civil government will have its own laws which will deal with the external behaviour of the individuals. The civil law will punish the blasphemy, idolatry and calumnies. The state (or government) will ensure that a public form of worship may exist among Christians and humanity among men. The civil government will thus discharge double functions—one spiritual and the other secular. Though Calvin admits the separate existence of two governments and to some extent the separate functions of each government, ultimately he has suggested that the civil government has definitely certain amount of responsibility towards the discharge of several functions which fall within the domain of religion. He has clarified his stand in the following way :

Calvin says that some people think that the duty of the magistrate is confined entirely to the administration of justice as if God has appointed him to settle secular controversies and he has nothing to do with religion and God. Calvin thinks that this is an erroneous conception about the functions of the magistrate. A magistrate cannot disregard what is of greater importance. This greater important thing is religion. He must see that individuals are religious-minded and they are properly worshipping God. He has further said, "in describing the office of the magistrates in this treatise, my design is not so much as to instruct magistrates themselves ...we see that they are constituted the protectors and vindicators of the public innocence, modesty, probity and tranquility whose sole objective it ought to be to promote the common peace and security of all." To this end Calvin vindicates for the civil authorities the right to inflict capital punishment, to carry on war and to raise money by taxation. The magistrate will punish the vice and reward the virtue. This he must follow simultaneously, otherwise he will not be able to maintain discipline in the society.

Calvin rejected the Zwinglian concept of amalgamation of state and church, and on this ground he dissociated himself from Zwingli. Calvin and his supporters strongly opposed the union of church and state in England. The reason was not that the state would be independent of the church. It was otherwise. He wanted to see the independence of the church. In spiritual affairs, the church would be allowed to discharge its duties freely. It would set its own standards and decide the principles according to the rules of the scriptures. The secular authority would have no say in the spiritual questions. It will create an external atmosphere in which people will get full freedom for exercising religious rights and duties. Calvinism "stood for the primacy and independence of spiritual authority and the use of secular power to give effect to its judgments about orthodoxy and moral discipline" (Sabine, p. 363).

At Geneva, Calvin attempted to put into practice his theocratic and aristocratic ideas of government. But immediately he was faced with several problems. He could not separate the ecclesiastical authority from a secular one according to his own conviction and concept. The moral code was made the basis of law, an ascetic form of life was enjoined by severe penalties and the secular authority was made the instrument of ecclesiastical council.

Passive Obedience or Non-resistance

The theory of passive obedience or non-resistance occupies a very important place in Calvinistic thought system. In the *Institutes* he says :

The first duty of the subjects towards their magistrates is to entertain the most honourable sentiments of their function, which they know to be a jurisdiction delegated to them from God and on that account to esteem and reverence them as God's ministers and vicegerents... Because the obedience which is rendered to princes and magistrates rendered to God, from whom they have received their authority.

The point Calvin emphasises here is that since the princes and magistrates are representatives of God on earth and their function is to carry out the order of God and translate his wishes into reality, it is a must for all citizens to comply with them in all respects and by doing this they will show honour and reverence not to magistrates but to God. Further, God has not given them any power to judge the activities of magistrates and princes. Elsewhere Calvin writes :

Even an individual of the worst character, one most unworthy of all honour, if invested with public authority, receives the illustrious divine power which the Lord by his *word* devolved on the ministers of his justice and judgement, and accordingly...in so far as public obedience is concerned, he is to be held in the same honour and reverence as the best of kings...it is not in our province to remedy the evils of the princes and magistrates and that nothing remains for us but to implore the aid of the Lord.

If we go through the observations of Calvin we shall find that he did not recognise people's right to criticise the principles and functions of the princes because this does not fall within their jurisdiction. Even, they cannot withdraw their obligation to the princes. It is the duty of the subjects to perform their duty and carry out what the princes say. Needless to say that Calvin announced this dictum exclusively in the background of religion. The administrators of the civil government are simply the representatives or nominees of God. And again :

We will never entertain the seditious thought that a king is to be treated according to his deserts, and that we are not bound to act the part of the good subjects to him who does not in turn act the part of a king to us.

The men who furiously strive to overturn the divinely established order of government are, according to Calvin, the insane and barbarous men. He has compared the disobedience with insanity and barbarity. He also calls it outrageous barbarity. The disobedient persons are also fanatics. To disobey an ordinance of God is really an insane and barbarous act. Only fanatics can venture to do it. How a prince rules and in what way he rules that is immaterial. All these are indicators of the fact that Calvin viewed and judged everything in the perspective and light of theology.

From the above passage it is obvious that Calvin had no interest in the desirability or non-desirability of the functions of civil authority and the acceptibility and non-acceptibility of these function by the people. The simple fact is that people will unhesitatingly endorse the functions of authority and carry out the orders. He conceives in Aristotelian vein that a system compounded of aristocracy and democracy far excels all others. In this connection Calvin brings the point to our attention that there are various forms of magistracy. But there is no material difference between these forms, because all the forms are regarded as ordained by God.

As to the limit to the power of kings Calvin does not recognise any right of the people. Their only duty is to surrender to the authority of the king. The power of the ruler is limited by the law of God. This fundamental concept must be accepted by all. Gettel writes : "Calvin favoured an authoritative attitude and disbelieved in freedom. He had a great contempt for the mob and preferred an aristocratic form of government. His point of view was that of a strong ruler and a uniform system of government" (p. 161).

8 MACHIAVELLI

Modern Political Thought

A cursory glance of political events reveals that it is difficult to divide the events into various periods such as ancient, modern, or medieval etc. In spite of this problem scholars and political scientists have divided the history of political thought into several periods. These are ancient, medieval, early modern and modern. The ancient and medieval periods are betw-een 400 B.C. to 1500 A.D. Important political philosophers of the ancient period are Socrates, Plato, Aristotles, Augustine, Justinian (not exclusively political thinker), Aquinas etc. The important events of ancient and medieval periods are Hundred Years' War (1337–1453), Renaissance in Italy (1450–1550), French Invasion of Italy (1494–1495), Start of Protestant Movement (1517). The early modern period is between 1500–1800. The important political thinkers are Machiavelli and his important work is *The Prince* (1513), Martin Luther was another important thinker. He authored several books, his important work is on *Secular Authority* (1523). Calvin published *Institutes of Christian Religion in* 1559. The exponent of modern doctrine of sovereignty is Jean Bodin and his important book is *Six Books of the Commonwealth* published in 1576.

Hobbes, Pufendorf and Locke are all contract philosophers, all of whom believed that contract among the people of the state of nature was the primary reason of the origin of state. But their lines of argument were quite different. Rousseau is also a contract thinker. Rousseau was the author of several important books and the important ones are *Social Contract* (1762), *Discourses* (1749–1755). French philosopher Montesquieu belonged to early modern period and his famous work *The Spirit of the Laws* was published in 1748. David Hume was both a philosopher and political thinker. He was famous for his work *Essays Moral and Political* published in 1741. The early modern period started, according to John Morrow, in 1520 and ended in 1820. In this period there was Hugo Grolius whose *The Law of War and Peace* published in 1625 created ripples in the academic world. The book chiefly deals with the legal aspects of relations among the nations. There were also other thinkers in the seventeenth and early eighteenth centuries. The nineteenth century almost started with a "new philosophy" and it is Utilitarianism whose chief propounder was Jeremy Bentham. Several works of high credit were produced by his pen and the important ones are Fragment on Government (1776). Introduction to *the Principles of Morals and Legislation* (1789). Immanuel Kant was a nineteenth century philosopher and his Metaphysics of Morals was published in 1797. Towards the end of the eighteenth century Mary Wollstonecraft published *A Vindication of the Rights of Men and A Vindication of the Rights of Women* were published in 1791 and 1792 respectively.

An interesting continuity of political thought is to be found in the cases of James Mill and J. S. Mill. The father and son were philosophers of the nineteenth century. James Mill, father of J. S. Mill, published *Essay of Government* in 1820. He was the friend of Jeremy Bentham who propounded the doctrine of Utilitarianism. His son J. S. Mill published several works and important of them are *On Liberty* (1859), *Representative Government (1861), On the Subjection of Women* (1869). Bentham was famous for propounding the doctrine of Utilitarianism and J. S. Mill is still remembered by the students of Western political thought for his revision of utilitarianism and concept of liberty. The nineteenth century is really famous for it produced a good number of famous philosophers. Apart from J. S. Mill, there were at least three utopian philosophers—Saint-Simon, Robert Owen and Charles Fourier. All of them are generally labelled by many as early socialists. The fact is that both Marx and Engels followed in their footsteps regarding socialism and elaborated many of their basic concepts about socialism. From 1840s to 1890s the European political thought centred around the Marxist philosophy. Evolutionary socialism of Edward Bernstein and Fabian socialism of Fabian Society were also the products of Marxist socialist thought. There is no doubt that evolutionary socialism, Fabian socialism are different from Marxist socialism. But these two types are undoubtedly the by-product of Marxian socialism.

In the twentieth century we find anarchism and strong criticisms of Marxism. Rosa Luxemburg Kautsky and many other Marxist thinkers have enriched Marxian philosophy by their critical analysis of Marxism. Mention may be made about Antonio Gramsci whose noted work is *Prison Notebooks* (1937). The late twentieth century has not been able to produce any new political philosophy. But old ideas have been reformulated in the light of new situation. F. A. Hayek, John Rawls and Robert Nozick are the most prominent personalities of the domain of political science who have viewed the subject in the background of social, economic and political incidents that are frequently taking place. Hayek, Rawls and Nozick are famous for revising liberalism that was propounded by John Locke and subsequently elaborated by a host of thinkers. Chinese revolutionary leader Mao was not in the strictest sense an original thinker. But in the list of socialist thinkers his name has got a special position because of his stand in Marxist philosophy.

Different Aspects of Modern Political Thought

Scholars of Western political thought are of opinion that both Renaissance and Reformation have contributed a lot to the emergence of modern political thought. These two released political theory or thought from the octopus of religion and superstition. It is true that these two movements could not establish secularism in politics, but as a result of Renaissance and Reformation the church was forced to give up its claim over politics. Church and papacy were forced to remain satisfied with their truncated authority. Political affairs of the state got ample opportunity to travel on their own way. Political ideas were suppressed or could not get ample opportunity to flourish in the Middle Ages when the church was all-powerful. After Reformation various strands of political ideas spontaneously developed and this is an aspect of modern political thought.

The downfall of Feudalism was a spectacular aspect of modern political thought and this appeared after Reformation. Feudalism was incongruous for an atmosphere (both political and economic) that appeared after Reformation. Trade and commerce developed and a new economic order emerged. Economic nature of society changed considerably. Cottage and small scale industries of the past were replaced by comparatively large sized industries. Agriculture society of the past was replaced by the industrial society. The contradictions of the feudal society gave way to new types of contradictions that characterised the industrial society. In such situation we find new types of political ideas. Marx and his followers strongly emphasised this new development and this many people call Marxian politics.

In the new political and economic situation two important classes appeared and their interest were poles apart. This situation created an atmosphere of contradiction and conflict. The industrial society was characterised by class conflict and this according to Marx and Engels—led to class struggle. Marxian politics is a prominent part of modern political ideas and class struggle occupies a central position of that politics. Marx, Engels and their followers focused their attention also on the materialism aspects of philosophy. Before Marx, idealism was one of the important aspects of politics. Marx challenged it. In the Theses on Feurbach Marx said, The standpoint of the old materialism is "civil" society, the standpoint of the new is human society or socialised humanity. He further said : The philosophers have only interpreted the world, in various ways, the point, however, is to change it.

The political thinkers of the modern age are thinking to change the materialistic aspects of society. so as to make it relevant for the new materialistic situation. But this will not be done in Marxian way. In 1884, Fabian Society was set up to fight the evils of Industrial Revolution. Attempts were made to give economic and other reliefs to the poorer and downtrodden sections of the society. So far as political thought or ideas are concerned the whole society is divided into two broad groups—Marxian politics and non-Marxian politics.

In his concluding observations about the foundation of modern political thought Skinner (Vol. II, p. 349) says "By the beginning of the seventeenth century, the concept of the state—its nature, its powers, its right to command obedience—had come to be regarded as the most important object of analysis in European political thought." The implication is the appearance of Renaissance and Reformation brought about sea changes in the vast field of political thought and it is interesting to note that this change is advancing. Skinner feels that though the basis of modern political thought appeared after Renaissance and Reformation, the actual foundation was laid by Aristotle in his *Politics.* In Book I of *Politics* Aristotle said *Communicatio* politica which means political community. After Aristotle scholars and philosophers have attempted to focus their attention on politics. In the Middle Ages people forgot to think seriously about politics and some critics think that it was buried in oblivion. After Reformation its revival appeared.

A very important segment of modern political theory is the rise of the bourgeoisie and capitalist state. The unprecedented growth of trade and commerce enabled few persons to harvest huge amount of profit and this made them strengthen their position in society. Ultimately the bourgeois class began to control politics and economics of society and, finally, an unholy alliance was established between the persons holding power and the capitalist class. Governmental control over economy and politics, in a considerable way, was discouraging the growth of *laissez faire* and in such a situation the capitalise class urged upon the government to slacken its control over society and economy. The modern liberalism started its journey from John Locke and received enough impetus in the hands of Adam Smith. He strongly advocated *laissez faire* in his *The Wealth of Nations* which was published in 1776. Liberalism and individualism travelled simultaneously. In the midst of all these religion was relegated to an ignoble position. Contrary to Middle Ages, people began to think more about economics and less about religion.

Machiavelli and Modern Political Thought

We shall now turn to an analysis why Machiavelli is called a modern political theorist or scientist. Machiavelli wrote few books, *The Prince* was the most important. But this book discusses very little about political science or political theory and hence the question is why he has been called so. The chief reason for giving him the rank or status of modern political theorist is he was the first thinker who freed political science or theory from the clutches of religion and morality. He was not interested in high moral or religious principles. His main concern was power and the practical or political interests of the state. It would be the primary concern of the prince in particular and government in general to protect the interests of state. In this connection R. N. Berki writes : "He is also renowned for being exceptionally outspoken and candid in his views, writing with a clinical detachment or sometimes even cynicism about issues. Such as the use of violence and deception in politics" (p. 119). In other words Machiavelli was the first thinker who took an unequivocal stand in regard to the relationship between religion, morality and virtue on the one hand and politics on the other. He adopted a very clear stand about politics, religion and morality. He never denounced virtue, morality and religion. But what he emphasised is that the domain of morality and religion is quite different from that of politics and the prince must maintain it in his treatmental of politics.

Machiavelli strongly advocated a dichotomy between morality and religion on the one hand and politics on the other. But Skinner is of opinion that (Vol. I, p. 125) : This dichotomy is not Machiavelli's own creation or discovery. Aristotle in his *Politics* adopted such form of dichotomy and Machiavelli scrupulously adopted Aristotelian method. Aristotle held the view that the "qualities which deserve admiration in a prince may be different from those which deserve admiration in a private citizen" (Skinner Vol. II, p. 125). Even many other thinkers following Aristotle and Machiavelli said that "the virtues of the rulers are one thing, the virtues of the people are another." In this way Machiavelli established a separate set of virtues for the prince or the ruler. In *The Prince* he emphasised that the prince must follow a virtue which is "*creative*"—creative in the sense that the virtue of the prince would be able to maintain the state. With the help of his virtues the prince would "fight off" his enemies. We, therefore, find that Machiavelli used the word "virtue" not in any conventional sense. The supreme objective of a prince is always to maintain the unity of his state and to bring it under good administration. People of the state always demand that they are not to be oppressed and exploited. It is the primary duty of the ruler to look after it and if any ruler fails to achieve it he is unfit for the post of ruler or to be called a prince. At the same time Machiavelli declared that if a prince or ruler fails to achieve this objective he cannot demand obligation from his subjects. In this way Machiavelli had established a new norm for politics and that norm is politics has nothing to do with the conventional type of morality or ethics. We further observe that Machiavelli denounced his contemporary political theories because they failed to emphasise the importance of power. In his opinion power is the most important aspect of political theory. Even today we cannot deny this concept power politics or practical politics does not give full recognition to morality or religion. Last of all we hold the view that he built up a wall between politics and religion not guided by personal preference but by the prevailing situation of his time.

Life and Time

Niccolo Machiavelli, one of the most controversial figures of Western political thought, was born in 1469 and passed away in 1527. At the age of 29 he enrolled in the public service of his native state Florence. His services lasted only for fourteen years. Machiavelli was one of the top policy-makers of the state. He had close connection with the highest echelons of state administration and this enabled him to come in contact with the inner circles of policy-making and policy application of state administration. He was so important figure of state administration that he was very often sent for diplomatic missions to France and Germany. But as ill luck would have it he was accused of serious crimes and for this he had to suffer punishment. In 1512 he lost his job. But his removal from job appeared to him as blessing in disguise. He fully utilised this forced retirement in constructive work. During the forced leisure he wrote his famous book *The Prince* which was published in 1513. He ardently hoped that he would get back his earlier job but his hopes remained unfulfilled. Naturally Machiavelli remained a jobless person or, we may say, in forced retirement. But he utilised it for academic purposes. He published another book *The Discourses. The Prince* is called by many as an advice book because it contains number of advices to a prince in respect of what he should do and should not do. Do's and don'ts are the central idea of *The Prince.* But the *Discourses* is an attempt to dissect and analyse the state or body politic. It also discourses the philosophical and historical aspects of contemporary politics.

Speaking about the content of *The Prince* Ebenstein writes : The most revolutionary aspect of The Prince is not so much what it says as what it ignores. Before Machiavelli all political writings—from Plato to Aristotle through the Middle Ages to the Renaissance—had one central question : *the end of the state.* Political power was assumed to be a means only—a means in the service of higher ends—such as justice, good life, freedom or God. Machiavelli ignores the issue of the end of the state in extra-political terms. He assumes that power is an end in itself and he confines his inquiry into the means that are best suited to acquire, retain and expand power" (p. 280).

Dunning, a noted interpreter of Western political thought, writes : "In no system of political philosophy is the influence of environment more manifest than in that of Machiavelli. The brilliant Florentine was in the fullest sense the child of his time" (p. 285). The impact of contemporary events always falls upon the thinker and this is more prominent in the case of Machiavelli. The Renaissance brought about an upheaval in the social, political and to some extent in the economic sphere of many European states and Machiavelli's Florence or other states were no exception. Machiavelli's contemporary Italy was divided into the following five states—Kingdom Naples in the south, Milan in the north west, Venice in the north-east, the Republic of Florence, and the Papal state. This division of Italy, Machiavelli was convinced, was the root cause of the backwardness and numerous ills from which Italy suffered. So the unification of Italy was the burning question because it was strongly felt that without unification any progress was impossible. Not only this, the whole of Italy was under the strong grip of corruption and mismanagement. A strong and powerful ruler was the need of the time and Machiavelli focused his attention to that. His conviction was that only a powerful prince could save Italy from disunity, profligacy and debauchery.

Machiavelli and Absolutism

At the beginning of the 16th century we see a very important aspect of modern political theory which can simply be stated as modern absolutism. In the opinion of Sabine, Machiavelli is the father of this absolutism. He suggested the separation between religion, morality and politics. In political matters the king will have the last word to say and all other centres must submit to political power. In the words of Sabine (p. 333) : "Absolute monarchy overturned feudal constitutionalism and the free city-states, on which medieval civilisation had largely depended. ....Ecclesiastical rulers were everywhere subjected more and more to royal control, and in the end church's legal authority disappeared". Both Renaissance and Reformation drastically cut the wings of church and papacy which created vacuum in social and political fields and this was forthwith filled up by the emergence of absolute royal power. Hence absolute royal power became the order of European politics. The growth of absolute monarchy, like that of feudal constitutional monarchy, took place in almost every part of western Europe" (Sabine, p. 333).

The question is why the absolute monarchy came to be the order of the day of European politics. In the medieval period the church or the Ecclesiastical authority in all possible ways discouraged the people to ignore the financial issues which ultimately resulted in the complete stagnation of economy. Both Renaissance and Reformation enlightened people's mind, thought and outlook and this, in turn inspired them to go out in search of money and wealth. In the new situation and atmosphere the medieval institutions were remodelled and partially revolutionised to cope with the new situation. Before Renaissance and Reformation trade and commerce were local and they operated in certain fixed routes. After these two, both trade and commerce became international or, we can say, the operation of trade and commerce expanded considerably. The wealth of many nations increased beyond imagination and simultaneously many people having considerable enterprise came to be the owners of newly created wealth. That is wealth, power and enterprise were in the hands of few persons and they came to be called capitalist class or bourgeois class. Before Renaissance and Reformation, in European society there was class of nobility and after these two there arose a new class—the capitalist class and finally the old class of nobility was forced to submit to the class of capitalists. The capitalist class saw that the citadel of wealth and property would face insecurity if military power and administration remained out of its control. In other words, the bourgeois class was very much eager to control the power and military of the state. The power of the kings in all practical senses must be absolute but it must remain under the control and supervision of the capitalists.

At the time of Machiavelli the capitalists were rising quite rapidly and they sought royal protection for the growth of trade and commerce. The meteoric rise of the power of kings appeared to be salubrious to the bourgeoisie. This class thought that with the help of the royal power it would be able to secure its wealth, because the king was the authority of military and bureaucratic administration. Machiavelli fully understood the social, economic and political situation of Italy and at the same time he thought that only an absolute monarch or prince with enormous power could save Italy. Democracy, liberalism, people's rights etc. had very little importance to him. Only an absolute monarchy was the need of the day.

Machiavelli was a great patriot and nationalist. He was convinced that only a powerful king could unite divided Italy. A powerful prince could hasten the economic progress. A united Italy was badly needed and a prince with enormous power at his disposal could achieve it. Like other Italians Machiavelli held the church responsible for the miserable condition of Italy. So we hold the view that the prevailing situation forced Machiavelli to strongly argue for a strong monarchy. Machiavelli was a practical man and he had wide interests and curiosity in politics. Italy of his time was weak politically and militarily. She was cornered in European politics. This ignoble position of Italy pained Machiavelli and he decided that Italy must be saved at any cost. Installation of an absolute power was the only solution. Absolute power of the prince was the only way. In support of his conclusion Machiavelli drew examples from ancient history of various European states. It means that at first he took a decision or selected a way and after that he gathered facts in support of his decision. This some people call Machiavellian. The word Machiavellian is also used to denote "some action on the part of a state, a politician or even a friend. By calling an action Machiavellian we mean that it is selfish, cunning and without any moral justification" (J. R. Hale : *Machiavelli And the Self-Sufficient State in Political Ideas*, p. 22). Though Machiavellism is used in pejorative sense we think that it is unjust because his method of analysis and objective cannot be subject of denouncement. The objective situation compelled him to advocate for an absolute power and separate politics from morality and religion. Many people may not like him or even may denounce him but a neutral assessment will support him.

Machiavelli and Renaissance

Many critics of Western political thought prefer to call Machiavelli as the child of Renaissance. W. T. Jones says "Machiavelli was the child of Florence and of the Renaissance. All the qualities which characterise his city and his age appear in his own personality". An important aspect of Renaissance is that, coming under its influence, man began to judge and value everything, specially politics, in a new light. Even they scanned the values such as morality, justice, religion. In the Middle Ages man was mesmerised by the church, Pope and, above all, by religion. He had no independent thinking power. But the advent of Renaissance changed this situation and man began to think of religion, values etc. by applying his own reason. Machiavelli also adopted it. He broke the traditional path. He analysed social, political conditions in the light of new thought, reason and perspective. So both ordinary men and Machiavelli changed their line of thinking and way of values. He thought that man was not created simply to follow the advice of church and adopt certain religious principles. He also observed that the orthodox religion has considerably dwarfed his power of thinking and ability to follow or adapt reason. This created a precarious situation in the Italian society. He observed that Renaissance everywhere of Europe created a new thought and advancement of learning. Renaissance inspired man to know more and to advance forward. But the people of Italy remained in darkness. Machiavelli arrived at the decision that the people of Italy must be saved from this position and new thought shall be injected in their "blood". Being influenced by Renaissance he thought in this line.

The study of history inculcated a new idea in his mind and that was the service and loyalty to God and church could never be a factor of social upliftment. For this purpose it is required that man must serve society and man. The influence of religion, ethics and morality must be removed and people must be made practical. He declared that in public affairs religion, morality and ethics must have no status. Only a powerful prince with absolute power at his disposal can achieve this. W. T. Jones writes : "A product of Renaissance, such as Machiavelli repudiates the old medieval nation of an objective moral order, determined by God, and in accordance with whose prescriptions men live best. On the contrary, for him that life is best which brings fame, distinction, honours, and reputation to a man" (p. 27). Needless to say that Machiavelli received his materialistic outlook from the Renaissance. The Renaissance taught man the important lesson that if man desires better living and better situation he must look to the material situation—and not to God or religion or morality. All these are subjective and cannot help man to attain overall upliftment.

Before Renaissance man was the doll at the hands of Pope and this resulted in the loss of reason and rationality. But he must think that he is endowed with reason, rationality, power of judgment. By applying all these qualities he can considerably improve his material condition. The subservience to God, morality, religion has no power to change and improve man's material condition. People of post-Renaissance period acquired this idea and Machiavelli thought it prudent to apply it for the general improvement of Italian society. This is materialism, and we also call it Machiavellism.

Machiavelli and the Reason of the State

The most revolutionary aspect of Machiavelli's idea about politics is the *reason of the state*. Ebenstein writes : Before Machiavelli all political writings—from Plato and Aristotle through Middle Ages to the Renaissance—had one central question—*The end of the state.* Political power was assumed to be a means only—a means to the service of higher ends such as justice, the good life, freedom or God—Machiavelli ignores the issue of the end of the state in the extra-political terms. He assumes that *power is an end in itself* and he confines his inquires into the means that are best suited to *acquire, retain,* and *expand power*" (p. 280). The fact is that the central concept of Machiavelli's political philosophy is the power of the state and, without power, the state is almost nothing. Studying history he formed the conclusion that only power can save Italy. If there is any message in *The Prince,* then it is that the sole objectives of the prince shall be to acquire power to make the state self-sufficient in all respects so that it can compete with other states. This is called the reason of the state.

The concept—reason of the state—is regarded by many—constitutes the central idea of Machiavelli's political theory or ideas. It means that a state may have many ambitious aims but the most important one is to strengthen its position by acquiring power because without power a state is almost nothing. A true prince must accumulate physical power by any means and apply it for the sake of the state. In the *Discourses* he said : "A prince must build on sound foundation, otherwise he is bound to come to grief. The main foundations of every state are good laws and good arms" (Quoted by Hale *Political Ideas*, p. 27). Why so much emphasis on arms and power? Machiavelli had a thorough knowledge about human nature. In order to fight human beings of this nature a prince must have enormous power. The power of the prince means the power of the state. Hobbes also held the same view. The point, however, is, these issues or aspects have met at a signle point and this point is—the nature of society, the nature of human beings and the duty of the prince. These three have combinedly constituted the concept of reason of the state.

Speaking about the reason of the state (or *regione di state*) Skinner maintains "Machiavelli's *The Prince* was first printed in 1532, and thereafter the Machiavellian defenders of *regione di state* showed an increasing disposition to argue that if the main aim of the political theorist is to offer genuinely useful advice on how to maintain one's state, then the less edifying aspects of prevailing political practice ought to be acknowledged and even recommended rather than merely outlawed" (Vol. I, p. 250). Skinner also observes that many have condemned his concept—reason of the state. But it is to be well-remembered that there was no alternative way. He wanted to save Italy from further deterioration and, in order to achieve that ambitious goal, the state of his imagination must have a positive and clear role. He did not think of a state in Platonic background. Some critics also say that Machiavelli's attitude towards religion, ethics and morality is unpardonable. But his idea of state and reason of the state are impressive. He possessed a clear conception about human nature and for such nature a powerful state is essential. Here lies the reason of the state. From history he collected numerous instances why a very powerful state is needed. Machiavelli was a practical man and he was not guided by any sentiment. That built up his reason of the state.

Power Politics and Self-Sufficient State

Machiavelli's two concepts—power politics and self-sufficient state—are closely connected. J. R. Hale in his article—*Machiavelli and the Self-Sufficient State*—observes : It is noteworthy how much Machiavelli sees politics as a battle—a constant struggle for power. All politics, in his sense, are power politics (p. 29). After the Second World War the whole world was in the grip of power politics which means most or all the big powers converted the whole world into a battle-field. The leaders of the super or major powers believed that war was the only way to solve all the problems. Machiavelli, almost in the same way, treated war as the only instrument capable to solve social and political problems. He writes in *The Prince* "Therefore, if a prince wants to maintain his rule he must learn how not to be virtuous, and to make use of this or not according to need. Everyone realises how praiseworthy it is for a prince to honour his word or to be straight-forward rather than in his dealings; nonetheless contemporary experience shows that princes who have achieved great things have been those who have given their word lightly, who have known how to trick men with their cunning, and who, in the end, have overcome those abiding by honest principles." In the theory of power politics there is no place of honesty and scruples. The sole aim of the prince or ruler of the state would be to achieve the goal. This goal is the interest of the state. To make the state powerful so that it can fight any ill-design of another state.

In the thought and action of the prince the only idea will get priority : The state must be made powerful at any cost because without military power the state is quite incapable to achieve its objective. In *The Prince* Machiavelli has elaborately discussed the concept of power : "There are two ways of fighting : by law or by force. The first way is natural to men, and the second to beasts. But as the first way often proves inadequate one must needs have recourse to the second. So a prince must understand how to make a nice use of the beast and the man. .....Prince must know how to act according to the nature of both, and that he cannot survive otherwise" (Machiavelli : *The Prince*). Machiavelli advised his prince to make a proper use of both law and brute force and in this way he was supposed to achieve success. He advised his prince to sacrifice honesty, morality, religion for the benefit, or, more generally, for the cause of the state. It would never be regarded prudence on the part of the prince if he sacrifice the interest of the republic at the altar of honesty and religion. This is regarded as the reason of the state. The interest of the state will be achieved if it is made all-powerful. He could not see anything of the state outside or beyond power. Both for survival and development of state power is indispensable. In the *Discourses* he has elaborated this idea. He supported his contention by drawing instances.

Another part or aspect of Machiavelli's contribution to politics is his idea of self-sufficient state. His idea of power politics reason of state and self-sufficient state are all closely related. J. R. Hale in his illuminating article—*Machiavelli And the Self-Sufficient State* has thrown ample light on this aspect. He says that Machiavelli did not appeal to the Christian morality or religion for the benefit of the state. To him the state was all-in-all and he was not prepared to sacrifice a small part of the interest of the state. Without a powerful state people's progress and welfare would remain unfulfilled. It is the reason of the state or *raison d'tat*. If the *raison d'tat* is achieved or successfully established the state will achieve the status of self-sufficiency. So behind the concept of power politics there was an idea of a self-sufficient state in his mind. The word self-sufficient is really a comprehensive term. But to Machiavelli it had a definite connotation. In order to be self-sufficient a state first of all must be powerful so that it can defeat the ill-motives of foreign states. After a state has achieved self-sufficiency in power (specially military power) it can land on other activities. The military power is at the top of all considerations.

In the concluding part of his analysis J. R. Hale writes "Machiavelli's assumption that the state must pursue a policy of self-interest in terms of *raison d'etat* is not a Bible morality, was later echoed by theorists like Hegel, and men of action like Bismarck and Hitler. Today the problem which Machiavelli stated is as urgent as ever" (p. 32-33). We think that what was true at the time of Machiavelli is still correct. Today the big or super powers are continuously fighting to establish their over-all supremacy. They do not know where they will reach. Machiavelli thought that the accumulation of military power was the most prudent way to establish one's supremacy. It was wrong. Even today the big or super powers think in the same line. It is also wrong. However, Machiavelli of Florence is not dead, he is still alive in the minds of the leaders of today's big powers. Hale concludes : We can throw away Machiavelli the bogey, but, if we are to think realistically about politics, the state and the super-state perhaps we still need the pugnacious common sense of Machiavelli the man" (p. 33). Both in national and international fields, power and politics are all-in-all. So we cannot blame Machiavelli.

Politics and Religion

Renaissance, Luther, Calvin and Machiavelli are almost contemporary. Both democracy and individualism are the products of the Renaissance. But simultaneously despotism emerged along with them. Church and papacy were forced to surrender their supremacy and dictatorial manner or functioning and the vacuum created in this way was forthwith filled up by the rise of monarchy. The dominating power of kings became absolutely prominent. Out of democracy, individualism and despotism, only despotism was able to draw special attention of Machiavelli. McClelland aptly observes : In the *Discourses* Machiavelli makes it perfectly clear that the ruthless rule of a new prince is only one of the forms of government (p. 154). Machiavelli was quite acquainted with various forms of government including democracy or republicanism. But he preferred dictatorship or despotism as the most suitable form of government. It is generally observed that he was the chief supporter of despotism because in his judgment only a despotic ruler could save Italy from the despicable condition. Somehow he arrived at the conclusion that a strong and powerful ruler was needed for Italy. Democracy could not save her. To Machiavelli politics was an end and its mechanism was military power.

He was chiefly concerned with the mechanics of government. He studied history of many European states and the knowledge he gathered was that Italy needed an autocratic government. "He was not a prisoner of indecision. It was his conviction. He writes almost wholly of the mechanics of government, of the means by which states may be made strong of the politics by which they can expand their power" (Sabine, p. 339). According to Sabine and many others political and military measures are of primary interest because Machiavelli thought that only these two had the power to save a state. He strongly advocated a separation between politics and religion and without this separation the state could not reach its goal. His open declaration was that the purpose of politics was to preserve and augment political power. He was so adamant in this respect that he was not prepared to make any compromise. The policy adopted by the prince may be cruel, faithless or lawless, but that, is quite immaterial. The point is whether it could help the prince to achieve success. The policy of the prince is quite moral or ethical and he is religious-minded but it is useless so far as its capacity to achieve success is concerned.

Machiavelli was not against morality, religion, ethics etc. Rather, he was indifferent. That is, he adopted an indifferent stand or attitude towards these. It is called **moral indifference.** In *Discourses* he made the following observation "our religion places the supreme happiness in humility, lowliness, and a contempt for worldly objects, whilst the others on the contrary, places the supreme good in grandeur of soul, strength of body. These principles seem to me to have made men feeble and caused them to became an easy prey to evil minded men". In this passage we find that he did not suggest to be immoral or anti-religious. He was of opinion that religion, morality etc. should be kept aside for special and personal use. If a prince wants to achieve success he must make serious efforts to separate religion and morality from politics. He should use these for his personal use only. The prince must not hesitate to use immoral means and unethical ways and corrupt practices to achieve success in political fields. A prince should not run after admiration. His subjects may throw him eulogy and admiration for being honest and religious minded. But they will never forgive him for his failure in political affairs.

Machiavelli recommends a double standard of morality and ethics—one for the ruler and the other for the private citizens or persons. The reason suggested by Machiavelli is that the supreme objective of the prince is to achieve success in political fields. Religion, morality and ethics should not be allowed to stand on the way of success. But the private persons have not such objectives and naturally they have the freedom to follow moral and religious ways. Machiavelli has suggested that the *virtu* of a prince is different from that of an ordinary person. Skinner observes "the whole of Machiavelli's advice is governed by a highly original sense of what should be taken to constitute true *virtu* in a prince. ....With Machiavelli the concept of *virtu* is simply used to refer to whatever range of qualities the prince may find it necessary to acquire in order to maintain his state and achieve great things" (Vol. I, p. 138). It is clear that morality, ethics and religion in the case of a prince are combinedly called *virtu* and the prince must adopt this *virtu* honestly. He should be least concerned with what happens in religion or morality.

By recommending the above Machiavelli clearly indicated the separation between politics and religion. This may also be called the "autonomy of politics", which implies that the politics has an exclusively different world. This is called secularism of politics or secularisation of politics. Machiavelli thought that politics and religion are different because their fields are separate. He had a firm belief that for all sorts of corruption in politics, religion is absolutely responsible. A prince or a political man could never achieve success by scrupulously following religious, moral and ethical means. If a man becomes prince he should avoid moral and religious ways by all means. There is emotion in morality and religion. A prince true to his name must give no recognition to the religious and moral feelings. Explaining the stand adopted by Machiavelli Skinner observes (p. 134) "if a ruler is genuinely concerned to maintain his state he will have to shake off the demands of Christian virtue, wholeheartedly embracing the very different morality which his situation dictates." It is to be noted here that "to maintain the state" and reason of the state are concepts of immense importance and Machiavelli took these seriously. A state must be maintained in the face of all odds or adverse situations and a judicious prince must reject the conventional religion and morality. This is the fulcrum of Machiavellian concept of secularisation of politics. If a prince honestly follows the Christian virtue that will stand on the way of success. Hence he recommended two separate compartments—one for politics and the other for religion.

His clear view was that when the safety of our country is absolutely at stake there need be no question of what is just or unjust, merciful or cruel, praiseworthy or disgraceful, but all other considerations set aside, that course alone is to be taken which may save our country and maintain its liberty. To him religion, ethics and morality were mystical concepts but the state was a real element. He was out and out a materialist and for that reason he refused to give proper recognition to the mystical elements such as religion and morality. State or politics has a separate and at the same time real or concrete domain. Florence was the birthplace of Machiavelli and birthplace of several celebrities. But this Florence was in an ignoble position or situation which he could not tolerate. His idea was that Florence or any other state was reality and in that sense politics was also a reality. But religion is not a reality. Hence state and politics are reality.

Machiavelli's Idea About State

It would be wrong to brand Machiavelli as a systematic political philosopher or thinker or a theoretician about state. His main concern was his birthplace Florence and overall progress of Italy, especially Florence, an important centre of art and literature. In The Prince he said : "A prince must build on sound foundations of every state, new states as well as ancient or composite ones, are good laws and good arms." But above all the prince must focus his attention on building up a powerful army. Only an army can make a state self-sufficient. We have already discussed this aspect. Here we like to note that Machiavelli's state was mainly a military state, it is not liberal or democratic state. He was not interested in democracy at all. He thought that with the help of military strength a state can achieve its object. He was out and out a materialist and wanted to build up the concept of state on materialism. He did not run after idealism, philosophy, morality etc. Even he did not think in those lines and this was the special characteristic of Machiavelli's state. G. W. Allen says : "He was really concerned only with the actual states of his day. He had crude notions of how the states came into being and he had the idea that all institutions tend to corruption owing to inherent defects arising from the nature of man. He believed that out of corruption comes, or may come, new healthy growth and that all tend to move in a circle. He conceived the state as something very unstable" (A History of *Political Thought in the Sixteenth Century*, p. 479).

Machiavelli's state was not only a military state, it was an absolutist state and above all it was a secular state. It was a state quite indifferent to morality, to religion, to ethics. We can say he predicted a twentieth century state—a state of power and politics. Let us again quote Allen : "Not only has it no vital relation to church it has no relation to God or to any cosmic purposes." He had a firm conviction that religion, politics and ethics could not cohabit. The area of politics is absolutely separate from that of religion and morality. Today we frequently talk about secular state. But it is to be remembered that several centuries ago Machiavelli, the son of Florence, laid the foundation of such a state."

Some interpreters of Machiavelli's political thought are of opinion that he had an idea of nation-state. He wanted to demarcate the boundary of each state to ensure the proper administration and jurisdiction. In the opinion of a critic "That Machiavelli perceived the advantage to a government of having subjects similar in language, customs and habits of life, is quite clear." In the last chapter of *The Prince* he had suggested that all the foreigners were to be ordered to leave Italy. He had the intention to convert Italy into one nation one state. This demand was revived in twentieth century. Today we frequently talk about right to self-determination—Machiavelli perhaps had that idea. Machiavelli had an apprehension that the foreigners were responsible for the present condition of Italy. He had an apprehension that if the prince proceeds to drive away all the foreigners from the soil of Italy then armed conflict with other states was inevitable and, for that reason, he suggested that a prince must proceed to build up a strong army to strengthen his defence and must not depend on mercenaries because they are useless and dangerous. Some critics may say that Machiavelli was a narrow-minded political thinker. May be so. But it is true that he was a patriot and loved his motherland more than any other contemporary politician.

Omnipotent Legislator

Machiavelli's concept of state or his philosophy is closely connected with his notion of omnipotent legislator. He makes the following observation in ***Discourses*** : "But we must assume, as a general rule, that it never or rarely happens that a republic or monarchy is well-constituted, or its old institutions entirely reformed, unless it is done by only one individual, it is even necessary that he whose mind has conceived such a constitution should be alone in carrying it into effect (Quoted by Sabine, p. 344). We have already observed that Machiavelli's main concern was a well-ordered and properly constituted state and he was fully conscious that law was the main instrument which was capable of achieving this objective. His belief was that only a good prince was unable to bring his state under proper administration. Two instruments were necessary—one is good law and the other is well-regulated army. The prince first of all will try to administer the state with the help of law and, where necessary, army will be called. Interpreters of Machiavelli's political thought are of opinion that he advised his prince to rely mainly on law. Sabine observes "The law-giver is the architect not only of the state but of society as well, with all its moral, religious and economic institutions" (p. 345).

Machiavelli received the importance of law from Greek political thought. In ancient Greece Solon (B. C. 638–559) was of opinion that law was the chief instrument which could ensure justice. Needless to say that Solon was a famous legislator. He relied on good law and legislator on the ground that human nature was not always up to standard—men are corrupt and self-interest seeking. To cope or fight with them good laws are essential. In his opinion human beings are selfish and egoist. To bring such persons under the administration, law was essential and for that reason he heavily relied upon law. To sum up, in Machiavelli's view, law was the most important part of state administration.

But the question is why an omnipotent legislator. We have already quoted a long passage from *Discourses*. He said "it never or rarely happen a republic is well-administered unless it is done by only one individual." So we can easily conclude that he had no faith on any legislative body or legislature. His prince had no limit to what extent he could go and similarly his law-giver had unlimited power to make law. Machiavelli does not clearly say whether his omnipotent legislator and king are the same person or not. But from his different comments in *Discourses* and *The Prince* it appears to us that he wanted to entrust the powers of law-making and administration in the same hands. An able prince, he hoped, would be able to make good laws which would build a solid foundation for a prosperous state. Sabine observes : "He can tear down old states and build new, change forms of government, transplant populations and build new virtues into the character of his subjects" (p. 345). A good administrator is also a good legislator. Machiavelli advised his prince to focus attention to both making of law and streamlining general administration. We can say that all his contemporaries were thinking of a good and all-powerful administration. Like Plato, Machiavelli did not think of a philosopher king, but the idea of an able and powerful administrator was quite active in his mind. This is an interesting aspect of Machiavelli's political thought which we can call "Machiavellism". Of course there are other aspects of Machiavellism but Sabine is of opinion that it is an important aspect. Finally, Machiavelli says that to what extent a person is a good administrator and legislator that requires to be judged by his success.

Assessment

The assessment of Machiavelli's political thought can best be described in the words of Sabine. He says : "No man of his age saw so clearly the direction that political evolution was taking throughout Europe. No man knew better than he the archaism of the institutions that were being displaced or accepted more readily the part that naked force was playing in the process. Yet no one in that age appreciated more highly the inchoate sense of national unity on which this force was obscurely based. No one was more clearly aware of the moral and political corruption that went with the decay of long-accustomed loyalties and pieties" (p. 335). This assessment of Sabine is perfectly correct.

Machiavelli had profound knowledge about social and political conditions of Italy and that created a lot of frustration and agony in his mind. He was a great patriot and he thought that Italy could be saved from this ignoble condition. He, for that reason, adopted an uncompromising stand. He, it is true, took an uncompromising attitude towards religion, morality and ethics. The dominating role of church and papacy was primarily responsible for the all-round deterioration of human society. He pinpointed it and suggested a way out. We may not agree with his suggestion, but the mere fact is that he had no other solution. "Indoctrinated as he was in the pagan revival in Italy he was unable both by training and temperament to grasp the constitutional and the moral ideals that European politics would carry over from the Middle Ages" (Sabine, p. 335). At the beginning of the sixteenth century constitutionalism was not highly rated as a good palliative for social and political malady. He understood the malady and applied his knowledge and experience. We may not agree but we cannot blame him.

He was a materialist and, at the same time, realist. Berki says that Machiavelli had clear conception about all the aspects of his contemporary society. Let us quote few words from Berki : of course, in truth Machiavelli's cynicism and practical concern are not the most important things about him, what we have to realise is that he had a clear and by no means ignoble, *political vision*" (italics mine, p. 20). Every political philosopher is the product of his time and Machiavelli is no exception. Plato, Aristotle, Marx all luminaries fall within this category. He believed that only a powerful prince could save Italy.

If we judge Machiavelli in a conventional way it will be found that he was guilty—guilty in the sense that he advised prince and politician to ignore morality and ethics. But he is to be judged in the background of his time and if we do this our conclusion will be of different nature. He is a thinker par excellence. His knowledge about contemporary political situation was really laudable. What he said is quite natural. He was a patriot, he was a practical man. Applying the best of his knowledge he advised the prince in such manner.

Dunning said "The influence of Machiavelli upon the history of political theories can hardly be exaggerated. Not only the method and substance of his philosophy but also the marvellous literary art with which it was expressed served to win for its universal attention" (p. 322). We appreciate Dunning's assessment. His literary art is praiseworthy, but more praiseworthy is his good command over real situation of his contemporary Italy.

His idea of power politics is absolutely pragmatic. His advice to the prince was—if he wants to achieve unity and progress of his state his sole aim would be to make his state militarily powerful and to that extent he must ignore Christian values, moral considerations and ethical judgements. Interesting to note that in the second half of the twentieth century the leaders of the superpowers followed the same track which created several crises. We do not know whether Machiavelli's prince followed his advice. But politician of seventies and eighties of the twentieth century exactly did the same thing. Machiavelli's state is the real state. It is never the embodiment of Christian values or morality. The state has an autonomous value and that value is the power of the state. This is the reason of the state or *raison d'tat*. He advised his prince to make the republic as strong as possible so that it would have not to depend upon others. We know that erstwhile Soviet Union and United States did the same thing in the fifties and sixties of the last century. In 1969 the 500th birth anniversary of Machiavelli was observed in many parts of the Western World. This indicates that Machiavelli's political thought has lasting value and this relates to his concept of power and particularly power politics.

Machiavelli was quite aware that maldistribution of poverty was the chief factor of conflict among the various classes of society. Both Marx and Engels recognised it. He believed that a powerful prince with enormous military power could save the society from this evil. He did not think of revolution. But it is not his fault. At the beginning of the sixteenth century the socio-economic-political condition of Italy was not ripe for a revolution and for that reason he did not lay emphasis on revolution.

"Machiavelli anticipates Hobbes in believing that the glory of a prince can consist of nothing but the prosperity and contentment of his people" (J. S. McClellend, p. 166). If a prince succeeds in unifying and strengthening his republic that will ensure the all-round prosperity of the state. We can remember that Thomas Hobbes also thought almost in the same line. In his opinion the anarchy of the state of nature was not congenial for the progress of the society and for that reason he suggested that a new society would be built up at the head of which there shall be a powerful sovereign authority. The sovereign authority will rule the state with law and sword. There is hardly any difference between Machiavelli's prince and Hobbes' Leviathan. In the strictest sense, both are of the same category.

Some critics charge him as the founder of fascism. The Michigan University has published a collection of essays under the title—"*Communism, Fascism and Democracy—The Theoretical Foundations.* In one of the essays Machiavelli has been depicted as the supporter of fascism. Fascism does not understand anything other than power and, more particularly, naked and unscrupulous power. Machiavelli advised his prince to adopt such power. Like Machiavelli, Hegel was also the worshipper of absolute power. Hitler was the disciple of these two thinkers.

Machiavelli was also a supporter of the bourgeoisie. As a result of Renaissance the trade and communication among nations expanded at a meteoric rate and some adventurist people earned a lot of money from trade and business. These people constituted a class called the capitalist class. Although, this class at the time of Machiavelli was just emerging or in nascent condition. He thought it his duty to support the cause if this class. His conviction was that an absolute monarchy would be the best possible form of government. This led him to support absolute monarchy.

9 JEAN BODIN

Life and Time

In the strict sense Machiavelli and Jean Bodin were not contemporary but both of them were the products of almost same circumstances—they were the products of Renaissance, religious strife and nascent capitalism and this is one of the reasons of the similarity of thought. Sufficient materials are not available about the various aspects of life of Bodin. He was born at Angers in France in 1530, three years after the death of Machiavelli. He studied law and other related subjects at the University of Toulouse and after receiving degree he became a Lecturer of jurisprudence of the same university. His close relation with law and jurisprudence made him a votary of constitutionalism. He viewed various aspects of political concepts in the light of law and jurisprudence. Particularly his famous theory of sovereignty falls within this category.

There are number of political thinkers who can rightly be called one-book genius and Jean Bodin falls in that category. His most important book *The Six Books of the Commonwealth* was published in the midst of the series of civil wars that broke out in 1562 and continued for the next thirty years. So Bodin's political ideas and thoughts can duly be called the product of tumultuous situation that erupted at the later half of the sixteenth century. The political and religious situation of France that emerged in the second half of sixteenth century considerably moulded his thoughts and ideas. Particularly the religious incidents created a great impact upon him. Bodin, we know, was a great supporter of absolute monarchy and this was due to his close association with the royal family of France. Bodin was a friend of the king's younger brother. He was sure that the religious fanaticism was "largely a product of inadequate political will and restricted military capability" (John Morrow, p. 30).

The massacre of St. Bartholomew that took place in 1572 considerably influenced the thought of Bodin. There were severe religious conflicts between two sections or groups of Christianity. The Huguenots could not accept many of the tenets of Christianity and their differences created ripples in the Christian community. The most vital stand adopted by the Huguenots was that every person has the right to follow his own faith and belief in religion. But this attitude of the Huguenots towards religion was unacceptable to the other faction. The strategy of the French government was quite peculiar. Instead of taking a neutral position the french government supported a particular section and this aggravated the situation. Skinner writes (Vol. 2, p. 241) "During the early stages of the religious wars, the basic strategy adopted by the Huguenots was that of avoiding as far as possible any direct confrontation with the government of Catherine de Medici. They insisted on upholding the fiction that they were merely opposing the government's enemies, and continued to pin their hopes on the possibility of wining an official measure of religious toleration as a by-product of Catherine's efforts to pacify the various warring elements in the kingdom."

But instead of religious toleration the intoleration became the most prominent picture of France and religious compromise became simply a dream. The weak position of the government and the adamant stand taken by different groups aggravated the religious condition. The religious animosity reached the culmination at the massacre of St. Bartholomew's Eve in 1572 that involved the slaughter of several thousand innocent Huguenots in Paris and other places of France. The religious intoleration was the basic cause of this infamous massacre. At the same time the weak position of the government was also a factor. Simultaneously the French might have adopted a neutral stand. But the government did not do that. This plagued the mind of Bodin and he strongly felt the necessity of a powerful monarch with absolute power at his disposal. Bodin supported absolute monarch as a palliative to the absolute situation of his time.

Chris Harman in his a people's history of the world (Orient Longman, 1999) has said that in the second half of the sixteenth century the French society was clearly divided into opposing classes that invariably resulted in class conflicts and Bodin was an eye-witness of this situation. The religious conflicts and class antagonisms created tension and Bodin thought that a constitutional remedy must be devised. Since Bodin was a student of jurisprudence and was a legal luminary of his time he could not think otherwise. It is generally observed that both the religious and class conflicts really created the most tantalising instability in French society. Machiavelli suggested the permanent separation between politics and religion, Bodin perhaps thought almost in the same line. Following Machiavelli's line of thought Bodin suggested that an absolute king must take steps to control the various sections of society. The difference between Machiavelli and Bodin is that the former did not like to depend on constitution or constitutional law, the latter heavily relied upon the constitutional system. Hence Bodin was the product of his time. Maxey rightly says : "Bodin was truly a child of the paradoxical age in which he lived, an age that was neither medieval nor modern, but displayed striking characteristics of both" (*Political Philosophies*, p. 163). The influence of contemporary events can still be viewed from another angle. John Morrow says (p. 252) "Bodin's focus on order can be explained by his experience on the dehabilitating effect of civil war in late sixteenth century France. ...Bodin's theory of absolute government was designed to undercut the position of Catholic magnates."

Bodin, Aristotle and Machiavelli

Though Bodin was tremendously influenced by his times and events, it is also true that the influence of his predecessors cannot be ignored. Allen, an interpreter of political thought of medieval period, is of opinion that though Bodin does not frankly recognise his indebtedness to Aristotle, a cursory glance of his *Six Books on the Republic* reveals that he throughly studied Aristotle's *Politics* and that put indelible mark on his thought and ideas. Almost identical view has been expressed by Dunning. In the opinion of Dunning Bodin has arranged his *Republic* in the line and style of *Politics.* Even Bodin has indiscriminately borrowed many words and phrases from Aristotle's *Politics.* We know that in Aristotle's *Politics* state is the centre stage of all discussions. Similar is to be found in Bodin's Republic. Both Aristotle and Bodin were influced, in a large way, by contemporary events. The indebtedness of Bodin does not imply that Bodin was not the originator of new and impressive ideas. There is lot of innovation in Bodin's political thought, the most important being his concept of sovereignty. In the opinion of Dunning both Aristotle and Bodin adopted historical method for their analysis. But Bodin was influenced by Aristotle does not mean that he copied Aristotle's *Politics*. The fact is that Bodin was more influenced by his contemporary events than by any other person or situation. The most important influence upon Bodin came from Machiavelli.

Allen writes : "The debt of Bodin to Machiavelli was considerable but in unimportant ways. But we do not think that in important respects Bodin was not influenced by Machiavelli. So far as the absolute power of the state is concerned Bodin was considerably influenced by Machiavelli. It is true that like Machiavelli Bodin did not specifically talk about prince and his enormous power. But the absolutism of the sovereignty is tantamount to the absolute power of the prince. Both believed that the supreme power vested in the hands of a prince or king could solve the ills of society. The central idea in the writings of both is absolute monarchy. If we thoroughly study *The Prince* and *Republic* we shall come to the conclusion that the objectives of both is almost same. Only an all-powerful ruler can ensure law, order and, above all, unity. Like Machiavelli Bodin did not speak about unity of state. But the revolution (this term has been used by Skinner) launched by Huguenots, according to Bodin, threatened the very integrity of the state. He lamented that if there were a very powerful king in France the state would not have faced such a revolution or religious conflict. Both Machiavelli and Bodin were confirmed that religious conflicts and disunity among the people were the great impediments to the overall progress of society. Machiavelli laid the foundation of a state (and more specifically nation-state) and Bodin placed the crown of sovereignty on the head of the state and this in a way completed the journey of the state or nation-state. Sabine is of opinion that "Bodin's thought was amalgamation of superstition, rationalism, mysticism, utilitarianism and antiquarianism" (p. 401). On the contrary, Machiavelli's thought was free from all these. He was mainly concerned with the unity of Italy and its progress. For that purpose he wanted to ban religion from political field. Sabine says that Bodin believed that he was following a new method the secret of which consisted in amalgamating philosophy with history. In Machiavelli's political ideas there is no such thing. Bodin thought that this was a glaring drawback of Machiavelli's political thought. Bodin attributed immorality to the political ideas of Machiavelli (Sabine, p. 401).

Bodin and *Politique*

From the sixties of the sixteenth century a good number of lawyers, politicians, administrators and even intellectuals appeared to propagate that the religious toleration or religious freedom were endangering the national unity of France and they even went to the extent that the religious freedom was about to "wreck the State". For the unity of state as well as for its prosperity they demanded "one faith, one law, one king" (*une foi, une loi, un roi*). This was the stand adopted by the *Politiques.* The term politique has been defined by Skinner in the following way : "The politique case was mainly presented by those who had no belief in religious liberty as a positive moral value, but merely believed in the unfortunate necessity of conceding it as the only alternative to endemic civil strife" (Vol. 2, p. 250). The *politique* has a very important influence upon the policy makers of France and it became the policy of French government. Bodin was a strong supporter of the arguments of *Politique.* Bodin openly advocated the importance of religious uniformity and unity. If this is not accepted, the republic would face great danger. To him the unity of the state was more important than religious freedom. Explaining Bodin's view Skinner writes : "his public doctrine always took the form of claiming that there can never be any question of accepting the natural right of minority religions to be tolerated. He insists that since all disputations of religion tend more than anything else to bring about the "ruin and destruction of the commonwealth" (p. 253). This is the position of Bodin in respect of religious freedom. He was against any type of religious freedom because it would wreck the unity and existence of the republic. Law will be enacted to forbid all types of religious freedom.

Bodin and Absolutism

There is a contradiction in Bodin's political thought and this is : he was always a strong supporter of constitutionalism and this he received from his attachment to jurisprudence. But though a constitutionalist, he was a strong supporter of absolutism and in this respect his stand was uncompromising. Skinner writes "Abandoning the constitutionalist position he had adopted in his *Method for the Easy Comprehension of History,* Bodin reveals himself in the *Six Books* as a virtually unyielding defender of absolutism, demanding the outlawing of all theories of resistance and the acceptance of a strong monarchy as the only means of restoring political unity and peace" (Vol. 2, p. 248). Bodin was an eyewitness of the St. Bartholomew Massacre and he attributed this to the Huguenots' stand of religious freedom. He, therefore, adopted two positions—there shall be only one religion which will be called unified religion and the other is all religious discords shall be strongly dealt with and this requires a strong king with absolute power. This is the foundation of Bodin's absolutism.

Bodin regarded the Huguenot theory of religious freedom and Althusius's theory of popular sovereignty as the greatest threat to the unity and stability of France. In the prefaces of the successive editions of *Six Books* he expressed his horror about religious freedom. He thought that religious freedom set the commonwealth ablaze and this threw common people into ruin. Establishment of an absolute monarchy was the major ideological task of the *Six Books.* In unequivocal terms he attacked the Huguenots argument and theory of resistance and toleration. He also said that if the Huguenots' were allowed to pursue their religious principles that would provide the greatest threat to the very physical existence of the well-ordered monarchy of France. He candidly admitted that his chief objective of writing the book was to give proper reply to the dangerous men who were threatening the welfare of France. In the name of religious freedom, "popular liberty", the rebels were opening the door to a "licentious anarchy which is worse than the harshest tyranny in the world." Bodin always strongly supported the unity of religion because religious conflicts were endangering "the health and welfare of the commonwealth." It is the primary duty of an able ruler to see that the order of the state and the unity of the nation are properly maintained. Skinner says (p. 254) "The duty of the prince is to ignore and avoid all such arguments as for as possible, separating the welfare of his kingdom entirely from the fate of any particular religion, and thereby ensuring that he is never driving to make himself a party, instead of holding the place of a sovereign judge." So far as the absolutism of Machiavelli and Bodin is concerned there is a fine difference. Machiavelli made his prince absolute and he advised the prince to strictly maintain a difference between religion and politics. Machiavelli's prince was not empowered to interfere with the religious affairs. On the other hand, Bodin's king must have power to control the religious affairs to maintain the health and welfare of the commonwealth. When the Bartholomew Massacre took place Bodin was just 42 years old and this left behind an indelible mark in his mind. He thought that if there were a powerful king with absolute power France would have been free of such incidents. Finally we hold the view that type of monarchy was not responsible for this St. Bartholomew incident. The real factor was the worst type of religious intoleration. The Huguenots did not demand anything unnatural. They simply claimed to pursue their own religious faith.

Theory of Sovereignty

Bodin defines sovereignty in the following words : "Sovereignty is the absolute and perpetual power of the state, that is the greatest power to command. ...This power is perpetual, for absolute power may be given to one or several for a certain time only. ...Whatever power and authority the sovereign prince confers upon others, his own person remains excepted. He retains more authority than he gives away, and he is never divested of his right to command and examine his officials. ...Only he is absolutely sovereign who, after God, acknowledges no one greater than himself. ...We thus conclude that the principal aspect of sovereign rule and absolute power consists in making general laws for the subjects without their consent." We have liberally quoted from Bodin's *Six Books*. Our purpose is to make clear about the concept of sovereignty defined by Bodin.

If we go through the above definition we shall find that the definition of sovereignty has few characteristics. One such characteristic is his sovereign power or sovereignty is **absolute** and **perpetual**. The sovereign power is not subject to any other authority. Absolute means sovereignty is the highest authority of the state. Bodin calls it the greatest power to command. It also means that only the sovereign power is entitled to command his subjects and by virtue of the fact that all his subjects are bound to carry out the commands which indicates that the subjects are not entitled to challenge the order or command of the sovereignty.

Another feature is soveign power is perpetual. The sovereign authority, if it pleases can give certain of his powers for a defined period of time as lease or loan. It means that soveign power cannot transfer his authority to any of his subordinates permanently. The soveignty can take back the power he transferred to others.

The sovereignty never transfers all the power. The sovereign authority never transfers all his powers to his subordinates. It implies that he retains more authority than he gives away. He retains the power to command. Bodin further says that since the power of the sovereignty is absolute he can take away the power which he earlier conferred to his subordinates.

The sovereign authority is all-powerful. He may receive power from citizens, but that does not mean that the citizens are more powerful than the sovereignty. Bodin has further observed that the absoluteness of power means that he is not accountable to anyone; of course the sovereignty is accountable to God.

Bodin has given a short explanation to the word "perpetual". He says "perpetual means the lifetime of him who has the power. "He has given an example. If the sovereign magistrate is elected for a year he will continue to exercise the power only for that period. During that period he will not be accountable to anybody.

Explaining the term "absolute power" Bodin in the form of explanation says that no terms and conditions are to be attached with the office of sovereignty. Again, he will not be accountable to anyone for his functions. Absoluteness also implies that the sovereign power or prince himself is not subject to his own laws—he is above his own laws. He has cited an example. Pope never ties his hands with anything even he may wish so. Similarly a sovereign power or prince cannot tie his hand although he may wish so. A sovereign prince is not bound by the law of his predecessor. Bodin's sovereignty is the maker of laws or ordinance. But he is not subject to this law or ordinance.

Limitations

Bodin's theory of sovereignty as depicted in the previous pages is highly acclaimed by the students of Western political thought. But it is unfortunate that he put a number of shackles on the body of the doctrine of sovereignty and because of this the theory suffers from a number of **"confusions"**. Bodin said that the sovereign power is perpetual, humanly unlimited, and unconditional right to make interpret and execute law. But in the same breath he said that the sovereign power is limited by law of nature and law of God. There is a glaring contradiction in this statement. An unlimited power can never be limited one. "The law is at once the will of the sovereign and an expression of eternal justice, yet the two may be in conflict" —Sabine.

There is another confusion in Bodin's theory of sovereignty. He said—"only he is absolutely sovereign who, after God, acknowledges no one." His fidelity to God and at the same time to constitutional law are contradictory. If a sovereign power is absolute how can it be limited by the law of God? Constitutional law is an object of real world which is not connected with the idea or law of God. If sovereignty claims that he is absolute, he need not be limited by the law or will of God. By incorporating the idea of God into his analysis Bodin has deliberately invited a confusion. Again, he has said that sovereign power cannot challenge the authority of constitutional law. His allegiance to constitutional law is quite conceivable because he was a student of jurisprudence. In our judgment it would have been better if he did not openly declare the sovereignty as absolute. Here lies the confusion.

The source of Bodin's confusion on the limitation of sovereignty is he was the prisoner of two situations. One was the prevailing religious conflicts which vehemently threatened the stability and peace of French society. He had a conviction that if there were proper consolidation of power in the hands of French monarchy the St. Bartholomew massacre could not get the opportunity to happen. He blamed the Huguenots for such tragic incident. He was of this opinion that absolute power in the hands of king was the panacea to all evils. This, however, is far from truth.

Bodin wanted a peaceful coexistence between divine law and man-made law and here lies the main source of confusion. In one place of his *Republic* he said : "If we should define sovereignty as a power *legibus omnibus soluta,* no princes could be found to have sovereign rights, for all are bound by divine law and the law of nations and also by the common law of nations which embodies principles distinct from these" (Quoted by Dunning, p. 98). Bodin's Republic was published in 1576. We all know that in the second half of the sixteenth century there was tremendous importance of religion in French society and it was impossible for him to deny its role. In that background Bodin formulated the theory of absolute sovereignty and that was the chief reason of confusion. Bodin wanted a juxtaposition between absolute sovereignty, law of God, law of nature and constitutional law. But he failed to realise the impossibility of such an attempt and finally this led to confusion.

Another source of confusion or limitation is his idea about the inviolability of private property. We have already noted that in his time capitalism was on the way of development. More than this is in his view private property is the foundation of family and its well-being. Hence destruction of the right to private property means destruction of family. He knew that right to family is an important right and it also constitutes the foundation of state. Hence to deprive an individual of the right to private property means the destruction of family, state and the right to live comfortably. Above all, Bodin has sympathy for the bourgeoisie and that impelled him to argue in an indirect way for the cause of the bourgeoisie. Normally the sovereign power is not bound to keep his promises or to abide by the decision of his predecessor. But in certain circumstances he may keep the promises or abide by the decision of his predecessor. Pointing out the distinction between law and contract Bodin has pointed out that the sovereign power may not obey his own law and in that case nobody can force him to do that. But contract is of different nature. The contract is a mutual obligation between prince and his subjects and it binds them reciprocally and it cannot be altered except by mutual consent. This is also a limitation on the absoluteness of king's sovereignty.

We have discussed the limitations of Bodin's theory of sovereignty. In this regard we quote here a passage from Skinner's book to throw light on the issue. He says (Vol. 2, p. 293) : Bodin's concept of sovereignty has come to be the centre of a considerable controversy amongst interpreters of the *Six Books*. The problem is to determine how far he intended that the powers of the sovereign should be taken to be absolutely unlimited. The consensus amongst the older commentaries was that Bodin totally extinguished the idea of constitutional state. It is arguable that if we approach Bodin's analysis with the traditional checks of la police, la religion and la justice in mind. We find that a number of significant elements of these constraints on absolutism will appear to be consciously retained. Bodin was a student of jurisprudence and an avid spectator of all contemporary events. He thought that only an absolute power could save France from religious conflicts and instability. But such a power has to abide by the constitutional law, religions, right to property.

Modern State or National State

J. S. McClelland observes that the "modern state came out of the feudal order. Of course it is a long story, but we can trace its progress from about 1500 to 1800 in the works of Machiavelli, Bodin, Hobbes and Adam Smith" (p. 280). Machiavelli's prince laid the foundation of modern state by making it all-powerful. The Prince did not allow all religious, moral and ethical considerations from the purview of politics and state affairs. The scholars of Western political thought are of opinion that this is the starting point of national state which is also the modern state. But Machiavelli's modern state suffers from one drawback—he did not pay proper attention to a very vital element of modern state, this is sovereignty. We are all aware that without sovereignty we cannot imagine of a national or modern state. But he had other aspects of modern state in his mind. For example, proper administration, importance of law etc. It is generally observed that Bodin removed the lacuna. He is the first political philosopher who strongly emphasised the importance of sovereign power. His theory is very simple. He said all well-ordered states must have an absolute sovereign authority.

Bodin well understood that all political organisations, specifically state, are destroyed by religious factionalism. Hence in order to be a modern or national state it must be an integrated one. But political or religious factions are to be worn out or removed at any cost. Machiavelli for that purpose strongly recommended a powerful prince with absolute power at his disposal. Bodin installed an absolute sovereignty at the top of the state and this completes the concept of modern state.

There is a big problem in Bodin's theory of modern state. While analysing the concept of state and sovereignty Bodin remembered the Aristotelian classification of states—lawful and unlawful. The picture of the state which he had in mind is primarily unlawful because only in such states the religious fanaticism and conflicts can dominate the situation. But many scholars are of opinion that the unlawful states can hardly be categorised as modern states. So in order to be modern state in the strictest sense a state must be lawful in all senses and for that purpose Bodin suggested an absolute sovereign power whose function would be to ensure law and order and to remove all factions and conflicts from the state.

Bodin was quite conscious of the importance of lawfulness. This can be justified by his definition of state. He says : "The state is a lawful government with sovereign power of different households and their common affairs." He wants to emphasise that if some robbers and pirates form an organisation that cannot be called state because robbers and pirates are involved in unlawful activities. The idea of lawfulness has an important place in the thought system of Bodin. He had an important attachment to jurisprudence and we think that such a person cannot prescribe unlawful activities. In order to remove the stigma of unlawfulness Bodin had prescribed an absolute government.

The critics of Bodin's thought believe that he had no intention to lay unconditional support to an absolute government. This he did to serve a definite purpose and that purpose is to bring about peace and order in the state. Bodin believed that the outward nature of government is not very important. The important point is how and in what way the government discharges its responsibilities that should be brought under proper consideration. Explaining Bodin's consideration J. S. McClelland says : As Bodin tellingly points out, the most absolute government or monarchy can rule popularly by delegating its authority widely, while the most popular democracy can, as in the ancient world, act despotically (p. 284). The point is, according to Bodin, the outward structure of a government is not important. The method of functioning is to be judged. We have already pointed out that Bodin recommended an absolute monarchy for bringing about law and order in the strife-torn France.

There is a beautiful observation about Bodin's concepts of sovereignty and modern state. This we find in McClelland's writing. He writes : "That Bodin describes the guts of the modern state there can be no doubt, but whether he has theory of the sovereign state is another matter. Bodin's theory of sovereignty is a theory waiting for an equivalent view of man and an equivalent sociology. ... The motives of Bodin's sovereignty are clear enough, but the arguments are merely formal" (p. 284). McClelland supposes that there is a subtle difference between modern state and sovereignty concepts. But we are not concerned with this subtle difference. We are fully confident that Bodin's method of analysis and objection confirm that he had an idea of the modern state. The most spectacular drawback of his analysis is he did not specifically mention the idea of the modern state. Like Machiavelli's Bodin's state is also a national state and by emphasising the sovereignty he made it modern. We further point out that it is not necessary that in order to be modern a state must be democratic. Many of the modern states are autocratic. Both Machiavelli and Bodin prepared the blue-print of state in sociological perspective.

Assessment

So far as the time and situation are concerned Bodin may duly be termed a modern thinker. We generally say that modern political thought starts from Machiavelli. But some critics of political thought hesitate to call him a modern political thinker. Sabine, however, has adopted a middle way. He says (p. 400) "Bodin's political thought was a singular mixture of the old and the new, as all philosophical thoughts in the sixteenth century were. He had ceased to be medieval without becoming modern." He said that law is to be studied in the background of environment, climate, topography and race. Such view was held by medieval lawyers and thinkers. His thought was a clear amalgamation of superstition, mysticism and antiquarianism.

He openly declared that an absolute sovereign power must give due importance to the law of God and law of nature. Such view occupied predominant position in the political thought of medieval thinkers. His allegiance was to many issues. He wanted to save France from religious turmoils, political problems etc. But he had also an allegiance to constitutional law and divine law. He could not remove the garment of religion from his body. He incorporated the concept of divinity and religion into the main body of his political thought. This invited contradiction and inconsistency in his entire thought system.

In spite of the above shortcomings Bodin is still remembered by the students of Western political thought for his important contribution to the theory of sovereignty. Sabine says : Bodin's political philosophy was a work of no slight importance. Compared with any other work of the second half of the sixteenth century it was broadly conceived and impressively executed" (p. 413). The students of Western political thought primarily remember him for his doctrine of sovereignty. But "he was not a man of one idea". We can remember Mooney's glowing tribute to Bodin. He says : "He was one of the first to appreciate the distinction between the state and the government of the state. ...He points out that the form of government does not necessarily conform with the form of state at all" (p. 169). Bodin had a clear idea about revolutions and in this regard he did not agree with Aristotle. It indicates that Bodin studied Aristotle thoroughly. It is noteworthy that Bodin's mind and outlook were quite scientific.

We can criticise him for his concept of sovereignty because such a theory of sovereignty is a precursor to absolutism. But we also remember that such a government was essential for the volcanic situation that prevailed in the second half of the sixteenth century. Bodin did not accept the communistic ideas of Plato and More. But he was at pains to see the glaring inequalities in economic field that prevailed in his time. He realised that the gross inequalities would threaten the stability of republic. Bodin is regarded as a political thinker of the modernity of the modern state. Maxey is of opinion that citizenship is an important element of the modern state. Bodin threw light on this issue. He viewed unconditional loyalty to the government as very important. Today we may take it as antidemocratic, but in his time it had enough relevance. We cannot accept his attitude towards the Huguenots. He did not recognise man's right to pursue his own faith and belief. But simultaneously we remember that to him state was more important than the democratic rights. It we do that our grievance against Bodin will invariably cool down.

10 REVOLUTIONS AND POLITICAL THEORY

Emergence of Overall Change

Both Renaissance and Reformation turned the academic, intellectual and even the political worlds of whole Europe upside down. The superstition, religious conservativeness and narrowness of mind and outlook underwent drastic changes. It has been observed by a critic that Renaissance and Reformation Movement penetrated at every level of superstitious beliefs. People of all walks of life changed their belief and outlook. They did not, it is true, throw away their beliefs about God and religion but the obstinacy in attitude was considerably relaxed and this was due to Renaissance and Reformation. The scientists and social reformers challenged the time-old views and ideas. People began to view everything with inquisitiveness and scientific mind. Unscientific views and concepts were faced with unprecedented challenge. There was also a change in the political world. People were conscious of their right and obligation. They demanded more and more rights and privileges from the authority.

Religious beliefs and faiths were replaced by materialistic outlook and in this field Thomas Hobbes is really a harbinger. According to several scholars of Western political thought he was the first man who introduced materialism or materialist outlook in political science. Chris Harman says : "The conservative political theorist Thomas Hobbes published a thoroughly materialist book *Leviathan* which combined attacks on the notion of religious miracles" (p. 240). Severe attacks against superstition, conservativeness, unscientific views and concepts began to pour and all these combinedly built up a solid foundation for new world of thought, faith and belief. Renaissance and Reformation ruthlessly removed superstition and enlightened the faith, belief and outlook. New thought and outlook were not confined in any particular field, it spread almost to all the sections of society and some people call it catch-all effects. That is, not a single sector or part of society remained out of the catch-all effects or category. Natural scientists, philosophers, historians, economists and political scientists and theorists all made sincere and serious efforts to make contribution to their respective fields. Their contributions were radical in nature. People of all walks of life began to think and feel that their society was defective and it must be changed. This feeling was almost universal and serious people came under its influence.

Voltaire's *Candide* caricatured brilliantly the existing situation, beliefs and faiths. Philosophers Decartes in France, Spinoza in Holland, Leibniz in Germany were all convinced that reason would prevail everywhere and guide all activities and thoughts. This inflicted a serious attack upon the prevailing thought system. This is called rationalism or rationalist philosophy. Many thinkers declared that every conclusion must be based on empirical observation. That is, every decision must be supported by facts or physical incidents. Voltaire and Montesquieu of France supported empiricism (Harman, p. 243). In the period of Enlightenment, Voltaire once said : *encrasezl' infame*—crush the infamy. These words he uttered against the superstition of religion. Gibbon in England wrote a pioneering work *The Decline and Fall of the Roman Empire* which was a scathing attack on the influence of the Christian church (Harman, p. 244). All these thinkers were unanimous at least in one respect and that was everything was changing and therefore society must be changed to cope with the new situation.

INDUSTRIAL REVOLUTION

Causes of Industrial Revolution

The analysis we have just concluded reveals that the entire society of European continent was absolutely ripe for change and the governments of several European states took steps. They introduced reforms to meet the challenge of new outlook and physical situation. The governments of European states felt that any negligence would invite disorder and chaos. Compared with the past, mind of men was quite scientific. Harman says : "Changing ideas was not the same as changing society. It would require another cycle of revolutions and civil wars to bring that about" (p. 246). In the second half of the eighteenth century in Britain and several other countries of Western Europe there was a revolution in the industrial world. Several factors jointly contributed to the emergence of the revolution in the industrial and commercial worlds and the intellectual factors being the prominent of them.

It has been asserted that evolution in thought and outlook was the chief factor that contributed to the rise of revolution in the industrial field. Before the emergence of revolution in industrial fields people earned their livelihood from agriculture and other fields. But agriculture was incapable to provide livelihood to everyone. People began to devise new scope for livelihood. Alternative occupations were to be found out and this feeling inspired them to go out in search of alternative ways. In the medieval period the life of the people centred around religion which taught them to be other-worldly minded. Under the impact of the new atmosphere people became materialist minded. They before long realised that agriculture could not satisfy their material demands and fulfil economic necessities. This caused Industrial Revolution.

In the second half of the eighteenth century a number of discoveries took place with rapid succession and all these brought about radical changes in the industrial and production fields which ultimately led to the unprecedented rise in production of commodities. Jointly it is called revolution in the industrial sector. The discoveries of Kay in 1733, Hargreaves in 1768, Arkwright in 1769 and Crompton in 1779 revolutionised in various ways the industrial picture in general and weaving industry in particular. There was a remarkable impact of scientific discoveries on transport and communication and agriculture. The farmers began to apply the discoveries in agriculture and this led to the rise to the production of agricultural commodities. The discovery of steam engine brought about change in the production of iron. In a word, the series of scientific discoveries change the industrial scene of several countries of Europe.

Many people were encouraged to invest in industries because they felt it highly profitable. Particularly the landlords sold their agricultural land and invested in industries. This resulted in the huge production of industrial goods that was practically unimaginable before Industrial Revolution. The setting up of new industries, at the initial stage, required labourers. The persons engaged in the production of agricultural commodities left villages and thronged in the cities and centres at which industries were set up. At the preliminary level there was no problem of getting jobs in industries because there was great demand of labour. We all call it Industrial Revolution because the successive discoveries of instruments practically changed the industrial picture. This change is called the Industrial Revolution.

If we look at the history and other aspects of Industrial Revolution we will find that it first originated in Britain. The pertinent question that peeps in our mind is that why did it first originate in Britain? (1) In sixteenth and seventeenth centuries, it has been observed, there were tension and instability in the social and political life of Britain and this situation prevented the rise and growth of economy in general and industry in particular. Thomas Hobbes writes in his *Leviathan* (1651) "Whatsoever, therefore is consequent to a time of war, where everyman is enemy of every man...wherein men live without other security, than what their own strength, and their own invention shall furnish them. In such a condition, there is no place of industry, because the first thereof is uncertain, and consequently no culture of the earth, no navigation, nor use of commodities that may be imported by sea, no commodious building, no instruments of moving" (p. 186, C. B. Macpherson (ed), *Leviathan*). This type of instability was to some extent absent in eighteenth century and this helped considerably the growth of industry. (2) Some people point out that the British people were to some extent invention-minded. They want to devise techniques for their work. (3) Before the onset of Industrial Revolution (H. G. Wells calls it *machanical revolution. A Short History of The World*, p. 269) feudalism collapsed in Britain. The attachment of the landlords to landed property practically came to an end and they went out in search of new ventures. This was one of the causes of Industrial Revolution. (4) New inventions and discoveries were applied in agriculture and this resulted in a revolution in agriculture. Scholars are of opinion that revolution in agriculture, in an indirect way, helped the Industrial Revolution. Raw materials were need for the furtherance of industrial progress. Thus both industry and agriculture got favourable opportunity for progress. (5) The production of industrial goods needed new markets and Britain got that opportunity because of its colonies that spread in Africa and Asia.

Consequence of Industrial Revolution

Before Industrial Revolution (hereafter only I. R.) the labour was "unproductive" because he had no instrument to help him in work. But I. R. made a labourer productive because he now got the help of new instruments in his activities. Adam Smith and many other economists have said that new machineries have transformed the unproductive labourer into productive. Harman observes (op. cit., p. 258),

"Productive labour helped create durable products which could be sold either to be consumed by those engaged in other labour or as capital to be used in producing more goods. In either case its output helped to create more output, making the "wealth of the nation" expand." This is a very important consequence of I. R. and it has far-reaching ramifications in the whole economy. Adam Smith has rightly said that it has helped the expansion of the wealth of nation. In fact, the wealth of the nations could not get any opportunity to expand without I. R.

Adam Smith has thoroughly studied the various aspects of I. R. and has arrived at the conclusion that it is this revolution that produced unimaginable amount of commodities. Not only this, it later on created opportunities of distribution and marketing. The producers made arrangements for the sale of all the industrial goods. With the meteoric rise of production, the manufacturers went out in search of new markets and in this task they sought the help of their government. This finally stood at colonialism or colonisation as is popularly called. Colonialism and I. R. in fact, went hand in hand.

The I. R. created, within very short time, fabulous amount of wealth and the maximum part of this wealth was gobbled by the capitalists or manufacturers because they always played the leading part in the process of industrialisation. But penetration into the entire process will reveal that the labourers—the real actors of the whole productive process—were practically deprived of the fruits of the I. R. That is, they were not getting their due share of the profit. Polanyi has rightly observed : the labouring people had been crowded together in new places of desolation, the country folk had been dehumanised into slumdwellers, the family was on the road to perdition and the large parts of the country were rapidly disappearing under the slack and scrap heaps vomited forth from the satanic mills (*The Great Transformation*, p. 39). This was the inevitable consequence of I. R. Man was converted into lifeless machine which finally led to the nefarious dehumanisation of labour. I. R. may rightly be termed as the father of both poverty and opulence.

I. R. practically created a moribund situation for the century-old cottage and small-scale industries that developed in the country-side and created employment opportunities for millions of people. In comparison with quality and price, products of cottage and village industries were far different than machine goods. The result was that while the demand for machine goods was high the same for the cottage industry goods lagged far behind. In many cases the age-old cottage industries were faced with destruction. This was inevitable.

The consequences of I. R. were not confined within the geographical boundaries of the countries of its origin. The manufacturers set up markets in foreign countries for the sale of their goods and this finally crippled the small industries of the colonies. The industrial magnates of Britain and other imperialist countries in all possible ways discouraged the industrialisation in colonies and this is one of the reasons of the industrially backwardness of the colonies.

Political Ideas of I. R.

The division of society into classes is the inevitable consequence of Industrial Revolution. The I. R. radically transformed the social, economic and political situation of all countries that came under its influence. "There was a transformation of the working and living conditions of millions of people. They began to crowd into town and cities on a scale unknown in history" (Harman, p. 319). People in rural areas left their ancestral homes and gathered around the factory and mills in search of jobs. Harman, citing few statistics, observes that in 1750 there had been only two cities with more than 50,000 inhabitants—London and Edinburgh. By 1851, just after a century, there were 29 cities and the majority of people lived in towns. There was a transformation of the whole society. Needless to say that most of the inhabitants of the towns were labourers. They lived in slums and led a life full of poverty, diseases and, above all, deprivation. These people worked hard from sunrise to sun-set for meagre wages which was insufficient for livelihood. "The new labour force was the source of massive wealth. But it was wealth for others" (Harman, p. 321). The fruits of I. R. (that is wealth and profit) went to the capitalists or the owners of industries. Whereas, the labourers who were the source of wealth were deprived of the benefit of I. R. To sum up, the I. R. divided the entire population into two broad classes or groups—propertied class and non-propertied class. Or, to put it in other words, capitalist class and working class.

With the progress of industrialisation the gap between these two classes began to widen. The propertied class was not prepared to allow benefits to the working class and the main reason behind this was that any attempt to alleviate poverty will undermine the discipline. If poor people get more financial benefits and concessions they would become idle, lazy and worthless. The actual reason is any extra benefits will cut the volume of profits and the capitalists were not prepared to accept it. The net result was the division of society into two classes. Now this division of society into two classes led to class conflict because the interests of the opposing classes was opposite. The purpose of the capitalists was to maximise the volume of profit and the objective of the workers was to earn enough wage so that they can lead a comfortable life. We conclude the conflict between the two major classes, the product of I. R., is the chief characteristic of an industrialised society. Class struggle later on came from this class conflict.

The class conflict or the bitter relation between the two major classes created another situation. In the thirties and forties of the nineteenth century the labour trouble in the industrialised countries assumed new dimensions and this forced the capitalists to think of reorganisation of public administration. They wanted to control state administration so that they could win over the working class. They believed that a definite control over the administration would enable them to check the labour trouble. Police, army and bureaucracy were the chief weapons by which the labour trouble could be checked and since all these were under the direct control of state administration the capitalists were determined to control administration in their favour. After the I. R. the capitalists constituted the dominating section of the society. Economically they were dominant. Finally, academically and politically, they finally became dominant. An unholly alliance was formed between the capitalist class and the government. Government wanted more money for running the administration which could be provided by the capitalists. The capitalists were prepared to part with a portion of profit and the government was prepared to help them to control the working class. Gradually the control of the state machinery went to the hands of capitalists. The bureaucracy, army and police practically were converted into puppets. There was a state in an industrialised nation whose chief objective was to safeguard the economic and other interest of the dominating section of society.

The I. R. completely changed the character of state administration. In the feudal age the state was controlled by the feudal lords and in the industrial period the state came to be dominated by capitalists. Ultimately the state was converted into a machine of exploitation. The machine was used by the capitalists to protect their financial interests. It is generally observed that the character of state assumed a new character and we call it the class character of state. Before I. R. there existed the class character of state but that was not so much prominent. This particular nature of state brought about numerous ramifications about politics. The state came to be called a machinery, its abolition was strongly advocated by Marx and his followers, and establishment of socialism and finally of communism. All these concepts are political-economic and, to some extent, sociological. Whatever it may be, they are definite by products of I. R.

Utopian socialism and Marxism are the products of I. R. The three utopian socialists, Saint-Simon, Charles Fourier and Robert Owen, first drew our attention to the miserable conditions of the working class and for the first time they suggested a way out. Of course Marx and Engels did not agree with their suggestion. Later on Marx and Engels went into the depth of capitalist society and scanned it thoroughly. The I. R. created miserable and intolerable conditions which were inextricably associated with the contradictions of capitalism. They drew the conclusion that the contradictions were the inevitable products of I. R.

Laissez faire may be regarded as an important product of Industrial Revolution. The father of this doctrine was Adam Smith (1723–1790). He elaborated this doctrine in his *Wealth of Nations* (1776). The English equivalent of the term is a policy of non-interference, especially abstention by governments from interfering in the workings of the free market. Before Adam Smith, the physiocrats strongly advocated the idea of non-interference in the economic affairs and in the seventies of the eighteenth century. Smith drew the attention of the larger section of the community by arguing that economic progress was dependent upon the establishment of the independence of the industrial capitalist. In his opinion any form of governmental interference in the economic activities of private persons or individual capitalists will thwart the progress of commerce and development of economy. This is popularly known as *laissez faire*. This is also called "economic liberation" (the term is frequently used by Eric Roll). This is also called the political philosophy of Adam Smith. The main emphasis of Adam Smith is that it is always the natural order that human beings prefer to work or to pursue their own policies or activities without being restrained. According to Smith it is "the obvious and simple system of natural liberty." He also said that if a person is permitted to follow his own policies and activities that will finally result in grand success. But governments restrictions will result in catastrophic consequences. Summarising Smith's observation Eric Roll makes the following comment : "The consequences of the belief in the natural order are simple. Government can rarely be more effective when it is negative. Its intervention in human affairs is generally harmful. Let it leave each member of the community to seek to maximise his own advantage and, compelled by natural law, he will contribute to the maximisation of the common good (*A History of Economic Thought*, p. 147).

The concept of liberalism was first enunciated by John Locke and subsequently it was elaborated by many. Adam Smith saw that being pressurised by various sectors the government was imposing restrictions upon the freedom of industrialists and this was hampering the overall economic progress. His *Wealth of Nations* was published in 1776 and by that time the governmental interference was prominent. Smith apprehended that if it were allowed to continue the concept of free market will face dire consequences. Apprehending this he enthusiastically built up the doctrine of *laissez faire*. In clear terms he declared that it is not the business of government to restrict the economic activities of private entrepreneurs in the pursuance of their economic policies and activities. Adam Smith argued that if freedom of activities is restricted (in the case of individuals) that will inevitably curtail their freedom and dampen their enthusiasm. Applying this general concept to economic liberalism Smith concluded that the I. R. has opened the door of industrialisation and progress and this can be achieved through the *laissez faire*. The government has no business of interfering in the policies of activities of private persons. Our point is the I. R., at least for a short period, invited the governmental interference in the economic fields and Adam Smith's *laissez faire* doctrine put a very powerful check upon that. Some scholars are of opinion that the I. R. rejuvenated the political doctrine of liberalism and practically it goes in the name of Adam Smith.

AMERICAN REVOLUTION AND POLITICAL IDEAS

"The World Turned Upside Down"

In the foregoing analysis we have briefly discussed the political ideas of Industrial Revolution. Almost contemporaneous of the I. R. is American Revolution. This Revolution has unequivocally enunciated certain basic ideas of modern political theory. About the American Revolution that took place in 1776 five words have been used and these are : The World Turned Upside Down. Why? The I. R. changed the economic picture of several states of Western Europe and the economic changes subsequently created strong influences upon politics and other branches of social science. About American Revolution Chris Harman has observed : "The military band played the tune The World Turned Upside Down as British forces departed from Yorktown in 1781. With this departure thousands King George's supporters also left America. Britain built up an economy in America which is called Britain's Atlantic Economy. An important part of Britain's national wealth came from America. There is no doubt that America was exploited by the British Government. Year after year the farmers, artisans, merchants, landowners and others were exploited by the British government. But the Americans were strongly reluctant to continue this exploitation indefinitely. So a clash between the colonies and the British government was inevitable.

The British government fully controlled the American economy. But the spread of Adam Smith's doctrine of economic liberatism considerably enthused the Americans to pursue an economic policy free from all sorts of governmental control (Harman, p. 226). The people of American colonies were confirmed that if they were allowed to follow their own economic policies and harvest the benefits that will guarantee the progress of the economy. That was the bone of contention. Resentment piled up in the minds of Americans and they were determined to come out of the strong grip of British domination. The colonies argued that in economic and political matters and problems they had hardly any freedom to take any decision. The British House of Commons was the final authority and this enraged the political leaders and common people. They also thought that their fundamental liberties were being trampled. They demanded that like British people they must have fundamental liberties. This feeling was quite widespread and people mobilised against Britain. Numerous groups and organisations were formed to fight against British domination. These groups called themselves "Sons of Liberty". The members of these groups or organisations were not sons of rich merchants or landlords, or resourceful planters. They were educated persons and many of them were intellectuals. Their chief demand was freedom of America at any cost. "The Sons of Liberty" practically formed a political party and organised meetings and protest march against "foreign rulers". Their main demand was freedom from foreign rule. The Americans knew it quite well that the British rulers would not grant freedom under normal circumstances and, in that background, they intensified their agitation through generating consciousness among ordinary Americans. There were frequent clashes between freedom fighters of America and British soldiers. The relationship between the freedom fighters and the British soldiers finally reached a culmination which means that freedom fighters were determined to free themselves or their motherland from British domination. The historians of American Revolution say that the revolutionaries were not rich merchants or big landowners but ordinary people.

Several Aspects of Political Ideas

If we go through the various aspects of political ideas that emerged from American Revolution the following can be treated as main. Locke's social contract and constitutionalism had a resounding impact upon the Americans and their fight for independence. The following observation has been made by a person who had thorough knowledge about American Revolution (henceforth only A. R.). He writes : "Jefferson copied Locke and Locke quoted Hooker. In political theory and in political practice the American Revolution drew its inspiration from the parliamentary struggle of the seventeenth century" (Carl Becker. *The Declaration of Independence* 1922, p. 79). But the influence of Locke was not confined to the Declaration of Independence, it was felt in the ideas and often the phrasing of State Declarations and Constitutions. He was quoted in the Federal Convention of 1787. Indeed there was a natural harmony between Locke's ideas and those of the nineteenth century United States. The mere fact was that the freedom fighters and constitution makers—all-drew their inspiration from the political ideas of Locke. In fact, John Locke was the invisible architect of the American constitution.

Maxey in his *Political Philosophy* observes that when the settlers covenanted among themselves, as in the Mayflower Compact and the Fundamental Orders of Connecticut, there was no doubting the contractual character of the mutuality of obligation between subjects and rulers (p. 405). The British king exercised his monarchical power over the Americans through his various agencies and they were forced to accept the monarchical sovereignty. But the argument of the Americans was that the king could not exercise his sovereign power in this way that unilaterally. Both the exercise and the acceptance of the sovereign power depend upon the willingness of the Americans because it is a type of mutual covenant between the subjects and the ruler. Unilateral exercise of power was strongly resented by American.

There is another aspect of political ideas that came out of A. R. Maxey says (op. cit., p. 405) : "Political authority was both ascending and descending phenomenon. By compact it ascended from the governed through the consent of will, by delegation from the sovereign it also descended from the above." The American colonists viewed the power of the British king in this perspective. They never thought that the power of the king is absolute. The exercise of the power by the king depends upon the terms and conditions of the contract. The law of the body politic is the final authority and hence it is binding on all. Maxey again writes : "the colonists came to think of sovereignty as vested, not in a certain person or body of persons, but in the fundamental law of the body politic" (p. 406). This view of the colonists is the basis of the constitutionalism. That is, both the ruler and the ruled are under the same law of the body politic. We can remember that Locke was the father of constitutionalism. A very important aspect of his social contract is, men, coming from the state of nature, formulated certain basic laws and it was categorically stated that both the government and the governed would abide by the laws. This is also called the sovereignty of the constitution which practically constitutes the central idea of American constitutional system. Even today we have accepted it.

The concept of civil society can also be regarded as the product of A. R. Following Locke the colonists said the they had already formed a civil society which was far better than the state of nature. In that state of nature there was neither liberty nor security to life and property. For the attainment of these basic needs they have formed civil society. But the activities of the British government had thrown them to utter despair. Again, the British government had no right to scuttle the very idea of civil society. Again, through civil society they want to achieve democracy. Through the formation of civil society and establishment of constitutionalism the Americans were determined to achieve the fruits of democracy. But the autocratic manner and functioning of British government was about to frustrate the noble objectives of colonists.

Locke also stated that the obligation to authority is not unconditional, but conditional—which implies that so long the government or authority discharges its functions according to the constitution, the citizens must show their obligation to the authority. The leaders of the American Revolution once again emphasised it. Their clear view was that the British monarchy or its representatives had no right to take decision and to implement it without the consent of the inhabitants of colonies. Particularly the British Parliament has no right to neglect the views of colonies. In his Commonwealth of Oceana (1656) Harrington categorically stated that obligation can never be unconditional.

There are also other important ideas that came out of the A. R. and these subsequently formed the basis of their constitution. The revolutionaries of America learnt some very important lessons from their long struggle against the foreign power. One such lesson is that there is nothing like absolute truth. Everything passes through trial and error. What is right and what is wrong will be decided by the people in a democratic method. No outside power can impose anything upon the people. Barack Obama in his *The Audacity of Hope* has said that people's voice is the final authority and this has been incorporated in the Constitution. He further says that the constitution is based on the concept of "deliberative democracy" whose main constituents are separation of powers, checks and balances, federalist principles and Bill of Rights.

Maxey has drawn our attention to another aspect of A. R. : "Democracy gained a place in the colonial political thought not through the preference of colonists for democratic principles in theory but through their actual experience in community life. ...No political or ecclestastical hierarchy was allowed to mediate between the individual and his God" (p. 406). The freedom fighters were largely influenced by the democratic thought and ethos. In fact, democracy was their guiding force. In his above-noted book Barack Obama has drawn our attention to this aspect.

Another aspect of American democracy is federalism or the federal structure of the United States. The colonies enjoyed freedom before the formation of the United States and even after the formation they will continue the freedom. Nothing will be imposed upon the colonies. We know that the revolutionaries were against any type of application of force and after freedom/independence that has been kept intact. Today we say that American federal system is ideal and this ideality is enshrined in the constitution.

Locke said that in the state of nature people were not quite happy though it was not nasty and brutish. They (people of state of nature) were passing through certain inconveniences such as there was no impartial authority to decide right and wrong to protect the natural rights. The great fathers of the constitution have made an elaborate arrangement for the protection of the basic human rights through the institution of an impartial judiciary. Locke thought that the government of the civil society would perform the job, the architects of the constitution authorised the highest court to do the job. Being influenced by Locke and Montesquieu the framers introduced the separation of powers into the constitution. Hence we hold the view that the basic principles of political thought were derived from Locke and Montesquieu as well as apathy to British imperialism.

FRENCH REVOLUTION AND POLITICAL THEORY

Causes of French Revolution

Like Industrial Revolution and American Revolution the French Revolution was also the originator of few but important political ideas or concepts. But before embarking upon that aspect it is necessary to throw light on several causes of the French Revolution (hereafter only F. R.). In most of the states of Europe there were absolute monarchies and absolutism reached the final stage of toleration or patience. The general nature of autocratic rulers was to declare war against other states and to meet the expenses of war their normal behaviour or method was to impose heavy dose of taxes upon the people including the aristocrats and the wealthies sections of the community. The victims of the heavy taxes raised their arms against the king and particularly the nobles flatly refused to pay extra load of taxes. This flat refusal embittered the relations between the king and nobles. The nobles further argued that the authority had no power to levy taxes without consulting the Estates General.

The French society was divided into three "estates"—the clergy, the nobles, and the rest. The king summoned the representatives of these three estates to find out the solution of the problem regarding raising of taxes. The "third estate" was the largest one and the members of this estate proclaimed themselves as the National Assembly. The members of the National Assembly refused to cooperate with the king and demanded that he must first of all give them a constitution. The king refused to accept this demand. This forced the people to revolt. People revolted against the monarchy and surrounded the palace and Bastille fortress. All the attempts of the king to save himself met with a complete failure. "After threatening to blow up the fortress, the commander surrendered the Bastille to the masses. Revolution had taken hold of the Capital" (Harman, p. 279).

The experts of the French Revolution are of opinion that there are certain deep-rooted reasons behind this and one of them is the division of French society into a number of opposing classes. The old society of France was known as *ancien regime* which was divided mainly into monarchy and nobility. There were various types or classes of nobility and most of the them were influential. The nobles controlled the administration and the judiciary. Besides the nobles in French society there were large number of merchants who earned big profits through trade and commerce. Before the F. R. there were large number of capitalists who formed a separate class—popularly called bourgeoisie. In respect of influence the bourgeoisie was inferior to nobles, but in respect of financial power the bourgeoisie was much above the nobility and this was a potent cause of conflict between nobility and bourgeoisie. Again, there were several groups within the bourgeoisie and because of this there was clash in this class. This is not all. There were many people who were not satisfied with their present position and made attempts to raise their financial status and social position. They were generally called the "men on the make". This can be treated as a reason of conflict.

Finally, there was the biggest class in France and it was the peasantry. The peasantry was exploited in various ways. But as the peasants were not organised they could not revolt against the autocratic rule in France. The French peasants were exploited in a number of ways. For example, they had to pay heavy taxes to the feudal lords. They were forced to bear the effects of the fluctuations of markets. From 1780s the French monarchy was involved in war and to meet the expenditure the king imposed taxes upon all and the peasants were the worst sufferers. The French society was under great turmoil.

In the eighteenth century the French society was divided into a number of classes and even in one class there were several groups. Bourgeoisie, nobility and peasantry all were divided and there were conflicts among them. In the earlier decades of the eighteenth century, for one reason or other, the conflicts were in latent condition, but towards the end of the eighteenth century the bitter relations between the classes or groups surfaced and in the eighties of the century the class conflicts were severe and that became the most powerful cause of the revolution. This however, was the opinion of the majority people. But some thought that the complex and bitter relationship between the groups cannot be the primary reason of F. R. This, of course, is the "revisionist" approach to the F. R. and is not accepted by majority historians of F. R. (Harman, p. 288).

Maxey says that the professional and commercial classes were in privileged position in French society. Through their profession and business they amassed huge wealth and they were not active actors of a revolution. The financial condition of the working class and peasants was not better at all. But it cannot be said that they were exploited. The crown abused his power and position and that made him highly unpopular. But this cannot be treated as the main cause of F. R. Even the revolution was not caused by the unbearable condition of the masses. If so, why did the F. R. occur? According to Maxey the cause of the revolution was in the institutional structure of the French society. Let us quote him. "The French Revolution came because the institutional structures which for generations had held in equipoise the dynamic forces of society rotted and crumbled. When these retaining walls went down, the tumultuous stream of social forces leaped its banks and swept all before it" (p. 342). In the opinion of Maxey the poverty, class conflict or the autocracy were not the chief causes of the F. R. The social structure of France had lost its adhesive power and because of this it could not hold all sections and parts together. The critics criticised the function or behaviour of many but they had not the power to provide alternative arrangements to run the French administration. The reason given by Maxey holds good no doubt. But after reviewing all the aspects of F. R. we observe that injustice and tyranny had reached the zenith and large number of people revolted against the established authority.

At this juncture of time, views and writings supplied sufficient fuel to the aggrieved sections of the French society. The writings and opinions of scores of people inflamed the emotion. Let us quote few lines from Maxey : "There was no lack of writers whose appeal was principally to the emotions. Voltaire, with his bitter shafts of satire; Diderot, with his effervescent brillance, Helvetius, with his contagious irreverence, Hobbach, with has solemn sincerity" passionately desired to set everything right. The most important person who inflamed the emotion of the revolutionaries was Jean-Jacques Rousseau. He has been termed by many as the Father of F. R. His *Social Contract* provided sufficient reason to the revolutionaries to revolt. Rousseau said : Man is born free, and everywhere he is in chains. These few words, it is said, changed the mind and feeling of the French people. We are of opinion that the F. R. took place at a particular juncture of time, but it was not caused by any single factor.

Other Views

A large number of renowned persons have recorded their opinion on French Revolution and in the following analysis we mention few of them. Edmund Burke was a famous orator and he supported some right issues. But in the case of F. R. he has been found to oppose it strongly. He admitted that in France the monarchy was autocratic and its autocracy crossed all limits of toleration. The people were pressed by poverty caused by heavy dose of taxation and sky rocketing price level. Notwithstanding he could not support the revolution because it in a well-calculated way destroyed the well established tradition, culture and system of France. In his judgment he was not opposed to any change but that change must protect the tradition, culture and system that was built up on the experience of several centuries. Burke was out and out a conservative and his inordinate love for conservatism prevented him from supporting the Revolution in France. But the views of Burke is not acceptable. Simply for the sake of conservativeness the tyrannical way of king's administration and the intolerable situation of France is not acceptable.

Narrating the cause of F. R. Alexis de' Tocqueville states that irreligion produced an enormous public evil. The autocratic rule of the French government was the potent source of public resentment and people—particularly the peasants and workers—reached the last stage of patience and they felt that revolution was the only remedy. He said, "The social order destroyed by a Revolution is almost always better than that which immediately preceded it and experience shows that the most dangerous moment for a bad government is generally that in which it sets about reform." In his opinion the growing impoverishment of the general public cannot be blamed for the revolution because in the *ancien regime* people were not becoming more and poor. The real cause of F. R. is, in the later half of the eighteenth century the middle class people were getting wealthier and becoming powerful and this led them to aspire for share in general administration of the state, but they were not getting it. The existing set up could not accommodate them and this led them to revolution. Maxey also supports this reason.

Rude does not fully support the view of Tocqueville. But in his opinion the French monarchy dismally failed to meet some of the basic demands of the general public and finally they wanted a respite through revolution. There were sporadic and half-hearted attempts on the part of the ruler to give relief to the public. But the tragedy is that the reforms introduced by one ruler were not followed by his successors. But the reforms failed in some cases to meet the exigencies of the common people. All these combinedly, in the opinion of Rude, invited F. R.

France's participation in war and involvement in several arm conflicts drained away a considerable portion of her wealth and to replenish the state exchequer the king levied huge taxes which irritated people of all walks of life. The bourgeois thinkers may or may not agree. But it is a fact that the overall condition of the French society was quite ripe for a change and that feeling was adequately inflamed by various factors and circumstances. Economic, social, political, cultural and numerous other factors contributed to the cause of the French Revolution. It is impossible to assess the contribution of each factor or cause, but every cause had a contribution. We shall now turn to the contribution of the F. R. in political theory.

Political Ideas of F. R.

In the far-flung field of political ideas the contribution of the F. R. is quite worthy. We, in this section, want to point out some of them. Let us first deal with human rights and liberty. The French National Assembly declared certain rights which may rightly be called very important and fundamental rights : (1) Every citizen is entitled to have liberty, property and security. No authority can deprive a citizen of these natural rights. (2) French people are entitled to all those rights and privileges which are granted by all civilised societies. (3) The state authority has no power to imprison or punish a French citizen illegally. That is, unlawful punishment in any form must be abolished. (4) Only court of law has the power to convict a person. But before that everyone has the right to think himself innocent. (5) According to the revolutionaries, man is born free and he is entitled to enjoy freedom throughout his life. (6) Exchange of views, opinions and ideas is another basic right and must be granted to all citizens. (7) Echoing Rousseau's views, the revolutionaries said that law is the expression of general will and every citizen must be allowed to participate in the lawmaking process of the state. (8) An important right found its place in the famous Declaration of Rights of Man and Citizen and this right is when the government violates the rights or infringes them the citizens have the right to protest through insurrection. It is a sacred and very important right. (9) People must have the right to protest and criticise the activities of government. (10) In one way or other, the authors of the Declaration of Rights of Man and Citizen gave utmost priority to the popular sovereignty or the direct participation of the people in all the affairs of state. This we call popular sovereignty or direct democracy.

The Declaration contains a very important aspect of modern political theory and it is separation of powers. We have already noted that there was clear and important influence of Locke, Rousseau and Montesquieu upon the revolutionaries. The revolutionaries believed that only through the application of separation of powers among the various branches of government the freedom and rights of the people could be protected. The revolutionaries further said that, of all the three organs of the government, the legislature must enjoy supremacy. The revolutionaries clearly stated that no compromise is to be entertained regarding the separation of power. Subsequently this idea got a place in the French system of politics.

The secularisation of politics is to be rightly called as contribution of the F. R. Throughout the Middle Ages, European politics, particularly the politics of Western Europe had no special status. It was controlled by the church and the Pope. Rather religion and politics were mingled together. A clear line or demarcation was drawn now between religion and politics. The separation of politics from religion allowed political authority to exercise power independently. That was the dawn of a new era of politics in France.

Emergence of classes and division of society into classes are still important contributions of the F. R. Rude, in his *Revolutionary Europe,* says that the revolution to a large extent consolidated the class structure of French society, particularly the bourgeoisie. Although the common people took the active part in the revolution, after it the capitalist managed to strengthen its position and finally harvested the benefits in its own favour. Engels in Socialism : Utopian and Scientific writes : "The French Revolution ensured the political triumph of the bourgeoisie in France" (Selected Work, Vol. 2, p. 108).

Towards the end of the eighteenth century the quantum of work force employed in industrial sector was really high. We quote here few statistics from Harman's book : "According to a recent estimate the economy grew at 1.9 percent a year throughout the 18th century. Textile output grew 250 percent, coal output seven or eightfold, and iron output from 40,000 tons to 140,000 tons. By 1789 a fifth of France's population was employed in industry or handicrafts" (p. 286). All these figures indicate that there was sizeable increase in the total work force in France. But at the same time their impoverishment also increased. Therefore, when in the eighties and nineties of the eighteenth century there was a general mass upsurge in France, the workers joined in that movement.

With the growth of rapid industrialisation in France a new moneyed class developed and gradually it began to gather strength. Simultaneously there arose a good number of monopolists. This situation, in normal course, aggravated the class relations. The bourgeoisie and the nobility both were quite active to "purchase" the favour of the king because the objective of both was to strengthen hold over the society. Marx, Engels and subsequently Lenin repeatedly emphasised this aspect of political concept. They wanted to say that the chief purpose of the bourgeoisie was to capture state power chiefly to exploit and control the working class. We can say that this started on the eve of F. R. or before the revolution.

Abendroth in his *A Short History of the European Working Class* has said : "French Revolution had paved the way for the recognition of human rights and the realisation of democratic ideals in Europe." We have already noted that the revolutionaries—through the charter of demand and in various ways—demanded certain basic rights. It is true that they got inspiration from the writings of Rousseau. To get freedom the revolutionaries revolted against the French monarch. The French people and society were not quite prepared for a large scale mass upsurge but it arose at least in embryonic form before or immediately after the F. R. The rise of class, the class structure of society and the relations among the classes—all practically constituted the major part of the political ideas that dominated the active and passive political scene of Europe in the nineteenth century.

A very important contribution of the F. R. is it cleared the way of the full-fledged development of capitalism. Let us see what Rude, a noted interpreter of French Revolution, says. He writes : "Declaration of Rights is remarkable in that it neatly balances a statement of universal principles and human rights with an evident concern for the interests of the bourgeoisie" (op. cit., p. 107). A simple cursory glance of the Declaration of Rights reveals that the Declaration highly emphasises the grievances of the Third Estate expressed in the *Cahiers*. These rights reflect the philosophy of the natural law school. Outwardly viewed, these rights are quite innocent. But inwardly viewed these rights carry different meaning. The Declaration gives more emphasis on the political rights. But our point is only the political rights cannot ensure the allround development of the common people. Declaration throws no light on the emancipation of people from the economic bondage. The members of the Third Estate were poor people and they took active part in the revolution. The economic hardship was one of the immediate causes of the F. R. and the Declaration must have thrown light on this issue.

It is also said that the F. R. invited the domination of the bourgeois class. The economic equality did not receive special attention of the revolutionaries or the Declaration. The emancipation of the members of the Third Estate from the abject poverty and hardship might have occupied the top position of the Declaration. That has not happened, on the contrary, the right to property is treated as an inviolable right and it is the sacred duty of the state to protect it. The critics claim that on this issue there is a clear influence of Locke over the framers of the Declaration. Locke also made it clear that it is the first and foremost duty of the body politic to protect the property. Rude finally concludes that in the F. R. : The bourgeois class was given a freehand in all affairs of the post-revolutionary France. The feudal lords were uprooted. The impediments to trade and commerce were removed. In various ways capitalists purchased the favour and support of the king or authority, the wings of the nobility were trimmed. The sale of sequestrated properties, the sweeping away of the old feudal enclaves and communities, the opening of careers to men of talents, the creation of a new class of civil servants, the liberation of internal market from restrictive tolls and guilds... all helped to promote the growth and raise the social status of the bourgeoisie (Rude, p. 290).

An important contribution of the F. R. is that it considerably raised the level of consciousness of the ordinary people. It is a fact that they were not adequately rewarded by the revolution. But they realised that only through struggle something could be achieved. This lesson of the F. R. spread to various parts of Europe. People propagated liberty, equality and fraternity and even today these are catchwords and inspire millions in various parts of the world.

11 SOME RADICAL REPUBLICAN THINKERS

The Levellers

In the past political views were propagated through pamphlets, debates, discussion and agitation. Another vehicle was the Radical and Republican thinkers. The authors and participants of the pamphlets and discussion were also radical and republican minded. The leadership of the discussion, debate and agitation was provided by Levellers and Diggers of Europe. Particularly the pamphlet-debate was very attractive and popular among larger sections of the community. Sabine calls it the first-great experiment in popular political education (p. 478). The discussion and propaganda of the Levellers and Diggers were not quite coherent. The leader brought home the fact that freedom and other democratic rights of the people could not be ignored. They propagated the natural right and the right to resistance. From their attitude, mentality and the content of the propagated ideas it appears that the Levellers and the Diggers were out-and-out anti-royalists. They adopted this stand because they believed that absolutism was the greatest enemy of freedom and individual rights.

The term Leveller means the levelleing or obliterating all differences. The Levellers wanted to do away with all sorts of social, economic and political differences that gripped the prevailing society. Even they raised their objection against the holding of vast amount of property. The Levellers were communist-minded and supported democratic radicalism. It was their belief that the inequality in all its forms and manifestations was the root cause of evils and, therefore, it must be eradicated. Nature has made all men equal and his given them liberty and right. No authority in the earth can deprive them of these privileges. By constantly propagating all these "communist" ideas they succeeded in establishing their credibility that they were against the special privileges enjoyed by a small group of persons. The monopoly of power and wealth must be destroyed.

The Levellers contended that the political structure was such that only a handful of persons received the undue advantage and by dint of their special position they reaped the benefit and amassed vast amount of property. The majority people had no voice because of their inferior political status caused by poverty. There was law but not the equality before law. Rich people used law for realisation of their class and sectarian interests. It was not acceptable to them and the Levellers wanted to bring about an end to this system. The Levellers treated every man separately and not as a member of organised group. In this respect they were individualists. In their manifestos the Levellers emphasised the individualisation of natural rights. The political philosophy of the Levellers was democratic liberalism and not socialism. Their main concern was the attainment of natural rights and political freedom and not economic equality although very often they advocated for it. This radical democratic liberalism irked Cromwell who opposed them and thwarted their projects in the council of the army.

The Levellers had very little respect for Scriptures and Revelation. Their main interest was in right reason. It has been said that the Levellers avoided the Scriptures and ignored the supernatural truths. A man cannot be questioned not the question or penalised for going against the Scriptures or disobeying the dictum of religion. His activities can be judged only in the light of nature and right reason. People will be governed by civil laws and constitution and not by religious principles and decisions of the church. In Levellers' view, both the king and the people will live under the same umbrella of law. The Levellers thus openly declared their *jehad* against the medieval system of law, justice and religion. The behaviour of the Levellers created a widespread sensation and ripples in the religion-dominated society and the religious fundamentalists did not take the situation lightly. Rather they challenged the standpoint of Levellers.

John Lilburne was the most important leader of the Levellers and a great political agitator. Concepts of popular sovereignty and people's democratic rights occupied a major portion of his political ideas. He was fearless and never hesitated to express his views. Lilburne was out-and-out an anti-royalist. He never thought of the rights of parliament or prerogatives of the king but the liberties, rights and privileges of the common people. He once said that all men are equal by nature. There is no difference in dignity and majesty. The function of the authority is to ensure comfort and peace. The power and authority of the government are based on the consent of the people. Both poor and rich people shall have same rights and privileges and there shall be no discrimination. Sabine observes : "The interesting and distinctive feature of the Leveller philosophy is the new form which it gave to the ancient conceptions of the natural rights and consent. They interpreted the law of nature as endowing human individuals with innate and inalienable rights which legal and political institutions exist only to protect... They argued that the only justification for society is the production of individual advantages" (p. 484).

During the Puritan Revolution the sovereignty of parliament was widely discussed. But the Levellers were not party to this discussion. They desired the supremacy of parliament over the two other branches of government and not its overall sovereignty. The protection of individual's rights and privileges was of paramount importance to them. In their view the parliament was simply a delegated authority. It would act on behalf of the people. They were in favour of constitutional devices which would guarantee the rights as well as would safeguard them. In the Agreement of the People it was laid down that there are certain rights which no authority can abrograte. The Levellers firmly stood for this provision. In the light of this they also announced that the parliament had no power to take away the right to property and personal liberty. In the declaration as well as implementation of rights no sorts of discrimination would be allowed.

To the Levellers, parliament was a kind of trust body. People's faith was its only property and loss of faith will throw it before a question mark. Outside people it had no separate entity. John Locke drew his inspiration from Levellers' political thought, particularly conception of parliament. Locke did not make parliament absolutely sovereign. He imposed certain restrictions upon its authority. The movement of the Levellers thus emphasised several aspects of political theory which later on were regarded as the basic concepts of liberalism and democracy. Not only this the movement created a great impact upon the political thought of subsequent period.

THE DIGGERS AND WINSTANLEY

Levellers' emphasis on political rights, side-tracking of economic miseries of common people and Lilburne's categorical denial of any connection with the communists created suspicion in the minds of some communist-minded radicals about the sincerity of the Levellers and the efficacy of their weapon to free the working men from exploitation. The misery of small farmers, tradesmen and artisans distressed the communist-minded men. The communists of the mid-seventeenth century wanted to utilise revolution as an instrument of emancipation from poverty, misery and exploitation. These persons were known as Diggers.

By the middle of the seventeenth century a small group of communists made attempts to take unenclosed common land for cultivation. Their purpose was to distribute the produce among the poor men. That is why they were called Diggers. The objective of the Diggers was no doubt noble but their technique of forcible occupation of land was not approved by authority and a sizeable section of the community. They were confronted with stiff opposition and were harassed by the legal authorities. The inevitable consequence was the premature collapse of the progamme. The Diggers, like the Levellers, were also agitators. The Diggers confined their programmes within the pamphlets. Gerrard Winstanley was the most important figure.

Winstanley accorded maximum importance to economic changes and reforms because without this the political reforms would before long prove their hollowness. So Winstanley and his followers insisted upon the economic transformation of society and this could be achieved by distribution of uncultivated or unused land among the farmers. On this point the Diggers differed from the Levellers. The Levellers interpreted the law of nature as a source of individual rights. But to the Diggers it was a source of subsistence. The land is the gift of nature and everybody has the right to use or cultivate it to earn livelihood. Its accumulation in the hands of few persons deprives the majority people of their right to livelihood. This, according to the Diggers, is against the law of nature. The land is the common property of all men. In one of their pamphlets we find the following : None ought to be lords or landlords over another, but the earth is free for every son and daughter of mankind to live free upon.

This view is a clear indication of the fact that the Diggers were thinking of primitive communism where there was no private property. The produce of the land was commonly consumed by all of the primitive society. There was no corruption and abuse of the land. Winstanley and other Diggers contended that private ownership of property was the root cause of all social evils. Only few greedy persons mis-appropriated the land which is the gift of nature. The result was that the majority were deprived of land. But this deprivation was the root cause of economic inequality as well as other inequalities. Class conflict arose out of it. This view of the Diggers reminds us of the later-day socialist and communist thought which blames private property as the prime cause of social malady. The fact, however, is that they failed to represent their views comprehensively and consistently.

Diggers and, more particularly Winstanley, realised that without abolishing the private ownership of land the exploitation could not be abolished. But they were not in favour of using force or dispossessing the landlords of their land or other property. The Diggers were also against revolution. In this sense they can be called utopians. By appealing to the landlords and other property owners they wanted to bring about radical social and economic changes. They believed that the hearts of the exploiters would soften one day.

Now we shall deal with Winstanley's concept of **freedom.** After Thomas More, Winstanley is another utopian thinker who imagined of a commonwealth based upon righteousness and perfect freedom. Poverty, according to Winstanley, is the cause of bondage and the best way to remove poverty is to ensure equal distribution of wealth among all. This is again possible when all will have equal access to the use of land and its fruits. True freedom consists in this. Self-interest and common interest are the two opposite motives which work in human mind. The former makes man covetous and tyrannical. In all sorts of tyranny freedom becomes the first victim. The tyrannical ruler is least concerned with the freedom of people and does not look after their welfare. His sole objective is to remain in power and to fulfil personal desires. Only common interest can establish a Commonwealth. Both the weak and strong are equally protected and a favourable atmosphere for freedom prevails.

Winstanley had suggested that the buying and selling of land is to be prohibited in a Commonwealth aiming at freedom and equality. The unclaimed land shall be distributed among all for their use. Common ownership of land means the common ownership of produce. In the Commonwealth there shall be a common store of all necessary goods and all will receive the quota. The able-bodied persons will work. This will free man from economic bondage.

The right to form family shall be recognised because it is the primary unit of social organisation and the most favourable place for the cultivation of freedom and inherent qualities. Winstanley has prescribed universal suffrage. Through this people will get the opportunity to exercise their political rights. The tenure of office will be limited to one year only. The implementation of all these reforms will enable men to exercise their various rights including participation in the affairs of state.

Winstanley had no faith in medieval religion. Divinity is the doctrine of the weak and sickly spirit. The divinely spiritual doctrine is a cheat. The Pope allured men to the happiness and comfort of heaven and advised them to forget the sorrows and sufferings of the worldly life and to practise austerity. The chief purpose of the church was to befool the people. Consciousness should be aroused in the mind of the people so that they can realise their own position. This view indicates that Winstanley was a strong supporter of social change by peaceful means. He could not support social change through revolution. He was also the supporter of spontaneity.

JOHN MILTON (1608–1674)

Short Life-History and Works

John Milton was born in 1608. Milton's grandfather was a Roman Catholic, but his father embraced the Church of England. This made his grandfather angry and deprived him of property. Milton was an extraordinary meritorious student. At an early age he was sent to school and at the age of 16 he was sent to Oxford and then to Cambridge. Thus Milton got the opportunity to have the best of education of the two leading universities. He obtained his M. A. degree and decided to devote his life and energy to the cultivation of intellect. Though Milton was reared in an orthodox atmosphere he had very little interest in religion.

At the age of twenty-nine he went out for a long tour of continental Europe. After two years he returned to England to find his native land completely plunged in civil war which moved his mind and thought remarkably. Milton was a strong supporter of Parliamentary system and very often advocated it. At the initial stages of the Puritan Revolution Milton did not take any side and he tried to maintain his neutrality. But the course of events prevailed upon him which forced him to give up the political neutrality and he joined the Puritan side. Milton began his political career and wrote several pamphlets and books on politics. At the age of thirty-two he was appointed a secretary to the council of state for the Commonwealth which he held till he was 52. During these twenty years he made very little contribution to intellectual product. His "poetic output shrank like a stream in a drought-smitten land" (Maxey, p. 237).

The people of English speaking world primarily know him as a man of poetic genius. He generally expressed his political views and ideas through literature and due to this people know him as a great personality of literary world. His most memorable work on politics is *Areopagitica.* It was published in 1644. In this book he defended the freedom of publication. It is to be noted here that John Milton said nothing new in this book. But his mode of expression and assertion drew the attention of the then society. This book contains the classic argument for freedom of speech and this can be compared with John Stuart Mill's *On Liberty*. It is said that his *Areopagitica* was written in the background of ordinance promulgated in 1643 whose purpose was to impose restrictions upon various freedoms including freedom or speech. This order failed to receive his support. Rather, he strongly opposed. When he was in service his another important work *Tenure of Kings and Magistrates* was published. Here Milton defended the execution of Charles. He also wrote several books on republican ideas.

Political Ideas of Milton

The importance of Milton in the history of Western political thought lies in the coherence of political thoughts and views. Maxey says (p. 241) "In Milton's political writings there was little that was original and novel, but his ideas were the outgrowth of a consistent philosophy of liberty and were fused into a potent body of thought. The major premise of his libertarian doctrine was the ancient postulate of natural freedom and natural rights." In the *Tenure of Kings and Magistrates* he has argued that all human beings are by nature born-free and are endowed with the reason and the right to work on their own accord. That is, reason and spontaneity are the chief traits of human character and no authority can curb this. Peoples have formed government for their own benefit, that is defence. And the foundation of the government should be mutual understanding between the ruler and his subjects. People must have the right to select their rulers or which may be called magistrates. This indicates that Milton was in favour of people's democracy and he had no faith on conventional form of democracy.

From the above it transpires that, according to Milton, the powers of the kings and magistrates are derived from the people and not from God. In his own words—"The power of kings and magistrates is nothing else but what only is derivative, transferred and committed to them in trust from the people to the common good of all, in whom the power yet remains fundamentally, and cannot be taken from them, without a violation of their natural birth-right." Every man has the right to defend and also to preserve himself. The public authority is created by the people unitedly for this purpose. Hence the kings and magistrates derive their power from them, they are not their lords and masters, but to be their deputies and commissioners, to execute, by virtue of their entrusted power, the justice. The kings and magistrates have, therefore, no indefeasible rights but are accountable to the people and they can remove them from offices when they think fit. Milton further argues that the king has the right to his crown and dignity. If anybody deprives him of that right he must protest or resist. Similarly, every individual in the Commonwealth has certain birth-rights to which he is entitled and any deprivation will lead to resistance. In Milton's republican thought the king, magistrates and mass are on the same plane. The implication of this contention of Milton is that king's right ends only in claiming the crown and monarchical status, but he cannot claim to have prerogative or arbitrary power. He was, in other words, supporter of limited monarchy.

Milton has also emphasised the importance of law. The kings and magistrates may be perverted, that is, they may adopt tyrannical methods which will go against the interests of men. As an antidote to this misuse of power Milton prescribed the prevalence of the administration of law which subsequently came to be known as rule of law. The rules must be framed or consented to by all to limit the actions of the governors. They are not above laws and cannot violate them. That is, their actions are limited by the laws. By making law the supreme authority in the Commonwealth Milton has ruled out the importance of divine right theory. To say that the kings are only accountable to God is overturning all laws and government. Milton writes : "For if they may refuse to give account, then all covenants made with them at coronation, all oaths are in vain, and mere mockeries; all laws which they swear to keep made to no purpose." So the kings are bound by laws and oaths given at the time of coronation. What Milton emphasises is that law is the determiner of everything and none is above law or outside the purview of law. This indicates the progressiveness of Milton's.

Milton's political philosophy is the clear manifestation of popular sovereignty and individualism. John Milton had no interest in the form or type of government. His main interest centred on popular sovereignty. He recognised and emphasised people's right to dislodge any government which clearly fails to serve the cause of society as a whole. Like Hobbes and Rousseau, Milton did not elaborate the concept of sovereignty, but the spirit of his analysis reveals that popular sovereignty was of prime importance to him. He vindicated people's right everywhere. His idea of liberty also convinces us that he was radical minded and this idea, in the background of his time, is highly attractive. Dunning says (p. 244) : "Milton is the earliest great prophet of that individualism which came to be almost a philosophic fetish in the nineteenth century. It is, however, the foundation and not the content of his doctrine that suggests the recent system of *laissez faire*". He advocated individual's freedom in economic affairs and he was against governmental interference. Milton was not only a great prophet of individualism but also of liberal philosophy which was subsequently developed by number of thinkers.

From his concept of liberty and individualism can be deduced his attitude to religion and church-state relation. The Protestant principle that every individual had the right to interpret the Scripture in his own way was accepted by Milton. Church had no right or power to impose its own religious principles or faith upon men. Its main concern was only with the ethical acts and state's concern was with outward acts. Both should try to confine each within its own sphere. He treated church and the state as two different institutions.

Milton's political philosophy is a curious mixture of contradictory views. He was a supporter of democracy and popular sovereignty. But at the same time he was in favour of the "best men" who would rule and hold office for life. He had little faith on the electorate. Like Plato and Aristotle he was of opinion that common people were not capable of shouldering the responsibility of managing the administration of the state. If man were not capable of taking the responsibility of administration how could they enjoy liberty? Sabine's comment in this respect is quite pertinent : "He wholly failed to see that individual liberty is an impracticable ideal if men are unfit to be trusted with a voice in government. Like all who idealize the early stages of revolution as a new birth of civilization, he was ill-prepared to face the realities of its last stage" (p. 512).

JAMES HARRINGTON (1611–1677)

Introduction

We have just now completed the analysis of the political ideas of John Milton, the great republican thinker of the seventeenth century. But he was not the solitary luminary of this century. There were also others, such as James Harrington, the English country squire, Bendict de Spinoza—the Amsterdam lens-grinder, and Samuel Pufendorf—the German university professor. Maxey says that political thought is ever prone to be the hand-maiden of political causes. In the seventeenth century the development of political thought was more articulate and rapid than any previous century. This century also fostered the awakening of the scientific spirit in political thought. Spinoza proposed to investigate the science of politics with the same freedom as we generally use in mathematics. The chief credit of Harrington and Pufendorf lies in the fact that they unhesitatingly travelled into the important fields of political science and recorded their valuable opinions which are duly respected even today. These great thinkers of the seventeenth century said very little new, but their approach is laudable. Spinoza, Harrington and Pufendorf were the representatives of pure intellectualism of the seventeenth century. If not as to specific doctrines, certainly as to spirit and approach, these thinkers must be counted among the most influential forebears of the modern political science

(Maxey, p. 266). It is true that Spinoza, Harrington and Pufendorf said nothing or very little that might be regarded as novel. But their emphasis of republican concepts are very important and the students of Western political thought still respect them for this.

Life and Work of Harrington

Harrington was born at Exton, Rutlandshire, in January, 1611. His father was the owner of a large estate and after the death of his father he inherited that estate. This made him economically solvent. In earlier centuries many educated and intellectuals had the tendency to travel to various parts of Europe. Milton and Harrington were no exception. Even Aristotle extensively toured different parts of Europe and Asia. Returning to England he threw himself into the management of the inherited property. He also developed a personal relationship with King Charles. He had no interest in the long drawn controversy between king and parliament and this disinterestedness kept him away from the platform of the great polemics. Harrington acted in different capacities in royal family and because of his personal relation with Charles I the antimonarchists suspected him. The behaviour of Harrington created suspicion in the minds of many people and they suspected him as a supporter of absolutism of the monarch.

After Charles I was beheaded, Harrington retired from politics and started to write his famous work *The Commonwealth of Oceana* which was published in 1656. This single book brought for him a lot of eulogy and reputation and he is called one-book genius. *Oceana* is still read by many who desire to be aquainted with the republican thought of the second half of seventeenth century. Though Harrington's *Oceana* was not a solitary one the book sincerely propagated the basic ideas of republican philosophy.

Political Ideas of Harrington

Before entering into the details of Harrington's political ideas let us make a glance over the plan of the book—*Oceana*. The book is divided into five sections. The first is called the "Preliminaries". This is the most important part of the book in the sense that it contains the gist of his political ideas. The second, called "The Council of Legislators", deals with the composition and procedure of the constituent body of the imaginary Commonwealth of *Oceana*. The name of the third section is "The Model of the Commonwealth called Oceana." The subject matter of this section is the constitution of Oceana. This section is full of imaginary narratives of the legislators. "The Corollary" is the fourth section. There are several things in this section, such as the proposed constitution of Oceana, its adoption and inauguration. The form of the new government is also discussed in this section. The final section is named "Description of Oceana." It is a short postscript depicting the unexampled felicity and prosperity of Oceana under her ideal government.

While Harrington was framing *Oceana* the picture of England was in his mind. He wanted that England would be governed by sound principles and right reason. Otherwise its stability would be at stake. In the guise of fiction he had re-written the history of England and had prepared a horoscope for the future. This approach of Harrington created immense interest in the minds of people and a large number of people read it. Interpretation of the book began to be different from person to person which became a source of controversy.

James Harrington, with great acumen, has elaborated the economic basis of republicanism. Here he has followed the policy and method of Aristotle. According to Harrington, not the tyrannies of monarchs, the ruthless behaviour of the ruling class, religious intoleration of different religious groups or the all-pervading corruption were the real causes of civil war. It was the unequal distribution of property—that is, land, which contributed to the emergence of civil war. That is, there was no economic balance in English society and this fomented the dissension. Harrington has said that domestic empire is founded upon dominion and the dominion is property real or personal; that is to say, in lands of goods or money. If the distribution of property is in proportion or balance then the empire or commonwealth is in stable condition. But if the balance is disturbed or upset then there will be disturbances in the state. It is now obvious that Harrington has blamed economic inequality as the primary cause of revolution and in this respect he borrowed Aristotle's idea. But we are of opinion that economic inequality is not singularly responsible for revolution. Other factors are also responsible.

The central idea of the above is that if the total amount of land is held by a few persons, the majority of the people will be both economically and politically dependent upon the nobility, that is, the economically powerful class, and this dependence will cause dissension among the members of this class. But if the land is distributed among the masses, the power and influence of the nobility will be curtailed and the Commonwealth will be saved. Harrington wants to emphasise that a powerful nobility is inconsistent with a republican form of government. There is also a striking resemblance between Harrington and Machiavelli, both held that there is inconsistency between nobility and republicanism.

Let us highlight another aspect of Harrington's economic basis of republican state. He classifies the states according to the distribution of land. If one man is the sole owner of the entire landed property he is grand signeur and his empire is absolute monarchy. If the few or a nobility with clergy be landlords or overbalance the people to the like proportion, it makes the Gothic balance and the empire is mixed monarchy. And if the whole people be landlords or hold the lands so divided among them that no man or number of men overbalance them the empire is a commonwealth. The law which determines the distribution of land is called agrarian law and any government which has no agrarian law can never be stable. England at the time of Harrington was an agricultural country and this inspired him to deduce the conclusion that in the agricultural sector there shall be balance. This again reminds us of Aristotle's influence upon Harrington. But his economic balance was not limited to the agrarian country, it was extended to non-agricultural states. His contemporary Holland and Genoa were not agricultural states. The source of wealth of these countries was trade. It is believed that he was also thinking of these states.

Harrington's ideal state is the ideal balance of economic forces. This ideal can be attained only by the establishment of an equal Commonwealth. Harrington's doctrine of economic balance is, no doubt, novel and, in the opinion of Sabine "He stood alone among the political writers of his time" (p. 498). The almost same idea has been expressed by Maxey (p. 272) when he says that he was a new departure in political thought. The ultimate bases of political authority, according to Harrington, are not social contract or covenant in its various forms of the divine right theory or the military force. These bases are misleading and false.

Harrington's equal Commonwealth does not imply equalitarianism. He has insisted upon the balance of economic forces, and not on the distribution of land or wealth among individuals. Harrington was a believer of natural aristocracy. That, from the standpoint of wisdom and capacity, all men are not equal. Some possess higher abilities than others. This must be recognised. In the equal Commonwealth the natural inequalities must be given due importance and, on the basis of the natural inequalities, the mutual relationships should be determined. Laws will be framed and government institutions are to be erected upon this ground. Harrington, it is now clear, was emphasising upon artificial inequalities created by the maldistribution of agricultural land and this type of imbalance was the root cause of various forms of discord. But in his frame of commonwealth there shall exist natural inequalities and he did not regard them harmful for society.

The distribution of land among all individuals was not all. The government should be organised for that purpose. Harrington has recommended that in the imaginary Commonwealth there shall be a senate to initiate policies and enact laws, a council consisting the mass of population or their representatives with the function of rating upon the recommendations of the senate and a magistracy to execute the policies and laws. Though Harrington clearly specifies the idea of separation of powers, his analysis, we believe, focuses that idea. He was thinking of dividing the powers of government among several organs for the purpose of ensuring good administration.

The characteristic feature of Harrington's Commonwealth is that it is an "empire of laws and not of men". This is typical Aristotelian principle of constitutional government. Aristotle distinguished between constitutional government and tyrannical government. The former looks after the public interest and the administration of the state is run on the basis of laws or constitution. There is hardly any scope of arbitrariness. In the latter, arbitrary rule and personal interest predominate. Hobbes's Commonwealth was the "empire of men and not of laws". Harrington has criticised Hobbes from different angles. He has said that "Hobbes was guilty of mere confusion."[1]

Harrington agrees with both Aristotle and Machiavelli on the point that politics is an art. So its management or organisation is a difficult task. Everyone cannot acquire this art. For the smooth running of the Commonwealth the balance between the economic power and political power is no doubt necessary, but it is also necessary that there should be predominance of laws and not of men. The absolute monarchy is essentially a government of men and that is why this type of government is not stable. In the monarchy there is no scope of rotation of power. One man holds power permanently. This goes against the stability of the state. He has suggested that the laws of elections will be framed in such a manner that every able and qualified person gets the opportunity to serve.

Importance of Harrington

Harrington was not an outstanding philosopher of the seventeenth century. Nor there was any radically new idea in his entire thought system. Notwithstanding, the students of political thought enthusiastically read his *Oceana* because it contains certain republican as well as utopian ideas.

---

1. Sabine—p. 502.

Harrington was a political philosopher, a utopian thinker and a theorist. *Oceana* was his dream-child. The dream or the imagination of a man cannot immediately be applied to practice. "But" observes Maxey "many of ideas and principles he wove into his dream have been translated into reality and are extant in the world today as living political institutions (p. 275). Particularly, his repeated emphasis on economic equality and rule of law constitutes the kernel of today's political thought. Dunning comments "Harrington has been preserved from oblivion only be appreciation of a small circle of readers. Yet to the few who have got to the essence of Harrington's thought it has been very rich in practical suggestions; and so it happens that the actual institutions in which the Commonwealth ideas has been realised in England and America present a remarkably large aggregate of resemblances to the establishment of Oceana" (p. 253–254).

Harrington created a profound influence upon the later day political thought. "He laid the foundation of modern political theory". Locke, Montesquieu, Hume, Burke and a host of other European thinkers and publicists of eighteenth and nineteenth centuries were indebted to Harrington. John Adams and Daniel Webster of USA were inspired by Harrington. He gave a very brief outline of the doctrine of separation of powers, which was later on developed by Locke and fully elaborated by Montesquieu. This again has constituted the central idea of the American constitution. The principle of rotation in offices is really interesting and no doubt a great check upon the misuse of power and corruption. Harrington supported the system of secret ballot which was unheard of in his own days. The system of popular ballot today is popular and part of election.

We shall conclude with the observation of Sabine : "Harrington was a political thinker of quite unusual power and independence, the only philosopher of Puritan Revolution who had any philosophical group of social causes behind it" (p. 496). His analysis of Puritan Revolution in the light of economic factors evoked considerable interest in those days. His approach to revolution and, above all, to politics, is systematic and scientific. Harrington was less interested in liberty than was Milton, but he was more practical. He had a good understanding of the real situation. His analysis of economic and political facts is still worth remembering. His name is connected with three revolutions—Puritan Revolutions, American Revolution and French Revolution. The economic factors acted behind these revolutions.

SPINOZA (1632–1677)

Introduction

After Hugo Grotius—the great interpreter of international law and sovereignty—another Dutch who held position and prestige of Holland high is Benedict de Spinoza and he did this through his remarkable genius. Spinoza was born at Amsterdam on November 24, 1632. He belonged to the Jewish community and his family lived in Portugal. To escape the Roman Catholic persecution his parents fled from Portugal and settled at The Netherlands. He received education here and developed his philosophy. But his philosophy was in a large measure determined by the conditions of his life. Spinoza's scientific mind and proclivity towards intellect incurred the displeasure of the Jewish authority. The Jewish community adopted several measures so that he could amend his attitude towards religion and when all attempts met with failure the Jewish community was finally compelled to excommunicate him. This happened when he was only twenty-four years old. He took up his residence with his friends and started his culture of philosophy independently.

Philosophers and historians have investigated the background of his intellectual and philosophical development. They have found the most conspicuous influence of Descartes. Descartes's conception of homogeneous substance underlying all forms of matter and another homogeneous substance underlying all forms of mind attracted him. Descartes explained all of the world except God and soul by mechanical and mathematical laws. During Renaissance and afterward machinery and industry developed remarkably and this created an impact upon Descartes's mind.

It is held by many that the excommunication from Jewish community was blessing in disguise for Spinoza. He got the opportunity to think freely. He earned his living at first by teaching children and then by polishing lenses. He had learned the optical trade while living in the Jewish community. His earning was meagre, but his living was very plain. So he did not face any financial difficulty. He devoted himself to intensify his thought and study. Few friends and admirers gathered around him. With them Spinoza formed a small school of thought. Many times he stayed in his room for two or three days together, seeing nobody and having his modest meals brought up to him.

His first famous treatise on politics[1] was published in 1670. The author, printer and publisher were kept in secret. The book immediately earned the wrath of the authority. In 1671 it was officially damned by the Synod (religious council) and in 1674 it was banned by the States-general of Holland. "Finally the book gained the accolade of the free-thinking books... Thus assured of a wide circulation, the book went through a long series of bootleg editions and enormously added to the prestige of its author."[2] His last work on politics is *Tractatus Politicus or Political Treatise.* It was published after Spinoza's death in 1677.

Spinoza on Social Compact

"Since fear of solitude exists in all men, because no one in the solitude is strong enough to defend himself and procure the necessaries of life, it follows that men by nature tend towards social organisation. To guard against danger the force or strength of one man would hardly suffice if men did not arrange mutual aid and exchange. Men are not by nature equipped for mutual forbearance of social order, but danger begets association, which gradually nourishes and strengthens the social instinct. Men are not born for citizenship, but must be made fit for it. The state of nature is insecure and without mutual help it is impossible to sustain life or cultivate the mind. Men must agree to live under the laws of society. Without law and government right and wrong cannot be determined and wrong-doers cannot be punished. In order to enjoy the freedom to the fullest extent men must unite themselves. It is not possible for them to forego freedom which is their natural heritage."[3] This observation of Spinoza clearly reveals that an environment was in

1. Theological-Political Treatise.
2. Maxey—op. cit., p. 279.
3. Quoted by Maxey—p. 283.

his mind which may be called state of nature. His state of nature may be compared with a situation where there is no government or administration.

In such an environment people decided to enter into a contract in order to set up a civil society or state whose primary function would be to enforce law and order which would restrain their harmful passions and unsocial behaviour because all these were against the interest of others. With the help of the compact people will be able to defend their rights and freedom and all men will come to the aid of each other. But it is difficult to enter into a pact when one cannot trust one's neighbour, and so each man must transfer all his power to the society. The supreme power will be vested in the society to decide everything and it is obligatory for everyone to show allegiance to the supreme power and accept the decision. The whole society is sovereign and not any person.

The compact theory of Spinoza is different from that of Hobbes and Locke. Instead of men transferring their natural powers to a sovereign ruler, they transfer them to the whole society and the state is created a democracy. Hence Spinoza's sovereign power is not Leviathan. He has not depicted a gloomy picture of human nature. He recognises that men have natural sympathy and pity and they feel the necessity of mutual assistance. Enmity and friendliness both are present in human nature. Of course, the former is stronger. Like Hobbes he does not think that man is always guided by selfishness. Generosity is also a motive force. Locke's state is an emasculated one. It has no power to go against the terms and conditions of the compact. Spinoza's compact is made valid by its utility without which it becomes null and void. Spinoza says that it is foolish to expect or require a man to keep a compact that does him more harm than good, or to keep a compact when the violation of it does him less harm than good. This consideration should have great weight in forming a state. To put the matter in other words, according to Spinoza, the aim of social compact should be a state in which each man or majority of men will have more to gain than to lose. It can be inferred from Spinoza's conclusion that it is the prudence of man and the desire to expand the quantum of liberty that led the people of pre-political society to lay the foundation of civil society. So we can say that the civil society depicted by Spinoza is of different nature. It will have many functions and the main function is to protect liberty and rights. The contracting individuals have also kept the controlling power in their hands. This is really a new aspect of contract theory. It may be compared with Locke's thought.

Republican Philosophy of Spinoza

In Spinoza's republican philosophy there is no place of Hobbesian absolute sovereignty or any sort of absolutism. Since all power rests with society, people are the sources of governmental authority. The whole society is now entrusted with the task of the protection of individual's liberty. Previously people could not protect liberty and enjoy other privileges on their individual capacity. So the main utility of the social compact lies in the enhancement of liberty. What place the concept of liberty occupies in Spinoza's thought can best be illustrated by the following passage.

"The last end of the state is not to dominate men nor to restrain them by fear; rather it is so to free each man from fear that he may live and act with full security and without injury to himself or his neighbour. The end of the state, I repeat, is not to make rational things into brute beasts and machines. It is to enable their bodies and their minds to function safely. It is to lead men to live by, and to exercise, a free reason; that they may not waste their strength in hatred, anger and guile, nor act unfairly towards one another. Thus the end of the state is really liberty."[1]

The above passage is self-explanatory. In the opinion of Spinoza the supreme aim of the state is the realisation of liberty. Without liberty people cannot lead a peaceful and comfortable life and needless to say that it is the supreme goal of every individual. The state will promote a rational rather than bestial life in men. Spinoza had a very clear and rational concept about liberty and this is evident when he announces that liberty is never a license, it is always conditional and must be a controlled one. The purpose is to enable the largest number of men to enjoy the fruits of liberty. According to Spinoza the perfect state will limit the powers of its citizens only as far as these powers are mutually destructive. In other words, for the greater interest of the society the state will have the power to limit the freedom of the citizens. Otherwise it cannot rule. Spinoza analyses the ideal of freedom from another angle. It is the most important precondition of growth.

The freedom of speech and expression is very important. It enables man to express what he thinks. Education and culture have taught him to think freely. If any law curtails that liberty man will resist the attempt. If freedom of speech creates inconveniences to others then that should be decided through free discussion and not through the application of draconian laws. Laws against free speech are subversive of all laws. For men will not long respect laws which they may not criticise. Needless to say that Spinoza's emphasis upon freedom of speech and liberty makes him a republican-thinker of the first rank. About the control of the state he has said the less control the state has over the mind, the better for both the citizen and the state.

In *Theological-Political Treatise* Spinoza has strongly argued for giving sufficient freedom to various political, social and religious institutions so that they can perform their duties without any obstruction. Spinoza thought that it was essential for the development of democracy. Spinoza was also in favour of religious freedom and toleration. Every citizen will have the liberty to pursue his own faith and the state cannot impose restriction. Though he was against state interference with individual liberty in political and religious affairs, he was not at all in favour of radical democracy.

There is a striking similarity between Spinoza and Milton in respect of their attitude towards liberty and few other liberal concepts. In Milton's view, liberty is the birth-right of the individual and the state cannot control it. For the sake of individual's liberty Milton proposed a popular sovereignty. We also find Spinoza championing the cause of liberty and rights. But the crucial difference between the two republican thinkers is Milton's liberty was individual-centred, whereas Spinoza's liberty is state-centred. Dunning writes (p. 316) : "To the Jewish philosopher the conclusive argument is that freedom of the thought and expression are essential to the preservation and welfare of the commonwealth, while to the Englishman this freedom has for its permanent justification the guarantee it carries of the supreme excellence of the human reason and the dignity of manhood."

Spinoza's attempt to view liberty in the background of the whole complex of society, his tendency to treat the state as an organic unity and his effort to regard

---

1. Quoted by Will Durant in *The Story of Philosophy*, p. 192.

sovereignty as resting upon the common reason of general mind of its members remind us of Rousseau. Like Spinoza, Rousseau makes a reconciliation between individual liberty and state authority. Spinoza does not find any conflict between individual and state. Frankly speaking, in this respect Spinoza's view is modern. He strongly argues for individual's freedom. But where the individual is unable to make his position suitable for the protection of liberty the state will come forward. Hence no question of conflict between the two does arise. Purpose of both is almost the same. Even modern political scientists hold the same view.

Spinoza's republicanism is again manifested by his preference for popular monarchic institutions. Spinoza's conclusion is that monarchy is efficient but an oppressive and militaristic form of government. The will of the king is all-powerful and there is no place of alternative opinion. So it ultimately leads to slavery and barbarism. In his words "if slavery, barbarism and desolation are to be called peace, men can have no worse misfortune." Democracy is the most reasonable form of government. For in it everyone submits to the control of authority over his actions, but not over his judgement and reason i.e., all cannot think alike, the voice of the majority has the force of law. The defect of democracy is its tendency to put mediocrity to power and there is no way of avoiding this except by limiting office to men of trained skill. As to the type of government, Spinoza's opinion is to some extent peculiar because, being a republican thinker, he did not hesitate to support monarchy. However, the monarchy must not be oppressive. A good and efficient monarchy is better than an inefficient democracy.

Assessment

Spinoza sees the state as a purely natural phenomenon. It is the product of human nature acting in response to varied factors, forces and conditions which make human nature what it is and not what it ought to be. He has viewed the origin of the state from a realistic point of view. The motives which guide men are self-preservation and self-satisfaction and not any ideals. Law is made by men to achieve these two prime objectives. This is, comments Maxey, crass materialism; for others it is sordid realism; but for the objective student of political phenomena it is simply an attempt to come to grips with facts and no derogation either of God or humanity.[1]

Spinoza is not the victim of imagination or wishful thinking. He has explained things as they are and how he sees them. Under the existing circumstances how man can adopt the best methods to reap best advantage. He has depicted human nature as neither noble nor depraved. On this point he departs from Hobbes. In his analysis we find man as a political creature and, consequent upon this, it is natural that he will form political organisations for his maximum advantages. It is quite natural for a political animal that he will make the best efforts for the protection of his liberty and rights. As a political animal he is endowed with reason and consciousness. He cannot make the sovereign absolute. Spinoza's men have not made sovereignty all-powerful. Materialism of Spinoza can be compared with that of Machiavelli and Hobbes. But Hobbes's materialism is of quite different type. "Spinoza was a truer scientist and a more penetrating philosopher than any of his materialistic predecessors."[2]

1. Maxey, op. cit., p. 290.
2. Maxey, op. cit., p. 291.

Maxey further observes (p. 292) : "The world was no more ready for his political than his religious philosophy. It did not welcome his ideas, but could never ignore them. No great iconoclast is ever acclaimed as a prophet and teacher by contemporary generations. Nor is he ever passed over in silence. His radicalism and irreverence always draw fire from the snipers of the Old Guard...... No cult of political pragmatism bears his name, but his utilitarian concept of the state gradually permeated the thought of the world and later, through the genius of such theorists as Bentham and Mill, was evolved into a dynamic system of political philosophy. His name is not associated with the monistic doctrine of sovereignty, but 19th century jurists such as Austin and Jellinek built largely on the foundations that he prepared." In the history of Western political thought—particularly republical thought—Spinoza has a special place. He was not a propagator of radical democracy but his attitude towards republicanism is still remembered by the students of political thought. Many scholars have discovered materialism in his thought. It is, however, some what controversial.

PUFENDORF (1632–1694)

Short Life-History and Works

We shall now discuss the world's first professor of international law, Samuel Pufendorf. He was born near Chemnitz in Saxony on January 8, 1632. In the same year Spinoza and Locke were born. His parents were devoted to Lutheran theology. At an early age he was sent to the University of Leipzig to study theology. But the narrowness of religion created apathy in his mind against religion and he rebelled. Pufendorf left Leipzig and went to the University of Jena where he studied jurisprudence. After completing his study at Jena he went out in search of a teaching post which he failed to get. Because of political turmoil he was sent to jail where he spent eight months. In order to free himself from the drudgery of solitude he engaged his mind to the serious study of philosophy and other related subjects and the solitary life in jail opened new vistas of thought.

Being released from jail Pufendorf went to Holland and joined the University of Leyden, where he showed the manuscript on *Two Books on the Elements of Universal Jurisprudence* to some of his friends and urged upon them to publish it. This was published in 1660. Immediately after the publication of the book the attention of the intellectual circles was drawn to the scholarship and wisdom of Pufendorf. All on a sudden he sprang into prominence. After the publication of the book the University of Heidelberg appointed him to the newly created post of professorship in natural and international law.

After the publication of the above-noted book his luck began to show favour and the first instance was that he was invited by the king of Sweden to join the professorship at the University of Lund. While at the University of Lund Pufendorf published his famous book *Eight Books on the Law of Nature and of Nations.* From Sweden he went to Stockholm to take the post of royal historiographer. This change in occupation curtailed his interest in jurisprudence and the enrichment of the subject at the hands of a renowned scholar ceased. This is a great loss. He became an archivist and historian. But the world remembers Pufendorf as a great scholar of international law and jurisprudence. He held the post of historiographer until his death in 1694.

In order to understand the political ideas of Samuel Pufendorf we shall have to go through his *Elements of Universal Jurisprudence.* His other treatise *The Law of nature and of Nations* is also important. But it is an elaboration of the contents of *Elements.* In these two books Pufendorf has said little new or original. Of course he has acknowledged his debt to Hugo Grotius, the propounder of international law, and Thomas Hobbes, the great author of social theory.

The State of Nature and Law of Nature

The starting point of Pufendorf's political and philosophical analysis is the *state of nature.* The term state of nature may be used in two senses. According to the interpretation of Dunning (p. 319) the first sense is the residual attributer of the concept humanity, when abstraction is made of the qualities and conditions which are due to civilisation and enlightenment. The second sense designates an actual condition which has prevailed at sometime among each of the various races of men, though not necessarily among all at the same time. In the *Law of Nature and of Nations* Pufendorf defines the state of nature as a condition in which there is no civil or political organisation, though in a qualified sense the term may be applied to the relation of families or states that have no common superior. The state of nature is a wretched and intolerable condition, but not a permanent state of war as Hobbes imagined. In his own words : His state of nature is in-between absolute disorder and anarchy and abode of heavenly peace. Due to the absence of civilised law and administration normalcy in life and living was absent.

"The state of nature is a condition of liberty, but must have been uncomfortable and dangerous. Nature itself wishes there to be some *cognatio* between men enjoining them not to kill, but rather to assist one another, but this *cognatio* has little effect among those living in natural liberty. Therefore, though a man need not treat his neighbour as his enemy, he must nevertheless regard him as an uncertain friend"[1] So in the view of Pufendorf the state of nature is not characterised by indiscriminate war but by peace. But there is a dark side of the state of nature to which Pufendorf does not forget to draw our attention. The state of nature is not a state of perpetual and absolute peace. From the above passage of Pufendorf it is obvious that in his judgment the people of the state of nature did not feel comfort and were not free from danger. From the picture of state of nature depicted by Pufendorf it is clear that people ever primarily moved or guided by passions and unreasonable motives and all these created some troubles and problems.

In the state of nature prevails the law of nature which acts as a brake to the indiscriminate behaviour of men meted out to others. What is the law of nature? In his definition of the law of nature Pufendorf follows Hugo Grotius. It is the dictate of right reason determining what is right and wrong in human conduct. Like Hobbes he has conceived that the first law of nature is that a pacific and social life must be maintained. That is, self-interest is the working principle of the law of nature. We thus find that in his analysis of the law of nature Pufendorf has combined the views of Grotius and Hobbes. But in one respect he has departed from Grotius and leaned to Hobbes. The distinction made by Grotius between the law of nature and law of nations has been rejected by Pufendorf. He shares Hobbes's dictum that the law of nature and law of nations are the same thing. Pufendorf holds as against

1. Quoted by J. W. Gough in *The Social Contract,* p. 119, Footnote No. 5.

Hobbes that men are naturally sociable and this sociability or natural inclination to join societies is the foundation of the law of nature and necessary conditions for forming society. We shall now turn to that.

Social Compact

Pufendorf has argued that the sociable nature of man was the primary cause of the formation of the society but it was not the only cause. Due to certain problems and unavoidable conditions the life of the people of the state of nature was not quite comfortable and peaceful. People of that situation sought a way out. The primitive people knew it very well that by forming a civil society and becoming its member they would have to sacrifice their natural liberty. They would get something as members of society and simultaneously lose something as individuals. So the genuine and chief reason why the partiarchs abandoned their natural liberty and formed states was in order to provide safeguards against the injuries which men may suffer at the hands of their neighbours. Somehow the people of the state of nature came to the conclusion that the formation of a civil society based on contract could fulfil their requirement, that is availability of safeguards against the misuse of power resulting in injuries and miseries. People regarded the civil society as a powerful weapon to fight the uncalled for behaviour of some persons.

Men of the state of nature decided to form a new social order or society which would give them permanent relief from the problems of state of nature. They thought that a mechanism was required and that was social compact. The state is crerated by a contract and according to Pufendorf this is the first contract. People have finalised the terms and conditions of the contract unanimously and the dissenting voice will remain outside the contract as well as the civil society. But only one contract is not sufficient. So they have made another and this is between the individuals as members of the corporate body and the would-be ruler. By enunciating the idea of double contract Pufendorf departs from Hobbesian concept of contract where there is the provision of only one contract.

His doctrine of double contract is characterised by liberalism or republicanism. The government contract reveals his anti-monarchic feeling. The king will have no scope to resort to arbitrary rule. Contract with the ruler imposes limitations upon the activities of the monarch. There is another aspect of his republican philosophy. The first contract is based upon the consent of each individual. This rules out the possibility or existence of coercion. Men are convinced of the utility of the contract. They are further convinced that only the state can bring about security and welfare. The government also promises to promote the common welfare of the body-politic.

Sovereignty of Pufendorf resembles that of Grotius and not of Hobbes. His sovereignty is supreme (*summus*) but not absolute (*absolutus*). Sovereignty performs his functions within the limitation imposed by the corporate body. What are the limitations? (a) The laws of God and of nature, (b) custom and ancient usage, (c) duties of the sovereignty are determined by the contract and, finally, laws are to be interpreted not by the king but by the sane and intelligent persons. Let us summarise Pufendorf's views of double contract theory. "Pufendorf argued that the creation of political authority involves not merely one agreement and a gift but two agreements. Once, heads of the families create an association through a contractual agreement specifying that they will seek a form of common leadership that will ensure their safety. Two, the members of the association issue a decree stipulating the form of government they think will secure this end. Three, the association enters into an agreement with a person or persons upon whom they confer sovereign power" (Morrow, p. 264). Pufendorf's agreement is *reciprocal*. The people undertake to obey the sovereign and to cooperate with him on the condition that the sovereign will make all arrangements for the safety of the state and their own safety. The sovereign will exercise power in accordance with conditions and constraints of the contract.

Conclusion

Pufendorf does not give any cognizance to the time-old divine right theory which was in past very popular. His love for republican thought led him to build up a theory of popular sovereignty which means that the power of sovereignty it derives from the people. This view found its place in Rousseau. A very interesting aspect of Pufendorf's thought is that the authority is always accountable to the general mass. This, we know, constitutes the main pillar of republicanism. We say that through the instrumentality of social compact Pufendorf has built up the foundation of liberalism and republicanism. His another credit is he has freed political thought from the closed compartment of religion and has made people the supreme authority.

Pufendorf's contract is individualist in nature. He has made the consent of everyone as essential. But like Locke he is persuasive, coercion plays no role in his thought system. Considering the utility of the civil society people will agree on its formation. This view brings Pufendorf nearer to Locke. The civil society and its constitution are both democratic. His concept of safety lacks clarification. But it is not difficult for us to understand what he means. In the state of nature there were several uncertainties and one such related to liberty. So we can easily surmise that men have formed society to protect their liberty. We thus come to the conclusion that through the social contract theory, Pufendorf maintains the liberal or republican tradition of the seventeenth century. In no sense he can be called an advocate of absolute monarchy.

There is a very interesting difference between contractualist Hobbes and republican thinker Pufendorf so far as the contract theory is concerned. Hobbes advised his people to surrender all their liberties and rights to the supreme authority. He did not accept the objection that the sovereign might be oppressive which could be the cause of people's misery. He believed that nothing could be worse than the state of nature. But "Samuel Pufendorf thought that human beings could create forms of government that would save them from hazards of the state of nature without requiring submission to an absolute sovereign" (John Morrow : *A History of Political Thought*, p. 77-78).

12 SOCIAL CONTRACT THEORY

Definition and Meaning of Social Contract

In social science and particularly in political science the concept of social contract is very wellknown and popular though many question (and quite reasonably) its historicity. Still today many renowned political scientists want to base social contract theory as the starting point of their theories. For example John Rawls believes that social contract can be taken as the major focus of his theory of justice. This is the social contract theory.

An authentic definition of social contract has been given by Michael Lessnoff in his introductory part of *Social Contract*. He says : "A social contract theory can be defined as one which grounds the legitimacy of political authority, and the obligations of rulers and subjects on a premised contract or contracts relating to these matters". There is another definition—"A contract between persons in a pre-political or pre-social condition specifying the terms upon which they are prepared to enter society or submit to political authority." Social contract can be defined as an instrument or mechanism with the help of which people enter into a new society. Or, it is a medium of transition from one stage to another and more specifically from the state of nature to civil society or political society. This transition is guided by certain conditions or terms and the social contract embodies those terms and conditions.

We have already noted that social contract is an instrument—which provides certain terms and conditions. Some people claim that they are not legally bound to carry out the directions of higher authority or the authority may say that it not legally bound to do such and such duties. In that situation social contract theory may be used as a weapon. The authority has already promised to perform such and such duties or, again, the contracting individuals are bound to obey certain rules as laid down in the contract. We can thus say that it is a document which contains certain conditions that bound both the rulers and the ruled. We, therefore, find that social contract contains some terms and conditions which bind both the ruler and the ruled. But this is not all. These conditions are *legitimate*. This is because at the time of finalisation of the contract both the parties promised to obey the terms and conditions and they did it assembling in an open place. In other words, pure democratic methods were used to finalise the contract. Naturally nobody can violate the terms and conditions of the contract.

Social contract theory is also defined as a foundation of political authority. What does it mean? The authority or the ruler or the government performs certain functions and the general public may raise the legitimacy or the utility of those functions. As again the ruled may refuse to cooperate with the authority or the government in respect of cooperating with the ruler. All these questions are easily solved by invoking the terms and conditions of the social contract. Naturally the social contract may be regarded as a source of political authority. Government will claim that it has been authorised by the contract to do this. Or the general public may claim that their functions are supported by the terms laid down in the contract.

Contract is the vital or most important source of consent. In the Middle Ages or even before that it was generally believed that all men are equal and naturally one cannot impose his will or decision upon other. If one wishes to perform certain duties with others then he must seek their consent or opinion. Since it is not possible to seek opinion on every issue there shall exist a general agreement or contract which will provide the guidelines. This general contract rules out the scope of repeated agreement. One general agreement will be the guiding star for all future actions. Therefore social contract can be defined as the holder of a general consent.

A social contract is a *legal document*. It has been signed and finalised by both or all the parties. Since everybody gave consent it was not possible to deny or refuse to give consent. But the question of consent is never unilateral, it is always bilateral or multilateral. That all the parties to the contract are *legally bound* to act in accordance with the terms of the contract. Naturally the two most important aspects of the contract are *consent* and *legality* or, in other words, *legitimacy*. Hence we can say that the social contract is a legal document based on the consent of all parties who were present at the time of finalisation of the terms and conditions of the contract and a society or political organisation that was created by this legal contract is also a legal political organisation. Thus one legal document comes to be the potential source of many other legal aspects. Some may raise the question on the importance or authenticity of contract as the source of the foundation of political society. This question or objection is very old. Still many believe that behind its foundation there is some sort of contract. Today almost all the states have written constitutions and these may be treated as contracts. Hence a social contract is a legal document which is based on consent and it is legal.

Origin and Development

From the study of history we come to know that the social contract is quite old. In the *Mahabharata* (*Shanti Parva*) there is a clear reference to social contract and this *Mahabharata* was written several thousand years from today. In the days of the *Mahabharata* in some places there was anarchy which in those days meant rule of the jungle or idiometically it was used that the small fishes were indiscriminately attacked and devoured by big ones. To bring an end to this anarchy an agreement was reached and all were parties to this agreement. This is a form of social contract.

Several scholars have asserted that the origin of the social contract can be traced to the eleventh century. Manegold of Lautenbach, after studying many things, arrived at the conclusion that there was a contract between the ruler and the people or ruled. That is, the contract was entered into between only two parties. The historians have cited several instances of earliest forms of social contract and one such form is in the writing of an Alsatian monk. In the contract it was said that in a society there shall be a ruler who may be called king. The king or kingship is just a title of office. Anyone who holds that office may be called a king. A contract was reached between the ruler and the people and simultaneously the terms of the contract were decided. The ruler or who might be called the king will administer in accordance with the terms laid down in the contract. He cannot be a tyrant by violating the terms agreed upon by both parties. It was also stated in the contract "he govern and rule according to right reason, give to each one his own, protect the good, destroy the wicked, and administer justice to everyman." Hence it is quite clear that it is the primary duty of the ruler to protect his subjects from all sorts of odd situations and any type of attack. For this purpose the contract was made and the post of ruler or king was created. "But if he violates the contract under which he was elected, disturbing and confounding that which he was established to set in order, then people is justly and reasonably released from its obligations to obey him" (Lessnoff, *Social Contract Theory*, p. 5). This is the most realistic version of social contract theory so far as origin is concerned. There is no trace of God, religion and divinity. The ruler will rule following right and any sort of aberration will be associated with the obligations of the people to the ruler.

If we go through the numerous political, social and other aspects of Middle Ages, especially fourteenth century, we shall come across the existence of embryonic form of social contract. Manegold in his idea of contract talked about a ruler, obligations of the subject to the ruler and prevalence of right reason. But in the fourteenth century Engelbert thought that there was some type of contract and the society was ruled in accordance with the terms of the contract. But the concept propagated (or elaborated) by Engelbert we find a new idea which is political authority. In other words, the contract was made by different parties (Engelbert thought so) to establish a *Political authority*. Not only this; in Engelbert's version the state or political authority originated from this contract. In Lessnoff's version : "all kingdoms and principates originated when men following nature and reason chose a ruler and bound themselves to obedience in a "contract of subjection" (*pactism subjecsonis*), made in order to be ruled, protected and preserved" (Lessnoff, p. 7). If we carefully study Engelbert's version of social contract we shall find that he imagined of two stages of society—one is pre-political or pre-social and the other is political which came into existence after the social contract. An interesting aspect of Engelbert's contract theory is he was the "first to enunciate an idea destined for a long career—what would later be called the *original contract*" (p. 7). This implies that subsequently people formed another contract. But the original contract was the source of political organisation and political authority.

The concept of social contract received further encouragement in the sixteenth century. Mario Salamonio, a Roman jurist, focused his attention on social contract. But he viewed the entire idea from religious point of view. Originally there was no political organisation as it is today. Perhaps Salamonio was thinking about state of nature. But he stressed that God had created all men and women equal and His intention was that all would enjoy equal privileges. But subsequently people strongly felt the necessity of establishing a kingdom or political organisation for the general betterment of people. Salamonio thought that this could be done by means of contract. Salamonio was a Roman Jurist and naturally he viewed everything in the background of Roman law. In Roman law political organisation was generally called *civilis societas* which means a society of partnership. "Thus for Salamonio political or civil society is a partnership among individual citizens created by contract among them... The terms of the contract are the laws of the state, without which no state can exist and which are binding on all its members—including the prince or the ruler" (Lessnoff, op. cit. p. 7). In the hands of Salamonio the idea of contract received a better treatment and it assumed an incomplete modern form.

Reformation, *Vindiciae,* Huguenot

From history we come to know that Reformation movement was chiefly a movement against maladministration and irreligious functions of church. But during the long course of movement it released certain basic concepts of politics and social contract theory is one of them. The Calvinists (of Reformation) in the 1550s believed that there existed an unwritten covenant or contract in all societies and it was the duty of both ruler and the ruled to obey the terms and conditions of these covenants. "Luther and Calvin both stressed the idea of a covenant between God and the people" (Quentin Skinner : The foundations of modern political thought, volume two, p. 236). But the king and higher officials were entrusted with the responsibility of carrying out the order of God and act in accordance with the terms of the covenant. But if there was any large scale disorder and transgression and also the violation of the basic rules of the covenant, people must have the right to protest the violation or trangression. Calvin's idea of covenant related to the Ten Commandments of the New Testament. Skinner says : "Since Calvin believed that in each case the essence of the covenant consisted of an agreement to obey the Ten Commandments, he went on to teach that it must be possible at any time for a group of godly men formally to reaffirm their contractual relationship with God" (op. cit. p. 236). From this it appears that the contract or covenant theory played a very important part in the Reformation movement.

The *vindiciae contra tyrannos* was published in 1579. It was a small but very powerful pamphlet which propagated the antimonarchism in the second half of the sixteenth century. The English translation of the pamphlet is A *Defence of Liberty against Tyrants.* This small book contains many explosive ideas whose central idea is that the king had no absolute power. But its most remarkable contribution (for the present purpose) is it contains the central idea of social contract theory. We can remember the opinion of Sabine : "In its main outline the theory of vindiciae took the form of twofold covenant or contract. There is first a contract to which God is one party and king and people jointly the other party.... Secondly there is a contract in which people appear as one party and the king as the other. This is specifically the political contract by which a people becomes a state, the king is bound by this agreement to rule well and justly" (Sabine, pp. 378–379). The *vindiciae* is an explicit assertion of the famous social contract theory.

Lessnoff makes the following observation about the contribution of *vindiciae* to the social contract theory. He says : The *vindiciae* is interesting both for what is old in it and for what is new. Junius Brutus reiterated the existence of a contract mutually obligatory between the king and his subjects which requires the people to obey faithfully and the king to govern lawfully" (p. 8). The *vindiciae* wants to assert that the king had no scope to act or govern the state whimsically, he is bound by the conditions of the contract. If the prince violates the faith or any part of the contract people will have right to withdraw obligations. In the sixteenth century the *vindicial* made a remarkable contribution to the antimonarchical movement and in order to strengthen the agitation the covenant theory was strongly emphasised. From *vindiciae* we obtain a few important threads of modern political theory and social contract theory is by far the most important of them.

The St. Bartholomew Massacre of 1572 opened the floodgate of several political and non-political issues. In this inhuman massacre more than two thousand Huguenots of Paris were brutally murdered. The Huguenots belonged to different religious faith and that was their "Unpardonable sin." The Huguenots and their spokespersons tirelessly propagated that every religious faith had the right to hold and propagate that faith peacefully. They further said that it was the duty of the king (or queen as might be) to protect every religious faith from the wrath and displeasure of an opposite faith. It is the constitutional duty of the authority. It is a type of contract. The authority will protect every religious sect and, in exchange of that, the sect will release obligation to the authority.

The Huguenot writers particularly Hotman said that the ruler even the hereditary ruler, had no right to deny its responsibility towards people. Its right to rule depends upon the tacit consent of the general public. Political authority is derived from "immemorial practices inherent in the community. ...the consent of the people, expressed in such practices, is the rightful basis of political power, and the Crown itself derives its authority from its legal position as an agent of the community" (Sabine, *History of Political Theory*, p. 376). The Huguenot writers wanted to emphasis that the king had no arbitrary authority, he must share his powers with the people of the society and, if he does this, people will show their obligation. This is the basic principle of contract theory and it is unfortunate that the French Government did not follow this basic principle. The Huguenot writers were at pain to note that the French government showed no respect to the immemorial practices and its responsibility to protect citizens.

Other Contributors

Althusius was the important contributor to the social contract theory. The contract theory, according to Sabine, figured in his analysis in two ways (p. 417). He believed that there was a relationship between the ruler and the ruled or subject people. He calls it the political role of the ruler. Again, in the view of Althusius, there exists a sociological role of the ruler. Sabine calls the first role as the political one and it is related to the contract of the government. The sociological role implies there is a tacit agreement between the government and the people as well as among the people themselves. A large number of people reside in a society and, according to Althusius, they are bound by contract and by virtue of it they form a community. Long ago Aristotle spoke of this type of community.

Sabine says (p. 418) that Althusius thought of several contracts that existed in society and all the people were bound by the terms of the contract. "The most important aspect of Althusius's theory was that he made sovereignty reside necessarily in the people as a corporate body." People as a body create law and the authority rules according to that law. Naturally the authority had hardly any opportunity to go against the law of the people. It is a type of popular sovereignty and the foundation is the contract. We think that Althusius's political theory is based on social contract and Sabine is right when he says that Althusius's political ideas are based on one idea or concept which is political and social relationships are guided by a single view and it is principle of consent or contract. The contract binds both the rulers and the ruled.

Samuel Pufendorf (1632–1694) was a seventeenth century jurist who supported the social contract as the basis of state or political society. From his writings we come to know that he thought of a double contract. There was a first contract which founded a state or political community. But to him a mere foundation of a political community was not all. It must be well-administered and serve the purposes of the members and, for that purpose, a second contract was necessary which would make provision for a ruler. He writes : "On the whole, to join a multitude, or many men, into one compound person, to which one general act may be ascribed."

In ancient Indian literature there are traces of contract as the basis of state. Ram Sharan Sharma in his noted work *Aspects of Political Ideas and Institutions in Ancient India* makes the following observation : "The first faint traces of the contract theory of the origin of the state are to be found in two *Brahmanas*, which refer to the origin of kingship through election among the gods on account of the compelling necessity of carrying on successful war against the asuras. ...Although the contract theory of the origin of the state is anticipated by early brahmanical literature, the first clear and developed exposition of this theory is found in the Buddhist canonical text Digha Nikaya, where the story of creation reminds us of the ideal state of Rousseau followed by the state of nature as depicted by Hobbes" (pp. 63-64). We thus see that in both West and East social contract was thought as a basis of state creation. But the difference is in the West the theory was very popular and widely conceived. In the East it was sporadically used.

Modern Version of the Theory

The revival of social contract theory in recent decades—specifically from the seventies of the last century—is astounding. Some people began to interpret it as the origin of utilitarianism because in their opinion people began to feel that well-organised and well-ordered state is far better than anarchical state, that is the state of nature. Many critics challenge the very historicity of social contract as the source or origin of state. But still they regard that in the process of evolution of state its importance is undeniable. It is believed that there existed at certain period of time anarchical situation and, in order to get rid of it, people laid the foundation of modern political organisation.

The most remarkable version of social contract theory has been provided by John Rawls in his *A Theory of Justice.* Lessnoff says : "More recently, social contract theory has been explicitly and self-consciously revived by the leading political philosopher of our day, John Rawls. Largely thanks to Rawls, social contract theory is now again a major focus of systematic and original political thought" (p. 1). Lessnoff says that the social contract is even more current. He cites an example. The British Labour Party in an election manifesto talked of social contract in different form. The manifesto said that in order to save the nation from the crisis a type of social contract was needed. It meant contract or agreement among different groups or parties. The purpose of the contract was to reach agreement which would save the nation from a number of economic crises. In every aspect of our social, political and economic life there is immense importance of social contract. Agreement is to be reached to find out ways of how to come out of various crises. The contract may not be in Hobbesian or Lockean way or formula, but contract is found.

John Rawls' *A Theory of Justice* was first published in 1971 and its revised edition in 1999. He says : "My aim is to present a conception of Justice which generalises and carries to a higher level of abstraction the familiar theory of social contract as found, say in Locke, Rousseau and Kant" (p. 10). Rawls has not used the social contract in its original form or the entire concept. But he adopts only some relevant portions for the analysis of justice as fairness. John Rawls is the propounder of the Justice Theory and he has said that certain aspects of social contract may serve his purpose. He writes : "the guiding idea is that the principles of justice for the basic structure of society are the objects of the original agreement" (p. 10). Rawls has assumed that the architects of the contract were "free and rational" persons. They started their activities from an original position and in that position all were equal. That is the starting point. After that they began to decide principles and formulate policies for further steps and actions. The main purpose is : all the future actions must be taken in a manner so that none will be in a disadvantageous position. That is, no one will suffer injustice. Rawls wants to say that at the initial position people will decide certain principles which may be called fundamental principles and these will "regulate all further agreements." Rawls is sure that in this way justice can be established in society. To use his language : "This way of regarding the principles of justice I shall call justice as fairness" (p. 10). Even Dr. Amartya Sen supports the approach (justice through social contract). He says in his *The Idea of Justice* "Even though the social contract approach to justice initiated by Hobbes combines transcendentalism with institutionalism, it is worth noting that the two features need not necessarily be combined" (p. 6, footnote).

Rawls further observes : In justice as fairness the original position of equality corresponds to the state of nature in the traditional theory of the social contract. This original position is not thought as a actual historical state of affairs. ... It is understood as a purely hypothetical situation characterised so as to lead to certain conception of justice" (p. 11). Rawls also refers to state of nature on another ground and it is "veil of ignorance." He says that the state of nature can be regarded as embodiment of "veil of ignorance" because the residents of state of nature had no clear idea of contract, civil society, government administration etc. Naturally, it was quite easy for the architects of contract to start from a position. One very powerful plus point is when the builders of the contract started from state of nature there did not arise any question of advantage or disadvantage.

Lessnoff says : "The Rawlsian contract is a hypothetical contract, but with a difference. ... Rawls's innovation has been to adapt contract theory to the problem of conflicting interests. To resolve conflicting interests in a way that adequately protects the interests of all is to ensure justice. Hence Rawls's contract theory is a theory of justice" (p. 18). Robert Nozick in his *Anarchy State and Utopia* has whole-heartedly supported Rawls idea of justice based on contract. But he has advanced a step. Nozick feels that for the proper realisation of justice at first what is required is institutionalisation of society and, to achieve this end, a scheme like contract is essential. All these clearly reveal that a theory which was first imagined several centuries ago has found its revival and this revival is quite interesting.

13 THOMAS HOBBES

Life and Times of Hobbes

Recent biographers of Hobbes say that "Hobbes and fear were born twins." He was born prematurely in 1588. On his birth there was the news of The Spanish Armada. There were also other disturbances at the time of his birth and historians are of opinion that he survived all the fears and vicissitudes of the seventeenth century Britain. In the last few decades, especially from 1580s, there were severe political turmoils. There were also economic and social instabilities. His span of life was quite long, as long as ninety-one years, which means that 1679 was the year of his death.

Historians are of opinion that when he was just fifteen years old James I ascended the British throne and clamped absolute rule upon the British people. James I strongly advocated absolute monarchy by reviving Divine Right theory. His absolutism immediately created a long and penetrating schism between monarchy and parliament. Because, by the end of sixteenth century, British parliament had already accumulated power and it wanted to establish its authority and, at the same time superiority over the king.

The war and other factors imposed unprecedented pressure upon the British administration in general and the treasury in particular. The British treasury was practically empty and in order to fill it up the king made attempts to impose taxes upon the British people. This was faced with stiff opposition from the parliament because its argument was that since its members were elected by the people the monarchy had no authority to ignore it. But James I refused to give due cognisance to the view or argument of parliament and this ultimately aggravated the relationship between king and parliament. Thus the reign of James I was full of conflict between king and parliament but somehow he managed the whole affair without any amicable settlement. His son Charles I ascended the throne and the conflict continued even during the rule of Charles I.

As an administrator James I was a failure, but he managed to carry on. Charles I was, again, most inefficient. His father was involved in the long quarrel with parliament and even during Charles I this did not die. The tragedy was that Charles I was directly involved in the conflict between Puritan and Conservative branches of English Church. At the time of Charles I there was also the Catholic question and this created troubles for Charles I because of his mismanagement. Thus the political and religious conflicts completely engulfed the entire British society and Thomas Hobbes was the witness of all these exciting drama. since he was not an inanimate object all these events created serious impact upon his mind and thought. His biographers are of opinion that the events helped him to form his opinion.

Let us turn to another aspect of Hobbes's contemporary situation which was also quite remarkable. When he was a student of the university Plato and Aristotle were taught within a very short time, Hobbes observed that various branches of knowledge, especially science, had remarkably developed and his university was far away from those developed branches of knowledge. There was significant progress in mechanical science. For example there were discoveries of Kepler, Galileo and Descartes and serious attempts were made to enter into new domains of science and knowledge. New light was thrown on physiology and magnetism. Newton's *Principia* created sensation in the academic world. In a word there was miraculous discovery in material science. Materialism took the place of philosophy.

Hobbes's mind, from the very beginning, was quite scientific and reasonable. The result was that, though he was the son of a clergyman, religion failed to create any positive impact on his mind. This is because during his student life he seriously studied mechanical and materialist science and subjects. He was also acquainted with geometry, calculus and other material subjects. He studied Leibniz and Newton. His inquisitiveness was also deep and wide. He not only studied various subjects of science and philosophy, he had an intention to know the world, peoples, society and culture around him. He extensively toured various parts of Europe and mixed with men of various walks of life. He was also a part of many educational tours and this quenched his thirst for knowledge. He also got the opportunity to mix with many celebrities of his time. This also broadened his mind and outlook. He got the scope to mix with great people of science, geometry and literature. It is said that during one tour he came in contact with Euclid's ideas. His biographers claim that he finally fell in love with geometry. In fact this love with geometry considerably moulded his academic life. This geometry is a material science. Hobbes thought that geometrical principles and formula could easily be applied to practical situations. He also arrived at the conclusion that material world and situations could easily be studied with the help of geometry. The study of geometry influenced him in various ways and one such is social and natural phenomena can be studied geometrically. He thought that behind every social action and incident there is movement. In this world, nothing is static or fixed. Everything moves from one point to another and if one fails to grasp it he will never be able to know the material world.

FACTORS THAT DIRECTLY INFLUENCED HOBBES

In *A Review and Conclusion* section of *Leviathan* Hobbes makes the following observation : "And thus I have brought to an end my *Discourse on Civil and Ecclesiastical Government*, occasioned by the disorders of the present time, without partiality, without application, and without other design than to set before men's eyes the mutual relation between protection and obedience of which the condition of human nature and the laws of divine (both natural and positive) require an inviolable observation" (p. 728). This observation of Hobbes is the best proof of the "fact" that his political and other observations contained in the *Leviathan* were strongly influenced by the circumstances he was confronted with or about which he had first-hand experience. We can naturally say that he did not have the habit of roaming in an imaginary world. He witnessed so many incidents which were not to his liking mark in his mind. The incidents also pained him. He had a bright and prosperous picture about his motherland he loved so much and he thought that the incidents would destroy the future of his motherland.

We know that Machiavelli was the son or product of Renaissance. In the same breath we can say Hobbes was the product of embroiled political, social, economic and religious situation that he witnessed. Particularly the gradual deteriorating political situation of Britain made Hobbes extremely thoughtful. Britain's long involvement in war created serious impact in his mind because he thought that the war had completely exhausted the treasury. The king imposed heavy taxation upon the common people. The entire economy was in shambles, trade and commerce were on the verge of collapse.

Apart from this the tentacles of corruption were spread in every nook and corner of society. Maxey says : "the corruption of justice to which James had resorted to accomplish his ends Charles carried to the point of outrageous tyranny, the bitter quarrel with parliament" (p. 212).

Maxey also writes : "The intellectual life of the country was correspondingly disturbed. ... The role of the printing press was as significant as that of the sword" (p. 213). The culture of art and literature was seriously affected. Hobbes himself was a great intellectual of his time. He was a genius and had the full ability to traverse almost all the branches of knowledge. Naturally when he found the miserable condition of art and literature and collectively of the intellectual world he decided to suggest a way out. Hobbes believed that the battle among the ideas could ensure the advancement of knowledge and intellect. But he saw that there was no battle of ideas, but a conflict among various religious faiths, which may reasonably be called religious fanaticism and intoleration and according to Hobbes all these completely dwarfed the progress of knowledge and intellect. Cultivation of knowledge was the first priority to Hobbes and when he saw its absence he was extremely disheartened. He desired an overall prosperity of Britain. He was not against religions but against its domination. He wanted individual freedom, but it was not all. The general progress of society was far more important and crucial than the progress of freedom of individuals. He paid less importance to any particular type of government. This particular philosophy of Hobbes practically inspired him to suggest a type of government with absolute power at its disposal. This is Hobbes.

SCIENTIFIC MATERIALISM

As a political philosopher Hobbes is remembered by the students of western political thought not simply for his theory of social contract, but chiefly for his contribution to scientific materialism. He made this scientific materialism as the basis or foundation of civil society which will be based on absolutism and secularism. Bodin's theory of sovereignty was absolute. He strongly defended absolute monarchy and he did this in the background of St. Bartholomew Massacre of 1572. His belief was that if the monarchy had absolute power at his disposal such a heinous incident would not happen but Hobbes viewed the idea of absolution in the perspective of materialism. Machiavelli was also a proponent of absolutism. But he founded his theory on different ground. According to Machiavelli the growing strength of opposing forces and the war among them created an atmosphere of extreme form of political instability and according to Machiavelli that retarded the over-all progress and political unity of Italy. Viewed in this light he prescribed absolute monarchy.

Hobbes studied geometry and other noted scientific works of his time. All these moulded his thought, ideas and outlook in a considerable way. Not only this, he applied his scientific knowledge and outlook to the study of political, social and all other situations. The logic and geometrical ideas helped the formulation of political ideas. It is a fact that there is no place of historicity in the theory of social contract. But his method is scientific and based on logic. The result is Hobbes's political philosophy is scientific. Sabine, the renowned interpreter of Western political thought, makes the following observation : "The defence of monarchical absolutism formed therefore a very superficial part of his effective political philosophy, and though the civil wars occasioned his thinking and writing, they account only in a small degree for the importance of what he had to say. Hobbes was in fact the first of the great modern philosophers who attempted to bring political theory into intimate relation with a thoroughly modern system of thought...on scientific principles" (p. 457). This assessment of Sabine about Hobbes is perfectly correct.

He had developed an inordinate passion for geometry which he studied and later on applied for the study of political phenomena. His purpose was to start from simple propositions and on the basis of these propositions he built up complex theoretical structure. He needed a two part method and arrived at the conclusion that the Euclidian method could not help him. The Galilean method might come to his help. Galileo adopted the resolutive-compositive method. The resolutive part was the way to reach the required simple basic propositions, the compositive part was the way to build the complex one from those. He adopted the resolutive part of Galilean method to the study of the main issues of political science. Hobbes found out the motions of political society and wanted to solve the political problems. He developed great love for motion and applied it to the study of political problems and issues. According to Hobbes man is not an inanimate object. He thinks, observes, hopes and plans for further action. In other words, he proceeds from one step to another and selects the most suitable alternative. In this way he arrives at the final stage of his programme. This is called motion and this he borrowed from geometry.

Hobbes's bold hypothesis was that the motion of individual beings could be reduced to the effects of mechanical apparatus consisting of sense organs, nerves, muscles, imagination, memory and reason. The apparatus did not have the capacity to move on its own accord. Its motion was created by external forces or objects. By applying the concept of motion to the study of political issues he introduced a new thought—the thought of motion and this thought he borrowed from geometry and other branches of mechanical science. It is said that here lies the credit of Hobbes. He imported the basic ideas of contemporary science and Euclidian geometry in order to enrich the study of political ideas.

The whole vs parts is another aspect of Hobbesian study of political issues. He could have started with the whole and then arrived at the conclusion, or the reverse could have been : He could start from the parts and then finally arrive at the whole. The fact is that his love for geometry led him to adopt the latter method. He started his survey of political concepts with the state of nature and its inhabitants whom he called natural men. Since they were the members of the state of nature it cannot be expected that they will have civilised behaviour. Rather, they possessed all the uncivilised or rustic maners. This is quite logical and natural.

Society is inhabited by human beings. But they are complicated, more intelligent than other members of society such as beasts or animals. The society is built up with human beings and, therefore, any study of society must start with the proper analysis of various aspects of human nature. Naturally a society inhabited by human beings must be studied in its proper perspective and this proper perspective is the study of human nature.

Hobbes started his analysis with man. But his man has reason, feeling, motive and emotion. He moves, works, acts or behaves being guided by all these. The interpreters of Hobbes' thought and philosophy are of opinion that these characteristics of man are simply the background factors of motion. In other words, man works because he has motive or feeling or reason. From here starts the concept of motion. Explaining Hobbesian philosophy Sabine rightly observes : At bottom every event is a motion and all sorts of natural processes must be explained by analysing complex appearances into the underlying motions of which they consist. ...Thus he conceived the project of a system of philosophy in three parts, the first dealing with body and including what would now be called geometry and mechanics" (p. 458). In the second part we find physiology and psychology of the individuals. It means that when individuals act both body and mind are in active position. In other words, both guide each other and this is a very important manifestation of motion. Finally there appears the civil society or body-politic or state. The body-politic, though artificial, is a part or manifestation of motion. The members of the state of nature founded such an artificial organisation and, at the root of this organisation, there was motion. If we thoroughly study Hobbes's materialism few basic points will emerge. One is, matter is the real thing and there is nothing real except matter. Morality, religion etc. are all of secondary importance. Second is, there is no hidden hand behind the rise and fall of society. Practical or material factors guide everything. We conclude that motion was the central idea of Hobbesian political philosophy and he explained it scientifically.

EVALUATION

Simply stated the premises of Hobbes's scientific materialism are the following : He was extremely dissatisfied with the prevailing situation of England, and wanted to save British society from the turmoil. He had a desire to lay the foundation of a new society, he studied geometry and other branches of science and finally he wanted to build up the foundation of a new society on the basis of knowledge he culled. The tragedy is that he did not enter into the details of the matter. That is, whether the application of scientific principles to the foundation of a new civil society will be relevant or not. The human society and geometry or mechanical science are separate subjects. The people of the state of nature abandoned that and proceeded to build up a new civil society. Hobbes discovered motion in this simple act. It is amusing. Human society and political philosophy have nothing to do with politics and Hobbes failed to understand this. Tom Sorell says : "Hobbes's idea is closer to the Baconian one that philosophy or science can contribute to the relief of man's estate." Philosophical knowledge may be helpful for the study of science or viceversa. But it is not at all correct to hold the view that science is at the root of the foundation of human society.

In our analysis of Hobbes's scientific materialism we have noted that he has taken the help of motion which is chiefly a Galilean principle for the study of politics. But many interpreters of Hobbes's political philosophy term it as "Coercive philosophy". Hobbes was a great scholar of his time. He studied various subjects. He very carefully and intelligently arranged the arguments and the readers are so mesmerised that they are compelled to buy his arguments. Some critics say that Hobbes has given no scope to his readers to think in their own way and apply their own view. He has arranged everything in such a manner that the readers are indirectly forced to accept his views. This attitude is not a welcome feature of his thought.

Tom Sorell says that the purpose of Hobbes's scientific materialism or science of moral and politics is to correct people's untutored belief of right or wrong and harmful behaviour and attitude. Hobbes speaks of the "prospective glasses" civil society makes available to counteract our natural short-sightedness in matters of moral politics. People are generally ignorant of the rules of peace. They are not well acquainted with what to do at the time of crisis such as war or general crisis. They are not also capable of dealing with love, passion etc. In all these cases the application of science or geometrical motion will not come to any assistance. Hobbes was overconfident that the application of motion or other principles of science will rectify people's harmful behaviour or bad attitude. But this is not the case. Rectification of people's undesirable behaviour requires different technique. His analysis of state of nature or human behaviour is not based on historical facts. Or these are not empirically tested. Even he does not claim that his study is empirically tested. Finally we hold the view that modern political scientists do not admit that there can be definite and scientifically tested morals and these can be usefully applied to political science. At least Tom Sorell thinks so. So we conclude that Hobbes's scientific materialism is not fully scientific. The credit of Hobbes is he did not base his theory on religion, ethics and morality.

HUMAN NATURE

Hobbes's social contract may not be fully historical or question may be raised about the scientificity of his thought, but one cannot question the logical consequence. People may question why did the inhabitants of the state of nature decide to set up a civil society? He has not given any scope. He has started his analysis with the depiction of human nature and this he has done in chapter XIII of *Leviathan* (1651). Let us quote few lines from this chapter :

Nature has made men so equal in the faculties of body and mind as that though there be found one man sometimes manifestly stronger in body or quicker in mind than another, yet when all is reckoned together, the difference between man and man is not so considerable. ... Men are in the point of equal than unequal. There is not ordinarily a greater sign of the equal distribution of anything. From this equality of ability arises equality of hope in attaining of our ends. If any two men desire the same thing they become enemies. They endeavour to destroy or subdue one another. In the nature of man we find three principal causes of quarrel, the competition, diffidence and glory. The first makes men invade for gain, the second for safety and the third for reputation.

Hobbes says that competition, glory and diffidence are the three characteristics of men who lived in the state of nature. These features of men created an atmosphere of animosity and there was none to stop or check it because there was no power to put an end to that undesirable situation. These three features of men created a condition of war. It was a war of everyman against everyman. The war was caused by man's desire to win the desired goal.

Hobbes has admitted that everyman in the state of nature was not rebellious; that is, he was not prepared to declare war against another. The real situation was some people were quarrelsome and this attitude instigated others which finally created a warlike situation. Again, every man thought that in no respect he is inferior to others and this mentality created unhealthy atmosphere. Man in the state of nature thought that he was not inferior to another man and this feeling led him to be involved in quarrel. Again, there was no end to the desire of man and because of this man jumped from one action to another. Since in the state of nature there was no recognisable power or authority to put restraints on the unbecoming behaviour of man, competition and quarrel continued to dominate the entire atmosphere of the state of nature.

Hobbes treated good and bad as subjective concepts and they fall within the private domain of individuals. Naturally, state has nothing to do. W. T. Jones says : "No man's judgment of value can be mistaken since his judgment "this is good" or "this is bad" is simply an expression of the motion of his body towards or away from object about which he makes judgement." In other words the decision of a men is not separate from their activities. By saying this Hobbes has imported the idea of motion into his analysis of human nature. The idea of motion thus works in the activities or behaviour of every man. We say that the behaviour of one person is the reaction to the behaviour of another man. Again, man is not concerned with the satisfaction of momentary desires. He wants his own preservation. To achieve this goal man seeks to get power and, in fact, there is no end to this desire.

STATE OF NATURE

We have just now concluded Hobbes's depiction of human nature. We shall now land on his description of state of nature. Needless to say that both these are well-connected. He has said that in the state of nature people were involved in continuous quarrel and according to him competition, diffidence and glory were the principal causes of quarrel. Hobbes very often called it war. However, it may not be actual war, it is warlike situation. This was war of everyman against everyman which means that the entire state of nature was in the brink of war or warlike atmosphere. In other words, the state of nature was not a place of peace and tranquillity, but tension and animosity. The animosity created a sense of insecurity of life. One man believed that another man was his enemy, but actually this was not. The ill-feeling and suspicion actually controlled the general atmosphere of state of nature.

After saying all these Hobbes opened his "Pandora's box" (I use it in special sense. His depiction of state of nature opens floodgates of issues). He says : In such a condition, there is no place for industries, because the fruit thereof is uncertain, and consequently no culture of the earth, no navigation, nor use of the commodities that may be imported by sea, no commodious building, no instruments of moving and removing such things, no knowledge, no account of time, no arts, no letters, no society, and which is worst of all, continual fear, and danger of violent death and the life of man, solitary, poor, nasty, brutish, and short (p. 186, Ch. 13). This was the picture of the state of nature. Hobbes admits that the picture of the state of nature depicted by him may not be universally correct. But in many places of America that situation prevailed.

Hobbes admits that all may not agree with his analysis of state of nature. But it is supposed that the state of nature will assume that picture because there was no general way of living and common manner to which everyone will have obligation. Again, in the state of nature there was no common power whom everyone will fear. Hence anarchy and warlike situation were the inevitable consequences. According to Hobbes, state of nature lacked the following : there was no well-defined law, there was no power to implement any decision, again, no authority to take decision. Most of the people were obstinate and competitive. They loved reputation or glory. Their nature was quarrelsome. In such an atmosphere there cannot prevail peace and security.

Critics generally argue that Hobbes's depiction of state of nature is full of sheer imagination, that is, it has no practical value. But on this ground we cannot reject Hobbesian conception of state of nature. He has said that in many places of world there was savage-like situation. Hobbes's depiction may not be fully correct, but the prevalence of anarchical situation cannot be denied. It has been asserted that in the state of nature there was law of nature and inhabitants followed or adopted this law of nature. Grotius, the noted authority of international law, at least claims so. The independent states sincerely followed the law of nature. The prevalence of law of nature cannot create any anarchy. We are, however, not interested in the historicity of the state of nature. It is said that he offered us this particular picture of state of nature keeping in mind the picture of his contemporary Britain.

SOCIAL CONTRACT

We have noted briefly the state of nature depicted by Hobbes. The question is how men "managed to get themselves out of the awfulness of the state of nature into civil society with its law and its reasonable degree of social stability"—J. S. MacClelland *History of Western Political Thought* (p. 194). By frightening or controlling other men the evils of the state of nature could not be avoided or overcome. It was thought that if all men were brought within the "orbit" of a single organisation and put under the administration of law the evils of the state of nature could be avoided. This is the best way. The "fear of punishment for breaking laws would be strong enough to secure obedience, then all might be well" (McClelland, p. 195). Hence the most powerful palliative to the evils of state of nature is the creation of a civil society along with a sovereign power of laws. Then the state of nature would never appear to be miserable.

After considering all the aspects of society Hobbes arrived at the conclusion that if a "common power" could be created through the instrument of covenant the awfulness of the state of nature could be overcome. He mentioned several things simultaneously. A covenant or contract would be finalised and all the members of the state of nature would be the party of the contract. Once a civil society is formed the separate existence of each member would be lost. All will create one person or one great multitude and the entire civil society would be a single unit. Hobbes writes : "The only way to erect such a common power, as may be able to defend them from the invasion of foreigners, and the injuries of one another...is to confer all their power and strength upon one man or the assembly of men" (Leviathan, p. 227, Part II, Chapter 17).

The central part of Hobbes's contract can be stated in the following words : "I authorise and give my right of governing myself to this man or to this assembly of men, on this condition, that thou give up thy right to him, and authorise all his actions in like manner. This done the multitude so united in one person, is called the commonwealth : in Latin Civitas. This is the generation of that great Leviathan or rather of that mortal God, to which we owe under the immortal God, our peace and defence" (p. 227).

If we go through the details of the social contract we shall find certain interesting **features** of the contract :

(1) The covenant created a society or body-politic which can be called a **legal institution.** In the state of nature there was no existence of such a legal institution because people did not create such body.

(2) The commonwealth or civil society is a common power and Hobbes calls it so. It is because different people may have their separate opinions but the commonwealth will be governed by one single opinion. That is, unanimity shall be the basis of commonwealth. It is not only a collective body but one person.

(3) The covenant created a new political organisation which is called state and this destroyed the past concept of society. In other words, in Hobbesian covenant, there is no legal status of society. The natural society, through the mechanism of contract, was converted into civil society.

(4) The contract establishes the idea that the principle of transition acts very actively. In the state of nature men were self-interest seeking creatures, unreasonable and quarrelsome. The contract completely changed their character. Again, there was a transition from anarchy to civil administration.

(5) In Hobbesian theory of contract there is no scope of divided opinion. One surrenders his earlier views, scope and rights on the condition that others will do the same. So we can say the foundation of the commonwealth is unanimity. Hobbes understood it very well that division of opinion would be detrimental to the foundation and interest of the civil society.

(6) Somehow the inhabitants of the state of nature realised that for the general security and welfare a commonwealth or civil society was indispensable. If some-one question why did the people of the state of nature realise this—there is no answer to this reasonable question. However, Hobbes has argued the whole concept in that way.

(7) Hobbes arrived at the conclusion that the creation of a commonwealth with unlimited power is panacea to all evils. But it is sheer naivety. It is the imagination of Hobbes that the erection of "Common power" will solve all the problems. But the matter may be looked from different angle. The anarchical condition of the British society he witnessed forced him to draw such a conclusion. Jean Bodin also thought that if there were an absolute power in France the most heinous Massacre could not get any opportunity to happen. So we do not find any unreasonability in the belief of Hobbes.

(8) There is a very reasonable and interesting point in Hobbes's contract theory. This is the transition from uncertainty to certainty, from lawlessness to lawful atmosphere, from physical power to reason. All the contractualists have spoken loudly about this transition though their language and techniques of analysis are different. Hobbes, Locke and Rousseau have all specially emphasised the idea of transition. Of course the society is always in the process of transition.

SOVEREIGNTY

The concluding para of chapter 17 makes the following announcement : "That person or assembly of persons is sovereign who is empowered to bring about peace and common defence." He uses the two words—sovereign and sovereign power—at the same breath. The attainment of sovereign power may take place in two ways—one is by natural force. This is the application of force. It means that a person with superior force may compel others to submit obedience to him. The application of natural force may assume the form of war. Other than the application of natural force there is another way of creating sovereign power, and it is, some men may agree among themselves to submit to some man or assembly of men voluntarily, on confidence, to be protected by him against all others. This second type of sovereignty is the characteristic feature of political commonwealth. Thus we see that two types of sovereign were quite active in the mind of Hobbes—sovereign created by institution and sovereign created by acquisition.

In Hobbes's theory sovereignty is absolutely an indispensable part of commonwealth. In chapter 18 Hobbes has further announced that the institution of commonwealth will never be complete without the creation of sovereign power. The creation of sovereign power will be completed in the manner the commonwealth was created or instituted. Hence we can say that the sovereignty is definitely an *integral part* of the commonwealth. The rights, responsibilities, powers and other "faculties" of sovereign are derived from the covenant. Since this sovereign is instituted it is different from the sovereignty by acquisition. It is interesting to note that Hobbes was in favour of sovereignty by institution though he finally made it absolute. It is again to be noted that Hobbes spoke of the institution of sovereignty by another covenant. He says : "From the institution of commonwealth are derived all the rights and faculties of him on whom the sovereign power is conferred by the consent of the people assembled." We thus find that after setting up of the civil society the contracting individuals proceeded to create sovereign power and there was the consent of the assembled men in this regard. "The consent of the assembled man" may be defined as a particular form of covenant.

Mere establishment of civil society is never the guarantor of the unity of people. The real and workable unity can be achieved through the institution of sovereignty. We think that this is an important part of Hobbes's theory of sovereignty. This particular aspect has been emphasised by J. S. McClelland in the following words : "The unity of a thing consists not in the thing represented but in its representor. A civil society acts only as a unity though the sovereign unity does not arise spontaneously, but is the deliberate creation of disparate human wills. ...It is important to remember that Hobbesian men do not come into civil society in order to change their natures. On the contrary, they enter civil society to fulfil their natures as rational egoists in so far as that is possible within the bounds of law" (p. 198). We, therefore, see that Hobbes's men were quite calculative. Their main purpose was to rationalise their irrational or unreasonable behaviour that was prevalent in the state of nature. They had no intention to abandon their egoistic attitude but to rationalise or civilise it through the instrumentality of sovereign power created by them.

Features of Sovereignty

1. The most important attribute of sovereignty is the new contract creating sovereignty and civil society would repudiate all the earlier contracts (if any) that people made in the state of nature because those contracts were not capable of fulfilling people's aspirations.
2. Sovereignty is not a party to the covenant and naturally he is not bound by the terms of the contract. People transfer their rights and other privileges which they enjoyed in the state of nature. That is, they make the sovereign their agent at large. They authorise the sovereignty.
3. Sovereignty is incapable of injuring anybody—why? Hobbes says that the state of nature has a law of nature to govern it and the law of nature is God's command and in the civil society nobody has any power to disobey the command of God that prevailed in state of nature.
4. Some critics say that the covenant may not have the support of everyone. Hobbes had a belief that the covenant must be supported by majority of men and it will make it voted.
5. The sovereign has no power to kill or invalidate his subjects and, in the same way, the subjects cannot kill sovereign.
6. The sovereign has been empowered to settle all matters regarding internal peace.
7. An important job of sovereign is to censor all religions opinions and decide on forms of worship. Sovereign cannot change the inner form of faith, but it can determine the expression for public interests.
8. All courts in the land shall be his courts and the decisions of the courts shall be treated as sovereign's decision.
9. It is not possible to perform all the activities of the state by the sovereign himself. He can take help and advice from others. Others will discharge functions on his behalf, but they will be in the name of sovereignty.

ASSESSMENT

Hobbes's theory of sovereignty is absolute in the sense that people or members of the contract who lived in the state of nature made him all-powerful almost in all respects. Let us quote few words, in support of our view, from *Leviathan* : "And covenants, without swords, are but words and of no strength to secure a man at all." He continues : "The bonds of words are too weak to bridle men's ambition, avarice, anger, and other passions, without the fear of some coercive power." He has also said that in one hand of the sovereign authority there shall be a law book and in the other hand he will hold a sword. He will first of all try to rule with the help of law and any failure will force him to use the sword. The simple implication is, according to Hobbes, sword is the best way to put everything under control. The law book is simply a symbol. This is the picture of absolute sovereignty. Hobbes has called his sovereign Leviathan and the dictionary meaning of the word is : a sea monster, a very large aquatic creature, something very large and powerful, an autocratic monarch.

Critics are of opinion that Hobbes has depicted the picture of sovereignty in this way deliberately. He had somehow formed the opinion that in order to control the unruly behaviour of the people of state of nature a ruler with absolute power was needed. An ordinary ruler would be an inappropriate selection. We, therefore, hold the view that the creation of an absolute sovereignty is not an unthoughtful creation. There was enough thought and plan.

J. S. McChelland has assessed Hobbes's theory of sovereignty from different perspective. He says : Hobbes's account of sovereignty is sovereignty on the grand scale. It is worth repeating that Hobbes infers all the attributes of sovereignty from the original case of voluntary contract by institution, and only then does he say that conquest sovereignty by acquisition would enjoy the same rights" (p. 208).

The idea that resided in the topmost place of his mind is that a weak sovereign power with a lot of limitations might be a welcome venture but it would never be a welcome suggestion for the stability and general well being for the common-wealth. Therefore J. S. McChelland is right when he says—"Hobbes is above all concerned with laying the ideological groundwork for an undisputatious and therefore stable commonwealth" (p. 208).

Hobbes's sovereignty is outside the contract, that is, he is not party to the contract and on that ground he is not obliged to obey the terms and conditions of the contract. He will govern according to the rules of the contract, but he may not obey the rules and this condition makes him absolute. War making is the ultimate act of sovereignty—*ultima ratio regis*—the king's final argument. Since sovereign resides above everything else the subjects have no legal right or power to accuse him of doing or not doing anything. It is the primary responsibility of the sovereignty to keep the law and order of the commonwealth within contract. We think this is the basic duty of the sovereign. He may seek advice of others, but he is not bound to act in accordance with the advice. Arguing in this way Hobbes reminds us the political and administrative situation in England that prevailed in his time. English monarch had a group of advisers, but he did not always act in accordance with their advice. Hobbes's sovereign simply repeats it.

ABSOLUTISM AND INDIVIDUALISM

Hobbes's concept of sovereignty reveals certain basic elements of absolutism and on the ground his critics have arrived at the conclusion that he was a supporter of absolutism. This allegation is not without any reason. We have stated that the sovereignty is not a party to the contract and, naturally, he is not legally bound by its terms. This automatically makes the sovereign power absolute which means that in his idea of sovereignty there are powerful elements of absolutism. According to Hobbes, subjects are bound to show obligation to the sovereignty. But the sovereign's accountability to people is not admitted. His love for absolutism can be argued from another angle. Hobbes ruled out the division of sovereign power. The division of sovereign power would have ruled out the possibility of absoluteness.

Hobbes's absolutism can be justified from another angle. He did not endorse people's right to express opinion freely. The sovereign power may censor opinions, particularly religious opinions. He has also the power to lay down lawful rules for public worship. This means that freedom of faith and worship has no place in Hobbes's philosophy. The sovereign will have power to interfere in the judicial system. In Hobbes's state system, public opinion has no place. The sovereignty will rule the state with law and sword. This is nothing but sheer absolutism. It is generally argued that Hobbes gave maximum importance to the unity and integrity of civil society and in his mind there was no place of man's freedom and opinion. Integrity of the state is very important no doubt, but for it individuals freedom cannot be sacrificed. The fact is that Hobbes has done it. These are the chief elements of absolutism in Hobbes's thought.

Hobbes's political thought is full of several anomalies and one such anomaly is he was a great worshipper of absolutism and simultaneously he was an individualist, or at least there are several elements of individualism in his thought. There is an important chapter in his *Leviathan*—Chapter XXI of *Part II which deals with, inter alia,* the individualism. The headline of the chapter is of the Liberty of Subject. He has defined liberty in the following words : "Liberty or freedom signifies the absence of opposition. By opposition I mean external impediments of motion" (p. 261). According to Hobbes a freeman is he who is able to do and is not hindered to do what he has a will to. So we find that in Hobbes's thought system persons on individuals were not reduced to insignificant elements. People may have their own thoughts and plan to work and when they are given full opportunity to perform those works, it will be taken for granted that they have freedom. It is interesting to note that in the second half of the seventeenth century Hobbes was quite alert of individuals' freedom and the proof of his alertness is he has devoted a chapter for the analysis of individuals' freedom.

Hobbes says that to get rid of the drawbacks of the state of nature people created an "artificial man" and this artificial man is the commonwealth. He wants to say that in creating a commonwealth people exercised their freedom. That is, they were not forced or induced by others to set up a commonwealth. Again, along with the creation of commonwealth, or, in his word, artificial man, they also made artificial chains, that is civil laws. It is to be noted that people deliberately created artificial chains, that is laws, for the proper management and stability of the commonwealth. They were quite aware that the laws would curtail the quantum of liberty; notwithstanding they made some civil laws. Hence the laws cannot be treated as impediment to freedom. He has further defined liberty in the following manner. The liberty of a subject lies, therefore, only in those things which, in regulating their actions, the sovereign has permitted, such as in the liberty to buy and sell and otherwise contract with one another, to choose their own abode, their own diet, their own trade of life and institute their children as they themselves think fit and the like" (p. 264). In this passage Hobbes has stated in no uncertain terms that in several spheres individuals will enjoy unhindered freedom and none has any authority to prevent him.

There are also other aspects of individualism. For example, the sovereign cannot order any person to kill or wound himself. Or, if anyone attacks, the person shall have the right to defend himself. That is, every individual has the right of self-defence. Individuals have the right to live and for that purpose they can take food, medicine and other necessary things that they require. The sovereign has no power to force a man to confess something. Another aspect of his individualism is the sovereign cannot force a person to join army if he provides a substitute. In case of any controversy with the sovereign the individual can demand justice and the method of demanding justice shall be decided by the person concerned. The individuals have the right to earn property and enjoy the benefits.

J. S. McClelland thinks that it is unreasonable to brand Hobbes as totalitarian. McClelland's arguments run as follows : When the people of the state of nature decided to set up a civil society, they did it without being forced or influenced by anybody. In other words they did it on their own volition which means that the individuals enjoyed autonomy. Naturally we can say that Hobbes admitted individual's freedom of thought and action. McClelland further argues that Hobbes met Descartes and Galileo. He was impressed by Harvey's discovery that blood circulated. We have already noted that he came under the influence of motion and gravity. Both internal and external motion control human happiness. He cannot pursue happiness endlessly. So these types of persons cannot be totalitarian-minded. They know how far to proceed. Hobbes also never indulged in totalitarianism.

C. B. Macpherson is also a well-known interpreter of Hobbes's political thought. His *The Political Theory of Possessive Individualism, Hobbes to Locke*—is a well-read and widely discussed book. Hobbes's men are aggressive, self-interest seeking marketmen. His men are possessive individualists. They always want realisation of their own interest and these interests relate to economic interests. Economic problems were of great importance to them; such persons are not generally totalitarian-minded. Hobbes was chiefly concerned with such persons and he has pictured their nature keeping in mind their basic nature and primary objective. Hobbes's men were aggressive no doubt, but that aggressiveness does not fall into the category of absolutism or totalitarianism.

WAS HOBBES A TOTALITARIAN ?

The critics of Hobbes's philosophy have discovered the shadow of totalitarianism in his analysis. Ebenstein believes that this is mainly due to the reason that his critics or opponents were great believers of parliamentary form of government. Particularly the people of the English speaking world were against absolutism. Naturally they had no intention to endorse the absolutist philosophy of Hobbes. Ebenstein concludes : "yet to call Hobbes one of the spiritual fathers of totalitarian fascism or communism is more untenable than would appear from a cursory glance at several key phrases in the Leviathan" (*The Great Political Thinkers*, p. 363). His certain uses carry the idea of totalitarianism. For example the parties to the contract handed over all the powers and authority to the sovereign. Only in a totalitarian form of government this can happen. Hobbes's sovereignty is all-powerful. His other comments carry the meaning of totalitarianism. But Ebenstein says that *Hobbes's state is authoritarian but not totalitarian.* Hobbes's sovereign authority is a supreme administrator and, at the same time, a lawgiver. In earlier centuries the supreme administrator was more or less a lawmaker. But this need not make a man totalitarian. The term totalitarian has a different meaning in political science. Hobbes has made enough scope for freedom of action and exercise of thought. He never made his subject slave. Finally we argue that Hobbes was not a totalitarian, but this does not imply that he was a democrat. Let us again quote Ebenstein : "The Hobbesian state finds its realisation in neither the modern democratic state nor the totalitarian dictatorship of the Nazi, Fascist or Soviet communist brand" (p. 365).

BOURGEOIS PHILOSOPHY

In recent years Hobbes's political philosophy has been scanned from various perspectives and one of the perspectives is : Hobbes wrote *Leviathan* to support the cause and economic interests of the nascent bourgeois class or capitalists. C. B. Macpherson is the pioneer in this field. J. S. McClelland also falls in the same category. McClelland says (p. 224) that Hobbes was thinking of a market society. Its implication is men's requirements are fulfilled by the market. C. B. Macpherson observes : "We live in market society, our behaviours our values are largely shaped, directly or indirectly, by the requirements of the market. We are bourgeois men. So were the men Hobbes described and analysed. ...His scientific method required him to build up a model of man and of society and the models he constructed were bourgeois models" (C. B. Macpherson edited *Leviathan, Introduction*, p. 12). Hobbes built up the model of a bourgeois society and it is perfect bourgeois. Hobbes apprehended that if there was no law and its proper application, if anarchy could be the prevailing characteristic of society industry, trade and commerce would be the greatest victim. That is, all these were to be adversely affected. We hold the view that Hobbes was seriously thinking of the industrial development under the stewardship of the rising capitalists.

Macpherson has argued that Hobbes's system of taxation is absolutely bourgeois. He supported the taxation on the ground that if sovereign power imposes heavy tax that will finally augment the government treasury and at the same time private businessmen will be financially benefited. The authority must make arrangement for the collection of taxes and remove the loopholes of evasion. He was a supporter of the concept that the policy of the state must aim at the development of capitalism. Keeping this in mind he prepared a model of a civil society based on capitalism. Apparently his civil society or commonwealth or mortal god is political. But beneath this political image there lies a perfect economic model. Hobbes has treated labour as a commodity and the same thing we find in capitalism. The following statement may be cited in support of the above : "A man's labour, also, is a commodity exchangeable for benefit, as well as any other thing." This comment of Hobbes is in complete similarity of capitalist conception.

Hobbes did not accept the theory of distributive justice. The central idea of distributive justice is there shall be arrangement for equal benefit to all men of equal merit. That is, all the persons of the same merit or work will get equal reward and any variation of this principle will mean violation of distributive justice. Hobbes rejected the concept of distributive justice. Commenting on Hobbes's idea about distributive justice and other related views Macpherson says : "From his treatment of distributive it is clear that Hobbes accepted not only the fact but also the justice of market society. The sovereign state he has justified is a bourgeois state" (*Introduction to Leviathan*, p. 51).

Hobbes has asserted that in the state of nature there was no security of life and property. Both these were too dear to the members of the state of nature. So for the clear purpose and enjoyment of property people created a civil society whose head will be a sovereignty with unlimited power. Hence the chief function of the sovereign power is to protect property of citizens. Elsewhere he has said that there are many things which are dear to man but the dearest of these are man's limbs, riches and property. If the sovereign power fails to provide proper security to property its utility will face a big question mark. In other words, the sovereign power must make arrangements for the protection of riches and property. This is undoubtedly a bourgeois mentality. That is why Macpherson has said that Hobbes's state is a bourgeois state and the safety of the people means the safety of the property.

Hobbes believed that the perpetuation of absolute sovereignty would facilitate the growth of bourgeois interests or capitalism. In this regard his suggestion is the sovereign power whether single person or an assembly will have the power to nominate its successor. That is, a sovereign power before its departure will select the successor. Even the assembly will have the power to select its successor. In this way the perpetuation of one sovereign power will be properly done. This is called self-perpetuating sovereign. The growth of capitalism and perpetuation of sovereign are closely related ideas in Hobbes's political philosophy. Macpherson says that for the realisation of capitalists interest perpetuation of sovereignty was required and he understood it fully.

UTILITARIANISM

Some interpreters of Hobbes's political philosophy claim that he may be regarded as one of the founders of utilitarianism. It is true that, like Bentham and J. S. Mill, Hobbes did not specifically deal with utilitarianism. But if we go through his analysis of state of nature and foundation of civil society we shall find that the concept of utility was quite active in his mind. The people in the state of nature were faced with certain insurmountable problems and these ultimately made their lives hell. Therefore they decided to leave that atmosphere and lay the foundation of a civil society which would be able to meet their basic needs such as the protection of life, riches or property and ensure all sorts of security. So in Hobbes's model we find two societies—one is society that existed in nature. Some people may refuse to call it a society. We, however, call it a nature society where there was no administration, no government, no law etc. Because of this the life in the state of nature was not peaceful at all. This situation forced the members of the state of nature to find out an alternative and that is why they set up a civil society. They somehow gathered the idea that the civil society could meet their basic requirements. In other words, the civil society has utility. So the idea of utility arose in the mind of Hobbes or in the minds of the people of state of nature. But civil society without law is a misnomer and for that reason the members of the new society decided to make law, and the law-making power was absolutely vested in the hands of the sovereignty. Hence Hobbes gave a short outline of the famous theory of utilitarianism. But the fact is that he did not think the concept in that line. We have deduced the idea of utilitarianism from his analysis.

MACHIAVELLI, BODIN AND HOBBES ON SOVEREIGNTY

Machiavelli (1469–1527), Bodin (1529–1596) and Hobbes (1588–1679) dealt with the most important and vexed issue–the sovereignty. But Machiavelli did not directly analyse the idea. The interpreters of his political ideas, however, have deduced certain features of sovereignty from his long and variegated advice to the prince. On the other hand, Bodin and Hobbes directly dealt with the concept. We have noted that Jean Bodin, the great sixteenth century French philosopher, was of opinion that the religious and civil problem as well as conflicts could easily be solved if there were a sovereign power with unlimited authority at his disposal. Because with the help of this unrestricted power he could control the unruly behaviour of some groups of persons or individuals. Bodin concluded this because he was the witness of the great Bartholomew Massacre (1572). Bodin thought of a well-ordered government with absolute sovereign power. Bodin had an idea that the French Government of his time was not capable of controlling the recalcitrant elements. He was of opinion that a government must have enough power to control any problem that might threaten the peace, and harmony of society. Again, the sovereignty must have unlimited power to make law. He in his *Six Books on Commonwealth* made the following observation : "There are none on earth, after God, greater than sovereign princes, whom God establishes as His lieutenants to command the rest of mankind" To sum up, Bodin's sovereignty is absolute and enjoys unlimited power.

Machiavelli did not directly deal with the idea of sovereignty. But we think that he was a great supporter of absolute power and he always advised his prince to exercise absolute power to achieve his objective which is the unification of Italy. Machiavelli thought that the sole objective of the prince must be to unify the various warring states of Italy. It was his belief that the main cause of backwardness of Italy was the internecine conflict among the several parts of Italy. Whatever might be the cause of disunity or division, Machiavelli's chief concern was to unify Italy and if this could not be achieved the progress would remain a distant hope. Machiavelli advised his prince to apply absolute power whenever necessary and in this regard he must not hesitate.

Machiavelli's concept of sovereignty is not well built and academically of high standard. David Held (*Political Theory and the Modern State*, p. 220) says : Bodin was a critic of Machiavelli's defence of centralised power—a defence of which, Bodin held firmly placed the ends of the state or community above these of individual subject and uncritically affirmed that "reasons of state" held priority over the rights of individuals. In contrast to Machiavelli, Bodin sought to show that a sovereign authority could only be properly established if the body-politic was regarded as being composed of both ruler and the ruled. To Machiavelli sovereignty was simply a type of power which the prince could use. On the other hand, to Bodin, sovereignty was an element of state. Bodin was a man of jurisprudence and that is why he viewed it from the standpoint of law. Whereas Machiavelli was a statesman. For this reason we find differences in the approaches of two persons. It is, however, interesting to note that both Machiavelli and Bodin emphasised the unity of state. Machiavelli advised his prince to neglect or deny morality and religion. But Bodin never said so.

Machiavelli's theory of sovereignty is not well-argued and elegant. But we witness all these qualities in the theory of Bodin. Almost all the characteristics of "classical' theory of sovereignty are found in Bodin's theory. But Hobbes's theory is better than Bodin's. It is logical and well-structured. People in the state of nature suffered a lot of insecurity and other hazards in day-to-day life and that made their everyday life miserable. This led them to find a way out and for that reason they set up a civil society and placed an absolute power at the top of the organisation that is body-politic. Drawing a comparison between Bodin and Hobbes David Held makes the following observation : "Hobbes provided one of the most elegant rationales for the primacy of the state....and for the necessary unity of the state as the representative of the body-politic, and for the necessity of the state as the creator and maintenance of positive law. Like Bodin, he wrote against the background of social disorder and political instability, in this case, the English civil war. Like Bodin, he sought to establish the necessity of an all-powerful sovereign capable of securing the conditions of peaceful and commodious living" (p. 221). We thus find that both Bodin and Hobbes wrote their theory of sovereignty being influenced by prevailing circumstances and they also thought that only an absolute sovereign power was the real remedy to the undesirable and harmful situation.

Hobbes's sovereignty is the product of the covenant. There were several stages. At the preliminary level the people of the state of nature abandoned that atmosphere assembled together, decided to set up a body-politic; created a sovereign power and at the penultimate stage handed over all the civil, legal and various other powers at the hands of the absolute sovereignty. No conditions of serious nature were imposed upon the exercise of sovereign power. Of course, there were few exceptions and those were not supposed to curtail the power of the sovereignty considerably. Bodin's sovereignty had to face certain limitations.

So far as the concept of sovereignty in these three cases (Machiavelli, Bodin and Hobbes) is concerned there is a very interesting similarity among the three. This is, all the three were great admirers and supporters of the nation-state. Machiavelli could not tolerate the multiple divisions of Italy. He wanted a strong and powerful nation-state and it was his firm belief that such a state was the powerful precondition of progress. We know that the most vital elements of nation-state are specific geographical area, a government with absolute power, and a well-ordered administration. Machiavelli, Bodin and Hobbes have all emphasised these three vital elements of nation-state in one way or other. Machiavelli strongly supported a strong and unified Italy. In Bodin's mind the picture of a strong and well-administered France was very active and clear. Hobbes laid the foundation of the nation-state. Before the setting up of a state people lived in the state of nature and the state of nature in the remotest sense cannot be regarded as a state or nation-state. Bodin was perhaps convinced that the religious strife and other troubles posed dangerous situation for the very physical existence of a state. All of them were led to believe that only the erection of absolute sovereign power could act as a saviour.

ASSESSMENT

There are divergent assessments about Hobbes, a political philosopher, and Maxey has offered us some of them (Maxey—*Political Philosophies*, pp. 230-231). Dunning's opinion is : "His work placed him at once in the front rank of political thinkers and his theory became from the moment of its appearance the centre of animated controversy and enormous influence throughout Western Europe." But other interpreters of Hobbes's political philosophy do not agree with Dunning. The language of their criticism is unpalatable. For example H. R. Murray (*The History of Political Science From Plato to the Present*) writes : "Hobbes's biographer could only find a solitary supporter, while his assailants were countless. Hobbism stood for atheist materialism, despotism or indeed for any other 'ism' that the fancy of the age suggested." In evaluating the importance of Hobbes's thought R. G. Gettel writes : "The theory of Hobbes had little immediate following in English political thought, although it probably influenced Cromwell to assume dictatorial power. His doctrines were not revived in England until the second half of the eighteenth century in the works of Bentham and Austin."

C. B. Macpherson in his *Introduction* to *Leviathan* has raised a very pertinent question which runs as follows—why, in the second half of the twentieth century, do we still read Hobbes who wrote three centuries ago? He has also raised few other questions and has given replies. Macpherson's opinion is—the world in which we live is highly preoccupied with numerous problems related to power. Now if we go through the *Leviathan* we shall find that Hobbes's analysis chiefly deals with power. Although Hobbes has analysed the various aspects of power he did throw enough light upon how to harness power or how to utilities it for proper development of society.

Hobbes, we know, also applied science to the study of politics and this approach has been appreciated by a large number of the interpreters of Hobbes's philosophy. Finally, Hobbes wanted to establish peace in a highly disturbed society. So there were three main concerns of Hobbes, power, science and peace. Today we are also concerned with these three. C. B. Macpherson rightly says : "So we may say that the twentieth century has brought us closer to an appreciation of Hobbes on three counts : power, peace and science" (*Introduction*, p. 11). In both national and international spheres there is problem of power. The nations are struggling for power. In the sphere of national politics there are numerous groups which are either directly or indirectly involved in power and power politics. Hobbes's love for science and motion and their application in political science really impress us. Sabine has rightly said that he was the first man to apply science to politics.

David Held has appreciated Hobbes's importance from another angle. He says (*Political Theory and the Modern State*, p. 225-226)—Hobbes drew a direct comparison between international relations and the state of nature. He described the international system of states as being in a continuous posture of war. Today the peace-loving people of the world have set up United Nations for the maintenance of international peace and security and has armed the key organ of the United Nations—the Security Council—with enormous power. In the middle of the seventeenth century Hobbes created a civil society and placed a sovereign power at the top of the civil society. He prescribed that in one hand of the sovereign there shall be a sword and in the other a law book. All these arrangements are for the sake of peace.

Today Hobbes's political ideas have relevance in the field of international politics. Held writes : In the study of international affairs Hobbes's account has become associated with the realist theory of international politics. Realism posits, in the spirit of Hobbes's work, that the system of sovereign states is inescapably anarchic in character and that this anarchy forces all states to pursue power politics in order to attain their vital interests. The approach of Hobbes can suitably be termed as *Real politik.* Hobbes's concern was neither morality nor religion but simply security; and he openly declared that without security and absence of anarchy there was no scope of development in economy, progress in commerce and advancement in transport and communication.

"Nor did any political thinker ever formulate better grounds than Hobbes for the suppression of revolution and rebellion. Abraham Lincoln of necessity fell back on the Hobbesian conception of social compact and sovereignty in order to find justification for the use of force in quelling the secession of the South" (Maxey, op. cit. p. 233). Maxey continues : "If Hobbes was a materialist, he was also a rationalist, and rationalism, not to say realism, in copious doses was needed to shock political thought out of the academic obfuscation in which in Hobbes's time it tended to become enveloped." To sum up, Hobbes's *Leviathan* is really fascinating. We may not agree with his observations, conclusions and methods. But there is no doubt that in the prevailing circumstances his suggesting or recommendations were by far the best. While evaluating Hobbes's contribution we must remember it.

14 JOHN LOCKE

Introductory

We have discussed Hobbes's version of social contract. We shall now turn to another eminent interpreter of social contract and he is John Locke. Locke was born in 1632 (44 years after the birth of Hobbes) in a well-established famous family and died in 1704. His father was an Orthodok Christian and he wanted his son to study and cultivate religion. But Locke showed least interest in religion. He began to study medicine. Some of his biographers say that his study of medicine helped him to be associated with the royal family. He had a chance of first meeting in 1666 with Anthony Ashley Cooper and later on Cooper became Earl of Shaftsbury. He also came in touch with other important families and persons. All these helped him to build up his career. But Locke's relation with the royal family did not last long. A sort of bitterness developed between Locke and the royal family on religious and political grounds and this disheartened him. He went to Holland and stayed there some time. While in Holland he developed cordial relationship with William. When William became king of England Locke was appointed a commissioner of commerce and plantation. From his life we come to know that he came in contact with trade, commerce and administration and from all these he earned huge experience. At the age of 54 he first established himself as an author. His important works include *Essays on Human Understanding, Letters Concerning Toleration*. His most famous book—*Two Treatises on Civil Government* was published in or around 1690. Many people are of opinion that Locke wrote this book to justify the Glorious Revolution of 1688. But this view has been contested by some.

Maurice Cranston in his noted essay published in Thompson-edited *Political Ideas* says that much before the Glorious Revolution the book was written. Let us quote few lines from Cranston's article. He says : "There is the idea that the book was written to justify the Glorious Revolution of 1688." Cranston further observes : "It now seems that the book was written something like ten years before the Glorious Revolution" (p. 74). According to Cranston this date is interesting. Of course the book was published after the Revolution. Some people are of opinion that the Glorious Revolution did not take place abruptly. Discontent was simmering and favourable situation for the Revolution was developing. Locke was acquainted with it and it may safely be assumed that he had sympathy for the Revolution. He became known as the philosopher of the Glorious Revolution—Cranston observes in this way.

It is said that Locke's *Two Treatises* is to some extent a polemical work. But Cranston is of opinion that it is immaterial. It is a good book of politics and philosophy. Particularly it has left behind a message of liberalism and a responsible government. Locke's *Two Treatises* is not an ordinary book. It is at par with Plato's *Republic* and J. S. Mill's *Essay on Liberty*. "Locke's work is both theoretical and didactic. He passes from the particular question of his own duty to his own king to the general question of any man's duty to any ruler and so to the problems of obligations and of sovereignty at the highest level of abstraction" (Thompson—Political Ideas, p. 75). The basic problems Locke dealt with are to be found today. His concepts of consent, responsibility of the ruler to the people, constitutionalism, basic liberties—all these still haunt us. Today in the twenty-first century we remember Locke for his ideas about rulers' obligation to the ruled.

LOCKE'S VERSION OF STATE OF NATURE

Like Thomas Hobbes, Locke starts his analysis with a hypothetical state of nature and in chapter II consisting of 12 sections (sections 4 to 15) he has discussed various aspects of the imaginary state of nature. In Locke's opinion the state of nature was a state of perfect freedom. They had the liberty to do anything and everything. But according to Locke it was not a state of license because in the state of nature law of nature was quite operative. This law of nature which was the embodiment of reason prevented men from doing harmful work. "The state of nature has a law of nature to govern it, which obliges everyone, and reason....teaches all mankind....being all equal and independent, no one ought to harm another in his life, health, liberty or possession. Locke says that none shall be deprived of life, health, liberty and possessions or property. But in actual situation this did not happen.

In the state of nature everybody had full freedom to do whatever he desired. They were guided by law of nature and its reason. But the problem is what is exactly the law of nature and its reason that was not known to the inhabitants of the state of nature. Since the law of nature and its reason were not properly clarified and executed every man has a right to punish another man and very often that happened. It is due to the fact that in the state of nature there was no authority to explain and execute the law of nature. People of the state of nature enjoyed unlimited freedom. But this unlimited freedom of some stood on the way of enjoying freedom for others. Locke has said that the people of the state of nature sometimes inflicted harm or injury upon others. But this they did not out of any bad motive but out of ignorance. But this does not mean that they were perfectly honest.

From Locke's version we come to know that they were in-between morality and immorality. Though the people of the state of nature observed the law of nature, what was exactly this law was that created the problem. Locke claims that in the state of nature there prevailed peace and order but that in a limited scale and because of this in the state of nature disorder very often raised its head. Locke is of opinion that it was the problem.

G. N. Gough is a renowned interpreter of Lockean philosophy. Gough says that he never meant that the law of nature was the supreme authority and everyone had clear conception about it. In Gough's view that was the problem. Misuse of the law of nature was quite rampant or prevalent. Gough has cautioned us by saying that we must not be emotional or over-enthusiastic about Locke's law of nature. Gough has said : The law of nature is for him the moral standard to which all men, including governors themselves, should conform, and his insistence on it is the foundation of his case for limited constitutional government instead of the arbitrary power so dreaded and hated by contemporary Englishmen (*John Locke's Political Philosophy*, pp. 25-26).

Locke has claimed that in the state of nature there were several inconveniences. Dunning has beautifully stated that the state of nature as conceived by Locke is a pre-political rather than pre-social condition. In this single and small sentence Dunning has stated the real picture of Lockean state of nature. The state of nature imagined by Locke was never the heaven on earth. But it was not definitely hell. Hobbes imagined that the state of nature was a hell—nasty, brutish and short. In this regard Locke differs from Hobbes and this he clearly stated in sections 19 and 20. In section 19 Locke says : "The plain difference between the state of nature and the state of war which however some men have confounded are as far distant as a state of peace, good-will, mutual assistance, and preservation. Men living together according to reason, without a common superior on earth with authority to judge between them is properly the state of nature." It is clear that Locke in this passage has unequivocally clarified the nature of state of nature. His words "some men" mean Hobbes. Hobbes depicted the state of nature but Locke states that it is a state of peace, goodwill, mutual assistance and preservation. Locke has further stated that in the state of nature there was no common judge with authority. There were aberrations or violations of law of nature. But without a common superior authority, there was none on earth to appeal. This was the most important inconvenience of the state of nature.

Locke has also admitted that the people of the state of nature were very often guided by reason and good motive and in that situation they wanted to settle the disputes among themselves. But mere attempts or gesture were not sufficient. Barker, explaining Locke's view, says that the people of that atmosphere ardently desired to get rid of the difficulties of the state of nature and this thought finally motivated them to set up an authority who will implement the law of nature, to judge whether the implementation is impartial and proper. They also decided to institute an authority whose function would be to enforce same law in a uniform manner. If all these steps are adopted the state of nature will not be an abode of disunity and trouble, it will be an abode of peace and tranquility.

SOCIAL CONTRACT

In section 13 Locke says : "I easily grant that civil government is the proper remedy for the inconveniences of the state of nature, which must certainly be great where men may be judges in their own case." The proper remedy to the inconveniences of the state of nature is the erection of a civil government and the civil government alone cannot be the provider of remedy, a civil society was necessary. The members of the state of nature felt that a judge was badly needed because only a judge with sufficient authority can put everything in order which was lacking in the state of nature.

Though Locke refuted Hobbes's idea of state of war in the state of nature we hear him saying "men living together according to reason, without a common superior on earth with authority to judge between them, is properly the state of nature. But force upon the person of another, where there is no common superior to appeal for relief, is the state of war. ...To avoid this state of war...is one great reason of men's putting themselves into society and quitting the state of nature, for where there is an authority, a power on earth...there the continuance of the state of war is excluded (Sections 20 & 21). We thus see that Locke is, here, quite clear about his intention regarding the erection of civil society. Power was the best remedy to all evils that plagued the people of the state of nature. Why? In section 3 he says : "Political power, I take to be a right of making laws with penalties of death and consequently, all less penalties for the regulating and preserving of property and of employing the force of the community in the execution of such laws and in the defence of the commonwealth from foreign injury."

If we go through the entire process of social contract we shall find certain basic **features.** It was felt by the people of the state of nature that setting up of a civil society was the proper remedy to all inconveniences that people witnessed. Hence we can conclude that social contract was a sort of mechanism that was used by the people to save from certain difficulties. Hobbes also saw this in the same light. In the opinion of Dunning the Lockean social contract was *pre-political but not pre-social*. That is, people of the state of nature maintained amongst themselves social behaviour and manner which means that there was sociability among them. Contract politicised the society. Social contract was itself a mechanism or weapon. Again, the contract empowered the people to control the government to act in accordance with the conditions laid down in the contract. According to the term of the contract people may or can demand security in various forms. If we go through the contract we shall find that everyone gave consent to the preparation of the contract and it is called the tacit consent. Some interpreters of Locke's philosophy argue that the inhabitants of the state of nature did two contracts—one is written and the other is unwritten. Before making social contract people did an unwritten contract among themselves and the objective of that contract was they desire to set up a civil society through a contract for better and safe living.

Recent interpreters of Locke's political thought have said that Locke thought of double contract. The source of this idea comes from the words stated in sections 95, 97 and in several other sections. In section 97 we find him saying : "everyman, by consenting with others to make one body-politic under one government, puts himself under an obligation to everyone of that society to submit to the determination of the majority and to be concluded by it, or else, this original compact whereby he with others incorporates into one society." Here the two words—"original compact" are very significant. We can easily assume that he had in mind the existence of another contract, otherwise he could not use the word "original". We can assume that after making one compact, the people made another compact. The first compact set up a body-politic or civil society and the second compact enabled them the *modus operandi* of the management of body-politic.

Locke was not satisfied by setting up a body-politic or commonwealth or civil society. The civil society to him was not simply a state, it must be a complete democracy and it is assumed that to achieve this another compact was made. Let us see what he says in section 132 : "By commonwealth it must be understood to mean not a democracy or any form of government but any independent community which the Latins signified by the word *civitas.*" According to Locke the word *civitas* means commonwealth. The administration and control of the body-politic shall be in the hands of the people. Perhaps this was in the mind of Locke and in order to do this there arose the necessity of another contract and Locke has done this. Locke was out and out a democrat. He had no intention to follow the footsteps of Hobbes, that is, to set an absolute power through the contract. One compact will lay the foundation of a civil society and another compact will make it a *civitas* or commonwealth.

LIBERALISM

J. S. McClelland (*History of Western Political Thought*, p. 242) writes : "Liberals have always shown a certain fondness for Locke, and it is easy to see why. Certain assumptions which Locke makes, certain attitudes which he held and certain arguments which he uses, fit in well with the doctrine which at the beginning of the nineteenth century came to be called liberalism." J. S. McClelland wants to say that in the *Second Treatise* Locke makes several comments which clearly lay the foundation of liberalism.

He says that property is a natural right and simultaneously it is inviolable. Property can, however, be taken but behind this there must be free and voluntary consent of the owner. Locke has said that in the state of nature people enjoyed the facilities of private property but because of certain inconveniences of the state of nature the enjoyment of the benefits of private property very often faced interruptions. This situation inspired them to set up a system of administration that could give guarantee right to property. The right to property was so important to Locke that without the consent of people or owner of the property nobody had any right to levy taxes on property. That is levy of tax must be preceded by owner's consent.

Locke wrote a book *Letter Concerning Toleration*. This book conveys his idea about liberalism. He has said that everybody should practise toleration about others and this toleration will teach people not to intervene in the private affairs of other individuals. To put it in other words, the right to privacy is a basic right and the democratic states have admitted it and made it a part of the constitutional rights.

Rationality or rational behaviour is an essential feature of liberalism and its existence in Lockean philosophy has encouraged them to find out liberalism in Locke. The liberals claim that in the Lockean analysis of contract there is enough emphasis on rationality. The individuals are well-aware of their rights as well as responsibility to other fellow citizens and society. The liberals call it rationality. Another manifestation of Locke's idea of rationality is that they formed a civil society for the proper protection and utilisation of natural rights and somehow they were confident that only in a *civitas* it is possible and for that purpose they made a second compact. It indicates their rationality. It is also said that to live in a civil society implies obligations. That is, in the state of nature the people had no feeling of obligation. But in civil society everyone must have the feeling of obligation, Locke's people had that feeling.

Another element of Locke's theory of social contract is "Lockean model of society is competitive capitalist model. Men are free to acquire and are encouraged by God to do so." Free competition and capitalism are important parts or aspects of liberal philosophy. In Locke's time capitalism was in embryonic stage and its proper development required congenial atmosphere and Locke, through the instrumentality of contract, wanted to ensure this.

A very important element of Locke's liberalism is to be found in his concept of *state as a fiduciary trust*. He thought that the general public was the source of government's power. Again, the government is always accountable to the people for all its policies and acts. The people have also the power to dislodge the government if it fails to act according to the terms and conditions of the contract. Locke's concept of fiduciary trust is unique and this has introduced the famous idea of *constitutionalism* which is the main feature of the American constitution. Its central idea is that both the rulers and the ruled are bound by the principles laid down in the constitution.

Locke's *separation of power* is another important part of his liberalism and needless to say that it is an important part. In section 134 he has said that men left the state of nature and set up a civil society for the purpose of protection, and enjoyment of property peacefully. But this cannot be done without laws and it is the chief function of the legislature to enact laws. Its implication is that legislature constitutes a branch of state and supreme power is vested in this organ. But the execution of laws shall be vested in a body of persons which is separate from the legislative body. The legislative and executive power are separated from each other. Though these two organs are separate from each other both are governed by the same laws. Locke says that after the formation of civil society a state or body-politic will have to establish relation with other states to deal with war and peace and for the purposes of making alliances. Locke calls this function *federative*. In other words what we call today international or foreign affairs function Locke calls it federative. We thus, in Lockean model, get three departments or organs of government—legislative, executive and federative. Hence we find that much before Montesquieu (1689–1755) Locke initiated the idea of separation of power. The framers of the American constitution later on made it a part of their constitution. In the eighteenth century the idea was regarded as key to the principle of bringing state authority under control. It was also thought that if powers are separated from each other that will put proper check on the government.

Democracy is a part of Lockean theory of liberalism. We want to mention few features of Locke's idea of democracy : (1) Locke has said that the contract has been finalised by taking the consent of everyone. Subsequently some may differ from others but this difference of opinion may be taken as normal. (2) The opinion of the majority shall be the principle of day-to-day administration. (3) The state shall be administered by the principle of law and terms laid down in the contract. This is the *constitutionalism*. It is believed that constitutionalism is the basic aspect of democracy and the liberals of all types emphasise it as a very crucial part of democracy. (4) An important aspect of Locke's idea of democracy is that people are the real source of government's power. Today many may call it as a type of popular sovereignty. Implication is the entire state shall be managed by the will of the people. (5) Locke has called the newly created civil society as a trust. It means the state acts only for the benefit and welfare of people. In other words, it is the custodian of people's interests. Locke thought of a continuous relation between the ruler and the ruled. Government cannot do anything against people's interests. (6) In today's democracy we talk about the protection of certain basic rights and Locke said so. To him right to property, security and life was essential and any authority worthy of its name must make arrangement for the protection of these three basic rights. (7) Locke was quite cautious of the rights and privileges of citizens and in a democratic state all these are quite safe but not in an autocracy. That is why we find that from the very beginning he framed principles which will control the state authority. He did not think about making sovereign power absolute.

LOCKE'S BOURGEOIS IDEAS

C. B. Macpherson and many others after painstaking research, have discovered Locke's sympathy with the capitalists. J. S. McClelland says (p. 243) "The Lockean model of society is a competitive, capitalist model—Men are free to acquire and are encouraged by God to do so." Macpherson says : "Locke's constitutionalism is a defence of the rights of expanding property rather than of individuals against the state." Another critic's opinion runs : "Locke deliberately intended to lead up to a justification of unlimited capitalist appropriation and the resultant unequal distribution of property. What made this possible along with the invention of money, was the fact that he regarded labour as alienable property, which a man could sell for wages."

We have quoted three observations of three eminent persons who are experts of Lockean philosophy. From three different angles they have viewed Locke's bourgeois concept. In numerous places of *The Second Treatise* Locke has said that one of the reasons of abandoning the state of nature was the insecurity of property. The implication is in the state of nature people were deprived of the adequate use of property, that is, property was quite insecure in that natural atmosphere. This feeling was so intense that they decided to abandone the state of nature. It is interesting to note that the concept of state of nature is simply a symbol. What he wanted to emphasise is that protection and personal use of property was very important to them. The idea of state of nature is simply a fiction. In the natural condition people will be highly concerned about property—is simply an imagination. Only in a developed and well-ordered society people's concern for property can be imagined. We can say Locke was actually thinking of a capitalist state. It may be that Locke's capitalist society or state was purely in primary condition. But it is out of our consideration. Locke's model of state is a capitalist state.

C. B. Macpherson has said that Locke was uncompromising supporter of capitalism. He further observes that the transition from state of nature to civil society, in the opinion of C. B. Macpherson, is not simply the product of an idle brain, it is a calculated step safeguarding the interests of capitalists or owners of the vast amount of property. This occupied the mind of Locke and setting up of a state was the best possible way. Lockean state may have manifold functions but the most important one is to protect the property which was insecure in the state of nature. Macpherson says : "Locke's whole theory of limited and conditional government was essentially a defence of property. The view of Locke's state is in effect a joint stock company whose shareholders were the men of property" (p. 95). He was so much interested in acquisition and protection of property that he has allotted a complete chapter—Chapter 5 consisting of 27 sections.

Locke was quite concerned about the security of people. Macpherson has explained it differently. Only the property owners or wealthy persons seriously think of their security and safety. Again, those who think in this way are rational. It is quite natural that the propertied person will always try to be conscious of the proper security of property. Locke has interpreted is as rationality. Macpherson has interpreted it in this way. Macpherson says : "When man, in general is thus conceived in the image of bourgeois rational man, the natural condition of man is eminently rational and peaceable" (p. 245). Rich and poor people, according to Macpherson, living in the same society cannot be equally rational. It is not that the poor people are not rational. Their rationality is of different type. Macpherson says that Locke's idea of rationality is chiefly the rationality of rich people.

Locke has categorically stated that man owns property through his own labour and he has every right over it. But when he found that some people here conspire to misappropriate his property through unfair means or by means of physical force, these people decided to create an institution whose one of the important functions would be to protect property. Furthermore, he has said in his chapter on property that the individuals have every right over the property and it cannot be taken away without their consent. The framers of the American constitution borrowed this concept from Locke and they have made right to property a fundamental right.

One of the main features of capitalism is a state or society is always a class state. Now J. S. McClelland raises an important question—Is Locke's state a class state or society? Locke never tells us in the *Second Treatise,* but there are broad hints elsewhere in his works, especially in his draft *Constitution for the Carolina,* where he refers to his "American Polity as a democracy of God's proprietors" (p. 244). According to Locke the state is a regulating mechanism. It will regulate the state affairs for the protection of property. In the opinion of Macpherson—"The whole theory of property is a justification of the natural right not only to unequal property but to unlimited individual appropriation" (p. 221). Only the property-owners took the leading part in setting up of new state or civil society.

CIVIL SOCIETY

John Dunn in his illuminating essay *John Locke's conception of civil society* claims that only two genuinely great political thinkers—namely Locke and Hegel—have used the term civil society. This claim has solid reason. In a number of places Locke has used the terms civil society or civil government. In section 13 he writes : "I easily grant that civil government is the proper remedy for the inconveniences of the state of nature." Again, in section 95, we find him saying "The only way whereby anyone divests himself of his natural liberty and puts on the bonds of civil society is by agreeing with other men to join and unite into a community." Here I have cited two instances to establish that Locke was conscious of the idea of civil society. There is a difference between civil government and civil society but in Locke's ideas both were used almost in the same sence.

Locke has clearly stated that the civil society is the proper remedy for the inconveniences of the state of nature. Locke thought that the civil society had two important advantages over the state of nature. One is the civil society is governed by civil laws which are far better than the laws of nature or natural laws. He thought that the laws of a civil society are clear and certain and can be easily applied. In a civil society there are impartial judges. Locke thought that for the protection of life, liberty and property impartiality of judges was indispensable and the state of nature lacked this. For the implementation of laws there shall be a political power. In section 3 he has said that the political power is the proper authority to make and implement laws. Needless to say that only in a civil society this is possible.

Sunil Khilnani in his article *The Development of Civil Society* makes certain observations about Locke's idea on civil society. "For Locke, the fundamental contrast defining a civil society was the state of nature : a predicament in which deeply held individual beliefs about how to be collided and where there could be no authoritative answer to the question "Who will be judges?" A civil society was one purged as effectively as possible of this condition. Locke made no separation between civil society and political society. ...Rather, a civil society was a "benign state", a legitimate political order. John Dunn has repeatedly used the term benign state by which he means to state that Locke's state is actually a harmless state or civil society and state are both used by him interchangeably. John Dunn has repeatedly used the term *benign state* in place of civil society.

Locke's civil society is simply a *Civilised Society* which is an aggregation of some "civilised" people. Locke has not categorically used the word civilised in his long analysis. But it has been assumed by his interpreters that only disciplined men can think of forming a civil society by throwing away their uncivilised behaviour which they displayed in the state of nature. Their dissatisfaction about the state of nature is a clear indication of the fact that they were guided by reason and not by emotion. At the same time we can note that Locke's people loved democracy and hated autocracy.

John Dunn has thrown ample light on Lockean theory of civil society. He observes that Locke's "civil society does not refer to a political or social substance that can be set over against an existent state. What he refers to in modern terminology is essentially the state liked the non-pathological state. Dunn's term the *state liked* is really innovative. It means that Locke's state is not an all-powerful state with absolute sovereign power. But it is not simply a conglomeration of discrete individuals. So Locke's civil society is *benign state,* state liked. Locke had no intention to prepare the framework of a state in modern sense or in Hobbesian way. He could have done it but he did not do that. Hobbes's state was the claimant of coercion and effective monopoly of power (Dunn, p. 55). It is to be noted that both Hobbes's and Locke's men were very clever persons. Hobbes's people gave consent to the absoluteness of sovereign power. On the other hand, Locke's men gave their approval to the democratic process to be followed by the authority of the civil society or, to use Dunn's phrase, *state liked.*

Analysing Lockean concept of civil society John Dunn further observes that the civil society in Lockean conception is the "optimal remedy for the state of nature." In the background of social, political and economic condition of Locke's contemporary society the concept of civil society was the best solution. "But Dunn further adds that it is necessarily an "imperfect remedy." In Dunn's judgment there were imperfections in his plan of civil society. But in one sense Locke's plan of civil society is really wonderful. He did not place an absolute sovereign power at the top of the administration of civil society. Like Hobbes he could easily do that, but he did not do. By making it democratic he paved the way for constitutionalism and liberalism. Here lies his credit.

POPULAR SOVEREIGNTY AND RESISTANCE

The name of the last chapter of Locke's Second Treatise runs—*Of the Dissolution of Government.* Locke was an eyewitness of the political turmoils that took place in the last two decades of the seventeenth century. Particularly the autocratic rule of some rulers moved his mind and thought. Several questions were raised in his mind. He was thinking about the consequences of tyrannical rule. In the background of these incidents he wrote the above chapter. John Morrow in his *A History of Political Thought* : A Thematic Introduction writes the following words : "Locke produced an account of sovereignty as a form of *trusteeship* and he argued that when the terms of the relationship are breached the bonds of civil society are dissolved."

An interesting point in Locke's analysis is that there is no *illegitimate political rule.* It means that whenever an existing government loses confidence of the general mass that government is removed from power. Since the legislature is the holder of supreme power, any violation of the terms and conditions of the contract will lead people to dissolve the assembly. Moreover this dissolution will free the people from showing their obligation to the assembly. That is why Locke has said there is nothing like misrule or illegal administration. Locke has repeatedly said that the assembly or legislature is the *trustee* of the people. It implies that the primary duty of the legislature is to act in accordance with the terms laid down in the compact.

Explaining Locke's views about rights and duties of the people John Morrow says : "Locke regarded resistance as an individual right, but he also thought that individuals have a *duty* to resist unjust governors. But since resistance takes place in a situation where government has already been dissolved, the duty to resist is one that individuals impose on themselves" (p. 318). "At the outbreak of the religious wars in 1562 the Prince de Conde, as leader of the Huguenots, issued a declaration justifying his decision to resort to arms" (Quentin Skinner. The foundations of modern political thought-II, p. 302). The clear purpose of this observation is that in the second half of the sixteenth century religious intoleration reached its zenith and the innocent people were indiscriminately murdered. These innocent people were known as Huguenots. They demanded that for the sake of self-defence they had the right to resist. Naturally the right to resist was not new when Locke was writing his *Second Treatise.* What is new is that the right to resist an autocratic ruler or a person who had violated the terms of the contract and was administering the civil society in an autocratic way. Several thousand Huguenots were killed because of the insistence of the fact that they had the right to practise their religious faith and several thousand people were murdered in the Bartholomew Massacre in 1572. We think that Locke was acquainted with this incident and keeping this in mind he strongly emphasised the right to resistance.

There is a very important aspect in Locke's theory of popular sovereignty and resistance. In section 241 he has raised a very vital question—Who shall be judge? The background of this question is if the people have the right to dislodge a government from power on the ground of its failure the pertinent question is who shall judge the failure of the government. In the previous section (section, 240). Locke says—who shall be judge whether the prince or legislative act contrary to their trust ? To this I reply : The people shall be judge, for who shall be judge whether his trustee or deputy acts well and according to the trust reposed in him but he who deputes him and must have still a power to discard him when he fails in his trust ? The five words : The people shall be judge—clearly establish that Locke was thinking of popular sovereignty. The final authority shall be vested in the hands of people and popular sovereignty says so.

Locke was a very intelligent man and his thought achieved full maturity when he published his Second Treatise in 1689, because by that time he was 57 years old.

Naturally he could not think that resistance or revolution could be the normal way of any civil society. That on any flimsy ground an elected government cannot be dislodged from power. In several places he has said that the subjects should be prepared to tolerate both "minor mismanagement" and isolated "great mistakes." Mistakes, violations of rules and numerous other mismanagements may occur. Locke does not advise his people to ignore, but to tolerate and if necessary they may resort to legal avenues for redressal. Locke calls this toleration. He apprehended that if governments are repeatedly removed from power that would create an anarchical situation. He was of the view that, in a civil society, there should exist law and order and, at the same time, peace. If governments are frequently removed from power peace shall be the victim. The point however remains that people have the right to judge the right and wrong of the government and have the right to resist.

NOZICK'S ASSESSMENT

Robert Nozick in his *Anarchy, State and Utopia* has assessed John Locke's political ideas from various angles. In Chapter 2 Nozick says that Locke's civil society may reasonably be called protective association. The term protective association (or protection association) is quite significant. In the state of nature there were inconveniences and groups of people assembled together to find out or remedy to these inconveniences and the consequence was that they formed an association (in Locke's language civil society). This association protects them from the difficulties and Nozick calls it a protective association. The members will form a protective association does not mean that this association will be at the beck and call of the members to deal with all problems and find out solutions. Again, this association will not follow a policy of non-intervention. The exact role of the protective association will be to adopt certain rules and procedures which will find out solutions to the grievances raised by the members of the association.

The protective association is not a state with absolute power. The main function of such association will be to protect the people from the feuds or irrational behaviour. The protective association will follow or adopt a middle way. Its policy will never be a policy of non-intervention or to intervene in all affairs of citizens. The associations will save the members from anarchy and, in the words of Locke, the inconveniences. The members of the state of nature formed such protective associations on the basis of voluntary arrangements. So we find that the voluntary arrangements constitute the main part of the protective association.

INFLUENCE OF LOCKE

It is little bit difficult to assess the importance of Locke who is considered as a controversial political philosopher. But he was also very popular notwithstanding his inconsistencies. We shall quote here several observations made by eminent persons.

On the occasion of Locke's tercentanary in 1932 Ernest Barker wrote an article which was published in The Times Literary Supplement. In this article Barker wrote "It was the political theory of Locke which affected the nation at large most deeply. Nor did it affect England. It penetrated into France and passed through Rousseau into the French Revolution, it penetrated into the north American colonies.

We find a tremendous impact of Locke's book—*The Two. Treatises*—on the American Constitution. The framers of this constitution borrowed several ideas from Locke's book—such as separation of powers, constitutionalism, right to property, life and liberty. Maxey rightly says : The Declaration of Independence is but a Thunderous transcript of this mighty book" (Political Philosophies, p. 260).

Let us now turn to another assessment. In the political philosophy of Locke the Whigs in England found a justification for their regime. At the same time it provided agrarian reformers. Locke had a number of admirers in France. Voltaire was both a critic and supporter of Locke. In fact, Voltaire popularised many ideas of Locke and Locke got French supporters.

I have already noted the influence of Locke on the preparation of the constitution. Again I want to point out another aspect of his influence. A critic observes in the following words "So close is the Declaration of Independence to Locke in form, phraseology and content that Jefferson was accused of copying the *Second Treatise*. Not only this." Several states of America copied verbatim the words and ideas from Locke in the preparation of their constitution. Locke is treated by many as the father of modern liberalism and United States is perhaps the first state which borrowed Locke's liberalism and implemented it. Hence we can say that the foundation of American liberalism is Locke's political philosophy.

Plamenatz, a renowned critic of political philosophies, makes the following observation : "His writings do not conclusively prove that he was a democrat. But the principles which he proclaimed in an era of aristocratic resistance to absolute monarchy are used in the West to justify liberal democracy. We may find many of Locke's argument inconclusive, we may think of him too careless and superficial. But his heart is in the right place, for that place is pretty much where our heart in the West is today." Plamenatz wants to say that the words and phrases used by Locke are sometimes misleading. But if we study his heart or what he wants to say we shall find that his heart really longs for democracy, liberty and rights. These are the most valuable concepts of political science.

The best tribute, I think, comes from C. L. Wayper : "His is the last great voice of one great generation and first great voice of another great generation." He could not bring himself out of medieval atmosphere. But he did not accept it. But he laid the foundation of a new era of politics—era of liberalism, democracy, popular sovereignty.

15 JEAN JACQUES ROUSSEAU

Life and Time

The Everyman's edition of *The Social Contract* notes the following short life history of J. J. Rousseau (henceforth only Rousseau) : "Jean Jacques Rousseau, born at Geneva in 1712, the son of a watchmaker. Attended a seminary at Turin and obtained favour with Madame de Warens, who supported him for ten years. He left her in 1740 and in 1756 went to live in Montmorency with Madame d' Epinay. David Hume (1711–1776) invited him to England in 1766, and he returned to France in 1770. Died in 1778."

There is a gap of eight years between the death and birth of Locke and Rousseau. His birth place was Geneva which was Calvinist, that is, it was under the tremendous influence of Calvin. Rousseau was a bohemian. He did not settle anywhere, rather roamed from one place to another. He spent a larger part of his life in Paris. He went to Paris in 1743 and by 1746 he came in contact with Diderot. There was an exchange of academic matters between the two. He wrote an essay on "Has the revival of arts and sciences done more to corrupt or purify morals?" Rousseau wrote an essay and sent it to the organisers. He was adjudged for the first prize and got 300 francs and a gold medal. He wrote another essay but it failed to bring a prize for him. Rousseau, however, was able to establish himself as an author or writer at the age of thirty eight. The winning of prize lifted him from obscurity and placed him at the centre-stage of the academic circles of Geneva.

Rousseau wrote several books : *A Discourse on the Arts and Sciences*—In Everyman's edition and with an Introduction by G. D. H. Cale, there is no hyphen between Jean and Jacques. But majority writers use hyphen. *A Discourse on the Origin of Inequality.* These two books were published, respectively, in 1750 and 1755. His next work *Political Economy* was published in 1758. The most important work *The Social Contract* in 1762. He also authored few other books such as *Emile* and *The Letters from the Mount*. Rousseau is read and remembered for *The Social Contract*.

We know that every thinker or philosopher is more or less influenced by the events and ideas that develop and flourish around him and Rousseau is not an exception. Though Geneva was his birth place he travelled France and lived there several years. So we can easily say that he was a piquant observer of various events and especially political ones that grew around him. France was the heaven of autocracy and the autocratic rule of French rulers created an intolerable situation in French society. The irresponsible activities of the autocratic ruler drained huge amount of money from the state treasury and, in order to replenish it, the ruler levied taxes upon the masses of men. Autocracy was the system of the day when Rousseau started his political and other writings.

The absence of democracy and the shortening condition of liberty created a tremendous impact upon the mind of Rousseau. From the very childhood Rousseau was a great worshipper of liberty. Immediately after his birth his mother died. His father was not fully normal. He lived few years under the guardianship of an educated and aristocrat lady. But this guardianship was intolerable to him. He was, in fact, a nature's child. It is quite natural that such a man would be the lover of liberty. But the physical environment around him was not favourable for liberty and democracy. This disturbed his mind and thought considerably.

Literally, the Industrial Revolution started its journey in the sixties of the eighteenth century and Rousseau's Social Contract was published in 1762. Many critic are of opinion that there were favourable conditions of industrialisation in various parts of Europe. In this situation Rousseau observed that there was generation of wealth and accumulation of property in society. Particularly in agriculture and commercial sectors there was large amount of wealth and property. But it was not properly distributed among various sections of the population. Because of this, inequality came to be the main feature of society. This inequality not only drew his attention, it disturbed his mind considerably. He wrote a small book entitled : *A Dissertation on the Origin and Foundation of the Inequality of Mankind*. It means that Rousseau was quite conscious of the inequality with which he was confronted. Again, this book has another title *What is the Origin of Inequality Among Men, and Is it Authorised by Natural Law ?* All these are proofs of the fact that he seriously thought about inequality and it is also true that he did not approve of this inequality. The fact is that the second half of the eighteenth century was characterised by the unequal distribution of wealth. Rousseau thought that the unequal distribution of wealth was also the cause of political discontent. He thought that this inequality was one of the causes of unrest.

In France and several other countries there were religious conflicts among various religious communities. He could not tolerate this. He also saw that the church and other religious organisations were eager to establish their own identity and to control the behaviour of the general public. All these led to the curtailment of people's liberty. Rousseau could not accept it as normal. Rather, he raised his voice. He was the great worshipper of liberty and its loss or curtailment was a source of great anxiety to him.

The general condition of Britain was not acceptable to him. He vehemently criticised the British form of parliamentary democracy. Even he did not hesitate to say that the British people were free only at the time of election. Rousseau saw that the British politics and economy were fully controlled by aristocrats, capitalists and feudal landlords. General public was far away from the real platform of democracy. In some parts of Europe the impact of Enlightenment was perceptible and he strongly felt the influence of Enlightenment. Being under the influence of Enlightenment, general people longed for more liberty and various opportunities. But because of the domination of propertied class and influential politicians they could not get their due share.

There is an interesting similarity between Plato and Rousseau. The thought of these two philosophers was enormously influenced by contemporary events. The downward movement of democracy, morality, ethics etc. disturbed Plato and, as a remedy, he planned for an ideal state. Rousseau was also influenced by Plato. He observed that morality, dignity of man, liberty and several other eternal values are at stake and the advancement of sciences and arts was primarily responsible for this. Ebenstein rightly says : "Rousseau sees a direct causal relation between luxury, constantly expanding needs and the rise of art and science, after which true courage flags and the virtues disappear." He thought that poor and simple Rome commanded respect. Wealthy and luxurious Rome failed to achieve that.

REVOLT AGAINST REASON

Rousseau viewed and analysed the contemporary society in his own way and his way was a different one. He wanted the revival of freedom and simplicity that prevailed in the state of nature. He squarely blamed the progress of arts and sciences for the loss of morality, freedom etc. Again, for the loss of freedom and morality the development of reason is responsible. He thinks : "A thinking man is a depraved animal." Sabine says : "Rousseau did not appeal to reason, on the contrary he turned the contrast into an attack upon reason" (p. 577). He revolted against intelligence, the growth of knowledge and progress of science. In his judgment all these are responsible for the general deterioration of society. Naturally men should not be moved or guided by reason. Rather, they should act in accordance with emotion, feelings and instincts.

According to Rousseau the feelings, affections and bond of family life, the joy and beauty of motherhood, man's love for arts and beauty are of eternal value and man should cultivate all these seriously and sincerely. The cultivation of all these will give man real joy and satisfaction. He believes that there is no place of reason in all these things. He believes that science cannot give man proper satisfaction in life. "Science is the fruit of idle curiosity, philosophy is mere intellectual frippery, the amenities of polite life are tinsel" (Sabine, p. 577).

The development of trade, commerce and the general economic condition drastically changed the physical condition of society and, at the same time, gave birth to a new and wealthy class which may be called bourgeois. In the observation of Sabine we find the following remark : In *A Discourse on the Arts and Sciences* Rousseau has openly denounced the negativeness of the progress of arts and sciences . In this book he has said that the progress of arts and science has not been able to contribute anything to the augmentation of human happiness. Rather, because of the progress of these, man's mind, thought and action are vitiated and corrupted. The simplicity of mind and action as well as thought is lost and, in the opinion of Rousseau, this is a great loss. Man is actually helpless in the rapid progress of arts and science. In order to save and revive the honesty, simplicity and virtue of man the best way is to stop the progress of science and arts. Rousseau has said "Those whom nature intended for her disciples have not needed masters—Bacon, Descartes and Newton, those teachers of mankind, had themselves no teachers" (*Social Contract and Discourses*, p. 141).

Rousseau could not accept the progress of arts and science on the ground that these made man reasonable and a reasonable man is corrupt and complex-minded.

Commenting upon Rousseau's view on the bad effect of progress Sabine says : "In short, intelligence is dangerous because it undermines reverence; science is destructive because it takes away faith, reason is bad because it sets prudence against moral intuition. Without reverence, faith and moral intuition there is neither character nor society" (p. 578). So it is obvious that morality, ethics, reverence and faith were much more important than the progress of arts and science. Somehow Rousseau arrived at the conclusion that morality and reverence had the power to make man perfect and honest. Hence reason be abandoned.

STATE OF NATURE AND SOCIAL CONTRACT

When Rousseau was the Secretary to the French Ambassador in 1743-44 he planned to write a comprehensive book on various aspects of body politic. But the adverse circumstances forced him to abandon the project. But the prize awarded to him by the Academy of Dijon inflamed his thought of writing a book and he started the implementation of the idea.

Like Hobbes he started his analysis of the state of nature but his depiction of the state of nature is in direct opposite to Hobbes's depiction. In *A Discourse on the Origin of Inequality* he directly criticised Hobbes's view : "Hobbes contends that man is naturally intrepid and is intent only upon attacking and fighting. ...Such circumstances, however, rarely occur in a state of nature, in which all things proceed in a uniform manner, and the face of the earth is not subject to those sudden and continual changes which arise from the passions and caprices of bodies of men living together" (p. 165). Self-preservation was the primary concern of man and this thought sometimes forced him to be involved in conflicts with other. But this did not take place at large scale. Few incidents of conflicts cannot be treated as the general feature. Men were subject to sickness and other problems in the state of nature. Since no remedies were available in the state of nature they were faced with many problems.

Rousseau also says : "Let us not conclude, with Hobbes, that because man has no idea of goodness, he must be naturally wicked, that he is vicious because he does not know virtue, that he always refuses to do his fellow-creatures services which he does not think they have a right to demand" (p. 181). Hobbes has further said that a bad man is a robust child. But it remains to be proved whether man in the state of nature is this robust child (p. 181).

So we find that he does not agree with Hobbes about the real situation or condition of the state of nature. His own idea about the state of nature has been succinctly stated in the following words : "Being subject to so few causes of sickness, man, in the state of nature, can have no need of remedies and still less of physicians, nor is the human race in this respect worse of than other animals, and it is easy to learn from hunters whether they meet with many infirm animals in the course of the chase" (p. 167). What Rousseau wants to say is that in the primitive atmosphere (what may be called the state of nature) the life of man was not easy. They had to pass through numerous hurdles and the people could not face or solve these problems single handedly. Men of the state of nature were not generally bad but the solution of the problems was beyond their capacity. He has also said that people of the state of nature loved each other and they had a desire to create a congenial atmosphere.

Rousseau has said that in the state of nature people were alone. That is, each individual was separate from another and this was the greatest weakness. He says : "the obstacles in the way of their preservation in the state of nature show their power of resistance to be greater than the resources at the disposal of each individual for his maintenance in that state. The primitive condition can then subsist no longer and the human race would perish unless it changed its manner of existence" (*The Social Contract*, p. 11). The prediction of Rousseau is quite simple. Either the people of the state of nature change their mode of living or they shall be prepared for perish. They, however, did not want the latter consequence.

He thought that it was not possible for the people of the state of nature to generate or create new force. What they can do is to unite the existing forces and this unification will be far stronger than the existing single force. In other words, the aggregation of the existing forces can solve the problems. This will enable them to ovecome all the problems. Rousseau, therefore, suggests that all the existing forces will be brought under one umbrella and the new combined force will be far greater than the former force. Rousseau says : "The problem is to find a form of association which will defend and protect with the whole common force the person and goods of each associate, and in which each, while uniting himself with all, may still obey himself alone, and remain as free as before" (p. 12). By creating a new society through the instrumentality of social contract the problems or inconveniences of the state of nature are thus solved. The social contract thus creates a new association and the problems are solved.

Rousseau further observes that the association creates a moral and collective body. The association created by the compact is both a moral and collective body. Again, this association may be termed as *Republic* or *body politic*. The members who formed the association also call it *state* or *sovereign*. His state has several names—body politic or republic or sovereign. It means that all have the same meaning. In his time all these terms carried almost identical meaning. He also used the *power* in place of state or body politic.

If we go through Rousseau's *Social Contract* and the formation of state we shall find some **features** which are narrated in the following way : (1) The contract enables each person to submit himself and the power he possesses under the common authority. (2) This common authority will be guided by the general will. The body politic will be administered by the general will. The opinion of any single person will have no importance. (3) In the state of nature people acted or behaved in *individual capacity* and in his opinion that was the root cause of problem. In the newly created society which is called the body politic all the individuals will act in *corporate capacity.* He has used two words—corporate body and collective body. Both have been used to mean the same idea. (4) The people met together and adopted collective decisions. In other words, all the individuals were parties to the decisions and, hence, nobody can modify or change any decision according to his sweet will. (5) An interesting feature of Rousseau's social contract is the goods and persons are put under the authority of association or body politic. But the contracting individual does not surrender his freedom to the authority of the body politic. He says : "While uniting himself with all, many still obey himself alone and remain as free as before." Rousseau's *Social Contract* opens a flood gate of controversies and the above comment is one of them. But David Held (*Models of Democracy,* 1996) says that Rousseau saw the individuals are involved in all the activities of the state (p. 57). The participation in the activities of the body politic is complete and universal.

The words "remain as free as before" are significant. The formation of the new society cannot curtail the freedom of the people. They will discharge their duties and responsibilities without being forced or influenced by other persons. They enjoyed complete freedom in the state of nature and that will remain intact. Here we may say that Rousseau has imagined three stages. There was originally the state of nature. It was absolutely not ideal.

The development of arts and science changed the social structure and people were faced with some problems. There were also problems in the state of nature but the development of arts and sciences aggravated the situation and this condition forced the inhabitants to build up a new society. He says that the society will be of different type but this new society must not curtail the freedom and other privileges which they enjoyed in the state of nature. He has openly declared his intention. The people, after forming the new society, will remain as before. He uses the words "everywhere the same." The formation of the new society will enable them to regain original rights and natural liberty.

The special identity which they had in the state of nature will be lost. It means that instead of being different all the contracting persons will be differently identified. Rousseau says (p. 12) "the total alienation of each associate, together with all his rights to the whole community." They surrender everything and make them as integral part of the new society on the condition that earlier privileges will be regained. In this way new body politic will be a perfect one. The members of the new society will get everything and they will have nothing new to demand. Again he declares : "each man, in giving himself to all, gives himself to nobody" (p. 12). Being a member of the new society individuals will, no doubt, lose something which they enjoyed in the state of nature. But at the same time the new society gives him something which he did not have in the state of nature. The gains are equivalent to losses. The new society will create a new force and it is capable of preserving the gains he has got from the body politic.

ROUSSEAU'S CONCEPT OF STATE

Different scholars have interpreted Rousseau's theory of state from different angles. But all of them have arrived at almost the same conclusion. If we seriously study his plan of state and other aspects we shall find that the entire structure of the body politic is modelled as *republican.* His individuals are directly and "ideally" involved in the creation of law, its application, and, finally, in the management or administration of the state they have created. G. D. H. Cole writes (*Introduction to The Social Contract*, p. XXXV) "Active will, and not force or even mere consent, is the basis of the 'republican' state." Cole wants to say that at every stage of the new society or social order there exists people's participation or consent. Individuals will obey themselves and are not directed or dictated by others. Cole further says that Rousseau's "state is not a mere accident of human history or mere device for the protection of life and property, it responds to fundamental need of human nature" (XXXVI). Rousseau planned a state for the fulfilment of special purpose and that purpose is realisation of democratic principles through direct participation in the law making and administrative process. This is purely republican system.

David Held has interpreted Rousseau's republicanism in a slightly different way. He says, in Rousseau's account, the idea of self rule is posited as an end in itself, a political order offering opportunities for participation in the arrangement of public affairs should not be just a state, but rather the formation of a type of society, a society in which the affairs of the state are integrated into the affairs of the ordinary citizens. In Rousseau's state, sovereignty originates in the people, that people are the source of power and authority. This is Rousseau's republicanism as well as popular sovereignty.

Rousseau is characterised as the progenitor of modern nation-states. This aspect has been analysed by Alfred Cobban in his thought-provoking book *Rousseau and the Modern State* (1934). "Here Rousseau is regarded as the progenitor of the modern nation-state characterised by homogeneity of culture and language, by a certain territorial integrity, and by a state which at least in principle treats all its citizens in the same way by giving them all equal rights and duties" (J. S. McClelland, p. 254). There are several reason why Rousseau has been called the progenitor of modern nation-state :

1. Rousseau has called his body politic as a "moral person." If it is a 'moral person' like every other person Rousseau's 'moral person', that is, the state, has certain rights and duities. Though he has not designated the rights and duties of his body politic or moral person, from his analysis we can easily formulate an idea about these. The modern nation-states claim obligation from the citizens, Rousseau's state also claims obligations from its citizens.
2. In every nation-state individuals have more important as well as responsible role and Rousseau thought that his citizens are responsible. This appears in his analysis of general will which is formed in open assembly. In this assembly the participation of individuals is compulsory. One person cannot represent another person. That is, there was no proxy.
3. J. S. McClelland says that modern states are characterised by uncomplicated patriotism and Rousseau painted the picture of such a state. There were several states in his time such as Corsica and Poland. These states were ideal to him. He thought that his state which will come out of contract will be of this same type—that is, the nation-state. His state will have clear boundary and special administrative structure. Because of these reasons his state is called a nation-state.

ROUSSEAU'S IS A TOTALITARIAN STATE

Rousseau is really a controversial person. He has been regarded by a good number of scholars as a great apostle of liberty or freedom. Simultaneously he has been depicted as a supporter of totalitarianism. These two terms are like pole apart. J. J. Talmon first draws our attention through his well-known book *The Origin of Totalitarian Democracy* published in 1953. Explaining Talmon's argument McClelland maintains : "Talmon thinks that the totalitarian state can demand unquestioning obedience, and the right to interfere with what it pleases" (p. 255). Totalitarianism implies that the words and authority of the government or person or the party are final and nobody can question. This type of government is based on an ideology. So whatever the government does is supported by the ideology. It has been claimed that Rousseau propagated an ideology and that ideology has been briefly stated by J. S. McClelland : "Rousseau's insistence that the history of all hitherto existing societies is the history of force and fraud is an ideological statement." To fight against this fraud and deterioration of morality, ethics and general values Rousseau wanted to make the state or its administrative system all-powerful. In Rousseau's time there were no party governments or—like today—all-powerful bureaucracy. His state and general will are all-powerful.

There are few elements of totalitarianism in his writings and one such element is "forced to be free." He has said that if anyone refuses to accept the decision or directions of the general will he will be forced to accept it. His firm belief was that the general will represents the real will of all. The welfare of all individuals contain in this general will. This will can never be wrong. All the individuals, participating in an open assembly, decided the general will. So such a will can never be wrong. If it is the exact nature of general will every individual is bound to obey or accept it. Any refusal will be followed by application of force. That is why he has used the very controversial words—"forced to be free." The coexistence between force and freedom is practically impossible. It is unfortunate that Rousseau has made that coexistence. In other words, force and freedom can never be bed-fellows. The result is that Rousseau has been depicted as a totalitarian.

Why Rousseau is called a totalitarian thinker is quite manifest in his observation he makes in Chapter VI (*The Limits of the Sovereign Power*, p. 24). "If the state is a moral person whose life is in the union of its members, and if the most important of its cares is the care for its own preservation, it must have a universal and compelling force, in order to move and dispose each part as may be most advantageous to the whole. As nature gives each man absolute power over all its members also." The passage is quite lengthy. What I want to emphasise is that the seeds of totalitarianism are to be found in Rousseau's writing and this allegation is not baseless. Knowingly or unknowingly, Rousseau made certain statements or comments which have made his readers or commentators brand him as a totalitarian.

But there are many scholars who claim that Rousseau was not totalitarian, though there are certain aspects in his thought which hint at his totalitarianism. The renowned scholar Plamenatz is of opinion that Rousseau was a democrat in toto. A totalitarian minded person cannot start his book—Man is born free and everywhere he is in chains. A totalitarian cannot suggest an open assembly for law making and administrative purposes. He was a great supporter of popular sovereignty and direct democracy. In his *A Discourse on the Origin of Inequality* he unequivocally condemns the gross inequality. His most controversial phrase—forced to be free—is treated as a vital source of totalitarianism. But many thinkers are of opinion that the real meaning of the term is none will be allowed to do any harm to society. Once the general will is formed, everyone is legally bound to obey its conditions because he was a participant in the process of general will. Even today, in all democratic states, once a law has been enacted by the law-making body it is binding on all. But do we call it totalitarian ?

Maurice Cranston is of opinion that it is very difficult to find out the seeds or elements of totalitarianism in the writing of Rousseau. J. S. McClelland says that though Talmon has said that Rousseau was a totalitarian there is doubt about it. There are enough elements of democracy in the writings of Rousseau. From his writings we come to know that he did not like the British model of parliamentary system. He, on the other hand, thought of periodic system of open general assembly and the formation of general will. In his opinion society is evil, irrational and corrupt. In such society there are inequalities. These are to be corrected with a strong hand and that has been suggested by him. It has been said that all the socialists of subsequent ages are called the grandchildren of Rousseau. It is admitted on all hands that there are certain perceptible aspects of totalitarianism in socialist thought and in that sense he might be called a totalitarian.

GENERAL WILL

G. D. H. Cole in his *Introduction* writes the General Will (hereafter only G. W.) is the most disputed and certainly the most fundamental of all Rousseau's political concepts. But it is a matter of great surprise that none has found any clear and acceptable definition of what is G. W. In *A Discourse on Political Economy* Rousseau says : "The body politic is also a moral being possessed of a will; and this general will, which tends always to the preservation and welfare of the whole and of every part and is the source of the laws, constitutes for all the members of the state, in their relations to one another and to it, the rule of what is just or unjust" (pp. 236–237). Again in Chapter II (p. 21, footnote) he makes the following comment : "To be general, a will need not always be unanimous, but every vote must be counted, any exclusion is a breach of generality." This condition is very important.

Rousseau has already announced that the body politic or state that comes out of the social contract is a moral being. Here he compares the body politic with human being and since every human being has his own will the body politic being a moral being cannot be an exception. The will of the body politic (also a moral being) can reasonably be called a general will. The General Will is not the will of any particular person or group of persons. It is the will of the entire body politic. Harmon says that G. W. is an expression of public mind. In other words, when the individuals of the body politic assemble at a public place and participate in the discussion they take certain decisions. These decisions finally form the body of G. W. Rousseau has added a powerful condition. A G. W. need not be unanimous. It means that it may be the majority will. But everyone must participate in the will.

In Chapter III—whether the general will is infallible—Rousseau has drawn our attention to some features of G. W. He says the general will is always right and tends to the public interest or public advantage. Such a generalisation may appear to us peculiar. But to Rousseau it was not so. All the members of the body politic decided the general will and they did it after long and thorough discussion. Moreover, the actors of the general will are people themselves and, since they are not corrupt, their decision can never be wrong. Eulogising the nature of people Rousseau has further maintained that though they are not corrupted, they are very often deceived.

He has drawn the attention of his readers to a complicated feature and this can better be stated in his own words : "There is a great deal of difference between the will of all and the general will, the latter considers only the common interest, while the former takes private interest into account, and is no more than a sum total of particular wills. In the G. W. the private interests have no dominating place. Only the will that aims at the common interest and the General Welfare that can claim to have a place in the general will."

Rousseau speaks of a peculiar nature of the G. W. He says (p. 23) that when there is only one society there can exist only one G. W. His state is undivided like a nation-state. Within the boundary of the body politic there is no place of groupism or partial or small societies where the members will be preoccupied with their own sectorial interests. This was unacceptable to Rousseau. The agreement among all the citizens regarding their interests helps the formation of G. W. It is now obvious that he understood different thing about the G. W.

In *A Discourse on Political Economy* his analysis about the G. W. is "brief and lucid and furnishes the best guide to Rousseau's general meaning." In support of this view we quote a passage from this book : "Every political society is composed of other smaller societies, of different kinds, each of which has its interests and its rules of conduct, but those societies which every body perceives... are not the only ones that actually exist in the State" (p. 237). All individuals are united by a common interest. Rousseau wants to say that in states there may exist smaller groups or societies and the formation of the general will may create problem. But he assures us that in all the small groups and societies there exists common interest and the commonness of interests is the vital aspect of the general will.

In the body politic there is no place of partial or particular will. Rousseau admits that in the body politic there may exist smaller types of G. W. But he assures his readers that the existence of the smaller wills need not be a cause of worries and anxieties because ultimately all these wills will merge together and form a G. W. We here find a difference in his approach. In *The Social Contract* his approach was against the particular wills. But in the *A Discourse on Political Economy* he argues that in the process of time the smaller general wills will merge together and form a greater and effective G. W. This change is due to the fact that while writing *A Discourse on Political Economy* he studied the political systems of his contemporary states and admitted the existence of smaller general wills. He had the belief that these will merge.

In Book IV, Chapter I, Rousseau has said that the General Will is indestructible. If the body politic is a united and single body or organisation then there is no scope of division in the G. W. If the body politic is well organised, if the fissiparous tendencies are not allowed to develop and, if all the members aim at general welfare, there cannot exist partial interests and suctorial outlook. The people are happy and live together peacefully. In such type of society the formation of general will is quite easy. Needless to say that Rousseau always imagined the existence or formation of such society. In this type of society the formation of G. W. is easy and once such a will is formed, it exists for pretty long time. In such society once the G. W. is formed that exists and he says that it is indestructible.

Rousseau has said that a very important precondition of the formation of G. W. is cordial and intimate relationship among the members of the state. The people will always regard themselves as the members of the state and there is friendship and brotherhood which is of extremely high standard. There is no relaxation in the friendship. Naturally there is no scope of deficiency in relationship. So good relation and high standard of friendship are indispensable for a good G. W. That is why he has said that when the social bond begins to be relaxed and the state to grow weak, when particular interests begin to make themselves felt, the common interests changes and finds opponents, opinion is no longer unanimous. We, therefore, find that complete agreement or unanimity is the most vital element of general will. When these disappear G. W. also faces critical situation.

EVALUATION

The General Will is the most favourite subject of Rousseau and simultaneously it is the most controversial or disputed concept. Barker, in his *Social Contract : Locke, Hume and Rousseau*, says : There is a logical difficulty in his concept of General Will. It is distinguished from the mere will of all. The G. W. is a true collectivity. How is it to be done? His reply is that if there are no parties in the open deliberations and if the discussion is held without party line the G. W. is bound to be correct. In his time party was infested with factionalism or groupism. This condition of party generally misguided the general public. Today, however, party has appeared to be indispensable for any political system. The point is that his approach to party is not acceptable to us.

Rousseau makes common good as the fulcrum of his General Will. The question is what is exactly meant by common good? The idea may differ from person to person—and in that case the formation of G.W. may create problem or even it cannot be formed. Let us quote Barker : "To distil the requirements of general good in something which requires both an intellectual effort of sustained reflection and a moral effort of abstinence from private and sinister interests, it will not come of itself, through the automatic cancellations of private interests by one another."

In the opinion of Sabine : "The development of the theory of general will was involved in paradoxes, partly because of the candidness of Rousseau's ideas, but partly because he had a rhetorician's liking for paradox" (p. 587). Sabine is of opinion that his idea of contract is unrelated with the rights and powers of government. Furthermore, there is another paradox. The state or society is formed by an imaginary act. This imaginary act has no capacity to create and enforce rights and other things. Still there is another paradox. Rousseau's contract has formed an association and not an "aggregation." So in an association the formation of G. W. in the formula prescribed by Rousseau is impossible.

Plamenatz has severely criticised Rousseau's theory of G. W. in the following way. A critical analysis of Rousseau's statements reveals that there is no clear definition of the idea. He has stated several ambiguous statements and the meaning of these statements is not clear. Plamenatz says that such a concept of General Will is sheer nonsense. He has suggested the formula of plus and minus. This may have importance in mathematics or other sciences, but no value in social science or in Rousseau's theory.

His theory of G. W. is applicable only in small societies. Because, in such societies the population is quite small and people can assemble in open place and can form G. W. through free deliberations. But its application in large societies is impossible. There is no scope of any open assembly and people cannot arrive at any unanimous decision.

In every society people express their opinion in the background of their political views or opinions. There may not exist any political party but people may hold political opinion and there is no bar to it. If so how could they arrive at a unanimous decision which is called the G. W.? The difference in opinion may stand on the way of G. W. It is unfortunate that Rousseau failed to consider this aspect. The problem is Rousseau was very much influenced by Plato and, naturally, he had no intention to look into the practical aspects of general will.

G. D. H. Cole supports Rousseau's G. W. from a different angle. He says that the General Will is "essentially ethical." "It is a principle of moral conduct applied to political behaviour" (XXX). Rousseau was influence by ethics and morality and wanted to apply these eternal values to politics. Plato planned for an ideal state knowing well that this could never be realised. Similarly Rousseau wanted to build a body politic whose foundation would be morality and ethics. In the contemporary city states he got the opportunity to witness the activities of direct democracy and to this system he added morality and ethics. Cole further maintains that the G. W. aims at applying freedom to political institutions. He wanted to say that people must have freedom and they must be given full opportunity to apply this freedom in their day-to-day life. For that purpose Rousseau selected the G. W.

Rousseau's general will is not only the central part of his theory or philosophy, it is the "most original and most interesting and historically the most important contribution which he made to political theory" (W. T. Jones, p. 318). Whether it is practicable or not is a different issue. But our point is the citizens must have full scope to exercise their opinion and participate in the affairs of state. This is the main point and even today we cannot deny the importance of this point. Even today many political systems try to arrive at a consensus. It is said that every opinion has value and that opinion must be allowed to express. Rousseau did that.

David Thompson in his article *Rousseau and the General Will* observes that the general will is a panegyric outburst and it throws light on several aspects of democracy. It is a qualitative idea. It has a patriotic spirit at the time of crisis. People must for sake parochial interests when needs demand. The fault with Rousseau is that he wanted to make it a permanent feature of the body politic. We are not concerned whether G. W. shall be the temporary or permanent feature of the state, our main concern is whether it has any validity or not. During the last two world wars a number of states knowingly or unknowingly took the help of G. W. to arouse the feeling of patriotism. In other words, the crisis of a state demands the application of the concept of G. W. embodied in the general interest of the state. That is what the overall interest demand—the citizens must be prepared to surrender the private or sectarian interest and Rousseau wanted to emphasise this.

David Thompson in his article further claims that the G. W. "makes Rousseau a great democratic theorist. He argues that sovereignty cannot be surrendered or delegated to any one person or group of people. It cannot be exercised at all through elected representatives" (p. 98). By advocating the open assembly and making people's participation at the meeting Rousseau succeeded in establishing his reputation as a great democrat of extremely high standard. He did not support the representative system of democracy of the British type and this form of government earned his wrath. It is to be added here that though he was the worshipper of democracy he was doubtful of its realisation. He said "were there a people of gods, their government would be democratic. So perfect a government is not for men" (p. 56).

It is said that Rousseau planned to write his book *The Social Contract* keeping in mind a particular philosophy which may briefly be stated as morality, ethics or, in general term, idealism. In his view people were basically moral and honest but due to the advancement of arts and science all these were lost. Hence his chief concern was the revival of these values. For that purpose he planned to set up a new society. It is clear in the following passage : "The passage from the state of nature to the civil state produces a very remarkable change in man, by substituting justice for instinct in his conduct and giving his actions the morality they had formerly backed" (Book I, Ch. VIII, p. 15). The attainment of morality was the important thing people gained from the setting up of the body politic. Cole says the same thing.

Rousseau advised the people to sacrifice the personal interest for the sake of general interest of the state. This is not anti-democratic or totalitarian though the tone is totalitarian. Swami Vivekananda also advised people to sacrifice personal interests for the sake of general interests. Should we say that he was totalitarian? It is a general idea that the interests of the community must precede the interests of the individual. The priority of the personal interests and fostering it will lead to the balkanisation of the state or community.

It is said that in the general will Rousseau did not recognise the freedom of the individuals. But this allegation has no value at all. The man who chalked out a plan for the revival of human freedom he cannot suggest its loss or destruction. There shall exist difference of opinion but he thought that his people will settle all disputes remembering that by submitting to the G. W. their objectives will be achieved. They would also realise that insistence on personal interests would ultimately be harmful for the body politic. Remembering all the aspects of the general will, we hold the view that it is a unique creation of Rousseau that influenced subsequent generations.

LIBERTY AND AUTHORITY

Rousseau's theory of liberty is, again, a controversial issue because in his analysis of G. W. he suggested to surrender the private will and interests to the general will and interests and this is clearly in opposition to human liberty. But in recent years the scholars have thoroughly investigated the various aspects of Rousseau's idea on liberty and have arrived at the conclusion that he was unquestionably a champion of liberty. J. S. McClelland in his scholarly work *History of Western Political Thought* says : "Rousseau's concept of liberty is a 'positive' concept of liberty in the classic sense outlined by Sir Isaiah Berlin in his celebrated essay *Two Concepts of Liberty*" (p. 264). If so we shall try to show what is exactly meant by positive idea of liberty.

Berlin defines positive liberty in this way "The positive sense of the word 'liberty' derives from the wish on the part of the individual to be his own master. I wish my life and decisions to depend on myself, not on external forces. I wish to be the instrument of my own, not of other men's acts of will. I wish to be a subject, not an object, to be moved by reasons, by conscious purposes, which are my own" (p. 131). The positive idea of liberty also consists in the freedom which consists in not being prevented from choosing as I do by other men." This is Berlin's positive meaning of liberty, on the other hand, negative liberty means the absence of restraints.

Rousseau's theory of positive liberty implies that liberty is a form of self-coercion. It means that individuals have the freedom to take steps for the realisation of his goals but, at the same time, he feels that his steps will not stand on the way of the fulfilment of others goals. The individuals will follow self-coercion. The pursuit of liberty will adopt a rational method or number of rational methods. Hence the idea of positive liberty is closely connected with rationality and self-coercion. Self-coercion means people adopt certain resolutions and promise to follow them with all sincerity. These resolutions form the part of self-coercion and positive liberty.

If we properly analyse his view of liberty it will be found that it has a close relation with G. W. Rather, positive freedom is part of the G. W. Therefore, in Rousseau's view, the liberty is a part of the whole body politic. It is a collective venture. Something *We* do, not something *I* do. The positive freedom rests on the idea that the individual is an integral part of the whole and everything concerning him is part of the whole. He does not decide anything that goes against the general interest of the state or civil society. Again, the whole body of society will not do anything that will destroy the real will and interest of the individual who is an integral part of the state.

Rousseau was sure that there was no conflict between G. W. and freedom of the individuals because Rousseau speaks of the G. W. as if it were something like Kant's "good will." The will of the people will not aim at the sectarian benefits. Gettell says : "Rousseau believed that there could be no conflict between authority vested in the people as a whole and their liberty as individuals" (p. 254). Gettell is right. The G. W. is not something different from people. In the G. W. there is the real will of every man and, naturally, when the members of the body politic start to implement the decisions or objectives of the G. W. they are not expected to do anything that will go against the G. W. as well as the interests or liberty of the members. The amalgamation of individuals will or welfare with the G. W. and common welfare is not slavery. He wanted to emphasise this.

We have already stated that, to Rousseau, liberty is positive. That is, he looks liberty in the positive sense. If so, the authority of the state can interfere with the freedom of the individuals when it is faced with problems : "The freedom which is realised in the general will is the freedom of the state as a whole, but the state exists to acquire individual freedom for its members" (Cole, op. cit., p. XXXI). Hence it is not correct to say that the state's interference in the affairs of individuals is designed to curtail freed on of men. Rousseau definitely did not mean that. He wanted to enhance the amount of freedom through the leadership of the state. The true purpose of Rousseau will be clear from the following comment made by him : "The sovereign cannot impose upon its subjects any fetters that are useless to the community, nor can it even wish to do so." Rousseau's sovereign power has moral and ethical sense and, because of this reason, it will not impose any restrictions upon its subjects mainly for the purpose of curtailing their freedom. He has said that, while the members of the body politic are uniting with others they will keep their freedom in safe custody. They will never surrender their freedom which they enjoyed in the state of nature. But, for general and greater interest, the members may sacrifice their liberty. But this special situation cannot be treated as curtailment of freedom. Herbert Spencer was a great individualist and champion of human freedom. Even he accepted—at limited scale—the interference of the state in individual affairs. In modern times, the state interferes with the affairs of some persons or institutions to prevent the loss of freedom of some persons. Rousseau also thought in the same line.

ROUSSEAU AND MARX

In recent years, scholars have started to investigate the importance of Rousseau and have found that Marx is indebted to Rousseau in many respects. The thought-provoking work has been published by the renowned Italian Marxist Lucio Colletti.

His *From Rousseau to Lenin* has recharged our interest about Rousseau in the sense that Rousseau foretold many revolutionary ideas which are found in Marx's writings. Here I quote few words from Colletti's above-noted book : "Revolutionary political theory, as it has developed since Rousseau, is already foreshadowed and contained in the *Social Contract*, or to be more explicit, that so far as political theory in the strict sense is concerned, Marx and Lenin have added nothing to Rousseau except for the analysis of the "economic bases for the withering away of the state" (p. 185). This assessment of Colletti—though an exaggerated one—is very important.

Lucio Colletti says that how Marx is indebted to Rousseau is to be explained by Marx's critique of *Hegel's Philosophy of Rights*. Here Marx speaks of dissolution of the state and, at the same time, the dissolution of civil society. The purpose of Rousseau's social contract was to dissolve the state. It is because the civilised state, a product of arts and sciences, is responsible for the moral degeneration and alienation of people from the mainstream of society. Rousseau wanted to replace the perverted state by a right, moral and ethical political organisation. In Rousseau's judgment the new state produced by the social contract shall be the right and most desirable state. Marx has said that the proletariat—through class struggle and revolution—will set up a new state which will be called a proletariat state. Colletti believes that Rousseau's just state and Marx's proletarian state have almost similar features.

In Book I, Chapter IX Rousseau makes certain observations which are indicative of the idea that he foreshadowed Marx. The caption of the chapter is Real Property. I want to quote certain observations of Rousseau :

1. "The state is the master of all their goods by the social contract, which within the state is the basis of all rights." In Marxian sense the state is the owner of all property or natural resources and, naturally, these are to be used for the benefit of all members of the body politic.
2. Every man has naturally a right to everything he needs; but the positive act which makes him proprietor of one thing excludes him from everything else... he can have no further right against the community.
3. In his *A Discourse on the Origin of Inequality* he said "I have endeavoured to trace the origin and progress of inequality. ....It follows from this survey that, as there is hardly any inequality in the state of nature, all the inequality which now prevails own its strength and growth to the development of our faculties and the advance of human mind, and becomes at last permanent and legitimate by the establishment of property and laws" (p. 221).
4. Since it is plainly contrary to the law of nature that children should command old men, fools wise men, and that the privileged few should gorge themselves with superfluities, while the starving multitude are in want of the bare necessities of life (p. 221).

All the above observations of Rousseau amply prove that Rousseau had a soft corner about the non-privileged section of the society. It is true that, like Marx and Engels, he did not systematically and scientifically state everything. This may be his shortcoming. But it is undeniable that he clearly understood the miserable condition of the have-nots section of the civil society. Marx is also indebted to Rousseau for the concept of alienation.

INFLUENCE OF ROUSSEAU

Almost all the political philosophers are more or less controversial, but in the list of the controversial thinkers, most probably Rousseau occupies the top position. In spite of this the students of Western political thought read his political ideas with all seriousness. The simple reason is his ideas still evoke our thought and interest. The French philosopher Voltaire did not like him. On the contrary, the German philosophers were influenced by his thought—especially his general will and idealism. Marx borrowed the concept of alienation from Rousseau. Marx's socialist thought can be traced to Rousseau's ideas about inequality and its origin.

The German idealism was enormously influenced by Rousseau's idealist philosophy. In this connection we can remember what Gettell said. In Germany, Rousseau exerted a mighty though contrary, influence. The school of German idealism was much influenced by Rousseau's concept of general will. His concept of general will served as a basis for German nations of the "will of the people" (p. 257). Kant has admitted that while studying Rousseau's *Emile* he formed several important conclusions which influenced his entire thought system. Both Rousseau and Kant desired to establish a conciliation between politics and morality. Both were convinced that there was no conflict between politics and morality. This idea was first pronounced by Plato and after him Rousseau revived it. Kant has said that in the field of natural science the discovery of Newton was epochmaking. The place of Rousseau in social science may easily be compared with Newton. The German philosophers have used the term 'the will of the people'. This term is borrowed from Rousseau's general will. The will of the people and G. W. are all assimilated in the will of the state.

The English idealists were also not free from the influence of Rousseau. Rather, their inspiration was chiefly drawn from Rousseau. T. H. Green's noted work *Principles of Political Obligations* contains a chapter known as *Sovereignty and General Will.* This chapter contains the main ideas of Rousseau. Green made an effort to reconcile between Rousseau's idealism contained in the G. W. and Austin's realism. To what extent Green achieved success is a different question but Rousseau's influence on Green is undeniable. Green has said—Will, not force, is the basis of the state. This is Rousseau's idea.

The impact of Rousseau's philosophy upon the French Revolution is inestimable. In the opinion of Burke the works of Rousseau were the ideal source of action for the French revolutionaries. He has been called the Godfather of the French Revolution. It is said the Parliament of Rennes quoted almost textually from Rousseau. Rousseau's idea of liberty created a tremendous impact upon the thought and activities of the French revolutionaries. Berki says, France saw tremendous eruptions, the overthrow of the whole social system, the appearance of a truly radical, truly disturbing doctrine in the centre...it is undeniable that there is some resemblance between his formulations and the pronouncements as well as actions of some of the most outstanding revolutionary leader" (*The History of Political Thought,* p. 166). The leaders of the French Revolution uttered the words from *A Discourse on Inequality* and *Social Contract.*

Plamenatz says that Rousseau's idea about liberty is really unique. According to Rousseau, men are not guided or controlled by impulse of appetite. His concept of freedom is not simply political or economic, it is moral and ethical. They want to get this freedom through the mechanism of G. W. or, more specifically, the body politic. But Rousseau's state is different from other ordinary states. It is a moral person. G.D.H. Gole said that the *Social Contract* is by far the best of all textbooks on political philosophy. Cole continues : Rousseau's political influence, so far from being dead, is everyday increasing and as new generations and new classes of men come to study his work, his conceptions, often hazy and undeveloped, but nearly always of lasting value, will assuredly form the basis of a new political philosophy, in which they will be taken up and transformed" (*Social Contract and Discourse. Introduction*, p. XLI).

Rousseau is regarded by many as the grandfather of modern socialist thinkers. There is a certain amount of exaggeration in this opinion, but it is true that in his writings there lies socialist thought in embryonic form. He was quite worried about the pitiable condition of the unprivileged people of society and growing inequalities among various people. For this undesirable condition he squarely blamed the growth of civilisation and sciences. Loss of morality, ethics and values are also to be blamed.

Dunning observes : "In the field of politics, Rousseau's teaching was suggestive rather than conclusive, but the stimulating force of his suggestions long remained a cardinal fact of literature and history. His fancies, fallacies and quibbles often appealed more strongly than the sober observations and balanced reasoning of Montesquieu to the Zeitgeist of the later eighteenth century. But the pure philosophy of politics and the practical statesmanship of the time clearly illustrate this. His spirit and dogmas are seen everywhere both in speculative system and in organisation" (pp. 38–39).

16 HOBBES, LOCKE AND ROUSSEAU COMPARED

Nature of State : Hobbes

In the previous three chapters we have discussed the social contract theory of three contractualists—Hobbes, Locke and Rousseau. But it is necessary to make a comparative study of the three contractualists because they differ from each other regarding the important aspects of the social contract. All the three philosophers held the view that the state or civil society or body politic was the product of contract made by men who lived in the state of nature. There are few similarities among them, but differences are more prominent. In this comparative survey we first deal with the nature of state as it is revealed in the writings of these three writers.

Hobbes conceived of an all powerful state which is also called an autocratic or collectivist state. Why did he propound the idea of such a state? The chief factor is, in his opinion, the people in the state of nature were quarrelsome, hostile with each other and restless. Moreover, there were no peace and security. All these led to the non-development of art, literature, trade, commerce and transport. Hobbes believed that a very powerful state with absolute sovereign authority could restore peace and security and bring about general progress.

To Hobbes the state is a machine. He depicted a gloomy picture of state of nature which was analogous to the picture of the British society of his time. In order to change the picture an all-powerful state was required and, in that case, the state will act as a machine. Except state no other organisation had the capacity to fulfil this demand. He reposed his confidence only on the state, to him any other organisation had no imprtance. People could rely upon the state. The consequence of Hobbesian logic is a despotic state. To him there was no difference between monarchy and tyranny.

Hobbes thought that only a state with on absolute sovereignty at the top of power could free the society from anarchy. Naturally, individual freedom had no importance to him. The individuals must surrender to the wills and authority of the absolute sovereign power. After the formation of the civil society the individuals surrendered all their rights to the sovereignty. Even they had no right to resist the state. Hobbes denied sovereign power's accountability to the people. We conclude that the *Hobbesian state is not democratic, it is absolutist.*

But Ebenstein observes that Hobbes cannot be called a totalitarian or collectivist thinker because he made special provisions for individuals. He said that none could force a person from taking food or medicine. Individuals have freedom to pursue their own faith.

Hobbes's is a utilitarian state. It was set up to achieve certain special purposes—specially peace and security. Peace and security are both collective and individual matters. Hence we can say that Hobbes made room for individuals.

Hobbes envisaged of a secular state. In the *Leviathan* he said that there was no place of a separate government for religion or church. The church was a spiritual organisation under the temporal authority and on that ground it was obliged to show loyalty to the king. Dunning has said that in the opinion of Hobbes there was no room for separate authority of church. This is obvious in his exaltation of political sovereignty. From the analysis of Hobbes it appears to us that he was thinking of a state which would be free from the authority and influence of the church. This is nearer to the idea of a secular state. The concept of a secular state was envisaged by Machiavelli.

Nature of State : Locke

Commenting upon the difference in approaches of Hobbes and Locke towards the state Prof. Harold Laski (*The State in Theory and Practice,* p. 43) has said "Hobbes's immense edifice is built, in the last analysis, upon the dual foundation of a belief that human nature is evil and that only an irrestible sovereign can maintain order against its inherent tendency to evil. Locke starts with a belief in the goodness of human nature and the danger of any government which can act without regard to the wishes of its subjects". Here lies the basic difference between Hobbes and Locke so far as the state is concerned.

According to Hobbes the state of nature lacked peace and security and, for that purpose, people of the state of nature entered into a contract for laying down the foundation of the state. But Locke has observed that the people of the state of nature were happy, but they were confronted with certain inconveniences which they could not remove. Important inconvenience, according Locke, was absence of man-made laws. This resulted in partial anarchy and loss of life, liberty and property. The chief objective of the state would be to protect these. The chief function of the state would be to provide security to life, liberty and property.

Pointing out the characteristic of Lockean state C. L. Wayper has said the state exists for the welfare of the people and not the opposite. Locke has said that the end of the government is the good of the community. The failure of the state to attain this goal will not justify its existence. It is an indication of the fact that Locke's state envisaged a welfare state which was absent in Hobbes's philosophy.

Locke's state was a machine. This is the opinion of C. L. Wayper. Locke said that the state was created by people to fulfil certain specific purposes. People of the state of nature somehow came to the conclusion that only through the machinery of the state could they protect their natural rights—that is, right to life, liberty and property. The human factor is the most important element of a state. Locke ruled out divinity from the arena of state. In this way state was converted into a machine.

So far as the formation and day-to-day functioning of the state are concerned Locke has introduced the ideas of consent and majority decision. The latter indicates how much a practical man Locke was. Day to day administration would be an impossibility if it were allowed to persist. For that reason Locke recommended majority opinion. This is a practical suggestion. Hobbes ruled out people's participation in the administration. Sovereign authority's will was final. People were deprived of contradicting that will. We can say that while Hobbes's state was autocratic, Locke's was democratic.

From Locke's contract theory we can draw the conclusion that his is the constitutional state because the government must follow the rules and principles laid down in the contract. This is called constitutionalism. The relationship between the governor and governed would be determined by the rule of law and not by arbitrary orders. The basis of the government and governance would be law. In Hobbes's state there was a place of law, but the law was nothing but the dictate or will of the sovereign authority. Hobbes had no intention to allow people's participation in the law-making process.

The theory of state envisaged by the contract is also a limited state. Some political scientists also call it a state like the night watchman. It means that the state will perform the duties prescribed by the contract. This concept influenced Bentham, Mill and many others. On the other hand, Hobbes's state is not limited, but an unlimited one. Hobbes did not think of limiting the power of the state.

Locke's state is negative because it does not intend to improve the character of the people. Wayper has said that it is a *transformer* state, because it seeks to transform the self-interest into public good. Locke's state is active and ebullient.

Locke did not recognise that the state should play definite and positive role in religious affaris. He was also against the interference of the church in the political affairs of the state.

Since Hobbes's state was absolute he advised people to show unconditional allegiance to the state. While in the case of Locke the obligation to the state is conditional. So long as the state will be able to fulfil the terms of contract people will not hesitate to show obligation to the state. But the failure of the state will definitely invite resistance against the state.

While analysing the various aspects of state both Hobbes and Locke were considerably guided by bourgeois philosophy. Hobbes's concept of the maintenance of peace and security and Locke's theory—the attainment of natural rights—right to life, liberty and property—constitute the core of bourgeois philosophy. Both Hobbes and Locke did not think about the problems of common people. The state was a machine to both—but it was a machine for the attainment of privileges of well-to-do people. Common, people deprived of basic necessities, cannot think of peace and security or life, liberty and property. This is the opinion of C. B. Macpherson.

Nature of State : Rousseau

The nature of state as well as the other aspects of state as found in Rousseau are different from those of Hobbes and Locke. Rousseau's state was created not to ensure peace and security or to protect life, liberty and property its purpose is more sublime that is ethical and ideological. Rousseau was influenced by Plato. Rousseau's state is a moral body or organisation and its duty is to make its citizens moral and ideal. Only through the membership of state can individuals become moral persons and exercise moral principles and objectives. Rousseau believed that the morality and idealism of a state are not different from those of the individuals. This is the idealist version of a state. About 2,000 years after Plato, Rousseau revived idealism oridealist theory of state.

It is very difficult or, so to say, impossible, to separate state from the g.w. Rousseau's state acts or discharges its function through the g.w. Again this g.w. is the product of the people assembled in an open assembly. The general administration of the state, under no circumstances can violate the principles of the g.w. If necessity arises to change anything about the g.w. the people assembled together will do it, the state administration has no jurisdiction in this regard.

This relationship between state and general will leads us to conclude that Rousseau's state is not only democratic but also republic. The general will is arrived at by the people's direct participation in open assembly. In his state there is not only democracy, but his democracy is of direct type. We may say Rousseau thought of a state in the line of the Greek city-state. In both places there was direct democracy.

Behind the formation of general will there is a social process. It implies that Rousseau's state is always active and never in hibernation. Harold Laski observes "Rousseau sought a formula of state which, in its operations, would secure an equal interest for all citizens in the result of the social process" (*The State in Theory and Practice*, p. 44).

Rousseau's state stands for the full realisation of freedom. In Chapter I of *Social Contract* Rousseau made the following remark : "Man is born free; but everywhere he is in chains". Outside the state, man cannot achieve freedom. In an oblique way we can say that Rousseau treated state as a kind of machine—a machine for achieving freedom. So far as this aspect is concerned he is not very much different from Hobbes and Locke.

Hobbes and Locke thought of establishing a state through the contract and this state was simply a political organisation. But Rousseau's state is a moral organisation and public person. It is not simply a political organisation. Rousseau had no intention to give a political colour to state. His state will fulfil political and other objectives as well. Rousseau said "The problem is to find a form of association which will defend and protect with the whole common force the person and goods of each associate".

According to Rousseau, absolute power will be vested in the state. This resembles Hobbes's view about state. But Rousseau thought that the power must come from the people through the means of general will. Hobbes—in the furthest sense could not imagine of a general will. This means that the administrators had no power to go against the general will. Locke made the state a fiduciary trust. People could not dislodge a government from power so long it honestly obeyed the terms and conditions of the contract.

The state envisaged by Rousseau is of organic character. All the individuals are integral parts of the state. They will lose their significance when separated from the main body of the state. In other words, their significance lies in the fact that they are members of the body politic. Rousseau's state is a "moral and collective body".

Sovereignty : Hobbes

In *Leviathan* Hobbes declared—"I authorise and give up my right of governing myself to this man or to this assembly of men". Another statement runs "Covenants without sword are but words and of no strength to secure a man at all". Interpreters of Hobbes's philosophy treat these two statements as basic sources of his concept of sovereignty. Hobbes was so much preoccupied with the maintenance of peace and security that he had no time to think of any other thing. His ideas about the state of nature (though imaginary) and the social economic condition of contemporary Britain inspired him to arrive at the conclusion that a sovereign authority with absolute power could be the only remedy to the uncalled-for situation. For this reason Hobbes made the sovereign power absolute. Not only it is absolute, it is indivisible and inalienable. Since Hobbes, these are being treated as the most important characteristics of sovereignty.

The sovereign power may be vested in the hands of a single person or group of persons. But Hobbes had always a preference for one person because it is quite easy for one person to exercise absolute power. Even Austin and several other thinkers have supported that sovereign power is to be vested in a single person. When one man is sovereign his will and decision are final.

Hobbes has suggested that the sovereign will rule with the help of law or terms and conditions of the covenant and when these will establish their inefficiency or insufficiency he will not hesitate to use arms or sword. It is said that he had no weakness or special preference for law. The use of arms or laws fully depends upon the gravity of the situation. Some critics say that Hobbes had special preference for weapons.

Sovereignty : Locke

Commenting upon Locke's theory of sovereignty, Barker (*Social Contract : Locke, Hume and Rousseau*, p. XXXII) has said "Locke has no clear view of the nature or residence of sovereignty. He speaks at one time of the supreme power of the people or in other words the community; he speaks of another supreme power of the legislature". This indicates that Locke had no clear concept about sovereignty. On the question of sovereignty Hobbes's stand is transparent though highly debatable. In regard to sovereignty Hobbes is to some extant nearer to Bodin and Locke is nearer to Rousseau. Both Hobbes and Bodin are the joint "proprietors" of the modern theory of sovereignty.

J. W. Gough (*John Locke's Political Philosophy*) has said that Locke in his earlier writings was influenced by Hobbesian concept of absolute sovereignty but for unknown (or known reason unknown to us) reason he changed the "phraseology". This opinion of Gough is controversial. To what extent and why Locke was influenced by Hobbes in respect of sovereignty is not known to us. His different writings prove that he was not in favour of an absolute sovereignty.

Hobbes was the staunch supporter of absolute sovereignty and we think that it is fully consistent with the main currents of his political philosophy. His chief purpose was to banish disorder and anarchy from society and thereby set-up peace and security. Only an absolute power could achieve that objective. He had no sympathy or weakness for democratic government. This apathy to democracy led him to formulate the theory of absolute sovereignty. On the contrary, Locke, on the other hand, was an ardent supporter of democracy and constitutionalism and all these are not consistent with the absoluteness of power in the hands of a single man. That is why he vested powers in the hands of persons or their representatives.

In Section 135 Locke has said that the legislative power may be placed at the hands of one or more persons, but it is always supreme power in the commonwealth. Therefore, all other powers or bodies are subordinate to the legislative authority. In Section 149 he has said the same thing. The commonwealth may be constituted according to its own nature, but there shall be provision of supremacy of legislature.

Hobbes has always used the word sovereignty, but Locke is evasive. He sometimes says sovereign power and sometimes supreme power. Of course, in general terms, both carry almost the same idea. However, we may draw an inference from this. Hobbes had a determination about the meaning and use of the term which Locke has not. This makes a clear difference between the two architects of social contract.

From Hobbesian theory of sovereignty we cannot deduce any idea of popular or parliamentary sovereignty. But it is possible from Lockean philosophy. He attributed sovereign power to the legislature. That means parliament will exercise supreme power. The term parliamentary sovereignty is quite known to the students of political science and perhaps it would not be unreasonable to attribute the status of father of parliamentary sovereignty to Locke. He did not directly use the term, but we believe that most probably he had the idea or an idea nearer to the concept. It is also possible to draw another inference from this. Parliament is constituted by the representatives elected by the people. Hence popular will is reflected in parliament. Thus parliamentary sovereignty may be called popular sovereignty. He, of course, does not use the term.

Hobbes's sovereignty had unlimited power over all persons and society. On the other hand, Locke had no intention to grant unlimited power to sovereign authority. He has said in Section 135 "it is not, nor can possibly be absolutely arbitrary over the lives and fortunes of the people". The reason he cited was—legislative, being only fiduciary power to act for certain ends, these remain still in the people supreme power. It means that the legislature—though supreme authority was nothing but a fiduciary trust. It was entrusted by the people to function in accordance with the terms and conditions of the contract.

We have already noted that while Hobbes is consistent in the analysis of sovereignty Locke is not. The latter has shifted his stand frequently. According to Hobbes supreme power would be vested in one person or group of persons. This much Locke has said that the same may be vested in (a) legislature, (b) the people; and (c) the community. The last word (i. e., community) is available in Section 49. We, therefore, conclude that it is very difficult to arrive at a definite conclusion so far as sovereignty is concerned.

Though Locke is full of inconsistencies, we are of opinion that we always prefer Locke to Hobbes. This is due to the reason that absolute sovereignty is another name of autocracy and we do not like it at all. The logical consistency of Hobbes has been the source of dislike and the logical inconsistency has led us to like Locke. Since political science is a normative science we cannot neglect this liking and disliking.

Sovereignty : Rousseau

Four Chapters (1 to 4) of Book II of *Social Contract* have been devoted to analysis of sovereignty. Rousseau has dealt with the subject sporadically in other parts of his book. According to Rousseau the general will is sovereign. Let us quote him

"...the general will alone can direct the state according to the object for which it was instituted, i.e., common good" (Book II, Chapter I). In other words, the sovereign power is vested in the general will. And the purpose of the general will is to translate common good into reality. So every one of the body politic will be governed by the common good. It would be the sole basis of the governance of society. He has further said "Sovereignty being nothing less than the exercise of the general will can never be alienated." We thus see that Rousseau's sovereignty is inalienable. In Chapter II he has noted that it is also indivisible. Rousseau's sovereignty is, further, absolute, as well as infallible. The general will being arrived at in an open assembly participated by all (or almost all) can never do any wrong. From the analysis Rousseau made in the above-noted Chapters in regard to sovereignty, three salient features can be deduced—sovereignty is inalienable, indivisible and absolute.

So far as the concept of sovereignty is concerned Rousseau stands very close to Hobbes. In fact there is very striking similarity between the two. But this similarity is a misnomer. There are more differences than similarity between the two and the differences have made Rousseau popular to his readers. Rousseau's general will is sovereign and it is again the embodiment of common good which aims at the general well being of the body politic. In fact, this is the central idea of his theory of sovereignty.

In Hobbes's opinion the will of the sovereignty is absolute and all other wills are subordinate to it. But he is silent on the wishes or wills of all individuals are reflected on the will of the sovereignty. Whereas, in Rousseau's judgment, general will is the embodiment of all wills of the society. It is never the particular will of a particular person. Therefore, in Rousseau's concept, there is no scope of the prevalence of any individual will.

In this connection it may further be observed that both Hobbes and Rousseau strengthened the foundation of nation-state through their formulations of sovereignty. In the Middle Ages the sovereignty was divided. Power was exercised simultaneously by the church, the king and the feudal lords. But the division of sovereignty practically leads to nothing about it. Hobbes, Bodin and Rousseau made remarkable contribution to the concept of sovereignly. But the point is to be noted that Rousseau's sovereignty is both absolute and popular.

If Rousseau is closer in certain respects to Hobbes he is also closer to Locke in other respects. In fact, Rousseau, in his formulation of sovereignty, combined both Hobbes and Locke. Dunning's comment is worth quoting : "Rousseau, with his characteristic boldness, proceeded to reconcile the absolutist with the liberal doctrine. He defined sovereignty with the fullness and precision of Hobbes and gave it an abode and an operation that satisfied the feeling of Locke" (Vol. 3, P. 21).

Locke's theory of sovereignty was not a full-fledged popular sovereignty, but it was not at all the absolute sovereignty envisaged by Hobbes. However, in Locke's theory of sovereignty, there was a place of popular will. Rousseau made his sovereignty popular by introducing the concept that the general will is the determiner of everything. Assembling at an open place, people form the general will. We can, therefore, say that Rousseau has removed all doubts about the fact that general will or, so to say, the common good, is the sovereign power.

Locke has said, "The community perpetually retains a supreme power of saving themselves from the attempts and designs of anybody". The implication is, if the existence of community is not threatened the community will go on exercising its power. But if any other organ of the government proceeds to threaten the unity or existence of the community it will withdraw its support to it. From Locke's idea it appears that the constitution is sovereign. He does not directly refer to this but we can form such an idea from his analysis. But if the authority obeys the constitution or law none can dislodge the authority from power. In the case of Rousseau the g.w. is absolute and its decision is final. Even if the g.w. commits mistake or violates rule none can remove it from power. This difference between Locke and Rousseau is vital and interesting.

Finally it may be pointed out that though Rousseu's sovereign power is absolute it has no authority to infringe the right and liberty of the people. He has in clear language stated that people formed the association to combine the power of all members so that the joint force could protect the liberty of all. But this condition does not weaken the idea that sovereign is absolute.

Obligation and Resistance : Hobbes

Hobbes has not directly dealt with the concept of obligation in his great work *Leviathan*. But an in-depth analysis of the various aspects of contract reveals that he had an idea about obligation. The state of nature was infested with war, suspicion against each other, involvement in war or conflicts centering around pretty interests. The residents of the state of nature were quite eager to find out a way out and finally they decided to set-up a commonwealth which could defend them from the invasion of foreigners and the injuries of one another. It is now obvious that the inhabitants of the state of nature on their own accord decided to form a political organisation.

Explaining Hobbes's stand on obligation, D. D. Raphael (*Problems of Political Philosophy*, p. 88) says "The citizens are obliged to obey the laws both because they have promised to do so, and because the alternative to a politically organised society is the state of nature". This obligation of Hobbes is of two types—moral and prudential. It is moral because leaving the state of nature they formed commonwealth and framed laws. Since these were their own creation they had no moral right to withdraw obligation from these conditions and rules. It is also prudential obligation because the only alternative to civil society is the state of nature which is tantamount to disorder and chaos.

Another aspect of Hobbes's idea of obligation is because of the unfavourable situation the state of nature lacked peace and security, but these were indispensable for peaceful living and progress of society. But they thought that a sovereign with absolute power was the only remedy and thinking in this line people of state of nature thought it prudent to show unconditional obligation.

We believe that Hobbes's emphasis is more upon prudential obligation than on moral obligation. A state with absolute sovereignty is preferable to anarchical state. This can be viewed as the utilitarian character of obligation. People forming the commonwealth were sure of maximising benefit from such organisation. Naturally, withdrawal of obligation would lead to the collapse of a commonwealth. There must be unconditional obligation to the state authority. It may be pointed out that Hobbes was conscious of conditional and unconditional obligation and he was in favour of the latter.

Generally speaking Hobbes's idea of obligation is viewed as unconditional. But he had some feeling for people and that feeling led him to make some concession for the people. In Part II, Chapter 21 he has said "The obligation of subjects to the sovereign is understood to last as long and no longer, than the power lasts, by which he is able to protect themselves. When none else can protect them, ...The end of obedience is protection; which wheresoever a man sees it either in his own or in another". Moreover, if the sovereign prevents the subjects from taking medicine or food, in that case they may refuse to show obligation. We thus see that Hobbes's view on obligation is associated with some sort of give-and-take policy. The sovereign must do some thing for the individuals and in exchange of that he can demand obligation. In this sense it is to some extent conditional. We have already noted that there are few and sporadic views about individualism in his writings and his idea of conditional obligation strengthens that stand.

Obligation and Resistance : Locke

John Locke is quite explicit about his approach to obligation and resistance. But if we analyse the various stages or the process of contract which brought about civil society we shall find that he had an idea about the two concepts. Like Hobbes he did not depict gloomy picture of the state of nature. People left the state of nature and entered into a contract to build up a body-politic chiefly on the ground that the state of nature suffered from certain inconveniences which they could not remove. In the state of nature individuals could not fully get life, liberty and property and pursuit of happiness was affected and this was due to clear positive law's absence. Moreover, there was no impartial authority. People finalising the contract imposed responsibility upon the government to achieve these things.

The idea of obligation emanates from this view of Locke. People will judge whether their life, liberty and property are adequately protected and pursuit of happiness is enhanced. The non-fulfilment of these requirement would lead them to withdraw their obligation to the government. The support to the government which they formed was conditional. In this respect Locke stands on the opposite pole held by Hobbes. Hobbes made no provision for withdrawing obligation in the situation of non-fulfilment of peace and security. In a sense Locke's view about obligation is prudential in the sense that it would be the primary duty of the authority of civil society to ensure the removal of drawbacks of the state of nature and in that field the success of authority will invite obligation. Any failure will be followed by the withdrawal of obligation. It is in this sense prudential.

In Section 97, Locke hints at "original" compact which is an indication of the fact that there was non-original contract. Interpreters of Lockean thought system have argued that there was another contract between people and the government. The central theme of any contract is either party shall have the freedom to withdraw in the case of failure of fulfilment of terms. Scholars are of opinion that, as per the second contract, people reserve the right to withdraw their support when the government fails to translate the conditions of the contract into reality.

According to Locke the state is a type of fiduciary trust which means that it is always accountable to the people. The failure to follow the terms of the contract will be followed by the withdrawal of obligation. The judgment of the people whether the state is doing according to the terms of contract is final. Hence people may express its noconfidence against the authority. But before that they must be sure that the authority has failed. This conditional type of obligation is really unique in all constitutional systems of government.

Raphael has drawn our attention to another aspect of Locke's theory of obligation. He says (*op. cit.* 102) that our obligation to state laws depends upon their ability to meet or achieve justice. If the laws fail the individuals are not obliged to obey laws that is to show obligation to the authority. Raphael has further observed that justice can be attained through the realisation of natural rights. These natural rights, according to Locke, are life, liberty, property and the opportunity to pursue happiness. He was of opinion that the people of the state of nature were deprived of justice because of the non-fulfilment of these natural rights which were also "absolute moral rights". Raphael concludes "Locke's view was that the state is designed to guarantee and protect natural rights. ...We may expand his doctrine and say that the state is designed and guarantee justice i.e., established rights plus fairness" (p. 103). Raphael has viewed Lockean idea of obligation in greater and deeper perspective. Justice is achieved through natural rights and their protection or realisation is the duty of state. Any failure in this regard will affect justice and people will think whether they will continue to display the obligation.

Locke's theory of resistance is closely associated with his theory of obligation. In general there is a subtle difference between the two. However, Locke was of opinion that if any foreign power by means of military strength could conquer a territory the individuals might rise against the authority. The individuals would have every right to resist any sort of foreign aggression. The right to resist enunciated by Locke is the product of his conception of contract and establishment of civil society. People coming from the state of nature unanimously decided to set-up body-politic and also formed the rules for its management. If any external power proceeds to destroy their creation they cannot accept the power. In Sections 185 to 190 of The *Second Treatise* of Government Locke has elaborated resistance.

In Sections 220-223 he has also explained the resistance. If the legislature or prince violates the trust reposed upon it people would not hesitate to resist that. "Governments are dissolved... When the legislative or prince act contrary to their trust" (Section 221). Locke has also stated other situations which are the reasons of resistances. These are if the authority forcibly deprived people of their legal property, if it is involved in corrupt practices, forfeits the power of the people and tries to satisfy the high ambition.

A section of critics holds that an important drawback of Locke's theory of obligation is it is conditional. But we do not agree with this view. The constitutional structure of a civil society was alive in his mind and in such a system people cannot act whimsically. In one fine morning they cannot withdraw their support to the government and cannot create anarchical situation. For every small mistakes people cannot withdraw support. The relation between the ruler and the ruled must be cordial and this is a reason why the obligation is conditional. Only in the case of major and far-reaching consequences resulting from the governmental act people may think of withdrawing support.

Rousseau on Obligation

Rousseau has not directly and elaborately analysed the concept of obligation. But the theory of general will contains practically all the major aspects of obligation. Let us start with the contention that there is a very small similarity between Hobbes and Rousseau so far as obligation is concerned. Both Hobbes and Rousseau were in favour of unconditional obligation. Hobbes advised his people to show unconditional obligation to the sovereign authority without which there could not be peace and security. Rousseau also advised his people to obey the general will because herein lies the welfare of all men and it cannot do any wrong. Naturally the obligation to such a will should never be conditional. Again, if anybody refuses to show obligation he will be forced to show obligation.

The chief difference between the two philosophers is that obligation of Hobbes's people was to a single person whereas obligation of Rousseau's people was towards the general will and people themselves were the architects of that will. So by showing obligation to general will Rousseau's men practically showed obligation to themselves.

In order to make a comprehensive analysis of obligation conceived by Rousseau we want to quote a lengthy passage from his *A Discourse on Political Economy.* "The body politic is a moral being possessed of a will; and this general will, which tends always to the preservation and welfare of the whole and of every part and is the source of the laws, constitutes for all the members of the state, in their relation to one another and to it, the rule of what is just or unjust". It emphasises the following aspects :

(a) To him the general will was a moral being.

(b) The general will always aims at the welfare of the whole society. Its purpose is also the preservation of the body politic.

(c) General will is the source of all laws.

(d) There is a close relation between general will and members of the body politic.

This nature of the general will forces the people to be obliged to it unconditionally. An alternative course of action will lead the body politic to destruction. But people will refrain from adopting that extreme and dangerous path. It was beyond the imagination of Rousseau that his individuals (i.e., the individuals of the body-politic) would take that action. This is the very foundation of Rousseau's theory of obligation. Moreover, laws are enacted to realise the welfare and preservation of the body-politic. Behind the enactment of law there was the active participation of people to disobey such meant to disobey themselves. The general will, again, is the manifestation of morality and, naturally, non-obligation cannot arise.

We have noted elsewhere that Rousseau imagined a state resembling human body. "The body-politic, taken individually, may be considered as an organised, living body, resembling that of man. The sovereign power represents the head, the laws and customs are the brain." As individuals are the parts of the body politic, there is hardly any scope for any particular individual to non-cooperate with the body politic. This observation of Rousseau regarding the organic character of state is similar to Plato's theory of state. Different parts of state are interdependent. Since Rousseau's body politic possesses the features of living body the obligation to such an organisation appears to be unconditional. All the parts of the organisation are closely related with each other and in such a case obligation is bound to be unconditional. Rousseau apprehended that a conditional obligation may lead the state to collapse.

G. D. H. Cole in his *Introduction* to *Social Contract* has interpreted Rousseau's idea of obligation in the following way. Since his general will is rational and infallible and men are also rational they are supposed to show unqualified obligation to the general will. Any aberration will expose the irrationality of the people and this is in opposition to Rousseau's main contention. So in the vortex of arguments Rousseau's concept of obligation has come to be an unqualified one.

It would be quite wrong to treat Rousseau's view of obligation as a mere conjecture or wishful thought. It is far more than that. It embodies a very high ideal. Through the instrumentality of general will he wanted to state that the members of the body politic would keep themselves above narrow and personal interests. He was of firm belief that the deviation of people from showing obligation to general will would threaten the very foundation of the body politic. His rational people would not resort to that technique.

He did not consider the obligation simply as a relation between the governor and governed. It is far more sublime and full of ideals and morality. The main pillar of Rousseau's political thought is general will and the core of the general will is obligation. He has viewed it from a comprehensive perspective. It is backgrounded by Plato's idealism. It constituted the central theme of direct democracy. It reveals people's rationality and pursuit of happiness. Rousseau adopted a sublime and universal outlook. So we can say that Rousseau kept himself above narrowness of personal interest. Mere attainment of certain rights was not important to him. Neither Hobbes nor Locke thought of morality or idealism. Nor did they treat obligation as a weapon for the advancement of welfare and preservation of the state. While considering obligation of the three philosophers we should keep this in mind.

It may further he added that through the general will and civil society Rousseau made a modest attempt to revive Plato's idealism to which he was attracted. Plato made all the citizens as integral parts of the ideal state and he kept no scope of difference between citizens and ruler. Plato's ruler is not an ordinary person—he is a philosopher-king. There is hardly any scope of raising allegation against such a ruler. General will is the manifestation of morality, idealism and the best wishes of all men. Naturally, there is no question of withdrawing obligation.

Resistance and Rousseau

Hobbes was a staunch advocate of autocracy and he left no scope for the people to resist any decision or action of the authority which was not of their liking. This recommendation of Hobbes created lot of criticism. If we study Rousseau's political ideas we shall find that there was no opportunity for the individuals to criticise the general will. In Book I, Chapter 7 Rousseau has made the following famous observation : "In order that the social compact may not be an empty formula, it tacitly includes the undertaking, which alone can give force to the rest, that whoever refuses to obey the general will shall be compelled to do so by the whole body. This means nothing less than he will be forced to be free."

It is interesting to note that Rousseau's concepts of obligation and resistance are intrinsically related with each other. He has formulated the general will in such a manner that he has given no scope to the members of the body politic to withdraw obligation. On the same consideration people cannot resist the functions or the policies of the general will. If they are allowed to resist any move or function of the general will its entire fabric is bound to collapse. Hence the argument of withdrawing obligation or the right to resist general will is logically inconsistent. He emphasised people's liberty but did not recognise the right to resist.

Another reason of not recognising the right to resist is because the general will was formed at an open assembly participated by all the members of the body politic. He even he did not allow proxy system. Once the general will was agreed upon by all and in the next stage it was objected by some. Rousseau possesed the intelligence to understand that the coexistence between unanimity and scope of resistance would invite inconsistency.

The social compact entitled people to enjoy moral freedom. Through the authority of the general will individuals could enjoy moral freedom. But if right to resist makes the general will unworkable the moral freedom will remain unrealised. Naturally people must show obligation to general will and all the laws made by state.

Hobbes did not recognise the right to resist. The decision of the sovereignty is final. Locke admitted the right to resist only in exceptional circumstances. Hence resistance is conditional. In Rousseau's analysis there is no scope of resistance. We thus find that there is slight similarity between Hobbes and Rousseau on the issue of resistance. But this is superficial. Rousseau's idea of general will is sublime and this has spread its wings all over the thought.

Hobbes wanted to give top priority to peace and security and he believed that resistance to authority's decision would threaten their attainment. Locke did not want to embarrass the government on any flimsy ground. On major aberration he permitted resistance. To Rousseau unity and integrity of body politic and moral freedom were most important. Any allowance to resistance would encourage groupism and invite narrow and harmfull politics in the state. Rousseau wanted to introduce values. Locke wanted to achieve natural rights and Hobbes wanted to ensure peace and security. These three different premises created impact upon the concept of resistance and have forced it assume different colours.

Hobbes on Democracy

To support the absolute monarchy in unequivocal language and the surrender of all rights to the sovereign authority, it is said, provide the powerful weapons for collectivist administration. The collectivism advocated by Hobbes has kept no room for democracy and for that reason Hobbes has never been regarded as an worshipper of democracy. Perhaps he did not intend to be so. If we study his *Leviathan* from top to bottom we shall not find him to be *very much sympathetic* with individual freedoms and rights. A king with absolute power was a model to him.

But one-sided evaluation must not be allowed to preoccupy our mind. It is not final that he was the staunchest advocate of collectivism. In his analysis we witness certain passages which display his sympathy for democracy. In other words it may be said that he had sympathy for democracy. Harmon, Sabine and Ebenstein are of opinion that he was not an out-and-out collectivist thinker. In the words of Harmon "Despite Hobbes's proposal to vest enormous powers to the hands of the sovereign, he did not advocate a totalitarian state". Ebenstein writes "yet to call Hobbes one of the spiritual fathers of totalitarian fascism or communism is more untenable than would appear from a cursory glance at several key phrases in *Leviathan*" (p. 363). There is reason behind this comment. Hobbes makes certain comments which are contradictory or convey different meaning at the same time. In spite of this, the fact remains that he had sufficient weakness for absolutism because he thought that this could save a turmoiled society. At the same time he had soft corner for individuals' life-saving needs. So both absolutism and democracy co-exist in his political philosophy.

Oakshot is of opinion that the source of modern individualism is nominalism. Its central idea is reality which is to be judged by the individual, society and social events. The central theme of Hobbesian thought system was individual and his interests. He categorically said that without peace and security development of arts, literature, trade and commerce was not possible. Needless to say that all these were related with the overall progress of individuals as important units of society. He thought for development not for any other purpose. If so, how can we jump upon the conclusion that he directed his arrow against the welfare and interests of individuals?

By emphasising upon the development of the environment of society and individuality Hobbes had strengthened the foundation of democracy. Modern democracy thinks about both individual and society. It is observed that both Plato and Aristotle neglected the individuals and idolised the state. But a deeper analysis will reveal that a proper ideal state—also properly administered—was capable of meeting the requirement of men. Hobbes focused on absolute sovereignty and he thought that if law, order and proper administration were restored, life and living of all individuals would be normal and the purpose of democracy—to some extent—is this.

Hobbes's sovereignty is very powerful, but his covenant is more powerful. Modern interpreters of Hobbesian thought are of opinion that by making the covenant powerful Hobbes has acted as the forerunner of the sovereignty of constitution. It is known to all that in democracy (if it is proper) the constitution is always supreme.

In democracy, individual's rights are always in prior position and Hobbes gave priority to right. Let us quote Ebenstein again : "Hobbes recognises the inalienable right of the individual to resist when life is at stake". If so, on what logic should we say that he was against democracy? He gave recognition to individual.

Locke on Democracy

Hobbes vis-a vis democracy is controversial. Locke's case is different. He is regarded as the symbol of democracy and constitutionalism. Starting from the foundation of civil society right up to the day-to-day administration Locke has adopted a liberal attitude which makes the way for the arrival and functioning of democracy. His love for democracy is undiluted and receives accolade from all corners of society.

In Section 96 Locke has observed that the residents of the state of nature built up community taking the consent of all persons. The repetition of the same thing is to be found in Section 97. Since behind the establishment of the community there was the consent of each and every individual, each is bound to obey the law of the community.

Locke was a clever man and he had experience of administration. Though unanimity was the factor of foundation of body politic, it could not be treated as an important factor of day-to-day administration. He, for this reason, introduced majority opinion—which constitues the main part of parliamentary rule.

Locke's main preoccupation was with the preservation of natural rights which people in the state of nature possessed. He regarded these as embodiment of justice and for the sake of justice he thought that these rights must be protected. To him these rights were also moral rights. However, the attainment and preservation of rights are the core of democracy. Locke said that the government must take measures for the attainment of life, liberty, property and pursuit of happiness. It would be no business of the government to neglect the individual by neglecting the natural rights.

Locke's contemporary society became the victim of absolute monarchy. Absolutism is the greatest enemy of individual freedom and democracy. We, therefore, see Locke to throw his unqualified support for constitutional government. He accompanied William and Mary from Holland to England and during their reign British Parliament passed the Bill of Rights which is a landmark event in the history of democracy in Britain.

As to the holder of supreme power the opinion of Locke is confusing. In a number of places he has said that the supreme authority of the civil society is vested in the legislature. It is all right. Elsewhere we find him saying the entire community is the holder of supreme power. The readers are in dilemma. Wherein exactly lies the supreme authority. Some critics are of the view that Lcoke had strong preference for parliamentary sovereignty.

If we go through the entire book *Second Treatise* we shall find that he had great sympathy and lot of feelings for individuals and this makes him an individualist. On this issue his position is direct opposite to Hobbes's stand. His heartfelt sympathy for common men is beyond question. At least Gough, the noted interpreter of Lockean philosophy, thinks so. This estimate, we believe, is an oversimplification. He was a democrat.

Rousseau and Democracy

From the past study we may frame the following conclusion. Hobbes was not a hundred percent autocrat, nor was he a perfect democrat. He was less a democrat and more an autocrat. To Locke both the legislature and the community were the holders of supreme power. But Locke is an inconsistent thinker. The legislature and community both cannot be holders of supreme power at the same time. But the stand of Rousseau in clear. The g.w. is the supreme authority and people assembling periodically decide the next course of action as well as policies. This is perfect democracy.

It is believed that his analysis of general will contains the idea of democracy. In Book II, Chapter IV Rousseau makes the following remarkable observation : "The general will, to be really such, must be general in its object, as well as its essence, that it must both come from all and apply to all; and that it loses its natural rectitude when it is directed to some particular and determinate object...what makes the will general is less the number of voters than the common interest uniting them". The central theme of democracy is that particular interest will never get any priority and Rousseau talked about that. In a democratic state the general welfare of the society will be placed above the personal interest and in the above passage Rousseau emphasised that. David Thomson in his eassy *"Rousseau and the General Will"* has said "It is this that makes Rousseau a great democractic theorist" (p. 98).

Rousseau did not judge democracy by number. In a society majority may be guided by personal interests while the minority may consider the general welfare and in that case minority's stand will be given approval. Even J. S. Mill (1806–1873) did not recognise majority rule as the criterion of successful democracy. Rousseau frowned upon British parliamentary democracy and said the British people are free only at the time of election.

It has been observed by many critics that while penning *Social Contract*, the memory of Greek city states was highly active in Rousseau's mind. But such a picture is quite irrelevant in our time. Naturally his conception about democracy cannot be accepted. But it is to be remembered that he thought of Greek city states or of his native Geneva to facilitate the personal involvement of all citizens in the law-making and decision taking process of the state and Rousseau considered this personal involvement as the vital aspect to democracy. So suspicion cannot be raised against Rousseau's view about democracy.

Rousseau thought that balkanisation of body politic is against the interest of society and he makes this point quite clear in Book II Chapter III where he said : "It is therefore essential if the general will is to be able to express itself, that there should be no partial society within the state." The implication is the division of society into small parts is against the proper functioning of g.w. and again if the g.w. does not function properly people's democratic right and its realisation will be adversely affected. In support of his contention Rousseau quotes Machiavelli. Machiavelli once said : "In fact there are some divisions that are harmful to a Republic". His apprehension was that if the g.w. cannot get scope to work properly, then people's democratic right turns into a fiasco.

Rousseau's love for democracy is revealed from his view expressed in Book IV, Chapter II where he has said that behind every law there shall be consent of all citizens. That is he wanted to make the law of the state unanimous. In the same chapter he has said that it is the duty of citizen to give consent to a law. The citizen shall have the right to express their opinion about any law but once it is accepted observing the norms of the general interest the dissenters must give their consent. We may say that by advancing this argument Rousseau had made the laws of the state really broad-based. His intention was to bring the minority into the fold of majority, and to stop the division of society into majority and minority sections. In any case minority will have to consider whether the law consented by majority is in conformity with the objectives and principles of general will.

In *A Discourse on the Origin of Inequality* Rousseau has maintained that in the state of nature there was hardly any inequality. This has been created and developed by the human faculties. Human nature and mind have made it legitimate and permanent. What Rousseau has not explicitly stated is that inequality is the creation of man for the gratification of parochial interests. This inequality is responsible for the deterioration of democracy. The state of nature was free from this sort of harmful inequality and he wanted to banish this by general will. Even today we treat inequality in status and wealth as the great enemy of democracy. We are surprised at the farsightedness of Rousseau who eloquently talked about inequality more than two hundred years ago.

Rousseau was not a statesman or a powerful leader of any mass party. With a deep insight he viewed the nature and working of government of his time. After this he came to the conclusion that the social evils are due to the social inequality.

The greatest worshippers of today's world say the same thing. There is no doubt that Rousseau was extremely anxious on seeing the condition of democracy. His anxiety is reflected on the last few lines in *A Discourse on the Origin of Inequality* : "Since it is plainly contrary to the law of nature, however defined, that children should command old men, fools wise men and that the privileged few should gorge themselves with superfluities, while the starving multitude are in want of the bare necessities of life". This view also reveals Rousseau's love for democracy. Democracy cannot thrive in a society divided into rich and poor because the former will dominate the latter. This is against democracy. His idea was that a real democracy should be preceded by economic equality.

We have briefly stated Rousseau's view on democracy. Whatever may be his love for democracy he was quite apprehensive of its practical side. He thought that real democracy could never be seen in actual life. In Book III, Chapter IV he said "It is unimaginable that the people should remain continually assembled to devote their time to public affairs". This means that he was quite conscious of the limitations of people. That is why he thought that democracy could not be achieved in real life. The last two lines of this chapter is worth quoting : "Were there a people of gods, their government would be democratic; so perfect a government is not for men." A question may arise why did he devote so much space to the analysis of general will and democracy? The most probable answer is he was very much influenced by the political idealism of Plato's *Republic* and he ignored the practical aspects of his thought.

17 EDMUND BURKE

Life and Works

This book contains the political philosophy of eminent thinkers. But Burke does not fall within this category. He was basically a politician and he is still remembered because of certain political ideas but these do not form a political philosophy. We also study Machiavelli because he took a stand on political matters that still evokes our thought. He clearly stated that politics had nothing to do with religion. Burke's views of French Revolution and role of people's representative are still remembered by students of Western political thought. In this connection we remember Maxey's considered opinion : "Edmund Burke is one of the best known figures in English history, and one of the few politicians of the eighteenth century England whose renown has not faded" (*Political Philosophies*, p. 372).

Edmund Burke was born in Dublin in 1729. His father was an attorney and a Protestant by faith. His mother was a Roman Catholic. These two streams of religious faith met together in the family of Burke. Burke's two brothers followed father's religion, while their sister followed the faith of mother. He was educated at Trinity College, Dublin, and received his degree from this college. In 1750 he went to London to study law, but as it was against his liking he gave up the study of law, and devoted himself to literary work. Two Essays—*A Vindication of Natural Society* and *Philosophical Inquiry into the Origin on our Ideas of the Sublime and Beautiful*—were published and he came to be known in the academic circles of England.

In 1759 Burke came in direct contact with Gerard Hamilton who became the Secretary of Ireland and he appointed Burke as a member of his staff. This post helped him to acquire a lot of experience about the practical affairs of government. In 1765 he was made private secretary to Lord Rockingham, the newly appointed Prime Minister of England. The association with the Prime Minister enable him to win a seat in the House of Commons and he entered Parliament in 1765. He delivered his first speech in 1766. The first speech appeared to be very promising and contained the seeds of a good parliamentarian. The death of his son and other family troubles disturbed his mind. He was also faced with financial problems. However, during his long career as a member of Parliament he was able to establish himself as an orator and, in fact, he was a legendary figure in the field of oration. He was the leader of the Whig Party until his retirement in 1794. Three years after, he died.

The important writings of Burke are—*Thoughts on the Cause of Present Discontents* (1770), *American Taxation* (1774), *Conciliation with the Colonies* (1775), *Affairs of America* (1777), *Reflections on the Revolution in France* (1790).

After he became the member of Parliament his first objective was to preserve the constitution. Burke was a number one conservative. He was against any sort of compromise with despotism and for this reason he supported the Irish, American and Indian standpoints regarding freedom movement and fight against imperialism. But he could not support the French Revolution. His *Reflection on Revolution of France* created a sensation. Eleven editions of the book were sold within a year. Within a short span of time more than 30,000 copies were sold. He carefully analysed the different aspects of the Revolution and also his point of view.

Burke retired from British parliament but he did not retire from studying, analysing and expressing different hot and current political views and burning issues. That was the characteristic feature of Burke. Towards the end of the century a peace treaty between France and England was about to be signed and when his attention was drawn to it he immediately expressed his view in *Letter on Regicide Peace.* But before the publication of the letter he breathed his last. About Burke's thought Plamenatz's comment runs as follows—It he is among the least systematic, he is also among the more consistent of political philosophers.

Burke on Social Contract

Burke was primarily a conservative thinker and because of his conservativeness he never recognised any abrupt or radical change for the upliftment of society. Because of his conservatism he could not lend his support to the French Revolution. Throughout the world there prevails a unique discipline and continuity. With the help of the well-articulated laws created by God the society achieves and maintains its mobility. These divine laws are also moral laws. In every civil society there are moral laws and the consciousness and wisdom of individuals facilitate the application of these laws. Membership of the civil society entitles man to enjoy certain rights and privileges. Society changes and develops, reforms are introduced. People continue to enjoy these rights and privileges and when attempts are made to impinge them they resist. It is the thought, action, accumulated knowledge and wisdom that help the human society to march forward. In other words, the past helps the present generation and simultaneously helps it to go ahead. Abruptness has no place in Burke's thought.

"Society is indeed a contract. Subordinate contracts for objects of mere occasional interest may be dissolved at pleasure—but the state ought not to be considered as nothing better than a partnership agreement in a trade of pepper and coffee, calico or tobacco or some other such low concern, to be taken up for a little temporary interest and to be dissolved by the fancy of the parties. It is to be looked on with other reverence; because it is not a partnership in things subservient only to the gross animal existence of a temporary and perishable nature. It is a partnership not only between those who are living...those who are dead, those who are to be born... It is a partnership in all science, a partnership in all art, a partnership in every virtue and in all perfection. Each contract of each particular state is but a clause in the great primeval contract of eternal society linking the lower with the higher natures, connecting the visible and invisible world, according to a fixed compact sanctioned by an inviolable oath which holds all physical and moral natures each in their appointed peace."

Here Burke seems to be playing a rhetorical game with the familiar contractarian phraseology; or rather to be reading into it such new depths of meaning as to transform it out of all recognition. If such are the real truths of politics could they not be better expressed by frankly abandoning the contract altogether and openly adopting an organic theory of the state? But he was addressing an audience accustomed to think in terms of the original contract. He deliberately intended to direct their thoughts away from of the errors usually advocated by its adherents. Party sympathy and dislike of revolutionary radicalism led him to defend the Whig settlement of 1689 and with it the idea of original contract. He made it a matter of practical politics rather than of theoretical solution.

Rights and Liberties

About natural rights and liberties Burke held different view. Hobbes and Locke believed that natural rights and liberties meant people of the state of nature possessed and enjoyed these. But Burke is of opinion that natural rights mean rights indispensable for the general development of all faculties of man and the government has responsibility to protect and implement these rights and it cannot deny its responsibility. In Burke's own words : "If civil society be made for the advantage of man, all the advantages for which it is made become his right. Such rights are the right to justice to the fruits of one's industry, to the acquisition of one's parents, to instruction in life and to consolation in death. In the partnership of society all men have equal rights but not have equal things." On the subject of natural rights what he wants to say is :

"Government is not made in virtue of natural rights which may and do exist in total independence of it and exist in much greater clearness... By having a right to everything, they want everything. Government is a contrivance of human wisdom to provide for human *wants.* Men have a right that these should be provided for by this wisdom. Among these wants to be reckoned the want, out of civil society, of a sufficient restraint upon their passions. Society requires not only that passions of individuals should be subjected, but that even in the mass and body, as well as in the individuals, the inclinations of men should frequently be thwarted... The restraints on men as well as their liberties, are to be reckoned among their rights. But as the liberties and restraints vary with times and circumstances, and admit of infinite modifications, they cannot be settled upon any abstract rule."

Burke's views on rights and liberties are really excellent. According to Burke people formed civil society primarily for the purpose of enjoying fights and liberties. Because only in such a society there is a legitimate authority and his responsibility lies in safeguarding these rights. In a society where there is no authority to implement rights men are absolutely helpless and rights face greate jeopardy. That is why he felt the necessity of the formation of a civil society. Here it is also to be noted that Burke did not tract the term civil society in ordinary sense. He was an eighteenth century intellectual and towards the end of his life he observed that the concept of civil society was gathering momentum and Burke could not keep him away from this popular and powerful trend.

In Burke's thought system there is no place of abstract philosophy of liberty. He has judged liberty from the practical point of view. Liberty is also a product of history and inheritance. Both liberty and authority in Burke's idea are subject to limitation. Unlimited liberty is equivalent to licence and unlimited authority is inimical to liberty. So both require to be restrained. Burke has conceived of liberty in the perspective of the whole society. The well-being of the society is to be placed at the highest point and all are to be adjusted with this ideal. One end ought not to be pursued at the detriment of the interests or other persons. Enjoyment or rights and liberties must stem at the common well being of society. Liberty is valuable no doubt, but also valuable are justice, order and peace of the society. They are even indispensable to the reality of liberty itself. Liberty is also the product of evolution. He says :

"You will observe, that from Magna Carta to the Declaration of Right, it has been the uniform policy of our constitution to claim and assert our liberties as an *entailed inheritance* derived to us from our forefathers and to be transmitted to our posterity—as an estate belonging to the people of this kingdom, without any reference whatever to any other more general or prior right."

Liberty thus is not a claim of people at a particular moment of time. It has a long background. So, to what extent people will enjoy liberty and exercise rights depends upon the history and civilisation of the state. Rights and liberties are parts of the whole civilisation. The above observation of Burke reveals that he did not treat rights, liberty and privileges as the product of contemporary situation. They are derived from the past conditions as well as they are the products of civilisation. In this view it is abundantly clear that Burke explained the ideas of rights and liberties from the standpoint of his favourite conservative philosophy or conservatism. Rights are not the products of any particular moment of time. They must have a history and tradition.

Democracy and Aristocracy

Like Plato and Aristotle Burke had no faith in the administrative ability and quality of masses of men. Administration requires special ability and all men do not possess it. In other words, only few people have the capability to shoulder the burden of managing the affairs of state. This approach of Burke does not corroborate the general attitude of people towards democracy. Of course this does not mean that Burke was an anti-democrat. Commenting on Burke's concept of democracy Ebenstein says (p. 469) : "Burke denies the validity of the central doctrine of democracy : that only the governed have the right to determine who is govern them and that all votes count equally. He opposes this democratic method as an *arithmetic* devoid of meaning and thinks of representation in terms of historic interests, such as the Lords, the Commons, the monarchy, the established church rather than in terms of individual citizens. Burke adheres to the medieval idea that the man is significant, not as an individual citizen, but solely as a member of a group to which he belongs socially or economically." Burke thus speaks of the corporate identity of the individual. A man outside the group is insignificant. His views and opinions, if expressed individually, are all perverted. Hegel has expressed the same view. Man always acts in corporate capacity. Individual identification or importance is both unnecessary and harmful. Burke's view on individual is precursor to totalitarian state of Hitler. Burke treated aristocracy as a necessary feature of constitutional monarchy. To him it was not a pure form of government. He laid faith on aristocracy on two grounds. Its members were wealthy and exerted influence on society. The aristocracy formed a political culture. In his opinion this would facilitate the administration of state.

Burke's View on Constitution

Every or almost all the political views of Burke are intrinsically parts of his conservatism and his idea about constitution is no exception. The accumulated knowledge and culture of a nation is reflected in the constitution. On this ground he vehemently opposed the attempt of French revolutionaries attempt to introduce a new constitution. By a constitutional policy, working after the pattern of nature, we receive, we hold, we transmit our government and our privileges, in the same manner in which we enjoy and transmit our property and our lives. The institutions of policy, the goods of fortune, the gifts of providence are handed down to us, and from us, in the same course and order.

The constitution is a repository of the past experience and it guides the future course of action. It is a continuity. "The whole scheme of our mixed constitution is to prevent any one of its principles from being carried as far as, taken by itself and theoretically, it would go" (Burke).[1] Checks and balances are the essence of the system. Each part limits and controls the other parts. Hence in the "British constitution there is a perpetual treaty and compromise going on, sometimes openly, sometimes with less observation."[2] Burke thus attempts to establish a philosophical justification of constitution. Traditions, morality, experience etc. all are carried over and all these together enrich the civilisation. In this way the fund of knowledge and experience expands. This is ultimately embodied in the constitutions, institutions and political processes.

Burke then speaks of the *prescriptive type* of constitution. Let us quote him : "our constitution is a prescriptive constitution, it is a constitution whose sole authority is that it has existed time out of mind... your king, your lords, your judges, your juries, grand and little all are, all are prescriptive... Prescription is the solid of all titles, not only to property, but to government. It is a presumption in favour of any settled scheme of government against any untried project, that a nation has long existed and flourished under it... A nation is not an idea of only of local extent and individual momentary aggregation, but it is an idea of continuity which extends in time as well as in numbers and in space. This is a *choice* not of one day or one set of people, not a tumultuary and giddy choice, it is a deliberate election of the ages and of generations, it is a constitution made by what is ten thousand times better than choice; it is made by peculiar circumstances, occasions, tempers, dispositions, and moral, civil and social habitudes of the people which disclose themselves only in a long space of time".[3]

"As to the theory of constitution, Burke has nothing positive to offer beyond the exposition and eulogy of the constitution of England. In this he sees social and political forces operating with the regularity, ease and effectiveness of nature itself. The organs of the government—king, parliament and courts—have their authority from the law and custom of the land."[4] We do not agree with Dunning's view. Burke has emphasised that the constitution of a country must contain in itself the characteristic features of social, political and economic conditions of the country concerned. It is true that while he was talking about constitution the picture of the

1. Burke—Quoted by Dunning (Vol. III), p. 183.
2. Op. cit., p. 183.
3. Quoted by Sabine, p. 609.
4. Dunning—op. cit., p. 182.

British constitution was quite alive in his mind. Till now no country of the world has framed her constitution completely ignoring the past history and tradition as well as the peculiar social, economic and political situation. Hence there is nothing objectionable in the view of Burke. Again, it is not surprising that a large number of countries have adopted the British constitution as their model, of course with some modification and variation.

Sabine says that Burke's theory of constitution is based upon the actual settlement of 1688 by which the effective political control passed into the hands of the Whig nobility.[1] Burke was against all sorts of reforms of parliamentary system and this was due to his loyalty to the British system of government. He lent his unqualified support to the then British parliament on the ground that it would be able to fulfil the needs of the people and augment the welfare of society. It is to be noted here that though Burke was dead against the incorporation of new elements in the British constitution the British Government could not resist people's persistent demand for introduction of new thoughts and elements into the main body of the constitution. But since the British constitution is unwritten it is not always easy to make distinction between old elements and added new elements. However, the entry of new elements into the body of the constitution is undeniable.

Representation and Political Party

For pretty long time Edmund Burke was a member of the House of Commons and he established himself as a successful and able parliamentarian. In this regard he favoured certain ideas. Particularly, he had definite conception about territorial constituency and responsibility of the representative towards the voters of his constituency. He held that the constituency was not a numerical or territorial unit. It is not simply a territorial area consisting of certain numbers of voters or citizens. Virtual representation, that is, representation in which there is a communion of interests and a sysmpath in feelings and desires, he thought, had most of the advantages of representation by actual election and was free from any disadvantages.

Burke criticised the existing system of representation and mentality and outlook of the representative. He was of opinion that English representative form of government was not functioning satisfactorily due to the defective system. In his address to the voters of his Bristol constituency Burke defended the independence of the representative. In this famous address Burke rejected the time-old conception of territorialism. Once a man is elected from a particular constituency, he is to be regarded as a member of Parliament, and not as a representative of that particular constituency. He receives by virtue of his membership, the right to represent the whole country. He is also to be allowed to exercise his own judgment and freedom.

A member of Parliament is not a spokesman of his constituency, although he is bound to look after the interests of his constituency, he is not bound to do it at the cost of national interests. He is not the ambassador of the constituency. He has his own view, outlook and attitude. He must adhere to his own principles. No representative can sacrifice all these things and it is quite unjustified to ask him to do that. The constituency is not a school where the members will go to take lessons from the the voters and advices his future course of action. He will have full freedom

1. Sabine—op. cit., p. 609.

to express his views in the Parliament and it may so happen that this may contradict the interest of his voters. He cannot take lessons about the law and government from the voters. What Edmund Burke asserts here is that a member of Parliament must have freedom of thought and expression and though he represents a territorial area he must see the national interests.

The view of Burke regarding the duty and responsibility of a representative has been a subject of a good deal of controversy. But this view is still a subject of serious discussion. Burke refused to accept that a representative was the spokesperson of the constituency. He cannot neglect the interests of the constituency he represents and simultaneously he cannot go against the national interests. He argued that it is the primary duty for the representative to give priority to the national interests. Today the situation has undergone changes. A prudent representative must make a balance between local and national interest. If he completely ignores the legitimate interests of the constituency he represents, the next election will not produce results that will go to his favour. Particularly in weak and developing democratic systems the representatives have been found to be serious about the issues and problems of their own constituencies. So far as the holistic approach to the representative system is concerned Edmund Burke is hundred percent correct. But his approach has certain practical limitations.

According to Burke—Party is a body of men united, for promoting by their joint endeavours, the national interests, upon some particular principle in which they are all agreed. Burke strongly advocated in favour of a party system. In his time the party system of the House of Commons had acquired a clear picture and this created a favourable impression about party functioning in his mind. He realised that British representative system could not work successfully without the proper development of party system. He also supported the loyalty of every statesman to the principles and ideology of the party. Private consideration, in his opinion, would not be allowed to break the loyalty to the party.

It is interesting to note that though Burke supported the independence of thought and judgment of members of Parliament he did not allow the same thing to the members of political parties. Burke emphasised the observance of party principles and ideology and he did not support any aberration. It is due to the fact that Burke had a great respect for the constitutional government of England and his clear opinion was that without a well-organised party this would collapse. So government was more important to him than individual freedom.

Conservatism

It is generally observed that Burke's criticisms of the intense political movements on behalf of democracy in Europe during his time constitute the basis of modern political tradition usually called conservatism. *Reflections on the Revolution of France* (1790) contains the conservative political philosophy of Burke. No attempt should be made to destroy the old tradition and civilisation of any society. The government and constitution both are the products of old tradition.

Burke's attitude to towards ideology is helpful to an understanding of conservatism. Burke was against ideology as such because ideologies oversimplify and exaggerate actual social conditions. Worst of all the slogans such as freedom, liberty and natural rights are dangerous to society and weapons of the revolutionaries and reformers who have scant respect for the tradition and civilisation of the country.

They do not also care for the consequences of their revolutions. In his *Reflections on the Revolutions of France* Burke has raised the following questions whose answer is *'No'*.

Am I to felicitate a mad man who has escaped from the protecting and wholesome darkness of his, on his restoration to the enjoyment of right and liberty? Am I to congratulate a highwayman and murderer, who has broke prisons upon the recovery of his natural rights? These two questions reveal Burke's attitude towards abstract rights and liberties as well as to ideology. Wasby comments that Burke's conservatism represents an anti-ideology. At the least it is strongly critical of most political ideas, especially those which urge social reform and social change.[1]

But even an anti-ideology cannot be expressed without ideas. The primary notion of Burke's conservatism is that to conserve the past. To destroy the past and introduce a novelty is harmful. Burke felt that there were certain "truths" about which there could be little doubt. One of such truths is that men are *naturally* unequal and society requires orders and classes for the good of all men. Man is the creature of appetite and will and is governed more by emotion than by reason. Burke also believed that the constitutions, institutions and other political forms had history or long background and tradition. They are necessary for the society and must be preserved at any cost. Burke, because of his conservativeness, did not approve the revolutionary attempts and he strongly criticised the French revolutionaries. We shall now turn to his view of French Revolution.

Burke and French Revolution

"The French revolutionaries seemed to Burke to be using the doctrine of the rights of man for a quite different purpose : not to justify resistance in defence of traditional freedom, of acquired rights, not even to support new claims intended to make that freedom more secure, but to subvert society. They were making claims incompatible with the existing social order, the system of existing rights; they were challenging those rights in the name of the principles such as equality, liberty taken in the abstract."[2]

The French revolutionaries, according to Burke, were fanatical. They could not attain their avowed purposes nor did they have that capacity. They had only ruined an ancient country having a long tradition, culture and civilisation. Burke called them ignorant surgeons. They were making preparations for major operations of the human body without any knowledge of anatomy. The French revolutionaries did not know that without any knowledge of the body any operation could not be done at all. All of them were incompetent persons. Their eagerness for change was the evidence of foolishness. The society is hard and complex. It is not soft clay which the potter can use to make any article or pot according to his own choice. They adopted a wrong path and the whole nation had to pay for it. From this observation of Burke it appears to us that he castigated the French revolutionaries in the strongest language. The chief reason behind this is the revolutionaries did not give any credence or recognition to the past history, tradition and culture of France as well as to its centuries old civilisation. That greatly hurt Burke's sentiment along with his conservatism. To him the past civilisation, culture and tradition are more

1. Stephen Wasby—*Political Science—The Discipline and Dimensions*, p. 293.
2. Plamenatz—*Man and Society*, Vol. I, p. 341.

important than mere political change. His belief was that the desirable change could be achieved keeping the past tradition and civilisation intact. But this could not be done.

Burke even did not spare the philosophers from whom the revolutionaries received inspiration and lessons. The philosopher were eager to destroy the old prejudices on the ground that they were irrational and were obstacles to progress. Burke said : "We know that we have made no discoveries, and we think that no discoveries are to be made in morality, nor many in the great principles of government, nor in the ideas of liberty which were understood long before we were born... Instead of casting away our old prejudices, we cherish them because they are prejudices and the longer they have lasted, and the more generally they have prevailed, the more we cherish them."

Burke realised that the French Revolution was more than an internal affair of France. It was a revolution of doctrine and theoretic dogma, and he attacked the state that emerged from it as a college of armed fanatics, for the propagation of principles of assassination, robbery, fraud, faction, oppression and impiety, Burke, therefore, called for a European crusade to crush the revolutionary spirit by force of arms. He was convinced that no monarchy would be saved as long as this strange, nameless wild, enthusiastic thing is established in the centre of Europe.

Importance of Burke

Maxey makes the following observation (p. 382) on the importance of Burke : "As a creative and systematic political thinker Edmund Burke cannot be rated high. An unrelenting foe of all theories and dogmas, of all reforms and innovations, and indeed of all principles not verified by actual experience, his mind declined airy flights of speculation and deprecated all attempts at the systematic rationalisation of political institutions." The observation of Maxey is quite correct. Burke was primarily a politician. He was not a philosopher or an academician nor a scholar of high repute. His views about French Revolution and his thought or the role of a parliamentary representative still evoke interest in the mind of his readers. He has been painted as a reactionary conservative thinker and propagandist. This is the view of a good number of his numerous readers.

His attitudes towards French Revolution have been strongly criticised by historians and scholars. His view that the French revolutionaries were against tradition and their purpose was not progress of society and their efforts would ultimately lead to anarchy has been vehemently opposed by various critics. After the Revolution, anarchy did not swallow the French society. It is said that the Revolution laid the foundation of a new society and the post-Revolutionary situation of France belied the prediction of Burke. The military power and the image in international field both increased after the Revolution. His call for the unity of European powers to crush the revolutionaries reveals his counter-revolutionary and reactionary mentality.

Burke saw only the destructive effects of French Revolution. We agree with Burke that revolutions do not always proceed smoothly and produce desired results. But our question is if the present system cannot be reformed by constitutional methods what is the way out? Unfortunately Burke does not enlighten us on this matter. Reforms and revolution are the two chief ways of change. When one fails the other remains. The French society reached an explosive situation and there was no other way than revolution. It is unfortunate that an experienced man of the stature of Burke failed to understand it.

In comparing the French Revolution with the English Revolution, Burke always pointed out to the violent and radical character of the first contrasted with the peaceable and conservative character of the second. But this comparison is untenable. In all the stages the English Revolution was not bloodless. Execution of Charles I cannot be termed a bloodless act. Ebenstein observes : "In cutting off the head of their monarch the French were no more than good disciples of the English and their Revolution was much more peaceful than the Puritan Revolution" (p. 473).

Burke also failed to see that the revolution is not necessarily the result of metaphysical fanaticism, but may spring from the soil of experience, the experience of protracted suffering. The breakdown of social and political institution and democratic values and norms forced a section and really a considerable section to resort to revolutionary method. Their judgment and their evaluation must be given due consideration. Another pathetic side of Burke's view of French Revolution is he had not the patience to analyse impartially the results of the Revolution. As if he knew what would happen. His analysis of French Revolution reveals that he played the role of an astrologer. He drew conclusions according to his own frame of mind.

In spite of all this his contribution to political thought cannot be underestimated. Maxey observes (p. 382) : "he made a very substantial contribution to political thought". "He takes a rank" continues the same critic "as one of the ever-luminous orbs in the galaxy of political thought. When Burke appeared...political thought had almost succumbed to the maudlin romanticism of Rousseau. Montesquieu was in eclipse, likewise Hume, Spinoza, Hobbes and other great realists of the past. History was "bunk", reason despised, and facts mere obstacles to be swept aside." Burke appeared on the political scene of England and Europe in general to sprinkle cold water upon the idealist thoughts and made serious efforts to abnegate the influence of past experience.

Burke makes it clear that both political and social life are extremely complex and their problems cannot be solved with the help of any easy formula or technique. The tradition of the political organisation, the attitude and temperament of people and many other things are to be brought under active consideration before suggesting any solution. Reckless destruction of old and established institutions and values has, according to Burke, never produced salutary results. It is not irrelevant to say that Lenin, the great revolutionary of the twentieth century, was very much cautious about the selection of revolutionary tactics and timing of launching revolution.

C. W. Parkin in his article *Burke and the Conservative Tradition* writes—"In the era of worldwide Marxism, Burke's polemic against the revolutionary idea—the utopianism, the canonisation of dualism and conflict, the search for some final political solution—has not lost its relevance or cogency. And for Britain's needs, cultural as much as political, the fruitfulness of his position has not been exhausted".[1]

Edmund Burke is regarded as the best interpreter of the traditional principles of *British political life.* It is interesting to note that his justification of British tradition

1. Thompson (ed.)—*Political Ideas,* p. 128.

prevails today. He has not been proved wrong or unjustified. A strong current of social change has flown over British society. But the continuity and tradition of which Burke spoke can still be identified. New changes have been grafted on to the old, but the old has not been thrown into the dustbin. The principles of the old were adopted to those of the new. This prevails almost everywhere. For example, in the working class movement or in the working of the ancient institutions, some critics belittle him as the spokesman or philosopher of British system of political party. But the actual position is not that. "Burke is not the philosopher of the British conservatism, but of British political life from Right to Left. His spirit informs the progressive movement as much as it informs the Conservative Party" (Thompson, p. 128).

Burke is not an exception so far as the political thought is concerned. There is always conflict in history, the conflict between old and new, between haves and have-nots, between pro-changers and no-changers. This conflict will never come to an end. We know Burke as the spokesman of the old tradition. This is not his fault. There is no dearth in his argument, there is no vagueness in his thought. Harmon writes : "In any event there is much in Burke's theory to support the stand of those who wish to keep things as they are. And his is an impressive contribution that cannot be ignored. Much depends, in any appraisal of Burke upon the circumstances surrounding those who agree or disagree with his theory" (p. 339).

Edmund Burke was absolutely fearless while expressing his views. He did not hesitate to denounce the misdeeds of Warren Hastings. His famous speech delivered in the British House of Commons still invokes our interest about him and kindles our respect to him. He impeached Warren Hastings on the ground that as the Governor General of India his activities and administrative policies violated the "eternal laws of justice". Commenting upon Burke's speech Amartya Sen in his *The Idea of Justice* says : "he spoke eloquently not on one misdeed of Hastings but on a great many, and proceeded from there to present simultaneously a number of separate and quite distinct reasons for the need to indict Warren Hastings" (p. 1). Burke in one place of his speech said : I impeach him in the name and virtue of those eternal laws of justice which he has violated".

18 THE ENGLISH UTILITARIANS

Definition and Nature of Utilitarianism

In C. L. Wayper's analysis of utilitarianism we find the following observation : "perhaps it was neither Hobbes nor Locke, but a school which owed something to both of them, which made the greatest English contribution to political thought, though paradoxically it never produced a thinker as great as typically English as the other. This was utilitarian school which for over hundred years from the middle of the eighteenth century to that of the nineteenth, dominated English political thought" (p. 82). The term 'English utilitarians' is slightly a misnomer because there were utilitarians in other countries. But the main theory of utilitarianism was assiduously propagated by Bentham and J. S. Mill and for that reason it is so called. It is to be noted that all the utilitarians did not propagate the same or identical principles. There are wide varieties which cannot be faithfully reconciled. Again, though the doctrine is associated with the names of Bentham and J. S. Mill, there were also a number of thinkers who directly and indirectly advocated the principle of utility and also its application to politics and government. First we shall deal with the definition of utilitarianism.

The term utilitarianism has not been clearly defined. However, it is not difficult to understand what does it mean. The COD says : the doctrine that actions are right if they are useful or for the benefit of the majority. It also says that the greatest happiness of the greatest number should be the guiding principle of conduct. Plamenatz in his *The English Utilitarians* makes an attempt to elaborate the idea in the form of four propositions : (i) Pleasure is alone good or desirable for its own sake; or else men call those things good that are pleasant or a means to what is pleasant. (ii) The equal pleasures of any two persons or more are equally good. (iii) No action is right until it produces greatest happiness to the person for whom it is made. (iv) The obligation to the government is not related to its power, but its capability to produce happiness.

The interpreters and critics of utilitarianism have found out two meanings of the doctrine. One is it is an *ethical theory* and the other *is it is a practical movement.* As an ethical doctrine it means universal Hedonism. It is unethical or immoral in the sense that since individual is the sole authority to decide his own course of action, he cannot be forced to act against his will. If anything is painful or undesirable nothing can compel a man to do or accept that. Every man has full freedom and authority to do something which is useful to him and not painful. To sum up, an individual is the sole determiner of everything. Pain and pleasure are his personal concern. It is also a *practical movement* in the sense that before enacting a law or taking a decision the government must see its utility to its subject. If the government fails, it shall be the duty of the citizens to oppose the measures adopted by it. Throughout their analysis the utilitarians have emphasised that utility is the determiner of every action the authority proposes to take.

Utilitarianism thinks that there are two opposite concepts in the mind of man—idealism and realism. Man adores idealism and tries to follow it. But in practical life he gives more importance to realism. He judges everything in the light of his own practical experience and the ability of a thing or piece of legislation to give pleasure. When there is a conflict between idealism and realism he gives precedence to realism. In the opinion of utilitarians man is always practical and highly conscious of his own interests.

Utilitarians have also been called Philosophical Radicals. The purpose of the Philosophical Radicals was to prepare a scheme of legal, economic and political reforms aiming at the greatest happiness of the greatest number. The Philosophical Radicals thought that this principle must guide both the public and private affairs as well as the politics of the government. The chief purpose of the Philosophical Radicals was to bring about radical or overall changes in economic and political sectors of society as well as to solve the problems of public administration through the implementation of a policy known as the greatest good of the greatest number. For the first time the utilitarians emphatically suggested this principle.

The Philosophical Radicals provided the intellectual structure of early liberalism and also its programme. The Philosophical Radicals were more interested in practical programme and less in doctrines and idealism. Prof. Sabine says (p. 647) : "The early liberals, though they were often provincial and doctrinaire, were also profoundly and sincerely public-spirited men who turned a defective social philosophy to purposes which in a large measure were socially beneficent and were never in intention merely exploitative. It was for this reason that liberalism could transform itself into an intellectual bridge between individualism of its earlier period, which was the heritage from the philosophy of the Revolutionary Era, and a recognition of the reality and the value of social and communal interests, which tended in general to put themselves forward anti-liberal forms."

Though the utilitarians were very few in number, it is surprising to note that these few persons dominated the political thought of England for a long time and stimulated the thought and ideas of subsequent periods. They, in the opinion of Wayper (p. 83), were too coldly intellectual too frigid and scholastic, and men were not flattered by their view of mankind. But for long they were without competitors. Because of the overwhelming influence of utilitarians over the intellingentia great contemporaries—Rousseau, Kant, St. Simon and Marx were unhonoured in England.

Utilitarianism never thinks that man is the symbol of a single interest or attitude, he is the bundle of diverse interests, attitudes and principles. Very often these are self-contradictory. This is due to the fact that man's actions are caused by real situation and he is a pleasure-seeking and pain-avoiding creature. Naturally it is useless to make any attempt for finding out consistency in his behaviour. The utilitarianism does not take seriously the contradictory behaviour of man. To the contrary, they hold the view that behind every human action there is reason and rationality. In its opinion man is the embodiment of these two qualities.

The utilitarians were also individualists. They treated every individual as a reasonable unit and all the units are equal. The society consists of these units and if each unit is allowed to pursue his own interest and welfare that will pave the way of general welfare of the society. This individualism of utilitarians is also called liberalism. But is to be noted at this stage of analysis that utilitarians' individualism makes a compromise with the need of the society. The individuals shall pursue their own interests but not at the cost of others' interests. So utilitarians' liberalism is enlightened individualism.

For the first time the utilitarians strongly advocated that any administrative policy—big or small—must take into account the issue that individuals' interest cannot be neglected. This stand of the utilitarians appealed to the large number of people—specially the members of the middle class. Both Bentham and J. S. Mill had sympathy for the middle class people and primarily for that they argued for them.

Origin of Utilitarianism

The utilitarian philosophy (though found its best treatment at the hands of Jeremy Bentham) is not his discovery. Even Bentham did not use the terminology. It is described as the nineteenth century revival of classical hedonism of Epicurus. Maxey says (p. 456) : "Benthamite cult was a revolt against the vapoury idealism of eighteenth century rationalism. For an absolute idealism it sought to substitute an absolute empiricism. Its leading expounders were individualists who, convinced of the utter sterility of such concepts as absolute right, absolute sovereignty and absolute justice, and come to believe that in human affairs there was one possible absolute, namely absolute expediency."

The interpreters of Western political thought say that utilitarianism is both a movement and protest movement because the political ideas of earlier century were not capable to meet the intellectual and other demands of quite large number of people whose thoughts and outlook had undergone radical changes due to the economic, social and other factors. Political institutions were not according to the people's choice and needs as well as to the proclivity of their mind. So a new philosophy was needed which would be based upon reason, rationality, experience and ambition of individuals. The rising magnates, products of Industrial Revolution, were sore with the old aristocratic order of society. They were not getting any avenue to express their displeasure and, ultimately, a scope was offered by the utilitarians. They found in the concept of utility a splendid weapon of attacking the old order. They did not directly attack the absolutism of monarchy, but said that achievement and utility would be the guiding principle of every action of government and every piece of legislation.

From the social, economic and political history of Europe we come to know that the Industrial Revolution completely transformed the society. Technological progress and scientific discoveries enabled men to harness the untapped resources of nature. A new professional and wealthy class appeared in the society. Simultaneously there was created a middle class. In the scientific and technological fields this class always assumed the leadership. In fact, the acceleration of growth was possible because of the hard as well as intellectual work of this class. But unfortunately this class did not find any recognition either in the economic sphere or in the field of general administration. Its zeal to mould the policies and principles of government made it restless. It is better to describe in the words of Sabine :

"More influential than any theoretical consideration were no doubt the changes that naturally occured in the outlook of the commercial and industrial middle class as its position and influence became more assured. This class everywhere formed the spearhead of liberal political reform in the nineteenth century, and the trend of industrial and commercial development made the expansion of its political power a foregone conclusion" (p. 670).

The emergence of the middle class was to some extent acted as a potent factor behind the rise and growth of utilitarianism. Its main interest fell on the management of state affairs and not on ideology. The members of this class were practical men and they wanted to see new institutions which would be able to cater to the demands and needs of the new age and new society having new values and outlook. Economically the capitalists formed the dominant class. But the proletarians—in the Marxian sense—were yet to emerge as a conscious and well-organised powerful class. The middle class was, therefore, the most important element of Britain's industrial society. Having both money and energy it was determined to ascertain its inroads into the political fabric of the society. It threw its full weight for the propagation of constitutional government and personal liberty. The middle class took no time to realise that without comprehensive reforms the political fate of this class could not be changed at all. It chanelled its advocacy towards the improvement of legal procedures, reorganisation on the judicial system, creation of judicial system, creation of sanitary code and expansion of suffrage system.

Ebenstein says (p. 497) : "The rising middle class in Britain inevitably developed a new social and political philosophy that was clearly distinct from Burke's adulation of landed aristocracy as well as from Paine's radicalism and Godwin's anarchy. Burke was too conservative, pessimistic and traditional, whereas Paine and Godwin were too radical utopian and revolutionary." The middle class had no interest in ideology and philosophy. Its chief aim was to protect its interests through the participation in the affairs of state. It also observed that the rising bourgeoisie played the active role in the industrial and economic sectors. The middle class selected the administrative and political affairs as its target.

It would be an erroneous conception if we treat the Industrial Revolution as the solitary source of utilitarianism. Thomas Hobbes and David Hume are also great exponents of utilitarianism. Both Hobbes and Bentham have held that man of intelligence and virtue is the best calculator and judge of the events with which they are faced. Again, his calculations are not different in nature. Bentham's legislator will enact law to ensure the greatest happiness of the greatest number. But the legislator cannot destroy the selfish motives of man. The purpose of Hobbes's sovereign is to ensure that every individual shall get the opportunity to maximise happiness and his happiness will remain unmolested by others. The terms and the language of the two philosophers are different, but the purpose of them is the same.

In the sphere of political philosophy Hobbes has direct and obvious influence upon the utilitarians. The utilitarians—like Hobbes—regard the state as a means of reconciling man's selfish interests. Apparently the purpose of Hobbes's state is to protect the natural rights. But the ultimate objective is to augment the happiness and raise it to the maximum level. On this point Bentham's view is akin to Hobbes's. It is true that Hobbes does not state all these things clearly. In the opinion of Plamenatz[1] Hobbes does not use the concept of natural rights in the traditional sense.

According to Plamenatz the Hobbesian theory of contract is a convenient fiction and the convenience is this. People assembled together to set up a body-politic for the purpose of preserving their interests. Hobbes has compared the body-politic with the state of nature and he has found the superiority of the former over the latter. So the political association has utility or, to put it in other words, political society in all respects is more convenient than the state of nature. Therefore, the difference between Hobbes and utilitarians is matter of language and use of terms and not of content.

The difference between Hobbes and the utilitarians is that the former supported the absolute government as the most effective weapon for the realisation of people's interests. The latter did not share this view. They wanted to limit the power of the government. Hobbes was afraid of anarchy and the utilitarians were afraid of misgovernment. Plamenatz concludes : "The utilitarians argued that because men are selfish, vain and naturally abusive of power, only a democratic government could secure them against each other's ill-usage. They accepted the opinion of Hobbes that the great function of government is to conciliate interests and they did not quarrel with his estimate of mankind. But they did not share his fear of anarchy ...Hobbes used a traditional vocabulary ...and it was precisely this vocabulary the utilitarians abandoned" (p. 16).

We shall now discuss the contribution of Hume to the development of utilitarianism. John Plamenatz says that David Hume is rightly regarded as the founder of utilitarianism (p. 22). In support of his view he quotes from Leslie Stephen's *History of English Thought in the Eighteenth Century.* Stephen said : "essential doctrines of utilitarianism are stated by him with a clearness and consistency not to be found in any other writer of the century and that from Hume to J. S. Mill the doctrine received no substantial alteration." Utilitarianism has a number of varieties in its formulation. But the essential form of the doctrine narrated by different adherents is the same. In our definition we have clearly stated the essential doctrines under four different propositions.

Hume's concept of utilitarianism can be briefly stated in the following words. He maintains that men normally approve of those states of mind or actions that are pleasant or a means to pleasure, and disapprove of those that are harmful or a means to pain. The simple implication is man is a pleasure-seeking and pain-avoiding creature. Hume observes that man has many motives or feelings, but he always attaches primary importance to pleasure and pain. Pleasure is good and pain is evil. To Hume the status and qualification of person, so far as pain or pleasure is concerned, are not a matter of importance. From most ordinary person to most famous one this concept is universally correct. Every quality that gives pleasure is virtuous and that produces pain is vicious. According to Hume this pleasure and pain may arise from different sources. Such as—we get pleasure from the view of a character which is naturally fitted to be useful to others, or to the person himself, or which is agreeable to others to the person himself (Plamenatz, p. 28).

1. *The English Utilitarians*, p. 13.

Besides Hobbes and Hume there are also others in whose writings the traces of utilitarianism can be discovered. For example, in Locke's theory of morality there are certain hints of utilitarianism. Locke asserts that there are no moral laws whose validity is immediately recognised without regard to their consequence. Plamenatz even goes far by saying that Locke's political doctrines contain a lot of utilitarianism. His social contract theory is a strong hint to that direction. Its utility, whatever its form be, induced men of the state of nature to build up the foundation of a civil society. In the ideas of Priestley, Hutchison and Helvetius some direct hints of utilitarianism are also available. It is, however, unnecessary to bring them under an elaborate discussion. The fact is that, except Hume, none of them directly and clearly stated the doctrine. In a roundabout way the critics have discovered the source of utilitarianism. We shall now turn to Jeremy Bentham the real 'father of the doctrine'.

JEREMY BENTHAM (1748–1832)

Life, Interests and Works

The man who controlled the English political thought for one hundred years is Jeremy Bentham. Although there were several exponents of the doctrine of utilitarianism, the name of Bentham tops the list. In fact, the doctrine is so much associated with Bentham that one cannot be separated from another. "He did for utilitarianism" comments Plamenatz, "what Sidney and Beatrice Webb did for British socialism. But intellectually he was superior to the Webbs" (p. 59).

Bentham was born just one hundred years before the publication of *The Communist Manifesto,* that is, in the year 1748, and he died in the year 1832 when the Reform Bill was passed by the British Parliament. Bentham's parents saw in their child the markings of an intellectual prodigy. While other children of his age spent their time in playing games, he read classics. He started reading at the age of three. The result of all these was that he could not receive formal education. He came of a very well-to-do family of lawyers. There was no dearth of money, mentality and material atmosphere necessary for education. Different classics of Latin were stocked in his father's library.

His early life was quite uneventful. He had no acquaintance with the real world. Since his father and grandfather were successful lawyers and built up a big fortune through their vast practice, young Bentham entered Lincoln's Inn after his graduation in 1763. Young Bentham did not feel any compulsion to earn his daily bread through practice of law. Moreover, because of his disinterestedness in the practice of law he could not follow it seriously. His interest was shifted to jurisprudence. He listened to famous judgments and lectures of Blackstone and Mansfield.

Bentham's interests were many and varied. Economics, logic, psychology, penology, theology, ethics and politics—nothing escaped his attention. But his main interest was law and government. Bentham viewed the activities of judicial department and public administration with a censorial outlook. In fact, the government and law motivated him to write books or propound theory. Throughout his life Bentham had advocated reforms of the legal system. He thought that this department had become irrelevant and failed to meet the demands of an industrialised society. However, he is better known for his doctrine of utilitarianism.

His first work was published in 1776 and this is the *Fragment of Government.* In 1789, one hundred years after the Glorious Revolution, Bentham's second work *Introduction to the Principles of Morals and Legislation* was published. His third book *Draught of a Code for the Organization of the Judicial System of France* was published in 1790. The French Revolution could not evoke much interest in him. He had no support for the revolutionaries. But he, like Burke, did not condemn them. "Hume anticipated the utilitarianism of Jeremy Bentham. He held that there were strict limits to the lengths to which human reason could go, and that to postulate a state of nature antecedent to society in which isolated individuals came together to forge a social contract was a fiction that was of no use in explaining how or why men behave as they do in society."—Dante Germino—*Machiavelli to Marx—Modern Western Political Thought*, p. 163.

Principle of Utility

Though Bentham, in the strictest sense, was not the father or originator of the doctrine of utilitarianism, there is no denying the fact that he is the greatest and best interpreter of the principle of utility or utilitarianism. His clear dictum is : each and every government—while formulating any policy or taking any decision or implementing any action regarding the management of state—must remember that whether or to what extent that policy or action or principle is capable of maximising comfort or pleasure of the people. This announcement of Bentham is clearly individualistic in tone. The comfort or pleasure of the people is of primary importance for any government worthy of its name. At the beginning of his *An Introduction to the Principles of Morals and Legislation* Bentham writes :

Nature has placed mankind under the governance of two sovereign masters—*pain* and *pleasure...* In words a man may pretend to adjure their empire, but in reality he will remain subject to it all the while. *The principle of utility recognises* this subjection and assumes it for the foundation of that system, the object of which is to rear the fabric of felicity by the hands of reason and law.

He further says—

To them...we refer all our decisions, every resolve that we make in life. The man who affects to have withdrawn himself from their despotic sway does not know what he is talking about. To seek pleasure and shun pain is his sole aim, even at the moment when he is denying himself the greatest enjoyment or courting penalties of the most severe kind. This maxim, unchangeable and irresistible as it is, should become the chief study of the Moralist and of the Legislator. To these two motives the principle of utility subjects everything.

These two observations of Bentham clearly state what he wants to say about the doctrine of utilitarianism. In every sphere of life and in every action man's sole guide is the calculation of pain and pleasure. So it is a must for the legislator or administrator to see that men are getting pleasure or will get pleasure while taking any action. What Bentham emphasises is that it would be unwise and undesirable to adopt any policy that will not be able to cater to the interests of general public or will not be able to avoid pain and augment the quantity of pleasure. In a word, the avoidance of pain and attainment of pleasure shall be the guiding principle of any governmental policy.

By the principle of utility is meant that principle which approves or disapproves of every action whatsoever, according to the tendency of which it appears to have to augment or diminish the happiness of the party whose interest is in question. The action may be of any private person or it may be any measure of government. The acceptance or rejection of every action or measure depends upon its ability to provide pleasure or pain.

Bentham then defines *utility. By utility is meant that property in any object whereby it tends to produce benefit, advantage, pleasure, good or happiness or to prevent the happening of mischief, pain, evil or unhappiness to the party whose interest is considered.*

Sources of Pleasure and Pain and Measurement

There are generally four sources of pleasure and pain which are distinguishable from each other. These are physical, moral, political and religious. These may combinedly be sanctions. The physical or natural sanction comprises the pains and pleasures which we may experience or expect in the ordinary course of nature, not purposely modified by any human interposition. The moral sanction comprises such pains and pleasures as we experience or expect at the hands of our fellow beings prompted by feelings of hatred or goodwill or contempt or regard; in a word, according to the spontaneous disposition of each individual. This sanction may also be styled popular, the sanction of public opinion or of honour, or the sanction or pains and pleasures of sympathy.

When the political authority as well as its laws and decisions happen to be the source of pain and pleasure for the individuals we call it political. Sometimes religion or religious authorities—through different acts and decisions—create both pleasure and pain or any one—we term it religious. The scrutiny of the value of pleasure reveals that it depends on generally four circumstances and, in the view of Bentham these are : intensity, duration, certainty or uncertainty and proximity or remoteness. While the individuals measure or estimate pleasure or pain they bring these four circumstances under consideration. But when the value of any pleasure or pain is considered for the purpose of estimating the tendency of any act by which it is produced, there are two other circumstances to be taken into account. These are its fecundity and its purity. The fecundity and purity are, in strictness, not deemed the properties of pleasure and pain.

An important part of Bentham's theory of pleasure and pain consists of calculation or what may be called measurement. If pain and pleasure cannot be measured, it would not be an easy task for the individual to take decision or arrive at conclusion. Bentham's suggestion runs as follows. Begin with any one person whose interests seem to be most affected by any act of the authority. Then we are to calculate the value of each distinguishable pleasure and as well as the value of each distinguishable pain. Sum up all the values of all the *pleasures* on the one side and those of all the *pains* on the other. If the balance is on the side of *pleasures* then the act or decision will be treated as good. The individual will give his consent to it. If the balance is on the side of *pains* the tendency is bad and the person concerned will argue against the implementation of the policy or act. Take an account of all the persons whose interests appear to be concerned and if we sum up the pleasures and pains according to the above process then we shall see whether the tendency is good or bad.

Bentham tells us that the value of a lot of pleasure or pain varies with its intensity, its duration, its certainty, its uncertainty, its propinquity, its fecundity, its purity and its extent. We have already pointed out all these. These are what Bentham calls the seven dimensions of pleasure and pain and he believes that by operating with them we can assess the value, by which he means the quantity or any sum of pleasure or pain. He admits that, in practice, such calculations can seldom be made with accuracy, but he supposes that they are, in principle, possible. He further observes that it is not to be expected that this process should be strictly pursued previous to every moral judgment or to every legislative and judicial operation. It may be always kept in view and as near as the process actually pursued on these occasions approaches it, so near will such a process approach the character of an exact one.

Features and Significance

It has been claimed by renowned scholars that Bentham has not categorically used the term utilitarianism though he was the father of the term. J. S. Mill, son of James Mill, has been found to use the concept liberally. It is, however, undeniable that the structure of the doctrine was built up by Bentham. Again, the analysis of the concept provides an excellent picture about the theory and some characteristic features. *Theory of utilitarianism is a "felicific calculus" or it is also called a "Hedonistic calculus."* Why? In Bentham's opinion both pleasure and pain are measurable and the amount of one offsets that of another. Since both of them are calculable they can be summed up. The balance will determine what is pain and what is pleasure. In this calculation four dimensions or phases are to be considered—the mention of which has already been noted. These are intensity, duration, certainty and remoteness. We have stated Bentham's method of measurement. In his judgment man is rational and this enables him to decide what will give him pleasure and from what source he will get pain. If we study Bentham's theory of utilitarianism we shall find that the entire fabric of the concept is buttressed by the idea that man is quite reasonable and rational. Though there is considerable doubt about this over-simplification, it is a fact that he accepted it.

Bentham further says that happiness has a sacred side and that is most desirable. That is why no one wants to neglect the pleasure and, to the contrary, makes all efforts to maximise pleasure or happiness. The concept that happiness is measurable is based on certain inferences, though these are questionable. He states that happiness may be both stable and unstable. Due to this, rational man desires to have stable or permanent pleasure. As to the measurability of pleasure Bentham has categorically indicated the special importance of the legislator. If we thoroughly and carefully analyse Bentham's views regarding the measurement of pleasure and pain it will appear that utility can be measured mathematically. That is, through calculation, man can know how much pleasure he has got. In other words, both pleasure and pain are mathematically calculable.

If we go through the various aspects of Benthamite theory of utility we shall find that he has not given recognition to the concept of natural rights because he believed that there could not be anything like natural rights. These rights are unrelated to real situation, they are simply metaphysical or unreal. The foundations of American Declaration of Independence or the French Declaration of Rights are the natural rights. They are not related to the utility or happiness of the citizens. Even the natural rights do not account how much pleasure people will get from them. Bentham has said that even after independence not a single slave got emancipation. So what is the value of natural rights if they do not find their implementation in actual life?

According to Wayper (p. 90) the doctrine of utility is a doctrine which is concerned with results and not with motives. Utilitarians, particularly Bentham, hold the view that the goodness or badness of an action cannot be determined from the motive. Only the results will say whether the decision is good or bad. Of course, Bentham and his followers have agreed to make a compromise in certain exceptional circumstances, but the motive cannot be accepted as a general principle. Wayper concludes (p. 91)—according to the doctrine of utility we cannot say whether an action is good until its consequences are known.

The doctrine of utility is universal in the sense that all the conducts of man are expressed in one form or other of utility. That is, there is utility behind every conduct. Bentham says of the principle of ascetism : Asectics derive their perverted pleasure from ascetism. Ascetism has painful consequences. It is explicable in terms of hedonism, while hedonism is not explicable in terms of ascetism.

Wayper has drawn our attention to another feature of the principle of utility. The doctrine is supposed *to be objective, verifiable, unequivocal and clear* (p. 93). Bentham does not support the view of the founding fathers of the American Constitution and the writers of the *Federalist Papers.* The authors said that justice was the basis of government as well as its end. In Bentham's consideration this is improper. Why not happiness? he asks. Every man knows quite well what is happiness. But the idea of justice is subjective and it varies from person to person. On the contrary, everyone knows what is happiness and, according to Bentham, on rare occasions dispute arises on the question of happiness. Hence it is a worthy criterion of policy determination. The doctrine of utility is not an imaginary one. It is based on solid foundation. It is applicable and ascertainable, since it is measurable.

The Industrial Revolution that took place in the second half of the 18th century changed the economic, social, political and cultural aspects of society and, simultaneously, certain deep rooted consequences and evils. An overall change in the entire structure of society was badly needed. Bentham thought that changes were to be made, but behind every change there must be consent of individuals. Again, they will give consent on the basis of utility they are supposed to get from the proposals. The individuals will calculate utility and after that they will give consent. The individuals are intelligent enough and capable of giving correct opinion. Whether a city will be made clear of slums, that may create heated controversy and it may happen that no definite decision can be taken. But if both evils and advantages are placed before the general public or policy-makers a decision could easily be taken. People will easily understand the exact picture of slum life.

Sabine says (p. 678) : "The theory of pleasure and pain and also the sensationalist psychology associated with it, had for Bentham another value besides that of enabling him to calculate the effects of legislation. He believed that by using the psychology he could track down and neutralise the "fictions" which he saw everywhere in social studies and political reasoning."

Bentham classifies pleasures and pains *into simple and complex.* According to Bentham there are at least fourteen simple pleasures and twelve simple pains. Pleasures of health, sense, power and piety, etc. are instances of simple pleasure. Privation, enmity, etc. are simple pains. Simple pains and pleasures are the foundations of complex pains and pleasures.

Criticism

W. T. Jones (p. 372) criticises Bentham's doctrine of utility on the grounds that it is *ambiguous*, it is *insufficient* and, finally, it is *inapplicable*. Let us see what Jones says. The principle of utility is full of ambiguities, because it does not clearly state and define what does it mean and ultimately to what it leads. What is meant by the greatest good of the greatest number? The number may be the greatest, but the happiness may not be greatest, or the vice versa. There is no certainty that both number and good will happen in reality. That is, good of the greatest number may not be the greatest good. Again, suppose a case. A can produce 100 units of happiness for each of his five companions and the total happiness is 500 units. B can produce 100 units of happiness for each of his four companions and the total happiness stands at 400. Who is acceptable? Who is better? It is very difficult to decide. Jones comments : "What appears on the surface to be a single self-evident exhortation is really two separate exhortations, which contradict each other."

Bentham's theory of utility does not provide us sufficient explanation of human motives. Men may generally seek pleasure and try to avoid pain. But it is not correct to generalise this motive. Men are guided by a number of motives and seeking pleasure and avoiding pain are one of them. Bentham does not recognise this. In fact, it is an over-simplification of human motive. Human nature and motives are so complex that these cannot be explained in simple terms. Even a cursory analysis of human character reveals that. Men want many things and with the passage of time his wants change. His want is not permanently fixed on Bentham's formula or simply pleasure and pain. Even he does not want these at the cost of other's interest. It is unfortunate that Bentham overlooks this.

The intensity of pleasure cannot be measured against its duration, nor its duration against its certainty or uncertainty. Of all the dimensions mentioned by Bentham only two couples are commensurable duration with extent and fecundity with purity. We can say that a pleasure or pain of a given intensity experienced by a person for two minutes is equal to that same pleasure or pain experienced by two persons for one minute. We can also say of a pleasure that its fecundity exceeds its purity. In other words, all his dimensions are not equally applicable to practical situation.

Criticising Bentham's principle of utility Plamenatz (p. 74) points out that he also confused measurements of quantity with comparisons of effects. When a man has to choose between two alternative pleasures, one of which is mild and lasting and the other intense and brief, he never can choose the greater for the simple reason that neither is greater.

Bentham has said that while calculating pleasure and pain people generally estimate the possible consequences of various actions and make comparisons among them and after that they take decisions. They also think about alternative proposals. In substance, people do not take hasty decisions. They apply reason, past experience etc. The inference that can be drawn from this is that his people are enlightened and aware of all the aspects of society and its functioning. But the fact is that Bentham's presumption is not true to fact and unsound assumption. His inordinate sympathy for middle led him to propound such a theory.

Moralists and idealists have united in denunciation of its "base" materialism. He judged human beings as though they were swine. Murray complains that if we take away conscience as Bentham does there is no such thing as a moral or an immoral action though there may remain acts that are generally useful or the reverse. As there is no individual conscience there is no collective conscience. The culprit does not feel the censure of the community.[1]

His method of reconciliation between the individual and community is unsuccessful. He has taken it for granted that there cannot be any contradiction between the individual and the state. But the policy of the state cannot always ensure hundred per cent materialisation of the pleasures of all individuals comprising the community. It is impossible. However, any attempt of reconciliation between individual and community is an impossible adventure.

It is unfortunate that Bentham forgot to take note of several other factors on which pain and pleasure depend. For example, in a class society, the attitudes of poor and rich towards pain and pleasure will considerably vary. Again, people's attitude towards pain and pleasure will vary with the change of social, economic and political conditions. The calculation of pain and pleasure is related with rationality of individuals. But it is not correct that a rational person does not always think about pain and pleasure. His aim may be more noble than mere pain and pleasure. Pain and pleasure are also subject to change when persons come in contact with other persons of foreign countries.

Legislator and Theory of Law

Since Bentham was a man of jurisprudence and had special attachment to it, it is quite natural that legislation will receive added significance in his political writings. The theory of law is a consequence of that. It is, therefore, expected that he would have great respect for law. Individuals' obligation to law is to be determined by its capacity to satisfy the utility. So the law is to be enacted in such a way as to fulfil this basic demand. Naturally, the person who takes the leading part in the enactment of law must know the people's requirements. In Bentham's society the legislator had a very crucial part to play. Now we shall quote him :

"The end and aim of legislator should be the happiness of the people. In matters of legislation, *general utility* should be his guiding principle. The science of legislation consists in determining what makes for the good of the particular community whose interests are at stake, while its art consists in contriving some means of realisation. To apply this principle with complete efficiency, that is, to make the very foundation of a system of reasoning."

The legislator is the most effective instrument for realising the greatest happiness of the greatest number. As to his skillfulness he is to be universally recognised. With the help of his skillfulness he can rear the fabric of felicity by the hands of reason and law. The legislator needs to know only the special circumstances of time and place that have produced peculiar customs and habits. The legislator with his weapon of law-making power can control the customs and habits by imposing penalties.

Why did Bentham want a complete subordination of customs and habits to man-made laws? In fact, this constitutes a major part of his theory of jurisprudence. He believed that history was full of crimes and follies of mankind. So the habits and

[1] Quoted by Maxey—p. 467.

customs behind which there was no reason and which were not guided by the principle of utility could not be the basis of scientific jurisprudence. In his judgment connection between law and utility is essential because only this can give law a scientific foundation. It also makes law practical.

How is the utility of legislation to be measured? Bentham's categorical reply is it is to be measured in terms of its effectiveness, the cost of its enforcement and, in general, by its consequences. That is, how much a law is advantageous or disadvantageous to a community that shall be decided by the consequences created by law. The chief function of the law is to allocate the penalties to produce desirable results. Law, in other words, prevents the undesirable activities and enhances the scope of pleasure.

In this connection we can refer to Bentham's views of obligation. The citizens are bound to obey law if it is in conformity with their utility. That is, it gives them pleasure and saves them from pain. But Bentham does not forget to point out that the legislator cannot enact a law which is going to violate morality and even if he legislates such a law the citizens are not obliged to show respect to such laws.

Bentham recognises the right to property because it provides security and enables men to calculate pain and pleasure. But law should be so enacted as to ensure a comparatively equal distribution of property. If it is not possible the law can make attempt to stop the arbitrary inequalities. It implies that Bentham was not strictly in favour of equal distribution of property. Bentham's contemporary socio-economic political situation was not ripe for equal distribution of property. However, the purpose of property would be to provide security and law must aim at that.

The law will check the criminal activities through the imposition for penalties. He asserts that in all cases the pain of punishment shall exceed the gain received from violating the law or committing the crime. If it is possible to introduce this the criminal activities will come down. Bentham wanted to abolish the savage methods of penalties which were quite ineffective.

Commenting on Bentham's theory of law Sabine says (p. 680) "Bentham's jurisprudence, which was not only the greatest of his works but one of the most remarkable intellectual achievement of the nineteenth century." Bentham's theory of law consists of systematic view of civil and criminal law and also procedural law. He wanted to reform the entire judicial system so as to meet the needs of a changing society. In his theory of law we find clear influence of the middle class standpoint. From Bentham's theory of law and other concepts we can make certain views about his attitude towards obligation. An individual is obliged to carry out the order of authority or obey the law if both meet the requirements of pleasure and avoidance of pain. If citizens find that the law of the legislator or decision of the authority go against the attainment of pleasure and in favour of the enhancement of pain they may refuse to show obligation. Though Bentham has not clearly stated this in clear terms, we can formulate it from his analysis. He has said that the aim of the legislator is to augment pleasure. But, if he fails, what will happen? The silence of Bentham is quite significant.

Bentham's Concept of State

The state, according to Bentham and his followers, *is a group of persons organised for the promotion and maintenance of utility—that is, to achieve greatest happiness or pleasure of the greatest number.* Bentham had no interest in the investigation regarding the origin of state. He started his analysis with the presumption that there existed a political organisation—state—by name. He then proceeds to explain what would be its function. He had no interest in the metaphysical, religious or ethical pursuits of state. The state should focus its attention to the enhancement of citizens' pleasure or happiness. This is stark materialism. Later on Harold Laski said that the primary duty of state is to meet the effective demand of citizens. Though pleasure and effective demand do not follow in the same category there is a fine and interesting link between the two.

Bentham elsewhere said : "The community is a *fictitious body* composed of individual persons who are considered constituting, as it were, its members. The interest of the community is what? —The sum of the interests of the several members who compose it. It is vain to talk of the interests of the community, without understanding what is the interest of the individual. A thing is said to promote the interest or to be for the interest of an individual, when it tends to add to the sum total of his pleasures or, what comes to the same thing, to diminish the sum total of his pains."

The most important duty of state, according to Bentham, is promotion of happiness and alleviation of pain and the state performs this duty through the implementation of laws that are enacted by the legislator. Like Hobbes or Austin, Bentham does not assign the law-making function to the absolute sovereignty. The legislator will do the job and the administrative sector will implement it. Therefore the law of the state is supposed to be an instrument which enables authority to increase pleasure and avoid pain. He also observes that the function of the state may curtail the freedom of individuals. But this is to be accepted because, according to Bentham, happiness is more important than liberty. We, therefore, find that there is nothing in this world which may be compared with the pleasure of the individuals. Law is a restraint on the unwanted functions of some elements or persons. We, therefore, find that the law and the state are the chief actors in the field of attaining happiness and avoiding pleasure.

It has already been indicated that the state is the only creator of law. So the state is the supreme authority. We can say that Bentham's state is the sovereign state. In the words of Wayper : "It is the hallmark of a sovereign state that nothing it does can be illegal" (p. 95). Bentham assumes that neither the law of nature nor the law of reason can limit the power of the state. His apprehension is that if the power of the state is limited, the greatest happiness principle may be affected. If the state fails to fulfil the demand of happiness its very justification will be at stake.

The state is not only the source of law; it is also the source of rights. In his opinion there is no such thing as natural rights, it is simply a figment of imagination. Natural rights are, simply, nonsense. Without state there cannot be any existence of rights. Again, without state the realisation of rights is impossible. This view of rights has been highly acclaimed by many.

We may add a few words to his view on obedience to state. As such, the individual has no right against the state or he cannot defy the order of the state on any flimsy ground. But if he finds that his continued obedience gives him more pain and less pleasure, he can disobey the state. Only on this ground he admits disobedience. The obligation of the individual to the state depends upon to what extent the latter is able to give pleasure and alleviate pain.

In Aristotle, the state was prior to individual. In Bentham, the individual is prior to state. His individual is endowed with reason and rationality and can make distinction between pain and pleasure, right and wrong. He can also calculate pleasure and pain. He even existed before the state. So the place of the state cannot be higher than that of the individual. The individuals do not exist for the state but the state exists for them. Bentham's state is, therefore, a trustee for the individuals.

Bentham's state stands for equal rights and equality in other respects. People enjoy not only equal rights, but they are also equal before law. He also suggests equality of property. When he speaks of equality he does not mean that there can be no inequality in the state. The inequality is inevitable in any real state, but too much of inequality is a hindrance to the attainment of happiness. "He recognised, and he was right in recognising, that a society which is without gross inequalities of fortune is happier than one which is not" (Wayper, p. 98).

Bentham's state is fundamentally a **negative one**. Its task is to maximise the happiness or pleasure and the state does it through the splendid weapon of law. But the state does not take any step to change the character of the individual. He does not recognise that happiness can be augmented by taking some positive steps which will change the character of the individuals. The state imagined by Bentham is not a place to develop what is best in him. He does not assign that function to the state. Wayper concludeds : "For it is not the state that moulds the citizens, it is the citizens that mould the state" (p. 99).

Bentham's Idea of Democracy

From the writings of Bentham we come to know that he wanted a powerful state. But this does not lead one to conclude that he was a supporter of autocracy. He was democratic-minded. His state is a democratic state. We have already noted that he did not believe in natural rights. He spoke of the rights created by the state. Every individual has equal rights in his state. This means he also admitted equality. Every man has the right to claim the greatest happiness and it is the primary duty of any state worthy of its name to fulfil that demand. It will be a useless institution if it fails to perform this fundamental task.

Benthamite democracy proceeds from the assumptions that every man has right and that he is a rational being and so he can judge what is his real happiness and how he can get the greatest happiness. He also assumed of equality—although not in its absolute from. Two kinds of equality were active in the mind of Bentham. The first is one man's happiness must count for as much as another's. This is an equality of right. Second, every man is apt to be the best judge of his own interest which is a sort of natural equality. This indicates that so far as right and equality are concerned Bentham has made his position clear and this makes him in the eyes of his readers a great democrat.

Bentham wanted to reduce the interference of the government with individual's affairs to the lowest level. That is, his government is a limited one. It cannot control all the spheres of human activity. He believed that an all-powerful state cannot ensure the greatest happiness for its citizens in the largest number. In this sense his government is a negative one—the role is not constructive but negative. The first duty of the government is to ensure that men get in each other's way as little as possible. The government cannot directly increase the happiness of its subjects.

What it can do is that it will remove the hindrances by ensuring the proper implementation of laws. When the government interferes with individuals' affairs, it does it for the benefit of the entire society, not for particular person or group of persons. It forbids certain kinds of behaviour and encourages others.

His attitude towards democracy and allied ideas reveals that he was in great favour of representative form of democracy. Of course, it is quite natural for him, because in the second half of eighteenth century this type of democracy was accepted by British people and was very popular. He also believed that this type of democracy would be able to meet the requirements of people. Only such a government is able to conciliate the individual interests with common interests. Moreover, the representative government will take active interest in furthering general welfare or happiness of the people on the ground that if they fail to do it, they will lose power. In the representative form of democracy, people will get chance to test their power of judgment and exercise the in political right. He also believed that a representative democracy would not dare to work for the benefit of any particular section.

He did not stop in suggesting a representative democracy. He strongly argued for radical reforms in the electoral system, votes for women, annual Parliament and secret ballot. The members of the Parliament should be mere delegates and the Prime Minister should be chosen by the Parliament. He recommended the appointment of civil servants through competitive examination. The government, according to Bentham, is a necessary evil. He advised his countrymen to keep a watch upon the activities of the government. People must see that the government is doing its duties. As Bentham grew older his suspicion for government's ability to meet the demands and to follow the democratic values and norms increased considerably. Though he had great faith in the British type of representative democracy he was quite suspicious of its inability. A powerful government might jeopardise the realisation of basic rights and thereby attainment of pleasure and alleviation of pain. His suggestion was that people must always be alert and watch the activities of the government. He said that it was the duty of the people to protect their own rights and to see that their happiness is not jeopardised.

If we look at what Bentham had said about democracy, happiness and pain, it will be found that his attention was always focussed on the interests of the rising middle class. He had unlimited sympathy for this class. In his time there were middle class, capitalist class and also working class. There were large number of educated men in the middle class and the members of this class were eager to have a share in the administration. This inspired him to support representative form of government. Bentham was against the House of Lords, because its members were not elected by the people. His theory of utilitarianism was built up to protect the interests of the middle class. Common men generally fight for the maintenance of their physical existence and not for the enhancement of pleasure.

Influence of Bentham

While estimating Bentham's influence we are faced with a clear paradox. He is not an outstanding philosopher. Nor did he invent any principle nor propound any theory. In spite of this he occupies an important place in the history of political thought. This is the paradox. Wayper remarks : "He took his theory of knowledge from Locke and Hume, the pleasure and pain principle from Helvetius, the notion of sympathy and antipathy from Hume, the idea of utility from any of half a score of writers. Lacking originality and full of prejudice in his speculations, he is as confused and contradictory in his own theoretical adventures as he is complacent" (p. 99). Wayper has also criticised the opening sentences of the *Introduction to the Principles of Morals and Legislation.* In his view, these sentences make no meaning. Bentham tries to remove confusion but, instead, creates chaos. He never explains what is exactly meant by the sovereign mastery of pleasure and pain. Yet this concept constitutes the central part of his political philosophy.

Maxey observes (p. 467) that the weakest points of Bentham's philosophy are that his psychology is inadequate and his reconciliation of individual and community satisfactions is unsuccessful. He has failed to go into the deep of human psychology. He has probed only a part of it. In this sense we cannot say that his diagnosis is a complete one. Even some critics say that he had not the intellectual capacity to draw a comprehensive picture of human psychology. Others hold the view that he was clearly biased to the middle class interests. In fact, his political ideas have centred around the aims and ambitions of the British middle class people which arose out of Industrial Revolution. Bentham's philosophy and reform proposals are for the rising middle class, not for the entire society. The capitalist class was already well-established.

It is the opinion of other critics that, like Hobbes and Locke, Bentham lent his support to the bourgeois class. The persons who are completely free from every problems and necessities can think of pleasure and pain. Only these persons can pursue their happiness. He wanted to reduce the interference of the state to a minimum level considering the interests of the bourgeoisie. His argument for equality of property is simply an eyewash. He never wanted it sincerely and he also knew that it was impossible.

Like Hobbes, Bentham has emphasised upon security. He wanted the security of property. His main concern was pleasure and pain. He has not uttered a single word against the evils of industrialisation. Bentham has not suggested anything about how to save the society from these evils. Some people say that he had an intention to redistribute property for bringing about equality. But this cannot be said that he was an advocate of socialism. Rather, he was the classical supporter of bourgeois state.

When all this is said about the drawbacks of Bentham something and even far more than this can be said in his support. Maxey says (p. 469) that here was a doctrine to rock the foundations of all accredited political theory. With the help of ruthless logic Bentham brushed aside the radical and conservative thought. He denied the feudal right, divine right, historical right, natural right and contractual right. In his view there is only one type of right and this is constitutional right or the state, created right, In this sense—Bentham is, no doubt, a radical philosopher.

Bentham's contribution in the field of jurisprudence is worthy of mention, particularly his criminal jurisprudence. In this field his influence was immediate and lasting. "No man did more to unravel the complexities of medieval law or introduce simplicity, clarity and practical good sense into legal thinking" (Maxey, p. 470).

Though Bentham's theory of utility suffers from a number of drawbacks its importance cannot be ignored. It paves the path of a welfare state. A government cannot ignore the welfare of its citizens. What we call welfare of general public,

Bentham has called it happiness or pleasure. When the welfare is achieved people will be happy. Bentham thought that the growing influence of capitalists cornered the middle class people and men of other sections. He was sure that this process must be stopped, otherwise the progress of society would be a simple myth. This also indicates that the state can claim obedience from citizens if it can meet their requirements. In this way men can get happiness. The interpreters of Benthamite philosophy have stressed the point that his views must be treated in larger perspective and not simply in the formula of pleasure and pain. That is why Maxey correctly observes that it is the duty of the government to justify itself through its functions and responsibility towards the citizens. In other words, it is the duty of the government to serve the people in the maximum possible ways.

Ebenstein has paid high tribute to Bentham. He says (p. 505) that one of Bentham's richest legacics of government is his awareness that good government is more than a matter of tradition, common sense etc. ...it needs a foundation of preliminary research and investigation. Any government of the modern age gives more emphasis upon research and investigation and, in fact, the investigation has become the fourth organ of the government. Bentham was the first philosopher who carefully treated the investigative aspect of the government. A government is no longer the day-to-day affair of simple dimensions confining itself to the maintenance of law and order. It must see the consequences of its policies and approach. He applied an empirical and critical method of investigation. Here lies the credit of Bentham.

In 1948, the bicentennial of Bentham was celebrated in England and *Times* of London made the following observation : "Bentham still exerts a posthumous despotism over English politics and on the whole it is a benevolent despotism." From the beginning of the nineteenth century Bentham's idea and philosophy worked behind all the reforms and policies of the British government.

Bentham's influence crossed the territorial boundary of England. The procedure of the French Assembly was based largely on a sketch by Bentham. The political and legal proposals of Bentham influenced many French thinkers and statesmen. His doctrine created enthusiasm in America and Russia, Portugal and Spain. The legal codes of many countries were revised according to the advice of Bentham. He proposed to the President of USA in 1811 to draw up a scientific code of law.

The English and American lawyers throughout the nineteenth century strictly followed the analytic jurisprudence and they knew that John Austin and his school were the founders of this system. But, in the words of Sabine (p. 684), Austin did little more than bring together systematically ideas that were scattered through Bentham's voluminous works.

Towards the end of his life Bentham was a great critic of monarchy and aristocracy. In these two forms of government, Bentham thought, the personal interests of the governors always got precedence over the collective interests of the society. These two types of government neglected the welfare projects and from this he came to the conclusion that it was impossible for monarchy and aristocracy to implement the radical changes aiming at the common good of community. Only a democratic form of government can do it. Liberal democracy, it is said, received the best treatment at the hands of Bentham.

Wayper observes that the great captains of Industrial Revolution were demanding that the efficiency, cheapness and uniformity—which they worshipped in their industrial undertakings—should also be introduced into government and law. But they were unwilling to accept the conservative philosophy of Edmund Burke and his respect for landed nobility. They had, of course, no respect for anarchism of Godwin and Shelley. They did not like Jacobinical principles and Natural Rights. They wanted reforms which would be sensible and practical and far-reaching without being too far-reaching, reform which would acknowledge the movement of power from the aristocracy to themselves without doing anything to encourage its further movement from themselves to masses. Bentham and his followers were also demanding uniformity, cheapness and efficiency. The captains of Industrial Revolution got their answer in the writings and proposals of Bentham (Wayper, pp. 101–102).

JOHN STUART MILL (1806–1873)

Life and Works

Three persons built up the structure of utilitarianism. They are Bentham, James Mill, and John Stuart Mill. James Mill was the friend of Bentham and father of J. S. Mill. James Mill was born in 1773 and John Stuart Mill died in 1873. There was a gap of a century. About this gap Dunning says : "The century covered by these two lives fixes very fairly the chronological bounds within which Benthamite utilitarianism rose, flourished and passed away by absorption into later philosophic growth" (Dunning, p. 235). We can reasonably say that utilitarianism is confined within Bentham and the two Mills—Though it is an "ism", it is different from other isms, such as liberalism, Marxism or idealism. It is not debated or thoroughly discussed. Though it was the joint product of Bentham and the two Mills, it was the product of Bentham and J. S. Mill. The contribution of James Mill is very insignificant. Again, there are wide differences between Bentham and J. S. Mill so far as the basic tenets of the theory are concerned. Bentham was interested only in utilitarianism while J. S. Mill's interest was wide. The theory of utilitarianism was one of them. Today J. S. Mill is remembered not simply for utilitarianism but for many others.

John Stuart Mill was born in 1806. At the age of three, John began to learn Greek and at seven Latin. The acquaintance with Greek enabled him to know the Greek philosophy. He also learned history and arithmetic. J. S. Mill went thoroughly in Latin literature. He started his study of political economy at the age of thirteen and completed Adam Smith, David Ricardo. Before he reached the seventeenth year he finished the study of Benthm's utilitarian principle. He died in 1873.

By 1823, Mill earned a good command over different subjects and he came to be acquainted with the academic circles of Britain. He also succeeded in establishing himself as a scholar. Mill joined the East India Company as an ordinary clerk. Thirty-three years later, in 1856, he became the chief of the office at an annual salary of £ 2,000. Two years later he retired. Most of his academic output was produced by that time. In 1856, J. S. Mill was requested by the voters of Westminster to contest the parliamentary seat and he kept their request and won the election. Next term he contested and was defeated. Victory was more surprising to him than his defeat.

When J. S. Mill was in his teens he published a number of articles on philosophy and politics. *Westminster Review* was the official organ of Philosophical Radicalism and he contributed to it. At the age of twenty-eight his first major work and still classic work on philosophy was published. This is the *System of Logic*. In 1848, the same year *Manifesto* was published, he brought out *Political Economy*. In order of importance it was next to Adam Smith's *Wealth of Nations*. Thus, two principal works on economics and philosophy were published long before his retirement. But his works on politics and morality were the results of his mature intelligence and thought. He completed his essay on *Liberty* before his retirement and the death of his wife delayed the publication. It was published in 1859. His *Utilitarianism* and *Representative Government* both were published in 1861.

Bad health and protracted illness stood like a big mountain on the way of his achievement in academic affairs. He was really a genius. Plamenatz[1] says that the three essays (*On Liberty, Utilitarianism* and *Representative Government*) exhibit all his defects as a thinker, because these were written by him when he was sick. Lack of clarity and inconsistency have characterised these three essays. According to the same critic the most defective is the *Utilitarianism* in which Mill seems to lose control of his argument at every turn. But it is the product of an intelligent and honest but an exhausted mind. *Liberty* and *Representative Government* are comparatively much better, but still are not free from defects.

The younger Mill could not accept many of the ideas of Bentham and his father. He thought their views irrelevant and incomplete. But his illness prevented him from contributing to politics and philosophy. Though Plamenatz says that his major works suffer from several drawbacks, we think that these three books are still classic in the whole gamut of political sicence. The students of political science still read his books with a lot of interest. Even he is regarded as progenitor of feminism which was a burning issue in the sixties, seventies and eighties of the last century.

Liberty and Democracy

We have already noted that Bentham, towards the fag-end of his life, was convinced that in the English society the sinister interests were extremely active and they were eating into the vital of democracy. So, with the help of all strength and energy, democracy could be established and safeguarded. This was one of the main objectives of Bentham. His utilitarian friend James Mill shared this view. The Industrial Revolution in England failed to make the foundation of democracy solid and broad-based. Rather, the American democratic system drew, at the time, attention of every serious thinker of the first half of the nineteenth century. Attention took a better turn after the publication of de Tocqueville's *Democracy in America* in 1835. It is to be noted here that from the 1830s the British government embarked upon certain reforms to strengthen the basis and periphery of democracy. The credit of this should go to Bentham. However, it was admitted on all hands that democracy in all its manifestations should be the ruling concept. But John Stuart Mill began to look at it from a quite different angle. His love for democracy was not less than anybody's. But he was also a great realist. He did not think in terms of avoiding democracy. His objective was always to rectify it. Plamenatz comments (p. 125)—His object in *Liberty* is to warn men of democracy's attendant evils and to show them how they can be diminished.

Mill says that in the present form of democracy the rule of all does not mean the rule of each man by himself. Some people rule the others. Again, what is

1. *The English Utilitarians*, p. 123.

commonly known as the will of the people is, in practice, the will of the majority. The will of the minority is neglected. Mill calls this rule of the majority the oppression or dictatorship or despotism of majority which, according to Mill, is anathema of democracy. This shortcoming of democracy is deplorable but it is a fact and democracy must be saved from this. Besides the oppression of majority there is the tyranny of opinion which is equally condemnable. Mill says : "whenever there is an ascendant class, a large portion of the morality of the country emanates from its class interests and its feeling of class superiority." Mill knew that, in practice, it is not possible for all people to rule; only the rule of majority is possible. But here he cautioned by saying that majority rule does not mean the suppression of minority opinion. The view of the minority must be given due importance. Both the majority rule and the domination of a powerful class are enemies of real democracy which he denounced in clear language. Democracy does not mean the rule of all; but real democracy will give credence to the opinion of all.

Mill was the first thinker of England who doubted the love for freedom of the English people. His cogent argument is it is not the love for freedom that is a great feature of Englishmen, rather they are very suspicious of the encroachment of organised power over the individual freedom. The same mentality encouraged the Americans to revolt against England. But Mill admits that tyranny of opinion is perhaps stronger among them than elsewhere (Plamenatz, p. 125).

In the essay *On Liberty* Mill states that the sole end for which mankind are warranted, individually or collectively, in interfering with the liberty of action of any of their number, is self-protection. That is, for the protection of the members of the community power can be rightly exercised by the authority, and in that case the particular will of any individual cannot be a hindrance. This is compatible with the concept of utilitarianism.

In the second chapter of the essay Mill discusses liberty of thought and expression. He assumes that it is to the advantage of mankind that knowledge should increase among—and should be possessed by—as many of them as possible. In the last two chapters Mill analyses the proper limits to the authority of society over the individuals. The whole essay undoubtedly reveals Mill's zeal for the protection of liberty. He did no approve of the dictatorship of the majority or the social stigma the purpose of which is to curtail the freedom of man.

In the essay *On Liberty* Mill asserts that liberty is not simply a way of pursuing happiness or avoiding pain. If anybody treats liberty in that light he will be quite unjustified. For the development of personality, liberty is indispensable. It is necessary both for the individual and for the society as a whole. For the maximisation of happiness, Mill contended, men should have maximum liberty. In this way utility and liberty are combined together.

Mill was the greatest champion of human liberty and he could not tolerate its curtailmaint. It is said the he was inspired by the Greek ideal of self-government. In such type of system people enjoyed maximum liberty. He believed that through the participation in the functioning of democracy people get the opportunity to enrich their political knowledge and experience. This is a great asset of democracy. Custom, tradition and others should not be allowed to stand on the way of gaining experience through the participation in democratic process. In his *on Liberty* he emphasised this. Let people earn experience. He has also said that people will develop their moral faculties through participation in democracy. It appears to us that, to Mill, democracy was the man-making workshop.

The greatest contribution of Industrial Revolution was the creation of uniformity. Before it there were small scale and cottage industries which earned remarkability or heterogeneous character. Mill treated it as the symbol of liberty. But the Industrial Revolution destroyed this heterogeneity. Man became the slaves of machine and they were subjected to the wills and whims of industrial tycoons. In his judgement this uniformity was against the development of personality and exercise of liberty. The concept of liberty is to be viewed in this background and that was his contention.

On every subject or issue every man has full freedom to know and analyse the various aspects of the matter. It is absolutely unjustified to deprive a man of his right to think the matter in his own way and by applying his own intelligence. If a society deprives a man of this opportunity that society cannot be called a free society. In a word he has supported the freedom of thought.

There is a very common notion that Mill was the advocate of absolute freedom. What he actually meant is difficult to say. The interpreters of his political philosophy hold the view that he was the victim of contradiction. We can say that though Mill was a staunch supporter of freedom he never wanted the interest of the society to be spoiled. He desired a reconciliation between individual freedom and interest of the community. We have already quoted him. The sole purpose of any civilised community is the protection of its members and, to that end, the authority will be justified in interfering. This is his utilitarianism and also his realism. Absolute freedom is never salubrious for society, that Mill had fully realised. His men are not selfish and he did not want them to be so. Naturally, his men are concerned with their own welfare as well as the welfare of the community. Here lies the credit of J. S. Mill, and on this point, again, he is different from other liberal thinkers.

Mill admits that the state shall have power to impose limitations upon the activities and behaviour of individuals. But this power cannot be unlimited. *State has no right to interfere with the religious freedom and freedom of speech and expression.* Let us put it in his own words : "If all mankind minus one were of one opinion, and only one person were of the contrary opinion, mankind would be no more justified in silencing that one person, than he, if he had the power, would be justified in silencing mankind." A state cannot deprive a man of his right to oppose the view of mankind. It may so happen that the opinion which has been suppressed is right and in that situation mankind will be deprived of a valuable opinion. Out of his experience Mill came to the conclusion that the juxtaposition of several opposite views would produce the truth. Moreover, he thought that in self-regarding activities the state had nothing to interfere. Only in other-regarding affairs state interference would be welcomed. This observation of Mill is oft-quoted as well as classic. It simply indicates his in unlimited love for freedom. He was of opinion that no power in the world can silence the view of an individual.

Why Mill was against the suppression of opinion requires to be elaborated. In his judgment there is nothing like permanent or eternal truth. What we call permanent today may not have any trace of existence in future. So, in the name of eternal truth, man's opinion cannot be suppressed. Suppression of opinion could not earn the approval of Mill and so he thought it quite unjustified. If we were to find out the truth, Mill observes, freedom of thought and expression must be recognised. No society can be termed civilised which does not recognise it.

From the above it appears to us that Mill was the champion of unrestricted freedom. But a large number of critics refuse to accept the view of Mill. They think that every person must have freedom and he should be allowed to enjoy it freely. But if his freedom goes against the general interest of the civil society he cannot be allowed to enjoy freedom. It is a matter of great regret that Mill failed to consider this aspect. He refused to accept the view that every freedom must have limitation. Notwithstanding, Maxey says that Mill's chapter on freedom of thought and discussion is one of the finest things and he can be equated will great luminaries such as Voltaire, Rousseau, Spinoza, Milton, Jefferson.

Mill had no faith on the intelligence and ability of the common people. He thought that they were moved by self-interests. Even the governors were not free from this. In spite of this, Mill strongly supported the democratic form of government. Though he supported democracy he did not like the existing form and functions. He wanted its reforms. His advocacy for proportional representation and woman suffrage is directed to that end. He has also suggested under what circumstances the democratic form of government can work successfully. All these things he has discussed in his *Representative Government*. The representative government must be helpful for the proper development of man's personality and enrichment of freedom.

In his view, only the wise and able men can make democracy a successful form of government. But if it is left to the whims and lack of consciousness of unwise and illiterate persons nobody can check its degeneration. Ability and wisdom could be achieved only through cultivation and the government would have to take the full responsibility. "The first element of good government is the virtue and intelligence of human beings composing the community. ...The most important point of excellence which any form of government can possess is to promote the virtue and intelligence of the people themselves" (Mill). This view of Mill reminds us of Plato's concept of ideal state. Plato had no faith on the intelligence and ability of general public. Mill wanted to say that intelligent and able persons will rule but everyone shall have the opportunity to express his opinion.

Mill did not support the alienation of people from the general administration. This would discourage them about the affairs of the state. Disinterestedness would breed corruption and that would signal the death of democracy. So, for the sake of democracy, people must be educated and enthusiasm be created in their mind. In order to check the despotism of the majority Mill suggested that there would be provision for political parties and the number of parties must not exceed *two*. In a proper democratic set-up the minority must have sufficient opportunity to express its opinion. It must not think that its opinion is being suppressed. To speak the truth, Mill's democracy is really an ideal one. It is not a democracy of a section of the society, it is for the entire society. It is for the proper development of the mental faculties of all individuals.

J. S. Mill thought that representative government was the most suitable form of government and for that reason he wanted to make it an ideal form. Such a form of government must have good manner, honesty and must show enough interest in public affairs. In the administration of such a government there must be wisdom.

These qualities of Mill's ideal type of representative government remind us of Plato's ideal state. He had suggested that a good form of representative government must educate its citizens or members to make them suitable for it. Plato, we can recall, suggested almost the same thing. He had a strong belief that a bad representative government will make the lives of human beings intolerable and hell.

Barker[1] says Mill, in his *Representative Government*, "Spiritualised the Benthamite defence of democracy. Instead of regarding popular self-government as freedom for the people to pursue its own self-interest at the expense of the "sinister interests' of classes and sections, he conceived representative institutions as the necessary condition of that individual energy of mind and character which must be developed all-round and in all things, and can only be so developed if the area of individual thought and will is extended to embrace the affairs of the whole community. His philosophy found room for trade unions ...it even admitted the possibility of social regulation of the laws of distribution."

Mill has been highly appreciated for his unadulterated attitude towards representative democracy and even today people of all walks of life adore him as a prophet of democracy. On this question the view of Wayper is different. He calls Mill a *reluctant democrat*. It was beyond his imagination that the mission of democracy could be achieved by the illiterate and politically unconcious people. So he invested his energy more in the discussion of the reforms than in the discussion of nature and other aspects. Even this has not been able to remove the loopholes. He did not support the popular sovereignty. He was in favour of wise men's rule. Today we call it the rule of the elite. He wanted reforms in the electoral system, but he did not want universal suffrage. A man with so much farsightedness could not imagine that a universal suffrage could free the society from numerous evils which could not be done otherwise.

Finally, we can again quote Barker : "Mill was the prophet of empty liberty and an abstract individual. He had no clear philosophy of rights, through which alone the conception of liberty attains a concrete meaning, he had no clear idea of a social whole, in whose realisation the false antithesis of "state" and "individual" disappears" (p. 4). This shortcoming is due to the fact that although Mill could not accept Benthamism in toto, he failed to come out of the Benthamite circle. A revision of liberalism was needed and that need was met by T. H. Green. Whatever may the opinions of the critics be, there is no doubt that his love for democracy or representative democracy is beyond any question.

UTILITARIANISM

Utilitarianism : Acceptance and Revision

It is admitted by all critics that J. S. Mill had a sincere intention to vindicate Bentham's theory of utilitarianism. But ultimately his theory has rejected the main tenets of utilitarianism advocated by Jeremy Bentham. Sabine observes : "The importance of Mill's philosophy consisted in its departures from the system which it still professed to support and hence in the revisions that it made in the utilitarian tradiion" (p. 707). Almost the exact opinion has been expressed by C. L. Wayper.

1. *Political Thought in England* : 1848–1914, p. 3.

He says : "In his desire to safeguard utilitarianism from the reproaches levelled against it, Mill goes far towards overthrowing the whole utilitarian position" (p.110).

However, it is a fact that he accepted the principle of utility propounded by Bentham and few other thinkers. Particularly he lent his full support to Bentham's 'greatest happiness' theory. In *Utilitarianism* Mill has said : "The creed which accepts as the foundation of morals, utility or the Greatest Happiness Principle, holds that actions are right in proportion as they tend to promote happiness, wrong as they tend to produce the reverse of happiness. By happiness is intended pleasure and absence of pain, by unhappiness, pain and privation of pleasure. To give a clear view of the moral standard set-up by the theory much more requires to be said, particularly what things it includes in the ideas of pain and pleasure."

The above opinion of Mill reveals that he accepted the central idea of utilitarianism but he did not accept all the aspects of the theory. He revised it so much that the theory has assumed new forms and for that reason many critics doubt whether Mill's utilitarianism and Bentham's utilitarianism are same. This doubt is quite reasonable and, on that ground, many argue that Mill has revised utilitarianism. Now the question is why did he try to include certain things into the original theory? It is a small point and we shall now deal with it. So long James Mill was alive he could not come out of the gripping influence of his father. He felt suffocation, but he had no courage to revolt against his father. The death of James Mill in 1836, four years after the death of Bentham, opened to him the floodgate of new light and opportunity and he did not hesitate even for a moment to view and review Benthamism in new light and perspective. This is the primary cause of his change in a attitude.

Berki has supported the idea that J. S. Mill has considerably revised the Benthamite theory of utilitarianism and in this connection he makes the following observation : "Bred on the utilitarianism of Bentham and his father James Mill he came later to be influenced by the romantic poetry of Wordsworth and the writings of Coleridge and Carlyle, through whom he got to know about and appreciate German philosophy, with particular reference to Germanic historical approach" (p. 182). In 1838 and 1840 he wrote several articles in London and Westminster Review. These articles were the starting points of his attempt of emancipation from the influence of James Mill. Therefore, though bred in the tradition of Bentham and James Mill, ultimately he succeeded in freeing himself.

In *Utilitarianism* Mill says—It is compatible with the principle of utility to recognise the fact, that some kinds of pleasure are more desirable and more valuable than others. It would be absurd that while, in estimating all other things, quality is considered as well as quantity, the estimation of pleasures should be supposed to depend on quantity alone. Mill wants to say that the qualities of all pleasures are not identical. Some pleasures are more desirable and valuable. While others do not fall in this category. That is, their quality is doubtful and, on that ground, their desirability is not high. Thus Mill makes a difference between the qualities of pleasure and this single criterion utilitarianism propounded by his father's friend. This we call the **revision of utilitarianism**. But Wapyer thinks that Mill's view on utilitarianism is to be termed non-utilitarian. Hence the entire issue is complex and controversial.

Mill says that men who have experienced higher and lower pleasures will agree that there is difference and they will always prefer higher pleasure. In Mill's own words : "It is better to be a human being dissatisfied, than a pig satisfied, better to be Socrates dissatisfied than a fool satisfied. And if the fool or the pig is of a different opinion, it is because they only know their side of the question. The other party to the comparison knows both sides." Here we fully agree with Mill's view. There is a difference between different types of pleasures. In comparison with Bentham, Mill is more practical.

If pleasures are qualitatively different then people will always want higher or better pleasures and the principle of utility falls on the ground. Mill has observed that pleasures are different both in quality and in quantity and by saying this he has not only revised Benthamite theory of utility, he has established his own theory. Even man cannot get equal amount of pleasure from all articles. *He makes gradations of them.* Sabine writes : "The distinctive characteristic of Mill's utilitarianism was that he tried to express a conception of moral character consonant with his own personal idealism" (p. 708). Hence Bentham's pronouncement that pushpin is as good as poetry, if it gives the same pleasure is "simply vulgar nonsense."

One important difference between the utilitarianism of Bentham and Mill is the former gave egoism the central place—egoism is the determiner of happiness. But in Mill's concept there is hardly any place of egoism and it is evident in the following comment of Mill. "Assumed soical welfare is a matter of concern to all men of goodwill and regarded freedom, integrity and self-respect and personal distinction as intrinsic goods apart from their contribution to happiness. Moral convictions of this sort underlay Mill's whole conception of a liberal society" (Sabine, p. 798).

Mill has made two wide breaches in his father's and Bentham's system. He has asserted that some pleasures are qualitatively superior to others and he has implied that the felicific calculus is absurd. We have discussed the first, now we shall discuss the second. Men have always relied upon the testimony of those most competent to judge. "There is no other tribunal to be referred to even on the question of quantity. What means are there of determining which is the acutest of two pains or the interest of the two pleasurable sensation except the general suffrage of those who are familiar with both" (Mill). Here Mill asserts that the *felicific calculus is really an absurd concept.* If we accept Mills contention then we must say that he has abandoned Bentham's theory. Mill is right in his view but the breach in Bentham's system is clear beyond doubt.

Bentham's theory of utility is not a separate concept. It has close relationship with politics. It is the duty of the legislator to enact laws which will help the people to get pleasure. But laws alone cannot help. The government must take steps to implement the laws. So we find that Bentham's utility is primarily a political concept. If the law, legislator and government do not appear in the picture, pleasure will remain beyond the reach of public. But *J. S. Mill considers the idea of utility in ethical terms.* It is more a guide of personal activities in the field or morality and less a political guide. In his essay on *Utilitarianism* Mill makes the following observation :

In the golden rule of Jesus of Nazareth, we read the complete spirit of the ethics of utility. To do as you would be done by, and to love your neighbour as yourself, constitute the ideal perfection of utilitarian morality. As the means of making the nearest approach to this ideal, utility would enjoin, first that laws and social arrangements should place the happiness or interest of every individual, as nearly as possible in harmony with the interest of the whole.

Here J. S. Mill makes it clear that apparently happiness is a personal matter, but in ultimate analysis it is not so. On the part of an individual it is immoral and unethical to be happy at the cost of happiness of others. Bentham treated pleasure of a man as completely separate issue. But at the hands of Mill it is not an individual or isolated matter but a social issue. The happiness of one is connected with the happiness of others.

According to Mill the spread of education and the proper cultivation of mind can change the character and outlook of man. The education established in the mind of man is an indissoluble association between his own happiness and the good of the whole society. Bentham was a social reformer and he thought of reforming the society from various angles. But he could not see the concept of happiness from the broader perspective of the whole community. Man can be educated so as to improve his idea of happiness and to enhance his power of adjustment with the rest of society. Only the rare personality of Mill can think in that term. Man is not alone, he is part of a great society. Education inculcates this idea in his mind.

Wayper says that *Mill's treatment of moral obligation converts him into a non-utilitarian.* Bentham had conceived of moral obligation as the product of past association of the selfish desires. According to Mill the idea of moral obligation is a quite different thing. Fear, memory, self-esteem play their part in its composition. Moral obligations cannot be explained in term of utility. Wayper concludes (p. 113) : "Thus while his ethics are certainly more satisfying than Bentham's, Mill is responsible for yet another important alteration in Benthamism."

Bentham's utilitarianism is individualistic. But Mill's utilitarianism, if it is at all utilitarianism, is less individualistic. Barker says : "in his hands utilitarianism begins to be less individualistic and assumes more and more socialistic quality. Social utility is the goal, and to this it may be the supreme duty of the individual to sacrifice himself" (p. 12). That is why Mill emphasises upon education and cultivation of social consciousness.

According to Bentham and his followers that state or society is happy which succeeds in maximising the happiness of its subjects. To put it in other words, the chief function of the state is to make its largest number of citizens happy and that happiness must be maximum. If the citizens receive maximum utility from the actions of state then it will be taken for granted that they are happy. On this fundamental question of utilitarianism Mill differs from Bentham. Not only this, Mill criticises the argument of Bentham. Mill treats the state not simply in terms of happiness but in terms of ethics and morality. A moral state can make its citizens happy and the citizens will be happy if they get their own dignity. In elaborating his view on utilitarianism Mill upholds his original stand—the quality of a state depends on the mental and ethical standard of individuals. If this is low or unacceptable the state can never be of high standard. Again, on this very important issue, Mill never makes any compromise. Emphasis on ethics and morality undoubtedly makes him an idealist utilitarian philosopher. *On Liberty* he has been found to give stress. Moreover, Mill was a socialist-minded thinker. Naturally he did not treat individuals separately from each other. He was led by a noble view—an individual must not think his own pleasure as absolute, but relative. If it is strictly followed the pleasure of the individual and the progress of the state both will be achieved.

Bentham has thought that the *justification of the state lies in its ability to maximise utility.* But Mill does not agree with the view of his father's friend. *The justification of the state lies in its capacity to develop the personality of its subjects.* Hence it is the duty of the state to take into account of that. Only a *liberal state* having representative government can ensure it. "He did not defend popular government because it is efficient. He had grave doubts whether it always is, and he had quite lost his father's confidence that the apparatus of liberal government, such as the suffrage, would always be rationally used for beneficial ends. The real argument for political freedom is that it produces and gives scope to a high type of moral character" (Sabine, p. 709).

Harmon raises a pertinent question : Is Mill's argument for freedom truly a utilitarian one? He further observes that J. S. Mill at least claims that. But his claim is not justified. Barker comments : "But Mill belongs to an old tradition, though he gave that tradition a deeper and more spiritual interpretation and he must be regarded as the last of the great utilitarians, rather than as the first among the new prophets who have arisen since 1848."[1] *His revision of utilitarianism has created a new theory which is not utilitarianism in the strictest sense of the term.* Wayper calls it *non-utilitarianism.* "In all these alterations" comments Wayper "that he makes in Benthamism, Mill may think he is defending it, but in fact he is destroying it."[2]

Maxey[3] writes : "In this interpretation of utilitarianism very little of Bentham remains. Bentham was concerned not with the *ought* but he is in human motivation and behaviour. His objective was a rule of legislation that could be applied to things as they are level of morality or any stage of civilisation." Mill saved the face of Benthamism, but confessed its essential fallacy. There is not much left to Benthamic utilitarianism when J. S. Mill has completed his defence of it. What is left is not utilitarianism at all (Plamenatz, p. 144). Mill borrowed the concept of utility from Bentham and completely idealised it with the precepts of ethics and morality borrowed from Greek thought and philosophy. In the hands of Mill utilitarianism has become a new concept.

Mill and Qualified Collectivism

Mill, we know, is the prophet of individual liberty and a great advocate of extreme individualism. But in spite of the fundamental premises there are certain comments and statements which force us to believe that he was not an individualist out and out. He had sympathy for socialism. Mill has repeatedly said that the individuals will pursue their happiness and pleasure in such a way as that will ultimately result in the happiness of the whole society. It is because the individual is an integral part of the society. But in his *Political Economy* he came to realise the hollowness of this assumption. In a society, all the individuals are not of equal ability. Naturally, the pursuit of happiness is bound to be different. It may be that the total happiness will increase, but its distribution among the individuals will be unequal. Again, there will be differences in physical environment which may affect the pursuit of happiness. Above all, the gross economic inequalities create the insuperable hindrances to attainment of happiness.

---

1. Barker—*Political Thought in England 1848 to 1914*, p. 70.
2. Wayper, op. cit., p. 116.
3. p. 479.

Mill had great interest in economics and he studied the subject thoroughly. This considerably helped him to arrive at the conclusion that the Industrial Revolution produced huge amount of wealth. But this wealth has not been properly distributed which had resulted in the gross inequalities and injustice. This again created impediments to the attainment of happiness. Land, industry and knowledge, he saw, were the monopoly of a few persons who constituted the minority. The majority was deprived of the fruits of wealth. These inequalities placed the *haves* of the society in better position and pursuit of happiness for them was quite easy. Rather, the wealthier section of the society made the pursuit of happiness its supreme goal. The *have-nots* were far behind them. Further, the whole legal system was so built up as to benefit the minority. Mill felt the necessity of overhauling the entire judicial structure. The small minority reaped the fruits of everything. All these progressive ideas cropped up in the mind of Mill in his later years.

"This being so, Mill shows a good deal of sympathy for socialism and urges to use the state to remove the obstacles in the way of individual's development and to make life tolerable for the masses."[1] In Mill's account we do not find any sympathy for Bentham's theory of property. Nor is the right to property sacred. The right to property is to be judged by its utility. Mill comes to the conclusion that though property has utilities if it is owned by a minority of individuals and the majority is deprived of this right, it is gross unjustice. It produces utility only to the owners of property and propertyless persons are deprived of utility. Private ownership is not expedient. In a society where there are no inequalities or less inequalities will the pursuit of happiness lead to the social happiness. What is apparent is that Mill has treated the theory of utilitarianism from the holistic standpoint. The theory of utilitarianism is not a completely separate issue. Its association with other concepts and matters is undeniable. We firmly believe that Mill fully understood it and for that reason he was thinking of the curses of the Industrial Revolution—maldistribution of wealth, inequality, improper holding of property by handful of persons. This represents his sympathy for the common people which is called socialism.

Mill says that there is a sphere of human activity in which the individual is supreme and the state is not permitted to interfere. But still there is another sphere in which the activity of the individual affects the behaviour and activity of others and the state, if required, shall interfere. This is a simple statement and Mill in his essay *On Liberty* has stated it several times. The trouble is that Mill cannot wholly accept this view. He vacillates between different conclusions. In other words, his account of liberty and also the intervention of state are full of contradictions, and these have made his analysis not always plausible. However, he has narrated certain activities of the state or, to put it in other words, what the state should do for the welfare of its subjects :

1. The state may insist upon the education of children even against the indifference or hostility of their parents, on the ground that the uncultivated cannot be the competent judges of cultivation. That is, in order to be better judges of the activities of representative government, the citizens must be educated or cultivated.

2. Public enterprises—which by nature of the circumstances are monopolies—may properly be subject to public regulation.

---

1. Wayper, p. 116.

3. The law may justly enforce a limitation on hours of labour, since, without its intervention, such a limitation could be effective only in the unlikely event of unanimous agreement among the workers.

4. Scientific research and exploration and various aids to navigation may properly be supported by the state, since they are of value to society and yet exceeds the resources of private individuals. Moreover, all these activities or measures do not make profit and naturally individuals will not find any initiative.

5. J. S. Mill was in favour of enhancement of wages whenever necessary and this could be done by the trade unions or any other labour organisations.

6. He strongly advocated the abolition of the principle of primogeniture (inheritance by first-born). He also supported the form of single tax on economic rent.

7. After the Second World War the Labour Government of Britain launched a number of welfare measures for the upliftment of the weaker sections of society. But it is amazing to note that Mill much before that had suggested several measures for the betterment of poor and unprivileged people. He narrated all these in his *Political Economy* and other writings. This undoubtedly proves that he had great sympathy for the poor people. He further suggested that factory owners or any other concerned authority must pay compensation for all accidents.

The above proposals made by J. S. Mill are no doubt novel in character and they also augur socialism or—what the liberal political stalwarts call—welfare state, the foundation of which was laid in the middle of the eighties of the nineteenth century by the Fabian Socialists. We can, therefore, legitimately say that Mill in a sense was the *father of Fabian Socialism*. It is further to be noted that the ills against which Mill wanted to fight were the products of Industrial Revolution. Benthamite doctrine of pursuit of happiness or extreme individualistic approach to social and political problems, or the reform proposals could not provide powerful palliatives against these evils. The interference of the state into the political and economic lives of people were badly needed. But a basic problem remains unsolved. How to make a reconciliation between individualism and *qualified collectivism*, to borrow the term coined by W. T. Jones. We, the readers of Mill's political philosophy, do not know. We are not researchers of consistency. We naively hold the view that Mill is both an individualist and a qualified collectivist or socialist. He is definitely not a socialist in the Marxian sense.

Berki points out that Mill suggests "qualified socialism" as a concrete solution to the problems of civil society. In his *Autobiography* (1873), he explains the nature of the qualified socialism in which he and his wife attained after a lifetime spent in intellectual exertions : we, as he puts it, looked forward to a time when society will no longer be divided into the idle and industrious and further the social problem of the future we considered to be, how to unite the greatest individual liberty of action with a common ownership in the raw materials of the globe and an equal participation of all in the benefits of combined labour (p. 186). It is not unnatural that J. S. Mill will have sympathy for ordinary men which is called socialism. Towards the fag end of his life he came in contact with socialist philosophy because Marx and Engels published their *Manifesto* in 1848. In the second half of the nineteenth century the intellectual section of Western Europe was flooded with Marxist philosophy and that might have touched J. S. Mill. His sympathy ran for socialism or welfare of deprived sections of the community.

Assessment of Mill

It is extremely difficult to assess the importance of J. S. Mill, the champion of liberty, reviser of Bentham's utilitarianism, forerunner of Fabian Socialism and, above all, the great philosopher of nineteenth century Britain. But in spite of that we shall have to take the venture. What he thought in the nineteenth century and how we think about him that must be assessed. Berki beautifully remarks : "Mill, like Marx, is too proximate to us in terms of time as well as issues to allow for a balanced, independent stance vis-a-vis his arguments. His ideas have proved a fruitful source of inspiration in a number of directions...Mill's ideas continued to fertilise the Left and the Right and the Centre. His *Systems of Logic* constituted one of the most important foundations of sociology and political science in Anglo-Saxon countries" (p. 187). Moderate social democrats and Fabian Socialists drew inspiration from Mill.

Some people raise questions on Mill's sympathy for socialism. We do not question it. But it is undoubtedly true that the issues he has raised are quite pertinent. The Industrial Revolution generated wealth and simultaneously inequality and numerous other evils. For the rectification and removal of evils the role of the state is badly needed. That was the central point of Mill's thought. Marx's communist society is a welfare state. Fabian socialism also wanted to build up a welfare state. Mill's conception about socialism is not basically different from all these. Mill believed that through the implementation of socialist principles people could achieve required amount of happiness, enjoy liberty and, finally, set up a self-government which is a representative government.

Bentham and James Mill thought that only certain reforms in electoral system would be sufficient for improving the lot of the British people and this conviction led them to advocate for the reforms. But by the fifties of the nineteenth century it became apparent that these reforms could not solve the basic evils or problems eating into the vitals of British social and political life. A tremendous responsibility fell upon J. S. Mill. The problem shall be viewed in a new light and more practical solutions shall be devised. That Mill did. In the words of Sabine : "What Mill recognised, and what older liberalism had never seen, was that behind a liberal government there must be a liberal society" (p. 710). It is the credit of Mill. *He viewed liberalism in the light of changed economic and political circumstances.* His liberalism is quite different from the older liberalism. In his hands a new liberalism was born and it is modernised liberalism. Barker says (*Political Thought*, p. 182) : "A transitional thinker, full of the inconsistencies natural to a period of transition, but supremely candid and generous in all his inconsistency, Mill prepared above all others the way for the new development of English thought which appears after 1880."

Barker is of opinion that Mill was one of the finest minds of the nineteenth century. In his writings he has been able to establish a balanced view of human nature. He clearly stated the duty of the state and role of individuals. Mill's concept of freedom combines both the internal and external worlds of individuals. Particularly his emphasis upon the spiritual aspect of freedom makes it more sublime. Mill's individuals are not simple instruments always busy in the pursuit of happiness at any cost. Men want happiness, and, at the same time, they want many other things. Only a sublime and liberal thinker like Mill can think in that way. That is why Barker calls him one of the finest minds of the nineteenth century.

The inconsistencies from which Mill suffer are many. But all these have not succeeded in eroding his importance as a great philosopher and thinker of the nineteenth century. Bowle observes "He was the prophet of his own age." We cannot imagine the political thought of the nineteenth century without a thoroughgoing analysis of Mill's political ideas. He was not the sole representative of this century, but he was in a very high position.

The editor of Mill's *Autobiography* says : "He was constantly in search of ways to help in the improvement of humankind, and if his "doing" was fundamentally that of a thoughtful writer with a clearly discernible influence on practical life, the appropriate response is not regret but celebration. His major deeds are discerned in his careful attention to what, why and how of his major writings, which detail his self-realization. Mill's *Autobiography* serves his purposes well, and also, if quietly, demonstrates his greater growth from the roots he eulogises"[1].

Wayper's estimate about Mill is that he remains far and away the most satisfactory of all utilitarians. He has looked at the concept from so many angles that it assumes real importance. If J. S. Mill were not its interpreter the principle of utility would not have achieved so much popularity. He goes into the depth of the doctrine which Bentham and his father failed to do.

Wayper has drawn our attention to another side of his influence. Like Locke he is writing with Englishmen in mind, and his individual men and women are recognisable Englishmen. Mill was a practical man. He observed the miserable conditions of the common people with an open mind and heart. After considering everything and all aspects of an issue he arrived at the conclusion that it is the duty of authority to do something for the removal of misery of the people belonging to the lowest strata of society and for that purpose the state will have to play a positive and pro-poor role. This may force the government to play a collectivist role. It means that the state will adopt measures for the poor. This is commonly called collectivism. At the closing years of his life Mill came to believe that the consistence between individualism and collectivism is not possible. Because of this and his great love for the poor people he sided himself with socialism or collectivism. The interesting point is that his sympathy for the poor did not lead him to throw his favourite concepts—individualism, liberty and representative democracy. He was fully convinced that by safeguarding democracy and liberty collectivist measures for the general upliftment of the poor could be taken. This is the central aspect of Mill's political thought. We conclude that Mill was a great individualist, but the individualist Mill had a lot of feeling for the poor people. The same feeling we find in the heart of idealist philosopher Thomas Hill Green.

LIBERALISM

Nature of Liberalism in its Early Form

It is very difficult to ascertain the exact time of the origin of liberal political philosophy. Some thinkers hold the view that it originated in the Reformation Movement. But most of the thinkers agree that liberal political ideas were prominent in the writings of Locke. We have discussed it earlier. The revival of political

1. J. S. Mill—*Autobiography*, Edited with an Introduction by John Robson, p. 23.

liberalism, we find, again, in English utilitarians. Bentham, James Mill and J. S. Mill—these three utilitarians have treated the doctrine with the best of their intellectual capacity. But the political liberalism of Bentham and James Mill does not resemble that of J. S. Mill on every point. There are several differences. Sabine calls liberalism of Bentham and James Mill early liberalism and J. S. Mill's modernised liberalism. "The division of liberalism into two periods somewhat more than an expository convenience...The dividing line can best be drawn perhaps at John Stuart Mill because his philosophy stood curiously on both sides of the line" (p. 674).

A caution is to be noted here. Liberal philosophy, though started much earlier, reached its culmination in the hands of the Philosophical Radicals. But it started to follow a different direction when the younger Mill appeared in full-fledged form in the academic world of England. We shall now see the nature of political liberalism of Bentham and James Mill's era. Bentham showed no special interest in political theory. His main interest was the principle of utility and jurisprudence. But the latter was a part of the former. For the maximisation of happiness the law and legislator were both essential. Bentham also expressed his great liking for *laissez-faire* economy. The self-regulated economy restricted the role of the state or government. The spontaneous economic activities could enrich the economy of the state and Bentham advocated it. Of course, Bentham was not the inventor of economic liberalism, he borrowed the principle from Ricardo and Adam Smith.

In an article published in the *Westminster Review* James Mill estimated that about two hundred families effectively controlled the entire House of Commons. The members of the House were chosen directly or indirectly by these two hundred families. They were the clergy of the Established Church, legal profession and landed aristocrats. That was the nature of the monopoly of political power. There were two political parties who controlled the politics of England. James Mill said that, in fact, there was no basic difference between these two parties. One exercised power and another remained in opposition. Both shared all the benefits of political power. The general mass had no say in the organisation and functioning of the state. There was the rule of coterie in every party. In fact, according to James Mill, the English politics was absolutely the organ of class interests. James Mill proceeded in a determined way to break this monopoly of power. His purpose was to open the door of the House of Commons so that people of all classes, particularly of middle class, could get an opportunity to enter the House. He wanted to reform the electoral system.

In his *Fragment of Government* Bentham insisted upon two principles. The power of the government shall be limited. To put it in other words, the accountability of authority to the people should be ensured. The other is that the liberal government must not be weak. Bentham suggested that this could be materialised through the sovereignty of parliament. In order to make the parliament broad-based Bentham proposed wide-ranged reforms of parliament and the representative system. Through the parliament, people could exercise their authority. The ultimate power in this way could be entrusted to the people. Bentham believed that it was not enough. Individuals must take active interest in social and political affairs and for that purpose other reforms, particularly reforms of suffrage, were imperative.

The political thought of Enlightenment left behind an impact about liberty and other related issues. The most important contribution of Enlightenment is the rise and development of reason. This influenced men to claim that they must have sufficient liberty for the proper development of their mental faculties. And this is not all. The liberty must be safeguarded and the state will have to take that responsibility. When this happens the government could be called a good one. Thus we find that the early liberals were considerably concerned with the attainment and protection of liberty. But they were against handing enormous powers to state.

The early liberals fought hard to effect a compromise between private and general interests. Without this harmony the greatest happiness of the greatest number of persons would never be a fact. James Mill argued that the education should be spread so that people with certain amount of general education can easily understand their own private interests and to reconciliate them with the interests of the community. Education also makes people politically conscious—which is a definite limitation upon the whimsical or arbitrary power of state.

The Philosophical Radicals or liberals were not active politicians nor did they form any party. They were intellectuals and they wanted to create pressure upon the government through their forceful writings. Sabine comments (p. 697) : "The liberalism of the Philosophical Radicals was an intellectual force of enormous political importance in nineteenth century politics. Without themselves attaining the proportions of a political party, they disseminated ideas in the light of which a vast amount of antiquated political lumber was swept away and legislation, administration and judicial process were made both more efficient and more democratic. The reform of parliament, the repeal of obsolete restrictions on trade and industry and the reorganisation of the judicial system were the conspicuous examples of this process." These are only few examples. The nineteenth century judicial and political processes underwent drastic changes as a result of the writings of Philosophical Radicals. An important aspect of early liberalism has ultimately become a confluence of several contemporary burning issues. Many of the early liberals had great interest in personal happiness, some of them were not against the general welfare of the community. They claimed liberty and wished to see the state to play a positive role. The early liberals wished to make a compromise between private and public interests but with a clear leaning towards the individual's interests. There are inconsistencies in this approach. But this is the situation.

The early liberalism is not free from criticism. It is commonly observed that the Philosophical Radicals had no clear philosophy nor any assumptions. Reform of judicial or administrative system does not constitute any philosophy at all. The early liberals claimed to be empirical. But, unfortunately, they never tried to check their premises or conclusions. They had no clear conception of social good. They relied too much upon the importance of education and reason of men. Education is important no doubt, but it is not Aladdin's Lamp which can solve each and every problem of the society. The liberals of the early period wanted to change the nature of politics without changing the economic base. Remaining within the capitalist structure and influence the early liberals wanted a thorough change of society. But this is an impossible adventure. They might have sympathy for the working people but the way of real emancipation was not known to them.

Modernised Liberalism

The liberal policies or reform proposals advocated by Philosophical Radicals proved their insfructuousness even during the first two decades of the nineteenth century. The unregulated industrialism produced undesirable consequences and misgivings and their reaction became quite obvious. Economic disparity crossed all marks of decency and toleration. C. B. Macpherson says : "The condition of the working class was becoming so blatantly inhuman that sensitive liberals could not accept it as either morally justifiable or economically inevitable." Engels has portrayed a very pathetic picture of the working class in his famous book *The Conditions of Working Class in England*.

In the year 1841 a Royal Commission was appointed by the British Government to investigate the conditions of the working class and numerous other aspects of the industrial world of Britain. The reports published by the government created a countrywide sensation. The report revealed the miserable conditions of workers—particularly women and children. They were forced to work long hours and without break. There was no system for equal wage for equal work. There were no safety devices and sanitary conditions in the work place. The women workers were exploited in all the ways. The Royal Commission primarily focused its attention on mining industries, but the conditions in other industries were not better at all. Large number of people began to think that the big and powerful industrialists were no doubt responsible for the appaling conditions, but the state also has a responsibility. It was forcefully argued that the state cannot absolve of its responsibility. It must do something for the alleviation of unbound miseries of common men. These people did not want to to make the state all-powerful in the Hobbesian frame. The state will have to play a positive role and, at the same time, people's liberty will get scope to flourish.

England was flooded with novels and other types of literature criticising the evils of Industrial Revolution. Mrs. Gaskell's *Mary Barton*, Disraeli's *Sybil* and Kingsley's *Alton Locke* were published in the decade of 1840. The sky of England was rent with vociferous criticisms of industrialism. Many people began to look askance at the efficacy of the liberal policies. Everyone felt that a change was necessary. Change in what? A change in the attitude of the government, a change in the policy of the government. We can in this connexion quote the pertinent remark of Sabine (p. 701): "As the nineteenth century advanced the volume of social legislation steadily increased until, in the opinion of the competent observers, by the end of the third quarter of the century parliament had in effect discarded individualism as its guiding principle and had accepted collectivism. Liberalism as it had been understood was on the defensive and by a curious anomaly legislation passed in the interest of social welfare and therefore of the greatest happiness, ran counter to accepted liberal ideas." In plain language the early liberalism was thought inadequate to meet the peculiar and complex situation of the nineteenth century. A new creed, a new ideology was badly needed. It was strongly felt that the state could not be a helpless onlooker of social events and deteriorating conditions.

The stage of British conservative society was not set for accepting any new dogma and rejecting root and branch the doctrine of liberalism. Liberalism occupied a major part of the public mind. A shift from liberalism to any other doctrine such as socialism meant the destruction of the old tradition and existing political system. British people were not prepared for that. They were always in favour of a compromise or adjustment. Onslaught against liberalism was growing no doubt. But nobody was thinking of eschewing it. Liberalism would remain, but a thoroughgoing revision was needed. Law, political system and the role of the government were to be changed to meet the new demands and situation.

The modernisation of liberalism assumed two shapes : One was provided by J. S. Mill and, to some extent, Spencer, and the other by the Oxford idealists whose leader was T. H. Green. Barker writes : "Not a modification of the old Benthamite premises, but a new philosophy was needed, and that philosophy was provided by the idealist school, of which Green is the greatest representative."[1]

Mill revised utilitarianism, attributed new role to the state. He recommended several reform proposals to improve the economic conditions of the workers. All these are regarded as "qualified socialism." In his *Autobiography* he admits that his weakness for socialism was influenced by his wife. We have, however, discussed all these things earlier. It is needless to repeat them.

1. *Political Thought in England*, p. 4.

19 UTILITARIAN THEORY OF LIMITED STATE

Introduction

Both Bentham and J. S. Mill laid stress on the idea that so far as the attainment of happiness and avoidance of pain are concerned the state has a crucial role to play. But this does not lead one to conclude that the state is the holder or should be the holder of enormous power. Both have been found to hold the view that the sphere of the state activities is considerably limited. In the last years of his life Mill has been found to support socialist functions of the state. But he did not support the expansion of the sphere of state activity beyond certain limits and these limits indicate that the role of the state is quite limited. From the analysis of Bentham we come to know that if the state helps its members in attaining required happiness and avoiding pain the duty of the state is more or less finished. The junior Mill thought of some welfare functions, Bentham and senior Mill did not think in that line. Naturally the utilitarian state is limited state—limited in the sense the role of the state is limited. Mill's inordinate emphasis on liberty indirectly is an espousal of limited state. The less the role of state is more is the sphere of personal liberty. It is generally observed that Bentham and Mill laid the foundation of limited state which is the originator of liberalism—in the second half of the twentieth century. Robert Nozick reemphasised this concept and the theory of limited state received accolade from wider circles of new liberalism.

Thomas Hobbes

Hobbes's sovereign was no doubt endowed with absolute power. But he was extremely cautious about the reason and calculating power of the individual. The sovereignty had no authority to deny the individual to deprive him this quality. Hobbes believed that each man had the right to pursue and maximise his happiness and none could aggress upon this right of man. To pursue one's own happiness unhindered or unmolested by others is nothing but selfish motive. But this was the view of Hobbes and it was subsequently shared by Bentham.

Now if the person were to be allowed to pursue his own happiness with complete freedom it is quite obvious that the authority of the state must be curtailed. Hobbes did not directly channelise his thought in that direction but one can reasonably draw such an inference. If the sovereignty were allowed to exercise its power over individual's efforts to maximise happiness it would definitely be affected.

Hobbes and other utilitarians have regarded the state as a means of reconciling men's selfish interests. Its implication is that the state is not for the fulfilment of certain ethical or heavenly desires and ambition. Attainment of happiness is an earthly desire and the residents of the state of nature planned to build up a civil society for that purpose only. It shall never be the function of the state to prevent individuals from that effort. Commenting upon Hobbes's view on utilitarianism Plamenatz observes (*The English Utilitarians*, p. 12) : "It (the state) exists not to protect their rights, but to give men more abundantly the happiness they always seek. Hobbes, it is true, speaks of natural rights that men possess before they enter political society, but he does not mean by this phrase what others have meant who used it. When Hobbes says that in the state of nature, men had an unlimited right to acquire whatever takes their fancy provided they have the strength to do so, he can only mean that, outside there is no sense in saying that it would be wrong for them to take it."

In the state of nature people had enough power to fulfil their desires because in that atmosphere there was no authority to curb the demands or unnatural desires. Hobbes believed that this was contrary to civilisation. He devised a technique of contract through which the foundation of a civil society was laid. The laws of such a society and the command of sovereignty will put curbs on the functions of individuals. The theory of contract envisages that people have very little to do beyond the contract. The contract has set up a civil society and sovereign power is its supreme authority. Though his power is enormous he cannot exercise this power because he has not that scope. The contract is again a "convenient fiction" —Hobbes thought of a civilised society and in such a society the desires of people must be limited and along with it the power of the civil society is to be limited.

Hobbes thought that in an atmosphere of anarchy people's personal or self-interests will be seriously affected and for this reason he wanted the sovereignty to ensure peace and security. If he had in mind a conception of unlimited power of state he could have designated them. Hobbes's *Leviathan* does not throw any light upon it. As to the absolute sovereignty it may naively be observed that the government will enjoy absolute power only in respect of the maintenance of peace and security. Other affairs or aspects of society will remain outside the jurisdiction of sovereignty. So we come to the conclusion that Hobbes had in mind the limited power of state and this is not a figment of imagination. We may quote several passages from his *Leviathan* but such an attempt will over-burden the analysis.

Hume and Limited State

David Hume—another founder of utilitarianism was not directly associated with the theory of limited state. It is observed that utilitarianism clearly envisages that beyond the attainment of utility the state has very little functions to do. That is, it is the mandatory duty of the state to help individuals to attain pleasure and avoid pain. Again, in this regard, the decisions of the individuals are final. Hence the state cannot do whatever it likes. Many critics are of view that the idea of utilitarianism is reasonably a theory of limited state and Hume falls into this category.

Explaining Hume's idea about utilitarianism Plamenatz says that men normally approve of those states of mind or actions that are pleasant or means of pleasure and disapprove those that are painful or means to pains no matter whose the pleasure or pain. Pleasure or pain is the determiner of action or policy.

Bentham on Limited State

The theory of limited state received a better treatment in the hands of Jeremy Bentham. It is generally observed that he was the first exponent of the theory. He expounded the theory of utilitarianism with the avowed purpose of limiting the functions of the state. In his opinion the state cannot claim unlimited authority and power over the individuals. The definition of state suggested by Bentham is it is a group of persons organised for the promotion and maintenance of utility. By propounding this concept Bentham was in line of several 18th century thinkers, specially Boalingbroke, Montesquieu, Hume and Burke. Since Bentham has clearly stated that the functions of the state is confined in the attainment of pleasure, its functions cannot be wide-ranging and at the same time numerous. This is simply the theory of the limited state.

He has said that it is the primary responsibility of every government to see that the greatest good of the greatest number in the society is achieved through its activities. This is due to the fact that every person always tries to get maximum amount of pleasure and, for that reason, his objective is to avoid painful actions. If individual fails to avail the required amount of happiness he desires because of the unfavourable circumstances the existence of the state authority will appear to the citizens unnecessary. He has said that when the greatest happiness or the greatest number is realised the concept of public good will find its proper nourishment. If the government neglects the greatest happiness principle it will neglect the public good.

Common people because of their limited knowledge and experience cannot always determine what is pleasure and what is meant by pain. It is because their knowledge about these are very limited. Naturally people's preference can never be the determiner of states policy or decision. But this should not be a bar to the enunciation of the doctrine or principle and government's determination of policy in accordance with the principle. He has maintained that people understand what pleasure, pain and happiness mean. This is due to the fact that individuals are quite reasonable and they possess sufficient reasoning and understand their own interests. Bentham's clear opinion is it is not the function of the state to make thorough enquiry about people's knowledge and understanding about pain and pleasure. The government cannot also determine the extent of power and reasoning. His argument is—every man has certain amount of common sense and that enables him to have conception about pain and pleasure.

Bentham categorically stated that the government ought to interfere with the activities and purposes of individuals as little as possible. His belief was that bringing the governmental interference to a minimum level would ensure the attainment of happiness in its maximum form. This type of state function envisaged by Bentham can be called a negative one.

What is the role of the state in realising happiness? Since according to Bentham the state cannot interfere with all the aspects of human affairs the role is limited to the task of removing the hindrances to the attainment of pleasure and avoidance of pain. The state will maintain peace by keeping law and order within normal condition. The state authority will prevent certain behaviour and activities and encourage others. For the prevention of activities harmful for happiness the government will sanction punishment.

Bentham has said that since the motto of every good government and good citizen is the greatest happiness of the greatest number it is within the right of every good citizen to "censure" the principles, policies and activities of government. He has further maintained that the censure may be ill-founded. But that does not matter. Such censure may help the reform. He believed that the existing institutions and structure of state were not helpful for the greatest happiness of the greatest number principle. These are to be reformed. Bentham's implicit assumption is that the existing set-up has given power to the state. This is to be curtailed. He was highly critical of the political and other systems of social life. Viewed from this angle Bentham is regarded as a radical thinker but his radicalism aims at curtailing the power of the state. To sum up, Bentham had enough faith on the reason and power of judgment of individuals. He believed that in order to implement the greatest happiness of greatest number principle the social and political structures are to be reformed and laws are to be enacted.

In the *Fragment on Government* he has admitted that the political power is always limited and it is shared by several agencies. By sovereignty he does not mean the unconditional obedience to the authority. The citizens shall have the full right to criticise and watch the activities of government. If the citizens are deprived of this right government's procedures and actions may not be able to ensure pleasure and avoid pain. Though it is the duty of government to enact laws, the citizens will judge them.

The proper function of various laws is to promote and maximise happiness of the subjects. These laws are mainly of two types—moral rules and laws made by the legislator. Bentham apprehended that there might be conflict between these two laws and in that case that law is to be preferred which maximises happiness. Thus the reasonability and utility of a law is to be decided not by the criterion that behind it there is sanction of sovereignty but by the criterion that it is capable of promoting happiness—that is, ensuring maximum pleasure and reducing pain to the lowest level. While the government (or the legislator) is enacting law it must bring this aspect into active consideration. Bentham, in this way, rules out freehand of the law-maker. Law making thus emphasises the limited nature of state authority. When law is endowed with such characteristic the subjects will show obedience to these laws. Any deviation will inspire people to withdraw allegiance.

The critics have cast doubt on the whole concept of Bentham. If the power of the state is limited how can it be possible for such a state to ensure happiness of individuals? Sufficient power may be required to do the job. Bentham, perhaps, was not worried at all. He had enough faith on the reasonability of people and ability of the legislator to enact good laws. These two combinedly could ensure the happiness of individuals and the state could not face any trouble. Besides this he believed that the separation of state functions could check one organ against another. This idea he borrowed from Montesquieu. Finally, we hold the view that he did not make any concession about his idea on the theory of limited state.

Bentham's idea about the theory of limited state is revealed from his concept of supremacy of legislature. He has clearly stated that supreme legislative authority does not mean it will have unlimited power. Its power must be limited by morality and fact. "It is not true that subjects ought to obey any law which the supreme legislature may choose to make, nor is it true that all its laws are in fact habitually obeyed" (Plamenatz, op. cit., p. 19). The law of the state must aim at protecting and furthering public good and if any legislature which has supreme power makes any law with the purpose of curtailing or adversely affecting the public good that will definitely be an immoral act on the part of the legislature. It is clear that Bentham has mixed morality with law and it is somewhat surprising and inconsistent. He says that the legislature is supreme and it is capable of making good laws that will ensure happiness. But in the next stage he has talked about morality. A good and supreme legislature will not venture to make bad laws because it believes that such an act would be immoral. Being an enlightened man it is unbecoming on his part to talk about morality. The legislature is mainly concerned with the legal aspects of anything and politics. It has nothing to do with morality.

Bentham has thus viewed the concept of sovereignty from the spectacular standpoint of limited state authority. This obviously results in a bit of confusion. However, if we try to follow what he actually wants to say, this confusion will forthwith evaporate. He did never attempt to prepare a well-knit theory of absolute sovereignty. It is just an aspect of his political idea. His chief objective was to build up a theory of limited state which, in his opinion, could ensure happiness. Plamenatz has stated : "Bentham does not, as some theorists have done, assume that in every well-regulated state there must be a sovereign legislature, nor does he treat sovereignty as monopoly of power." In fact, after Locke, Bentham has succeeded in projecting the state as a truncated political organisation. It is not the Hobbesian state.

James Mill and the Theory of Limited State

James Mill (1773–1836) was another utilitarian thinker who strongly advocated the Benthamite utilitarianism and its associated concept theory of limited state. All the interpreters of Western political thought are of the view that James Mill practically added nothing to Bentham's utilitarianism. But, as Maxey says : "He was a genius in dressing those ideas to achieve the best effect". His credit in this field also lies in illuminating Bentham's chief concept of utilitarianism.

He believed that the happiness of individuals could be raised to the maximum level through limiting the powers of the governors. But the senior Mill (J. S. Mill is called junior Mill), could not lay his faith on the separation of governmental powers. Like Bentham he insisted upon the supremacy of the legislature. The interests of the legislature are identical with the general interest of the state. The members of the legislature might have no motive to gratify personal interests through the usurpation of state power. Again, if power in full form is vested in the legislature that will be able to control the executive organ of the government.

Elder (or senior) Mill has said that the greatest happiness of the greatest number shall be the motto of every society. But he was suspicious about the attainment of this lofty goal. He believes that is general human nature that a man wants to seize as much fruits as he can and thinks nothing about others. A man desires to make other men subservient to his pleasures. But elder Mill says that if this process is allowed to continue it will never be able to produce the greatest happiness for the largest number of persons. Hence there is a suggestion of senior Mill and this can be better said in the words of Plamenatz : "It is, therefore, desirable, if the means of happiness are to be produced in the greatest abundance, that every man should retain as much as possible of the fruits of his labour. But this he can only do if all men unite together and delegate to some few of their number to protect them all.

Those who exercise this protective power are the government" (*The English Utilitarians*, p. 105).

How can the powers of this government be limited? Elder Mill had no faith on general government—that is, monarchy or its variations. There remains always the possibility of the abuse or misuse of political authority leading to the deprivation of pleasure and enhancement of pains. The device suggested by James Mill is the introduction of representative government, because in such a government the governors are always responsible to the governed. So elder Mill thought that representative government is a limited government and its rule is favourable for attainment of greatest happiness of the greatest number. This theory of senior Mill resembles that of Jeremy Bentham.

James Mill advocates a wide franchise so as to intensify and ensure people's control over the government. No class of people will be excluded from this franchise. Through their right to vote electors will be able exercise control over the government. In the opinion of senior Mill a narrow ruling elite always acts badly and keeps itself busy in protecting its own interests at the cost of other's interests.

In conclusion few words may be said. Both Bentham and James Mill reposed their faith on the system of representative form of government and both were convinced that only a representative form of government that prevailed in Britain could ensure maximum amount of pleasure for the greatest number of people. Though Britain had a monarchical form of government, theoretically parliament was all in all and this parliament consisting of people's representatives could provide a brake on the functions of the executive and make the entire structure of state limited—both theoretically and practically. The boundary of British electorate was gradually expanding. This created enthusiasm in the minds of the educated people that parliament could provide enough check to the power the of government. Bentham and James Mill were no exceptions. We thus see that utilitarianism and the concept of limited state and representative form of government all are inextricably related with each other.

UTILITARIAN THEORY OF LIMITED STATE AND CLASSICAL ECONOMISTS

Adam Smith (1723–1790)

Two famous classical economists, from the standpoint of economics, supported utilitarianism along with limited state. Particularly Smith was pioneer in this field. Ricardo also thought that the state must perform its functions within certain limits and the limits are to be decided by law.

Smith penned two works—*Theory of Moral Sentiments* and *The Wealth of Nations.* The latter work is relevant for the present purpose. Smith heavily emphasised upon the importance of *natural order* which relates to the spontaneity and natural inclination of human character and behaviour. That is, what human beings want or desire to do should be left to them, and they should be allowed to enjoy the non-interference of government.

Smith has devised six manifestations of human nature. These he calls *motives.* They are : self-love, sympathy, the desire to be free, a sense of propriety, a habit of labour, the propensity to truck, barter and exchange one thing for another. By exercising these motives the individuals judge the activities, policies and decision of the state authority and practically they reach the real, reasonable and beneficial conclusion. *Smith calls this the natural order.* If they are forced to leave this natural order there will emerge undesirable consequences. He pointed out the perfections of the natural order and imperfections of human institutions. Smith said (*The Wealth of Nations*)—Take away artificial preferences and restraints and the obvious and simple system of natural liberty will establish itself. Again that order of things which necessity imposes is promoted by the natural inclinations of man. Human institutions only too often thwart these natural inclinations (Quoted by Eric Roll. *History of Economic Thought*, p. 146).

So far we have obtained two points from Smith's views : human beings have certain inborn motives and the natural order of society should not be disturbed by artificial institutions and governmental interferences. Naturally each man is the best judge of his own interest and he should be left to himself to attain his best interests. If everyman is allowed to do this that will ultimately benefit the entire society and common good will be benefited. The implication of Smith's observation is that individuals understand their utility. If any external authority proceeds to guide them and to impose restrictions that will create a great damage to their spontaneity. For this obvious reason the power of the state should be reduced to the minimum level.

Smith believed that disturbance of the natural order by the governmental interference would result in the following consequences. Interference of the government would be harmful. The negative approach of the state authority could bring about positive results. Eric Roll, summarising the benefits of non-intervention, makes the following observation : "Its intervention in human affairs is generally harmful. Let it leave each member of the community to seek to maximise his own advantage and, compelled by natural law, he will contribute to the maximisation of common good." According to Smith the natural law specifies three important duties of government and beyond this it has nothing to do for society. These three duties are duty of defence from foreign aggresions, the duty of establishing an exact administration for jutice, and maintenance of public works and institutions for peace and security. In all other spheres the individuals will enjoy full freedom. Particularly in economic affairs the subjects will pursue their interests.

It is obvious that Adam Smith was a strong opponent of any form of government intervention. The natural order or the natural law is so arranged or made that it cannot do any harm to the utility or advantage of individuals. On the contrary, if too many man-made institutions are permitted to function that will ensure corrosive effects upon the spontaneity of men. Smith has also said that governmental regulations regarding wages and other matters are treated with suspicion. Both Bentham and Adam Smith viewed the role of the state from the standpoint of advantage or utility which the individuals expect from non-intervention of government. Bentham emphasised upon the political aspects, Adam Smith upon the economic aspects. But the objective of both was to limit the duty of the state for the sake of utility.

Adam Smith is the 'father of *laissez-faire* doctrine'. Its central theme is—people should be left alone to pursue their own policies and principles and if the government does not interfere with the functions of the individuals that will lead to the generation of highest amount of utility and economic benefit for the people. Moreover, individuals are the best judges of the economic policies and their effects. State interference will create a haphazard situation. So we find that for the economic betterment of society Smith forcefully prescribed non-interference of the state. It is true that Adam Smith did not directly talk about utilitarianism but one can definitely draw certain interferences from his famous *laissez-faire* doctrine. But Smith's involvement in or association with utilitarianism is not direct and not worthy. Some people think that Adam Smith had a soft corner for Bentham's utilitarianism.

Ricardo (1772–1823) and the Idea of Limited State

David Ricardo, a classical economist, was a supporter of utilitarianism. Following Adam Smith he drew the conclusion that the real objective of a government would be to achieve greatest pleasure of the largest number of people and this could be achieved through the minimum interference of the government in the economic and other private affairs of individuals. Bentham's *Fragment of Government* was published in 1776 and Ricardo's *Principles of Political Economy & Taxation* in 1817.

What idea of limited state function do we get from Smith and Ricardo? Let us put in the words of Plamenatz (op. cit., p. III) : "Don't do what we tell you not to do and men will be the happier for your abstinence, you need only look at the methods whereby they produce and exchange goods and services and you will see that we are right. The classical political economy, ... from 1776 until middle of the next century, was the theory behind the advice given by utilitarians to the successive governments".

Ricardo advised the government to keep itself aloof from the day-to-day functions of the individuals which may be political, social and economic, or anything else. This will help individuals to reach their coveted goal and this will ultimately help them to reach the zenith of happiness. The point to note is that both Smith and Ricardo emphasised the economic aspects while Bentham selected legislation and governmental function as weapons. The common factor is the limitation of the states functions. To sum up, Bentham, J. S. Mill, Adam Smith, Ricardo and scores of other's thinkers advocated liberalism as a broad way to ensure maximum happiness.

J. S. Mill and Theory of Limited State

Mill's political philosophy is a multi-faceted one. He is a great individualist, a great utilitarian, a renowned liberal philosopher, and also a "qualified socialist". Above all, he was a staunch supporter of the limited state activities. He valued the thought, belief and opinion of individuals so much that he was not in a position to tolerate governmental intervention. Only in limited and special circumstances he allowed the state to interfere with the personal affairs of individuals. His strong support for individuals has made him a great advocate of the limited function and role of the state. His theory of utilitarianism may also be cited as a support for it.

J. S. Mill strongly believed that every individual must have the freedom of opinion and the reasons advanced by him are the following : One, any opinion we silence may be the true opinion and by silencing that opinion the authority of the state deprives the society of a true opinion. This is unjustified. Nobody has any right to deprive one of any true opinion. Two, the silenced opinion may be partly correct and the prevailing opinion may not be completely correct. From the conflict between these two the final truth may come out. In that case, it would not be prudent for any civilised society to silence an opinion. There should be proper arrangements in every society for the ventilation of all sorts of opinion. The simple implication is that the activities of the state shall be limited. Three, Mill finally observes that the prevailing opinion may be completely true. But such a complete truth is nothing but a dogma and it must be challenged by the society. Only the uncontrolled opinion can challenge such a dogma. As to the expression of opinion Mill thus came to the conclusion that it is not the business of the government to seek to control the opinion of individuals. They must enjoy full freedom.

The complete freedom of body and mind was of prime importance to J. S. Mill and he was not prepared to make a large amount of relaxation. Only for the sake of self-protection the intervention of the state can be allowed. Let us put it in the words of Mill : "The only purpose for which power can be rightfully exercised over any member of the civilised community, against his will, is to prevent harm to others." Mill thus sanctions state interference only for the purpose of self-protection. He comes to the view that in the present set-up of society the persons may not be in a position to protect or defend himself from the assault of others. And, in the absence of state intervention, and in the case of his inability, the person will face destruction which any civilised community cannot allow. By propounding this concept in a quite bold manner Mill proceeds to advocate a limited state role. Mill prescribed that the state can interfere with the activities of individuals which are likely to affect the interests of other persons. Mill divides the functions of persons into self-regarding and other-regarding.

Mill's attachment to and love for utility is beyond all sorts of doubt. But the interpretation of the concept is different from Bentham. This has added new meaning to the whole concept. Some critics say that Mill's interpretation has created interest in the minds of his readers. He says : "I regard utility as the ultimate appeal on all ethical questions, but it must be utility in the largest sense, grounded on the permanent interests of man as a progressive being." Utility is the guiding and motivating force of every action launched by the individual or the state. Hence any measure devoid of utility cannot be entertained. To what extent a measure or policy is capable of producing utility is to be judged by the individual himself and not by the state. Because, he believed that individuals possess sufficient reason and intelligence. So it is the duty of the state authority to allow persons to exercise their intelligence and freedom so that they can reach any fruitful decision regarding the capacity of a policy in producing utility. It is not the function of the state to decide beforehand which measure has utility and which has not. So Mill's concept of utility is designed to curb the functions of the state in a considerable way. It is a fact that Mill's utility is different from Bentham's. So far as the present issue is concerned the difference between Bentham and J. S. Mill is quite immaterial. Both Bentham and J. S. Mill wanted to curb the authority of the state.

The idea of self-development inspired, in a spectacular way, to propound a theory of limited state. This point has been emphasised by Ebenstein (*Great Political Thinkers*, p. 533) : "In championing iiberty Mill has a broad goal in mind : the "Greek ideal of self-development." It is the privilege of every human being to use and interpret experience in his own way, and the act of choosing between alternatives brings man's moral faculties into play". The point to be emphasised is that only proper freedom can be a help for the individual in his efforts of self-development. If he is obstructed by the authority his spontaneity will be discouraged, thus harming his own development. His argument for freedom is for the development of moral character. Mill thought that only in an atmosphere of limited state proper or real freedom gets the opportunity of progress. Self-development, proper freedom, greatest happiness of the largest number and limited power and function all are closely related.

In the opinion of Mill the state is for the individuals and the individuals are not for the state. So it is the primary responsibility of the state to ensure the all-round development of individuals. In the last few lines in *On Liberty* Mills says : "The worth of a state, in the long run, is the worth of individuals composing it and a state which postpones the interests of their mental expansion and elevation, to a little more of administrative skill or of the semblance of it which practice gives, in the details of business; a state which dwarfs its men in order that they may be more docile instruments in its hands even for beneficial purposes—will find that with small men no great thing can really be accomplished : and that the perfection of machinery to which it has sacrificed everything, will in the end avail it nothing, for want of the vital power which, in order that the machine might work more smoothly, it has preferred to banish." Mill has said : "state which dwarfs its men". These five words are very significant. He had firm belief that the state generally dwarfs the interest, energy and activities of individuals through its cumbersome process of administration. This makes men disinterested in his own mental and intellectual progress and also the also social progress. So dwarfing men is a phrase that carries a volume of weight. Mill disapproved this type of state's functions from the core of his heart. He openly declared that under no circumstances the state shall be allowed to impede the mental and all other types of growth of individuals. He further maintains that the state is very often misguided by wrong ideas and this is harmful for those who are at the receiving end—that is, individuals.

Why was Mill fervently advocating for the limitation of state power? In his judgment the state is a "necessary evil". He does not deny the importance of state as a political institution in certain affairs—such as defending the state from external aggression and defending the individuals from doing harm to other persons. Barker has said that, according to Mill, the state has no right to interfere with the "self-regarding" activities of the individuals. Only the "other regarding" functions come within the jurisdiction of the state. This is a clear proof of Mill's idea on the limited state activities.

Mill was also very much apprehensive about political tyranny. The authority of the state in the name of majority imposes its decision upon the people without giving due importance to their opinion. This is not only, according to Mill, unfair but also detrimental to the spontaneous development of individual freedom. He, therefore, comes to the conclusion that the power of the state should be curtailed and on the question how that can be done he suggests two procedures—(1) the formulation of the doctrine of rights, and (2) the establishment of constitutional checks.

Mill has said that large scale participation of people in the governmental affairs can necessarily control the excesses of government's functions. The objective—popular participation can be achieved in a representative form of government. His another suggestion is—various institutions are to be formed and nourished within the social framework with the help of which people can develop their inherent qualities. He believes that augmentation of consciousness through the spread of education can put the authority within the desirable limits.

Conclusion

We have analysed the concept of limited state in the background of utility. But in the hands of J. S. Mill it has received a deeper and wider meaning. Mill's theory of limited state can pertinently be regarded as the foundation of liberalism—whose father was John Locke. I do not think that Mill's politics was chiefly concerned with the greatest happiness of the greatest number. His main concern was freedom of the individuals. He also wanted all-round progress of people. He developed the idea that unlimited power of the state will build up a Himalyan barrier. The state is a necessary evil and yet he had great faith in it. But we cannot deny that there is some evilness in every state. Mill was afraid of it. He thought that there was no place of supremacy in the entire gamut of state and on that consideration he did not favour Bentham's idea of supremacy of legislature. Neither state nor legislature nor any other organ shall have absolute power. Through the enjoyment of liberty people can have maximum happiness because this liberty enables them to realise what is happiness and where it resides.

Helvetius (1715–1771) is also regarded as a utilitarian thinker but unfortunately there is practically nothing about the limited sphere of state activity in his writings. He says : "Corporeal pleasure and pain are the real and only springs of all government." If it were the chief aim of all governments to maximise pleasure and minimise pain then understandably the functions are bound to be curtailed. But Helvetius did not rule out the active role of the state in the affairs of the realisation of maximum pleasure. Interpreting Helvetius thought Hallowwell (*Main Currents of Modern Political Thought*, p. 206) has observed : "He believed that society, by providing rewards for socially beneficent behaviour and punishment for socially destructive behaviour, could make morality attractive. Men are not born with innate principles of virtue or with natural compassion but they can be made to approximate them by method of education and legislation." So in the inculcation of virtues and other good qualities, Helvetius recommended a positive role for the state. What would be the exact role of the state that has not been properly ventilated by Helvetius? He has also maintained that since it is the primary objective of a state to promote happiness, it can promote freedom to that end. The state has also a responsibility in curbing undesirable happiness. "Helvetius hoped that these principles might be adopted by an enlightened and benevolent prince and accordingly dedicated one of his essays to Catherine II of Russia" (Hallowell. op. cit., p. 207).

20 GERMAN IDEALISM

Origin of German Idealism

Idealism in politics during the eighteenth century originated from the doctrines of natural law, natural rights and social contract. There was also idealism in *laissez-faire.* But the events and facts of the nineteenth century deflated the principles of idealism. Maxey writes (p. 490) "The nineteenth century saw revolution degenerate into chaos and reaction, saw democracy itself betray the grand ideals of the eighteenth century, saw economic freedom converted into an instrument of power and acquisition specially fitted to the hands of rapacious industrial moguls." Bentham built up the doctrine of utilitarianism in support of the cause of the English middle class. He wanted that the middle class should come forward and directly participate in the political and other affairs of state. From this he developed the idea of utilitarianism. His premises of thought were that men are reasonable, they seek their own interests and happiness and if such men are allowed to pursue their own activities and policies without state intervention or minimum intervention, then they will be able to maximise their pleasure. But the Industrial Revolution completely changed the political, economic and social milieu of European society and it has been asserted by many, especially Barker, that utilitarianism was incapable to cope with this new situation and a new philosophy was required. The utilitarian philosophy—idea of limited state—required to be replaced by a new philosophy.

Some university professors of Germany and England did not make any attempt to modify utilitarianism. They wanted to lay the foundation of a new philosophy. They thought that the nature, functions of state, role of individuals, their relation to state and many other related issues should be reviewed in the background of the new situation. These philosophers formed a school and we call it the idealist school. The idealist school formed by the Oxford professors is called Oxford Idealist School. Kant, Fichte and Hegel are German philosophers and the idealism professed by them is called German Idealism. The best known English idealists are T. H. Green, Bradley, and Bosanquet. But the Oxford Idealism drew its inspiration from German Idealism. *The idealism in politics as a whole is voluminously indebted to Greek philosophy, specifically Plato and Aristotle. These idealists are called metaphysical idealists.* The doctrine of these metaphysical philosophers is understood by very few, but their influence on modern political thought is enormous.

The ultimate bases of idealist philosophy of the state is thus to be found in the writings of Plato and Aristotle and in a steady tradition of study and teaching of *Republic* and *Ethics. From Greek philosophy the idealist adopted the view that political philosophy was essentially an ethical study which considered the state as a natural society and which inquired into the methods by which it sought to attain its moral aims.* Man is a member of a state as a political association and his membership is for *the purpose of fulfilling moral objectives.* The state is the highest manifestation of morality and ethics. So no individual can think of giving up the membership of the political association. Furthermore, according to Greek idealism, the law is the expression of pure reason. So no question of withdrawing obligation from the state or disobeying the law does arise. The primary objective of every individual is to perform his duties assigned by the community.

The noted German philosopher Kant borrowed from Rousseau's 'general will' and the concept of moral freedom. We find a close relation between the general will of Rousseau and the moral imperative of Kant. Rousseau thought that members of the body politic are guided by morality and this is more or less self-imposed. Kant's individuals are also guided by moral imperatives. In both cases, authority does not impose moral principles upon the members of society. Kant also borrowed Rousseau's general will. Kant said that individuals thought it to be a moral duty to be an integral part of general duty. Needless to say that it is Rousseau's theory. Hegel also accepted (though in different form) the general will of Rousseau. The former said that general will is the will of the national state. Strictly speaking, Rousseau's body politic and Hegel's national state are different. But Hegel's philosophy is based on dialectics. Hegel's national state is the culmination of family and civil society and, in the whole process, dialectics has worked.

To Kant, to perform a self-imposed duty is morality and the right to will—a self-imposed duty—is freedom. Man cannot be politically free if he is not morally free. Man must think that he is an integral part of the whole. The decision of the whole is his decision. Rousseau's moral freedom insists that an individual is not permitted to do whatever he thinks. It is said that with Kant freedom has a negative, limited and subjective meaning.

Rousseau revolted against reason. In his view, the development of art, science and civilisation was responsible for moral degeneration. To him, emotion was more important than reason. The German idealists did not give much credence to scientific intelligence and truth. They sought a higher kind of truth. There was a distinction between truth discovered by observation of phenomena and truth arrived by abstract thought. In this process, political theory became a part of transcendental metaphysics.

German Idealism and French Revolution

It is commonly argued that the German idealism has been the theory of French Revolution. The implication of this comment is not that the German idealist philosophers set out to interpret the French Revolution in terms of idealist philosophy. But they (Kant, Fichte, Schelling and Hegel) wrote their philosophy largely as a response to the challenge from France to recognise the state and society on a rational basis so that social and political institutions might accord with freedom and interest of the individual.[1]

---

1. Herbert Marcuse—*Reason and Revolution*, p. 3.

The ideas of the French Revolution constitute the core of German idealism. It abolished the feudal absolutism and replaced it with the economic and political system of the middle class. The most important contribution of the French Revolution is the emancipation of man from the enslavement of thought imposed upon him by others. After the Revolution man began to treat everything with reason and learnt the technique of self-reliance. Man is a thinking being. His reason enables him to recognise his own potentialities. He does not take events and facts as they are, but subject them to the acid test of reason. He accepts those which reason allows him to do. He is not at the mercy of anybody.

Though Rousseau revolted against reason, Hegel held the view that in every sphere of life there were inequality and unreasonableness. In the opinion of Hegel all these dominated French society. In fact, the lack of reason and courage and absence of freedom froce man to surrender to irrationality and servitude. Hegel argues that the French Revolution had succeeded in asserting the dignity of man. He can now understand what is right and what is wrong. Reason dominates his action and conduct. This reason is, again, central to Hegel's philosophy. In order to recognise individuality and give it proper scope for its development several things require to be done. Feudal absolutism is to be abolished and free competition is to be established. The Revolution did these two things. After the disintegration of feudalism, industrial capitalism came to occupy that place and, with it, free competition was ensured.

Hegel thinks that the French Revolution asserted the supremacy of reason over reality and this is an important part of Hegel's idealism. The German idealists--and particularly Hegel—state that thought or reason ought to govern reality. What men think to be true, right and good ought to be realised in actual organisation of their social and individual life. But the thoughts of different individuals will vary and a cohesive and well-knit social organisation will be impossible. Hegel says that certain universally accepted principles and concepts are required to be properly emphasised.

Philosophical Foundation of German Idealism

German idealism rejected empiricism and British empiricism is the root of the general doctrine of empiricism. The root of empiricism is that there is no single concept of law of reason and universality of reason. The British empirical thinkers said that there was no such thing as unity of reason, but there is unity of custom and habit. Locke, the great British empiricist, said that the general ideas were the invention and creatures of understanding. The generals are the products of particulars. At the beginning people study particular events and form certain views on the basis of observations. On the basis of these observations they form—at subsequent stages—general opinion. The general cannot be separated from the particular and this forms the basis of empiricism. David Hume, another great empirical philosopher, expressed identical view. The empiricists further said that there was nothing like universal thought and reason. If the particulars differ, the general idea or conclusion will also differ. German idealism rejected the empirical philosophy of particularism and proceeded to universalise everything. Some critics say that the German philosophers started their analysis primarily to challenge the British empirical philosophy of the eighteenth century.

According to the German idealists, the "empiricist attack jeopardized all efforts to impose an order on the prevailing forms of life. Unity and universality were not to be found in empirical reality" (Marcuse, p. 18). Fact is concerned with what is. But the existence of something is not all. There is something beyond the existence of reality or matter. According to German idealism, reason deals with that. It says what ought to be. German idealist does not intend to confine man or his ability within "the given". "The given" is temporary and limited. But the universality of concepts and principles goes beyond "the given". Reason crosses the boundary of "is" and embarks upon the vast field of "ought". German idealism argues that, if experience and custom were to be treated as the sole source of knowledge, then men will have no weapon to fight custom.

In the opinion of German idealist philosophers, human psychology is subject to change. There is every possibility of uncertainty and chance and from this no necessity and universality can be derived. But necessity and universality are sole guarantees of reason. Unless the general concepts that claimed such necessity and universality could be shown to be more than the product of imagination, they could be shown to draw their validity neither from experience nor from individual psychology, unless, in other words, they were shown applicable to experience, reason would have to bow to the dictates of empirical teaching (Marcuse, p. 20-21).

IMMANUEL KANT (1724–1804)

Life and Work

Immanuel Kant was born at Konigsberg, Prussia, in 1724. He came of a very poor family. His forefathers lived in Scotland. His parents were religious—minded and this influenced young Kant. He was also a regular visitor to the church. He received very little formal schooling or education. Kant lived in the age of Rousseau, Voltaire and Hume. All of them profoundly influenced his thoughts and ideas, though he wanted to refute their thought.

Kant led a very regulated and disciplined life. Heinrich Heine in his *Religion and Philosophy in Germany* has said that it is very difficult to portary the history of Kant for he had neither life nor history. His life was so mechanical that there was no change or variety. Everyday, at a fixed time, irrespective of summer, winter or rainy season, he went out for walk. Rising in the morning, coffee-drinking, writing, reading, dining and walking all were done according to time. There was no change in his style or dress. He was a bachelor. Inhabitants of the street of Konigsberg knew this man. Rather, he was a popular figure, though they understood very little of his philosophy.

In 1755 Kant began his life as a private lecturer at the University of Konigsberg. He remained in the post for fifteen years and twice his application for the post of professorship was rejected. Finally he was made professor of logic and metaphysics in 1770. He died in 1804.

His *Critique of Pure Reason* was published in 1781 at the age of 57, and *Critique of Practical Reason in* 1788. Kant established himself as an author at an advanced age. Kant's political ideas are chiefly found in his *Metaphysical First Principle of the Theory of Law* published in 1796. He wrote two essays : *The Principles of Political Right* and *The Natural Principle of Political Order.*

Commenting upon how Rousseau influenced Kant, Durant writes : "When Kant read *Emile* he omitted his daily walk under the linden trees, in order to finish the book at once. It was an event in his life to find here another man who was groping his way out of the darkness of atheism, and who boldly affirmed the priority of feeling over theoretical reason in these suprasensual concerns. Here at last was the second half of the answer to irreligion; now finally all the scoffers and doubters would be scattered. To put these threads of argument together, to unite the ideas of Berkeley and Hume with the feelings of Rousseau, to save religion from reason, and yet at the same time to save science from scepticism—this was the mission of Immanuel Kant" (p. 261). Besides Rousseau, Voltaire (1694–1778), John Locke (1632–1704), George Berkeley (1684–1753) and David Hume (1711–1776) moulded his thought system in one way or the other.

Political Ideas of Kant

Like Rousseau and many others Kant was not, in the strictest sense, a political thinker. His main interest centred on philosophy and he is known to us as a great idealist philosopher. Scholars have discovered his indebtedness regarding political ideas to Rousseau and the French philosopher Montesquieu. Analysis of Kant's political ideas reveals that he supported the contract as the origin of state and separation of power as the key to the individual's freedom.

Kant thought that there was an atmosphere like state of nature where men were not quite happy and their freedom very often faced danger and hurdles. They, in this situation, decided to ensure freedom this and decided to set up a civil society or state which could secure freedom. Thus, according to Kant, the state is the product of a contract and people voluntarily made the contract. If we enter into the details of Kantian contract theory we shall find that Kant followed Rousseau in this regard. Kant was a great worshipper of natural rights and human freedom. He thought that putting all these under the governance of the body politic would enable men to enjoy them with full satisfaction. Kant was not interested at all in the historicity of the social contract. He used it as a weapon for legalising the natural rights which people enjoyed in the state of nature, but were not always secure there.

Kant's political ideas, to a large extent, *were influenced by the prevailing political situation of Germany.* Germany of his time was a feudal state and feudalism was absolute. She lagged far behind England in industrial progress. Economically, she was backward. He could not support the royal absolutism. In every sphere of life there were disorder and anarchy. Equality before law or obligation to law was scantily addressed to.

On, concept of sovereignty, Kant followed Rousseau. *He believed that sovereignty in a state resides in the people as a whole and their will,* which is called general will, *is the source of all authority.* Following Rousseau, Kant argued for the popular sovereignty and thought that this general will was the source of law. It means that like Rousseau, he thought of open assembly where all people met and took decisions regarding the state administration. This is direct democracy. We can say that Kant was not concerned with the possibility of direct democracy in Germany but Rousseau's influence inspired him to accept the concept of direct democracy.

Kant accepted the principle of the separation of powers elaborated by Montesquieu. The functions of the government can be divided into legislative, executive and judiciary. He did not favour the doctrine of the balance among the different organs or branches of government. He supported the supremacy of legislature over the two others organs. The supreme will of the people is expressed through the legislature and, naturally, the executive and legislative powers cannot be combined in the same body of person. The legislature shall have power to remove the executive from exercising authority. He also recommended that the judiciary should be allowed to discharge its functions independently of the two other organs of state.

The prevailing conditions of Prussia led Kant to find out a reconciliation between Rousseau's theory of popular sovereignty and the Prussian system of monarchical government. "The general will of the people is sovereign, but the sovereign power could be exercised through a monarchic form of government" (Gettell, p. 357). Kant's theory of popular sovereignty is not a consistent one. If people's will is supreme, people will have the absolute power to decide any issue. But in Kant's ideas we do not find that. Even men are helpless when the legislature exercises the sovereign power. Furthermore, popular sovereignty and monarchical form of government cannot make any logical combination. But Kant has done that.

Gettell has drawn our attention to a very interesting aspect of Kant's political thought. Rousseau's influence led him to support direct democracy and popular sovereignty. These two are features of the Rousseauist model of ideal state. There are also other features. In practice Kant was faced with a practical state that prevailed in Prussia and there are polar-like differences between the two. The fact is that Kant could not ignore Rousseau's ideal state or Prussia's practical state. He even believed that there was reason behind the practical state of Prussia. He thought that there were reason and historical incident behind the rise and development of Prussian state. Our view is that Kant could not give us a clear conception about state. He was—in a sense—a prisoner of indecision.

Because of his attachment to moral philosophy and idealism Kant showed scant interest in practical politics. However, whatever he has said about politics and related issues can be said as an integral part of his philosophy. Law is a part of morality. Since people's will is the source of all laws it would be immoral to disobey those laws. According to Kant, laws are divided into two parts—private law and general law or public law. Marxian critics have discovered that Kant had deliberately drawn this distinction. The society in which he lived was a bourgeois society. There were two things—the private ownership of the means of production, and the market economy. In such a society, private law was necessary. However, in Kant's opinion, the private law determines the relationship among rational individuals. The private law also deals with the man and property relations, and also the distribution of property. The purpose of the public general law was to control the relation between the individual and the state or among the several states.

Kant's view on religion is not directly related to his political ideas or conception of state. But he has specifically identified the role and sphere of action of the church. He has analysed religion in the light of morality. Since religion must be based not on the logic of theoretical reason but on the practical reason of the moral sense, it follows that any Bible or Revelation must be judged by its values for morality, and cannot itself be the judge of moral code. Churches and dogmas have value only in so far as they assist the moral development of the race. Kant once said "Christ has brought the kingdom of God nearer to earth, but he has been misunderstood, and in place of God's kingdom, the kingdom of the priest has been established among us". Here Kant clearly indicates that the chief function of the church is to help the moral upliftment of people. It cannot interfere with the political activities of the state. To put it in other words, the church and the state are two different units or agencies and each will have its own area of action and influence.

Kant's political ideas are combination of several contradictory opinions. He supported Rousseau's general will in which there is the will of every individual. But he could not support the people's right to revolt. He cherished a wrong idea that the monarchy of Germany could not do any work that might go against the interest of common men. In general term this view of Kant is unacceptable. But behind his apathy to revolution there was a reason. His apathy to revolution can be traced to the violent and cruel activities of his time. He was alarmed at the execution of Charles I and Louis XVI. The revolution, in his view, was always destructive. In his opinion a revolution destroys normal life, morality and natural order of society. To him all these were more important than a revolution. On this ground he refused to lend support to a revolution. He thought that change in political system could be btrought about not by revolution but by reforms. But if revolution at all comes and a new political order is established, people must show their obedience to it.

Kant's concept of freedom is to be judged not from a general perspective but from the background of idealism. He thought that freedom meant the right to will and this will must be moral in all respects. Again, an individual will have a desire, but that desire must be guided by self-imposed imperative of duty. Naturally-man cannot desire to have anything. Behind the doing and desiring must have moral reason or moral purpose. Kant further said that the pursuit of freedom must not create an anarchical situation in the state, because this will obstruct the enjoyment of freedom by others. From Kant's analysis we conclude that freedom is based on morality and it exists in an orderly state.

The forms of state, according to Kant, are autocracy, aristocracy and democracy. Forms of government are two : republican and despotic. Any form of government that is not representative, Kant declares to be out of rational consideration. In England, a tradition of representative system developed and the British people accepted this and adjusted themselves with it. In fact, in England, the representative form of government, worked through these institutions. So they were the integral parts of the British representative system. Earlier we have noted that there were no such representative institutions in Germany. So both Kant and Hegel indulged in a kind of distrust against numerous representatine institutions. Barker makes the following observation : "Even Kant distrusts representative institutions, though he is less full of the zeal for undivided sovereignty than Hegel, he fears that the representatives will tend to be unduly dependent on ministers" (*Political Thought*, p. 21). To sum up, *the state, law, sovereignty, institutions and everything else are, Kant thinks, manifestations of morality. Even freedom is a moral concept.*

The struggle for existence, according to Kant, is not altogether an evil. Nevertheless, men should perceive that it must be restricted within certain limits and regulated by rules, customs and laws. Its simple implication is that Kant has not ruled out competition among the states but that they must abide by certain rules and they must be limited. In order to keep the competition within limitations, Kant held, the nations should, like the individuals, enter into a contract. The whole meaning and movement of history is the ever greater restriction of pugnacity and violence, the continuous enlargement of the area of peace. The history of the human race, declares Kant, viewed as a whole, may be regarded as the realization of a hidden plan of nature to bring about a political constitution.

In his *Eternal* published in 1795 Kant said : "Standing armies excite states to outrival one another in the number of their armed men which has no limit. Through the expense occasioned thereby, peace becomes in the long run more oppressive than a short war : and standing armies are thus the cause for aggressive wars." Much of this militarism, in Kant's judgment, was due to the expansion of Europe into America, Africa and Asia, with the resultant quarrels of thieves over their new booty. He said, "if we compare the barbarian instances of civilized, and especially the commercial, states of our continent, the injustice practiced by them even in their first contract with foreign lands and peoples fills us with horror" (Quoted by Durant, p. 284).

JOHANN GOTTLIEB FICHTE (1762–1814)

Introduction

Johann Fichte was born in 1762 and died in 1814. He was a short-lived philosopher of Germany in whom German idealism found its fertile soil of growth. In the history of Western philosophy Fichte is not a very well known and influential figure. But his thought occupies an important place in the whole arena of Western philosophy. He was the brilliant disciple of Kant and his philosophical preeminence is worthy to be noted. "Fichte's dialectic subtleties" writes Dunning (p. 137) "was more refined than Kant's and his criticism and modification of the latter's metaphysics made a sensation in the learned circle of Germany".

An an idealist philosopher Fichte is not at par with Hegel but his philosophy is not to be neglected. His philosophy relating to politics centred on selected and practical problems. What he saw around him he thought about, and recorded his feelings. We know that in the eighteenth and nineteenth centuries it was a form of "hobby" of European rulers to be involved in war; and in Fichte's time there a war between Prussia and France and in this war Prussia's loss and disasters were quite heavy. This situation created a deep mark in the mind of Fichte and he formed a negative view about war. So far as religion is concerned his views incurred the displeasure of authority. His attitude on politics was also not acceptable to the then authority. The result was that he was forced to leave the post of professor of the University of Jena.

Maxey says that Fichte started his academic career as a disciple and interpreter of Kant. But he did not agree on all points to Kant's philosophy. He contended that the strictly subjective activity of the mind is itself the cause of all our ideas about the external world and, hence, the mind alone is real. The individual mind is merely part of the universal and absolute mind—which is nothing but God.

Political Ideas

The two works of Fichte contain his views regarding politics : *Closed Commercial State* and *Theory of State*. Clear influence of Rousseau and Kant is to be found on his political thought as well as philosophy. In his earlier life he was influenced by the law of nature, the natural rights, the individual's freedom, sovereignty of the people. Particularly the last mentioned issue was borrowed from Rousseau. In his later years he changed his view regarding political issues. He, however, did not build up a complete system of political science.

In the above-noted two works Fichte insisted on the unity, integrity and power of the national state. He also strongly argued for the extension of the power of such a state : He wanted to see a powerful state encompassing almost all the aspects of the individuals life. Fichte's ideas ultimately led to the advent of state socialism and fascist doctrines.

Dunning says that Fichte's political thought and ideas start with the rational self-consciousness of the individuals. He assumes that rational consciousness of all individuals creates a system of social regulation which in German is called *Recht*. In Fichte's system of thought this rational consciousness plays an important part. Consciousness of one leads to think about the problems of other and in this way the freedom of all men is limited. Fichte says that only consciousness creates social regulation and experience and education have no part to play. How is the unity arrived at? Following Rousseau, Fichte says that this is achieved through the social contract. The social contract is thus the basis of reapprochement among the individuals of the community. But he did not regard the social contract as the cause of the origin of state. In Fichte's opinion, the contract is a process by "which the private will and general will are synthetically united." The terms of the synthesising process are those of Rousseau's contract.

Though Fichte does not use the contract as an explanation of the origin of state, it has been accepted as an explanation of the structure of rights and duties within the state. Three distinct agreements are involved in the social pact. The first is the property contract, by which each individual agrees with all others on what property, rights and liberties he is to have and what he is to cede to others. Fichte does not recognise natural rights. This agreement must be made individually and in person with all others as individuals—the other party. Fichte includes the whole sphere of individual freedom under the concept "property" which he defines as rights of free action in the world of sense. The boundary of each one's property is fixed by the terms of contract.

The second type of agreement is protection contract which is a sequence of the first. In this contract each individual agrees with others to protect their specified property and all other rights, on the condition that they will likewise protect his. The first contract was a "negative will" because everyone promised from invading the right and property of others. This negative will is now converted into a positive will.

The third type of contract is union contract. This secures and protects the two previous contracts and, in union with them, forms the fundamental contract of state organisation. The effect of this is that each individual becomes a part of an organised whole and melts into one with it. This union contract completes the social pact and constitutes a sovereign.

In his earlier life Fichte held that it could never be the function of the state to make men happy, wealthy and God willing. People cannot expect that the state will protect the property and rights of individuals. It has numerous other functions and the state should perform them. But in later yeas of his life he changed his opinion about the functions of the state. Summing up the views of Fichte regarding the functions of state Dunning says : "To give to each for the first time his own, to install him for the first time in his property and then first to protect him in it". His changed position puts him nearer to the utilitarian philosophers. It is the duty of the state to see that citizens are capable of getting sufficient pleasure and happiness. A large number of political philosophers felt that it is the primary duty of the state to protect the property of citizens and Fichte was no exception. Fichte was a contemporary of Industrial Revolution and capitalism was the product of this revolution. It is quite natural that Fichte will have sympathy for capitalist class. He also could not avoid the influence of religion. It has been observed that he was to some extent a capitalis-minded philosopher.

Fichte was also influenced by the prevailing conditions of Germany. He believed that each state should be economically self-sufficient. The state should distribute its population among different classes such as farmers, merchants, artisans, producers etc. The state must take care that the total national incomes is proportionately shared by all people of the state. The critics are of opinion that this suggestion of Fichte is simply an imagination and naturally has no practical importance.

Fichte viewed the concept of national state from a different angle. He was opposed to free trade. Free trade was the chief cause of economic rivalry and competition and, finally, of war. So a national state should always try to avoid free trade. If it is at all unavoidable then the state should take the leading part. To be economically exclusive and self-sufficient was of precisely the same significance politically as to be exclusive and independent in legislation and judicature. So political and economic exclusiveness was essential for the national state. The idea of national state was active in his mind. Once he said, "certain parts of the earth's surface, with their inhabitants are evidently determined by nature to form political units. River, sea and mountains determine the natural boundaries of state. These natural boundaries are important for national state."

In his later years, Fichte propagated certain socialistic doctrines. It was the duty of the state to guarantee the material existence and comfort of all citizens. He categorically announced that the government must provide every individual with work and it must also see that each person is getting his share of national wealth.

Fichte offers us a consistent analysis of government and constitution. Laws are the expression of the sovereign will of the people. He did not separate executive organ from the judiciary. Both the executive and judicial functions were to be performed by the same group of persons who were to be representatives. The government might be monarchic, aristocratic, or hereditary. But people as a whole could never act as administrators. The implication is that he never thought that common people could work as good administrators. In other words, he thought of a separate class of administrators. This brings Fichte nearer to Plato. To ensure that the sovereign will of the people as embodied in the laws forming the constitution should not be overridden by the government, Fichte conceived an institution named the ephorate that he regarded as indispensable to a rational constitution. The right of final judgment upon the conduct of the government must inhere necessarily in the people as a whole.

The cause of Prussia's defeat in war with Napoleon was, according to Fichte, the lack of political consciousness of the people. So he appealed to the people to arouse their sense of patriotism and raise their political consciousness. German unity, he believed, was to be achieved and maintained at any cost. As every man has a mission in life, so a nation has a mission and that can never be achieved when the nation faces disintegration. Every nation must do something for the progress of civilisation.

GEORG WILHELM FRIEDRICH HEGEL (1770–1831)

Hegel and German Idealism

Behind the development of German idealism there was a chequered and colourful background. It originated in the idealism of Plato and Aristotle of about 4th century B. C. and then for about 2,000 years it was in fact buried in oblivion. It was Rousseau who lifted the concept of idealism from the thick darkness of oblivion. But in Rousseau's hand the resuscitation of idealism (that received elaborate and finest treatment in the hands of Plato) was not complete. His chief interest was to build up a civil society based on morality and which could assure freedom. From Rousseau it went to the German philosophers Kant and Fichte. "The climax of German idealist political thought" thus comments Gettell "was reached in the writings of Georg Wilhelm Hegel". The same opinion has been expressed by Dunning. The climax of German idealism in political philosophy was reached in the speculation of Hegel. The profound knowledge and extraordinary genius of this German philosopher not only enriched the idealist philosophy, but also raised it to the pinnacle of glory. But the dark aspect of Hegel's philosophy is it is very very difficult to understand. A critic once said that Hegel and selected few persons understood his philosophy.

Hegel borrowed the central idea of idealism from Plato and Aristotle. Some of Rousseau's thought are to be found in Hegelian idealism. He also culled few materials from the French Revolution. All these he combined with his attitude towards German nationalism, history, German state and prevailing politics of Germany and other European states. So we find that Hegel's philosophy in general and idealism in particular are not monolithic constructs. Rightly speaking, it is the confluence of various ideas and incidents. The entire political and economic situation of Europe created an indelible mark on his thought system. He wanted to analyse politics in the background of all these. Personal pleasure or pain could not make any impact on his mind. Absolute idea, world spirit etc. occupied his thought world.

Herbert Marcuse has traced the origin of German idealism and also of Hegel's idealist philosophy to German Reformation. Since the German Reformation the German people had become accustomed to the fact that liberty was an "inner value" which was compatible with every or any form of bondage and the obedience to any existing authority was an important precondition to everlasting salvation. The Reformation leaders taught that toil and poverty were the blessings of God. One of the decisive functions of Protestantism had been to induce the emancipated individuals to accept the new social system created by the Reformation movement and to divert their claims and demands from the external world into the inner life.

Out of this new outlook in Germany there developed the German culture the central idea of which was beauty, morality and freedom. German idealism immediately received it and made it a part of it. Ultimately both German culture and German idealism were mixed together and it is difficult to make any separation between them. "Culture was then essentially idealistic, occupied with the *idea* of things rather than with the things themselves. It set freedom of thought before freedom of action, morality before practical justice, the inner life before the social life of man. This idealistic culture, just because it stood aloof from an intolerable reality.....served as the repository of truths which had not been realised in the history or mankind" (Marcuse, p. 15).

In order to understand Hegel's philosophy we must remember that he judged and analysed everything in the background of one integrated whole. Remembering this Marcuse has rightly said that Hegel's idealism or philosophy is the culmination of the entire tradition of Western thought. Politics, culture, civil society, state, tradition, civilisation etc. are all integrated together. He analysed this idea with the help of dialectic. The progress of civil society and its culmination into a national state is the result of dialectic. Even the progress of civilisation is the product of dialectic. There are always conflicts between negative and positive forces and in this process, finally, the positive forces win, the absolute idea it reaches the final stage. But it is to be remembered that behind everything there works an idea. The idea is first; and from that comes the reality. The importance of man comes from his membership of the state and he has no importance outside the state or away from the state. Completeness or indivisibility is the central idea of Hegel's philosophy. This concept of indivisibility has been a very important source of criticism against Hegel.

Kant was always in favour of an all powerful German state. This type of state in modern language is called an autocratic state or an absolute state. His sympathy for an all powerful state led him to oppose or creticise Locke's philosophy of liberalism. For this reason he supported the absolutism of Hobbes and Rousseau. Hegel's idealism accommodated this philosophy of Kant. His idealism teaches that man must show unconditional obedience to the state. We have already pointed out that this he got from the Reformation. Rousseau's moral freedom and general will influenced both Kant and Hegel. The morality, freedom and will of the individual are not separate from those of the state. So Hegel's idealism veered around the state. Here he follows both Kant and Fichte. The three great German philosophers thought of institutions as repugnant to the all-round development of human personality and idealism. We, therefore, conclude that German idealism found its greatest manifestation in Hegel's idealism.

Hegel and the French Revolution

No philosopher of any worth can avoid the influence of contemporary events and Hegel is no exception. The political situation and events of the then Germany created an important impact on his mind. In both France and England there were absolute monarchies. But people's continuous struggle checked the oppression of absolutism. Liberal and democratic institutions flourished in these two countries and people fostered very carefully the democratic values. Moreover, democracy in these two countries was successful. The political situation in general and situation in particular were quite different in Germany.

The French Revolution and the invasion of Napoleon's army were supposed to bring about liberty, equality and universal brotherhood. But ultimately success was not achieved. There remained an atmosphere of authoritarianism. The German ruling class did not like the democratic and liberal values of the "West". Moreover, since Germany did not show any sympathy to France and French political ideas and principles she thought liberalism as her national enemy. Ebenstein remarks (op. cit. p. 590) : "The political experience of Germany has been preponderantly authoritarian, its orthodox tradition of political theory has been chiefly though not wholly, antidemocratic." In this atmosphere of authoritarianism Hegel was born. He could not think anything outside authoritarian politics. Even he did not like the democratic institutions of England and France.

Initially Hegel supported the French Revolution. Both Hegel and Schelling defended the Revolution with forceful arguments. But later on Hegel freed himself from the illusion. The violence and terrorism of the Revolution were disapproved by him. Moreover, the Napoleonic wars left devastating effects upon many small countries of Europe. The reconstruction of these countries was a major problem. Hegel came to the conclusion that the problem would not be solved by appealing to the abstractions, like rights of man, that had proved so disruptive. Sabine writes "more and more Revolution was felt to be destructive and nihilistic and its philosophy was pictured as a doctrinaire effort to remake society and human nature according to caprice. Substantially this was the estimation in which Hegel came to hold the Revolution and individualism of its political philosophy" (p. 621).

National reconstruction, integrity of nation and overall progress of the state were prioritised by Hegel and for that reason he could not support individualism and the rights of the individual. National solidarity, he thought, could not be sacrificed at the altar of individualism. The continuity of civilisation, culture, history and tradition could be maintained at the cost of anything. Many people call this attitude of Hegel reactionary. But, in fact, it was not reactionary. It was constructive and conservative creative forces of the nation state. So it was the national state which received maximum treatment in the hands of Hegel. Theory of the national state, to Hegel, was the embodiment of political power. Real political and economic factors influenced the political ideas of Hegel. He was not against the rights of individuals. But to him national reconstruction and progress of Germany were more important than the personal rights. He had the firm belief that if the nation remains in poor or deplorable condition and remain unattended there cannot be any development of individual. His philosophy was—whole is more important than parts. Naturally the interest of nation must remain much above the interest of the individuals. Hegel observed that the Industrial Revolution could not make any perceptible impact on Germany. The result was the she lagged behind other European nations. He wanted to reverse this situation.

Life and Works

Georg Wilhelm Friedrich Hegel was born at Stuttgart on 27th August 1770. His father was a subordinate officer in the department of finance and Hegel himself grew up with the patient and methodical habits of those civil servants whose modest efficiency gave Germany the best governed cities of the world. A solvent financial position enabled his father to give young Hegel the best possible education. He was sent to Grammar School at Stuttgart. At the age of 18, Hegel entered the university of Tübingen to study theology. But this was not his subject of interest and naturally he began to neglect it. He studied the Greek and Roman classics.

He graduated from Tübingen in 1793. He then went to Berne in Switzerland as a private tutor. In 1799 his father died and he inherited certain amount of money which he thought sufficient. He gave up the job of private tutor. He then went to Jena to get a chance in that university. In August 1801 he was appointed a private teacher and began lecturing on logic and metaphysics. As a teacher he earned wide reputation and in 1805 he was given the post of Professor which was highly coveted in those days.

While at Jena, in 1806, Napoleon's army invaded Prussia and the French army threw the scholarly city into confusion and terror. French soldiers invaded Hegel's home and he took to his heels like a philosopher, carrying with him the manuscript of his important work *The Phenomenology of Spirit*. The University of Jena was closed and Hegel was in great financial crisis. For sometime he was the editor of a newspaper. He was later on offered the professorships at several universities including Heidelberg and he accepted this. He was there until 1818. Then he went to Berlin to take the chair of philosophy left vacant by the death of Fichte. At Berlin, Hegel's fame reached far and wide and within a short time he became an international figure. In this connection a famous incident may be noted here. "While at Jena in 1806 he saw Napoleon—the world soul—on horseback. Prussia's defeat at the battle of Jena established French hegemony in Germany. That hegemony only lasted a few years. Neverthless, it was Jena and its aftermath that made Germany one of the key players in world history in Hegel's sense"—J. S. Mcclelland—*History of Western Political Thought*, p. 520.

His *Phenomenology of Spirit* was published in 1807. But this book did not bring for him wide reputation. He wrote *Encyclopedia of Philosophical Sciences* in 1817. For the students of political thought his important works are *The Philosophy of Right* (1821) and *The Philosophy of History* (posthumously published in 1837). He died suddenly on November 1831 after oneday's illness of cholera.

From his days at Berlin to the end of his life he ruled the philosophic world as undisputably as Goethe the world of literature, and Beethoven the realm of music. His birthday came on the day after Goethe's and proud Germany made a double holiday for them every year. After his death his influence was very great, not only in Germany but also in England and America.

The Hegelian Dialectic

Hegel has analysed his philosophy and other related ideas with the help of dialecties and to him the dialectics means the embodiment of reason. Even history progresses from one stage to another in dialectical process. He believed that there is always change and behind every change dialectics works. That is why he calls dialectics or reason as the "motor force of history". He has also said that "the dialectic operate in individual mind". Both history and intellect, in the view of Hegel, work according to dialectics.

The word dialectic is derived from the Greek word *dialektike* and according to Concise Oxford Dictionary the word dialectic means the art of investigating the truth of opinions. Plato adopted this method and a number of other philosophers followed Hegel. Dialectic is a process by which, in controversy, one proposition is set over against another and out of this confrontation a new proposition emerges. This unites the truth contained in the original proposition. Hence dialectic is a method to find out the truth. Hegel adopted this method to explain the movement of Reason in human affairs. The dialectic helps us in arriving at truth. The ultimate reality is reason and the process by which it is unfolded is dialectic.

Stated briefly, the "dialectic in Hegel's hands is not merely a description of the way in which opposing tendencies are adjusted in political life and history. He is not talking about any law of the pendulum or saying only that historical change proceeds by opposites. For him the dialectic had to be a law of logic. The dialectic is the mechanism by which thought propels itself on the way in which Reason progressively embodies itself in institutions or in series of propositions, no one of which is the truth, but each of which contains a part of the truth along with error."[1] The dialectical investigation proceeds by stages and at each stage of the argument a position is advanced. In Hegel's dialectic it is also found that nothing is fully true or completely false. Naturally nothing is wasted. The truth of one stage proceeds to a higher stage. Again, truth or false will emerge, again. Both truth and false are the product of argument and do not come from outside. The truth comes from the argument and for that reason it is said that the truth is discovered and not invented nor is it created. The dialectic suggests no short-cut method. Both history and intellect are to proceed stage by stage and dialectically. Hegel thinks that historical dialectic always works in this process.

The Reason (or what he calls Idea or Spirit) passes through three stages and Hegel calls them Thesis, Antithesis and Synthesis. So any assertion or proposition which one makes is never perfectly true or correct. Because as soon as the assertion is made, contradictions or opposites emerge. Hence a conflict between the true and false becomes inevitable. This is Antithesis. But the conflict between truth and falseness does not exist indefinitely, it is resolved. This is due to the fact that the dialectic is self-propelling. That is, it is a self-regulatory system. It has the capacity to resolve the conflict. It is a characteristic feature of the dialectic. Again, the Antithesis does not last long. It passes over into Synthesis. In this way the idea or Reason is constantly changing until a final state arrives. Hegel states that the Synthesis is not the final stage. It contains the germs of opposites and, therefore, it very soon is converted into Thesis. It is called new Thesis. The Synthesis is not imposed by any outside force, it is inherent in Idea, Reason, Spirit, the Absolute—Hegel uses these terms.

This view of Hegel's dialectic is not very unlike that of Socrates. But Hegel may deny that his dialectic is similar to the dialectic of Socrates. The point is that for Hegel the contradictions are not obstacle to the way of progress. Whereas Socrates thought that they were creating obstacles to progress. In Hegel's opinion the contradictions are essential conditions to progress. They are essential to our understanding of truth. If there is no contradiction there cannot be any tension, there cannot be any struggle between right and wrong, truth and falseness. The contradiction—according to Hegel—is the motivating force.

Hegel claims that this is his new logic of dialectic. Contradiction is not blemish or deficiency or fault in a thing. Rather, the contradiction or conflict is life-blood. It helps the Reason or Idea or Spirit to move from one state to another. Contradiction is concrete and there is determination in it. It moves until it is settled. *Contradiction or the dialectic is, therefore, a self-generating process.* The world or history or civilisation moves because there are contradictions. Hegel has said that Synthesis will not be a compromise between Thesis and Antithesis. Nor it is a victory of one over another. Thesis and Antithesis are present in Synthesis. It is the nature of dialectic that out of the tension the truth will come out. So there is no question of defeat of one and victory of another.

Dialectic, History and Civilisation

According to Hegel the true subject of history is universal, not the individual; the true content is the realisation of self-consciousness of freedom, not the interests, needs and actions of the individuals. The history of the world is none other than

1. W. T. Jones (ed.)—*Masters of Political Thought,* Vol. III, pages 25-26.

the progress of the consciousness of freedom—thus declares Hegel. The universal law of history is, in Hegel's formulation, not simply progress to freedom, but progress in the self-consciousness of freedom. A set of historical tendencies becomes law only if man comprehends and acts on them. Historical laws, in other words, originate and are actual only in man's conscious practice, so that if, for instance, there is a law of progress to ever higher forms of freedom, it ceases to operate if man fails to recognize and operate it. "Hegel's theory of history is progressive, more and more people are actually coming to understand what freedom is and more and more people are actually coming to enjoy freedom as the form of state changes. But Hegel still has to deal with the sceptic who might say : It is one thing to say that the world is freer today than it was yesterday, but how can we be sure that the world is going to be freer tomorrow than it is today? Hegel seems to be saying that we can never know the present, let alone the future, in the way we can know the past". J. S. Mcclelland, p. 529.

Hegel further observes that the history of civilisation is the unfolding or the progressive realisation and materialisation of the world spirit in time. When civilisation gradually unfolds itself dialectically the efforts of particular individuals, whoever they may be, are of little importance. Hegel admits that the individuals may have their own desires, ambitions and gratifications. But so far as the progress of history or civilisation is concerned they have no special importance. All these are sacrificed for the sake of civilisation or for the fulfilment of the requirements of the nation. In this way Hegel has explained the necessity of history.

In the progress of history or human civilisation only the impersonal or general forces are important and they act. No particular incident or person has very little to contribute. If a person's contribution happens to be highly important in the background of entire civilisation or history only that accounts for. In other words, the contribution of a person is to be judged in the light of whole history and civilisation. If Hegel's theory is accepted we should say that the individual is insignificant. Is it correct? We believe that every man has something to contribute to the whole progress of human civilisation. Of course Hegel's theory stands upon the denial of man's individual contribution. The critics such as Mccelland say so.

He cites the example of Caesar's struggle for power. Caesar, guided by personal ambition of power, overthrew the traditional Roman Senatorial Power. But in satisfying his personal desires or of the ambition he fulfilled a necessary destiny in the history of Rome and the world; through his actions he achieved a higher, more rational form of political organisation. A universal mission is achieved through the personal activities of a man. A particular individual can change the destiny of a nation. Hence a man can play an important and necessary phase in the development of truth. Absolute Spirit or Idea uses a particular man as a tool. In the dialectical progress of history the importance of individuals is not continuous and unilinear.

Opposition and contrariety are the essential characteristics of Idea or Reason as well as of nature. This is also the law of cosmos and of thought. In Hegelian logic the entire world is a moving equilibrium. This is due to the fact that there is a tussle between the positive and negative forces of Idea or Reason. Opposite forces provide the dynamism of history. That is, history of the world, or, for that matter, civilisation, moves towards perfection and it passes through contrary forces. Sometimes equilibrium emerges, but it does not last long. This is disturbed by the appearance of new forces. So there is no permanent equilibrium. The disturbance of balance is not unnatural, rather it is an indicator of change and continuity. One positive or one negative in Hegel's system is never correct or permanent. But it does not mean that any one is wrong. Both are partly wrong and partly right.

The dialectic and contradiction are the most important things of progress of civilisation and history. Because there are problems in every society there are also contradictions. The contradiction leads problems towards solution. But he cautions us by saying that no problem can ever be solved permanently. If a problem could have been solved permanently then history and civilisation would have no scope to advance forward. But, in his opinion, this is not so. Interpreting Hegel's logic Sabine says : "It is like a spiral that mounts as it turns. The driving force he called contradiction. In Hegel's logic contradiction means the fruitful opposition between systems" (p. 641).

Hegel applies the dialectic to the study of the progress or change of society. It has several parts in its structure. They are laws, morals, religions, institutions. All these are principal parts. There are also secondary parts in the structure of society. All these parts are moving endlessly and, therefore, there is a continuous tension between them. The movement is, of course, not fruitless. The different parts are adjusting and readjusting among themselves and, as a consequence of it, equilibrium is reached. But this balance is disturbed by the emergence of new opposite forces. In the process of dialectic, when one stage is arrived, the next step can easily be surmised.

Hegel adopts the method of dialectic to explain the social change. There are two interpretations or adoptions. One is in the realm of social change—the negative and affirmative or positive forces come into conflict and in this way society proceeds towards higher and higher stages or progress. There is still another interpretation. The social change may be continuous or gradual; or it may be radical or violent. The gradualness of change is the symbol of positive or affirmative force and the radical or destructive or violent change is the symbol of negative force. There is conservativeness in continuity or gradualness. In this change, old tradition is maintained and everything proceeds on the basis of 'wait and see'. The violent change negates the past and advances to vamp the whole society anew. What method will be applied to explain the social change that depends upon the philosopher's outlook? Conservative Hegel and his followers were in favour of gradualness or continuity.

According to Hegel the key to social change is dialectic. This dialectic has two movements—one is negative and the other is positive or affirmative. Every thesis contains within itself certain contradictions. In the process of movement these become explicit that become active and destroy the original thesis. When the dialectic is positive or constructive in the conflict between negative and positive forces, the first is destroyed, and positive force wins. This results in the emergence of higher stage or level.

Abstract Rights and Morality

Hegel discusses abstract rights, morality, the relation between them, the contradiction and reconciliation. He says that, as rational being, every man makes certain claims for the development and assertion of his individuality and these claims are called abstract rights. Hegel does not treat man as simply a creature of appetite. Man is rational and moral conception guides his activities. Now, by morality, he means that rational man has some feelings and intentions. He has some rights and obligations. Also, he possesses conscience. Man exercises the rights for the development of personality and, while doing this, he applies his maximum conscience. That is, he feels that his exercise of rights does not create any problems to others. So, in every act, conscience guides him. This is morality. His life is purposeful only as a member of society and in society the individual leads an ethical life. Hence, abstract rights, morality and membership of the social order are closely connected with each other. A moral being cannot ignore the difficulties of others. It is to be recalled that Rousseau thought almost in the same line. In his theory of general will there is no place of a will which aims at the interests of a particular person. Again, in the civil society of Rousseau, every men will get freedom and right. But he will not enjoy or exercise his freedom or right at the cost of other's freedom and right. Rousseau's civil society is a moral society and everyman is guided by morality. Hence the influence of Rousseau upon Hegel is quite explicit.

In the *Philosophy of Rights* he has emphasised that man is rational and moral. This results in the fact that exercise of rights by man does not involve any loss or injury upon the exercise of rights and enjoyment of freedom by others. The question may arise—how did he come to the conclusion that every individual is rational and moral? We have no answer. We believe that the idealist philosophers are accustomed to think in this way or line.

Hegel also discovers the contradiction between abstract rights and morality, because the relation is part of his theory of dialectic. The abstract rights and morality may be incompatible and Hegel asserts that they are very often in conflict. How does this conflict arise? In all societies, including primitive and static, rights are violated or infringed. But this violation or infringement goes unchallenged. People of these societies have not acquired the moral sense to argue that the infringement of rights is unjustified on moral grounds. Only in developed society—where self-consciousness has fully blossomed—the violation of abstract rights faces severe criticism. However, Hegel's point of view is that very often contradiction arises between abstract rights and morality.

Hegel has said that there may arise a contradiction between abstract right and morality. But since this contradiction is dialectical it can never be permanent. The conflict will jump upon the next stage and, finally, a reconciliation will arrive. Summarising Hegel's views Plamenatz observes : "Abstract right and morality, when they do conflict, can only be reconciled in ethical or communal life. This ethical life is their *synthesis*, not only in the sense that they are inseparable spheres in which the tension between them is resolved" (*Man and Society*, Vol. II, p. 231).

Family and Civil Society

We have discussed the triad of abstract right, morality and ethical life. The tension between abstract right and morality is resolved by ethical life. Hegel then discusses another triad and it is the family, the civil society and the state. But this triad is not the same as the earlier one. Abstract right and morality are connected but the family and civil society are not so connected. We may state Hegel's view in the language of Plamenatz "Where there is a right of any kind, there is also some kind of morality, and the two are mere aspects of social life. But it is not true that where there is any community of family type, there is always some form of civil society, and that neither family nor civil society is ever found outside the state" (*Man and Society*, Vol. II, p. 232).

Let us see what Hegel means by family. The family is a *natural* foundation for the order of reason that culminates in the state. The family has its external reality in property but property also destroys family. When the children grow up they separate themselves from their parents and establish their own families. The property is also divided. Thus, the amount of original property becomes small. Breaking of property and disintegration of family go side by side.

Following Hegel, we can define civil society in the following words. It is a community of producers of the kind described by classical economists together with the public services needed to maintain order inside it. In primitive times, there were societies but they were not civil societies. Civil society is a particular product of the development of history. In ancient times there were tribes and clans. In the process of time the tribes, clans etc. disintegrated and out of this emerged civil society and state.

There are few reasons as to why Hegel gave emphasis on civil society. First reason is—He was out and out a bourgeois-minded philosopher and had lot of sympathy for the bourgeois class. The control of civil society was at the hands of bourgeoisie and for that he was eager for the development and protection of civil society. Secondly, Hegel's state is the final stage of dialectical process. Before state there were family and civil society. Naturally the civil society is an important phase of rational development. For that reason civil society occupies an important place in Hegel's thought. Thirdly, Hegel believed that civil society is the manifestation of reason. In fact, reason is present everywhere in his thought. He said "in a political constitution nothing should be recognised as valid unless its recognition accorded with the right of Reason" (*Civil Society*, p. 106). Finally, the state is the highest embodiment of the development of the spirit of the people and in the process of development civil society occupies an important place. That is why he emphasised civil society.

In Hegel's contemporary Germany there were many guilds and corporations. There were also various types of associations and local communities. All these had great contribution to the moulding of human character and behaviour. Hegel was fully acquainted with this picture. That is why he made civil society as part of his philosophical analysis.

Hegel was an abstruse philosopher, but he did not stay at the top of the ivory tower. He was a close observer of all the social, cultural and political events which thrived in his contemporary society of Germany. He realised that without associations and communities individuals would be formless agents of society. They must realise the worth of personality and importance of social life, and this was possible only in civil society. He further held that the individuals must be made fit or suitable for the state. They must be mediated through a long series of corporations and associations before they arrive at the final dignity of citizenship in the state (Sabine, p. 660). The life in civil society is educative. People learn the values as member of the civil society and these values find their manifestations in the state. People learn the technique and value of collaboration in the civil society.

Civil society does not challenge the family. In Hegel's judgment there is no contradiction between family and civil society nor there is any tension between civil society and state, they are complementary. The civil society makes citizens eligible for the state. It educates and moulds their lives. The civil society, according to Hegel, is the intermediate position between the individuals and state. The civil society is not independent of state, it works under it. It has not separate will, but it plays an important role (Plamenatz, p. 232).

Hegel's Theory of State

We have prepared a background for a comprehensive analysis of the theory of state. Now we shall start with what Hegel says about state. Stated briefly, his theory of state is an integral part of his whole philosophy, and it is the final stage of the dialectical process. History, in Hegel's view, is the manifestation of Absolute Idea or World Spirit and this history is embodied in the state or, what Hegel frequently calls, national state. The national state is the greatest manifestation of morality ethics and civilisation. This is his state.

Originally, man was like many other animals. But through dialectical process he has reached the final stage of evolution and he is the best of all animals. He is not alone or he does not like to live alone. He likes to live with others and to form associations. Hegel says that the earliest form of association or institution is the family which is built up on the feeling of love and affection. Family is not only the most elementary institution, it is the smallest institution with extremely limited capacity to meet the requirements.

However, Hegel calls family the Thesis. It is unity and all the members of the family are held together by the bond of love and affection. Withing the family there is no conflict or tension and so no place of contradiction or disunity. In our earlier analysis we have seen that the family is not the only institution and it is not permanent. When the children become adult and self-dependent they form separate families.

To meet their growing demands people move for better and greater society. They land on wider environment. This society is bourgeois society. While the family is Thesis the bourgeois or the civil society is antithesis. Wayper writes : "Unlike the family which is a unity regarded by its very members as being more real than themselves, bourgeois society is a host of independent men and women held together only be ties of contract and self-interest. Whereas the characteristic of the family is mutual love, the characteristic of the bourgeois society is universal competition" (*Political Thought*, p. 162).

The family according to Hegel is the primary unit of state which passes through dialectics. But with the development of trade, commerce, human habit and man's necessity the family failed to meet the growing and varied demands of man. Particularly in development of capitalism there occured a significant change in trade, commerce as well as habits and outlooks of the common people. In this situation the family proved its inefficiency and there arose a gap. A new society called civil society controlled by the bourgeoisie emerged. The new society made laws for its own management. There were also other processes of the civil society which was also bourgeois in nature. In bourgeois or civil society of Hegel's time there were guilds and corporations. The owners of these guilds and corporations developed a type of affinity and they began to control the state administration sometimes in clandestine ways. In the civil society there were capitalists as well as the common people. But the latter practically had no say in the management of society and state. This was the nature of civil society that prevailed in Hegel's time and he was overwhelmingly influenced by this civil society.

In support of the above view we quote few lines from Wayper : "The thesis the family, a unity held together by love, knowing no differences is confronted by the antithesis, bourgeois society, an aggregate of individuals held apart by competition knowing no unity, even though it is manifestly struggling towards a greater unity which it has nevertheless not yet atained. The synthesis which preserves what is best in thesis and antithesis, which swallows up neither family nor bourgeois society, but which gives unity and harmony to them, is *State.* It does this because it is a super-organism" (p. 162-163).

The final stage of the dialectic process is the state. In Hegelian formulation there can be no change. It is not only the super-organism, but also the highest manifestation of the Idea or World Spirit or Reason. In the words of Hegel : "The essence of the modern state is that the universal is bound up with the full freedom of particularity and the welfare of the individuals, that the interest of the family and bourgeois society must connect itself with the state but also that universality of the state's purpose cannot advance without the specific knowledge and will of the particular, which must maintain its rights. The universal must be actively furthered, but on the other side subjectivity must be wholly and vitally developed. Only when both elements are there in all their strength can the state be regarded as articulated and truly organised." The state of Hegel is, thus, the meeting point of both particularity and universality.

Characteristics of State

It is a divine state. Hegel's state is a mechanism, but it is a mechanism for different purpose. It is not an instrument to maximise the happiness of individuals. Nor it is an institution to preserve the life, liberty and property of men. It is a *super-organism.* "It is the institutionalization of perfect public spirit and complete disinterestedness and the guarantor of folk custom, with the demands of which individual desires are in perfect harmony."[1] *Hegel's state was not only real but the highest form of reality.* It was the God Himself. "The State is the Divine Idea as it exists on Earth."[2] "We must, therefore, worship the state as the manifestation of the Divine on Earth and consider that, if it is difficult to comprehend Nature, it is infinitely harder to grasp the Essence of the State..... The State is the march of God through the world." To sum up, Hegelian state is the highest embodiment of Divinity or Spirit.

In all its essentials *Hegelian state is an organic state.* "The state must be comprehended as an organism. To the complete state belongs, essentially, consciousness and thought." If we go through Hegel's view about state it will appear to us that the state is a natural growth. It has passed through several stages of evolution. The final stage is state. There is dialectic and the evolution indicates that the next stage is better than the former. All the stages or parts are closely related with each other. But it is to be remembered that the state is a complete whole. This is because when the evolution is complete all the parts forming the state are fully merged with it and the parts cannot claim their separate identity. If the state is destroyed various parts

1. Lancaster—*Masters of Political Thought*, Vol. III, p. 43.
2. *Philosophy of History*, p. 39.

will lose their existence. When the question is put "Why should I obey that state"? There is a very simple answer. Summarising Hegel's view Wayper says (p. 170) : "My hand is fulfilled in me, and I am fulfilled in the State, and there is nothing more to be said about the matter." The hands are under my control and I am in the control of the state. So no question of disobedience arises. The morality and freedom of the individual are not separate from those of the state. The worth of the individual is ascertained only as a member of the state or social order. Moreover, *Hegel's state is an end in itself and never a means to an end.* The individuals exist for the state, and not vice versa.

The moral law cannot bind the state, because the state is the creator of morality. The state fixes the standard of morality for its individuals. Man moves, acts and decides guided by conscience. Conscience tells us to do what is right, but it cannot tell us what is right and just. That decision is to be taken by the state. Man is just like a machine to perform his duty. What to do and whether the "doing" is justified—that never falls within the jurisdiction of the individual. A man does not possess the wisdom to challenge the morality or ethics or the state. The wisest men of antiquity have laid it down that wisdom and virtue consists in living conformably to the customs of one's people which are indeed the collective wisdom and reason of the past. The state is the best interpreter of the tradition of the community, only it can tell us what is good, and conformity with its decrees or social ethics, is thus the highest morality.

Another feature of Hegel's theory of state is, it is sovereign both in national and in international spheres. In relation to other states is own safety is of prime consideration. Hegel has categorically stated that it cannot make any compromise about its own safety and security because with these two the highest interest of citizen is connected. For the sake of its safety what it decides that is law and it is the highest law. Hegel, in his *Philosophy of Right,* declares "It is a generally acknowledged and well-known principle that particular interest of the state is the most important consideration." To safeguard its own interest and protect its own sovereignty is the highest morality. Any plea against it is not allowed. What is good and bad, right and wrong—that is to be decided by the state and no interference by any other agency can be tolerated. International relations mean the relation among the sovereign states and, in that sphere, every sovereign state has the right to protect her own interests. Negligence to perform this duty is a sin. We believe that this view of Hegel regarding the status of state in international arena is wrong. A state is sovereign in international field does not mean that the state has the absolute right to do whatever it likes. But the fact is that every state will have to observe and obey the international code of conduct and law of nations. But he ignored this aspect. The picture of an all-powerful German state was so much active that he forgot the law of nations and international code of conduct. He wanted to see an all-powerful German state. Rather, he was a blind supporter of a powerful Germany. For such a view Hegel was squarely blamed and castigated.

The Hegelian state has the absolute right to declare war. How does he justify it? The fundamental proposition of international law is that the treaties, as the ground of obligations between the states, ought to be kept. But since the sovereignty of the state is the principle of its relations to others, states are, to that extent, in a state of nature in relation to each other. These rights are actualised only in their particular wills and not in a universal will. It follows that, continues Hegel, states disagree and their particular wills cannot be harmonised, the matter can only be settled by war. War is not to be regarded as an absolute evil, but as a purely external accident. War is the state of affairs which deals in earnest with the vanity of temporal goods and concerns. War has the higher significance that, by its agency, the ethical health of people is preserved in their indifference to the stabilisation of finite institutions, just as the blowing of the winds preserves the sea from the foulness which would be the result of prolonged calm, so also corruption in nations would be the product of prolonged perpetual peace. The successful wars have prevented the civil broils and strengthened the internal power of the state.

The discovery of gun and gun powder has contributed liberally to the furtherance of civilisation. Evil doings and corruption of nations can be removed only through the declaration of war. If we deeply go through the argument of Hegel we shall find that so-called uncivilised and weak nations have no right to exist. Only the powerful nations have the right to preserve their own interests. The weaker nations, being deprived of power, are also deprived of the right to preserve their national interests. Hence these nations have no right or opportunity to uphold the morality or ethical principles.

In Hegel's thought and philosophy war had a sublime position. Like many other thinkers he did not view war as a menace to civilisation and annihilator of man and property. Explaining Hegel's position Lancaster observes : "War ennobles the individual by showing him the variety and triviality of everyday preoccupation." Hegel was a great nationalist and a patriot. The concept of state occupied his thought and he believed that only through the state individuals could find the fulfilment of all their ideas and ideals. Hence they must be prepared to make all sorts of sacrifice for the sake of the state. Naturally the individuals must be enthused or inspired for the cause of the state and in this situation war is the most potent means. The war can also ensure the loyalty of citizens to the state.

The above analysis of Hegel's theory of state establishes the fact that he had no confidence on or respect for the famous social contract theory of state. It is the product of dialectical process or evolution. It may also be called the evolutionary theory of state and, in this sense, Hegel comes nearer to Aristotle. Of course, he has philosophised the theory of state in an abstruse way not comprehensible to common people. Hegel has said that just as it is impossible to subsume marriage under the concept of contract so it is equally far from the truth to ground the nature of the state on the contractual relation whether the state is supposed to be a contract of all with all or of all with monarch or the government. The state is the "actualization of Reason", it is the mind objectified. It is the product of long evolution and this evolution passes through several stages dialectically. "The real is rational and the rational is real." The rationality is realised in the state.

Totalitarian Features of Hegel's State

We have discussed the central idea and salient features of Hegel's theory of state. Time is now ripe to point out the totalitarian features of his theory of state. It is to be mentioned here that not all critics share the view that Hegel's state contains the totalitarian elements. First we shall see to what extent Hegel's state can be called totalitarian. Next we shall place the counter-arguments.

Karl Popper in his celebrated work *Open Society and Its Enemies* (Vol. II) passes the following remark (p. 62) : "Nearly all the more important ideas of modern totalitarianism are directly inherited from Hegel, who collected and preserved what A. Zimmern calls the armoury of weapons for authoritarian movements. Although most of these weapons were not forged by Hegel himself, but discovered by him in the various ancient war treasuries of the perennial revolt against freedom, it is undoubtedly his effort which rediscovered them and placed them in the hands of his modern followers."

(i) The modern totalitarian doctrine of state says that the state as such is not the highest end. It views the state from different perspective. This is the Blood, the Race, the People. The higher Races or Peoples possess power and subjugate the rest of the state. Hegel's Spirit can be substituted for Blood. Hegelian state is totalitarian. Its might must permeate and control the whole life of the people in all its functions. "The state is the basis and centre of all the concrete elements in the life of a people : of Art, Law, Morals, Religion and Science. The substance that exists in the concrete reality which is the state, is the Spirit of the people itself." Hegel further comments, "Nations are what their deeds are. A nation is moral, virtuous, vigorous, as long as it is engaged in realising its grand objects."

We, therefore, see that *Hegel developed the historical and totalitarian theory of nationalism.* A nation is all in all, it is supreme. All individuals are subordinate to it. His theory of nationalism has also psychological bearing. He speaks of German nationalism. Germany was superior to all other nations. Particularly he had a feeling of contempt for England. This narrow nationalism was followed by many of his adherents.

(ii) Hegel had justified and glorified war on another ground. He said that apparently there was good or cordial relation among the states. But this is not the real picture. The states are enemies with each another and there is a struggle for power and position among the states. Particularly the big states are involved in this struggle. This problem, Hegel held, could be solved only by war. He said : "War is not only a practical necessity, it is also a theoretical necessity, an exigency of logic. The concept of the state implies the concept of war, for the essence of the state is *Power.* The *State* is the *People* organised in sovereign *Power.*" This *glorification of war is to be found only in totalitarian states.* Mutual good relationship or friendship and peaceful coexistence are not generally to be found in the lexicography followed by the adherents of totalitarianism.

(iii) Hegelain state is characterised by another feature. Without any ambiguity Hegel declared that the state is above all types of law and morality because it is the embodiment of morality and the state is itself a law and creator of law. Many other totalitarian thinkers treated state and law in the same line. Naturally the state should not be bound by law and morality. Karl Popper observes (p. 66)—"Its only judge is the History of the world. The only possible standard of judgement upon the state is the world historical *success* of its actions. And this success, the power and expansion of the state, must overrule all other considerations in the private life of the citizens; right is what serves the might of the state. This is the theory of Plato, it is the theory of modern totalitarianism; and it is the theory of Hegel : it is the Platonic Prussian morality."

"The state is the realisation of the ethical Idea. It is the ethical Spirit as revealed, self-conscious and substantial will." The violation of treaty or agreement is quite immaterial. He says that, if this violation ensures the success of the nation or enhances the power, then violation of treaty is not immoral. Success counts much. A state cannot surrender to any other will or decision of another state.

Plamenatz does not agree with the view that Hegel was the believer or propagator of totalitarian state. In his view—"This is an ambiguous and misleading charge. The word totalitarian is not to be found in Hegel's writings; his varied and peculiar vocabulary does not include this particular epithet, which belongs to our century" (*Man and Society*—II, p. 262). What Plamenatz wants to say is that his emphasis on state, compulsory membership of state and several other views about it cannot be treated as yardstick of totalitarianism, or it cannot be said that he was a great supporter of totalitarianism. He viewed the state from a particular standpoint and in the background of special circumstances. He wanted to see his Germany a powerful, developed and self-sufficient state. This mentality inspired him to draw the picture of state in this way.

Hegel has said that the individual must obey the established laws and conventions of the state when the state is at its highest stage of development. This obedience to the laws and conventions of the state does not indicate that he will not have any freedom to criticise those laws and conventions. He can both obey and criticise. If we interpret the opinion of Hegel in this light there is no harm or illogicality.

His view on war is not completely illogical or irrelevant. He defended war as a preventive of slackness and corruption and of checking domestic slackness. Even today, in the second decade of the 21st century, we find the validity of Hegel's argument of war. Many states use it as a technique of checking people's unrest resulting from maladministration and inefficiency.

The state which Hegel described in his *Philosophy of Right* and the actual Prussian state are both undemocratic. The state in which Hegelian freedom is realised fully is not democratic. We can say Hegel had no faith in democracy. Hegel was not a great votary of democracy and this has been interpreted that he was a totalitarian. Since he was undemocratic or illiberal he was definitely totalitarian. But this oversimplification is unjustified. A man is undemocratic—is not to say that he is totalitarian. His argument against democracy was based on the belief that in a democracy the majority party controls the government and party government means the government of a faction of population. We may not share his views. But we cannot blame him as a totalitarian.

Although Plamenatz does not accept that Hegel was believer of totalitarianism, he admits (p. 264) that he made excessive claims for the state which have supplied fuel for the arguments in favour of totalitarianism. "It cannot be denied that he makes extravagant and false claims for the state. It may be that man is rational, moral and free only as a member of society, but it is not true that he is so only as a citizen—a member of the state." There are family, civil society and various other ethical or religious organisations which mould the conduct and guide the activities of the individual. It is not true that he does not know it. What we can say about Hegel is that, for one reason or another, he had excessive sympathy for the state.

It is commonly argued that Hegel was the official philosopher of German government and the godfather of Hitler. Hitler quickly accepted the Hegelian doctrine of absolutist state and applied it in toto. It cannot be denied that there is a similarity between Hegel's approach to state and Hitler's Fascist state. But this similarity must not lead us to conclude that Hitler was influenced by Hegel. There were scores of undemocratic theories and Hitler might have been influenced by them. Modern historians are of opinion that the then social, economic and political situation of Germany and the international situation influenced Hitler.

It may be that Hegel, in mind or feeling, was not totalitarian. We have already noted that special circumstances that prevailed in his time encouraged him to depict the picture of state in this way. Again, if we look at the Western political thought we shall find that apart from Hegel many idealist philosophers had soft corner for totalitarianism. In Plato's political ideas there are many elements of totalitarianism. Rousseau is also not an exception. Almost all the totalitarian thinkers always give priority to whole and not to parts. The position of society or state is much higher than that of the individual. They believed that all-round progress of individuals is possible only through the general progress of bodypolitic. The most serious charge against Hegel—so far as his idea of state is concerned—is that he has glorified war and the state is the actor of war. Today we despise war from the core of our hearts. We are making numerous efforts both at national and international levels to stop war or to discourage any efforts of making war. His weakness for totalitarianism cannot be severely criticised. But we cannot forgive him for holding a brief for war. War is the most dangerous and vicious enemy of human civilisation and even for the mere existence of mankind. We do not know why did Hegel fail to understand the devastating consequences of war.

Theory of Government

Hegel's theory of government is to be understood only in the background of his philosophy, particularly his theory of dialectic. He has said, "what is rational is actual and what is actual is rational." The state and the government both are actual. Their existence cannot be denied. So they are rational. If the state were not the highest embodiment of rationality or ethical Idea it could not have reached that stage at all. The state is the actuality of the ethical Idea. The state is not only absolutely rational but also the actuality of the substantial will which it possesses in the particular self-consciousness. The state is *Whole* and it is *Real*. "The state is organism, that is development of the idea to its distinction."

In every fully developed state, which is an *organic whole*, there is a government. Since the state is the synthesis, that is, the contradictions are resolved in it, the government also takes the character of the state. If the state is rational and real the government is also bound to be rational and real. It is also the manifestation of Reason. It guards the universal will and prevents the particular will from its encroachment upon the universal will.

The organism, according to Hegel's logic, is the constitution consisting of distinct powers so correlated as to sustain and strengthen the unity of the whole. The constitution, as Hegel conceives, is the complex of habits and responses produced by generations of living together under the same social and political institutions. These habits and responses are grounded in reason.[1] Hegel says, "The constitution of any given nation depends in general on the character and development of self-consciousness. The constitution is unity of explicit differences, i.e., of individuality,

1. Lancaster—*Masters of Political Thought*, Vol. III, p. 53.

particularity and universality, i.e., of the crown, the executive and the legislature. Since these form a concrete unity, each of them has reflected into the characteristics of the other two".

In his *Philosophy of Right* Hegel writes "The state as a political entity is thus cleft into three substantive divisions : (a) the power to determine and establish the universal—the legislature, (b) the power to subsume single cases and spheres of particularity under the universal—the executive, (c) the power of subjectivity, as the will with the power of ultimate decision—the crown. In the crown the different powers are bound into an individual unity which is thus at once the apex and basis of the whole, i.e., constitutional monarchy". We can form certain conclusions from this classification : (1) He was in favour of monarchical form of government and the interpreters of his political thought say that this monarchy is constitutional. (2) Among all the divisions—the legislature holds the most important position that is it is the most vital organ of government. (3) He did not suggest separation of powers. This is probably due to the fact that he had no interest in the liberty of individuals. Montesquieu prescribed separation of powers as key to individual freedom. Hegel had no intention to follow Montesquieu. (4) So far as the classification of government is concerned, it may be observed here, there is hardly any seriousness. (5) This type of classification is Hegel's own.

The legislative power is vested in the Assemblies of Estates. We call it legislature. Hegel finds no ground in support of the universal adult franchise, because people do not know or cannot fully realise the public interest. So popular assemblies comprising the representatives have no place in the Hegelian system. The Estates has two houses—one composed of landowners entitled as of right to be called. The other house is a functional body. This bicameral legislature reminds us of the composition of the British Parliament. One is House of Lords and the other is House of Commons.

Assemblies of Estates are *whole* and the real reflection of the state or government. It is a *unity* and a perfection. The obedience of the citizens is to the Assemblies of Estates and not to the civil societies or associations since they represent only the particular or partial interests. These "partial associations" stand between the individuals and the state. Hegel does not assign specific and elaborate function to Estates. He makes certain sporadic remarks. He says that the legislature will act as an advisory body to the executive or bureaucracy. It cannot act as a check upon the bureaucracy.

We now come to Hegel's second organ of government—the executive. To Hegel the executive was the most important organ of government and in this regard he differs from many other political thinkers. It consists of the civil servants. According to Hegel, the civil service is the universal class which is the synthesis of two subordinate classes—farmers' class and manufacturers' class. The former is called substantial and the latter is called reflecting class. The farmers' class is characterised by family life where particular interest predominates. The manufacturers' class is aware of public interest and gives priority to universality. In Hegel's view there is, thus, a contradiction between farmers' class and manufacturers' class and this contradiction or difference is a logical necessity and not a matter of accident or convenience.

Hegel's belief is that the civil servants have deeper and more comprehensive insight into the nature of state's organisation administration and requirements. They are also well acquainted with the necessities and administration of the government. The members of the civil service are educated and possess greater skill. So they should be entrusted with the responsibility of the state. The function of the legislature is to advise the civil servants. The proposals of laws are to be made by the civil servants. Since the outlook of the civil servants is universal and they aim at general interest, the purpose of the state would be better served by them.

Hegel's special interest in civil service is really interesting. This is probably due to the fact that in Germany the civil service was well-organised and played crucial role in administrations. The famous German scholar Max Weber (1864–1920) took a lot of interest in civil service system and he is treated by many as the first man to throw enough light on it. It is held by many that the civil service system in Germany was of high quality. The civil service system of Germany which was an autocratic state was the backbone of state administration and Hegel was aware of it.

Concept of Sovereignty

It is difficult to formulate a clear concept of sovereignty from Hegel's huge works. Even he does not feel it necessary to deal with this matter in a categorical way. Some discussion is available in his *Philosophy of History* and *Philosophy of Right*. But the analysis is far from being systematic. In his division of power we have seen that there is an organ called crown or monarchy. Planenatz (*Man and Society*, Vol. II, p. 255) explains Hegel's theory of sovereignty in the following way. In his classification of government there is a branch which is called monarchy and sovereignty resides in monarchy. It means that sovereignty hold is the power to utter the last word on any issue or matter. Both legislature and executive are the two other branches of government but so far as the ultimate power is concerned monarchy is above two other branches. The monarchy is not only the authority to utter the last word, he is the reconciler and restorer of harmony. Hegel has depicted the picture of sovereignty in this way. But it is far from satisfactory.

Hegel's view that sovereign power is vested in monarchy does not give us a full picture of the subject. Rather it is partial. Why? He has argued that the state is indeed the sovereign, because in the state Reason, Idea, Spirit and Freedom are represented. Or, the state is the manifestation of the *Weltgeist* or World Spirit. So outside the state there cannot be any freedom or morality. If such is the nature of state it is quite obvious that it should be the symbol of sovereignty.

The state sovereignty requires a personification and that is to be found in monarchy. Granting that sovereignty in conception may properly be said to be an attribute of the state as a whole, be contends that sovereignty in reality and in action consists in the final decisive indication of an individual will. If the state be sovereign, yet an expression of the sovereign will must necessarily involve in the last analysis a determination by some person (Dunning, p. 162).

The Hegelian conception of sovereignty resembles the British system. Many critics blame him as an advocate or believer of totalitarianism. But they will be frustrated to see that he did not recommend unfettered prerogative powers for the sovereign authority. To him it was simply one of the formal organs of the government. He argued, however, that the acts of the state are the acts of ministers who are responsible, whereas the personal majesty of the monarchy is above all answerabilit for acts of government. Even the sovereignty of the state is not such as to deny the rule of law under ordinary circumstances.

Explaining the Hegelian theory of sovereignty Maxey says (op. cit., p. 498) that it proceeds directly from his exaltation of state as the external manifestation of ultimate consciousness and will. His theory of sovereignty is not the outcome of contract, it is the necessary unity of state itself. Moreover, Hegel's sovereignty is *absolute and indivisible.* In his judgment people are formless and not fully conscious. So they cannot have power to exercise sovereign authority. Hegel thus rules out the possibility of popular sovereignty. By doing this he makes his philosophical analysis more consistent.

Theory of Freedom

The contemporary social, political and economic situation of Germany was one of the chief sources of political thought of Hegel. Germany was ravaged by corruption in all levels of society, chaos, indiscipline, provincialism and groupism. Integrity of the nation was at stake. But Hegel, we know, was the staunchest supporter of nationalism and national state. The unity of Germany received highest priority in his analysis. The prevailing contemporary situation of Germany inspired him to form the opinion that individualism stands on the way of attaining and perpetuating national integration. People must first of all show unconditional allegiance to the authority. The general interest of the state must come first and must be protected at any cost. Individualism was to him another name of provincialism and particularism. Parochialism and groupism had no place in his philosophy. So he did not intend to give the individual's private interest prime importance.

Hegel, according to Sabine, also identified individualism with Jacobinism, violence, terrorism, fanaticism and atheism of the French Revolution. Moreover, his assessment of the individual was very low. The individual is merely capricious, an animal governed by brute instinct with no rule of action higher than his own impulses, appetites and inclinations with no rule of thought higher than his own fancies. Analysing the background of Hegel's theory of freedom J. S. Mcclelland makes the following observation : "Perhaps the best approach to Hegel on freedom is to regard the theory of freedom as a philosophical commentary on the epoch of the French Revolution and its aftermath, particularly in Germany. Before 1789, Germany was little more than a geographical expression. There were over three hundred German states, duchies, free towns, seigneuries. The effect of French Revolution was to rationalise the German state system. Hegel was enthusiastic about the French Revolution" (p. 533). The reorganisation and restoration of units of Germany were of prime importance to him.

The importance of the individual is due to the fact that he is a member of society and also an integral part of it. The attainment of freedom and development of personality are possible only through the membership of the state. Modern civilisation is embodied only in the national state. Not only civilisation, Protestant Christianity, Absolute Idea and Reason are also embodied in it. Outside the national state the worth of the individual will not be recognised. Most important of all is—individual will find his freedom only in the national state. It reconciles authority of the state with the freedom of the individual. Hegel himself says : "The essence of the modern state is that the universal be bound up with the complete freedom of its members with private well-being." Hence, from Hegel's analysis, we conclude that freedom of individual and the state cannot be separated from each other. He says : "The state is the actuality of concrete freedom. But concrete freedom consists in this, that personal individuality and its particular interests not only achieve their complete development and gain explicit recognition for their right, but, for one thing, they also pass over of their own accord into the interest of the universal, and for another thing they know and will the universal. They even recognised it as their own substantive mind; they take it as their end and aim and are active in its pursuit."

Hegel has elaborately analysed his favourite concept—the state is the actualisation of freedom. Freedom of the individual is not an abstract choice, but only the willing of what is rational, of what the Spirit or Reason or Idea would desire and what the state intends. So the individual can have freedom only through his membership of state and obedience to it. Why will the individual obey the state? The state is represented by the absolute Idea. It is his real will to the dictates of the state. What the state dictates that is his real will. The state cannot dictate anything wrong or unjustified. The state has the right to command and the individual must obey those and in this process he will find the fullest freedom.

The individual may obey the state still for other reasons. Hegel rules out the existence of freedom in the case where the individual obeys the order of state out of fear. When the citizen will obey the dictates of state out of his own accord and when he thinks that the will of the state is real will, and it is also his will, then, and then only, he will have the opportunity to enjoy freedom. He will subject his will to the will of the state. The citizen will be fully convinced that what the state demands he also desires the same thing. The simple implication is that the individual will identify himself in all respects with the state. This is the essence of freedom. Hegel observes that the state is the form of reality in which the individual has and enjoys his freedom provided he recognises, believes in and will what is common to the whole. We now conclude that freedom for Hegel consists in obedience and this obedience must be voluntary.

Barker, doyen of political science, has compared the freedom theory of Hegel with that of Kant. Kant, according to Barker, interpreted freedom as the right to will a self-imposed imperative of duty, and he insisted that every man, possessing by his virtue of his reason such a will, existed and ought to be treated, always as an end in himself and never as merely a means. In the opinion of Hegel such a concept of freedom is negative, because it wears the face of duty. Again, Kant's freedom is limited, because he treats every man as an isolated unit. But, according to Hegel, every man is part of the whole and he cannot enjoy liberty or freedom in isolation. Third objection against Kant's theory of freedom is it is subjective, because it resides in the inner world of intention and conscience and does not find a free issue outward into objective life.

According to Barker, Hegel's freedom is *positive,* it is *expansive* and it is *objective.* Hegel's freedom does not mean absence of restraints. Since it is positive its aim is to develop the self of the individual. Man shows utmost obedience to state simply for the realisation of his self. It is expansion : it consists in the will to make my outward self adequate to the measure of the fullness of my thinking self. Hegel's freedom is outwardly expressed, so it is objective. Finally, another feature of Hegelian freedom may be mentioned. It is *creative,* because is expresses itself through law, through the rules of inward morality, and through the institutions.

Hegelian freedom is a social phenomenon. Kant compared the doctrine of freedom with individualism. Hegel removed that apparel and placed it in the midst of the vortex of society. The individual will enjoy liberty or freedom, but he will do it in cooperation with others. So it is absolutely *a social phenomenon.* This is the observation of Sabine. In his own words "Freedom must be understood as a social phenomenon, a property of the social system which arises through the moral development of the community..... Freedom consists rather in the adjustment of inclination and individual capacity to the performance of socially significant work" (p. 655). Freedom cannot be supported if the will or desire of the individual is not made to adjust with the general good supported by the general will. *Hegel's freedom is thus not an end, it is a means to an end and the end is public good.*

There is a very important reason why Hegel makes freedom a social phenomenon. We have earlier mentioned that unintelligent and uneducated man cannot enjoy freedom fully. Only educated and intelligent man can realise that all his desires will never be fulfilled, some will remain unrealised, and he must accept it. That is, the individual must have the mentality to make sacrifices whenever required. If anybody thinks that freedom means the ability to satisfy desires, then that will indicate an immaturity of thought.

Hegel was not a liberal philosopher and, therefore, in his philosophy there is no place of liberal concept of freedom. *Freedom is not the absence of restraints. Rather, limitations and constraints are imposed upon the impulses and desires of individual so that he can adjust with the rest of the society.* He must learn the techniqe or method of adjusting the private interests with the common good of the society. This is an essential precondition of freedom. He never treated freedom as the opportunity to pursue one's own interests exclusive of others. Man's real and substantive freedom as distinct from mere formal freedom consists in submitting it and identifying himself with the higher rationality of the state. This submission must be voluntary. Hegel has always emphasised that the individual is an inseparable part of the whole and his overall progress is to be achieved through his membership of the whole body. He is not separate from the whole. Commenting on this aspect Sabine says : "Hegel characteristically equated individual choice with caprice, sentimentality or fanaticism" (p. 656). It is now clear that Hegel does not consider man's freedom as an essential element. To claim freedom or to be away from the rest of the society is sheer madness. In his judgment an individual is completely merged with the state and by state he meant a unified reorganised state. The man cannot have any existence outside the state.

Submission to the state means submission to the law of the state, because the will of the state is expressed through the law. The law is made to actualise the general interests of the society. The law of the state can never be wrong or unjustified on the ground that Reason or Absolute Idea or *Weltgeist* (World Spirit) is embodied in the state. Hegel's individual is completely at one with the state. Though Hegel speaks of voluntary submission to state's laws, he apprehends that compulsion might be necessary and that is immaterial.

Individual and the State

In order to have a clear understanding of Hegel's attitude we are to remember that liberalism or liberal philosophy had no place in his thought system. In Britain and France there developed a liberal tradition and people were well acquainted with it. Naturally there was strong urge of general public for rights and freedom. But Germany was an exception. There were autocratic rulers whose first act was to suppress freedom of individuals. Hegel's acquaintance with this political atmosphere made him more or less anti-liberal or anti-individual. But he was not at all an enemy of individuals. In his view the state was first and after the state the position of individual.

The Industrial Revolution of England and French Revolution necessitated a *laissez-faire* doctrine which was another name of economic individualism. So the people of these two countries for several reasons were able to build up strong liberalism in both political and economic spheres. But the tradition of Germany was of different nature. Sabine comments (p. 648), "There had been and there continued to be little in the politics of Germany that could give to the idea of individual rights a hold upon the political consciousness of Germany as such. As a theory the philosophy of natural rights was of course fully known to Germans but it remained for them in a sense esoteric and academic".

The objective of life is the realisation of freedom and that objective can be achieved through individual's identification with the state. Hegel's state is an ethical whole and a march of God on earth. In order to reach the stage of the World Spirit the state is the only medium. In his account there is no contradiction between the individual and the state. Interpreting this concept of Hegel, Harmon observes (p. 35) : "As the state is necessary to be march of the World Spirit and is a means to that end, so the individual is a means to the end of the state which serves that purpose." Harmon further says that all men to Hegel are instruments but the ability of all men is not equal. Some men are more wise and able than others.

The individual is completely merged in the state and naturally there is no scope of demanding separate identity. This identification is indispensable for realisation of freedom. The liberalism went on emphasising the distinction between liberty of individual and authority of the state. Rousseau, by propounding the doctrine of general will, made an attempt to obliterate this distinction and ultimately he forged a reconciliation between the two. Hegel consciously or unconsciously followed the path of Rousseau. The difference between the two would, Hegel believed, invite anarchy. Rousseau said that individuals would be forced to be free. On the other hand, we are told of the identification of man with the idea of state in Hegel's theory.

Hegel refused to be one with those who supported the French Revolution on the ground that it vindicated the absolute individualism and advocated enmity between individual and state. It was thought by the revolutionaries that state was an evil and an anathema to individual liberty. So it was necessary to impose restrictions upon the authority of state so that liberty could expand. In Hegelian philosophy there is no place of abstract individualism. Sabine writes, "The fundamental error in its policy was its attempt to erect paper constitutions and political procedures on the assumptions of individualism" (p. 651).

Hegel's conception of the relationship between individual and state emerged from the fact that individualism could destroy the unity of state. He also believed that the individualism could ultimately become insuperable hindrance on the way of the realisation of Reason or *Weltgeist* through dialectic process and this was the most favourite doctrine of the German idealist. The disunity of the Italian state and also internecine warfare among the different parts disturbed his mind. Machiavelli also could not support individual freedom. To him there was not the question of individual versus state, it was the state alone which could be the final determiner of everything within its boundary. So both Machiavelli and Hegel thought almost in the same line so far as the relation between individual and state is concerned.

From our foregoing account it may appear to us that Hegel wanted to transform the individual into the slave of the state. But according to many critics this allegation against Hegel is devoid of any solid foundation. To Hegel, like many other idealist and absolutist thinkers, *freedom was a social affair and people could enjoy it only in collaboration with others.* Freedom can never be unilateral. Liberty in the modern state is never unconditional or unregulated. It is always regulated and the regulations are imposed by the state in the name of public interest. Needless to say that Hegel argued in the same line. So if the authority of the modern state can restrict liberty for common good and if we cannot blame it why should we blame Hegel? Harmon has said (p. 352) that Hegel's conception of individual and state relation has been wrongly interpreted and by doing this critics have done injustice to him. He thought of individuals' welfare from a quite different standpoint. Mill's society consisted of unrelated individuals each pursuing their own interests. Hegel's society was composed of individuals who constituted a complete whole and all were organically connected with each other. Identification of individuals with the state does not mean that the state is a dictator or autocrat. Hegel had no intention to award dictatorial power to the state.

We believe that Harmon's assessment of Hegel's idea about the relationship between state and individual is right. His only fault (if it is to be treated as fault) is that he thought that the general progress of Germany could be achieved through the machinery of a powerful state. Both Britain and France reached the goal of considerable development in industrial and commercial sectors and through this development individuals' rights, liberty and other things got the opportunity of adequate progress. Germany was deprived of this situation. For that reason Hegel has been found to give priority or maximum importance to the interest of the state. This does not mean that he vehemently opposed to individuals' cause. He believed that progress of individual could be achieved through the progress of the state. This view cannot be treated as wrong or anti-individual.

An Appraisal

There are three great pillars of German idealism. They are Kant, Fichte and Hegel. But the most important and widely read of them are Hegel. Hegel is both criticised and praised all over. But his number of critics has far surpassed the number of admirers. It is also said that the number of persons who actually understand his philosophy can easily be counted. It is because his philosophy is complex. Even those who praise his philosophy do not accept his worship of war and its idealisation as well as his overlordship of state. In this connection we can remember the observation of Durant : "The old philosopher denounced the radicals and dreamers, and carefully hid away his early essays. He allied himself with Prussian Government, blessed it as the latest expression of the Absolute and basked in the sun of its academic favours. His enemies called him the official philosopher" (Durant, p. 298).

Schopenhauer was a great admirer of Kant. He also knew Hegel. But his estimate about Hegel was not of high quality. He said, "Hegel, installed, from above by the powers that be, as the certified great philosopher, was a flat headed, insipid, nauseating, illiterate charlatan, who reached the pinnacle of audacity in scribbling together and dishing up the craziest mystifying nonsense. This nonsense has been noisily proclaimed as immortal wisdom by mercenary followers and readily accepted as such by all fools, who thus joined into a perfect chorus of admiration."

Hegel claimed that he had revised the law of contradiction and had substituted for it, in the dialectic, a new and fruitful logic. But this claim, Wayper thinks, is unconvincing. His dialectic is not a new form of logic. Long before Hegel the dialectic was discovered and fruitfully applied by Greek philosophers. One of the central concepts of Hegelianism is contradiction. He discovered contradiction and from that tension in everything and, on the basis of that, he made numerous propositions. We admit that there are oppositions in many things but those oppositions need not necessarily lead to contradiction or tension. The various oppositions can be expressed in non-contradictory statements. This aspect has been emphasised by many and it is a pity that Hegel overlooked it.

The dialectic is a wonderful instrument. Manifold social and political phenomena can be interpreted with the help of dialectic and on the basis of dialectic we can arrive at certain reasonable as well as acceptable conclusions. Dialectic also helps us to acquire mastery over the different stages of social and political development. That is, we come to know of their nature. But Hegel used this instrument in order to make the state or nation-state all-powerful. The German state, he declared, was the embodiment of Reason or World Spirit or, in his own words *Weltgeist*. Even according to Hegel, the German state is the manifestation of highest civilisation, morality, freedom and nationalism or nationalist feeling. This worship of the state is absolutely unacceptable. Wayper comments, "We may very well doubt the value of a method of analysis which enables Hegel to worship the state as God and Marx to damn it as the Devil" (p. 172). In the hands of the Greek philosophers the dialectic was used for the analysis of academic issues and it had earned undiluted praise. But Hegel used it to make the German state omnipotent.

Hegel's conception of freedom is not also above criticism. Freedom lies in the identification of the individual with the World Spirit embodied in the state. Hegel, by announcing this, denied the separate status to the individual. Barker calls Hegelian freedom positive, creative etc. From the standpoint of philosophy both Hegel and Barker are right. But to us it is still a mystery. How an individual will come to enjoy freedom by completely identifying himself with the state? How will he be able to get freedom by sacrificing his individuality at the later of all-embracing-Leviathan-like state? We do not deny the importance of obedience, but absolute and unconditional obedience can never constitute the foundation of freedom. Although Hegel does not deny the right to criticise the government, in his philosophy there is no such scope. Whom will he criticise? What will he criticise? The answers to all these questions are not available from the political philosophy of Hegel.

The concept of God has created a lot of enthusiasm from the dawn of civilisation. It is simultaneously a controversial concept. Notwithstanding, the idea of God is live in the mind of everyone. But the tragedy is this controversial and even physically non-existent idea constitutes the central part of Hegel's philosophy. From the study of Hegel we come to know that God is an earthly matter and everyone can get access to it. He has unsuccessfully mixed the unreal idea with a real idea—the state. This is the greatest part of the weakness of his philosophy. Furthermore. Hegel's argument for absolute sovereignty both in national and international sphere, if implemented, will create a great damage to the survival of mankind and growth of civilisation. "The Juggernaut" writes Wayper "passing in triumph over the crushed bodies of its devotees, has become an offence to civilized consciences, and the Deity incarnate in sovereign states which are strongly attached to the practice of mutual throat-cutting and who can therefore only advance through the suicide as it were of different forms of itself, is not a Deity which can command our respect" (p. 172).

Another serious allegation against Hegel is his utterances that the state, individuals, their rights and privileges are absolutely undemocratic. He vehemently opposed people's participation in the law-making process. He had great doubt about the consciousness and ability of persons. To allow all persons to participate in the affairs of the state is irrational. He was the forerunner of corporate organisation of modern fascist state by his emphasis that the individual should be politically articulate only as a member of the social group or class. According to Hegel, individual as an isolated ordinary citizen had no recognition. He did not think that isolated individuals should have any importance. Hitler and Mussolini thought in the same line.

Speaking of the sovereignty of the people Hegel said, "So opposed to the sovereignty of the monarch, the sovereignty of the people is one of the confused notions based on the wild idea of the people. Taken without its monarch and the articulation of the whole which is the indispensable and direct concomitant of monarchy, the people is a formless mass and no longer a state." The democratic doctrine that people are the state is rejected by Hegel as a "perversity" and "rule".

Indirectly, Hegel was the believer in anarchism. How? He wanted to build up a strong state. But if all states were strong that would lead to anarchy in the international arena. All would try to exert power by virtue of sovereign authority. In support of this view we may quote Ebenstein—"Hegel advocates the strong state—on the model of the Prussian police state of the nineteenth century. Yet when it comes to the question of how states are to live together, Hegel is an enthusiastic anarchist. In fact, he is nihilistic enough to deny relations between states have anything is common with morality such as regulates conduct between individuals" (p. 593).

"Though garbed in high-sounding philosophical term, Hegel's political theory contains all essential elements of fascism, racialism, nationalism, the leadership principle, the government by authority rather than consent, and above all, the idolisation of power as the supreme test of human values" (Ebenstein, p. 595). It is definitely not the question whether he believed in totalitarianism. But the mere fact is that his various arguments clearly state that he had sufficient weakness for an all powerful or omnipotent state and he believed that such a state could solve all the deep-rooted problems which plagued the German state from various directions. It is not important what was in his mind, it is more important what he has written.

So far we have criticised Hegel. But something can be said in his favour. Sehopenhauer, who released a vitriolic tirade against Hegel, even admits the importance and worth of this giant philosopher. He has said that Hegel exerted tremendous influence on German literature. His logic and argument stupefied Germans. Even the highly educated Germans could not avoid his influence. Many have thought to combat his influence, but unfortunately none has come forward. Nobody thinks in a constructive way how to challenge the philosophy of Hegel.

The two most important ideologies of the twentieth century is communism, or, according to many, totalitarianism and fascism. Hegel is regarded as the father of these two antagonistic ideologies. The basis of the materialistic interpretation of history is dialectic and Hegel is the modern interpreter of the dialectic method. Marx, it is true, freed dialectic from the clutches of Idea or *Weltgeist*, but the principle of dialectic remains the same. Marx has acknowledged his indebtedness to Hegel. From historical materialism comes communism. Hence Hegel's dialectic, Marx's dialectic and communism—all are tied with the same rope. Thesis, antithesis and synthesis of Hegel are not basically different from those of Marx. Hegel borrowed the concept of dialectic from the Greek philosophy and applied it in the analysis of state, civil society etc. He also explained civilisation and other concepts with the help of dialectic. The central part of Hegelian dialectic is contradiction. It is interesting that Marx borrowed both dialectic and contradiction from Hegel and applied it to the interpretation of progress of society and not to the progress of Idea or Spirit.

There are also other aspects to Marx's indebtedness to Hegel. R. S. Peters, in his article *Hegel and the Nation State*, makes the following observation "Hegel's conception of nations as dominant expressions of what he called the self-developing self-consciousness of the world mind, was transformed by Marx into the conception of social classes fulfilling a historic mission. And just as Hegel thought that individual's interests and ideals were identical with those of this state, that there could be no morality between states, and that states would be at war with each other, so Marx thought that the individual's interests and ideals were those of his class, that there could be no morality between classes....and that class war is inevitable, the dynamic of social change" (*Political Ideas*, p. 140). The influence of Hegel upon Marx is really tremendous and such an influence of one philosopher upon another is seldom found. In his *Thesis on Feurbach* Marx has said that philosophers have interpreted the society and history but the point is how to change it. That is, the main concern of Marx was to change the society and also the nature of history. We hold the view that both Hegel and Marx have done it. Hegel has interpreted the nature of history and civilisation through the glasses of Idea or Reason and he has done it with the help of the instrument of dialectic. Marx proceeds to recommend the technique of social change. In both cases, R. S. Peters says, clarity and truth have been sacrificed.

Assessing Hegel's political philosophy, Maxey observes that his views and methodology have deeply affected the social sciences. His rejection of social contract theory has opened a new gate of world-thought. Social and political institutions including bodypolitic are not the creation of a particular contract, that is, they are not artificial, but they are a natural growth. The contract theory dominated the political thought of Europe for several centuries. Hegel's rejection of social contract theory as the origin of state has created a new horizon in the realm of political science and partially other branches of social science. It is now believed that society has evolved and the evolution has brought society to the present stage. The credit for this should go to Hegel.

Both liberals and conservatives received inspiration from Hegel. The emergence of *laissez-faire* doctrine after the Industrial Revolution was a landmark. It assiduously advocated for non-intervention of the state in the economic activities of the individuals. But when the fruits of industrialisation were grabbed by a microscopic faction of society and growing disparity went to the point of intoleration a number of men pondered over how to save the society from the evil consequences of industrialisation. At that crucial moment Hegelian theory of state appeared as a great saviour. He attributed a new role to the state—as a plausible basis for programmes of reforms. He thought that the state must do something positive for general welfare. Hegel's concept of nationalism was interpreted by conservatives as economic nationalism. Many have interpreted his nationalism as parochial. But it can be pointed out with certainty that his nationalism was not meant for Germany alone. We may not agree with his philosophy of theory of state and conception of freedom but we must admit that he was a great patriot.

There is no shadow of doubt that the Oxford Idealist philosophers T. H. Green, Bradley and Bosanquet were in one way or other influenced by Hegel. Sabine maintains "Hegelianism was an important factor in the revision of English liberalism by Oxford idealists" (p. 667). English liberalism of the earlier period could not meet the demands of the post-industrial society of England. A new liberalism was needed and it was combined with idealism. A major part of Hegel's idealism was absorbed into Oxford idealism. Absorption of Hegelianism into idealism gave it a new philosophy. Green gave the leadership of the revision of liberalism. Green observed that the utilitarians reduced the state to the status of social events. But the industrial society of Britain wanted that the state should play a more positive and constructive role. We do not want an all embracing nature and power of state. But at the same time the state should not be a helpless spectator in the face of numerous social, political and economic issues and problems. It has something to do and idealism has said this.

Hegel was a philosopher of extraordinary mind and intelligence. Schopenhauer's estimation that he was an illiterate is absolutely baseless. Sabine observes that his mind had an extraordinary breadth of grasp. He was mainly a philosopher, but he had clear conceptions of different branches of knowledge. He knew history and he had a good command over literature. In Hegel was united the 'common good' concept of Rousseau and tradition and religious vision of Burke.

Conclusion

In the form of conclusion few more words may be said. Berki has said (p. 179) that Hegel's thought "represents one of the biggest watersheds in the entire intellectual tradition." His "giant shadow over our horizon after 150 years." There is an "immence influence" of Hegel's thought on modern political thought. Berki further observes that liberalism through the views of Green, Bernard Bosanquet and some others "has absorbed into itself a large does of Hegelianism." Even Marxian socialism is heavily indebted to Hegelianism.

Hegel glorified the state. But what we see in the present day is nothing but Hegelian concept. The Industrial Revolution of Britain made the state powerful and she established colonies throughout the world particularly in Asia and Africa. The United States is the most powerful state in the present world system. There is a glorification of state in the present day world system though in different form. But that is immaterial. The Cold War or conflict between USA and erstwhile Soviet Union centred around the idea of all-powerful state. So what is the wrong with Hegel? Many critics say that Hegel was the Godfather of Hitler. But this estimation is unjustified. If there were no Hegel, Hitler could have been a great dictator. Hitler used Hegelian theory of state in order to subterfuge his real motive.

The first decade of the twentyfirst century has just passed and in this era we find the revival of Hegel's glorification of state and war. In the second half of the twentieth century there was bipolarism—the division of the world into two power blocks. After the fall of Soviet Union the world came to witness the domination of a single superpower and it has come to be called "unipolarism." Here again there is the overwhelming preponderance of a single state—USA. This particular state is controlling the military and financial affairs of the world. Most of the states of the world are—in one way or other—subservient to USA. Politicaly they are sovereign. But in the strictest sense of the term they are incapable to taking independent political and economic decisions. The small and weak states of the globe are dependent on USA. Literally, none is glorifying USA. But everyone hesitates to call a spade a spade. USA declares war and after that it justifies its action. We blame Hegel, but are we blaming USA for its declaration of war against Iran? Hegel did not denounce war. Bernard Shaw, the top ranking member of Fabian Society, hesitated to denounce war. Why should Hegel alone be blamed?

STATE AND INDIVIDUAL IN GERMAN IDEALISM

Introduction

Our foregoing analysis has depicted various aspects of political philosophy of three German philosophers—Kant, Fichte and Hegel. It is needless to say that state and individual constitute the very core of Western political thought. Various manifestations of state such as sovereignty, society, relationship between state and individual, rights of individual, individual's obligation to state subsequently emerge to occupy important place of analysis. But the state and individual always remain at the top place. We study Plato for his idealist view of state and concept of justice. Aristotle followed the footsteps of Plato, but he made remarkable deviations in some respects from his teacher. We, however, study him for his views, inter alia, on classification of constitution, origin of state and political idealism. We thus see that state always remains a central theme. Contractualist Rousseau borrowed a major part of his philosophy from Plato and after that he built up the fabric of his political thought independently.

The German idealists based their philosophical thought in the background of Greek philosophy and the philosophy of Rousseau. Naturally state and individual will occupy a major part of their philosophy. But the treatment of state and individual in the writings of Kant, Fichte and Hegel is not uniform, Still these different treatments constitute as a whole the German idealism. It is, therefore, required that a comparative analysis is to be made.

Kant on State and Individual

Being influenced by Rousseau's political thought Kant came to the conclusion that the state was the product of contract. And in other respects practically there is no difference between Kant and Rousseau. In order to give freedom its full realisation Kant, following Rousseau, observed that a civil society through the machinery of contract was formed. The civil society or, as it is called, state, was a moral organisation to both Kant and Rousseau. But to Kant it was more than that. This was also a legal organisation.

Rousseau talked about a different type of sovereignty better known as popular sovereignty. The functioning and image of Greek city-states were quite alive in his mental world. And since he was the great lover of human freedom he built up the fabric of general will which will ensure popular sovereignty and individual's liberty. Kant followed Rousseau and accepted his general will. Many other concepts of Rousseau also influenced Kant.

We find a great amount of influence of the prevailing condition of Germany or Prussia upon Kant's idea on state. Germany was ruled by absolute monarchy and Kant was not in favour of such type of government though he did not come forward with a denouncement of absolutism. Perhaps he believed that absolutism was not in consonance with people's liberty and rights.

Kant, however, was in search of a reconciliation between the prevailing monarchical structure and Rousseau's general will. The sovereign power will exercise its authority through the general will and in this way Kant effected the compromise between people's sovereignty and Prussian monarchical system. But we think that Kant's solution is not a practical one. There is hardly any scope of peaceful co-existence between monarchy—which is absolute in character—and general will's authority.

Kant could not support the imperialist and expansionist designs of state because he believed that the "standing armies excite states to outrival one another in the number of their armed men, which has no limit" (Quoted by Will Durant, p. 284). Kant wanted peace and hated militarism. He witnessed how military expansion destroyed the natural political, social and ethical situation of both home and abroad. His love for freedom led him to support a republican form of government and constitution. This view of Kant establishes the fact that he wanted a good relationship between the state and the individual. He did not recognise the state's right to declare war. If war were to be declared at all it should be based on plebiscite. Hence people's will is the ultimate determiner of state affairs. Kant had not the courage to declare openly the imperialist motives and functions of the German state. But if we read his mind and thought we shall find that he was against all sorts of military preparations and imperialist motives. He wanted peace for the survival and progress of mankind.

Kant's acceptance of Rousseau's general will once again makes us to believe that individual and his will are never to be neglected and that freedom must be given, in all cases, priority. He never thought that the relationship between the individual and the state is not of the master and slave relationship. Though state is a legal organisation its duty is to create an atmosphere in which individual can develop his morality. Both Rousseau and Kant viewed politics, individual and other related ideas from the standpoint of morality and ethics. Man performs his duties not for the maximisation of utility or happiness but for the attainment of morality and ethics. He cannot sacrifice morality and ethics for the sake of happiness or material gain. Particularly, Rousseau emphasised on morality and ethics.

Fichte on State and Individual

Like Kant, Fichte was not very much interested in the origin of state. But he thought and said something about the state and along with it about individual and his freedom. He wrote two books on politics—*Closed Commercial State* and *Theory of the State* and from these two books it is evident that he was in favour of national state which must have sufficient power encompassing almost all the aspects of individual life. The interpreters of Fichte's philosophy draw conclusion from this that his ideas practically laid the foundation of a fascist state. Also Hegel drew inspiration from Fichte's conception of state, because both thought of a powerful national state.

Why did Fichte support a national state? His contemporary Germany was not economically self-sufficient. Industrial progress was quite unsatisfactory—such could never be the true state of a national state. He wanted to introduce the idea of exclusiveness into the concept of national state and for that purpose he vehemently opposed free trade. He was of opinion that a free trade leads to commercial and economic rivalry among the states creating an atmosphere of war. Sometimes a real war is the cause of keen competition among the states.

The idea of exclusiveness indicates that a state should always make efforts to achieve self-reliance in economic sphere and for that purpose it should produce all commodities which it requires. Dependence of a state upon others is likely to weaken a state. Fichte's argument behind such conception was to make Germany self-dependent and powerful. Once he said that some states have their natural boundaries such as river, mountain etc. and these make the states national states. He also believed that national states must have political self-reliance which means that it must be capable of making its own political and other regulations.

Summarising Fichte's ideas about state Maxey makes the following observation : "In his mature political writings Fichte argued that the principal function of the state is to make individuals free by establishing in the outward world the conditions necessary to further identification with the universal. This meant that it was the rightful business of the state not only to remove obstacles which might stand in the way of this communication but to compel people to follow proper courses of action to that end" (op. cit., p. 492).

Fichte believed that the individuals could realise their freedom and other goals only through the state. The state was an end in itself. Without state the individuals had no opportunity to achieve their objectives. For this reason Fichte argued for the identification of the individual with the state; and the state was again identified with the universal.

In such a state the individuals cannot have separate status and importance. They have been advised by the state to sacrifice to the state for the development of personality. This view of Fichte resembles that of Greek idealist philosophy. His exaltation of state has reduced the individuals to a very insignificant position. In other words, in Fichte's political philosophy, the term individualism has no place. The state is all-powerful and the individuals must display their unconditional obedience to it.

What has been said above is the reflection of Fichte's maturity of thought in respect of philosophy and politics. But in his earlier days he showed special interest in individual's rights and duties. He thinks about contract for the realisation of certain rights. The idea of natural rights has no place in his thought system. Through the contract people will be entitled to some rights such as right to property. There may be contract among the people. Under such contract each individual will agree to protect the rights of others. This gesture of people is associated with the consciousness which they possess. Without consciousness people cannot make such sort of contract. Nobody can violate the contract in his own sweet will.

Rational consciousness constitutes a basic aspect of Fichte's theory of rights of individuals and their relationship with the state. Because the individuals are in possession of rational self-consciousness they cannot ignore the interests and requirements of other persons of the society.

One very interesting aspect of Fichte's views regarding state, individual, their relationship, possession of rights, realisation of those rights etc. is that he wanted to bring all these under one umbrella. State, individual, rights and their realisation—all these are not separate from each other. They constitute a complete or undivided whole and this is the national state. Fichte also thought of a reconciliation between individual rights and the rights of other persons. For this purpose he envisaged of a contract the mention of which has been made earlier. Only through a contract a compromise will be made between private will and general will. For this idea Fichte is indebted to Rousseau.

Though in his later writings Fichte wanted to make a state powerful, in his earlier works he made ample scope for individual volition. Following Rousseau he said that people assembling in a common place would decide the political and other issues which is an indication of the fact that people are the source of sovereign power. Behind the law of the state there shall be the consent of individual. So Fichte did not deny individual freedom. According to Fichte, rational consciousness enables man to think of others, as well as to think about the national interests. This is the source of patriotism. Thus Fichte places every person at the centre of political and other activities.

State and Individual in Hegel's Thought

We know that Hegel had no sympathy for liberalism or liberal political philosophy which was highly prevalent in Britain and some other parts of western Europe. In Germany the liberal tradition did not develop. For that very reason he did not keep any special place for individual's rights and privileges. He did not consider that rights were essential for the adequate development of man's personality. To him state and individual are not two distinct entities between which there was a Chinese wall. Rather, the individual must unconditionally surrender to the authority of the state because only through it could he find his progress in freedom.

According to liberal thinkers rights, freedom etc. are personal and the role of the state is negative. It is in the sense that the duty of the state ends in hindering the hindrances to the attainment of freedom. On the other hand, according to Hegel, rights and freedom are social in character and these can be achieved through the legal protection adopted and ensured by the state and, in that sense, the state is never an enemy of individual freedom. Hegel did not support the liberal concepts of Locke and many other liberal thinkers. His belief was that liberalism had the only objective and that was to curb the power and authority of state. Since he was not brought up in a liberal tradition he had no sympathy for liberalism. On the contrary, his firm belief was that growth of liberalism would lead to dwarf the function of state. This will ultimately stand on the way of all sorts of progress. This idea he built up in the background of economic backwardness of Germany.

Kant developed a weakness for Rousseau's philosophy—particularly general will. But at the same time he could not embrace liberal political philosophy. The concept of German national state in an embryonic form occupied place in his mind.

But in ultimate analysis he has been found to effect a reconciliation between general will and monarchical form of government. Whether in practice it is possible or not that not our concern. The point is, Kant could not ignore the concept of a national state. Fichte, in his later year, voted for the national state. Kant could not view the idea of national state from broader perspective which Fichte did. He was of opinion that the self-reliance of state (in his opinion of Germany) in economic and political spheres could strengthen the foundation of a national state. Fichte rejected competition among the states on commercial interests and also war. But Hegel glorified war.

All the three German philosophers—Kant, Fichte and Hegel had discussed the idea of national state. But Hegel's analysis on the subject is comprehensive. He has discussed it from the wider perspective. Here lies his credit. In earlier life Hegel showed his sympathy for the French Revolution. But in the later years he revised his earlier views. The destructive and violent aspects of the Revolution forced him to reject the previous ideas. Hegel's main interest was national state and then its various aspects such as integrity, unity, construction, progress. He believed that war had the potentialities of halting the advance of civilisation and to him the national state (and in his case the German national state) was the greatest manifestation of highest civilisation. Kant and Fichte did not spend so much time and energy as well as space for a comprehensive analysis of national state.

Kant said that general will or people was the source of sovereignty. This is Rousseau's view. General will is the source of all power and authority. Hegel differed from Kant. Sovereignty in Hegel's state vested in the monarchy. Monarchy, according to Hegel, is the symbol of unity and integrity and it is the ultimate decision-making authority. People's will has no place. We may call Kant's sovereign power as popular while it is absolute in the case of Hegel. Hegel has personified sovereign power with the state and in this way Hegelian state is totalitarian. When the state is so, people's special status is neglected.

Kant's acceptance of the separation of powers is an indication of the limitation of state power and proliferation of individual's liberty. Hegel had no business to deal with special attention the liberty of persons. According to Hegel, individual will find the proper flourishing of liberty or freedom through the ultimate authority of state since it is the manifestation of Absolute Idea or World Spirit. Hegel has called the limiting of the state power for the realisation of man's freedom as negative. Man is an insignificant part of the national state and he cannot claim separateness. Separation from state will lead to the destruction of freedom. Kant believes that freedom is the right to will a self-imposed imperative of duty. But this approach of Kant has been termed by Hegel as negative and he calls his own approach to freedom as positive.

The concept of national state has assumed clear position in the hands of Hegel because in such a state there is a clear location of sovereignty—is an essential ingredient of state. Kant was influenced by Rousseau and by emphasising general will he has clouded the concept of national state.

21 ENGLISH IDEALISM

Source of English Idealism

Any analysis of idealism or idealist philosophy will remain incomplete without proper and elaborate mention of English idealism or what is also called Oxford idealism. The English idealists drew their inspiration from German idealists. But German idealists were not the single source. A. D. Lindsay in his Introduction to T. H. Green's The *Principles of Political Obligations* makes the following remark : "Green and his fellow idealists represent the renewed liberalism of the last quarter of the nineteenth century. They were all of them, for all their Platonism and Hegelianism, in the succession of utilitarians. They were all fundamentally individualists and democrats. But they were convinced that utilitarianism had become barren as a political creed because of the inadequate philosophy upon which it was based" (p. VII). Marcuse, an important member of Critical Theory group, says : The British movement was still connected with the principles and philosophy of liberalism and for this very reason lay much closer to the spirit of Hegel than did the Italian" (*Reason and Revolution*, p. 390). So it can be maintained that Oxford or English Idealism had several sources—Platonism, German Idealism, Utilitarianism and, above all, British liberal tradition of democracy and parliamentary system of government.

The persons who were influenced by Hegel's idealism were Thomas Hill Green, Bosanquet, and D. G. Ritchie. Bosanquet's famous work *Philosophical Theory of the State* was published in 1899. D. G. Ritchie, who came under the influence of Hegel's idealism, wrote *Darwinism and Politics, Principles of State Interference, Darwin and Hegel,* and *Natural Rights.* All these were published between 1889 and 1895. The most important idealist philosopher was T. H. Green. His famous book is *Lectures on the Principles of Political Obligations.* The Lectures were delivered by Green in 1879 and were published in 1882 after his death. A. D. Lindsay writes "They represent the most important contribution to political theory of the school of thought sometimes known as the "Oxford Idealists.[1] Edward Card, William Wallace and Arnold Toynbee were also members of the school."

We have already seen that Kant and Hegel did not attach too much importance to the representative institutions of England. They were accustomed to the authori-

1. *Introduction to Political Obligation*, p. VII.

tarianism of Germany and saw the disunity and constant fight among the various independent units of German states. Liberal tradition had no scope to develop in Germany. Even Hegel castigated the representative institutions of England. People of that country could not test the freedom which was to be realised by monarchy and on this ground he branded England as the most backward country of Europe (Barker, p. 21).[1] Kant also believed that the representatives had no scope to work independently, because they had to depend on the ministers. This was the academic situation on the eve of the emergence of Oxford idealism.

Barker writes (p. 21), "Some modification of the theories of Kant and Hegel is thus obviously needed to make the idealist theory of the continent square with the representative institutions of England and to adjust a theory which emphasises the majesty of the state to a practice which emphasises the liberty of the subject." The ongoing economic, political and other situations of Britain influenced the Oxford idealists to think about society in a new way. They thought that the attitude towards the activities, role etc. of the state required to be amended or might be made suitable for the changed situation. In the post-Industrial Revolution period the British society was in the grip of crises and problems relating to social, economic, and political matters. The authority of a state cannot play the role of a helpless onlooker and leave everything to fate or God. This can never be the duty of a responsible government. It must exercise power to arrest the crises in order to free the citizens from problems. But, at the same time, the democratic institutions which took centuries to assume proper shape must be given adequate importance and place. In other words, the English idealists felt the need for a reconciliation between the authority of state and democratic values and principles.

Green and other Oxford idealists were convinced that a new political philosophy must be found out in order to tackle the situation arising out of the Industrial Revolution. The sixties and seventies of the nineteenth century saw the heyday of Utilitarianism. The only important member of the Benthamite school was J. S. Mill. The size of the school was very small, but its impact was very great. In fact, utilitarian philosophy dominated the English academic and political world for a considerable period of time. But it took no time for the Oxford idealists to discover the barrenness of the philosophy. Utilitarianism had reduced the individual to a bundle of pleasures and pains. The state, to the utilitarian thinkers, was simply a collection of independent individuals. One individual was completely indifferent to the weals and woes of another person. This philosophy of utilitarian thinkers was inadequate. No further progress could be made in such an understanding of politics.

We have so far discussed how Hegel's idealism and Benthamite utilitarianism influenced Oxford idealists to evolve a new political philosophy. But this is not the end of the matter. Carlyle's influence on them can be remembered here. It is said that Carlyle was a bitter critic of the creed of "each for himself and the devil take the hindmost." The growing misery of the poor disturbed their mind and they pondered over finding out a solution. That is why the Oxford idealists leaned to Carlyle's thought. In a great society, an individual cannot remain alone. He cannot make himself busy with his own affairs. The social problems must be treated as a whole. In society each man is not up to himself. This philosophy of Carlyle led the Oxford idealists to think in terms of a new philosophy. But they did not share

1. *Political Thought.*

Carlyle's aristocratic ideas and anti-democrat leanings. It is due to this fact that the Oxford idealists were democrats and individualists.

They felt that a new start had to be made and a proper conception of human nature and action acquired before an adequate political theory could be constructed. That is why none of them were concerned only with political theory. Their politics were to be the outcome of a view of human nature and of the world—of moral philosophy and of metaphysics (A. D. Lindsay).

We again turn to utilitarianism to trace the origin of Oxford idealism. The utilitarian thinkers wanted to make politics a science of achieving happiness and pleasure and avoiding pain. Simultaneously they thought that the individuals had sufficient reason and intelligence to know what is pain and what is meant by pleasure and how to achieve them. The generalisation about human nature as well as ability had no scientific basis. It was a sheer imagination of the utilitarians. The impractical and unfounded assessment of human nature made the thought system of utilitarians unsuitable for the post-Industrial Revolution British society. They did not think about numerous common men. On the contrary, the idealists woke up for the common people. The fruits of democracy and the benefits of social wealth must be made available for the poorest of the poor. So the attitude of Green and other fellow idealists differed fundamentally from that of the utilitarians.

In the 1870s and 1880s there was a change in public opinion. Legislation, in Dicey's phrase, was passing from an individualist to a collectivist trend. The state was no longer confining itself to securing the free play of competition and vindicating freedom of contract, but was addressing itself to the more positive function. Public opinions already awakened and it demanded alertness of the state. The Oxford idealists echoed the sentiment of the mass of men. They abandoned their academic recluse. They roamed in the dark and narrow lanes of London City and mixed with the denizens of those lanes and by-lanes. This enabled them to be acquainted with the economic and other conditions of those hapless men. Particularly T. H. Green did this. They were idealists, wanted to idealise politics. But they were also realists. They, through serious efforts, came to be acquainted with the down to earth condition. The Oxford idealists were humanists and, at the same time realists. This differentiates them from German idealists and utilitarians.

A few more words may be added to clear the nature of Oxford or English idealism. Herbert Marcuse (*Reason and Revolution*, p. 393) points out that mention has sometimes been made that the development of British idealism from Green to Bosanquet was one in which the liberal philosophy of earlier epoch was abandoned. Of course the abandonment took place very slowly. So far as the terms and words of British idealism are concerned it is purely Hegelian. But if we consider the spirit or inner meaning of Hegel's idealism we shall find that the Oxford idealism is far removed from it. There are several points of departure. Bradley's metaphysics, notwithstanding its Hegelian concepts, has a strong irrationality that is alien to Hegel.

"From its beginning the renaissance of idealism showed a definite anti-materialist tendency, a quality it shares with the tendencies accompanying the transition from liberalism to authoritarianism. The ideology accompanying this movement prepared the individual for more labour and less enjoyment, a slogan of the authoritarian economy. Gratification of individual wants had to give way before duties to the whole" (Marcuse, p. 394). Bosanquet has said that an imperative is imposed upon us by the concept of social good. Liberty of the individual can be realised only through the obedience to that imperative. Thus, Oxford idealism is a combination of new liberalism and authoritarianism. What the Oxford or English idealists have emphasised is that man no doubt seeks pleasure and tries to avoid pain. But his is not the only feature of human character. Many people have feelings for other and try to do something for them. They follow an ideal and try to implement it. They do not always achieve success but they do not always abandon the ideal. We may call Oxford idealism as realist idealism. It is an idealism that thinks about ordinary men and renewed role of state. From this has emerged the concept of welfare state.

T. H. GREEN (1836–1882)

Green : Life and Source of Political Thought

Thomas Hill Green was born at Birkin in the West Riding of Yorkshire in 1836. His father was an Anglican parson and was a well-known personality in the Church of England. Young Green was educated at home and in 1855, at the age of nineteen, he was sent to Balliol College, Oxford, and there he spent the rest of his life. During his days at Balliol College, Green could not establish himself as a preeminent scholar. However, he could not confine himself only within the studies of subjects. He exhibited his varied interests.

He was elected a Fellow of the Balliol College in 1860 and continued in tutorial capacity until 1878. In that year he was appointed the Whyte Professor of Moral Philosophy. At Oxford he taught several subjects, such as ethics, history of philosophy, metaphysics, logic etc. In Balliol College he established himself as a successful teacher. His popularity spread wide.

Green was also interested in public affairs. He joined the Liberal Party and participated in its campaign. In fact, his participation in public and political affairs brought about dramatic changes in his academic and public life. He was member of the Oxford Town Council and School Board. Green was stricken with blood poisoning and died in March 1882 at the age of forty six. His important works include *Prolegomena to Ethics* and *Lectures on the Principles of Political Obligations*.

His membership of the Oxford Town Council and participation in the public affairs of London created lot of interest in his mind on the growing problems of the day. He urged upon the state to regulate the liquor traffic. His membership of the Town Council brought for him the opportunity to travel the narrow and dark lanes and by-lanes of London city and he observed the mode of life of the people living in the unhygienic conditions of slums. He also observed from a very close distance the impact of industrialisation upon land cultivation.

When T. H. Green was writing his books on philosophy and politics, the Industrial Revolution crossed the mark of century and its effects—both good and bad—upon all aspects of life became prominent. Green, a piquant observer of social problems, began to think of them. As a close observer, Green saw the injustice, both moral and economic, which prevailed in his time. He also discovered a relationship between moral injustice and economic injustice. Economic misery led people to be involved in immoral activities.

In *Political Obligations* he says : "To an Athenian slave, who might be used to gratify a master's lust, it would have been a mockery to speak of the state as a realisation of freedom; and perhaps it would not be much less so to speak of it as such to an untaught and underfed denizen of a London yard" (p. 8).

According to Green, abject poverty is the root cause of moral degradation. So, for the self-development of the poverty-stricken people, what is first of all required is the removal of poverty. He did not speak too much for economic equality. This term to him was vague. What he saw was poverty and what he felt was its removal. He further believed that the end of the liberal society was an essential precondition for achieving such a goal. He did not prescribe three different chambers for economics, politics, and ethics or morality. He believed that fight against poverty can make men moral and this fight can only be launched by the political authority of the state.

Green and other fellow idealists drew inspiration from the study of Greek classics. The idealist thoughts of Plato and Aristotle created a tremendous impact on the mind and ideas of the Oxford idealists. The *Republic* of Plato and *Ethics* of Aristotle were parts of the main texts of Oxford University. Students, generation after generation, acquainted themselves with the ideas contained in these two classic books. Man, by nature, is a political animal and he is also a member of the political community, state is a partnership of life in virtue, law is always the manifestation of reason—all these utterances instilled faith in the mind of students studying at Oxford. Green and other members of his school were not exception. Once Gilbert Murray said : "If you take English political thought and action from Pitt and Fox onwards, it seems to me that you will always find present....strands of feeling which are due—of course among many other causes—to this germination of Greek influence; an unquestioning respect for freedom of life and thought, a mistrust of passion. ....a sure consciousness that the poor are the fellow citizens of the rich, and that statesmen must as matter of fact consider the welfare of the whole state."[1] To sum up, the political idealism of Plato and Aristotle dominated the English political thought for several centuries and the members of the Oxford idealist school could not avoid that influence.

Mention of the influence of Hegel on Green must also be made. The philosophical theory of state elaborated by Green and Bosanquet was first expounded by Hegel and other German idealists. Green said that Hegel's account of freedom as realised in the state does not correrspond to the actual facts of society. But in spite of this the state has certain amount of responsibility and it performs that in realising the freedom. The state does not always directly do it, its various agencies perform the duty on its behalf. Again, Green's state, like Hegel's, is a community of communities. Like Hegel, he concludes that the state is supreme over all other communities. Both Hegel and Green have held the view that individuals derive their rights only as members of state, and they have no right against it. The state of both Hegel and Green differes from all other associations within it.

Wayper has drawn our attention to other aspects of how Green was influenced by Hegel. Like Hegel, Green believed in the existence of Divine Spirit or Reason or Idea. He borrowed from Hegel the idea that the Divine Spirit was constantly pushing forward to its goal (p. 175). There is an interesting similarily between Hegel

1. Quoted by Barker in *Political Thought*, p. 16.

and Green so far as the concept of freedom is concerned. Both viewed it from the standpoint of idealism and morality. Good, moral and ethical persons have the right to claim freedom. But in general sense a member of body politic can claim freedom. Hegel and Green thought if an individual performs moral and ethical duties he can claim freedom. Both of them had a belief that state has a duty to protect freedom.

Green was profoundly influenced by Rousseau. In his *Political Obligation* he has said (p. 90), "It does not follow...that there is no truth in the conception of the state or sovereign as representing a general will, and as authorised or entitled to obedience on that account. It is this conception, as the permanently valuable thing in Rousseau." Green further points out that Rousseau's conception of the sovereignty of general will holds good only in small cantons of Switzerland. Even where it works the private interests work in the name of general will. But this loophole can be removed by dividing the sovereignty into *de jure* and *de facto*. Green also agrees with Rousseau that pure disinterestedness prevails in the society. Every citizen acts with the intention of safeguarding common interests or objects. Always he gives priority to common good.

Theory of Freedom

What T. H. Green really thought about freedom can best be explained in his own words and for that reason I quote a lengthy passage from his book : "We shall probably all agree that freedom, rightly understood, is the greatest of all blessings, that its attainment is the true and of all our efforts as citizens. But when we thus speak of freedom, we should carefully consider what we mean by it. We do not mean merely freedom from restraint or compulsion. We do not mean merely freedom to do as we like irrespectively of what it is that we like. We do not mean a freedom that can be enjoyed by one man or one set of men at the cost of a loss of freedom to others. When we speak of freedom as something to be so highly prized, we mean a positive power or capacity of doing or enjoying something with doing or enjoying and that too; something that we do or enjoy in common with others. We mean by it a power which man exercises through the help or security given him by his fellow-men and which he in turn helps to secure for them."

A close scrutiny of the above passage reveals certain characteristics of freedom and these are stated below. In the first place, Green's concept of freedom is not negative. He says freedom does not consist in the absence of restraint or compulsion. It is not the unlimited freedom of one and no freedom or very little or another. Green does not accept the situation where the freedom of one depends upon the activities or enjoyment of freedom of others. In his theory, everybody will have the opportunity to enjoy freedom. Green was in favour of state intervention in the realisation of freedom and he stated it clearly. Barker maintains, "The one thing the state must not do is to check its self-determination, either by repressive interference or by paternal government; the one thing the state must do is to liberate its energies by removing the obstacles to their action."

Green's theory of liberty, secondly, is a positive thing. It is a positive power of doing or enjoying something *worth doing or enjoying*. Individuals will enjoy freedom in cooperation with other fellow-citizens. Whenever a man demands freedom and after getting it proceeds to enjoy it, he must consider that other people can claim the same thing. So freedom is something which is to be enjoyed in common with others. This public spirit or altruism is vital to freedom. But this spirit or feeling comes when consciousness arises in the mind of people. There is a famous and beautiful observation of Barker : "Human consciousness postulates liberty, liberty involves rights, rights demand the state" (*Political Thought*, p. 23). This famous and oft quoted observation of Barker clearly states that right, liberty and state are all related and interdependent concepts. Without state people cannot have any scope to enjoy liberty and exercise rights.

Man must be conscious of what he should not do. He must also be conscious of the idea of common good or interest. He will enjoy his freedom only in a way that will help the progress of common good. Pursuance of interest at the cost of others' interest is no freedom, *Green's theory of freedom is, therefore, determinate.* Man is permitted to do only those things that will come to the benefit of the whole society, not any part of it. This determinate character makes freedom more idealistic and moral.

Green had a deep feeling for the masses who were untaught and underfed. He was not a socialist, but he was a great humanitarian. The freedom of one influential person or economically dominant class does not indicate the freedom of the whole society. He said : "But we rightly refuse to recognise the highest development of an exceptional individual or exceptional class, as an advance of the true freedom towards man. If the ideal of true freedom is the maximum of power for all members of human society alike to make the best of themselves, we are right in refusing to ascribe the glory of freedom to a state in which the apparent elevation of the few is founded on the degradation of many." Green never recognised the freedom of a particular person or a class means the freedom of all. All the people must have the opportunity to enjoy freedom and from this condition there can arise morality. Again though Green did not talk about the equitable distribution of wealth he was the believer of the idea that proper distribution of wealth among people can ensure freedom. In his book Green has indirectly discussed it.

Green then proceeds to discuss the freedom of contract as a part of his whole concept. He says that the freedom of contract, freedom in all forms of doing what one will with one's own is valuable only as a means to an end. That end constitutes the positive end of freedom. This is the liberation of powers of all men equally for contribution to a common good. No one has a right to do what he will with his own in such a way as to contravene this common good. According to Green, the concept of common good is the supreme guide for all persons. It may also be called the supreme authority. Every individual must conform to the idea of common good. Freedom lies in the obedience to it. Green does not, like Rousseau, say that any recalcitrant individual will be forced to obey the dictum of general will which represents the common good. Green's men are rational and possess public spirit. So the application of coercion under normal circumstances does not arise.

Green does not view freedom in legal perspective. The state has a role no doubt, but this is not legal. This is due to the fact that his freedom is viewed in a positive sense. Pointing out to this aspect Sabine remarks : "Freedom must therefore imply not merely a legal but an actual possibility, in view of existing circumstances, of developing human capacities, a genuinely increased power on the part of individual to share in the goods which a society has produced and an enlarged ability to contribute to the common good" (p. 729).

Theory of Right

Green was concerned not only with freedom of individuals but also with their rights. He understood the close relationship between the two. For the proper development of human personality both freedom and right are essential. Again, he has viewed these two in the light of idealism. When the consciousness of man develops fully, then—and then only—the question of liberty arises. When liberty comes, rights will not remain far away. Then we can roughly conclude following Green that the *development of human consciousness is the foundation of both liberty and rights. But the self must be interpreted in a broader and idealistic perspective.*

The self must know itself. It is the first phase of achieving consciousness. Again, the will of the self must conform to the common interests of society. That is, the will of one will not be at variance with the general will of the society. When these two conditions are fulfilled then it will be assumed that self-consciousness has been achieved. Green's self-consciousness, therefore, means the consciousness of others. The consciousness implies that individual is not alone in the society and, therefore, he has no right to pursue his own good. He has every right to seek his own good. But it is his duty to remember that his goodness depends upon the goodness of others. In this situation every individual claims that other persons in the society must recognise him.

What others will recognise? Green wants to emphasise that no individual, whoever he may be, can unilaterally pursue his own interests. Pursuance of self-interests, according to Green, is the forerunner of anarchical situation. The society is always to be treated as a whole. The implication is that the right and liberty of one individual are dependent upon the right and liberty of another person. The society is a complete whole and the pursuance of exclusive self interest has no place. While a person makes claims he must remember that these claims must not stand on the way of raising and realising claims by other fellow citizens. Barker writes : "Claims thus recognised are translated into rights, and it is such recognition that constitutes them rights."

We have now reached a very important phase of our analysis. Rights have two aspects. One is it is claim and the claim is made by individual guided by self-consciousness. Another aspect is claim must be recognised by the society or state as the case may be. A man can claim certain things and the claims have no conflict with the common good. But if the society does not recognise the claims it will never be translated into reality. So the intervention of the state is important. A man may claim right to work and it is a right. But if the state does not recognise the right, the claim remains unfulfilled or useless. There are many states where right to work is not yet recognised. Its another implication is men can claim rights only as members of society.

The word recognition requires clarification. When Green speaks of recognition he does not mean legal recognition. His rights are not legal but ideal rights. If the citizen does not fulfil moral conditions, if he does not identify his interests with the general interests, then he cannot claim rights. Hence the validity of rights comes from the self-consciousness of the individuals. The duty of the state is to provide safeguards, that is, men will not face any hindrances in enjoying rights. Common moral consciousness recognises rights. Green, by recognition, does not mean legislature or executive. Moral rights need not be legal rights. Barker points out—"The rights are relative to morality in the sense that they are the conditions of the attainment of the moral end; and the recognition is given by the moral consciousness because it is known that they are the necessary conditions of its own satisfaction" (p. 26). An interpretation of Green's theory of rights asserts that he did not treat this concept in the background of legality. According to Green rights, liberty etc. are to be viewed in the light of morality and idealism. Recognition of state also falls in this category.

Green was the professor of Moral Philosophy and he viewed rights from the standpoint of morality, but he never ignored the question of rights in relation to law. He was fully conscious of the relationship between rights and law. *Rights, according to Green, are embodied in law. That is, they are expressed in the form of law. This does not imply that rights are exclusively legal.* In Green's view rights are more moral than legal. But when the question of the enforcement of rights arises the issue of law becomes inevitable. Only the sovereign authority enforces the rights. Barker's cogent remark in this connection is to be remembered : "Rights are enforceable and indeed have to be enforced" (p. 27). Jethro Brown distinguishes three types of rights. Let us put the matter in his own words "Law defines existing legal rights; ethics defines moral rights; politics defines those moral rights which would be legally enforceable if law were what it ought to be." Political rights are, therefore, different from ethical and legal rights.

The rights envisaged by Green may be called natural rights. But the term natural rights has a different connotation in the context of Green's theory. By natural rights we ordinarily mean rights enjoyed by the people in the state of nature and those people were isolated individuals and their self-consciousness did not develop. So rights had no moral meaning to them. Green's rights are the products of self-consciousness. His rights are innate and inherent rights. All people are endowed with moral sense. Hallowell observes "We can speak of such rights as natural only in a sense that they are claims that the state should recognise because there is a common consciousness, that the individual ought to have such rights; they are not natural facts but ideals." From the above analysis we come to the conclusion that in Green's philosophy rights are moral, ethical, and, at the same time, legal. If rights are not enforced they are practically useless and, again, if they are not enforced by legal authority they have hardly any value. He did not recognise natural rights in ordinary sense.

There is another feature of his theory of right—simply stated this is rights are not to be treated as permanent because nothing is perennial. *Common consciousness is central to the conception of rights.* Now, in a dynamic society, this common consciousness changes. And, therefore, rights are subject to change. People claim more and more new rights and if these new rights are backed by common moral consciousness, the state is bound to embody them into laws and these laws are ultimately enforced. In this process of evolution the old rights take leave from society and new rights fill up the vacuum.

We now come to a very important aspect of Green's theory of rights. What is the exact position of state in respect of rights? Position of Green is quite clear. In every society there is a supreme coercive power and this is the characteristic feature of the society. The function of the sovereign as an institution is to protect the rights from invasion either from withing or from without. The state is made a state by the functions which it fulfils in maintaining the rights of its members as a whole, in such a way that none gains at the expense of another. Thus the state, or the sovereign as a characteristic institution of state, does not create rights, but gives fuller reality to rights already existing.[1] Green further observes that the exercise of supreme coercine power is not arbitrary. The sovereignty strictly follows the laws and customs and also unwritten conventions. It is now obvious that Green has not lowered the importance or role of the state in the field of maintaining rights. When Green admits that the state has a positive role in the field of recognition of rights he was not thinking of any arbitrary power of the state. Nor did he think that a state will exercise its powers whimsically. The picture of a responsible state was active in his mind. Simultaneously the citizens are supposed to be moral and conscious. Thus Green's theory of rights in really a multifaceted one.

Theory of State

In our analysis ot the theory of rights we have seen that the state does not create rights, but gives fuller reality to rights already existing. The implication is the chief function of state is to remove the hindrances which stand on the way of implementation or enjoyment of rights. Green felt that any other association could perform the job. But he had doubt about the capacity or eligibility of those associations. Only a society having supreme coercive power can resist the aggression or disturbance from within or without which may intensify the assault upon the rights. The state has the supreme coercive power and it exercises that power whenever necessary. Green says : "It is not a state unless it does so" (p. 138).

The word "state" is the one naturally used for the purpose controlling disturbance and preserving rights. The exact degree to which the process must have been carried before the term "state" can be applied to the people in which it has gone on, cannot be precisely determined, but as a matter of fact we never apply it except in cases where it has gone some way and we are justified in speaking of the state according to its idea as the society in which it is completed. So the state is a definite association with definite purposes.

The concept of state in Green's philosophy has a special and meaningful connotation. He did not treat state in general sense. In Section 134 he says, "A state presupposes other forms of community, with the rights that arise with them, and exists as sustaining securing and completing them. In order to make a state there must have been families of which the members recognised rights in each other." The members of the family recognised rights of each and all those rights aimed at the common good of the family. But the relationships were not confined to small familes. They grew bigger and out of them more and more families were created. Communities or tribes were formed. Relationship between the tribes was established and this was a natural development. Different tribes or communities recognised rights for them. But the definiton, reconciliation and also recognition required a general law. Only the general law can regulate ther conduct of all communities. Particularity was removed by generality, and some sort of enforcement appeared. Green emphatically uses the term general law. He believed that the law of the state must be general in the sense that it is to be applied for all categories of persons. The state must free itself from all types of sectarian behaviour.

1. *Political Obligation*, Section 132.

"When such a general law has been arrived at, regulating the position of members of a family towards each other and the dealings of families or tribes with each other; when it is voluntarily recognised by a community of families or tribes and maintained by a power strong enough at one to enforce it within the community and to defend the integrity of the community against attack from without, then the elementary state has been formed." This is the origin of the state. What factors according to Green contributed to the origin of state? —Rights, law and enforcement of law by a common authority having supreme power. We have already mentioned Barker's famous opinion which states that without consciousness there can never exist liberty. It means that people must ardently desire to have liberty and for this they must be prepared to make all sorts of sacrifice. Again, the real source of rights is liberty. It means that only free people (free in all senses) can demand rights. Rights cannot be automatically implemented. For the enjoyment of rights intervention of the state is indispensable.

What is the position of the state vis-a-vis the individuals? This question we shall discuss later on. For the sake of convenience it may be noted that Green does not fully authorise the individuals to disobey the state. He draws a distinction between natural rights acknowledged by common social consciousness and the rights not acquired in this status. The natural right is the necessary condition of full general welfare of the society. Now if a state makes and enforces any law towards the implementation or preservation of natural right, it is the duty of every citizen to obey that law simply on the ground that interest of the whole cannot be sacrificed for the part only. From the above it now appears that if a right is not based on common consciousness people have the right to disobey a right. So behind every right there shall exist common consciousness.

We now come to another aspect of Green's theory of state. It maintains a good relation with all the groups and associations which exist within its boundary. There may be small and insignificant groups like families or bigger groups aiming at universal brotherhood. The state makes no discrimination. It makes adjustment with them all and creates an atmosphere for their proper development. In the words of Green the state is a society of societies. Although the state represents the highest good, the realisation of this passes through all the groups and tribes. Green's state is not *Leviathan.* It aims at the general welfare and seeks the help of all. The state has not grown in vacuum and does not develop in solitude. It always seeks cooperation of all other associations. He acknowledge the importance of the associations in forming the rudimentary step of social intercourse.

Green had an idea of universal brotherhood in his mind and this leads us to discuss his conception of the relationship among the states. Barker calls Green's concept of universal brotherhood the "most distinctive". It makes clear what he thought about war and the relationship between the states. Every individual of the national society has a right to live. Bitterness or conflict ultimately leads to destruction and in that situation the right to live is violated. All the peoples of all countries of the world have the right to live. This universal right needs universal recognition and without universal brotherhood it is not possible. That is why we find Green emphasising upon universal brotherhood.

While analysing Green's views about state Herbert Marcuse makes the following observation : "The material arena in which the common good has to be realised is not the state as such, but this or that particular state which might perhapes not fulfill the purpose of a true state and therefore have to be swept away and superseded by another. Hence there is no ground for holding that a state is justified in doing whatever its interests seem to require. In contrast to Hegel, Green holds war, even just war, to be a wrong against the individuals' right to life and liberty. In opposition to Hegel's fundamental concept of supreme sovereignty of national state, Green envisages an over-arching organisation of mankind" (p. 392-393). It is now absolutely clear that Green differs from Hegel regarding his stand on state and war. This difference of opinion makes Green an idealist philosopher of a quite different category. Green is an idealist of liberal tradition and Hegel of absolutism.

Green felt that war is not the solution of any problem, rather, it has exceptional ability to aggravate situation. The war situation can be avoided by increasing intercourse between the individuals of different nation-states and by opening new avenues of trade and commerce and, finally, by creating new organisations. As it has been maintained by Green "The more completely the organisation becomes, the more the motives and occasions of international conflict tend to disappear, while the bonds of unity become stronger" (p. 177). The best way to get rid of war is to enhance the scope and possibilities of brotherhood on international level.

Green has also viewed the war from a quite different angle. War cannot be regarded as a right of every state, nor it is an absolute right. Again, it is an attribute of an imperfect state. Some states may resort to war in self-defence, and Green admits that right. That is why he has said that a war may be the relative right of any particular state and to what extent that right is to be exercised depends upon the particular situation. If the states are well-organised and brotherhood is established and fully cultivated all the imperfections and misunderstandings will evaporate. From this it appears that Green had consciously propagated a particular type of liberal philosophy in which there was practically no place of war or animosity among nations or even groups of people. He was always speaking about universal brotherhood or brotherhood at smaller level or range.

Better organisation of state means free scope to the individual. This again means free intercourse between members of one state and those of another and, in particular, more freedom of trade. All restrictions on freedom of wholesale trade are really on special class interests and must disappear with the realisation of that idea of individual right, founded on the capacity of everyman for free contribution to social good which is the true idea of the state.

Though Green viewed the state from an idealistic point of view, his state was never absolute or all-embracing. His state is not an end in itself, it is a means to an end and the end is moral upliftment of all citizens and attainment of common good. The primary duty of the state is to hinder the hindrances to moral development. So the power of the state is limited, but it is not an emaciated state. The utilitarians advocated for a limited state action and by this they meant the state would ensure the attainment of pleasure and avoidance of pain. J. S. Mill advanced a step. The state had nothing to do with the self-regarding activities. Green correlated the development of the nation-state and the development of individuality. He never believed in the sacrifice of the individual at the alter of the state. To Green, to ignore the individual and to give prominence to the state is equivalent to putting the cart before the horse. He said, "To speak of any progress or improvement or development of nation or society or mankind except as relative to some greater worth of person is to use words without meaning." Green did not ignore the cause or interest of the individual. Hegel thought that through the development of nation state the individuals would find the fullest development of freedom and everything related to the cause of individuals. But it is Green who travelled along a different path. Without the proper progress of individuals the progress of state is never possible and the opposite is true. What Green has said is correct in all respects.

There is another salient feature of Green's theory of state. It is both negative and positive. It is negative because the state cannot make man moral. Morality consists in the "disinterested performance of self-imposed duties." The duty of the state is to remove the obstacles. This, according to Wayper (p. 179) is the negative function of the state. But it has also certain positive function. The state must do something for the untaught and underfed denizen of a London yard with gin-shops on the right hand and on the left. It was the duty of the state to see that mental and physical malnutrition were removed. The state must ensure that no man is used for the private gain. Any and every sort of tragic event must be controlled. The state shall create an atmosphere in which everyone will have enough opportunity to contribute to the common good.

In the light of what Green has said about state and its functions he may rightly be called the progenitor of a welfare state. The welfare concept primarily emphasises the material development of all individuals along with the full realisation of liberty. Green adds morality and idealism to the concept of progress. A worshipper of idealism and an advocate of individualism, he believed in the material progress of man. Material progress followed by Industrial Revolution could not solve the basic problems of English society—alleviation of poverty and removal of illiteracy and disease. Green's primary concern was with these. He thought that to spread education among the masses, to check adulteration in foods, to solve land and revenue problems, to enact new law for workers, state intervention was badly needed. He had unending interest in social problems. He delivered lectures on Liberal Legislation and Freedom of Contract.

So long there is illiteracy, poverty, alcoholic habit, ignorance and indiscipline there cannot be morality. But all these evils emanate from the indifferent attitude of the state towards these problems. The state interference, Green believed, did not depend upon any ideology, but upon the practical situation. State's supreme objective is liberation of human capacity for self-determination. It may have certain amount of connection with ideology, but is not the sole determiner of state activity. The implication of this view is that Green, as much as sober realist a a soaring idealist, addressed himself to eliciting and explaining the presuppositions implicit in the contemporary life of the English state (Barker, p. 22).

Although Green supported the intervention of state to augment the welfare of people, he cannot be called a collectivist thinker. He was a liberal and he revised liberalism by idealism. He was all along an individualist. Any encroachment upon the freedom of people was beyond Green's imagination. The central theme of Green's philosophy is proper and full development of individuality. Hence the question of neglecting the individual does not arise at all. Like the utilitarians, Green thought of the limitations upon state action and indeed he strictly defined them.

Right Against State

The theory of political or simply obligation is a very old issue and it has stimulated thoughts and ideas of thinkers in various ages. Green's book *Principles of Political*

Obligations deals with the issue from several standpoints, but the chief of these standpoints are morality and idealism. The people have the right against the state or they can resist a move of law of state if it is found that the state or its law or any approach stands on the way of realisation of idealism or morality and, above all, attainment of common good. He has allotted a special chapter consisting of eleven sections (from 137 to 147) and the title of the chapter is *Has the Citizens Right Against The State?* At the very outset he has raised a question. Since all rights are derived from the sovereign no one can have any right against the sovereign or state. But Green has raised a question. If the consciousness of the individual demands that he should resist the function of the state or its law then what will be the course of action of the individual? Here Green does not confine himself within the legality of the issue. He has discussed the matter from the idealistic and moral point of view. Here is the novelty of Green's theory of Right Against State.

In the opinion of T. H. Green the rights enjoyed by people—although to some extent natural rights—are not so completely, because they are entitled to rights only as members of civil society or state. That is, in Green's conception, people not living in society cannot enjoy rights. The rights are also recognised by human consciousness. When does this occur? His view is that people enjoy rights in conformity with others. They cannot act unsocially. In Green's own words "A right, then, to act unsocially, to act otherwise than as belonging to a society for which such member keeps the exercise of the powers within limits necessary to the like exercise by all other members is a contradiction. To sum up, if the basis of rights is the mutual recognition and if all other persons show obligation to the society, a particular individual's right against the society cannot be granted." Green says, "Right against society as such is an impossibility" (p. 145).

State does not create rights. But that should not be a ground for disobeying the order of state. Rights are derived from social relation and protected by the general law. The state is the complex of those social relations to be regulated and harmonised according to a general law. The state is the harmoniser and regulator of all social interests. Without this harmony and regulation the citizens cannot enjoy rights. He further observes that the citizen cannot have any right against the state in the sense of a right to act otherwise than as a member of some society, the state being for its members the society of societies, society in which all their claims are mutually adjusted.

What does the assertion that he can have no right to act otherwise than as a member of his state amount to? Does it mean that he has no right to disobey the law of the state to which he belongs—whatever the law may be? These and several other questions Green has raised in Section 142. The discussion of Section 100 draws our attention to the concept of common good. It any law of the state comforms to the common good the citizens have no right to disobey that law. The common good must suffer more from resistance to a law or to the ordinance of legal authority, than from the individual's conformity to particular law or ordinance that is bad, until its repeal can be obtained (p. 111). Here Green wants to point out that the citizens must obey the law even if it is bad or harmful, because by disobeying the law they will do more harm to the common good. Common good is social, rights are social, so obedience to law is also social. Hence obeying or disobeying a law depends upon to what extent the law serves the purpose of common good. Green has said that it is the "social duty" of man to conform to the law and by doing this he can fulfil the common good. But the individual must observe that the common good is not really common or defective and in that case he should raise his voice against the common good and, at the same time, against law.

In Sections 100 and 101 he discusses the legal aspects and related issues regarding right against state or the issue of political obligation. The conscious citizen may feel that the prevailing law is defective and the common good has certain loopholes or it may be that the sovereignty is disputed. All these are valid reasons of resisting the authority. But he reminds his readers that the citizens are moral and ideal. At the same time, law-abiding. So he advises his readers that the citizens will obey and protest. It clearly indicates that Green was not in favour of anarchy or revolution. His theory of resistance or withdrawing obligation depends upon the judgments of citizens and their affinity to morality, idealism, assessment of functions and nature of common good. This implies that Green's individuals are reasonable and rational.

The common good or public interest is the supreme motivating force in the society. It guides both the state authority and public in general. Legislature of state cannot enact any law or introduce any policy violating the common good. "A right against the society as such, a right to act without reference to the needs or good of society is an impossibility, since every right depends on some social relations." So we find that in Green's theory of obligation there is hardly anything such as illegal law. Green thinks that law may be illegal, but even then, if that law is helpful for the furtherance of social well-being or common good, it is the duty of individuals to obey that law. He will do more good and justice by obeying the harmful law, than by disobeying it. Of course, he can start a movement for abrogation of that law.

If we analyse Green's view on individual's right against the state we shall find that he has emphasised only two or three points—(a) the state is the harmoniser of public interests, hence he must obey the law. (b) The state's purpose is to protect the common good and so we must obey the order of what it says. Anything against common good is practically an impossibility and finally the right against the state is permitted when its law is contrary to general public interest and, in that case, the individuals must build up a strong public opinion against that policy or law of the state. The individual alone is not entitled to disobey the law. He must gather other fellow citizens in his favour. We should say Green wants to discourage the public to disobey law. He permits the individual to judge the common good and to start a movement. But here is a big lacuna. If the person concerned acts as a representative of a particular economic class and he happens to be an influential man, he, in collaboration with his class, will force the government to abrogate the law. It may be that the repealed law really aims at the common good.

It is unfortunate to note that Green has failed to see the whole idea of resistance to state in its proper perspective. Green feels proud to announce that, in his own country, with representative set-up, an agitation is easy to start. But the actual situation of the British society offers us a quite different picture. It is a class society having an economically dominant class which controls the superstructure as well as the whole system of government. In such a society, the idea of common good is really a misnomer, or, if it is a real concept, the common good means the good of the powerful class. We do not think that Green was not in the know of this but he was helpless.

Theory of Sovereignty

In his analysis of Green's theory of rights Barker says : "Rights are enforceable, and indeed have to be enforced" (p. 27). This short comment opens the gate of state intervention. Rights are to be recognised by the common moral consciousness, but simultaneously it needs the recognition of the state. State recognition does not indicate legal recognition. State authority must come forward to preserve the rights when they will be in peril. This notion leads the conception of rights from the domain of common moral consciousness to the domain of state authority. In ultimate analysis the state will have to put forward its supreme coercive authority, if necessary, for safeguarding the rights.

But Green's theory of sovereignty differs from the Austinian theory of sovereignty. Austin viewed sovereignty completely from legal point, but Green views it from idealistic point. "If the consciousness" writes Barker "creates rights it creates the sovereignty which is the condition of their maintenance" (p. 28). It is not the absolute power of sovereignty nor its legal status that guides the political action. The moving force is spiritual force. Behind the action of sovereign power acts the common moral consciousness. It is to be stated differently. The sovereign power of the state acts or discharges its full power on behalf of the common conviction. Sovereignty simply implements the law. But the laws and rules of the state are the manifestations of the common conviction or conscience. Hence there is hardly any scope on the part of the sovereign power to act arbitrarily. Needless to say, Green leaves no opportunity for that.

Green devotes maximum space to the analysis of the theory of sovereignty. In all, thirtythree sections deal with the idea of sovereignty. According to Green, only Austin provides us with a clear definition of sovereignty. Austin conceived of sovereignty in a determinate person or persons and the essence of sovereignty lies in the political power. On the contrary, the essence of Rousseau's theory of sovereignty is the general will or *'volonte generale'*. This cannot be identified with the will of any determinate person or body of persons. It has no legal implication or, if any, that is minor. In the opinion of Green, Austin's doctrine seems diametrically opposite to one which finds the sovereign in a *volonte generale*.

Neither the opinion of Austin nor that of Rousseau is fully acceptable to Green. He comes to this conclusion. The central idea of Austin's theory of sovereignty is supreme coercive power. On the other hand, general will, in Rousseau's view, is sovereign. There is no place of coercion. Both are partly true. Green admits that coercion is an essential element of sovereignty, but it is not all. In Green's own words "It is not this coercive force that is the important thing about it or that determines the habitual obedience. By raising the bayonet the sovereign cannot always claim obedience from men. To show or not to show obedience is to some extent a psychological matter and emanates from the core of heart. Its course is not always and unilaterally determined by coercion."

Green concludes that the two views—view of Austin and that of Rousseau—are required to be combined if we want to build up a complete picture of the doctrine. "The two views thus seem mutually exclusive, but perhaps it may be by taking each as complementary to the other that we shall gain the truest view of sovereignty as it actually exists. ....the sovereign power should be regarded, not in abstraction as the wielder of coercive force, but in connection with the whole complex of institutions or political society. It is as their sustainer, and thus as the agent of general will, that the sovereign power must be presented to the minds of the people if it is to command the habitual obedience, and obedience will scarcely be habitual unless it is loyal, not forced." Green thus successfully combines the two theories—theory of Austin and theory of Rousseau. The sovereign power must be endowed with coercion. People shall demonstrate habitual obedience. But its foundation shall be the will or consent of the people. If the government and its administration are based on the consent of the people—that is, the general will—they will spontaneously show their allegiance to the authority. So both coercion and consent of general will are required for a complete theory of sovereignty.

The basis of Green's theory of sovereignty is—the will not force is the basis of state. He has always propagated that nothing should be imposed upon the citizens against their will. The implication is behind every application of force there shall lie the consent of individuals. In this way Green has made his theory of sovereignty democratic. But democratic aspect of sovereignty is not all. Once the sovereignty has received people's consent it will exercise coercion. Green has further observed that it is undemocratic to use coercive power without the consent of general public. Here we are of view that so far as the idealistic aspect of his theory is concerned he is perfectly right. But from the practical aspects we conclude that it is impractical. At the time of emergency or during crisis the authority of state exercises sovereign power without considering how much the steps of the state will be acceptable. The national interest is of primary interest, democracy is of less importance. Because of this reason, in the field of theory of sovereignty, Austin is still regarded as the final authority and not Rousseau or Green.

The above reformulation reveals that Green wanted to reform the concept of sovereignty in the background of idealism and morality. It may be called a realistic approach, but in the strictest sense it is not so. Only the coercive power does not always succeed in demanding allegiance from the mass. He was both an idealist and a democrat. Behind the legal sovereignty there is the general will. This is true irrespective of government the state may possess. Green thinks sufficiently highly of the general will. But this is no metaphysical or vague definition of it. He writes of that impalpable congeries of the hopes and fears of people bound together by common interests and sympathy which we call general will. He calls it common consciousness of the common good. Green keeps sufficient scope for the application of force since he knows that actual states do not always conform to ideal principles. If force is completely ruled out, the practical situation may be alarming.

Green and Revision of Idealism

Both J. S. Mill and Herbert Spencer are known to the students of Western political thought as staunchest advocates of individualsm. But Spencer was an orthodox and extremist individualist. His extremist individualism proposed that the management of post, telegraph, health, education, security, welfare and even the mint should be left to the private management. He believed that these services under private management could provide better or efficient services. But J. S. Mill was not an individualist of extreme type. Sabine aptly observes : "Indeed Spencer's theory of the state was very largely a test of functions that the state should at once abandon, since they had been assumed in the first place by some of the innumerable 'sins of legislators' or of functions that will be made unnecessary by the progress of evolution" (p. 724).

Clearly the private interest and the individual's welfare were given the priority by Spencer and, to some extent, J. S. Mill. In their conception the well-being of individuals will lead to the general welfare of the society. But it was found that both Spencer and Mill and all other individualists were basically wrong. They had very little idea about the exact position of human nature. Above all, they calculated common good mathematically. Sum total of all good does not lead to common good. Man is basically egoist and not altruist. Leadership of the state, clear conception of common good and inculcation of public spirit through idealist thought must be the ingredients of political activity. The state cannot make people moral, but it hinders the hindrances.

"Clearly, in certain circumstances the appeal from a less to a more adequate conception of the common good and its requirements might take the form on insisting on greater measure of individual liberty. For human beings cannot develop themselves as persons unless they have scope for the exercise of such liberty. But Green is actually concerned with opposing *laissez-faire* dogmas. He does not advocate curtailment of individual liberty by the state for the sake of such curtailment. Indeed he looks on the social legislation which he approves as a removal of obstacles to liberty, that is, the liberty of all citizens to develop their potentialities as human beings. For example, a law determining the minimum age at which the children can be sent to work removes an obstacle to their receiving education. Private, sectional and class interests, however hard they may mask themselves under an appeal to private liberty, cannot be allowed to stand in the way of creation by state of conditions in which all citizens have the opportunity to develop themselves as human beings and live truly human lives."[1]

The above remark of Copplestone clearly states that Green was a liberal, an individualist and above all a great idealist and his idealism has roots to the real situation. Here lies the credit of Green. He had clear knowledge about the real situation and on its foundation he built up his castle of idealism. This makes him a different idealist. According to Sabine (p. 726) Green accomplished two-fold objectives. One is, he converted liberalism into a movement which dominated Anglo-American philosophy for a full century. On the other hand, after the Industrial Revolution, only the economically dominant class controlled both the base and superstructure (to use Marx's phrase) and this jeopardised the stability and security. Green did these two things. This is the "operative ideal of the movement." It started it journey towards the closing decades of the nineteenth century. Coppleston observes (p. 178) : "His formulation of a theory may be open to some criticism. So it was certainly preferable not only to *laissez-faire* dogmatism but also to attempts to retain this dogmatism in principle while making concessions which were incompatible with it."

The individual is an integral part of the mainstream of society and he enjoys rights and liberty only as its member. But he keeps his own identity although he is a part of it. Green's idealism and even his individualism do not build up any wall between the state and individual. He does not conceive that individual is completely merged in the state. Green has viewed individual from realistic point of view. He desires man's moral development, but he does not think that morality is unrelated to material conditions of society. Abject poverty is largely responsible for moral

1. Coppleston : *A History of Philosophy*, Vol. VIII, p. 177.

degradation. Analysing Green's views Sabine remarks (p. 728) : "Full moral participation in social life was for Green the highest form of self-development and to create the possibility of such participation was the end of liberal society." Sabine has beautifully summarised Green's views on people's participation in the political and other affairs by using the phrase "moral participation." Needless to say that Green has used the word moral in his analysis in broader perspective and not in orthodox sense. Green's men are moral and ideal and they are highly conscious. The conscious and moral participation of such people will undoubtedly heighten the society in all respects.

Moral development is the supreme end of every individual and it is the first and foremost duty of the state to help the individual in this regard. Politics, according to Green, is not an end in itself, it is a means to an end. It shall create social conditions that will make moral upliftment a possibility. The state will see that a man is never used for the attainment of personal gain of another man. We do not know whether Green was an orthodox Christian but he had great respect for the values and principles of Christianity. He argued for the rise and moral development of all. He had support for Aristotle's idealism, but he did not accept the weakness of Aristotle for the privileged class. Opportunities, Green thought, should be made available to all classes of men.

Interpreters of Green's political philosophy are of the opinion that his lecture on "Liberal Legislation and Freedom of Contract" is a great symbol of his revised idealism. He admits that employer and employee or tenant and landlord all have equal freedom to finalise a contract. But Green out of his practical experience has observed that this freedom is not positive. Freedom is not simply legal, it is moral and positive. It must aim at the development of human capacities. The exercise of freedom must contribute to the common good. But the freedom of contract does not serve this purpose. Parties to the contract are in unequal position. The terms of the contract place the powerful or dominant party in favourable position. *The contract ultimately makes way for greater oppression. It makes no contribution to the general well-being of the society. Such contract can never be encouraged.*

Green was an idealist and he had great respect for ideology. But none can blame that he was an orthodox thinker. He had no sympathy for inflexibility. The society always changes and the authority must formulate policies to accommodate all the changes. This attitude makes him liberal. But simultaneously his love for idealism and morality remains unaffected. This is the most important aspect of Green's philosophy. It has been pointed out by Sabine (p. 730) "Liberal policies have to be flexible to meet changes of circumstances and if they are genuinely liberal they have always to follow the guidance of moral purposes." Green speaks of what should be the standard of legislation. He does not accept Bentham's dictum that maximisation of pleasure should be the *leit-motif* of every legislation. On the contrary, his view is that the moral development of general well-being shall be the standard of legislation.

Green has revised earlier liberalism with the help of his new concept of law. To an orthodox individualist every law was harmful. Bentham treated law as an instrument of maximising pleasure and any contrariety to it was not acceptable to him. Green consents to neither of these views. Green says : "A law is not good because it enforces natural rights, but because it contributes to the realisation of certain end" (p. 41). Again, there is no conflict between law and liberty. Law removes the obstacles to the realisation of liberty. The function of law is to promote the habits of true citizenship and law does it by removing the obstacles. A true citizen will participate in the promotion of general welfare. Hence, law has a positive role to play here. Green admits that a conflict may arise between law and spontaneity. But the authority of the true state will have to consider the greater and better interest of the society. The parents may be reluctant to send their children to school and in that case a law of compulsory education will force such parents to send their children to school since without education moral development is impossible. Here, in this case, law is meant not to dwarf the spontaneous activity but to enlighten the mind essential for freedom and consciousness.

The essentiality of Green's liberalism can be stated in the following words. It is to be noted here that his liberalism may be traced to Rousseau's philosophy. He has stated that behind every policy or law of authority there shall be the consent of people. Rousseau's people met in an open place and decided policy and formed general will. Green says that a government cannot make any law or decide any policy against the opinion of general people. A law must aim at the general welfare of the people and they will decide what really constitutes their welfare. Naturally people's will is the determiner of everything. Through law and policy the authority will ensure justice, equity and humanity. This is the sum and substance of his liberalism. The essence of Green's liberalism is nothing shall be imposed on the people against their wishes. But this cannot be called *laissez-faire*. Government has a positive role to play. The state shall create an atmosphere in which people shall get full opportunity to develop their morality and idealism but the state cannot force them in this affair.

When Green speaks of people's control over state activity and their consent to law he uses these terms or words in a different sense. He always emphasises the social conscience. Mere numerical majority is not important. People, while giving consent, must be guided by social conscience. Sabine comments (p. 733) "The most characteristic element in Green's liberalism was his belief of a social conscience which both regulates law and is supported by law... Every man must follow his intelligence and his conscience, and a liberal society is one which respects his right to judge and also enhances the probability that his judgments will be socially trustworthy."

Green touched two burning issues of his time—the freedom of the individual and the exact role of the state in the midst of ever-increasing problems or evils created by industrialisation. To what extent he had been able to provide a solution, that is a different issue. What is important to us is that through his revision of liberalism he made sincere efforts to tackle the problem. Contrary to utilitarian thought he believed that individuals enjoy liberty only as a member of the society. Isolation from society does not enable him to have freedom or to develop morality. To arrest the evils of society concerted efforts are required and in this regard the initiative must emanate from the state. J. S. Mill in his *Autobiography* gave a hint of state legislation for collective benefit, Green dealt with the matter directly. Green was anxious to find out a compromise or an equilibrium between individual freedom and collective state action. David Thompson in his *Political Ideas* (p. 199) says : "Green's political thought was an unstable equilibrium between the appeals of the community and of the individual."

Through the idealistic revision of liberalism Green initiated not only economic and social welfare, but also "moral welfare". Without moral upliftment social and economic progress is bound to fail. A separate compartment cannot be earmarked for morality only. Common moral consciousness is a potent factor of social progress. Man must be conscious of self at first and then of others. Without this consciousness, progress cannot be expected.

Right to Property

Green's right to property is not different from other rights. That is, the basis of all rights is the moral development of individual and the purpose of property should be the common good of society. Property, according to Green, is the sum of instruments necessary for the free play of self-realising principle in man and contribution to the common good. Property is an instrument for the "emancipation of the individual from all restrictions upon the free moral life, and his provision with means for it" (p. 219). Green was not satisfied with the property system that prevailed in various states of Europe. He, of course, knew that the European property system was the product of Industrial Revolution and behind this the capitalist class played the dominant role. The property was primarily used for personal gain and the notion of common good was neglected. This system of property was strongly disliked by Green. Like every other right the right, to property must be associated with morality, idealism and common good.

The rationale of property, Green announces, is that everyone should be secured by society in the power of getting and keeping the means of realising a will, which, in possibility, is a will directed to social good. Whether anyone's will is actually and positively so directed, does not affect his claim to the power. This power should be secured to the individual irrespectively of the use which he actually makes of it so long as he does not use it in a way that interferes with the exercise of like power by another.

So far as the concept of private property is concerned, there are two extreme views. One group of people holds the view that there is nothing wrong in private property and in all respects it is justifiable. On the other hand, there are many people who hold the view that the system of private property is unjustified and on that ground this right to property should be abolished for the sake of justice. Again, the system of private property violates the principles of common good and morality. Green adopts a middle way. Generally private property is a means of realising a will potentially directed to social good. But this should not be strictly and in an orthodox manner be held. The simple implication is the violation of the principle may be permitted. Private property may not always fulfil this condition, that is, may not aim at social good. To put it in other words, it is not anti-social. In that case, should not the provision of private property be allowed? Green says that the private property may not directly help social good, but indirectly helps. The capitalists invest money to manufacture commodities, employ workers for that purpose. In this way they facilitate distribution of wealth and performing yoeman's service to the society. This is also contribution to social good.

Green had practical knowledge about the political, social and economic structure of British society. He was well-acquainted with the unequal distribution of property. This plagued his mind and he believed that this unequal distribution of property was an important source of many evils. He says, "Once admit as the ideas of property that nature should be progressively adapted to the service of man by a process in which each, while working freely or for himself, i.e., as determined by a conception of his own good, at the same time contributes to the social good, and it will follow that property must be unequal. If we leave a man free to realise the conception of a posible well-being, it is impossible to limit the effect upon him of his desire to provide or his future well-being" (p. 221). What Green wants to say here is that all the individuals cannot contribute to the social welfare in a uniform way. Varieties shall be allowed to persist. Again, if each man is allowed in his own way to contribute to the social good then he should be permitted to own different means, that is different amount of property. Out of this notion comes the concept of inequality of property. Green further argues that only through the free play of individual wills the attainment of social good is possible. The right to private property, therefore, must be admitted and its inequality is an inevitable consequence.

Property is required for the realisation of free will, but if this realisation is at the cost of the interests of many and if the common good is adversely affected, then the concept of property shall be condemened. Barker observes : "Thus any kind of property which realises the will of one man at the expense of stopping the realisation of will of many, is instantly condemned" (p. 44).

Assessment of Green

It has already been pointed out that the source of Green's philosophy is Greek idealism, and Hegel's idealist philosophy which passed through Rousseau's general will and morality. But he interpreted idealism in the background of English political thought, social and economic conditions and institutions. He had great respect for and attachment to English representative institutions. He had a deep sense of right and freedom which marked the tradition of English political thought. Here is the credit of Green. His main concern was individual's freedom. But his men are not unrelated and isolated atoms. The realisation of freedom is possible only as a member of social order. Green built up a revision of liberalism on the foundation of English tradition which was more important to him than any other orthodox political ideology. In other words, his revision gave priority to practical situation.

We come to know from his writings that he had unbound feeling and sympathy for untought and underfed denizens of London city and he thought about their upliftment. Green was an idealist, he was an individualist, but above all he was a great humanitarian. Abject poverty and unbound moral degradation pained his heart to a considerable extent. He was against any domination and could not approve exploitation of one for the benefit of others. He was not a professed socialist. But the feeling of Green for the downtrodden mass was not less than that of a professed socialist.

Bentham founded his doctrine of utilitarianism on the basis of pleasure and pain calculation. Even the government action was to be measured by this criterion. Spencer was the orthodox protagonist of *laissez-faire* doctrine. He applied Darwin's 'survival of the fittest' theory of the social progress. Marx rejected Bentham's pleasure-pain calculation and openly challenged the individualism of J. S. Mill. To him socialism was the only way which had the power to change radically the entire structure of society. "It was the peculiar service of Thomas Hill Green to inject into this turbid conflux of ideologies a liberal political philosophy in which social expediency was the dominant principle, a philosophy in which the concept of social expediency was raised to an ideal by the insistence of its author that expediency be determined by moral obligation of the state to create an environment favourable to the full realisation of what is best in every individual" (Maxey, p. 510).

Green has made a strong plea for the interference of state, but like Hegel and Plato he does not idealise the state, nor does he make it all-powerful. He does not say that the state is the march of God on earth. There are innumerable social and political institutions within the state which mould the character and behaviour of the individuals. So there is no scope to establish the majesty of the state, it is limited from within. It is also limited from without. It does not enjoy absolute sovereignty in international sphere.

Green draws a distinction between the outward and inward activities of the individual and, according to Barker, this is the true distinction. The state will regulate the outward actions to secure the rights for the individuals and the state does it through its laws. On the other hand, there are certain actions which proceed from the inward will and the external force of the state has nothing to do with the inward will of man. In Barker's judgment (p. 47) this distinction between outward and inward action is far better than Mill's self-regarding and other regarding actions of individuals. Green's distinction between outward and inward aspects of life is still prevalent. Even today social scientists in general and political thinkers in particular emphasise this idea. They are of opinion that a state should refrain itself from interfering in the activities of man which are exclusively inward; of course to distinguish between outward and inward is very difficult. But this should be treated as a norm.

Green's political philosophy was not confined within the four walls of classroom, it created a positive impact upon the policy of the government. We have already mentioned that Green was the founder of the idea of "moral welfare". His schemes and proposals laid the foundation of the welfare state. Fabian socialists were in various ways indebted to him. Pension for the old, insurance scheme for the unemployed persons and compensation for the workers—in all these matters Green was the pioneer. In his assessment of Green, David Thompson has said : "In the quarter century before 1914, during which much social legislation was passed by the liberal governments, Green's ideas permeated social thought in England..... They spread wide and sank deep because they were in the direct evangelical tradition of philanthropic humanism" (*Political Ideas*, p. 199).

It is necessary that our assessment about Green must be balanced and to that end the drawbacks from which he suffers are to be ventilated. The central theme of idealism in general—and Oxford idealism in particular—is the general will. All the idealists assume that in every society there is some kind of general will in respect of policies and values. The general will is good will, it aims at the common good, it is the practical guide to every policy. All the good citizens always identify their own real will with the general will. But the question is : Whether all these attributes of general will correspond to the real situation? Is it easy to locate the general will in every kind of society? Can it be formed in a big state like ours? Even in a small state having few million people the existence of general will is difficult to ascertain. Hobhouse once said, "In so far as it is will, it is not general, in so far as it is general it is not will." If this is the nature of general will, how can it be guide to policy and action?

If we go through the views of Green we shall find that the concept of common good constitutes the central part of Green's political philosophy. As such, the concept is quite plausible. But as soon as we embark upon its detailed analysis we shall be quite disheartened. Some of the pertinent questions raised about the common good are—What are the elements of common good? Can it be defined? Who will decide that common good has been achieved or not? Who will decide the differences of opinion? All these are vital questions and a thorough study of Green's political philosophy does not offer us convincing replies.

In our analysis of utilitarianism we have seen that it is basically an impractical concept. Green's theory of common good and idealism fall in the same category. Each and every individual runs after pleasure and is anxious in avoiding pain. This is not correct. Similarly, behind every action of man there is consciousness is not correct. People's actions very often proceed from the subconscious. It is not also correct to hold that man's actions aim at common good. Green has oversimplified human nature. They are not absolutely egoist, but not absolutely altruist. They are mixture of both.

Green's concessions to people for the right against the state are, in fact, extremely limited and, in ultimate analysis, these come to nothing. Green has advised that people must exhibit obedience to law and authority even when they are not satisfied with it. Their right to resist is permitted only when this resistance will be advantageous for the common good. Another concession is that the dissenting citizen will build up a strong public opinion against the proposal of the government. If he succeeds then he, along with other citizens, can disobey the state's order or policy. Green assures us that the political set-up of his own country is favourable for such a move. But what about other countries?

Green was not free from bourgeois mentality. He has repeatedly emphasised upon self-consciousness. But our humble submission is : Can the untaught and underfed citizens of London slum area attain this stage of consciousness? Only people having strong economic foothold can claim to have achieved consciousness. Green himself admits that spread of education is precondition of self-consciousness and morality. In Green's time education was neither compulsory nor universal. Green was quite aware that the accumulation of wealth in the hands of a few persons was singularly responsible for the growing misery of the working class. It is unfortunate that we do not find Green to utter a single word against that class. He might have enough sympathy for the wretched denizens of London city, but we want to know what concrete measures he has suggested. The evils of industrialisation were so deep-rooted that any piecemeal attempts might not prove fruitful.

In Green's time, the British society was not free from the influence of pressure groups. If an influential pressure group prevails upon the government and forces to take decision in its favour and accept its interpretation of common good then what will happen? What is apparently common good in actual practice is the good of a particular class of group of people. Green suggests no palliatives as to how a bourgeois and pressure group influenced society can get rid of it. Green's political philosophy suffers from a number of drawbacks. But it is true that perhaps he was the only idealist philosopher whose idealism was firmly rooted to the practical situation of the then British society. He was the only idealist philosopher who strongly felt the necessity of the role of state in the field of the alleviation of poverty and misery of common people.

FRANCIS HERBERT BRADLEY (1846–1924)

In political philosophy there is very little contribution of F. H. Bradley. He is still remembered by students of history of political thought because of his connection with the Oxford idealist school. His famous book *Ethical Studies* was published in 1876. T. H. Green was then alive. There is a chapter in this book—"My Station and Its Duties." It was in the philosophy, remarks Copplestone, of Francis Herbert Bradley that emphasise on the subject. Object relationship was decisively supplanted by the idea of supra-national one, the all-embracing Absolute (p. 187).

Green was Hegelian no doubt but Hegelianism reached its culmination in Bradley. Bradley develops the idea that the state is a moral organism and the individual is a part of it. He performs all his duties simply as a moral unit. In the chapter "My Station and Its Duties" Bradley says that one's duties are specified, by one's station, by one's place and function in the social organism. This announcement leads him to assert that morality not only is but ought to be relative. "That is to say it is not simply a question of noting the empirical fact that moral convictions have differed in certain respects in different societies. Bradley maintains in addition that moral codes would be of no use unless they were relative to given societies" (Copleston, page 193). To put it in other words, the morality or moral actions are to be judged in the background of particular society. Bradley wants to emphasise that what a man will do is decided by his position in the society. Besides, he is an integral part of the social organism. Naturally, he has very little freedom in respect of what he will do.

Bradley borrows the conception of moral organism from Plato and Hegel. According to Plato, there is a function for every man appropriate to his position and it is his righteousness to perform that function. This function is also commensurate with the structure, nature and purpose of the society. So to refuse to perform the socially ordained duty is immorality. Again, Hegel says that the spirit of the nation (which is a spirit of social righteousness), controls and entirely dominates from within each person, so that he feel to be his own very being and looks upon it as his absolute final aim.[1]

In Bradley's conception the state is an organic unity. The functions are determined by the state and the individual performs them. His morality, his freedom, his righteousness and everything else lie in his ability to discharge those duties. Bradley has said : "In fact what we call an individual man is what he is because of and by virtue of community, and communities are not mere names but something real." The identity and character of the individual are determined by the community in which he is born and brought up. We quote Barker : "Already at birth the child is what he is in virtues of the communities : he has something of the family character, something of the national character, something of the civilized character which comes from human society. As he grows, the community in which he lives pours itself into his being in the language he learns and the social atmosphere he breathes, so that the consent of his being implies in its every fibre relations of community" (p. 50).

The individuals find their fullness of character if they sincerely cultivate their specific duties. Bradley says : "The breadth of my life is not measured by the multitude of my pursuits, not the space I take up amongst other men, but by the

1. Barker—*Political Thought*, p. 50.

fullness of the whole life which I know as mine." Bradley's state is a "moral organism". Its parts are the citizens. But there is a difference between the parts of the body and those of the state. Parts of the state are self-conscious.

BERNARD BOSANQUET (1848–1923)

Introductory

Bernard Bosanquet was born in 1848, the year of publication of the *Communist Manifesto,* and died in 1923. He was educated at Harrow and at Balliol College, Oxford, where he came under the influence of T. H. Green. In 1871 he was elected Fellow of the University College, Oxford. In 1881 he went to London to reside there and his purpose was to deliver lectures for adult education movement. He had also an intention to devote his energy to social work. From 1903 to 1908 Bosanquet was the professor of Moral Philosophy of the St. Andrews University. In 1911 and 1912 he delivered his famous lectures at the university of Edinburgh and the subject was *The Principles of Individuality and Value.* Bosanquet was connected with many philanthropic organisations.

He was a versatile thinker and prolific writer. His well-known and best-known work *The Philosophical Theory of the State* was first published in 1899 and its fourth edition appeared in 1923, the year of his death. His other works include *Logic as the Science of Knowledge, Logic or the Morphology of Knowledge, Companion to Plato's Republic, Essentials of Logic, The Principle of Individuality and Value.*

Different contradictory opinions are expressed about Bosanquet. A critic has called him the greatest of English idealists. On the other hand, Copleston, a renowned interpreter of philosophy, says that, like Bradley, Bosanquet is rarely mentioned today and this is due to the fact that he has not said anything new which his contemporary thinkers have not said. His theory of state, relationship between the individual and state, legislation etc. all were elaborated by Hegel, T. H. Green, Rousseau. Naturally he did not say anything new. In spite of this we still remember Bosanquet and the naive reason is that he was the leading member of Oxford idealism. He forcefully vindicated the central principles of Oxford idealism.

Bosanquet was indebted to both Green and Rousseau. He adopted many of the principles of Green but he modernised them in the light of new data found out by experience. He also abandoned some of the limitations of Green. These limitations relate to liberalism. On this point we like to quote Barker : "He would thus bring Green's philosophy to a point where it approaches close to, if it does not altogether blend with, the full Hegelian conception of the state" (p. 57).

Theory of State

Idealism originated in the thought of Plato and Aristotle and for about 2000 years it was buried in oblivion. It was then resuscitated by Rousseau which was elaborated by German idealists. Oxford idealists were subsequently influenced by Rousseau's idealism. Particularly Green and Bosanquet borrowed heavily from Rousseau. Barker says (p. 57) : "In constructing his own theory of state Bosanquet starts by a vindication of Rousseau." He accepted Rousseau's theory of general will and conception of individual's liberty. Finally, like Rousseau, he reconciled the will or liberty of the individual and the general will of the state.

Following are the points of agreement between Rousseau and Bosanquet : Like Rousseau, Bosanquet hold that the individual is not a self-enclosed unit, he is a part of the society and integrally connected with it. The individual's real will is identical with the general will and in this identification we find the true account of political obligation. In obeying the state the individual is obeying himself and his real will. When he is constrained to act in a certain manner, he is constrained to act in accordance with his real will and so to act freely. Thus announces Bosanquet. This opinion of Bosanquet reminds us of Rousseau's famous phrase "forced to be free".

Following Rousseau, Bosanquet says that the will of the individual is completely merged with the general will of the state. To put it in other words, the individual imagined by both Rousseau and Bosanquet is moral and rational and, therefore, he never hesitates to forge an identification between his will and the will of the state. He fully realises that the fulfilment of his moral ideals is possible only as a member of a political organisation. The following comment of Bosanquet is worthy to be quoted : "The human mind can only attain its full and proper life in a community of minds or more strictly in a community pervaded by a single mind, uttering itself consistently though differently in the life and action of every member of the community."

There is another point of agreement between Rousseau and Bosanquet. Only the membership of the political organisation enables a man to be moral and civilised. The membership removes the animal and impulsive nature and makes him real. The ultimate aim of the state, as of its members, is a moral end, the attainment of the best life, the life which most develops man's abilities as human being.

Both Rousseau and Bosanquet hold the view that the state cannot always use force or resort to force on every occasion to make men moral. As it has been pointed out by Copleston : "Individuals can be compelled to refrain from certain actions; but they cannot be compelled to refrain from them for high moral motives. It is indeed clearly conducive to the common good that people should refrain from murder, even if their motive is simply the avoidance of punishment" (p. 228). The point of emphasis made by Bosanquet is that people's altruistic mentality, which he achieves through the membership of the state, induces them to follow moral motives. That is, they, on their own accord, refrain from those actions and motives which are contrary to common good and morality. To both Rousseau and Bosanquet the state is a moral organisation.

From the above analysis it is now clear that in Bosanquet's concept there is hardly any conflict between the individual and the state. The authority of the state does not approve the freedom of the individual. The anti-thesis between the individual and state is really a false anti-thesis. Copleston maintains "And it follows that the alleged problem of justifying interference by the state with private liberty is not a genuine problem" (p. 227). The state is not there to curtail the freedom of persons but to enhance it by hindering the hindrances.

Green's theory of the state is negative in the sense that its chief function is to remove the impediments to moral development. This negative view of the state has been accepted by Bosanquet who says that the state helps the individual in achieving the good life by enacting new laws and other ways. He also agrees with Green on the positive role of the state. The state removes illiteracy and liquor traffic etc. and by doing this ensures the general welfare of the society. *Both Green and Bosanquet admit the autonomy of the good will and this can be ensured through the freedom of the individual.*

The state in both cases is the guarantor of external conditions. Both Green and Bosanquet hold the view that the external conditions which the state guarantees are the rights and without these rights the free action of the goodwill is not possible.

Bosanquet also shares the view of Green in another aspect. Locke has traced the origin of the state to contract. But even after the establishment of the state, people reserve the right to take action when actions contrary to contract or general welfare are performed by the state. This is the individualistic character of state. Neither Green nor Bosanquet agrees with this nature of state. A government cannot be removed from power according to whim or alleged inefficiency by the subjects. Moral upliftment or attainment of good life is not possible outside the state. Moreover, the state has different sorts of activities. It simply removed the obstacles to good life.

Bosanquet endorses another view of Green's theory of state. Following Green he has drawn a very clear picture of the relation between the state as a political organisation to use physical force, but a general organisation which synthesises the activities of individuals and coordinates the relationship among them. This is the bigger and nobler view of state. In such a state the society exists. Within the state there are various associations which mould the character and guide the behaviour of the individuals. Both Green and Bosanquet agree that state is a society of societies. Summarising the views of Bosanquet Barker writes "The state is a group of groups, a community of communities embracing and sustaining the whole field of social cooperation" (p. 58). Hence the state is a driving wheel and motive power. It adjusts the several organisations and invigorates its citizens.

Bosanquet's state as a synthesis of life and all other organisations existing within the state is much closer to the Hegelian state. This closer approximation of Bosanquet's state to Hegel's state reveals few features. Bosanquet abandons Green's conception of free play of individuals' wills. Green holds the view that the state might have a will but under no circumstances it will absorb all the wills of its subjects. It implies that Green admits the individuality and this makes him a great votary of individualism. To the contrary, Hegel recommends the absorption of individual's will in the state. Bosanquet follows Hegel. The significance and justification of community lies in the fact that it exists within the state. A common consciousness pervades the entire state. In this connection the opinion of Herbert Marcuse may be noted here. Bosanquet's *Philosophical Theory of the State* (1899) has features that make the individual a victim of the hypostatized state universal, so characteristic of later Fascist ideology. The average individual is no longer accepted as the real self or individuality. The centre of gravity is thrown "outside him" (p. 393). "Outside him means to Bosanquet outside his own private interests and amusement, outside the sphere of his immediate want and desire."

From psychological point of view Bosanquet comes nearer to Hegel. Hegel imagined of a state as a self-conscious, a self-knowing and self-actualizing individuals. Bosanquet does not admit the separate or independent existence and spirit of social institutions. All the institutions are connected by living minds in a living way. He views the six hundred members of British Parliament as a complete whole. The members are not separate units. The minds of six hundred members are connected by common purpose and common experience. Barker says : "Parliament in the last resort is neither bricks nor mortar, nor flesh and blood, it is the substance common to six hundred minds. It is, as we say, common mind. All the institutions of a country, so far as they are effective, are not only products of thought and creations of mind; they *are* thought and they *are* mind" (p. 60-61).

The concept of group mind is further elaborated by Bosanquet. It is a sheer mistakes to take Oxford College as a group of buildings, though outwardly it is so. There are several buildings, but in those buildings many people are engaged in different types of work. These men have formed a group and all of them are connected by a mind which may properly be called a group mind. The minds of all men are united by an idea. So the group mind or united idea is all the same. The fact is that all the works of an institution or organisation are conducted by a single idea. In this sense there is a trade union mind or there is a public mind.

In similar way we can postulate a national mind. The nation-state is not something inhabited by millions of men and women engaged in their respective works. A common idea passes through all men and women and that constitutes national mind. The national mind resembles the group mind, but it is bigger. The government and all its subjects both are guided by a single idea. Men are also conscious of such an idea. Externally subjects are all different but internally they are one and united by the idea.

The state and its subjects are permeated by an idea of good life or it may be called the best life. People are conscious of it. The state is there to remove the external hindrances to good life. Bosanquet believes that the state cannot make man moral or it cannot make good as such. It simply hinders the hindrances. This is the primary duty of the state. The state synthesises all the individuals and institutions. In this way a group mind or national mind is created.

Bosanquet concludes that the single idea that guides the activities of all men is the ethical idea. The institutions and the state have ethical idea. But the state is an institution. So it has an ethical idea. Let us see what Barker says on this point : "The state is an ethical idea, or rather it is *the* ethical idea, since it is the final working conception of life as a whole" (p. 62).

Criticism

In his "*Crisis in the Theory of the State*" Laski observes "The idealist theory of the state in its famous formulation by Bosanquet remains a formulation of a conceptual state *in posse* rather than of the states we know." This is the most powerful criticism against the idealist or philosophical theory of state. Bosanquet and other idealist thinkers have built up the foundation of state in heaven and not in earth. The state imagined by Bosanquet or even T. H. Green is not to be found in the real world. The same view has been expressed by Barker : "The state of which it conceived resting on the free consent and cooperation of the moral will of every citizen, may be up in heaven, and it is not established on earth" (p. 66).

However, the idealists alone cannot be blamed for elaborating an impractical theory of state. The utilitarians can also be criticised on the ground that their idea of pleasure and pain calculation does not tally the exact situation. Moreover, politics is a normative science. It is not always concerned with what is, but what ought to be. The idealist thinkers have simply done that. The idealists have conceived of what ought to be established in every civilised society. So it is quite natural that reality and ideality will not travel on the same track.

It is observed that the purpose of the idealists was not to construct an ideal state or society but to idealise something. For example, Aristotle idealised the slavery, T. H. Green idealised the capital. Idealism, as such, is not condemnable. But when we find that war is idealised, as Hegel has done it, then the purpose of the idealists raises suspicion. T. H. Green fails to see the pernicious effects of capital. Hegel does not recognise or he overlooks the destructive effects of war. If this is the mentality of idealists, we humbly submit that we are not with idealism. We reject it root and branch.

Barker points out another criticism against the idealist theory. "The idealist thinkers ascribe too much to the conscious will and reasoning mind. There *is* a sphere of will and reason; but there are also other spheres. Man is a part of nature set in the midst of all the play of selection and survival and evolution; and the biologist must have his say in any full political theory.... Man is the creature of compact emotions, inpulses and instincts as well as of conscious reason" (p. 68). It is, therefore, quite wrong to think of man as the embodiment of particular will or reason. Moreover, he constantly adjusts the different wills and impulses as well as emotions.

L. T. Hobhouse criticises the philosophical theory of state from the following standpoint. He says that the metaphysical or philosophical theory of state can be stated in the following propositions : (a) the individual attains his true self and freedom in conformity to his real will, (b) this real will is the general will, and (c) the general will is embodied in the state. The state is thus identified to all intents and purposes with the entire social fabric. Within the state may institutions and organisations may exist. But they have no different personality of their own apart from the state. The state, in other words, encompasses them all. Moreover, Hobhouse proceeds, the state is the highest embodiment of morality and social development. Hobhouse asks why the national state is the highest product of morality and social development? Why not the universal world society? "In this sense idealist political theory is unduly conservative."[1]

Hobhouse criticises metaphysical theory of state sill from another angle. If the state is regarded as the guardian and expression of morality and as the highest moral entity, the logical consequence is a disastrous moral conformism. If the state is really a moral entity of higher order than the individual moral agent, it is very odd that these sublime moral entities, namely different states, have not succeeded in regularising their mutual relations according to moral standards. In brief, "To confuse the state with the society and political with the moral obligation is the central fallacy of the metaphysical theory of state" (Hobhouse).

Bosanquet's philosophy of state puts the individual into the complete control of society as such or state in general. "Whereas, in reality, the individual always has to carry on his life in some particular historical form of society and state. This "central fallacy" is of utmost importance, for in it is implied the confusion between contingent relations and moral obligations" (Marcuse, p. 395).

Another criticism of the idealist theory of the state is the following. In a class society there is always one class which is economically dominant and this class controls both the base and superstructure. In such a society the interests of this class pervade the whole society and the economically weaker class which is also the

1. Copleston : *A History of Philosophy*, Vol. VIII, p. 231.

majority has no influence. Such a society or state cannot be called the expression of real will of all individuals. Hobhouse himself comments "Whereas a community is governed by one class or one race the remaining class or race is permanently in the position of having to take what it can get. To say that institutions of such a society express the private will of the subject class is merely to add insult to injury."[1] The central point highlighted by Hobhouse is the welfare of the individual is more important than the expression of morality in the universal society.

Harold Laski in *The State in Theory and Practice* has drawn our attention to another weakness of the philosophical theory of state. In his view the theory fails to understand the nature of individuality. It finds its essence not in the ultimate isolation which all of us daily experience, but in the contribution that isolation makes to the life of the whole in which the individual shares. The isolation of an individual is unreal. Unity does not arise from sharing a common world. It arises from taking the same kind of view about the action which the meaning of that common world seems to render desirable. History becomes meaningless unless we can assume that men can legitimately differ about the facts and events which occur in the society. Unity is not something which is imposed or given. Men discover it through their continuous efforts in seeking their ends. But this discovery is made in isolation. Man will not be advised to be merged in the whole. Rather, he will be allowed to pursue his goals in isolation. Of course, the common good must always be given priority. They must be made rational and intelligent. This is the duty of society. Economic emancipation is a must to make life and will real. Unfortunately, the metaphysical theory does not enlighten this aspect.

One of the fundamental concepts of philosophical theory of state is common good. But the phrase covers a number of different ideas. Laski suggests the following meanings : (a) It may mean the good achieved by the definition in the ideal state. The ideal state is not actual state. So the common good cannot be the guide of actual states. (b) Another meaning of common good is the principles of well-being which the state is to aim. Here is a problem. Whether any actual state has ever attempted to achieve this well-being? Experience shows that state has never made any attempt to achieve that end !! (c) Finally, common good may mean those habits, traditions and purposes which a society aims at preserving.

UTILITARIANISM, IDEALISM, AND DEMOCRACY

The chief exponents of utilitarianism are Bentham and J. S. Mill and the central theme of this doctrine is that individuals are quite reasonable and rational and, hence, they are capable of estimating what is pleasure and pain. On the basis of their rationality and reasonability individuals start to judge the policies and law of the government. This sole aim is to decide the acceptability or non-acceptability of the law or policy. The purpose is how much pleasure they can get. This principle, when adopted in practice, can solve the frictions from which a society normally suffers, because the laws and institutions are so framed as to achieve that goal successfully. It is the view of the utilitarians that state and society are corporate bodies and are fictitious. For that very reason they are not in a position to enable the individuals to maximise pleasure. It should conveniently be left to the individuals.

1. Quoted by Marcuse, p. 396.

The central idea of utilitarianism has failed to enthuse, in a considerable way, the English idealists-specially Green-who is regarded as the leading personality of English idealism. A. D. Lindsay in his Introduction to T. H. Green's *The Principles of Political Obligation* makes the following observation : "Green and his fellow idealists were all fundamentally individualists and democrats. ... They were all convinced that utilitarianism had become barren as a political creed because of the inadequate philosophy upon which it was based" (p. VIII).

What is the "inadequate philosophy' of utilitarianism? The main charge of idealist philosophers against the utilitarians is that the latter have treated the individuals simply as a bundle of pleasures. In other words, the persons of the society have no other objective than maximising their happiness in one way or other. Utilitarianism also believes that society or state consists of completely separate atoms who are individuals. They do not indulge in any other feeling or objective except happiness. This self-centred character of people has not succeeded in receiving approval from idealists. Idealism is of opinion that this type of depiction of human character is unreal and disappointing because pleasure may be one of the objectives of individuals but it is not the only one.

We now turn to a very vital aspect of the relationship between utilitarianism, idealism and democracy. It is generally believed by utilitarianism—though not fully correct—that both the state and society are fictitious organisations. Even the utilitarian philosophers did not hesitate to call the state a necessary evil. Because of this attitude of the utilitarians, it was propagated that such a state was incapable of doing any commendable work for the welfare of public. For this attitude it was held that the interventions of state should be reduced to the minimum level. It has been the conviction of utilitarianism that the removal of restrictions will facilitate people in getting the required amount of pleasure. On this point idealism and democracy differ from utilitarianism.

By arguing the removal of state restrictions the utilitarian thinkers have neglected the case of democracy. Real democracy needs state intervention in the affairs of individuals. A great evil of Industrial Revolution is the gross inequality of income. A larger part of wealth produced by this Revolution is in the control and use of few people who have constituted a class.

We do not like to jump to the conclusion that the utilitarians had no sympathy for the poorer section of the community. But the fact is that if their doctrine is implemented that will fail to alleviate the growing poverty and sufferings of common people because this can be done only by proper state intervention. Utilitarianism cannot ensure democracy. One of the main concerns of idealists is the emancipation of poor people from sufferings and they have favoured state initiative. Green was not simply an idealist philosopher, he was also a practical man. He was moved at the sight of the impoverished and miserable condition of the poor people of various parts of London. The poverty was a positive factor of the deteriorating conditions of the dignity of man which is not conductive to real democracy.

By giving utmost priority to the reason and rationality of individuals and advocating restrictive state activity the utilitarians have endeavoured to build up an unsound political theory. A new role of the state conducive to the enhancement of the dignity of man and establishment of social justice through the alleviation of poverty is to be emphasised through the construction of an adequate political theory.

This has been provided, it is claimed, by the idealists of Oxford group. Idealists argue that if each man pursues his happiness and if each counts one and not more than one that will never succeed in establishing justice. Here is a difference between utilitarianism and idealism. Idealism gives proper importance to the dignity and requirement of each individual and simultaneously acknowledges the role of the state.

Lindsay has drawn our attention to another aspect of difference between utilitarianism and idealism and their approach to democracy. Utilitarianism believes that if the individuals are left to themselves and if no restrictions are imposed that will generate harmony among the individuals. In this way unity and integrity will be achieved. This doctrine further believes that if each individual is permitted to pursue his own happiness that will ensure the happiness of all. But idealism rejects this stand of utilitarianism : Its standpoint is—some people may be intelligent and better equipped than others and these persons may be able to ensure their happiness. But what about the others? These people will be deprived of happiness because they are ill-equipped and the state intervention is essential for these persons—which utilitarianism does not permit. Hence utilitarian democracy is only for a section of people and not for all persons; and idealism says that this is not real democracy. By advocating state-interference for the greatest good of all individuals, idealism has endeavoured to establish real democracy in the society. This is especially evident in T. H. Green. A true democracy says that it is the purpose of the state to serve the ordinary citizens and all citizens and not part.

A. D. Lindsay observes (p. XII), "T. H. Green and his school were idealists, but they were under no illusions about the human nature. ...Their idealism consisted in regarding the state from the point of view of what could be made out of it. They had learned from Plato that the nature of any social organisation .... is best understood by looking at it from its highest realisation downward rather than from its rudimentary beginnings upward. The justification of the state, and indeed, of any institution, depended for them on the opportunities which it awarded men for their good use of it." We have inserted a long quotation from Lindsay with the sole purpose to show that utilitarian thinkers were under a great influence of illusion that the individuals are intelligent and scientific minded. But this is far from reality. This illusion has built up a theory and, naturally, the theory cannot be real. There is justification of any organisation because of its services to people.

The comparison between utilitarianism and idealism may be viewed from another angle. The former is of opinion that obligation to law is due to its ability to generate pleasure. But the idealism of Green and other English idealists says that there is a moral function or purpose of any law. By compulsive measures the state cannot make persons moral because it is contradictory. But Green has said that the business of law is to maintain certain conditions of life and, through the maintenance of these conditions, the individuals can lead a moral or virtuous life.

However, on one vital issue both utilitarianism and idealism agree and this is the state or any other organisation cannot make men happy or moral by resorting to compulsive measures. The primary responsibility is to remove the hindrances which stand on the way of achieving happiness or being moral. In other words, both doctrine, want liberty of thought and action.

If we look at the real world of state activities and their relation to human welfare we shall find that idealism is more relevant (idealism of Oxford idealists) than the utilitarianism of Bentham and J. S. Mill. Government policies and decisions are never decided by their ability to produce utility. Moreover, the term utility is abstract and ambiguous. By reducing the state interference to a minimum level the greatest welfare of human society cannot be achieved and democracy cannot be established. The presumption that some people are rational and reasonable—cannot be the basis of state activity. In the words of Lindsay this is definitely an "illusion" and this should be abandoned. It is a matter of great gratification that idealists reject this. The utilitarians were guided by a misconception. Non-interference of state can never be the surest guarantor of greatest happiness of the greatest number. The view of English idealists is a ground-to-earth real approach to the problem. The English idealists are democrats and moralists. We know that the impractical approach of Bentham was revised by J. S. Mill and towards the fag-end of life he recommended state intervention which, we think, brings him near to T. H. Green. For the greater benefit of the whole society the intervention of the state is being felt strongly and this feeling is multiplying day after day. So we can say that in the background of the present day situation utilitarianism has very little relevance.

We are of opinion that utilitarianism and idealism are parts of liberalism. The former wanted to restrict the functions and role of the state for the benefit of individual. Utilitarianism feels the less the intervention of state, the more is the freedom of individuals in their choice of pleasure and avoidance of pain. Green's idealism prescribes for state intervention for the general upliftment of the people. Needless to say, democracy wants this. The utilitarianism have depicted the self-interest seeking character and nature of men which is not always correct; on the contrary a state in a class society cannot do justice to all types of men. This lacuna of Green's idealism cannot be ignored. Neither utilitarianism nor Green's idealism did utter a single word against the class structure of society though it was quite prominent in Mill's days or Green's time. Both Mill and Green accepted the ascendancy of the capitalists as an integral part of British society. Democracy should be viewed in this backdrop.

22 THE ENLIGHTENMENT AND POLITICS

Definition and Nature

Different scholars have defined enlightenment in their own ways. Let us start with the COD's definion. There are two definitions in this dictionary. One is the general meaning of enlightenment which is specially related with Buddhism and the other is the enlightenment. We are here concerned with the latter meaning. The COD's definition is that enlightenment is a European intellectual movement of the late seventeenth and eighteenth centuries emphasising reasons and individualism rather than tradition. J. S. Mcclelland has elaborately discussed several aspects of this concept and its relations with political theory. The impact of enlightenment fell on almost all the sections of society but the most spectacular effect fell on the entire thought system. Let us take different important definitions.

The great German Philosopher Kant said enlightenment means "dare to know." It means to throw away the stigma of ignorance and the determination to move forward. Following Kant Mcclelland defines it in the following words : "The enlightenment is characterised as being in revolt against ignorance and superstition ...It is an umbrella opened so wide that as many thinkers as possible can shelter under it" (p. 300). Elsewhere in the same book Mcclelland says that enlightenment is an attempt that tried to expand the principles of toleration and moderation into general principles of individual life and the life of both society and politics (p. 298). Enlightenment means to remove ignorance and darkness from the mind of men and society. The revival of morality and ethics in all spheres of social life.

Dante Germino (*Machiavelli to Marx : Modern Political Thought*) has defined the idea in the following way. It is a coherent period in the history of political thought or it has become a slogan to be defended by political writers who see merit in the principles it embodies. Peter Gray has offered us a thoroughgoing research on this subject. He says : The enlightenment—the age that extends from Locke to Condorcet—was one of the most creative ages in the history of political theory. Its leading writers brought the conception of natural law to its culmination, created the foundation of modern sociology, developed utilitarianism, anticipated socialism and gave democratic theory the most profound formulation it has ever received.

Maxey's explanation of enlightenment runs as follows : civilisation has its seasons of sowing and its seasons of harvest. The seventeenth century was for the most part a time of planting and germination; the eighteenth was preeminently a century of fruition and reaping. This was true on well-nigh every front of human enterprise, and notably so in the spheres of science and philosophy. The scientific rationalism which had its birth and adolescence in the seventeenth century came to maturity in the eighteenth. This growth of enlightenment, this movement to enlarge the area of human understanding and enthrone reason as the sovereign guide to human affairs was by the Germans called the *Aufkarung,* by the French *Eclaircissement,* and by the English the Enlightenment.

Rousseau revolted against reason and he had enormous faith on emotion, belief etc. Enlightenment declared the almost opposite and held that reason is the sovereign guide to every action. Whether beliefs and emotions have any importance or not the enlightenment does not consider. Human thought shall be guided by reason. Kant in his *What is Enlightenment?* (1784) wanted to emphasise the revolt against ignorance and superstition. Before the advent of enlightenment superstition, ignorance, belief, emotion etc. were the guiding force of social and political life of individuals. Hence enlightenment wants to assert that not belief and emotion should be the determiner of human activities, the reason shall be the supreme guide. Mcclelland says (p. 298) : "Voltaire attempted to popularise and spread the teachings of Newtonian physics as the true constitution of the universe." Voltaire, we know, was the most important personality of the enlightenment period. He, along with many others, revolted against superstition and other unscientific behaviour and acts.

Enlightenment does not want to treat society as it is, it wants to change the whole structure and functions of society. Its method is to remove ignorance from the mind of people. The chief "function" of ignorance is to stop the growth of knowledge or the urge to know. Mcclelland, that is why, correctly says : all societies left to themselves were necessarily bound to go through the same processes of growth, maturity and decline. I say, "left to themselves" because an important part of enlightenment consisted of devising ways in which that apparently ineluctable process of development could in fact be changed into necessary and inevitable progress, and all this without a word from God" (p. 298). People dared to know, they threw a challenge to what was happening. The irresistible desire of man wanted to know the unknown and to get what has yet not been achieved. In this indomitable desire there was no place of invisible power or, specifically, God. It was believed that human force and knowledge were capable of doing or changing "anything". Enlightenment had also another meaning—to know itself and to know the surrounding.

Rise of Enlightenment

Different scholars have analysed the emergence of enlightenment from their respective outlook. For example, Chris Harman (*A People's History of the World*) says that the rise of class society was a potent factor of the emergence of enlightenment. He says that the intellectually conscious sections of society came to believe that the prevailing structures of the society were defective, that is were not up to mark, and, because of this, they must be changed or restructured. These conscious people, Harman believes, belonged to the middle or upper classes. For one reason or other these people were fully dissatisfied with the mode of functioning of the present society. A major section of these people were highly educated or they were intellectuals. They attacked the prejudice or superstition that dominated the society.

Naturally these people wanted a complete overhaul of society. Harman says : "This catch-all category included a range of thinkers and writers—natural scientists, philosophers, satirists, economists, historians, essayists, novelists, political theorists and even musicians like Mozart" (p. 242). It is not that people of all categories of men held the same view, but all of them came to believe that the existing structure of society must be changed. The outlook of approach of all these categories of people was quite different. But at least on one point they were unanimous. Let us again quote Harman (p. 242) : "What they shared was a belief in the power of rational understanding based on empirical knowledge. This had to be applied to the world, even if it meant challenging existing myths and established beliefs." Such an approach represented a challenge to many of the institutions and much of the ideology of existing European societies. The root cause of enlightenment lies in this approach and outlook.

The origin of enlightenment can also be traced to the idea of John Locke and the Glorious Revolution of 1688. It is said that the Glorious Revolution introduced a change or number of changes which made way for enlightenment. This Revolution made people politically conscious of their own political and other rights. Again, Locke is also regarded as a great precursor to enlightenment. He asserted that "innate ideas" were not the source of knowledge. Only empirical observation could reasonably be regarded as the real source of knowledge. Towards the end of seventeenth century, capitalism was proceeding slowly but steadily and Locke observed that the leading members of this class were eager to ensure their position in society and they began to advance new arguments and place data in favour of their intention and argument. Some believe that this was also a reason of the rise of enlightenment. There is no doubt that the members of the wealthy and powerful class played a leading role in the emergence of enlightenment in several parts of Europe.

Rise of democratic feeling and rationality can be regarded as the cause of enlightenment. Democratic feeling made men conscious of themselves and simultaneously of the society. Along with it came rationality. People observed that superstition and ignorance unreasonably dominated the society and numbed the mind and thought of people. This produced disastrous effects. There was hardly any place of rationality; reasonability and consciousness. A critic observes : "rationality is considered to result in the enlightenment and the development of modern knowledge systems especially in the natural sciences, though it also took an economic form intrinsic to the development of capitalism, industrialisation, modernisation" (*Civil Society*, Edited by Sudipta Kaviraj & Sunil Khilnani, p. 151).

Enlightenment and Political Thought

J. S. Mcclelland says : ...it is no exaggeration to say that all that is best in the Western liberal tradition comes from Enlightenment" (p. 298). Here "liberal tradition" generally means liberal political ideas such as civil liberties, institutionalism, the abolition of slavery, gradualism and moderation etc. All these various concepts have built up the structure of modern liberal political theory. Mc clelland points out that. Mcclelland is not alone, another authority on Enlightenment has expressed almost the same view. He says : The Enlightenment—the age that extends from Locke to Condorcet—was one of the most creative ages in the *history of political theory*. In fact, the important aspects of political theory were the products of enlightenment. Peter

Gay in his *The Enlightenment : An Interpretation* says that without Enlightenment the major aspects of political theory could not get any scope to rise and flourish. So far as modern age of political theory is concerned, Enlightenment has a very important role to play. Modern age starts from the Enlightenment.

The most important contribution of Enlightenment is the development of reason and reason is singularly responsible for the rise and growth of liberal political ideas such as democracy, liberty, rights etc. Prof. Amartya Sen in his recent and noted work *The Argumentative Indian* has observed that Enlightenment has inspired men to follow reason and act accordingly and, again, the reason encourages him to make "intellectual enquiry." The urge to enquire everything by applying reason has given birth to many political concepts.

Reason and liberalism are inseparable concepts. An individual under the influence of reason tries to follow and act. In other words, whenever a man acts or intends to act he does it by applying his reason and from this has emerged the basic aspect of liberalism. Liberalism implies to act anything in accordance with reason. A man cannot use another man as his slave. Both are the creatures of God. There is no reason behind the system of slavery. This feeling finally led to the abolition of slavery. **Hence an important contribution of Enlightenment to the political theory is liberalism.** Dante Germino in his *Machiavelli to Marx : Modern Western Political Thought* writes : "Many of the Enlightenment spokesmen were liberals." The liberal thinkers of the Enlightenment period were liberal-minded and this feature influenced them to view the political ideas and concepts form this background. In France, Enlightenment was very active and that generated the liberal thought. It is observed that Enlightenment forced the autocratic government to adopt certain liberal measures. But the autocratic nature of the French Government survived. There was practically no change and this frustrated the liberal thinkers of the eighteenth century.

Another aspect of liberalism can be stated in the following way. This laid great faith on institutionalism and all sorts of liberty—particularly civil and political liberty and right. Being under the influence of reason and rationality people began to demand more and more rights and liberties because they thought that without these there was no possibility of developing unblossomed qualities of man. Enlightenment had hardly any faith on revolution or armed struggles. It believed that political, economic and social goals could be achieved through constitutional and democratic methods. This is called gradualism. Liberalism had no confidence on abrupt and violent change. Gradualism has also a relation with moderation. The time-old behaviour social structures and manners can be changed or reformed with the help of gradualism or liberal methods. There is another aspect of liberalism. The rule of law must prevail in every sphere of social and political life. Each person must have full freedom of thought and expression and to form association. The liberalism simultaneously extended its wings even to the domain of internationalism. There shall exist cordial relation and good understanding among all nations—big and small—Progress in all its manifestations shall be achieved through mutual understanding and cooperation. There also developed an interesting idea in the age of Enlightenment and this can be stated in the following manner—People will enjoy both rights and liberties. But all these must not hinder the enjoyment of these by other people as well as the smooth functioning of democratic government.

Enlightenment duly recognised the importance of natural rights and natural law. The importance of natural rights and natural law did not start their journey during the period of Enlightenment. Actually the journey started during Aristotle's time and the journey reached a very important stage in the writings of contractualists Hobbes and Locke. Several Enlightenment thinkers thought that only proper emphasis on natural law and natural rights could ensure people's interests and position and enhance the boundary of democratic rights. The following comment, it is expected, will throw enough light on the subject. "In the evolution of the concept of natural law emphasis is shifted from duties to rights, from the natural basis of the community to the inviolable claims of the individual, from a theologically related natural law to norms that emanate from world—immanent autonomous reason." Dante Germino : *Machiavelli to Marx : Modern Western Political Thought*, p. 156.

Another contribution of Enlightenment to political theory or thought was that it helped people to be conscious of their own position in society. Chris Harman refers to the class. He says that the rise and development of reason enabled men to be conscious of their status or position (specially in regard to economic status) in society. Harman claims that before the advent of Enlightenment men were not quite conscious of this aspect. It means that during and after Enlightenment people came to realise that there are different classes (judged from economic criteria) in society. Mainly there were two classes—wealthy class and poor people. In between these two were also other classes. But these two were prominent. Harman (through statistics) says that only very few people were capable of leading luxurious life and the largest numbers were deprived of bare necessities. This implies that even before the onset of Enlightenment the division of society (into rich and poor) was almost complete. But the Enlightenment thinkers were not revolutionaries and not eager to change the structure of society. Even the great intellectuals did not think of changing the society. The division of society into classes did not go unnoticed. Large number of people were vociferous of the nature and ill-effects of the division of society into classes. But it took more than half century to be widely discussed. In the hands of Marx class society received maximum treatment.

An important aspect of Enlightenment's contribution to political thought is serious attempts were made by many to free politics from the clutches of church and religion. Gibbon's famous book *Decline and fall of Roman Empire* contains a scathing attack on the influence of religion and church on the political affairs of state and government. It is perhaps not unresonable to say that secularism in politics started (at least in embryonic form) during the period of Enlightenment. Though Machiavelli was pioneer in this field, his achievement was not spectacular. David Hume was also very vocal about the dominating influence of religion. Voltaire was also very vocal about the ill-effects of religion and he called it infamous. His famous slogan in this regard was "Crush the infamy" "So Voltaire could rage against the superstition of religion and subject Biblical accounts of miracles to devastating critiques. Voltaire vehemently opposed (and also criticised) the behaviour and activities of the Pope and the priests of the church. This attitude of Voltaire immediately antagonised the Church fathers and they in numerous ways tried to heckle Voltaire. The growth of Enlightenment, however, put a powerful brake on the forward journey of religion and its dominating influence upon politics and other aspects of society. The Enlightenment thinkers further argued if God created laws for the physical world, the same God also made laws for human world and this world would be administered by these laws. All must be governed by these laws and no discrimination should be allowed to work. This implies a very important aspect of modern political theory and this is the rule of law. Later on the British Constitution adopted this concept and Britain the constitution followed.

Montesquieu

Montesquieu's full name is baron de la Brede et de Montesquieu—popularly known as Montesquieu. He was born in a French noble family in 1689 and died in 1755. He loved to read and write and, like the utilitarian thinker—he spent his life in reading and writing. He was really a great intellectual of eighteenth century France, and not only France, his name and fame crossed the border of France and spread in other parts of Western Europe. Three important works of Montesquieu deal with political theory. These are : *The Persian Letters* (1721), *Consideration on the Causes of the Greatness and Decline of Romans* (1734), and the most important and widely read book *The Spirit of the Laws* (1748).

I have already noted that Montesquieu was the most important figure of the Enlightenment. Let us throw light on this issue. He once said that there was no second opinion that people should be enlightened because without this their prejudice and ignorance would never vanish. Again, he believed that both prejudice and ignorance were the greatest enemies of man, progress and, above all, civilisation. In this connection Dante Germino says : "Enlightenment was Montesquieu's goal. By enlightenment he meant the liberation from prejudice of both rulers and the ruled. By prejudice he meant not what makes men ignorant of certain things but what makes them ignorant of themselves. He shared the Enlightenments confidence in the power of education to liberate man" (p. 169). Through the machinery of Enlightenment Montesquieu wanted the overall progress of society. Some of his biographers and critics of his political philosophy claim that he used Enlightenment for the purpose of new political ideas and concepts.

Separation of Powers

Montesquieu is famous in the history of political thought for his famous formulation of separation of powers as the most important precondition of political liberty and this idea he stated in his famous *The Spirit of Laws.* About this book Marxey says (*Political Philosophies*, p. 305), "It would be hard to name a book that has ever achieved speedier, wider or more lasting fame than *The Spirit of the Laws.* In this book he dealt with number of political concepts which are still of prime importance. One such concept is *separation of powers* and the other is *laws.*" Let us quote liberally from *The Spirit of the Laws* :

"In every government there are three sorts of power—the legislative, the executive in respect to things dependent on the law of nations, and the executive in regard to matters that depend in the civil law. By virtue of the first, the prince or magistrate enacts temporary or perpetual laws. By the second, he makes peace or war, sends or receives embassies, establishes the public securities. By the third, he punishes criminals and determines the disputes that arise between individuals. The latter we shall call judiciary power." This is the clear formulation of separation of power stated by Montesquieu. He visited several European countries including Britain and there he "found" that the British people enjoyed liberty because of the separation of power. In other words, the separation of powers was the recipe of political liberty. Let us again quote him :

"When the legislative and executive powers are united in the same person or in the body of magistrates, there can be no liberty. Again there is no liberty, if the judiciary power be not separated from the legislative and executive. Were it joined with the legislative, the life and liberty of the subject would be exposed to arbitrary control. Were it joined to the executive power the judge might behave with violence and oppression. There would be an end of everything, were the same men or the same body, whether of nobles or of the people to exercise those three powers, that of enacting laws, that of executing the public resolutions, and of trying the causes of individuals. We have quoted a lengthy passage from Montesquieu's *The Spirit of the Laws.* In the opinion of Montesquieu the key to political liberty lies in the separation of powers. He was so impressed at the sight of the quantum of political liberty enjoyed by the British people that without going into the depth of the matter he forthwith arrived at the conclusion that this was due to the separation of powers. But, in reality, this is wrong.

Montesquieu gathered a very wrong conception about the structure and working of the British administrative system. Being an Enlightenment man he was a great lover and worshipper of freedom and the amount of liberty enjoyed by Englishmen impressed him. But the fact is that in his time and even today there is no trace of separation of powers in Britain. Notwithstanding, British people enjoy political liberty. Why and how? Let us quote few lines from Maxey's book : "British liberty had been achieved by the erection of constitutional barriers against arbitrary power and there was a feeling that the courts should be independent and the crown and parliament balanced against one another, though full organic separation had not taken place and never did" (p. 319). He believed that without liberty people could not get any scope to enlighten his thought and achieve success in life.

Montesquieu and Law

Montesquieu has treated laws as simply social facts. Laws are the crystallisations of social experience and byproducts of social adjustments. In human society, people live, and they are to make adjustments among themselves. Laws are the products of those adjustments. Let us elaborate the matter. At some period of time people lived in unorganised societies and the relationship among them was not controlled by law because there was no law worth its name. The formation of society was actually the originator of law. He writes : "As soon as man enters into a state of society he loses the sense of his weakness, equality ceases and then commences the state of war". Social life makes men conscious and courageous. They prepare themselves to face any situation. But the society does remain static in a particular situation. It moves forward, which means that, with the change of time and physical environment, society also changes. This change brings about change in the nature and structure of law. Summing up Montesquieu's stand Maxey says (p. 310), "These two states of war give rise to positive law; the law of nations, governing the relations between individuals within societies." Behind the formation of law there was always the active role of reason. Let us see what Montesquieu says about law. He says :

"Laws, in their most comprehensive signification, are the necessary relations which derive from the nature of things, and, in this sense all beings have their laws, the divinity has its laws, the material world its laws, intelligences superior to man their laws, beasts their laws, man his laws" (Quoted by Dante Germino, p. 170).

If we thoroughly study Montesquieu's view about law we shall find that there are several factors behind every law; one such factor is reason. Since he was an Enlightenment man he always thought that behind every act or gesture there must be reason. In other words, the laws are always the manifestations of reason. Laws, again, are built upon the relations among men. In his view the relations are practically built upon reason and, finally, on law. Explaining Montesquieu's view about law Plamenatz makes the following observation. His definition of law "is meant to cover all uniformities of behaviour as well as moral rules, custom and civil laws. It, therefore, treats descriptive and prescriptive laws as if they were of the same general type."

Montesquieu divides law into three classes corresponding to three sets of relations. When the law is between the nations, it is the law of nations. When there is the question of the relation between ruler and the ruled it is called political law. The relations among the individual citizens are decided by civil law. His classification of law is unique. Today there exist all these three types of law. Even there are other types of laws. But Montesquieu had noted three basic form of laws. Here lies his credit. His view about law has been criticised by Sabine. He says that Montesquieu's theory of law is based on a vague formula and he makes no attempt to clear his definitions. Plamenatz says that it is easy to pull his theory of law to pieces. But many of his innumerable facts and conclusions have proved true or close to the truth. Though Voltaire did not like him he thought that Montesquieu's opinion about law was correct.

David Hume

Hume was born in 1711 and died in 1776. This year is famous in Western history. Adam Smiths *The Wealth of Nations* was published in 1776. The American Declaration of Independence took place in 1776 and, finally, Bentham published his *Fragment of Government* in this year. Hume was an important part of the Enlightenment. 1748 was a memorable year for Hume. He published the third edition of *Essay.* Hume had a great friendship with Enlightenment thinker Montesquieu. Hume presented a copy of the third edition of *Essay* to Montesquieu and in return Montesquieu presented a copy of *The Spirit of Law* to Hume. This paved the way of friendship between the two great thinkers of the Enlightenment.

Hume has been regarded as an iconoclast in the philosophical world. He thought that religion made man bad—individually and collectively. This is the opinion of Maxey. He thought that man was generally misguided by religion and, in fact, there is no reason in religion. Man is moved by sentiment and emotion and these are generally the products of religion. Some critics say that Hume was a turncoat on account of his apparent swing from Whigism to Toryism. But Maxey does accept this charge against Hume. He says, "The integrity of his fundamental political ideas was never compromised" (p. 331). Hume was always under the influence of particular incidents and these forced him to change his opinion. About him Plamenatz's assessment is interesting : "Hume's would surely be a broom. Not that he liked to boast or threaten. He was the most polite as well as most ruthless of critics. He used his broom deftly and quietly, raising little dust, but he used it vigorously" (p. 299).

Hume on Social Contract

Hobbes, Locke and Rousseau, the three great apostles of social contract—have assiduously argued that the civil society or the body politic or the state was the product of contract. But Hume—the great figure of Enlightenment and ardent believer in reason, was against the contract theory. He was also historically-minded. In our analysis of contract theory we have shown that behind it there are no historical facts. It is simply an imagination that at certain period of time men lived in an imaginary situation called the state of nature and the unpleasant or anarchical situation forced them to leave that situation. But Hume rejected the social contract root and branch. He was of the view that a social contract might be the cause of state, but such a contract must, for all practical purposes, be *historical* and *sociological*. He says, "no compact or agreement was expressly formed for general submission; an idea far beyond the comprehension of savages."

About the origin of state Hume said :

"Examination of the world today affords no support for the view that government rests on contract. On the contrary, everywhere we find princes who claim their subjects as their property and assert their independent right of sovereignty from conquest or succession and subjects acknowledge their subordination. Almost all the governments which exist at present or of which there remain any record in his story, have been founded originally either on usurpation or conquest or both, without any pretence of a fair consent or voluntary subjection of the people". So we find that in Hume's judgment the state was not the product of social contract. He also did not accept the tacit consent.

Hume concludes that all the governments whose records are available in history were founded without any voluntary consent of the people. "It is vain to say that all governments are or should be founded on popular consent, as much as the necessities of human affairs will admit I maintain that human affairs will never admit of this consent, seldom of the appearance of it. My intention here is not to exclude the consent of the people from being the one just foundation of government where it has place. It is surely the best and most sacred of any" (Quoted by Maxey, p. 331). So it is quite clear that Hume did not accept the social contract as the foundation of state. If so, what, according to him, is the real cause of the foundation? According to Hume, the **social evolution is the real cause.** He has explained the stages of social evolution and in a stage the state or human society has finally come into existence. In the various stages of evolution human consent has very insignificant role to play. Stage by stage and step by step society has evolved and, naturally, the consent has nothing to play. Human society is always in the condition of change or flux. In such a situation consent has no scope to play any constructive role. He has, however, admitted that consent might have a very insignificant contribution. In the opinion of Plamenatz (*Man and Society*, Vol. 1, p. 316) according to Hume the state is merely a contrivance in the public interest. The more we accept it and less we tamper with it, the more useful it is likely to be.

Assessment

Many modern critics are not quite sympathetic about the contribution of Enlightenment. For example J. S. Mcclelland makes the following comment :

"Enlightenment's critics seem to be unanimous that the Enlightenment was deeply subversive. ...Enlightenment came to be a byword for shallow and pretentious over-intellectualism, naively deductive, geometrical in spirit, indifferent to anything about men except their natural rights. It was this superficiality which led enlightenment thinkers to attack, or at least ridicule, all existing forms of authority in the name of individualism" (p. 310).

The chief contribution of Enlightenment is it has always appealed to reason. It has vehemently opposed religious bigotry and superstition. Its main appeal was to reason and intellect. It is correct. But reason or intellect of very limited and educated persons. In the days of Enlightenment the percentage of literacy was miserably low and, naturally, very few persons had the ability to be guided by reason. That is why Mcclelland rightly maintains : "Enlightenment was not populist. Its audience was the literate bourgeoisie and aristocracy, neither of which could be called naturally revolutionary classes" (p. 311).

Enlightenment had immense faith on reason. Reason, no doubt, has power to guide men properly and correctly. But this power is very very limited. Men must be properly educated and there shall exist enough congenial atmosphere to express opinion fearlessly. It is quite unfortunate that Enlightenment has not brought all these into active consideration.

The bright sides of Enlightenment must be equally considered with due importance. Peter Gay (*The Enlightenment : An Interpretation*) says, "Enlightenment philosophers had a set of ideals. They championed free enquiry, they upheld the right to free thought and expression, they believed in diversity, they were secular, they despised superstition and fanaticism, they believed in the possibilities of reform and they were passionately humane. Indeed, if Enlightenment thinkers could be summed up in one phrase. I would call them 'the party of humanity'."

The most important contribution of Enlightenment was liberalism and specially the rights and liberties of men. In 18th century, people's will, feeling and rights were mercilessly suppressed. The writers of the Enlightenment period were quite vociferous about these rights and liberties and they tirelessly propagated that all the people must have liberty and right. They were revolutionaries but they supported the right and genuine cause of men. The Enlightenment thinkers of France and other European states propagated that every individual must have natural rights. The political philosophy of Enlightenment is clearly reflected in the American Declaration of Independence. The constitution of US declares all men are created equal and they have right to life, liberty and property. It is said that this is the message of Enlightenment. The French declaration of the Rights of Man of 1789 is also representative of Enlightenment.

23 HERBERT SPENCER (1820-1903)

State vs Individual

The cult of the state is the dominating thought of both German idealism and Oxford idealism. T. H. Green is a small variation because of his emphasis on individuals. But in the writings of Bosanquet the state appears to us as the most powerful institution. It is the highest embodiment of goodwill, morality, spirit or idea and the individual achieves his morality and freedom only through the membership of state. Against this cult of state there also developed in the nineteenth century the cult of the individual. Not the state but the individual is the central figure of the social *milieu*. He keeps and safeguards his independent existence within the state. The will of the individual in certain respects is subject to that of the state, but he never loses his identity within the state.

The cult of the individual may aptly be called the product of rationalism and industrialism. It was believed that rationality made men reasonable which enabled him to judge every act, principle and policy with reason. If policy, principle and actions appear to be reasonable people think of accepting them. Since men are the holder of reason and rationality authority, cannot take any policy ignoring their arguments. To sum up, men form the central position of the entire social structure. Hence the cult of the individual means man is the final determiner of everything. The individual is rational and this helps him to decide what is good and what is bad. Through the independent and rational efforts of all individuals general welfare of the society is possible. The interference of the state in this field is uncalled for.

Industrialisation changed the economic and commercial picture of Europe. Rapid progress took place. Huge amount of commodity was produced. Simultaneously, state intervention began to increase day by day. This was not favourably looked by many. The state intervention in economic affairs is obsolete and anti-progressive and it is simply obstructionist. For the maximisation of economic progress the individuals shall have sufficient freedom so that they can exercise free will. Individual liberty came to be a strong principle in both economic and political fields.

Herbert Spencer (born April 27, 1820) was an uncompromising advocate of extreme form of individualism. Though he was a nineteenth century thinker his arguments still create interest in the minds of students of Western political thought. His father was a poor school master and unable to provide Spencer proper education. Because of poverty he could not finish his school education. But his father always encouraged him to act and think according to reason and adopt scientific methods in his study and thought. With the help of his father J. S. Mill had acquainted himself with Greek and Latin when he was just three years old. In comparison, Spencer was unfortunate. Even when he was thirteen he had no knowledge of Latin and Greek. At the age of sixteen he acquired working knowledge of mathematics and other subjects. He, with the help of his knowledge, was able to get a job in a school. But he did not continue as a school teacher. He was appointed a civil engineer in Birmingham Railway. His service was terminated with the completion of the Railway construction.

After he was sacked he shifted to London in order to establish himself as a man of literature. This he did in 1843. He wrote many articles on economics, philosophy, science, sociology etc. By 1848 Spencer succeeded in establishing himself as a writer. In 1848 he was appointed a sub-editor of the famous *The Economist*. By virtue of his position as a sub-editor he came in close contact with many noted personalities such as Huxley, George Eliot etc. Since 1848 he devoted his time and energy to writing and reading. Maxey observes (p. 556) "Spencer's social background and irregular education had not a little to do with his dissident approach to philosophical problems. All his life he remained keenly class conscious and manifested positive dislike for the upper classes and all their works".

In 1851 he published *Social Statics* and in 1855, at his own expense, *The Principles of Psychology*. Spencer's health at this time did not run well. He undertook several excursions to France. In 1858 he brought out *A System of Synthetic Philosophy*. His other works *The Principles of Biology, The Principles of Sociology, The Principles of Ethics* were published between 1862 and 1892. He also wrote several other books such as *Justice, Nature* and *Reality of Religion*. His most important work on politics, *The Man Versus the State*, was published in 1884.

Spencer's Method

It is said that the method applied by Spencer for the analysis of political phenomena and related ideas is called scientific method. This is because Spencer claimed that he applied scientific method and principles of natural science for the analysis of political issues. He did not follow utilitarianism which in his opinion is nothing but "expediency philosophy". But he did not rule out the idea of utilitarianism. He supported it in an indirect way. Each and every man must be able to maximise his happiness in the social system. Laws should be framed keeping this general idea in mind. He had no weakness for morality which was assiduously propagated by Green and other Oxford idealists. He was of opinion that morality is essentially one with physical truth—is in fact a species of transcendental psychology.

Spencer's chief objective was to synthesise all the scientific knowledge. He was least interested whether this was possible or not. But his inclination to scientific method and his determination to apply it to ethics, politics and above all philosophy augmented his position as a philosopher and secured for him a very high place in the philosophical world of the nineteenth century. He deeply involved himself into the exploration of knowledge contained in metaphysics, ethics, theology, biology, psychology and sociology. He failed in this field no doubt, but he differed from his predecessors.

In his analysis of political ideas and issues he applied the general principles of evolutionism and for that reason he was called an evolutionist . There is no doubt that he was tremendously influenced by Charles Darwin. Six years before the publication of Darwin's *Origin of Species* Spencer published several essays and books on the nature of evolution. Spencer's attitude to evolutionism brought him nearer to Darwin, Wallace, Huxley and Lewes. An evolutionist though he was, he disagreed with Darwin on some points or conclusions. "He did not agree with Darwin that natural selection takes place through accidental variation, but held that variation and adaptation were manifestation of purpose" (Maxey, p. 557).

Spencer's political thought is the manifest product of his scientific knowledge, particularly his theory of evolution. He applied his theory of purposive adaptation and selection to political theory. Spencer also believed in the organic character of society. That is, society is analogous to biological organism and it is subject to the same law of evolution. In his view, as society evolves so also human thought and specifically the political thought. To sum up, Spencer attempts to apply the theory of evolution to all spheres of knowledge. The characters of human beings come under the influence of evolution. The human qualities are transmitted though natural selection.

An important aspect of Spencer's method is he applied systematic and scientific method for the analysis of the various issues of politics and chiefly for this reason he has been called a system-builder. He believed that without systematic and scientific knowledge political issues can never be properly explained. His study of biology, psychology and other subjects enabled him to arrive at this conclusion. He also applied strict disciplines for the analysis of political ideas. He is generally called a system builder. But many of his critics do not agree. His sole purpose was to arrive at a single formula.

Spencer's systematisation is an outgrowth of his theory of evolution. By evolution he means "an integration of matter and concomitant dissipation of motion, during which matter passes from a relatively indefinite, incoherent homogeneity to a relatively definite, coherent heterogeneity and during which the retained motion undergoes a parallel transformation." This process of evolution is to be found everywhere—in highly organised complex living bodies, in the growth of language and also in the evolution of social and political organisations. Spencer says that these organisations move from relative indefiniteness to relative definiteness, from incoherence to coherence. With the evolution, structural and functional differentiations also surface. In this way, Spencer systematises and unifies the philosophy.

Barker strongly criticises Spencer's attempt to view politics in the light of natural science. His purpose was not to enrich politics with the principles of science or to elicit the political lessons which science might teach. He had no intention to improve the teachings of politics by applying scientific principles to the field of politics. On the contrary, he formed certain political preconceptions and then he wanted to establish and justify them with the help of the examples and analogies of science. He sketched the plot and then justified it. Barker observes (p. 71) "The fundamental confusion which he never surmounts is due to the fact that the *a priori* conceptions of individual right with which he starts do not and cannot accord with the organic and evolutionary conception of the state which he attains through the use of natural science. His philosophy consequently begins and ends as an incongruous mixture of Natural Rights and physiological metaphor."

Spencer was extremely obssessed with the freedom of the individual and consequently with the limitations of state power. The power of the state should be cut to size for the purpose of enhancing the liberty of the individual. He came to the conclusion that the evolution of human being has reached the apex stage and because of this reason he should be given maximum freedom. Only in this way a desirable level of social development can be achieved. Spencer was thus one of the chief exponents of *laissez-faire* doctrine.

Theory of Evolution

We have already stated that Spencer applied principles of evolution in the study and proper analysis of political principles. Now let us see what did he mean by the principles of evolution. In the principle of evolution he has shown how the material world is changing constantly. It evolves from one stage to another, from indefinite to definite, from incoherent to coherent, from incoherent homogeneity to coherent heterogeneity. The earth also develops from uniform liquid mass to diversified form and structure. The law of evolution also works in the development of society. According to Spencer, the primitive society was incoherent and simple. Complexity and coherence have become prominent in the developed state of society. In the *Social Statics* Spencer has elaborated the concept of evolution.

The process of evolution results from the perpetual antihesis of two great forces of nature—the dynamic tendency towards change and the static tendency towards equilibrium. This is a very important principle of the theory of evolution. Darwin discovered it and Spencer borrowed it from him and applied it to political studies. Spencer writes in *Social Statics* "All evil results from the non-adaptation of constitution to conditions. Equally true is it that evil perpetually tends to disappear. In virtue of an essential principle of life, this non-adaptation of an organism to its conditions is ever being rectified; and modification of one or both, continues until the adaptation is complete. Whatever possesses vitality, from the elementary cell upto man himself, inclusive, obeys this law."[1]

Applying the general principles of evolution Spencer has said that as animals have adjusted with changes in environment and in this way both animals and society of animal have evolved, so men will have to adjust with the environment that exists around them. The success of men in the process of adjustment will finally result in the setting up of an equilibrium—equilibrium among all the forces or element that exist. When such an equilibrium appears it will be assumed that perfection has arrived. In other words in a perfect society man and his environment are both in a balanced position. Spencer further observes that such a balanced and static position may not be fully achieved, but the concept of evolution may be approached from this angle. If we accept the principle of evolution this conclusion is inevitable.

It has been argued by Spencer that the growth of society is accompanied by a progressive differentiation of structures, which results in progressive differentiation of functions. The principle of evolution states that the "state of homogeneity is an unstable state; and where there is already some heterogeneity, the tendency is towards greater heterogeneity." From this it follows that the movement of evolution is greater in a heterogeneous society. A society with greater and deeper differentia-

1. Quoted by Maxey, p. 558.

tion is subject to bigger dynamic changes. So contradiction or differentiation is a vital aspect of social change.

Coherence and incoherence; homogeneity and heterogeneity are very important terms of Spencer's theory of evolution. Armed with these terms Spencer distinguishes between militant society and industrial society. He assumes that in the former there is coherence of homogeneity. In other words, uniformity is the characteristic feature of militant society. Various stringent regulations control the conduct of individuals and they have no freedom of action and thought. Because of great homogeneity the militant society naturally does not achieve spectacular progress. The individuality of each member has to be so subordinated in life, liberty and property, that he is largely or completely *owned* by the state. Militant type of society aims at self-sufficiency, political autonomy tends to be accompanied by economic autonomy. By industrial society Spencer means a society dominated by the principle of *laissez-faire*. In Spencer's judgment, in an industrial society there is ample scope of evolution. Heterogeneity and differentiation lead it to greater amount of perfection. Again, such societies are rich in experience. Differentiation and heterogeneity act as inducement to progress.

Spencer has said that the concept of evolution is not confined only in the physical world. He has said that the experience, knowledge and ideas all change through the process of evolution. The consequence is the idea, knowledge and experience of one epoch are higher and developed from the previous epoch. In this process experience and knowledge proceed towards higher or better stage or quality. The experience of one generation is transmitted to the next. The human faculties, through the process of evolution, achieve more and more perfection. Spencer's theory of evolution thus encompasses both external and internal factors. With the process of evolution the adaptation and adjustment also takes place. Experience and knowledge enable man to adapt with the new environment. So the development of knowledge and experience is essential to evolution. What Spencer asserts is that without knowledge and experience neither progress nor evolution is possible and an industrial society assures it.

Survival of the Fittest

The survival of the fittest can reasonably be called the product of the theory of evolution. Darwin said so. But some scholars are of opinion that Spencer coined the phrase–"survival of the fittest". It however goes with the name of Darwin. The possibility to survive depends upon the ability to adapt or adjust with the physical environment. The weak or sick incapable of adjusting with the environment becomes victim of extinction. So the first and foremost condition of survival is fitness. Spencer says that a labourer incapacitated by sickness from competing with stronger fellows should have to bear the resulting privations. In other words, adaptation and adjustment is the primary condition of survival and it is corroborated by history.

In his opinion, philanthropic organisations and kind-hearted persons are giving continuous help to disabled persons and by doing this they are entailing greater misery and misfortune upon the society. Spencer is a logical thinker and because of this he has illustrated his contention. When a mother, disregarding the advice of doctor, gives sweets to her child that cannot be treated as kindness. If a doctor considering the pain refrains from operation, surely he is not doing benefit to the patient. Under the natural order of things the society is constantly excreting its unhealthy, imbecile, slow, vacillating faithless members. In this natural way the society purifies itself. But if this purification is stopped by artificial means the society will become filled up with underserving persons. The venture of the philanthropists discourages the multiplication of competent persons.

His extreme love for the theory of evolution inspired him to frame certain conclusions which have been vociferously denounced by many. He said that the philanthropists or state authority adopt several welfare measures for the improvement of physical and economic conditions of the weaker or poorer sections of the community. Apparently these measures improve their conditions but ultimately these welfare measures are doing more harm than benefit. How? Spencer says that man constantly adapts himself with the environment taking the help of his acquired knowledge and experience. But, being helped by others, man loses the urge to adjust. That is, power of adaptation fails to develop. This is a dangerous tendency. The dependence of weak persons is making them more and more weak and this is multiplying the burden of society. The creative faculties are discouraged and inefficient faculties are encouraged. This never produces salutary results. Spencer, therefore, concludes that nature should be given a free hand in the selection of persons who are fit for the society. After studying all the aspects of evolution and natural selection Spencer was confirmed that the state interference or the activities of the philanthropists were halting the process of natural selection and this led to the halt or demise of survival of the fittest. The result was that the equilibrium among the various sections could not find any opportunity to develop. He also said that everyman has certain creative faculties and these develop through the process of survival of the fittest. To sum up, Spencer adopted Darwin's theory to the study of social as well as political phenomena and framed conclusions.

Spencer was to some extent influenced by German idealism and this led him to propagate the theory of universal evolution. In the entire universe different forces or energies are constantly proceeding towards perfection and to achieve that goal they are adjusting with the environment. The perfection may be termed as equilibrium. To make the universal equilibrium a possibility it is necessary that the power of government should be curtailed. Spencer emphasises that the whole universe is under the process of evolution and no part can be separated artificially.

Theory of State

Plato and other idealist philosophers viewed the state as an organic whole in the sense the individuals constituting the state are its integral parts. Hobbes's state was an all-powerful Leviathan. But Spencer's analysis of state does not fall in this category. He treated the state as an organism and he uses the word in a metaphorical sense. He says that organic bodies are all subject to the laws of growth and decay. Birth, growth and decay all are the characteristic features of every organic body. Spencer asserts that the state, like an organic body, is also subject to the same laws of birth, growth and decay. It is interesting to note that Spencer borrowed this idea from biological science and applied it to the theory of politics.

Let us note some of the aspects of similarities between human body and state as conceived by Spencer. There are various parts of every human body, so also has the state manifold parts. There are farmers, workers, retail traders, wholesalers, manufacturers, professional persons, engineers, lawyers, bankers, priests and academicians. All these persons constitute the structure of the state and participate in its administration. They have their different functions as the different parts of the human body discharge different duties

Elaborating the analogy between the state and organic body he further observes that the population of the state increases—that is the indication of its growth. Sometimes foreign territories are added to a state through aggression which is also a sign of growth. It is also found that new states are created. Due to political turmoil or other factors some states are merged with others, that is called decay. How the birth, growth and decay characterise the human body require no elaboration. Both human body and state pass through evolutionary process.

Spencer says that the growth of both human body and state passes through complexities and differentiations as well as long process of time. In other words according to Spencer evolution works behind both of man and state. The primitive state was coherent and simple. This is not the case with the modern state. The same also applies to human body. The growth of the body invites both complicacies and differentiation. In developed industrial societies the division of labour is strictly adhered to. As different parts of the human body are dependent on each other and the whole body functions because of the cooperation of these parts, so also the several parts of the state are dependent upon each other and the non-cooperation of any one part or department or section can throw the entire state into disarray.

All the parts of human body are not of equal importance—some are more vital than the others. The same thing applies to the state. In a state, there are several departments without which the normal functioning of the state will be an impossibility—military or defence, finance and railway. The normality of both body and state depends upon the proper functioning, healthy conditions and the spontaneous cooperation of all the vital organs. That is why careful attention is always focussed to these vital organs.

Spencer in his *Principles of Sociology* has drawn our attention to other aspects of similarities between human body and state. He says that both human body and state have passed through several stages to reach the apex position. The primitive societies were very simple. When it became industrial society, new feature cropped up, making it a complex one. Similarly, primitive man was not intelligent and their inventive power was not of high quality. Evolution has made him intelligent and inventive. But, at the same time, his life has become complicated.

The similarities between state and human body need not lead one to jump upon the conclusion that both the state and human body are almost identical in many respects. There are vital dissimilarities between the two. The units or organs of the state are not fixed in size and function. With the progress of state, different organs grow in size and the functions also assume complicacy. On the other hand, the parts of body are always fixed. In the society there is no single centre of consciousness but in body there is such a single centre.

Functions of State

The state conceived by Spencer is basically an individualist state which means that the state is an independent unit like an individual and it discharges its responsibilities independently. Each individual is a separate centre of consciousness and he claims that individuals should be permitted to have distinct identity. Many societies have not made any provision of this basic requirement. One unit cannot function with complete independence. We find Coplestone to make the following observation : "Spencer's determination to use the idea of evolution throughout all fields of phenomena leads him to speak of political society, the state, as a super organism. But as he is a resolute champion of individual liberty against the claims and encroachment of the state, he tries to deprive this analogy of its sting by pointing out essential differences between the organic body and the body political. And he does this by maintaining that while political development is a process of integration in the sense that social groups become larger and individual wills are merged together, it is also a movement from homogeneity to heterogeneity, so that differentiation tends to increase" (pp. 131-132).

According to Spencer it is the impact of evolution that has enabled man to develop and exercise separate identity and due to this heterogeneity has become a feature of society. Heterogeneity is the basic characteristic of man. This is the source of Spencer's individualism. There is another potential source. Spencer sprang from a family essentially dissenting and, as such, opposed to authority; and his nonconformist instincts and non-conformist training in his youth left an abiding mark (Barker, p. 72). He had formed a firm belief that the absence of any hype of state control upon people would invariably lead them to reach the maximum level of pleasure. He, of course, endorsed the governmental interference for maintaining law and order.

Commenting on Spencer's elaborate account of the functions of state Prof. Ernest Barker makes the following succinct comment "Spencer's account of the function of the state is mainly an account of what the state ought not to do." On an earlier occasion we pointed out that Spencer was not a utilitarian in the sense Bentham was. But he believed in utilitarianism. Only the minimum "governance can ensure maximum happiness". That means Spencer's state has practically nothing to do except maintaining law and order. Spencer was an advocate of *laissez-faire* doctrine. Free play of individual's freedom in economic field would ensure profit and growth of industry. So a government with a minimum amount of reason should not try to interfere with the activities of the industrialists. In order to allow the natural selection to operate, it is the duty of the state not to provide relief to the poor. The persons who are incapable to fight away the odd situation would ultimately succumb and finally this will bring about a great relief for the entire society and it will be benefited. The man who cannot compete with others has no right to live. The society is meant for the fittest persons. In religious affairs, state interference cannot be tolerated. If the state launches welfare projects to give relief to the poor and disabled persons they will be completely dependent upon state, will not be able to adapt with the environment, and, finally, will never learn the discipline. What appears from Spencer's account of the functions of the state is that he was in favour of limiting its functions. It is also the duty of the state to see that the society is capable of maintaining its competitive character which is a criterion of growth.

Spencer is also against state-sponsored education system. He proposes that the entire system of education shall be fully controlled by individuals or organisations existing beyond the control of all types of control of state. Man will purchase his daily necessities from open market and he will educate his children according to his own choice. State-controlled education is always conservative in character. Education of the state has no power to check crime. Nor can it broaden the human mind. Spencer even goes further when he observes that it is unnecessary for the state to set-up mint or to erect a lighthouse. Barker writes (p. 88) : "It has, in a word, no business to interfere with the wise severity of nature's discipline, which makes us better when we do things for ourselves, and what is more—makes the things which we do for ourselves better done than those which the state does for us."

Herbert Spencer is quite meticulous in regard to what a state cannot do. In fact he has given a long list of areas in which the state has practically no role to play. He has, however, said that the state has something to do. In his view the chief function of the state is to make the process of evolution obstacle-free. *Laiseez-faire* is the only way to social progress and scientific development. People will be able to enrich fund of knowledge and experience from trial and error, but will learn very little if doctored by others. So the process of evolution should not be stopped and, on the contrary, by all means it should be encouraged.

In the *Social Statics* Spencer enumerates the following functions of the state :

"It is clear that any being, whose constitution is to be moulded into fitness for new conditions of existence, must be placed under these conditions. This granted, it follows that as man has been, and is still, deficient in those feelings which prevent the recurring antagonisms of individuals and their consequent disunion, some artificial agency is required by which their union may be maintained. Only by the process of adaptation itself can be produced that character which makes social equilibrium spontaneous. And hence, while this process is going on, an instrumentality must be employed, firstly to bind men into the social state, and secondly to check all conduct endangering the existence of that state. Such an instrumentality we have in government."[1] While analysing the functions of state Spencer always emphasised that the state interference must not dwarf the intelligence, reason and initiative of individuals. They are the final authority to take a decision about what action is to be performed or decision is to be taken.

In the opinion of Spencer a state has chiefly two roles to play—a protector and an aggressor. The activities of the state are limited only to the protection of individuals. Beyond that, the state cannot do anything. But if it exceeds that limit it is to be regarded as an aggressor. In Spencer's own words "For, if regarded as a protector, we find that the moment it does anything more than protect, it becomes an aggressor instead of a protector, and if regarded as a help to adaptation, we find that when it does anything more than sustain the social state, it retards adaptation instead of hastening it."

Spencerian theory of the nature of the state has very little to do with the controversy between capitalism and socialism. According to Spencer the basic issue is not who owns the means of production, rather it is whether the ownership succeeds in producing more wealth and ensuring greatest happiness. The purpose of social wealth is always to maximise the happiness of individuals. If the ownership of the wealth goes to the state and not to individuals this objective will remain unfulfilled. Hence there is no question of state ownership. Gradual expansion of state power is always inimical to individual freedom and also to the production of wealth. Spencer also treats *laissez-faire* or private enterprise as the potential precondition of internal and international peace and prosperity. If we analyse Spencer's analysis about the functions of state we shall come to the conclusion that he had

1. Quoted by Maxey, p. 559.

no respect or sympathy for socialism. To him socialism meant the loss of individual's initiative and expansion of state intervention in the economic activities of men. Again, according to Ebenstein, socialism meant to him a sure return to pre-industrial type of military society. He was against the militarisation of society through the intensification of states activities and role.

Spencer's Man versus the State

Spencer's political ideas are sporadically stated in many of his voluminous works but in two books *Social Statics* and *Man versus the State* we find a clear picture. Ebenstein calls the *Man versus the State* his most famous work on politics. This book contains his forceful arguments on *laissez-faire* and liberalism. It is a fact that we do not agree with his views. But still there is worth in his arguments and these have made him famous. In 1884 Spencer wrote four essays for the publication in the *Contemporary Review,* and these were assembled together in the form of a book entitled *Man versus the State.*

The title of the first essay is "The New Tories." In this essay Spencer attacks the English liberals for abandoning the historical individualism in favour of social reforms and welfare state. He says that the English conservatives originally adopted the principles of militancy and status and English liberals' extreme individualist policies. But their roles have turned upside down. Spencer noticed that economic individualism had been adopted by the conservatives. He foresaw that the British Conservative Party would in future be the party of free enterprise and economic individualism.

He criticised the liberal party on the ground that it was in favour of welfare programmes for the benefit of the weaker sections and people. His reasons can be briefly state in the following way. He thought that the welfare programmes would ultimately lead to socialism and he was so much against socialism that this might pertinently be called socialism-phobia. In his judgment "all socialism is slavery." His main argument against socialism is that it creates the greatest assault on individual's freedom. Under socialism or communism the individual is enslaved to the wishes of the authority. Spontaneity becomes the greatest victim of socialisation of the means of production.

Spencer admits that there are numerous problems and difficulties in society and all or most of them are created by human nature. But he thinks institutional changes cannot free the society from these difficulties. Spencer's main objection against socialism is it allows sick and incapable persons to occupy their places alongwith the able and well-equipped individuals and this process discourages the latter. This defective procedure leads to the greatest inefficiency. Spencer himself says : "There is no political alchemy by which you can get golden conduct out of the leaden instincts."[1]

Spencer observes that governmental control over the process of evolution and determination to check the manifestation of spontaneity is extremely harmful for society. This facilitates the advent of slavery. According to Spencer a slave is a person who labours under the coercion to satisfy another's desires. This is the summary of his second essay "The Coming Slavery." Spencer calls state-sponsored system a slave-system because in it persons have no freedom and spontaneity.

1. Quoted by Ebenstein—p. 617.

In the third essay "The Sins of Legislators" Spencer says that before embarking upon any enactment of law the legislator must know the laws of social progress and the laws of society as a whole. In this essay he further states that the guiding principle of family is generosity. Whereas, the same of the state is justice. Here the weak and disabled cannot be favoured or fostered at the cost of the rich or able or healthy persons. By favouring the sick the government is inflicting injustice on the society as a whole. In other words, in the calculation of Spencer, any sort of favour shown to the weak and incapable persons is an indicator of gross injustice. It is injustice because the state cannot favour one at the cost of another. Piety and kindness is absolutely an individual affair.

Spencer announces that all the small and great discoveries until now have not been made by the government. People's painstaking research work is behind all these. Again, in navigation, arts, literature and science, the government's contribution is nothing. If this is so, why should a government interfere with the spontaneous activities of individuals. The government he defines as a "begotten of aggression and by aggression". So, he abhors state interference. On this point Spencer is perfectly right. Only individual initiative and hard labour produced most of revolutionary discoveries. If the government were allowed to conduct the scientific affairs discoveries and inventions would never happen.

Turn now has come to deal with the final essay "The Great Political Superstition." Spencer equates the divine right of kings with the divine right of parliament. He says that in the past it was thought that the monarch was the representative of God on earth and because of his divinity he was above all. This is a political superstition. Today, it is thought that parliament is supreme and it is also a political superstition.

Spencer rejected Hobbesian theory of absolute sovereignty and Benthamite concept of rights on the ground that both clearly aimed at enhancing the power and authority of the state. But he was not in favour of proliferation of state activities. This again means the invariable loss of individual's freedom. Spencer, the orthodox champion of individual liberty, wants to assert that justification of state authority is the abnegation of individual liberty. Even before the existence of state there were rights and people enjoyed them. So the rights are not due to the state, but they are simply sanctioned by it. Particularly, right to property existed before there was any law. The reverse picture is rather true. As the state grows, people lose their rights. In other words, the rise of state power goes with the rise of slavery. In practice, a state is never sympathetic to the rights of the people.

We have presented here a very short survey of Spencer's famous work. *"The Man versus the State."* The reason may be stated very briefly. The book was published in the eighties of the nineteenth century. At that time it had a good deal of relevance and even the modern age has not proved that it is irrelevant. We are strongly advocating and fighting for democratic government, democratic values and, above all, democratic society. But, at the same time, the power of the state is increasing. We are alarmed at this gargantuan increase of state power, but not alert how to stop it. The purpose of *Man versus the State* is to inflame our feeling for democracy and to make us cautious of the enormous rise of state power.

Spencer was alarmed at the unprecedented rise of power of some European states. He cited the case of Germany. After the Franco-Prussian War the expenses and strength of the army and the interference of military into the administration of the state increased so much that Spencer was forced to raise his stentorian voice against the authority of the state. The German military leaders and bureaucrats also propagated the *Kultur Kampf* at this time which relegated the church to a subordinate position of the state. Police surveillance over ordinary citizens was made compulsory. It is to be stated that the unprecedented rise of the power of state and its allied organisations created an alarm in the mind of Spencer who was a great individualist. He was not an anarchist or in favour of abolition of state. But he thought that every state must confine itself within certain limits so that the individuals can enjoy liberty and maximise their happiness.

Theory of Rights

If we go through the writings of Spencer regarding his ideas about rights, freedom etc. we shall find that he has viewed all from a broader perspective. According to Spencer freedom is the antecedent of government. Freedom is its standard. Freedom means that everyman shall enjoy his natural rights. Denial of freedom means denial of natural rights and justice. By justice Spencer meant that everyman shall be free to do what he wills provided he infringes not the equal freedom of any other man; what he wants to say is that all the individuals shall have freedom, natural rights, and, when these are fully achieved, only then people will have the opportunity to enjoy justice. So we find that in the absence of natural rights and freedom there cannot be justice. Again, by freedom he meant the absence of all restrictions. His clear argument is that even before the creation of government there were rights and freedom. Naturally, it is beyond the authority and power of a government to control rights and freedom. Spencer wants to make the state almost powerless chiefly for the sake of freedom, right and justice. To him all these were extremely important.

Rights are "nothing but artificial divisions of the general claim to exercise the faculties." He calls the rights natural because they are pre-social rights. The rights are inherent properties of human constitution as divinely ordained. From this account we can frame certain features or rights. Rights are the inherent properties of every man. Man is the creation of God and by virtue of that he is entitled to enjoy rights. Then, therefore, the rights are the artificial divisions of claim made by man. These claims are essential for the development of faculties which a man possesses. Since rights are pre-social they are not created by the state.

Then Spencer proceeds to draw the distinction between private rights and public rights. Private rights of citizens relate particularly to property and family. Whereas, public rights are concerned with his relations to the state. Barker thinks that Spencer's private rights have certain peculiarities (p. 84). He does not recognise any private right in land. That is, right to land-property is inadmissible. Why? Everyone has equal freedom to land. So there shall be public and national ownership of land and law is to be enacted to that effect. But although private property in land is not allowed, private ownership of products is to be permitted. Man will cultivate the soil and before that he will obtain the permission of the society. Once he obtains the permission he has every right to be the owner of the product.

The above conception of Spencer as to the recognition of right by society is incongruous to his original view that natural right is independent of social recognition. It is very difficult to reconcile these contradictory views. Everyone shall have free and equal access to land but that does not debar one from enjoying private right to land. National ownership of land is recognised only in socialist societies. But Spencer is a prime critic of socialism. However, this view of Spencer is revolutionary.

Spencer's conception of private right to family is even more revolutionary than his right to property of land. He successfully established himself as the champion of woman's liberty. He, in unambiguous language, attacked the subjection of women and this he did even decades before J. S. Mill. Women should have right to vote. He did not also approve the subjection of children and was against coercion applied to them. He advocated the extension of liberty to children. There should not be any difference between adults and children so far as rights are concerned.

Spencer's theory of public rights is based on his attitude to government. The government is a temporary social institution. In the primitive society, when men were uncivilised and selfish, there was the necessity of government. The cage and the government are of the same category. The purpose of both is to control. But for civilised people the government is a necessary evil. To such people it is a vicious and immoral institution. It simply interferes with the free exercise of human faculty. This conception of Spencer reminds us of anarchist theory of state. The anarchists believed that at the primary stage of evolution there was the necessity of state. Since society and individuals have reached the final stage of evolution, there is no necessity of state.

The state can assert its importance or existence in the following fields. First, the state will justify its existence by allowing its citizens to ignore it. The implication is, that the state will do as little as possible. In the rest of the spheres the state will not exert its influence. Barker calls it effacing itself. The state will not bestow benefits and even if it does the citizens will abandon them. Secondly, the state admits that every one has equal freedom and the restraints it imposes upon its citizens will be shared equally by them. Partiality and the part of the state is quite unjustified and it should not be allowed to spread its roots. Finally, the state must clearly state its function. One function of the state, says Barker (p. 87), is protection—administration of law of equal freedom—maintenance of natural rights. It has been pointed out by Spencer that the state is a "joint stock protection company for mutual assistance."

Criticising Spencer's theory of natural rights Barker observes (p. 79) "the doctrine of natural rights is simply a doctrine of the blessedness of final anarchy." This is a serious charge against Spencer's concept of natural rights. How does Barker come to this conclusion? According to Spencer, evolution comes to an end when equilibrium is reached. It is a future stage. However, it is an absolute standard or norm. It is also a social ideal. When society, through the evolutionary process, reaches that equilibrium, people will perfectly adapt themselves with the environment. They will be perfectly intelligent, wise and rational. They will do what they ought to do. The government will be rejected just like a used vesture.

Since, in the perfect equilibrium, there will be no necessity of government, Barker apprehends that will create anarchy. So the social ideal is another name of anarchy. Social ideal or perfect equilibrium is a utopia is always far from reality. So Spencer's social ideal is simply an idle conjecture. The concepts of social ideal cannot be taken too seriously. Spencer is quite wrong is assuming that the evolution of human behaviour will ever attain a state of perfect equilibrium and it will permanently stay there.

It is now as clear as broad daylight that the state has very little positive to do with the rights of people. The state provides protection to its citizens through the enactment of law. In the stage of perfect equilibrium the state will lose that importance. In Spencerian dogma there is hardly any place of rights in relation to state. In fact, his apathy to state has impelled him to adumbrate certain inviolable rights. For this reason Spencer has imagined social ideal or perfect equilibrium in which the state will be reduced to absolute insignificance.

Spencer's natural rights are also called ethical rights. People voluntarily part with a portion of their rights so that their fellow citizens will enjoy these rights. Spencer's men will not claim something depriving other people. This is morality or ethics. T. H. Green spoke of the rights in the same idea. Right is a social concept and any one man cannot claim all the rights. But here is a confusion. According to Barker, if rights are ethical they cannot be natural (p. 104). There is a clear difference between the approaches of Spencer and that of us. Spencer did not think that in the realisation or attainment of rights state or any other authority has anything to do or contribute. People come to enjoy freedom, exercise rights and attain justice as a result of evolution. The evolutionary process, Spencer concluded, creates an equilibrium among different elements or forces as a result of which people enjoy all these. How evolution makes possible all these, that is a different issue. We simply hold the view that Spencer believed this. If rights, freedom and justice are the products of evolution the state has no contribution in the creation and realisation of all these. In the assessment of Spencer the state is a political organisation which is good for nothing. That is why Barker has challenged the view of Spencer.

Spencer's Liberalism

Herbert Spencer is undoubtedly a very important figure in the history of Western political thought and this importance is due to his contribution to liberal thought and philosophy. The central theme of his liberalism is the establishment, recognition and development of individuality and, to that end, the role of the state should be as far as practicable non-functioning or, if at all functioning, it should be limited to the minimum. Spencer's division of society into militant and industrial is significant in more than one respects. The important point is—in the militant society there is uniformity. The nation is one and the army is all and the individual is nothing. Opposite to this is the industrial type of society. This type of society is famous for its heterogeneity, differentiation in function, and emphasis on individuality. Emphasis is shifted from totality to individuals. "Under the industrial regime the citizen's individuality, instead of being sacrificed by the society, has to be defended by the society. Defence of his individuality becomes the society's essential duty" (Spencer).

Spencer applies the principle of evolution to the interpretation of the progress of society. He thinks that the evolution of society ultimately leads to the creation of an industrial type of state. He optimistically says that the industrial state is comparatively a peaceful state. In Spencer's judgment, this is the most desirable state since it is characterised by individual's freedom and minimum state interference.

In The *Man versus the State* Spencer has said : "The great political superstition of the past was the divine right of kings. The great political superstition of the present is the divine right of Parliament." In this oft-quoted statement Spencer wants to emphasise that the supremacy, in both cases, is harmful for freedom. The all-powerful parliament has replaced the all-powerful king. Otherwise there is no difference. Freedom of people in both cases was at stake. In Spencer's liberalism, therefore, there is no place of parliament or monarchy—the individual is the central figure of all social activities. In the same book there is another comment : "The function of Liberalism in the past was that of putting a limit to the powers of the king. The function of the true Liberalism in the future will be that of putting a limit to the powers of Parliaments." What transpires from the above comments is that to Spencer neither the king nor the government nor parliament is above criticism. Even they are not to be regarded as divine institutions. They are created by human beings for the fulfilment of certain specific objectives. Therefore there is no divinity in all these institutions. Man constitutes the central part of the entire organisational structure and the chief function of this organisation is to make all men happy. All sorts of organisations are for the general welfare or benefit of all men. Spencer started his analysis about liberalism from this.

One of the main assumptions of Spencer's liberalism is the principle of harmony and equilibrium. If all the individuals are allowed to pursue their own interests and free economic activities that will ultimately promote the general good of the society and no amount of state intervention will be required. The free competition among the entrepreneurs is the best guarantor, according to Spencer, of the economic progress. The free competition has a self-adjusting and self-regulating mechanism which eliminates the sick, weak and disabled elements from the field. The interference with the economic activities by the authority appeared to Spencer—economically and morally—unsound and unacceptable. The law of evolution—and concomitant with it is the law of the survival of the fittest—operate in both animal world and society. But in the latter case the law of evolution ensures all-round progress and posits it on solid foundation.

But all did not go well. Capitalism towards the end of the nineteenth century was faced with a number of crises. Spencer thought that it was free from crisis and would remain free. Subsequent events belied his hope. Public pressure was heaped upon the government to take action to arrest the crisis. It was forced to believe that the primary duty of any and every civilised government is to provide its citizens minimum necessities such as clothing, food, housing etc. The government cannot shirk off its responsibility. Spencer's liberalism, based upon natural science, was felt inadequate. Government adopted several welfare schemes. All these irritated Spencer and towards the last years of his life he wrote "The Coming Slavery" condemning all government measures. Spencer's liberalism was no doubt an extreme form and because of this it has been revised again and again but it has never been rejected. The liberal thought started its journey from the writings of Locke and still it exists. But it has changed its colour and—to some extent—contents. Needless to say that demise of socialism has strengthened liberalism.

Assessment of Spencer's Thought

We have made a survey of Spencer's political ideas. It is now high time to make an assessment of his political philosophy. It is to be noted at the outset that no thinker—whatever may be the magnitude of his thought and contribution—is above criticism and Spencer is not, and cannot, be an exception. We shall here try to assess his contribution.

Maxey observes (p. 562) "No reputable political thinker of the present time acknowledges Spencer as his master. For the critical mind of today he is an amateur scientist and a pseudo-philosopher. Science has learned a lot about evolution since Spencer's day, and very little of what has been learned tends to confirm the over-confident dogmas with which he assumed to settle the great problems of human society... Science now teaches that evolution is a process wherein each adaptation creates conditions calling for new adaptations, and *so ad infinitum* to ends that no man can hope to know—which completely explodes Spencer's synthetic theory and demolishes his political postulates."

Copleston, a renowned interpreter and critic of philosophy, observes (p. 121) "Spencer is little read nowadays. It is not merely that the idea of evolution has become common coin and no longer arouses much excitement. It is rather that after the brutal challenges of the twentieth century we find it difficult to see how the scientific hypothesis of evolution, taken by itself, can provide any adequate basis for that optimistic faith in human progress...which was a characteristic feature of Spencer's thought. On the one hand positivism has changed its character and fights shy of explicit and comprehensive world visions. On the other hand, those philosophers who believe that the trend of evolution is in some real sense beneficent to man generally appeal to metaphysical theories which were foreign to the mind of Spencer."

There are several confusions and inconsistencies in the political thought of Spencer. But in this respect Spencer is no exception. Many great thinkers suffer from this. Our objection is he was an individualist to the stage of extremity. This position of Spencer made him extremely unpopular. He believed that men were capable of ensuring their own good and naturally there was no necessity of any form of state interference. But this is not the actual situation. Social evolution teaches us that step by step the state will have to take the responsibility of the weaker sections of the society. The conflict between individualism and social organism are simply imaginary. The presence of state in the large number of social and welfare activities does not mean the loss of individual's freedom. Rather, through the activities of state the people will be in a position to realise freedom. In the opinion of Hearnshaw "the course of social development naturally tended to display itself as a gradual movement away from primitive, anarchic individualism towards the unity of a complete communism."

As an individualist Spencer's excessive zeal for preserving rights of man is quite reasonable and consistent. But we cannot reconcile this with his assertion that the private property of land cannot be permitted. He postulates national and public ownership of land. Again, though private ownership of soil is not granted private ownership of product is allowed. These are contradictory proposals. Moreover, the national ownership of land is destructive.

Spencer was not a farsighted philosopher or thinker. He saw the state simply as an evil. He might have understood that it was beyond the capacity of any individual to solve the growing economic crises. His orthodox individualism had no limits and for that reason he ruled out the possibility of state intervention. Towards the end of his life he saw the state to interfere with the free play of economic activities and this stopped the aggravation of economic situation. Spencer vehemently opposed it, but it was welcomed by all sections of society. It is evident that Spencer's liberalism was unsuitable for the contemporary situation.

Concluding Remarks

Herbert Spencer was the chief protagonist of the highly criticised doctrine—the survival of the fittest. Today it is the belief of all over the world that, it is not birth of a person which is the determiner of his subsequent fitness or unfitness. There is a tremendous impact of environment upon the character building of an individual. It is a tragedy that Spencer forgot to notice this fact. By changing or improving the environment human ability and character can be remarkably changed and remoulded.

Experience tells us that under favourable circumstances man can exhibit his fitness or ability and in the opposite situation the failure of the same person will appear. A true humanitarian cannot rely on the survival of the fittest doctrine. Moreover, science cannot accept this doctrine. It believes in change and progress and this it wants to do by changing the physical environment. Science can never surrender to fate or to any supernatural element.

If we surrender to this theory we shall never be able to build up a welfare state and improve the lot of the people. It is further observed that the acceptance of the theory will halt the progress of civilisation. As civilisation progresses physical environment also changes. The reverse is also true. Civilisation means overall progress of society. It also removes the distinction between fitness and unfitness. Its purpose rather is to bring all into the mainstream of social progress.

Sabine calls Spencer (p. 723) a "reactionary". In his judgment some persons are fit and, therefore, are entitled to survive. While the rest are unfit and are not entitled to survive. This *fatwa* is definitely a reactionary thought. Sabine has further concluded that Spencer's belief is baseless and a source of endless confusion about the nature of culture and social changes. When the social change takes place it makes no distinction between fit and unfit. If there are any unfit persons social change brings them under its huge and comprehensive fold and this is the exact nature of social change. So it is true that Spencer's philosophy is really the source of a lot of confusion as well as a reactionary one.

However, some people have made attempts to protect Spencer from criticism. They are of opinion that the chief objective of Spencer was to make people hard-working and self-dependent. If the weaker people are allowed permanently to depend upon the government subsidy and help that populist measure will make these men idle. It is argued that Spencer disliked this very much. Keeping this in mind Spencer strongly opposed any move on the part of the government with the sole purpose of protecting the unfit persons. It shall be the duty of any rational government to remove the hindrances which stand on the way of social progress and encourage the spontaneity of individuals. If it were the real motive of Spencer we think that he gets a plank to keep his feet for standing straight.

It cannot be said that Spencer was quite indifferent to the general welfare of society and its residents. We are of opinion that he indulged in a different view about welfare. He believed that every person should be taught that it is his duty to build up his own fate. Permanent dependence upon the state cannot ensure the improvement of human condition. Today the government of welfare states are giving lot of material help to the weaker sections of society. But this is mainly on populist considerations. The purpose of a true welfare state must be to help its citizens to be self-sufficient and we think that Spencer wanted this.

Many people felt that the state should play an increasing and positive role for the consolidation of the benefits of Industrial Revolution and because of their insistence the post-Industrial Revolution state started to play greater and crucial role. Spencer treated it as a definite aggression upon the freedom of individuals. From the standpoint of his own philosophy he could not accept it and for that reason he declared a *"jehad"* against state intervention. His inordinate love for Darwin's love for evolution theory led him to propound such an extreme form of individualism.

24 FABIAN SOCIALISM

Establishment of Fabian Society

Only after a century of Industrial Revolution its undesirable and harmful consequences were so pervasive that almost all the people of the weaker sections came under these consequences. They were more or less deprived of the benefits of Industrial Revolution and began to think about a way out. It was a type of nightmarish situation. People were deprived of bare necessities such as food, residence, health facilities etc. Specially the working class was the victim. In a word, all-round deterioration gripped the British society. In this situation it was thought by a large number of men that the setting up of a socialist society could save men from this situation. Some of the historians conclude that in the year 1883 Thomas Davidson, an American school teacher, took the initiative of forming the Fabian Society. But this view has been contested by many others who hold that practically the society came into being on January 4, 1884 and Frank Podmore was the founding father. Other persons who got the opportunity to celebrate the birth of the society were Edward Pease, and granddaughter of Robert Owen, Dale Owen. Subsequently Bernard Shaw, the Webb couple, H. G. Wells and Graham Wallas with their efforts and intellect graced the Fabian Society.

The term *Fabian Society* was coined by Frank Podmore. In ancient Rome there was a famous and brave general whose name was Quintus Fabius Maximus Vemecosus, also known as Cunctator ('Delayer'). There is a common and interesting story that Fabius Cunctator was an intelligent and cautious military general. Before taking any decision he thought of its various aspects of consequences and justifiability. His advice was à man must wait for the right moment patiently. It might cause delay, but cautious and prudential methods are always fruitful. Frank Podmore and few others who participated at the opening of the society took the advice of Fabius Cunctator to their heart. They fully realised that in order to mitigate the sufferings of toiling masses, capitalism would be overthrown. But one must wait for the right action moment. A right action in a right moment would never go in vain. In other words, it was thought that everyone must wait for the most opportune moment. Otherwise success would never be achieved.

Studying the various aspects of British society the Fabians came to believe that a strong action was to be taken against capitalist oppressors and exploiters. But that situation had not yet arrived. Naturally they must wait for that situation. They must study the nature and activities of capitalists, their strength and purposes. It was necessary to bring people into confidence. So they wanted to launch an intensive propaganda against the wrongs of capitalism. The Fabians declared that their purpose was to establish socialism and it was not an overnight job. Lichtheim has said that the Fabians whole-heartedly supported the advice and technique of Fabius Cunctator and that is why they paid maximum emphasis upon caution. Because of this cautiousness the Fabian approach was evolutionary, gradual and moderate. There is no place of revolutionary tactics in their approach.

Origin of Fabian Socialism

Towards the end of the nineteenth century, particularly during the seventies and eighties, on the one hand, Herbert Spencer, with all his intelligence and enthusiasm, was advocating the non-intervention of state for the sake of individual's liberty. On the other hand, a vast section of the British populace was fighting tooth and nail to save themselves from growing miseries and sufferings created by the Industrial Revolution. During the fag end of his life John Stuart Mill gave, to some extent reluctantly, permission to state interferences. Then appeared the renowned Oxford idealist and professor of Moral Philosophy—T. H. Green. He unequivocally announced that the rapid moral degradation and miseries suffered by the people were chiefly due to the economic poverty and deterioration of all sorts of values and principles. So resuscitation of all values and ideals was of primary importance. The state must intervene in favour of the untaught and underfed denizens of London city. It is the moral responsibility of the state to consider whether the opening of wine shops was necessary at all. Green and his fellow idealists reached a firm conclusion that politics, morality and economics were not elements of watertight compartments. The prevailing objective social, economic, political and other conditions inspired some intellectuals to search for a new ideology on the basis of which a new society could be built up whose sole purpose would be to free common people from all sorts of miseries. Fabian society circulated its brand of socialism which is known to us as Fabian Socialism. It is so called because the Fabian society fathered it.

Laissez-faire, individualism and state's non-intervention in man's economic and other activities were the guiding principles of the economic and social order of the Victorian Age (1837–1901). But the slow movement of economic growth, the gradual and rapid increase of competition among the capitalists of different nationalities and the adoption of protective tariffs questioned the justifiability of free trade. Moreover, intermittent depressions and critical unemployment situation created deep-rooted and widespread suspicion in the minds of the people about the efficacy of capitalism as a progressive economic system and its potentiality to fight the evils that had been created by the prevailing economic system—capitalism. In a word, capitalism was faced with challenges in the last decades of nineteenth century.

We shall focus our attention on the dismal picture of the economy. There was a remarkable slow growth rate from mid-1870s to mid-1890s in England and this has been termed by many as the Great Depression. "Economically its most pronounced feature was a deceleration of economic growth and a fall in prices of commodities."[1] Between 1850s and 1870s (early part) the average growth rate was 3 percent. But after 1870s it was halved. The impact of this depression was not

1. Ben Pimlott (Ed.)—*Fabian Essays in Socialist Thought*, p. 17.

confined within the British Isles, it spread far and wide. As a result of depression the prices of agricultural commodities fell considerably, the wages of the agricultural labourer came down to miserable level. This sector of the economy was looked upon as unremunerative. Millions of people left the village to swell the urban population and industrial labour force. The economic depression hit hard the people of both rural and urban areas. There was a clear imbalance between the rural and urban areas. This was not a healthy sign for Britain.

"The depression had its effects on industry too. Growing competition from overseas rivals, a heavy export of capital and consequent under-investment at home, and a growing deficit on a trade balance were features which began to erode some of the self-confidence." Although England was industrially developed its technical education system was not up to mark. There was a gap between England and other West European countries, particularly Germany, so far as technical education was concerned. The British capitalists wanted to expand foreign trade but there it had to face keen competition and it was difficult for them to reap the fruits of foreign trade fully. The depression might have been fought away. But the ways were beyond the reach of the authority. The foreign trade could be expanded. But for this was required political subjugation. The growing national liberation movements in the Third World states stood on the way of political subjugation. In the home front there was very little scope of the expansion of market because depression and other factors had considerably curtailed the purchasing power of the people of urban areas. The rural people were comparatively poor. Particularly the economic condition of the agricultural labourers was miserable. All these combinedly made the British economy miserable.

The unregulated capitalist economy was largely suspected as the root of the evils. The spread of Marx's thought and ideas, on the one hand, evil effects of capitalism, and the failure of the Industrial Revolution to meet the necessary requirements of common and working people convinced the general mass of the necessity of governmental intervention. Parliamentary commissions, factory legislations and social investigations were suggested as remedies to the evils of post-Industrial Revolution society. Welfare schemes were needed to meet the growing demands. It was strongly felt and admitted that any civilised government must do something to give relief to its toiling and helpless masses. During the last decades of the nineteenth century, a sizeable section of the British society came to the conclusion that if the natural resources were properly utilised and wings of capitalism were cut, the miserable conditions of the poor people could be arrested. Material condition could also be improved. Private enterprise should have freedom to conduct the economy but in the case of its failure the government must come forward to ensure the desired results. That is, private control over the economy cannot be allowed *ad infinitum*. In this connection we can quote an observation of a Fabian socialist :

"All seemed to point to the fact that free market principles, the religion of economic individualism and *laissez-faire* could not coordinate the vast interdependent organisation of modern industry. In many areas an extension of public responsibility was required and the setting up and funding of public administration which could provide the collective services the society required, and which it would not otherwise get."[1]

---

1. Quoted in Ben Pimlott's book, p. 23.

The Fabians formed a part of a ferment of social and political thought which began to reassess the ethical basis and effectiveness of both capitalism and liberalism in providing for the spiritual and physical needs of society. Amidst the many voices which addressed the social and political questions of the day, the early Fabians emerged as a group. This group wanted political and administrative changes which were not directed to *socialism* but to a *Socialist direction*.

Very few enthusiastic persons took active interest about how to come out of the crisis. Those who took interests finally decided to set up a new society whose objectives and ideals would be to set up a socialist society. In January 1884, a year after Marx died, handful of persons set up the Fabian Society and the socialist ideas propagated by it are known as Fabian Socialism. The founding Fabians published the first Fabian tract under the title "Why Are the Many Poor?" The tract sold like hot cake. Within a year of its formation a number of great intellectuals joined the Fabian Society and most important of them were the "Big Four"—Sidney Webb, George Bernard Shaw, Sidney Oliver and Graham Wallas. These Big Four took the leading part in the Fabian movement. During the first two or three years the Fabian Society confined its activities within discussion, analysis and debate. It could not make much headway in the practical field. After 1886, the Fabian Society decided to participate in the metropolitan politics. It realised that propaganda among the people was necessary to their consciousness. The society was urged upon to define its purposes. The purposes were defined in the draft of "*Basis*."

Fabian Socialism and Evolutionary Socialism

After a thorough analysis of the recorded history of the world Marx (1818–1883) and Engels arrived at the conclusion that the working class was always oppressed and exploited by the economically dominant class. They also said that since the interests of the two principal classes—proletariat and bourgeois are irreconcilable. The inevitable result is the struggle between these two classes. After the struggle the proletarians will set up a socialist society. So we find that socialist society can emancipate the people and, without struggle, socialist society can never come into existence. Exploitation, struggle and setting up of a society with the avowed purpose of achieving socialism are all related issues and capitalism is associated with these concepts. Rather capitalism is the central figure or concept. But there are two vital issues—emancipation of the working class and without struggle this is not possible.

The Fabian socialists of England admitted the necessity of a new socialist way which would combat the evils of society. But they firmly announced their disapproval of any revolution or destruction of capitalism. Only the evolutionary tactics such as factory legislation, parliamentary commissions, reforms could be adopted to serve the purpose. They also thought that these methods were more effective than the revolutionary methods. Socialism achieved through these evolutionary tactics or gradual methods or reforms may aptly be called evolutionary socialism. In the evolutionary socialism there is no place of Marx's class struggle or armed revolution. Nor could the Fabian Society rely on coercive method. Only through gradual tactics could socialist goals be achieved.

For the Fabians themselves, the aim remained the *gradual transformation* of capitalism into a form of welfare state which would find it necessary to take into ownership and control the means of production. It is obvious that the Fabians realised that capitalism was the cause of post-Industrial Revolution evils. It could be rectified and amended and not destroyed and ended. The gradualism to them was the only way. Almost in the same tone G. D. H. Cole and Rayomond Postgate have said "Fabianism was the new Benthamism, seeking the greatest happiness of the greatest number, not by means of *laissez-faire*, but through the collective control of the economic forces of society, and regarding socialism as simply the logical consummation of a progressive policy of social reform."[1] It may naively be stated that Fabian socialism in an indirect way combines both Benthamise utilitarianism and Marxian socialism. It says that by setting up a socialist society through evolutionary methods the lofty ideal—the greatest good of the greatest number—could be achieved.

The methods of the Fabians were reformist, permeative and evolutionary. Persuasion and not coercion was the method advocated by them. G. D. H. Cole elsewhere says : "It envisaged socialism as a heap of reforms to be built by the droppings of a host of successive swallows who would in the end make a socialist summer." The method of the Fabian socialism is the peaceful way. Persuasion, parliamentary intervention and many other peaceful means will ensure the transition of society from capitalism to socialism.

The Fabian Socialists borrowed the idea of evolutionism from Darwin and Comte—who were its great advocates. The development or change of society, they viewed, in the light of evolution. It has been observed by Lichtheim that the British socialists were positivists in that they regarded themselves as disciples of Comte. Comte does not make it clear that capitalism is to be destroyed or at least it should be controlled. Of course, he has indirectly said that it should be progressively used. But his followers have asserted that a compromise between capital and labour is to be effected and, in that case, the destruction of capitalism will not be required. The Fabian socialists believed that the reformers and Parliament would have to take the leadership. Evolutionary methods are time-consuming, but, ultimately, they pay.

A pertinent question may arise here. Why did the Fabians select the reforming and evolutionary methods to achieve socialist goals? The simple answer is that in Britain there was a tradition of parliamentary democracy and liberalism. The liberal institutions were not the instruments of achieving socialism, but they were always used to fight social, economic and political injustice. The Fabians realised that only socialism could save the country and to that extent they were influenced by Marx. But simultaneously they realised that revolution or armed struggle was not the way. The Fabians were brought up in the tradition of liberalism and democratic forms and they did not want to throw them away. The socialism envisaged by the Fabian Society is generally called evolutionary socialism because in this type of socialism there is no place of revolution or armed struggle or abruptness. Socialism is the goal but it could be achieved step by step or gradually. It means that the democratic process is the best way to reach the socialist goals.

At the time of foundation the members of the Fabian Society were middle class people. Bernard Shaw once said : "We were than middle class all through. We know the middle class people are generally not in favour of revolution. Their weakness is for gradualism and reformism." Moreover, members of the society thought that

1. Quoted in Pimlott's book, p. 23.

revolution would ultimately lead to the predominance of working class. Bentham's utilitarianism was meant for the participation of middle class people in the affairs of the state. These middle class people towards the last decades of the nineteenth century came forward to establish their influence and to curtail the power of the capitalist class. For one reason or other, middle class men were firmly convinced that the capitalists would not be allowed further to control the society. Fabian Socialism is the direct by-product of that mentality. Translation of middle class aspiration originated with Bentham and it, to a large extent, reached a comfortable position during Fabian movement. This was encouraged by the contemporary intellectuals of England. Besides Bernard Shaw, there were professor Graham Wallas, noted author H. G. Wells, Annie Besant, Sidney Webb and his wife Beatrice Webb. There were many other academicians. All of them did not look at the growth of capitalism with a favourable eye. It is interesting to note that the persons who were associated with the founding of Fabian Society were all great intellectuals and prominent personalities. This indicates that these great luminaries of the nineteenth century Britain were, for one reason or other, dissatisfied with the activities of capitalism. They sincerely wanted an end not of capitalism but the activities of capitalism. They wanted the reforms and to some extent the rehabilitation of capitalism but not its abolition. Because abolition of capitalism meant armed struggle and revolution.

"Basis for the Fabian Society"

The Fabians agreed that "the competitive system assures the happiness and comfort of the few at the expense of the suffering of the many and that the society must be reconstituted in such a manner as to secure the general welfare and happiness." To this end they proposed the following principles which were issued in 1887 as the "*Basis for the Fabian Society*." The "*Basis*" is a document containing the objectives and programmes of the Society. From the writings and activities we can draw the conclusion that the Fabians were quite serious about the function of the Society. They thought that the setting up of a socialist society in the Fabian way could emancipate people. Naturally they did not take the issue of socialism lightly or half-heartedly.

The "*Basis*" starts with the declaration : "The Fabian Society consists of socialists." This declaration is significant. The members are all socialists and, therefore, their only goal is socialism. Only the socialist path is the way of emancipation. The working of capitalism during the past centuries, particularly the century after the Industrial Revolution, was the chief cause of miseries and sufferings of masses of men. The socialism which the Fabians professed to achieve was based on the obvious evolution of society which existed around them. It was not based on the speculation of German philosophers. It was not prefixed by "scientific". The edifice of Fabian Socialism was built upon the foundation of political and social institutions which existed in England. So when the Fabians pontifically declared themselves as socialists, the term had a particular connotation. The Fabians had no intention to alienate themselves from the tradition.

What are the objectives of the Fabian Society? The Society aims at the reorganisation of society by the emancipation of land and industrial capital from individual and class ownership, and the vesting of them in the community for the general benefit. In this way only can the natural and acquired advantages of the country be equitably shared by the whole people. Here it is clear that land and capital are the two important factors of production and these two must be released from the private ownership and be placed under the management of society for the common benefit. Feudalism and industrial capitalism both deprived the masses of their legitimate share in national wealth.

The society accordingly works for the abolition of private property in land and of consequent individual appropriation, in the form the rent, of the price for permission to use the earth, as well as for the advantages of superior soils and sites.

The society further works for the transfer to the community of the administration of such industrial capital as can conveniently be managed socially. For, owing to the monopoly of the means of production in the past, industrial inventions and the transformation of surplus income into capital have mainly enriched the proprietary class, the worker now being dependent on that class for leave to earn a living.

If these means be carried out without compensation (though not without such relief to expropriated individuals as may seem fit to the community), Rent and Interest will be added to the reward of labour, the idle class now living on the labour of others will necessarily disappear, and practical equality of opportunity will be maintained by the spontaneous action of economic forces with much less interference with personal liberty than the present system entails. This general objective can be divided into three parts : there shall be no provision of paying compensation when the property, i.e., land and capital, is taken away. In special circumstances, compensation may be given. Next, if land and capital are placed under the management of society, labourers will get the benefit of rent and interest. Finally, if the above objectives are carried out successfully the systems of idle class and unearned income will come to an end resulting in the emancipation of the exploited people.

For the attainment of these ends the Fabian Society looks to the spread of socialist opinions, and the social and political changes consequent thereon, including the establishment of equal citizenship for men and women. It seeks to achieve these ends by the general dissemination of knowledge as to the relation between individual and society, in its economic, ethical and political aspects.

A cursory study of the above objectives reveals that so far as the objectives of Fabian Socialism and Marxian Socialism are concerned there is very little difference between the two varieties of socialism. But this should not lead one to jump upon the conclusion that both are without any difference. The aim of both is the nationalisation of the sources of production and to ensure the collective management. This will terminate the system of unearned income. The collective management will open the opportunities for the common people to share the reward derived from land and capital. The fundamental point of disagreement between Fabian socialists and Marxian socialists relates to the method of attaining the socialist goals. Fabians insisted upon the evolutionary techniques whereas Marxists thought that only a class struggle leading to revolution could make an end of the system. Marx did not treat socialism as an end. To him it was an intermediate stage between capitalism and communism. But to Fabians it was the goal or final stage. The Fabian socialism can be called the extension of socialised liberalism or idealised liberalism propounded by Thomas Hill Green. Marxian socialism was indebted to Bitrish political economy, German idealism and Utopian Socialism.

From Individualism to Socialism

It was widely claimed that the undesirable consequences of Industrial Revolution were primarily due to individualism. People's consciousness was growing and they felt that establishment of socialist society was the only antidote. But the spokespersons of social change were against revolution. They were of view that socialism through evolutionary method was the only way. This principle was borrowed by Fabians from Charles Darwin and Spencer. People's distrust on individualism was rapidly growing and faith on socialism was gradually increasing. The transition from individualism to socialism was inevitable. They also believed that this transformation, though at times distressingly slow, was all the more substantial because it had not entailed violence, but grew out of the sober conviction as to its efficiency and justice.[1] The common people and socialists both were convinced that the British society was ready to welcome socialism through evolutionary methods.

Though British democracy achieved maturity, it remained incomplete because of the prevalence of gross economic inequality and extreme form of exploitation. Individualism and even liberalism emphasised on political liberty and rights. The Fabians proceeded to introduce socialist measures to fulfil the aspirations of people. In this connection a very apt remark of Webb may be quoted : "In the teeth of the current political economy and in spite of all the efforts of the mill-owning liberals, England was compelled to put forth her hand to succour and protect her weaker members." Here the intention of Webb is quite clear. The government must be invited to intervene to make an end of the deterioration of economic condition. In one of the *Fabian Essays* we find the following lines :

Advocates of social reconstruction have learned the lesson of Democracy and know that it is through the slow and gradual turning of the popular mind to new principles that social reorganisation bit by bit comes. All students of society who are abreast of their times, socialist as well as individualists, realise that important organic changes can only be (1) democratic, and thus acceptable to a majority of the people; (2) gradual, and thus causing no dislocation; (3) not regarded as immoral by the mass of people and not demoralising to them; (4) and, in this country, constitutional and peaceful.

In the eighties of the nineteenth century there emerged a large-scale consensus among various sections of British society that democracy includes people's control over the main instruments of production, gradual substitution of organised cooperation for the anarchy of the competitive struggle. A new and appreciable idea developed in the mind of a large section of British people that political principle of democracy was to be combined with people's control over the means of production and that would give birth to Socialism. Fabian Society's conclusion regarding the inevitability of socialism is based on the fact that the events of post Industrial Revolution and the growing miseries of people will mount pressures upon the government to adopt socialist measures for alleviation of sufferings. We conclude that behind the emergence of Fabian Socialism a good number of factors were quite active. Briefly stated, these are the curses of Industrial Revolution, British people's apathy to armed revolution, the inordinate love of British people to parliamentary system of government.

---

1. Lancaster—*Masters of Political Thought*, Vol. III, p. 314.

Fabianism and Imperialism

Before 1900 the Fabian Society did not display any enthusiasm in the foreign affairs of Britain and this is chiefly due to the fact that in its formative years it wanted to preoccupy itself in economic and to a lesser extent political and domestic affairs. Foreign affairs failed to draw its attention. Some members of the society expressed sporadic opinion on particular international issues but that did not form any part of the Society's declared policy or principle. Only in 1900. G. B. Shaw's *Fabianism and the Empire : A Manifesto* was published. The immediate factor that occasioned the publication of *Fabianism and the Empire* was the South African War. The members of the Society saw the war with a different outlook. They regarded it as inevitable. The imperialist powers of Europe were engaged in partitioning the globe and the Fabians, particularly Shaw, thought that this could not be resisted. The main reason behind this support to imperialist expansion was to provide moral support to British imperialism. Shaw and other co-Fabians in clear language stated that in the process of imperialist expansion she gobbled up many nations and this was unfortunate. But she could not allow others to gobble up her. However, imperialism was not immoral because it was based on "*inefficiency*".

The members of the Society came out with a straight-forward suggestion that there was no question of dissolving the empire. The empire should be fruitfully utilised for greater and noble purpose : the establishment of a socialist "Commonwealth". Shaw in the *Manifesto* said, "the socialist commonwealth be exploited for the public good rather than for private gain." Some of the Society's members categorically announced that they should not make any effort to reverse the imperialist expansion, but try to swim with it. That is, they must support imperialism. G. B. Shaw made this point more emphatic by saying that the peculiar business of the Fabian Society was to supply progressive aspirations with practical methods. In 1900 the most practical method was to hitch it to the rising star of Liberal imperialism. The society decided to do that.

Shaw in his *Manifesto* claimed that the colonies were inefficient to conduct their own business. To remove this the imperialists brought them under efficient administration. This is popularly know as "overriding claim of efficiency". For the domestic administration Shaw also argued for efficiency. In his judgment only efficiency could make socialism a grand success. Shaw further said that it was the moral duty of all efficient nations to help all the inefficient colonies. Shaw also divided the nations into higher civilised and lower civilised categories. The lower civilisations were to be raised to the higher civilisations and for the attainment of that goal the imperialist powers were engaged in dividing the globe among themselves. In his view it was not wrong. While many imperialist powers and personalities talked of the "white-man's burden" in support of their imperialist designs, Shaw advanced the argument of colonies' inefficiency to support his theory of imperialism. He, however, wanted to camouflage his real intention.

Society's stand on imperialism was not based on pure expediency. From 1900 onwards few other pamplets were published by the Society. These productions show that the Fabians were deeply plunged into the question of imperialism. So expendiency was not the factor of their active interest. Bernard Porter in his article *Fabians, Imperialists and the International Order*[1] aptly observes (p. 56) "If the Fabians

---

1. The article is included in Ben Pimlott's *Fabian Essays in Socialist Thought*.

had merely wanted to *use* imperialism there was no reason for them to plunge in quite *so* whole-heartedly as this. Clearly it appealed to them for other reasons too. One reason was the nature of their socialism. Fabian socialism was fundamentally a statist, interventionist kind."

Sidney Webb also made a lot of contribution to the Fabian concept of imperialism. In Margaret Cole's words Sidney Webb was a "natural bureaucrat in the best sense of the word." He wholeheartedly supported Fabian philosophy of imperialism and also enriched it with his characteristic style of argument. He had no sympathy for self-government of colonies. The establishment of world government—through imperialism—was their sole objective. They also treated it as part of their theory of evolution. In the domestic field the transition from individualism to socialism was inevitable because of the evolutionary process. This evolutionary process would ultimately lead to world or international government and that would facilitate the emergence of socialism. The concept of inevitability impelled them to support imperialism. Most of the members of the Society were so much intoxicated by imperialism that they refused to give due recognition and support to nationalism and nationalist feeling. Economic and political interests of Britain were more important to them than democracy and self-government.

In *Fabianism and Empire* Shaw argued that in the present imperialist era the old nationalism was obsolete and that would be replaced by international government. It was not difficult for Shaw to realise that the nationalist feeling was anti-imperialism. The spread of nationalism meant to Shaw dissolution of the British Empire. G. B. Shaw dreamt of a world government and that would be, if we can study his mentality properly, under the leadership of Britain. Interpreters of Shaw's political ideas are of opinion that he had been all along opposing the principle of nationality. As it has been pointed out by Bernard Porter, "It began with a repetition of Shaw's old strictures on the principle of nationality and ended with a tribute to the British Empire as the closest approximation to an ideal international authority yet achieved" (p. 60).

Shaw was a rank imperialist. He was so much convinced of the higher civilisation of Great Britain and also of France, Germany and USA that he did not consider any other nation as highly civilised. This conviction may aptly be called dogmatism or racism. The hegemony of particular race or civilisation was later on propagated by Hitler and he made it the main plank of his propaganda and political activities. We normally blame Hegel as the godfather of Hitler. But Shaw was not less responsible for racist ideology.

During his lifetime (1856–1950) Shaw witnessed the disintegration of the British Empire and his flamboyant announcement of world government shattered. Shaw did not hope that it would ever come into reality. However, he thought that the unrealisation of world government was due to the lack of vision of the British statesmen. The disintegration of the British empire impelled few members of the Fabian Society to ponder over their attitude towards imperialism. Few members found no rationality and justification in the arguments of Shaw and other orthodox supporters. Some of them resigned from the Society on the issue of imperialism. Some called the book "crude and frivolous". Many Fabians branded the book "as a youthful aberration or a piece of political manoeuvering that went wrong or just another example of its author's odd little ways". But modern researchers hold a different view. They are of opinion that it was not the personal view of G. B. Shaw, it was the philosophy (if the word is to be used at all) of Fabian Society. This view appears to be more reasonable. Sidney Webb and many other Fabians were in favour of British imperialism. Shaw had expressed the view in a straight-forward language.

Among all the leading members of the Fabian Society G. B. Shaw was the most vocal person who supported imperialism. He was born and brought up in an atmosphere of imperialism and he knew that imperialism protected British economic and political interests. The decaying condition of British imperialism was very much painful to him. The national liberation movement in the Third World states threw a severe challenge to British imperialism and Britain's economic interests. Because of these reasons Shaw strongly supported imperialism. His advocacy for imperialism had ill-designs though he expressed his viewpoints with sufficient intelligence and lot of finesse. Not Shaw alone, many other intellectuals argued for imperialism.

The Fabian State

Rodney Barker in his essay *The Fabian State* writes, "Fabian socialism, by repute, is state socialism. Not the socialism of some abstract or idealised state, nor of revolutionary dictatorship of the proletariat, but a socialism which sees in the English state, duly extended and reformed, the engine of all those misty purposes which it implies rather than explains" (p. 27).[1]

So far as the position of state in Fabian socialism is concerned there cropped up a problem. In the British political system the state was out and out a bourgeois state—ruled and fully controlled by the capitalists. But, on the contrary, in the socialism sponsored by Fabian Society the state must play a vital role and the common people and working class must have a say. If the prevailing bourgeois state were to be kept intact, the state-sponsored socialism proposed by the Fabian Society would create conflict and problem. Some of the leading members of the Fabian Society were aware of it and sought a solution to this complex situation. H. G. Wells thought that in the proposed system of socialism the state must play a dominant role and this state must start with the capital letter "S". H. G. Wells and others were sure that if the state were not allowed to play the dominant role in the building up of socialism there is hardly any scope of achieving socialism. The interesting fact is that the actual role of the state in Fabian type of socialism was not clearly defined.

At the very beginning of the society its members took very little interest about the various aspects of state. Though it was set up in 1884 it took long thirtysix years to publish a book on the social welfare state. In 1920, Sidney Webb and Beatrice Webb published their famous book *A Constitution for the Socialist Commonwealth of Great Britain.* The Webbs made serious attempt in the *Constitution* and also in their earlier work *Industrial Democracy* to describe the various functions of the state or, what they sometimes called, the political organisation of society. According to the Webbs there are three general and very significant functions of state or political institutions of society. The first is that the state is the repository of the coercive power. It is minimum and essential power. With the help of this power the state exercises its authority to defend the sovereignty and integrity, maintains law and order and, finally, establishes justice. The state is the final arbiter of all disputes. There is a second function and it is the "administration of public services and

1. Ben Pimlott : *Fabian Essays in Socialist Thought.*

nationalised industries." To the Fabians it was an important function. One of the goals of Fabian Society was the nationalisation of industries. After nationalisation the state will take the full responsibility of the management of all nationalised industries. Finally, the state was to them an instrument for building up a future society. The state must promote a civilisation commensurate with socialist ideals.

The Webbs and many other front-ranking members of the Fabian Society were against the coercive power of state and, because of this, they were in favour of state without coercive power. In the earlier centuries the state was mainly treated as the source of police power. The utilitarians and many other thinkers, in their inordinate zeal to safeguard individual freedom, recommended a considerable curtailment of the state authority. The Webbs decided to traverse the same track. In their *Industrial Democracy* we find them saying :

"With the change of time and the manifold objective conditions of society the character and functions of authority have undergone spectacular changes. What was originally the police powers has become increasingly administration of public services—in fact merely house-keeping on a national scale. The Government has passed from an autocratic monarch, whether a person, a class or an official hierarchy, to whom we owe loyalty and obedience and has become, in these departments of its work, a busy house-keeper, whose object is to serve the citizens and to whom we owe only such adherence to common rules and such mutual considerations as will permit the civic household to be comfortable" (Pimlott, p. 30).

To put the state within certain limits so that it cannot create obstructions to the attainment of socialist programmes the Webbs suggested a twofold division of functions. One part would deal with criminal law and political dominion and the other part with the social and economic administration. The Webbs have no faith on civil service. The bureaucrats are conservative and secretive. The administration of nationalised industries is not to be vested in the hands of bureaucrats, but in a board of directors. The Webbs also proposed a social parliament.

The picture of the Fabian state drawn by the Webbs suffer from several shortcomings. First of all, Webbs's reply to the question who govern Britain was "the bureaucracy." Who ought to govern? The Webbs said—everybody or nobody. The last answer indicates nothing. Actually, in Webbs's time, the elites ruled Britain and even today they are ruling. Only a handful of persons coming out of Oxford and Cambridge universities are at the helm of state administration. Secondly, the Webbs thought that only a coordinating body or a board of directors would be able to manage the nationalised industries. This is quite wrong. The management is so complex that untrained board of directors or coordinating body cannot properly shoulder the responsibility of management. The dream of a socialist state will come true if a group of persons whose number will be quite adequate with proper training and missionary zeal were vested with the task of administration. Here again the concept of elite appears. Whatever it may be, training is a vital part of the management of socialist state. The objection of the Webbs couple against bureaucracy is quite justified. But it is unfortunate that these learned members of the society failed to offer any pragmatic solution. What would be replaced in the vacant place of bureaucracy?

The controversy that raged the leading members of the Fabian Society still is to be found. If the intellectuals try to control the socialist system the entire administrative system will face problem because a well managed administration requires able and expert administrators who are called bureaucrats. Many of the Fabian socialists were wary of the dubious role of the bureaucrats. The Fabian Society failed to offer an alternative to bureaucracy. The result was that in the socialist system of Britain (if it is to be called a socialist system at all) the bureaucracy came to control the entire political and economic systems. Even in the former Soviet Union the bureaucracy played the most crucial role in state administration.

Fabians' Political Economy

Socialism embraces both economics and politics. We have just now completed our analysis of Fabian ideas of the state. We shall now analyse what the members of the Society thought about economic science. A common charge generally levelled against the Fabians, and it is correct, that they did not approach the subject coherently or systematically, rather electically. Some of the members of the society adhered to the market economy, others flatly rejected it. In the thirties of the twentieth century, when Keynes adumbrated certain principles to fight depression and arrest growing unemployment, some Fabians did not hesitate to show allegiance to the Keynesian economics. Simultaneously, others were sceptical about it. Some of the Fabians were convinced that state control was the only way out and hence planning was essential. Many refused to pin their hopes on planning and state control. Elizabeth Durbin is perfectly right when she says in her essay *Fabian Socialism and Economic Science* that there is no consistent body of thought which could properly be described as Fabian economics (p. 39).[1] Nonetheless, continues Elizabeth Durbin, a distinctive Fabian approach to economics can be traced.

In the middle of the eighties of the nineteenth century Sydney Oliver, Bernard Shaw and Sidney Webb first made a concerted effort to thrash out certain principles which would guide the socialism of Fabian brand. But at the very outset the point they made clear was that they were rejecting Marxian economic principles. Graham Wallas later joined the group and whole-heartedly supported the anti-Marxian approach. The leadership fell upon Webb and Shaw. Originally, Shaw laid his faith on Marxian economics and later on he shifted his allegiance. The tangible result of the efforts was *Fabian Essays.*

In the introduction to the essays Shaw categorically announced that the writers of the essays were all social democrats. Shaw also explained in the introduction the Fabian economic basis for socialism. He said that the members of the society proceeded "with a common conviction of the necessity of vesting the organisation of industry and the material production in a state identified with the whole people by complete Democracy."[2] Shaw propounded the theory of marginal productivity. He accepted the Ricardian theory of economic rent or surplus value. He said that rent or surplus value could accrue to all the factors of production, to land and labour. He rejected the labour theory of value and advocated the exchange value. He wanted to say that the value of commodity was determined by the free play of demand and supply and not by the amount of labour needed for its production. What Shaw said about Fabian political economy is nothing new. He took the side of Ricardian economic theory and rejected Lockean labour theory of value. Whereas, Marx accepted it. The fact is that Shaw's views about economic functions of state do not suggest socialism.

---

1. Ben Pimlott (ed.) *Fabian Essays in Socialist Thought.*
2. Quoted by Durbin, p. 41.

Shaw has summarised the Fabian socialist economic policy in the following words : "What the achievement of socialism involves economically is the transfer of rent from the class which now appropriates it to the whole people. Rent being that part of produce which is individually unearned, this is the only equitable method of disposing of it." What is the method which purports to transfer the wealth concentrated in the hands of a few to the hands of the whole society? This is the common ownership of property. Let us quote Webb "the gradual substitution of organised cooperation for the anarchy of competitive struggle."

Webb's words "anarchy of competitive struggle" are very significant. The Fabians admitted the evils of capitalist economy and monopolistic competition. Capitalism, according to Fabians, was the chief source or cause of large scale poverty and suffering of men. But they did not predict that capitalism would collapse. They had no intention to recommend an intensive class struggle for its destruction. Socialism could be achieved through gradual process, parliamentary initiative and, finally, people's conscious efforts arising out of propaganda launched by Fabian Society. The Fabians admitted that capitalism was associated with periodic slumps and recesses. But because of these slumps capitalism could not be overthrown. It would meet a natural death or be cut to size if socialist programmes were implemented successfully.

Both Shaw and Webb conceived that socialism would be achieved through nationalisation, municipalisation and expanding governmental control over the economic affairs. These three methods were designed to signal the end of *laissez-faire.* Democracy to the Fabians was not simply political—it was both social and economic. Particularly, they emphasised the economic aspect of democracy. A society characterised by exploitation cannot be called truly democratic. Shaw described the aim of social democracy in these words—"to gather the whole people into the state, so that the state may be trusted with the rent of the country, and finally with the land, the capital and organisation of the national industry—with all the sources of production, in short, which are abandoned to the cupidity of irresponsible private industrialists."

Summarising Fabians' approach to *neoclassical economics* Elizabeth Durbin contends "Neoclassical analysis was central to the Fabian case against Marx and for collective ownership. However, there were problems with this approach which a more sophisticated understanding would later reveal. For it is impossible to measure rent, and the early Fabians were confused between the payments due to the factors of production and the income going to families" (p. 42).

The Great Depression of the thirties of the 20th century threatened the economic and political stability of capitalist countries. At the same time, the then Soviet economy, through state control and planning, achieved miraculous success and that impressed a number of Fabians. The Webbs were so much impressed with Soviet success in the economic field that they wrote a book *Soviet Communism : a New Civilization?* In this book they advocated state controlled economy and adoption of planning as potent methods of attaining socialism.

In the thirties of the twentieth century the Fabians were influenced by another thought. In 1936, J. M. Keynes published his epoch-making work *General Theory of Employment, Interest and Money.* As a result of depression the expansion of economy shrank to a considerable extent. People's purchasing power fell remarkably. The unemployment reached a stage that was unprecedented. The growth of economy was so discouraging that common people and even the big policymakers and administrators could not find a single ray of hope. At this juncture of time the Fabians thought that J. M. Keynes's suggestion could provide solution and they forthwith accepted his proposals. The Fabians accepted the Keynesian theory of full employment. To arrest growing unemployment Keynes urged upon the government to expand spending. The Fabians saw in this Keynesian proposal the intervention of government and also the cornering of capitalism. The Fabians further thought that the government spending would offset the insufficient private spending. However, Fabians did not share Keynes views on capitalism. There were many Fabians who opposed Keynes's individualism.

After the Second World War (1939–1945) the economic condition of Britain underwent drastic changes. The unemployment and inflation were mounting day by day. The Labour Party came to power in 1945 after the war and it showed no resistance to Fabian philosophy. The socialist principles of Society were incorporated by the Labour Government into its future programme. Side by side the post-war economic situation created an atmosphere for free discussion. The Fabian Society commissioned Arthur Lewis to write a book on the economic perplexities of the moment. Lewis performed the duty by writing *The Principles of Economic Planning*. Lewis argued that the crucial issue was whether the state should operate through the price mechanism or in supersession of it. The real choice was between "planning by inducement" and "planning by direction". The Labour Government, guided by Fabian philosophy, ultimately decided to make enough room for the private enterprise and this signalled the advent of mixed economy. In fact the Fabian Society was the creator of mixed economy which was later on accepted by India's Planning Commission and politicians. The central idea of such a system is both the state and private enterprises will be allowed to play important role.

Fabian Socialism and Marxian Socialism

From the above analysis the general conclusion that we can frame is that the Fabian Society thought that socialism was the only way of coming out of the evils of capitalist society. But Fabian brand of socialism and the way of setting up of a society are different from Marxian socialism and the techniques of building up of this socialism. Hence a comparison between the two brands of socialism, we think, will sharpen our thought. We can fruitfully remember Lichtheim's cogent remark in this connection : "Fabians' fundamental assumption was that socialism would be introduced not through class conflict, but by way of democratic welfare legislation administered by civil service." Here is the fundamental difference between Fabian socialism and Marxian socialism. Though both Fabians and Marx believed that capitalist system of economy was the chief cause of the common people's misery, the latter insisted upon class struggle and also its intensification which would ultimately lead to the overthrow of capitalism and establishment of dictatorship of the proletariat. This, according to Marx, is the only way of emancipating the oppressed people.

A good number of Fabians thought of the collapse of capitalism but they were lackadaisical in their approach to this and many members of the Society did not subscribe to it. The Fabians did not envisage any class conflict or class struggle. Even, they did not imagine of any revolution on which Marx pinned too much hope. Reforms, parliamentary initiative, governmental legislation, the active role of the political and social institutions based on democratic values and principles and, above all, people's consciousness were, according to Fabians, the most effective weapons to reach socialist goals. Hence there is a fundamental difference as regards the methods of these two types of socialism. We can put it in other words—*one is evolutionary and the other is revolutionary.*

In the middle of the eighties of the nineteenth century some socialist-minded people called Fabian socialists set up an organisation and started movement to free the common people from economic hardship and sufferings. So far as organisational aspect of Marxian socialism is concerned Marx and Engles did not pay any attention to set up an organisation for the intensification of the movement. Their primary concern was academic. They interpreted history by applying dialectical materialism which is also called materialist interpretation of history. In this interpretation they have shown how the production relations in different periods of history have changed and how society assumes different shapes in different periods—such as primitive communist society, slave society, feudal society and industrial society. Nobody brings about any particular type of society by deliberate efforts. Historical determinism operates. Analysing development of society and facts recorded in history Marx has come to the conclusion that socialism is inevitable. It is not to be brought, it will come. Marx calls his socialism 'scientific' because both Marx and Engels have analysed everything scientifically.

The Fabians had no interest in social development nor had they any intention to interpret history materialistically. They were top-ranking intellectuals and they had heartfelt sympathy for the toiling people. They wanted immediate relief for them. That is why they did not rely on the inevitability of socialism. They urged upon the government, the people, the parliament to rise to the occasion. The Fabians believed that socialism could not be achieved overnight. There was no Aladdin's lamp at their disposal. They believed so. Slow and steady process would ultimately ensure the advent of socialism. That was the firm belief of the Fabians. Revolution and struggle they disliked from the core of their heart.

To Marx and Engels communism and not socialism was the ultimate goal. In the critique of the Gotha Programme Marx has stated it in clear language. In socialism the importance of the state will decline, but it will not wither away. The socialist state will be quite different from bourgeois state. It will no longer be an instrument of exploitation or symbol of class rule. The communist society will be a classless society and the state as an instrument of class rule and expolitation will prove its futility and, finally, it will wither away.

The Fabians have argued that in socialism (not in the Marxian sense) the importance of state will gradually decline but it will not wither away. But what appears from their arguments is that the state, in ultimate position, will be able to keep its status intact. The socialist state envisaged by the Fabians will be stronger than the liberal state. The Fabians never dreamt of its withering away. Nor did they, like anarchists, think of abolishing the state. The Fabian state was an instrument to achieve socialism. In Scientific Socialism, party and proletariat play the predominant role.

The application of Fabian Socialism in practice appears to us not very encouraging. The acceptance of Fabian Socialism by the Labour Party was its only success. In fact, there was a time when majority of the Labour Party M. P.s were intimately related with the Fabian Society and were believers of Fabian Socialism. In the

General Election of 1945, 229 of the 394 Labour M. P.s were members of the Society. It has been observed by many that even the members of the bureaucracy were sympathisers of Fabian Socialism.

On the contrary, after two decades of Engels's death (1895) Marxism was applied in Russia under the dynamic leadership of Lenin. After the Second World War, in 1949, China went to communism. Today Soviet communism has collapsed and the Soviet Union has disintegrated. China, North Korea, and Cuba yet hold the torch of Marxism-Leninism. The interesting point is that Marxian socialism is a complete ideology based on scientific principles. It is claimed by its adherents that is a living ideology. We may agree or may not agree with its practical application, but we must agree with its principles. On the contrary, compared with Marxian Socialism, Fabian Socialism is not a complete ideology.

Evaluation

The main factor behind the rise and growth of Fabian Socialism was to counteract the emergence of Marxian Socialism on the British soil. *The Communist Manifesto* was published in 1848 and all the major works of Marx and Engels were published between 1850 and 1883—when Marx died. Fabian Society came into being at the very beginning of 1884. By that time, Marx's works were widely read and his brand of socialism was a much-talked subject. The major works of Marx and Engels were translated into various European languages. The British people were determined to "save" their system of culture, tradition and politics from the "invasion" of Marxism or, more definitely, Marxian socialism. On the contrary, they felt that socialism was the only way which could lift the people from the squalid condition and give them a decent living standard through the eradication of unemployment and exploitation. The Fabian socialists wanted a type of socialism which would be in tune with the time-old tradition of Britain. This tradition is parliamentary democracy. Marx and Engels were philosophers and theoreticians. They were not serious at all how to popularise their doctrine of socialism. This task was performed by Plekhanov, Lenin and a score of other leaders. But in Britain the Society shouldered the responsibility to propagate the basic principles of socialism and it also brought to light the evils of capitalism. Both Marx and Engels assertively predicted that—because of its inherent contradiction—capitalism would ultimately collapse. The proletarians will fully utilise this situation and through revolutionary methods they will precipitate the collapse of capitalist system. The Fabians, on the other hand, were not at all eager in the collapse or breakdown of the capitalist system root and branch. They wanted to control it. The publication of dozens of Fabian Tracts aroused sympathy and consciousness for and of socialism. In April 1884 the first Fabian Tract "Why are the many poor?" was published and within next few years 100,000 copies of this Tract were sold. The sale of a pamphlet or a book might not always be a barometer of the popularity, but it is definitely a barometer of people's interest about the idea contained in it.

There were top-ranking intellectuals and leading personalities behind the emergence and growing importance both of Fabian Society and Fabian Socialism. This considerably enhanced the prestige of the Fabian Society. The popularity was not imposed from above, it was spontaneous. The association of persons like G. B. Shaw, Annie Besant, Graham Wallas, H. G. Wells and the Webbs with the Society raised its status to a very high place.

The credit of the Society shall be counted from another angle. The necessity of planning for economic development or, more specifically, eradication of poverty, was strongly felt by the Society. The Society's interest in planning was, of course, a sequel to miraculous success of the Soviet five year planning. On the one hand, the Webbs wrote *Soviet Communism : A New Civilization* and on the other hand, W. Arthur Lewis wrote a memorable small book *The Principles of Economic Planning*. Besides these two books there was another book on planning and price system. It was *Planning and Price Mechanism* and the author was Meade. Needless to say that, in a bourgeois democratic state, planning is generally looked with suspicion. But for the first time in history Great Britain created an exception by giving serious and active thought to economic planning and this was done under the stewardship of the Fabian Society. In the thirties of the last century the erstwhile Soviet Union adopted planning system for the purpose of time-bound economic development and, subsequently, several other countries of the Third World adopted planning system as a technique of economic development. However, the Fabian Society was the first in this field.

The Fabians' contribution to political theory or political thought is less pronounced, but their contribution to practical working of government, efficient administration and economic activities of the state is really significant. The overall deterioration of British society was an aftermath of the Industrial Revolution. Widespread evils of Industrial Revolution, mismanagement of economy and maladministration created indignation and suspicion in the minds of both Marxists and Fabians and this led them to think in terms of an alternative system. So, instead of harping upon political obligation or the like, they concentrated their attention on how to build up an efficient administration and the foundation of a welfare state.

There is no doubt that the members of the Fabian Society seriously thought about the problems and miseries of the common people and the working class. One credit we must give to Fabian. They thought of the growing miseries of the people and started to find out a solution. In a sense the Fabians were, to some extent, practical-minded because they set up a society to implement the programmes. The weakness was they wanted to keep the capitalist state structure intact and within it they desired to achieve socialist goals. And this was impossible. They failed to understand this simple truth. J. S. Mill, T. H. Green and several others were thinking about improving the economic conditions of the working people. But they did not start any practical programme. Only the Fabian Society came forward with a well-chalked-out programme and clear policy, clarity which surpasses the ambiguities.

The Fabians viewed the state mainly as an administration of public services and nationalised industries. This is the most practical and useful function. As the source of coercive authority it will settle the disputes. But this was the secondary function to them. Today the enhanced role of the state envisaged by the Fabians may appear insignificant, but towards the end of the nineteenth and at the beginning of the twentieth century it was not insignificant, because there was a great wave of *laissez-faire*.

Many eminent persons have criticised Fabianism from more than one angle and many of these carry weight. Critics are of opinion that it is rather unfair to exaggerate the contribution of Fabian Society or importance of Fabian Socialism. A comparison between Fabian Socialism and Marxian Socialism will reveal the unscientific character of the former. In a class society there shall always be an economically dominant class under whose control the base will always work and this base will determine the character of the superstructure. Reforms, parliamentary initiative or factory legislation, experience teaches us, make certain concessions for the working class. But all these cannot free them from exploitation. Researches have shown that the British Labour Party is dominated by Fabians and this party has come to power several times. The Fabians believed that the emancipation of the working class was possible through evolutionary and parliamentery procedures. Many eminent persons rediculed at the Fabian Society's policy and programme. But the collapse of the Soviet system at the beginning of the last decade of the twentieth century has to some extent confirmed the objective and programme of the Fabians.

During the last one hundred years there had taken place remarkable progress in the financial conditions of the working class. This was chiefly due to the political consciousness and collective bargaining of the workers. In all the capitalist countries the workers—by exerting pressures upon the industrialists—have been able to ameliorate their economic conditions. The capitalists understand only one thing—that is profit. They have no obligation to socialist principles or no sympathy for the sufferings of the workers.

In our earlier analysis we have shown how the Fabians in general and G. B. Shaw in particular supported imperialism on flimsy and reactionary grounds. The subjugation of one nation by another nation was absolutely a non-issue to the Fabians. The absence of national self-government never aroused any feeling or emotion in their mind. Shaw and Webb were impressed by the argument of efficiency and evolution. The backward nations, in their opinion, would be benefited by their association with the civilised nations. This argument today is untenable and highly condemnable. In 1895 the Webbs established the London School of Economics and Political Science and a staunch supporter of imperialism was appointed its director. Shaw once said "A Fabian must be an imperialist." The Fabians lent their unqualified support to the British policy towards South Africa. Their approach to imperialism was very much closer to Halford Mackinder's theory of geopolitics. Shaw once said that the gobbling of nations was unfortunate but not immoral. The Webbs were so much obsessed with imperialism that for a pretty long time they forgot Fabian Socialism and devoted their energy to the course of *realpolitik*.

Concluding Observations

Marx died in 1883 and the Fabian Society was set up in 1884. By that time the intellectual giants of various parts of Europe had come across the main tenets of Marxism in general and Marxian socialism in particular. Industrial Revolution had passed a century and quarter and its far reaching evils became prominent in several countries of Europe, specially Britain, where Marx spent more than thirty years of his life. Marx and Engels built up the fabric of their theory from the lessons of the consequences of Industrial Revolution. But it is surprising that the application of Marxism could not find any place in Britain. However, a number of intellectuals and statesmen were convinced that only socialism could save the oppressed masses and the tangible result was the establishment of the Fabian Society—the creator of Fabian Socialism. So Fabian Socialism can be called an off-shoot of Marxian Socialism. The fathers of Fabian Socialism detested violent measures essential for establishing socialism.

Alter the First World War the Fabian Society was associated with the British Labour Party and a good number of intellectuals became its members. "The Fabian Society has always embraced a range of socialist viewpoints but the broad disposition of its members has often been characterised as democratic socialist" (Oxford Concise Dictionary of Politics, p. 175). *We may,* therefore, *hold the view that there is a very close relation between Fabian Socialism and Democratic Socialism,* the precise meaning of the latter being the pursuit of socialism by democratic means. Reforms of capitalist system and the laws enacted by parliament are regarded as the best means of achieving socialist goals. Parliamentarism is placed ahead of socialism. We know that violence and class struggle have no place in Democratic Socialism. In other words, peaceful means are the only ways for construction and administration of socialist society and this type of society may also be called democratic society.

The Fabian Society laid enormous faith on parliamentary means and democratic methods for achieving socialist goals. Class struggle, class conflict, armed revolution have hardly any place in a country imbued with the advantages of parliamentary system. Fabian socialists are also called "moderate left" because their leftism or leftist attitude is different from Marxists who believe in violent methods. Fabian socialists believe that violence begets violence and solves no basic problems or issues. Rather, it creates animosity among several sections of society. Hence both Fabian Socialism and Democratic Socialism scrupulously adhere to the democratic and peacefull means for the establishment of socialism. Marx and his followers have devalued the importance of parliament and reforms because all these aim at compromise with the capitalist class which is the enemy of the toiling masses of men and cause of their great misery and endless sufferings.

Fabian Socialism, Democratic Socialism and Evolutionary Socialism fall almost in the same category. The supporters of all these think that armed struggle must be avoided because this is not suitable. Fabian Socialism is based on the presumption that the talents of the individuals can be developed only through the free exercise of various democratic rights and this makes good and responsible citizens. Only democratic means can ensure social welfare. On the other hand, Marxian Socialism purports regimentation and curtailment of political freedom. This aspect of Marxism dwarfs the spontaneity of the individual's intellect. Fabian Society, because of this apprehension, kept itself aloof from Marxism and the Marxian path of arriving at socialism.

Several governments of post-Second World War countries have given recognition to Democratic Socialism which contains the chief characteristics of Fabian Socialism. It is a belief of many people that Fabian Socialism or Democratic Socialism is quite capable of delivering social democracy while Marxian Socialism is not qualified for that purpose. Because, in Marxian Socialism, there is enormous regimentation. Regimentation and force are rank enemies of democracy. Both Fabian Socialism and Democratic Socialism lay their undiluted faith on election for setting up a government. This preference for elected government constitutes the core concept of Fabian Socialism and Democratic Socialism. We, thus, see that Fabian society is progenitor of Democratic Socialism. Today Democratic Socialism or attainment of socialism through democratic means has earned large scale applaud and approval from wide varieties of states, people and organisations. If any credit is to be awarded to anybody then it is undoubtedly to the Fabian Society.

Fabian Socialism rejects the orthodox aspects of liberalism. Liberalism aims at reducing the state activity to a minimum level. Individual's initiative and spontaneity are regarded as the sole criteria of social progress and social harmony. But the prominent defects of the Industrial Revolution convinced the intellectual members of the Fabian Society that there was a great need of state intervention for the alleviation of people's sufferings. Of course, J. S. Mill (1806-1895) and Thomas Hill Green (1836-1882) recommended state intervention for the greater interests of social welfare or common good. Perhaps the last word has been uttered by the Fabian society of Democratic Socialism. Some may object to the term "last word" because there is nothing like "last". Spencer's (1820-1903) or Mill's liberalism has proved maximum inadequacy to tackle the situation of the modern world. The collapse of the Soviet Union has practically drawn a curtain upon Marxian Socialism.

Today the thinking people of both academic and intellectual world have pinned their hope upon Democratic Socialism as a panacea for various economic and political ills from which society suffers. This Democratic Socialism resembles some of the basic features of Fabian Socialism, but it is not all with it. It does not completely deny the Marxian brand of socialism. Though socialism is passing through changes, we think, the Fabian type, because of its peaceful and evolutionary bias, will be able to survive.

25 REVISIONISM AND BERNSTEIN (1850-1932)

Introduction

Immediately after the death of Marx and during the life-time of Engels their scientific socialism underwent changes. The revolutionary character of Marxian or scientific socialism was faced with criticisms from various corners of intellectual world and practical persons. The critics belong to several groups, but for the sake of analysis they may be divided into two groups—one group comes to be known as Fabian socialists and the other group is called German revisionist. In our last chapter we have discussed the various aspects of Fabian Socialism. In this chapter we shall try to throw light on revisionism headed by a German socialist for which it is called German revisionism. The spokesman of the German revisionism is Eduard Bernstein. Both Fabian socialism and German revisionism are connected by a common thread which is called evolutionary socialism. Class struggle or armed revolution are no longer treated as the only ways of establishing socialism. Evolutionary methods are more effective. According to evolutionary socialism parliamentary methods, democratic ways, reforms, laws and pursuasive techniques can profitably be used to achieve socialist goals or set up a socialist society. Urging upon revolution Marx had selected an erroneous way. Socialism cannot be attained all on a sudden. Towards it people will have to proceed step by step. Both society and socialism are the products of evolution.

Eduard Bernstein was the leader of German socialist movement and by virtue of his position he came in close contact with Engels and subsequently became a leading Marxist. He then revised his views and this revision branded him as revisionist.

Eduard Bernstein was born in 1850 *two years after the publication of Manifesto of the Communist Party*, in a poor family of Berlin. His parents were Jewish. Because of poverty his parents could not give him proper education. He was sent to a very ordinary school and even there he could not complete his education. Severe poverty and other factors stood on the way of the continuation of studies and Bernstain was forced to put an end of study. After receiving the training of banking service he was appointed to a post of clerk to it. He then served the bank up to 28. While in service he studied literature on socialism and developed an inclination to it. He then became a member of German Social Democratic Worker's Party. In 1874 he was influenced by Dühring's philosophy. He then attended the Gotha Congress of 1875 as a delegate of the Social Democratic Party.

The ever rising influence of socialists and the growing number of socialists created a nightmarish situation in the mind of Bismark and in 1878 he made an anti-socialist law. The purpose of this law was to curtail the influence of socialists. The organisations, magazines, and journals all were banned by this law. Before the promulgation of the Anti-Socialist Law, Bernstein left Germany and went to Switzerland to act as a private secretary of Karl Höchberg. Höchberg was a wealthy businessman and philanthropist. Towards the end of 1870s Bernstein actively associated himself with the Social Democratic Party of Germany and assumed all the financial liabilities of the party. In 1879, the Anti-Socialist Law of Germany came into force and the S.D.P. was declared illegal.

Socialist party, newspapers and all socialist outfits were banned by the Anti-Socialist Law of Germany and the Social Democratic Party was faced with crisis. It was difficult to run the day to day activities in the midst of stringent anti-socialist laws and stiff government opposition. Marx and Engels advised Liebknecht to set up an underground paper abroad and assisted in determining its political orientation and selecting its editors. Marx and Engels adopted this way because they were convinced that the socialist ideas must reach the largest number of people. Otherwise the goals of socialism will never be achieved.

In the second half of 1879 Marx and Engels kept in close touch with the German Social-Democrats and held discussions with them for setting preliminaries regarding the publication of a paper—*Sozialdemokrat* whose head office would be in Zurich : The paper commenced its publication from Zurich and in the editorial board there were Höchberg, Karl August Schramm and Eduard Bernstein. This Marx and Engels considered unacceptable, because they knew the attitude and character of every person. Höchberg was a social reformist and bourgeois. Bernstein and Schramm were enthusiastic admirers of Eugen Dühring. In a letter to Bebel in 1879 Engels in clear language stated that it was not possible for him as well as for Marx to make them associate with the paper which was financed by Höchberg, a bourgeois and social philanthropist.

Under the intellectual guidance of Bernstein and financial leadership of Höchberg the paper was published. A remarkable article was "*The Socialist Movement in Germany in Retrospect.*" This was virtually a manifesto of the right opportunist elements. Engels complained that the paper published by three Zurichers was practically the personal property of Höchberg.

While in Switzerland he developed friendship with Kautsky. He was then expelled from Switzerland and after that he went to London and he also shifted his editorial activities to London. In London Bernstein came in contact with the Fabian Society and he shared with its views and ideas. All these happened at the beginning of the nineties of the 19th century and those were the years of the heyday of Fabianism. In London there occurred another interesting incident. Bernstein's friendship with Engels became deep although the latter indulged in critical notion about English socialists, particularly Fabians.

During Engels's life-time the political ideas of Bernstein did not assume explicitly revisionist nature. In London he maintained friendship with the Fabians and also with Engels. He was also an executor of will. However, after Engels's death in 1895, Bernstein began to express his own political and academic views and opinions. He published several essays under the title "*Problems of Socialism and the Tasks of Social Democracy*". The purpose of these essays was to attack Marx's materialism and other theories. His most famous work was *Evolutionary Socialism : A Criticism and Affirmation.* After propagating revisionism for about four decades Bernstein died on 18th April 1932. Eduard Bernstein was undoubtedly a flamboyant propagator of revisionism and he welcomed all sorts of hardships for the propagation of revisionism. But after his death revisionism was practically a forgotten political ideology. It was satisfied with its confinement only in intellectual circles.

Revisionism : Definition and Nature

The term revisionism is used in a pejorative sense. People use the word revisionism to deprecate some ideas, ideology and concept. The German synonym of this word is *durchsehen.* It is to be noted here that to revise or review something is not bad or condemnable at all. But in the Marxian literature it carries a special connotation. The Marxists use the term revisionism or revisionists to condemn those who have deviated from orthodox Marxism.

The term revisionism has a broad meaning. At different times different persons or group of persons were nicknamed revisionists. Trotsky, Kautsky, Tito, Carrillo, Lukacs, Korsch and even Mao were called revisionists. The broadness of the term originated from the variety of interpretations of Marx's philosophy. Different persons interpreted Marx's principles in their own ways and that gave rise to variety of opinions sometimes leading to contradictory lines. When the principles, policies, programmes and ideology of some persons were in conflict with those of the official line the former were called revisionists. In narrower sense the opposition to Marxism is revisionism. Some intellectuals and socialist minded people questioned the economic philosophy and principles of Marx and Engels and expressed their doubt about the practical importance of Marx's ideas. These people came to be called revisionists. The interesting point here is that the revisionists did not intend to abandon Marx's ideas but they questioned the applicability of his principles. However, they agreed with his socialist philosophy.

The revisionists agreed with some of the fundamental principles of Marx and Engels, but disagreed with others. The social, economic and political conditions are changing rapidly and in the background of this change the revisionists strongly felt the need of changing the basic tenets of Marxism. They felt that attachment to any particular principle would lead to failure. This approach is generally called revisionism. A recent critic has explained the term in the following words : "Revisionists were not the people who abandoned Marxism completely or never had been Marxists, but those who sought to modify the traditional doctrine or who held that some of its essential features were no longer applicable in the present state of society... Later the term was also applied to those who attempted to supplement Marxism in Kantian line." So any change of or supplement to Marxism held by the official line came to be treated as revisionism.

Revisionism is used in both wider and narrower sense. In wider sense it is integral to Marxist theory and practice, "predicated as that must be on a social ontology which has self-creation through labour as the fundamental characteristic of being human" (Bottomore p. 475). But the term is rarely used in wider sense "Marxism became canonised and revisionism gained a narrower, negative and shifting connotation. Before 1914 revisionism became synonymous with those writers and political figures who, while starting from Marxist premises, came by degrees to call in question various elements of the doctrine, especially Marx's prediction as to the development of capitalism and the inevitability of socialist revolution" (Kolakowsky quoted by Bottomore, p. 475).

Herbert Marcuse, in his noted work *Reason and Revolution*, observes that Marx's various principles began to undergo changes immediately after his death. So long Engels was alive he resisted this change by offering "authentic" interpretation of Marx's ideas. Let us, for the sake of clarity, quote Marcuse : "The history of Marxism has confirmed the affinity between Hegel's motives and the critical interest of the materialist dialectic as applied to society. The schools of Marxism that abandoned the revolutionary foundations of Marxist theory were the same that outspokenly repudiated the Hegelian aspects of the Marxian theory, especially the dialectic. The revisionist writing and thought, which expressed the growing faith of large socialist groups in a peaceful evolution from capitalism to socialism, attempted to change socialism from a theoretical and practical antithesis to capitalist system into a parliamentary movement within the system" (p. 398).

In the opinion of orthodox Marxists the change or amendment of original views of Marx is sheer opportunism. Because Marx arrived at certain conclusions after studying history scientifically. At least the Marxists viewed it in that light. Some of the revisionists termed Marxism as the remnants of utopianism. Revisionism replaced the revolutionary action by faith in natural evolution and reformism. Bernstein called the dialectic as the treacherous element in the Marxian doctrine, the trap that is laid for all consistent thinking. He declared that the "share" of dialectic consists in its inappropriate abstraction from the specific particularities of things. He defended the matter of fact quality of the fixed and stable objects as against any notion of their dialectical negation. Bernstein's revisionism attacks not only certain principles of Marxism but its very root. The dialectical method is the centre-stage of Marxian philosophy. In fixed and stable condition, according to revisionism, the state of affairs evolves towards a rational society.

Origin of Revisionism

It is generally believed by some scholars of Western political thought that Bernstein is the originator of revisionism. This is partially correct. It is true that Bernstein's interpretation of Marxism gave birth to revisionism in a large scale but its true origin can be traced to the anti-socialist laws that were implemented in the eighties of the nineteenth century. A good number of socialist thinkers published articles in socialist journals to ventilate their own views. But these writings were not in consonance to the views of Marx and Engels. Revisionism practically originated from this.

It has already been indicated that Höchberg, Bernstein and Schramm published a journal. This journal published the views of the authors which contained ideas about socialism that were not to the true spirit of Marx and Engels. These surreptitiously revised the original idea of socialism. The "Three Zurichers" berated the Social Democratic Party for being a one-sided workers' party. In their journal Bernstein, Höchberg and Schramm made the following suggestions : (a) They wanted the Social Democrats to cease their attacks on the bourgeoisie, (b) to open up the party to bourgeois elements, (c) bourgeois intellectuals will be allowed to hold party posts in view of the workers' lack of education, (d) Marx and Engels along with all Social Democrats must renounce the revolutionary methods and aims,

(e) finally they must use legal, parliamentary methods and reforms. These five suggestions constitute the core of Bernstein's revisionism. Bernstein and two other Zurichers concluded that if these five "principles" are strictly followed socialism will be achieved and there would be no necessity of Marx's class struggle and armed revolution.

Marx and Engels were highly indignant. Marx said that the three-star constellation were out to denigrate Social-Democrats. The purpose of Bernstein, Höchberg and Schramm was to abandon the revolutionary struggle and to surrender unconditionally to the police regime of Bismarck. Marx and Engels also vowed at this time that the ulterior motive and revisionism of Bernstein and company must be fought tooth and nail. Marx and Engels issued a "circular letter" criticising the Right opportunism of Three Zurichers. Marx and Engels wrote in the "circular letter" : "It is the representatives of the petty bourgeoisie who are here making themselves heard, full of anxiety that the proletariat, under the pressure of revolutionary position may go too far."[1]

Bernstein's disagreement with Marxists was widening day after day. He made all-out efforts to launch a polemical onslaught against the Marxists and the death of Engels brought for him the opportunity. In 1897-98 he published few articles under the title "*Problems of Socialism and the Task of Social Democracy.*" In these articles he attacked the theoretical basis of Marxism. Bernstein proclaimed himself a true socialist and he wanted to prove that his was the true method. He criticised Marx's concept of matter in the light of Kant's idealism.

On March 6, 1895, few months before his death, Engels wrote an *Introduction* for the reprint of *The Class struggles in France 1848-50*. In this *Introduction* he made the following polemical observation which is regarded as the potential source of revisionism "History has proved us wrong. It has made it clear that the state of economic development on the continent at that time was not, by a long way, ripe for the elimination of capitalist production; it has proved this by the economic revolution which, since 1848, has seized the whole of the continent, and has caused big industry to take real root in France, Austria, Hungary...while it has made Germany positively an industrial country of the first rank."

"The franchise has been transformed from a means of deception which it was before, into an instrument of emancipation. In election agitation it provided us with a means, second to none, of getting in touch with the mass of the people where they still stand aloof from us; of forcing all the parties to defend their views and actions against our attacks before all the people. It provided our representatives in the Reichstag with a platform from which they could speak to their opponents in parliament."

"With the successful utilization of universal suffrage an entirely new method of proletarian struggle came into operation, and this method quickly developed further. It was found that the state institutions...offer the working class still further opportunities to fight these very institutions. The workers took part in elections to particular Diets, to municipal councils and to trades courts; they contested with the bourgeoisie every post in the occupation of which a sufficient part of the proletariat had a say. And so it happened that the bourgeoisie and the government came to be much more afraid of the legal than the illegal action of the workers' party."

1. Quoted in Engels : A Biography, p. 322.

"The conditions of the struggle had essentially changed. Rebellion in the old style, street fighting with barricades, which decided the issue everywhere up to 1848, was to a considerable extent obsolete. A real victory of an insurrection over the military in street fighting, a victory as between two armies, is one of the rarest exceptions. The most that an insurrection can achieve in the way of actual tactical operations is the proper construction and defence of single barricade...Hence passive defence is the prevailing form of fighting; the attack will rise here and there; but only by way of exception, to occasional thrusts and flank assaults." (All these excerpts are from *Marx-Engels—Selected Works,* Vol. II, pp. 129-131)

Engels further observes that earlier it was thought that a small group of persons with revolutionary zeal could throw a surprise attack and achieve object. The large scale participation of masses was not thought as a part of revolutionary activities. In the *Introduction* Engels has changed his earlier view. This *Introduction* has introduced a new controversy which is whether a revolution requires a few dedicated and well-trained revolutionaries or large scale mass participation. Engels was a practical man and a close observer of political events that were happening in several parts of Europe. He saw that the political incidents that took place during the then last fifty years (1846-1895) clearly revealed that for a successful revolution large scale mass participation was a "must". General public must be well-acquainted with the important aspects of revolution and its keys to success. It is not possible for few revolutionaries to achieve success. He also said that there had occured sea changes in political arena which cannot be dismissed as silly affairs. The leaders of revolution must bring them into active consideration. This clearly indicates the change in view that Engels held earlier and what he held in 1895. This is treated by many as the origin of revisionism.

Slow and intensive propaganda through pamphlets and booklets, mass meeting close contact with the public, to propagate the necessity of revolution and parliamentary tactics are recognised as the immediate task of the party. This general principle is applicable to all countries. Engels has announced that the pressing conditions always require the revision of tactics. The revolutionary situations everywhere are never uniform. What would be the exact method that depends upon the particular situation, Engels concludes, whatever may happen in other countries German Social Democracy, as the vanguard of international movement, must continue to pursue the above tactics. We have extensively quoted Engels's view in order to trace the origin of revisionism.

Bernstein's Criticisms

Bernstein had criticised Marxian philosophy from several standpoints. These may be arranged under the following points. Bernstein's first objection is that "Engels had written of a revision of *tactics,* but in fact this was a revision of *strategy,* a revision of the premises of theoretical Marxism. The errors denounced by Engels were not merely a result of contingent factors; they derived from essential points of doctrine" (Colletti, p. 49).

Bernstein's another objection is that in Marxian theory, there is no coordination between theory and reality. To make a theory acceptable and useful there must be a unity between the two. So far as the theory is concerned, Marx is quite right. But the theory has very little connection with practice. In one of his letters Bernstein wrote "The doctrine (i.e., Marxism) is not sufficiently realistic for me. It has lagged behind the practical development of the movement. It may still be all right for Russia...but in Germany we have outgrown its old form." In this observation Bernstein clearly indicated that he had no quarrel with Marx's theory. He framed conclusions and made predictions on the basis of Marx's analysis of history based on dialectical materialism. But he observed that the political and economic situation in Germany and several other West European countries differed from what Marx said.

In the third place, the difference between theory and practice is due to the fact that Marxism is mainly outdated and utopian. He had said that the tactics and methods of workers' movement had changed remarkably and naturally Marxian *tactics* were irrelevant for the prevailing conditions of Germany. His purpose was to liberate workers' movement from the encumbrances of old theory and methods. Then the movement would be able to achieve its goals. "The defect of Marxism" says Bernstein "lay in its excessive abstraction and theoretical phraseology." This is the greatest defect of his *Capital.* In spite of scientificity the *Capital* does not evoke considerable interest because of the excessive abstraction.

Bernstein's another criticism against Marxism is that it is based on "a priorism". The proletariat will seize power through revolution or through political catastrophe. This idea or notion, according to Bernstein, is based on an "a priorism". That means proletariat will or must revolt or the capitalist system must face the inevitable catastrophy. The assumptions are : the society will be polarised between two main classes—bourgeois and proletariat, there will emerge the growing immiseration of the proletarians, economic conditions will progressively worsen. Ultimately, the revolution will overthrow the regime.

Bernstein observes that the study of history reveals that the events of society have not proceeded according to the predictions of Marx and his "a priorism". If so, Marxism and the predictions of Marx have faced with a very big question mark. But Marx's predictions constitute the most vital aspect of his theory. Bernstein claimed that he made this observation on the basis of his studies of economy. Bernstein in support of his view also said that even Engels, his lifelong friend, did not hesitate to admit that the earlier assumption regarding the activities of capitalism had proved false. Here it is to be noted that the economic situation of many countries of Europe had undergone rapid changes after the death of Marx in 1883 and Engels curiously and seriously observed those changes.

Collapse of Capitalism and Theory of Breakdown

Colletti in his *From Rousseau to Lenin* (p. 52) says, "The pivot upon which the whole of Bernstein's argument turns is his critique of the "theory of breakdown". The "theory of breakdown" is Bernstein's own discovery. Marx or Engels never uttered such words. From Marx's collapse of capitalism Bernstein derived this theory. In volume one of *Capital* there is a chapter "Historical Tendency of Capitalist Accumulation". In this chapter Marx says that at a certain stage of development the capitalist accumulation brings forth the material agencies for its own dissolution. From that moment new forces and new passions spring up in the bosom of society, but the old social organisation fetters them and keeps them down.

The development of capitalism is accompanied by the centralisation of capital. With the progress of capitalism the competition among the capitalists becomes keen and keener. The small capitalists are forced to retreat, that is, to close their units or they are merged with the big capitalists. This leads to the centralisation of capital. Along with the constantly diminishing number of magnates of capital, who usurp and monopolise all advantages of this process of transformation, grow the mass of misery, oppression, slavery, degradation, exploitation; but with this too grows the revolt of the working class.

In *Capital* (Vol. I, p. 763) Marx says : "The monopoly of capital becomes a fetter upon the mode of production which has sprung up and flourished along with and under it. Centralisation of the means of production and socialisation of labour at last reach a point where they become incompatible with their capitalist integument. Thus integument is burst asunder. The knell of capitalist private property sounds. The expropriators are expropriated." This is Marx's historical tendency of capitalist accumulation. The capitalist accumulation begets its own negation. It is the negation of negation. This negation is due to the inexorability of the law of Nature. The capitalist, whatever may be the extent of his power, cannot escape from this inexorability of the law of Nature. That is, capitalism is bound to collapse. So far as the collapse of capitalism is concerned Marx arrived at the above conclusion on the basis of his study of capitalist development.

Eduard Bernstein challenged Marx's observation regarding the collapse of capitalism and he claimed that his opinion was based on his study of the functioning of capitalism. In his judgment it is a "purely" "speculative anticipation". He not merely rejected a certain form of collapse, he also rejected the very possibility of collapse. According to Marx, the capitalist order is a historical phenomenon, a transitory and non-natural order. There are contradictions within capitalism and these lead to its own breakdown. Bernstein rejects all these. Capitalism is endowed with self-regulatory mechanism and this saves capitalism from any collapse. Bernstein admits that there are contradictions within capitalism. But with the improved methods of communication, credit system and also various other ways, the capitalists are able to fight against the forces of imminent collapse. Interpreting Bernstein's view Colletti observes (p. 54), "Cartels, credit, the improved system of communications, the rise of working class, in so far as they act to eliminate or at least mitigate the internal contradictions of the capitalist economy, hindering their development and aggravation, ensure for the system the possibility of unlimited survival."

About the establishment of socialism or a socialist society Marx said that the roots of socialism contained in the development of capitalist economy. In capitalist development the impoverishment and oppression of working class will rise and at the peak of capitalist development poverty and oppression will reach a stage of intoleration. The working class will launch a struggle that will lead to the setting up of a socialist society. According to Bernstein, socialism is based upon ethical ideal. The higher form of civilisation ingrains in the mind of people the feeling for a socialist society. When man will be confirmed that socialist society is better than any other society he will be morally or ethically bound to set up such a society. It is not due to the inherent or internal contradictions of capitalist system. It is simply a speculation. Again, he does not agree with Marx that socialism is inevitable. Here we note that so far as the establishment of socialism is concerned Bernstein differed from Marx. He did not believe that advent of socialism was connected with the capitalist's own view and has no real basis.

Bernstein also rejected Marx's concept of "Centralisation of Capital". He admitted that industrialisation had resulted in the concentration of industry. This concentration, according to Bernstein, was due to the availability of the factors of production or due to extraneous factors. But he did not accept the view that concentration of industry was the concentration of property. On the other hand, he concluded there was remarkable diffusion of property. The big industrial units did not gobble the small units. The actual picture was that the small industrial units existed side by side of the big industrial establishments. The history of capitalism had shown that the number of property owners was increasing day by day which had falsified Marx's prediction or speculation.

Bernstein said that Marx's prediction of imminent crisis was farthest from reality. Through the new tactics and strategies the capitalists had been able to resist the advance of crisis and to ensure their survival. At the same time the workers were able to mitigate their sufferings by means of collective bargaining and concerted trade union activities. Bernstein said that Marx knew all these things, but he did not recognise the impact of worker's collective efforts. Here is the unfortunateness of his theory. Capitalists' rate of profit had increased, but that did not lead to the decline in wages. The fall in employment, Bernstein said, was not always due to the exploitative nature of capitalism. Bernstein also spoke proudly of the progressive democratisation of the capitalist system.

Theory of Value

In criticising Marx's theory of value Bernstein pointed out that there was enough confusion between what had been said in the third volume of *Capital* and in the earlier volumes. In the third volume Marx makes the following observation : market value is represented as equal to the cost of production including average profit. In the earlier volume the exchange value is represented as measured solely by the amount of necessary labour used in production. Bernstein criticised Marx's theory of value on the ground that labour-created value was untenable as a basis for discovering a just system of distribution. That is, Marx's theory of value (or labour theory of value as it is called) does not solve the problem of distribution faced by the economy. In the following opinion Bernstein makes his stand clear : "The theory of value gives a norm for the justice or injustice for the partition of product of labour just as little as does the atomic theory for the beauty or ugliness of a piece of sculpture. We compare today the best placed workers just in those trades with a very high rate of surplus value, the most infamously ground-down workers in those with a very low rate. A scientific basis for socialism or communism cannot be supported on the fact that only the wage worker does not receive the full value of the product of his work."

He has criticised Marx's labour theory of value from another standpoint : "Labour value is nothing more than a key, an abstract image, like the philosophical atom endowed with a soul—a key which, employed by the master hand of Marx, has led to the exposure and presentation of mechanism of capitalist economy as this had not been hitherto treated, not so forcibly, logically and clearly. But this key refuses service over and above a certain point." Marx has borrowed the concept of labour theory of value from his predecessors. He himself did not propound it. What Marx has said is that he treated the theory for building up the concept of surplus value which is a very important part of capitalist exploitation. On this issue again Bernstein differed from Marx.

His own view is this : Value is mere thought-construct : it is, in Marx's word, a formal principle which serves to bring system and order to the complexity of the analysis, but itself has no real existence. Bernstein comments, "In so far as we take into consideration the individual commodity, value loses any concrete content and becomes a mere mental construction...Hence it is clear that the moment that labour value is only valid as a mental formula or scientific hypothesis, surplus value also becomes a pure formula, a formula based on a hypothesis."

On his interpretation of labour theory of value Bernstein cannot claim any credit because, before him, Wenner Sombart and Conrad Smidt held this view. Value, according to Sombart, is not an empirical but a mental and a logical fact. In Smidt's view, the law of value within the capitalist mode of production is a pure—although theoretically necessary—fiction.

Bernstein opposed Marx's labour theory of value still from another angle. He wanted to consider value as function of utility. He said that the value of a commodity depended upon the utility which the consumer expected to derive from it. The value is also decided by the upward and downward movements of demand and supply.

Bernstein and his fellow revisionists "rejected Marx's theory of value in so far as the theory involves the principle that the exchange value of commodities is measured solely by the efforts of the wage earners and that the surplus value absorbed by the capitalists is measurably only by the excess of what labourers produce over what they receive. But they did not reject the contention that there is surplus value or that the surplus represents generally the excess of what capitalists receive for the sale of commodities over what they contribute the value of those commodities. And they held to the belief that the effort of capitalists to increase the surplus supplies the propelling force in the natural development of capitalism and creates an exploitation of wage-earners" (Coker, p. 109).

Nature of Society

Bernstein rejected Marx's class structure of society. In *The Communist Manifesto* and in several other works Marx and Engels have said that the society is divided into mainly two classes—bourgeois and proletariat. Marx and Engels admitted the existence of other classes but so far as capitalist development, inherent contradictions in capitalism and conflict between the classes are concerned the importance or existence of other classes is of no real value. Marx emphasised the existence of two classes keeping in mind the idea of class struggle. In Bernstein's opinion the class structure depicted by Marx and Engels suffers from oversimplification. Bourgeois and proletariat are not two main classes and there is no clear evidence of gradual proletarisation. In every industrial society there is a powerful or influential middle class. He admits that there is no fixed character of middle class. But in spite of this the existence and importance of middle class is undeniable. Particularly in industrial society, intellectual development comes from the middle class.

Marx has said that the additional wealth produced by capitalist development has been captured by the capitalists. But the workers and smaller classes have a microscopic fraction of the huge wealth. Bernstein again did not agree with this contention of Marx. He is of opinion that the workers, middle class people and other persons have got a share of this wealth. The workers have got greater share of wealth which they have acquired through the technique of collective bargaining. The improved economic conditions have raised them to the status of the middle class. In his own words "The enormous increase of social wealth is not accompanied by a decreasing number of large capitalists but an increasing number of capitalists of all degrees. The middle classes change but they do not disappear from the social scale." Bernstein has further observed that what is generally called working class is not a homogeneous group of people. There are different categories of people in the working class.

In any industrial society the proletarians form the majority. But among them there are diverse interests, outlooks and cultural affinities. According to Bernstein these diversities create the most powerful stumbling block to any revolution. It is unfortunate that Marx failed to take it into active consideration. His "constructive" suggestion is that the working men should patiently wait for their supremacy over economic and political affairs and they can achieve it through democratic or parliamentary methods.

Bernstein does not agree with Marx's theory of class struggle. The existence of classes does not imply the struggle or conflict between them. Things do not always proceed according to the line prescribed by Marx and Engels in the *Manifesto*. In past there were conflicts between classes but the repetition cannot be predicted for the future. The workers, on the contrary, have realised quite well that a cooperation is needed for their survival as well as development. In the view of Bernstein the workers regard as indispensable the cooperation of those among the bourgeoisie who—if not repelled by an antagonistic attitude on the part of the workers—are disposed to make common cause with them in restricting capitalist exploitation and abolishing political privileges. In this connection it may be maintained that the sociologists have assertively said that the existence of classes does not always lead to conflict among them, Rather, there is cooperation.

Bernstein's conception of non-antagonistic classes and the coordination between them constitutes an important aspect of revisionism. Marx thought that, because of the antagonism, class struggle was inevitable. Bernstein thought that class collaboration was the basis of social relationship. Marx, according to Bernstein, committed a blunder by elaborating the class antagonism. Moreover, progressive democratisation of society would obliterate the ill-feeling among the classes. While Marx ruled out any *rapproachement* Bernstein used it as the main issue of analysis of the nature of society. Bernstein held that only the proletarians were not fighting for their cause, even some people of middle class supported their cause.

After a prolonged struggle against the capitalists the working class would ultimately capture political power and then set up a social democracy. Bernstein threw an open challenge to this view of Marx. Social democracy, a different form of socialism, could never be set up by class struggle. Nowhere in the world Marxism technique has succeeded in this regard. Rather, people are more and more inclining to parliamentary ways and tactics for building up a social democratic society. Moreover, parliamentary ways are more safe than class struggle. It is to be held that there is nothing new in this contention of Bernstein since he was against any type of revolutionary struggle.

Dialectical and Historical Materialism

Bernstein challenged the core of Marxian philosophy by rejecting the dialectics which he regarded as the offshoot of Hegelianism. The dialectic method was termed by him as the "treacherous elements in the Marxian doctrine, the trap that is laid for all consistent thinking." Marx used dialectics to show the process of the development of society. There are opposite forces in every non-socialist or non-communist society and these forces are proceeding towards perfection through dialectical method. The conflict between the forces will come to a halt at communism when there will be no existence of opposite forces. So, in Marxian philosophy, dialectics is an integral part of socialism. Bernstein does not accept this contention. Bernstein emphatically states that there is no remotest relationship between socialism and dialectics. It emerges neither through revolution nor through conflict of forces, but through democratic processes.

Dialectic is harmful to socialism. It misleads people. They fail, being under the illusion of dialectics, to understand the nature of social forces as well as their activities. Bernstein defends the matter of fact quality of the fixed and stable objects as against any notion of this dialectical negation. He maintains "If we wish to comprehend the world, we have to conceive it as a complex of readymade objects and processes." Here the main point of difference between Marx and Bernstein is according to the former progress of society takes place dialectically and it is not possible for few or many people to change the dialectic course. On the other hand, Bernstein does admit the importance of dialectical method. It is man whose efforts and intelligence have enough power to change the social process as well as its progress. This basic difference cannot be solved easily.

Bernstein strongly criticises Marx's materialist interpretation of history. In his judgment, Marx put the progress or evolution of society into the steel frame of dialectics and by doing this he denied the importance of man's rationality, intelligence. There is no place of man's creative role in determinism and fatalism. Bernstein held "With the developing intelligence and insight of mankind, individuals and nations acquire increased freedom in shaping their progress. He contended generally that intellectual or ideal factors operate as coordinate causes with economic factors in determining the course of history."

"To be a materialist means, first and foremost, to reduce every event to the necessary movements of matter." Secondly "movement of matter takes place, according to the materialist doctrine, in a necessary sequence like a mechanical process. Since this movement is also that which must determine the formation of ideas and the orientation of the will, it follows that the historical and human world is represented as a chain of predetermined and inevitable events. In this sense the materialist, Bernstein concluded, is a Calvinist without God" (quoted by Colletti, p. 63).

The innovation of economic determinism is the most important part of materialist interpretation of history and Bernstein criticised Marx and Engels for their concept of economic determinism. In a letter to Block, Engels made certain critical observations which has to some extent exonerated him and Engels from criticism. In this letter Engels observes, "According to materialist conception of history the *ultimately* determining element in history is the production and reproduction of real life. More then this neither Marx nor I have asserted." Bernstein regarded this self-criticism as a substantial relaxation of the original "determinism." But his charge is that the concept *per se* remains. His revisionism asserts that the "*autonomy*" of non-economic factors is more important than that of economic factors. Virtually the non-economic factors determine the course of social progress. Bernstein said, "the point of economic development attained today leaves the ideological, and especially the ethical, factors greater space for independent activity than was formerly the case." The ideological development of modern society has reached such a stage that it has considerably eclipsed the economic factors.

In the opinion of Engels economic factors largely determine the political, religious, judicial, philosophical, literary and artistic progress. But this is never one-way. Again all these determine or influence the economic factors and at the same time economic development. Bernstein in clear language states that he does not agree with this contention of Marx. His opinion is that it did more harm than good to historical materialism. He rebels against doctrinaire attitude and he always favours reason. Doctrine in his opinion fetters the thought. One must try to see what is happening in the real situation. Less dependence on doctrine and more dependence on reason and the desire to judge everything with an eye to the facts make our analysis more and more coherent and reasonable. Unfortunately, Marx and Engels have neglected that.

If we go through the writings of Bernstein we shall find that he makes certain amount of relaxation in his contention regarding the relationship between economic progress and philosophical and artistic progress. He admits that sometimes capitalist mode of production influences the advent of socialism. But this influence is not quite spectacular. He has associated the value judgments with the emergence of socialism. Socialism is not something that *must be* but something that *ought to be.* Socialism is preferable to any other type of system and men by concerted efforts will bring it about. It will not come on its own accord due to the inherent contradictions of capitalism. Moral and ethical forces impel people to seek for socialism. Voluntaristic stance is more important than any hypothetical and speculative stance. To fulfil their ethical and moral demands and desires people will set up a socialist society.

Other Political Ideas

Bernstein once said, "what is generally called the ultimate goal of socialism is nothing to me, the movement is everything". Bernstein dealt exhaustively with issues like the right of the people, role of the parties and democracy. In his famous letter to the Stuttgart Congress he expressed his views on these subjects : The party at the present time should not rely on a great cataclysm. According to Bernstein the parliamentary ways, democratic movement, the consciousness of people and their consistent demand for the proper realisation of democratic rights can ensure the working men's emancipation. In this regard, he further observes Marxian theory of class struggle has hardly any importance. It achieves practically nothing but invites disorder or chaos. To capture power cannot be treated as an end in itself, nor democracy is an end. Power and democracy are instruments to attain the goal. Democratic means, he asserts, are more powerful than the armed struggle. Bernstein had arrived at this conclusion on the basis of his experience which he gathered from the working of several governments of western European states. This is the tall claim of Bernstein. This claim of Bernstein is, however, not above criticism.

Bernstein criticises Marx's theory of revolution still from another angle. In his view the mental preparation and physical environment of workers were not congenial for any revolution. But they were capable of adapting to peaceful ways of movement. Some people might have reservations about revolution, but there is no difference of opinion about democratic movement, Revolution is generally followed by repressive measures, but there is hardly any scope of repression in peaceful movement. Summarising Bernstein's views Kolakowski comments (p. 110) : "The socialist movement was capable of fighting successfully for many changes which would mean the realisation of more and more socialist values, if it were to live merely on the expectation of an once-and-for-all cataclysm, it would not be serving the interests of the proletariat" (*Main Currents of Marxism*).

Let us slightly recapitulate. The Fabian Society of the mid-eighties of the nineteenths century laid the foundation of evolutionary socialism or gradualism and, after the death of Engels, Bernstein got an opportunity to bring the evolutionary socialism in the limelight. He claimed that his experiences about the economic functions of German economy do not corroborate Marx's view—class struggle and armed revolution are not the surest ways to establish socialism. But he admitted that in many parts of Europe there were sporadic revolutionary movements. He was not, however, sure of the success of these revolutionary movements. He observes that the sporadic and rapid revolutionary movements are not the guarantor of the coveted or ultimate goal of the working class. This goal, in general terms, is emancipation of workers. In every revolution there is a possibility of counter-revolution and this is more powerful than the revolution itself. But the peaceful agitation is unaccompanied by any risk. In democratic movement there is rationality, perspicacity and intelligence. In revolution there is emotion and irrationality. He says that, in legislation, intellect dominates over emotion in quiet times, during a revolution emotion dominates over intellect. But if emotion is often an imperfect leader, the intellect is a slow motive force. Legislation works as a systematic force, revolution as an elemental force.

Bernstein had expressed doubt about the nature of society created by revolution. The society coming out of the revolution was always dominated by revolutionary ideas. The proletarians were deprived of exercising legitimate power. Democracy and democratic institutions appeared to be the greatest victim of revolution. In pre-revolutionary society, the capitalists dominated the entire situation, after revolution the control of the society goes to the hands of the professional revolutionaries and few intellectuals. Revolution never guarantees power to the common people. Bernstein emphatically points out that the rule of the few is always the characteristic feature of both pre-revolutionary and post-revolutionary societies. Elitism, hated by Marxism, appears in different guise. Virtually the "dictatorship of the proletariat" was a meaningless concept in a socialist society. This view of Bernstein clearly indicates that he wanted a socialist society based on liberal democratic principles. Liberalism and socialism must exist side by side. Whether this is possible or not that we do not know. But Bernstein thought in this light.

Bernstein's view of liberalism and its relation to socialism is worth mentioning. It is to be recommended that some moderation should be kept in the declaration of war against "liberalism". It is true that the great liberal movements of the modern times arose from the advantage of the capitalist bourgeoisie first of all, and the parties which assumed the names of liberals were, or became in due course, simple guardians of capitalism. Naturally, only opposition can reign between these parties and Social Democracy. But with respect to liberalism, as a great historical movement, socialism is its legitimate heir, not only in chronological sequence, but also in its spiritual qualities. So in Bernstein's judgment socialism is the real consequence of liberalism. We may not like liberalism, but, if there were no liberalism, socialism would never come.

There is actually no liberal thought which does not also belong to the elements of the ideas of socialism. Even the principles of economic personal responsibility which belongs apparently so entirely to the Manchester School cannot be denied in theory by socialism nor be made inoperative under any conceivable circumstances. To sum up, socialism is the actualisation of liberalism. It is even called the "organised liberalism".

Bernstein's view of liberalism and its relation to socialism amply proves that he was enormously influenced by Fabian Socialism of Great Britain. In fact, both Fabian Socialism and Bernstein's socialism fall in the same group—evolutionary socialism. This type of socialism is fundamentally different from scientific socialism of Marx and Engels. Marxian socialism is the product of revolution and embodies revolutionary thought.

Bernstein also rejected the formula contained in the *Manifesto* that the workers had no definite nationality or fatherland. This was correct in the 1840s when Marx and Engels were writing the *Manifesto* and other books. Workers in those days were not politically conscious and did not enjoy any rights. They were not even an organised force to fight the capitalist forces. So the workers, for the sake of emancipation and to keep their physical existence running, were advised to forget their individual nationality and extend helping hand to all the fighting workers of different countries and they were also advised to build up a common force on international level. Bernstein criticised Marx's view regarding workers' nationality concept. Every individual or worker is quite conscious of his own nationality and feels a deep attachment to his fatherland. There is a difference between what Marx said and what really exists.

The darkest aspect of Bernstein's political ideas is his unstinted support to colonialism. On this issue he comes very much closer to many Fabian socialists. Territory was not simply to be conquered, it was to be economically used and developed for the benefit of all. This objective was to be achieved by the civilised nations. "Civilised peoples who could cultivate the land to advantage had a better right to it than savages" (Kolakowski, p. 110). British colonialists had performed yeoman's service for Indian people. This view indicates that he fully realised the traditional theory of colonialism. As to the theory of colonialism, Bernstein comes closer to Fabian socialism. G. B. Shaw also used the same argument in support of colonialism. The nineties of the past century was the heyday of colonialism. Neither Shaw nor Bernstein could keep themselves away from the current tendency.

Evaluation of Bernstein's Revisionism

Although Bernstein rejected Marx's "historical tendency of capitalist accumulation," according to Colletti (p. 53) "this is the most verified of all Marx's predictions; the capitalist concentration and centralization he forecast." The eminent American economist Leontiev, espousing Marx's theory, said :

"The record is indeed impressive; increasing concentration of wealth, rapid elimination of small and medium sized enterprises, progressive limitation of competition, incessant technological progress accompanied by evergrowing importance of fixed capital and last but not least the undiminishing amplitude of recurrent business cycles an unsurpassed series of prognostications fulfilled, against which modern economic theory with all its refinements has little to show indeed."

Rosa Luxemburg and Kautsky both have rejected Bernstein's criticism. Luxemburg and Kautsky have said that by rejecting Marx's theory of collapse of capitalism Bernstein abandoned the nucleus of Marxism. So it is not Bernstein's revisionism, it is abandonment of Marxism. Bernstein rejected not only Marx's theory of capitalism along with its collapse but also many other important theories of Marx. Kautsky has said, "capitalist society has failed; its dissolution is only a question of time; irresistible economic development leads with natural necessity to the bankruptcy of the capitalist mode of production." Even in the eighties of the twentieth century and in the first decade of the twenty-first century capitalism has been found to face crises. This clearly indicates that Marx's analysis of capitalism is correct. On the other hand Bernstein fails to assure us that his analysis is true to the fact. By advancing queer logic he rejected the collapse of capitalism, but facts of actual situation offer us a different picture. Let us quote a small passage from Colletti's book.

"In the Great Depression lasting from 1873 to 1895 all the fundamental categories of Marx's analysis came fully into play : the tendency of the rate of profit to fall due to the organic composition of capital, stagnation and partial saturation of outlets for investment, unimpeded action of competition, which apart from affecting profit margins, resulted in spectacular fall in prices" (Colletti, p. 56). Engels got the opportunity to witness the catastrophic consequences of the crisis of capitalism predicted by Marx and also by him. Even in the twentieth century there were also a number of depressions—both small and big. So Bernstein's contention that capitalism would never collapse because of its self-regulatory mechanism does not hold good in practice. Rather, Marx's predictions are more correct.

Bernstein did not agree with the inevitability of socialism propounded by Marx and Engels. Engels was also aware that progress of socialism or its inevitability was faced with a big question mark and he also advanced the reasons. According to Engels, when colonialism was at its zenith the British capitalists earned unimaginable amount of profit through the sale of its product in the larger areas of the markets of Asia and Africa and the British workers got a share of this profit which satisfied them. Naturally they were not concerned with socialism. The disinterestedness of the British working class was a major factor of why socialism could not make any advancement. Engels called it the privileged position of the British working class. He repeatedly pointed it out to Kautsky when the latter in London in 1885.

Bernstein vehemently criticised Marx's theory of the autonomy of economy and, again, this can be repudiated in the following way. In his letter to Bloch (1890) Engels said, "If anybody twists this (economic determinism) into saying that economic elements are the *only* determining one, he transforms that proposition into a meaningless, abstract phrase." After this assertion of Engels there cannot be any doubt what Marx and Engels wanted to say. They categorically denied the accusation of "fatalism". Kautsky also said that both Marx and Engels specifically acknowledged the importance of human factor and human invention in history. The overthrow of capitalism, Marx said, could never be performed by purely economic causes. We thus see that Bernstein levelled fabricated and ill-conceived charges against Marx.

Bernstein repeatedly said one thing "What is generally called the ultimate goal of socialism is nothing to me; the movement is everything." Kolakowski says that (p. 109) what Bernstein exactly wants to say is not clear at all, rather it distorts the ideas of Marx elaborated in *The Civil War in France* and in *The German Ideology*. Marx said that the scientific socialism did not offer the working class a rosy picture of a perfect socialist society nor even a perfect society. The purpose of Marx in these two books and in other writings was to show and ascertain the economic and social tendencies and to arouse the consciousness of the workers and activate them so that they could change the existing social order. It was necessary to study natural historical tendencies in embryo or, as he put it in 1843, to force these petrified relationship to dance by playing their own tune to them. This attitude of Marx was certainly opposed to all sentimental and moralizing utopias, but not to the hope of a single violent revolution (Kolakowski, p. 109).

Marx had said that so long there was capitalism, workers would not be able to improve their economic condition. Bernstein rejected this important premise of Marx. He said that, even in the worst form of capitalism, through concerted efforts and agitations, the workers can improve their lot. If we accept Bernstein's contention then socialism as a revolutionary doctrine immediately loses its importance. The implication is : socialism is no longer a revolutionary doctrine. But the Marxists are not prepared at all to make any compromise.

Bernstein's thought suffers from a serious contradiction. If the workers can improve their economic conditions under capitalist system through democratic processes and parliamentary initiative then socialism is definitely unnecessary. Why should the workers strive for socialism? Socialism is not a superior system to capitalism. Let capitalism be a permanent system and workers enjoy heavenly peace and comfort. It may be asked naively if capitalism is endowed with self-regulatory mechanism to cure the ills of over-production, why did capitalism fall into the great depression in the last quarter of the nineteenth century? Again there was great depression in the thirties of the current century. Why did the self-regulated mechanism fail? Bernstein was quite aware of the earlier depression and he could not provide any satisfactory explanation.

Rosa Luxemburg criticised Bernstein on the following ground : If we accept Bernstein's logic that capitalism can be reformed from within, the consequences of anarchical production can be removed and finally, by all these means, the sufferings of the workers can be mitigated, then there is no necessity of revolution at all. Does the working of the capitalist system assure us in the light? The answer is an emphatic no. Reforms are impossible in the capitalist system. The workers are exploited and they continue to be exploited. The only way out is revolution. It is true that in same countries or in some industries the workers may get higher wages or certain other fringe benefits, but the Marxists firmly hold the view that this is not the solution of the problem. Explaining Luxemburg's view Kolakowski says : "The state of things cannot be eliminated or be improved without expropriating the capitalists. There is a qualitative difference between revolution and reforms of any kind" (p. 112).

Kolakowsky has correctly differentiated revolution from reforms. Reforms of capitalism can definitely change the economic conditions of the working class in a very limited scale but these have no capacity to bring about radical changes. Bernstein committed a blunder. He thought that piecemeal changes in economic and other fields could bring about a large amount of economic progress. But this is not correct. First of all, the capitalists and their cohorts will not allow any important change that could improve the conditions of the working class. Secondly, in capitalist system there was very little scope to fight against the capitalists as well as the state administration. Both the capitalists and the state are bound by an unholy alliance.

Luxemburg further observes that three consequences are associated with the development of capitalism : (a) Break-down of capitalism is inevitable because of the anarchical conditions in production. (b) Gradual socialisation of the productive process augurs the advent of a future social system which will be free from exploitation. (c) Maturity of workers' consciousness and organising capacity will make revolution inevitable. All these three facilitate the avdent of scientific socialism. Unfortunately, Bernstein rejects these basic principles of Marxism. The rejection means to throw out Marxism. In Luxemberg's own words : "But if one admits with Bernstein that capitalist development does not move in the direction of its own ruin, then socialism ceases to be objectively necessary." The ruin of capitalism and the emergence of socialism are the fundamental premises of Marxism. Bernstein refuses to oblige the Marxists by showing allegiance to these premises.

We can criticise Bernstein for his anti-Marxist stance, but we cannot excuse him for his blatant espousal for colonialism. If he were a real socialist he could keep himself above the parochial German interests. His contemporary Germany was a big colonial power and much of her economic interests was connected with the colonies—for that reason Bernstein supported colonialism. He had no sympathy for the people exploited by German colonialism. Some critics are of opinion that he supported both capitalism and colonialism because his numerous friends who were capitalists wanted capitalism and colonialism. Again, these persons wanted to capture and retain state power. Bernstein was quite conscious of it and, perhaps mainly for that reason, he supported capitalism in a roundabout way.

Bernstein also could not free himself from illusion and utopian thought. He had great faith on reforms and parliamentary enactments. If all these were so powerful then Britain would have been the first country in the world to achieve socialism. History tells us the opposite. Bernstein's revisionism or evolutionary socialism is the German brand of Fabian Socialism of Britain. In Bernstein's time the German workers succeeded in getting some benefits from the capitalists by employing collective bargaining and other trade union methods. This encouraged Bernstein and he thought that socialism could not be equated with attainment of certain economic gains since it was not its chief objective. Socialism aims at the complete emancipation of workers and all-round progress of society. Reforms might have the capacity to alleviate the sufferings of workers, but general upliftment is impossible. Moreover, the utopian socialists, particularly Robert Owen, left no stone unturned to change the heart and outlook of capitalists, but the petrified heart showed no sign of melting. So Bernstein's hope is simply utopian.

Bernstein was fundamentally a man of bourgeois mentality. He was allured by the ever-increasing popularity of socialism. His association with Engels made him sympathetic to socialism. But at the same time, because of his bourgeois mentality, he could not dissociate himself from the bourgeois system. He attempted an effort for a compromise—compromise between bourgeois system and socialist goals. The tangible result is evolutionary socialism. But socialism understands no compromise, it makes no room for the rehabilitation of moribund capitalism. In fact, it is ruthless, it wants capitalism's collapse. Peaceful coexistence between capitalism and socialism is impossible.

A FEW WORDS ABOUT REVISIONISM

Bernstein's revisionism has been vehemently criticised some of which have been noted in the previous pages. But something still may be said in its support. Revisionism of Bernstein, it has been noted, is not without any root. Engels has already acknowledged the futility of agitational techniques for the realisation of demands or mobilisation of forces for the seizure of political power. Engels himself admitted the utility of parliamentary tactics, reforms and other democratic methods of movements. Bernstein also emphasised upon these methods for the attainment of worker's demands. Hence in the strictest sense Bernstein cannot be blamed for advocating revisionism.

Since the death of Marx in 1883 the political scenario of Europe was undergoing rapid changes. Elections were held in many parts, workers were participating in those elections, in many places movements were very peaceful and industrialists were cooperating so far as the demands of workers were concerned. Bernstein witnessed all these incidents and from that he came to the conclusion that violent agitation or revolutionary struggle against the capitalists had lost sharpness and, according to Bernstein, time had arisen to review the old method and think about new methods.

Workers in many parts of western Europe laid their hope upon reforms as a means of realising demand. This encouraged revisionism. Kolakawski has observed : "The history of revisionism does not suggest that the working class is naturally revolutionary because it is forced to sell its labour power and is incurably alienated in consequence. Thus it was not only in the doctrinal field that revisionism called into question the traditional belief in the revolutionary mission of the proletariat, the belief was challenged, perhaps more effectively still, by the success of revisionism as a social phenomenon, which robbed socialism of the glamorous prospect of a final battle for universal liberation". We think that Kolakawski's assessment of revisionism is quite correct.

Kolakawski arrived at this conclusion in the background of the failure of socialism in Eastern European countries. We know that Stalin imposed communism in East European states, but after few years they were faced with crisis and ultimately the communist governments collapsed. The mere fact is that the people of these states did not cooperate with the dictatorial communist governments. Many of them felt that the economic condition of common men could be improved through democratic ways. There is a good amount of force and violence in revolution which is the way suggested by socialism for the radical change of society.

It is a fact that the rise in the popularity of revisionism was chiefly due to the drawbacks of orthodox doctrinaire Marxism and people's strong apathy to violent methods of class struggle. For some reason the workers at the beginning of the 20th century came to the conclusion that violent class struggle and class animosity would lead nowhere and because of that "conviction" they came to lay faith on traditional parliamentary means and reforms as weapons for the realisation of demands. It can also be added that after the Second World War both the workers and the capitalists have changed considerably. The capitalists thought that for industrialisation workers were indispensable and for that they began to meet the basic and reasonable demands of workers. Again, the workers abandoned the militancy of agitation. They launched peaceful agitation and adopted collective bargaining to fulfil their demands. This is one of the causes of the declining condition of Marxism.

It is said that Marxism has two broad aspects-theoretical and practical. So far as the former in concerned there is no place of revising or amending the basic tenets. It is perfectly right. But the theoretical aspect of a doctrine of social science is not all. It ought to be tested by the events of real world. That is, the theory must be applied to reality and if it comes out with flying colours then the theory shall be accepted. The practical aspect of Marxian doctrine, it is said, is not above criticism. Lenin and many of his successors wanted to implement Marxism in erstwhile Soviet Union. Particularly Lenin was serious in regard to the application of Marxism on the soil of Russia. In several fields during the regime of Communist Party Russia achieved miraculous success but ultimately, in 1991, the Soviet Union collapsed leading to the creation of several independent sovereign states who subsequentlly formed the Commonwealth of Independent States—CIS. Many critics hastily conclude that the inherent defects of Marxism might be considered as the chief factor of disintegration of Russia.

Today in the 21st century and at the beginning of a millennium we are of opinion that theoretical Marxism has lost a major portion of its sharpness or validity. In the present day world situation practically there is no place of applying orthodox Marxism. Even China who claims to be a communist state has adopted many enonomic and other policies which do not corroborate Marxian doctrine. Particularly China's acceptance of capitalism's liberal economic policies do not, in the remotest way, support orthodox Marxism and critics conclude that this is sheer rejection of Marxism. If Bernstein were alive today he would have danced at the sight of these two memorable incidents—fall of Soviet Union and entry of liberal economic policies into China.

At the beginning of the eighties of the nineteenth century Fabian Society was convinced that only socialism could save the British working class from increasing poverty and squalor of life. But under no circumstances it could be Marxian socialism, because the British working class had already developed a strong apathy against violent revolution which was the only way of achieving socialism. Moreover, people's consciousness and victory of numerous democratic methods have blunted the sharpness of Marxian techniques. Fabian Society in this way laid the foundation of a socialism which is popularly called evolutionary socialism. Bernstein's revisionism is also directed to that purpose. Today in many parts of the world there is to be found either evolutionary socialism or any of its variety. Theoretical Marxism, to use a mild term, has been kept in abeyance. There is no place of lamentation so far as this miserable fate of orthodox Marxism is concerned. There is a gulf of difference between capitalism of Marx's time and capitalism of the twentyfirst century. The capitalists have changed, amended, and in some cases have rejected their means, so also has socialism. The capitalism of 19th century will dismally fail (if it were alive today) to solve the problems of the 21st century. For its own survival it has adjusted itself with the changed situation. The same is applicable to socialism. Today there is nothing like "agmark" capitalism or socialism. Both are subject to change for the adjustment of changed situation.

The orthodox capitalist countries have been found to adapt some socialist methods. The reverse is also true. The case of China may be cited as an example. One may call it a compromise between capitalism and socialism and many may refuse to be in the line. But the mere fact is that in a social science there is hardly any place of any orthodox ideology. A compromise or adjustment between different "isms" or ideologies is always found and that is the trend and the trend is a realistic one. If amelioration of people's condition through the implementation of any political ideology is the *leitmotif* then adjustment or compromise between different ideologies is indispensable. This is the cause of the emergence of revisionism or evolutionary socialism. This was spearheaded by Fabian Society in England and Bernstein in Germany. It they were not, other persons could have performed the job. A method or technique or person is the product of a practical situation. Marx and Engels were the products of Industrial Revolution. Fabian Socialism and Bernstein's revisionism were the products of the economic, political and other conditions of the twentyfirst century. Hence Bernstein cannot be blamed.

The revisionism created a foundation of a new social democracy. Let us quote Kolakowski "This new doctrine was a compromise between liberalism and Marxian socialism or socialist variant of liberalism. It was applied to situations other than those envisaged by classical Marxism and appealed to different psychological motivations" (p. 114). There is no doubt that, compared with theoretical Marxian socialism, the appeal of evolutionary socialism is quite broad and far-reaching. Its appeal spreads to many sections of society. Here lies the credit of evolutionary socialism in general and Bernstein's revisionism in particular. Even revisionism or the revised form of socialism is not the last word. Today we are seriously thinking about "welfarism". Both big and small states of all the continents are adopting policies and strategies for improving the economic and other conditions of people. These are collectively called welfare policies. Many of the principles of socialism are included into it.

CONCLUSION

The controversy between Marxism or Marxian socialism and revisionism is not yet over. During the last three or four decade renewed interest in Marxism is being seen among the highly educated people and intellectuals of Europe and America and it proves beyond doubt that Marxism is not dead or revisionism has completely eclipsed Marxism. Hence we cannot say that it is needless to say anything in support of Marxism. Many eminent persons believe that Marxism with all its branches provides food for thought and, on the contrary, revisionism is almost a forgotten concept. It is discussed only in academic circles.

It is difficult to ascertain what is exactly the purpose of revisionism. It wants socialism and, at the same time, capitalism. It is impossible to say that socialism will be established without revolution because the capitalists will not surrender their interests. On the contrary they will create counter-revolutionary forces to defeat the advent of socialism. Once Kautsky called revisionism a type of "vulgar socialism". Let us quote him :

"The talk about their revisionism leaves me cold. They have nothing to revise, for they have no theory. The eclectic vulgar socialism to which the revisionists would like to reduce Marxism to something beyond which they (the Belgians) have not even begun to advance" (Quoted by David Mc Lellan—*Marxism after Marx*, p. 21).

It is further to be noted that the theory of revisionism is confined in Germany and some parts of Europe, whereas Marxism is still lively discussed throughout the world. David Mc Lellan says that very few persons have strongly opposed Marxism. It is said that Marx once said that he himself was not a Marxist. According to David Mc Lellan this comment inspired many to criticise Marx's doctrine (p. 22).

26 ANARCHISM

Definition and Origin

The English word anarchism; it is said, is derived from the Greek word *anarkhia.* Or anarchia may be the root of anarchism. According to COD anarchy means "absence of government; disorder and confusion." Utter lawlessness or complete disorder are used to indicate anarchy. However, the term anarchy is used to indicate several situations all of which mean lawlessness or disorder. We, therefore, say that confusion or lawlessness is closely associated with anarchy. The term anarchy has a special relevance in civil society or civilised society because it is generally believed that in every civilised society there shall exist rule of law which means that only law will control the society—both ruler and ruled. Its absence means the anarchy. It is thus obvious that the term anarchy is associated with law. The anarchical condition is never desirable and to this situation Hobbes first drew attention of his readers. He imagined of a state of nature which was unfit for human habitation and in order to get rid of it, the inhabitants of the state of nature decided to build up a civil society in which law and its administration would prevail. So administration of law is opposite to anarchical situation. But when the law and the authority of state went beyond certain limits some people advocated that anarchy was more preferable to the all-powerful state system. Since then anarchism has managed a place in the vast field of political science.

The term used in politics does no differ considerably from the above meaning. Sebastien Faure defines it in the following way : "Whoever denies authority and fights against it is an anarchist." To deny authority and to propagate it continuously is called *anarchism.* Anarchism may be said to be a faith or belief. It is sometimes called an ideology. Of course all do not subscribe to the last meaning.

The *Concise Dictionary of Politics* precisely says that the specialised usage of the word differs markedly from common usage, which takes anarchism as a synonym for moral and political disorder. In general terms the word is used in a pejorative sense.

George Woodcock, a well-known authority on anarchism, has defined the concept in the following words : "Historically anarchism is a doctrine which poses a criticism of existing society; a view of a desirable future society; and a means of passing from one to another" (*Anarchism,* p. 7). The said authority further says that it is chiefly concerned with the relationship between man and society. When the normal, orderly and civilised relationship between man and society deteriorates or collapses it is considered as anarchy. Hence anarchy may be treated as an attitude to any particular situation.

Anarchy or anarchism is a normative concept because it is held that the prevailing condition about law and order and deteriorating condition between man and society in not desirable. Something better or different is desirable. To put it in other words, anarchism indicates that people are dissatisfied with the prevailing situation and condition and they desire something better than the existing one. So anarchism speaks of difference between present and future.

Anarchism is also compared with nihilism. Nihilism means the abandonment of all current doctrines and faith. Anarchism believes that prevailing political situation is not conducive to the development of individual's qualities and for that reason it is to be rejected.

Some critics have bracketed anarchism with terrorism on the ground that both have declared their strong opposition to the rule of law and apathy against it. Both believe that strict application of law or adherence to it is against the normal functioning of general public and human organisation. But today terrorism is used in a different sense. It aims at destablising the prevailting system by means of armed struggle or violent means. Anarchism openly declares its apathy to civil administration whereas terrorism does not do this.

It is generally believed by a good number of scholars that origin of anarchism can be traced to the French Revolution. Though some think that the anarchical situation prevailed even before the French Revolution and people were acquainted with it. In seventeenth century the term received wider circulation and later on it was discussed in both academic and political circles. During the revolutionary period common people squatted on the streets and agitated against the failure of the government to check the sky-rocketing condition of disorder, turmoil and food prices. They also demanded the overthrow of the Girondins and the establishment to the Jacobin dictatorship. In fact, during the Revolution there was no normal condition of law and order and harmonious relationship between the ruler and the ruled. There was practically no authority to implement the existing rules and regulations because people lost their faith on these rules. They believed that these could not serve their purpose and on that ground they violated the rules. In other words, people reached the end-point of their patience. To explain this situation the term anarchy was used. It has been observed by James Joll (*The Anarchists*) that the anarchist was the term adopted by Robespierre to attack those people on the left whom he had used for his own ends but whom he was determined to be rid of.

Originally the term anarchism was associated with the dismal economic situation. It was said that when ordinary men were deprived of day to day necessities and the prices of necessary goods were beyond their reach that could not be considered as a normal condition. It was definitely an anarchical situation. Anarchy also meant the absence of law and order in every sphere of life and that was clearly evident during the French Revolution. In eighteenth and nineteenth centuries many people (some call them misguided) came to believe that the absence of government and strict application of law were far better than the prevailing system of governance with the help of law and police.

Basic Concepts of Anarchism

It is very difficult to state in a precise form the basic tenets or concepts of anarchism because of the fact that there is no single exponent of the theory. Woodcock has rightly said, "To describe the essential theory of anarchism is rather like trying to grapple with Proteus for the very nature of libertarian attitude—its rejection of dogmas, its deliberate avoidance of rigidly systematic theory and above all its stress on extreme freedom of choice and on the primacy of individual judgment—creates immediately the possibility of a variety of viewpoints inconceivable in a closely dogmatic system." Several exponents of the doctrine have stated the theory in their own ways which have created a lot of confusion about it. In spite of this primary problem certain basic concepts have been devised.

In the first place anarchism states that individual is the sovereign and he is the sole determiner of everything. Any sort of intervention in his affairs will be treated as harmful and undesirable. So anarchism may be regarded as an extreme form of individualism or liberalism. Both these do not recognise the importance of state or any other organisation.

Secondly, anarchist theory of individualism is a different one. It never says that individual is a completely isolated unit and selfish. Rather he is cooperative-minded. Like Bentham's utilitarianism he does not think of his own good at the cost of other's good. He gives priority to both and effects a compromise.

Thirdly, anarchism believes that development of the inherent qualities of the individual is possible only through the recognition of his sovereign status. The meddling of any other authority or organisation can achieve this goal. This is because of the fact that according to the anarchist thinkers the individual is quite reasonable and he understands what is good and what is bad. So the individual should be left alone and, if done so, that will generate the greatest welfare in the society.

Fourthly, there are some extreme anarchists and Max Striner (1806-1856) is one of them. He says that each person should be given unrestricted freedom to do whatever he likes because in this way he can develop his own intellectual capacity. He is the centre of all activities and he is responsible for everything. Max Stirner rules out any sort of state interference in the affairs of the individual. For this reason he is called an extreme anarchist.

In the fifth place, a thorough study of anarchism reveals that it is in strong opposition to collectivism and communism because they do not recognise individuals' worth and freedom. Collectivism does not say that individuals are capable of making remarkable contribution to the progress of society. This view has been held by Benjamin Tucker (1854-1939). Tucker advocates no compromise with collectivism or communism.

In the sixth place, anarchism has laid great confidence upon the reasonability of individuals. The doctrine stresses that there shall be laws and regulations in any society but the individuals will on their own accord obey these laws.

Seventhly, it envisages an all-round social progress but the only actor of this process will be the individual and not the state.

Anarchism and the Concept of State

The most important aspect of anarchism is its attitude to state. It has thrown its vitriolic tirade against the all pervasive character or affairs of state system. Its attack against the state is so vehement that it is not prepared to make any compromise. It has been observed, "While supporters of the state see it as necessary to solve problems of security and order (and in many cases, to provide other services), anarchists reverse the argument" (*Dictionary of Politics*, p. 11). The anarchists believe that the so called problems of security and order are chiefly due to the concentration of power in the hands of few persons who are members of the state government. If there were no government the problems of law and order as well as of security would never arise. The authority has deliberately created the problems and in the name of solving these problems it demands unconditional obligation from people. It accumulates power.

William Godwin (1756-1836) was the earliest anarchist thinker whose writing *An Enquiry Concerning Political Justice* (published in 1793) contains that it is the state power which corrupts and misleads the people. The authority of state dwarfs individual judgment and reasoning. It is not necessary at all for individuals to show obligation to the state. On the contrary, they can defy the state authority which will ultimately benefit them.

It is generally believed by the anarchists that the state is the manifestation of supreme coercive power and violence and the sole usurper of individual liberty. The anarchists have asserted that the coercive power of state destroys the spontaneity of individuals, their urge to perform constructive work and not only this the authority of state imposes various restrictions that discourage people to work spontaneously. The result is the progress of society is halted. Hence the authority of state can reasonably be regarded as a great enemy to human progress as well as the progress of society. This view of anarchism should not lead one to conclude that anarchism is supporter of *laissez-faire*. Laissez-faire supports restricted state activity, anarchism talks about abolition of state.

The above reasons have induced the anarchist thinkers to challenge the authority of state and even to annihilate it. The modern state is nothing but an organisation managed by very few persons. Minority imposes its rule and authority over the majority. Such a state can never be called a democratic one. In fine, it is a state controlled by elites and for the benefits of elites.

According to anarchism, the modern state is a complex machinery. The machinery is so complicated that it is beyond the capacity of ordinary men to be acquainted with its functions. Such a state cannot do any benefit for the common people. The state machinery is controlled by few intelligent persons. In this way an alienation is created between different classes.

Anarchism emphasises that the numerous functions are not alone performed by the state. There are many organisations and state-sponsored bodies who do the job on behalf of the state. The state and all organisations exercise coercive power. The result is that individuals do not get any scope to exercise their initiative. This is harmful for individuals. People hardly get any opportunity to exercise their reason and intelligence. In earlier stages of the development of state there were many associations, that is, the state had federal structure, but with the passing of time the federal character came to be lost. The state became omnipotent and omnicompetent. It has been stressed by anarchism that in the Middle Ages there were communes and associations but they were devoured by the gigantic nature of modern state. Anarchists' viewpoint is that two diverse tendencies went side by side. One is the rapid decline of the spontaneity and importance of the individual. Second is the meteoric rise in the importance of the state.

Anarchism has advanced an interesting argument in support of its contention. In the preliminary stages of social progress the mental development, ability and intelligence of individuals were not sufficient and because of this they were not capable of shouldering the responsibility of the management of state. So they had to depend on the authority and guidance of state. But modern people have reached the highest stage of evolution and, at such a stage, the guardianship of state is not necessary at all. People do not require the power of state. If state authority is accepted that will be to put the cart before the horse, to stop the progress of human civilisation. This is not possible.

The modern state, according to anarchists, stands for uniformity. But the nature of individual prefers variety and abhors uniformity and regimentation. The state through its overriding power tries to destroy the variety of human nature, attitude and behaviour and in this way destroys the scope of development.

Neither in short term nor in the long term management or affairs of state the individuals have no scope to exercise their judgment and reason. Even the state imposes taxes upon people without considering their ability to pay. In the Middle Ages the kings or emperors did the same thing and they invited wrath and rebellion. If the state is replaced by cooperation and mutual association the system of taxation will no longer exist.

The above analysis reveals that the anarchist thinkers has offered us a very gloomy picture about the very nature and function of state. For various reasons they came to the conclusion that the state was the enemy of individual's overall progress and hence there is no reason to justify the existence of state. It would be better if the state is destroyed. For this reason the anarchists strongly advocated for the annihilation of state structure. They were convinced that peace and progress could never be achieved so long there would exist a state. Anarchists' all attention was concentrated upon state versus individual and in this controversy they unhesitatingly took the side of the individual. They could not believe that state might come to any benefit of individual. The utilitarians thought that by limiting the powers of state and keeping it at a desirable level the happiness of people could be maximised. On the other hand, for almost the same objective, the state system should be abolished. But the interesting point is that both the utilitarians and the anarchists were extremely concerned with the welfare of the individuals, though their scheme and approach were different.

Anarchist View of Society

The anarchists have been found to strongly support the federalisation of society which visualises that there shall not be any single authority in any society—rather, there shall be multiple centres. This multiplicity of centres implies the decentralisation of power in all its manifestations. State will be denied any sort of overriding control over society. The federalisation of society will facilitate individual's participation in the affairs of society. It means that the society will be divided into small groups and all shall have scope to manage the affairs in their own way.

According to anarchists the federalisation scheme will ensure three things : (a) individual participation in the various affairs of society, (b) brotherhood among all the members of society and harmonious relation among all the groups, and (c) each group will have sufficient autonomy. If the anarchist scheme of federalisation of state or society is implemented into practice the only consequence will be the state will invariably be deprived of its absolute power. This may be called a stateless condition. Because when a state is deprived or forced to be deprived of absolute power it no longer remains a state at all. Anarchist suggestion finally leads to a type of stateless society. Again, there is doubt whether this condition can at all be called a state.

Since human society is the product of a long process of evolution there is no role of human factor or human contribution in this evolution. Simply stated, according to anarchism there is no human contribution to the origin of state. This view of the anarchists goes against the social contract theory which believes the contribution of human factor behind the origin of state or society. If so, every society shall be emancipated from the control of higher authority.

The anarchists have also dealt with the organisation of society. They have said that the society will be organised in the line of mutualism. Proudhon has defined the term mutuality as involving and constituting economic right or the application of justice to political economy. "In terms of organisation society would be composed of workers' associations or cooperatives. Within each mutualist association the workers would be joint owners of the productive apparatus and entitled to a share in its product. Each mutualist cooperative would exchanges its product with other cooperatives. They would develop their skills and educate themselves" (Schwarzmantel : *Structures of Power*, p. 242).

Anarchists have also dealt with the organisation os society in which we find the following scheme. The whole society will be divided into several stages from bottom to top. The whole society along with all the stages shall be free from all sorts of control. They have suggested that the division of society will create communes. Marx also thought of such schemes. The communes shall be free from external control and in several respects shall be self-dependent. This will nullify the state system. Social organisation is also called workers' organisation. In both function and organisation the principle shall always be cooperation and harmony. Each member of society will share a part of whole responsibility. The day-to-day administration will be conducted by the members of the society. Nothing will be imposed upon members of society. It has been observed by an anarchist that if this self-management scheme is realised there shall be no necessity of a government of one set of persons which will rule upon the rest of the society. In social organisation there shall be no place of governmentalism. So anarchism once more rules out the guardianship and control of the government.

Anarchist View of Revolution

We shall now focus our attention on the anarchist theory of revolution. Almost all the anarchists were in favour of changing the society through revolution. Because they believed that compromise or reforms could not be relied upon for the purpose of changing society in a radical way. Among all the anarchist thinkers perhaps Bakunin was the top so far as the idea of revolution is concerned. Ailein Kelly in his noted work *Mikhail Bakunin* has aptly said, "Through his battle against the state and authority in all its forms Bakunin has come to be regarded as one of the greatest champions of individual in the history of political thought. Few thinkers have been so uncompromising and extreme as Bakunin in their demand for the liberation of men from the bonds and constraints imposed on them by political, religious and philosophical systems" (p. 1). Bakunin thought that this emancipation could be achieved only through a revolution. Not only Bakunin, several other anarchists held the same view. Any type of compromise would spoil the purpose of the common people in their attempt for radical change.

The anarchists out of their experience came to the conclusion that the emancipation of the workers would never be possible without the destruction of state structure and revolution could do that. First of all a revolution will destroy the existing structure of state and in that place will be set up autonomous units in the form of association. These units will be self-sufficient in all respects. In other words the existing state structure will be replaced by the autonomous association and they will discharge the functions of state.

According to anarchists in the present system of state what is prominent is that corruption has spread to every nook and corner of society and this situation cannot be remedied by piecemeal attempts such as reforms or parliamentary procedure or revisionary methods. A radical change of society is essential and only revolution can bring about. The existing structure of society would be destroyed by a revolution. Compromise or parliamentary procedure would lead to adjustment with capitalists. Compromise means replacement of one exploiting class by another. So in ordinary change the emancipation of working class will remain a far cry. But anarchism envisages of a radical change of society. That is why the revolution has been so much emphasised in anarchism.

In the opinion of the anarchists the system of private property is the root of all evils and this system of property should be abolished to free the society from evils. Proudhon once called the private property as nothing but theft. Marx and his followers were also against the system of private property. Apart from this the system of private property encourages and brings about inequalities. In ordinary way private property cannot be abolished, for this is required a revolution.

Who will be at the helm of revolutionary struggle? This is a very piquant question. The Marxists have held the view that mass participation in revolutionary struggle is an essential pre-condition of the success of revolution. But party shall be at the leadership. Leadership of party means leadership of very few persons. Both Proudhon and Bakunin were against this approach to revolution. Strongly opposing the Marxist approach to revolution the anarchists have observed that common people will have full control over management and leadership of revolution and this will ensure their participation.

The anarchists have also considered the ends and means of revolution. Emma Goldman, a noted anarchist, has said that in launching a revolution both ends and means must be given due importance. The Russian Revolution gave priority to ends and this is improper. The means used by the revolutionaries must be duly considered. She has said that "no revolution can ever succeed as a factor of liberation unless the means used to further it be identical in spirit and tendency with the purposes to be achieved" (Quoted by Schwarzmantel, p. 247). Emma Goldman has further said that in a revolution, means cannot be separated from purposes. This implies that a revolution must be very straight-forward in its approach and method. Bakunin held the same view. He advocated for an honest and real revolution. In such a revolution both means and ends are properly emphasised. If purpose is given priority that will make a revolution dishonest. Ultimately such a revolution can never the successful.

There was controversy in regard to the techniques or methods of revolution. Some anarchists have been found to suggest terrorism or terrorist ways for running or conducting a revolution. But many anarchists have been found to disapprove terroriasm. However, under special circumstances, terrorist means may be resorted to but not in all cases. Schwarzmantel has said "Where an autocracy pushed oppression to its extremity and the hopelessness of the political situation drove people to despair, as happened in pre-revolutionary Russia, anarchists resorted to individual acts of terrorism and àssassination... Such tactics were also tried by some anarchists in France from 1892 to 1894" (p. 247). But these terrorist methods could not achieve desired results. Terrorism was foiled by more oppressive measures adopted by reactionary power. Some anarchists have advocated "direct action".

Anarchism and Marxism

Both anarchism and Marxism as isms are almost contemporary. Both aimed at establishing an exploitation-free society. The exponents of both these isms cherished to set up a future society through revolution. Anarchism and Marxism blamed capitalism for the exploitation of workers and the overall miserable conditions of society. Both the isms thought that due to the system of private property the inequalities in income were increasing at a galloping rate. The two isms believed that the state is the instrument of exploitation and the instrument is used by the owners of capital. Both anarchism and Marxism are quite sympathetic to the miserable conditions of the people in general and the working class in particular. Both believe that the emancipation of people from all sorts of exploitation is possible only by a revolution or class struggle. But in spite of these similarities there are number of spectacular difference between the two. These differences are to some extent polar.

In the first place, the assessment of anarchism about past and future society is imaginary and unscientific. The noted scholar on anarchism, Woodcock, makes the following observation in this respect : "In its (anarchism) attitude towards social development anarchism often seems to float like Mohammed's coffin suspended between the lodestones of an idealised future and an idealised past. The peasant communism of the Russian mir...the free cities of the European Middle Ages...the sharing of goods implied in customs of certain primitive tribes...all these attract anarchist theoretician as examples of what can be done without the apparatus of the state" (op. cit., p. 22). Marx studied history with the help of dialectical materialism and framed the conclusion that in the primitive society there was communism. With the passing away of time the economic, political, social and other aspects of society underwent radical changes. The study of the evolution of society convinced Marx and Engels to form such conclusion. The materialist interpretation of history convinced Marx that the changes or evolution of society will continue until there was communism. This conclusion of Marx is not imaginary or wishful thinking but based on scientific analysis. But anarchist's analysis of social development is not scientific. The picture of future society depicted by the anarchists is not based on any scientific foundation. It is guided by sentiment.

It is very often alleged (and of course correctly) that anarchism is reactionary whereas Marxism is progressive. Let us explain. Anarchism has stressed upon the customs, habit etc. of past society, which were conservative in nature, as well as guiding forces. It is strange that these conservative forces have been highly appreciated by the anarchists. Marxism does not recognise any conservative element because they inhibit the progress of society. In other words, conservativeness is enemy to progress of society.

Though both anarchism and Marxism hold the view that the revolution is the only way of changing the society along with the emancipation of working class there spectacular differences between the two regarding the techniques, management and other aspects of revolution. Anarchism says that common people will be at the helm of leadership of the revolution and among the masses peasants will the foremost section. In other words, anarchist's confidence was concentrated upon peasants. On the other hand, Marxism has said that redundant proletariat will take the leading part in revolution.

Anarchism rules out party and its importance in revolutionary process. Marxism believes that revolution can be successful only through the party. Anarchist's apathy to party is based on the conception that it is an authoritarian organisation. Schwarzmantel says, "A libertarian society cannot be produced by an authoritarian organisation." Hence follows the rejection by anarchists of the Marxist emphasis on political parties as necessary elements in the revolutionary process.

Anarchists exalt spontaneous mass action. They are critical of what they regard as an elitist and authoritarian organisation. They are hostile to political parties, whether they are of the Leninist vanguard type or social democratic mass parties (Schwarzmantel, p. 244). Here lies the basic difference between anarchism and Marxism. Though Marx and Engels did not give special emphasis upon party as a potential weapon for realising revolution, in this respect Lenin did not fail. Anarchists' viewpoint that people *en masse* will participate at all the stages of revolutionary process and that participation shall be spontaneous. No vanguard organisation shall be there to guide and motivate them.

There is another difference between anarchism and Marxism. The former refused to accept any form of participation in state institution including electoral process. "Anarchists called for "abstentionism" which meant rejection of the vote and party politics. Participation... would seem to legitimise the system and help to perpetuate it" (Schwarzmantel, p. 244). But these arguments of the anarchists have been strongly opposed by the Marxists. They point out that mass participation in political activities and party organisation are essential parts of revolutionary process. The working class gets ample opportunity to ventilate their views through this participation.

Both Marxists and anarchists had different views about capital and state. This difference was so prominent that there was polar difference between the two. Engels pointed out this difference in his letter to Cuno which was written on 24 January 1872. A portion of the letter is quoted here : "Bakunin has a peculiar theory of his own, a medley of Proudhonism and communism. The chief point of which is...that he does not regard capital—and therefore the class antagonism between capitalists and wage workers which has arisen through social development but the state as the main evil to be abolished" (*Marx and Engels : Selected Works*, Vol. II, p. 467). Engels has further observed that Bakunin has failed to realise that the state is nothing more than the organisation of the ruling classes and they utilised it for harvesting their own privileges and benefits. Bakunin maintains that the state has created capital and capital has all the evils. If state is destroyed capitalism will go to blazes of itself. On the contrary, Engels says that if capitalism is done away with and the concentration of wealth in the hands of few is stopped the state will collapse. So we see that there is a basic difference between anarchism and Marxism as to the role of state and capitalism.

There is another difference. The abolition of capital will not lead to the abolition of state as had been imagined by the anarchists. Engels has maintained that without a previous social revolution the abolition of state is a nonsense. Only a social revolution can help the abolition of capital and the abolition of state will follow. This difference in approach is due to the fact that Marxism believes that the state is the product of capitalism. On the other hand, anarchism says that the state has created capital. We think that the Marxian analysis is more scientific because before the creation of capital practically there was no existence of modern state apparatus. Moreover, Marx and Engels have come to this conclusion from an in-depth analysis of social development. Their conclusion is not *a priori.*

The anarchists vehemently opposed the state because the state means authority and it again means loss of freedom of individuals. So the individuals can have full freedom in the absence of state. But in his letter to Cuno Engels has raised a very pertinent and practical question. If there is no authority how a factory or railway or any organisation will be managed? There shall be one authority to take a decision or utter a final word in regard to management. Engels's argument is perfectly right. In every human society there must exist a type of organisation which will be empowered to take a decision for the settlement of all disputes. By criticising anarchists' standpoint of the abolition of state the Marxists have shown a good deal of intelligence and reason.

There is a very important difference between anarchism and Marxism as regards the abolition of state. Lenin in his famous work *State and Revolution* has elaborated this aspect. The anarchists have advocated the abolition of state. But Marxism is of opinion that *the state is not destroyed or abolished, it withers away.* Marx and Engels have emphasised that a revolution abolishes a bourgeois state, and, after this revolution, the proletarian state is established. Let us put the matter in the words of Lenin : "As a matter of fact, Engels speaks of the proletarian revolution abolishing the bourgeois state while the words about the state withering away refer to the remnants of the proletarian state after the socialist state revolution. According to Engels, the bourgeois state does not wither away, but is abolished by the proletariat in the course of the revolution. What withers away after this revolution is the proletarian state or semi-state" (*Selected Works*, Vol. II, p. 315). Lenin's interpretation of state and Engels's theory of "withering away of state have created a lot of heat and controversy and these have not yet died down. It is, however, held that the state has neither been destroyed nor abolished nor withered away. It still exists and will continue to exist.

Lenin says "Marxism differs from anarchism in that it recognises the need for a state and for state power in the period of revolution in general, and in the period of transition from capitalism to socialism in particular (*L.S.W.* II, p. 65). Anarchism does not recognise the importance of state at all, whereas Marxism recognises its importance.

Anarchism and Utopianism

Schwarzmantel in his *Structures of Power* makes the following remark..."anarchist theory contains utopian elements and is of little relevance to the practice of everyday politics" (p. 248). This is a very remarkable observation and this requires to be explained. There was a time when anarchism drew a good deal of public attention. Superficially, the anarchist doctrine is attractive, but if we enter into its details we shall find that it is purely utopian and full of impractical ideas.

There are three stages of anarchist theory : the state as a political organisation is oppressive. It forces the individuals to show their obligation to the state and any refusal is followed by punishment. The state is the source of all sorts of corruption and evils. Such an organisation is to be abolished. Secondly, the state is to be abolished by means of revolution. So long the state exists there cannot be any emancipation of people. If the state is forcibly abolished capitalism will not be the source of any evil and individuals will be in a position to enjoy full freedom. Finally, after the abolition of state, there will be set up a new society based on harmony and cooperation among all individuals. The new society will be free from all evils, bondage and corruption.

Let us explain the utopianism or utopian aspects of anarchism in details. There is nothing wrong in the anarchists' argument that state, the ownership of private property and capitalism are the main sources of evils and misery of the working class. Anarchists' argument is also not wrong that only revolution can emancipate the people. But their contention is that only masses of men can make revolution a reality. The anarchists have ruled out the question of leadership. They were apprehensive of the appearance of the elitist element. We do not contradict this viewpoint. But it is utopian to think that common people will be able to provide the adequate leadership which will make revolution successful. History does not record of any such incident. Furthermore, without party and leadership no revolution can be successful. Hence anarchism is utopian. In no country of the world masses have been found to possess intelligence, capacity etc. necessary for managing or conducting a revolution.

By advocating that in the future society there shall be cooperation and harmony, anarchists have dismally failed to understand the proper nature of man. Basic tendency of individuals is selfishness and, in this content, a harmonious society cannot be set up. To ignore the basic nature of man is an indicator of utopianism. Utopian socialists also wanted to build up a socialist society on the basis of cooperation and harmony. But from the records of history we gather that utopian socialists' attempt to construct a harmonious society based on goodwill, cooperation, rationality and harmony never came into existence though there was no flaw in the attempts of utopian socialists.

The anarchists rule out any type of authority—which is another side of utopian thought. How is it possible that in future society no conflict will ever arise? If conflict arises—and it is bound to arise—there must be an authority to settle the conflicts. If there is no authority who will settle the disputes? Even for the management of any factory or organisation the existence of an authority is a must. The simple fact is that in all forms of human organisation there must exist an authority. Even in a family there is head of family and he guides the whole family.

Both society and civilisation are progressing. But it is unfortunate that the anarchists planned for creating a society of primitive type. For example "Proudhon envisaged a society in which men's products would be directly exchanged for the other goods they needed, and in which such institutions as might be required for this purpose would be provided by negotiations between the groups concerned" (James Joll, p. 59). The contemporary society of anarchists was quite advanced and in spite of this they—particularly Proudhon—suggested that a primitive type of society would be established. How could they succeed we do not know? Could they convince people that the modern society could be replaced by an old society based on exchange?

In spite of the shortcomings of the existing state system, its indispensibility is beyond any doubt. Modern life is practically impossible without a state. The anarchists failed to realise this fundamental aspects and importance of state. No other organisation can act as an alternative to state. Marx and Engels also predicted the withering away of state. But in no part of the world, and even in a socialist state, the state has withered away. It is a fact that importance of state is increasing day-by-day. Hence the plan to destroy state is simply a utopian thought, nothing else.

The utopian character of anarchist thought is revealed in a statement of Kropotkin : "Common possession of the necessaries of production implies the common enjoyment of the fruits of common production...an equitable organisation of society can only arise when every wage system is abandoned" (quoted by James Joll, p. 139). This picture of a future society is absolutely utopian in nature. Marx and Engels as well as their predecessor utopian socialists also imagined to build up such a society and it is needless to say that such a society has never been set up and will not be set up in future. One of the utopian ideas of anarchism is that anarchists strongly argued for the abolition of all laws and regulations because all these tend to curb human freedom. The anarchists have further argued that instead of laws there shall exist harmonious relation and cooperation. These will rule and manage society. Such an approach is impractical from top to bottom. Laws are essential for the proper management and administration of society.

Anarchism in Modern Times

Though anarchism, like Marxism, failed to create a lasting impact upon the mind of the academics, it cannot be said that as an ism it completely failed. In the earlier decades of the 20th century the revival of anarchism does not surprise us at all. "Gandhi (1869-1948) and his followers responded to Kropotkin's populist message and his ideas of natural village communities sportaneously springing up. Oscar Wilde was impressed by his personality and message" (James Joll, p. 142). This is an indication of the fact that the main tenets of anarchism did not die down. In several West European countries we witness the continuity of anarchist thought.

The most important aspect of anarchism that has impressed quite a very good number of men of the academic and political world is the freedom of choice and the absence of central coercive authority in a society. Gustav Landauer was a German non-violent anarchist. He said that social revolution must come through the voluntary cooperation of all people. He opposed the existing state structure and party system. In the first three decades of the 20th century Gustav Landauer participated in revolutionary activities of several European countries.

The countries which have not yet experienced the European or American type of industrialisation have been found to be under the impact of anarchism. But this conclusion cannot be treated as a general one. In many countries of Asia and Africa anarchist thought regarding state and economy has found a large number of supporters. James Joll writes, "In India Gandhi himself and subsequently Jayprakash Narayan and Vinoba Bhabe have dreamed basing Indian society on self-sufficient, self-governing village republics." Gandhi, Narayan and score of other thinkers did not support the prevailing state system with supreme sovereign power because all of them thought that absolute power of state was inimical to individuals' freedom of action and thought. To all of them individuals' liberty was of utmost importance and this cannot be dispensed with. They have denounced the Western type of absolute sovereignty and, in support of their contention, they recommended decentralisation of power to the grassroot levels. Both Gandhi and Narayan viewed state as embodiment of violence and coercion. For that very reason they have strongly advocated for the establishment of village republics or gram panchayat system which will ensure people's participation in all affairs.

James Joll concludes, "The 1960s and 1970s were marked by number of episodes and movements which showed that the anarchism was not dead" (p. 262). The student movements of the sixties and seventies of the 20th century and the terrorist movements of several countries show that anarchism is still popular among a section of people. It is true that there are variations of anarchism, but it is also true that the core idea of anarchism—freedom of choice and absence of absolute state authority—has not yet lost its appeal to the both educated and politically conscious people of many parts of the globe.

The first decade of the twentyfirst century may be said is at crossroads. The growing importance of state is being strongly felt. But at the same time it is being emphasised by many that the freedom of individual must be properly protected. It is a time-old idea that the state is for the individuals and not the opposite. The absolute power of state had certain amount of meaning and relevance in earlier centuries, but with the passing away of time the absoluteness of power has lost importance. Today we look to the state as friend, philosopher and guide. In the light of this thought we have come to think the entire idea of anarchism anew. There shall remain the state but, at the same time, the freedom of people must be given utmost priority. When the anarchists revolted against the state they had reason because the state was omnipotent and omnicompetent. Even persons like Robert Nozick admits the importance of state. He has clearly stated it in his book *Anarchy, State and Utopia.* We think that there shall exist a harmonious relationship between state and various organisations that exist within the jurisdiction of state.

SOME ANARCHIST THINKERS
PROUDHON (1809-1865)

Proudhon's Life

Pierre-Joseph Proudhon was born in 1809 and died in 1865. His forefathers were peasants and financially they were not well-to-do. They belonged to the lower middle class group and on that consideration Marx once called Proudhon *petit-bourgeois.* His father at the beginning of life was an artisan and later on became a brewer. In this trade he was never successful and poverty was the constant companion of the family. Moreover, Proudhon's father was really a scrupulous brewer and this was the main cause of poverty.

Proudhon's mother possessed all the virtues of a peasant family. She was also an independent spirited lady. The virtues of his mother's character considerably influenced Proudhon. He wrote "My ancestors on both sides were all free labourers...famous for their boldness in resisting the claims of nobility. As for nobility of race, I am noble." In his boyhood years Proudhon worked as a cowherd.

Proudhon was entirely a self-educated man. It is very difficult to discover coherence and consistency in his writings. A critic has said "his writings are full of the odd and unexpected pieces of unsystematic knowledge of the autodictat." Proudhon also worked as a printer. He learnt Hebrew, Latin and Greek and studied extensively religion and philosophy. Throughout his life he was a relentless critic of existing social and political systems.

Human Nature

Proudhon's conception of human nature is an important aspect of his philosophy. He deals with this issue succinctly, but it is clear what he wants to say. For Proudhon, work was the characteristic of man's nature. If a man did not work, he could not be a full man. Now what is the exact nature of man? Proudhon said, "Man is a tyrant or a slave by his own will, before he is made a tyrant or a slave by fortune, the heart of the proletarian is like that of the rich, a cesspool of babbling sensuality, a home of faith and hypocrisy." Men are not fully disciplined and are guided by egoism. These are the obstacles to the attainment of equality. It is wrong to assume that the institutions will have to be changed in order to bring about a corresponding change of human nature. Man's nature is to be changed at first. Man is to be reformed morally. Why? Proudhon's answer is this : Man is by nature a sinner, that is to say—not essentially a wrongdoer, rather wrongly made.

On the above point Proudhon differs from utopian socialists and Marx. The former held that if physical environment were changed, man's nature would also change. Marx thought that nature of man, particularly his moral conception, was totally conditioned by material circumstances. Proudhon rejected the influence of external forces upon the formation of human nature. He was confident that men could do it only by their individual efforts. That is, individuals must be conscious of their own weakness. Only through positive and constructive efforts men could establish themselves as moral beings. This view of Proudhon about human nature was subsequently taken up by all anarchists.

Violence and irrationality are the inherent features of human character. These traits of human character, according to Proudhon, were the chief causes of war. If man could not convert his irrationality into rationality the possibility of war could not be removed. Proudhon, that is why, emphasised upon the psychological origin of war. Efforts were made to avert war, but they were in vain because of the militant attitude of man. James Joll in his book *The Anarchists* (p. 53) remarks, "War would only end after the social revolution, which would provide an adequate method of diverting the instincts of hatred and revenge into support for a system of law which would be mutually respected." It is interesting to note that Proudhon's view of war is even relevant today. UNO emphasises upon the psychological factors as the chief causes of war and on that ground it aims at changing people's heart. Proudhon's emphasis on human nature and its relation to politics is not anything new. A good part of social contract theory—particularly the Hobbesian version—is connected with the psychological aspects of men. Machiavelli also built up a fabric of politics on the basis of human nature. What is new in the case of Proudhon is that he thought of a social revolution for the change of human nature and that change will build up the foundation of a new society.

Conception of Society and State

According to Proudhon, family was the basic unit of every society. Assembly of several families gave the formation of association. Several associations were formed to give the state a shape. In every stage man was the central figure. For him man was the manifestation of certain virtues and vices and also a working unit. It has been observed by James Joll that importance of Proudhon's work lies not so much in their theoretical arguments, but in his whole conception of the nature of man and society. In his judgment every man must work. This working man is the basis of society. Only work can free a man from bondage. If we go through Proudhon's analysis about society as well as the role and importance of man we shall find that he consciously made man the central figure of society and its functions. Through a social revolution the nature of man first of all will change and after that man will work hard with all sincerity for an overall change of society. Hence man is the chief catalyst of social change. He did not allow religion or any other factors to intervene in the process of social change and specifically building up a new society.

Proudhon's was not a homogeneous society. It was not also a unitary one. Society must be based on small units. Once he said, "If the family was the basic element of feudal society, the workshop it the basic unit of the new society." Proudhon conceived that these small units would develop among themselves a good relationship. These units of society, he further pointed out, would be associated in communes. The communes would finally form a bigger federation. A portion of the commune's power would be delegated to the central authority. That is, powers must be considerably limited.

His critics are of opinion that Proudhon was to some extent a reasonable-minded person and for that reason he did not accept the social contract the origin of state. But he utilised the contract for different purpose. He said :

"The idea of contract excludes that of government...Between contracting parties there is necessarily a real personal interest for each; a man bargains with the aim of securing his liberty and his revenue at the same time. Between governing and governed no matter how the system of representation or delegation of the governmental function is arranged, there is necessarily an alienation of part of the liberty and means of citizen."

Proudhon was always in favour of multinational states and on that consideration he vehemently opposed the unity move of Mazzini and Garibaldi. He also rejected the demand for national state on the basis of right to self-determination. Federalisation of society was the only way to safeguard liberty. Proudhon did not suppress his anger against the reactionary aristocrats. He opposed the independence of Poland on the ground that after independence the country would fall in the hands of reactionary aristocrats. To sum up, any type of society other than federal type was disliked by Proudhon.

Proudhon on Government

For Proudhon the government was the symbol of all sorts of restrictions. To be governed is to be watched over, inspected and spied on, directed and legislated at, regulated, docketed, indoctrinated, preached at, controlled, assessed, weighed, censored, ordered about, by men who have neither the right, nor the knowledge, nor the virtue. To be governed means to be, at each operation, at each transaction, at each movement, noted, registered, controlled, taxed, stamped, measured, valued, assessed, patented, licensed, authorised, rebuked and arrested. In the name of the general interest common people are taxed and exploited, extorted and robbed. If people complain against these measures they are repressed, harassed, beaten and bullied, imprisoned and fined. These are the very common methods to punish the innocent citizens. On every footstep men are mocked, ridiculed, insulted and dishonoured. Their voice is very feeble, they are not always organised. Naturally they cannot protest the repressive measures of the government. Despite all these the government claims that it is maintaining utmost justice and protecting morality from the public assault. This is nothing but mockery.

Let us quote few lines from Proudhon "To be governed is to be watched, inspected, spied upon, directed, law driven, numbered, regulated, enrolled, indoctrinated, preached at, controlled, checked, estimated, valued, censured, commanded, by creatures who have neither the right nor the wisdom nor the virtue to do so. To be governed is to be at every operation, at every transaction noted, registered, counted, taxed, stamped, measured, numbered, assessed, licensed, authorised, admonished, prevented, forbidden, reformed, corrected, punished. It is under pretext of public utility and in the name of general interest, to be placed under contribution, drilled, fleeced, exploited, monopolised, extorted from... That is government, that is its justice, that is its morality" (Quoted by Robert Nozick. *Anarchy, State and Utopia*, p. 11).

What would be the exact type or nature of government? What would be its sphere of action? Proudhon says that if there is a government, it can only result from a delegation, convention, federation, in a word, from the free and spontaneous consent of all the individuals which make up the people, each one of them insisting on and canvassing for the guarantee of his own interests. Thus the government, if there is one, instead of being *Authority* as hitherto, will represent the relationship between all the interests created by free property, free labour, free trade, free credit and will itself only have a representative value, just as paper money only has value through what it represents.

The affairs of the government will be conducted not by laws but by contract. In Proudhonian concept of state or government there is no place of man-made laws. Laws mean restrictions and curtailment of spontaneity. In place of laws we will put contracts. Whether laws are voted by majority or by all that is immaterial. Each citizen, each industrial unit and each town will make its own laws. In place of standing armies there shall be industrial associations. In place of political centralisation there shall be economic centralisation. To Proudhon law means extortion, control, restrictions and all these ultimately lead to the loss of freedom of the people. Some interpreters of his political ideas have said that he was not against law or government. Both may exist but there shall be no restrictions on the spontaneous activities of individuals. But this is not possible.

Revolution

Proudhon's *The General Idea of Revolution* was published after the great political upheaval of 1851 and the book is considered as an important work. Woodcock maintains that *The General Idea of Revolution* is a study of revolutionary process and Proudhon prersents it as a necessary phenomenon. Proudhon himself was allergic to revolution but he believed that the revolution in certain circumstances might be unavoidable.

A revolution is a force against which no power—divine or human—can prevail and whose nature is to grow by the very resistance it encounters. Any resistance to revolution makes its action and advance irresistible. The revolution advances with sombre and predestined tread, over the flowers strewn by friends, through the blood of its defenders, over the bodies of its enemies.

This is Proudhon's view of revolution and it is an anarchist view. People will spontaneously participate in the revolutionary process. Party organisation or leadership cannot guide revolution. The revolution will set up a society free from the influences of government or authority. It will make people all-powerful. The Marxian and Proudhonian revolution are different in many ways.

Concept of Property and Other Economic Ideas

In 1840 Proudhon published a book under the title *"What is Property?"* And through this he came to be known as a serious thinker. In this book Proudhon mounted attack upon the ownership and accumulation of property. The very institution of property was disapproved by him. The ownership of property, he said, could only be supported on the ground of equality. That is, everyone in the society would be allowed to own equal amount of property. Although this was a utopian thought he propagated in with all his zeal and earnestness. In *What is Property* there is the following paragraph :

If I were asked to answer the question what is slavery? and I should answer in one word "Murder", my meaning should be understood at once. No further argument would be needed to show that the power to take from a man his thought, his will, his personality, is a power of life and death and that to enslave a man is to kill him—why, then, to this other question : What is property? may I not likewise answer "Theft". That is, property is nothing but theft. There is some justification in treating property simply as "theft". He believed that for the maintenance of life man needs very small amount. But whenever a man is found to amass large amount of property it is assumed that he has acquired that property not by honest means. People earn property to satisfy his urge to get more and more property and this feeling leads him to be involved in unfair means. In this sense property is a kind of theft.

In his *What is Property?* Proudhon has said that every man must work to earn something without which he cannot fulfil the mission of his life. The right to work is his absolute right. So he has every right to what he produces. But the man has no right over the means of production. The right to products is exclusive and the right to means of production is common. When a man comes to control the means of production an inequality automatically crops up. The raw materials are provided by nature and no man can own them exclusively for his personal pleasure.

Exclusive right over property in the means of production creates inequality and invites injustice. Both injustice and inequality are impediments to the proper development of individuality. Communism condemns the private property in the means of production. But Proudhon treats communism as annihilator of human freedom and spontaneity. So both communism and system of private property over the means of production are to be exiled from the surface of society. Anarchy is the only way. It eliminates the deficiencies of both communism and private property. Only in an anarchical system equality, justice, independence and individual merits can flourish. In Proudhon's judgment only anarchy is an ideal system.

Woodcock says (p. 105) : "Property is a Theft was to become one of the great political catchwords of the nineteenth century and to hang like a symbolic on the popular image of Proudhon." Property to him was a sum of abuses and that is why he denounced it. One man exploits another and in this way property is accumulated. So exploitation is always associated with property. Speaking about property and communism Proudhon said, "Property is the exploitation of the weak by the strong, communism is the exploitation of the strong by the weak... In communism inequality springs from placing mediocrity on the level with excellence. Communism is oppression and slavery."

Explaining the nature of society and government and their relation to economic affairs Proudhon said, "Government is the public economy, the supreme administration of the labour and the assets of all the nations." Elsewhere he said : "Free association, liberty, limited to maintaining equality in the means of production and equivalence in exchange, is the only possible form of society, the only just, and the only true one. Politics is the science of freedom, the government is the oppression. The high perfection of society consists in the union of order and anarchy."

From the analysis of Proudhon's economic ideas we come to know that he did not support the establishment of largescale industries. His main argument was that such big industries generally exploit the workers. The owners of industries generally employ sophisticated machines and people do not get jobs. So the largescale industries are not at all helpful for the interests of people, specially the workers. Hence for the benefit of the general public there shall be set up small scale industries and the old exchange system should be revived. He argued for the revival of the old exchange system to uproot exploitation and corruption. Men's products would by directly exchanged for the other goods they needed.

Proudhon's *What is Property*? is regarded as the founder of libertarian doctrine and the principle of economic decentralisation. Proudhon has concentrated his attention on the analysis of peasants, workers and small craftsmen. He neglects the importance of big industrial units.

To restore the direct relationship between what a man produces and what he consumes, the first condition prescribed by Proudhon is the abolition of the whole existing structure of credit and exchange. If banking system and financial institutions are destroyed the economic relations between men will return to a healthy natural simplicity. That is, the whole economic system will be managed by the people themselves.

Utopianism of Proudhon

We know Charles Fourier as a great utopian thinker and Proudhon as the 'Father of Anarchism. But modern researchers have said that Proudhon was also a great utopian'. His ideas contain many seeds of utopianism. He wanted to lay the foundation of society which would be free from exploitation and which would be based on the principles of liberatirianism. His chief concern was the emancipation of people and this he fervently believed could be achieved through revolution. We have already mentioned that Proudhon's revolution is basically different from Marxian revolution. Proudhon rules out the interference of party and role of the leader. People will spontaneously conduct the revolution and in Proudhon's view this is ideal revolution. But in our judgment it is sheer utopian thought. Nowhere has Proudhon's conception of revolution succeeded.

Proudhon's insistence upon the revival of primitive exchange system has thrown him again into the utopian domain. We know that Proudhon's contemporary France or England was in the grip of deep economic crisis. But his recommendation of the abolition of banking and credit system was not the master solution to the deep-rooted crisis. These utopian suggestions could not even touch the problems at all. Proudhon had comprehensive knowledge about social, economic and political conditions of society that existed around him. But it is unfortunate that though he was aware of the situation he dismally failed to suggest any practical remedy. Rather he roamed in an imaginary world and this is his utopianism.

Other by-products of Proudhon's fertile brain were the establishment of Exchange Bank and the abolition of interest system. He treated taking of interest as another way of exploiting people and hence it should be abolished forthwith. There should be the provision of lending money to the people but not against taking of interest. Monetary transaction would be done by the Exchange Bank. The administrative authority would have no control over this Bank. It is true that the system of interest is a way of exploiting the poor persons because these persons borrow money to meet their day-to-day needs but they fail to repay the loan. The interests multiply and this leads them to extreme impoverishment. But if the system of interest is abolished how is it possible for industrialists to invest? Industrialisation and development will stop due to the shortage of capital because nobody will lend money without interest.

In his *Theory of Property* published posthumously in 1866 he went so far as to propose the retention of private property in its existing form with its power to use and destroy mitigated only by equilibrating guarantees. The balance of contradiction is achieved and the power of exploitation is abolished when property is parcelled out and agriculture and industry are carried on by numerous small producers. Similarly, by expressing his anger and dislike against machinery, Proudhon proposed a retrograde step.[1] It is a retrograde step because without machinery industrialisation is impossible and without industrialisation no sort of development is possible. We come to know from his views that he wanted progress but was against the use of machinery. This is out-and-out contradictory or utopian.

The political organisation of this ideal society should also reflect the equilibrium of forces or, as Proudhon calls it, the social mutualism. The state must disappear. Society would be based on the principle of voluntarism. Administrative restrictions would be given a permanent farewell. Proudhon's idea about the capability of independent social and political organisation is really utopian. Not to speak of its relevance in modern times, even in Proudhon's time it had no relevance at all. We can safely say that he was completely devoured by utopian thought and conjectures.

1. Eric Roll—*History of Economic Thought*, p. 242.

"Proudhon's socialism," observes Eric Roll, "becomes an unrealistic dream of the golden age, to be achieved by the abolition of interest. It may be said that Proudhon lived in an environment in which the power of exploitation seemed symbolised in finance. But Proudhon's failure to analyse the principles of capitalist production and to understand the quality of capital and the function of money make his practical proposal as ineffective as his ideal retrograde" (p. 244).

Proudhon had great sympathy for the poor. His zeal for establishing justice is really praiseworthy. But the methods he suggested are not up to the mark. Like Robert Owen, Charles Fourier and Saint-Simon he was a utopian. His political and economic ideals are replete with utopian dreams. Did he know that his unrealistic suggestions would never be transformed into reality? We do not know. He gleefully roamed in the world of imagination. A man with the slightest amount of realism cannot suggest abolition of interest, machinery, banking and all sorts of financial institutions. Without organisation a revolution is not possible. People will spontaneously be involved in a revolution, but they must be guided by an organisation. Of course many of the great philosophers and thinkers were utopians.

MICHAEL BAKUNIN
(1814-1876)

Introduction

It is generally observed that Proudhon has stated in a succinct form the central theme of anarchism and the subsequent thinkers of this doctrine have added little to the main body of the doctrine. There may be slight exaggeration in this assessment, but it is more or less right. Proudhon thus provided the ideas and inspired the anarchist movement. It was Bakunin who gave later anarchists an example of anarchist fervour in action. Bakunin has given us a systematic and thorough-going analysis of the various aspects of anarchism, though his writings are not systematically arranged.

Bakunin was born in 1814, 150 miles away from Moscow in the province of Tver. He was the son of a diplomat and studied in the universities of St. Petersberg and Moscow. From his very childhood he was violently rebellious. He received this violent and rebellious character from his mother who was despotic by nature and she always wanted to impose restrictions upon him. Bakunin spent twelve years in prison and was twice sentenced to death. He was mainly an organiser and political agitator. He believed in movement because he thought that without movement people could not be aroused to action. After an eventful career Michael Bakunin died in 1876.

It has been said by many critics about Bakunin that he was a monumentally eccentric rebel. His every act or gesture was the symbol of anarchy. He was the first aristocrat to be an anarchist, but he never lost interest in aristocracy. All his appetites were really enormous. He was a voracious eater and non-stop talker. He could drink profusely. In one month he smoked 1,600 cigars in jail. Bakunin had no sense of propriety and proportion. He had no regular source of income. He lived on the gifts, helps and loans from his friends, well-wishers. He never hesitated to borrow money without thinking of repayment. He also gave generously what he received. He was intelligent and learned; naive and cunning; loyal to the last degree but sometimes appeared to be imprudent. He possessed an unbound enthusiasm for revolution. He could easily inspire other people with his ideas and could lead them to his public meeting.

Some people say that Bakunin gave a systematic shape to the body of anarchism and he analysed it from various aspects most of which were quite practical. Many, however, doubt the practicality of his suggestions. Here lies his greatest contribution. He was an anarchist from top to bottom. His activities, attitude, ideas and life-style all were in fine tune with anarchist philosophy.

State and Private Property

Like other anarchists Michael Bakunin believed that the human society was the outcome of a long evolutionary process and the present state of affairs is the penultimate stage. In his opinion this is purely scientific because state or society is not created in a day or two. At the very initial stages of evolution men led a life of beast and to control his bestiality external authority, checks and restrictions were created. The purpose of all these was to put man in a framework of rationality. In the primitive stage of society, therefore, there were state, private property, religion and other artificial institutions. Bakunin also believed that, in the lower stages, man's intelligence was not enough to make him self-dependent and self-sufficient in all respects. Men were always subject to impulses, physical desires and fears. As a safeguard against all these there was a strong necessity of external control and private property. But at higher and upper stages of development or evolution all these are redundant. It is here evident that Bakunin was a great believer of the theory of evolution. He somehow arrived at the conclusion that the present stage of society has reached maturity and people's intelligence is also mature. Naturally external guidance and help are redundant.

Bakunin thus holds the view that while the society is the product of evolution the state is a human creation to serve particular purposes. Any artificial institution embodies external control and it is always exercised against the will of man. The state is the biggest and most powerful artificial institution and, therefore, its control is all-pervasive. In his generalisation and oversimplification of the nature and purpose of the state Bakunin is uncompromising and explicit. This view of Bakunin regarding state is not above criticism because if the whole society which he analysed was the product of evolution how can the organisations or institutions of such a state be fully artificial? The organisations are also the products of evolution. Certain amount of artificiality may be in their body but ultimately they are the parts of evolution.

Explaining the nature of the state Bakunin further observes that all the states—democratic, autocratic and theocratic—are same so far as their control is concerned. Every type of state is desirous of intensifying its control over the inexperienced and innocent but not unintelligent citizens and, when obstructed, resorts to repressive measures. It is argued that the state based on universal suffrage accommodates the desires of people. But according to Bakunin the universal suffrage is nothing but a hoax. *It is beyond the capacity of universal suffrage to change the character of state and because of it even after the introduction of this system the character of state has remained as before.* He has said : "Despotism lies not in the form of state but in its essence, and the most democratic devices are of no avail whatever in modifying this essential character of the state." In no form of state all men are allowed to share power. Naturally, few will control many.

Bakunin has said that economically powerful class controls the economy for its own benefit. But it does not stop at that stage. To ensure its control over the economy it controls the state machinery through its pervasive control over the political affairs of the whole state. This is the general nature of all capitalist states. The *raison d'etre* of political authority is to confirm and organise the exploitation of workers by property owners. The state perpetuates an opprerssive economic condition. The state always avoids the path of persuasion and enlightenment and eager to adopt repressive measures. The activities of the state only ensure the moral debasement. The *state is,* therefore, *the most condemnable political institution,* hence it must be destroyed and not be seized.

In all types of state the decision of the few is forcibly imposed upon the many and this is the normal process. There are, in many states, innumerable avenues of ventilating the grievances. But very little action comes out. The very existence of the state dwarfs the morality and intelligence of individuals. It is due to the fact that man performs work under the sole guidance of the state. People's personal judgment, rationality and reason are not given due importance. So these do not get any scope to flourish.

Interpreting Bakunin's view Coker writes (p. 204) : "private property which is both the ground of existence and the consequence of state, creates physical and moral evils of all kinds. To the millions of workers, it brings economic dependence, laborious toil, ignorance, and social and spiritual immobility, for the few wealthy, in provides superfluous luxury and special opportunities for physical pleasure and artistic and intellectual enjoyment." We are of the opinion that Bakunin correctly diagnoses the ills of the capitalist system. Right of the few over the means of production is the source of all evils. It creates gross economic inequality, debases morality, restricts intelligence, curtails freedom, blocks the road to enjoyment and retards the growth of artistic genius. Immobility is the only tangible result of state activity. In order to smash this immobility the state is to be destroyed. Many cannot be exhorted to sacrifice their interest and welfare for the comfort of few.

There is always a tendency on the part of many to capture political power for the harvest of more and more benefits and this is abundantly found among the capitalists because they know that without full or intensive control over the state authority the full control of economy is not possible. The tendency to grab more and more power does not always follow scrupulous means or ways. Honesty, morality, reason and scruples ultimately are sacrificed. Bakunin was aware that the capitalists were exploiting the whole society, specifically the poor people. But they use the state as an instrument of exploitation. This character of state is so much prominent that general people know the state as an instrument of exploitation. Marx and Engels exposed this character of state and Bakunin supported it. The state was not only an exploiter but also an evil. So it must be destroyed. Here lie the seeds of anarchism. The capitalists and the capitalist state both aim at depriving individuals of their freedom in all its manifestation—that is economic, political, social etc.

Revolution

Bakunin led a Bohemian life. He visited almost all the countries of Europe and wherever he went he was always surrounded by friends, anarchists and revolutionaries. He was the centre of discussion, conspiracy, plan, projects and programmes. He was the inspirator of anarchist movement. His firm conviction was that without a revolution the emancipation of masses was not possible. All his efforts and plans were, therefore, on materialising a revolution. Few people could not make a revolution. Participation of masses, he concluded, was essential. He said :

Two great questions were posed from the first days of the spring (1848) : the social question and that of the independence of all nations, the emancipation of all people internally and externally at once. It was not a few individuals, nor was it a party, but the admirable instinct of the masses which raised these two questions above all others and demanded their prompt solution. The whole world understood that liberty was only a lie where the great majority of the population is condemned to lead a poverty-stricken existence and where deprived of education, of leisure and of bread, it is destined to serve as a stepping stone for the powerful and the rich.

The emancipation, in the opinion of Bakunin, is possible even through evolutionary process. But evolution does not assure us a quick result. The movement of evolution is so slow that lot of time is required to reach the destination. But the exigency of social condition cannot wait for that. Hence, common people cannot be advised to wait for an indefinite period of time. It is of no use waiting for the slow processes of evolution to make the people aware of their own interests. "We must not teach the people but lead them to revolt" announced Bakunin. The act of revolution would be sufficient educational itself. Many bourgeois socialists preached "Let us instruct the people first and then emancipate them." Bakunin contradicting this said, "Let them emancipate themselves at first and they will instruct themselves of their own accord."

Evolution may come to the assistance of revolutionary process. But the ultimate goal will be achieved through launching a revolution. An anarchist revolution means the destruction of all that is commonly understood in the expression of public order. The possibility of violence cannot be ruled out from revolution. But peaceful or reformation methods are ineffective. Parliamentary tactics are of no help. Personally Bakunin disliked violence and revenge. But in large scale destruction violence is unavoidable.

Bakunin proposed the formation of voluntary organisation of faithful anarchists in every capital or key city. These associations would be organised by "barricades" (grouped by streets or quarters of the city). The task of the revolutionary organisation will be to execute thoroughly the programme of destruction. What will be destroyed? All the political institutions which perpetrated repression on people. The revolutionary organisation will then distribute all the productive properties among the workers' societies. The revolutionary organisation will not make any attempt to set up authoritative institutions. The organisation then will send representatives and agents to the countryside to awaken the masses. Intensive propaganda will be launched throughout the country to secure the participation of people.

Bakunin thought of building up a new society. But without destroying the old one a new society cannot be built up. The entire scheme has been viewed by him in the light of morality. In his opinion to destroy the old society which deprives men of their freedom is a moral duty of individuals. Again it is also their moral duty to build up a new one. All these are to be performed by revolution. It is the moral duty of people to participate in revolution and lead it to success. According to Bakunin morality is not an imaginary idea and never resides in vacuum or world of imagination. It is closely associated with practical world. To start a revolutionary movement is not all. It is the primary responsibility of revolutionaries to lead it to success. It is to be mentioned here that in this particular issue Bakunin shared his views with many renowned revolutionaries. He also thought that victory in revolution shall be the ultimate goal of all revolutionaries, but the participation with all sincerity is also very important. Again, he held the view that revolution means the absence of all compromise. It is said that this view made Bakunin a true revolutionary. Bakunin could not tolerate the prevailing bourgeois system of economy and capitalist state structure. So revolution is needed.

Marx and Bakunin

In order to get a full picture of the revolutionary movement of the nineteenth century it is necessary to draw a brief comparison between Karl Marx and Michael Bakunin since both were great revolutionaries. Both of them had unfathomed sympathy for the toiling masses of several European countries. All their efforts and energies were channelled to the emancipation of the working class. Marx and Bakunin held that the capitalist system of production was solely responsible for glaring inequality and of all evils. Revolution, to both of them, was the only way of emancipation. Bakunin differed from Proudhon and agreed with Marx by announcing that revolutionary organisation would be set up to provide leadership to people. But these apparent similarities are not enough. The two great revolutionaries differed on several vital issues which require elaboration.

Marx was convinced that revolution could only take place in industrial societies and by means of class-conscious industrial proletariat. On the contrary, Bankunin completely disagreed with Marxian conception of revolution and he said that revolution could take place even in non-industrial societies such as Italy and his native Russia. Coming to Italy he saw that there was no privileged class of workers. So a revolution could be spear-headed by a well-organised working class.

There was an international organisation called League of Peace and Freedom and in September 1867 Bakunin came in contact with it. For several reasons he was not satisfied with its activities and he formed an alternative organisation—International Social Democratic Alliance. There was another organisation—International Association of Working Men. Marx and Engels from the very beginning were connected with it. Bakunin also joined this Working Men's Association and a distant relationship with Marx was formed. He admired Marx's profound learning and intelligence. He also believed that Marx's leadership could emancipate the workers. But Marx had no high regards about Bakunin. In his estimate Bakunin was a man devoid of all theoretical knowledge.

Towards the end of 1868 Bakunin heavily depended upon International Social Democratic Alliance, because he believed that it would inspire the revolutionary fervour of workers. Several branches were set up. But Marx and Engels did not take it lightly. They suspected that Bakunin had been hatching a conspiracy. Marx also expressed his hostile attitude to him and this surprised Bakunin. To speak the truth Bakunin never thought himself as a rival of Marx nor did he want to have any antagonistic relations with him. He had high regards for Marx. It is observed by interpreters of the history of socialist thought that Marx always suspected Bakunin and the he showed intransigent attitude towards him. Despite this hostile attitude of Marx, in December 1868 he wrote an apologetic letter to Marx. In this letter he wrote "I now understand better than ever how right you have been in following and inviting us all to tread the high road of economic revolution...I an now doing what you started to do more than twenty years ago...My fatherland is now International, of which you are one of the main founders."

The relationship between Marx and Bakunin got soured on an issue which was very minor, Bakunin decided to wind-up his Alliance and to participate wholeheartedly in the International. But there arose a controversy and the nature and control of the organisation. Both these were rated by Marx as very significant while by Bakunin unimportant. Again, Marx began to suspect that Bakunin was out to challenge his authority and leadership in the International which was not true. Marx then was determined to destroy the influence of Bakunin.

The difference between Marx and Bakunin surfaced at the Congress of the International at Basle in September 1869. Bakunin wanted to know the exact position of the General Council on matters of policy and doctrine. A controversy also cropped up on the issue of the abolition of the right of inheritance. He had strong feeling about this. "For him the hereditary property, far from being one of the many comparatively unimportant evils that would vanish with the transformation of society, was the basis on which the whole of existing society rested".[1] Bakunin was determined to give priority to this issue. The abolition of hereditary property was most important to him. Bakunin, we know, was a great worshipper of equality. It was not desirable that hereditary property would be a source of inequality. The Marxists, on the other hand, argued that it was a minor issue and would be settled after revolution. The controversy became intense.

Bakunin and his supporters defeated the International's General Council proposal sponsored by Marx's followers. Marx and Engels took this defeat somewhat lightly but the rift with Bakunin widened. Bakunin had a number of enemies and they secretly collaborated with Marx and Engels on the issues of the nature of organisation utilising people's revolutionary mentality and aims of movement. Marx's insistence upon centralised organisation was rejected by Bakunin. He believed that it would frustrate people's revolutionary zeal and spontaneity.

The hearts of both Marx and Bakunin profusely wept for the miseries of the working class and both worked hard to emancipate them from the in miseries. The problem, however, remained elsewhere. Bakunin was convinced that anarchist way was the best for the purpose of emancipation. Anarchism shall be the chief aim of any revolutionary movement. Marx and Engels, on the other hand, differed from Bakunin. They thought of a proletarian revolution which would abolish the bourgeois state and in that place at first stage the proletarians would set up a socialist society and after the final stage there shall be communist society. In both cases there was no scope of anarchism. Bakunin's anarchism and Marx's communism are quite different. Bakunin thought that emancipation would come through anarchism and to Marx it would come through communism. Moreover, Bakunin could not tolerate communism. He made the following caustic remark about communism :

I detest communism, because it is the negation of liberty and because I can conceive nothing human without liberty. I am not a communist because communism concentrates and absorbs all the powers of society into state, because it necessarily ends the centralisation of property in the hand of the state, while I want the abolition of state.

---

1. James Joll : op. cit., p. 85.

Criticising Marx's concept of liberty Bakunin said that he had no clear conception of liberty. Rather, Proudhon understood it more clearly. Marx was an authoritarian from head to foot. In authoritarian system, liberty can never thrive properly. There are only two systems—the anarchist system of Proudhon envisaging people's freedom and initiative and Marx's system of authoritarian communism.

James Joll in *The Anarchists* contends "The difference of temperament between Marx and Bakunin also led to the fundamental difference in the methods by which they believed the revolution could be achieved. For Marx the revolution would come through the ineluctable processes of history and through the gradual realisation of the proletariat of their place in the inevitable class struggle. For Bakunin, on the other hand, the revolution could be provoked by a handful of devoted and fanatical leaders who would exploit the potentialities for revolution already existing." "Few hundred young men," wrote Bakunin, "of goodwill are certainly not enough to create a revolutionary power without the people but they will be enough to reorganize the revolutionary power of the people." The preference for loosely organised secret societies over the mass political parties which Marx's followers were organising led to a radical difference in the tactics and organisation of the revolution.

In what exact way a true revolution would come is a very controversial and unpredictable issue. There was a revolution in Russia under the leadership of Lenin. But the pertinent question that peeps in our mind is did Lenin strictly follow Marx and Engels? On the other hand, Bakunin's anarchist way could not get any scope. His anarchism remained confined within the four walls of analysis, lecture and theory. Today the situation has dramatically changed and people show no sign of interest about revolution. The attack of both Marx and Bakunin was against nineteenth century capitalism. But after Second World War this capitalism began to show signs of change and today's capitalism has radically changed.

PETER KROPOTKIN
(1842-1921)

Introductory

Prince Peter Kropotkin was born in 1842 and breathed his last in 1921. Kropotkin was a Russian noble. He was educated for army and at the age of twenty he became a military officer in Siberia. Kropotkin's great interest in science developed from his military training which he received to get a job. This moulded his life in future. He had a scientific mind and devoted his time and energy to the study of books on science. As a military officer in Siberia Kropotkin got ample opportunity for geographical survey and expedition. Thus his shift from military service to geographical survey and expeditions enriched the subject profoundly. He contributed many articles to different journals.

Kropotkin was a man of different mentality and attitude. His stay in military service could not satisfy his academic and intellectual requirements and desires and after serving several years he relinquished the job, and entered the university of St. Petersberg in 1867. His vast knowledge in geography brought for him the post of secretary of Geographical Society. Even this vital administrative post could not detain him for long time. He moved to radical political movements.

In 1872 Kropotkin joined the International Workingmen's Association. Later on he was deeply involved in subversive and anarchical activities. This led him to imprisonment in 1874. He escaped from prison in 1876 and went to England. The England of the second half of eighteenth century was the centre of revolutionary activities, although she never experienced any revolution. He also travelled to Switzerland and Paris. While in Paris he was again arrested by the French government in 1883. Released from prison in 1886 he went to England and settled there. He remained in England until the Russian revolution in 1917. The rest of his life was spent without political activity.

Kropotkin was an evolutionist anarchist. But his evolutionism was more scientific than that of his predecessors. He wrote several books on anarchism such as *The Place of Anarchy in Socialist Evolution* (1886), *The Conquest of Bread* (1888); *Its Philosophy and Ideal* (1896). *The State : Its Part in History* (1898) and *Modern Science and Anarchism* (1903). His deep interest in science, particularly biology and anthropology, opened before him new and enchanting vistas of knowledge and all these inspired him to study biological science with added interest. He applied concept of evolution to the study of political ideas and this finally ended in the emergence of evolutionist anarchism. Maxey writes (p. 588), "He was a student of biology and anthropology...and his geographical work was much influenced by his knowledge of those subjects. His theory of anarchism revealed the same influence. He believed and marshalled an array of biological and anthropological data to prove that anarchy was in harmony with the true principles of natural social evolution."

Theory of Evolution

Kropotkin's theory of evolution is based on scientific principles. As a student of geography, biology and anthropology Kropotkin studied the development of both animals and human beings. Urge to survive forced both man and animal to adapt to the circumstances. Through adaptation and adjustment man makes himself suitable for environment. Failure to adapt is the chief cause of destruction.

Kropotkin argues that under normal circumstances man and social life pass through the natural process of evolution and this process is smooth. But when the artificial activities or human volition interfere with the natural process of evolution of social life, it becomes abrupt and violent. Violence comes from resistance. Sometimes the sudden appearance of new ideas and new events makes the evolutionary process abrupt.

According to Kropotkin's reasoning—when impediments are placed on the natural process of evolution force is applied to neutralise or remove the effects of impediments. Kropotkin calls it revolution. So evolution and revolution are not to be separated from each other. Revolution is a natural aid to evolution. So revolution cannot be viewed as abnormal and destructive. Kropotkin has drawn instances from history in support of his view.

The most important aspect of Kropotkin's theory of evolution is his emphasis on cooperative mentality of men. Kropotkin accepts the central idea of Darwin's theory of evolution. The animal world has passed several phases of evolution to reach the final phase. But some evolutionists have argued that there was an intense fighting among men and animals and in this struggle only the fittest ultimately survived. This latter theory finds no place in Kropotkin's theory of evolution.

Instead of using fighting as the main plank of evolution he emphasises upon cooperation as the basic motive of human being.

Kropotkin studied biology and anthropology and nowhere he could find the trace of Hobbesian picture of human nature. In the primitive society, Kropotkin held, there was a law of nature and this was also a law of cooperation and not contradiction or animosity. There was the law of mutual aid, fellow-feeling and sympathy. The primitive society was not the society of war of all against all, not the fighting mentality. The primitive people developed a lot of cooperative mentality amongst themselves and in the opinion of Kropotkin that was the cause of their survival. Kropotkin's *Mutual Aid : A Factor of Evolution* deals with cooperation. The higher the species the more perfectly developed are the dispositions and capacities for cooperation. Kropotkin has culled innumerable instances from history in support of his conclusion. Throughout the numerous stages of evolution there was always cooperation. People behaved among themselves cordially. But the creation of artificial organisation like state or government unnecessarily interfered with the cooperative mentality and behaviour of man. This led to the loss of liberty, justice and goodwill. Kropotkin raised his voice against this situation and that laid the foundation of anarchism.

Theory of State

Kropotkin has argued that the natural goal of social evolution is the attainment of principle of equality, justice and social solidarity. The higher the evolution the more perfect is the natural goal. The question then is what obstructs the attainment of this natural goal. The artificial institution and human volition are the most powerful hindrances to the natural goal. Kropotkin says that the state is the most potential source of all these hindrances.

So far as theory of evolution is concerned the state has no connection with it. It is man-made. Whereas, the society is the product of an evolutionary process. The state is regarded by Kropotkin as the embodiment of coercion and restriction. These are necessary to settle the conflict. So in the general theory of state there is no recognition of the cooperative instincts and spirit of individuals. The existing state is based on certain false assumptions—man is unsocial, quarrelsome and engaged in incessant competition. The actual situation is quite different.

Kropotkin has argued that the evolution of human faculties is still in the process of evolution, that is, human faculties are changing. But the establishment of state or any other artificial organisation means the interference with this natural process of evolution. Again, in this evolutionary process there works spontaneity. The present system of political authority denies the importance of spontaneity. Every man should be given full freedom to pursue his own methods for the development of his faculties and in this way the overall progress of society will be possible. Here he emphasises the spontaneity of individuals. Kropotkin claims that his special emphasis on the freedom and spontaneity of individuals is not based on imagination but is a realistic one. The freedom and spontaneity—if properly nurtured—would lead to sufficient development and he experienced it as an army officer of Russia. He saw that if people are allowed to work freely and spontaneously better results are to be found. But, on the other hand, if they are forced to carry out the order of others, and if this against their will, progress will be affected. For this reason Kropotkin strongly objected to the creation of artificial authority. He has further observed that spontaneity and freedom enable men to overcome very tough situations. But authority destroys the spontaneity and freedom.

According to Kropotkin the study of primitive society reveals that there was no government or coercive power. Notwithstanding, these primitive societies were well administered and there was no lack of obedience on the part of subject people. How was it possible? asks Kropotkin. His reply was mutual aid and cooperation. Cooperation should be the basis of every society and people will cultivate it spontaneously. Out of cooperation comes mutual aid. We can say one complements the other. In short, he says that cooperation, mutual aid and spontaneity shall be the basis of any human society. If restrictions and coercion are invited to interfere that will lead the society to destruction or anarchy.

Kropotkin investigated the origin of state as a political organisation. His view is stated in the following way. It is relatively a late historical development. Originally there were various social and cultural organisations based on voluntary principles and cooperation. When the economic forces and conditions divided the society into classes the interests of these classes became antagonistic. A force or power was created to settle the hostility. This is the state. This conception of Kropotkin reminds us of Marxian concept of origin of state. Laws were also enacted to serve the interests of the dominant class. The cooperation and mutual aid which prevailed in earlier societies were buried in oblivion. Customs and conventions were displaced by man-made laws.

Kropotkin makes no distinction between different forms of government so far as their repressive nature is concerned. Even in democratic states based on universal suffrage few rule on behalf of the majority. Coercion and exploitation both are characteristic features of such states. All states are repressive and their activities as well as laws are sources of injustice and suffering. Labourers and peasants are exploited. Again, the institution of private property is the source of dissension, strife and inequality. Thus, in Kropotkin's judgment authority, law and private property are enemies of people and their cooperation.

Revolution, Terrorism and Violence

Why the state-power is to be destroyed is now clear. But how it is to be done we have not yet analysed. We shall do it now. In order to establish freedom, justice and equality, he asserted, the private property and its ally—state—must be destroyed. The state and its ally—the capitalist class—have created religion to hoax ordinary people and to make exploitation thorn-free. So religion and its institutionalisation must be abolished. This can be performed only by revolution.

Kropotkin's theory of revolution is quite different from what his predecessors had talked about. In the words of Woodcock "He is considering the revolution, not in the apocalyptic form of a vast inferno of destruction...but as a concrete event in which the rebellious workers must be aware of the consequences of their actions, so that revolt will not end in the establishment of new organs of power that will halt the natural development of free society." *The raison d'etre* of revolution, in Kropotkin's view, is to build up a new society based on the principles of liberty and equality. It will have before that to destroy the old society. It is to be remembered that destruction can never be the *leitmotif* of any revolution. But destruction is unavoidable.

In the theory of revolution enunciated by Kropotkin there is no place of gradualism which is fatal in all its aspects. Gradualism is reformism, it is compromise. But Kropotkin is explicit and uncompromising. Only revolution can ensure substantial advance towards social equality. Gradualism accommodated old forms and private property system. It keeps the state structure as it is and permits additions and alterations. This is not enough. A new society is to be constructed and so revolution is indispensable.

So far as revolution and terrorism are concerned the position of Kropotkin is different from that of other anarchists. He thought the revolution was the only way to change society. But his idea of revolution is not fully connected with terrorism. His apathy to terrorism is quite known to his readers. He thought that the terrorist way might be used as last weapon. Explaining Kropotkin's viewpoint James Joll observes (p. 133) : "In fact, Kropotkin believed that in certain situations violence was justified and that it might well be the only means of revolution." Kropotkin said, "A frightful storm is needed to sweep away all this rottenness, to vivify torpid souls with its breath, and to restore to humanity the devotion, self-denial, and heroism, without which a society becomes senile and decrepit and crumbles away."

Kropotkin had suggested that a violent and pervasive revolution was needed to free the society from all evils and undesirable elements. It was beyond the capacity of gradualism to cure the disease. But the question is : Can terrorism be accepted as part of revolution? Personally Kropotkin disliked terrorism or revenge. Revenge, moreover, can never be the aim of the revolutionaries. But the importance or significance of revenge or terrorist activities lies elsewhere. Kropotkin has said that in the present structure of state the workers are the victims of all types of tortures, exploitation and persecution. This is really a sorry state of affairs and they must be freed. Kropotkin has said, "In fact we have not suffered from the persecution as they...we are not judges to those who live in the midst of all this hell of suffereing...personally I hate these explosions, but I cannot stand as a judge to condemn those who are driven to despair...one single thing—that revenge must not be erected into theory. That no one has the right to incite others to it, but that if he keenly feels all that hell and does a desperate act, let him he judged by those who are peers, his equals in bearing those pariahs' sufferings."

Kropotkin was faced with a complicated problem. Without a violent revolution the working class of Russia could not be freed from the present situation. But he did not like a violent revolution because the government of Russia was extremely reactionary. People will have to face severe penal measures for their involvement in violent revolution.

So far as use of violence is concerned there was a clear difference of opinion between Kropotkin and Tolstoy. Tolstoy was also an anarchist and he wanted the abolition of state or political authority. But he was convinced that this objective could successfully be achieved through non-violent methods. Tolstoy's doctrine has been called a Christian anarchism. Both the state and private property, according to Tolstoy, are incompatible with true Christianity. The state demands obligation from its citizens and executes its will through coercion. Tolstoy argues that this act of the state is against the principles of Christianity. Christianity further maintains that evil cannot be resisted by force. Tolstoy believed that anarchism could be attained by non-violent methods.

Personally Kropotkin had no quarrel with Tolstoy. They also never met. Points of disagreement centred around Christianity and use of violent methods. Kropotkin was scientific minded. He had a great respect for history. He buttressed his theory of anarchism by scientific argument. Kropotkin's love for scientific argument and reason prevented him from agreeing with Tolstoy who based his theory of anarchism on religion. Kropotkin viewed anarchism in the light of evolution and not of Christianity. Kropotkin also did not like violence. But in final analysis he thought that it depended upon the situation.

Anarchist Communism

Kropotkin's anarchism is different from Bakunin's collectivist anarchism and Poudhon's mutualist anarchism. Kropotkin is an anarchist communist. In his anarchism there is compulsion. His anarchism is no longer compatible with voluntarism in a hundred percent way. The whole theory of communism in anarchist form is developed in his *The Conquest of Bread* published in 1892.

Kropotkin enthusiastically propagated the anarchist communism though he was not the first man in this field. Long before him several persons advocated it. Anarchist communism was advocated by Sir Thomas More in the sixteenth century and Winstanely in the seventeenth century. Campanella's *City of the Sun* contained seeds of anarchist communism. Kropotkin was, however, its great apostle and populariser.

In the Jura Congress of 1880 Kropotkin presented a report—The Anarchist Idea from the point of view of Its Practical Realisation. This report for the first time stressed anarchist communism. The objective of the anarchist communism was the expropriation and collectivisation of the means of production. He did not specifically mention the word communism nor did he speak of communist method of distribution. However, what he suggested was nothing but anarchist communism.

Kropotkin said : "To make prosperity a reality, this immense capital–cities, houses, tilled fields, factories, means of communication, education—must stop being considered as private property which the monopolist can dispose of as he likes. This rich productive equipment, so painfully obtained, constructed, developed, invented by our ancestors must become common property so that the collective spirit can draw from it the greatest advantage for everyone. We must have EXPROPRIATION. PROSPERITY for all as an end, expropriation as a means." The expropriation clears the way of the appearance of anarchist communism. The system of private property would be abolished. Communism would fill up the vacuum. With the private property, political authority and exploitation would also go.

In *The Conquest of Bread* we find Kropotkin saying "All things are for all men, since all men have need for them, since all men have worked in the measure of their strength to produce them, and since it is not possible to evaluate everyone's part in the production of world's wealth. If the man and the woman bear their fair share of the work, they have a right to their fair share of all that is produced by all, and the share is enough to secure their well-being."

The basic principle of anarchist communism is—from each according to his ability, to each according to his needs. It is not, says Kropotkin, possible to allocate the fruits of labour according to the work done by man. However, it is enough that each labourer will get what he requires. Kropotkin observed that capitalist society is the heartland of all sorts of exploitation. Naturally in order to bring about an end of exploitation it is necessary to uproot capitalist system. How could it be done that is the problem. Let us see what he says :

"Common possession of the necessaries of the production implies the common enjoyment of fruits of the common production; and we consider that an equitable organisation of society can only arise when every wage system is abandoned and when everybody, contributing to the common well being to the full extent of his capacities, shall enjoy from the common stock of society to the fullest possible extent of his needs.

The communists share this ideal of the anarchists. But the communists believe that this can be achieved through the centralised system of production and distribution. On the other hand, Kropotkin and his followers believe that the ends can be obtained by mutual cooperation and free association. The central idea of Kropotkin's anarchist communism is a communist society can be built up through decentralisation and diversification. Whereas Marxism thinks of centralisation is anathema to freedom, equality and to some extent justice.

Arguments against Anarchism

The anarchists of all shades of thought have declared crusade against state and all types of authority and it is generally observed that this declaration smacks of utopianism. The scheme of society prepared by the anarchists has hardly any relevance to the real world. It is unfortunate that in spite of their intense agitation and continuous propaganda the anarchists have not succeeded in doing away with the state. Rather, even during their lifetime, it had assumed enormous power. Russia and Spain were the best possible states for success of anarchism. But in those states the governments were not only powerful, the powers and authority were highly centralised. Nowhere in Europe there was any chance of replacement of state by voluntary organisation.

The anarchists did not at all favour the party system and for that reason they strongly argued for the abolition of all types of party. They believed that political parties are the usurpers of human freedom and do not acknowledge equality. Naturally in a revolutionary struggle parties will have no role to play. Because of this impractical attitude to political party they were alienated from the common people and this was discernible particularly in the twentieth century. People's increasing inclination to democracy all over the world, their inordinate zeal to set up democratic institutions and determination to use political parties as a platform are regarded as the greatest onslaughts on anarchism.

Their criticism of the misuse of coercive power of the state, ineffectiveness of political institutions and representative system in a society where sources of production are controlled by a handful of persons is quite valid and any reasonable man will admit that the representative system is not working up to full satisfaction of the people. But this is followed by big question mark : What about the workability of the scheme made by them? The scheme itself and the workability both are impractical. Who will settle the disputes when the state is destroyed? Even in the tribal societies about which Kropotkin speaks a lot there was an authority whose decision was in all cases final, that is, it was binding to all. So for every society authority is essential to utter the final word.

The anarchists are extremely critical of the large-scale industrial enterprises and the existing system of economic organisation. But it is unfortunate that they failed to understand the trend of economic development. After Industrial Revolution there spontaneously developed the big industrial system. Even the small industries merged together to build up a big industrial enterprise. This was chiefly due to the economic compulsion. Hence the arguments of anarchists against big enterprises is fully unrelated to the economic compulsion and real economic situation. Viewed from this perspective we can say that the anarchists were to some extent emotional and lacked farsightedness.

Anarchists' portrayal of future society and nature of people is couched with romanticism. In this connection we can quote the relevent portion of James Joll's analysis : "the basic assumptions of anarchism are all contrary to the development of large-scale industry and mass production and consumption. When it comes to the point, the anarchists are all agreed that in the new society man will live on extreme simplicity and frugality and will be quite happy to do without the technical achievements of the industrial age. For this reason much anarchist thinking seemed to be based on a romance" (p. 259).

Woodcock in his book has drawn our attention to the following point. He says, (p. 443) : "Clearly, as a movement, anarchism has failed. In almost a century of effort it has not even approached the fulfilment of its great aim of destruction and build Jerusalem in its ruins. During the past forty years the influence it once established has dwindled...Nor is there any reasonable likelihood of a renaissance of anarchism."

As a theory anarchism appeals to people of all classes. Particularly its appeal to the intellectuals is more articulate. Educated persons, intellectuals and freedom-loving people have bitter experiences of authoritarianism which is vested in the state. But as a practical movement its appeal to people, even where it is strong, is transitory. To destroy the state is easy, but to build up an alternative is extremely difficult or practically impossible. Drawing illustrations from primitive system Kropotkin comes to the conclusion that if primitive people can conduct their political and social function without the authority of state, modern people can do it easily. But this comparision is quite untenable. Modern problems are more complex and relationships between man and society and man and man have assumed new configurations. The innocuous character of primitive men cannot be compared with the complex living and character of modern men.

Distinguishing revolution from rebellion Woodcock points out that theoretically anarchists were revolutionaries. In practice, theirs was a movement of rebellion. Revolution aims at radical social, economic and political changes. Whereas, rebellion is an organised armed resistance to established government. We may also call it a protest movement. Their needle of suspicion was aimed at the state. Woodcock's assessment is to the point. Marx and Marxists thought of revolution. They wanted radical change of society and only such a change is capable of bringing about an emancipation of the common people. Rebellion has not that capacity.

Marxism, Fabian Socialism, and Anarchism all were contemporary ideologies. But of all these, Marxism had a clear edge over all other. Moreover, Marx and Engels analysed the development of society from materialistic and scientific points of view and this had a greater appeal to all people. Again, knowledge of Marx far surpassed that of Bakunin or Proudhon or Kropotkin. Even Bakunin admitted the dynamic leadership of Marx and his vast knowledge. But the difference of temperament exacerbated the relationship between the two. Proudhon's *The Philosophy of Poverty* was pilloried by Marx. A substantial portion of the workers of European countries was so much influenced by the towering personality and vast knowledge of Marx that it was not possible for Bakunin, Proudhon and Kropotkin to counteract that influence. Marx called Bakunin a *petit-bourgeois* because of his attitude, although by birth he was not. He delivered an all-out attack on Proudhon's economic theories contained in his *System des Contradictions.* Ridiculing Proudhon's book *The Philosophy of Poverty* he wrote *Poverty of Philosophy.* The overwhelming influence of Marxism, to sum up, thwarted the success and advancement of anarchism.

Marxism had only two spokespersons—Marx himself and Engels. Later on Lenin, Stalin and large number of thinkers have explained and interpreted it in their own way. On the contrary, anarchism cannot claim that it has been explained and propagated by a single man. Bakunin was one of the spokesmen of anarchism and he was at the forefront of many an agitation. But in different countries he propagated different ideas and dogmas. Critics say that in Russia he was the leader of elitist and terrorist movements. In France, Belgium and Switzerland Bakunin was an orthodox follower of Proudhon. In Italy he was a radical reformist. Peasants lent their support to Bakunin's movement in the hope that they would get land. Kropotkin mingled anarchism with communism and it became anarchist communism. Unfortunately, this alchemy of Kropotkin could not provide any respite to exploited people of late nineteenth and early twentieth centuries. Tolstoy's anarchism was based on Christianity. So anarchism had not one shade, one banner and one manifestation. Lichtheim correctly observes : "All this somehow started under the black flag of anarchism on the black and red banner of syndicalism" (p. 143).

Woodcock says (p. 24) : "anarchists have tended to welcome as natural rebels the de 'classe' elements whom Marx despised most of all because they fitted nowhere into his neat pattern of social stratification; as a result the anarchist movement has always had its links with that shadowy world where rebellion merges into criminality...These elements unite mainly in their opposition to the modern state and the modern capitalist or communist economy. They represent a rebellion, not necessarily in favour of past, but certainly in favour of an ideal of individual freedom which belongs outside the present in which they find themselves."

Case for Anarchism

No ism of political ideology is above criticism—and anarchism is no exception. But there is no doubt that the hearts of anarchists bled profusely as the sight of the miserable condition of common people. On this issue, Marxian and anarchism stand on the same ground. Today many people view anarchism from the standpoint of modern situation. This is wrong. The state and government of twentieth and twentyfirst century have radically changed. This change has made anarchism an irrelevant ideology. It is correct when Kropotkin says that "the state is an institution which works to shackle the development of local and individual initiatives to crush existing liberties, to prevent this new blossoming". The anarchists have exaggerated the destructive and anti-individual role of the state. Even today we see the anti-individual attitude of state. Hence the anarchists cannot be blamed.

Schwarzmantel (op. cit., p. 249) says : "The anarchist critique is especially relevant with respect to socialist ideas and projects and it should be heeded by the Marxists. The ultimate aim of anarchism is socialism. Marxism also wants the same. The difference between the two lies in the methods of achieving socialism. Marxism recommends the seizure of state power first and when this is achieved everything will come to normalcy. Anarchism thinks of destroying capitalism first and then state. This, however, is a matter of priority. The objective is same."

"The anarchist perspective functions as a corrective and it contains a warning against the misuse of political power. It criticises state power and exposes the tendency of any state system to perpetuate itself. It exphasises the fact that the powerholders will always try to maintain their power. Anarchists also have pointed out the possibly corrupting and deliberating effects of parliamentary as well as bureaucratic party politics" (Schwarzmantel, p. 248). This view of the anarchists has been supported by many others who are nor anarchists. Even today the various agencies of state are corrupt, particularly the bureaucracy. This corruption is crippling the functions and role of the state. If anybody asks what is the state the real answer is it is an organisation which is controlled by some self-interest seeking politicians and bureaucrats who are corrupt from head to foot. If this the real picture of the state we can easily support the view of anarchists.

Both Marxism and anarchism have evolved. Today there are several interpretations of Marxism. Similarly, Bakunin is not the sole authority of anarchism. It has undergone radical changes. Herbert Read is of opinion that anarchism is no longer the anarchism of Bakunin and Kropotkin. "Since Kropotkin's time anarchism has evolved to meet modern conditions." This is the opinion of Read. When we call Gandhi and J. P. Narayan anarchists we do not use the term in Bakunin's sense. Gandhi did not want to destroy state, but to limit its power to the minimum.

Hobsbawm is not surprised at the revival of anarchism. He says that there are two powerful factors behind the revival of anarchism : the crisis of world communist movement after the death of Stalin and the rise of revolutionary discontent among students and intellectuals. Particularly the latter is found in many parts of the world. Even the students and intellectuals of western Europe have revolted against the all-embracing power of the state.

The existence of anarchists provides a clear warning to the holders of state power. There must be limit to the state power. Modern anarchism wants to emphasise that. In the modern social structure there is no place of absolute sovereignty. In international politics, state has no scope to exercise absolute power. In domestic field the authority must exercise power with the consent of the people. If there is aberration the authority will have to face protests from individuals and various organisations.

An interpretation of anarchism is—there must be harmony between the ruler and the ruled. For that purpose power shall be decentralised. Anarchists have simply said that. But since power corrupts and absolute power corrupts absolutely anarchists have suggested the destruction of state power to destroy corruption. We must admit that state is the source of all forms of corruption.

An important contribution of anarchism is that it initiated the stress upon the importance of mass movement as a powerful remedy to the antipeople or undemocratic activities of government. Anarchism also talked about spontaneous movement. In the absence of agitation or movement, oppression on the general public will continue. Drawing our attention to the importance of anarchist movement Maxey says that if there were no movement launched by the anarchists in the second half of the nineteenth century the autocratic functions of some states would cross all barriers. We cannot deny this contribution of anarchism. It propagated a very valuable lesson. Without a militant movement the antipeople activities of governments could not be brought to an end.

27

EARLY SOCIALISTS

Origin of Socialist Idea

The origin of the term "socialism" is controversial though the contents of socialism were present even before the use of it. The earliest reference may be made about Plato who advocated communism in family life and property. According to Lichtheim, *The Cooperative Magazine* in the November issue of 1827 first used the word socialist. Almost at the same time, Robert Owen used the term socialist or socialism. In Kolākowski's account we find that a follower of Saint-Simon claimed that he used the word socialism in the journal *Le Globe* in 1832. The uncontroversial matter that now stands is that the term appeared in the writings between the end of twenties and the beginning of thirties of the nineteenth century. In many religious books, though in an oblique form there are hints about socialism. The Bible may be cited as an example. Plato thought of communism in his analysis of ideal state. Marx and Engels claimed that before them many thought and said about class struggle and setting up of an oppression free society.

The writings of Thomas More, Campanella and many other writers contained the ideas of socialism or communism or any of its varieties, sometimes directly, sometimes obliquely. But it would be a wrong notion to hold that all these early writers viewed the term socialism in the modern sense. In fact, it has passed through several phases and forms to reach the modern phase. Kolakowsky rightly points out "From the sixteenth to the eighteenth century socialists ideas were generally inspired not merely by the reflections of the sufferings of the downtrodden classes, but by a philosophical or religious belief that antagonisms and conflicts of interest, inequality and oppression were contrary to God's plan or Nature's which intended men to live in a state of peace and harmony" (p. 184). The anarchist thought of Kropotkin was based on Christianity. God wishes that in every society there shall be perfect equality, justice and complete uniformity. Any violation of this principle will go against the pious wishes of God. We want to draw the curtain over this point by quoting a passage from Lichtheim : "Nevertheless, there is a sense in which socialism like democracy (from which it stems) is rooted in sentiments as ancient and permanent as human society itself" (p. 11).

Rousseau is one of the controversial figures in the history of political thought. But still he is regarded as one of the early socialists. A French economist, Bastiat, once said that socialists are "grandchildren" of Rousseau. While Bastiat was generalising this he had in mind the thoughts and works of French socialists. But the mention he made here is that the French socialists did not acknowledge their debt to Rousseau. Plamenatz is his *Man and Society* (Vol. II) says "yet the early socialists, French and English, held two beliefs which we associate more with Rousseau than with any one else because he was by far the most eloquent exponent of them—the belief that man in his wretchedness is the victim of society and the belief that freedom is impossible except in a community of equals." Political philosophers before Rousseau thought of equality. But none of them spoke so eloquently that inequality was the root cause of the major evils from which common people suffer. In this connection few lines from Rousseau may be quoted here. "Society is evil, irrational and corrupting because it allows of great inequalities unconnected with differences with ability or merit." This is one of the two recurrent themes of Rousseau's philosophy : "The other is that freedom is grounded in an equality."

Rousseau in *A Discourse on the Origin of Inequality* said "it is plainly contrary to the law of nature that children should command old men, fools wise men, and that the privileged few should gorge themselves with superfluities, while the starving multitude are in want of the bare necessities of life" (p. 221). Rousseau deplored inequality on the ground that it was contrary to law of nature. Whatever may be the cause the central theme is inequality must be sent to exile.

A major part of Rousseau's political thought bears the imprint of socialist and revolutionary ideas. Plamenatz observes (p. 37) that he was the revolutionary of all critics of the established order. But he was not revolutionary in the Marxian sense and never intended to destroy the existing social system by force. He wanted to abolish a social system based on inequality through the creation of a new body-politic guided and administered by general will.

Some people say that Rousseau was the "grandfather" of the modern socialists. We admit that Rousseau believed in socialism but he did not extend his socialist thought and made no concrete proposal about setting up a socialist society. He was confined within an analysis. Plamenatz however, admits that Rousseau inaugurated a line of thought which in later years enabled the early socialists to differentiate themselves from the liberals (p. 28). He was not a socialist, because socialism was the by-product of industrial capitalism and in Rousseau's time that had no trace at all. Whatever may be Lichtheim's view there is no denying the fact that Rousseau's political philosophy contained the seeds of socialism. For example, his concept of equality and his emphasis upon it are regarded as basic ideas of socialism. Moreover, he developed a theory of democracy which was not liberal and individualist in the Lockean sense. We have already quoted a passage from his *Discourse* where he said that it is unnatural that few wealthy persons will control the many poor persons.

Interests of Early Socialists

The term early socialists may be misleading. The socialist thought started more or less from Rousseau. Marx and Engels gave it a concrete shape and they proclaimed their socialism as scientific. In order to distinguish Marxian socialism from the socialism or socialist thought that prevailed before them the term early socialists is used. The socialist predecessors of Marx did not elaborate the socialist policies, principles and philosophy, nor did they view it with a scientific outlook. But all of them had a heartfelt feeling for the downtrodden masses. They deplored capitalist system as the root cause of sufferings. Hence, we can say that the concept of socialism or socialist thought gathered momentum after Industrial Revolution achieved maturity to some extent.

An important feature of early socialists is that they believed in setting up of a socialist society through peaceful ways such as appearing to the capitalists that they should refrain from exploiting and oppressing the workers. They further developed a nation that the dark sides of capitalism and the brighter aspects of socialism shall be intensively and extensively propagated among the workers and under-privileged section of the society. All these are peaceful ways and part of evolutionary socialism. They viewed the state with great suspicion on the ground that it was a party to exploitation. The unholy alliance between capitalists and state never produced any salutary results. The suspicion made them uninterested about the state. Plamenatz thinks that all the early socialists were hopeful men and they believed in progress (p. 38). All of them had plans of future society based on socialist principles. But these principles were not well-calculated, scientific and realistic. That was the great drawback of the early socialists.

The early socialists believed that it was poverty and ignorance which led men to commit crime and violence. An important precondition of the removal of crime and violence is to banish poverty and ignorance from society. Because of inequality men were deprived of adequate opportunities to develop their good qualities. We can, therefore, say that the notion of early socialists was uniformly focused on the evil effects of inequality. They squarely blamed it. Robert Owen, Charles Fourier, Saint-Simon and Proudhon—all these early socialists held the view that if all the persons get proper scope to improve their economic condition it will be possible to destroy poverty and ignorance. It is thus quite manifest that the early socialists were eager to change the material condition of society and Marx accepted their view.

Plamenatz maintains that the study of the writings of the early socialists reveals that they had some sense of history. In their various writings they emphasised that in past the rate of progress was very slow. This was due to the fact that very few persons controlled the means of production and they were excessively preoccupied with their own betterment keeping aside the general progress of society. Their knowledge of history enabled them to know what was the condition of society in the past. On the contrary, many political philosophers such as Hobbes and Locke had no interest in history. Saint-Simon, it is said, studied history exhaustively and developed his own conception about history. He had shown how European society had changed from the eleventh century. But all the early socialists did not possess the same amount of interest in history. For example, Robert Owen displayed very little interest for history. On the other hand, both Marx and Engels were serious readers and critical analysts of history. From the study of history of several centuries they gathered certain facts and on the basis of these they built up certain conclusions and ideas. They studied history from the standpoint of materialism and arrived at the conclusion that appeal to the capitalists would never bring about emancipation.

All the early socialists acknowledged that the society was divided into rich and poor and the former controlled the entire wealth of the society for its own benefit. To defend the private property the rich needed the help of the state and thus it became the ally as well as guarantor of property. Without the help and protection provided by the state it would have been impossible for the capitalists to protect their property or wealth. So the capitalist system was not the only caûse of the untold miseries of the working class, the state is also equally responsible for this. The early socialists did not think about replacing the bourgeois state system through violent upheavals. They preferred to appeal to the capitalists to show mercy to the workers. They also believed that if the capitalists voluntarily part with a portion of their wealth for the upliftment of the conditions of workers, their economic conditions would invariably improve and importance of state would diminish.

An interesting point may be allowed to interfere with our analysis. Hobbes, Locke and Rousseau did not raise their arms against the society and organised force created by people. They did not regard man as victim of society, but it was the society which was their saviour. Both Plato and Aristotle and several other philosophers thought of the state as the reformer of individuals, behaviour not congenial to the ideal symbolised by the state. Rousseau viewed a state or society consisting of equal persons and in such a state there would neither be contradiction nor animosity. People will be the integral part of the mainstream of society. Furthermore, he envisaged the existence of coercive power in a society. The early socialists developed a state-phobia..

There is a difference between Rousseau and the early socialists. He deplored the multiplication of wants. Nor did he preach austerity. His naive view was that a society should not create wants which people could not satisfy. The unfulfilled desires contaminate the social atmosphere. But the early socialists were not against desires. To them more desires meant more production and more progress. So they did not deplore the multiplication of wants. Moreover, the multiplication of wants would lead to greater collaboration among the people.

Socialist Thought and Two Revolutions

It is now quite manifest that before the advent of Marx and Engels in the political scene of Europe in the nineteenth century the socialist ideas were not unknown to people. So we can say quite reasonably that Marx and Engels were not the originators of socialism. Kolakowsky says (Vol. I, p. 182) : "The mainspring of socialist ideas that arose under the combined influence of the Industrial and French Revolutions was the conviction that uncontrolled concentration of wealth and unbridled competition were bound to lead to increasing misery and crises, and that the system must be replaced by one in which the organisation of production and exchange would do away with poverty and oppression and bring about a redistribution of the world's goods on a basis of equality." The two Revolutions, it is said, generated socialist thought in the minds of people and after the Revolutions they began to grow speedily. The progress of industrialisation created more and more economic disparities between rich and poor and along with it there emerged antagonism between the two classes—capitalists and workers. The French Revolution created a sort of consciousness—about rights, equality, freedom and above all economic conditions. Now-a-days it is said that Rousseau was the philosopher of French Revolution because the revolutionaries received inspiration from his writings.

The above point has been beautifully expressed by Lichtheim in the following words : "A simplified account of the birth of socialism might begin with the statement that the Industrial Revolution furnished the thesis, the French Revolution the antithesis, while socialism brought about a synthesis of these two parallel but unconnected phenomena" (p. 41). The Industrial Revolution created large amount of wealth and this was ultimately captured by a very small number of capitalists. The workers and other sections of society were deprived of their legitimate share of wealth which generated large scale dissension among the masses of men. People began to feel increasesingly that the Industrial Revolution did not appear as a blessing to them. It was rather a curse. It was the source of sufferings, miseries and gross economic inequalities. The hands that controlled the industry also controlled the political power. So the concentration of wealth and power went almost simultaneously. The hostility to capitalism became pronounced. Hobsbawm says that hostility to capitalism was extremely prominent with the rise of people's suffereings. Many people wanted to set up a just society which would be progressive. It must envisage freedom and equality. Justice would be the basis of the new society.

The Industrial Revolution was the father of the new class structure of society. After industrialisation the industrial society was divided into two great warring classes—bourgeois and proletariat. In earlier phases of social development there were also classes and class conflicts. Industrial Revolution gave them new dimensions. At the same time the French Revolution dramatised the issue of social conflict, thereby encouraging a surge of feeling which evolved into utopian socialism. The Industrial Revolution was the abnegation of liberty, equality and fraternity. Its main contribution was social conflict. The philosophy of the French Revolution was liberty, equality and fraternity.

These two Revolutions together produced a diversity of thought, principles and proposals. But a single current passed through all these variety of proposals and principles and that was socialism or any one of its forms. Many people openly supported the cause of the working class. They highlighted the sufferings and advanced the remedies. This was socialist principle. Some proclaimed the necessity of revolution whose purpose would be the abolition of inequality and injustice. Several persons pointed out the class conflict and its gradual intensification. They predicted the collapse of capitalism and advent of the dictatorship of the proletariat. Some imagined of a perfect society which they desired to set up by appealing to the capitalists. Others wanted to destroy the state and private property. Some people studied the course of historical evolution in order to identify the natural laws which would ensure the advent to socialism. Thus, these two Revolutions are to be regarded as the mainspring of socialist thought.

In this connection it may be pointed out that on the one hand some people thought of destroying the capitalist system through revolution and set up a new social order. On the other hand, some people and great intellectuals thought of emancipation of the working class through the expansion of the role of state. The state will take initiative to make laws which will curtail the motive of capitalists to make more and more profit. At the same time law will ensure wage, working hour and other benefits of the workers. It is called socialism through democratic or parliamentary process.

Central Idea of Utopian Socialism

The dictionary *meaning of the term Utopia is imaginary island with perfect political and social system; ideally perfect place or state of things.* The word "utopia" is derived from the Greek word *"eutopia"* the meaning of which is good place. There is a similarity between the original Greek word *"eutopia"* and the English word "utopia". Sir

Thomas More in 1516 wrote a book *Utopia* and from that year the concept gained publicity and popularity. A complete one hundred years—from the middle of the eighteenth century right up to the middle of nineteenth century—the utopian thought largely dominated the European political scene. As agitators or revolutionaries, the adherents of utopian socialism did not set up any record of success. But their ideology—comprising politics and economics—left a legacy which imbued the generation following them. The legacy may be called the political and economic doctirne of utopian thinkers.

The important premise of the Utopian Socialists is that human beings everywhere are part of humanity and they are the holders of the same degree of dignity. As to the merit and ability there are differences among men. But that cannot be the basis or reason of inequality. This prescription of Utopian Socialists is normative. Any future society must acknowledge it. Corollary to it is the concept of equality. If all the individuals possess same dignity they can legitimately claim equality in various spheres of social life. The utopians or early socialists held the view that none can be deprived of the right to equality. Rather, it should be the basis of every society. If it is proclaimed as the basic aim of society then conflict in all forms will come to an end. Mutual love, brotherhood and fellow-feeling will ultimately rule the society. There will be no place of exploitation and oppression. This is the picture of future society according to the utopian socialists.

The early socialists or utopians never regarded socialism as a free ideal. That is, it could not be achieved easily or without any effort. Socialism was bound to come but that must be preceded by arduous efforts. Socialism, according to the utopians, would finally conquer the world. Why did they come to the conclusion? They believed that everywhere the system of private property and capitalist mode of production had created intolerable and chaotic conditions causing great hardship to the toiling masses. Mass awakening would lead them to work for socialism. Utopian socialists thought that emergence of consciousness does not stay at any single place or condition. History shows that knowledge, consciousness idea etc. move from one stage to higher stage. The material conditions of society also help this movement. Naturally, when people realise that they are oppressed or exploited they will be in search of a proper remedy and finally they will discover that only a socialist society is capable of emancipating them from all sorts of evils. In other words, socialism is the saviour.

The utopians never conceived of achieving socialist goals by revolutionary means. They believed in the economic objectives—that is, mitigation to inequality in economic sphere and redistribution of wealth in order to give every man his due share of wealth. The political revolution was not treated by them a master means. Rather, they had no intention to use or adopt revolution. The early socialists were not revolutionaries. But they cannot be mistaken as counter-revolutionaries. They were convinced that socialism could be achieved by spreading education, intensifying propaganda and adopting reforms. To put it in a different language, peaceful ways are the best methods for achieving socialism.

The utopians were convinced that the capitalist system of production was solely responsible for the large-scale chaos in the economic world. Both the numbers of capitalists and the competition among them had increased enormously. The inevitable consequence was over-production and in order to save themselves from this crisis the capitalists were forced to retrench workers and to adopt other anti-worker policies. But these failed to provide the effective cushion. Poverty and unemployment began to increase by leaps and bounds. These created suffocating conditions for the people living in a capitalist society. The growing crises forced the capitalists to find out ways of survival. They devised ways. But these could not help them because the crisis in capitalism was deep-rooted. The result is the crisis continued; on the other hand the working class was also the victim of the crisis of capitalism. Unemployment increased by leaps and bound. The economic hardship went on. The workers everywhere were forced to work at nominal wage. The purchasing power of the workers decreased. The multiplication of hardship and crisis became the characteristic feature of almost every capitalist system.

The utopians have prepared a scheme of future society based upon certain ideals. These ideals may be attained either by reforms or individual efforts such as appealing to industrialists. However, mutualism has been emphasised by them. They had no intention to exacerbate the relationship between classes. So it was also their goal to effectuate social harmony. In the scheme of future society we find the following ideals. The private property is to be abolished. A planned economy on a national scale is to be accepted. Without planning a society cannot be freed from anarchy. The right to work is to be admitted. Abolition of the existing class structure of society is essential. The manufacturers would form cooperatives on a voluntary basis. All distinctions between men and women and also between different religious sects are to be abolished. The arts and science will be allowed to flourish with complete freedom. Universal education at public expense will be introduced. This is the scheme of a future society. If all these are translated into reality there will be no exploitation in the society. So socialism is the only way of emancipation.

SIR THOMAS MORE
(1478-1535)

Life and Works

It is generally observed by the scholars of socialist thought that Sir Thomas More was the first utopian socialist thinker. He was born in 1478. He received his primary or early education from the Archbishop of Canterbury. More was sent to Oxford and after completing studies he went to London to study law. He then became a Member of Parliament and his charming qualities and personality attracted many top-ranking persons of his time, including Henry VIII. In rapid succession he was awarded knighthood, made a member of the Privy Council, treasurer of the Exchequer, Speaker of the House of Commons and, finally, in 1529 he was appointed to the most coveted post of Lord Chancellor.

But this meteoric rise did not last long. He fell from the grace of the monarch because of his failure to support the king on the controversial issue of divorce. It has been said by his biographers that he always performed those acts which his conscience permitted. Because of this he could not support every act of the king. This created a rift between him and the king. He was removed from office and was convicted of treason and finally beheaded in 1535. More published his *Utopia* in 1516. He coined Utopia from the Greek word "nowhere". While Machiavelli was writing *The Prince* More was composing the *Utopia*.

Utopianism of More

Thomas More has portrayed satirically the decadent condition of the contemporary British society. He investigated the reason of the decadent condition of the British economic and social system and formed the conclusion that the entire British social and economic structure must be completely overhauled. His attack was focused at the capitalist structure of British economy. In the capitalist system, More said, only few had the opportunity to be the owners of the means of production. The working masses were allowed to share a very small portion of the wealth. In this way inequality came to be the characteristic feature of the society. He observed that along with inequality there was boundless exploitation of the toiling people.

In the imaginary island of More there shall be no place of exploitation. The island shall be surrounded by natural boundaries. Every man and woman will learn trade and must labour six hours a day. None shall work more than the stipulated hour. Every child will be trained in the arts of agriculture. All the products of the *Utopia* shall be stored in the common place and from there each citizen will receive his requirements. In the *Utopia* there shall be no government and no control. Complete brotherhood, equality and liberty will be the dominant features of *Utopia.*

The family is the basic unit of social organisation and economic activity. In the *Utopia* parents, children and grand-children will live together and in large family mansions. The children will receive this education from teachers appointed by the parents. The organisation of the society will be hierarchical. People will elect their magistrates and all the magistrates assembled together will elect a chief magistrate. The chief magistrate is called the prince. "One might say the prince is nominated by the people and elected by the magistracy. He holds office for life but may be removed for cause."

People of the *Utopia* will have the opportunity to enjoy all sorts of democratic rights and privileges. There shall be a system of open general assembly and all adult citizens will participate in the assembly. All decisions shall be taken in the meeting of the open assembly. Though More thought of an imaginary utopia, we think that this was in the line of Greek City-states. More has also made provision for a national assembly. Each city and its adjacent farm territory sends each year three representatives to the national assembly. National assembly is the supreme governing body of the *Utopia.* The members of the imaginary island will lead a communistic way of life. The members have their noon and evening meals together in the common refectory. Maxey says (p. 147) : "There is plenty for all and nothing that one may have that another may not likewise possess. Hence there is no disposition to accumulate."

Campanella and Winstanley

Thomas Campanella was another utopian thinker who was born in 1568 and died in 1639. In his philosophy Campanella combined materialism with narrow Christian theology. He always insisted on the synthesis of philosophy and theology. His important utopian work is The *City of Sol* or *The City of Sun.* The book contains the description of an imaginary commonwealth.

The City of Sol or *Sun* was represented as an absolute monarchy whose ruler was designated as Sun. The king would rule the state for life. He would be elected by a college of magistrates. Since Campanella had a strong fascination for theology or religious activities the monarch of the commonwealth would perform both political and religious functions. He prepared a scheme of administrative organisation of his commonwealth. He divided the functions of the government into three. The functions relating to war and diplomacy; to superintending public instruction and public works and finally, to physical improvement of people.

The utopian aspect of Campanella's politics is that commonwealth or city of Sun was free from exploitation and slavery. Campanella's commonwealth resembled More's *Utopia.* Both were planned to offer a heavenly peace and happiness to all the citizens. Both More and Campanella wanted to combine intelligence with science to maximise the welfare of the people. He did not make any provision for private property and accumulation of wealth. All the citizens would take their meals in the common dining hall. Campanella, of course, like Plato, recognised the existence of three classes. He envisaged of a priest-magistrate which corresponded to Plato's philosopher guardians or king.

In the seventeenth century the Levellers and Diggers launched a movement which may appropriately be compared with utopianism. Although the movements of Levellers and Diggers was called republican, some of these ideas were really utopian. They emphasised upon people's consent and wanted to exterminate the system of private property because it was the source of corruption. The leader of the movement was Winstanley. In 1652, his *Law of Freedom* was published. His utopian society based on exchange system. Selling and purchasing he did not allow. People would draw their necessities from the public store. None would be allowed to take more than his requirement.

GRACCHUS BABEUF
(1760-1797)

Gracchus Babeuf was an eighteenth century socialist thinker who propagated the basic ideas of socialism. He believed that only socialism could save toiling masses from all types of misery and hardship and in this respect he was at par with Saint-Simon. Immediately after the French Revolution he jumped upon the task of propagating the socialist ideas. Upon the socialist ideas of Babeuf and his co-socialists there was a clear influence of Rousseau. Of course all the revolutionaries were inspired by Rousseau. Babeuf and his followers wanted to set up a society in which there would be no exploitation and private property because they believed that the system of private property sanctioned by the state and possessed by the capitalists was the root cause of corruption and inequality. Let us quote few lines from Kolakowski's monumental work : *Main Currents of Marxism*. Babeuf and Babouvists took their philosophy in the main from Rousseau and utopianists of Enlightenment and regarded themselves as the successors of Robespierre. Their basic premise was the idea of equality as Bounarroti wrote "the perpetual cause of the enslavement of the peoples is nothing but inequality and as long as it exists the assertion of national rights will be illusionary" (p. 152).

In Babeuf's judgment, though the French Revolution brought about an end of despotic rule in France, its success in ending the capitalist system was nil. But so long capitalism would continue to exist emancipation of people would remain a distant hope. The constitution of 1793 proclaimed the right to equality and Babeuf demanded that that must be translated into reality. It must be removed from the confinement of the constitution.

Babeuf and his followers were convinced that the forcible removal of the despotic ruler could ensure a free, fair and equal society. So in Babeuf's philosophy we find an endorsement of armed revolution. In order to reach the final goal his followers preferred secret activities and on that ground they were generally called conspirators. The fearless conspirators would be endowed with undaunted spirit. Under the Directory a conspiracy hatched by Babeuf and his followers was detected. He was tried and guillotined in 1797. In this way the life of a revolutionary and a utopian came to an end.

The students of Western political thought, especially the socialist thought, will remember Babeuf and his comrades for their bold step and firebrand leadership. They revolted against autocratic rule and openly challenged the anti-people policies of the government and powerful ruling class. Babeuf dreamt of a future society which will be free from exploitation though the dream never saw the light of sun. Kolakowski sums up the importance of Babeuf and Babouvist in the following language (p. 185). "The Babouvist movement is important because it reflected for the first time a conscious conflict between the revolutionary ideal of freedom and that of equality. Freedom meant not only the right of assembly, but the abolition of legal differences between estates of the realm but also the right of every man to carry an economic activity without hindrance."

Babeuf and Babouvists assumed that the poverty and sufferings of the workers were due to the luxury and excessive consumption of the rich people. The privileged classes enjoyed the wealth depriving the larger section of the society. If the wealth were distributed properly among all the people, the ideal prosperity for all would then appear. The early socialists including Morelly and Mably based their socialist principles on the normative theory. They said that every man had identical right to whatever nature provides. Sometimes they supported their view with the help of quotations from the New Testaments and sometimes with the help of materialism. But the argument was always that the inequality of consumption was to be done away with.

What is the contribution of Babeuf? He, at a very tender age, was guillotined. But with his death the movement for socialism or communism did not end. The movement rather gathered momentum. Marx and Engels were inspired by the utopian socialism. He was the first revolutionary. The term "socialism" may be associated with the names of Saint-Simon or Fourier or Owen, but communism is identified with the name of Babeuf. He disliked to confine himself within the boundary of democracy and wanted to embark upon the vaster field of communism. In fact, the revolutionary movement started with Babeuf. He failed, but not his ideas.

SAINT–SIMON
(1760-1825)

Career and Works

Claude-Henry de Rouvroy, Comte de Saint-Simon, was born in 1760 in one of the great families of France. At the age of seventeen he entered the military service and participated in the French campaign of American Revolution. As an army officer he went to Mexico and was engaged in peculiar activities. He then returned to France but was disgusted with the intellectual sterility of military service. He decided to devote his energy and time to intellectual activities. He had a great ambition to be an academician. He also felt that his selection of military service was inappropriate. He finally decided to relinquish the military service. The biographers of Saint-Simon say that he attained these two things. Within a very short time he acquainted himself with the leading intellectual circles of France. He also earned a lot of money from the speculative business of land.

Saint-Simon was both liberal and radical minded. He wanted to be known as a revolutionary. Saint-Simon renounced all his titles of nobility. He earned a lot of money and spent it liberally for hospitality to scientists and scholars. Saint-Simon was specifically interested in science and political issues and he published several papers on these subjects. He wrote a number of books many of which were published after his death. The important works of Saint-Simon are *Letters of a Resident of Geneva* (1802), *The Reorganization of European Society* (1814), *The Industrial System* (1821) and *The New Christianity* (1825). It is unfortunate that all his writings could not create any impact on the contemporary mind. He had also few converts. His personal life was not happy. During the last years of his life he was faced with abject poverty. He lived on the donations from few philanthropic friends. In both adversity and prosperity he never lost his courage and laboured manfully to make his mission successful.

Although Saint-Simon could not get any recognition in his lifetime, death brought for him great honour. Maxey-says that (p. 545) Saint-Simonism became a fashionable creed. He was the enunciator of several doctrines and they were disseminated among the people. His doctrines created new hopes in the mind of the younger generation disilusioned by Rousseauism, Bonapartism and Legitimism. Younger men found in his doctrines the answer to the age-old problems of government. Saint-Simon had the genius to express one idea in various forms and his doctrines catered to the interests of many people.

Saint-Simon on Social Change

Saint-Simon studied history in order to understand the historical development of society and the study reveals that in the Middle Ages the society was controlled by feudal landlords or specially by feudalism. Moreover, theology had great influence upon the functioning of society. But at the same time he found that the development of science and scientific mind of people changed the society. Previously religion and superstition controlled the social behaviour of men and the individual relationship. Advent of science and its influence on men made their outlook reasonable. They lost their faith on supernatural elements and people's outlook gradually became scientific.

As a result of the development of science a new power—industrial power—was created. The society witnessed the unprecedented flow of wealth. In the Middle Ages the leadership of society was provided by the church and feudal lords. Now the industrial magnates assumed the leadership. Saint-Simon further observes that in the past both the feudal lords and the church demanded obedience from the commons. But the leaders of the industry and the teachers of the academic institutions could not demand unconditional obedience. "Thus the spirit of the old society" comments Plamenatz "was quite contrary to the spirit of the new classes growing up inside it, the new society centered in the chartered towns and in the universities founded on them."[1] Plamenatz is perfectly right. There was a conflict between the spirit or idea of the old regime and the philosophy as well as materialism of the industrial society. This conflict was quite inevitable. Saint-Simon was the first man to draw our attention to this contradiction between the old and the new. Later on, Marx explained it more elaborately.

The new class had an outlook and objective, but it was weak. So the conflict between the old and the new could not surface. In the sixteenth century the old order was openly challenged by the new order. According to Saint-Simon this change was caused by the emergence of three factors—the discovery of America and route to India; the invention of printing, and the theories of Copernicus and Galileo. All these together helped the expansion of trade and commerce. "The theories of Copernicus and Galileo, offering simpler and clearer explanations better supported by facts, were fatal to the anthropomorphic theology of the church."[2] In the eighteenth century the development of science and the rise in the consciousness of the commons threatened the old order. Both the temporal and spiritual authority faced the greatest attack. This is a type of Enlightenment. The development of science removed darkness from the mind of people. The immediate impact was people began to lose their faith in religion, belief and host of supernatural elements. Men's mind was under the strong influence of reason and they began to see everything with an enlightened and reasonable outlook.

The expansion of industry and progress of science changed the very structure and functioning of society and also its authority. The feudal lords and church receded to the past. Industrialists, middle class and intellectuals came forward to guide the society. New authority, new hierarchy and new systems were created. Old systems collapsed. Saint-Simon maintains that this is inevitable. The old system had not the power to face the challenge of the new order. So it had to bow to the new one. The transition from the old to the new took place smoothly says Saint-Simon. In the transition the lawyers and metaphysicians took the leadership. But Saint-Simon disapproved of it on the ground that these classes of people always misguide the general mass.

The French Revolution, according to Saint-Simon, overthrew the despotic rulers. But it failed to fulfil the economic, political and other aspirations of the people. A false notion about liberty and equality was created by the leaders of the Revolution. Saint-Simon called them negative conceptions of liberty and equality. He said that the principle of liberty and equality in an industrial society must be positive. Positive principle meant to him the following. From everyone according to his capacity to everyone according to his contribution. This principle gives every man his proper reward. The services of each individual must receive due recognition from society. But the growth of industry and the volume of wealth could not bring any relief for the toiling masses. Their poverty and sufferings multiplied in geometrical progression. He was in great dilemma—his mind was overwhelmed with sorrow and, on the other hand, he had no power to save the people. Being helpless he fervently appealed to the big industrialists to change their outlook. Saint-Simon wanted to say that the industrialists must give a part of their huge profit to the workers. He appealed to them to change their outlook. But this did not happen.

1. *Man and Society*—Vol. II, p. 69.
2. *Man and Society*—Vol. II, p. 70.

Plan of Future Society

Saint-Simon studied history, understood the root causes of the misery and extent of exploitation and as a remedy he appealed to the capitalists. This went in vain. He thought that a future society was to be discerned in the light of past historical changes and trends. *He has interpreted the development of society in the light of historical materialism.* Marx has recognised this approach of Saint-Simon and has expressed his indebtedness to him in this regard. In past the society underwent changes and all these related to system of production. Saint-Simon has asserted that the political changes have been due to the evolution of the instruments of production. He relates the economic conditions to the system of production. Free competition, anarchy—all are the causes of poverty and economic crises.

"The future society", comments Kolakowski, "to which industrial concentration was leading, would be one in which industry was to be managed by the producers of wealth, production would be planned and measured by social needs, and private property would change its character, as its use would be subordinated to the general good and not left to the owner's whim; inheritance would be abolished." Saint-Simon says that competition will be replaced by emulation. In his future society a conciliation between private interests and common good is to be effected. But under no circumstances private interests will be given priority. Saint-Simon, for this conception, is indebted to Rousseau. Indeed, many early socialists are indebted to Rousseau.

Saint-Simon does not abolish the social hierarchy. But this must be made commensurate with the general welfare of the community and this will never be hereditary. He emphasises that the worth of every man must receive due recognition from the authority. The task of transforming the society will be carried out by bankers, scholars, manufacturers and not by workers themselves. But he has cautioned us by saying that their responsibility is to transform the society for the benefit of the poor. They must not be given any power or authority to control and exploit the working class and other common people. In the future society the concept of political power will undergo considerable changes. The persons in power will administer the state and will never govern the people. The purpose of this proposal is to utilise in the best possible way the gifts of the nature which few people possess. All persons have not the genius or ability to shoulder the burden of administration. If implemented this will ensure the maximum benefit.

Classes and Class Struggle

Saint-Simon and his followers have interpreted history as a continual progress in which two phases alternate. The phases are organic and critical. Organic phase of history is characterised by the unity and integrity of faith and principles. In the society there is a clear-cut hierarchy. All the parts are closely connected with each other. But the critical phase or period is the most important for our analysis. In this period there are dissentions and conflicts among the various sections of the community. From the unity point of view the nature of the community is lost. Bonds are relaxed. Saint-Simon, studying the development of European history, comes to this generalisation. The disharmony, says Saint-Simon, is both religious and economic.

Saint-Simon has correctly diagnosed the character and functioning of capitalism. Even Marx and Engels have endorsed the analysis of Saint-Simon. He observes that the competition among the capitalists is the chief cause of economic anarchy. The privatisation of the means of production is the source of all troubles. The workers are exploited. Moral degradation is the result of this exploitation. A recent critic has observed, "He linked exploitation with the institution of private property. He saw the defects of the social system based on private ownership as the main cause of crisis and production anarchy inherent in capitalism." The working class is the victim of this crisis and anarchy. The worker is exploited materially, intellectually and morally as the slave once was. The workers sell their labour because they have nothing to sell and also they own nothing except their ill-fate. And in exchange of labour they are given a wage which is not sufficient to lead a comfortable life. On the other hand, the owners of capital or the industrialists live a quite comfortable and luxurious life and the monetary source of this life style comes from the huge profit produced by the workers. This is not only an inequality but gross injustice. Workers are the source of profit but they are deprived of it.

Saint-Simon had a lot of sympathy and feeling for the workers. Even Marx has admitted it in his *Capital* (Vol. 3, page 591) : "Just as in the writings of the physiocrats the *Cultivateur* does not stand for the actual tiller of the soil, but for the big farmer, so the *travailleur* with Saint-Simon, and continuing on through his disciples, does not stand for the labourer but for the industrial and commercial capitalist... In fact one should bear in mind that Saint-Simon speaks directly for the working class and declares their emancipation to be the goal of his efforts." We find its reverberation in Engels's writing. Engels writes that the lot of the working class is his main interest, because this class is the most numerous and exploited.

Saint-Simon has said that before the Industrial Revolution there was practically no working class and hence no conflict between workers and the capitalists. The Industrial Revolution not only created these two classes, but also inequality in wealth or mal-distribution of wealth. The society was infested with class conflict. Saint-Simon calls capitalists as idlers because they do not perform any physical labour. The workers were quite aware that the income of the capitalists was derived from their labour. But due to lack of organisation they could not protest.

Let us sum up the views of Saint-Simon. Industrial Revolution created capitalism and the system of private property. A new class—working class—came out of the industrialisation. Contradiction surfaced between the capitalists and workers because of the capitalists' motive to give labourers less than what is their due, leading to the exploitation. Finally, the degradation in all its forms is the offspring of exploitation. A new society is to be built up based on equality and freedom.

Saint-Simon's Utopianism

The general impression about Saint-Simon's socialist thought is that it is utopian in character. John Plamenatz, a noted interpreter of political thought, is of opinion that Saint-Simon's socialist principles are quite unrealistic. But on that ground we cannot call it utopian. Plamenatz's argument is that Saint-Simon's idea about the transformation of society is based on illusions. He assiduously appealed to the leaders of industry to change their hearts and methods of activities so that the labourers could get their legitimate share of national wealth. But they took no notice of it. It is pity that though Saint-Simon discovered the cause of illness, he failed to prescribe the correct medicine. Rather, he resorted to a wrong and illusive path. That is utopianism. He was under the influence of illusion that his appeal to the industrialists would bring about a change in the hearts of capitalists. Why did he believe the capitalists? Saint-Simon had sufficient knowledge about social development and the nature and functioning of capitalists. In spite of this why did he keep faith on the capitalists—Did he not know that without application of force the capitalists would never stop exploitation? The impracticality of his suggestion (appeal to the capitalists) makes him utopian.

Saint-Simon knew it quite well that as a result of Industrial Revolution the society was divided into two opposing classes and an innocuous appeal had no power to change merciless hearts of the capitalists. One or two particular industrialists might have a soft corner for common men but this is not the general case. Naturally class interest prevented them from giving any benefits to labourers. Saint-Simon failed to realise the class character of capitalists. We are forced to say that Saint-Simon understood the nature and development of society but he failed to enter into the depth of the heart of the heartless capitalists. This failure constitutes the centre of his utopian thought.

Marx and Engels have called him utopian on two grounds. He laid too much confidence upon the benevolent character of capitalists. Secondly, he believed that socialism could be achieved without revolution. Many people of his day were convinced that the leaders of the industry could not be entrusted with the management of economy, because it was not possible for them to keep themselves above personal interests. But he believed the industrialists. Adam Smith, Ricardo and Sismondi—the classical economists of his time—realised the class interests.

The transformation of society required the destruction of privileges enjoyed by the few. In that case, Saint-Simon might have appealed to the workers or the unprivileged. There was only one effective way of ending exploitation and that was to enlighten the workers through the spread of education and by encouraging them to organise themselves until they are strong enough to launch a decisive fight against the leaders of industry and privileged section of the community.

Contribution of Saint-Simon

Acknowledging the debt to Saint-Simon, Engels says that in Saint-Simon we find a comprehensive breadth of view, by virtue of which almost all the ideas of later socialists that are not strictly economic are found in him in embryo. If the assessment of Engels is correct, and there is no ground of it being wrong, then we should say that Saint-Simon may aptly be regarded as the harbinger of the latter day socialism. Marx has also expressed his indebtedness to Saint-Simon. This is not courtesy or formality. The indebtedness is a fact.

Saint-Simon's conception of history, which is called historical materialism, is akin to Marx's materialist interpretation of history. Saint-Simon assumed that the leaders of industry would take the leadership in transforming the society. Marx also assumed that the proletariat would play the historic role in the realm of transformation. Both the industrialists and the proletariat would be enlightened by a sublime thought. Saint-Simon and Marx admitted that the workers are exploited by capitalists and private property is the root cause of dissension and inequality. "Just as Marx treats political history as essentially the record of a struggle for influence and power between classes, some of which are growing stranger and others weaker through the operation of causes of which they are unconscious, so too does Saint-Simon" (Plamenatz—Vol. I, p. 83). In all these respects Marx comes closer to Saint-Simon than to any other of the early socialists.

The socialist movement of France and several other countries of Europe started with Saint-Simon. We do not agree with his method and mode of presentation. But the fact is that he was the icon of socialism. He considered the socialist way as the only saviour of the working class. Anikin's observation may be quoted here : "Nevertheless the influence of Saint-Simonism on the future development of socialist ideas in France and to a certain extent, other countries, was extremely great. For all the defects of their religion, the strength of Saint-Simonists lay in the fact that they had a bold and consistent programme of struggle against bourgeois society."[1]

Saint-Simon was the first man who drew our attention to the fact that economic issues control political affairs and general administration of state. This view of Saint-Simon later on built up a famous conception known as base-superstructure relation. Marx and Engels elaborated this but Saint-Simon, in an indirect way, was the originator of the concept. Saint-Simon deplored the industrial civilisation for social injustice and negative principles of private interests. The formula "From each according to his ability to each according to his needs" was taken over by the Marxist socialism from Louis Blanc, who modified Saint-Simon's doctrine on this point.

Kolakowski concludes "of all pre-Marxist doctrines, Saint-Simonism had the strongest effect in diffusing socialist ideas among the educated classes. It was chiefly due to the Saint-Simonists that a belief in socialism spread to the intellectuals of the great European countries, including German Romantics, British utilitarians, and Russian and Polish radicals."

Some critics have called Saint-Simon an over-ambitious socialist. But Gide and Rist—noted critics of economic thought—hold different opinion. They have argued that his desire to achieve equality was not the outcome of his over-ambitiousness. It was very much a down-to-earth expectation. He raised his voice against the inhuman consequences of Industrial Revolution. He did not hesitate to criticise the barons of big industries. He also challenged liberalism. He did not want its modification but its overthrow.

In Maxey's estimate Saint-Simon was not in the rank of Descartes, Bacon and Newton. It may be that he had not unparallel brilliance, intelligence and genius. But he was unquestionably the first nineteenth century thinker to envision a fully rounded science of society. We crown him with the glory of foreshadowing some of the notable ideas of modern political thought, including socialism, positivism, technocracy and internationalism (Maxey, p. 544).

Saint-Simon believed that science would rule the world and in that case universal peace would be feasible. Saint-Simon proposed a plan for international federation of politics and economics. A supranational parliament might also be created to regulate the affairs of the world. It embodied the dreams of internationalism. The scientific socialism of Marx and Engels also envisaged internationalism. Saint-Simon strongly emphasised the correlation between world peace and efficient industrial production.

As a thinker he had both plus and minus points. Needless to say that nobody is free from limitations. Naturally he cannot be an exception. Marxey's valued judgment is "though he is ticketed as a precursor of modern socialism, it is doubtful

1. Anikin—*A Science In Its Youth*, p. 351.

whether Saint-Simon should be called a socialist at all. Saint-Simon argued that there could not be real progress so long there existed private property. But he did not suggest any method of confiscating private property. Here there is a great inconsistency. Private property and socialism cannot peacefully coexist. He had no proposal of universal collective ownership of property. Pious hope or pontifical declaration cannot ensure the advent of socialism. Concrete programme, scientific outlook, well-built organisation and revolutionary zeal can make socialism a great success. Needless to say, Saint-Simon's plan lacked all these. His heart was magnanimous, objective was noble, knowledge about history and development of society was of high quality. But his suggestion for achieving socialism was impractical. He failed to study the character of the capitalists and this failure bracketed him within the utopian socialists.

ROBERT OWEN
(1771-1858)

Introductory

While Saint-Simon was spearheading his attack against capitalism in France, Robert Owen, his contemporary, was sharpening his sword in order to cut the wings of the British capitalists. In the middle of May 1771 Robert Owen was born. His parents were so poor that they could not bear nominal expenses of his education. When other boys of his age spent their time and energy in reading and playing Owen went out in search of job to earn money. At the age of eleven he was apprenticed to a businessman. The rest of his life was a record of phenomenal success in business. He then borrowed a meagre amount of money from his brother to open a shop for machinery parts required for cotton textile industry. Goddess of wealth blessed him.

At the age of twentythree he started a cotton textile factory on a partnership basis and he became its manager. This business brought for Owen both wealth and recognition. Within a short time Owen was elected the leader of the business community to which he belonged. He did not want to confine himself only in the business world. He displayed increasingly his interest in the social problems. Just then he got an opportunity. There was a cotton mill at New Lanark. He purchased the entire cotton mill as well as the village where it was situated. He started to improve the lot of the village.

Owen implemented certain welfare schemes and achieved success forthwith. This brought for him international success. In 1813 he wrote a series of essays entitled *A New View of Society.* In 1817 he was requested by a Parliamentary Committee to prepare a report on the relief of the manufacturing poor and he did it. In the report he analysed the economic and social conditions of machine production and he proposed plans to alleviate the sufferings of the poor. Owen, it is said, was a rational secularist. He did not mingle religion with politics and welfare activities. He announced his view publicly and this offended many of his fellow industrialists and politicians. They used it for political gains. Though Owen was against religion he was not against Christian ethics and morality.

Robert Owen died in 1858 at the age of 87. The students of socialist thought still remember him for two reasons. One is, even being a big capitalist his heart wept for the suffering and toiling masses of the British industrial society. For the emancipation of the working class he tried heart and soul to build up a socialist society. The other reason is he was the owner of vast amount of wealth and it is amazing that he spent the entire amount for the benefit of the working class and at the fag end of his life he became practically pennyless.

Social Programmes and Performance

Robert Owen was dumbfounded seeing the ugly, insanitary and impoverished conditions of New Lanark where there was a cotton mill which he purchased. The other mill towns were no better than New Lanark. But Owen was a man of different type. The appalling conditions of the inhabitants of New Lanark pained his soft heart. The children above six had to work from six in the morning to seven in the evening. The wages in the factory were miserably low. The low-paid wage earners were also cheated by local shopkeepers at every point. They had no education, no healthy environment. Diseases, drunkenness, degradation and debauchery were their all time companions. They were plunged from head to foot in poverty and debt. Death rate increased in astronomical proportions.

The situation was intolerable to Owen. He proceeded with strong determination to save the workers and villagers of New Lanark. Owen was a socialist both in his mind and activities. He decided to convert New Lanark into a socialist model. He had an apprehension that this small attempt may not help him to achieve his ambitious goal. But he was not worried. He believed that small is beautiful and every big project starts with the small. So he began to implement his programmes. He reduced working hours, stopped employing children under ten, introduced free primary education and relatively hygienic conditions, eliminated drunkenness and theft by persuasion and not by punishment. Owen was not a theoretical or declared socialist. But he showed that by improving the physical environment the health and mental conditions of the workers could be changed and production of the mill could be remarkably increased. This he achieved. It was a miraculous success. Many criticisms and obstructions were thrown upon him but he overcame them with stone-like determination. In 1806 an acid test came to him. Government drastically cut the import of cotton and as a consequence all the mill owners closed the mills and retrenched the workers. Robert Owen did not follow the path of the fellow-industrialists which was quite uncommon in his days. Though he closed the mill, he retained all his employees and gave them wages. We do not know any other better socialist principle than this. After the crisis was over he introduced other socialist measures, such as old-age pension.

The activities of Owen drew the attention of various sections of society as well as government. Being requested by the government he submitted the *Report to the Committee for the Relief of the Manufacturing Poor.* In this *Report* he mentioned that the immediate cause of the large scale distress among the workers was the depreciation of human labour. This was due to the introduction of mechanism into the manufacture of objects. The rapid advancement of mechanism reduced the demand for labour. Labour power came to be cheap. This made their condition more miserable. Mechanism also dominated the labourers. The capitalists were not interested in the psychological or social problems. Their main concern was profit. Impoverishment and degradation in all its forms took alarming shapes.

Owen worked hard to get his different schemes implemented, he particularly wanted to stop the employment of children in all factories. On this issue he faced stiff opposition from other manufacturers, because child labour was remunerative to them. With great difficulty he succeeded in obtaining the passage of the Factory Act of 1819, the first law in England to limit child working hours in the textile industry. This can be treated as a great success on the part of Owen. He created a public opinion in favour of the abolition of child labour and—being excessively pressurised by Owen and the people—government was forced to enact the law.

Owen then launched an attack against the established church for keeping masses in poverty and superstition. Although Owen did not pronounce it publicly that religion was opium, by action he showed that. His objective was to save the masses from the clutches of the church. We have earlier said that he was a socialist, now we see that he was also a materialist. Owen was convinced that both church and religion were squarely to be blamed for religious superstition. Church was misguiding the common people and befooling them. So long church and religion were controlling or misguiding the general public no progress was possible. Both church or religion and capitalists would continue to exploit people. Owen's assessment of church and religion was accepted by Marx.

Utopian Programmes

Owen was really a great benefactor of common people and philanthropist. He did not like to confine himself within the four walls of welfare activities. He planned to build up a new society where there would be no exploitation, no inequality and, finally, no antagonism. Owen said that millions of suffering people could not be left to their fate, because in that case the result would be disastrous. Owen thought that since mechanism was the cause of depreciation of human labour, the progress of mechanism must be stopped. But according to Owen that would be an impractical suggestion. The only practicable way open to the society to devise a plan which would provide security for the working classes against the vicissitudes of machine production.

Owen proceeded to set up cooperative villages. All the able-bodied working men shall be employed. One section of the working men shall work in industry to produce industrial goods and the other section shall be engaged in the agricultural sector. And when this scheme is fully implemented every cooperative village shall be self dependent and self-sufficient. Every cooperative village would contain about 1,000 men and 1,200 acres of cultivable land would be allotted to every village. Ownership would be common. Production would be stored in a common store house and each will draw his necessaries from that store. Each village would have a common kitchen, common dining room and dormitory. There would also be provision for worship and education. All members of the cooperative village—irrespective of sex, age, and ability—would be employed in various occupations such as farming, manufacturing and different establishments of the community. Wealth would be distributed according to ability and experience.

Every cooperative village or society would be self-sufficient in all respects. The internal administration of the copperative village will be managed by the members on cooperative basis. The *raison d' etne* of Owen was to make man completely self-dependent so that they do not fall to the prey of self-interest seeking persons. Throughout his life Owen fought for the elimination of poverty, unemployment, crime and exploitation and for that purpose he wanted to build up a communistic system of society. He was somehow convinced that private property is the chief cause of social ulcer and in order to cure it the very system of private property is to be abolished. His cooperative society was fashioned in that light.

Owen gave priority to education since he believed that only education could change the mind of man. Education would inculcate love of the community from the child's earliest years. Fellow-feeling, brotherhood and other traits of human character should be ingrained in the mind so that real community feeling can grow. For this purpose Owen wanted to set up a communist society. Education, self-consciousness and financial stability, Owen believed, would remove the social evils such as illiteracy, drunkenness, diseases, debauchery. Communist way of life can save society from exploitation—that was the firm belief of Robert Owen.

It is worthwhile to note that Owen wanted to change the mind of man and his character through the improvement of physical environment. Socialism, Owen believed, could do that. He insisted upon augmentation of wealth as well as its proper distribution. Both would be left to the management of society. Private management in production and distribution would entail corruption and all sorts of inequality. Once inequality takes final leave from society spontaneous development of personality would not be impossibility.

It was the intention of Owen to materialise the various programmes through comprehensive reforms. Owen himself believed that the workers were the real source of wealth and, if so, it was the primary duty of the industrialists to adopt measures for the improvement of the in economic condition. That is, the owners of industry must give a share of profit to the workers. By doing this the capitalists will do their own benefit. But it is unfortunate that the capitalists took no notice of this. By giving meagre wages the manufacturers put the severest assault on the purchasing power of the workers. Low purchasing power leads to the minimum consumption and this creates over-production. Owen argued to the capitalists that low level of wages was not profitable to them, rather it was the cause of their ruin. It is also a self-defeating process. They should, for their own benefit, protect the interests of the workers and refrain themselves from exploitation. It was his pious hope that noble sense and rationality would ultimately prevail upon them.

The various programmes launched by Owen proved that he was a great critic of capitalism and a socialist. He admitted that there were inconsistencies in capitalism, but these were the products of ignorance and confusion. Spread of education among the workers and dawn of rationality could function effectively in the removal of exploitation and other harmful consequences of industrialisation, violent armed struggle or revolution was unnecessary. Owen was also not eager to convince his readers that he was a believer of class struggle. He was rather afraid of it. His insistence upon class collaboration reveals his love for utopianism. He failed to realise that privileged and unprivileged would never cooperate to free the society from the curse of exploitation. Clear conception of human nature he never nurtured.

The communistic proposal of Owen was not received cordially by his countrymen, co-manufacturers and people in authority. Some exhibited lukewarm attitude to his efforts. The *Report* he submitted was also kept in abeyance. Owen was disheartened. He realised that the social and political structure of his country was not ripe for launching a comprehensive reform scheme. But Owen was a great dreamer and activist. He was fully convinced of his own potentialities. In order to translate his dreams into reality Robert Owen went to America and purchased a 30,000 acre tract at the price of 150,000 dollars in the new state of Indiana. There he started his experiments. He called the colony New Harmony. It was constructed in the model of New Lanark colony and he also intended to implement fully the communistic principles. He made every effort to make New Harmony a grand success. But all his efforts were in vain. He recruited brilliant individuals for the implementation of the project. Maxey comments, "This was his mistake. There was too much brains in the colony and not enough brawn, too many brilliant individuals and not enough plodding cooperators" (p. 518).

Discontent on theological and other issues began to brew within a short time. The whole New-Harmony was divided into different warring factions. Owen gave in to the demands. The New Harmony no longer remained a united and cooperative society. When Owen accepted the contradictory demands of conflicting groups and factions that signalled the death of the communistic society. The New Harmony started in 1824 and its end came in 1827. He wound up the project and returned to England in 1829 almost empty-handed. He spent four-fifths of his fortune behind the project of New Harmony.

Everywhere the utopian scheme of Owen met with failure. But he did not give up hope because he was optimistic. He was a great dreamer and he liked to dream. He had unbound faith on rationality and good-will of man. He believed that the oppressor and the oppressed could live together, employer would sacrifice his profit motive to widen the benefit of the employees. The collaboration and cooperation among all classes of people would be able to eliminate poverty, inequality, disease and debauchery. This was Owen's lofty idealism. His dreams and idealism were never translated into reality. As a philanthropist he was successful, but as a utopian socialist his failure knew no bounds. In spite of the series of failures history remembers him. Why? We shall discuss this in our next section, i.e., Owen's contribution to utopian socialist thought.

Contribution of Owen

Engels in his *Socialism : Scientific and Utopian* says that the new mode of production, created by Industrial Revolution, was the herding together of a homeless population in the worst quarters of the large towns, the loosening of all traditional moral bonds, of patriarchal subbordination, of family relations, overwork—especially of women and children—and complete demoralisation of working class. At this juncture, there came forward a reformer and a manufacturer. Robert Owen adopted the teaching of materialist philosophers : that main character is the product, on the one hand, of heredity, on the other, of the environment of the individual during his life-time. Needless to say that Owen supported the influence of environment. In the Industrial Revolution all other manufacturers saw the chaos and trouble and they utilised it as an opportunity of fishing in the troubled waters, but Owen saw in it the opportunity of putting into practice his favourite theory. He saw the chaos as an indication of a new era. He wanted to build up a new society out of it.

Owen was an uncompromising fighter. He fought relentlessly for the emancipation of workers from exploitation. His fight was against all the evils of industrialisation. How much sympathy he held for his men is quite evident from his gesture or behaviour meted out to them. Without depending upon what other industrialists would do Owen unilaterally adopted certain welfare and socialist measures and these incurred for him their displeasure. The untiring efforts of Owen may only be compared with those of Marx and Engels. Owen, no doubt, was a big industrialist and he had accumulated a vast amount of wealth. But he spent the entire amount for the fructification of an ideal-socialism. He did not succeed. But he was the forerunner of Marxian socialism. This is no small a contribution.

Owen was convinced that only mass education could ignite consciousness against exploitation. So he insisted upon the spread of education and he wanted to inculcate education among the children. He set up schools. The Marxian socialists on this point are not at all different from him. Education is viewed as the foundation building factor of socialism. Owen once said, "the best governed state will be that which shall possess the best national system of education."

Kolakowski, a noted interpreter of Marxian thought, makes the following observation on Owen's contribution : "Owen's doctrine initiated a new phase of the British workers' movement, in which it *ceased* to be merely an outburst of despair and became a systematic force which in the end brought about immense social changes. Moreover, his attack on capitalism and his plans for a new society contained enduring features although some of his ideas—for example, that of a labour and currency were soon discarded as they proved to be based on entirely false economic diagnoses" (p. 197).

Every social movement in England was associated with the name of Owen. Even Marx admitted the importance and contribution of Owen to the socialist movement and that is why Marx sought his help to make International Working Men's Association a success. Both Marx and Engels were profoundly influenced by Owen. When Engels was in England he contributed to Owen's *New Moral World*. In several places of *Capital*—Marx points out Owen's importance, specially his conception of social revolution. In this respect Owen occupies a higher place than Saint-Simon. After his conversion to communism Owen concentrated his attack upon the main obstacles which prevented the transformation of the bourgeois social order into a communist social order.

He was a hard-shelled materialist, and based his theories upon the idea that human character is the outcome of exterior influences, that man does not possess any innate ideas or qualities or moral sentiment or conscience and that none of these things are instilled into his mind by any kind of supernatural power. "The fact is that conscience is just as much a manufacture as cotton or any material." This observation has a far deeper significance than all the thoughts of ordinary non-historical materialists put together.[1] Owen was also pioneer in many other activities, such as labour legislation and introduction of education for the children working in factories.

In spite of all these remarkable contributions Owen remained basically utopian and his utopianism was the prime cause of his failure. His faith on class collaboration, reforms, appeal to big industrialists and other conciliatory moves as the modes of attaining socialism proved in his lifetime ineffective. Anikin says (p. 376), "Owen's system is utopian, and hence full of contradictions and inconsistencies." He spent enough resources to implement his scheme, but even that was insufficient.

Apparently Owen's utopianism was responsible for the failure of all his schemes. But we are to think the whole issue from a different perspective. Marx and Engels have claimed that their socialism is scientific. Has that socialism succeeded? No. People, government and industrialists of Owen's time were not prepared to walk on the road of socialism. Particularly the government and the capitalists were

1. *The Communist Manifesto* of Marx and Engels—D. Ryazanoff, p. 193.

against socialism. People were not prepared. Under the leadership of Lenin a "socialist" state was established in Russia. The Soviet Union disintegrated in 1991 and that brought about an end of socialism. There are few socialist states in the present day world. Question is are they in Marxian model? Many still firmly believe that socialism is not the only system that can emancipate the people from oppression. Today capitalism has radically changed and so also people's attitude. They think that emancipation from oppression may be possible through parliamentary procedure.

CHARLES FOURIER
(1772-1837)

Preliminary Remarks

The scholars of Western political thought—specially the socialist thought—are of opinion that Charles Fourier weaved the fabric of socialism or, more particularly, its utopian variety, in a grandiose scale than others and if we enter into the details we shall find that there is ample truth in this observation. He had first-hand knowledge about the French Revolution and had a thorough knowledge about the economic and other conditions of French society. This considerably helped him to form opinions and arrive at conclusions. Fourier was the son of a wealthy French merchant and all their wealth was lost in the Revolution. His father wanted to make him a businessman but he had no liking for it. He developed a keen interest in social problems and deeply studied books and journals to enrich his knowledge and ignite his enthusiasm and insight. He then started to write books and articles on various social problems which drew the attention of many educationists and well-known persons. A number of persons became his disciples and they enthusiastically disseminated his ideas.

In the early years of his life he spent his energy and efforts to earn money but good luck did not favour him. The last four decades of his life were spent in elaborating and publicising the ideal of a perfect society. Fourier frequently said that he was in great need of large amount of money to implement his scheme of new society. He began writing in 1800 and he left behind a volume of manuscripts.

Fourier was different from other utopian socialists in more than one respects. Both Saint-Simon and Owen were extremely moved by the exploitation and suffering of poor people. Surprisingly Fourier remained unmoved. Maxey writes (p. 520), "What did shock him to smoking indignation was the disorder and wastefulness of the competitive system. The exploitation of the unprivileged was too bad, but the waste of labour, materials, money, time—those were atrocious, damnable and ought to be corrected. So Fourier became an evangel of order, efficiency and economy in societal process."

Fourier had formed the belief that in the kingdom of God there always prevailed harmony and rule of law and because of this there was no anarchy. He ardently desired that in the human society the same thing must reside. Man has been created by God giving him certain instincts with the help of which he can build up a new and perfect society. These instinct or passions according to Fourier are—sight, hearing, smell, taste, touch, friendship, love, ambition, paternity, emulation, alternating, composite. In the existing society these could not be implemented, a new society was required.

Nature of Society

The twelve instincts or passions we have just now pointed out may be divided into three broad categories—five passions or senses tend to luxury. They aim at gratifying the desires of man. Four passions are affective and these make man sociable. The last three passions are distributive. Fourier believed that the evils of society are largely derived from the fact that men's natural instincts and their social environment were constantly opposed to each other. That is, there was no reconciliation or adjustment between the passions and social environment. He proposed to set up a society which would make adjustment. Before giving a picture of such a society we need to see what were the evils of society.

Society, we are told by Fourier, is both repressive and wasteful. Parents are very often strict. They want to prepare their children for the society and for that purpose restrain the passions of their wards. Children resent the attitude and behaviour of parents. This difference of attitude destroys love, affection, pleasure and respect. Fear and resentment become the dominant characteristics of every society. Normal functioning of society is adversely affected. The production of society is disorderly, because it responds to the speculation of middlemen. The middlemen, in one way or other, exploit both the producer and the consumer. In this way the normal relationship is destroyed. Fourier also observes that the producers also monopolise the production and the distribution. The consumer is helpless. The production of the commodity is determined not by the necessity of the consumer but by the profit-motive. This attitude of the producer affects the interests of the consumer and aggravates their suffering; wealth and power of the industrialists increase and, on the opposite side, the poverty and misery of workers also increase. The state hardly comes to their help. The gap between the poor and the rich widens. Waste is enormous because there are idlers, because there is inefficiency and because much is produced which is not wanted or does not satisfy" (Plamenatz, p. 105).

In all human societies there are several undesirable characteristics—or these may be called crises. These are speculation, crises in various forms. Above all, weaker sections of the population are variously exploited by the richer and powerful sections. He concludes that these evils are inevitable because of the social structure. There are few rich people and innumberable poor men. So long as the prevailing social structure remains intact these evils will continue to exist. But in order to banish them it is necessary that the entire social structure be completely overhauled. He was of opinion that the system of labour and exchange was singularly responsible. One cannot eradicate the passions or instincts of human beings. The society is to be organised in such a way as to adjust with these passions. There is is a gap which we have already pointed out. Modern civilization is contrary to the natural order as established by God. Fourier's categorical suggestion is society is to be organised in accordance with nature's order.

Plan of the Future Society

In order to free the society from numerous evils and shortcomings Fourier devised a plan and it is known as *phalanx*. It is no doubt a unique creation and constitutes the vital aspect of Fourier's utopian thought. Phalanx is a type of community each consisting of 1,000 to 1,600 members of different age, fortune and experience. In the phalanx all work will be voluntary. Every worker or member will do the work according to his choice or liking. In such a community there is no place of force or compulsion. None will be forced to do any work against his liking. Man will find his passions fully realised. In other words, Fourier's community will be the meeting point of passions and functions. The absence of discrepancy will make life pleasant.

The whole work-system of the community will be divided into several groups and there will be a group of members for each type of work. The members will decide what types of work they will do. The basis of the community is the division of labour. Fourier further suggests that the groups doing similar works will be arranged in series. A competition between the groups doing similar work is inevitable and Fourier thinks that this competition will lead to better performance. The competition is also healthy and cordial. Some workers may be interested in more than one work and the phalanx will make arrangement to allow them to be members of more than one groups. This arrangement furthers the incentive to work and also augments pleasure. Fourier expects that there will be fifty to sixty groups in the series. In some cases the number of groups might be higher.

Plamenatz says—The system aims at making the best use of the three distributive passions : the butterfly passions for variety; the composite passion for blended or multiple satisfaction; and the cabalistic passion for intrigue. These are reprobate passions in actual society, repressed and harmful, but in the phalanx they are respectable and useful. There is both cooperation and competition. The competition is not out of ill-motive. All the members of the phalanx cooperate among themselves. The work performed by members satisfy their desires and increases pleasures. Absence of compulsion makes them feel free. The arrangement leads to the betterment of community. Fourier has further stated that ill-feeling and harmful rivalry will be removed for ever. There should prevail harmony, fellow-feeling and, above all, healthy competition. This atmosphere will inspire men to work and devise new plans for betterment. Since every group is the rival of other groups there is constant scheming and ample of persuasion and manoeuvre and the passion for intrigue is satisfied.

Fourier suggests that in the *phalanx* the unpleasant jobs such as killing of animals, cleaning sewers and drains are to be performed by children since they like to play and work in the dirt. Life in the community will be both private and communal. Women will enjoy equality with men. Family life will be abolished. Children will be brought up at public expenses. In the phalanx there will be two units—agricultural and industrial. These two units will be organised in such a manner as to meet the demands of the members. People may live monogamously if they like, but love will be free.

In Fourier's *phalanx* there shall be no place of forced labour. Again, none will be idle. In capitalist society large number of men work hard to earn their daily bread and very few men—are the owners of capital—are idle. But these few men capture the almost entire profit and the toiling people are deprived of the benefit of production. In Fourier's scheme there shall be no repetition of this system. Everyone will have to do work to earn his daily bread. In the scheme of phalanx there shall be no scope of forced labour and, as a result, the work will be a potential source of pleasure. The community will provide to every member the minimum subsistence. His hope is that by force private property will not be abolished, but if the phalanx succeeds it will be ultimately unnecessary. Because, if everyone gets his necessaries from the community, none will go to take the trouble of making private property.

Production will be made on cooperative basis. Each will be paid according to his ability. A man having various experiences will earn more. Fourier assures us that this will not generate unhealthy and envious feeling.

In the perfect society there will be provision for large buildings in which the members will live together, and take their meals and leisure together. In Fourier's term it is called *Phalanstery.* This is the communal aspect of the perfect society. But there will be arrangements for privacy. Love, affection, friendship or brotherhood all will develop in the phalanstery. In the phalanx all groups are harmonious. There will also be provision for entertainment. So in all respects the community or phalanx will be an ideal one.

Phalanx will welcome all classes of persons and none will be forced to make any sacrifice. The rich will enter the phalanx with all their wealth and capital and will be given the opportunity to invest. The return or profit will be distributed among the various factors of production, but the return on capital will gradually diminish. Fourier expects that when the phalanx will be a growing concern the rich will lose all their interest in saving more and more and investing it. They will prefer a life of leisure and comfort to a life of anxiety. We have already noted that in the phalanx there will be difference of income, but that will have no significance. It will never be a cause of discord. Everyone will work and ability will be the sole criterion of reward.

Assessment of Fourier's Utopianism

James Joll in *The Anarchists* makes the following observation. Fourier's communist society "is a truly anarchist society. Fourier at no point requires the intervention of a state to regulate the relations within and between the various phalansteries. He condemns the use of force. All that is founded upon force is fragile and denotes the absence of genius" (p. 36). Joll's observation is correct because Fourier wanted to do away with the importance of any type of central or administrative system or organisation. A community without a central organisation to enforce law and control the relations among the citizens is anarchical in nature. Fourier holds a very unreal and idealistic view of human nature. It is true that the external environment moulds the character and behaviour of man. But only change of environment cannot make man good or ideal. Hobbes's depiction of human nature may not be hundred percent correct. Fourier makes no provision to deal with that character.

Because of the extravagance and naivety of perfect society Kolakowski calls him a "hopeless crank." The sexual promiscuity and gluttoning are no signs of any healthy society. Long before Fourier a Greek philosopher thought of communism of wife and children. But that was rejected by Aristotle. Such a proposal is absolutely absurd. Fourier offers that absurd proposal.

Fourier is a controversial figure of utopian socialism. Though the thought of Fourier contains originality it is not free from inconsistency and unclarity. He conceived of a compromise and adjustment between employer and employees without giving any specific plan or scheme. So we can say his view of compromise is simply a pious hope. Anikin writes (p. 356), "In depicting capitalism's crimes, he could not discover their basic cause, for he did not have a clear understanding of production relations and class structures of bourgeois society."

Both Owen and Fourier were really friends of the working class and both had genuine sympathy for them. Both of them wanted a radical change of the existing social, political and economic structure of the society. But the scheme they prepared was absolutely impractical. Owen wanted to build up a perfect society and behind this he spent all his resources and prime part of his life. This made him a pauper, but he gained nothing. Fourier's *phalanx* is out and out utopian. Fourier's scheme is suitable only for the gods and not for human beings. Only Saint-Simon had a clear conception of history and certain amount of practical knowledge. "By comparison with Saint-Simon, Charles Fourier cuts a lesser figure, though nor for originality. He was the great eccentric of the early socialist movement, the inventor of fantastic cosmology, he was also the descendant of Rousseau."

However, the loopholes and absurdities of Fourier's utopian socialism do not make it absolutely worthless. It has several bright and illuninating aspects which need clarification and emphasis. Kolakowski correctly writes, "Despite the absurdities, Fourier's critique of civilization and his ideas of a future harmonious state contain many elements that became part of the socialist tradition. His view that exploitation and poverty are due to discrepancy between social conditions and developed instruments of production appears in a more precise form in Marx's writings. Fourier pointed out the parasitic nature of trade in conditions of economic anarchy, and also the harm done by the tiny land holdings" (p. 201).

He argued that more and more introduction of machinery increased the misery and poverty of the porletariat. Fourier correctly diagnosed the exact role and consequences of private property. Fourier was against the system of employing labour and forcing him to do a job which he dislikes. In his phalanx everyone will have full freedom to choose any job according to his own choice and inclination. It is interesting to note that modern public administration emphasises upon workers' personal liking and disliking.

"His utopia was the antithesis of the monastic imaginations of the Renaissance and Enlightenment; he held that ascetism was contrary to nature and that the liberation of man signified the liberation of his passions" (Kolakowski, p. 202). In this respect Fourier's utopian socialism is different from the socialistic ides of others. He is more close to Marxian socialism than any other utopian socialists. Fourier was sure that it was impossible to change the nature of man. But the nature of society or physical environment could be easily changed and for that purpose he wanted to set up a communist society in which people could find realisation of passions. Fourier thought that if physical environment is changed that will have a positive and far-reaching impact upon the mind of people. This conception is correct. Modern behaviouralists and many others—including materialists—believe that men's nature, mind, outlook and, above all, behaviour, cannot be changed overnight. But all these can be amended by reorganising or remodelling the social system. Recently Robert Nozick in his *Anarchy, State and Utopia* makes a modest attempt to throw light on this aspect.

Extolling Fourier's contribution to the socialist thought Engels in his *Socialism : Utopian and Scientific* has said that we find in Fourier a criticism of the existing conditions of society, genuinely French and witty, but not upon that account any less than thorough. Fourier takes the bourgeoisie, their inspired prophets before the Revolution, and their interested eulogists after it, at their own words. He lays bare remorselessly the material and moral misery of the bourgeois world.

His conception of history of society is an exceptionally realistic one. Engels calls it his greatest contribution. Fourier divides the evolution of society into four different stages—savagery, barbarism, the patriarchate and civilisation. He says that civilised state has every vices practised by the barbarian society. He has cited so many illustrations.

We do not find in Fourier's analysis the realistic interpretation of capitalist system. But he never forgot to point out that capitalism was the cause of exploitation and according to him the remedy lies in setting up a communist society. Anikin has aptly pointed out—His genius consists in the fact that, basing his argument on his analysis of capitalism, he showed a number of true laws of socialist society (p. 356).

Both Marx and Engels have expressed in unequivocal language their indebtedness and also his contribution to the socialist thought. He was not the father of scientific socialism, but he sincerely attempted, and largely succeeded, to free political and economic ideas and principles from the confinement of liberalism. Fourier was not alone in this respect, but he helped the acceleration of socialist ideas and decay of liberalism. We do not agree with his views, but he was relevant in his own age.

PROUDHON
(1809-1865)

Utopian Ideas of Proudhon

In the Western political thought Pierre-Joseph Proudhon is known both as an anarchist and a utopian socialist. We shall, however, focus our attention on his socialist ideas which are classed as utopian. His character is eccentric. He wrote volumes and most of these writings have no importance or substance. Both Marx and Proudhon developed friendship for short period of time and this friendship was chiefly due to Proudhon's socialist ideas. But within a very short time schism developed between the two—one reason is Marx did not give importance to the socialist ideas of Proudhon and the other factor is Proudhon did not know German quite well. In the nineteenth century the autocratic governments of several European countries did not allow people to propagate socialist ideas and since Proudhon believed in socialism (though it was utopian) he was imprisoned several times and each time he was acquitted.

After 1848 Proudhon took an active interest in political and economic matters He studied the economic life of people and economic conditions of society. He was well-aware of the miseries and exploitation of the workers. He believed that property was nothing but theft. So he wanted to do away with the system of property. He was a great believer of reforms. Only reforms and mutual adjustment, he believed, could bring about emancipation of the workers. He had no faith in revolution which is generally used in the Marxian sense. Kolakowski says : "His plan belongs to the category of socialist utopias in so far as it is purely normative and invokes ideal of justice and equality."[1]

Proudhon was a sympathiser of the workers and poor people. He was himself poor and, therefore, his feeling for the poor was genuine. But he had no clear conception of class antagonism or the reactionary character of the bourgeois government. After the Revolution of 1848 he appealed to the republican government to implement his reforms programme. He was elected to the Constituent Assembly,

---

1. Kolakowski—*Main Currents of Marxism*, Vol. I, p. 204.

but there he could not stay long. He was arrested because of his criticism of Louis Napoleon. In 1851 there was a *coup d' etat* in France and he hoped that the Prince-President might carry out his socialist plans. But, again, his hopes could not see the light of the sun, it remained in darkness.

Proudhon believed in the inalienable rights of man. These rights are—right to freedom, right to equality, and right of individual sovereignty. These rights were prescribed by God and, therefore, could not be abrogated by any system—economic and political. But he saw that the existing economic and political systems were not helpful for the fulfilment of these inalienable rights. Inequality, competition and corruption were rampant. Workers were exploited to the point of intoleration. He blamed the existing economic system for all these evils. If all the natural rights were fully realised a natural social harmony could be effected.

Proudhon has said that property is a physical and mathematical impossibility. Here he wants to emphasise that every man will have to work to earn his bread. His income will be proportionate to his labour. Under such circumstances a man cannot get any scope to a mass property and, if anybody does it, then we must say that he has certain amount of income behind which he has no labour. Such income—or it may properly be called property—is quite unjustified and immoral. A man cannot enjoy the benefits of dividends, interests, rent etc. on the ground that he owns wealth or capital. If a man enjoys something or gets something over and above the remuneration which he receives in exchange of his labour that is immoral.

He said that the contemporary economy was based on false premise. Capital or land was the factor of production. Neither capital nor land could produce anything. To produce, he said, a piece of article, labour was essential. So the owners of capital could not claim any extra privilege. In a just economy it could not happen that goods were bought and sold in accordance with the fluctuations of supply and demand instead of their true value.[1] The guiding principle of his economic utopia is that each man should receive what he produces. The value of his labour is to be measured in hours of labour. Since a man cannot claim anything more than his labour, the system of unearned income is to be abolished. In order to eliminate the concentration of wealth and gradual pauperisation of the poor the system of unearned income or, what Proudhon calls monopoly of income, is to be done away with. We therefore, see that Proudhon linked inequality and exploitation with the property or unearned income. These ideas of Proudhon are highly plausible. Though he was to some extent an eccentric, I believe, he fully understood the real nature of a capitalist society and mounting impoverishment of the workers. In one respects he frustrates us. A worker is a factor of production, but there are also other factors and naturally a worker cannot claim the entire profit of what he has produced. This is sheer utopia.

From his analysis it further appears that Proudhon was not against property. He was against that property which was the source of inequality, monopoly and impoverishment. If all men could get to which they were entitled then, in that case, property could not be regarded as immoral. This view of Proudhon has been interpreted by many that he cannot be called a real communist. He was simply pointing out the cause of poverty and exploitation. Like Fourier and Owen he did not have any plan for setting up a communitarian society. He expected that reforms could achieve the desired results.

---

1. Kolakowski—op. cit., p. 207.

Many critics are averse to calling him a real socialist. Rather, he can be branded as a utopian socialist like Saint-Simon, Owen etc. It is observed that he had no concrete proposals for the implementation of the socialist ideas. These were simply dreams. Every proposal must be accompanied by clear and practical plans. In this field he is to us a source of lot of frustration. He had no idea of class struggle or class antagonism. Nor did he recognise it. It is, therefore, evident that he would be opposed to revolutions. He thought that a violent revolution would lead to disorder and chaos and aggravate the class relations. He did not want class hostility. Proudhon did not believe in class antagonism and for that reason he always appealed to all class of people. To him both the oppressor and the oppressed were at the same level. He believed that human nature was always against any struggle or violence. So it would be unwise to resort to violent struggle.

Proudhon had so much faith on class collaboration that he repeatedly invited the capitalists to implement his reform proposals. There was an alliance between the property owners and the machinery of the state and for that reason he did not want the state. But Proudhon in this case suffered from a glaring inconsistency. He desired that the state should play an auxiliary role. For several years he propagated class cooperation. Cooperation between the classes was the foundation of his "mutualism". Besides class cooperation endorsement of decentralisation is to be found in his thought system. By this he mainly meant decentralisation in productive saystem.

Assessment

It has already been mentioned that Proudon was both an anarchist and an utopian socialist. The consequence emerging from this is that thought suffers from inconsistencies. A conciliation between anarchism and socialism is practically an impossibility. In some respects there are pole-like differences between the two. This is the main source of drawback of Proudhon's thought.

Commenting upon Proudhon's inconsistency Kolakowski writes : "In his early writings he takes an anarchistic view of the state as an instrument of possessing classes, to be replaced by a system of free agreements among economic cooperatives. Later he came to acknowledge state power, not as the weapon of class, but as the organiser of production for the common good." Ryazanoff has revealed another aspect of his contradiction. He says : "in his early writings he criticised bourgeois society from the point of view of the French minor peasantry, whereas at the later date, in his *Philosophy of Poverty,* his criticism was made from the outlook of the petty-bourgeoise, which was oscillating between the small producers and workers. Proudhon wished to refashion bourgeois society" (p. 148). Notwithstanding the numerous drawbacks of his socialist thought and programmes we humbly submit that in those days of nineteenth century to hold and propagate socialist ideas was a sort of "crime" and Proudhon committed that "crime". Here lies his credit. It is correct that his socialist ideas were not always straight-forward.

Weitling's Utopian Thought

Wilhelm Weitling (1808-1871) was a contemporary of Marx and propagated some utopian thoughts, but he was not a forerunner of Marx. Ryozanoff observes that Weitling was one of the most notable communists before Marx and Engels. He was a tailor by trade. His childhood passed through extreme poverty. He travelled to several countries as an itinerant tailor.

Weitling criticised the existing social order in the light of human passions. He recommended primitive evangelical communism. The existing economic and political system created a situation antagonistic to human freedom. Weitling claimed that since he was a very poor man he could feel the pulse of the proletariat. God has created all men equal. The resources of nature are to be divided among all. Inequality, exploitation and tyranny are man-made and against the wishes of God. We can in this background say that Weitling was a Christian communist. Weitling mixed socialism with religion and this in the characteristic feature of his socialism. But Marx was against this mixture. According to Marx, socialism is a materialist idea and religion or God is other-worldly concept and, hence, the amalgamation of the two are fully unjustified.

According to Weitling there are mainly two classes in every society—poor and rich. By virtue of greater power and position the rich people control the society in their favour. They are selfish and acquisitive. Poor men are exploited in every sphere of their life. The wealthy persons pass through luxury. He did not blame machine for the exploitation and worsening conditions of the proletariat. It is the misuse of machine that is responsible. Increasing use of machine is the indicator of progress. With the help of machine and other improved techniques the capitalists produce greater amount of wealth. The greater part of this goes to the pocket of industrialists or rich people. The resultant effect is gross inequality.

When the wealth is held in common through the communisation of ownership all sorts of inequality will disappear. In constructing his plan of a future society, he gave a leading position to the representatives of applied sciences. He considered that the best way of establishing the new social order would be to bring the extant social disorder to such a pass that the patience of the people would be exhausted. He could not reconcile himself to the notion of a transitional period during which the bourgeoisie would functions as the rulling class.

Etienne Cabet

Etienne Cabet (1788-1856) was another non-revolutionary utopian socialist who wanted to set up a communist society within the capitalist order. By profession, Cabet was a lawyer and participated in the revolution of 1830. His best-known work *Voyage en Icarie* was published from England where he stayed temporarily to escape prosecution. The publication of the book caused stir both in England and France.

At the beginning of 1849 Cabet sailed for America and settled there for some years to build up a communist society which he called New Jerusalem. His communism was also based on Christianity. He rejected violence or revolution as technique of establishing a communist society. His belief was that violence was against Christianity. There is a common point among all the utopian socialists. All of them believed in the class-collaboration and attainment of socialism through appeal. Cabet or Weitling are no exceptions.

Cabet first of all appealed to the bourgeois class to eschew their profit motive and to make considerable concessions for the alleviation of the workers' miseries. But when his appeal could not produce any results he advised the workers to collaborate with the capitalists. His hope was that this would be able to mitigate the sufferings. This again failed. He also appealed to the Communist Workers' Educational Society. But this Society did not take his appeal seriously. Some members of the society opposed his scheme.

What was the scheme of Cabet? Kolakowski says, "Cabet's *Icarie* is an egalitarian community with some totalitarian features, like many utopias of the Renaissance and Enlightenment" (p. 213). Like many other utopian thinkers he held the view that it is the maldistribution of property or wealth produced in industry which is fully responsible for all sorts of evil—especially exploitation of workers and unequal distribution of wealth. This he calls ulcer and in order to free the society from this ulcer it is essential that the system of private property is to be done away with. In his scheme of egalitarian community there is no place of monetary system. Society is the owner of all resources and all commodities are produced, under the full authority of the whole society. In this scheme no particular section of the population will have control. Naturally everyone must have a legitimate share in the produce. Every ablebodied individual must work according to his ability and then he will claim a share of the revenue behind which he has invested his labour. The share in revenue must be proportionate to his needs. All the socialists of the first half of nineteenth century held the same view. The community must see that all the members eat the same food, wear the same dress and live in the same type of building. The purpose of Cabet was to bring about a uniformity in the living conditions of all members of the egalitarian community. That is why it is also called totalitarian society.

There is a difference between Cabet and Babeuf as regards revolution. The latter was a revolutionary and favoured conspiratorial techniques to achieve socialist goals. But Cabet did not agree with him. In Cabet's political scheme we find that people as a whole is sovereign. It elects administrators to rule the territory for a very limited period. The administrators will look after both administration and production. Cabet does not envisage any political party or club.

Cabet has added a new point or aspect of socialist thought in his analysis. In his opinion the capitalists are oppressors no doubt. But for this they are not fully responsible. The defective education and other drawbacks have forced or encouraged them to be oppressors. We think that Cabet is partially right. The society makes some people oppressors. Again, these people have reorganised society to help in all sorts of oppression. He has also the workers to cooperate with the capitalists. He suggests the education system is to be reformed to meet the requirements of the larger section of the society. His excessive reliance on reforms differentiates him from revolutionaries. Like Proudhon he advocates gradualism. "As a widely read writer in a popular style he did much to spread communist ideals, he had no influence whatever on Marx" (Kolakowski, p. 214).

Louis-Auguste Blanqui (1805-1881)

Louis-August Blanqui was the son of a Girondin. He studied law and medicine in Paris. While a student he came in close touch with various socialist doctrines and studied them. He also participated in the July Revolution. In the history of utopian socialism or socialist thought the name of Blanqui is remembered not because he was the originator of any particular theory or principles. He was the sincere adherent of Babouvism. He always indulged in revolutionary zeal and liked conspiratorial activities.

In the thirties of the nineteenth century Blanqui organised several clandestine societies to achieve socialist goals. He was imprisoned for his so-called subversive activities. In the trial room he did not defend himself but, on the contrary, he accused the existing system. Blanqui launched an unsuccessful revolt against the French monarchy in 1839. He was sentenced to death. But the Revolution of 1848 liberated him. He then became the leader of the working class. From 1871 to 1879 he was in jail. When in 1879 he was released, he again jumped upon revolutionary activities.

Blanqui was not a writer and he did not make any attempt to establish himself as a writer. He was mainly a propagandist. He came under the influence of Enlightenment. It is said that Blanqui was the originator of the idea of "dictatorship of proletariat", though not the phrase. He criticised the activities of capitalism and its mode of production. But all these were stereotyped. "He shared the view that inequality and exploitation occur because goods are not exchanged at their true value as determined by labour orient; as to the future communist society...His chief role in the history of socialist movement is that he inculcated the importance of revolutionary organisation and helped to improve the technique of conspiracy." The term "Blanquism" in socialist parlance came to mean much the same as revolutionary voluntarism (Kolakowski, p. 215).

From the above analysis it appears that Blanqui was an agitator organiser. He did appeal to the working class and manufacturers for class collaboration. He ceaselessly fought against the oppressor. He never brought the oppressors and oppressed to the same level. He believed that conspiratorial activities could succeed in bringing about socialism.

LOUIS BLANCE
(1811-1882)

Louis Blanc was a prominent nineteenth century scholar, agitator and, above all, a socialist. He had great interest in socialist philosophy and principles. He was contemporary of Marx and Engels. He wrote a number of books and large number of articles. The most important of his books is *L' organisation du travail*. His another important work is *Le Socialism*. It was published in 1848, the year of the *Communist Manifesto's* publication.

In the socialist ideas of Blanqui and Blanc we find the combination of Babouvism and Saint-Simonism. Babeuf was the originator of revolutionary and conspiratorial tactics for achieving socialist goals. Blanqui derived his inspiration from Babeuf. Whereas Blanc followed the path of Saint-Simon who thought that exploitation and inequality could be eliminated through the implementation of reforms.

If we go through the revolutionary activities and principles we shall find lot of truth in the assessment of Kolakowski. He writes : "His classic work *L' Organisation du travail* argued that revolution was inevitable, but by this he meant radical social reform and not violent political change... Blanc set out to be a practical reformer and to indicate what steps might be taken on the basis of the existing state of affairs" (p. 178). Louis Blanc was a practical man. He did not believe in impractical or impossible plans and proposals. He suggested that the state should take immediate steps to stop unbridled competition among the capitalists. He never suggested the abolition of private enterprise by violent means. Competition with socialist ways will ensure their extinction.

To give a job to each unemployed person was of urgent necessity. Unemployment, poverty and exploitation had explosive power. The natural order of the state could be destroyed at any moment if all these three evils were not eradicated with proper method. Crime, inequality, disease, degradation, debauchery—all are the after-effects of the above evils. The competition among the manufacturers leads to all these harmful consequences. The management of state property should be placed under the authority of all people. The state with its accumulated experience and knowledge will help its subjects in the conduct of economic affairs.

The ultimate result of revolution is negative. The defeat of the revolutionaries is followed by repressive measures. It (revolution) invites pointless and ruthless slaughter. He has said that all these are not concocted stories. In can be supported by illustrations drawn from different revolutions. Revolution as a guarantor of socialism is quite unreliable. It is, therefore, better to rely upon the proposals of Saint-Simon, Robert Owen and Charles Fourier.

Everything will come under the aegis of public property. Industries will be set up on national loan. Remuneration of the workers will be determined by their productivity. Yes, that will lead to a great enhancement of wages. Poverty and inequality will cease to be the characteristic features of society. Kolakowski writes (p. 178) : "No more competition, no more crises, no more so-called over-population; technical progress, instead of harming workers' interests would lessen the weight of toil and shorten the working day. Free compulsory education would bring benefits to all. Wage rates would have to be differentiated for some time to come. The administrative hierarchy would be elective, and the units of production would enjoy autonomy. The right to work would be universally recognised as the basic principle of social organisation."

In the vast field of utopian socialism Blanc is comparatively a less-known figure, but his ideas are rich in contents. He did not travel in the imaginary world. He is called a utopian thinker but compared to other utopians he is less utopian. He was a practical socialist thinker. He knew quite well what was possible and what was not possible. Like Fabian Socialists he laid faith on reformism, gradualism and parliamentary practices. Perhaps because of this Kolakowski rightly maintains (p. 179) that "Blanc may justly be considered one of the chief precursors of the welfare state. He believed that it was possible, without violence or mass expropriation, to carry out peaceful economic reforms within a system of political and industrial democracy which would eliminate poverty and harmful competition and would gradually lead to social equality and the socialisation of the means of production." Here lies the real credit of Blanc. He is less-known but his ideas are rich and well-known. In today's world Louis Blanc is more relevant because we are inclined to welfare principles.

General Evaluation

We have so far discussed the ideas of the socialist thinkers preceding Marx and Engels. It is now high time to make a general assessment of the invariegated thoughts. But while doing this we must adopt utmost caution. Because, in the light of modern age, it is very easy to criticise them ruthlessly or we can simply deny their importance. But if we adopt that approach, we shall no doubt inflict injustice on them. The social, political and religious *milieu* is to be considered duly. The early socialists were not highly intellectual and talented persons, but they possessed impulses. Their sympathy for downtrodden persons was of high mark. If we extol Marx and Engels for their feelings and activities for the working class, we must do the same for the early socialists.

Marx and Engels have criticised their predecessors form several standpoints. They have also admitted their contribution. "The utopians' mode of thought has for a long time governed the socialist ideas of the nineteenth century, and still governs some of them. Until very recently all French and English socialists did homage to it. The early German Communism, including that of Weitling, was one of the same school. To all these socialism is the expression of absolute truth, reason and justice and has only to be discovered to conquer all the world by virtue of its own power."[1]

It may frankly be said that Marxian socialism descends from the socialist doctrines held by Marx's predecessors. Lenin's frank admission is in the direction to that point. "But early socialism" said Lenin in his *Three Sources* and *Three Component Parts of Marxism* "was utopian socialism". It criticised capitalist society, it condemned and damned it, it dreamed of its destruction, it indulged in fancies of a better order and endeavoured to convince the rich of immorality of exploitation. The idea of socialist thought was first ingrained by the earlier socialists in the mind of the people. They propagated the evils of capitalist system of production. They unequivocally noted that capitalism was the prime cause of corruption, inequality and all other evils.

We can safely say that of all the early socialists or utopian socialists Saint-Simon was the only socialist thinker who viewed socialism from a scientific and materialist point of view and in this respect he is compared with Marx. Marx has also highly appreciated him. The defect with Saint-Simon is he did not give us a complete programme and blue-print of a socialist society. Again, there is no denial of the fact that he had heartful sympathy for the downtrodden section of capitalist society. He had not the extraordinary genius of Marx but his sympathy for the poor may be compared with anybody's sympathy.

The utopian and other socialists were not hopeful of a revolution's success. Only Babeuf and Blanqui thought of revolution and conspiracy. But even Marx and Engels did not get the opportunity to see the success of revolution. It was Lenin who translated the hopes and doctrines of Marx and Engels into reality. Our humble submission in this respect is that the socio-politico-economic environment was not ripe for an armed struggle or revolution. There were contradictions but those did not reach the apex point when Saint-Simon, Fourier, Owen, Blanc or Blanqui or scores of other socialists were writing or agitating. Babeuf and Blanqui had to swallow the dire consequences for revolutionary and conspiratorial activities.

The thought of early or utopian socialists was circumscribed by historical conditions. They could not deny their influence, because it was not possible for them. Anikin aptly observes "utopian socialism, by virtue of historical conditions in which it emerged, could not rid itself of petty bourgeois illusions...all attempts to prescribe a certain method of action and behaviour of people of future and to regulate their life in detail are doomed to failure." We may not agree with them, but we must say that the early socialists were largely aware of the practical situation. Their dream of the future society was utopian. But their understanding of society and the practicability or impracticability of anything was realistic. Babeuf's revolution could not get the support of majority.

The foundation of socialism is reason and justice and that was fully acknowledged by the early socialists. The ulcerous aspect of capitalism is exploitation. The

1. MESW—II, p. 127.

raison d' etre of capitalists is to maximise the profit and this deprives the workers of their legitimate share of wealth. The socialist predecessors of Marx thought that it was quite unjust and unreasonable. Justice and reason demand that everyone must get his due share. Maurice Cornforth in his noted work highly speaks of this attitude. He says : "The utopians criticised the capitalist order of society as unreasonable and unjust. For them socialism was based on reason and justice...They contributed the first exposure and condemnation of capitalism and the first vision of socialism...But this vision was spun out of the heads of reformers" (*Dialectical Materialism,* p. 137). Their vision was correct but their path was wrong. It may reasonably be observed that the methods of early socialists could not ensure the attainment of socialism but their diagnosis of a capitalist society or the causes of the miseries of the large section of society were correct. Their sympathy for the poor is beyond question. Particularly Owen's love for the common people impresses us.

Admitting the contribution of early socialists Plamenatz has expressed his views in the following language : "The early socialists never lost sight of the goal which made the journey worth taking; it was never beyond their horizon. The world since their time has become even more complicated, with even greater concentrations of power than they knew, and so their fears are more than ever our fears. And we still, in the West, share their aspirations. We want the poor to live more abundantly, we want equality of opportunity, we want security and independence. Though we have abandoned all hope that state will grow weaker and disappear, we seek to make it our servant, rather then our master...we are, in some respect, petit bourgeois, we share some of the fears and some of the aspirations of the early socialists" (*Man and Society,* Vol. II, p. 127).

The early socialists were not impressed by the principles of ideas of *laissez-faire* principles. They firmly believed that the non-intervention of the state was no solution to the deep-rooted maladies of capitalism. Rather, the state has something to do. This was the message of the utopian socialists. Deliberate intervention with definite motive can make the purpose of the political process fruitful and welfare-oriented. Because of the automatic nature of social and political process of capitalist system the evils have cropped up. In order to free the society from all the evils created by capitalism the automaticity is to be abandoned. The early socialist, strongly argued for that abandonment. Like the anarchists they did agitate for the destruction of state but they moved for the curtailment of its absolute power. The state can never be our master, it should be our servant. It must work within the ambit of planning. The consciousness, deliberateness and planning have important parts to play. This was emphasised by the early socialists.

The early socialists, writes Plamenatz (p. 125), are not to be reckoned among the most profound or subtle or many-sided or lucid of social theorists. Neverthless, taken collectively, the early socialists are intellectually rich. They are also important. In the field of social theory it is they who, with Rousseau and Hegel, take us from the eighteenth to the nineteenth century.

Marxism and Utopian Socialism

Plamenatz says that most of the ideas that go to make up the social theory of Marx and Engels are already present somewhere or other in the early socialists' works. The early socialists anticipated several aspects of Marxian socialism. The early socialists on the one hand and Marx and Engels on the other hand have held the view that without changing the relations of productions and relations of property a radical change of society is not possible. Both Saint-Simon and Marx have interpreted the evolution of society almost in the same light. We can say, Marx is indebted to Saint-Simon for the materialist interpretation of history. Saint-Simon started from the primitive society. Marx also did the same thing. Like early socialists Marx holds the view that the overall progress of society is due to technological progress, although the technology has been misused by the capitalists for the fulfilment of their narrow and sectarian economic purposes. For that deliberate misuse technology cannot be overthrown. Rather, it is to be employed for common benefit.

Both early socialists and Marx thought that the capitalist system of production was singularly responsible for the miseries of the working class. Both also concluded that there were contradiction in the capitalist system and because of these contradictions the capitalist system would collapse—the vacuum would be filled up by the socialist system. However, as regards the collapse of capitalism and advent of socialism there are differences of opinion. The advocates of capitalist system argue that in capitalism there is a self-regulatory system or mechanism which would save it from crises. This controversy created a lot of heat and a schism grew among the socialists or Marxists. Later on Gramsci said that the civil society saved capitalist system from many crises.

Resemblance between them is to be found on another point. The socialist predecessors of Marx resented the amount of wage paid to the workers because it was quite insufficient for comfortable living. It was termed by them survival wage. Marx also has strongly criticised this minimum wage system. The workers cannot get any opportunity to raise their living standard. A large portion of the commodities manufactured by the capitalists remained unsold and because of that reason capitalism suffers from frequent overproduction. Anarchism comes to be the dominant feature of capitalism. So all socialists—utopian and scientific—came to the conclusion that private ownership of the means of production leads to poverty, unemployment and inequality. So this system is to be abolished at first.

As to the nature of future society, the early socialists and Marx share views. In the future society—which will be socialist—there shall be no system of private ownership and, hence, private property. All the early socialists agree on this point. Marx also accepts the proposal of the abolition of private ownership. Marx and his predecessors have endorsed the importance of planning in building up of future society. The Fabian socialists of the eighties of the nineteenth century also talked about planning. But there were differences between Marxian planning and Fabians' planning. The early socialists also thought of planning but that was absolutely of different type.

In the future society envisaged by Marx and his predecessors all able-bodied individuals will have the right to work and their remuneration will be based on their labour. The right to work and proportionate remuneration are really revolutionary concepts. For the removal of inequality and eradication of unemployment and exploitation the right to work and right to proportionate remuneration are to be recognised and implemented. These rights are also essential for the abolition of class distinctions, town and country differences.

Both early socialists and Marx have insisted upon the importance and spread of education. The emancipation of workers is possible only if they are ready to make sincere and concerted efforts. The spread of education in its proper form can enlighten the mind and outlook of workers. They must understand their position and must know the way out. Without education workers cannot raise themselves to the level of consciousness. Marx and Engels have repeatedly insisted upon indoctrinating the workers in order to raise their mental upliftment and to fit them for revolution.

The capitalist system is generally called a system of exploitation. It not only exploits the workers by not giving their due share, it simultaneously exploits the women. Both the early socialists and Marx were conscious of this heinous act and they wanted a way out from this situation. Early socialists and Marx have argued for the equal wage for equal work. The early socialists also have argued for the abolition of child labour and lessening of working hours. Particularly, we find Robert Owen take steps in this direction. In the ideal society the political power is to be replaced by economic administration. Exploitation of man by man or rule of one over another is to be stopped. To sum up—both the early socialists and Marx thought and planned of an ideal state where there would not be a place of animosity among various sections of people, no exploitation, no misery and nothing else. In a sense the future society, that is, a socialist society, will be ideal in all respects and aspects. We believe that it is utopian. Both early socialists and Marx were utopians.

The similarities between early socialists and Marx are quite impressive. But behind these similarities there are so many differences which are more impressive. We shall now discuss them. The utopians have imagined of a society which will have equality, abolition of private property, no exploitation, no poverty. All these are ambitious economic goals. But, according to them, these are to be attained without changing the political system. By appealing to the existing political authority and capitalists and adopting reforms all these economic objectives can be achieved. On this point Marx and Engels are at variance. First of all, the political structure is to be changed. In a bourgeois set-up, workers cannot improve their economic lot. Moreover, the state is the instrument of exploitation. So it would be the first task of the proletariat to capture state power.

Kolakowski has drawn our attention to another difference. The starting point of utopians reflections is poverty, which they are bent on relieving. But Marx enters into greater detail and depth. The poverty of the proletariat is not of prime importance. His starting point is dehumanisation. Let us quote Kolakowski..."the fact that individuals are alienated from the in own labour and its material, spiritual and social consequences in the forms of goods, ideas and political institution, and not only from these, but also, from their fellow beings and ultimately from themselves. The germ of socialism in capitalist society consists in the working class's awareness of dehumanisation, not of poverty" (p. 222).

The recognition and emphasis on dehumanisation is the most important aspect of Marxian philosophy. He believes that the capitalists are fully conscious of their profit, vital role in the productive system and their ability to control economy. So they will not voluntarily surrender their position and privileges. To resort to persuasion and peaceful means is sheer nonsense. According to early socialists, reforms and peaceful means are the best way to achieve socialism. Contradicting them, Marx asserts that revolution, which is a political action, is the only way to achieve socialism. Again, revolution is not possible without consciousness. Hence the consciousness of the capitalists can be fought by the consciousness of the workers. "Free human action cannot bring about a radical change of conditions if it is only a question of ideal and an attempt to reform society from outside it is constructive only when it proceeds from the society's awareness of itself as a dehumanised society and this awareness can only arise in the working class which experiences the acme of dehumanisation" (Kolakowski, p. 223).

Utopian Socialists' Attitude to Religion and Nationalism

Our brief survey of the various aspects of early socialists clearly reveals that their chief concerns were sorrows, sufferings and growing impoverishment of the working class. The medieval period and its thinkers consciously or unconsciously thought of religion of people and from their attitude to religion we come to know that religion was, in fact, a sort of determiner of political and other affairs or factors. The early socialists did not give much importance to religion and this may be due to the fact that they consciously neglected this aspect of human behaviour. People of post-Industrial Revolution had developed a materialist outlook and naturally they had less interest in religion. However, the utopians thought of religion and some expressed sporadic views above religion.

Robert Owen and Proudhon were extremely hostile to religion. It is asserted that Owen's mind was rational and enlightened like many others of the eighteenth century. He says that while men's consciousness and rationality did not develop adequately and were ignorant of the social phenomena, they were great believers of religion. Church and religious institutions played a very positive roll in building up faith in religion is general and Christianity in particular. Owen blamed church for people's attitude to religion and its evils in private and social life. The growth of science and education created a positive impact upon the mind of men and they were persuaded to believe that only environment could build up human character. "The church had taught that man is responsible for his own actions and can justly be blamed and punished for the harm he does. If was this doctrine that Owen believed to be the most pernicious of errors" (Plamenatz : *Man and Society,* Vol. II, p. 112).

Owen has also said that churches were diverting men's attention from real causes and preventing them from doing beneficial activities. This was responsible for the tardy progress of society during the medieval period. The bad and pernicious teachings of church, Owen says, forced men not to take any initiative in development. This type of attitude of Owen is quite expected from a person like Owen who was a great sympathiser to common people's woes and problems. He was very much materialist-minded.

This is an interesting aspect of Owen's political thought; like medieval thinkers he did not combine religion and politics. Even like Machiavelli he did not make any attempt for the separation between the two. He simply denounced religion and did not recognise its importance in the material world. Marx and Engels have said that Owen had developed a scientific teaching of materialism and real humanism. All these led to the logical basis of communism. We, therefore, conclude that Owen's attitude to religion was quite scientific and relevant to his political philosophy—socialism.

Plamenatz has observed that Proudhon too was quite apathetic to religion. But he is not sure whether this was his belief. In the opinion of Proudhon, in the early stages of social progress and evolution, man's consciousness and rationalism did not adequately develop and, in fact, they were ignorant of many happenings of society that led them to lay their faith on religion and other supernatural concepts. But at this developed stage of evolution and social progress religion has hardly any place.

But, like Owen, Proudhon did not blame religion for various social evils. Proudhon admitted that in that past religion had good effects. Being influenced by religion, people behaved well and brought about unity among sections of society. This was due to the fact that they were ignorant : "Perhaps he believed that while organised force was still necessary to maintain social discipline, religion provided supplementary sanctions. Perhaps he believed that at a time when men were still too ignorant to know how to remove the social causes of their wretchedness, it was good that they should have religion to comfort them" (Plamenatz, p. 113). But in the higher stage of social progress men do not require religion. It is an obstacle to social progress. Religion is responsible for the loss of self-confidence. Because of religion man failed to realise his dignity.

There is a difference between Owen and Proudhon so far as attitude to religion is concerned. While Owen blamed church, Proudhon blamed man. "He accuses man for taking refuge in God to escape his worldly responsibilities" (Plamenatz, op cit., p. 113). Here we witness a contradiction in Proudhon's thought. If men were ignorant how could they stand against religion? He should have realised that men were overpowered by the church in many affairs. In this respect Owen is more logical than Proudhon.

Saint-Simon stands apart from both Owen and Proudhon. He is of opinion that every society requires certain beliefs and religious principles which guide people in their day-to-day life. Without such beliefs and principles people will face numerous problems. According to Saint-Simon, theology and morality are interconnected. For the unity of the state, religion is also necessary. In the Middle Ages religion played a very constructive part. But Saint-Simon was conscious of the excesses of religion in those days. He was against the imposition of religious beliefs upon any person. For this reason he did not like the continuation of medieval system of religious practice. He has said that progress of science and other practical subjects has been a great cause of the decline of religion. During the later years of his life Saint-Simon observed the growth of selfishness in the minds of men and he was in dilemma whether the medieval practice of religion could be revived. He, however, came out of it and concluded that selfishness and egoism could be fought by enlightening the minds of men through the spread of liberal and scientific education. He thought of a compromise between religion and science.

Saint-Simon has said that people in the medieval period inclined to religion for comfort and peace. Now it is the duty of science and industrial development to provide this and if they succeed that will ensure the decline of medieval type of religion. It is interesting to note that Saint-Simon's ideas about religion constitute the important part of his main political philosophy. The growth of capitalism and rise in the inequality of distribution of wealth created frustration in the mind of the majority and these people were inclined to religion for solace. In a roundabout way he suggested that the state should shoulder the responsibility of balanced development of society—which will create an apathy in the minds of people towards religion. Plamenatz maintains that Saint-Simon's idea about religion is not fully consistent (p. 115).

The utopian socialists did not elaborate their ideas about nationalism. But a thorough study of their writings reveals that they had certain amount of conception on this subject. The three prominent utopian socialists were Saint-Simon (1760–1825), Robert Owen (1771–1858) and Charles Fourier (1772–1837). Needless to say that the utopian socialists had the opportunity to experience the development as well as evils of Industrial Revolution. When Charles Fourier died, the age of the Industrial Revolution was more than 75 years and naturally by that age the Revolution attained certain amount of maturity.

It has been pointed out by some that nationalism travelled alongwith Industrial Revolution. The industrialists sailed to far and wide areas to find out the markets for their products. It is interesting to note that they carried their language, religion, culture etc. along with the commodities. They sold the commodities in the markets and propagated their religion among the people of far-flung areas. They also made attempts to establish the superiority of their religion, culture, language etc. This is the characteristic feature of post-Industrial European societies. It was the belief of Saint-Simon that the growth of industry was making the nation states more and more dependent upon each other. The industrialists for the sale of the excess product went out in search of markets in the far-flung areas of the globe.

Nationalism made way for one type of cosmopolitanism. The geographical barriers were obliterated. There was hardly any place of militant or narrow nationalism in the wake of rapid industrialisation. Class divisions and distinctions were also on the decline. "The industrial class had interests transcending national barriers" (Plamenatz, p. 121). Saint-Simon believed that only an international order could bring about peace. "Saint-Simon believed that governments, constituted as they were in his day, were moved by ambitions surviving from an earlier type of society. These ambitions were both dangerous and absurd in an industrial age" (p. 122).

So, for an industrial age, a new outlook is necessary for an international order.

28 MARXISM

What is Marxism?

During his lifetime (1818-1883) Marx himself was not at all acquainted with the word Marxism. After his death Engels and his adherents circulated the term and since then we use the word Marxism. The interesting fact is that he once said, "all I know is that I am not a Marxist." But one cannot infer from this that Marx rejected the main tenets of his doctrine. The interpreters of Marxism say that Marx never claimed that he had presented a clear and correct view about the social political and economic conditions of the world. He studied the social, economic and political conditions of the various countries and specially the capitalist states of the world and on the basis of his study and investigation he drew certain conclusions. Behind every conclusion there are facts. Of course he has interpreted the facts and social-political-economic conditions. In general terms Marxism is the world view of social, economic and political conditions. He has interpreted the facts he collected in the background of the particular idea or thought or what may be called philosophy. This we call Marxism. So we quote Plekhanov : Marxism is a whole world view and this view has been explained by a method or principle which is called dialectical materialism.

Marx explained and interpreted the political economy of the entire capitalist world and arrived at the conclusion that the economically powerful class which is capitalist exploits the entire society for its own benefits. He had not only exposed the naked character of exploitation, but also pointed out vehement protest against this exploitation. The proletariat class is the victim of exploitation and naturally this class started to protest and the method of protest is revolutionary. Hence Marxism includes nature or various aspects of capitalism and revolutionary protest against it. He explained the nature of capitalist society in details and reactions against it. Marx explained nature of capitalist society consciously and those who protested against it, they did it quite consciously. Marx explained capitalism with the help of facts contained in history. He never resorted to imagination and for this reason Marxist method is called materialist method as well as dialectical method. So Marxism is interpretation of history or bourgeois society by way of dialectical materialism.

Marxism consists of three elements. First is a dialectical philosophy borrowed from Hegel but transformed into dialectical materialism, from which, in turn, historical materialism derives. In the second place Marxism is a system of political economy. It consists of labour theory of value and theory of surplus value. Marx drew his conclusions from these two concepts. The labour theory of value was first formulated by Locke. Finally, Marxism is a theory of state and revolution. Generally, Marxism includes all these three elements. Marxism is, therefore, a composite social, political and economic picture of bourgeois society viewed through dialectical materialism.

Karl Korsch (1886–1961) a German Marxist, has redefined Marxism in an essay published in 1935. The essay is entitled *"Why I am a Marxist"*. According to Korsch there are few important features of Marxism :

1. All the tenets of Marxism are particular and not general. It has not built up any general theory which is applicable in all places. Marx's concept of "base" and "superstructure is a real concept, but its application differs from place to place. The only statements that are valid are particular descriptions of particular phenomena at a given stage of history" (Kolakowsky, p. 1044).
2. Marxism is not science or philosophy. It is simply a critical and practical analysis of existing society. Naturally it can be called a praxis. Marxism is based on exact and verifiable knowledge. It can be empirically tested or verified. Hence it is an empirical doctrine.
3. The central subject of Marxism is capitalist society. Marx scanned almost all the important aspects of capitalist society by applying dialectical materialism.
4. Its chief aim is not simply to analyse the capitalist society, but to change it. Marx has said that the philosophers have interpreted the world, but the real task is to change the world or society.

In the Third World countries Marxism means a guide to national liberation movement. Up to the end of the Second World War, Marxism was generally confined within anti-capitalist and anti-exploitation thought. But during the fifties and sixties of the last century almost whole of Asia and Africa was plunged in anti-imperialist struggle and the leaders of the liberation movement were inspired by Marxism. In several cases Marxism was synonymous with anti-imperialism and anti-colonialism. In the light of Marxism (to some extent orthodox Marxism) colonial and imperial questions were being interpreted and this considerably enhanced the scope of meaning and definition of Marxism. Particularly Lenin's *National and Colonial Questions* was drafted in the light of Marxism. The ill-designs and conspiracy of imperialist powers were not only interpreted in the background of Marxism, but Marxism was treated as a powerful weapon to fight imperialist powers. In this way the purview of Marxism has increased perceptibly.

Fundamental Principles of Marxism

It has been asserted that Marx in all his works followed certain fundamental principles and Kolakowsky puts it more categorically in the following words. There are certain "fundamental principles of Marx's theory, from which he never departed. The whole of his work, down to the last page of *Capital*, was a confirmation and elaboration of these ideas" (p. 149). Let us briefly state (following Kolakowski) these fundamental principles :

1. Both Hegel and Marx have dealt with a basic question—How is man to be reconciled with himself and with the world? Hegel was of opinion that mind of man passes through history and finally comes to realise what is the world.

This realisation is truth. Hegel also speaks of Spirit and man understands it through his realisation of the world. But Marx did not support the contention of Hegel. The opposite view of Hegel was first formulated by Feuerbach and Marx borrowed it from him. According to Marx man is not concerned with Absolute Idea or Spirit but with the stark reality. This he tries to understand and explain in the background of his own life. He always interprets the world around him.

2. Both Hegel and Marx thought that man was the product of self-knowledge and he goes on reconciling with the world. But to Hegel the concept of self-knowledge is associated with Spirit or Absolute Idea. Marx has rejected it and has laid down the famous doctrine of alienation. That is, he tries to understand himself or the world around him through the alienation. The theory of alienation is the product of the alienated labour. In fact, alienation occupies a very important place in Marx's theory.
3. In capitalist economy there is a division of labour which means that a labour produces a single or small part of an article. The capitalist system has introduced this division of labour to have better results. But its harmful consequence is with the passing away of time man is gradually alienated from the whole production system and finally the society. He is ultimately converted into a machine. The division of labour no doubt helps the progress of industry of capitalist society. But man is the victim of its harmful effects. Again, this alienation is responsible for dehumanisation. According to Marx this dehumanisation is the greatest evil of capitalist society.
4. The general meaning of alienation is that it is the "subjugation of man by his own work, which have assumed the guise of independent things." The entire economic process including production and distribution is beyond the control of workers. They work just like machine. In other words, the workers are alienated from the mainstream of productive process and from here the dehumanisation starts. Hence alienation and dehumanisation are closely related and the entire capitalist system is absolutely responsible for this.
5. In the opinion of Marx, since alienation is the greatest evil of capitalist system the workers must be freed from this evil. But he has warned us by saying that there is no scope of freeing individuals from the curse of alienation because it is an integral part of the capitalist system. The only way is the curses of alienation are to be removed. But in a capitalist system there is no possibility of freeing man from alienation.
6. If we go through Marx's analysis we shall find that the only way of freeing man from alienation is the establishment of communism or communist society. Let us put it in the words of Kolakowski : "communism puts an end to the division of life into public and private spheres and to the difference between civil society and the state, it does away with the need for political institutions, political authority and governments, private property and its source in the division of labour. It destroys the class system and exploitation, it heals the split in man's nature and the crippled one-sided development of the individual" (p. 147). Hence communism and disappearance of alienation are almost same thing. That is why it has been rightly observed that the transcendence of alienation and communism are identical. The building up of a communist society will completely transform the existence of men and women.

7. Only in communism man gets the full opportunity to flourish his latent qualities and this makes him a perfect human being. In a capitalist society he is deprived of this. Man has many good qualities and abilities. Capitalism suppresses them. But in communism he gets full scope to develop them and ultimately he arrives at the stage which he desires. Only in communism man frees him from all sorts of exploitation and bondage. Communism creates an atmosphere which ensures the "realisation of freedom, not only from exploitation and political power but from immediate bodily needs. It is the solution to the problem of history and is also the end of history" (p. 148).
8. The utopian socialists "imagined" that communism could be achieved through the repeated and fervent appeal to the capitalists. But Marx did not accept it. He thought that only through an intense struggle against the bourgeoisie a communist society can be finally built up. In his opinion the present age (when Marx was writing 1845-1883) is quite ripe for an intense struggle. It is the duty of the working class to fully utilise the situation. The contradictions within capitalism have achieved the stage of maturity. There was maximum dehumanisation and this is intolerable. A worker is no more than a commodity. He gets no respect as a human being. In other words, the capitalists treat him as a commodity. This is an unimaginable humiliation—only communism can save him and to achieve it workers will have to fight. Kolakowski says, "The proletariat is not a mere agglomeration of suffering, degradation and misery but also the historical instrument by which man is to recover his heritage."
9. About consciousness Marx's opinion is clear. He says that the consciousness of the proletariat is not all. That is, it may be passive or active. If the consciousness is of the former type emancipation from exploitation will not be possible because the passive consciousness cannot do the job. The consciousness must be active and must have a revolutionary spirit. The proletariat must be prepared for all sorts of hazards. Workers must fight against these. Naturally, consciousness of revolutionary category is the only way of emancipation. What Marx means is that without struggle emancipation is not possible.
10. Marx also talked about various aspects of consciousness. For example, proletarians will be conscious of their own class. Again, be conscious of the fact that only struggle against the bourgeoisie is the way of freedom. Without prolonged struggle, communism cannot be achieved. Moreover, communism can be protected through continuous struggle.

Scientific Discoveries and Marxism

The Marxists have discovered a close relationship between the emergence of Marxism the several important scientific discoveries that took place in the first half of the nineteenth century. These scientific discoveries in a large way stimulated the growth of capitalism variously and again all these inspired Marx and Engels to think about social, economic and political conditions in the light of the new situation. There were three scientific discoveries that inspired Marx and Engels to think everything in a different and new way. One was the discovery of the law of conversion of energy. The second was the discovery of cellular structure of living organisms and, finally, Charles Darwin's theory of evolution.

In the forties of the nineteenth century the German physician Julius Robert Mayer explained the law of conversion and conservation of energy. According to Mayer certain quantity of motion in one of its forms is converted into an equal quantity of motion in any other forms. It was proved that heat, light and other states of matter are qualitatively definite forms of its motion and this motion cannot be created or destroyed but is constantly converted from one state to another. This scientific discovery is at the root of dialectical understanding of the change of social process. In the physical world there is motion and in society there is a change—and from this Marx and Engels established the theory of dialectical materialism.

Again, the discovery of cellular structure of living matter is at the root of materialistic understanding of the unity of life in all its diversity. A critic observes : The cellular theory proved the internal unity of all living beings and indirectly pointed to the unity of their origin. Dialectical materialist conclusions from the cellular theory were drawn by Engels in his *Anti-Duhring* and *The Dialectics of Nature*. Both Marx and Engels observed that nature is subject to incessant changes. The change is also taking place in human society. Both in nature and society constant changes are taking place and behind this change there is motion. But this motion is within nature and in society. There is a clear relation between motion and matter and this makes nature quite dynamic. Similarly, the society moves or changes from one stage to another. This helped Marx to explain how the human society changes. This is called historical materialism. The animal and vegetable cells have their birth, growth and death. Similarly, in human society, different sections or parts are closely connected with each other. But some parts or sections become inactive with the passing away of time. But at the same time new forces surface. Conclusion is—with the help of scientific discoveries Marx and Engels had explained the human society.

Darwin in his *Origin of Species* for the first time established the idea that God did not create man and other animals. Both are the products of nature and after passing through the evolutionary process of million of years their present stage has arrived. That is animal world is not the "divine creation". He proved the mutability of the species of animals and plants and the unity of their origin. Darwin proved that behind the present stage of animal world (including man) there is evolution. It is to be noted that Darwin's theory was not based on imagination or guesswork. Behind this conclusion there is a painstaking research. Through the evolutionary process the world of the animals has reached the present stage. Marx has said that the human society also evolves and the evolution is from bad to better. That is, one stage is better than the previous stage.

After a good deal of research work Darwin arrived at the conclusion that in the natural world there is a continuous process of change and evolution and both these are making some kind of change. That is, one stage or form of change is different from the previous stage and the latter stage or form is invariably better than the earlier stage. Darwin also observed that natural selection promotes a high degree of specialisation. Marx borrowed this conception from Darwin. The tools and machinery used by man are passing through improvement or development. Marx in his *Capital* said : The manufacturing period simplifies, improves and multiplies the implements of labour by adopting them to the exclusive and special functions of each kind of worker. In 1873 Marx sent to Darwin an inscribed copy of *Capital*. All these indicate that Marx was influenced by Darwin.

After Marx's death Engels delivered a speech at the graveside of Marx. He said, "Just as Darwin discovered the law of development of organic nature, so Marx discovered the law of development of human history." Some critics do not find justification in the observation of Engels. But we are of opinion that there is a close similarity between Marx and Darwin. Darwin explained the evolutionary progress of natural world and Marx—with the help of dialectical materialism—explained the progress of human society. Both drew conclusions empirically. The minds of both were scientific.

Indebtedness of Marx to Hegel

In 1913 Lenin published an article *Three Sources and Three Component Parts of Marxism.* This article is a landmark one so far as the emergence of Marxism is concerned. Marx repeatedly informed us that he had said nothing new. Whatever he has said is to be found in the writings of his predecessors. Though his indebtedness is unlimited specific mentions may be made about Hegel in special and German philosophy in general. It is generally said that the development of German philosophy reached the zenith in the hands of Hegel. Both Hegel and Rousseau admitted the "negative and harmful effects" of alienation. The alienation dehumanised man. Man is alienated from the mainstream of society and from his surroundings. This has negatively affected his morality, character and everything worthy of name. Both Hegel and Marx held that society passes through various stages of evolution. But in Hegels view behind this evolution there is an important role of Idea, that is according to Hegel the Idea passes through evolution and finally it reaches the stage of Absolute Idea or World Spirit. Marx accepts this process of evolution but the basic difference is in Marx's thought system there is no place of Idea. Matter is everything. Hegel emphasises the concept of Idea, but Marx talks about matter. This is materialism. The differences between Hegel and Marx are important. In Hegel's opinion Idea is of first importance because it arises at first and matter is of secondary importance. Engels says, "The Hegelian system is a colossal miscarriage."

Explaining Hegel's interpretation of history with the help of dialectics Hunt (*Theory and Practice of Communism*, p. 40) says : "For Hegel history was a process in which the Absolute progressively unfolds itself revealing more of its true nature in later periods than in earlier, and this more in the national state than in primitive communities. The dialectic provided clue to this development." Marx borrowed this concept of dialectic from Hegel and applied it to the explanation of society. He also said that dialectic was also the clue to progress but this progress is not history and the culmination of progress is neither history nor Absolute Idea not even the National State of Germany. Marx also differed from Hegel on another standpoint. Hegel had simply interpreted the history dialectically but he did not suggest how to change the history as well as society. In Marx's view, function of philosophy was not to interpret the world, but to change it. Hunt further observes (p. 41) "having found, as he believed, a convenient instrument in the dialectic, he went further than Hegel in applying it to the future."

Marx applied dialectic to "justify" the proletarian revolution and radicalism. Hegel idealised the state through dialectical method and ultimately it culminated to fascism. Marx's application of dialectic led to the proletarian revolution and establishment of communism. Marx had no interest in metaphysics. What is metaphysics? It is essentially an abstract way of thinking. Idea and metaphysics failed to allure Marx. To him matter was of primary importance. Both Marx and Engels had admitted that Hegelian dialectics had both idealistic and revolutionary aspects. Marx and Engels accepted the latter. In this background we can say that Marx and Engels have converted Hegelian dialectics into materialist dialectics and this is not only a method but also a theory—a theory of development of the most general laws of development of nature, society and knowledge. Marxist method is materialist as well as dialectical. In Marxism, dialectics and materialism are not separate from each other.

Finally, we say that Marx expressed his indebtedness to Hegel in regard to dialectics but simultaneously he categorically stated his differences with Hegelian dialectics. Let us quote few lines from his *Capital* (Vol. I, p. 19) : "My dialectic method is not only different from the Hegelian, but is its direct opposite. To Hegel the life process of human brain, i.e., the process of thinking, which under the name of idea he even transforms into an independent subject, is the demiurgos of the real world, and the real world is only the external, phenomenal form of the idea. With me, on the contrary, the idea is nothing else than the material world reflected by the human mind and translated into forms of thought." Marx agreed with the dialectics of Hegel but disagreed with the mystifying aspect.

In the thoughts of both Hegel and Marx there are seeds of revolution. For the first time Hegel pointed out that history is always in movement. It never stands at a particular pointer stage. Its movement is dialectical. "He insisted that it is not simply a bare sequence of events, but a gradual process of unfolding" (Hunt, p. 42). According to Marx the society also progresses and the method is dialectic. In the process of progress the latter stage is different from the former. Marx also said that the latter stage is developed from the former. Both Hegel and Marx insisted that there was reason behind the dialectical process and it is not guided and motivated by any external or any other force.

Hess, Feurbach and Marx

Marx (1818–1883), Moses Hess (1812–1875) and Ludwig Feurbach (1804–1872) all were contemporary philosophers. Marxists hold the view that Marx was considerably influenced by both Hess and Feurbach. First of all we shall focus on how or to what extent Marx was influenced by Hess. The family of Hess was Jew and he was brought up in a strict Jewish orthodoxy. In his younger age he was influenced by Rousseau who held the view everyone must be allowed to enjoy natural equality. Not only this, Hess was attracted to the socialist ideas of his time. In the middle of the nineteenth century in Germany capitalism had developed leading to the growing inequality between workers and capitalist class and he apprehended that this would lead to antagonism between the two classes. His conclusion was that only socialism could save society from this danger or crisis. In order to disseminate his socialist thought Hess wrote articles and pamphlets. This made him closer to Marx. Needless to say that both Hess and Marx in their young age were influenced by Hegel.

From 1830s Hess began to publish books and articles about socialism. In these works he portrayed a clear picture of communist society "and attempted a deeper analysis of the economic causes of contemporary ills of capitalist society. He remained convinced that the perfect society was simply the realisation of the essence of humanity" (Kolakowski, p. 91). His firm belief was that re-distribution of wealth and property is the only or primary precondition of ensuring peace and goodwill among various classes of society. In his opinion socialism is a social movement and the working class through revolution must build up a socialist society. He thought that if there were no glaring inequality in society there would not arise the necessity of socialism. Hence socialism can be treated as product of poverty. Kolakowski says : "Hess was the first writer to express certain ideas which proved especially important in the history of Marxism" (p. 93). The simple fact is that Marx borrowed some of his ideas from Hess and he expressed his indebtedness in unequivocal terms in several places of his works. In Germany there was socialist movement and Hess was in various ways associated with them. There was a personal relationship between Hess and Marx and a meeting was held between then in 1841.

Ludwig Feurbach (1804–1872) was another German philosopher whose influence upon Marx is quite discernible. Feurbach was older than Marx. In the socialist movement of Germany Feurbach's involvement was positive and deep and this encouraged Marx. In his various analyses Feurbach applied materialism. For instance he strongly criticised the idea of eternal life or the life beyond this world. His chief concern was the reality of the world in which people live. It is said that Feurbach did not give very much importance to the concept—materialism. But whatever he has said is stark materialism. In every analysis he adopted materialist standpoint. An important aspect of Feurbach's materialism was—he was opposed to God and all sorts of religious activities. He frequently said, "man is nothing but object". The objectivity is the essence of everything. He propagated several formulae and one such formula is : Man belongs to the essence of nature and nature to the essence of man.

A very important part of Feurbach's materialism contains in his approach to religion and God. He said that God is the product of man's imagination. When man loses his faith on his own capacity and on the importance of his surroundings he lays faith on any supernatural power like God and religion. Hence God is nothing but the product of man's imagination. It has no importance in reality. It is said that man's knowledge of God is an attempt to perceive himself in the mirror of exteriority. Both God and religion paralyse the creative faculties and intellectual capacity of man. He is not assertive of his own ability. Feurbach also says the religion destroys the feelings and even the reason which a man possesses. Religion creates a type of alienation and this alienation is evil and dangerous and it is even poisonous—All these evils are the products of religion and abnormal affinity to God. In his noted work *The Essence of Christianity* he vehemently criticised the various bad aspects and effects of religion and God. His idea about religion can be explained in the following words : "Religion is an ersatz satisfaction of human needs that cannot be met in any other way : men seek to compel nature to obey them by using magic or appealing to divine goodness" (Kolakowski op. cit., p. 96). According to Feurbach, "religion was the source and epitome of all the evils in history; and he expected that public enlightenment, sweeping away religious prejudice, would at the same time eradicate social servitude" (Kolakowski, p. 97). This type of devastating attitude to religion considerably inspired Marx. Before Feurbach no other thinker took or adopted such type of clear attitude to religion. Feurbach rejected not only Hegel's idealism as religious fiction, but also of Fichte and other German philosophers. He had no faith in Absolute Idea or Spirit—material world was of primary importance. Feurbach's view on religion and other matters provided the main stimuli that enabled Marx to reject Hegelian Categories in his own thinking. He also owed much to Feurbach as regards knowledge of history (Kolakowski, p. 97).

POLITICAL ECONOMY AND MARXISM

Definition of Political Economy

It is generally observed that one of the very important foundations or components of Marxism is British political economy or simply political economy. It is called British because its chief founders or propagators were by birth British. There are few definitions of what is exactly meant by political economy. An important definition is it indicates the area which studies resource allocation and determination of aggregate economic activity. Its more specific meaning in a Marxist context relates to the corpus of work of certain writers who dealt with the distribution and accumulation of economic surplus, and the attendant problems of determination of prices, wages, employment and the efficacy or otherwise of political arrangements to promote accumulation (Battomore, p. 426).

It is called political economy because the economy or economic affairs and policy making are associated with the art of government. The government is primarily concerned with the political affairs of the state. But a government cannot consistently ignore the economic aspects and because of this government generally takes active interests in the economic affairs such as the causes of the wealth of nations, price fixation, distribution of wealth. Since seventeenth century the term political economy is in circulation, particularly in the academic circles. A good number of scholars believe that for the general welfare of the people a government must see that the economy acts within certain conditions and these conditions must aim at general progress. Summarily, political economy wants to emphasise the general control of state over the functioning of economy.

Political economy has three broad traditions, one is, the tradition of classical political economy. Another is the Marxian tradition and, finally, the tradition of political economics which uses statistical and modelling techniques to test the hypotheses about the relationship between government and the economy.

Though the term political economy was widely known to academic circles Marx was the first person who gave importance to the concept. In Marxism the term means the corpus of works of several economists and writers some of whom are Adam Smith, David Ricardo, Malthus, James Mill and his son J. S. Mill etc. Marx focused his attention on the economic writings of Adam Smith (1723–1790) and David Ricardo (1772–1823). Adam Smith's *The Wealth of Nations* was a widely read and much discussed book. In it he said that the political economy is a branch of the science of a statesman or legislator.

An important aspect of political economy is commerce or economic prosperity and growth of political liberty are closely related. Adam Smith strongly argued that progress of commerce or economy as a whole could come if government regulations are relaxed considerably. If the producers or capitalists are not given sufficient liberty the growth of economy will be adversely affected. Naturally liberty can be regarded as the important factor of the growth of industry and commerce. This doctrine of Adam Smith is generally called the *laissez-faire*. Smith's another message was that individuals shall be allowed to pursue or implement their economic objectives and political interference shall have no voice at all. The economic policies must be free from political interference but all the policies shall have political purposes. This doctrine of Adam Smith drew the attention of Marx and he thought that Adam Smith's doctrine paved the way of unhindered growth of capitalism and exploitation of working class.

RICARDO AND MARX

David Ricardo is one of the renowned classical British economists whose influence upon Marx is quite clear. In the opinion of Marx, Ricardo was one of the greatest classical economists. Marx with some of the conclusions or opinions of Ricardo regarding economics, but he disagreed with many. Ricardo said that prices are regulated or determined by embodied labour. Marx accepted this view of Ricardo. But he raised another important point. Ricardo made no distinction between *abstract* labour and *concrete* labour. Abstract labour means value producing labour and concrete labour means use value producing labour. Ricardo also made no distinction between socially necessary labour and individual labour.

Marx was attracted to Ricardo's another view. Ricardo saw the conflict of interest between capitalists and wage earners. In his opinion the progress of science and technology might be the cause of the fall in employment, because the same amount of work will be done with the help of less number of workers. The volume of employment will fall and this will reduce the total income of workers. Relationship between Ricardo and Marx may also be viewed from another perspective. According to Hunt (p. 81) the British school had adopted the theory of value first outlined by Locke. He defended the concept of private property on the ground that a man was entitled to that to which he had given value by his labour. In other words, a man is entitled to that property which is the product of his labour. Many classical economists of Britain accepted this view and Ricardo is one of them. Following Locke he said that the value of a commodity depended on the relative quantity of labour necessary to its production.

The influence of British classical economists upon Marx can be best stated in the words of Kolakowski and we quote a lengthy passage from his *Main Current of Marxism*. "Marx regarded the works of the classical British economists as a model of unprejudiced analysis, endeavouring without sentiment to discover the actual mechanisms of social life. He understood that their doctrine was grounded in economic liberalism and the belief that it was natural for owners of land and capital to be rewarded for their share in production. But what interested him in Smith and Ricardo was their description of the interrelation between the various elements in the production process. ...Marx used the theory of value in a different way from any of the economists who preceded him. ...Marx arrived at the formulation of the theory of value by various stages" (pp. 221-222).

Though Marx was influenced by the theory of value propounded by Locke and Ricardo, he used the value theory in greater and deeper perspective. For example, he discovered in the value theory the seeds of exploitation. From the labour theory of value Marx has built up his famous theory of surplus value. Labour has the unique faculty of producing material value over and above what the worker needs to maintain himself and his family. The surplus value, simply stated, is the difference between what the capitalists receive from selling the commodity produced by the labourer and what he gives to the labourer in the form of wages. In the view of Marx, the surplus value finally leads to the exploitation of labourer. The worker sells his labour, but he gets less than what he gives. This is exploitation and unfortunately Recardo failed to highlight this very important aspect of his theory of value.

EARLY SOCIALISM AS SOURCE OF MARXISM

Rousseau and Socialist Thought

Plamenatz in his scholarly work *Man and Society* says that modern thinkers generally regard Rousseau as the progenitor of modern socialist thought. Plamenatz refers to the noted French economist Bastiat who once said that all the socialists were the "grandchildren of Rousseau." The analysts of socialist thought are of opinion that before Rousseau many thinkers talked about socialism in a sporadical way. But Rousseau clearly and assertively propagated socialist ideas in his writing. In his *A Discourse on the Origin of Inequality* he said : there is hardly any inequality in the state of nature, all the inequality which now prevails owns its strength and growth to the development of our faculties and the advance of human mind and becomes at last permanent and legitimate by the establishment of property and laws" (p. 221). In this oft-quoted passage lie the seeds of socialist thought of Rousseau.

Interpreting Rousseau's philosophy Plamenatz maintains that, in the judgement of Rousseau, the society is evil, irrational and corrupting because it allows of great inequalities, unconnected with differences of ability or merit" (*Man and Society* Volume Two, p. 37). Plamenatz supports this view. He is of opinion that Rousseau imbibed socialist ideas though he did not elaborate them. There are many views which Rousseau said and these are central to socialist thought. The French socialists expressed many socialist ideas whose roots can be traced to Rousseau's philosophy. Rousseau was the most revolutionary. Why revolutionary? "Revolutionary, not in calling for its destruction by force—for that he never did—but in expressing a horror of it so profound and persuasive as to make it seem hateful to many who might otherwise have resigned themselves to it." (pp. 37-38).

Origin of Marxian Socialism

In *Socialism : Utopian and Scientific*, Engels writes : "Modern socialism is the direct product of the recognition of the class antagonism existing in the society of today between proprietors and non-proprietors, between capitalists and wage-earners, on the other hand, of the anarchy existing in production. But, in its theoretical form, socialism appears ostensibly as a more logical extension of the principles laid down by the great French philosophers of the eighteenth century" (*Marx and Engels. Selected Works* II, p. 116). Saint-Simon and Charles Fourier were the two great utopian socialists who propounded the basic principles of socialist thought. Engels called them utopian because they failed to show the way of achieving socialist goals in a scientific or materialist way. The great French socialists of the eighteenth century could not go beyond the limits imposed upon them by their epoch. The epoch was not quite ripe for mass agitation or revolution. This was due to the fact that the contradictions in capitalist system were not severe. The workers were not mentally and physically prepared for revolution against the capitalists. But Engels admits that the physical and mental conditions were becoming more and more favourable for revolution.

Engels claims that in the writings of Saint-Simon and the letters he wrote the basic ideas of socialism are in an embryonic form. What Marx and others have said are to be found in Saint-Simon's works. He said that the science of production was under the complete control of politics. That is, political authority controls economic affairs for the preservation and progress of its own interests. Again, the bourgeoisie controls the entire economic world. Saint-Simon further held the view that private property system was practically the chief source of all evils which have overcast the whole society. On the other hand, Fourier had depicted the miserable condition of capitalist society. He said that there was exploitation in all forms. Women and children were exploited by the powerful men, workers were exploited by the capitalists. Fourier, however, said that if the whole society is emancipated both women and children would also be emancipated. Engels admits that both Saint-Simon and Fourier predicted some of the ideas which both Marx and Engels in later days accepted.

In the opinion of Engels, Robert Owen is another socialist thinker who said that only socialism could save or emancipate the working class or, in general, all exploited persons. According to Engels, Robert Owen was a great materialist philosopher. He analysed the social condition from materialist perspective. Robert Owen propounded certain basic principles of communism. He introduced several reforms and systems for the alleviation of miseries the workers were forced to suffer. Owen was a very popular man in Europe for his philanthropic activities. He introduced few communist principles for the general benefit of ordinary men. But success failed to greet him. According to Engels, because of three great obstacles Owen could not succeed. These were : the system of private property, religion, and the present form of marriage. Both Marx and Engels carefully studied the views of all the eighteenth century socialist thinkers and thought that these thinkers must be remembered for their outspoken views about socialism.

Three important works of three utopian socialist thinkers are important. Saint-Simon's *Letters from an Inhabitant of Geneva* (1802), Fourier's *Theory of the Four Movements* (1808) and Robert Owen's *New View of Society* (1812–1816). From these three books many formulate the basic principles of utopian socialism. Both Marx and Engels were influenced by the views of these three thinkers. But they thought that a socialist society could never be built up on the suggestions they gave or methods they suggested. Throughout the utopian literature few ideas have been emphasised, some of them are the following. Men are intended to live in a state of equality, love and goodwill. But the development of capitalism has gone against this most desirable situation. On the contrary, there is exploitation, oppression, conflict and ill-feeling among men. Only socialism can free society from this situation. The three thinkers wanted to construct a new society which could provide love, affection equality, goodwill etc. The utopian thinkers thought of a moral and ideological sphere and socialism can ensure this. Marx accepted this contention. The important aspect of Saint-Simon's thought is he squarely blamed the system of private property for all the ills, and this is correct. Robert Owen focused his attention on the miserable situation of post-war unemployment and this led him to find out palliatives. He wanted to construct new societies and made serious efforts on convince the ruling class of his project. But he failed. However, at various levels, the thought of these three socialist thinkers enthused people to think about socialism. In several writings Engels recognised the contribution and importance of these three utopian thinkers.

29 DIALECTICAL AND HISTORICAL MATERIALISM

Meaning and Definition

Though dialectic constitutes the central part of Hegel and Marx's analysis, both of them were not the discoverer of the concept or idea. Several hundred years ago it was first used by the Greek philosopher Socrates (470-399 B.C.) and after him Plato's (427-347 B.C.) method of analysis in *The Republic* is a clear example of dialectic and Mc Lellan in his *The Thought of K. Marx* writes : "To the ancient Greeks the dialectic was the art of discussing a problem by way of question and answer, and the development of the balanced point of view by means of such discussion." A good number of scholars have elaborately discussed the origin and development of dialectic and Kolakowski, the renowned scholar on Marxism is, one such person who has gone through the nook and corner of the idea. The traditional Christian theology used the art of dialectics in various forms to reach a conclusion. The Concise Oxford Dictionary explains the term in the following words : Art of investigating the truth of opinions, or testing of truth by discussion. Joseph Stalin in his wellknown work *The Problems of Leninism* writes (p. 714) "Dialectics comes from the Greek *dialego*, to discourse, to debate. In ancient times dialectics was the art of arriving at the truth by disclosing the contradictions in the argument of an opponent and overcoming these contradictions." The philosophers of ancient times believed that the disclosure of contradictions was the best way of arriving at truth. The dialectic to them was the motive force of progress of thought. If the contradictions remain unsolved the thought cannot progress at all.

The concept of dialectics used by ancient Greeks and Christian theologians subsequently became central to Hegelian philosophy. In his greatest work *Phenomenology* Hegel traced to development of Idea or Spirit or Mind. The Idea develops through dialectical method. The Idea proceeds from the simple to the complex and ultimately the Truth or Absolute Idea is arrived at. Hegel believed that Idea never remains static at any particular stage. It passes through several stages and when it reaches the stage of synthesis it becomes Absolute. The starting point of dialectics is Thesis. From this emerges the Antithesis and the final form is Synthesis. This is the process of dialectics.

The central idea of dialectic is that in every thought or idea there are opposite views or contradictions. The participants in the discussion always make attempts to find out a correct view and for that purpose they continue the discussion and when an agreed stage of discussion arrives the discussion of the particular discussion comes to an end. The German philosopher Hegel used it for academic purposes. He presented its general form of working in a comprehensive and conscious manner. But Marx did not apply dialectics to the analysis of Idea. His dialectics is material. Summing up the difference between Hegel and Marx on the issue of dialectics David Mc Lellan (p. 152) observes "Hegel certainly understood history as a process of dialectical development, but whereas labour in Hegel was always intellectual, in Marx it was material-designed to satisfy the material needs of men. For Marx the dialectical interchange between man and nature was conducted through a specific mode of production which itself generated new needs and the means to satisfy them."

Dialectical Materialism : Definition and Nature

According to Stalin "Dialectical materialism is the world outlook of the Marxist-Leninist Party. It is called Dialectical Materialism because its approach to the phenomena of nature, its method of studying and apprehending them, is *dialectical*, while its interpretation of phenomena of nature, its conception of these phenomena, its theory is *materialistic*. Hence, the process or method is dialectical and the object is materialism. To interpret the matter, to know the nature of matter the dialectics is used". Lenin has summed up the essential idea of dialectical materialism in the following words : "The idea is the recognition of the contradictory, mutually exclusive, opposite tendencies in all phenomena and processes of nature. That is, in all phenomena and processes of nature there are diametrically opposite forces or tendencies and they are at clash or conflict and this continues until a solution is reached. This alone furnishes the key to the self-movement of everything in existence. It alone furnishes the key to the leaps, to the break in continuity, to the transformation into the opposite, to the destruction of the old and emergence of the new. In its proper meaning dialectics is the study of the contradiction within the very essence of things" (Quoted by Cornforth, p. 47).

The idea of materialism or matter was first used by Feurbach who challenged the traditional concept of religion or unearthly ideas. He said that religion or related concept which has no factual or material basis cannot be regarded as the basis of analysis of worldly ideas or topics. This view of Feurbach highly impressed both Marx and Engels and they began to study society materialistically which finally constitutes materialism. Then they developed it into a philosophical theory of materialism and kept aside its idealistic-religious, ethical encumbrances. Basically Feurbach was a materialist, but surprisingly he objected to the use of the word materialism or materialist. Remembering this Engels once said that Feurbach was within the fetters of idealism. Joseph Stalin, a great interpreter of Marx's and Lenin's philosophy, has stated some of the important features of dialectical materialism and we now turn to them.

(1) *Dialectics does not regard nature as an accidental agglomeration of things*, of phenomena, unconnected with and isolated from and independent of each other, but as a connected and integral whole. Phenomena are organically connected. The action of one reacts upon another, and vice versa. This idea of Marxian dialectical materialism differs from metaphysics. The dialectical materialism clearly states that all the phenomena of the modern world are inextricably connected with each other.

Naturally any analysis of the material world or the society we live in must be taken as a whole. The isolation of one phenomenon from another is impossible. The dialectical materialism treats all the phenomena together and starts analysis. Isolation of one phenomenon from another will not help understanding the dialectical materialism. Failure to do this will make our attempt to analyse nature a meaningless venture.

(2) *The nature is not a stable or stagnant state and because of this continuous change is taking place.* There is a constant conflict between the negative and positive forces and out of the conflict emerges a new force which is also unstable till the final end is reached. In the process of continuous change something new is coming out and old things or forces are dying away. Hence, the dialectical materialism is characterised by interconnection among the various parts but also by the continuous movement. Engels wrote "All nature from the smallest thing to the biggest, from grains of sand to sun, from protista to man, has its existence in eternal. Coming into being and going out of being, in a ceaseless flux, in unresting motion and change."

(3) *The process of change and development which dialectics assumes is not simple and uniform.* It does not proceed along a predetermined path. The development passes from insignificant and imperceptible to open and fundamental changes, also to qualitative changes. The changes in dialectics are never smooth and gradual but rapid and abrupt. The change does not move in a circle but it is onward and upward. Engels wrote "Nature is the test of dialectics and it must be said for modern natural science that it has furnished extremely rich and daily increasing materials for this test, and has thus proved in the last analysis nature's process is dialectical and not metaphysical, that it does not move in an eternally uniform and constantly repeated circle, but passes through real history."

(4) According to Stalin final feature of dialectics is that *contradictions are inherent in all things and phenomena of nature.* Every thing or phenomenon of nature has negative and positive sides. All the elements of nature have two features—negative and positive which implies that there is a conflict between these two and this conflict leads to the death of the negative element. But the conflict does not stop at this stage. Conflict is a continuous process and it is also natural. Stalin says (p. 717) "The dialectical method holds that the process of development from the lower to the higher takes place not as a harmonious unfolding of phenomena, but as a disclosure of contradictions inherent in the things and phenomena." Lenin once said "In its proper meaning dialectics is the study of the contradictions within the very essence of things." The development of society and also of the idea is caused by the existence of two opposite forces. The development comes through the struggle. Matter and dialectic are two important issues and one cannot be separated from the other.

Marx and Engels took the help of dialectics for the explanation of the materialist condition—that is, the development or evolution of society. The Marxist dialectical method teaches us to understand the processes of development.

Materialism and Idealism

The use of the term materialism demands that there is something called idealism and a comprehensive discussion of both is essential. Materialist philosophy emphasises that its core idea is neither idea or idealism, but rather it is physical world. It stresses upon the matter or material condition of society and day-to-day life.

Materialism does not recognise anything beyond the physical world. In materialism or materialist philosophy there is no place of divinity or supernatural phenomena or elements or force. Man constitutes the nucleus of materialism. Along with man, the society enters into the materialist philosophy.

But there are many philosophers who deny this. They assert that only mind, thought, spirit and ideas are primary. Nature or the physical world is secondary. The physical world is derived from spirit, consciousness and ideas. Man thinks something first and out of that imagination or thought physical world emerges. Physical world is a piece of man's imagination. Hence the difference between materialism and idealism may be succinctly stated in the following words : "Those who consider that the material bases—nature—is primary and regard thought, spirit as a property of matter, belong to the camp of materialism. Those who maintain that thought, spirit and idea existed before nature and that nature is, one way or another, the creation of spirit and dependent upon it comprise the camp of idealism." From the early days of civilisation a controversy has been going on between idealism and materialism. If we look at the development of history of philosophy we shall find that a major part of it is covered by the conflict between materialism and idealism. But towards the middle of the nineteenth century Marx and Engels, through consistent and unassailable logic asserted that the matter or material world is real and idealism has no real basis, it is simply an imagination and, hence, it cannot be taken as the subject of any serious analysis.

Materialism or materialist philosophy is practically a protest against idealism or spiritualism. It is a guide to actual life and action. Materialism helps us to understand the nature, functioning and development of society. It does not proceed to ascertain happiness and pleasure of heavenly life. It teaches man to be practical. It further states that the change and development of society are the results of human efforts and not dictated by the wills or whims of supernatural power. Engels has said "Modern materialism is not a philosophy but a simple conception of the world (*Weltanschauung*) which has to establish its validity and be applied not in a science of sciences standing apart, but within the actual sciences."

An important aspect of materialism or materialist interpretation of history is that man with his intellectual capacity can enter into the deepest stage of matter and can know what the matter is. In other words, it is man's intellectual capacity that helps to unfathom the secrets of nature as well as matter, So we can say that man is the sole determiner of everything in the society. Idealism asserts that it is not man nor his intellectual power nor his consciousness which determines the happenings of the physical world. The ideal or the eternal spirit determines the movements of the physical world. As a result of this, idealism glorifies the death and also a life after death. According to philosophical idealism the external world is a misnomer. The only reality is the spirit or ideal. The simple difference between the two is idealism forcefully says that ideal is all-in-all and naturally it determines everything. The opposite view has been propagated by materialism.

Materialism is, in its essence, an optimistic, life-asserting and radiant philosophy. It is alien to pessimism. Materialism is the world outlook of progressive social groups and classes. The advocates of materialism always look ahead for a bright and enlightened future. It is imbued with optimism. The supporters of idealism generally argue that in materialism there is no place of morality, ethics and value judgment. But this charge against materialism is absolutely unfounded and motivated. "In their dialectical and historical materialism Marx and Engels, far from rejecting progressive ideas, moral principles and lofty ideas, lay great emphasis on them."[1]

The distinction between materialism and idealism is not simply theoretical but also practical. The idealist philosophers have advised us not to rely too much on science. Science deals with logic and realities of the world. But the real truth lies beyond this real world. The unseen world is more important and higher than the world in which we live. It guides men to lay their faith on superstitions and supernatural beliefs. The church in the Middle Ages did this. The clergymen ingrained an apathy in the mind of men towards the real world. The press and other media followed the line.

The idealists, through their continuous propaganda, assert that there are many things in the world which cannot be solved by science and technology. Only an inner and invisible power and regeneration of faith on the heavenly force can save mankind or emancipate man from sorrows and sufferings. The *raison d' etre* of this propaganda is quite manifest. The capitalists know it very well that if the mind of the common people become too much materialist the real nature of capitalism would be exposed to them and that will stand in the way of capitalist exploitation. Hence the best way is to divert the mind of people from the material world and help them to focus on the other-worldly affairs and idealism. Mainly for that reason there is an unholy alliance between capitalism and idealism. Marx and Engels challenged this and exposed the unholy alliance.

BASIC LAWS OF DIALECTICS

Law of Transformation of Quantitative to Qualitative Change

The authors of the *Fundamentals of Marxist-Leninist Philosophy* write "Dialectics, the most complete, comprehensive and profound theory of development, is the heart and soul of Marxism-Leninism, its theoretical foundation. The universal-laws of dialectics reveal the essential features of any developing phenomenon, no matter to what field of activity it may belong" (p. 97). The dialectical materialism does not treat the nature or universe as stable or immobile—the concept of development lies in this notion. There is a continuous struggle between the opposite forces and this struggle, according to Marx and Engels, is the key to all sorts of progress. Dialectical materialism further states that the change or evolution from lower to higher, from quantitative to qualitative is never slow or gradual or smooth. It is sudden or abrupt. The real development of society envisages such a transformation.

A. P. Sheptulin remarks "The totalities of properties that make a particular thing what it is, is called its quality. The totality of properties indicating a thing's dimensions or magnitude is called its quantity. Dialectical materialism is not content with asserting that everything develops. The development or transformation is from quantity to quality." Now let us explain what is meant by quantitative and qualitative change.

The first basic law of dialectical materialism is that *transformation of change may be quantitative or qualitative.* All change has a quantitative aspect. That is there may

1. *Fundamentals of Marxism-Leninism*, p. 28.

be decrease or increase of the thing. But quantitative change—decrease or increase cannot go indefinitely. It has its limitation. After certain point the quantitative change may turn into qualitative change. When the water is being heated it becomes hotter and hotter and after some time the water is converted into vapour. This conversion of water into vapour is qualitative change. Similarly, when the water is cooled and the temperature is brought down to the freezing point the water becomes ice. The water is converted into ice but both are not the same. Quantitative changes occur constantly and gradually.

What about qualitative change? Qualitative changes in a thing are a result of accumulated quantitative changes in it. So quantitative and qualitative changes in a thing are, in a sense, matter of stages. After a particular stage quantitative change does not occur. Again, qualitative change assumes the form of leaps. There is a break or discontinuity which is absent in quantitative change. Leap is a form of development that occurs much quicker than the continual development. Leap form of development is characterised by intensity. It is really a breakthrough. *Quantitative change is gradual, qualitative change is abrupt.*

Let us summarise what we have just now said about the transformation of quantitative change to qualitative change. The law states that there is an interconnection and interaction between the quantitative and qualitative aspects of an object thanks to which small, at first imperceptible, quantitative changes, accumulating gradually, sooner or later upset the proportion of that object and evoke the fundamental qualitative changes which take place in the form of leaps and whose occurrence depends on the nature of the objects in question and the conditions of their development in diverse forms. Knowledge of this law is vital to the understanding of development. It provides a guideline for examining and studying phenomena as the unity of their qualitative and quantitative aspects, for seeing the complex interconnections and interactions of these aspects, and the changes in the relationships between them.[1] Engels borrowed the concept of quantitative-qualitative change from science and applied it to society. With the rapid growth of industrial capitalism wealth in the form of money is accumulated in the hands of few and the number of propertyless proletariat begins to rise and this proceeds unabated. When enough people have proletarianised to make capitalism mature quantitative change gives rise to qualitative change.

Law of Unity and Struggles of Opposites

A. P. Sheptulin defines opposites and contradictions in the following words : "Aspects in which changes move in opposite directions and which have opposite trends of functioning and development are called opposites, while the interaction of these aspects constitutes a contradiction" (p. 251). Every phenomenon is characterised by certain opposites and contradictions. This is the property of the phenomenon. For example, in capitalist society there are two antagonistic classes—bourgeoisie and proletariat. The interests, objectives, attitudes of these two classes are diametrically opposite. But they exist side by side and this is due to the interdependence and interconnection and interpenetration of opposites.

The opposites have different aspects of functioning and development and have different directions of change. But in spite of this the opposites do not eliminate each

1. *Fundamentals of Marxist-Leninist Philosophy*, p. 109.

other, they co-exist in an unbreakable unity and interdependence. This is an interesting characteristic of all opposites. Let us illustrate our point. In all class societies, Marx and Engels have said, there are mainly two classes—proletariat and bourgeoisie or capitalists. There are conflicts and contradictions and in spite of these both the classes exist side by side and this coexistence is inevitable. One cannot exist without the other. But a situation arrives when the coexistence becomes absolutely impossible and this finally leads to revolution or class struggle. It has been claimed by Marx that after the revolution the proletarian class will establish its supremacy and create a classless society which is called a communism. Whether a communist society will bring about an end of contradiction is a debatable issue. But Marx and Engels have explained the matter from the standpoint of historical materialism.

The law of dialectics states that the struggle of opposites cannot be underestimated. Rather, it is the motive force of social development. Lenin once said, "Development is the struggle of opposites." This development or motion is self-development or self-motion. That is, the development resulting from the struggle of opposites is not caused by external forces. This motion is quite relevant to dialectical materialism. This principle of dialectics has its own laws of motion. This to be carefully remembered.

We have earlier noted that the contradictions are not immobile or immutable. Once they have arisen they develop and pass through definite stages. For the disappearance and replacement of contradictions two conditions are to be fulfilled. One is—contradictions must be fully revealed, and the other is, they must be fully developed. When these two conditions are fulfilled a situation for the leap will emerge. The old phenomenon will disappear and will be replaced by a new which will be qualitatively higher or better than the earlier.

There are two stages of this development. First is contradictions will unfold themselves and then they will be resolved. The contradiction first appears in the form of difference. Then this deepens into manifest contradiction. In order to maximise profit the capitalist develops his productive system. Wealth, in the form of money, is concentrated in the hands of the few. Workers are more and more proletarianised. Contradictions deepen. Ultimately demand is raised for the replacement of private property by the socialist property. When is such a demand made? The contradictions will arrive at a critical stage and the struggle between the opposites will reach the ultimate point. This is the stage of resolution of contradictions. Dialectical materialism attaches a good deal of importance to the resolution of contradictions.

In order to explain the law of struggle of opposites Cornforth cites (p. 78) an example. A cord will break when excessive load is put upon it. The qualitative change takes place as a result of the opposition set up between the tensile strength of the cord and the pull of the load. Another example is when a spring wheat is transformed into winter wheat, this is result of the opposition between the plant's "conservatism" and the changing conditions of growth and development to which it is subjected; at a certain point the influence of the latter overcomes the former.[1] Stalin said "the internal content of the process of development, the internal content of the transformation of quantitative changes into qualitative changes consists in the struggle of opposites."

1. Maurice Cornforth—*Dialectical Materialism*, p. 78.

The Law of the Negation of Negation

Marx has said "In no sphere can one undergo a development without negating one's previous mode of existence." Negation is an inevitable and logical element of development. Marx and Engels have said that a very powerful precondition of social development is the negation of previous existence. Now the question is what is negation? The authors of the *Fundamentals of Marxist-Leninist Philosophy* have defined it in the following way : "In ordinary consciousness the concept of negation is associated with the word "no", to negate to say "no" or to reject something." But dialectical materialism looks at the concept from different angle. Negation is an important element of progress. So it has deeper connotation. According to Engels "Negation in dialectics does not mean simply saying no, or declaring that something does not exist, or destroying in the same way one likes."

In the opinion of A. P. Sheptulin "Dialectical negation is objective. It is the negation of one qualitative state and the formation of a new one. It stems from the development of the internal contradictions of a phenomenon and result from the struggle between internal opposite forces and tendencies; it is a connecting link between lower and higher" (p. 268).

Dialectical negation is an important factor of progress or development. This is a feature of dialectical negation. Another feature is *it combines old and new.* That is it is a connection between the two. The negation of the old force by the new removes the obstacle on the way of development. Once development appears the new force does not stand disconnected with the old force. In this way a chain of connecting continues to exist.

The negation carries with it the potentialities of new force. Otherwise the negation is meaningless. It performs the function because it has the ability to create something new. Lenin wrote "Not empty negation, not futile negation, not sceptical negation, vacillation and doubt is characteristic and essential in dialectics—which undoubtedly contains the elements of negation and indeed as its most important element—no, but negation as a movement of development retaining the positive" (quoted by A. P. Sheptulin, p. 265).

The law of negation of negation is a law whose operation conditions the connection and continuity between that which is negated and that which negates. For this reason dialectical negation is not naked, "needless" negation, rejecting all previous development, but the condition of development that retains and preserves in itself all progressive content of previous stages, repeats at a higher level certain features of initial stages and has in general, a progressive and ascending character (*Fundamentals...*, p. 122).

HISTORICAL MATERIALISM

Historical Materialism Defined

"Historical materialism is the extension of principles of dialectical materialism to the study of social life, an application of the principles of dialectical materialism to the phenomenon of the life of society, to the study of society and of its history" (Stalin). To put it in other words the *historical materialism is nothing but the application of the principles of dialectics to the study of social life.* R.N.C. Hunt has defined the historical materialism almost in the same language. He says (p. 61) "Historical materialism or the materialistic interpretation of history is simply dialectical materialism applied to the particular field of human relations within society." In *Socialism, Utopian* and *Scientific*, Engels defines historical materialism in the following words : historical materialism is "that view of the course of history which seeks the ultimate cause and the great moving power of all important historic events in the economic development of society in the changes, in the modes of production and exchange, in the consequent division of society into distinct classes and in the struggle of these classes against one another." Explaining Engels's view, Kolakowski says, "Historical materialism is thus an answer to the question : What circumstances have had the greatest effect in changing human civilisation? This word being understood in a broad sense covering all social forms of communication from categories of thought to social organisation of labour and political institutions" (combined edition, p. 276). It is called historical materialism because the starting point of human history from the materialist point of view is the struggle with nature, the sum total of means employed by man to compel nature to serve his needs, which grow as they are satisfied. Man is distinguished from other animals by the fact that he makes tools (Kolakowski, pp. 276-77).

Historical materialism studies the laws of interrelationship between matter and consciousness and the general laws of being in their specific manifestations in the social life and discovers the general laws governing the functioning and development of society as a specific form of the motion of matter. We can generally say that the subject matter of historical materialism is the study of the general laws governing the functioning and development of society.

The historical materialism constitutes the nucleus of Marxist philosophy. Marx and Engels have rejected root and branch Hegelian concept of Spirit or Idea and have meticulously analysed the society exclusively from the materialistic point of view. Their interpretation of history is based on materialism in which there is no place of imagination, conjecture or subjective element. They have viewed history not through the spectacles of idealism but of materialism.

Historical materialism envisages that all the parts of social life are interconnected and any analysis of social life must seriously consider that. Historical materialism discusses the general laws and driving forces of functioning and development of society treating it as an integrated whole. There are contradictions and opposites in social life which are connected with each other and dependent upon each other. If we fail to recognise this a clear realisation of the development of society will remain a far cry. It is also to be noted that historical materialism combines both theory and method in one. The society or social development viewed dialectically and dialectical materialism furnishes all the solution to problems.

Marx and Engels did not use the term "historical materialism." They have used the term materialist conception of history. The coinage of the term or its discovery according to Engels is really a revolution and it stands parallel to Darwin's theory of evolution. In his speech at the graveside of Marx, Engels said "Just as Darwin discovered the law of development of organic nature, so Marx developed the law of development of human history : the simple fact, hitherto concealed by an overgrowth of ideology, that mankind must first of all eat, drink and have shelter and clothing, before it can pursue politics, science, art, religion etc., that therefore production of the immediate material means of subsistence and consequently the degree of economic development attained by a given people or during a given epoch form the foundation upon which the state, institutions, the legal conceptions, art and even the ideas of religion, of the people concerned have been evolved and in the light of which they must therefore be explained, instead of vice-versa as had hitherto been the case." Marx may be called the social Darwin of modern age. Darwin put an end to the view that animal and plant species are unconnected and fortuitous creations of God. So Marx put an end to the view that human society is an aggregation of individuals.

Marx's Formulation of Historical Materialism

In 1859 Marx published his *A Contribution to the Critique of Political Economy* and in the *Preface* to the book what he said has been regarded as the classic formulation and basic proposition of materialist interpretation of history or historical materialism. He wrote :

"In the social production of their life, men enter into definite relations that are indispensable and independent of their will, relations of production which correspond to definite stage of development of their material productive forces. The sum total of these relations of production constitutes the economic structure of society, the real foundation, on which rises a legal and political superstructure and to which correspond definite forms of social consciousness. The mode of production of material life conditions the social, political and intellectual life process in general. It is not the consciousness of men that determines their being, but on the contrary their social being that determines their consciousness. At a certain stage of their development, the material productive forces of society come in conflict with the existing relations of production. From the forms of development of the productive forces these relations turn into their fetters."[1]

In the above famous passage Marx has categorically said that in society there are two stages—one is base or what may also be called the foundation and the other is called the superstructure. If there is a change in the base or foundation of society there will take place a corresponding change in the superstructure. Marx discovered this relationship between base and the superstructure from the analytical study of society with an outlook of materialism. In considering such transformations a distinction should be made between the material transformation of economic conditions of production and the legal, political and religious, in short, ideological forms. Our opinion of a man is not based on what he thinks of himself. Similarly we cannot judge a period of transformation by its own consciousness. On the contrary, this consciousness must be explained rather from the contradictions of material life, from the existing conflict between the social productive forces and the relations of production.

In his letter to Bloch, Engels writes about materialist conception of history. "According to materialist conception of history the ultimate determining element in history is the production and reproduction of real life. More than this neither Marx nor I have ever asserted. Hence if somebody lists this into saying that the economic element is the only determining one, he transforms that proposition into a meaningless, abstract, senseless phrase. There is an interaction of all these elements in which amid all the endless host of accidents the economic movement finally asserts (Quoted by *McLellan, Marxism After Marx*, p. 14).

1. *MESW* I, p. 362.

Higher relations of production never appear before the material conditions of their existence have matured in the womb of the old society itself. Mankind always sets itself only such tasks as it can solve. When the material conditions for solution exist then—and then only—the tasks arise. The bourgeois relations of production are the last antagonistic form of the social process of production. It is not individual antagonism, but antagonism between the social conditions of the life of individuals and the productive forces developing in the womb of bourgeois society.

Principles of Historical Materialism

From the materialist interpretation of history certain principles are obtained and these may be stated in the following way. The first principle is that *social development is regulated by objective laws discoverable by science.* The second principle is that *views and institutions such as political, economic and cultural emerge from the development of material life of society.* That is, there is a close relationship between ideological institutional progress on the one hand and economic progress on the other hand. Marx and Engels have also said that the ideas, institutions and ideology considerably guide or mould the material life of human beings.

The first guiding principle of historical materialism is that change and development of society take place according to objective laws. Objective laws are those laws which are discoverable and which relate to the material world. Any divine law or concept is out of the jurisdiction of historical materialism. Materilism never recognises that inexplicable law is the cause of social change and development.

The development of society includes the development of views and various institutions—political, economic, social and cultural. Historical materialism asserts that the progress of views and institutions is determined by the material conditions of social life. According to Marx and Engels, matter can never act as a factor of social progress. Matter or material life is the primary thing. Materialism further states that views and institutions originate from the material conditions. We have already quoted a lengthy passage from Marx's *Preface to the Critique of Political Economy* where he has stated that it is not the consciousness of man that determines his being, but the social being determines the consciousness. The idealists make us believe that the idea to overthrow the feudalism arose in the minds of our forefathers. Materialists legitimately ask—why did the idea arise? The idealists have no answer. Materialists say that the change in material conditions led them to think of overthrowing the feudalism. Simply stated, the problem is one group—that is idealists—say that idea is supreme and it determines the course of action of man. Another group is of opinion that it is not idea, rather the material condition of situation is one only which determines everything in human society. This is the basis of controversy between idealism and materialism or materialist interpretation of history.

Marx and his followers have stressed the point that the ideas of material life play a very important part in the development of society. A carpenter has ideas about wood and a tool-maker forms ideas about metal. Without the ideas they cannot work. If they are not well-acquainted with the properties they will not be able to work. Cornforth observes (p. 159) "People do not work without ideas. Indeed when primitive men made his first stone implements, he was already demonstrating the role played by ideas."

For the maintenance of day-to-day life men require different types of articles or commodities and they produce them with their own brain or mental power and physical power. But without controlling nature people cannot do this job. It means that behind the production of every article there is the brain and along with it the labour of man. Behind all these there is the labour of man. Production is impossible without labour. The animals also work or they apply labour. But there is a fundamental difference between the labour of man and that of animal. Human labour is associated with his consciousness. Consciousness again originates from his social existence. Man applies his labour consciously. He starts his work with a definite purpose. In the case of failure, he ponders over it and tries to know the cause of failure. If necessary he modifies his method of work or he radically changes his method. Again, in case of success, he continuously makes his efforts to improve his method.

From the above we can draw another inference. The labour of man is always creative. Man applies his labour to produce something. That is why historical materialism stresses that man's labour is always creative. This creative labour transforms the society and makes possible the development. He is not guided by any invisible force. His only motive is to change his and society's material conditions. In human labour social consciousness and social existence are combined.

Productive Forces and Production Relations

How are commodities produced? The materialist conception of history reveals that the production of commodities is possible because of the interaction between man and man and between man and nature. Without this interaction the production would never be possible. Here there are two forms of relations or interactions. One is relations among men and the other is relation between man and nature. This relation is very vital in materialist interpretation of history. The relation among men, again, can be called a type of cooperation. Marx and Engels call these two forms of relationships as the nucleus of the productive system which includes forces of production and relations of production. In order to understand the mode of production the presentation of a clear picture of the productive forces and production relations is essential. It must also be presented how these two are connected.

According to the authors of the *Fundamentals of Marxist-Leninist Philosophy* "The productive forces are the forces by which society influences nature and changes it." Nature itself is not productive force. It is the universal object of labour. William Petty said that nature is the mother and labour is the father of wealth. Marx accepted this view of Petty. Nature is the source of the vast amount of wealth. Not entire nature is the subject of labour. Only that part of nature comes under the jurisdiction of labour which can ensure production or man can use it for productive purposes.

Stalin in his *Problems of Leninism* says (731), "The instruments of production wherewith material values are produced, the people who operate these instruments of production and carry on the production of material values thanks to a certain production experience and labour skill—all these elements jointly constitute the productive forces of society." We can, therefore, say that the term productive forces is comprehensive. It does not mean only labour or raw material or capital. The accumulated labour, the instruments, land, road everything which come directly or indirectly to the assistance of production is to be called force of production. Consciousness and inventive power of man enrich and sharpen the productive forces and also the instruments used for production.

G. A. Cohen in his celebrated work *Karl Marx's Theory of History* gives us a very simple formula of the concept productive forces. Productive forces mean means of production. It includes (A) instruments of production, (B) raw materials, (C) labour power. Labour power implies productive faculties of producing agents, strength, skill, knowledge and inventiveness. The catalogued terms are unified by the fact that each is, in a wide sense, *used* by producing agents to make products. A denotes what they work with, B what they work on, and C what enables them to work with A on B (p. 32). It is clear that while analysing the term productive forces a comprehensive idea was quite alive in Marx's mind. Before him nobody used the term in such a way.

The productive forces are only one aspect of production, only one aspect of the mode of production. Another aspect is relations of production. "Production" says Stalin "is at all times and under all conditions social production." In our formula we have seen that in order to make production possible a relationship between persons and means is a must. Cohen says (p. 31) : "persons and productive forces are the only terms bound by production relations. All production relations are either between a person (or group of persons) and another person (or group of persons), or between person and productive force. In other words, production relations bind at least one person and at most one productive force. The term production, Marxism says, is a very very wide idea. A particular commodity is produced at a very particular time. But behind it lies the accumulated knowledge of previous ages and the efforts of numerous people. We must remember it.

In producing material goods people interact not only with nature but with one another. In the process of production certain relationships necessarily arise between people. These are called relations of production. Marx in his *Wage, Labour and Capital* writes : "In production, men not only act on nature but also on one another. They produce only by cooperating in a certain way and mutually exchanging their activities. In order to produce, they enter into definite connections and relations with one another and only within these social connections and relations does their action on nature, does production take place. These social relations into which producers enter with one another, the conditions under which they exchange their activities and participate in the whole act of production, will naturally vary according to the character of means of production" (p. 89).

Though behind every production there is crucial role of machinery, it is at the same time true that there is positive role of individuals and, simultaneously, the roll of the entire society. Because of this, production is generally called a social process. Various sections or units of society are actively associated with production of commodities. The novel aspect of Marx's theory of materialist conception of history is he calls all sorts of production as social production and it is also a social process. Whole society including its past and present is closely connected with process of production. It is the production relations that tell us whether a worker is a slave, or a wage worker or whether machine serves as a means of exploiting the labourer, or vice versa. Production relations are economic relations. They are studied in detail by the science of economics.

Stalin says (p. 731) that the production relations may be of various types. Such as cooperative production relations. When people are quite free and participate in the productive system freely it is called so. In cooperative production relations there is no place of exploitation. It may be subordinate production relations. Finally, they may be from one form of relations of production to another. But whatever may be type of production relations, they always constitute the essential element of production.

Features of Production Relations

Marx has drawn our attention to a very important aspect of production relation. In his opinion it is never static. Commodities are produced. But in a dynamic society the demand for particular commodities is not static. From time to time the demand for commodities changes and corresponding to this production as well as productive system also change. Stalin has observed (p. 732) that changes in the mode of production inevitably call both changes in the whole social system, social ideas, political views and political institutions. In a word, change in production relations calls forth the change in the whole social system and political order. To put it in other words, the production relations constitute the central part of the whole social fabric. Change in production relations is accompanied by far reaching changes. If this is the position or characteristic of production relation then we can safely say that the history of the development of society is the history of the production relations and the history of the productive forces.

Another feature of the production relations is that its changes and development entail changes and development of productive forces. Productive forces are, therefore, mobile and revolutionary. They are the most important elements of production. "Productive forces of the society change and develop and depending on these changes and in conformity with them, men's relations of productions, their economic relations, change." This is one aspect of the dialectial change. Another side is, relations of production influence the development of the productive forces. The development of the production relations is dependent upon the development of the productive forces. Again, the former also react upon the latter. We can say both relations of production and forces of production are dialectically connected.

The above feature should not lead one to assume that the action and reaction between the two are always proportionate. It may so happen that the production relations lag behind the productive forces. Here may crop up contradiction. But Marx has stressed that this lagging behind is temporary. Let us put the matter in the clear language of Stalin (p. 734) : "However much the relations of production may lag behind the development of productive forces, they must sooner or later come into correspondence with the level of development of productive forces. Otherwise we would have a fundamental violation of the units of productive forces and production relations within the system of production as a whole." There will be crises and disruption.

Another feature of production relations is that the rise of new productive forces and production relations does not mean that correspondingly a new system will emerge and the old system will be completely destroyed. It takes place within the old system. It takes place not as a result of deliberate and conscious activity of man, but spontaneously and unconsciously of the will of man. This is due to the fact that man has no freedom to choose one mode of production or another. Productive forces and production relations of every generation are bequeathed to the next generation and it is so part and parcel of the economic and social system that the next generation cannot part with it. Another interesting thing about the dialectical relationship between the two is that when a new method or technique is introduced nobody knows about its repercussions. Man is forced to adapt himself with the new method. So, in the productive system, man can hardly claim any independence. To sum up in simple language, the productive system and productive forces of any particular age are not the exclusive properties of that particular age. The knowledge and experience about production of a particular age is carried over to the next period and this process is a continuous one.

Each form of production relations exists as long as it provides sufficient scope for the development of the productive forces. But gradually relations of production come into contradiction with the developing productive forces and become a brake on them. They are then superseded by the new relations of production, the role of which is to serve as the form of the further development of the productive forces. Marx observes that people never give up the productive forces they have brought into being, but this does not mean that they do not give up the production relations. In order to get better fruits of civilisation men form new relations.

The recent interpreters such as G. A. Cohen have wanted to establish a *"primacy thesis."* Its central idea is that the nature of a set of production relations is explained by the level of the development of the productive forces embraced by it.[1] Though the primacy thesis implies that the changes in productive forces bring about changes in production relations, yet some changes in productive forces are too limited in scope to have that effect. Nor is it possible to provide a general statement of how much productive power must increase for a consequent change in production relations to occur (Cohen, p. 135).

Marx and Engels have studied the relationship between productive forces and production relation in a different way. They have said that this relationship differs from age to age. Under the primitive communal system the means of production were socially owned. The system was free from antagonism between the two. Primitive people worked in common and enjoyed the fruits of their labour in common. They had no experience of any exploitation.

Antagonism between productive forces and relations of production, Marx and Engels have said, first surfaced in the slave society because the owners of slave were also the owners of sources of production and simultaneously they owned the workers of production. The slave owner was the sole authority of the slave. He could sell, purchase and even kill him. Such relations of production corresponded to the state of productive forces of that period. In the slave period there also appeared the exchange of products between individuals and societies, accumulation of wealth in the hands of the few and concentration of the means of production in the hands of the minority.

The basis of production relations under the feudal system was that the feudal lords owned the means of production. But like slave owners they did not fully own the workers of production who were serfs. The serfs were comparatively free. The feudal lords purchased the labour of the serfs They were given wage or certain amount of land for their own cultivation and use. They were also allowed to enjoy few rights. Notwithstanding, there was no perceptible improvement in the relation between productive forces and production relations. This was mainly due to the fact that feudal lords were the owners of the sources of production and the serfs were not well-organised and adequately conscious. But the rise of political consciousness

1. G. A. Cohen—*Marx's Theory of History*, p. 134.

led the serfs to demand for more rights and liberties which the feudal lords were not prepared to provide. An antagonistic relationship between feudal lords and serfs became inevitable. The exploitation also assumed greater dimensions. Sporadic fightings became the order of the day. In the words of Stalin (p. 737) : "A class struggle between the exploiters and exploited is the principal feature of the feudal system."

The Industrial Revolution completely changed the economic and political scene of the society. The means of production were controlled by the few industrial magnates. The age-old cottage and small scale industries were faced with extinction and in many cases were destroyed. Streams of people from the countryside flocked to the towns and cities in search of work. Before Industrial Revolution there were agricultural workers or farmers and feudal landlords. When there was no cultivation the agricultural workers or cultivators were engaged in off-season business activities. There were also people of small business. But after Industrial Revolution the society was primarily divided into two main classes—industrial workers and the owners of capital or industries. The industrial workers subsequently came to be known as proletarians. Rader in his Marx's *Interpretation of History* writes "under the spur of technology, the forces develop more rapidly and in direction incompatable with the relations of production" (p. 13). But the intense antagonism between the two classes did not surface at the primary stages of Industrial Revolution. The progress of industrialisation intensified the conflict. Rader observes (p. 13) : "The conflict between forces of production and relations of production intensified until a period of revolutionary upheavals, the social relations are reorganised so as to harmonise with the productive forces."

In *The German Ideology* Marx and Engels wrote "all collisions in history have their origin in the contradictions between productive forces and forms of intercourse." This was true for all societies except primitive communal society. "When this conflict between the relations and forces of production occurs, it signifies that the present society has exhausted the possibilities for developing productivity and that the time for revolution is drawing near.[1]

We have so far seen that Marx and Engels had an idea of the conflict between relations of production and forces of production. But some recent critics have come to the conclusion that from Marx's writing we cannot be sure of the contradiction. This suspicion or opinion, whatever may be, centres around an observation made by Marx in *Wage, Labour and Capital.* Men produce commodities by cooperating among themselves. From this observation it is easy to conclude that social relation is part of productive forces. That is, there is not always contradiction between the two. One may overlap another. "Social relations are to be counted among the productive forces. There is an overlap between the relations and forces, because both include the organisation of the work process and division of labour among the working personnel" (Rader, p. 25). Gordon Leff remarks : "If there is no actual distinction between forces of production and productive relations, the contradiction between them is not the motive force of change."

Rader does not agree with this opinion of Gordon Leff. According to Leff there shall be extreme contradiction between the two or there shall be no contradiction at all. This is not correct at all. The conclusion of Leff is unfounded. Marx has said

1. Alvin W. Gouldner—*The Two Marxisms*, p. 191.

that the contradictions between productive forces and production relations are sometimes found, but not always. Under normal circumstances, when the economy expands, production relations are productive forces. The cooperation between the two accelerates the economy.

We have analysed the important aspects of historical materialism because it constitutes the central aspects of Marxist philosophy. Harold Laski in his *Communist Manifesto : A Socialist Landmark* has said that this concept is not free from defects. But it is at the same time true that it has explained the social change in a correct way. Harold Laski and many other critics have said that if we want to enter into the depth of social change and related issues the historical materialism is the most potent means. The changes that are taking place in a society must be viewed or analysed from the standpoint of materialism. Lukacs says, "Historical materialism did not exist for its own sake, it existed so that the proletariat could understand a situation...armed with this knowledge, it could act accordingly."

30 CLASSES AND CLASS STRUGGLE

Definition of Class : Marx and Engels

The *Communist Manifesto*, called the Bible of the working class, starts with the classic statement—The history of all the hitherto existing society is the history of the class struggles. Hence, the history viewed by Marx and Engels is nothing but the history of the struggle between two opposing classes—slaves and slave owners, feudal lords and serfs, and, finally, bourgeois and proletariat. Such is the importance of class in Marx's thought-system. Marx's analysis centres around materialistic conception of history. History, in his view, is not the struggle of ideas, it is replete with incidents of class struggle. If such is the importance of class, it is expected that Marx and Engels will give us a clear definition and elaborate analysis of class. Unfortunately we are disheartened.

Critics have viewed it from a different angle. They think that the concept of class is so important that Marx and Engels have left it to the judgment and wisdom of readers. They will frame their own views. We, however, do not like to detain ourselves on the point why did they not give a clear definition and elaborate analysis? We simply hold the view that Marx perhaps had an intention to give a clear and rational analysis of class. Some critics are of opinion that sudden death of Marx was the cause. But this argument is not plausible—even after Marx's death Engels got enough time to define the concept. I think that neither Marx nor Engels did think it necessary to define the idea of class. Many political concepts have remained undefined and the idea of class is one of them.

The last chapter of third volume of *Capital* proposes to deal with the concept of class. He raises the question what constitutes the class?—and the reply to this follows naturally from the reply to another question, namely : what makes wage-labourers, capitalists and landlords constitute three great social classes? Marx may think it a reply to his question what is class? But in our consideration this is not a reply at all. Instead of defining a class he has simply offered to his readers a three-fold classification of class. He has further observed that there are three great groups of individuals who live on wages, profit and ground-rent. On the basis of the sources of revenue he wanted to distinguish three main classes. The individuals who sell their labour power and get wage are called workers. Those who invest capital and earn profit and live on it are called capitalists. Persons getting rent from land are to be named as feudal lords.

Marx and Engels may be disinterested in defining class. But their readers are not disinterested at all. From the vast literature of Marx and particularly *The German Ideology* and *Poverty of Philosophy* the readers have built up definitions about class. One such definition has been given by Plamenatz : "The class a man belongs to, ...depends on whether or not he owns property and on the type of property he owns" (Plamenatz—*Man and Society*, Vol. II, p. 293). The proletarian does not own property in the normal sense of the term. Nor does he own natural resources or instruments of production. But he has his own labour power which he can sell to others or if he so wishes he can refuse to sell his labour. The capitalist is the owner of the sources or means of production. He buys labour and invests capital. Some scholars of Marxism think that Marx and Engels have explained the concept of class in terms of property. If we interpret the concept in a wider sense we shall find that to define class in terms of property is quite relevant.

The industrial development of Britain in the first half of nineteenth century far surpassed that of other countries of Western Europe and Marx and Engels developed their thought primarily in that background. The concept of class is no exception. Engels wrote his *The Conditions of Working Class in England* in the background of the industrial progress of Britain. Kolakowski rightly observes that Marx analysed the concept of class from the standpoint of the conditions that prevailed in Britain in his time. Again, he writes "The definition of class is by no means a purely verbal or methodological question. The need for a definition arises from observation of the facts of the class struggle" (p. 29).

A very important aspect of Marx's theory of class is it shows "spontaneous solidarity in its opposition to other classes, though this does not prevent its members from being rivals to one another" (Kolakowski, p. 291). An important aspect of Marx's theory of class is he rejected utopian socialist classification according to scale of income or relative share in the whole social product. Marx has also categorically stated that the precondition of the existence of class there must exist the consciousness about class.

Two-Class Model and Marx

There is a common notion that Marx has envisaged a two-class model and this notion is primarily derived from the *Manifesto*. Marx and Engels in the *Manifesto* have said that the history of human society, history that is recorded, is replete with struggles between two classes. They say freeman and slave; patrician and plebian, baron and serf; and guild-burgess and journeyman—in a word oppressor and oppressed stood in sharp opposition each to other. The society was, therefore, directly divided into two opposite classes. In earlier epochs there were class divisions and antagonisms between classes. But with the progress and change of society this antagonism began to assume new shapes and dimensions. The bourgeois age is distinctly distinguished by a simplified two-class model. In their own words "More and more society is splitting into two great and directly contraposed classes—bourgeois and proletariat."

A pertinent issue disturbs the mind of students of Marxism. Does the two-class model suit the real situation of society? When Marx was writing *The Manifesto* in England the middle class was rising rapidly and was extremely eager to exert its influence on the administration. Jeremy Bentham, the great utilitarian, propounded his theory of utilitarianism to make a strong plea for this class. Moreover, the century-old Industrial Revolution has succeeded in establishing the middle class and other small classes in-between bourgeois and proletariat. There were also other small classes. Bourgeois critics generally charge Marx by saying that by highlighting the two-class model he has showed no respect to the existing condition and picture of the society. But we refuse to accept this contention. Nowhere in their writing Marx and Engels have said that there are only two classes. Central idea of the two class model is that if the classes are not posited in quite opposite directions there cannot be conflict. We have already noted that Marx and Engels have viewed the concept of class from the angle of struggle. There are conflicts among other classes, but these are not sufficient to aggravate a situation for an intense struggle.

In several writings we get reference to petty bourgeoisie, farmers and other small classes. There is also the mention of the middle class. He has criticised Ricardo for mentioning the middle class. There are large number of men who cultivate land, but are not farmers or proletarians. They constitute a class. Marx has also given a status of class to intellectuals. Marx has deprecated the role and functions of these classes—particularly the intellectuals and middle class. Intellectuals are the salaried spokesman of the bourgeois class. Their chief functions is to theorise the viewpoints of capitalists.

In his *Class Struggle of France* Marx points out a class—lumpen-proletariat. They are the dropouts of the society. The lumpen-proletariat is a reactionary class. The lumpen-proletarians have no fixed livelihood. Most of the time they take the side of the capitalists. Their chief aim is to harvest certain amount of immediate gain by taking side of the capitalists.

The concept of two class-model is, we now think, quite clear. The main thing is contradiction. In *The German Ideology* Marx and Engels have said that certain number of people will constitute a class only when their interests are opposite to those of other people. In the *Eighteenth Brumaire* the same idea with its elaborate form has been stressed by him. Here he includes the culture and environment into the ambit of contradiction. It is, therefore, quite manifest that Marxian two-class model has a deeper and very significant perspective and meaning. It should be understood what he actually wants to say. Many critics have challenged Marx's two-class model. But these critics have failed to go into the depth of Marx's view. He admitted the existence of more than two classes. But his chief intention was—in a capitalist society the class conflict was inevitable and, if so, there must exist only two classes whose interests are quite opposite.

Ruling Class Theory

In order to have preliminary ideas about the concept of ruling class and its special importance in capitalist state we quote few lines from *The German Ideology* which is a very important work of Marx and Engels. The ideas of the ruling class are in every epoch the ruling ideas, i.e., the class which is ruling the material force of society, is at the same time ruling its intellectual force. The class which has the means of material production at its disposal consequently also controls the means of mental production so that the ideas of those who lack the means of mental production are on the whole subject to it.

Explaining the concept of ruling class Gouldner maintains "What makes a group ruling class is in the part the needs it satisfies, how acute and widespread they are, on the one hand, and their ability to exclude others from satisfying this need, on the other. What makes a group ruling class is its ability to monopolise a necessary service, to inhibit others from providing this service, and above all to present those receiving help from helping themselves and satisfying their own needs. What makes a group ruling class is that it can satisfy acute and recurrent mass needs, and that it can prevent others from doing so."

The very term ruling class was most probably coined by Marx to throw light on the class structure and class domination system of capitalist society. The ruling class means—a class which is economically powerful and because of this it controls political system, needless to say in its favour. Not only this, it controls the economic and cultural sides of the state. Simultaneously it prevents others from the access to these needs. It controls the means of production and at the same time creates hindrances so that others cannot get any opportunity to control them. To put it differently, the ruling class rules out the possibility of competition. There may be competition among the members of the ruling class. But the members of the non-ruling class must not be allowed to enter into the domain of ruling class. That is, proletarians will always remain proletarians. The fact is that the bourgeois class wanted to divide the society into two water-tight compartments. They will not get any scope to improve their lot.

The ruling class monopolises the capacity to satisfy the basic needs. This is not all. Other classes, at the same time, although they are needy, are prevented from doing this. The ruling class will have full scope to exercise authority. While the minimum scope will never be offered to other classes. The ruling class subjugates all other classes to it. The leadership and control of the ruling class are final and uncontested. It not only controls the material world but also the intellectual world. The thoughts and ideas of the society cannot go against the thoughts and ideas of the ruling class. The ruling class achieves its objective not through military methods but through subtle propaganda and indoctrination. The dominant role of the ruling class is generally found in civil society. It controls almost all the important aspects of civil society.

Features of Marxian Concept of Class

David McLellan points out few features of Marx's theory of class. He says (p. 181) "Marx's definition of class seems to vary greatly, not only with the development of his thought, but even within the same period. Marx often uses the term, in common with the usage of his time, as a synonym for faction or group." What McLellan wants to emphasise is that Marx did not adhere to any fixed notion about class. He viewed this in the background of existing conditions. With the change of economic conditions, structure and composition of class underwent changes. Marx had to accept it and incorporate it into his definition.

In the third volume of *Capital* Marx points out three different classes—capitalists, landowners and proletariat. In Marx's time in England there were these three classes. The industrialisation created the former two classes and even the progress of industrialisation failed to obliterate the feudal system. So, considering Marx's time, this tripartite division is a realistic and rational one. In the second half of the nineteenth century feudal lords constituted an important class. But he prophesied that under the impact of industrialisation the land owning class would not be capable of surviving and practically that happened. Under the economic pressure it will, in course of time, disappear. Some of them will be capitalists and others proletariat.

Kolakowski and several other critics have observed that Marx viewed the class primarily in the background of struggle. Again, his class is associated with economic position or status. We here hold the view that the question of struggle cannot arise without the rise of consciousness. That is, class-struggle is possible only when the members of the class are conscious of their position and condition. The condition can be designated in simple language as suffering or exploitation. Consciousness again leads to hostility. A class according to Marx will always view its own interests and will give priority to the interests and when doing this a conflict with another opposing class becomes inevitable. Hence consciousness, conflict and struggle are inevitably connected with the idea of class.

From the analysis of Marx another feature of class can easily be deduced. Class divisions, in general, have nothing to do with the natural differences of sex, race etc. Even there may be different classes within the same race or sex. Marx and Engels do not subscribe to the bourgeois classification of class on the basis of political factors. In *Anti-Dühring* Engels says (p. 37) "the warring classes of society are always the products of the mode of production and of exchange—in a word, the economic conditions of their time."

Class-in-Itself and Class-for-Itself

Marx once said that he was not the first man to use the word class and the ideas related to it. We admit it. But it is undoubtedly true that two concepts—class-in-itself and class-for-itself were for the first time used by him. These two phrases or terms are significant. A group of people in Marx's view cannot be called a class. It must have certain features. In *The German Ideology* and *The Poverty of Philosophy* Marx and Engels have elaborately discussed the matter. *The German Ideology* contains the following uses on the formation of class : "The separate individuals form a class only so far as they have to carry on a common battle against another class; in other respects they are on hostile terms with each other as competitors. On the other hand, the class, in its turn, assumes an independent existence as against the individuals, so that the latter find their conditions of life predetermined" (p. 85). In *The Poverty of Philosophy* (p. 104) Marx says..."the proletariat is not yet sufficiently developed to constitute itself as a class, and consequently so long as the struggle itself of the proletariat with the bourgeoisie has not yet assumed a political character." Though Marx and Engels did not elaborate the idea of class a detailed study of the above-noted two books reveals that the concept of class occupied an important place in their entire thought system. Since they were seriously thinking of the emancipation of the working class both of them paid maximum importance to the formation of class and its prospective role.

In *The Poverty of Philosophy* Marx has further observed (p. 150) "The economic conditions had first transformed the mass of the people of the country into workers. The combination of capital has created for this mass a common situation, common interests. This mass is thus already a class as against capital, but not yet for itself. In the struggle this mass becomes united and constitutes itself as a class for itself."

Now let us explain the two phrases. The first phrase the *class-in-itself* refers to the objective fact of the class as an aggregate, defined by its position in the economy. The second phrase *class-for-itself* refers to the members of this class when they have become aware of this identity as a class, aware of their common situation, and of their role in changing or preserving capitalist society. Such class consciousness is not included in the objective condition of the term "class".

The ideas and ideology are determined by the economic bases of society. The class consciousness of the proletariat will follow this rule. The ideas men come to have are generally determined by the state of history in which they live and by the class position they occupy within it. In the capitalist society the ideas of the ruling class are the ruling ideas of the epoch. The proletarians are indoctrinated by the ideas of the ruling class. But in due course the class consciousness emerges among the proletarians.

The class-for-itself has deeper and wider implications which require clarifications. The proletarians must be fully conscious of their present condition (the extent and depth of exploitation) and they must also realise that the only way of emancipation is struggle against capitalists and bourgeois state administration. The struggle may be intense and long-drawn and may require a lot of sacrifice. This type of consciousness and realisation will make the proletarian class as *a class for itself.* But without political consciousness this realisation will never be achieved. In several works including *The Poverty of Philosophy* both Marx and Engels have strongly emphasised the immense importance of consciousness. In the *Manifesto* Marx has pointed out that the workers must be united without which there cannot be any political party. It is the consciousness which makes them hostile. In *The Eighteenth Brumaire of Louis Bonaparte* Marx says :

"In so far as million of families live under economic conditions of existence that separate their mode of life, their interests and their culture from those of the other classes and put them in hostile opposition to the latter, they form a class. In so far as there is merely a local interconnection among these small-holding peasants and the identity of their interests begets no community, no national bond, and no political organisation among them, they do not form a class. They are consequently incapable of enforcing their class interests in their own name, whether through a parliament or through a convention. They cannot represent themselves, they must be represented" (p. 334).

It is be noted here that Marx and Engels were quite confident that mere formation of a class was not enough for launching a fierce and longdrawn struggle against the very powerful capitalists and their state because the state was the instrument of exploitation and oppression. For that purpose Marx put so much emphasis on the distinction between class in itself and class for itself.

Concept of Class and Lenin

There is no second opinion about Marx as a great thinker. But he does not systematically analyse different key concepts and this is the greatest weakness of Marxian philosophy. One such concept is class. Nowhere has he clearly defined class. The third volume of *Capital* just starts to analyse. But it does not proceed further. *The Poverty of Philosophy* contains certain sporadic remarks. *The German Ideology* simply emphasises the importance of the ruling class. We find some discussions in *The Eighteenth Brumaire of Louis Bonaparte.* This is again inadequate. It is not difficult to form a coherent view about class. We have done that. The students of Marxism desire to have a clear definition of class and that has been provided by Lenin. His small book *A Great Beginning* offers us a clear definition. Let us see what he says :

"Classes are large groups of people differing from each other by the place they occupy in a historically determined system of social production by their relation (in most cases fixed and formulated in law) to the means of production, by their role in the social organisation of labour and, consequently, by the dimensions and mode of acquiring the share of social wealth of which they dispose. Classes are groups of people one of which can appropriate the labour of another owing to the different places they occupy in a definite system of social economy" (p. 248).

An analysis of Lenin's definition reveals certain features. Within every system of production, classes occupy different or diametrically opposed position. The positions are determined by their relationship to the means of production. The relationship, in turn, determines their role in the social organisation of labour. Classes perform various functions in social production. A society is divided into antagonistic classes, one class controls the sources of production and the distribution system as a whole. Other classes are engaged in physical labour. That is they make possible the production.

Class divisions form the whole of social life and whole system of social relations. The relations may be material or ideological. Classes are connected by certain economic relations which enable the exploiting classes to appropriate the labour of the exploited. The ruling class cannot keep its physical existence intact without exploitation. But the exploited class demands the end of exploitation. This demand is based on material and ideological ground. The wealth is created by workers and, therefore, they have a legitimate claim over the wealth. The rationality of this claim is based on ideology. Ideology of emancipation; ideology of communism.

Class Structure of Society

Marx has said that the capitalist mode of production has simplified the class structure of society and also the class antagonisms. In earlier epochs there were both classes and class antagonisms, but they were in complex forms. Then chiefly two types of classes in any antagonistic class divided society—*Basic classes* and *non-basic classes.* The basic classes are the classes which are engendered by the prevailing mode of production and without which such a mode would be inconceivable. The slave-owning mode of production conditioned the existence of slaves and slave owners. These two were the basic classes. Similarly, in the epoch of feudalism, peasants and landlords were two basic classes. Feudal mode of production was impossible without these two classes. The capitalist mode of production necessiated the bourgeoisie and the proletariat.

The relations between the basic classes determine the essence of society's socio-economic system and the form of exploitation. The transition from one mode of production to another also changes the relations between the basic classes in a radical way. In the slave society the slaves were the property of the slave-owners. While in the feudal system the peasants or serfs were no longer the property of the feudal lords. They were free. The landlord had a claim over the labour of the peasants. Under capitalism the relationship between the proletariat and bourgeoisie underwent radical changes. The workers were exploited but they were free and independent of the capitalists. The capitalists could not force the workers to sell their labour.

Interpreting history from the standpoint of materialism Marx has come to the conclusion that in any mode of production normally there are two basic classes. On the other hand, the number of non-basic classes is never two. The non-basic classes are also called transitional classes. With the arrival of new mode of production or any other factor the non-basic classes do not survive. In other words, the existence of non-basic classes is determined by different socio-economic structures existing along with dominant mode of production. In the slave-owning society there were small-scale farmers and handicrafts. In feudal society, as the towns developed, there arose new social strata comprising—craftsmen organised in guilds, corporation, merchants and so on. When capitalism was fully developed the old and one-time powerful feudalism ultimately disappeared. It is because feudal system was incongruous with the capitalist structure of society. But though feudalism was destroyed very few feudal lords remained. These few landlords, however, failed to constitute a basic class in the regime of capitalism. Marx has said that in capitalism there existed both basic and non-basic classes and this was an important feature of capitalist society.

Marx observed that in capitalist societies of some European countries there were many intellectuals who created influence among the educated section of society and they formed a separate class. In Sheptulin's language "Intellectuals, who are neither owners of the means of production, nor direct producers of material goods, make up the intelligentsia, which include researchers, writers, teachers, doctors, artists and some sections of white collar workers."

In capitalist society the intellectuals serve different purposes. Some of them take side of the capitalists and help capitalist production. They join hands with the capitalists in propagation and elaboration of bourgeois ideology. In other words, the main purpose of this section of intellectuals is to safeguard the interests of capitalists in all possible ways. The other section of the intellectuals throws in their lot with the working people. They fight workers' cause and voice their interests.

In the antagonistic class structure of society there is another non-basic class which is called petty-bourgeoisie. It is not a full-fledged bourgeois class. But as capitalism develops the petty-bourgeoisie also disintegrates. A small portion of it adds to its wealth and joins the capitalists while the larger part goes bankrupt and become proletarians or semi-proletarians. This is a regular process. So far as middle class and petty-bourgeoisie are concerned there is no stability. Change from one class to another takes place.

Forms of Class Struggle

The class struggle is not a transitory phenomenon. Throughout the recorded history of mankind there was always class struggle and only the establishment of a classless society will bring about an end to this struggle. Marx and Engels have said in the *Manifesto* "Freeman and slave, patrician and plebian, baron and serf, guild burgess and journeyman—in a word oppressor and oppressed—stood in sharp opposition each to other. They carried on perpetual warfare that invariably ended either in a revolutionary change or else in common ruin of the contending classes." The class struggle is not one but of various forms. What are the forms?

From the recorded history of the world Marx and Engels have discovered various forms of class struggle and they have also observed that the struggle among the classes takes place on reasons more than one. The most important reason of the class struggle, according to Marx and Engels, is economic. If we look at the history we shall find that the workers started a struggle against the capitalists to get some economic concessions. To put it in another way, to safeguard the economic benefits and interests the workers took arms. That is why it is called economic class struggle.

The workers fight for higher wages, reduced working hour, improvement of working conditions. To fight for the economic benefits the workers at first formed organisations. Trade union is such an organisation. Methods of struggle are strikes. Economic fight is of vital importance to the working class. This helps them to improve their economic conditions. But if the workers concentrate their efforts and energy simply on the fighting for economic benefits their emancipation from exploitation will never be realised. That is why the Marxists have always advised that the economic struggle will never be their sole objective. Marxists are of opinion that—significant though it may be—the economic struggle is not in itself enough to do away with the capitalist exploitation. To achieve this there must be a political struggle.

There are various forms of political struggle. Such as : participation in the elections to parliament, local councils and other state organisations. Political struggle may also assume the form of demonstration, mass protestations against the arbitrary and repressive activities creating barricades and launching agitation. The objectives of political struggle and economic struggle are different. The objective of the former is to overthrow the established government from power and seize political power while the purpose of the latter is to force the owners of industry and also the government to accept some basic economic demands. By means of both struggles the working class intensifies class struggle.

Marx and Engels have said that from history it appears that workers at first start movement for the fulfilment of certain economic demands and after that they start political struggle. But as to its importance it ranks first. The political struggle is more extensive and its repercussions are also greater. The whole political structure undergoes radical changes. The capitalists and workers are set against each other. The economic struggle makes workers economically conscious and trade union conscious. But political struggle creates a political consciousness. For the emancipation of workers, capture of political power is a must and that end can never be attained without political consciousness. Marx, Engels and their followers never have given too much emphasis upon trade unionism. It is a mode of struggle but trade unions are never the highest form of organisation. Political party belongs to that category.

Form the above analysis it is now obvious that political struggle is a must for the working class. It is also to be noted that, through economic struggle and formation of trade union, workers proceed towards political struggle. Political struggle is rather the highest form of class struggle. The economic struggle cannot be minimised. It helps the workers to gain confidence in their capacity of launching a fierce struggle against the capitalists. The economic lot of the workers, at first, be improved and then they will be encouraged for a further struggle.

The ideological struggle is also an important form of class struggle. Marx and Engels have repeatedly stressed that the working class must realise the extent of the exploitation, and the nature of class interests. In order to be acquainted with that a complete training in ideology appears to be must. Engels took steps to that direction. It is a must for the worker that they must know the laws of development of society, laws of the development of capitalism. All these they can get from the training or indoctrination of ideology. The theoretical and ideological struggle of the working class is aimed at freeing the workers' minds from bourgeois ideas and prejudices. Teaching of Marxist ideology raises the consciousness of the working class to a very higher level. So the ideological form of class struggle is just as essential for final victory of the proletariat as its other forms.

Marx and Engels have strongly emphasised the rise of consciousness, because only this consciousness can lead them to final victory. It is wrong to assume that only propagation of ideology will create a flood of consciousness in the minds of workers and practical activities are less important. It is to be asserted here that ideological training and various forms of economic and political activities supplement each other. Ideological training sharpens the political and economic weapons. Again, participation in struggle will never be fruitful without training. Lenin said "consciousness means the workers' understanding that the only way to improve their conditions and to achieve their emancipation is to conduct a struggle against the capitalist factory owner class." It is said that ideological struggle is a long and continuous process. The mind and thought of working class and other weaker sections of society cannot be changed overnight. The indoctrination or training in ideology will take time because while the workers and their leaders resort to this task their counter-forces or parties do not sit idly. They also participate in counter-propaganda and, in this way, the struggle in ideological arena continues.

Evalution

The above analysis of the forms of class struggle is not free form limitations. The economic class struggle is not completely separated from political class struggle. Workers very often resort to political methods of struggle in order to realise economic gains. It is to be pointed out that the purposes of economic and political struggles coincide. Emancipation from oppression is the main objective of any struggle which may be economic or political. Naturally a clear-cut line cannot be drawn between these two forms of class struggle. Sometimes it is found that the ultimate aim is the overthrow of government and economic factor evokes the determination to struggle.

One spectacular limitation of class struggle, in its economic form, is that it is not always general. Very often the workers of any particular industry or manufacturing concern launches a struggle against the owners and in that situation the workers of other industries may not ally with the agitating workers. If all the workers are not united a broad-based struggle will never be possible.

Marx and Engels have cautioned us by saying that the purpose of the class struggle will never be confined in the attainment of certain economic benefits or overthrow of government. The ultimate aim will always be to ensure the dictatorship of the proletariat. In his famous letter to Wedeymeyer (March 3, 1852) Marx said "What I did that was new was to prove that...that the class struggle necessarily leads to the dictatorship of the proletariat." When the proletariat will establish its overall authority including the capture of political power then there will no longer exist any classes. So the purpose of the class struggle will be to set up a classless society. Though in Marxism class struggle occupies a prominent place, it has been said that there is hardly any place of complacency. Even in socialist or communist society there is every possibility of emergence of counter-forces whose sole purpose is to scuttle the objectives of the working class; for that very reason some people think of permanent revolution or struggle. This type of struggle may also assume the form of class struggle.

Marx has also said that the proletarians shall use the class struggle as an instrument to achieve their goal. They must also release all sorts of efforts to intensify the class struggle. With the development of capitalism the contradiction between the capitalists and workers will increase. In that case the active role the workers must play. Mere existence of contradiction is not a sufficient factor of the class struggle. Marx and Engels had no faith on the goodwill of the capitalists. That is why they have placed their reliance on the class struggle. The workers must also be prepared to continue the class struggle.

Class Struggle as the Motive Force of Development

It has been held by Marx and Engels that the struggle between the owners of the means of production and the workers is a social, political and psychological reflection of objective conflicts. These conflicts lead to different reactions among the members of the different classes of bourgeois society. The objective contradiction within the capitalist economy has its subjective counterpart in the class struggle within the capitalist society. In this struggle the wage-workers represent the expanding forces of production and owners represent the maintenance of established relations of production and with them the exploitation of unpropertied class. The interests of these two contesting classes are diametrically opposite. The workers are determined to change or overthrow the existing system to bring an end of the exploitation. The bourgeois class is determined to safeguard at any cost the existing system which is conducive to their interests. The objective of one class is not to be exploited and that of the other is to perpetuate the exploitation. So, to speak the truth, this situation (the opposite interests of the two major classes of capitalist society) is the prime cause of class struggle.

History of human civilisation is the sequence of contradictions. It is a struggle between the classes. Marx has held that the revolution will result from the developing material forces of production as they come into conflict with the relations of productions. The economic contradiction is the prime cause of revolution and this revolution, in turn, leads to a radical change of society. The workers firmly believe that sporadic and piecemeal efforts cannot improve their conditions and lift them from the morass of exploitation. The class struggle or radical revolution is the only means which can save the working class from exploitation. Marx in this way has suggested that the class struggle is the motive force of development. The term "development" has a broader connotation in Marxism. It implies overall progress of the society.

The intensive class struggle will have the following consequences. There will be seen the development of productive forces. The struggle will ensure the productive capacity of workers. The owners of industries will introduce higher and improved technologies. All these will lead to further development of industries. The struggle will also force the industrialists to shorten the working hours. Various other developments will follow. The class struggle also gives an impetus to the development of production relations. Obsolete production relations are not automatically changed under the impact of productive forces that have developed within their framework. The ruling class will resist any change in the relations of production. This class will support the old production relations. In order to overcome the resistance of the ruling class a more powerful force is required and that force is class struggle.

Marx has said that the ruling class will not easily surrender to the struggle of the working class. It will employ all its resources and strength to defeat the struggle of the working class. It will always adhere to the outdated measures and techniques. Only a class struggle can bring about a change. The ruling class does not want any development, because that may not maximise its profit or surplus value. The bourgeois theoreticians enthusiastically plead for reforms and compromise. But Marx summarily discards them. Without a struggle leading to revolution, progress or development is impossible.

Although the ultimate purpose of class struggle is development, its history reveals that this was not achieved in past as a single event of class struggle. The class struggle proceeded step by step towards its apex goal. It can be illustrated in the following way. In the slave society the slaves fought against the slave-owners not for changing the ownership of means of production or relations of production but for the abolition of slavery. The uprisings of the slaves forced the slave-owners to accept the major demands of slaves such as ownership of land. That is, the slaves were awarded the ownership of land. This system converted the slaves into small peasants and serfs. Thus arose feudalism.

From history we come to know that in the feudal age the peasants struggle against the landlords to find out a way from exploitation. The end of slave-system and advent of feudalism could not draw a curtain over the exploitation. Hence the class struggle continued—though in different forms—and between different types of classes. It is to be noted here that the feudal system, in comparison with slave system, was a better and improved social system. The class struggle made this possible. The peasants' struggle in the feudal period played a very important part since it promoted the abolition of feudal mode of production and feudal production relations. Thus the peasants' struggle against the feudal lords created certain positives steps for the advancement of society. The slaves in the earlier epoch even could not imagine to change the relations of production and overthrowing authority.

Then came industrialisation which completely changed the economic, political, social and cultural picture or situation of society. The industrial proletariat appeared and asserted itself as an independent force. The misery leads the proletarians to demand for the abolition of private property. When the property is released from private control its full utilisation becomes possible. The whole system of property or the sources of production are used for the development of society as a whole. Only the class struggle makes it possible.

Economic struggle is the first form of class struggle. It grows spontaneously out of the economic plight of the workers and is waged mainly for improvements in the terms for selling labour power, rather than for the complete abolition of such conditions. The importance of the economic struggle is great since it gave raise to the first class organs of the proletariat—the trade unions.

The proletarians, with the maturity of consciousness, come to realise that mere class struggle in economic form cannot free them from exploitation. Capture of state power is essential. This leads to the revolution. The state as an instrument of exploitation loses its importance and ultimately it withers away. The whole force of society is employed for the development of all. And it is possible only in socialism. It is because socialism is the only form or social system which stands for the development of all irrespective of any difference.

The contention of the bourgeois ideologists is that the class struggle takes a heavy toll of life, property and cultural values and upsets the normal rhythm of society's life. It is negative and inhibits mankind's all sorts of progress. Marx and Engels summarily reject this contention of the bourgeois ideologists. One of the important advances of the materialist understanding of history is the conclusion that, far from being an inhibiting factor, the class struggle is a great motive force of the development of antagonistic societies. Without a class struggle there cannot be a transition from the old socio-economic system to a new one.

Some critics say that any uprising of peasants and workers cannot be called a class struggle, because for a clear-cut class struggle there must be a clear and well-defined class. Marx and Engels express the view that theoretically this may not be properly class struggle, but it creates a foundation of class struggle as well as of progress. Speaking of the peasant war of 1524-26 in Germany, Engels noted that it "pointed prophetically to future class struggles, by bringing on to the stage not only the peasants in revolt—that was no-longer anything new—but behind them the beginnings of the modern proletariat, with the red flags in their hands and the demand for common ownership of goods on their lips" (Zotov, 119).

Causes of the Class Struggle

We have so far discussed several aspects of class struggle. Now time has arrived to explore the causes of class struggle. The struggle, which occupies such important place in Marxism, is not due to the cantankerous nature of classes or people. The bourgeois ideologists admit the existence of classes, but do not say that these classes are involved in irreconcilable conflicts, though there might be sporadic clashes. The prime cause of this clash is the misunderstanding and it is resolved without disrupting the normal functioning of society. The bourgeois theoreticians particularly the sociologists, admit the existence of classes and differences in interests, but they do not admit that these differences will ultimately result in serious class conflict or struggle between the classes. They are of opinion that all the conflicts are amicably settled by means of negotiations or mutual understanding. They also propagate that peaceful coexistence among the classes is rather the characteristic feature of society. The bourgeois scholars further claim that in spite of the conflicts among the classes the total development of society has never been adversely affected. Rather it has progressed satisfactorily. Hence struggle between the classes can never be treated as a potent force of development.

Marx and Engels have held that mere communication gap is not the cause of conflict. The class struggle is caused by the diametrically opposed social positions and contradictory interests of the different classes. What is class interest? It is determined not by the consciousness of the class but by its position and role in the system of social production. In the capitalist system of production the proletariat is deprived of the ownership of the means of production and is thus deprived of all privileges. The workers are also subjected to exploitation. So the workers feel that it is capitalism which is the source of misery and suffering. Not any particular worker is victim of capitalist exploitation, but the working class as a whole. But the consciousness cannot be exiled from the domain of class interest. The working class must be conscious of the extent and nature of exploitation and must also be conscious that only the overthrow of capitalism can emancipate this class. Hence the class interest and consciousness are inextricably connected.

The cause of the class struggle is the opposite nature of the interests. The interest of the capitalist class is to maximise the profit, whereas the interest of the working class lies in the enhancement of wage sufficient for comfortable living. Workers' demand is quite rational in the sense that wage must always be proportionate to the contribution to production. To put the matter in simple language—maximisation of profit is the objective of one class and maximum wage is the aim of another class.

These diametrically opposite interests cannot be reconciled. The socialist predecessors of Marx, particularly the utopian socialists, heavily depended upon the goodwill and philanthropic mentality of the capitalists and they believed that the capitalists would concede some of the basic and legitimate demands of the working class voluntarily. Adjustment and conciliation, they thought, were sufficient weapons to improve the economic conditions. But Marx and Engels have discarded this as absurd. It is impossible to think or assume that the capitalists will part with a portion of their profit. The capitalists cannot deviate from the path of profit motive. The surplus value is the source of capital formation. Again, the exploitation swells the surplus value. On the other hand, the working class resorts to struggle not simply for survival but for the realisation of their legitimate demands. Which the capitalists are not prepared to concede.

Class struggle in antagonistic capitalist society is not the result of any single factor. The immediate cause is the exploitation. But not always. There was exploitation in feudal society but this was free from class struggle. The intransigence of the capitalists, the determination of the working class to abolish exploitation, rise of consciousness, the maturity of contradiction and the inability of the capitalists to provide long-term palliatives against the erosion of influence—all these combined together to precipitate class struggle.

Appraisal

The class struggle constitutes the core of Marxism and the novelty lies in the fact that this leads to the dictatorship of the proletariat. The simple meaning is that the struggle of the proletarians against the bourgeoisie is not the sole objective, they must, after the struggle, establish the predominance over all. Now to what extent the proletarians have been able to set up the dictatorship is an issue of great polemics. We have no intention to enter into the controversy because for academic purposes that will be a fruitless adventure. The scholars and critics do not agree on the causes of the failure of the proletarian movement.

About 100 years ago Lenin said "the proletariat economically dominates the centre and nerve of the entire economic system of capitalism." This observation still holds good. The scientific and technological revolution has changed the economic conditions of both workers and capitalists. But the major portion of the benefit has gone to the capitalists. V. D. Zotov in *The Marxist-Leninist Theory of Society* writes "In the conditions created by state-monopoly capitalism and the scientific and technological revolution significant changes are taking place in the working class. These changes are not leading to the "disappearance' of the working class, to the deproletarianisation of capitalist society. The tendency towards the steady growth of the working class, of its proportion in the population continues. In 1980 the working class totalled nearly 80 percent of the gainfully employed population in the USA and Britain, 77 percent in France, 60 percent in Italy and roughly 62 percent in Japan" (p. 121). The capitalist mode of production is also proletarianising the peasants. In order to get better economic facilities the peasants are relinquishing their traditional farming and joining the army of industrial workers. This is ruining them gradually. In U.K., USA and France there are no peasants in the traditional sense. It is a clear indication of the falsity of bourgeois plea that the number of proletarians is declining. If the number of proletarians increases the class struggle is inevitable. Analysing the exact nature of capitalist society, V. D. Zotov has come to this conclusion.

The concept of class struggle propounded by Marx, Engels and subsequently elaborated by Lenin has been called 'scientific' on the ground that all of them have explained it from the background of historical materialism. According to Marx and Marxists to explain any idea or concept in the light of historical materialism is scientific. In every eopch of social progress there were classes and also conflict among them. Marx made this revolutionary conclusion by gathering facts from the study of history covering several centuries. It is very much unfortunate that the bourgeois scholars and theoreticians did not pay proper attention to this aspect of class struggle. It is the credit of Marx and Engels that they have viewed it scientifically. They have said that the class struggle will lead to dictatorship of the proletariat. This is a logical and scientific conclusion. If the workers are serious of their own emancipation—and Marx believes that they are serious because they are conscious—then they cannot stop at class struggle. They will make all efforts to establish their dictatorship.

Gouldner in *The Two Marxisms* says "Marx's very conception of class struggle reveals the characteristic ambivalences between the structural scientific socialism, on the one hand, and his voluntaristic critical Marxism on the other. On the voluntaristic side, Marx argues that while capitalism's development will make ever greater encroachments on the working class, pushing the value of labour power down to a minimum, nonetheless, the workers have a duty to keep on struggling, even for improvements that can only be temporary" (p. 204). It is the historical duty of the workers to go on struggling until capitalism is completely annihilated. If they stop struggling they will be cowards. In this voluntaristic mood, Marx holds, workers have a duty to struggle against capital.

The importance of class struggle can be viewed from another angle. So long as the wage system remains there is very little scope of the improvement of the workers' conditions. The intransigent attitude of the capitalists is not solely responsible for this. The structure of the capitalist society is so built up as not to allow considerable concessions to labourers. Under such circumstances the workers are forced to fight against the capitalists. Gouldner observes (p. 205) "Given its basic structure, there was little workers could do to improve their conditions in any fundamental way under capitalism and its wage system. Yet, they were to continue struggling, partly as a duty to themselves and history, partly to educate and to transform themselves in preparation for their overthrow of capitalism and its limits."

Karl Marx's observation—all struggles are class struggles–has been challenged by his opponents. In any society there are several classes and conflicts frequently arise among them but these cannot be categorised as class struggles. It may be religious conflicts. On cultural grounds conflicts may arise among different cultural groups. Conflicts may also arise between the ethnic groups and this is not rare at all. The religious conflicts were the characteristic features of the Middle Ages. But the religious and ethnic struggles cannot be called class struggle.

Marx thought that the rapid rise in the number of working class or proletarians was the prime cause of antagonistic relationship between the classes—particularly two major classes. Unfortunately he forgot to note that with the rise of the number of proletarians they have also increased their status in the field of collective bargaining which has increased enormously. It is unfortunate that Marx did not bring this aspect of capitalist society into serious consideration. The capitalists have also modified their behaviour and attitude towards working class. This has not led to the abolition of antagonism. But the workers today are in better position. Today we are faced with a peculiar situation which Marx and Engels could not foresee. They thought that if the profit of the capitalists rises the miseries of the workers will also rise. Today we find a different picture. Profit has risen but not the misery. The workers through collective bargaining have succeeded in enhancing their wages. The system of capitalism since Marx has undergone tremendous changes.

"Society as a whole is more and more splitting into two great hostile camps, into two great classes directly facing each other; bourgeoisie and proletariat." This is the observation of Marx and Engels. Critics hold the view that the relationship between bourgeoisie and proletariat is not always bitter, though most of the time this is so. At present the capitalists adopt different methods to placate or appease the workers. The workers are not only organised but also militant. Their unity can throw the capitalists into great troubles. The representatives of the two antagonistic classes sit round a table to find out the solution to outstanding problems. The real situation forces them to come to a settlement. The pragmatism of these two classes does not allow the interests to be irreconcilable. The bourgeoisie has nowhere been overthrown due to class struggle. In every capitalist society the bourgeoisie and proletariat are living side by side. Miliband in *Marxism and Politics* (p. 21) says "This of course raises the whole question of the validity or otherwise of Marx's and Engels's belief in the inevitability of revolution." The workers will go on fighting against the bourgeoisie—this conception is not supported by actual situations.

Marx nowhere has elaborated the notion of class, though it is a central part of his philosophy. The term proletariat has been explained by Engels in his *Principles of Communism.* But it is so brief that the whole discussion does not throw sufficient light on the subject. Miliband (p. 22) has said that we do not know what exactly Marx and Engels meant by these two terms. This deficiency of Marx has encouraged bourgeois theoreticians to interpret the terms in their own way which harms Marxism. Marx might have been more cautious.

In the third volume of *Capital* Marx said "the stratification of classes does not appear in its pure form." In spite of this frank admission, the pertinent question which crops up in our mind is—Is his classification a realistic one? The modern states are ruled by a large number of bureaucrats and officers. To what class these persons belong? Similarly the army and police cannot be classified according to Marx's specification. But the modern states cannot be imagined without army, police and bureaucracy. There are also various groups and subgroups in every capitalist party. Any analysis of class struggle minus these suffers from deficiency.

Marx's theory of class and class struggle is not applicable to the Third World countries. The socio-economic condition of the Third World countries is different from that of developed countries. Miliband writes "The class profile...refers to the advanced capitalist countries. The very large question which arises is how far that profile and the propositions have application to other types of society—the countries of the Third World...In regard to the Third World countries class relations are central determinant of their mode of being. But it is equally clear that classes involved in these relations are in some major ways different from those in advanced capitalist societies" (p. 29). Marx's theory of class and class struggle has raised many eyebrows. Even Mao of China interpreted the term in the socio-economic and political atmosphere of China. The result is that Marx's theory of class and class struggle and Mao's idea on the same issue are different. The interesting point is nobody has been able to challenge Mao's theory of class struggle. Again, in the second half of twentieth century Marx's theory of class struggle has faced few basic questions such as what is exactly a class? Does the existence of classes lead to conflict? What are the elements that constitute class? According to Marx, economic element constitutes class and he derived this idea from the study of history. But from the same source we derive that there are many elements that form the structure of class. There are differences of opinion, but those differences did not result in class struggle. Hence the concept of class and class struggle is extraordinarily complex. We believe that Marx did not pay sufficient thought and pay attention to the analysis of class and class struggle.

Class Interests, their Irreconcilability and Exploitation

In the just concluded analysis we have dealt with various aspects of classes and class struggle. In this regard certain points need further clarification. Such as, does the existence of classes lead to class struggle? What is exactly meant by irreconcilable class interests? When the irreconciliable class interests lead to class conflict? If we study the vast literature of Marx and Engels we shall find that Marx was quite aware of the issues raised above. In *the Eighteenth Brumaire of Louis Bonaparte* Marx clearly stated that the existence of two opposite classes does not mean a class conflict or it does not mean that there is a class and so the class will enforce its interests. There are many a gap between the lip and the cup.

From the record of history we come to know that there were two classes whose interests were opposite and one class was exploited by another, still the exploited class did not revolt. Another case may be cited. Irreconcilability of interests between two classes in past did not lead to exploitation. For example, the interests of the bourgeois and feudal lords were irreconcilable but one was not exploited by the other. In spite of the irreconcilability of the interests between these two classes there was cooperation. There is thus a point to ponder over. It is further to be noted here that even in a class constituted in Marxian sense there may exist several subgroups based on group or parochial interests. There are classes but there are no subgroups—is practically an unimaginable idea. We surmise that Marx realised this nature of class.

It is not expected that every class (in Marxian sense of course) shall be absolutely homogeneous. In such class there may exist small groups or factions and the interests of these groups or factions may be incompatible and sometimes may be irreconcilable. But this does not create an atmosphere of class or group conflict because either they are suppressed or do not get scope of exposure. All the groups live under the big umbrella of a large class. In any society such sort of picture may be available.

Society is always dynamic. With the change of economic, social and political situation the interests of the class as well as those of groups change and this change is not a potential reason of class struggle. It is said that for a class struggle the incompatibility of interests must be stable, that is, it will continue for pretty long time. The members of the class must realise that further continuation of irreconcilability will cause irreparable damage to the interests. Unfortunately such type of situation does not always arise.

Again, irreconcilability is not always a reason of conflict. Let us explain it. The members of the class may hold different attitude to the idea of justice, interests and origin of classes. This difference creates a disunity among the members of the classes making, difficult for class struggle. Because there must be strong unity among the members of the class. It may be held by some members that by launching a struggle justice may not be achieved. Question may arise about the justification of this reason, but the members have the full freedom to adhere to different view. If the class is intimately associated with the structure of society and if the members are of opinion that without changing the social structure a class struggle is impossible they will be quite reluctant to launch a struggle.

Marx and Engels have also talked about the *objective class interests.* It has been found that many people do not possess clear conception about class interests. What they hold are momentary interests or some impractical or imaginary interests. Marx and Engels have said that the members of the class must have clear conception about the interests. Cloudy conception cannot act as an important factor of class conflict. If people are guided by momentary impulses the irreconcilability cannot produce results.

An important aspect of class struggle is that in any class struggle—what ever may its form and magnitude be—the most crucial role is always played by consciousness and along with it by spontaneity. If it were not so the slaves could have revolted against the slave owners or there could have occurred fierce struggle between landlords and serfs. There were sporadic conflicts, but the class struggle in Marxian sense never occurred. We have already referred to Marx's observation in *The Eighteenth Brumaire of Louis Bonaparte.* The French peasants formed a class and their interests stated in opposition to the interests of other classes. But they lacked two things—political organisation and, above all, class consciousness. The peasants of France were incapable of working and acting together. The absence of unity among them stood in the way of launching a revolution. Here is the role of class consciousness. Every class must be fully conscious of what it is getting, what it wants to get, the difference between the two and, finally, must be prepared to get it.

Plamenatz (*Man and Society* II, p. 307) says "The bourgeois have class consciousness; they work together to further their interests. They do not merely know what they want as individuals, they do not merely have personal ambitions. They have demands which they make in common they know what they want done on their behalf as a class, or if all of them do not know they have leaders who do know and whose leadership they accept. They are organised to make collective demands, and could not even decide what demands to make unless they were organised". This is the consciousness. The word consciousness is not a mere mouthful word—it has several vital aspects. The consciousness leads the members of the class to exert their demands to the proper authority. It creates organisation. Through the machinery of consciousness the workers are united. Through unity demands are placed collectively.

The importance of class-consciousness may be illustrated by an observation made by Marx in *The Eighteenth Brumaire of Louis Bonaparte* : "But let there be no misunderstanding. The Bonaparte dynasty represents not the revolutionary, but the conservative peasant; not the peasant that strikes out beyond the condition of his social existence, ...but rather the peasant who wants to consolidate this holding...not the countryfolk who want to overthrow the old order through their own energy, but on the contrary, those who want to see themselves favoured by the ghost of the empire. It represents not the enlightenment but the superstition of the peasant, not his judgment, but his prejudice; not his future but his past" (*MESW* I, p. 335). We have given here a long quotation simply to prove that Marx was quite aware of the role of consciousness in the various stages of class struggle.

The purpose of class struggle is to end exploitation. "Exploitation is appropriation by some social classes or groups of the product of the labour of other classes, without compensation. It is engendered by the appearance of private ownership of the means of productions which brings about a division of society into antagonistic classes." We thus see that the emergence of exploitation is due to the rise of private property and division of society into opposite classes whose interests are incompatible. But the nature and extent of exploitation is not one-dimensional. There are various types of exploitation. If the householder does not pay proper salary to his domestic help or driver of his car it is also form of exploitation. If an employer forces his subordinate to do extra work without additional payment it is also an exploitation. So we say that in every society there are various forms of exploitation. But every exploitation does not lead to conflict or struggle.

The economically powerful class, that is, the bourgeois, employ workers for the purpose of production. But the capitalists deceive or exploit the worker by giving less than what they should get in exchange of the labour. The capitalists make more and more profit through the appropriation of surplus value. The capitalists do not apply any coerceive measure for the appropriation of greater profit. They force the workers to sell their labour at comparatively cheap rate.

Marx and Engels have analysed various ways adopted by the capitalists for the purpose of multiplying profit that is exploitation. One such technique is the application of the division of labour. The capitalists introduce division of labour for safeguarding and increasing their own monetary interests, but ultimately this method throws labourers into competition among themselves and narrows down the scope of employment. Moreover, the workers are faced with monotony of work and they do not get job satisfaction. But they are forced to work for livelihood. According to Marx this is one type of exploitation and it is found in every industry.

Introduction of new and improved machinery makes many workers surplus. Competition among the workers rises considerably and they are forced to sell their labour at a lower level of wage and in this way wages decrease. Marx in his *Wage, Labour and Capital* sums up the whole matter in the following words : "The more the productive capital grows, the more the division of labour and the application of machinery expands. The more the division of labour and the application of machinery expands the more the competition among workers expands and the more their wages contract" (*MESW* I, p. 104). Industry develops, machinery improves and unemployment increases. This leads the workers to work at less and less wage. On the contrary, rapid industrialisation and application of sophisticated machinery enables capitalists to bag higher and higher profit.

Industrialisation in this way clearly divides the society into two distinct opposite classes whose interests are not only antagonistic but irreconcilable. Sporadic protests and agitation sometimes take place and the workers resort to these in order to realise their legitimate demands. The capitalists, in order to fight the protests and agitation, take the help of state machinery such as police and military because these are state-controlled. The rise in consciousness among the workers and building up of organisations ultimately make the struggle between workers on the one hand and the capitalists and state on the other hand a practical possibility, the chief aim of which is to bring about emancipation of workers. We thus conclude that, in Marxian philosophy, classes, class struggle and exploitation all are well-linked concepts.

31 BASE AND SUPERSTRUCTURE

Base and Superstructure : Defined

A simple analysis of the productive forces and production relations cannot reveal the real nature of historical materialism. For that purpose it is necessary to enter into the discussion of basis and superstructure. In several books Marx and Engels have elaborately dealt with the matter. Marx's *Contribution to the Critique of Political Economy* contains an exhaustive analysis of the concept—Base and Superstructure. We shall, however, first see what is meant by base or basis? Stalin's version is "the basis is the economic structure of society at the given stage of development. The historical materialism states that there are various stages of social development and each stage has its own economic structure." This is called basis.

In Bottomore's book the following version of base and superstructure is to be found. "The building-like metaphor of base and superstructure is used by Marx and Engels to propound the idea that the economic structure of society (the base) conditions the existence and forms of the state and social consciousness (the superstructure). One of the first formulations of this idea appears in *The German Ideology* Part I where a reference is made to the social organisation evolving directly out of production and commerce which in all ages forms the basis of state and of the rest of the idealist superstructure (p. 44).

In the *Anti-Dühring* Engels says (p. 37) "the economic structure of society is always the real basis, starting from which we can alone work out the ultimate explanation of the whole superstructure or juridical and political institutions as well as of the religious, philosophical and other ideas of a given historical period." In this observation Engels has pointed out both base and superstructure. *Base or basis is the economic structure. Above it is built up a vast structure of philosophy, law, art, literature, religion, history and civilisation. In Marx's language it is called the superstructure.*

A. P. Sheptulin says (p. 334) "production relations are considered the economic basis of society, while the views and corresponding institutions determined by them are considered society's superstructure." But the basis consists not only of the production relations that are dominant in the given period, but also of a mass of other production relations, in particular those left as survivals of the old mode of production, as well as these associated with the new economic structure.

The basis according to Marxism is *the totality of the relations of production*, that is, the relations of property exchange and distribution. These are included into the basis because all these constitute the economic structure. It is nevertheless connected with the dominating mode of production. Only the dominant mode of production determines the character and essence of basis.

The best and most interesting explanation of the concept is available in Marx's famous writing—*Contribution to the Critique of Political Economy*. This is an oft-quoted and widely discussed writing. We quote here a part of the writing. Marx says : "In the social production of their existence, men inevitably enter into definite relations, which are independent of their will, namely, relations of production appropriate to a given stage in the development of material forces of production. The totality of these relations of production constitutes the economic structure of society, the real foundation, on which arises a legal and political superstructure and to which correspond definite forms of social consciousness."

Some Features of Basis and Superstructure

We have pointed out that the economic structure of society at a particular stage of social development is called the basis. But here the implication is not that the mode of production is to be called the basis. The Marxists have argued that the mode of production implies the unity of the productive forces and production relations. The productive forces do not come under the purview of the concept of base. Only the production relations figure in it. The economic basis consists of production relations and also all other factors or matters closely connected with production relations. It is to be noted here that in the economic system there are minor or insignificant production relations. The Marxists are of opinion that the predominant production relations determine the character of basis and form it. Let us be more explicit. The economic structure is not conceived as a given set of institutions, productive units or material conditions, it is rather the sum total of production relations entered into by men, or, in other words, class relations between them (Baltomore, p. 45). Marx says : "it is always the direct relation of the owners of the conditions of production to the direct producer."

The most important feature of the economic basis is that *its existence is represented by the material relations*. That is, *the economic basis is the result of material relations*. On the other hand, superstructure is not based on material relations. *The elements of superstructure are ideology, culture, art, literature, history etc.*

The base or basis has a general character. All the members of the society in one way or other are connected with the basis. The source of sustenance of the superstructure is the basis. This is due to the fact that the basis is economic and no one, small or big, is away from the economic influence of the basis. This general character of basis has made it more important. Another aspect of the general character of the basis is that all are participants in the activities of the basis. It is true that there is anomaly and inequality in the distribution of material benefits produced by the economic basis. But this is a different issue. The mere fact is that the economic basis is all-embracing.

One of the most important features of the basis is it has a class character in an antagonistic society. The totality of the production relations is based on private ownership of the means of production. So the capitalists or the owners of the means of production are the controlling elements of the economic base. In an antagonistic society, basis is bond to be controlled by the bourgeoisie

A. P. Sheptulin has pointed out another aspect of basis. He says (p. 336) "the basis represents a kind of intermediate link between productive forces and superstructure. Neither the productive forces nor changes in them have a direct influence on the superstructure or political, juridical and other social ideas and corresponding institutions. This influence is indirect, through the basis." The character of the relationship between base and superstructure is more complicated. Marx is aware that the determination by the base can be understood as a form of economic reductionism. That is why he further characterises this relationship as historical. Uneven and compatible with effectivity of the superstructure.

Interaction of Base and Superstructure

In the *Preface to the Critique of Political Economy* Marx writes "The mode of production of material life conditions the social, political and intellectual life process in general. It is not the consciousness of men that determines their being, but on the contrary, their social being that determines their consciousness." This observation of Marx clarifies the relationship between base and superstructure or the interaction between the two. The interaction between base and superstructure implies that one influences the other. It is said that base has a dominant and determining role. On the other hand, in some cases, the superstructure exerts its influence upon the base.

Generally the superstructure is the reflection of the basis. V. D. Zotov says (p. 103) "whatever the nature of the basis, such will be the nature and hallmarks of the superstructure. If one basis is replaced by another, the old superstructure will be replaced more or less rapidly by a new superstructure." In the feudal society the basis was feudal, that is, the production relations were feudal. The superstructure was also feudal. When the feudal basis was replaced by a capitalist basis the feudal superstructure also lost its relevance and, hence, was replaced by a capitalist superstructure.

The attention of the reader to an important point may be drawn here. Sometimes a revolution may destroy the existing base. But this does not mean the destruction of the old productive forces. The new base establishes an adjustment with the old productive forces. Similarly the new economic system or base does not forthwith invalidate or reject the old superstructure. The new base works with the old superstructure. This is a logical and rational consequence, because the new base cannot start its operation with a clean slate. It must utilise the old forces or elements.

Analysing the interaction between base and superstructure Engels writes "political, juridical, philosophical, religious, literary, artistic etc. development is based on economic development. But all these react upon one another and *also* upon the economic basis. It is not that the economic situation is *cause, solely active,* while everything else is only passive effect. There is rather interaction on the basis of economic necessity, which ultimately always asserts itself." We may put the matter in a slightly different language. The economic basis of the society always plays the dominant role and largely determines the nature of the superstructure built upon it. In turn, the latter also influences the nature and activities of the former. This is interaction. The relationship between basis and superstructure is never a one-way traffic.

This interaction between base and superstructure practically constitutes important aspects of historical materialism and many other aspects of Marxist philosophy. The concept of interaction may also be looked from different angle. In capitalism the capitalists control and guide the superstructure so that it can work in favour of the base—the capitalist system. Again, the superstructure influences the base in numerous ways. In this way the capitalist society functions. The interaction between base and superstructure has been elaborately analysed by Gramsci.

We have already noted that in an antagonistic society its class character is reflected on the economic basis. Again, the base embraces all the classes—oppressor and oppressed—though there is a difference in their roles. We know that the superstructure is the sum total of all ideas and institutions. So it includes the ideas and other things of both the oppressor and oppressed classes. Naturally its influence upon these classes is not and cannot be uniform. We come to the conclusion that like the base the superstructure has also a class character. In the words of Sheptulin "So in a class society the superstructure has a class character and becomes a battleground for a fierce class struggle reflecting the opposite interests that are determined and consolidated by the antagonistic basis" (p. 338). The struggle at the superstructure level is the struggle between ideas and ideologies. The capitalists utilise the various modes of expression for the propagation of ideas and ideologies. Particularly the audiovisual methods are under their control. The proletarians use their own methods. But they are at inferior position. However, that does not discourage them.

Active Role of Superstructure

Though the change of the economic foundation immensely transforms the superstructure, it is wrong to assume that the superstructure is a passive and completely dependent force. It is an *active force.* The superstructure, it is said, is a reflection of the base, but this never makes it a subservient force to the base. Rather, it bears upon the base. V. D. Zotov observes (p. 104) "The state, political parties, the various organisation and the scientific and other ideological guidelines expressing and championing the interests of the new ruling class are created for the express purpose of helping its basis to take shape and sink roots."

So far as the development of the society is concerned we witness an active and sometimes an independent role of the superstructure. The bourgeois superstructure, by utilising the various propaganda machines, severely criticises the various aspects of socialism in order to resist the downfall of the capitalist system. But all the elements of the bourgeois superstructure are not under the control of the bourgeoisie. The working class utilises a part, thought it might be a microscopic fraction, of the vast superstructure for the propagation of the socialist ideology, for the exposition of bourgeois exploitation and finally to make working-men conscious.

The capitalists always resort to repressive measures to stop the working men's movement. The records of history reveal that complete success has never greeted them. The methods and measures the capitalists adopt to secure their position are never free from defects. Part of the literature, history, law is used by the proletarians. The literature of every country and of every epoch exposes the real character of the bourgeoisie. Proletarians use them as weapon of progaganda.

It has been argued by Marxists that superstructure, though dependent on basis, has its own laws of development and operation. Moreover, various of its elements interact and influence each other. All the changes of the superstructure are not due to the changes of the economic basis of the society. Many changes of the superstructure are caused by the class struggle. Some decisions and politices of the ruling class are directly influenced by the class struggle. This is due to the fact that the ruling class, in order to save itself from further onslaught, concedes some of the demands of the proletarians. This is neither new nor rare. The rising consciousness and growing bargaining power of the workers have created positive impact upon the bourgeois behaviour. Needless to say that the proletarians have obtained this from the bourgeois superstructure.

V. D. Zotov and several other Marxist thinkers have drawn our attention to how in some cases superstructure works independently. There are a number of contradictions in the basis which are created by private capitalist property in the means of production. These contradictions "in effect split the political and ideological superstructure into two antagonistic parts—the ruling and the non-ruling" (p. 106). The ruling parts consist of bourgeois state, bourgeois party, bourgeois law and bourgeois theoreticians, and the proletarian parties, proletarian organisations and Marxist-Leninist ideologies are the non-ruling parts.

From Marx's analysis of base-superstructure relationship we come to know that a change in economic base brings about a change in superstructure. But there are many instances in history that the economic base has changed, while there has not occurred a corresponding change in the superstructure. Zotov observes "there are also superstructure phenomena that though they come to life on one basis continues to exist and develop on another and even several subsequent bases" (p. 106). For example, religion is an element of superstructure. Since Middle Ages the economic bases have changed several times, whereas the notions of religion have not changed considerably. Not only religion, the caste system, superstition and many habits and culture maintain their character and influence even after the economic base has undergone rapid changes. For example, in India, the economic conditions have radically changed after independence but people's attitude towards caste system and superstition has not changed considerably.

Economic Determinism and Relative Autonomy of Superstructure

We have so far discussed how both base and superstructure react on each other. In spite of their interdependence the critics of Marxism and some bourgeois theoreticians have propounded a theory of economic determinism. This notion they have derived from a famous comment of Marx made in the *Preface to the Critique of Political Economy.* Here he said "The mode of production of material life conditions the social, political and intellectual life process in general." This comment is the source of all trouble. Critics say that "conditions" means determines. That means the economic foundation of society determines the superstructure that is social, political and intellectual life process of people in general. Here is economic determinism.

A number of Marxist scholars have disapproved the standpoint of the bourgeois scholars on the ground that they have misinterpreted or have not properly interpreted some words of Marx. For example, Melvin Rador says that the term "condition" is the translation of the original German word *bedingen.* This means "to influence generally". To determine and to influence are not same. The German synonym of determine is *"bestimmen"*. He does not use the word *bestimmen* in this particular case. Hence we cannot say that the idea of economic determinism worked in the mind of Marx. Moreover, *determinism means there is a mechanical relationship between base and superstructure.* Base determines superstructure mechanically. Nowhere Marx and Engels have said that. Base simply influences the superstructure. We, therefore, conclude that *base and superstructure are not mechanically related.* In support of the view that both are interdependent Maurice Cornforth says (p. 222) "...modern British Parliamentary institutions are undoubtedly products of the capitalist system of Britain. But that does not mean that institution of parliament and what is does is of no importance. On the contrary, we know that the Acts of parliament have very great effect, not only in the political sphere, but in the economic sphere as well. To suggest the contrary would be indeed a "fatuous notion".

What Marx meant by economic determinism can be explained by Engels's letter to J. Bloch written in September 1890. The letter was written just five years before his death. Naturally it may be regarded as the product of Engels's mature thought. He writes : "According to the materialist conception of history, the ultimately determining element in the history is the production and reproduction of real life. More than this neither Marx nor I have ever asserted. Hence, if somebody twists this into saying that the economic element is the only determining one, he transforms that proposition into a meaningless, abstract, senseless phrase. The economic situation is the basis, but the various elements or the superstructure : political forms of the class struggle and its results, to wit : constitutions established by the victorious class...philosophical theories, religious views and their further development into systems of dogmas...exercise their influence upon the course of historical struggle. There is an interaction of all these elements in which, amid all the endless host of accidents, the economic element finally asserts itself as necessary" (*MESW* I, p. 488). There is no ambiguity in this observation of Engels. Economic element *ultimately* detrmines the superstructure. It simply implies that there is importance of all other elements but economic movement finally asserts itself. So it is not a correct proposition that Marx and Engels have propounded a theory of economic determinism.

Kolakowski is a renowned Marxist scholar. We state his viewpoint in support of our stand. Marx and Engels have replied to all the objections raised by critics though these have not been able to remove all the ambiguities. However, economic determinism "is not and does not claim to be a key to the interpretation of any particular historical event. All it does is to define the relations between some, but by no means all, features of social life" (Vol. I, p. 339). "Marx's account" continues Kolakowski "of the dependence of the superstructure on the relations of production applies to great historical eras and fundamental changes in society. It is not claimed that the level to technology determines every detail of social division of labour, and thus in turn every detail of political and intellectual life." It is, therefore, quite manifest that in great historical epochs and in the cases of fundamental changes the economic foundation appears to play an important or rather determining role. In all other cases its role is quite secondary. The same view has been expressed by Engels in his letter to Starkenburg.

Generally economic conditions influence views and institutions. But there is a problem. What exact form the views and institutions will take from economic conditions cannot be assuredly stated. That is, the exact impact of economic situation upon superstructure cannot be ascertained. The nature of influence as well as its extent depend upon variety of factors. The legal conceptions and code of law in England arose, not as a direct product of economic conditions, but by a process of working upon and adapting the already existing legal conceptions and codes, which belonged to the past epoch, into forms suitable for the new epoch (Maurice Cornforth, p. 223).

Individual and Society

The historical materialism or materialist interpretation of history deals with various material aspects of society and within this also falls the relationship between man and society. For fuller analysis of the entire concept this point requires to be properly explore. By stating that history of all the hitherto existing society is the history of class struggle Marx and Engels directly spoke against the historians who highly eulogised the heroic and talented persons. It is to be emphasised here that Marx and Engels had no intention to undermine the importance and role of individuals. The role of individuals envisaged by Marx and Engels must be viewed in the proper perspective. They have admitted the crucial role of individual having exceptional qualities in the making and remaking of history and also moulding the process of development. An outstanding individual like Oliver Cromwell or Napoleon Bonaparte or Marx himself has tremendous influence upon the course of history. An exceptional individual has certain traits of character which ensure his role in the progress of history.

To a very crucial point Marx and Engels have drawn our attention. Historical development took place at different periods of time. We also come to know that individuals gave leadership to these development processes or to this development. But Marx and Engels have said that these individuals are not ordinary persons, they are leaders to classes and movements. This is the key point to be properly treated. Individuals direct the movement of history as leaders of classes, representatives of the mass. Cornforth, in this connection, maintains "unless the individual bases his authority and his influence upon the support of some class, whose interests and tendencies he represents, he is impotent and can exert no decisive influence" (p. 102). As without the support of classes leaders cannot influence history, so without leaders the classes and movements cannot achieve success. The good leaders accelerate the movement and bad leaders retard it.

Marx regards individuals as a product of social being or product of materialistic situation. Individual does not come from the vacuum. He draws his inspiration from the society. This does not, of course, mean that a particular historical situation will produce identical individuals. Though the superstructure is the reflection of basis, it is not devoid of varieties. There are varieties of ideology, religion, art and literature. All these lead to the varieties of individual's character and attitude. Thus a capitalist base has various types of individuals. That is why in capitalist society some people relentlessly fight against capitalism and vow to overthrow it.

In capitalist society the individual is simply a wage-earner and a machine of surplus value, i.e., surplus value-creating agency. He sells his labour and in exchange of that gets an amount of wage which just helps him to survive. The workers are forced to stay and comfort themselves at subsistence level of wage. The greatest *"achievement"* of capitalism is that it has alienated and dehumanised individual. On his labour the great citadel of wealth is built. He is destined to sacrifice. Individual in capitalism is the victim of exploitation, misery, suffering and degradation. He is put to all sorts of subjection. He is supposed to have freedom, which is, in fact, a false one. Economic slavery makes freedom fully meaningless. Absence of economic freedom abnegates the political freedom. The creative activity of the individual, in capitalism, is retarded.

So what is the way out? Socialism, Marx believes, is the only way of emancipation. It opens the floodgates of opportunities for the individual sufficient for the utilisation of creative faculties which the individual possesses. He gets back his worth. Let us put the matter in the words of Kolakowski : "Socialism was vastly to enlarge the sphere of creative activity outside the production process, freeing consciousness from mystification and social life from reified forces" (p. 345). Forces of production will be released from private control. The contradictions, characteristic features of capitalist society, will cease to exist. Abolition of the antagonistic class society will radically change the character of base and superstructure. Man will no longer be subject of exploitation. Both alienation and dehumanisation will be buried in oblivion. "Socialist production" observes Cliff Slaughter "will provide an entirely changed basis for individual development. Social forces and cultural stimuli will come under individual's control" (p. 68).

From the above analysis of base and superstructure relation or interaction we conclude that Marx makes a very important contribution to social philosophy. Many of the concepts or ideas of Marx may be challenged or rejected but his in-depth analysis of base and superstructure has an everlasting value. In every capitalist society base generally controls the superstructure and sometimes the superstructure is found to influence the base. This view of Marx is found in many systems.

32 MARXIAN THEORY OF STATE

Introductory

Marxian theory of the state is basically different from pluralist and elitist theories. According to the former there are manifold agencies and groups in society and the position of the state is just like a neutral agency whose function is to settle disputes neutrally. But it is wishful thinking that the state maintains neutrality among the different conflicting groups and classes. Rather, it always acts in favour of economically dominant class. Marx and Engels reject this pluralist notion of state. The elitist theories hold the view that only a small group, called elite, having higher and better skill and ability, controls political power. Engels has said that the minority group qualified and called to rule by the given degree of economic development. The power base, then, is the ownership and control of society's productive resources. The elite group, that controls the forces of production, ultimately controls the political power. Marxism sees and interprets state from a quite different perspective which in final analysis is the rejection of both pluralist and elitist theories. It views the state in the light of classes and class struggle and believes that a classless society will be the final goal of the struggle. The classic view of Marxian theory of state is to be found in *Communist Manifesto.* Here Marx and Engels make the following observation : "The executive power of the modern state is but a committee for managing the common affairs of the whole bourgeoisie." Commenting on this view of Marx and Engels the writer of the article published in—Bottomore edited *A Dictionary of Marxist thought*, writes : "This is a more complex statement than appears at first sight, but it is too summary, and lends itself to oversimplification : however it does represent the core proposition of Marxism on the subject of the state" (p. 520).

It is to be noted here that what is popularly known as the Marxian theory of the state is nowhere clearly and elaborately stated by Marx. Only his life-long friend Engels has dealt with the matter in his *The Origin of Family, Private Property and State.* Later on, Lenin in his *State and Revolution* elaborates the contention of Marx and Engels. Besides, in numerous other works, Marx and Engels have made passing or cryptic remarks about state which provide potential sources or materials for building up a theory of state. A few more words may be added to our present analysis. In fact, Marxist theory of state of the sixties and seventies of the nineteenth century has been reformulated by the continental thinkers. So long Stalin was alive he did not allow any country or individual to commence research work about numerous aspects of Marx's and Engel's thought. After his death in 1953 tremendous enthusiasm was shown by scholars throughout the globe. The tangible consequence is that the scholars of various countries have started to interpret various concepts of Marx and Engels in new light and perspective. Marxism, today, is not the property of few blunt-headed and less educated politicians.

From the extensive research work *three views of state have come out. The state is the product of class divisions of society, the state is an instrument of class rule and finally when the society becomes classless there will be no need of state. It will wither away.* These three assertions build up the whole fabric of Marxian theory of state. All these are connected with each other.

Definition of State

In The *German Ideology* Marx and Engels have made the following observation regarding state—"out of this very contradiction between the interest of the individual and that of the community, the latter takes an independent form as the *State,* divorced from the real interests of individual and community." In such a state there are conflicts and struggles, but all these are illusory, that they are not real. Mere mock fighting. No one is interested in setting up a true government or democracy and in abolishing class division. They have further said in the same book (p. 99) that the state is the political form of class rule. In their own words "Since the state is the form in which the individuals of a ruling class assert their common interests, and in which the whole civil society of an epoch is epitomised, it follows that all institutions are set up with the help of the state and are given a political form."

There is an Introduction by Engels to *The Civil War in France* (1891) where he criticises the philosophical theory of state elaborated by Hegel. The state is neither the "realisation of the idea" nor march to the kingdom of God on earth. It is absolutely a *material conception devised by men to meet material needs.* These needs, of course, belong to a particular class or group of people. Engels writes in this Introduction "In reality the state is nothing but a machine for the oppression of one class by another and indeed in the democratic republic no less than in monarchy; and at best an evil inherited by the proletariat after the victorious struggle for class supremacy" (p. 485). *The state,* according to Marx and Engels, *is a machine of class rule and it is also an evil.*

In the *Eighteenth Brumaire of Louis Bonaparte* Marx points out that the state is a political or administrative unit consisting of bureaucracy and army. Elsewhere Marx and Engels have said three agencies combined together constitute a political form and this is called state. These agencies are bureaucracy, army and police. In fact, these are the three arms of any modern bourgeois state. In *The Civil War in France* Marx has added judicial organ to the three arms of bourgeois state. The Russian state, he said, was completely dependent on the police and army and with the help of these two the Prussian Government established autocratic rule. In *Grundrisse* Marx has said that state is a complex synthesis of multiple determinations. In *Politics Ideology and the State* Sally Hibbin writes (p. 59) "One cannot take the state as an unproblematic given nor reduce it to one of its multiple determinations...The state is both the point of departure and the point of arrival in political analysis since it can only be comprehended after a complex process of theoretical analysis and synthesis." Of all these definitions, I think the most significant one is the state is a complex synthesis. The concept of state can never be confined within certain specific denominations. With the change of economic, political and situations or conditions the managers of the capitalist state change the methods of administration and attitudes to various issues. It is because the sole purpose of the managers is to keep intact the supreme hold over the state.

Origin of State

Marx and Engels studied the views of the three contractualists and found their view unacceptable because the state could never be the product of any contract. From the study of history both Marx and Engels reached the conclusion that it was the product of class rule and the dominant class uses it to maintain its supremacy. That is, *the state is man-made and it was created to fulfil specific purposes*. Marxian theory of the state is based on the foundation of historical materialism. It has nothing to do with contract. It is the product of class antagonism. In *The Origin of Family, Private Property and State* Engels has surveyed the gradual development of state. It is man-made no doubt, but the artefact of the state is based on scientific reason and perfect logic. Here lies the novelty of their idea. They have not imagined of any state of nature which—according to Hobbes, Locke and Rousseau—was either intolerable or inconvenient. On the contrary, Marx and Engels have shown the development of state from the primitive communal stage to the industrial period. Only in the primitive period there was no state in modern sense because there were no classes and private property. To sum up, the state represents a particular class, used as a machine by that class and protects the interests of the economically dominant class. Both Marx and Engels have elaborated the rise and development of state as a political organisation in *The German Ideology*.

Summarising the views of Marx and Engels in *Anti-Dühring, The Origin of Family, Private Property and the State* Plamenatz (*Man and Society, II*, p. 352) says "The need for the state arises from the increasing size of the community and from the extended division of labour inside it. A close study of views expressed by Marx, Engels and Lenin in many of their works reveal that two factors are primarily responsible for the emergence of state. One is division of labour and the other is the class division of society. As the division of labour increases, the society divides itself into classes. With the increase of the size of the community the occupations within it became diverse and specialised. Complex rules and procedures were needed to control them. Complexity created ample room for varied disputes. Primitive way of settling the disputes proved its irrelevance and ineffectiveness. All these together needed an authority with controlling power. Maintenance became the primary function of state. The interests of the classes were irreconcilable." Following Engels we can admit that the form of the state depends on how the society is divided into classes. But the class structure is dependent on division of labour and system of property. Hence the institution of state has not emerged out of nothing. It is a reality and product of real situation. We quote here the famous observation of Engels :

"The state is, therefore, by no means a power forced on society from without : just as little is it "the reality of ethical idea", the "image and reality of reason", as Hegel maintains. Rather, it is a product of society at a certain stage of development, it is the admission that this society has become entangled in an insoluble contradiction with itself, that it is cleft into irreconcilable antagonisms which it is powerless to dispel...A power above society became necessary" (*MESW*, II, p. 318). It, therefore, appears that according to Marx and Engels the state is a reality and it is not an embodiment of Absolute Spirit. The state is the creation of men and it was created to meet certain specific demands of some people who formed a class which was economically most powerful.

The emergence of the state is characterised by the formation of a special group of people engaged only in government and using a special apparatus of coercion for this purpose. "When there appears such a group of man occupied solely with government, and who in order to rule need a special apparatus of coercion to subjugate the will of others by force—prisons, special contingents of men, armies etc.—then there appears the state." Lenin has said that the appearance of class and the emergence of state as an institution are almost simultaneous. If there were no classes and private property, there would been no necessity of state. This point has been elaborated by Lenin in his small pamphlet *State.* Of course Lenin's views are not different from those of Marx and specially Engels. Engels in his noted work *The Origin of Family, Private Property and State.* Engels has elaborately analysed the rise, growth and other aspects of state.

The organs of the state appear partly as a result of the transformation of the previous organs of government that took shape within the tribal system, and partly by means of the elimination of the management organs of the tribal system and their replacement by the new organs. Thus, the apparatus of the special public power of class society, the so-called state apparatus, gradually takes shape. Following Engels, Lenin has said that the origin of state can be traced to the emergence of economic classes in society and also to the creation of property system. The organs of the capitalist state also existed in tribal and feudal systems—though in different forms. Coercion was the characteristic feature of the tribal system of government and the bourgeois state system inherits that.

State and Irreconcilable Classes

It has been stressed by Engels that the *state is the result of irreconcilability of class interests.* Recent researchers have made attempts to show whether the irreconcilable class interests are exclusively responsible for the emergence of state or the state causes the interests of various classes irreconcilable. The issue is to be treated with all seriousness. The persons having free access to political power can use it to augment the quantum of property or wealth and it is a quite natural tendency on their part. Besides political power they use other means. However, political power is the chief source of accumulation of property. Accumulation of wealth enhances exploitation. Plamenatz writes (p. 357) "The owners of property acquire, in various ways, rights of property in other people's labour; they acquire slaves or serfs. Therefore, the exploitation of class by class arises, at least in great part, as a consequence of the emergence of state."

There is a famous sentence in the *Communist Manifesto* : "Political power, properly so called, is merely the organised power of one class for oppressing another." So far as the nature of bourgeois state is concerned this is a significant comment. In this short sentence Marx and Engels have portrayed the real picture of capitalist state. Political power is used to oppress or exploit class or classes. It is well-organised and used by a class. The economically powerful or dominant class creates access and avenues to the corridor of political power and subsequently uses it for the realisation of its own sectorial interests. The appearance of classes, irreconcilability of interests and the inequality between the classes are no doubt responsible for the emergence of state. Simultaneously the state is the cause of exploitation, oppression and aggravation of inequality. Mere existence of antagonistic classes cannot cause oppression. Or even if there is oppression it cannot assume alarming form. In this connection we can remember the observation of Plamenatz (p. 357) "Where there is no apparatus of power controlled by one class to the detriment of others there cannot be much class oppression."

There are two processes—the appearance of state and appearance of unequal classes. Do these two processes overlap? Plamenatz says that these two processes do not overlap. According to Engels the appearance of classes is the cause of the rise of state. But once the state appears and consolidates its power and position it begins to act in favour of the powerful class and the political or state power is used to widen the inequality. Plamenatz concludes "What Marx and Engels say about connections between two social processes does not accord with their actual description of these processes. They tell us that one process determines the other, when they come to describe one or other of the processes they admit that each has a powerful influence on the other...the rise of the state is as much a cause as an effect of the emergence of classes" (p. 358). •

State as an Instrument of Exploitation

The general and most popular formulation of Marxist theory of state is to be found in the Communist Manifesto. It is popularly known as the *instrumentalist model* or the state is an instrument of exploitation. In numerous place Marx and Engels have expressed that the state is used as a weapon by the bourgeoisie to exploit the proletarians. Two famous remarks of Marx and Engels may be quoted here in support of the above view. These are from the *Manifesto.* One is "The executive of the modern state is but a committee for managing the common affairs of the whole bourgeoisie." This remark I have already quoted earlier in reference to the definition of state. The second we have quoted in the present analysis several times. This is "political power is merely the organised power of one class for oppressing another." In the *Socialist Register,* 1968, Ralph Miliband says, "This is the classical Marxist view on the subject of the state and it is the only one which is to be found in Marxism-Leninism."

In regard to Marx himself, and this is also true to a certain extent of Engels as well, it only constitutes what might be called primary view of the state. But there is to be found another view of the state in his work. This is the *relative autonomy model.* This cannot claim equal status with the instrumentalist model. It is, nonetheless, of great importance.

The implication of the statement,—the state is an instrument of exploitation of class rule—is that if there were no unequal classes, with the superior among them needing to use force to maintain the social conditions of their superiority, there would be no state. Because of the unequal distribution of property, one class having the largest share of property or wealth and the dominating class having free access to governmental affairs, the exploitation by the ruling class becomes the characteristic feature of society. *The instrumentalist model of Marxist theory of state emphasises that the state is simply a weapon of class rule.* It never thinks of neutrality among the various classes of society. Whenever there is a conflict between proletariat and capitalists—the two most powerful classes of capitalist state, the authority or what may also be called the government always comes forward to protect the capitalists from all types of attack. It is because the interests of state and capitalists fully coincide. The bourgeois state always fights for the interests of capitalists. This type of state sometimes gives some concessions to the proletarians but it is infinitesimal. The state does it to establish its so-called neutrality.

We have earlier noted that *The German Ideology* and the *Manifesto of Communist Party* are the two primary sources of the instrumentalist model. Reference to *Manifesto* has already been made. Now we shall turn to *The German Ideology.* "By the mere fact that it is a class and no longer an *estate,* the bourgeoisie is forced to organise itself no longer locally, but nationally and to give a general form to its average interests...it is nothing more than the form of organisation which the bourgeois are compelled to adopt, both for internal and external purposes for the mutual guarantee of their property and interests." Miliband says that *this "general form" is nothing but state.* The capitalists use this general form of organisation to safeguard their property and other interests. It is simply due to the fact that army, bureaucracy and police—the three pillars of bourgeois state—are under the control of the authority of such state. In the *Poverty of Philosophy* published in 1847, Marx again states that political conditions are only the official expression of civil society. The state is always subject to economic conditions. Legislation reflects the will of those who control the economic affairs. If the state were not an instrument of exploitation there would never arise the necessity of class struggle—that is, the struggle between the two dominant or powerful classes of capitalist state. Hence the instrumentalist model of state occupies the most important place in Marxian theory of state.

Why did Marx and Engels say that the political power is an instrument of exploitation? It is observed that in their time there were mature and powerful capitalist states—Great Britain, France and USA. Of these three first two were European countries and when they were writing *Manifesto* both Britain and France established themselves as representative of powerful ruling class. The persons manning the various branches of state administration were recruited only from the powerful sections of society. Even today this system has not lost its importance. The economic and cultural background of the persons managing the state affairs is the same. Naturally these persons who are also called elites will make all efforts to use the state as a weapon of protecting the interests of the ruling class. Marx and Engels were so much convinced that they, in various ways, expressed the instrumentalist character of bourgeois state in *Manifesto* and *The German Ideology.*

In a developed capitalist economy the sources of production are in the complete control of the bourgeoisie and this control is intensified to consolidate the power and position of bourgeoisie. By setting up giant industrial organisations the capitalists control the production and also the productive system. In the capitalist-controlled world small business holdings have no place. Both the internal and external markets are under the control of the bourgeois. Particularly for establishing hegemony over the markets of other states the state machinery is used by the capitalists. The domains of politics and economy coincide. The capitalists form an organisation to press their demand and this acts as a powerful pressure group.

Because of the structural constraints the state is called the instrument of exploitation. What do we mean by these structural constraints? If the economy, in all its manifestations, is under the full grip of the bourgeoisie, the state will be the complete reflection of this particular class. Miliband has said that the state is the instrument of the ruling class because, given its insertion in capitalist mode of production, it cannot be anything else. The economic system or base will be capitalist and the superstructure will be socialist—that peculiar situation cannot be imagined. Even it is un-Marxian. There shall be a correspondence between base and superstructure. Antagonism might also appear, but not always.

A recent critic[1] has defined the state as an instrument of ruling class. He says, "The state is the institution or complex of institutions, which bases itself on the availability of forcible coercion by special agencies of society in order to maintain the dominance of a ruling class, preserve the existing property relations from basic change and keep all other classes in subjection." This implies that the state consists of an increasingly complex apparatus of domination to defend the existing property relations. This comment of Hal Draper is nothing but the repetition of the view that the state in bourgeois system always acts to protect primarily the interests of the ruling class. Our point is the instrumentalist model of state is a widely accepted notion of Marxist theory of state.

Evaluation

The instrumentalist model of Marxian theory of state has been criticised from various angles. Bob Jessop, a recent critic, observes that there is uncertainty in the formulation of the instrumentalist approach. This approach is accompanied by a short message and rhetoric. It suffers from objective analysis. The state, in all cases and in all epochs, is an instrument of the ruling class—this is an oversimplification of the whole issue. Bob Jessop is of opinion that it is unjustified to brand the capitalist state as an instrument of exploitation. It has other manifestations. It exploits and at the same time it performs welfare activities. Not a single bourgeois state has neglected the interests of the working class. It is true that its main sympathy is for the capitalist class. But the parliamentary forms and political consciousness have alerted the state about its primary responsibility towards the teeming millions. Sometimes the state plays the role of neutrality. It may be rare but it is a fact. In many political systems the bourgeoisie has not succeeded in controlling the politics and economic affairs up to its full satisfaction.

In the second half of the nineteenth century the rise of middle class, modification of liberalism and propagation of Fabian Socialism curtailed the meteoric rise of capitalism. Particularly the Fabian socialists were determined to cut the capitalism to size. The philosophers, intellectuals, politicians, statesmen and policy-makers could not keep them aloof from the growing misery and deprivation of the working class. They did not advocate for the introduction or Marxian socialism through class struggle and violent revolution, but they pleaded for state interference in the social and economic affairs of the state with the sole purpose of mitigating the misery.

Plamenatz has raised (p. 366) another objection against the instrumentalist approach. He says that in *The Origin of Family, Private Property and State* Engels says that the state arises to keep peace between the classes having irreconcilable interests. But the classes which exist when the state arises are not classes in the Marxian sense of the class, they are merely groups engaged in various occupations having

1. Hal Draper : —*Karl Marx's Theory of Revolution*, p. 251. Quoted by Schwarzmantel in *Introduction to Power*, p. 116.

divergent interests. The interests of various classes will be irreconcilable when they will be classes in the strictest Marxian sense. So when there are no classes in the proper sense of the term how can their interests be irreconcilable? In order to raise itself to the level of ruling class, it must be adequately powerful. Mere control of productive forces cannot make a class powerful. It must have sweeping control over politics, culture and other spheres of social life. These objections do not however make the instrumentalist model fully irrelevant. We are of opinion that sometimes the state decisions go in favour of the working class and common people. It is to be remembered that the capitalist state adopts this neutralist approach simply to camouflage its real motive and the real motive is to safeguard the most vital interests of the capitalists. This is not mere conjecture or fabricated allegation. History is replete with instances that in Marx's time and before him the state acted in favour of the ruling class.

Relative Autonomy Model

Although the instrumentalist approach to state occupies the prominent place in the domain of Marxian approach to state, the other approach—the relative autonomy model—is, nonetheless, of great importance. Since this concept carries sufficient weight we shall devote enough space to its analysis. The *Eighteenth Brumaire of Louis Bonaparte,* written between December 1851 and March 1852, offers a brief outline of this model. Ralph Miliband says (*Socialist Register*) "The extreme manifestation of the state's independent role is to be found in authoritarian personal rule, Bonaparteism." The pre-1789 French monarchy was not controlled by any class. The absolute monarchies of other European states were also not controlled by any powerful class. The first and second empires in France were also not states controlled by either the decayed nobility of the rising bourgeoisie.

Marx has said that the ruling class is not always well-organised and sufficiently assertive. Naturally, its extent of control over the state may not be far-reaching. The ruling class is also divided into various groups and factions. Under such circumstances it cannot fully control the state machinery. The ruling class is forced to make compromises with all other groups. The lack of organisation in the ruling class sometimes becomes a limiting factor in the way of its control over the working class. There is another limitation which comes from pressure group. In all the liberal democracies economically powerful class is under the influence of pressure groups. Homogeneity of attitude and approach between the ruling elite and pressure group may not be a normal feature.

Schwarzmantel in *An Introduction to Power* says "The idea of relative autonomy of the state was anticipated by a distinction which Marx made between the dominant class (*herrschende klasse*) and governing caste (*regierende kaste*). The holders of the state power who staff the state machinery and form the government are not normally the same people as those who control the means of production." The independent character of state, therefore, appears from the difference between the holders of power and holders of the productive forces. In 1855 Marx wrote, "The governing caste, which in England is by no means identical with the ruling class, will now be driven from one coalition to the next until it has given conclusive proof that it is no longer destined to govern."

In liberal democracy the class state functions to protect the interests of the dominant class. Marx calls the government elite a "Committee". The advocates of the relative autonomy model say that even the members of the committee are not always unanimous on all issues. The members of the committee who manage the common affairs of the whole bourgeoisie are not puppets who respond to every matter or whims mechanically. As Miliband rightly says, the state may well act on behalf of the ruling class, but that is not to say it works at their behest. To understand the state as an immediately responsive instrument or tool of a class would be a very "vulgar" form of Marxism. He further points out that the very notion of the state managing the common affairs of the whole bourgeoisie implies a process of selection. The holders of the state power have to decide which measures would, in fact, further the interests of the property owning class as distinct from the interests of a section of that class. The holders of state power are never the blind followers of the ruling class. They always give priority to stablisation of the ruling class and attainment of long-term benefit. In order to achieve these goals the state authority, if necessary, will contradict the ruling class. The central idea of the relative model is that generally the state power supports or protects the interests of the ruling class, but it is not always correct. The state authority sometimes maintains an apparent or so-called neutrality among the various groups who are on the one hand powerful and on the other fight for capturing power. The role of the state appears to be of an umpire. The ruling authority wants to prove its neutrality, stability in politics and to establish that it is not done at the hands of powerful groups.

The persons in power sometimes adopt such measures as shortening of working hour, paid holidays and social legislation. All these measures benefit the working class, but the *raison d' etre* of all these is to stabilise the capitalist system. The New Deal measures of the thirties of the 20th century USA were promulgated mainly to preserve the interests of capitalists. As Schwarzmantel writes (p. 120) "The government regulations were denounced by some spokesmen for industry as "creeping socialism". Nevertheless, the action of the state was in the long-term interest of American capitalism enabling it to recover from the recession without in any way imperilling the basic system." Same indepence of state action is to be found in Britain.

The *coup d' etat,* Marx wrote, was the victory of Bonaparte over parliament, of the executive power over the legislative power, of force without phrases over force of phrases. The nation made its general will the law, that is, it made the law of the ruling class its general will. Before the executive power it renounces all will of its own and submits to the superior command of an alien will, to authority. The executive power, in contrast to the legislative power, expresses the heteronomy of a nation, in contrast to its autonomy. France seems to have escaped the despotism of a class only to fall back beneath the despotism of an individual, and what is more, beneath the authority of the individual without authority. The struggle seems to be settled on such a way that all classes, equally important and equally mute, fall on their knees before the rifle butt (*MESW*, I, p. 332).

Marx then goes on to speak of this executive power with its enormous bureaucratic and military organisation, with its ingenious "state machinery, embracing wide strata, with a host of officials numbering half a million, besides an army of another half million, this appalling parasitic body which enmeshes the body of French society like a net and chokes all its pores" (p. 332). This bureaucratic power which sprang up in the days of absolute monarchy had first been the means of preparing the class rule of the bourgeoisie. While under Restoration, under Louis

Philippe, under the parliamentary republic it was the instrument of the ruling class, however much it strove for power of its own. But the *coup d" etat* changed its role. Only under the Second Bonaparte does the state seem to have made itself completely independent. As against the civil society, the state machine has consolidated its position so thoroughly that the chief of the society of December 10 (i. e., Louis Bonaparte) suffices for its head.

The above is the brief picture of the independent functioning of state. This he has portrayed in *The Eighteenth Brumaire of Louis Bonaparte.* The two models—instrumentalist and relative—are opposite to each other. But one should not forget to note that both these models depict the true character of capitalist state that prevailed in his time. A number of recent scholars are of opinion that the relative autonomy model is of great significance. It proves how Marx was sensitive to the functioning of the state. It also proves the piquancy of his observation. Miliband says, "This (analysis in *Brumaire*) would appear to suggest the *complete* independence of the state power from all social forces in civil society" (p. 85). It is to be noted here that though Miliband claims full independence of state authority, in capitalist system the state authority can never be fully independent because the most powerful class or group will never allow the state authority to function independently. If the state does so the vital interests of the dominant class would face erosion or danger. In one way or other the powerful class would prevail over the state authority.

Reasons of the Relative Autonomy

In the opinion of Schwarzmantel there are two main reasons of why the state must have relative autonomy. For the "ruling class cohesion" the autonomy of the bourgeois state is essential. There are numerous divisions within the capitalist class. Sometimes they fight against each other. Persons managing the state affairs are well aware of it. If this is allowed to continue, the rulers apprehend, the interests of the capitalist class will be seriously jeopardised. The authority must not be responsive to each and every attitude and demand of the economically dominate class. Administration will be a separate entity. If the members of the dominant class interfere with the process of administration conduct of government will be an impossibility. Moreover, the government must publicly show that it is neutral in the midst of various classes. That is, the image building purpose leads the state to pursue an independent policy. Peace in society is also an important precondition for uninterrupted growth of capitalism. Blatant partiality simply antagonises other classes. This is to be shelved. Again, class cohesion means integration of conflicting interests. This is also essential. Speaking of the nature of capitalist class Draper says, "No other ruling class is so profusely criss-crossed internally with competing and conflicting interest groups. Competing national groups are split by regional group interests, different industrial interests, antagonism within an industry."

Schwarzmantel's another reason is "the state, in a liberal democratic system, must have some autonomy in order to preserve its legitimacy. If the state was seen to be too closely bound up with and dominated by one set of interests, it would not be able to maintain the belief that it represents the general interests." Liberal democracy does not believe that the working class will have no influence on the policy and affairs of the state. The elites are very clever and understands the nature and functioning of state. This enables them to acquire control over the state affairs.

The liberal democracy permits the free political activities of all groups of persons. It the powerful class wants to capture power the active support of the working and middle classes is a must. Naturally the holders of power do not want any alienation of the working class from the ruling class. They want to establish a *rapprochement* between the classes. This necessiates independent functioning of state.

In Marx's time the state was not so much autonomous as it is today. Why? The increasing democratisation and rising political consciousness have created mounting pressure upon the state to follow an impartial policy. It the ruling class follows an uncompromising policy that will lead to an explosive situation detrimental to the general interest of the bodypolitic. So in Marx's time there was autonomy and it still exists though in greater amount.

Is the State Really Autonomous?

The liberal democratic state or the autocratic state of Marx's time maintains an autonomous status even in the midst of divergent forces—does not lead one to think that the state is absolutely autonomous and it is not an instrument of class rule. Under pressure of circumstances the ruling class may amend its policy or modify its attitude. But the *leitmotif* remains in all circumstances unaffected, to safeguard the class interest. Sometimes the ruling class pleads for a "strong state" and concedes to the erosion of its power. Military organ of state enjoys precedence in all cases. This naive concession is not to be treated as a permanent arrangement. When the state appears to be powerful the ruling class switches its allegiance from traditional bases or agencies to new elements. In every capitalist system there is an unholy alliance between the powerful class and the state structure and this alliance benefits both. As a result, if situation demands the powerful class utilises the state machinery in its favour which finds no resistance from state. Marx never assumes that the state power always maintains neutrality. In the *Eighteenth Brumaire of Louis Bonaparte* he has said (p. 333 in *MESW*, I) "And yet the state power is not suspended in midair. Bonaparte represents a class, and the most numerous class of French society at that, the small holding peasants."

Engels was well aware of the issue of relative autonomy of state and he has said that the state maintains its neutrality in some cases. He is conspicuous in the following comment made by him : "By way of exception...periods occur in which the warring classes balance each other so nearly that the state power, as ostensible mediator, acquires, for the moment, a certain degree of independence of both. Such was the absolute monarchy of the seventeenth and eighteenth centuries, which held the balance between the nobility and the class of burghers : such was the Bonaparteism of First and still more the Second French Empire, which played off the proletariat against the bourgeoisie, and the bourgeoisie against the proletariat." Commenting upon Engels's conception of relative autonomy Ralph Miliband says in *Socialist Register* "But the independence of which he speaks would seem to go much further than anything Marx has in mind. The vital point is that though Engels admits of the autonomy of state he never gives it too much importance. He says that *the autonomy of state is a rare occurence. It is never the primary character of the state.* He calls the *autonomy an exception.* The instrumentalist model is general. In the *Origin of Family, Private Property and State* Engels remarks that the fact is that the state is an organisation of the possessing class for its protection against the non-possessing class. Everywhere wealth plays the vital role in the political affairs of the state. This role is sometimes direct sometimes indirect. Both the relative and instrumentalist models are correct, but they do not offer the last words about the nature of bourgeois state. Such a state is always sensitive to prevailing situation. We have already noted that every bourgeois state wants peace and stability within its geographical boundary and for that purpose it is forced to make compromises with all prevailing forces. Up to the end of the nineteenth century the state was controlled by powerful class. But after the First World War (1914-1918) the situation began to change and today no capitalist state is absolutely controlled by any powerful class.

Some Recent Observations

Fyodor Burlatsky, a renowned critic of Marxian politics, deals with the concept of relative autonomy of state. It is interesting to note that he admits the existence and working of the autonomous bourgeois state. But he points out that to what extent a bourgeois state will admit the autonomy that depends upon the ability of autonomy to serve the purpose of bourgeoisie. There is a tendency on the part of the state to acquire autonomy. Burlatsky investigates the working of the American capitalist system and on the basis of investigation he says (p. 63) that enormous expansion of state's economic function, pressure on the state of class forces opposing and fighting against monopolies, increasing complexities of state's public administration, mass activism in social conflicts and international factors are responsible for the autonomy of state in capitalist society. He concludes "The does not mean that the bureaucracy is becoming an intermediary force in bourgeois society. Under any conditions it takes a stand in defence of the economic and sociopolitical system of bourgeois society" (p. 64).

United States is the most prosperous, powerful and reactionary bourgeois state. Its administration is so complex and policy-making system is so much connected with numerous departments that both these require a heavy does of specialisation. The ruling class as a whole cannot shoulder the entire responsibility of the complex system. Autonomy of state apparatus is, therefore, a natural consequence. But we must be alert about the fact that the policy-makers and administrators never betray the capitalist class. The ruling class is forced to take assistance of numerous pressure groups and interest groups and this it does reluctantly. It is true that the leaders of the ruling class give final touches to all policies but behind every policy or decision there work large number of experts. Naturally we cannot say that the powerful class is all in all. In every state various forces are quite active in numerous sections of state administration.

During the 19th century the economic, political and social conditions of all the capitalist states have undergone radical changes. What was simply capitalism in past, now it has assumed the character of State Monopoly Capitalism. Hence the economic functions of state have increased enormously. On the other hand, rise of people's demands are mounting upon the state authority at an increasing rate. The authority of state is busy in arriving at a compromise between the contending forces of the society and in doing this it maintains an autonomy. Whatever may be the extent of the power of the ruling class, the holders of power try to bypass some of the demands of the dominant class. *The relative autonomy of the state under present circumstances is not a myth, it is a reality, a stark reality.* Modern bourgeois state will proceed to disintegration if it neglects the interests of other classes, but it does not sacrifice the interests of the ruling class.

The present position of the relative autonomy of the state can be illustrated by several recent experiences. Hitler, with the help of capitalists, came to power. But he consolidated and strengthened his position with the help of bureaucracy and military and simultaneously he suppressed all elements of opposition. The German state became the most powerful totalitarian state. Dictatorship of Hitler was strengthened and autonomy of the party state and military mechanism considerably grew. Of course, there were crises in the ruling classes in Germany. However, in the thirties the German state under the leadership of Hitler became the most powerful autonomous state.

In the late fifties of the 20th century General de Gaulle captured power in France to tide over the rapid deteriorating conditions. He was the symbol of national power and was determined to pursue an independent policy both in national and international fields. He snapped relations with USA and other NATO states and established cordial relations with the then Soviet Union. All these measures considerably enhanced the prestige and image of France in international arena. Needless to say General de Gaulle wanted that.

What is the exact picture of the relative autonomy of state in the developing countries of the Third World? In spite of the autonomy of state, the dominant class enjoys certain amount of influence in administrative and policy-making affairs. But in developing countries the picture is quite different. In these countries it is very difficult to locate an economically dominant class. A number of classes vie with each other to capture power and this ultimately leads to political instability. The state as a balancing force exercises its power to settle the disputes. The state, in the last analysis, enjoys autonomy. This is relative autonomy of state. Kandai Seshadri in his *Studies in Marxism and Political Science* has said : "The administration of colonial and semicolonial countries representing a nebulous state may exercise a certain measure of independence. This is what could be called the relative autonomy of state" (p. 60). Base (production relations) and superstructure (state) are not mechanically related. It is a feature of the developing countries that economic base is backward, while the superstructure—that is law, courts and bureaucracy—are not backward, rather quite developed. The influence of pressure group and political consciousness of masses are not of high standard. State gets ample scope to discharge its functions independently.

WITHERING AWAY OF STATE

The Meaning

We have so far discussed two models of Marxist theory of state—the instrumentalist model or the state is an instrument of class rule and, simultaneously, an instrument of exploitation which means the economically powerful class uses it to exploit the proletarians. The other one is relative autonomy model. The first highlights the notion that the state always and everywhere acts as an agent of the powerful class. It has no other purpose than to protect the interests of the class. The other model emphasises that it tries to maintain its neutrality in the midst of various classes. Miliband says that in ultimate analysis there is no conflict between these two models. However, we are not concerned with it. Engels in his *The Origin of Family, Private Property and State* says that after setting up of a classles society there will be no need of state, it will wither away. This is a logical conclusion. If there are no classes its function to keep peace between irreconcilable classes will cease to exist. If society is classless the state will disappear. With the withering away of the state there will be no police force or army or any agency to suppress the proletarians. The withering away of state—according to Marx and Engels—is inevitable. The proletarians will overthrow the bourgeoisie from power which means an end of bourgeois rule and disintegration of state machinery. So the state does not wither away at the sweet will of anybody. It is a logical inevitability.

Engels's Version

In several of their works Marx and Engels have repeatedly emphasised the end of state but the classic formulation of the withering away of state is to be found in *Socialism : Utopian and Scientific.* In this famous pamphlet Engels writes : "The proletariat seizes political power and turns the means of production into state property. But in doing this it abolishes itself as a proletariat, abolishes all class distinctions and class antagonisms, abolishes also the state as state...The state was the official representative of society as a whole, the gathering of it together into a visible embodiment. But it was this only in so far as it was the state of that class which itself represented, for the time being society as a whole : in ancient times, the state of slave owning citizens, in the Middle Ages the feudal lords, in our time the bourgeoisie."

"When at last it becomes the real representative of the whole society, it renders itself unnecessary. As soon as there is no longer any social class to be held in subjection, as soon as class rule, and the individual struggle for existence based upon our present anarchy in production...are removed, nothing more remains to be repressed, and a special repressive force, a state, is no-longer necessary."

"The state interference in social relations becomes, in one domain after another, superfluous and then *dies out of itself;* the government of persons is replaced by administration of things, and by the conduct of processes of production. The state is not *abolished.* It *dies out.* This gives the measure of the value of the phrase a *free state,* both to its justifiable use at times by agitators and as to its ultimate scientific insufficiency and also of the demands of the so-called anarchists for the abolition of the state out of hand" (*MESW*, II, p. 159-151).

Engels concludes (p. 153) "Man's own social organisation, hitherto confronting him as a necessity imposed by Nature and history, now becomes the result of his own free action. The extraneous objective forces that have hitherto governed history pass under the control of man himself. Only from that time man will himself more and more consciously make his own history—only from that time will the social causes set in movement by him have, in the main and in a constantly growing measure the results intended by him. It is the ascent of man from the kingdom of necessity to the kingdom of freedom."

Lenin's Interpretation of Witherning Away of State

Lenin's *State and Revolution* published in 1918 contains by far the best exposition of Marxist theory of state. Lenin emphasises that the key idea of the withering away of state enunciated by Engels is that it differs from the anarchist view of the abolition of state. At the outset Engels has said that in seizing state power the proletariat "abolishes the state as state". Engels uttered these words in the background of the experience of the Paris Commune of 1871. The difference between the withering away and abolition is that the proletarian revolution will abolish the bourgeois state. After capturing power the proletarians will use the bourgeois state to further their own interests. That means certain remnants of the bourgeois state will find their place in the seized state. The proletarian revolution is not the final stage. After it there shall appear or occur another revolution with is called social revolution. Lenin states that only after the social revolution the remnants of the bourgeois state will wither away. In Lenin's own words—According to Engels, the bourgeois state does not wither away, but is abolished by the proletariat in the course of the revolution. What withers away after this revolution is the proletarian state or semi-state (*Selected Works*, Vol. II, p. 315).

The proletariat needed a dying state. Why? All the elements or aspects of bourgeois state are not to be destroyed or abolished. Only those which are not harmful for proletarian rule and conducive to the furtherance of proletarian interests will be kept. Bureaucracy and judicial system are such elements. Trotsky calls it dying state, because it is not bourgeois state in the strictest term. In *The Critique of Gotha Programme* Marx has said "communist society, not as it has developed on its own foundations, but on the contrary; just as it emerges from capitalist society, which is thus in every respect, economically, morally and intellectually, still stamped with the birthmarks of the old society from whose womb it emerges."

According to Engels the state is a special "repressive force". This characterisation of bourgeois state according to Lenin is a splendid and profound definition. The bourgeoisie uses the state machinery to oppress the proletarians. It is, in other words, the instrument of exploitation. After overthrowing the bourgeoisie from power the proletarians will abolish the exploiting character of the bourgeois state. The word abolition has a wider connotation. The proletarians through the seizure of power will destroy the repressive weapons. All the means of production are to be taken by the proletarians. The taking of possession will make the capitalist resourceless and powerless. It is self-evident that such a replacement of one (bourgeois) special force by another (proletarian) special force cannot possibly take place in the form of withering away (*LSW*, II, p. 315).

Lenin says that the withering away of state is directed against the anarchists and opportunists. The anarchists always spoke of the destruction of the state which Marx and Engels do not support. The opportunists have distorted the concept of withering away of state. They have said that at the very first stroke the proletarian revolution will put the state to such a level that it will practically cease to exist. According to Lenin one revolution is not sufficient for the withering away of state. A violent revolution will destroy the repressive character of bourgeois state but all the counter-revolutionary forces and agents acting against the interests of proletarians cannot be destroyed by a single revolution. The remnants of the capitalists will remain and they will gather forces and after some time these forces will try to stage a counter-revolution. To frustrate this revolution more than one revolution will be required.

Many criticisms have been levelled against the concept of withering away. Critics as well as opportunists have held that if the state disappears who will settle the disputes arising between the citizen and various state authorities as well as among the individuals. This objection has been partially met by Lenin in many of his works and also by other Marxists. They have attempted to draw a distinction between organised force that is government and administration. When Engels says that the state withers away at the classless society he means that the repressive character of state withers away. In a classless society the application of force will be redundant, because there will not be an economically dominant class. The proletarian state will always work for the benefit of the entire population.

In the classless society—which is another name of communist society—there will be disputes. Where there are disputes, the parties to them, if they cannot settle them amicably, will submit them to the arbitration and loyally accept the decisions of the arbiters. In the *State and Revolution* Lenin has said that in a communist society all the individuals will be quite free to pursue their own ideals and will be fully politically conscious. The repressive force being destroyed and freedom being established, people will voluntarily and spontaneously abide by the laws and rules created by the communist society. No extraneous force will be necessary to force them to show obligation to laws. In exceptional cases there shall be provisions for arbitration. In a communist society one man is not the subject of another man. The communist society is a just society and justice in all its forms prevails. A member of the society is just one of the equals and he enjoys all sorts of dignity. He is conscious and prudent and cannot inflict injustice upon others.

Stalin's Explanation

In the background of Soviet state the bourgeois theoreticians have said that state has not withered away. Therefore, Engels's concept is false. Stalin, a great interpreter of Marxism-Leninism, challenges this contention. Engels never used the idea of withering away in the case of any particular state. To put it in other words, when there is socialism or when its transition to communism is complete in any one country the state as an organised force of exploitation will never wither away. A socialist state encircled by a number of bourgeois states will not and cannot wither away. On the contrary, this particular socialist state will be more powerful to fight against the capitalist state. Stalin has said the purpose of all the capitalist states is to destroy the socialist state.

When all the states are socialist and capitalism is completely annihilated, the question of strengthening and consolidating the power of the socialist state will never arise. The antagonism between the capitalist and socialist countries will no longer be a live question. This suspicion of Stalin against the capitalist state is not unfounded and unreasonable. After the establishment of USSR in 1917 and till the Second World War the bourgeois states of Europe were determined to destroy Soviet communism. The political picture, of course, quickly changed. Soviet Union was included into Allied Power Group. France, England and America were convinced that only with the help of mighty Soviet Union could Germany and Italy be defeated.

Stalin admits that for the distortion and misinterpretation of withering away by the bourgeois theoreticians Marx and Engels can be blamed partially. They have not systematically explained the concept of state and interpreted the subtle distinction between withering away and abolition. This shortcoming has been misused by them. However, Stalin says, Lenin has clearly explained the issue in his *State and Revolution.* Stalin has further observed that when and at what stage the state will wither away the bourgeois academicians have not fully understood. Engels has clearly said that proletarians will abolish the state in its manifestation as a repressive force. In Stalin's judgment the capitalists do not admit that the state is an instrument of exploitation. Because of this the concept has been grossly distorted.

Evaluation

Plamenatz argues that in the ordinary sense Marx and Engels are not anarchists. They had no intention to get rid of the state. The main purpose of the worker was to capture state power so that they could destroy the bourgeois social relations and bourgeois mentality. But in a deeper sense they can by called anarchists because "they wanted workers to use the state to destroy the social conditions which made it necessary to have a state. They shared the belief common among all anarchists that class privileges and state power are corrupting" (p. 374). They are anarchists it another sense. They have depicted only one side of state—the state as an instrument of exploitation. They have not noted the utility of state—enforcing authority of law and arbiter of disputes. They have laid heavy faith on people's good sense and rationality. The practical situation offers a contradictory picture. Without casting any doubt on people's good sense we can humbly add that this is not a guarantee that all disputes will be settled amicably. The abolition of the state, we apprehend, will create an anarchical condition and it is unfortunate that Marx and Engels have not suggested any palliatives. The abolition of the state will be followed by anarchical situation.

Marx and Engels, so far as their theory of state is concerned, are charged of being utopians. After the abolition of state at first there will be set up socialism or which is called primary stage of communism. Then the appearance of classless society will make the state redundant leading it to wither away. *Dialectically or logically it may be correct but from practical point of view it is simply utopian.* Marx and Engels have held that in the old primitive society there was no state. The state is not only the product of class and property relations, it is also the product of civilisation and progress. It is associated with manifold evils, but its welfare activities or salutary aspects need not be minimised. Marx's classless society may aptly be compared with *Ram Rajya.* But *Ram Rajya* is an imaginary concept; so also the classless society. The abolition of state will make way for the creation of a classless society and class in Marx's own sense. But the abolition of class in Marxian sense does not mean that classes in other forms will never surface in society and reality has taught us that classes in various forms other than Marxian sense appeared in former USSR. The definition of class in Marxian sense may have relevance in a developed industrial society, but it has very little relevance in undeveloped or developing societies. So, abolition of state will not follow Marx's prediction. Hence, despite their repeated pronouncements that the theory of state is based on scientific logic, it is not free from utopian thought.

Critics point out that when Marx and Engels were writing i.e., in the second half of the nineteenth century, the state was largely an instrument of exploitation. This was chiefly due to the fact that the proletarians were not well-organised and fully politically conscious. In Marx's own words they were class-in-itself, but not class-for-itself. This condition of the working class encouraged the capitalists to exploit them. Their apathy to struggle was another cause of exploitation. Today the social, economic and political conditions of the capitalist states have come under radical changes. The emergence of Labour Party in England as a force to reckon with, its installation to power and determination to fight for the cause of the workers, have made the capitalists think that the days of naked exploitation have gone permanently and they will have to adjust with the new epoch which relates to the new demands and rise of consciousness of workers. Not only Great Britain, the authorities of several other capitalist countries were forced to take measures for alleviation of miseries and stop exploitation. The contribution of Fabian Socialism, in this connection, may be fruitfully remembered.

Modern state is generally called a welfare state the general meaning of which is the state adopts numerous projects for the upliftment of the improvement of the economic and social conditions of the public. The state is no longer an exploiting and repressive instrument. It initiates welfare measures. For reasons best known to readers the state cannot leave every important matter to the profit-making magnate of the society and cannot allow the hapless workers to be exploited by them. Even philosophers like Thomas Hill Green were pained seeing the unbound sufferings and degradation of the unfed denizes of London. The state is not simply a law-enforcing agency. It cannot maintain studied indifference to the growing misery of the workers. The changed circumstances have forced the state to adopt certain welfare measures. This can be traced to Fabian Socialism. In Marx's time workers were alone and unorganised. In the twentieth century they were organised and the state at least peripherally comes to their assistance. This is, no doubt, a victory of the workers.

The methods of agitation have undergone seachanges during the past century. The workers nowhere are interested in class struggle, revolution, abolition of bourgeois state and setting up a classless society. Parliamentary procedures, demonstrations, strikes, protest movements etc are treated as more effective means to fulfil their various demands. Even Engels towards the end of his life admitted the effectiveness of democratic methods. Workers want emancipation from exploitation, but not through the capture of state power or through its abolition. They feel the necessity of state and they think that it must come to their help. In past, the bourgeoisie used the state as an instrument of exploitation, the workers today want to use the state as an instrument to fight against the exploiters. The role of the state is thus reversed. If Marx and Engels were alive today, the critics point out, they would not suggest to abolish the bourgeois state and predict its withering away.

The withering away of the state has perhaps faced the severest criticism from a different angle. The critics have categorically said that the state has not withered away; on the contrary, it has become more powerful. No socialist state in the world has been found to wither away. There is practically no difference between the Chinese state and American bourgeois state. From military point of view the erstwhile Soviet state and the present American state were equal. Both were aggressive and both aggravated the Cold War. Both were superpowers. In this background it is absolutely utopian to think that the state will wither away in communism.

It is difficult to challenge the validity of the above arguments. But Marxists view the concept of state and other conceptions from a different angle. Marxian philosophy is a branch or part of social science and no concept of social science is in full conformity with the real situation. That is, a discrepancy between reality and concept is inevitable. But we are to remember that there is a logical consistency in all their views. The critics may say that the state is not an instrument of exploitation. Today it is not, but in Marx's time that was the chief characteristic feature of state. Every state has certain primary and secondary functions. A bourgeois state generally protects the interests of the capitalist class. Its other functions are in addition to it. It is unthinkable that there is a bourgeois state but it does not work as an instrument of exploitation.

Harold Laski is the chief protagonist of the liberal view of state. He has attacked the capitalist state on various counts. Any state in which the instruments of production are privately owned cannot provide a technique of peaceful change or satisfy the demands of citizens on the widest possible scale. To what extent a state will be able to meet the demands of its people depends upon the property relations. In a capitalist state the incentive to production is the making of profit. There is always a discrimination between those who own property and means of production and those who do not own anything. "Only the capture of the state, followed by the definition of its legal postulates, could remedy this conditions" (Page V)[1] Laski's conclusion is "the idealist theory of the state in its famous formulation by Bosanquet remains a formulation of conceptual state *in posse* rather than the state we know. The liberal and anti-idealist view, as expressed by L. T. Hobhouse, assumes but does not prove, that, given time, reason will always be victorious in matter of social conflicts. Neither Bosanquet's view, nor that of Hobhouse, fulfils the scientific canon of prediction. Broadly speaking, the Marxian view of the state has so defined its nature and functioning as to enable us to predict with assurance the course its operations will follow. As an index to the problems of our age it decisively, in my judgement, holds the field' (p. V).

During the last one hundred years the capitalist states have changed both in outlook and in methods of administration. But it has not changed to such an extent as to nullify the role of instrument of exploitation. Marxist's view in this regard is that the state remains more or less an instrument to exploit the working class. Its role will never assume a reverse character. The capitalists cannot be credited for this change. It is the growing pressure of the working class which has forced the capitalists to change the mode of action. The capitalists of the modern world have come to the full realisation that they cannot continue their production and business so long the workers will remain dissatisfied. They, therefore, are resorting to the 'policy of appeasement'.

In conclusion we want to make the following considered opinion. It is very easy to say that both Marx and Engels are wrong so far as their assertion that the bourgeois state will wither away with the advent of communism. But we must remember that Marx and Engels made this observation in the perspective of their analysis of capitalism and materialist interpretation of history. Their very simple version is if the state is an instrument of class rule and class exploitation, if there is no class this particular role of the state will no longer be a valid one. Again, since the role and nature of bourgeois state have changed, the withering away is invalid.

A Critique of Marxian Theory of State

Our survey of Marxian theory of state has dealt with several aspects of the concept. In this section few points are required to be highlighted. The discussion of this part is based on the essay—Marx and The State by Ralph Miliband which was published in *The Socialist Register*—1965. In this essay Miliband has analysed the Marxian theory of state from historical and contemporary reality. We think that this approach of Miliband is quite plausible because no thinker can overlook or ignore the influence of contemporary events. The events of contemporary Greek city states created an impact upon the political philosophy of Plato. Similarly Machiavelli or Hobbes or Locke kept in mind the prevailing incidents.

1. *A Grammar of Politics.*

Ralph Miliband observes that Marx has not made any detailed analysis of the theory of state. Marxian theory of state is based on the "interpretations and adaptations made by the Marxists and supporters of Marxism and above all by Lenin. Miliband says that these interpretations and adaptations cannot be taken to constitute an adequate expression of Marx's own views. This is not because these theories bear no relation to Marx's views but rather that they emphasise some aspects of his thought to the detriment of others and thus distort by over-simplification."

Miliband has said that it was not possible for Marx to avoid the influence of contemporary events of the capitalist states of his time—particularly of France and Britain. Marx wrote three important books—*The Class Struggle in France, The Eighteenth Brumaire of Louis Bonaparte* and *The Civil War in France. The Class Struggle in France* was written by Marx in 1850. The *Eighteenth Brumaire* was written between December 1851 to March 1852 and *The Civil War in France* in April-May 1871. So within a span of 21 years he wrote these three important books. The critics of Marxian theory of state garner materials from these three books. The political, social and economic conditions of France during the second half of the 19th century are quite well-known to the students of history. The authoritarian rule, political turmoil and instability in governmental affairs considerably influenced Marx's thought system. Miliband has emphasised that aspect.

According to Miliband, Marx had also studied the nature and function of states of Asia. He called the Asiatic states as despotic states where the political realm is nothing but the arbitrary will of a particular individual. Marx is quite right in his assessment about the nature of the Asiatic states. The administrative systems of Mughal emperors can be cited as illustrations. The will of the Mughal emperor was final and he was the ultimate source of authority and sovereign power. The despotic nature of Indian emperors is also revealed is their flamboyant claims that they were the representatives of God on earth. Marx closely observed all these things. Miliband writes "It is evident that Marx does view the state in the conditions of Asiatic despotism, as the dominant force in society, independent of and superior to all its members."

Miliband has dealt with Marx's "dictatorship of the proletariat". In the letter to Weydemeyer in March 1852 he said that the only new thing he said is that the class struggle necessarily leads to the dictatorship of the proletariat. But unfortunately he has not defined the concept in any specific way. The concept dictatorship of the proletariat constitutes a basic aspect of Marxian theory of state. So it is necessary to throw light on what Marx actually meant and Miliband had performed that job. In the words of Miliband : "The dictatorship of the proletariat is both a statement of the class character of the political power and a description of the political power itself; and that it is in fact the nature of the political power which it describes which guarantees its class character." The dictatorship of the proletariat would be the outcome of a socialist revolution. Marx pointed this out in the *Critique of the Gotha Programme*.

Lichtheim in his *Marxism*, published in 1961, said that Marx's theory of state is decidedly authoritarian doctrine. According to Marx the state was to assume dictatorial powers. But Miliband does not agree with this view of Lichtheim. He is of opinion that Marxian theory of state is "decidedly authoritarian" in character is not based on facts or evidence. Explaining Marx's stand on the nature of state Lenin said "If the political struggle of the working class assumes violent forms, if the workers set up this revolutionary dictatorship of the bourgeoisie, they commit the terrible crime of violating principles, for in order to satisfy their wretched, vulgar, everyday needs, in order to crush the resistance of the bourgeoisie instead of laying down their arms and abolishing the state, they give the state a revolutionary and transitory form".

Ralph Miliband concludes : "The fact is that, far from bearing any authoritarian imprint, the whole of Marx's work on the state is pervaded by a powerful anti-authoritarian and anti-bureaucratic bias, not only in the relation to a distant communist society but also to the period of transition which is to precede it. True, the state is necessary in this period. But the only thing which, for Marx, makes it tolerable is popular participation and popular rule. If Marx is to be faulted, it is not for any authoritarian bias, but for greatly understating the difficulties of the libertarian position".

All critics may not agree with Miliband's views. But it is a fact that there is a difference between Marx's words and his real intention. Particularly his term "dictatorship of the proletariat" has been misinterpreted and it has been source of all confusion. There is no doubt that Marx was democratic-minded out and out. It is inconceivable that a man who wanted to abolish the supremacy of capitalists will ultimately support the supremacy of another class. If Marx were alive for another one or two decades he could give reply to many of the criticisms raised against his theory of state.

33 MARXISM AND RELIGION

Definition of Religion

A fruitful and comprehensive analysis of Marx's political ideas and philosophy will remain incomplete without any reference to religion because it constitutes the core aspect of Marx's materialism in historical background in particular and political philosophy in general. In this chapter we shall focus our attention on his analysis about religion. He defines or explains religion in the following manner.

It is the considered opinion of Marx, which he formed on the basis of study of history, is that man makes religion, but religion does not make man. In other words, religion is the self-consciousness and self-feeling of man who has either not yet found himself or has already lost himself again. But man is no abstract being squatting outside the world. Man is the world of man, the state, society... Religion is the general theory of that world, its encyclopedic compendium, its logic in a popular form... It is the fantastic realisation of human essence, because the human essence has no true reality. The struggle against religion is therefore mediately the fight against the other world of which religion is the spiritual aroma... Religion is the sigh of the oppressed creature, the heart of a heartless world, just as it is the spirit of a spiritless situation. *It is the opium of the people (Contribution to Critique of Hegel's Philosophy of Right).*

In the above definition Marx has stressed few points about religion which require special emphasis. In his opinion religion has been created by man to meet his own requirements. It is not the opposite. It is secondly the fantastic realisation of human essence and this has no practical existence. Religion is associated with the other world. Thirdly, it is the sigh of persons who are exploited. Finally, we refer to his famous remark. It is like a sedative. Marx calls it an opium. Religion helps man to forget the real world. Persons having vested interests use religion for the attainment of their parochial and limited interests. Marx makes all these remarks about religion in the background of the role religion played in all the periods before him. Though religion was quite active in almost all periods of European history, it was super-active during the Middle Ages.

Explaining Marx's stand on religion Lenin says that religion is one of the forms of spiritual oppression. Religion is a weapon which blunts the sharpness of human intelligence and productive capacity of workers. He further observes that religion teaches man to be submissive and docile. Religion is a sort of spiritual booze, in which the slaves of capital drown their human image. According to Lenin common people have been taught religion to make them forgetful of the prevailing social, political and economic conditions. The approach to religion adopted by the ruling class is a way of exploiting the masses of people.

Marx, Engels and Lenin hold that religion must be treated as a private affair and state must not have any role in religious matter. The state should not interfere with the religious beliefs of individuals. It shall not be the business of state to encourage or discourage any religious belief. There shall be no provision of subsidy in any form to religious institutions such as church or ecclesiastical organisation. The citizens shall enjoy full freedom to form or join associations according to their own belief or faith.

Sources of Marx's Thought

For almost all the major aspects of his philosophy in general and political ideas in particular Marx is indebted to his predecessors and his thought on religion is not an exception. His indebtedness to Feurerbach and Hegel may be mentioned. At an early age Marx read Feuerbach's *Essence of Christianity* which created a strong impact upon his mind. In this book Feuerbach has stated that the ignorance of man fails to explain the natural and other phenomena and this leads him to take the help of religion. In other words man endeavours all the "unexplained" phenomena to treat as supernatural or religious and for this reason Feuerbach calls religion a "fantasy" which compensates his own inadequacy. Man feels that he is inferior to what he might be. In this way the idea of God appears in his thought system and imaginary world. Man thus creates God after his own image. Feuerbach has clearly stated that when man was in the depth of insecurity and helplessness he created an imaginary concept in the name of God and subsequently that became religious and this was not the reflection of the real world.

Feuerbach has also said that as man will be able to acquire more and more knowledge in accurate form and will be able to explain correctly the natural and other phenomena the idea of God and religion will become more and more indistinct and one day it will disappear. "Man will come into full possession of his humanity and will dispense with his illusion of God. Religion is a product of man's immaturity" (Plamenatz, op cit, p. 334). Feuerbach took this idea of religion from Hegel. There are of course differences between them. Hegel has used the word Spirit whereas Feuerbach speaks of man. Feuerbach's reality has become Spirit to Hegel.

Earlier thinkers treated religion as a *social phenomenon* and this impressed Marx considerably. We observed that religious beliefs and ceremonies were practised by men with a great fanfare and this practice provided social unity. People of all sections of society worked, lived and behaved in a disciplined way with the help of religious beliefs. Religion also strengthened social unity and obligation of man to society. Religion was thus a great cementing force. For this reason religion was a social phenomenon and Marx noticed it with great interest. It is to be noted here that to Feuerbach religion was a psychological phenomenon. Feuerbach's view did not impress Marx considerably. He inclined to those who regarded religion as a social phenomenon. Marx has said that under the influence of religion man has no freedom to implement his full potentialities, he becomes the victim of religious practices. Man's power and ability are limited and he does not possess the courage to challenge the religious practices according his own reason. In this way man is compelled by circumstances to surrender to the social practice.

Marx also took notice of the fact that religion gave man comfort and to some extent security. It also removed man's sense of fear. This is because man's rationality did not develop properly due to the inadequate development of education and science. Saint-Simon for that reason argued for their progress which would be able to remove the sense of fear and insecurity from the mind of man. We can, therefore, say that Marx's idea of religion is linked with Saint-Simon's thought on the same subject. Pointing out Marx's indebtedness to Saint-Simon, Plamenatz makes the following remark : "Though Saint-Simon does not call religion the opium of the people, he does say that theology flourishes while men are still incapable of explaining the world and themselves scientifically and that it holds together a society in which an unproductive ruling class live off the labour of others. Of these early socialists none had a greater influence on Marx than Saint-Simon (Plamenatz, p. 336). It is interesting to note that Saint-Simon has drawn our attention to the fact that the capitalist class uses religion as a weapon of exploitation. Whole society is held together with the help of religion and the capitalist class intensifies its control and exploitation over that society. In the case of any lack of obligation of working class the capitalist class uses religion to achieve its objective. We, thus, see that both Marx and Saint-Simon held similar views on the role and importance of religion as a social phenomenon. The capitalist class took active interest in the discipline and order of society because without this its exploitation could not become a reality. Marx noticed that in the Middle Ages the church and priests used religion for the purpose of utilising common people for their benefit. The Renaissance and Reformation brought about a change in the attitude of man towards religion. But these two failed to make the change radical. The capitalist class followed the path adopted by the church.

Religion as Class Ideology

We shall now deal with how and in what sense Marx considered religion as a class ideology. The term class ideology means religion is held or practised by a class and the religious beliefs flourish within the class structure. In this regard there is a lot of controversy. It is due to the fact that the definitions of class and religion do not always suit class ideology. For example, the primitive tribal people had their own religion. But the tribal communities were not classes in the Marxian sense because Marx used the concept in a special sense. Moreover, his definition of religion is not applicable to the religion of tribal communities.

There are two broad aspects of Marx's concept of religion. The advent and development of religion is due to the ignorance of man to understand the natural phenomena and their incapacity to solve his problems. When these two are overcome the importance and even the existence of religion will be in danger. The German philosophers Feuerbach and Hegel viewed religion as fantasy of alienated man and Marx subscribed to this view. The alienated man being "unable to live a full and satisfying life, seeks compensation for his incapacity" (Plamenatz, p. 337).

The above two elements of Marx's doctrine of religion are not compatible with class ideology. Religion interpreted by Marx is not practised by any particular class. But in spite of this his doctrine of religion can be called a class ideology. Let us quote Plamenatz again : "Yet both these doctrines are compatible with the belief that it is so (that is, its a class ideology-added). For religion, on either of these views, can be held to be a cement holding—society together, and if society is divided into classes, some of which exploit others, it is a cement which helps to make this exploitation possible" (p. 339). All the classes use religion, of course, for different purposes. Both the exploiters and exploited will use religious beliefs. It may be that any one class does not believe in religion, but uses it as a weapon for the attainment of any cherished goal. In a capitalist society the exploiting class with the help of religion exploit the proletariat. The working class practises religion and that helps the members to be united.

In the Middle Ages the powerful class used religion—that is Christianity—to exploit the common people. The feudal landlords, the priests and many other influential persons used religion for the simple purpose of exploitation. Common people were taught that the life of the other world was more covetable and desirable and for that life they should ignore this mortal world and abide by the sermons of the pope and other priests of the church. This was the way of strengthening their control over the community. On the other hand, common people out of the fear of punishment and to get rid of the wrath of God showed unconditional obligation to the church. The religious beliefs practised by different people before Marx were quite alive in his mind and in the background of that he drew certain conclusions. In fact, religion of his time can be called a class ideology, because no class was quite free from the influence of religion. Moreover, each class had its own approach to religion though, in broadest term, the religion of all classes was the same.

Religion and Science

In the previous pages it has been noted that religion originated due to the ignorance of man about nature and natural phenomena. Marx, Engels and their adherents have concluded that religion will disappear with the progress of science and the application of science and technology to the development of society. That is, when a society will achieve all-round development, religion will gradually lose its importance. The development of science will make minds of men scientific and rational with which they will be able to disprove the unscientific and absurd ideas of religion. Spread of scientific spirit will also cause the disappearance of religious faith and practices. This is due to the fact that the development of science and scientific spirit will inculcate a feeling in the mind of man to be indifferent to theology. Thus religion will not be forced to disappear, it will, like the withering away of state, wither away.

Marx and Engels have stressed that because of the development of science man will be able to realise his potentialities which will help the rise and strengthening of self-confidence. This will be a sufficient factor for undermining the importance of religion in society. The development of science has the capacity to destroy the alienation of man which previously caused the rise and growth of religion in society.

How the progress of science causes the disappearance of religion or theology can be viewed from still another perspective. The superior knowledge derived from science enables man to answer questions which were so long unanswerable, or man declares the questions simply as empty. Thus the role of religion on the solution of social problems is removed. It is gradually reduced to non-existence. Marx and Engels in this way have come to the conclusion that science and religion are incompatible. It has also been argued that the progress of science transforms the whole society which brings about a radical change in society. The existence of religion and progress of society due to the development of science will lead to the coexistence between the two impossibles. Thus the disappearance of religion or the decline of its importance due to the progress of science is not a concept characterised by oversimplification. Piecemeal progress of science cannot help a radical transformation of society.

It is necessary that science will lead the evolution to a stage where men will not feel the necessity of religion. This is a more plausible argument. In primitive tribal societies people depended upon science not only for comfort but for various other necessities. When science will meet all the requirements of society man will no longer resort to religious practices and adhere to religious beliefs and faiths. If the society reaches that stage the need for religion will decline.

The impact of the progress of science and scientific knowledge upon religion has another aspect. A very important property of scientific development and the emergence of scientific spirit is it involves man in multifarious activities. This phenomenon removes the idleness of mind and body. Man finds no time to contemplate about religion. He will concern himself with finding out avenues for accelerating material progress. This is evident when we look at the society that emerged after the medieval period.

Universality of Religion

Marx's concept of religion has been interpreted in a different light. He calls religion as the *fantasy of alienated man*. But if his ideas are thoroughly interpreted it will be found that it is more than that. It is not the "animism and magic of the simplest societies", it is also a "dogmatic theology" of the complicated and sophisticated societies. It is not true that only uneducated people of simple societies follow and adopt religious faiths in their day-to-day life, educated and wealthy people also practise religious faiths. Privileged people of society scrupulously follow religion. Plamenatz says "Theological religion, the type presented to us by Feuerbach and Marx as the religion of alienated man, is the religion of the sophisticated. It has been most fully accepted by the educated and the privileged" (p. 342). This indicates that religion has a universal appeal. The alienated worker may be attracted to religion, but the alienated man who is not a worker may also be attracted to religion. Explaining Marx's position critics say that whenever a man suffers from frustration or fails to solve the mysteries of nature he resorts to religious practices. Suffering from frustration or seeking comfort is not solitary to any particular man or group of men. Anybody can become the victim of circumstances and in order to get rid of that he may seek the help of religion. However, the unprivileged section is the victim of environment and for that very reason it is attracted to religion to a greater extent. It is said that all men in a class society are alienated and, naturally, the universality of religion will prevail.

Lenin and Religion

Lenin's view on religion is not basically different from Marx's. But he has explained it in a greater perspective. He has said that religion is absolutely a private affair and it must not be the business of the state to interfere in any form with the religion. He further observes that in a true socialist society there cannot be any place of religion. In an article published on 5 December 1905 he made the above and following observations. In this article he said "Religion must be no concern to the state, and religious societies must have no connection with the governmental authority. Every one must be absolutely free to profess any religion he pleases or no religion whatever, that is to be an atheist, which every socialist is, as a rule".

The point of emphasis is that, in a socialist state, the authority shall have no relation with religion or religious societies. The state will neither oppose or support any religion which is private. The most important thing about a socialist is he may be a believer of any religious faith or he may not be. He is above all an atheist. It means that a socialist is indifferent to religion. Even if he professes any religious faith he cannot be expected to be dogmatic. Orthodox attitude to religion is not expected from a socialist.

In socialism there shall be complete separation between state and church. If there is no such separation, Lenin says, proletarians will demand the separation. This is because in the name of religion some persons exploit the working class and in a socialist state there is no place of exploitation. Emancipation is the aim of socialism and if there is religion emancipation is not possible. Communist party is the vanguard of workers and peasants and its members are highly self-conscious and class-conscious. The members of the communist party, Lenin claims, are not the victims of ignorance and obscurantism in the shape of religious faith. He has further maintained that if church and other religious organisations are allowed to continue their normal functions that will before long contaminate the mind of the working class. For this reason he has demanded "complete disestablishment of church, so as to be able to combat the religious fog with purely ideological and solely ideological weapons."

According to Lenin the yoke of religion is merely a product and reflection of the economic yoke. Communist party will launch a propaganda to enlighten the mind of people regarding the true nature of the religious fog. Party will propagate that members must cultivate atheism. Once a man becomes a victim of religion he will not be able to come out of it. If people are not atheist, establishment of socialism will be a very difficult task. Lenin concludes the essay with the following remark : "The revolutionary proletariat will succeed in making religion a really private affair, so far as the state is concerned. And in this political system, cleansed of medieval mildew, the proletariate will wage a broad and open struggle for the elimination of economic slavery, the true source of the religious humbugging of mankind."

Criticism

Marx's theory of religion is faced with few criticisms. First of all, it is true that with the progress of science the influence of religion will disappear. Science and technology in the twenty-first century have reached a stage of unprecedented growth, but still there is influence of religion. It is true that today's people are not orthodox in their attitude to religion, but they are not absolutely unreligious or atheists. There is a fear of God or feeling of religion, more or less, in the mind of many people. So we can say that progress of science and religion coexist peacefully. It is not true that science contradicts religion. The fields of the two are different.

In the second place, the former Russian leaders claimed that they had succeeded in achieving socialism, but it is also true that they had not been able to banish religion. Religion became a completely private affair, but there was religion. We, therefore, see that Lenin's estimation that in socialism there cannot be religion is not true. If in former Soviet Union there were religion there were no socialism, or vice versa.

Thirdly, it is not correct to hold that religion is the fantasy of alienated man. In our previous analysis we have said that even the privileged and educated people of sophisticated societies practise religion, but how are these people alienated? If these people are alienated then the concept requires to be redefined. There is no such scope.

Few more words may be said in support of Marx. While Marx was writing about religion the position and influence of religion of Middle Ages was highly active in his mind. The students of Western political thought are quite aware of the all-pervading influence of Christianity in general and church in particular over all sections of society. Even the powerful emperors were not free from the influence. The pope could dictate the kings in their day-to-day activities. There was nobody to challenge the authority of the pope. It was the religion which was responsible for the economic backwardness of medieval Europe.

It is also true that there was a time when religion acted as opium. Religion reduced the consciousness of people to the minimum. In medieval society religion was so powerful that people failed to consider their own interests. They were forced to think about the other world which had no physical existence.

Today the orthodox aspect of religion has declined remarkably. There are several reasons behind this and the most important are the progress of science and the development of consciousness. Religion has not disappeared and will not disappear as Marx predicted. However, the educated people have developed a sort of indifference towards religion. There is today less orthodoxy, less fanfare and very less humbugging. There is religion in miniature form. Lenin is not correct when he says that a socialist must be atheist. Many socialist minded people have been found to practise religious principles and faiths. This is because we are interpreting religion in a liberal way.

34

SCIENTIFIC SOCIALISM

Definition and Origin

Maurice Cornforth defines socialism in the following words : "Socialism is the social ownership of means of production and their utilisation to satisfy the material and cultural requirements of the whole of society. Socialism is necessary because only by such a radical transformation of economic basis of society can the evils resulting from capitalism be done away with and new powerful techniques be fully utilised" (p. 135). This definition provides certain basic features of socialism of which Marx and Engels thought a lot. One is, the forces of production will be placed under the control of society which will ensure their proper utilisation. Socialism envisages a radical change or transformation of the economic basis of society. Third is, this radical transformation will cure the evils created by capitalism. Fourth is, capitalism may have some good effects. But these so-called good effects of capitalism are for the benefit of the capitalist class which is powerful almost in all respects.

Scientific socialism has been viewed as the "science about the proletarian class struggle and the socialist revolution, about the sociopolitical laws behind the building of socialism and communism and about the world revolutionary process as a whole" (*Dictionary of Scientific Communism*, p. 212).

As a science, socialism has its own laws and categories, reflecting the basic aspects of revolutionary transformation of capitalist into communist society. The laws relate to the socialist revolution, establishment of the dictatorship of the proletariat and the transition from capitalism to socialism and then to communism. How the working class will conduct a class struggle scientific socialism relates that. So it provides a guidance for revolutionary struggle. It contains the principles, laws and techniques of a new society—classless society. Scientific socialism is not a conceptual matter, it is an operative aspect of historical transition from capitalism to communism. Scientific socialism (henceforth S. S.) deals with the various stages of revolutionary struggle and nature of socialist society.

The evils of capitalism created large scale discontent in the minds of men and they were in search of a way out. People well aware to the evil effects of capitalism believed that only a socialist society could save the working class people and common men from all types of exploitation and oppression. How is socialism indebted to capitalism for its emergence that is to be briefly investigated. Engels has said (*MESW* II—116). "Modern socialism, in its essence, is the direct product of the recognition of the class antagonisms existing in the society of today between proprietors and non-proprietors, between capitalists, and wage workers, of the anarchy existing in production. But in its theoretical form modern socialism originally appears ostensibly as a more logical extension of the principles laid down by the great French philosophers of the nineteenth century." What Engels emphasises is that socialism is the logical consequence of historical development of society which is materialist interpretation of history.

Elaborating Engels's view Kolakowski writes, "Capitalism creates the precondition of the new society not only by revolutionising technology and evolving new forms of cooperation ..... joint stock companies in which property and management are separate, and likewise cooperative factories are to be regarded as transitional forms or instances of the abandonment of the capitalist mode of production within the system itself. In this sense socialism is not simply the negation of capitalism but also a continuation of it and of the socializing process based on the technological development of the present age" (Vol. I, p. 305). Capitalism creates the necessary preconditions of socialism.

The growth of capitalism has always been accompanied by unprecedented increase in wealth the major share of which goes to the hands of few. The toiling masses are plunged into unbound impoverishment. The growth of technology and harnessing of the natural resources have hardly come to the benefit of working people. All these evil aspects of capitalism have worked as potential source of discontent. People in general have formed the firm conviction that the continuation of capitalism cannot materialise the hope of emancipation. Capitalists will never direct science and technology to the overall progress of society. The only way to get rid of capitalism is to overthrow it. Summarising the evils of capitalism Maurice Cornforth says (p. 136), "The great capitalist monopolies of today subjugate everything to their drive for maximum profits, to secure which they step up the exploitation, annex other countries and plunder their resources, militarise the national economy and prepare for and wage wars."

Scientific Socialism and Materialist Conception of History

The term scientific socialism was coined by Engels in order to distinguish Marxian socialism from utopian socialism. There are a number of differences between the two forms of socialism. The socialism formulated by Marx and Engels is founded on materialistic conception of history whereas their utopian predecessors wanted to build up a socialist society in an imaginary and impractical way. The utopian socialists were very much under the influence of French materialist ideas that saw in man the product of nature and the environment in which he lived and had been brought up. They believed that to change society with its manners and customs it was necessary to change the conditions under which people lived. These conditions, they believed, could be changed if all the members of society were made to realised that the conditions did not conform to human nature, that they were corrupting and spoiling people by inculcating in them such ugly qualities as avarice, arrogance, greed, laziness. From this it follows that in order to change society its members must be re-educated. This, in turn, would only be possible when the conditions under which people lived were changed, for they determined the morals, customs and character of people. The utopians were, therefore, in a vicious circle. In order to change, morals conditions must be changed. Again, in order to change conditions, morals must be changed. This is the vicious circle.

In his *Socialism : Utopian and Scientific* Engels observes that Hegel had freed history from metaphysics—he had made it dialectic. But his conception was essentially idealistic. Now idealism was driven from its last refuge—the philosophy of history. At last the materialistic treatment of history has been propounded. According to Marx and Engels it is unscientific to interpret the progress of history and society as the struggle between ideas as suggested by Hegel. Rather it is a struggle between two historically developed classes—bourgeoisie and proletariat. The struggle between the two classes continues until a radical change or transformation of the old bourgeois society takes place. This happens only when the proletariat captures state power and place all the means of production under the management of society as a whole. This is socialism.

Engels says that, viewed in this light socialism is not the brainchild of any ingenious man. It is the necessary outcome of the struggle between two historically developed classes—the antagonism between bourgeoisie and proletariat are irreconcilable. The intransigence of both these classes leads to struggle which will ultimately lead to revolution. The emergence of two main classes and antagonisms between them are to be treated as primary causes of socialism. This is the materialistic interpretation of socialism. Some of the earlier socialists had an idea of history. Name of Saint-Simon may be mentioned in this connection. But they did not explain it in terms of matter and they took no help of dialectics. The socialism of the earlier days was incompatible with the materialistic conception. The earlier socialists criticised the existing capitalist mode of production and its consequences. They could not explain them.

The early socialists or utopian socialists particularly Saint-Simon thought that capitalism was the root cause of miseries, that is, exploitation and oppression of the working class. But the way out they suggested was absolutely impractical. They did not explain the nature of exploitation. The earlier socialists believed that under capitalism exploitation is inevitable, but they did not proceed further. They failed to suggest a way out from the exploitation for which capitalism was primarily responsible. They also failed in other respects also. They did not present capitalistic mode of production in its historical connection and its inevitableness during a particular historical period. The socialist predecessors of Marx had no clear idea about surplus-value. That was their great defect. The two discoveries—the materialistic conception of history, and surplus-value—have made socialism scientific.

The basic proposition of the materialistic conception of history that the production and next to production, the exchange of things produced, is the basis of social structure. From this point of view the final causes of all social changes and political revolutions are to be sought, not in man's brains, not in man's better insight into eternal truth and justice, but in changes in the modes of production and exchange. They are to be sought not in the philosophy, but in the economics of each particular epoch.

Because of the conflict between productive forces and production relations, feudalism collapsed. Similarly the same type of conflict has been the cause of the disintegration of capitalism. The germs of the conflict are within the capitalist mode of production. "This conflict engendered in the mind of man, like that between organised sin and divine justice. It exists objectively, outside us independently of the will and actions even of the men that have brought it on. Modern socialism is nothing but the reflex, in thought, of this conflict in fact, its ideal reflection in the minds, first, of the class directly suffering under it, the working class."

The division of society into classes is the inevitable consequence of unlimited growth of capitalism. Marx and and Engels have said in the *Manifesto* that bourgeois and proletariat are at loggerheads and this is due to the conflict of class interest. Engels writes in *Socialism : Utopian and Scientific* (p. 116) "Modern socialism is, in its essence, the direct product of the recognition, on the one hand, of class antagonisms existing in the society of today between proprietors and non-proprietors, between capitalists and wage-workers; on the other, of anarchy in production."

Anarchy in the productive system and contradiction in the capitalist system of production have led men to think that capitalism is unreasonable and not congenial to the interest and general well-being of the working class. Growing misery and dehumanisation have created heaps of discontent in the minds of men. So any discontent about capitalism is not the product of imagination or idealism. It is not divine thought divorced from reality. The interpretation of history with a materialist outlook and the working of capitalism in general and particularly after the Industrial Revolution have exposed the darkest aspects of the bourgeois system. The emancipation of the working class is possible if the present capitalist system is changed or overthrown. Here is the basic difference between utopian socialism and scientific socialism. Thought of socialism came from real situation of objective facts and it is to be achieved through class struggle. Thus socialism is closely related to materialistic conecption of history.

Nature of Socialism

From the above analysis we are now in a position to form the conclusion that its advent is inevitable, specially if we accept the materialist interpretation of history with the help of dialectic. Marx and Engels were sure that nobody desired the advent of capitalism. In the same way socialism must come. Capitalism calls for a certain versatility in the working class and thus creates conditions for an upheaval. "The growth of capitalism reaches a stage which the capitalists cannot control. There is too much civilisation, too much means of subsistence, too much industry, too much commerce. The productive forces at the disposal of society no longer tend to further the development of the conditions of bourgeois property, on the contrary, they have become too powerful for these conditions by which they are fettered ..... they bring disorder into the whole bourgeois society, endanger the existence of bourgeois property. The conditions of bourgeois society are too narrow to comprise the wealth created by them" (*Manifesto*).

The crisis of capitalism in this way appears and it clears the way of socialism. In support of this view I quote few words from Kolakowski (Vol. I, p. 306), "Socialism reaps the harvest of capitalism and without the latter it could only be an empty dream. The new society will arise out of the catastrophe towards which capitalism is swiftly yet unconsciously tending." The weapons with which bourgeoisie felled feudalism to the ground are now turned against the bourgeoisie itself. The weapons are not proletarians' own.

There is a common notion that socialism means the abolition of poverty or luxurious consumption of bourgeoisie. In socialism there exists neither poverty of many nor luxury of few. But it is more than this. It promises the growth of all and abolition of all inequalities. The characteristic feature of socialism is it abolishes human alienation. In capitalism labourer is alienated from the productive system. He is also alienated from nature, from himself, that is, from his own activity, and also from other men. Socialism does not imply the redistribution of wealth or income, while the old system will continue to exist. The old economic will be overthrown in socialism.

Socialism abolishes the wage labour system of capitalism. That is, there shall be no sale of labour power. The whole material production is devoted to use value. The scale and character of production in all branches will be governed purely by social needs and not by the desire or profit making. Socialism means that the vast resources of modern technique are developed and utilised to meet the needs of the people. The productive forces being released from private control will be used for the general welfare of the society.

Socialism promises increased productiveness and greater intensity of labour. They both augment the mass of articles produced in a given time. By suppressing the capitalist mode of production the length of the working day could be reduced to the necessary labour time. Again, in socialism the distinction between necessary and surplus labour will lose its importance and meaning. The surplus value derived from surplus labour will be abolished in socialism. Worker will get enough time for their own recreation. They will devote time to the cultural activities and finer pursuits.

Socialism not only assertively talks about the full satisfaction of material needs, but all-round development of human personality. Socialism promises to liberate human power from bondage. Capitalist system of production imposes manifold barriers through division of labour and many other ways. Marx, that is why, wanted to bring an end of the division of labour which was crippling workers both physically and spiritually. Socialism does not mean that human development and creativity cease to exist, but that there are no longer any social restrictions upon them. In socialism the realm of freedom will be considerably expanded. Being released from physical necessity human beings will invest energy for greater and nobler purposes.

Socialist Society

Though Marx was a great scholar and his knowledge was encyclopedic he failed to explain some key concepts which he frequently used such as class, state, socialist society etc. The last one is a very important concept and unfortunately it finds no explanation. *The raison d'etre* of proletarian movement is to set up a socialist society by overthrowing the bourgeois state. Here, again, we are faced with dilemma. His work lacks any systematic analysis. Two works deal with the subject—one is *Manuscript of* 1844 written when he was a young man of 26 and the *Critique of the Gotha Programme.* In Marx's judgment both these were not fit for publication. In fact, the *Critique of the Gotha Programme* throws light on the structure of the socialist society. But it is insufficient. Avineri is of opinion (p. 220) that these two books are full of sporadic and sometimes unconnected opinions about socialist society. For this reason "Marx's discussions of future society are, therefore, most austere and restrained" (Avineri).

Marx mentions two stages of socialist society or socialism—one is pure socialism and the other is communism. Socialism is the first phase and communism is the second or final phase of socialist society or scientific socialism. There is a qualitative difference between the two phases. Lenin in his *State and Revolution* has distinguished between the two phases. Marx was, of course, quite aware of the difference between communism and socialism.

A socialist society comes out of the contradictions engulfing a capitalist society and according to Marx the advent of socialism is inevitable. In every respect, economically, intellectually and morally it is stamped with the birthmarks of the old society from whose womb it emerges. A society which comes out of the womb of capitalism is called socialist society. This is not free from the defects or evils of capitalism. Immediately after the abolition of capitalism the proletarians will set up their own type of society. Naturally it will not be possible for them to remove all the evils of capitalist mode of production.

In the *Critique of Gotha Programme* Marx says, "Between the capitalist and communist society lies the period of revolutionary transition of the one into the other. There corresponds to this also a political transition period in which the state can be nothing but the revolutionary dictatorship of the proletariat." This dictatorship of the proletariat is the state. Marx emphasises that the transition from capitalism to communism which is higher form of socialism is not direct. In the *Critique of the Gotha Programme* Marx has unambiguously stated that there are number of important differences between socialism and communism. Socialism came through revolution and similarly another revolution will be required for building up of a communist society.

Nature of Socialist Society

Commenting on the nature of socialist society Marx says that it is an immature or crude form of communism. The ultimate purpose of the proletarians will be to bring about communism. The proletarian revolution has simply abolished the bourgeois state. The great fabric of bourgeois superstructure will not be completely eliminated. The first phase of socialism, as we have noted earlier, will carry with it all the birthmarks of capitalist society. In the *Critique of the Gotha Programme* he refused to accept the socialist ideas of Lassalle. What Marx wants to say here is that socialist programme is very much important, no doubt, but "every step to real movement is more important than a dozen programmes." Lassalle thought that in socialism worker would get the full reward of his labour. Refuting this contention of Lassalle Marx has argued that it is impossible, because a portion of wage will be kept aside for consolidated fund, for the depreciation of machinery and purchasing of new machines. Hence, remuneration will never commensurate with labour. The ideals, objectives and other aspects of communism will never be reflected in socialism. That is why he calls socialism an immature form of communism. Until communism emerges socialism will proceed or work with all the imperfections. This is inevitable.

Analysing the basic feature of the first phase of communist society Engels in *Anti-Dühring* writes, "In making itself the master of all the means of production to use them in accordance with a social plan society puts an end to the former subjection of men to their own means of production. The society cannot free itself unless every individual is freed. The old mode of production must, therefore, be revolutionised from top to bottom, and in particular, the former division of labour must disappear. Its place must be taken by an organisation of production in which no individual can throw on the shoulders of others his share in the productive labour." In the socialist society individuals will get the full scope for the development of all his faculties, physical and mental, in all directions. This is not an imaginary picture. The socialist society is created to fulfil the promises.

Capitalism divided the society not only into bourgeoisie and proletariat, but also into various other splinter groups. The chief reason of dividing the society into groups was to weaken the unity of society. The capitalists thought that a united society would pose a great challenge to the authority and domination of capitalists. Socialist society will abolish the manifold divisions. Such a society will assume the character of workers' cooperative. Lenin has beautifully said, "Socialism is merely the next step forward from state-capitalist monopoly. Or in other words, socialism is merely state-capitalist monopoly which is made to serve the interests of the whole people and has, to that extent, ceased to be a capitalist monopoly."

Marx has highlighted the basic nature of society in the following way : The individual producer receives back from society—after the deductions have been made—exactly what he gives to it. No one will be deprived of his just share of product. Marx and his followers have called it equality. Lenin says, "Equality apparently reigns supreme..." Some have called the system equal distribution of product. Others call it equal right of all to an equal product of labour. In the opinion of Marx in the first phase of communist society there shall prevail the principle of equal right, but in its higher phase it shall wither away. The idea of equal right is a bourgeois concept. Everyone shall have the equal right to exploit and capture means of production. In fact, all will not be able. That is why, he has pronounced that right instead of being equal would have to be unequal.

According to Marx the first phase of communist society will accompany with it some features of capitalism and according to him it was inevitable only one revolution was ineufficient for the obliteration of evils of capitalism. Specifically for that reason the Marxists talked about continuity of revolutions. The equal right will be one of its feature. Since the economic structure of the socialist society is not perfect, one cannot expect a perfect form of equality or right. People will have to be satisfied with imperfect forms. Marx writes (*MESW* I-24), "Right can never be higher than the economic structure of society and its culture development conditioned thereby."

Marx has categorically stated that even after the seizure of state power and establishment of socialism there would exist bourgeois laws and other things relevant to socialism. The proletarians will apply some parts or portions or aspects of bourgeois laws only to hasten the revolution and suppress the remnants of bourgeois counter-revolutionary forces. If necessary the bourgeois laws shall be made consistent with the socialist goals. Sometimes they may be amended. Here Marx wants to emphasise that the proletarians shall not be guided by any orthodox and impractical mentality. It is unnecessary to jettison all the elements of bourgeois state. To do it is sheer utopianism. The proletarians shall have to build up a new society out of the ruins of an old one. They, therefore, must proceed cautiously.

Lenin has reiterated two great principles propounded by Marx. These are to be applied in socialist society. One is—He who does not work shall be not eat. The other is—An equal amount of products for an equal amount of labour. The proletarians must materialise these two principles or objectives.

Planning is the core of socialism. Nothing would be done without any planning and naturally socialism rules out anarchy. It is the firm belief of socialism that the ownership of the means of production by private persons is the source of people's poverty and other evils. So it plans to dislodge the private individuals from the ownership of the means of production and place them under the management of society. The entire economy is to be managed in accordance with the principles laid down by central planning. Hence planning occupies a strategic position in socialist system. Huberman and May have remarked, "Just as public ownership of the means of production is an essential feature of socialism, so too is centralised planning." The adherents of socialism are of opinion that without central planning the success is never to be achieved. In capitalism there is no place of planning. Production of commodities in socialist society is to be done according to planning. Socialist economy is basically a planned economy. Only planning can ensure the proper management of an economy. It is to be remembered here that the utilities of planning was first realised by the Fabian socialists and for deciding the principles and programmes of planning they set up a cell of Fabian Society under the leadership of Arthur Lewis. Perhaps the Marxists borrowed the idea of planning from Fabians.

Classification of Socialism

Manifesto contains a precise but useful classification of socialism. According to this classification *socialism is of three types—Feudalistic socialism; Bourgeois socialism* and *Utopian socialism.* Before the Industrial Revolution the feudal lords and the aristocrats were combined together and formed a class which was the basic class. After industrialisation the emergence of bourgeoisie cornered the aristocracy and it became the basic class whereas the aristocrats were relegated to the non-basic class. This was not possible for the aristocracy to swallow. The aristocrats and landlords revolted against the bourgeois domination and in order to arouse the sympathy of the workers and peasants they indicated the bourgeoisie. The aristocrats were able to relieve their feelings by penning lampoons against their new masters and by uttering sinister prophesies of impending doom. Such was the origin of feudalistic socialism. The feudalists pointed out that the capitalists were exploiters, but they forgot that they were also exploiters. The aristocrats inspired educated people to write pamphlets exposing the nature and extent of bourgeois exploitation.

The second type of socialism is petty-bourgeois socialism. Petty-bourgeoisie is a class that stands between proletariat and bourgeoisie and is perpetually constituted as a supplementary component of bourgeois society. The members of the petty-bourgeois class have made a shrewd analysis of capitalist system and have exposed the contradiction. It blames capitalism for all evils. Petty-bourgeoisie further condemns the capitalism for introduction of machinery and division of labour. It emphasises the wretchedness of proletariat, anarchy of production, gross inequalities in the distribution of wealth, the industrial wars the nations wage for mutual extermination, and the break up of the old family ties. But in practice the petty-bourgeois socialism wants to re-establish the old methods of production and these with old property relations.

Let us deal with German socialism. In France there developed a system of socialist thought. The German philosophers borrowed the basic principles of French philosophical thought and adopted it to the soil of Germany. But the socio-political conditions of two countries were not identical and as a result of it the key concepts of French socialism were considerably distorted. The German socialists demanded political movement for realisation of socialist goals, such as abolition of repressive measures of government and bourgeois law, establishment of liberty and equality, protection of the freedom of press. But unfortunately the German socialists failed to champion the interests of proletarians.

The capitalist class is very clever. Sometimes this class takes measures to remove some grievances of people. But one should not think that this class does this out of benevolence, but simply to safeguard the interests. Economists, philanthropists, humanitarians and welfare workers fall within the category of bourgeois or conservative socialism. They want prevention of cruelty to animals and various types of reforms. They tacitly admit the evils of bourgeois society. But they think that class struggle is not the solution of grievances. Compromises, adjustments and reforms are the best ways of alleviating the miseries. They want the extant society without its revolutionary and disintegrating elements. They want the bourgeoisie without the proletariat.

Of utopian socialists the prominent figures were Saint-Simon, Charles Fourier and Robert Owen. They felt the miserable conditions of the working class and were also aware of the reasons of pathetic conditions. But unfortunately they failed to suggest any way out. Marx and Engels agreed with some of the views of the utopian socialists but disagreed with their suggestions.

Political Organisation of Socialist Society

After capturing political power the first objective of the proletarians would be to build up a new political organisation essential for building socialism and communism. They very foundation of the new political organisation is the state of the dictatorship of the proletariat. In the *Critique of the Gotha Programme* Marx says that between capitalism and communism lies a new political organisation which may aptly be called the revolutionary dictatorship of the proletariat. This is the state. Both the nature and function of this revolutionary state are quite different from those of the bourgeois state. It is so longer an instrument of exploitation. We also call it a socialist state.

Such a state is an instrument for uniting the masses and educating them in the spirit of communism, an instrument of building the new society. Here the term "dictatorship" creates a lot of confusion. The term is not used in ordinary sense. The functions of the socialist state are directed against the bourgeoisie. Socialist state democratises the entire society.

The bourgeois state is the instrument of exploitation of the workers whereas the socialist state is an instrument of power exclusively at the disposal of the working class. But this power is not for exploitation, it is for management of socialist state. It may be noted that the socialist state retains its suppressive function. The socialist political organisation suppresses the exploitation and counter-revolution. It also checks all the disruptive forces. The extent and forms of suppression depend on the nature and intensity of counter-revolution and exploitation. The socialist state will never be used for the furtherance of the interests of any particular class. It releases all efforts for the overall progress of society. In a socialist state uniform importance will be given to all the social and cultural activities. In a capitalist state these were treated perfunctorily. A socialist state will reorganise itself from top to bottom.

The external functions or aspects will also be reorganised. A socialist state never aspires to be an aggressor, rather it disdains aggression. But one socialist state is desirous of setting up cordial relations with another socialist state. At the same time a socialist state helps materially, intellectually and morally the socialist movement of other countries. It is the purpose of any socialist state to build up socialism in all countries of the world, because it is the only way of emancipation of the working class.

The capture of the state by the proletarians brings about an end of the predominance of bureaucracy. The socialist state will not destroy the bureaucracy but it will cut it to size. But as socialism becomes more and more perfect the importance of bureaucracy will tend to decline and with the arrival of communism the bureaucracy of the state will wither away.

The socialist political organisation will bring into being a new type of law. The bourgeoisie used the law to exploit the proletarians and further their own interests. The new state system promises to use laws to safeguard the socialist property and to frustrate the counter-revolution. The new legal superstructure of a socialist state will correspond the new base.

The bourgeois state was the state of a minority section of society, whereas the socialist state is the state of the whole people. The essential nature of the socialist state, born of the revolution, does not change. It is wrong to oppose the dictatorship of the proletariat to the socialist state of the whole people. The new stage of statehood corresponding to the victory of socialism does not alter the leading role of the working class in the life of society (*The Fundamentals of Marxist-Leninist Philosophy*, p. 305).

COMMUNISM

Definition of Communism

We have so far discussed various aspects of socialism and the nature of socialist political organisation. But according to Marx and Engels, and later on Lenin, socialism is not the final form of society which can ensure the complete emancipation of the working class. Moreover, the withering away of state envisaged by Engels and elaborated by Lenin in *State and Revolution* will never turn to a fact in the structure of socialist society. There is a higher form of socialism which is called communism. In common parlance we often forget to distinguish socialism from communism. But in Marx and Engels's lexicography there is a difference, though they are not different types of society. They are different stages of the same society.

We have already noted that socialism is the first stage of communism. If this is so what is exactly meant by communism? In *The German Ideology* Marx and Engels have defined communism in the following language : "Communism is for us *not a state of affairs* which is to be established, *an ideal* to which reality (will) have to adjust itself. We call communism the *real* movement which abolishes the present state of things. The conditions of this movement result from the now existing premise" (p. 57). To Marx and Engels communism was a movement whose sole aim was to convert the socialist society into a communist society. The proletarian revolution seized power from the hands of the bourgeoisie and set up a society. Another revolution will convert socialism into communism.

Communism is a movement in the sense that what principles will be adopted for a future society that has to be decided. Society is always dynamic and also communism. The principles of the future society may be called communism. Hence there is a question of revolution. The establishment of socialism through a proletarian revolution is not the end, rather it is the beginning. This revolution will be followed by other subsequent revolutions. In a communist society there will be no necessity of a revolution in its strictest sense. But the working class will remain vigilant so that the counter-revolutionary forces would not get any scope of come-back. This alertness was essential.

In *The German Ideology* Marx and Engels have further observed that communism differs from all previous movements in that it overturns the basis of all earlier relations of production and intercourse and for the first time consciously treats all naturally evolved premises as the creations of hitherto existing men, strips them of their natural character and subjugates them to the power of the united individuals. Its organisation is, therefore, essentially economic, the material production of the conditions of this unity. The reality which communism creates is precisely the true basis for rendering it impossible that anything should exist independently of individuals, in so far as reality is, nevertheless only a product of the preceding intercourse of individuals.

In the *Critique of the Gotha Programme* Marx has explained the nature of communist society in the following words :

In a higher phase of communist society after the enslaving subordination of the individual to the division of labour and therewith also the antithesis between mental and physical labour, has vanished; after labour has become not only a means of life, but life's prime want; after the productive forces also increased with the all-round development of the individual, and all the springs of cooperative wealth flow more abundantly—only then can the narrow horizon of bourgeois right be crossed in its entirety and society inscribed on its banners—From each according to his ability, to each according to his needs (*MEWW*-II—24).

Emancipation of individual from all sorts of slavery is the primary as well as sole objective of communism. In the opinion of Kolakowski it was never the purpose of Marx to lift the individual from abject poverty, but to stop the dehumanisation from which individual was suffering. Abolition of the division labour promises to bring about an end to moral and intellectual degradation—If dehumanisation is stopped and abundant amount of wealth is produced all-round development of individual will automatically emerge.

In the *1844-Manuscripts* Marx says, "Communism is the positive abolition of private property and thus of human self-alienation and therefore, the real reappropriation of the human essence by and for man. This is communism as the complete and conscious return of man conserving all the riches of previous development for man himself as a social, i.e., human being."

A communist society regulates the general production and nobody will have any exclusive sphere of action. All will get adequate opportunities for the full and proper development of all faculties. In the bourgeois society the elites were the determiners of everything—economics, politics and culture. The workers had no place in the social structure—they were simply wage labourers and in exchange of labour they got a paltry amount of wage which was absolutely insufficient for comfortable living. Communism, by abolishing the property and predominance of a group, will free the individual from this bondage.

Explaining nature of communism Marx in his *1844 Manuscripts* has said it represents the positive in the form of the negation of the negation and thus a phase of human emancipation and rehabilitation. Communism is the necessary form and dynamic principle of the immediate future, but communism is not as such the goal of human development, the form of human society.

Features of Communist Society

According to Lenin's definition communist society is a society in which all things—the land, factories—are owned in common and the people work in common. Not only the means of production in a communist society are common, but also all the commodities produced are to be distributed according to the needs of the members of the communist society. Thus, both production and distribution being free from private management will benefit equally all men. Discrimination is the first thing to be banished by communism.

It is a basic feature of communist society that every individual must perform his duties according to his ability. This is a very important feature of communist society. Every individual must perform some sort of duty. There is no compulsion that every person must do definite duty. He will do useful work and again it is according to his ability. A man who cannot do any work has no right to claim bread. It is the dictum of communism that he who does not work shall not eat. Communist society wants to abolish the leisure class and the system of unearned income. Work is compulsory does not mean that men will be forced to work. Lenin has said "We give the name communism to the system under which people form the habit of performing their duties without any special apparatus of coercion." Communism rules out any possibility of coercive method and emphasises on spontaneity. People will do their social duties voluntarily. Here lies the difference between capitalism and communism. Communism is the manifestation of moral and mental upliftment as well as the highest form of consciousness. People disfavour to live without work. They love and like work.

A communist society proclaims—Each according to his ability to each according to his need. This requires elaboration. Marxism admits that differences in intellectual capacity do not imply any differences whatsoever in the nature of the stomach and physical needs. The conditions of the communist society lead to the flowering of all the abilities of man and thereby make labour performed to the full measure of his ability much more productive. Furthermore, communist society promises that each person will get, irrespective of his position, what he needs. This is due to the fact that man's needs do not depend upon his position or intellectual attainment. So to do work and to get what he needs in exchange of his labour is a basic principle of communist society. The multiplication of demand and flowering of intellectual capacity both will proceed hand in hand.

The fullest development of all the inherent qualities of the individual is ensured by communism. Marx and Engels have repeatedly said that man is full of immense potentialities. He is not a slave to machine and the circumstances. It is the purpose of communist society to discover the potentialities and translate them into reality. In capitalist system the worker is faced with contradiction between mental labour and physical labour. Communist society, by shortening of working hour and introducing new and higher machinery, will free the individual from drudgery of work. Worker will get ample scope for recreation and the development of finer qualities. The charge of the bourgeois theoreticians—in communist society individual is neglected—is motivated and malicious. These persons do not know the nature and working of the communist society. Rather, communism gives the highest importance to the individual. It is to be stated here that in a communist society the progress of science and technology is channelled to the greatest possible development of individual's intellect and not to the swelling of profit and interest of few persons.

Communist culture is different from capitalist culture. Brotherhood, friendship and proper development of finer qualities constitute the communist culture. Freed from monotony and drudgery of day-to-day labour man will devote his time and energy to the development of culture and aesthetic qualities. Again, ideology is a part of communist culture. Communism teaches man to think of world culture and to inculcate universal attitude. One need not be confined to his own country or environment.

It is commonly said that a communist society does not approve morality. System of property is destroyed. Some men are illegally and forcibly deprived of their due share. Thus it can be said that communism is the negation of morality and ethics. But Marx and his followers do not subscribe to this baseless idea. It has been said about communist morality that it is a manifestation of ideological, political and moral unity and of its advance towards social homogeneity. Without moral values man's sincerity and sense of duties cannot develop at all.

In a communist society, observes Cornforth (p. 286), a new and enhanced role is played by human consciousness. For, the development of society is guided and controlled by people's consciousness of their own requirements. In every sphere of communist society consciousness of man has a definite role to play. It is so important that the very existence of communist society will face critical position without it.

What would be the exact nature of political organisation of communist society has already been elaborated in our analysis of the withering away of state. For the sake of convenience it is to be noted here that since communism envisages classless society there will not be any necessity of state. It will ultimately wither away. All the bourgeois elements will be fully redundant. Man will form his own social organisation according to his own need, will and choice. Force or coercion will permanently take leave from society. Man's subordination to higher authority is destroyed.

Communist society promises full liberty and proper democracy. Only in a communist society individual can enjoy the taste of real democracy. Class and coercion are not conducive to democracy and liberty. In capitalist system state imposes numerous restrictions on the behaviour of individuals. Spontaneous participation in the activities of state is a rare incident. In capitalism, only men of ruling class have freedom, whereas, in communism, all people enjoy freedom to the fullest satisfaction. Good relation and brotherhood dominate all aspects of social life. Communist society makes no distinction between town and country. Not only this, all artificial differences are removed from communist society. The state is an integrated and united whole. Difference of culture, language, race and religion will exist in communist society, but they will not assume ugly shapes and hinder the growth of society. All the individuals will get adequate and equal opportunities for self-development.

TRANSITION FROM SOCIALISM TO COMMUNISM

Transitional Character of Socialism

There is a confusion even among the serious students of Marxism that socialism and communism are one and same thing. It can be used interchangeably. But a deep study of Marxian literature reveals that two are separate concepts and separate stages of social development. Maurice Cornforth in his illuminating work points out certain transitional features of socialism. An analysis of these features is necessary in order to grasp the transition from socialism to communism. One such feature is, socialism abolishes all classes and class exploitation and also exploitation by man. Cornforth's interpretation is that abolition of classes and class antagonisms does not mean that classes will be completely abolished. The remnants of reactionary or bourgeois classes will remain in a socialist society. Even there may not be classes, there may be agents of classes. Holders of big private property will be forcibly expropriated, but the same method cannot be applied to small property holders. The small and middle peasants very often act as agents of capitalists and their extermination takes time. Engels said, "in effecting transition from private enterprise and private possession to cooperative ones, not forcibly but by dint of example and the proffer of social assistance for this purpose" (quoted by Cornforth, p. 259).

The second transitional feature is—socialism institutes a social ownership of the means of production and makes man the master of machine. But this ambitious objective cannot be achieved overnight. This is a long process. "It involves a thoroughgoing re-training of labour—to educate and train all-around people" (Cornforth, p. 246). The process of removal of subordination of labourer to the division of labour begins in socialism and the process continues until communism arrives. To remove the sub-ordination is the goal of socialism but it is not fully achieved in socialism. Because of this there is the question of transition.

Socialism aims that every requirement of man shall be satisfied. This objective cannot be realised immediately because of certain constraints from which socialism suffers. Particularly the satisfaction of the requirement wants immense advance of production and all-round development of the economy. Socialism coming out of the womb of capitalism cannot perform miracles. In socialism individuals receive a share of social product not according to the need of each, but according to the quantity and quality of work each has contributed. When all sorts of commodities are produced abundantly there will be a flood of commodities and people will get what they require. There may be difference in quality and quantity of labour, but needs will never remain unfulfilled.

Conditions for Transition from Socialism to Communism

Stalin said "in order to pave the way for a real transition to communism, at least three main preliminary conditions have to be satisfied. Briefly stated, these conditions are (a) to raise production to the level where the needs of all can be fully satisfied, (b) concentrate the whole of production and the whole product in the hands of a vast association of the whole people, and (c) create the necessary conditions for making labour life's prime want and eliminating all sub-ordination of people to the division of labour.

In the previous section we have pointed out that in order to meet all the demands of all people tremendous expansion of production is essential. All the means of production will be fully utilised and profit motive will not work behind production. The socialist society through scientific management and proper utilisation of science and technology will ensure the abundance of commodities. When this has been achieved communism will be at the doorstep. Communism thinks that fulfilment of requirement means end of misery and poverty. Both Lenin and Stalin emphasised the abundance of goods.

For the transition from socialism to communism, it is necessary that a central authority or socio-economic centre will control the production of commodities as well as the distribution. By doing this the authority will safeguard the interests of the society as a whole. The state control over production and distribution is to be achieved step by step and not by forcible measures. This is particularly relevant for agricultural and small manufacturing sector. The way between socialism and communism is long and complex. It cannot be negotiated by any shortcut formula or pre-planned technique. Prevailing situation will determine what procedure is to be adopted. Confiscation of small property by coercive measures and adoption of drastic measures may delay the attainment of supreme goal. It may also jeopardise.

Stalin said the third condition to be fulfilled for the transition from socialism to communism is "to ensure such a cultural advancement of society as will secure for all members of society may be in a position to receive an education sufficient to enable them to be active agents of social development, and in a position freely to choose their occupations and not be tied all their lives, owing to the existing division of labour, to some one occupation" (quoted by Cornforth, p. 256).

Some other conditions are to be fulfilled for the transition from socialism to communism. One such condition is the elimination of distinction between town and country. Socialism tries to eliminate the distinction. But since the roots of distinction are very deep, socialism cannot uproot them in a single attempt or venture. It is a long process and several stages have to be overcome. Full elimination of the social and economic distinctions between town and country is a task which is due to be accomplished in the period of transition from socialism to communism. The capitalist system concentrated on the urbanisation and industrialisation and application of higher technology in agriculture was neglected. Peasants economic progress lagged far behind that of industrial labourer. Development of the mechanisation of agriculture is one of the chief aims of socialism. Both industry and agriculture are the two sides or aspects of the same economy. In a capitalist economy it is normally found that peasants and other poor people migrate to the urban area in search of job and create congestion. The capitalists take its full advantage. Socialism—by effecting a balanced and continuous progress of all sections and parts of society—will stop it.

Another task is to be performed during the transition from socialism to communism and it is the abolition of differences between mental and physical labour. In every capitalist system of economy there are differences between brain workers and manual workers and this antithesis between work by hand and work by brain is to be eliminated so as to advance communism. This antithesis arose as an inevitable result of the division of society into oppressors and oppressed, when all the forms of mental labour were turned into a monopoly of the ruling classes. The members of this class advanced the argument that by nature they are possessors of higher calibre and intellectual capacity and also managerial ability. By dint of this self-made superiority of ruling class came to be a hereditary owner of all property.

Socialism wants to put an end to this situation. In this system the brain workers and physical workers have common interests. The purpose of both is the general progress and welfare of the society. There may be qualitative and quantitative differences between works or contribution. It is quite natural that some men will have more intelligence and ability and will form a group. Socialism cannot stop the culture of intellect and ability. In that case what would be the correct step of socialist society which will facilitate its transition to communism? The first task the socialist authority will take is to change the very nature of labour which demands constant intellectual development, a broad outlook, great knowledge and creative approach. "Socialist society proceeds from the premise that the all-round development of people takes place first of all through labour. It is labour such as it becomes in the process of transition from socialism to communism, that affords favourable conditions for intellectual development". The educational system will be modelled in such a manner as to enable the workers to develop their intellectual capacity. In this way socialism will eliminate the distinctions between brain worker and manual worker. Transition from socialism to communism will achieve this progress.

As a society draws nearer to communism, differences in the payment for worker and consequently in the living conditions of all classes and strata of population will gradually be smoothed out. Similarly, with the progress of socialism towards communism, the inequalities from which the women suffer will gradually be ironed out. These inequalities relate to the status and privileges of women. The socialist promises to free the women from the monotony of day-to-day household chores.

Role of Class Struggle and Superstructure

Point has already been made that class struggle in socialism does not cease though its intensity subsides. In the words of Lenin class struggle will not disappear under the dictatorship of the proletariat, it merely assumes different forms. The class struggle in socialism is necessary because there are still several remnants of bourgeoisie and agents of capitalist class. Naturally the question of disbanding class struggle does not arise. The end of socialist society is communism and it is to be achieved, in the words of Maurice Cornforth, not by gradually giving up class struggle, by gradually reconciling antagonistic classes and substituting class collaboration for class struggle, but by waging the class struggle to the end, that is to such complete and final victory of the working class over the exploiters that the latter are abolished as a class, leaving not a trace behind them (p. 262).

The superstructure has a positive role to play in the process of transition from socialism to communism. Though the superstructure is the product of basis and generally corresponds to it, it has some independent character in the sense that it acts independently in certain instances. The spread of socialist views among the workers is essential to arouse their consciousness. Mass organisations are to be set up to consolidate and strengthen the communist superstructure. The orientation of superstructure in the tune of communism can fight the recalcitrant elements of both base and superstructure. It has been stressed by Marx and Engels that mere overthrow of power does not ascertain communism. First comes socialism and then communism. In between two stages superstructure plays an active role. Commenting on the above point Maurice Cornforth says (p. 266), "Marxism always stresses the positive role of the superstructure in social development." In the building of socialism and communist socialist institutions and view play the most active role, in directing, organising and mobilising the people for the accomplishment of the social tasks. Marxists assert that both the base and superstructure must be socialist and then only building up of communism will be an easy task. Cornforth points out certain features of socialist superstructure. Such as socialist view and institutions are developed with the conscious purpose of helping people to satisfy their requirements, socialist views and institutions are developed to widen people's participation, socialist views and institutions are developed to facilitate the transition to communism.

Socialism and Communism : Differences

In several sections of our earlier analysis we have noted that socialism and communism are not two types of social system, they are rather two phases of the same society. Even Marx and Engels have not treated them as separate from each other in fundamental respects. They are simply two stages. Lenin says, "What is usually called socialism was termed by Marx the first or lower phase of communist society. In so far as the means of production become common property, the word communism is also applicable here, providing we do not forget that that this is not complete communism (p. 93 of *State and Revolution*). Notwithstanding, this socialism is in certain respects different from communism.

In the first place, socialism coming out of the womb of capitalism bears the birthmarks of capitalism. The superstructure of socialist society will have some vestiges of capitalism. It is not possible for socialism at the outset of its emergence to eliminate everything of capitalist society. But through an intensive and continuous struggle these elements are to be removed and communism will be free from all these defects. In the *Critique of the Gotha Programme* Marx writes, "These defects are inevitable in the first phase of communist society."

The principles of socialism and communism are not same. The principle of the first stage is "From each according to his ability to each according to his deeds." This is the socialist principle of distribution. But it is a defective one. Another principle of socialism is he who does not work neither shall he eat. These principles are realised in a socialist society. In such a society bourgeois right also exists. Lenin says that this is not communism. The principle of communism is "From each according to his ability to each according to his needs". This is the supreme objective of the communist society. Communism admits that ability and intellect of everyone cannot be same, but needs cannot be differentiated. Needs of every individual must be met.

There is a difference between the two in respect of production relations. Socialism eliminates private ownership over means of production, but the relations of production do not everywhere correspond to that. It has been said that socialism introduces production relations corresponding to the character of the productive forces developed under capitalism. Because of the correspondence of production relations to the capitalist productive forces a gap between demand and supply remains in socialism. The communist society removes this gap by freeing production from capitalist grip and raising it to the adequate level of development. Only communism meets all the requirements of people.

In socialism, the worker is emancipated. He no longer sells his labour power. He is an indispensable part of the social production and social progress. Enough time is left for him which he can utilise for recreation purposes. The greatest shortcoming of socialism is he does not get what he requires. Communism solves this. Each receives all he needs. As a result of this, new attitude of labour must have been generated. Then "labour has become not only a means of life, but life's prime want". People contribute according to ability, not as a necessity to obtain the means of life but because to take part in social production is life's prime want. Productive labour becomes a means to the emancipation. "In communism, whole of people's time is restored to them, the whole of their life is their own." We can say the emancipation of the worker starts with the arrival of socialism and finds its apex embodiment in communism.

Individuals have various faculties. In capitalism they do not get proper opportunities for the development of all the faculties. This is due to the fact that they are subject to the strict and monotonous division of labour and predominance of machine. In socialism division of labour, may be in a miniature form, exists. This retards the growth of individual's faculties. Communism is completely free from this drawback. In our analysis of transition from socialism to communism we have seen that continuous training and re-training makes the worker conscious of his position and objective to be attained. Communism, therefore, is absolutely conducive to the proper blossoming of the individual's personality.

How communism differs from capitalism and partly from socialism may be stated in Marx's and Engel's own words. In the *Manifesto* they have said, "communism abolishes eternal truths, it abolishes all religion and all morality, instead of constituting them on a new basis; it, therefore, acts in contradiction to all past historical experience ..... In place of the old bourgeois society with its classes and class antagonisms, we shall have an association, in which the free development of each is the condition for the free development of all."

35 CAPITALISM

Definition of Capitalism

The starting point of Marxian philosophy is capitalism. In fact capitalism is the by-product of Industrial Revolution and Marx's philosophy centres around the development of capitalism and its consequence. It is, at first, necessary to define capitalism, though the task of defining is not an easy one.

It is said that capitalism is a social system based on the exploitation of wage labour by capitalists in whose hands the means of production are concentrated as their property. So the term capitalism is associated with three notions. One is, capitalism means exploitation. Second is, the ownership of the means of production is concentrated in the hands of few persons. Thirdly, majority people are deprived of the ownership of the forces or means of production. The chief elements of capitalism are capital, means of production and labour. But these three elements do not normally constitute capitalism. The capitalist or the owner of capital brings them under one umbrella to manufacture something and this is commodity. In Bottomore's book capitalism has been defined in the following language. The term capitalism denotes "a mode of production in which capital in its various forms is the principal means of production. Capital may take the form of money or credit for the purchase of labour power and materials of production of physical machinery." ... The suffix "ism" can be used to denote a phase of history, a movement, a system of ideas or some combination of them (pp. 71-72).

Capitalism is the highest form of commodity production. Mere production of commodity is not capitalism. It is produced not merely for use, but also for sale from which comes profit. Hence the notion of profit is connected with the production of commodity. There is another side which is to be explored. If the commodities are produced under the guidance and authority of the whole society and the means of production under its control the production will not give rise to capitalism. One typical feature of capitalism is the domination of few persons in commodity production. Commodities are produced under the absolute authority of the owners of capital.

Capitalist production is the production of commodities. Commodity production is the production of goods for exchange or sale. It replaced the natural economy that was the dominant form of production under slavery and feudalism. Commodity production arose in the period of disintegration of the primitive communal society and gradually acquired increasing importance.

We have already noted that the Industrial Revolution signified the establishment of the material base corresponding to capitalist production relations. Capitalism becomes the prevailing mode of production. The capitalist mode of production requires that labour power is to be purchased or hired to facilitate production. The purchaser offers an amount to the labourer for the labour power and it is called wage. There is a gap between what the capitalist receives in the form of revenue from the sale of the commodity produced by worker and what he gives him in the form of wage. This gap is so wide that it forms the basis of exploitation.

What is Commodity?

It is now quite clear that commodity and commodity production are vital aspects of the rise and development of capitalism. It is, therefore, necessary to know what is commodity? In *Capital* (Vol. I, Part I, Chapter I) Marx analyses the concept in details. From his analysis it appears that not every product of labour is a commodity. If the product of individual's labour satisfies his own needs or those of his family, then it is only a product, a thing, but not a commodity. A product of labour becomes a commodity only when transferred to another for consumption through exchange. A commodity has a two-fold character. The capacity to satisfy some human want gives a commodity its *use value.* The capacity of a commodity to be exchanged for another commodity gives it *exchange value.* The use value of some commodities is important. Whereas the exchange value of some is important. However, the common characteristic is that they are all products of human labour. From this point of view, all commodities represent crystallised human labour. So a commodity is an object outside us, a thing that by its properties satisfies human wants of some or another. The wants spring from the stomach or fancy. Neither are we here concerned to know how the object satisfies the wants, whether directly as means of subsistence or indirectly as means of production.

Commodity Fetishism

G. A. Cohen in *Karl Marx's Theory of History* defines fetish or fetishism in the following words : "To make a fetish of something or fetishise it, is to invest it with powers it does not itself have. The fetish then manifests itself as endowed with a power which in truth it lacks. It has the power not in the real world...but in a world of illusion" (p. 115).

Marx identifies several fetishes in the sphere of economy. The commodity fetish is most famous. "The essence of commodity fetishism is that, in measuring the output of energy by labour-time, we introduce into the products of labour the measure which originally relates to the life-process itself...commodity fetishism is the inability of human beings to see their own products for what they are, and their unwilling consent to be enslaved by human power instead of wielding it. Fetishism contains in embryo all other forms of alienation" (Kolakowski, pp. 276-77). There are two phases of commodity fetishism. One is separation of exchange-value from its material basis. The other is attachment of exchange-value to the substance of commodity.

Marx analyses commodity fetishism in section four of chapter one. A commodity appears, at first sight, a very trivial thing. Its analysis shows that it is, in reality, a very queer thing, abounding in metaphysical subtleties and theological niceties. To far as it is a value in use, there is nothing mysterious about it. But as soon as it steps forth as a commodity it is changed into something transcendent. They mystical character of commodity does not originate in use value.

"A commodity is a mysterious thing because in it the social character of men's labour appears to them as an objective character stamped upon the product of that labour, because the relation of the producers to the sum total of their own labour is presented to them as a social relation. This is the reason why the products of labour become commodities, social things whose qualities are to once perceptible and imperceptible by the senses. The existence of things *qua* commodities, and the value-relation between products of labour which stamps them as commodities, have absolutely no connection with their physical properties and with the material relation arising therefrom. Here it is a particular social relation between men that assumes, in their eyes, the imaginary form of a relation between things. To find an analogy we must have recourse to the mist-enveloped regions of the religious world, where the productions of the human brain appear as independent beings endowed with life, and entering into relation both with one another and with human race. So it is in the world of commodities with the products of men's hands. This I call the Fetishism which attaches itself to the products of labour, so soon as they are produced as commodities and which is inseparable from the production of commodities" (p. 72).

DEVELOPMENT OF CAPITALISM

Collapse of Medieval Economy

From the standpoint of historical materialism the rise of capitalism as a social system was inevitable. During the second half of the fifteenth century medieval society, based on small-scale production, was in the active process of decay. The monetary economy replaced the old exchange system. This gave rise to mercantile capital. Trade and commerce developed at a rapid pace. A number of technical improvements in the realms of metallurgical production, textile manufacture, navigation, armaments, clock-making, astronomical instruments, invention of printing, all these gave a mighty impetus to the growth of productive forces, and encouraged persons to take new initiative and venture. So the growth of mercantile capital and productive forces resulting from scientific inventions and technical improvements accelerated the disintegration of medieval economy.

The merchants and manufacturers competed among themselves to capture new markets in different far-flung areas. Transport through navigation developed in an unprecedented way. The dark continent of Africa, regions of America and Asia were mapped by the brave navigators. "Thanks to the voyages and discoveries, the world market was greatly extended to absorb the growing production of the sixteenth century, the century which was the birth of contemporary capitalism" (Ryazanoff, p. 61).

Plundering, exploitation and extermination of native population by the conquerors started almost from the beginning of the sixteenth century. The purpose originally was to expand and consolidate commercial interests and subsequently assumed the form of exploitation and colonisation. With this also started the slave trade and it has been aptly observed by Marx that it was upon the foundation of the slave trade that Liverpool became a great city. The expansion of slave trade also reached North America, and by the nineteenth century slavery was treated as a national institution. The growth of manufacturing industry both in Europe and America and the development of agriculture were chiefly due to the slave-trade. Because slaves were cheap labourers big industrial units were set up in several parts of Europe and America. The small scale and cottage industries of medieval period were incapable of competing with these comparatively big manufacturing industries having world-wide markets and expansive commercial interests. So the economy of the Middle Ages declined and on the foundations of its ruins the structure of capitalism was built up.

Industrial Revolution and Capitalism

The manufacturing industries of the sixteenth and seventeenth centuries helped the progress of industrial capitalism. The Industrial Revolution of the second half of the eighteenth century provided a further impetus to the growth of manufacturing industry. Large-scale industrial production was made possible by a series of scientific inventions. The Industrial Revolution released countless workers and peasants from the feudal economy and small-scale industrial units and brought them within the four walls of big manufacturing industries. In the sixteenth and seventeenth centuries a new class—bourgeois—emerged. The members of this class were able, because of the new situation, to accumulate a considerable amount of capital and they were extremely eager to invest it in new enterprises and the Industrial Revolution opened that scope. The erstwhile landlords of earlier periods also joined hands with the newly created capitalist or bourgeois class.

The collapse of feudalism did not help the decay of agriculture. On the contrary, the direct impact of Industrial Revolution fell on it. Agriculture was rather industrialised. Modern method of rotational crop was introduced. The whole agriculture was mechanised. In fact, agriculture became a part of industrial capitalism. Capitalists also invested their money in agriculture.

Henceforth the society was divided into two major classes—bourgeoisie and proletariat. The bourgeoisie put the entire economy under its control. The capitalists exploited the workers by giving minimum wages and detaining them longer hours in factory. They had no scope for recreation and were made subordinate to machine. With the growth of industry the division of labour was introduced and the impoverishment and dehumanisation both went ahead. The greater the development of capitalism the greater the exploitation. Simultaneously there arose contradictions within capitalism. Again, the growth of capitalism accompanied with it class antagonisms.

The progress of capitalism revealed another feature of its class division. At the primary stage the bourgeoisie was not a well-articulated class. That is, it was to some extent subordinate to feudal lords. But the rapid growth of capitalism raised it to a clearly defined class and it immediately overthrew the feudalist social order, and set up a bourgeois system in the place of the old. The proletarians also organised themselves as a class. Capitalism did many evils to them, but one good thing it did and that was it aroused political consciousness of the workers.

Manufacturing System and Capitalism

According to Marx there is a very close relationship between industrialisation, progress of capitalism, and setting up of manufacturing industries. Capitalism is the greatest manifestation of establishment of manufacturing industries. Marx says (*Capital*, Vol. I, p. 641), "Along with the development of the factory system and of the revolution in agriculture, production in all other branches of industry, not only extends, but alters its character." The owners of manufacturing industries exploited the workers in various ways. The workers could not keep pace with the rapid technical progress of the manufacturing industry. Many of them were treated as unskilled workers and were given minimum wages. Large number of children and women were employed and they were subjected to poisonous gas and were forced to work in unhealthy atmosphere and environment. Any protest was accompanied by dismissal. These persons left their ancestral village home in search of better living.

With the introduction of new machinery capitalism makes a new stride in its own development. Marx says (*Capital*, Vol. I, p. 403), "If machinery be the most powerful means for increasing the productiveness of labour—i.e., for shortening the working time required in the production of commodity, it becomes in the hands of capital the most powerful means, for lengthening the working day beyond all bounds set by human nature. The lengthening of the working day allows the production on an extended scale without any alteration. Mechanisation helps the growth of capitalism in a double way. It reduces the cost of production and enhances the volume of products. On the other hand, in most cases, at the same wage it prolongs the working day. Capitalism thus strengthens its position. Machinery also produces larger amount of surplus value which swells the quantum of investment."

The capitalist employment of machinery supplies new and powerful motives to an excessive lengthening of working day, and radically changes, as well as the methods of labour, as also the character of the social working organism, in such a manner as to breakdown all opposition to this tendency. On the other hand, it produces, partly by opening out to the capitalist new strata of the working class, previously inaccessible to him, partly by setting free the labourers it supplants—a surplus working population, which is compelled to submit to the dictation of capital. Machinery sweeps away every moral and natural restriction on the length of the working day. The paradox is that instead of shortening the working day machinery lengthens it and places workers at the mercy of the capitalist.

Revolutionary Character of Capitalism

In the *Manifesto* Marx and Engels announce "The bourgeoisie cannot exist without constantly revolutionising the instruments of production and thereby the relations of production and with them the whole relation of society" (*MESW*—I—37). Capitalism cannot fix its position at a particular point. It must go ahead. Its *raison d'etre* is to create favourable conditions for its rapid expansion. To achieve that supreme goal the capitalists constantly revolutionise the modes of production and throw away the outdated and irrelevant ones. Capitalism makes all efforts to change the base and—corresponding to it—the superstructure.

Analysing the revolutionary character of capitalism Marx says in *Capital* (Vol. I, p. 485) "So long as the handicraft and manufacture form the general groundwork of social production the subjection of the producer to one branch exclusively, the breaking up of the multifariousness of his employment is a necessary step in the development. On that groundwork each separate branch of production acquires empirically the form that is technically suited to it, slowly perfects it, and so soon as a given degree of maturity has been reached, rapidly crystallises that form. What induces change here and there is a gradual change in the instrument of labour"..."The technical basis of modern industry is therefore revolutionary, while all earlier modes of production were essentially conservative. By means of machinery, chemical processes and other methods, it is continually causing changes not only in the technical basis of production, but also in the functions of the labourer, and in the social combinations of the labour-process... At the same time, it thereby also revolutionises the division of labour within the society, and incessantly launches masses of capital and work—people from one branch of production to another" (p. 486).

The capitalists revolutionise not only the means of production by introducing new machinery, but also the outlook, attitude and behaviour of people. Progress of capitalism will be seriously affected if people always feel antagonism to it. Capitalism constantly reorients law, philosophy, art, literature etc. through its paid theoreticians and intellectuals. Government controlled machinery is being progressively used by the capitalists to propagate the ideology and objectives of capitalism. While the owners of capital are hesitant to spend a paltry amount of money for the benefit of workers, a fabulous amount is being spent for propaganda purposes. They are utilising the revolution in communication and technology for the advancement and consolidation of capitalism.

Capitalism's Conquest Over Nature

The bourgeoisie felt that the growth of capitalism would be faced with the retardation if it failed to conquer nature and with the avowed purpose to accelerate the progress of capitalism concerted efforts were made to harness nature. It is to be noted here that capitalists did it not with a mind to society's welfare. The manifold discoveries expanded industry and created an industrialism. The chemical science with its discoveries revolutionised agriculture. Through the conquest of agriculture capitalism conquered nature. Marx says in *Capital* (Vol. I, p. 505), "Capitalist production completely tears asunder the old bond of union which held together agriculture and manufacture in their infancy. But at the same time it creates the material conditions for a higher synthesis in the future, i.e., the union of agriculture and industry on the basis of the more perfected forms they have each acquired during their temporary separation."

Agriculture was not only industrialised, it was put under constant and active surveillance. Science was used to raise the fertility of soil. When natural manure was insufficient, artificial manure was used. In this way the deficit in nature was compensated by the discoveries of science. The main purpose of the bourgeoisie was to harness nature with all its resources for the advancement of its own interest. Thus it raised nature from what it is to what it ought to be. Nature must help the progress of capitalism. With the help of science and technology distant parts of earth were brought under cultivation. Irrigation system was improved. The capitalists were not willing to depend on the whims of nature. The evils of natural calamities were lessened through various efforts. In all the capitalist countries agricultural production was raised to a very high level. Marx and Engels have shown with profuse statistics how—through the conquest of nature—agricultural sector was improved.

Before the development of capitalism the navigation system did not develop considerably. Waterways were old-fashioned. The capitalists found this incapable of meeting their growing demands. So they focused their attention to the digging of new canals, like the Suej and Panama, and improving the old ones. Ryazanoff says (p. 81), "The development of canals was due to the urgent needs of a growing commerce. As the technique of canal construction improved, the channels were deepened and widened to such a size as to accommodate sea-going ships. These ship canals have mostly been constructed either to shorten the voyage between two seas by cutting through an intervening isthmus, or they have been made in places to sea-ports."

Capitalism as a Global Phenomenon

It has been diagnosed by Marx and Engels that by the seventies of the 19th century the expansion of capitalism turned out to be a global phenomenon and capitalists can be credited with it. It spread its branches in the every nook and corner of the world. Why and how—let us see in the *Manifesto* :

"The need of a constantly expanding market for its products chases the bourgeoisie over the whole surface of the globe. It must nestle everywhere, settle everywhere, establish connections everywhere. Bourgeoisie has through its exploitation of the world market given a cosmopolitan character to production and consumption in every country. To the great chagrin of Reactionists, it has drawn from under the feet of industry the national ground on which it stood. All old fashioned national industries have been destroyed or are daily being destroyed. They are dislodged by new industries, whose introduction becomes a life and death question for all civilised nations, by industries that no longer work up indigenous raw materials, but raw material drawn from the remotest zones; industries whose products are consumed, not only at home, but in every quarter of the globe. In the place of the old wants, satisfied by the productions of the country we find new wants, requiring for their satisfaction the products of distant lands and climes. In the place of the old local and national seclusion and self-sufficiency, we have intercourse in every direction, universal interdependence of nations."

We have quoted a lengthy passage from the *Manifesto* which exposes the global character of capitalism. The urge for survival led the capitalists to establish markets everywhere in the world. The home market of the bourgeoisie was not sufficient to consume all the products. That is why the bourgeois class was forced to set up new markets. Not only capitalism created new markets, but it imposed a civilisation which it embodies upon the people of new markets. The sole purpose of capitalism was to change both the base and the superstructure. New commodities were exported which ultimately destroyed the indigenous markets and productive system. The old-fashioned industries were also destroyed. The capitalism of the late eighteenth century assumed a world character in the late nineteenth century.

Capitalism annihilated all the national and geographical barriers through its concerted efforts. The old fetters of transport and communication were thrown away and with the help of new technology the transport and communication system was revolutionised. All nations—even the most barbarians—were drawn together by the worldwide influence of capitalism. There was competition among the capitalists of various nations, but the character of capitalism was the same everywhere. European capitalism forced all nations to follow it in all respects, i.e., to adopt the capitalist mode of production, the capitalist way of life, and capitalist technique of exploitation. Capitalism exports both products and civilization. In the words of Marx and Engels, capitalism creates a world after its own image.

The poor countries came to be dependent on the developed capitalist countries of the West. The indigenous sources of production were destroyed by the capitalists. These nations had no means or managerial acumen to set up modern industries. Capitalism in its global appearance created a havoc. It changed the mode of living, outlook and taste. People of various parts of the globe come nearer to each other and this changed almost everything of human life. This was possible because of the rapid progress of transport and communication. The mode of living and outlook of the people of the Third World changed remarkably.

Imperialist Stage of Capitalism

For exploitation and accumulation capitalism expands which is not unlimited. However, it reaches a final stage of its expansion and this stage has properly been named by Lenin as imperialism. In his famous and classic definition he has said that imperialism is the highest stage of capitalism. We have already mentioned that capitalism in its mature phase of development becomes a world phenomenon. The capitalists, in order to keep the momentum of expansion and consolidation of power, seek to set up markets in the far-flung areas of the globe. But the economic interests cannot be fully safeguarded without the capture of political power. The collaboration between the capitalists and the home government becomes a very logical and natural way out. This government of the capitalist country subjugates the governments of other countries. Overthrow of the existing political system and the destruction of indigenous economy go hand in hand.

Lenin has also said that if it is necessary to give the briefest possible definition of imperialism we should have to say that it is the monopoly stage of capitalism. Let us explain it. The concentration of production and capital developed to such an advanced stage that it creates monopolies which plays a decisive role in economic life. The merging of bank capital with industrial capital creates the foundation of a new system which as called "finance capital". This is the new aspect. The industrialists of capitalist countries are not always in a position to provide necessary capital for the rapid growth of industries. Banks come forward to help the industrialists. This gives rise to a new dimension of capitalism. A holy alliance is effected between the banking authority and capitalists. Lenin calls it financial oligarchy. Banks and capitalists monopolise the entire capitalism.

At the commencement of capitalism as a world phenomenon it started to export commodities. But when it reached the monopoly stage it began to export capital. This is a distinguishing feature of capitalism. The national liberation movement of the Third World countries created impediments to the export of foreign goods. The capitalists then started export of capital. This feature of capitalism appeared towards the beginning of the twentieth century. In the export market of commodities the capitalists were faced with stiff competition from various quarters. When Marx and Engels were writing they were not fully aware of it.

Features of Capitalism

Capitalism has certain features. The first one is, *it is characterised by the private ownership over the means of production.* The state ownership is never a guarantee of economic development; rather, it hinders the growth. The private ownership is supported by another reason. The libertarian view is that the state control of the means of production ultimately leads to the control of private life of individuals. The classical thinkers of capitalism are of opinion that in a state control system the proper progress of science and technology is really a far cry. To sum up, private ownership is the only way and objective of capitalism.

Capitalism is called market-economy. Before the emergence of capitalism people generally produced their own requirement and the exchange system, as a means of meeting the demands, was unknown to them. The invention of market-economy by capitalism is a great landmark. This type of economy is normally credited with the introduction of two systems—system of division of labour, and production of commodities more than the requirement. For the sale of the commodities the capitalists develop a well-knit and well-organised distribution system under their own guidance and control. Another aspect of the market economy is that manufacturers produce the articles required by the consumer. The consumer sovereignty is the determiner of the movements of the market economy. The capitalists impose their decision upon the consumer. They also dislike to include the welfare motive into the economy. The decision of the consumer is final and that is to be accepted as the real guideline of production. The producers will always act according to the preference of the consumers. The market economy, in this connection it is to be noted, admits of crises and in that case it approves of state interference and even that on a very limited scale. In a word, market economy is to be encouraged and safeguarded.

The students of political science are sometimes misled by the argument that capitalism and its market-economy are analogous to the fascist system, because in fascism private ownership is the characteristic feature of economy. But the fact is that the fascist economy is called command economy. The government decides the manner and principles of employment, pricing, production and distribution. The producers are hardly left with any freedom. Capitalism's market economy is, again, different from communism in the sense that in the latter the decision of the authority or party is final. Economy of communist society is also planned. That is, there is enforcement and no place of persuasion which characterises capitalism.

Another feature of capitalism is competition among the manufacturers. Since the consumer is sovereign, capitalists compete among themselves to satisfy the consumers. Thus the principle of consumer sovereignty leads to the competition among the manufacturers. The champions of capitalism believe that consumer sovereignty and the competitive market economy are sufficient to safeguard the consumers' interests. The government regulations over production and distribution of commodities are against consumers' interests. Competition has also other good effects. Producers, in order to survive and develop, always try to reduce the cost of production. Experience tells us that the capitalists spend a lot of money for research and this is one of the many causes of the progress of science and technology in capitalists countries. After the Second World War the miraculous development of technology in Japan and Germany is normally treated as contribution of capitalism.

We can call profit—making and profit—motive as important features of capitalism. Profit acts as the greatest impetus of expansion. Moreover, out of the surplus value the capitalists build up the investment fund. Hence the survival of capitalism without profit is an impossibility. During the Middle Ages both profit and interests were highly condemned and because of that reason industry could not develop at all.

In capitalism this profit is the main source of dissension between capitalists and proletarians. Through the system of profit or surplus value capitalists exploit the workers. The emergence of proletarians as a class-for-itself confronts it with the capitalists and the struggle between the two classes becomes inevitable. We can, therefore, hold that we cannot imagine capitalism without class struggle. The bourgeois theoreticians have also admitted the existence of class conflict, though they speak of class collaboration.

The capitalists are panegyric of democracy and they feel proud that capitalism creates an atmosphere for the affluent blossoming of democracy. But, in fact, the picture of democracy in any capitalist society is absolutely gloomy. Rather, capitalism and democracy are contradictory. Real democracy exists in a society where there is no gross economic inequality and the state is not ruled by a particular class.

In capitalism the elites control the power of the state. So the fruits of democracy are enjoyed by the elites. The majority people are deprived of democracy. The elites always represent the economically dominant class and the laws are formulated at the behest of the elites. The capitalist democracy is called the democracy of the elites.

The most important characteristic of capitalism is that here the state is an instrument of exploitation. The capitalist class uses the state machinery for its own purposes—to suppress the agitation or movement of workers. It is a puppet at the hands of the bourgeoisie. In *Anti-Düring* Engels wrote, "The modern state, no matter what its form, is essentially a capitalist machine, the state of the capitalists, the ideal personification of the total national capital. The state is the representative of the bourgeoisie."

Capitalism admits of multiplicity of opinions and views. For this reason we find numerous groups and organisations and more than one political party in any capitalist system. There are also conflicts among groups and parties. There is, in capitalism, an economically dominant class, but there are also other classes and each class is represented by one party. Since the whole economic system is under the full control of the bourgeoisie the workers' party has hardly any scope to change their lot. The party of the powerful class controls both economics and politics. Again, the bourgeois parties have no ideological difference. In USA, the Republican Party and Democratic Party are two sides of the same coin.

The writer of the article published in Bottomore's book has summarised the features of capitalism in the following way :

1. Capitalism is characterised by production for sale rather than own use by numerous producers.
2. In capitalism labour power is bought and sold like any other commodity. In capitalism it is called labour market.
3. In capitalism the capitalists control the purchase of labour, production of commodities, the sale of these commodities, working hour and everything which is connected with production.
4. Capitalism also controls the entire financial system.
5. In capitalism there are various types of competition among the capitalists.
6. To tide off the undesirable effects of competition the capitalists spend huge amount of money for the invention of new machinery and improvement as well as innovation of the existing one.

CONTRADICTION AND CRISIS OF CAPITALISM

Origin and Nature of Contradiction

In the *Afterword to the Second German Edition of Capital* Marx wrote (January 24, 1873) : "The contradictions, inherent in the movement of the capitalists society, impress themselves upon the practical bourgeois most strikingly in the changes of the periodic cycle, through which modern industry runs and whose crowning point is the universal crisis." The central point is that, according to Marx, capitalism carries with its gradual progress all the potentialities of contradiction. So contradictions are inherent in every capitalist system. The capitalists leave no stone unturned to get rid of the contradictions, but there is no way out.

It has been maintained by Marx that the contradictions of capitalism have not come from outside, rather their seeds were within capitalism and the system is itself responsible. He has explained the capitalist system in the outlook of materialistic conception of history and have noted that, in the feudal system, property relations were incompatible with already developed productive forces. The existing relations of production and property were converted into so many fetters and they had to burst asunder. Into their place stepped free competition, accompanied by a social and political constitution adapted to it, and by the economical and political sway of the bourgeois class.

The development of capitalism under the guidance of the bourgeoisie has surpassed all past records of social progress. In all fields such as transport, communication, commerce, and, finally, productive system and production relations, the development of capitalism is really miraculous. But this is the source of crisis and contradiction. The development of capitalism is followed by the epidemic of over-production. Why? The capitalists, in order to earn more and more profit, produce more and more. On the contrary, the society is not well-equipped for the consumption.

The contradiction in capitalism is class contradiction. In every contradiction opposites co-exist and because of this opposition the contradiction becomes inevitable. Capitalism creates two basic classes—bourgeoisie and proletariat. The capitalists and workers exist side by side. Both of them are indispensable to each other. Capitalism exploits the workers and it is forced to do it for its own survival. On the other hand, workers are exploited by the capitalists. They cannot get rid of it. They are not the owners of the sources of production and in order to earn livelihood they are forced to sell their labour at a rate much below their expectation and requirement.

Marx points out another contradiction of capitalism (Vol. I, p. 487). He wrote, "But if Modern Industry, by its very nature, therefore, necessitates variations of labour, fluency of function, universal mobility of labourer, on the other hand, in its capitalistic form, it reproduces the old division of labour with its ossified particularisations... This contradiction between the technical necessities of Modern Industry and the social character inherent in its capitalistic form, dispels all fixity and security in the situation of the labourer." What Marx emphasises here is that the industrialisation recognises, as a fundamental law, the variation of work and consequently the fitness of the labourer for varied work. But capitalism creates manifold fetters for the workers, particularly the fetter of division of labour. Because of this fetter the labourers do not get adequate opportunities to develop their aptitude. The workers have no scope to come out of it. The capitalist system has created the division of labour for its own sake. We can rather say it is associated with capitalism's question of life and death. But the contradictions or antagonisms do not stay at a particular point, that is, they are not immobile.

Contradiction between Social Production and Private Ownership

In Volume III of *Capital* (pages 242-259) Marx points out the contradiction between social production and private ownership. There is a contradiction between the social character of production or social production and private ownership of the means of production. At the very rudimentary stage of capitalism the capitalist was just an organiser. With the development of capitalism various other agents came to be involved and became integral part of capitalism's development. To put it in other words, when capitalism assumes a social character, capitalist production also becomes a social production. What is known as the product of a particular capitalist is, in actual practice, product of several forces or agents. This is social production. On the other hand, the ownership of the means of production remains in the hand of the capitalists. To sum up, production is social and ownership of the sources of production is individual. "As production becomes more and more social in character, the private appropriation of fruits of labour is seen to be more and more anachronistic."

"...the growing accumulation of capital implies its growing concentration. Thus grows the power of capital, the alienation of conditions of social production personified in the capitalist from the real producers, capital comes more and to the fore as a social power, whose agent is the capitalist. This social power no longer stands in any possible relation to that which the labour of a single individual can create. It becomes an alienated, independent, social power, which stands exposed to the society as an object, and as an object, that is, capitalists source of power. The contradiction between the general social power into which capital develops, on the one hand, and private power of the individual capitalists over these social conditions of production, on the other, becomes ever more irreconcilable" (p. 159). By virtue of the ownership of capital the capitalists control the social production and the whole economic system. But the contradiction between social production of capital and private ownership remains. It is beyond the power of the capitalists to come out of the contradiction or remove it for good. The capitalists fail to realise that they can control the ownership of capital, but cannot control the nature of social production. So the development of capitalism creates its own real barrier. It is the capital and its self-expansion appear as the starting and the closing point, the motive and purpose of production.

Maturity of Contradictions

According to Marx the appearance of contradiction in capitalism does not mean that capitalism will face crisis or critical situation. For the collapse of capitalism it is necessary that contradictions must arrive at the stage of maturity which requires sufficient time and other favourable situation. In *Capital* (Vol. I, p. 503) Marx says, "By maturing the material conditions, and the combination on a social scale of the processes of production, it matures the contradictions and antagonisms of the capitalist form of production and thereby provides, along with the elements for the formation of a new society, the forces for exploding the old one."

Marx has studied the different stages of the development of capitalism and has observed how it is faced with contradiction as well as its maturity. The capitalist cannot exist without constantly developing his mode of production, intensifying domination and exploiting the workers. When all these reach an apex stage the contradictions get maturity. The capitalists and proletarians stand face to face. The contradictions become irreconcilable. Marx has said (Vol. I, p. 645), "Within the capitalist system all means for the development of production transform themselves into a means of domination over the producers. They mutilate the labourer into a fragment of man, degrade him to the level of an appendage of a machine. It follows that in proportion as capital accumulates, the lot of the labourer, be his payment high or low, must grow worse."

With the process of further accumulation or development of capital new forces and new passions spring up in the bosom of society. The old social organisation fetters and keeps them down. The contradiction between old and new forces surfaces. The conflict between the old and the new becomes prominent. Marx has said that (p. 762) when the old society becomes sufficiently decomposed from top to bottom, as soon as the labourers are turned into proletarian, their means of labour into capital the contradictions reach the point of explosion. The contradictions must explode.

"The monopoly of capital becomes a fetter upon the mode of production, which has sprung up and flourished along with and under it. Centralisation of the means of production and socialisation of labour at last reach a point where they become incompatible with their capitalist integument. Thus integument is burst asunder—The knell of capitalist private property sounds. The expropriators are expropriated" (p. 763). The maturity of contradictions is, therefore, essential for hastening the dissolution of capitalism. The working class cannot create contradictions or impose them upon the society or the capitalist mode of production. The important task the proletarians have to perform is to organise themselves in a dominant force so as to fight the capitalists.

Crises : Its Nature and Effects

The contradictions lead to crises and finally to the collapse of capitalism. Here we are concerned with the crises. The capitalist production process reproduces the social conditions that estrange the worker from his own labour and its product and perpetuates itself by depriving the producers of a share in the values they create. But the capital accumulation cannot proceed indefinitely. The tendency of growing capitalism is falling rate of profit and this induces capitalists to curtail the quantum of investment and retrench the workers. This measure further aggravates the crisis of capitalism. In the industrial market an artificial over-population is created. The capitalist adopts various measures to reactivate capitalism from recession. The paradoxical result is that the whole industrial market is flooded with an excess of capital and excess of workers.

Explaining the origin and nature of crisis in capitalism Marx and Engels have said in the *Manifesto* "Modern bourgeois society with its relations of production of exchange, and of property, a society that has conjured up such gigantic means of production and of exchange, is like the sorcerer who is no longer able to control the powers of the nether world whom he has called up by his spells. For many a decade past the history of industry and commerce is but the history of the revolt of modern productive forces against modern conditions of production, against the property relations that are the conditions for the existence of the bourgeoisie and of its rule. It is enough to mention the commercial crises that by their periodical return put on its trial, each time more threateningly, the existence of the entire bourgeois society. In these crises a great part not only of the existing products, but also of the previously created productive forces, are periodically destroyed. In these crises there breaks out an epidemic that, in all earlier epochs, would have seemed an absurdity—the epidemic of overproduction" (*Manifesto*, p. 57). Marx and Engels call it "monetary barbarism".

The materialist interpretation of history reveals that the emergence of capitalism and rise of bourgeoisie as a potential power have completely changed the social-economic-political environment of society. The capitalist society and civilisation are completely different from feudal society and civilisation. A new civilisation appears, and it is a great civilisation. It is far greater than all earlier civilisations. Commerce, industry, transport and communications all have advanced tremendously. The conditions of the bourgeois society are too narrow to comprise the wealth created by new industries. Naturally contradictions and crises are bound to crop up. It would be quite wrong to assume that the capitalists took no measures to fight the contradictions and crises. What measures did they take? On the one hand by enforced destruction of a mass of productive forces, on the other by the conquest of new markets, and by the more thorough exploitation's of the old ones (*Manifesto*, p. 58).

Kolakowski says that the economic crises involve the squandering of the community's wealth on a vast scale, demonstrating that capitalism cannot cope with its own contradictions. They are the expressions of a conflict between the techno-logical level and social conditions of technical progress, between the forces of production and the system within which they work. If the capitalists were not engaged in squandering the wealth of the society for their own interest, there would have been no crises or contradictions.

Some of the spokesmen of the working class argue that the crises could be averted by raising the wages and enabling the market to absorb the excess products. To put it in other words, by raising the purchasing power of the workers and other common people the economic crises could be arrested. But Marx in *Capital* (Vol. II) has said that this is not the case. Crises and contradictions are the inherent characters of capitalism. They regularly occur after a period of prosperity. Interpreting Marx's view Kolakowski maintains that (p. 299) the greed for expansion is such that the market cannot possibly go on absorbing the products of capitalism—especially the bulk of these. Lenin has said capitalist production cannot develop except by fits and starts—two steps forward and one step—sometimes even both—back.

Collapse of Capitalism

In the *Manifesto* Marx and Engels have said the weapons with which the bourgeoisie felled feudalism to the ground are now turned against the bourgeoisie itself (p. 58). Let us add few words to this famous comment. In feudalism the productive forces developed to such an extent that the feudal system and economy could not cope with this and the bourgeoisie used this development in its own favour to destroy the feudal system and to establish its domination. The capitalists, during the critical period of feudalism, asserted themselves as a basic class and, naturally, it was an easy task for them to destroy feudalism. It is to be noted that the credit should go to the seeds of destruction inherent in feudalism. In the same way the collapse of capitalism is inevitable. The striking difference is the bourgeoisie played the leading part in the destruction of feudalism and the working class has come forward in overthrowing capitalism.

It is not true that capitalists are quite indifferent to problems, crises and contradictions. The reverse is true—capital seeks frantically for new markets and endeavours to expand into non-capitalist areas, but the more the productive capacity increases, the more obvious is its conflict with the narrow limits of consumption. According to Marx the collapse of capitalism is inevitable because of the economic reasons. These economic factors cause class struggle. The workers are not responsible for the contradictions. For this reason Marx has ruled out the enhancement of wages as a way of averting crisis. In *Capital* (Vol. II, p. 410) Marx says, "It is sheer tautology to say that crises are caused by scarcity of effective consumption or of effective consumers."

Engels once said (in an article in *Democratic Review,* March 1850), "We have had many of these revolutions, happily overcome hitherto by the opening of new markets (China in 1842) or the better exploiting of old ones, by reducing the cost of production (as by free trade in corn). But there is a limit to this, too. There are no new markets to be opened now, and there is only one means left to reduce wages, namely radical financial reforms, and reduction of the taxes by repudiation of national debt. It is evident that, with no chance of further extending markets, under a system which is obliged to extend production everyday, there is an end to mill-lord ascendancy. And *what next?* Universal ruin and chaos, say the free traders. Social revolution and proletarian ascendancy, say we." Here Engels repudiates the palliatives of the crises of capitalism. The capitalists take all measures to avert crises and contradictions. But there are limits to these measures.

Marx and Engels have asserted that no outside force is required to destroy capitalism root and branch. There are contradictions within capitalism and when they reach the stage of maturity capitalism will automatically collapse. This was, of course, the prediction of Marx and Engels. Inconsistencies or contradictions are numerous, types are also many. However, the destruction of capitalism cannot be checked. In *Capital* (Vol. III, p. 245) Marx writes, "Capitalist production seeks continually to overcome the immanent barriers, but overcomes them only by means which again place these barriers in its way and on a non-formidable scale." The means of getting rid of contradictions are only of limited purposes. So the conflict between private ownership and the development of instruments of production and technical co-operation continues.

Lenin has beautifully explained how the collapse of capitalism for political reasons is inevitable. Because of the inadequacy of the internal market the capitalist countries proceed to capture territories and set up new markets. This creates an unhealthy competition among the capitalist countries creating all the potentialities of war. For the absence of an authority with sovereign power in international arena, the disputes among the competing powers remain, in most of the cases, unsettled. In fact, the countries belonging to the Third World are thrown into turmoil, instability and a situation of armed conflict. Lenin has said that the First World War is a war among the capitalist powers.

Taking the opportunities of the competition and conflict among the capitalist states the people of the Third World countries accelerate their national liberation movement, i.e., to liberate themselves from the shackles of colonial power. At the rudimentary stage of the development of capitalism the bourgeoisie propagated the messages of liberty, equality and fraternity. Now the liberation seekers use the same values and principles against the bourgeoisie. The capitalists are, therefore, confronted with two-fold dangers—self-destructive war and mounting liberation movements. The capitalists have hardly any weapon at their disposal to fight these two "evils".

At the imperialist stage capitalism faces the greatest disintegration, because all the avenues of progress are closed. That stage has been called by Lenin imperialism. The crises and contradictions are not only mature but on the point of explosion. The proletarians are waiting for this situation. Now it is their duty to use these for their liberation. It is to be noted here that the workers are not responsible for the crises, but they must be alert for their proper use. The limit and scope are to be decided by the proletarians. The moribund capitalism is to be thrown in a single assault. The integument is burst asunder. The death knell of capitalism sounds. Expropriators are expropriated.

Criticism and Evaluation

Marx and Engels published the *Manifesto* in 1848. During this last 160 years and more capitalism throughout the world has undergone radical changes and the picture portrayed by Marx and Engels in many a case appears to be irrelevant. The orthodox supporters of capitalism are of opinion that there may be contradictions and crises in capitalism, but these do not necessarily lead to the disintegration of capitalism. It will never reach the moribund stage. Why? It is generally argued that systems including capitalism have their own regulatory mechanisms and whenever any crisis arises these self-regulatory mechanisms save the system from crisis. Because of this self-regulatory mechanism capitalism has been able to save itself. This is particularly applicable to animal body. In the 1950s a number of behaviouralists had emphasised this through the input-output model. Because of this self-regulating mechanism, capitalism of Britain and USA has been able to withstand the crisis. We, therefore, conclude that contradictions and crises do not lead to the collapse of capitalism.

Lenin is hundred per cent correct when he says that the imperialist powers are involved in armed conflict among themselves. But we are of opinion that the capitalist world of Lenin's time or of the post-Lenin period has undergone sea changes. The capitalists have fully realised that competition and war cannot help the progress of capitalism. In order to consolidate capitalism and also to make it effective the capitalists of today's world are united. They have not completely eschewed the path of attrition (e.g. the Iraq War), but it is not a frequent one. There is polycentrism in the capitalist world, though we cannot treat it as the product of conflict.

Marx has repeatedly asserted that it is the first and foremost duty of the proletarians to utilise the crises and contradictions of capitalist society and in this way it will be able to dislodge the bourgeoisie from power and to establish their dictatorship. Emancipation or revolution will not fall from the sky. Marx and Engels were very much confident of the willingness of proletarians to launch a revolution and continue the class struggle until the classless society was established. But today, critics plead, the situation has changed. The workers want to change their economic lot not by resorting to class struggle, but by parliamentary tactics. Bernstein's revisionism succeeds in changing the outlook of working class towards class struggle. Moreover, capitalists have revised their attitude towards workers. They are more sympathetic. Simply through collective bargaining workers have been able to get a number of concessions.

We now look at the present situation of capitalism. The antagonism between the two basic classes of capitalist society, according of Marx, will be the cause of the collapse of capitalism. Evan Luard, in his noted work *Socialism Without State,* has observed that this prediction of Marx has proved false. Rather, the antagonism of classes in erstwhile Soviet Union and Eastern European countries has become the source of the fall of socialism. Whereas in Western European countries—particularly in Britain and France, capitalism becomes consolidated. In Luard's own words : "And it is perhaps not surprising that it was in the Communist East, not in the Capitalist West, as he had forecast, that antagonism between classes finally led to the collapse of the entire political system" (p. xix).

Luard further maintains, "There was a similar error in the doctrine's forecasts about economic development generally. Marx believed that capitalist system was incapable of developing in a way that would enhance the living standards of those who worked within it. It contained within itself the seeds of its own destruction... capitalism did not destroy itself with overproduction and declining profits." The governments of all the capitalist countries have come forward to help the growth of capitalism and resist the immanent causes of fall.

We have discussed Marxian theory of capitalism and also its drawbacks. The Marxists do not always agree with the criticisms or arguments put forward by the bourgeois critics. They are of opinion that the time has not yet arrived to throw Marxian theory of capitalism overboard. Some recent bourgeois theoreticians have come to the conclusion that the power and influence of capitalists have enormously increased. Ebenstein in his *Today's Isms* has said that (p. 132-133) in USA, five hundred big industrial corporations control the production and distribution of 80% commodities and 75% of the total profit is pocketed by these corporations. In fact, the entire American economy is controlled by these corporations alone. Again the power and influence of all these corporations are not of the same measure. Few are more powerful than the rest. However, the fact is that the profit of all the industrial corporations has increased considerably. Without exploitation this cannot happen. It may be that the industrialists are giving more and more concession to workers, but this does not mean that there is no exploitation. The moot point of Marxian Capitalism is that without exploitation there cannot be upward trend of profit. The monopolisation of power has strengthened the measures of exploitation.

The Marxists further argue that the collective bargaining of the workers has succeeded in raising the level of wages. But the condition of the worker should be viewed in broader perspective. The wages and inflation both have increased. Does it indicate the betterment of the workers? Minimum knowledge of economics does not say this. The workers may not be always exploited, but the general consumers are exploited. Through attractive advertisement and various other ways the capitalists are selling their commodities at higher prices and making abnormal profits. Consumers' choice are gradually becoming narrowed down. Our conclusion is—so long there is capitalism there is exploitation.

It is not true that workers' urge for struggle has declined. The Marxists always argue that the step to be taken by the proletariat depends upon the bourgeoisie. There is ample proof to hold that the capitalists of the modern world have softened their attitude and do not always resort to coercive measures against the workers, as the earlier capitalists did. As a result of this the workers have also taken a lenient attitude to the bourgeoisie. Furthermore, the modern state is not absolutely indifferent to the problems of workers. Innumerable welfare projects have been implemented to improve their economic lot. Various avenues are being explored for ensuring security. All these have outwardly polished the ugly character of capitalism.

So far as capitalism is concerned the basic of its key idea emphasised by Marx still remains intact. Capitalism cannot be dissociated from exploitation. It exploits either workers or consumers. Modern capitalism of anywhere of the world is exploiting workers and consumers. The latter have no choice in the face of capitalists' sovereignty is simply a high-sounding phrase with no practical value.

36 REVOLUTION

What is Revolution?

According to COD the term revolution means "complete change, turning upside down, great reversal of conditions, fundamental reconstruction especially forcible substitution by subjects of new ruler on polity for the old." This is not definition of revolution. These are the various meanings of revolution. One meaning is significant. It means fundamental reconstruction that brings about radical changes of the society. Lenin's remark about revolution is that in political and scientific sense it is the transfer of power from one class to another class. Even this is not sufficient. Macpherson defines revolution in an elaborate sense. *For the purposes of political, social and economic changes the forcible capture of political power is revolution.* He defines revolution in the light of Marxian concept of revolution. The objective of revolution is to bring about radical changes in society. If it does not take place, it is not revolution. The writer of the article published in the Bottomore-edited book defines revolution in this way. In the scheme of history first sketched by Marx and Engels in *The German Ideology,* the leading idea was that of a succession of eras—each based on a mode of production, and revolution in its fullest sense meant a cataclysmic leap from one of these to the next.

Herbert Aptheker, the renowned Marxist thinker, defines revolution in the following way : "I would define revolution as an historical process leading to and culminating in social transformation, wherein one ruling class is displaced by another, with the new class representing, as compared to the old, enhanced productive capacities and socially progressive potentialities" (p. 65). We can deduce several features of revolution from Aptheker's definition. One is, revolution is an historical process. Second, it brings about a radical change of society. That is, society is completely transformed. Third, one ruling class is displace by another ruling class. Fourth, revolution releases the productive forces from the grip of few persons. Finally, socially progressive potentialities are utilised for the welfare of the whole society.

Normally non-Marxist thinkers do not make any distinction between revolution and counter-revolution. Aptheker holds a different view. While the objective of revolution is radical change of society the purpose of the latter is to frustrate that attempt. Aptheker writes (p. 66), "any definition that would call both the victory of George Washington and the victory of Francisco Franco by the same name is bound to confuse more than define." Marx and his followers view revolution completely from different background. Revolution does not mean mere change of government. In normal sense, revolution means one class or party comes to power replacing another class or party. The economic foundation or base of the society remains unaffected. Few changes here and there in the superstructure take place. Marxists do not call it revolution. The chief purpose of revolution in Marxian sense is to attack the economic base of capitalist society. After that it will attack the superstructure. Economic, social and cultural changes occur as a result of revolution.

Inevitability of Revolution

With the growth of capitalism the power, influence, wealth etc. of the bourgeoisie have increased enormously. On the contrary, the proletarians have sunk into deeper pauperism, their conditions have become more and more miserable. Marx and Engels say in the *Manifesto* (p. 69) that the bourgeoisie is unfit to be the ruling class in the society and to impose its conditions of existence upon society as an over-riding law. It is unfit to rule because it is incompetent to assure an existence to its slave within his slavery, because it cannot help letting him sink into such a state. Society cannot live under this bourgeoisie, in other words, its existence is no longer compatible with society.

The rapid development of modern industry produces wealth on the one hand and on the other innumerable contradictions and crises. Capitalists adopt various curative measures to get rid of the crises, but they do not prove their effectiveness. The crises and contradictions multiply and aggravate day after day and irreconcil-ability also mounts. They ultimately explode, forcing the proletarians to revolt. Marx and Engels have said in the *Manifesto,* "Modern Industry cuts from under its feet the very foundation on which the bourgeoisie produces and appropriates products. What the bourgeoisie produces above all is its own grave-diggers. Its fall and the victory of the proletariat are equally inevitable" (p. 70).

The authors of the *Manifesto* have said that the proletarians must utilise the social conflicts so that these lead to an open revolution. The violent overthrow of the bourgeoisie will lay the foundation for the rule of the proletariat. So it is the inherent social conflicts of capitalism which will lead to the revolution. By using the conflicts the proletarians will precipitate the revolutions.

Marx and Engels have emphasised in their various works that the transfer of power from the hands of one group of persons to those of another group in a peaceful way cannot be regarded as revolution because it does not make way for radical changes of society and the emancipation of working class from capitalist exploitation. They have further said the proletariat cannot raise itself up without the whole superincumbent structure of official being sprung into air. The parliamen-tary means of solving workers' problems were despised by Marx. He called them "parliamentary cretinism". Moreover, it would not be a weapon for the proletariat, but a trap.

Pointing out the ineffectiveness of parliamentary system and inevitability of revolution Lenin once said this was "historically obsolete". The parliamentary system simply allows people to decide every few years which member of the ruling class was to repress and crush people through parliament. Peaceful and reformist transition to socialism is not merely philistine stupidity but also downright deception of the workers. Only the forcible overthrow of the bourgeoisie and the destruction of the entire bourgeois state can ensure emancipation. So it is not compromise between revolution and reformism, and parliamentary system and proletarians' class struggle.

In *Capital* (Vol. I, p. 762) Marx writes that the process of transformation has sufficiently decomposed the old society from top to bottom. New forces are emerging, labourers are turned into proletarians, the development of the capitalist mode of production has reached a maximum point after which there is no scope of expansion. Under such circumstances the whole society waits for a change. That is, the revolution is inevitable. In *The German Ideology* we find Marx and Engels saying both for the production on a mass scale and for the success of the cause itself, the alteration of men in mass scale is necessary, an alternation which can take place in a practical movement, a *revolution*, this revolution is necessary, not only because the ruling class cannot be overthrown in any other way, but also because the class overthrowing it can only in a revolution succeed in ridding itself of all muck of ages and become fit to found society anew.

Types of Revolution

From the study of history through the application of dialectic Marx and Engels were convinced that only one revolution was not enough for the formation of a communist society. A number of revolutions were required. When the relations of production appear to be incompatible with the existing forces of production a change becomes inevitable. When the change comes in a violent way or form, sometimes it is called revolution. One such revolution is bourgeois revolution. It is a way of transformation from the feudal to the capitalist socio-economic formation. To put it in other words, in feudal society there arose a bitter class struggle between the feudal lords or aristocrats on the one hand and the bourgeoisie or capitalists on the other hand.

The radical changes that take place within the feudal society are the objective prerequisites of the bourgeois revolution. The bourgeoisie, by increasing production, harvests larger amount of profit and to ensure the continuous flow of profit the bourgeoisie tends to control the political power. The power is used by the bourgeoisie as an effective weapon. Talking about bourgeois revolution Marx writes "Bourgeois revolutions storm swiftly from success to success, their dramatic effects outdo each other, men and things seem set in sparkling brilliance."

The French Revolution of 1789-94 was a classical bourgeois revolution in the forms of struggle, the scope of events and degree of participation by the working class. The French Revolution was the result and expression of the powerful popular anti-exploiter movements. That is why the big bourgeoisie, which came to power, was eager to clamp down on the masses after the first onslaught of the revolution. The urge was expressed in the declaration of *Right of Man and Citizen* (1789), which proclaimed equality for all people, but sanctified the right of property. The dictatorship of the Jacobins, the most revolutionary representatives of the bourgeoisie, was the pinnacle of revolution. The French Revolution could not satisfy the demands of the poor people nor was it able to do away with the division of society into rich and poor.

Before the publication of the *Manifesto* Marx seriously studied the various aspects of the French Revolution and this enabled him to form the following opinion—the

Revolution was purely a political one because there was a change of hands of political persons. It ended the rule of autocracy, but the bourgeoisie filled up the vacuum. The French Revolution could not emancipate the workers and peasants, only a socialist revolution can achieve the objective. In the *Eighteenth Brumaire* Marx observes that though the French Revolution was a political one subsequent revolutions would be socialist. *A political or bourgeois revolution ends in transfer of power, but a socialist revolution aims at radical change in the ownership of the forces of production and relations of production.*

Sources of Revolution

We have briefly analysed the types or forms. It is now necessary to throw light on various sources of revolution. According to Marx the conflict or contradiction is the main source of revolution. We shall here quote a portion of the famous passage in the *Preface to the Critique of Political Economy* : "At a certain stage of their development, the material productive forces of society come in conflict with the existing relations of production...with the property relations within which they have been at work hitherto. From forms of development of the productive forces these relations turn into their fetters. Then begins an epoch of social revolution." We, therefore, see that the contradiction between the forces of production and relations of production is the prime factors of revolution. In every capitalist society this contradiction is permanently and spectacularly found. This antagonism is irreconcilable and there a revolution is inevitable. The contradiction will end in social revolution. That is the prophecy of Marx. In *Capital* (Vol. I, p. 488) Marx writes, "the historical development of the antagonisms, immanent in a given form of production, is the only way in which that form of production can be dissolved and a new form established."

The contradiction, according to Marx, has two-fold effects. One limits the efficacy of the ruling class and the other raises the consciousness and organising capacity of the proletarians. How does the contradiction lead to revolution? In *Capital* (Vol. III) Marx has elaborated the issue. With the accumulation of capital both the exploitation and misery of the workers grow more and more. Sometimes some of the workers are paid high wages. But that does not help the alleviation of misery. The workers are also dehumanised, they become part of the machine. But the mere appearance of contradiction cannot create a revolutionary situation. Marx has cautioned us on this point. The antagonisms must reach the stage of maturity and this is possible only in developed capitalism.

In *Class Struggle in France* and other writings Marx has said that revolution is not a readymade thing which the workers will get on demand. Let us quote him "The working class did not expect miracles from the commune. They have no readymade utopias to introduce *par decret due people.* They know that in order to work out their own emancipation, and along with it that higher form to which present society is irresistibly tending by its own economical agencies, they will have to pass through long struggles, through a series of historic processes, transformation circumstances and men" (*MESW*, Vol. I, p. 523). Proper consciousness creates an atmosphere conducive to revolution. Consciousness about what? Consciousness about their position, about the utility of struggle. The Marxists hold that in this arena there is an important role of ideology to play. It makes people conscious to know the nature of antagonism.

In a mature capitalist system there shall exist contradiction and the workers are quite aware of it. But the awareness is not sufficient for revolution. This consciousness must inspire them to fight for their emancipation. However, the existence of contradiction and sufficient consciousness are essential elements of revolution. In the words of Aptheker, "The relationship between the two elements of the contradiction is dialectical" (p. 69). Here the two elements of contradiction are—it manifests the decay of efficiency of ruling class, and strength of consciousness.

The Marxists are of opinion that a revolutionary situation is an objective condition of revolution. It means the material condition of society must be quite ripe for a revolution. Only a revolutionary situation encourages workers to throw the severest onslaught against the bourgeoisie. Side-by-side a subjective condition also hastens the revolution. A critic observes, "A revolutionary situation merely creates the possibility of a victorious revolution. But to turn this possibility into a reality the subjective factor too must be ripe." People must be mentally prepared to make any sacrifice for the success of revolution.

"Revolution in Permanence"

Marx was more or less sanguine about the success of revolution, because it is inevitable. The proletarians are determined to change their economic lot. The contradictions make them conscious. Again, the revolution is a historical process. But how much time a revolution will take for its success that is undecided. That is, time factor remains beyond Marx's analysis. However, he is sure that a single revolution cannot put the crown of success over the heads of the workers. They will have to wait for a pretty long time. Marx's *Address to the Communist League* deals the question of permanent revolution.

In the *Manifesto*, Marx and Engels wrote, "The bourgeois revolution in Germany will be but the prelude to an immediately following proletarian revolution." This remark makes it clear that the proletarians must be prepared for a number of revolutions. The final stage of all revolutions is the proletarian revolution. In the *Address*, Marx advocates this idea of permanent revolution while the democratic petty bourgeois wish to bring the revolution to a conclusion as quick as possible, and with achievement of the demands, it is our interest and our task to make the revolution permanent, until all more or less possessing classes have been forced out of their position of dominance, until the proletariat has conquered the state power, and the associations of proletarians, not only in one country but in all the dominant countries of the world, has advanced so far that competition among the proletarians of these countries has ceased... For us the issue cannot be the alternation of private property but only its annihilation, not the smothering over of class antagonisms but the abolition of classes, not the improvement of existing society but the foundation of a new one." (*S.W.I.*, p. 110). Here Marx and Engels have given a long list of the objectives to be achieved by the proletarians through the continuous struggle against the capitalists. Marx and Engels have categorically pointed out the task of the workers is to make the revolution permanent. Within stipulated time this cannot be achieved.

For a different reason Marx and Engels wanted to make revolution permanent. During proletarian struggle and even after the establishment of proletarians' supremacy the petty bourgeois and reactionary elements of society may temporarily be hesitant, undecided and inactive. Any leniency or inactivity on the part of the workers will rejuvenate them. The reactionary elements will always raise a hue and cry about the excesses of revolution and try to divert people's enthusiasm to revolution.

Speaking of the permanent revolution in the *Address* Marx and Engels have further observed that the workers will not be the victims of the intoxication of power. There will always be possibility of the revival of reactionary elements and vested interests. The proletarians will continue their fight against them. The mistrust must be directed to them as well as to their previous allies. Marx has elsewhere said, "We tell the workers; you have to endure and go through 15, 20, 50 years to civil war in order to change the circumstances, in order to make yourself fit for power." One thing is to be noted here. *Raison d' etre* of proletarian revolution is to change radically the physical environment of society conducive to the attainment of socialism. Again, through the continuous revolution proletarians will prepare themselves so that they can exercise political power in the proper manner. Through the uninterrupted revolutionary process the proletarians will remove all doubts and apprehensions from people's minds and annihilate or check the counter-revolutionary forces. The last sentence of the *Address* is "Their battle cry must be : The Revolution in Permanence."

SOCIALIST REVOLUTION

Meaning and Essence of Socialist Revolution

Cornforth writes (p. 195), "The principal conclusion of the materialist theory of the laws of social development is that of the historical necessity of the socialist revolution." So it is historical necessity that the socialist revolution will appear at a definite stage of social progress. We have already discussed the inevitability of revolution. It is generally maintained that the socialist revolution is the most radical social revolution in the history of class society, a mode of transition from the capitalist socio-economic foundation to the communist foundation. The socialist revolution is, therefore, a great leap forward from capitalism to socialism. It is also a qualitative leap. The meaning of these two adjectives is that socialism in all respects is different from capitalism. The society as a result of socialist revolution changes and changes qualitatively. Moreover, these qualitative changes are decisive. Some Marxists call the socialist revolution a gigantic leap. It surpasses all past record of social changes. It does not envisage a simple change of political power. The whole state machinery is overhauled.

Socialist Revolution and Previous Revolutions

Marx's concept of revolution is completely different from the bourgeois revolution. The latter aims at the change of government while both the base and superstructure remain unchanged. Marxian revolution envisages a radical change of society. In *The German Ideology* Marx and Engels have said : "In all previous revolutions the mode of activity always remained unchanged and it was only a question of different distribution of this activity, a new distribution of labour to other persons, while communist revolution is directed against the hitherto existing mode of activity, does away with labour and abolishes the rule of all classes with the classes themselves, because it is carried through the class which no longer counts as a class in society, is not recognised as a class, and is in itself the expression of the dissolution of all classes, nationalities etc. within present society" (p. 60).

Marx and Engels have called the non-socialist revolutions or bourgeois revolutions as the revolutions of minorities. These were conducted by the capitalists or other petty bourgeois groups with the sole purpose of achieving limited and class objectives. The workers or peasants never participated in all these revolutions. A minority revolution cannot bring about general welfare of the society and in that sense the early or previous revolutions were always incomplete.

The pertinent question which may be raised at this stage of analysis is why did not the proletarians participate in revolutions? Marx's answer is they were not organised and prepared for a revolution. For that reason the bourgeois revolutions of earlier epochs achieved success. The workers were divided and the necessity of a revolution was not fully realised by them. Moreover, the bourgeoisie controlled both the base and superstructure and used the media for the propagation of their own ideology. The proletarians were deprived of it. It was also a factor of the success. Above all, the state as an instrument of exploitation was always in favour of the bourgeoisie.

Engels wrote a long *Introduction* for *Marx's Class Struggle in France* just before his death, i.e., in 1895. This *Introduction* is important for several reasons. A part of the *Introduction* deals with the nature of bourgeois revolution. Engels wrote, "All revolutions up to present day have resulted in the displacement of one definite class rule by another, but all ruling classes up to now have been only minorities in relation to the ruled class. One ruling minority was thus overthrown; another minority seized the helm of state in its stead and refashioned the state institutions to suit its own interests."

Lenin was also quite aware of the difference between bourgeois revolution and socialist revolution. According to Lenin, one of the fundamental differences between bourgeoisie revolution and socialist revolution is that, for the bourgeois revolution, which arises out of feudalism, the new economic organisations are gradually created in the womb of the old order, gradually changing all the aspects of society. The bourgeois revolution faced only one task—to sweep away, to cast aside, to destroy all fetters of preceding social order. The socialist revolution, according to Lenin, is quite different. The task of the socialist revolution is to set up new organisations and organisational relationships. It must perform certain complicated positive or constructive work for setting up of a new society. Since socialist revolution does not aim at a simple change of government, its actions are far-reaching. It has to face the resistance from reactionary elements and counter-revolutionary force. Analysing from this angle Lenin had said that all the previous bourgeois revolutions were very easy. The feudal lords or nobles were in decaying conditions. They had not enough capacity to resist the attack of the bourgeoisie or to check its growth. On the contrary, the position of the proletariat is different. The fight of the proletarians is a fight against the bourgeoisie, against the state which is an ally of the bourgeoisie and all other allies. At a single revolution all these cannot be annihilated. Revolution, that is why, is permanent.

There are also other differences. For example, when the bourgeois revolution began to emerge there was a feudal society; but in the womb of that society there arose a powerful capitalism with all its potentialities. So the bourgeoisie got a ready-made form prior to revolution. On the contrary, the socialist revolution started its task with a clean slate. The superstructure was under the domination of the capitalists. So a favourable condition for socialists revolution was either absent or almost absent.

Still another difference is that the purpose of the previous revolutions was never to destroy the antagonistic class relations, but simply the replacement of one class by another. Whereas the socialist revolution proceeds with the avowed purpose to destroy all class antagonisms and the exploiters. The old state machinery is not completely smashed, it is kept temporarily and subsequently it is replaced by a new one and, finally, the state withers away. Here is an important aspect of difference. After every bourgeois revolution the state becomes more and more powerful, the socialist revolution makes its annihilation precipitated. But it takes time. For this reason the socialist revolution is permanent, the bourgeois revolution is temporary.

Socialist Revolution and Development

It has been observed by Sheptulin (p. 399) that a socialist revolution does not limit itself of the destruction of the old, historically outdated order, its mission is to create new forms of property and new production relations that could not arise within the old society based on private property. Hence the destruction and construction both are simultaneously performed by the socialist revolution. This construction is of a new or better society. Socialist revolution signifies a new social order where there shall be no classes and class antagonisms. Unlike preceding revolution, the socialist revolution does not view itself as being the last. It envisages dynamism and change—change towards better and better society or social system.

As a first step towards better society or developed social order, the socialist revolution proceeds assertively to destroy elitism and all its manifestations. In every capitalist society few elites rule the nation and control the economy in the name of the majority. The socialist revolution's first attack falls upon the elites. They are dislodged from power. The adherents of socialist revolution deny that few have the exceptional ability which the majority claim. Aptheker says (p. 108), "this denial of elitism will apply also to varying endowments of talents or capacity."

The post-revolutionary society is opposed to elitism as well as racism. Racist tendencies, ideologies and activities have no place in a society created by revolution. Racism is outlawed in all socialist societies. Revolution does not recognise groups based on race. Socialist revolution abolishes all classes and groups. There shall be only one class in a socialist society and that is the proletariat. Racist groups are outlawed. The protagonists of socialist revolution say that racist feeling is a product of capitalism. Capitalism in the name of democracy also creates small national groups. The ulterior motive of capitalism is to divide society into small groups and to encourage the in-fighting. Lack of consolidation and strength enables the capitalists to harvest benefit. The golden rule of capitalist society is divide and rule. Developed society created by socialist revolution does away with the so-called golden rule. It is a better society based on the principles of brotherhood, goodwill and co-operation. Spontaneity dominates everything.

The better society—a product of socialist revolution—is full of promises. It has released all the productive forces from the grip of capitalists. Larger amount of goods and commodities flood the society. Scarcity and poverty are banished. In capitalism profit motive always worked behind the production of commodities. Welfare of the people was scantily treated. In capitalism there was always an apprehension about the availability of necessary articles. The better society removes that apprehension root and branch.

Aptheker says (p. 109) : "The socialist revolution has torn from the grasp of imperialism large area of the "backward" world and has in a matter of few decades transformed them into remarkably productive areas, challenging the advanced capitalist nations for productive supremacy."

Frequent crises and contradictions are the characteristic features of capitalism. Socialist revolution removes all these contradictions and crises and ensures an uninterrupted growth of economy. It also frees society from fear of war. The capitalists select war as the only way of setting disputes. War, in fact, is inevitable in capitalist system. For the sale of commodities the capitalists subjugate foreign territories and this creates attrition between the capitalist countries. The war, therefore, is a natural consequence. Socialist revolution—by abolishing classes and class antagonisms—draws a final curtain over colonialism and also on war. Along with the possibility of a war-free society the wastage of scarce resources—resulting from unhealthy competition—is stopped. People's consciousness about the destructive society, with consequences of war, reaches a highmark. "In place of old bourgeois, its classes and class antagonisms, we shall have an association in which the free development of each is the condition for the free development of all"—say Marx and Engels in the *Manifesto* (p. 88).

37 DICTATORSHIP OF THE PROLETARIAT

What is Meant by Proletariat?

The dictatorship of the proletariat constitutes practically a major part of Marxian philosophy. In his famous letter to Weydemeyer (March 5, 1852) Marx wrote : "What I did that was new was to prove (1) that the existence of classes is only bound up with the particular historical phases in the development of production, (2) that the class struggle necessarily leads to the dictatorship of the proletariat." It is, therefore, not enough to admit that there exists class struggle. A true Marxist must also admit that the class struggle ends in establishing the dictatorship of the proletariat. The purpose of every struggle between the classes and of any revolution is to overthrow the bourgeoisie from power and to fill up the vacuum by the proletarians' own supremacy. Since the term proletariat occupies a very significant place in Marxian philosophy it is imperative on our part to know who is proletariat?

The term proletariat has its origin in Rome. When the Roman state was at the pinnacle of its power and glory, its citizens were chiefly divided into two classes—owners and non-owners of property. The owners paid direct taxes to the state, whereas the non-owners had not the capacity in financial term to pay taxes. They gave the state their children. In Latin, children or offspring mean *"proles"*. "Proletarians", writes Ryazanoff, "constituted that class of citizens who owned nothing but the arms of their body and the children of their loins" (p. 236).

The proletarians of ancient Rome had nothing but their own children to offer. From this the modern term is derived. Today we mean by proletarian a man who has nothing but his labour power to sell. He is not the owner of any means of production. The proletarian of ancient Rome had neither freedom nor education. The proletarians were the hopeless fellows of Roman society. But the proletarians of our society are in a better position. Bourgeois system provides for them an education with which they can fight against the injustice. In the background of this analysis we can define proletarian.

D. Ryazanoff, the celebrated interpreter of *Manifesto*, offers us the following definition of proletariat : "The proletariat is that class of society whose means of livelihood entirely depends on the sale of its labour, and not on the profits derived from capital whose weal and woe, whose life and death, whose whole existence depend on the demand for labour, depend on the alterations of good times and bad, on the fluctuations which are the outcome of unbridled competition. The proletariat or class of proletarians, is, in a word, the working class of the nineteenth century" (p. 261). Proletarians, poor people, or working classes, do not mean the same thing. In the history of the development of capitalism the term proletarian has a special significance and meaning. However, the definition given by Ryazanoff is treated by both Marxists and non-Marxists as more or less standard.

Rise of Proletariat

The Industrial Revolution in England took place in the second half of the eighteenth century and the proletariat class can reasonably be called the product of this Revolution. Before the industrialisation there were poor people, but they were different from the modern proletariat. The series of scientific and technological discoveries rendered the age-old tools and machines irrelevant for an industrialised society of Europe. The introduction of new machines threw the users from jobs which made them unemployed. Again, since the installation of these machines required a fabulous amount of capital, only the wealthy persons could lay out the new machines. The other side of the picture was that the workers had no access to means of production. The invention of machinery handed over industry to the great capitalists. The society was automatically divided into two broad groups—one was the owner of the means of production and the other was the worker who had labour to sell.

The rapid progress of industrialisation was the primary cause of the rise of proletariat as a separate class. The number of proletarians swelled day after day due to the impact of rapid industrialisation. The manufacturing industry developed, peasants and workers of the rural area flocked to the city in search of new jobs because they had already lost jobs in rural areas. They had only their labour-power for sale. The expansion of the labour market threw the workers into keen competition among themselves, which was fully exploited by the capitalists. They paid minimum wage. The proletarians are different from peasants in the sense that the latter were owners of certain amount of means of production while the former were not.

Nature of Proletariat as a Class

In *The Eighteenth Brumaire of Louis Bonaparte* Marx said, "The Roman proletariat lived at the expense of society, whereas modern society lives at the expense of the proletariat." The only recognition of a modern proletarian is he sells his labour-power to the capitalist and, in exchange of that he gets a certain amount of money which is called wage. But this wage is insufficient for his livelihood. The capitalists earn profit from the sale of commodities produced by the proletarians. The whole structure of capitalist society stands on this unearned income or surplus value. To put it in other words, the proletariat is the producer of surplus value.

Marx, in several of his works, mentions the proletariat as a *universal class*. Scholars hold the view that Marx, of course, is not the inventor of the term. Analysing the nature of bureaucracy and also its role the German philosopher Hegel used the phrase universal class. To Hegel bureaucracy was the universal class. But Marx does not recognise it as a universal class. To him, proletariat is really a universal class. He analyses the universal class in the background of dialectics. In the process of social development there emerges at different stages new classes. The new generation welcomes this new class.

Marx says that at a particular stage of social development a particular class may be the universal class. But in the next stage that class may not be entitled to that status. In Hegel's time bureaucracy was the universal class. But the development of capitalism completely changed the economic and political scene of society. The bureaucracy is no longer a dominant or universal class. That place, according to Marx, has been occupied by the proletariat. He further says that throughout history the process of rise and decline of classes continues.

In *Introduction to the Critique of Hegel's Philosophy of Right* Marx has elaborately dealt with the concept of the universal class. Here he has said that, that class is to be called universal which represents the entire society and imbues it with new ideas and imagination. It must have definite objectives and look after the interests of the whole society. It must demonstrate the ways how to emancipate the society from the evils and, if necessary, it shall fight for the general welfare of the people. In The *German Ideology* Marx said that while a class is fighting or revolting, it is not doing that as a class, but as a representative of the society. In the words of Avineri "only because he sees in the proletariat, the contemporary and final, realisation of universality, does Marx endow the proletariat with a historical significance and mission." It is here to be noted that Marx's conception of proletariat is all-embracing.

Dictatorship of Proletriat Defined

In the *Critique of the Gotha Programme* Marx and Engels have made the following observation : "Between the capitalist and communist society lies the period of revolutionary transformation of the one into the other. There corresponds to this also a political transition period in which the state can be nothing but the revolutionary dictatorship of the proletariat." The establishment of the dictatorship of the proletariat is the *leitmotif* of the working class and this ambitious goal is achieved through a protracted revolution or a series of revolutions. Like many other concepts the dictatorship of the proletariat remains unexplained in the vast literature of Marx and Engels. However, the deficiency has been fully compensated by Lenin. He has explained the concept in several of his works, specifically in *State and Revolution*. Lenin's explanation covers all the aspects of the concept which Marx and Engels thought.

Generally, the concept means that *it is power in the hands of the working people for building up of a socialist society.* In the *State and Revolution* Lenin says : "the dictatorship of the proletariat is the rule unrestricted by law and based on force of the proletariat over the bourgeoisie, a rule enjoying the sympathy and support of the labouring and exploited masses." *When the proletarians are organised into a class and establish their supremacy over the bourgeoisie and the purpose of this is to emancipate the workers then that can be termed dictatorship of the proletariat.*

Elsewhere Lenin defines it in the following words : "If we translate this Latin scientific historical philosophical term dictatorship of the proletariat into a more simple language it means—only a definite class, namely that of the urban and industrial workers in general, is able to lead the whole mass of the toilers and exploited in the struggle for overthrow of the yoke of capital, in the process of the overthrow, in the struggle to maintain and consolidate the victory, in the work of creating the new socialist social system, in the whole struggle for the complete abolition of classes."

The dictatorship of the proletariat, according to Lenin, is a specific form of class alliance between the proletariat—the vanguard of the working class—and the numerous non-proletarians strata of the working people, on the majority of these strata an alliance for the final establishment and consolidation of socialism. So we can hold that *dictatorship of the proletariat is a specific form of rule and the dictatorship is an instrument for the attainment and consolidation of communism or socialism.* Proletarians use their dictatorial power for the suppression of the bourgeoisie as well as to destroy the citadel of power built up by the capitalists in collaboration with the state authority. The suppression of bourgeoisie and destruction of state power both are essential preconditions of the emancipation of proletarians.

The dictatorship of the proletariat used by Marx, Engels, Lenin and Stalin cannot be confused with the bourgeois or liberal meaning of the term. The bourgeois theoreticians use dictatorship to mean the rule of particular persons or party over the rest of the society. In other words, it is a rule and oppression of minority over the majority. In Marxian terminology the term means a form of government of the majority established to crush the capitalist rule and oppression. The dictatorship of the proletariat has a special meaning in Marxism. Through the establishment of the dictatorship of proletariat the advent of communism will be very easy. The proletarians may be allowed to exercise dictatorial power, but it is a temporary phenomenon. Once counter-revolutionary forces are destroyed and the state comes under the full control of the proletariat the meaning and significance of dictatorship will tend to evaporate. Dictatorship of the proletariat is a definite form of government.

Some critics of the dictatorship of the proletariat hold the view that whether the proletariat will set up dictatorship rule or not shall be decided by vote. Lenin was against all sorts of parliamentary tactics or methods. He says that the supporters of this view forget that voting system, parliamentary tactics, universal suffrage are all bourgeois policies and have thrived in bourgeois system. They are beyond the bounds of proletarians. Naturally, laying confidence on these policies will inevitably mislead the working class. Proletarians will have to set up their supremacy only through revolution.

Essentiality and Inevitability

Marx, Engels and Lenin in their various writings have dealt with the major aspects of the concept and this treatment reveals that dictatorship of proletariat is both essential and inevitable. Marx and Engels were convinced that the bourgeois state—an instrument of exploitation—could not be amended, but, at any cost, be destroyed. The emancipation of the proletarians is impossible so long the bourgeois state continues to exist and exercises its power over the proletariat. The bourgeois state machinery has to be broken, and smashed from top to bottom. To achieve this lofty ideal a gigantic machinery or institution must be created. This implies the essentiality of the dictatorship of the proletariat.

The whole theme is to be analysed still from a different angle. Bourgeois states are most varied. That is, the forms of government, administrative systems and judiciary are varied and many. But in one respect they are one : all bourgeois states are instruments of exploitation, and every bourgeois state is the dictatorship of the bourgeoisie. The logical conclusion, therefore, is proletarians require dictatorship or dictatorial power to smash the dictatorship of the bourgeoisie. Without dictatorial power the proletarians cannot destroy the bourgeois state and the remnants of bourgeoisie after the establishment of the first phase of communism.

The bourgeois freedom is the freedom of a minority, freedom of the elites. The great majority of the masses is deprived of the values and fruits of democracy. This is to be reversed and, for that, the proletarians must have sweeping power in every sphere of society. The abolition of capitalism gives real freedom and democracy to all. Simultaneously, the bourgeois system of private ownership of property is to be destroyed. Socialism and private property cannot co-exist. All the sources of production and the methods of distribution of these products shall be placed at the disposal of the whole society. Marx and Engels, out of their own experience and from the study of history, have come to the conclusion that sporadic attempts and lukewarm behaviour and lackadaisical efforts cannot fulfil the ambition.

As to the inevitability of dictatorship of the proletariat we can here refer to the letter written by Engels to Eduard Bernstein on 24th March 1884. The proletariat needs democratic forms of the seizure of political power. But if democracy is wanted as an *end* it is necessary to rely on the peasantry and petty bourgeoisie, i.e., on classes that are in the process of dissolution and reactionary in relation to the proletariat when they try to maintain themselves artificially. So with the help of petty bourgeois or peasantry democracy and freedom cannot be established. The proletarians must prepare themselves in all the ways to set up freedom and democracy and attain supremacy.

An Instrument of Revolution

Stalin has explained the dictatorship of proletariat in the following way. He has said that it is an instrument of proletarian revolution. Stalin observes that the question of the proletarian dictatorship is, above all, a question of the main content of the proletarian revolution. The purpose of the revolution is to set up a classless society and without a proletarian revolution this can never be achieved. The only means is political domination of the proletariat. Engels stated this unambiguously in a speech made at the London conference of the International Workingmen's Association in September 1871. Proletarians' revolution is the supreme political act and it has no alternative.

Echoing Engels's view, Stalin has said that it is the most important mainstay brought into being for the purpose of overthrowing exploiters. The dictatorship of the proletariat will launch a revolution for achieving socialism and the revolution will continue for its completion. The revolution can defeat the bourgeoisie, can overthrow its power, even without the dictatorship of the proletariat. But the revolution will be unable to crush the resistance of the bourgeoisie to maintain its victory and to push forward to the final victory of socialism unless it creates a special organ in the form of dictatorship of the proletariat as its principal mainstary (Stalin, *Problems of Leninism,* page 46).

Task of the Dictatorship of the Proletariat

In our definition we have noted that dictatorship of the proletariat is proletarians' rule coupled with force over the bourgeoisie. From this definition it is quite manifest that dictatorship of the proletariat cannot be assumed as a change of government, or a change of personalities. It is a change of the whole state—it is a new state, it is a state of the proletariat. It arises not on the basis of bourgeois order or to safeguard the bourgeois interests, but to rule over the bourgeoisie and to destroy gradually all the vestiges of bourgeois rule and economy. So one of the most important tasks of the dictatorship of the proletariat is to overthrow the bourgeoisie and to finalise the process of expropriation of the landlords and capitalists through the socialisation of principal instruments of production.

Another important function of dictatorship of the proletariat is to fight violently the reactionary and counter-revolutionary forces. Even after the revolution the bourgeoisie continues to gain and consolidate power and makes alliances with other counter-revolutionary forces. This is dangerous for proletarians' dictatorial power. By destroying all the remnants of bourgeois rule the proletarians must clear the deck for socialism. For building up a better society the proletarians will have to start afresh. They will get nothing readymade.

The dictatorship of the proletariat is both a form of government and an instrument of rule or administration. Capture of power or establishing ownership over the means of production cannot immediately bring success for the proletarians. The bourgeois superstructure is first to be destroyed and then to be rebuilt. New cultural and social organisations are to be created for the all-round development of the proletarians. A new superstructure is to be constructed in order to correspond it to the new economic base. Dictatorship will emphasise on the cultural and educational aspects of the proletarians.

The dictatorship of the proletariat has a responsibility in the international field. The revolution in one country is not enough. All the proletarians of all the countries of the world must be brought under one umbrella. The exploited masses of the world are to be united under the leadership of the dictatorship of the proletariat and their efforts for emancipation will be consolidated in a formidable manner. The dictatorship of the proletariat will always support people's struggle for emancipation and, if necessary, will help both materially, intellectually and psychologically. The *leit-motif* of the dictatorship of the proletariat is first to disintegrate both capitalism—and its highest form imperialism—and then to precipitate their destruction.

PROLETARIAN DEMOCRACY

Bourgeois Democracy

In order to understand the nature of proletarian democracy it is essential to know what is bourgeois democracy. Lenin with his great insight and acumen has scanned the nature of both bourgeois and proletarian democracies. According to Lenin and many other Marxists the bourgeois democracy is based on the principle of inequality in all its manifestations. Particularly, the bourgeois theoreticians emphasise the political nature of democracy. Economic oppression and inequality are, for them, quite immaterial. As a result of this deep-rooted notion in capitalist society we have a democracy that is curtailed, wretched, false, a democracy only for the rich, for the minority" (*LSW*-II, 374). Bourgeois democracy is the democracy for an insignificant minority. The nature of capitalist democracy, in Lenin's view (Ibid, p. 372), is there an emphasis on the details of universal suffrage, techniques and functioning of representative institutions and glorification of people's political rights. The bourgeoisie resorts to intensive propaganda in favour of this type of democracy forgetting that without an emancipation from economic bondage the political nature of democracy is simply a farce. Only dictatorship of the proletariat can fulfil the aspirations of the working class.

Marx on Proletarian Democracy

Marx grasped the essence of capitalist democracy splendidly and that is why he attacked this with all his vigour. In the *Manifesto* we read the following words—The first step in the revolution by the working class is to raise the proletariat to the position of ruling class, to win the battle of democracy (p. 85). The most important task of the proletariat is to capture power and then to free democracy from the grip of bourgeoisie. According to Marx, democracy will get full scope to thrive only in the atmosphere created by the dictatorship of the proletariat.

The proletarian democracy is the real democracy, it is the democracy of the majority, it is the democracy for the free and full development of all. Elaborating the Marxian concept of proletarian and bourgeois democracy Lenin has said that the bourgeoisie confined democracy within the elites or insignificant minority. Bourgeois democracy is the democracy for the rich. But real democracy is that which reaches the door of all, inspires all, and where there is no oppression and exploitation. All these ideals are realised only in a proletarian democracy. Democracy undergoes tremendous changes during the transition period from capitalism to communism. Proletarian democracy oppresses the oppressors and exploiters. The proletarians must suppress the oppressors in order to free humanity from wage slavery. The resistance built up by the bourgeoisie must be crushed. In the words of Lenin (*LSW*-II, 373) "it is clear that where there is suppression, where there is violence, there is no freedom and no democracy."

Marx and Engels were over-confident that only the dictatorship of the proletariat could defeat the reactionary and counter-revolutionary forces of the state, and then only could real democracy appear. In *State and Revolution* Lenin has said that the gigantic power of the capitalists can only be defeated by the proletarians. Through revolution the proletarians will expand the sphere of democracy. Marx, Engels and Lenin have held that the proletarians must do this. Democracy is an instrument of struggle for emancipation. Democracy will go on working until communism is achieved.

The capitalists use the state to protect their democracy, that is, the democracy of the minority. After overthrowing the bourgeoisie from power the proletarians will use the same state to protect proletarian democracy. That is why, at the first phase of socialism, workers will never try to demolish the bourgeois state. Thus, at the hands of the proletarians, the character of the state will be quite different. The proletarian state and proletarian, democracy will ensure the development of all. The dictatorship of the proletariat will hand over power, administration and the entire responsibility of the state to the proletarians. This process, attaining maturity, will reduce the importance of the bourgeois state and ultimately the state will tend to wither away. Lenin wrote (*S.W.* II, 384) "The more complete the democracy, the nearer the moment approaches when it becomes unnecessary. The more democratic the "state" which consists of the armed workers, and which is no longer a state in the proper sense of the word, the more rapidly the every form of state begins to wither away." What has been emphasised here is that the state (in the bourgeois sense of course) and real democracy are arch-enemies. Both cannot coexist. In other words, there is an antagonistic relationship between state and democracy. In the dictatorship of the proletariat there will be state, but this state will be different from the bourgeois state which means that the proletarian state will lose its character as an instrument of exploitation. The existence of the state in proletarian democracy will be a temporary phenomenon. The development of democracy will make the state redundant.

Lenin has said that the proletarian democracy and the dictatorship of the proletariat are synonymous. They are the two sides of the same medal. It is unimaginable that there is dictatorship of the proletariat and, at the same time, there is no democracy. That is why democracy finds the fullest development only in the dictatorship of the proletariat. Lenin has said that the opportunists and bourgeois theoreticians find contradiction between proletarian democracy and dictatorship of the proletariat.

Marx and Engels have categorically stated that the bourgeois democracy is not real democracy. It is the democracy of a minority. A particular class which is economically powerful controls both economics and politics for its own benefits as well as advantage. Proletarian democracy is not for few persons or class, it is the democracy of the whole society and of all persons. Proletarian revolution abolishes all classes and all other artificial divisions and that paves the way for fuller and perfect democracy. In the epoch of proletarian democracy the artificial distinctions made by the bourgeoisie between the rural and urban area is removed. All the political, social and cultural organisations are remodelled and reorganised to make them fit for building up socialism. All the people will be imbued to come under the banner of new construction of society. There will be no bar to national participation. Everybody will have freedom to work and express his own opinion on national and local issues. Proletarian democracy is called an integrated and united social system. Lenin has said that in order to make proletarian democracy universal the workers can form alliances with other small groups of persons and unorganised small manufacturers.

Proletarian democracy disdains the formal equality propagated and practised by bourgeois thinkers and politicians. The formal equality or the equality is only in the political arena while the forces of production are controlled by few. This is simply a farce. Proletarian democracy proceeds firmly to do away with this formal and farcical democracy and equality. By making the society—that is all members of society—the owners of the means of production, socialist revolution removes all inequalities and converts democracy into a real one. Formal equality will be converted into real equality or actual equality, i.e., to the operation of the rule "from each according to his ability, to each according to his needs."

An important aspect of proletarian democracy is democratic centralism. In capitalist system there is also a type of centralism, but that is bureaucratic centralism. Bureaucrats are completely alienated from the people and they enjoy supremacy in the decision-making process. Workers and peasants have no role to play in the making of decisions and administration of the state. Accountability—a recognised principle of democracy—is flatly bypassed or violated under bureaucratic centralism. In proletarian democracy there is centralism—that is, the whole administration of the state is run from a single centre. But there is a hierarchy. The decision-making process and administration is clearly divided into several stages and all the stages are connected with each other. One stage of administration is accountable to the other and in this way the concept of accountability has been raised to the level of utmost significance and meaningfulness. Democratic centralism of proletarian democracy opens the door for the participation of masses in all the spheres of state administration. This ultimately creates tremendous enthusiasm in the mind of the people.

In proletarian democracy there is no place of conspiracy and secrecy which is characteristic feature of bourgeois democracy. Marx and Engels have said in the *Manifesto* that the communists disdain secrecy and conspiracy. They do everything openly and declare their objectives publicly. People will participate in all the activities of the state—that is the *raison d' etre* of proletarian democracy. To deprive people from this fundamental right, in one way or other, is a great crime and also abnegation of democracy. *Proletarian democracy, therefore, enriches democracy's certain fundamental principles. It brings for the people a new hope, an ambitious future and promises a new way of life, a quite new type of society which was unimaginable by the bourgeoisie.*

Assessment

We have analysed various aspects of the dictatorship of the proletariat. We shall now make an objective assessment of the concept and its practical side. The revolutionary government in Russia under the leadership of Lenin in 1917, and the revolution was spearheaded by the Bolshevik Party. Only the urban workers took the leadership and played active role in the revolution. This raised a lot of suspicion in the minds of people. *It is alleged the peasants constituting the important section of proletariat had no role to play.* In December 1917 Lenin said that it could not be expected that the rural proletariat would be clearly and finally conscious of its own interests. Only the urban working class could be. The proletariat should become ruling class in the sense of being leader of all who work, it should be the ruling class politically. But this assertion of Lenin could not bring an end to the suspicion that the proletariat was not actually the ruling class.

Elsewhere Lenin admitted that not the proletariat but the Bolshevik Party was exercising dictatorial power, and he thought that there was no wrong in it. For several years the Bolshevik Party had been working for the workers and guiding them. It was their vanguard. The natural leadership of the workers fell upon the Party. So the dictatorship of party and the dictatorship of workers or proletariat were synonymous. This plea of Lenin is untenable. Because, under abnormal circumstances, the dictatorship of the party may be accepted temporarily. But this cannot be the permanent feature or solution. Proletarians should be the supreme authority. Miliband in his *Marxism and Politics* writes (p. 142), "the fact remained that the party had substituted itself for a ravaged and exhausted working class in a country gripped by civil war, foreign intervention and economic collapse." Whatever may be the reason the fact is that the Party—not the proletariat—exercises the dictatorial power. This is a clear departure from Marx's original concept of dictatorship of the proletariat.

Marcel Liebman, a renowned interpreter of Leninism, says (pages 348-356) that a lot of confusion has been generated by the term dictatorship of the proletariat. This is chiefly due to the fact that neither Marx, nor Engels not even Lenin have explained in unambiguous terms the concept. "The mechanisms and structures of such a dictatorship were never described" in details. Should the proletarians rule themselves? Should some other persons rule and proletarians will guide them? What would be the methods and tactics of the government? What would be the role of force in the dictatorship of the proletariat? All these questions remain unanswered.

Marx, Engels and Lenin generally refer to the Paris Commune. But this does not throw ample light on the vital questions raised by the critics. It is maintained that these questions are to be answered.

Kautsky believed that the proletariat as a class cannot govern. The parliamentary system should be revived. Retorting Kautsky's suggestion Lenin said "it is altogether wrong to say that a class cannot govern" and claimed that only a parliamentary cretin could say this (quoted by Leibman, p. 354). Although Lenin had great faith on the ability of the proletariat as a ruling class, in his lifetime the party was all in all, and this party constituted a microscopic fraction of the whole proletariat. So it is not true that the proletariat, in practice, was the ruling class. Even today, proletarians as a whole have no place in any administrative system.

Liebman concludes that the dictatorship of the proletariat "was an ephemeral thing that was unable to survive for long the exhaustion of the political or even simply physical energy of the proletariat" (p. 355). In 1919 Lenin identified the party with the proletariat. Earlier he said that the Bolshevik Party was substituted for proletariat to meet the exigency of the situation, later on he identified the party with the working class. "The thesis of the *identification* of the class with the party prevented the thesis of substitution from raising its head. Lenin had admitted implicitly that the dictatorship of the proletariat was a thing of the past. The replacement of the proletariat by the party has left nothing about the concept."

But the whole concept of dictatorship of the proletariat cannot be summarily rejected. It is said that both Marx and Engels have floated this concept to effectively counteract the supremacy of the bourgeois in economic, cultural and political spheres. They saw that the supremacy of the capitalist class was counter-productive in all respects and, in order to bring about an end to this, the proletariat class must establish its supremacy through the seizure of political power.

38 ALIENATION

Definition and Nature

According to COD alienation is the state or experience of being alienated. A state of depersonalisation or loss of identity in which the self seems unreal. Alienate means cause to feel isolated. Lose or destroy the support or sympathy. But the dictionary meaning of alienation—though paves the path for better understanding of the concept, it is not enough for forming a comprehensive idea. Rousseau and Marx used the concept in their political philosophies and in the twentieth century this has been widely analysed by a good number of thinkers. In this analysis we shall primarily confine ourselves within the Marxian sense. But before him Rousseau developed the idea in his mind.

The author of the article *Alienation* published in Bottomore's *A Dictionary of Marxist Thought* says : "In Marx's sense an action through which (or a state in which) a person, a group, an institution or a society becomes (or remains) alien (1) to the results or products of its own activity (and to the activity itself) or to the nature in which it lives or to other human beings... Thus conceived alienation is always self-alienation i.e., the alienation of man (of his self) from himself (from his human possibilities) through himself (through his own activity). And self-alienation is not just one among the forms of alienation but the very essence and basic structure of alienation" (p. 4). Alienation has another manifestation. It is not simply a concept but a real picture of a capitalist society. If it is so then we may treat it as an appeal for a revolutionary change of society. Marx intended to emphasise that alienation is the primary cause of dehumanisation and both alienation and dehumanisation are curse of a bourgeois society.

Meszaros in his noted work *Marx's Theory of Alienation* explains the concept in the following way : "Alienation is an eminently historical concept." If man is alienated from something, as a result of certain causes—the interplay of events and circumstances in relation to man as the subject of this alienation which manifest themselves is a historical framework." Meszaros calls it a historical idea or concept because it did not arise all on a sudden. In a capitalist society the system of production and the nature of the economy created an atmosphere which ultimately resulted in an alienation. Alienation is not a negligible aspect of a bourgeois society. Its tentacles spread almost every part of society and in that sense it is general. It is said that (a) man is alienated from nature, (b) from himself, that is from his own activity, (c) from his species-being, (d) and, finally, he is alienated from his fellow citizens. What is of importance is that there are foot-prints of alienation in every nook and corner of a capitalist society. In his *Economic and Philosophic Manuscript—*1844, Marx made the following remark : Man's species being, both nature and his spiritual species properly, into a being alien to him, into a means to his individual existence, his human being (p. 76). Man is estranged from the product which he produces with his own labour, with his own intelligence and physical capacity. He becomes, due to the curse of alienation, simply a machine. We here quote a part of Meszaros' comment he makes about Marx's idea on alienation : "Thus Marx's conception of alienation embraces the manifestations of man's estrangement from nature and from himself on the one hand and the expressions of this process in the relationship of man-mankind and man-man on the other" (op. cit. p. 15).

Rise and Development

Since alienation is an important part of Marx's philosophy the scholars have displayed active interest in its various aspects. George Lukacs is of opinion that Marx's theory of alienation can be traced to Hegel's *Protestantising Critique of positivity*. In this critique Hegel rejects as dead those human relationships or institutions in which persons give only an outward and constrained conformity, but concerning which they lack a freely given inward conviction. Gouldner says (*The Two Marxians*, p. 177) : "The roots of the theory of alienation, then, reach down into the rejection of "constraint" into the disjunction in which constraint is experienced as powerful but wrong; it is a response to the perception of this violation of grammar of societal rationality and an effort to overcome such an unpermitted social world. The spiritual world is a world of corruption and slavery. It is uncontrolled absolutely by few churchmen. Ordinary people are deprived of unhindered access to the temple of God. Naturally the church or temple or any holy place is alien to them. Neither protestation nor grumbling has any effect. Common people have no feeling for the world they live in. It is alien to them. This is the picture of alienation generally found in religious world.

Rousseau is the real progenitor of Marx so far as the idea of alienation is concerned, because he spoke of this concept in the most unequivocal terms. He started in *Social Contract* with the famous declaration : "Man is born free; and everywhere he is in chains. One thinks himself the master of others, and still remains a greater slave than they." Rousseau says that from the moment of his birth man is the victim of alienation. Man is born in a society and then he is alienated from it. This alienation is to be removed through the formation of a new society whose mechanism is social contract. A new body formed on the basis of certain principles can destroy the possibility of alienation. The formation of bodypolitic alone cannot remove alienation. The whole body politic will be administered by the principle of general will and this general will is the sovereign. In other words, introduction of direct democracy is the only way out from the menace of alienation. In Rousseau's judgment enlightenment and the all-round development of reason were the root causes of alienation, because these invited fraud and corruption. This led Rousseau to revolt against reason and progress of science and civilisation. In this connection I quote a beautiful remark of J. S. McClelland. "Rousseau's insistence that the history of all hitherto existing societies is the history of force and fraud is an ideological statement" (*A History of Western Political Thought*, p. 255).

Rousseau speaks of alienation from nature. He is of opinion that when a good thing is out of hands of God it finally comes to be vicious. Degeneration in all its forms steals the virtue of goodness and man comes to be its victim. Finally, civilisation comes to be the victim of this degeneration. Man is separated from his near and dear ones, from his environment. Man's most dear wishes remain unfulfilled. In the state of nature there was no existence of alienation. For that reason he suggested to build up a new society which would facilitate the revival of old state of nature and at the same time destroy alienation. Money and wealth are chiefly responsible for the alienation because these have corrupted man's mind and self-centred. The exorbitant love for money leads him to earn more and more money and this is a vital factor of the rise of alienation. We think that Rousseau rightly diagnosed the cause of alienation.

Ludwig Feuerbach (1804-1872) threw sufficient light on the concept of alienation and Marx agreed with most of the views of Feuerbach. We have already stated that Feuerbach strongly criticised the prevailing concept of religion and in that connection he opposed the religion-created alienation. Feuerbach said that "man is not a self-alienated God, but God is self-alienated man" (Bottomre, p. 12). God is created by man, but he is above man and is separated from man in all respects. He is estranged from man and Feurbach calls it alienation. In Feurbach's opinion religion is the best example of estrangement or alienation. He further says that it is peculiar that the religion or God is man's own creation and ultimately he is separated from it. Naturally if man wants to make him alienation-free, the best way is de-alienation.

Feuerbach confined himself within the religious alienation and Marx did not agree with this, because he was of opinion that alienation was of more than one form. This was first pointed out by Hess. Hess did not agree with Feuerbach's one type alienation. Marx also agreed with Hess and this he noted in his *Economic and Philosophical Manuscripts.* "Marx praised Hegel for having grasped the self-creation of man as a process, objectification as loss of the object, as alienation and transcendence of this alienation. But he criticised Hegel for having identified objectification with alienation and for having regarded man as self-consciousness and the alienation of man as the alienation of his consciousness" Bottomore (ed) *A Dictionary of Marxist Thought,* pp. 12-13.

Marx's Theory of Alienation

Both *The German Ideology* and *Paris Manuscripts* have elaborately analysed the theory of alienation. In the *Paris Manuscripts* Marx has used the term alienation of labour or alienated labour. What did Marx actually mean by alienation or alienated labour? We shall quote a lengthy passage from his *Paris Manuscripts.* He said : "The worker is related to the product of his labour as to an alien object. The object he produces does not belong to him, dominates him and only serves in the long run to increase his poverty. Secondly, alienation appears not only in the result, but also in the process of production and productive activity itself. The worker is not at home in his work which he views only as a means of satisfying others' needs. It is an activity directed against himself, that is, independent of him, and does not belong to him. Thirdly, alienated labour succeeds in alienating man from his species. Species life, productive life, life creating life turns into a mere means of sustaining the worker's individual existence and man is alienated from his fellowmen. Finally, nature itself is alienated from man, who thus loses his own inorganic body." Marx speaks of these four types of alienation.

The alienation, he describes, is primarily the product of capitalist system of economy. But if the capitalism is in its childhood stage the alienation does not seem to be its basic characteristic. When it sufficiently develops the alienation surfaces prominently. Explaining Marx's standpoint or view Kolakowski makes the following observation : "Private property is a consequence and not a cause of the alienation of labour..... In the developed conditions of capitalist appropriation the alienation of labour is expressed by the fact that the worker's own labour as well as its own products have become alien to him. Labour has become a commodity like any other, which means that the worker himself has become a commodity and is obliged to sell himself at the market price determined by the minimum cost of maintenance; wages thus tend inevitably to fall to the lowest level that will keep the workmen alive and able to rear children" (op. cit., p. 114). In other words, the worker works hard and this he does not for his own satisfaction or benefits but for the benefits of the capitalist. He grumbles, he remains dissatisfied. But he is helpless. Marx has also said : "The worker only feels himself outside his work, and in his work feels outside himself. He feels at home when he is not working, and when he is working he does not feel at home" (Quoted by Chris Harman—*A people's history of the world*, pp. 328-329).

Marx draws our attention to this point. He says that the working class alone is not the victim of alienation. The entire capitalist society comes under the evil influence of alienation. In the *Holy Family* he writes : "The propertied class and the class of proletariat represent the same human self-alienation. But the former feels comfortable and confirmed in the self-alienation knowing that this alienation is its own power and possessing its semblance of human existence. The latter feels itself ruined in the alienation and sees in it impotence and the actuality of an inhuman existence". Alienation produces double effects. The capitalist class, though alienated, produces wealth. The working class is alienated but is the victim of poverty and exploitation. There is hardly any good relation or coordination between the two classes though both are indispensable for production.

The German Ideology and Alienation

In *The German Ideology* Marx and Engels have discussed the alienation. But instead of using the word alienation they have used "estrangement' which also signifies alienation. In Section 14 we find the following sub-heading *Social Division of Labour and its consequences; Private Property, The State, Estrangement of Social Activity.* According to Marx-Engels one of the basic characteristics of capitalist society is the division of labour and within this there lie numerous contradictions. The worker is separated from family. But normally this should not happen. Again, in a capitalist society, families are opposed to each other. The produce is not properly distributed, that is, there is unequal distribution of commodities. This is also a type of contradiction and leads to alienation. The condition in the family, relations that grow within the family and other related matter are also the product of capitalist system. These are the potential sources of alienation. None gets rid of it because everything is inextricably related with capitalism. Marx-Engels write in *The German Ideology* :

"Out of the very contradiction between the particular and the common interests, the common interest assumes an independent form as the *state*, which is divorced from the real individual and collective interests, and at the same time as an illusory community. ...as long as man remains in naturally evolved society, that is as long as a cleavage between the particular and the common interests, as long as activity is not voluntarily, but naturally divided man's own deed becomes an alien power opposed to him which enslaves instead of being controlled by him. ...As soon as division of labour comes into being, each man has a particular, exclusive sphere of activity, which is forced upon him and from which he cannot escape" (pp. 52-53).

Some critics have alleged that compared with *Paris Manuscripts* Marx uses the word alienation or alienated labour less frequently in *The German Ideology*. But Kolakowski says that this allegation is baseless because in many places he and Engels has used the alienation or estrangement. In *The German Ideology* Marx and Engels have said that division of labour was the real villain, that it was the root cause of alienation. The improvement of tools has intensified and universalised the division of labour and this, in turn, led to the alienation. Kolakowski observes : "division of labour leads necessarily to commerce, i.e., the transformation of objects produced by man into vehicles of abstract exchange value. When things become commodities, the basic premiss of alienation already exists" (p. 141). Hence the real culprit is division of labour. Furthermore, without division of labour the modern industry cannot proceed at all. It is, however, evident that in *The German Ideology* Marx and Engels both were fully conscious of the alienation. Let us quote few lines from *The German Ideology* :

"Individuals have always regarded themselves as the point of departure, their relations are part of the real process of their lives. How can it be, then, that their relationships become independent of them, that the forces of their own lives gain control over them? The answer, in a word, is—the division of labour, the degree of which depends on the extent to which productive forces have developed." In *The German Ideology* they have further observed : "For the proletarians the condition of their life, labour and with it all the conditions of existence of modern society, have become something extraneous, something over which they, as separate individuals, have no control, and over which no social organisation can give them control" (p. 88).

Effects of Alienation

Marx and Engels have not consistently analysed the inhuman effects of alienation. The central idea of this alienation is it is the core of the entire capitalist system and it is the primary reason of the dehumanisation of man in general and workers in particular. As a result of alienation man simply becomes an instrument of production. All his good and artistic qualities are lost. "Alienated labour deprives man of his species-life, other human beings become alien to him, communal existence is impossible, and life is merely a system of conflicting egoism. Private property, which arises from alienated labour, becomes in its turn a source of alienation, which it fosters increasingly" (Kolakowski, p. 115).

The effect of alienation is it paralyses the entire society. Man is paralysed, he forgets social and ethical aspects of life. In society there develops social relation among men. This social relation based on mutual love, respect, and give-and-take relation is, in a sense, elixir of life. Man draws inspiration from the social relation. But the division of labour destroys all these aspects and man finally becomes a tool of production of various commodities. The worker is reduced to a mere animal or a lifeless instrument of production. Physiologically a worker is a man and this much only. In the real sense he is not a man. Again, the capitalist is not free from the bad effects of alienation. A capitalist is a human being no doubt. But as a consequence of alienation he is simply a money-making machine. He forgets social life. To a capitalist money is the supreme good and all other things are inferior to it. A worker is practically forced to think in the same line. Thus the whole society is dehumanised as a result of alienation.

Emancipation from Alienation

We have pointed out the harmful effects of alienation. It paralyses man's artistic aspects of life, it dehumanises him. Because of alienation man fails to establish himself as a man. Hence it is the primary objective of man to get rid of the alienation. But the problem is to think to emancipate from alienation and finally to transtate it into reality are very different issues. Only the abolition of private property cannot ensure the emancipation from alienation. The tentacles of alienation are spread far and wide and sometimes they have gone into the deep of society. The primary source of alienation lies in the system of private property. This was the opinion of Marx and Engels. Even before them Saint-Simon thought almost in the same line. The problem is how an emancipation from an alienation is possible remains a million dollar question.

The Economic and Philosophical Manuscripts were first published in 1932 and the *Grundrisse* in 1939 and they were republished in 1953. The Marxists are of opinion that the publication or republication have thrown profuse light on various aspects of Marxist philosophy but throws little light on the emancipation of alienation. In *The German Ideology* Marx and Engels casually mention Rousseau's *Contract Social*. Perhaps Marx and Engels thought of Rousseau's ambitious plan of establishing a new society which he called public person and we call it an ideal society based on Platonic model of idealism. Rousseau thought that setting up of such a society would be capable of emancipating people from alienation which was the consequence of the development of art, science and culture. But we are not sure whether Marx and Engels thought in the line of Rousseau.

There will be an end to all speculation if we look at the complete philosophical thought of Marx and Engels and their numerous suggestions. They were all along against the system of private property which, according to Marx, created disastrous effects in society. In other words, the system of private property is the root of all evils including alienation. It paralyses practically everything of man's "species-life". Hence the abolition of private property shall be the first step towards the emancipation from alienation.

Along with the abolition of private property Marx also suggested that religion must be abolished. Both private property system and the system of God were simultaneously responsible for the alienation. Private property system means capitalism. In *Economic and Philosophical Manuscripts* Marx elaborately analysed various aspects and forms of alienation. "The criticism of alienation was not an end in itself for Marx. His aim was to pave the way for a radical revolution and for the realisation of communism understood as the reintegration of man, his return to himself, the supersession of man's self-alienation and the positive abolition of private property" (Bottomore, p. 13). *The Communist Manifesto* ends with the following declaration : "The communists disdain to conceal their views and aims. They openly declare that their ends can be attained only by the forcible overthrow of all existing social conditions. Let the ruling classes tremble at a communist revolution. The proletarians have nothing to lose but their chains. They have a world to win." (*M.E.S.W.* Vol. I, p. 65).

Types of Alienation

In *Capital, The German Ideology, Economic and Philosophical Manuscripts* (1844) and many other works Marx, along with Engels, has discussed various types of alienation. These may be categorised as **political alienation, economic aleination, alienation of human power** etc. We shall start with **political alienation.**

According to Marx man plays double role—he is a member of society and, at the same time, he is a member of state which is also called political system. As a member of society he has his own views or conception about religion, morality, ethics, values and culture and he always endeavours for the fulfilment of these. An individual cannot avoid society or he cannot live outside it. He is also a member of the state or political system. The problem lies in the fact that though the individual is a member of the state, he is not fully free to do his duties. This is primarily due to the fact that the economy and administration of the state are dominated by the bourgeoisie and it is so controlled as to safeguard the interests of this class. In the state, common people are not free to take their political an economic decisions freely. It is because the capitalists control the entire state for their own benefits, and, in that situation, general public are practically alienated from the political and economic structure. Again, in capitalist system, people have very little or no scope of participation in the affairs of the state. Again, in the economic field, people are simply wage-earners and this wage is subsistence level, that, is somehow to maintain the physical existence of the wage-earner and his family. Again, the bureaucracy of the state is all powerful and the common people have no scope of participation. This is the central idea of political alienation as Marx and Engels witnessed in their contemporary society.

The *economic alienation* is the most important form of alienation and both Marx and Engels have emphasised it. In the *Economic and Political Manuscripts* (also called the *Paris Manuscripts)* and *Capital* (Vol. III) Marx elaborately analysed the economic alienation. He has said that in the primitive mode of production there was no division of labour because the productive system was not developed at all. But, with the progress of productive system and capitalism, division of labour ultimately came to be an integral part of capitalist economy. For the betterment of economy and other compulsive reasons the capitalists were forced to introduce division of labour and with the progress of the capitalist system the division of labour gradually intensified.

With the improvement of the division of labour there appeared spectacular loss of freedom of the workers. Because the workers of one industry had no freedom to move from one industry to another. Marx said : Since his own labour has been alienated from himself by the sale of his labour power, has been appropriated by the capitalists and incorporated with capitals, it must be in the production process, be realised in a product that does not belong to him. The labourer constantly produces material, objective wealth—but in the form of capital—of an alien power that dominates and exploits him. The capitalist also produces labour power in the form of subjective source of wealth separated from the objects in which it can alone be realised. In expansion of capitalism, growth of wealth creates only wage labourer. A barrier or alienation is created between capitalists and worker. The growth of capitalism only perpetuates alienation.

Marx further says : "Capital shows itself more and more as a social power and its agent is the capitalist. The capitalist enjoys the right to appropriate values created by the workers. On the contrary, the worker is not the owner of the product he produces. Capital becomes a strange, independent social power. It stands opposed to the society and opposed to the interest of labourers. The contradiction between capital as a general social power and as a power of private capitalists over the social conditions of production develops into an ever more irreconcilable clash." This clash or contradiction is basically due to the alienation of worker from the mainstream of productive system. Marx's special emphasis is that a capitalist system cannot get rid of alienation because there is contradiction.

Marx has also said that in the field of alienation technological progress has a special importance Machinery is not guided by man; rather man is guided by machine. Labourer has no opportunity to work with the machinery in accordance with his own will or advantage. Rather, labourer will have to cooperate with the machinery. It is a fact that machinery helps man to produce huge amount of commodities but its dark side is it has made man its slave. How the capitalist productive apparatus intensifies the alienation. Kolakowski beautifully says : "Work presents itself to him as an alien occupation, and he forfeits his essence as a human being, which is reduced to purely biological activities. Labour becomes only a means to individual animalised life and the social essence of man becomes a mere instrument of individual existence. Alienated labour deprives man of his species-life, other human beings become alien to him, communal existence is impossible and life is merely a system of conflicting egoism" (pp. 114-115).

If we go through Marx's writings we shall find another type of alienation and it is **alienation of human power**. Marx says "Man is directly a natural. As a natural being and as a living natural being he is on the one hand furnished with natural powers of life—he is an active natural being. These forces exist in him as tendencies and abilities—as impulses. On the other hand as a natural corporeal, sensuous, objective being he is a suffering, conditioned and limited creature, like animals and plants. That is to say, the objects of his impulses exist outside him, as objects independent of him. Yet these objects are objects of his need—essential objects indispensable to the manifestation and confirmation of his essential power." What Marx emphasises here is that as a natural human being he has certain desires, impulses, liking and disliking. He has the desire to fulfil his desires. But the tragedy of the capitalist system is man has no power to satisfy his desires, to translate the impulses into reality, because he does not possess the power. The capitalist system has snatched away that power.

Marx further observes "Man is not merely a natural being, he is a human being. That is to say he is a being for himself. Therefore, he is a species-being and has to confirm and manifest himself as such both in his being and in his knowing. Neither nature objectively nor nature subjectively is directly given in a form of adequate to the human being."

From the above two passages we can draw certain conclusion : (1) Man is a natural being. (2) As a natural being he has certain impulses and natural needs and he wants to satisfy them. (3) Man lives in a society. His life and all sorts of activities are performed and satisfied with the help of others and in association with others. But in the system of capitalist economy he is not getting these opportunities. The capitalist system virtually separates one man from another. The needs of man are not fixed, always changing, but he is not capable of keeping himself abreast of change. It is because the capitalist system has enormously truncated his power and ability. Suppressing his wishes and all sort of impulses he is forced to the power of the society—that is the authority of the capitalist system.

Marx is of opinion that alienation is peculiar to class, society workers are alienated from the mainstream of society (both politically and economically). They are the real agents of production. They create wealth but they are deprived of the benefit of wealth. The system of the division of labour has created an atmosphere of alienation. It is beyond the capacity of the workers to rectify or change it in their favour. The workers are alienated in the field of production due to the strict division of labour. Workers are converted into machine and they work just like machine. They have impulses but have no time to feel them. "In bourgeois society men acquire values in which they cannot find satisfaction, they are frustrated and are therefore, prone to actions which are wrong or illegal according to the moral rules and laws which embody these values. The morality of a bourgeois society is not a truly human morality, it does not allow men to make the most of their natural capacities" (*Man and Society*, volume Two pp. 376-377). Plamenatz, however, does not agree with Marx that the alienation is the product of capitalism and class society.

39 POLITICAL PHILOSOPHY OF LENIN

A Short Life History

The family name of this world famous revolutionary and a great interpreter of the political ideas of Marx and Engels is Vladimir Ilyich Ulyanov. He was born on 22 April 1870 (in old style or system of calculation it was 10 April). Simbirsk was Ulyanov's birth-place and it is now called Ulyanovsk. From the end of 1901 he came to be known as 'Lenin' because in his writings he used that pseudonym.

Vladimir's father Ilya Nikolayevich was an educated person and held the post of school inspector. He had also direct and strong connection with Russian particularly Tsarist bureaucracy and in bureaucratic circle he was a respected person. Ilya Nikolayevich took special care of his children's education. Though he was very much religious-minded and imparted religion-based education upon his children he was not a bigot. His elder brother Alexander was a student of Petersburg University and from his earlyhood he was revolutionary in his attitude and activities. This mentality led him to be a member of a terrorist and secret organisation popularly known as Narodnaya Volya. This organisation was involved in the assassination of Tsar Alexander II in 1881, and when Alexander's involvement was discovered he was hanged.

Lenin believed that his brother Alexander was innocent and when he was hanged for no fault of his own Lenin became furious and decided to take revenge. But Lenin's mother did not approve his decision and she wanted to divert the attention of Lenin. His mother took serious efforts to involve him in studies and because of her efforts Lenin was allowed to be a student of St. Petersburg University and by 1891 he became a law-graduate.

Lenin's membership of the university and mother's efforts failed to bring about a break on his connection with the secret organisations, particularly Narodnaya Volya. He was determined to end the autocratic rule of the Tsar and in order to achieve that ambitious objective he began to study the various revolutionary literature. By 1890 Lenin came in close contact with the works of Marx and Plekhanov. Before Lenin Plekhanov was a great Marxist and he published a number of booklets and articles explaining and interpreting the thoughts of Marx and Engels. Plekhanov's writings impressed Lenin and he began to study seriously the works of Marx. His attachment with revolutionary philosophy in general and

Marxian philosophy in particular began to increase in astronomical proportion and before the end of the 19th century his name appeared to be a very known figure among the socialist circles. The secret police and organisation of the Tsar intensified their surveillance over Lenin and he was not permitted in the academic affairs of St. Petersburg University. This, however, could not deter Lenin. With added enthusiasm he carried on his revolutionary activities.

Background of Lenin's Thought

In his letter to Weydemeyer on 5 March 1852 Marx wrote "And now as to myself, no credit is due to me for discovering the existence of classes in modern society, nor yet the struggle between them. Long before me the bourgeois historians have described the historical development of this struggle of the classes and bourgeois economists the economic anatomy of the classes." Needless to say that the same also holds good for Lenin. Lenin's political philosophy—or what is better known as Leninism—did not emerge accidentally. It is coupled with a long and multifaced background whose understanding is essential for a comprehensive grasp over Leninism.

When Lenin embarked upon the turmoiled political and economic situation of the then Russia (roughly in the middle of the nineties of the nineteenth century, he witnessed a host of revolutionaries and socialist thinkers such as Struve, Martov, Krzhizhanovsky, Potresov etc. There was also Plekhanov who built up a powerful group of Marxists and elaborated, interpreted and propagated the main currents of Marxist thought. Plekhanov's intellectualism created an impact upon the revolutionary zeal of Lenin. In the fifties of the nineteenth century Belinsky and Harzen launched, at a limited scale, the revolutionary movement in Russia which created a stir among the peasants, because they believed that only the Russian peasants could form a potential force to save Russia from the Tsarist misrule.

In the 1860s some Russian thinkers and revolutionaries believed that only a reform movement could be a right way. Chernyshevsky gave leadership to this movement. Though many people call Chernyshevsky's reform movement revolutionary, in practice, it was not so. Many people think that the purpose of this reform movement was to slow down the terrorist movement which was gathering momentum under the leadership of Lenin. His movement was partially anarchist and partially individualist. It was, however, anti-establishment.

Narodnik (Populist) and Narodnaya Volya (People's will) parties emerged in the seventies to press the cause of common people, particularly the peasants. The populist or Narodnik Party had no practical experience of revolution or leading the toiling masses to revolutionary activities and, as such, the Narodnik Party failed to achieve even moderate success. After sometimes the party gave the Slogan "Go to the people'. The activities of the party went off to the countryside to raise their enthusiasm.

The successive failures of the Narodnik Party split it into two groups—one terrorist and the other, to some extent, reformist. The former was called Narodnaya Volya and Lenin had weakness for this group. Lenin's elder brother was connected with this terrorist group and the group was responsible for the assassianation of Tsar Alexander II. Tsar police did not hesitate to adopt most repressive measures and some were hanged. This could not generate any deterrent effect upon the revolutionaries. Conspiratorial activities went unabated.

In the mid 1880s some Marxists in exile intensified their activities for the cause of emancipation of the working class and most prominent among them were Plekhanov and Axelrod. Plekhanov was rated as the key factor for transforming populism into Marxism. In has been observed by a critic that Plekhanov's writings not only converted Lenin but also reared a whole generation of Russian Marxists. Plekhanov emphasised that populists' method of terrorism was in bankruptcy and hence it could not be relied upon. He was sure that capitalism was rapidly developing in Russia and would create a vast army of proletariat who would overthrow the autocratic rulers from power. This analysis of Russian capitalism impressed Lenin and he took active interest.

It has been pointed out by Christopher Hill (*Lenin and the Russian Revolution*, pp. 17-19) that Russia during the Tsar rule was in fact divided into two opposite classes—landlord and bourgeois on the one hand, and toiling masses on the other. There was no middle class as it is to be found in other capitalist countries of Europe. In the midst of this terrorist and revolutionary movement the liberal philosophy of the 19th century could not get any scope to flourish in Russia. Moreover, the landed and industrial interests in Russia were chiefly dominated by the foreigners which created a strong resentment among the common people. This was quite favourable for the advancement of revolutionary movement and, needless to say, Lenin took the full opportunity of this situation. A large number of socialist thinkers and activities had already prepared an academic atmosphere by interpreting and propagating Marx's thought and ideas.

Lenin and the Russian Revolution

A number of Russian revolutionaries ploughed the field for sowing the seeds of revolution and Lenin was undoubtedly the most prominent personality. In fact, without the dynamism and bold leadership of Lenin the Russian revolution would never have been be a reality. The ruthless administration of Russia sent him to jail and exile for a number of times, but everywhere he continued his schemes of revolution with added zeal and enthusiasm. In 1893 he returned to St. Petersburg and made efforts to unite the various revolutonary groups. But Russian police did not allow him to remain outside jail to continue revolutionary activities. He was arrested and sent to Siberia.

Lenin was an inborn revolutionary and while in exile he continued his revolutionary activities which resulted in the formation of a revolutionary party known as Russian Social Democratic Labour party (R.S.D.L.P.). Under its leadership number of strikes in the textile factories of St. Petersburg took place. Lenin was at that time in Siberia and when he returned in 1900 he witnessed that Russian social and political situation was quite ripe for a revolution. At the same time he strongly felt the necessity of a journal to spread and inculcate the principle of revolution among the workers and with the help of Potresov and Martov he clandestinely published a journal called Iskra (The Spark) and immediately it was received by the workers and revolutionaries enthusiastically. Lenin thought that the publication of Iskra was a positive step towards the materialisation of revolutionary objectives.

The years following 1893 were years of confusion and indecision. In the Minsk Congress the RSDLP was formed, but it could not proceed rapidly towards the fulfilment of revolutionary goals. It simply organised few strikes. There were, moreover, dissensions among the revolutionaries. How to organise a movement?

What would be the objectives of revolution any movement? Some revolutionaries advanced the argument that the workers should form trade unions to press their demands upon the capitalists. The political objectives of any organisation will definitely divide the workers. But the core group set up by Lenin, when he was in Geneva, strongly opposed this move. His argument was trade union based on economic factors would make the workers reform-minded and enslave them to capitalists. So Lenin advised his followers to discard such trade unionism.

Before 1905 Lenin was convinced that the peasants and workers must understand the necessity of a revolution and in order to organise and unite them a party organisation is a must. Lenin once said—It is not sufficient for revolution that the exploited and oppressed masses understand the impossibility of living in the old way and demand changes... For revolution it is essential, first, that a majority of the workers (or at least a majority of the class-conscious, thinking, politically active workers) should fully understand that revolution is necessary and be ready to sacrifice their lives for it, secondly, that the ruling classes be in a state of governmental crisis. Lenin thought that if the government were in crisis that would encourage the backward and politically conscious people to assemble together and form a coherent movement against the government which will precipitate the fall.

This fundamental principle of revolution formulated by Lenin is not imaginary. The revolution of 1905 and two revolutions of 1917 corroborate Lenin's fundamental law. He was of opinion that the mere presence of objective situation was not enough for any revolution, it must be organised. Lenin fully realised that the prevailing political situation of Russia was quite congenial for a revolution. The Tsar government was weak and to cover up its weakness it resorted to repressive measures and for that purpose it employed a large number of agent-provocateurs. Lenin thought that intensive propaganda and large scale organisation of masses could be alienated from the government and simultaneously its misdeeds and weakness should be exposed to the people so that they can form an anti-government attitude. He also emphasised that the Russian economy was dominated by the foreign investors and capitalists. Lenin was convinced that for the emancipation of the working class it is necessary to seize political power because it is the cause of exploitation.

Lenin and the Revolution of 1905

In the 1905-war with Japan Russian army received a severe defeat at the hands of Japanese army and this brought about several setbacks for the Russian government. The autocratic and repressive rule of the Tsar already created an anti-government attitude and the abortive Russia-Japanese war fuelled that dissension beyond all sorts of pacification. People of all sections of Russian society adopted the agitative tactics to curb the governmental activities. The working class was more militant, Strikes, demonstrations and other tactics were adopted by them. The peasants also joined hands with them and, ultimately, the countrywide agitation made the Tsar rulers helpless. The workers, peasants and even the members of the bourgeoisie formed organisations to give concrete shape to their movements. In such a situation a revolution took place in Russia in 1905 (22 January). It is also called "Bloody Sunday".

Russian people demonstrated before the palace of the Tsar peacefully, but repressive and ruthless measures were perpetrated by the Tsar police upon them and this made the people furious. Waves of strikes and demonstrations flooded the

Russian Society. At the time of 1905 Russian revolution Lenin was in Geneva. So the revolution was absolutely spontaneous. The activities and the policies of the Tsar government crossed all the limits of toleration. But the revolution could not succeed, it was crushed by the Tsar Government.

On the question of leadership of revolution and the tactics to be followed in it severe differences of opinion developed between Lenin representing Bolshevik group and the Mensheviks. The main cause of the conflict between Mensheviks and Bolsheviks was that the former wanted to cooperate with the bourgeois democratic groups in their fight. Lenin said that the help of the bourgeois democratic liberals should be sought and on this issue he had no difference of opinion with the Mensheviks. But the moot question is are the members of the bourgeoisie liberal? He was convinced that the Russian bourgeoisie was not liberal at all and accepting the help of this bourgeoisie does not arise at all. During the reign of Alexander II, Zemstovs were set up. These were local assemblies and were given extensive powers for self-government. But the Zemstovs were in favour of autocratic rule and for that reason Lenin did not support any cooperation with them which the Mensheviks refused to accept. Lenin could not find any revolutionary trait among the members of the bourgeoisie and he thought that it was anti-revolutionary. It has been observed by Marcel Leibman (*Leninism Under Lenin*, p. 69) "Between the end of revolution of 1905 and the outbreak of war in 1914, Lenin's struggle against Menshevism became very largely a struggle against liberation and against all tendencies towards alliance between Social Democrats and Constitutional Democrats".

Lenin and the Revolution of 1917

Lenin investigated the causes of the failure of the revolution of 1905 and he stated his conclusions in *Lessons of Revolution* published in 1910. His analysis contains the followings points : (a) No cooperation with the so-called Russian liberals. (b) Only a revolutionary struggle of the masses can lead to victory. (c) Mere underestimation of Tsarism is not enough, all efforts must be made to destroy it. (d) Only the working class can provide proper leadership because the peasants are weak and unorganised. (e) Constitutional tactics adopted by the Tsar government should be discarded. (f) Mensheviks were the tools of Russian liberals and democrats and hence they cannot be relied upon.

Keeping the above lessons in mind Lenin wanted to launch a final strike against the Tsar authority. From the activities of the Tsar government he realised that it was gradually becoming weak and reckless and trying to save itself from complete disaster. The agitation of the masses was increasing rapidly. Lenin was determined to utilise the large scale mass discontent.

Lenin was convinced that it was beyond the capacity of the Tsar government to provide bread and other necessaries and ensure peace and allot land to the landless people and under such situation he gave a clarion call to the masses to rise against all sorts of odds and repressions. He openly declared that he would not accept parliament.

By October 1917 the weakness and inefficiency of the government reached their zenith and Lenin thought that the most opportune moment had arrived to launch a final attack and he did that immediately. The bold leadership of Lenin and the enthusiastic support of the people helped him to corner the Mensheviks. The Bolshevik group under his leadership marched ahead and in October 25, 1917 (New system 7 November), the Bolshevik party captured power. R. N. Carew Hunt writes (*The Theory and Practice of Communism*, p. 178) ..."both the social revolutionaries and the Mensheviks were outplayed by a party far more smaller, but better organised". The success of the revolution of 1917 demonstrates that the fundamental difference between Lenin, and the Mensheviks was that the former wanted to adopt a pragmatic policy to win the fight against the Tsar government and the latter were orthodox Marxists. They held that the Russian situation was not ripe for seizure of power. This orthodox attitude towards the Russian situation was the chief factor of debacle from which the Mensheviks suffered and from which they never recovered. Some critics (mainly form Western countries) accuse Lenin of distorting Marxism. But a proper assessment reveals that he possessed unbound acumen of dealing with practical situations and this made him victorious.

Lenin and the Party

During their lifetime Marx and Engels could not find sufficient time and scope to prepare a full-dress theory of party. In *Manifesto of the Communist Party* (henceforth *Manifesto*) they have said that the working class must form a party to seize political power and establish its dictatorship without which the in emancipation would never be possible. In his *Civil War in France* Marx clearly stated that the chief cause of the failure of the commune was workers' inability to form a party. But when Lenin appeared in the Russian political scene and decided to launch an uncompromising struggle against Tsardom, he felt the necessity of a party and this realisation came as early as 1901.

Two issues dominated Lenin's mind when he was seriously thinking about organising a party. One is, he thought that a political party of the Western type (bourgeoisie democratic party of western Europe) could never be able to fulfill the objective of the Russian working class whose chief aim was to overthrow the rule of the Tsar. Political parties of Western bourgeois democracies always follow a tactics of compromise and cooperation with the capitalists class. The second issue is on the role of the party. Lenin openly challenged the argument and stand of the economists. "The economists interpreted historical materialism as a theory of primacy of the proletariat's economic struggle as compared with political aims" (Kolakowski—*Main Currents of Marxism*—III, p. 385). The argument of the economists was that the material interests of the workers is economic interests and those must be met at first and after that they will spontaneously fight for political struggle and domination. To unite the workers, they held, this condition must be fulfilled.

In his famous work *What Is To Be Done* Lenin attacked this economism. He said that the chief objective of the workers would be to capture political power and emancipation from economic bondage would follow. He also refuted the economists' argument of spontaneity. The revolutionary principles shall be spread through various means among the workers so that they can form a definite opinion about the exploitation of the capitalists. Hence the theory of spontaneity does not hold good at all.

Lenin has said that without revolutionary theory there can be no revolutionary movement. Only a well-organised party can preach and propagate it among the workers. He has further observed that left to themselves the workers were not capable of attaining consciousness of the fundamental opposition between their class as a whole and the existing social system. The history of all countries shows that the working class, exclusively by its own efforts, is able to develop only trade union consciousness. But for a complete emancipation trade union movement and spontaneity cannot work satisfactorily. The role of vanguard fighter can be fulfilled only by a party that is guided by the most advanced concepts and ideas of the theory of socialist revolution.

While Lenin was channelising his efforts for organising a party for conducting revolution he simultaneously thought of spreading ideology among the workers. It is not true that the working class will develop an independent ideology of its own while guiding a movement. Only a struggle can form the foundation of an ideology. This naive contention of some persons has been challenged by Lenin. He is of opinion that no independent ideology can develop in the process of labour movement. In any society there can be only two ideologies—bourgeois and socialist—and the working class will have to select any one of these two. There is no middle course and hence there is no third ideology. It is the most important task of a revolutionary party to convince the workers of the necessity of socialist ideology, because only this course will convince them of the extent of capitalist exploitation. The task of the party is to combat spontaneity, to divert the working class movement from the spontaneous trade union movement to the umbrella of revolutionary movement.

At the beginning of twentieth century, in Russia, there were a number of revolutionary groups who were fighting against Tsardom. Lenin felt the necessity of a united party, because only such an organisation could succeed in capturing political power. He wanted to call it a homogeneous All Russian Party. A centralised and well-organised party was to him the only way. "As against the populists, he conceived of this party as proletarian, as against the legal Marxists, as a party of action as well as of theory, and as against the economists as a party with a political as well as an economic programme" (Carew Hunt, p. 186).

Lenin thought that in order to be the vanguard of the proletariat the party must be an "iron party", that is, it must enforce discipline and principles of revolution and protracted class struggle among the members. Without an "iron party" it was impossible to carry out the dictatorship of the proletarian. Party should be the highest form of organisation for carrying out proletarian struggle against the bourgeoisie. What Lenin wants to emphasise is that without a nod from the central committee or organisation regional branches cannot take any decision.

To fulfil the goals of revolution Lenin thought that *the party should be small so that it can function swiftly and quite effectively.* The central committee of the party will dominate the ideological and other aspects of the organisation and from this view of Lenin critics draw the conclusion that he was thinking about the dictatorship of party. From the political experience of Russia, Lenin formed the opinion that only a small party can work efficiently.

As regards the organisation of the party Lenin states that it will not only be small, but will consist of professional revolutionaries. These persons will take revolutionary activity as the in profession. The allegiance of these persons to both ideology and party shall be beyond all sorts of doubt and suspicion. Explaining Lenin's view Kolakowski (Vol. 2, p. 388), says that such a party of professional revolutionaries must not only gain the confidence of the workers and take over the spontaneous movement, but must make itself the centre of all forms of protest against social oppression. A small well-organised party will highlight the class interest and expose the class antagonism among the workers and peasants. It will warn the working class against any possible onslaught released by the capitalist and their puppet counter-revolutionary forces. It may suitably be called *general campaign of exposure.* Lenin laid great faith on the party. He believed that it was the duty of the party to expose the motives and character of religious fundamentalists and reactionary forces.

Lenin believed that the leadership of the party shall be at the hands of professional revolutionaries who may be workers or intellectuals. But his preference was always for the workers dedicated to the cause of revolution and emancipation of workers. It has been maintained by Christopher Hill (*Lenin and Russian Revolution,* p. 60) that he had very little faith on the intellectuals because they can easily be purchased by the capitalists. The latter offer them lucrative employment and other comfortable opportunities and amenities and this makes them oblivious of revolution. Even they may abandon revolutionary activities. The intellectuals prefer seminars and declarations. They very seldom think how to implement the declarations. This view of Lenin about the intellectuals was opposed by many of his own party. Even a number of top revolutionaries held the view that large number of intellectuals were in favour of revolution and they believed that only a revolution could emancipate the working class.

In 1920 Lenin laid down that the basis of the party should be "democratic centralism" which implies the combination of democratism and centralism or centralisation. Lenin elaborated the principles of democratic centralism under the new historical conditions when the age of proletarian revolution had come. Lenin wanted to apply the principle in the party congress of the Russian Social Democratic Labour Party. All organisations of the party, according to Lenin, are subordinated to the central authority, the decisions of the higher party organisation are obligatory for lower party organisations. All the units of the party are well-connected and the office-bearers are elected by the members of the party. All the important issues shall be threadbare by analysed in different units of the party and the final decision will be taken by the majority which will be binding on all.

Lenin's theory of party as well as its role in the Russian revolution may also be explained in the light of the relationship between the party and Soviets. In *State and Revolution* and other works he has stressed that the proletarian revolution will smash the bourgeois state and that will be replaced by the Soviets. "The decisive feature in Lenin's analysis, and those to which he attached the greatest importance were his insistence on smashing the old state apparatus, on replacing it by the dictatorship of the proletariat and his new vision of Soviets as the political machinery through which this dictatorship could best be exercised" (Hill, op. cit., p. 87). Lenin thought that after the revolution the proletariat will seize power and dictatorship will be established. All these were categorically stated by Lenin before 1919. In this year he said "the party must win for itself undivided mastery over the Soviets". Critics are of opinion that with the change of time and situation Lenin had jumped from one concept to another. Dictatorship of the Soviets, dictatorship of the party and dictatorship of the proletariat are not identical terms. Subsequently the matter was clarified according to the following line. The party will guide and lead the Soviets and will never replace them. That means the Soviets will be in full control of all the activities of the state and society.

Stalin in his *Problems of Leninism* has offered a slightly different explanation. He has said that the dictatorship is exercised by the proletariat which is organised into society and is led by the party. The party, in essence, exercises the dictatorship of the proletariat. The Soviets are the direct expressions of the dictatorship of the proletariat. Not a single important political or organisational question is decided by our Soviet without guiding direction from our party.

Criticism

Lenin's theory of party has been subject to severe criticisms by both Marxists and non-Marxists. He and his adherents have always assured us that Lenin is neither distorting nor amending the central principles of Marxism. But if we look at his theory of party we will witness a clear negation of this contention. Both Marx and Engels have all long advocated the establishment of dictatorship of proletariat after the seizure of power by the proletarians. Instead of advocating for dictatorship of proletariat, Lenin ultimately supported the dictatorship of party which Marx and Engels never wanted. His advocacy for the mastery of party over all the affairs of state clearly curtails the power and rule of the Soviets. Dictatorship of party undoubtedly makes Marxism a mockery.

His criticism of his opponents' view reveals that he was intolerant and very often used indecent phrases. Marcel Liebman (*Leninism under Lenin*, p. 59) has said—"one could go on indefinitely accumulating examples of the invectives indulged in by Lenin in his pursuit of what he himself called an "implacable campaign". Once he described Trotsky a Judas Trotsky. Though Lenin himself had sufficient sense of decency...Martov was also subjected to his thunderbolts. .....Lenin even went so far as to insinuate that Martov was in the service of Tsar". Such insinuations are unworthy for Lenin.

Social Revolution

Definition and Objective Condition :

In the last section we have discussed the theoretical aspects of party. Lenin was never an orthodox theoretician. His purpose of analysing party was to bring about a revolution for the emancipation of the working class. In his judgment only party could achieve this task. The revolution of 1905 taught him this valuable lesson. Now what we call revolution, interpreters of Lenin's political ideas and philosophy call it social revolution. Social revolutions are vital turning-points in history. They change the whole social, economic and political structure of society. *Social revolution means fundamental change in the whole social system. It implies a qualitative leap in the development of society resulting in the replacement of one social economic formation by another. It is a deep-going upheaval. It not only replaces one ruling class by another, but abolished old relation of production and introduces new ones and radically changes social views and institutions.*

Social revolution or revolution as it may also be called is quite different from ordinary bourgeois revolution. In the latter, one class of rulers is replaced by another class while the whole political and economic structure remains intact. A bourgeois revolution never touches the economic system of society and, more particularly, the relations of production. Lenin thought that social revolution could only be the goal of working class. In their writings both Marx and Engels gave primary importance to the objective condition of social revolution. Both of them were also convinced that subjective conditions were also necessary. However, Lenin elaborately discussed both the subjective and objective factors of social revolution. But it would be wrong to hold that both objective and subjective factors are quite different and they work separately. These two elements of social revolution are intimately connected.

Following Marx and Engels Lenin had said that to make revolution possible there must be a revolutionary situation. What is revolutionary situation? Revolutionary situation arises when the contradictions between classes became extremely actuate. Not only this, the working class will utilise this revolutionary situation. An interpreter of Lenin's philosophy says—"A revolutionary situation is a build-up of social political conditions necessary for revolution" (*The Fundamental of Marxist-Leninist Philosophy*, p. 323). The symptoms of revolutionary situation may change at various stages of history, but in all cases it presupposes a profound crisis in the old system. Lenin in his *The Collapse of the Second International* published in 1915 has defined these symptoms in the following way : (a) A crisis in the upper classes, a crisis in the policy of the ruling classes, when it is impossible to maintain their rule without any change. (b) The suffering of the oppressed classes and their wants have grown more acute. That is, suffering would be intolerable. (c) Because of the above factors there would arise increasing activities of the masses.

In some writings Lenin has also pointed out another objective element of social revolution. The rise and growing strength of capitalism forged an alliance which may appropriately be called unholy alliance between capitalism and state power. In order to overcome the growing and uncontrollable crisis, capitalism sought the assistance of state power. But this ultimately could not provide any relief. On the contrary, crisis in capitalism began to advance rapidly. Again, a contradiction became inevitable between the growing capitalist system and working class. This is chiefly due to the social character of capitalism and capitalist production relation. To sum up, *the conflict between the social character of capitalism and its old production relation produced the most favourable objective condition of revolution.*

The rapid progress of capitalism also brought about another situation. The capitalist world was divided. In order to maximise profits the capitalists came into conflict with each other and this to a considerable extent eroded their power of exploitation and domination. The conflict among the capitalists finally weakened the very foundation of the capitalist system. This appeared to the working class as an opportunity. The weakness of capitalism is the strength of the working class.

Subjective Conditions : Objective conditions are no doubt necessary but not sufficient for social revolution. Revolution may not always take place even in the presence of objective conditions. Lenin has said that there were revolutionary situations in Russia both in 1859–1861 and in 1879–1880, but no revolutions occurred in those years. This is due to the fact that for the occurrence of a revolution there shall be a juxtaposition of both objective are subjective conditions. Talking about the abortive 1905 revolution Lenin has pointed out that in that year the objective revolutionary condition existed, but the attempts of the revolutionaries could not succeed.

The defeat of a revolution may be due to several causes, including an unfavourable balance of class forces. But even with the balance well in its favour a revolution will not be victorious if there is not a sufficiently mature subjective factor. For the success of revolution the revolutionary class shall be prepared to make any sort and amount of sacrifice. This is the most important subjective precondition of social revolution. Lenin has cautioned that a revolution will never occur automatically. History has taught us that the workers shall organise themselves and must be imbued with a revolutionary zeal.

There are few subjective conditions and the important of them are :

(1) *Revolutioary consciousness of the masses, their readiness and determination to carry through the struggle to the end.* The readiness and determination of masses are vital because only the people carry out the practical tasks of revolution, while the leaders give them directions. The anti-revolutionary and counter-revolutionary forces first throw their attack against the common people to frustrate their courage.

(2) *The organisation of masses and their vanguard make possible the victory of revolution.* In our earlier section we have pointed out why Lenin was determined to form a centralised, strong, effective party for revolution. He was of opinion that left to themselves masses cannot do anything. They must be guided by a vanguard party. All the revolutionary forces must be united. This is an important subjective precondition. The capitalists forces may be divided, but in their attack against proletarians they are united. So to fight the capitalists the revolutionary forces must forge a unity.

(3) Finally, the *leadership of the party must be experienced and trained.* Otherwise the battle against the bourgeoisie shall be abortive. It is the duty of the leadership to find out a correct strategy and adopt pragmatic tactics. Lenin emphasised leadership on the ground that because of the lack of experience and political consciousness common people cannot select the night strategy.

Relation between the Two

A common allegation against Lenin's theory of revolution is that while Marx and Engels laid emphasis on the objective preconditions of revolution, Lenin emphasised the subjective preconditions and by doing this Lenin not only *revised* Marxism but also *distorted* it. This allegation is wrong root and branch. Both Marx and Engels were quite aware of the importance of both these preconditions. In many of their writings they have clearly stated that for the success of revolution objective conditions are essential no doubt, but they cannot be mechanically separated from the subjective conditions, and if any attempt is made in that direction that will be the grossest distortion of Marxism. They said that the crisis in capitalism alone could not bring about revolution. The working class shall utilise it and for that they must acquire consciousness and build up organisation. Engels pointed out this in 1889. He advised workers to form revolutionary party.

The authors of the *Fundamentals of Marxist-Leninist Philosophy* make the following observation : Social revolution demands unity of objective and subjective conditions. This law of social revolution had been confirmed by all revolutions and particularly by three Russian revolutions of the 20th century. After the First World War (1914-1918), revolution in some of the countries in Europe could not succeed although in those countries there were either objective or subjective condition. But the presence of both of them is essential for revolution. In those countries there could not form powerful and widespread mass communist parties or revolutionary parties based on communism. The absence of leadership, Lenin thought, was also another factor. The working class in these countries was exploited, but the powerful capitalist class through various techniques suppressed their discontent.

"In view of the historical conditions Lenin produced a comprehensive study of the role of subjective factor in the struggle for effecting a socialist revolution" (*The Fundamentals of Marxist-Leninist Philosophy,* p. 326). Some bourgeois ideologists acknowledge the growing role of subjective preconditions. But Lenin attacks this stand. He is of opinion that for a successful revolution the subjective preconditions must be combined with the mature objective preconditions. Lenin further says that subjective condition does not simply mean the conspiratorial activities of some terrorist groups. Behind every revolutionary step there shall be the approval of mass. *The basic law of social revolution is that the subjective factor shall be combined with objective conditions and no one can deny this basic law.*

Theory of State

A very important contribution of Lenin lies in his interpretation and elaboration of the concept of state of which Marx had said very little. The best treatment is found in Engels's The Origin of Family, Private Property and State. Lenin, borrowing the central idea from Marx and Engels, has expounded the Marxian doctrine in his *The State* and *The State and Revolution.* The latter was published in August 1917 and the former in 1919. *The State and Revolution* is regarded by many scholars as a very important writing of Lenin. What Engels did not say but wanted to say, Lenin has explained in *The State and Revolution.*

Following Marx and Engels Lenin says that in the primitive society there was no existence of state because there were no classes. When the society came to the divided into opposing classes as a result of the emergence of private property the necessities of state became inevitable. History shows that the state is a special apparatus for coercing people. One class uses this apparatus to coerce another class. The state is by no means a power forced on society from without...It is the product of society at a certain stage of development. This society has become entangled in an insoluble contradiction with itself. It is now clear that according to Lenin—also Marx and Engels—the state is a human product not bestowed upon man by any invisible power : *A product of irreconcilability of class antagonism.* Marx, Engels and also Lenin have viewed history from the standpoint of materialist conception. They have said that the study of history reveals that in different periods of time different classes arose and their interests were diametrically opposite; and because of this the in interests could not be reconciled. In the slave society there were slave-owners and slaves, in the feudal period there were landlords and serfs. Finally, in industrial society, there arose capitalists and working class or proletarians. In all these epochs these classes stood against each other. One class wanted to dominate another. But ultimately it was found that the economically dominant class got an upper hand and established its mastery over the weaker class which was in numerical majority. The powerful class with the help of police, army, bureaucracy and other coerce-enforcing machinery succeeded in controlling the weaker class. These forces are state forces and controlled and maintained by state. It may also be put in a different way. The economically stronger class created a machinery which could help it in exploitation. It is now obvious that if the interests of the opposing classes could be reconciled such an apparatus could not have arisen. Let us sum up the matter in the words of Lenin :

> The state is a product and a manifestation of the irreconcilability of class antagonisms. The state arises, where when and in so far as class antagonisms objectively cannot be reconciled. The existence of the state proves that the class antagonisms are irreconcilable. (*The State and Revolution,* p. 10).

The state is an organ for the reconciliation of classes. It has been maintained by Lenin that although the state represents the powerful class, it sometimes plays the role of arbitrator in cases of disputes and this the state does to show its neutrality. But ultimately the state fails to settle the disputes simply because these cannot be reconciled. When the settlement fails the real character of state is exposed, it takes the side of the dominant *class state.* The state is the *rule of a definite class.*

Immediately after October Revolution (November Revolution—New Style) Lenin castigated the Mensheviks and Socialist-Revolutionaries. They argued that the state could reconcile the classes. Lenin called this petty bourgeois theory. He also called it *petty bourgeois and Philistine reconciliation theory.* He concluded that the state is an organ of class rule and product of class antagonisms. This specific role of the state helps its alienation from the rest of the society. It keeps itself above the society and rule from above. Hence the emancipation of the working class shall be preceded by destruction of ruling class and seizure of state power.

An Instrument for Exploitation

The chief role of state according to Marx, Engels and Lenin is—it is an instrument of exploitation. The dominant class controlling the sources of production uses the state for its own benefits. So if there were no classes there could not arise the necessity of state. In *The State* Lenin makes the following observation : The state is a machine for maintaining the rule of one class over another. How the state plays the role of exploitation? It has a vast army of bureaucracy which from time to time make laws fulfilling the interests of the ruling class and again when these laws prove redundancy they are abolished or amended and in this way the process continues. In case of violation of state laws, army or police are pressed into service.

The state is a machine for the oppression of one class by another, a machine for holding the obedience to one class other subordinate classes. There are various forms of this machine. The slave owning state could be a monarchy, an aristocratic republic or even a democratic republic. In fact, the forms of government varied, but their essence was always the same. The slaves could not enjoy any rights. The condition of serfs in feudal state was better in comparison with slaves, but they were oppressed and exploited. The industrial workers in the same way were also oppressed and exploited.

In a democratic republic wealth exercises its power indirectly, but all the more surely, first, by means of the direct corruption of officials as in America and secondly by means of an alliance with government and Stock Exchange as in France and other capitalists countries. In all the capitalist countries, Lenin observes, banks and other financial institutions have developed exceptionally and these are controlling the financial world. Moreover, these financial institutions are in the full control of the wealthiest section of the community. These capitalist countries are called democracies or republics, but these terms are misnomers. People hardly enjoy any rights or privileges. The interests of Stock Exchange and financial institutions are fully protected by the various machinery of state. Political, economic and other interests of the working class and peasants received no importance at the hand of persons manning the state machinery. Some petty-bourgeois democrats, socialist revolutionaries and Mensheviks liberally eulogise the so-called democratic methods of bourgeois state. These are universal suffrage and party system. Lenin is of opinion that these petty-bourgeois democrats have dismally failed to understand the real character of the exploitative role of the capitalist state. These are subterfuges employed by the state.

Withering Away of State

Engels, in his pamphlet *Socialism : Utopian and Scientific*, says "interference in social relation becomes, in one domain after another, superfluous and then dies out of itself... The state is not abolished, it dies out." This is, in nutshell, the famous doctrine of withering away of state. This doctrine has been variously interpreted and the bourgeois theoreticians and sociologist have distorted the concept to suit their motives. Lenin in *The State and Revolution* has offered us a clear exposition of the theory. Lenin's clarification of withering away of state is :

First, Engels said in seizing state power the proletarial thereby abolishes "the state as state". This phrase of Engels is the source of a lot of confusion. Detractors of Marxism say that Engels advocated for an abolition of state and in that case he was at par with anarchists, because the anarchists also wanted to destory the state. Lenin's clarification is that after the proletarian revolution, the bourgeois state will be abolished. But such a state will not immediately wither away. Why? When the proletarian seizes state power, for its own convenience and benefit it will keep certain elements of the bourgeois state. Only the repressive aspects of bourgeois state will be abolished, not the whole structure of such a state. After the socialist revolution there will be no classes. The proletarian state will be a symbol of perfect democracy. *The phrase withering away means the remnants of the proletarian state will die or wither away.* Lenin emphasises that there is difference between the abolition of state as state and withering away of state. Bourgeois thinkers, because of their shallow knowledge, have failed to realise this difference.

Second, about the withering away of state Lenin says that the central idea of what Engels wanted to say had not been fully understood by the bourgeois thinkers. In speaking of the state as dying down of itself Engels refers clearly and definitely to the period after the state has taken possession of the means of production in the name of the whole society, that is, after the socialist revolution. A socialist revolution will abolish state as state. But when there will be a perfect democracy there will be no need of any state apparatus. The remnants of the bourgeois state will then wither away. In other words, the withering away of state is in full consonance of perfect democracy.

Third, Lenin says that the proposition the state withers away is mainly directed against opportunists and anarchists, particularly the latter. This is due to the fact that the anarchists raised a slogan that state should be destroyed to ensure maximum freedom of people. Engels threw a challenge to it. So long there would be necessity of state it could not be destroyed.

In *Manifesto* Marx and Engels have said—The proletariat will use its political supremacy to wrest, by degrees, all capital from the bourgeoisie, to centralise all instruments of production in the hands the proletariat organised as the ruling class. Commenting upon this observation of Marx and Engels Lenin says that (*The State and Revolution*, p. 26) this is the most remarkable and important formulation of Marx about state. Here they have also given a brief definition of state—*proletariat organised as ruling class.*

In order to suppress the counter-revolutionary forces and reactionary elements the proletariat will need a State. Let us put it in the words of Lenin : "The working people need the state only to suppress the resistance of the exploiters, and only the proletariat can direct this suppression, can carry it out." When the dictatorship of proletariat will be established there will no longer be any classes in society, that is, it will be a classless society. Lenin says that the chief role of the bourgeois state is to exploit the proletariat, and when the proletariat will seize power the role of the state as an instrument of exploitation will be redundant. By interpreting Marxian theory of state in his way Lenin was successful in removing all sorts of confusion and propaganda let loose by the bourgeois theoreticians.

Dictatorship of the Proletariat

Meaning and implication : Lenin took up the issue of dictatorship of proletariat (henceforth DP) very much enthusiastically from Engels' writing and Marx's famous work *A Critique of Gotha Programme.* Engels in his *Socialism : Utopian and Scientific* said—The proletariat seizes political power and turns the means of production into state property. But in doing this, it abolishes itself as proletariat, abolishes all classes and class distinctions, abolishes also the state as state. In this famous comment of Engels the concept of DP is hidden. The proletariat will not only capture political power by overthrowing capitalists, it will establish its supremacy over both economic and political spheres.

Lenin says that by coming to power the first task of the proletariat would be to abolish the state as state. That is, the proletariat will not abolish the state from top to bottom, only the coercive aspects of the state will fall under the scheme of abolition. Explaining the concept Lenin says that in *Critique of Gotha Programme* of 1875 Marx clearly envisaged of an ideal known as DP. He said that DP is the political form appropriate to the transitional period which lies between the abolition of bourgeois state and the establishment of communist society.

In *"Left Wing" Communism—an Infantile Disorder* Lenin defined DP in the following words—The dictatorship of proletariat means a most determined and most ruthless war waged by the new class against a more powerful enemy, the bourgeoisie, whose resistance is increrased tenfold by their overthrow not in the strength of international capital, the strength and durability of their international connection, but also in the force of habit, in the strength of small scale production (Marx, Engels, Lenin on the *Dictatorship of the Proletariat : A Collection*, p. 466). This is perhaps the most appropriate definition of DP Lenin has ever offered.

Explaining Lenin's views on DP Carew Hunt (*The Theory and Practice of Communism,* p. 180) says that Lenin has warned his followers that the DP does not mean the end of state, it will continue in the form of DP. He is at pains to point out that it will be a temporary order only. The exploitation of man by man will cease, but the utility of state will exhaust. The coercive function of state will be used by the proletariat to suppress the counter-revolutionary forces. Lenin in *The State and Revolution* has said—under communism there remains for a time not only bourgeois law but even the bourgeois state, without the bourgeoisie. Lenin claims that it is not paradox or simply a dialectical conundrum. He further says that a Marxist is one who extends the acceptance of the class struggle to the dictatorship of the proletariat. Thus DP constitutes the *very central part of Lenin's whole political philosophy.* He has explained it in his several works.

Nature of the Concept

Lenin conceived of DP as new form of the class struggle of the proletariat. It has already been pointed out that DP does not signify the end of the class structure of society and, if that be so, the DP will release all efforts to intensify class struggle. To put it in other words, the DP is the continuation of the class struggle—of course in new forms. Lenin thought that the proletariat is a special class and hence it is entitled to continue the struggle. In his view after capturing power the proletariat will utilise the state machinery for the purpose of class struggle. He has further observed that before the seizure of power proletariat also launched struggle, but in the post-capture stage the nature of the struggle will be different. In earlier epoch proletariat had no opportunity to use the state machinery. With the help of state the proletariat will take all steps to destroy or suppress the remnant of the capitalists.

Lenin has explained the concept of DP as an instrument of class struggle in different perspective. He says that the establishment of DP in one country is not an enough precondition of its survival and success. In international arena there might be several capitalist countries frustrating the DP and in that case the DP will have to take the cudgel against such eventuality. This is an important aspect of DP. Moreover, the aim of the DP would be not only to suppress the bourgeoisie but also to neutralise the counter-revolutionary efforts. The DP would also endeavour to utilise the progressive elements (because such elements are always there) of the bourgeoisie for the realisation of its purpose.

The DP will then proceed to destroy bourgeois democracy and establish or lay the foundation of proletarian democracy. The terms democracy of capitalist society and dictatorship of proletarians are contradictory. But a penetrative analysis reveals that there is no contradiction. Bourgeois democracy is for the few rich and property-owners. Working class and peasants which constitute the overwhelming majority are deprived of participation in such a democracy and for quite obvious reason this type of democratic system cannot be called perfect democracy. The proletariat is committed to overthrow this democracy and to set up a proletarian democracy which will be near the democracy of the majority.

DP has also a task in the field of fighting imperialism. The beginning of the 20th century witnessed the menacing advance of imperialism and Lenin hoped that the DP will fight imperialism earnestly. Seizure of power in one country was not enough. In order to ensure that seizure the imperialism which, according to Lenin, is the highest stage of capitalism, was to be uprooted and DP must assume the responsibility. National war must be converted into international war. DP shall support both materially and in other ways any struggle against imperialism.

DP and Socialism : The DP has a special and very important role in establishing socialism. This aspect of DP has been specifically emphasised by Lenin in several places. He says that socialism means the abolition of classes, but in order to do this it is necessary that the rich landowners and capitalist should be overthrown. It is also necessary that the difference between factory workers and peasants should be obliterated. He has further observed that this is a stupendous task and cannot be performed at a stroke. Continuous struggle against the vested interests and reactionary elements representing the landlords and bourgeoisie shall be cut to size so that they cannot become insurmountable barriers to the progress to socialism. The transition from capitalism to socialism, according to Lenin, is extremely protracted—the DP must move cautiously.

The DP will abolish classes for setting up socialism but the naked fact is that classes cannot be abolished all on a sudden. Classes will remain and it is the duty of DP to continue the struggle. Without the DP they will not disappear. In the era of the DP every class has undergone a change and the relations between the classes have also changed. The class struggle does not disappear under the DP, it merely assumes different forms. Under capitalism, the proletariat was an oppressed class, under the DP it will be a ruling class, it wields state power, it exercises control over the means of production.

Nature and Administration of State : Something needs to be said about the nature and administration of a proletarian state. Lenin is of opinion that one of the important tasks of the proletariat would be to overthrow the elements who are enemies of socialism. Lenin says that some utopians hold the view that bourgeois parliament should be abolished. He disagrees with this suggestion. The way out of parliamentarism is not the abolition of representative institutions and the elective principle but the conversion of representative institutions from talking shops "into working bodies". The role of the parliament should be reversed. It must act for the betterment of the community and welfare of its members. He believed that the members of the bourgeois parliament are engaged in "political prostitution". Lenin thought that representative institutions are the life-blood of proletarian democracy. The DP should take all steps to nurture the political institution so that democracy can smoothly flourish.

Lenin did not want the abolition of bureaucracy at once everywhere and completely. It is a utopia. But to smash the old bureaucratic machine at once and to begin immediately to construct a new one that will make possible the gradual abolition of all bureaucracy. This is not a utopia, it is the experience of the commune. It is the direct and immediate task of the DP.

Carew Hunt (*op. cit.*, p. 183) states that Lenin's observation about the state under DP are of an extreme naivety, because he has reduced it to "accounting and control". In *The State and Revolution* (p. 95) Lenin has said that after the overthrow of capitalist and bureaucrats the DP will proceed to control the production and distribution of commodities. Before this the DP will ensure its control over the sources of production. It will *keep account* of labour and products and in this work the trained section of population will be of considerable help. He has further said that the question of control and accounting should not be confused with the question of scientifically trained staff of engineers and agronomists.

Accounting and control is mainly needed for the smooth working, and the proper functioning of the first phase of communist society. He says that capitalism has simplified the accounting and control of the economy and this can be performed by any literate person. Sometimes special training for some specific works might be needed and that type of training shall be given on behalf of the state by any institution. Therefore, there cannot be any necessity of bureaucracy, it will be reduced to insignificance. If bureaucracy is made unimportant the system of awarding special remuneration would also be unnecessary.

Although Lenin categorically states that the task of accounting and control shall be undertaken by ordinary people he did not rule out the importance and special function of the technicians, specialists and industrialists. In fact, during the period of war communism, these persons performed yeoman's service. The DP must not hesitate to requisition the service of these persons. But it is important to note that here the position of Lenin is quite curious. He was desirous of getting special and important service from the technicians and specialists, but at the same time he refused to pay them extra remuneration. This attitude of Lenin made him ludicrous to all his critics. In fact, Lenin could never reach the goal of socialism—or whatever it may be called—without the specialist services of technicians and engineers. His orthodox and unpragmatic attitude towards the bourgeoisie impelled him to assume such a curious position. In the First Five Year Plan Stalin unhesitatingly received the help of bureaucrats and specialists. For building up of new society and new economy specialists are important. In 1920 Lenin however partially amended his views and attitudes towards specialists. He said "we have to administer with the help of people belonging to the class the we have overthrown." This he said in the 9th Party Congress of April 1920.

Criticism

Lenin's theory of DP has been variously criticised. If the proletariat establishes its own mastery over the whole of society then what would be the fate of democratic values and institutions? The central theme of *The State and Revolution* reveals that Lenin was a great worshipper of liberalism and democracy. But the dictatorship of the working class and democracy cannot peacefully and fruitfully coexist. The DP may have several "draconian manifestations" which may be contrary to democracy and liberalism and in that case the DP may be counter-productive.

If the proletariat established its dictatorship what would be the fate of rule of law? The concept rule of law is not a liberal propaganda or full of hollowness. It is a basic feature of democracy. The dictatorship is undoubtedly a negation of rule of law. We do not think that Lenin was not aware of this lacuna of his doctrine.

Liebman in his famous work has pointed out another drawback of the concept. He says (p. 354) that the working class may exercise dictatorial power, but at the same time may make arrangements with the bourgeoisie clandestinely and such a possibility cannot be ruled out. If this at all happens that will pose the greatest danger to DP. Lenin in 1920 said that the DP is in the period of transition from capitalism to communism. Liebman is of opinion that even this reformulation cannot bend the rigidity of the doctrine.

Liebman further observes (p. 355) that the dictatorship of the proletariat was an *ephemeral thing* that was unable to survive for long the exhaustion of the political or even simply physical energy of the proletariat. Lenin was quite aware of it and in 1919 he said that the dictatorship of the working class is being implemented by the Bolshevik Party. What is the position of DP? It means the dictatorship of the party. But the two are not same. Party is a microscopic portion of the whole proletariat. Critics say that Lenin might have said of the dictatorship of the Bolshevik Party. He further softened his stand by saying that, the proletariat is merged with the party. Principles, ideologies etc. of the party and the proletariat are identical. This interpretation again, is untenable, because this does not give any scope of difference of opinion.

In fact, the criticisms of Lenin's theory of DP were so severe and widespread that he could not find out a way. Once he said that the DP was a thing of the past. At different times Lenin gave different explanations and interpretations and all these substantially confused the concept. This shows that the very foundation of the doctrine was highly feeble. Marx and Engels thought of DP as an ephemeral phenomenon, it is a period of transition from capitalism to socialism. But they did not get time to overview it closely. What would be its fate after socialisms?

Lenin on Liberalism

Lenin's attitude to liberalism and specifically to liberal philosophy of the bourgeoisie has been a controversial one. Critics say that he did not hold any definite view. He expressed different opinions at different times. We are, however, not concerned with the details. In 1903, when the Russian Social Democracy was split into two broad groups—Mensheviks and Bolsheviks—the issue of cooperating with the liberals or accepting their assistance in overthrowing autocratic rulers of Russia was first raised and debated.

It was thought at that time that if the social democrats refused to take any help of the liberal elements of the bourgeoisie, they will be ultimately *isolated* in their protracted struggle against Tsardom, and in order to avoid this it would be prudent to make an alliance with the liberals. Lenin shared this view. The struggle against the reactionary and autocratic sections of Russia must be broad-based and, in order to isolate them from the majority of the masses, the progressive section must be brought into confidence. This opinion Lenin expressed as early as 1897. But subsequently he added "This support does not presuppose, nor does it call for, any compromise with non-socialist-democratic programmes and principles". The naive implication is alliance might be sought but not at the cost of democratic principles of the Bolshevik party.

In *What Is to Be Done?* Lenin said that the bourgeois democrats are the natural and desirable allies of Social Democracy, but the essential condition of such an alliance must be the full opportunity for the socialists to reveal to the working class that its interests are diametrically opposed to the interests of the bourgeoisie. From the above comments it is quite obvious that so far as the alliance with the progressive section of the bourgeoisie are concerned Lenin did not adhere to any orthodox stand. The only point he harped upon was that principles and ideology of Social Democracy could not be jettisoned, they must be strictly followed at any cost. It further means that Lenin had always indulged in distrust about bourgeois liberalism. Any alliance with it was absolutely for advancing class struggle and isolating the bourgeoisie.

But the Russo-Japanese war of 1905 brought about a radical change in the political scene of Russia. Russia's defeat exposed her bankruptcy in all spheres, and the working class and peasants, utilising the opportunity, intensified agitation throughtout the country and under such circumstances. Lenin was not in favour of any alliance with the liberals. On the contrary the Mensheviks decided to support the liberals and Zemostovs. Zemstovs were the local assemblies. Mensheviks believed that the liberals were part of the struggle against autocracy. Lenin discarded this contention and said that they were more counter-revolutionary.

Lenin's difference with the Mensheviks began to multiply after 1904 and assumed enormous shapes between 1905 and 1914. He differed from the Mensheviks on two issues—organisation of party and alliance with the liberals. His struggles against Menshevism was largely a fight against liberalism. He could not accommodate himself with the Constitutional Democratic Party, because in his view it was the symbol of reactionism and the bourgeoisie.

Again, the Mensheviks were in favour of participating in the Duma (Russian Parliament). Even they planned to forge an electoral alliance with the Constitutional Democrats. But Lenin rejected such a proposal outright. He believed that within the four walls of Duma, the Social Democrats would hardly get any scope to fight the Tsar rulers. Moreover, with their limited membership and practically no power they would not be able to force the autocratic government to concede to their demands.

It is not easy to assess the steps taken by Lenin and the attitude he adopted. Whatever he said depended upon the prevailing situation. But Lenin always held the view that the liberals could not be wholly relied upon and in no case could they be allowed to capture the leadership of proletarian struggle. He by saying this made clear his position, although to his leaders it was not always clear.

Lenin on Parliamentarism

In order to understand Lenin's views on the Russian Parliament (Duma) it is necessary to know what Mensheviks and other leaders held about it. We have already noted that one of the main planks of dissension between Mensheviks and Bolsheviks is the participation in the activities of the Duma, 1906 and years following it saw the intensifications of conflict between the two parties. Mensheviks and other leaders such as Plekhanov, Axelrod etc. held the view that the powers of the Duma were highly limited and in some cases fictitious. But in spite of this the socialists under the banner of Menshevism could easily participate in the activities of Duma and whenever any opposition to Tsarism would arise the socialists must not hesitate to utilise it for mass struggle and to expose the misdeeds of the Tsar. A section of Menshevik Party desired to convert the floor of Duma for socialist movement. In this way Mensheviks proceeded to reformism and parliamentarism which was strongly presented by Bolsheviks. The Menshevik leaders thought that in most of the European countries the socialist movement was graced by parliamentarism and naturally they cannot go against the tide.

This tendency of the Mensheviks was vehemently opposed by Lenin and he warned his comrades against the Menshevik trap. He advised them to go to the workers of factory and villagers and peasants of countryside and to propagate among them that without class struggle and revolution it was impossible to seize power. He told them of the "impossibility of achieving political freedom by parliamentary means as long as real power remains in the hands of Tsarist government and to show the people the utter uselessness of the Duma as a means of achieving the demands of the proletarian and the revolutionary petty bourgeoisie especially the peasantry" (*quoted by Liebman*, p. 70).

Though Lenin called the Mensheviks' decision to join Duma as opportunism, he was faced with a dilemma. A section of the Bolshevik Party was in favour of participating in the Duma and it was not possible for him to disregard it. Softening his rigid stand he said that the socialists must see that the participation in parliamentary activities was to further the socialist movement and the goals of the party. In other words, the objective of participation in parliament would be "debunking of parliamentarism". Socialists must remember that the Duma was the spawn of counter-revolution and that no real good could be expected from it.

The socialists or Social-Democratic members may join the Duma on the condition that they will carry out the task of criticism, propaganda agitation and organisation. They will use the general elections as broad and effective platform of propaganda. It would never be the purpose of the socialist members of the Duma to sincerely participate in the legislative functions of the Duma.

Lenin stressed another point about the participation in the Duma. He said that the socialist members must be preserved from contamination of bourgeois parliamentary members. How could it be achieved? Lenin said that cooperation between socialist and bourgeois members must be forbidden. The Social-Democrats must strictly adhere to the principles of revolution and militancy, any deviation of socialist ideology resulting from the participation in the Duma would be a suicidal policy.

Lenin also said that the Constitutional Democrats would adopt all possible steps to purchase or motivate the Social-Democrats. It would be the duty of the Bolshevik Party to keep a close watch over that. Because the maneuvering capacity of the Constitutional Democrats is superb and they would not hesitate to adopt any measure to disrupt the socialist programme. This proposal of Lenin emanated from the Menshevik move for a joint meeting between the Social-Democrats and Constitutional Democrats.

Lenin was also not in very much favour of electoral alliance with the Constitutional Democrats in all cases. He said that only under exceptional circumstances such electoral alliance might be forged. On this issue he differed from Mensheviks. He was of opinion that in order to fight the right wing and reactionary candidates alliance might be made. Lenin thus adopted a mid and moderate path so far as participation in parliament was concerned.

Right to Self-Determination

Marx and Engels on right to self-determination : Marx and Engels in their voluminous works did not specifically deal with the question of right to self-determination or what is popularly called 'one nation one state'. This is chiefly due to the fact that they were all along advocating internationalism. They were imbued with internationalism and the movement for setting up separate nation states on the basis of nationalism would encourage the imperialist powers to intervene in the national questions and finally subjugate the weaker nations. It is the foremost duty of the proletariat to foil the conspiracy hatched by the bourgeoisie. They also advised the working men of different nationalities to forget the differences of language, religion and geographical boundaries and to unite under a single banner. Their famous slogan is 'workers of all countries unite' and needless to say this clearly rejects the demand and movement for separate national states on the basis of language and geographical peculiarities.

Marx and Engels have given a vivid picture of how the development of capitalism gave rise to the cosmopolitan character of production in *Manifesto of the Communist Party*. The bourgeoisie has, through its exploitation of the world market, given a cosmopolitan character of production and consumption in every country. All old-fashioned national industries have been destroyed or are being destroyed. In place of the old wants satisfied by the productions of the country we find new wants. National one-sidedness and narrow-mindedness become more and more impossible. With the help of rapid growth of communication the bourgeoisie had drawn all nations—both developed and underdeveloped—together. The bourgeoisie keeps more and more doing away with the scattered state of population, of the means of production and of property in a few hands. The inevitable consequence of this was political centralisation. Independent or loosely connected provinces became lumped together into one nation, with one government, one code of laws.

Although Marx and Engels were against right to self-determination, Miliband (*Marxism and Politics*, p. 102) is of opinion that classical Marxism does not deny its importance. If the people of a region agitate for a national state to free themselves from bourgeois autocratic rule, such an agitation may be supported. They believed that the movement for self-determination precedes the socialist movement. The people of an area must first of all be politically free and then they will start a struggle for socialism. They also thought that nationalism might be treated as a weapon for raising political consciousness. We can thus say that Marx's view on right to self-determination was issue-based.

Lenin's Definition

We have explained the position of Marx and Engels in respect of right to self-determination. The stand taken by Lenin is not only different from that of Marx and Engels but Lenin's is a more pragmatic one. In his book *The Right of Nations to Self-Determination* published in 1914 he elaborately analysed both the theoretical and practical aspects. After the 1905 revolution the political scenes of many countries of Europe underwent rapid changes and the impact of that influenced the idea of nationalism. It was impossible for Lenin to keep mum on this new development and *The Right of Nations to Self-Determination* is the result. He defines the concept in the following words—Self-determination of nations mean the political separation of these nations from the national bodies and the formation of an independent national state.

In the *Socialist Revolution* and *The Right of Nations' to Self-Determination* Lenin makes the following observation. The rights of nations to self-determination implies exclusively the right to independence in the political sense, the right to free political separations from the oppressor nation... The demand for political democracy implies complete freedom to agitate for secession and for referendum on secession by the seceding nation.

What is manifest in these two definitions is that he viewed the issue from the standpoint of democracy and politics. If a particular individual can claim for democratic right and political freedom a nation consisting of millions of individuals can legitimately claim political separation or the right to secede from another nation. We are quite aware that Lenin was a great worshipper of democracy and for such a person it was not possible to overlook the burning question of right to self-determination. In general terms Marx and Engels were against right to self-determination, but to free a nation from bourgeois rule people can fight for self-determination. Lenin agree with Marx and Engels. The difference is (and the difference is significant) the issue received maximum importance in the hand of Lenin.

He also said that complete equality of rights for all nations, the rights of nations to self-determination, the unity of the workers of all nations—such is the national programme that Marxism, the experience of the whole world and the experience of Russia teach the workers. We thus find that like the equality among the individuals, the nations also have the right to equality. He did not believe in the difference between nations on the basis of wealth, industry, power and position. He wanted to build up unity in the midst of diversity. By destroying diversity, unity could not be achieved at all.

Lenin's Conditions

Lenin never advocated the right to self-determination unconditionally. He said that a group of people had the right to demand separate state or to secede, does not mean that it can be supported in all cases. The demand should be considered exclusively on the merits of each particular case, in conformity with the interests of social development as a whole and with the interests of the proletarian class struggle for socialism. This implies that the demand for separate state cannot be made for the fulfilment of narrow nationalist goals. Narrow nationalism has no place in Marxism. The proletariat assesses any national demand, any national separation from the angle of the worker's class struggle.

In *The Right of Nations to Self-Determination* Lenin writes—"The interests of the working class and of its struggle against capitalism demand complete solidarity and the closest unity of all the workers of all nations, they demand resistance to the nationalist policy of the bourgeoisie of every nationality. Hence, Social Democrats would be deviating from proletarian policy and subordinating the workers to the policy of the bourgeoisie if they were to repudiate the right of nations to self-determination" What Lenin emphasises here is that if a community of people is oppressed and harassed by the bourgeoisie in the name of nationalist policy, the proletariat should come forward in support of the oppressed nation for its demand for self-determination.

Lenin believed that if the oppressed nations were deprived of right to self-determination there could never be socialism. Emancipation from oppression and exploitation was the first step to the attainment of socialism. He also said that right to self-determination was synonymous to right to secede. But the working class must think of integration and cooperation. In *Socialist Revolution and Self-Determination* we find him saying—In the same way as mankind can arrive at the abolition of classes only through a transition period of the dictatorship of the oppressed class, it can arrive at the inevitable integration of nations only through a transition period of the complete emancipation of all oppressed nations, i.e., their freedom to secede (Marx, Engels, Lenin on *Dictatorship of the Proletariat*, p. 193).

Conflict with Luxemburg : In our previous analysis we have seen that Lenin supported the right to self-determination of nations, but made it conditional. This stand of Lenin as well as of the Bolshevik Party faced the greatest challenge from Rosa Luxemburg. She called it false, corrupt and a self-centred principle. It is a dangerous principle and, if pursued strictly, that will jeopardise the class struggle and amity among the working class of all nations.

From the difference of opinion between Lenin and Rosa Luxemburg it cannot be concluded that both were diametrically opposite. It cannot again be attributed to Luxemburg that she was not in favour of oppressed people's political independence. This has been aptly stressed by Miliband (*op. cit.*, p. 103)—"It is important not to draw false contradictions...The point is not that Lenin believed in national independence and statehood for subject peoples...Rosa Luxemburg did not. The point is that Lenin and Bolsheviks believed that Marxists could not deny the right to independence. As for Rosa Lusemburg she did not believe that the subject people should be devoid the right to independence; but that this could be achieved on the basis of international socialist struggle. She denounced the right of self-determination as hollow phraseology, as a diversionary, corrupting and self-defeating slogan".

We, therefore, find that so far as right to self-determination of subject people is concerned the difference between the two is related to the technique of attaining it. Rosa Luxemburg thought that if at first international socialist struggle is allowed to occupy a back seat that will pose greatest danger to working class interest.

Lenin's Theory of Imperialism

Introduction : Lenin's contribution to Marxism in its elaboration and interpretation is many-sided but the most important aspect of this is his view on imperialism. Lenin started his analysis with Hobson's theory. J. A. Hobson's *Imperialism* was first published in 1902 and Lenin wrote his pamphlet *Imperialism, The Highest Stage of Capitalism* in January-June 1916 and was published in April 1917. He was also indebted to Hilferding's *Finance Capital* (published in 1910).

What Lenin has said in this pamphlet is neither a refutation nor a denial of Marx's views on imperialism. He writes in his pamphlet that half a century ago, when Marx was writing *Capital,* free competition appeared to the overwhelming majority of economists to be a "natural law". Today monopoly has became a fact. The economists are writing mountains of books in which they describe the diverse manifestations of monopoly (*Selected Work*, I, p. 723). Naturally we cannot say that Lenin's theory of imperialism simply rejects Marx's theory. Lenin's point of emphasis is that in Marx's epoch capitalism was the dominant feature of bourgeois economy and that was confined to free competition. In his time, capitalism has assumed the character of monopoly, and this is the highest stage of capitalism which, according to Lenin, is the moribund stage.

Lenin's Definition

Lenin defines imperialism in the following words : If it were necessary to give the briefest possible definition of imperialism we should have to say that imperialism is the monopoly stage of capitalism. Such a definition should include what is most important, for, on the one hand, finance capital is the bank capital of a few big monopolist bank...and, on the other hand, the division of world is the transition from a colonial policy...to a colonial policy of monopolistic possession of the territory of the world (*op. cit.*, p. 871).

In this definition Lenin emphasises that when capitalism reaches the stage of monopoly expansion that is aptly to be called imperialism. In imperialism, export of commodities is not of prime importance, monopolists export capital which is called finance capital. This is the most important characteristic of imperialism.

Lenin further observes that an appropriate definition of imperialism includes the following features :

1. the concentration of production and capital has developed to such a high stage that it has created monopolies which play decisive role in economic life.
2. the merging of bank capital with industrial capital, and the creation on the basis of this "finance capital" of a financial oligarchy.
3. the export of capital as distinguished from export of commodities acquires exceptional importance.
4. the formation of international monopolist capitalist combines which share the world among themselves.

5. and the territorial division of the whole world among the biggest capitalist powers is completed.

He further states that imperialism dominates monopolies and finance capital. Particularly the export of finance capital has acquired a pronounced importance. The big powers—in order to capture the market for the export of finance capital—are set to divide the territories of the world. In fact the world is divided among the big capitalist powers.

Lenin in his definition has also called it a manifestation of parasitic or decaying or moribund capitalism. The monopolies and oligarchies are fighting tooth and nail to increase the number of colonies which are weak and backward nations of Asia and Africa. When Lenin was writing his pamphlet he witnessed that monopolies did not want to confine themselves to their own national territories. This led to the keen competition amongst themselves and Lenin called it decaying capitalism. Marx and Engels saw the growth of capitalism and during their life-time though capitalism was advancing towards decaying stage they could not invest their thought. So imperialism is nothing but decaying or moribund capitalism.

Imperialism and Finance Capital

The important credit of Lenin in explaining the nature of imperialism lies in the fact that he focused upon the unprecedented growth of finance capital which surfaced at the beginning of the 20th century. He says..."the twentieth century marks the turning point from the old capitalism to the new, from the domination of capital in general to the domination of finance capital." The implication of this comment is, according to Lenin, the industrialists do not control the financial market. They obtain the use of it through the medium of banks and few other financial institutions. Finance capital is concentrated in a few hands and exercise virtual monopoly over its use. Owner of finance capital also exacts enormous profits by exporting to other countries. In developed capitalist countries the emergence of financial oligarchies have became a *fait accompli.* The owner of finance capital harvests huge profit by exploiting society, but the benefits are received by monopolists.

One of the vital aspects of finance capital and its relation to monopolies and imperialism is that the ownership of capital is separated from the application of capital to production, the money capital is separated from industrial or productive capital. Imperialism, or the domination of finance capital, is that highest stage of capitalism at which this separation assumes vast proportions. In imperialism, capital had become a commodity. In earlier epochs, capitalists exported commodities and earned profit. In the imperialist stage, financial oligarchies started to export capital and they lived on profit earned from export of capital.

Why was capital exported? Lenin had charged that if the capitalists or owners of finance capital could invest capital in agriculture or to augment the standard of living of masses, then there could not arise the necessity of exporting capital. But this had not been done. For uneven development and starvation of masses the capitalists were responsible. If the capitalism could not change or mend its course of action, it would be forced to export capital to other countries for its own survival. Moreover, the purpose of capitalists was never the development of economic situation, but to harvest highest amount of profit—and this they achieved by exporting it to the colonies.

The export of finance capital had created an interesting impact. The exporters had created their own image (image of exploitation and suppressions) in the countries where this was exported. Lenin's argument runs : "Finance capital has created the epoch of monopolies and monopolies introduce everywhere monopolist principles" (*Selected Works*, Vol. I, p. 762). It is worthwhile to note here that Marx and Engels in their *Manifesto* uttered the same thing. The capitalists earned the character of cosmopolitanism through their activities and they obliterated the differences of geographical boundaries. The nation state and concept of national sovereignty appeared indistinct in most of the cases. This is the effect of imperialism resulting from the export of finance capital.

Kautsky's definitions is—"imperialism is a product of highly developed industrial capitalism. It consists in the striving of every industrial capitalist nation to bring under its control or to annex larger and larger areas of agrarian territory irrespective of what nations inhabit those region" (*Selected Works*, Vol. I, p. 783). Lenin calls this definition "utterly worthless" because it "arbitrarily" singles out the national question. He connects the national question with industrial capitalism. This is the political aspect of imperialism. He says that the political nature of imperialism is no doubt correct, but incomplete. More important aspect of imperialism is its *economic* aspect. Kautsky was quite aware of the economic character of imperialism, but it is unfortunate that he did not give due importance to it and as a result of this his definition remained incomplete.

Lenin observes that the vital aspect of imperialism is that it *is not industrial.* Imperialism had centred around the export of finance capital. The extraordinary development of finance capital in capitalist countries was not accidental but a product of deliberate efforts. In order to export finance capital, Lenin says, the capitalists from the eighties of the nineteenth century resorted to the policy of annexation; and with the passing away of time the annexation intensified. The capitalist annexed territories not for the sale of commodities but for export of finance capital.

Evaluation

Lenin criticised Kautsky's theory of imperialism as arbitrary and one-sided because of his emphasis on the political aspect. But Lenin's theory also suffers from the same fate. He concentrated his attention on the export of finance capital. But a true theory of imperialism, we think, must encompass both politics and economics. The capitalists of the eighties of the 19th century channellised their efforts for the export of finance capital, but they did not reject or neglect the export of commodities. For these two purposes the annexation of territory appeared to them inevitable. These three aspects of imperialism cannot be separated from each other.

However, Lenin's ability to assess the correct nature of imperialism is highly laudable. In his time imperialism assumed new dimensions, it became more powerful and wide-ranging. In every corner of the world imperialism spread its branches. He was also correct when he said that the First World War was an imperialist war. Disputes centred around the share of colonies or territories. In our earlier analysis we have said that Lenin, on principle, was not supporter of right to self-determination, but if it is fought for breaking the chains of imperialism then the struggle for right to self-determination could be supported. He also wanted to extend it to revolutionary war. He advised the proletarians to extend support to those who are fighting against imperialist powers.

Leninism : Definition and Nature

Joseph Stalin in his noted work *Problems of Leninism* has defined Leninism in the following words and this definition is still regarded as classic. He said "Leninism is Marxism of the era of imperialism and proletarian revolution. Leninism is the theory and tactics of the proletarian revolution in general and the theory and tactics of the dictatorship of the proletariat in particular" (p. 16). Stalin has further observed that Marx and Engels pursued their activities in the pre-revolutionary period in which imperialism did not fully develop and, because of this, proletarian's struggle against imperialism was not an immediate practical inevitability. But Lenin, on the other hand, was faced with the problem of developed imperialism and to fight against it he used Marxism as tactics. Hence Leninism is not different from Marxism but it is "the further development of Marxism".

It is the application of Marxism the purpose of which is the emancipation of the proletariat. Stalin does not agree with the view that Leninism is the application of Marxism to the conditions peculiar to the situation in Russia. He says that such a definition is partially correct. It is true that Leninism was applied to the peculiar conditions of Russia, but it is definitely not national, it is applicable to all countries ruled and dominated by imperialism. According to Stalin, Leninism was applied to the Russian conditions, but above all *it is an international phenomenon rooted in the whole of international development.*

He is not also in agreement with those who say that Leninism is the revival of the revolutionary elements of Marxism. In the opinion of Stalin "Leninism not only restored Marxism, but also took a step forward, developing Marxism further under the new conditions of capitalism and to the class struggle of the proletariat. Leninism is exceptionally militant and exceptionally revolutionary in character. Marx and Engels laid down the basic principles of class struggle and proletarian revolution. Lenin applied those principles to the peculiar socio-economic practical situation of Russia. But *Leninism is general in character, it is applicable to all situations of societies having the features of capitalism.* In his lifetime Lenin did not get the opportunity to apply his ideas based on Marxism to other areas of the world particularly to the areas of the Third World. It is the viewpoint of the disciples of Leninism that it is never a drawback or limitation of Leninism.

The character of capitalism that prevailed in the last few decades of the 19th century underwent radical changes in the first two decades of the 20th century and, in that changed situation of capitalism, Lenin applied the basic principles of Marx and Engels and here lies the credit of Lenin. To be more precise, Lenin made Marxism a realistic or practical ideology. Leninism is an instrument of proletarian revolution. In the words of Liebman "There is hardly any insurrectionary movement today, from Latin America to Angola, that does not lay claim to the heritage of Leninism." The point of emphasis is that Leninism can claim its role in every revolutionary movement of the world. Stalin is, therefore, right when he claims that Leninism is international.

Liebman has viewed Leninism still from another angle. He says "Leninism even in its mistakes and in spite of its failures, is one of the richest sources of inspiration in the fight for socialism, one of the most fruitful contributions to men's struggle for their emancipation" (Liebman, *Leninism under Lenin*, p. 448). That is, Leninism is not a simply a weapon for the struggle of emancipation it is also a source for establishing socialism. In other words, Leninism shows the way how socialism could be established.

Leninism is both a theory and an instrument for class struggle. A theory is essential for the guidance of workers. Marx, Engels and Lenin—all believed that the proletarians must have a sound knowledge about the development of capitalism, its nature and various aspects of contradiction and the nature and growth of imperialism. Above all, the nature and extent of exploitation. They must have sound knowledge about revolution. For this reason Lenin throughout his life emphasised upon the spread of theoretical knowledge about Marxism among the proletarians. Lenin believed that when the attainment of theoretical knowledge is more or less adequate they make preparations for a class struggle.

Leninism has also practical aspects. It is an instrument of revolution. Proletarians will derive lessons from Leninism how to launch and conduct a revolution. Leninism also stresses that the revolutionaries will try to establish the compatibility between tactics and real situation. The implication is that Leninism is not something rigid. But flexibility does not indicate opportunism. Leninism teaches that before any action every situation must be cautiously judged. Leninism is not adventurism. Before jumping upon any action Leninism advises to judge a situation in its proper perspective.

But there is difference of opinion about the exact nature and other aspects of Leninism. Kolakowski observes that the character of Leninism as a variant of Marxist doctrine has long been subject of dispute (*Main Currents of Marxism*, Vol. II, p. 381). Kolakowski wants to say that Leninism is a "variant of Marxist doctrine". It is not an explanation of the principles of Marx and Engels. It is to some extent a different theory. There is some truth in this characterisation. It is said that Lenin did not scrupulously follow all the principles of Marx and Engels. He changed or amended them to suit the special socio-economic conditions of Russia. This attempt of Lenin makes him subject of criticism. The critics say that Lenin cannot claim to be a faithful follower and interpreter of Marxism. One critic says that Lenin had been false to Marx's doctrine on many essential points.

It is true that Lenin deviated from some of the basic principles of Marx and Engels. For example, he laid maximum importance to the national question whereas Marx and Engels did not do that. Marx and Engels were out and out internationalists. Their clarion call was "Workers of all the world, unite". Lenin wanted to build up party organisation and he gave maximum emphasis upon it. Marx and Engels did not think the issue in proper perspective. Marx and Engels thought of effecting an alliance with the bourgeoisie in the phase of bourgeois revolution. Critics say that Lenin was in favour of making alliance with workers and peasants. But the protagonists of Leninism rule out any deviation of Leninism from Marxism. They argue that Lenin scrupulously adhered to the basic doctrine of Marx and Engels. He simply interpreted it to suit the peculiar situations.

Lenin's Contribution to Marxism

As to the contribution of Lenin to the development of Marxism there are two distinct groups of thought—one believes that Lenin amended the basic principles of Marx and Engels and, in certain cases, abandoned some principles to suit his own thought-system. Other groups holds an opposite view. It says that Lenin has interpreted Marxism and this is in full consonance with the central theme of Marxism. It further states that Marx and Engels are not always clear. There are a number of lacunae in their thought and philosophy. Lenin has simply filled up those with his own ideas—keeping in mind the basic philosophy of these two thinkers. This attempt cannot be treated as an amendment or abandonment of Marxism. The orthodox followers of Marxism-Leninism belong to this group. Lenin himself said in his *Our Programmes* "We do not regard Marx's theory as something completed and inviolable; on the contrary we are convinced that it has only laid the foundation stone of the science which socialists *must* develop in all directions if they wish to keep pace with life." This is more or less the prevailing idea about Lenin's contribution to Marxism and in the following pages we shall make attempt to show how Lenin developed Marxism.

The authors of *The Fundamentals of the Marxist-Leninst Philosophy* have said that Lenin developed Marxism in the new historical conditions which are mature development of capitalism, its conversion to imperialism, the fierce struggle among the imperialist powers and the intensification of class struggle. These conditions demanded that it is the vital duty of the Marxists to analyse and interpret the ideas of Marx and Engels and to throw light on them. The authors conclude "unless this was done, the philosophy of Marxism would cease to be a living theory, a method of cognition and revolutionary action". Lenin was not a great scholar like Marx and Engels. Nor was he a great theoretician. His contribution lies in developing the central idea of Marxism. The above-noted authors have said "Leninism is not an interpretation but a development of Marxism, that without Leninism the theory of Marx and Engels cannot correspond to contemporary historical conditions, which naturally could not have been reflected in the works of the founders of Marxism."

Now there is a controversy regarding interpretation and development. The orthodox Marxists adhere to the term *development*. We are of opinion that there is hardly any tangible difference between the two words. Without interpretation a social theory cannot be developed in the background of new conditions. Hence interpretation and development of a social theory go hand in hand.

R. N. Carew Hunt (*The Theory and Practice of Communism*) says p. 171) : "Marx never explained how his revolutionary objectives would be actualised and seems to have supposed that this was a matter for which the revolution would itself provide the solution. That Lenin, faced with practical problems of administration which had never entered into Marx's orbit, should have found himself obliged to adapt the classic theory according by was natural enough and whether we regard this as a distortion it will depend upon how far we regard Marxism as providing the basis of a genuinely democratic society."

R. N. Carew Hunt (op. cit.) has pointed out the fields in which the contribution of Lenin to Marxism is quite prominent. He says that under the leadership of Lenin there were two revolutions in Russia—one in 1905 and the other in 1917. In these two revolutions Lenin applied the theory and tactics of Marx and Engels and modified some of their principles as situation demanded. The purpose of these revolutions was to destroy the existing social and economic order and the establishment of the dictatorship of the proletariat. This was Marx's one of the fundamental principles. But the credit of Lenin lies in the fact that he applied the principles in the peculiar situation of Russia. Many people in these days accuse Lenin of distorting Marxism. But Carew Hunt says (op. cit., p. 179) that the same charge may be brought against his followers of western socialism. The fact is that Lenin fully understood the economic, social and administrative situation of Russia and adopted his tactics suitable for those conditions. He thus developed the principles of Marx and Engels.

Lenin's another contribution in the development of Marxism is his ideas about state and his classic work *State and Revolution* throws sufficient light on it. Engels in his *Origin of Family, Private Property and State* has said in seizing power the proletariat will put an end to State...as State and this state will ultimately wither away. But this observation of Engels raised plethora of objections and questions and many critics ridiculed the withering away of state. But in the *State and Revolution* Lenin has elaborated in great detail what Engels wanted to mean. He has clarified the point that there is difference between bourgeois state and the proletarian state after revolution. He has also explained what Engels actually meant by withering away of state. The elaboration of Marxian state is not to be found in the vast literature of Marx and Engels.

There was a misconception (before Lenin) that the proletarian revolution and the establishment of the dictatorship of the proletariat would end the very existence of state. Lenin warned his followers and detractors that it was a wrong conception. Only the establishment of communism will end the state. The proletarian state, according to Lenin, is the bourgeois state without the bourgeoisie. He also makes a distinction between anarchist theory of the destruction of state and Marxist theory of withering away of state. This is undoubtedly a remarkable improvement upon Marxian theory of state.

Lenin's another contribution lies in his definition of class. It is a great irony that a very good part of Marxism occupies class and class struggle, but neither Marx nor Engels has defined class in clear terms. In the last volume (III) of *Capital* Marx makes a good beginning to define class, but he has not been able to end the project. *A Great Beginning* is one of Lenin's famous works and here he defines class. This definition is in full conformity with the ideas of Marx and Engels. The students of Marxism treat this definition of Lenin as a standard Marxist definition of class. Lenin thus completes Marx's concept of class.

Marx and Engels spoke of the dictatorship of proletariat. They were quite aware that an organised working class could achieve that goal. But they could not enter into the detailed activities of the working class in the realisation of this objective.

While Marx and Engels were great scholars and philosophers Lenin was a great practical man and activist. He believed that the revolution could never be a reality without an organisation and, for that very fact, he channelised his efforts and energy for the organisation of a party. The party is the highest form of class association of the proletariat. It is also the instrument of dictatorship of the proletariat and embodiment of the will of unity. Lenin had a strong belief that without an iron party it was impossible to carry out the dictatorship of the proletariat. On the role and organisation of the party Lenin came into conflict with several leaders of Russia.

Marx and Engels were chiefly concerned with the development and evils of capitalism, but Lenin studied it in a broader perspective. He makes an elaborate analysis of imperialism in his *Imperialism, the Highest Stage of Capitalism,* Lenin felt that any analysis of capitalism without an elaborate analysis of imperialism would remain incomplete. The communists hold the view that Lenin's idea about imperialism is a notable advance in Marxist economics. In fact, in Lenin's time, capitalism advanced to such an extent that it assumed the character of imperialism and for that reason he focused his attention to imperialism. If Lenin did not do that the real character of capitalism and its ultimate fate would never have been exposed. Marx and Engels spoke about the contradiction in capitalism, while Lenin extended those contradictions to imperialism. This is not the distortion of Marxism but its development. The contradictions in capitalism forced capitalists to be involved in internecine war.

Lenin borrowed the principle of dialectics from Marx (and he borrowed it from Hegel) and explained scientific materialism. Following Marx and Engels, Lenin developed dialectical materialism not only as a world outlook, but also as a theory of knowledge, a method of thinking and of practical transformation of reality (A. P. Sheptulin—*Marxist-Leninist Philosophy*, p. 86). Lenin's further elaboration of materialistic dialectics, and his study of the dialectical materialist theory of knowledge are of everlasting importance.

We know that both Marx and Engels were immensely influenced by the contemporary developments in natural science—particularly the fundamental discoveries. These are regarded as great sources of Marxism. It is said that Lenin, following Marx and Engels, closely studied the fundamental scientific discoveries and moulded and generalised the revolutionary philosophy in the background of those discoveries.

Sheptulin observes (op. cit., p. 88) "Lenin developed the Marxist teaching on the character and motive forces of the bourgeois democratic revolution and its connection with the socialist revolution."

The above analysis does not prove that Lenin's contribution to Marxism's development is undisputed. The learned interpreter of Marxism, Kolakowski, says that the innovation that Lenin introduced into Russian revolutionary movement suggested considerable doubt as to his fidelity to Marxist tradition. This charge against Lenin is not exaggerated. He did not interpret or develop some of the basic principles of Marx and Engels but amended them. He replaced the dictatorship of the proletariat by the dictatorship of the communist party.

40 POLITICAL IDEAS OF MAO ZEDONG

Biographical Sketch

Mao Zedong (in Wade-Giles romanisation it is Mao-Tse-tung) was born on 26 December 1893 at Shaoshan of Hunan Province, China and died on 9 September 1976. He was born in a very poor peasant family. His family had a small business of rice and pigs and his parents had also a trade of money-lending. His father was quite capable of providing education to Mao but that did not happen. From the very childhood Mao joined the business of his father and, as a result, Mao was deprived of formal education. Mao had an indomitable thirst for knowledge and this led him to acquire knowledge from different sources. He began to neglect his father's business and in his father's opinion it was an unpardonable act. He began to beat Mao mercilessly. The cruel nature of Mao's father forced him to leave home. He travelled several places and this provided an opportunity to be acquainted with revolutionary thought. After some time he returned home and found his father a changed man. This opened his eyes. He came to believe that any type of protest and resistance had the power to produce results. His father surrendered to his rebellious nature and since then Mao decided to protest any type of wrongdoing.

In 1909 Mao enrolled in a secondary school and completed his studies of that standard. Finally he graduated. It is said that his upbringing enabled him to be acquainted with revolutionary thought along with Buddhism and Taoism. It is to be noted that the religious aspects of Buddhism did not appeal to him. Its dialectical elements attracted him. The dialectical nature and aspects of Taoism also impressed him. Needless to say that the revolutionary nature of Mao blossomed when he seriously studied the dialectics of Buddhism and Taoism.

Mao's indoctrination to Marxism began at the age of twentyfive when he got a job as an assistant librarian in 1918. In those days the Chinese had no interest in revolutionary thoughts because revolutionary literatures were not available in China. Even the writings of Marx and Lenin were not translated in Chinese. At the beginning of 1920s some news about the success of Bolshevik revolution of Russia reached China and Mao got access to them. This convinced him that if the Bolshevik Revolution could overthrow the powerful and autocratic ruler of Russia, a revolution of the same type could do the job in China. This conviction inspired Mao to make preparations for a revolution. In these circumstances the first task of Mao was to prepare the ground for a revolution. He was of opinion that the social, political and economic conditions of China were ready to welcome a revolution of the Bolshevik type.

"Nationalism emerged as a real force in 1919 with the May Fourth Movement in which there were widespread demonstrations and rioting when it was learned that the corrupt government had agreed to hand over to the Japanese the important province of Shantung in spite of the promises by the Western powers that it should revert to China" (David McLellan, *Marxism After Marx*, p. 218). Nationalism and revolutionary thought began their appearance almost simultaneously. The Western ideas of democracy and parliamentary system failed to appeal to the educated and political conscious people of China. They thought that Chinese society with all its aspects could be radically changed only by means of revolutionary methods propagated by Marx, Lenin and their followers. Keeping this in mind some people founded the Chinese Communist Party in Shanghai in 1921.

Crossroads in Chinese Society

For several centuries China was a stable society. There were very few or no political, social, economic and other upheavals. She was primarily an agricultural country as her land was fertile. Agricultural produce was sufficient to feed the hungry mouths. There were mountains and rivers which provided natural security. Besides agriculture there were handicrafts which provided parttime employment. China also had an official philosophy—Confucianism. Again, she was free from outside political interferences and this was another cause of internal stability. From the standpoint of modern civilisation China was definitely a backward country, but her civilisation was quite rich.

In the nineteenth century China was confronted with changes and some problems. She came under the administration of the Manchu Dynasty. The rulers imposed their rules and regulations upon the self-sufficient society of China. The self-sufficient and peaceful China was shattered. Outside connection was at the centre of China's entry into new world. Foreigners were lured at the natural wealth and resources of China and they began to plunder the resources. People of China were not prepared to resist foreign invasion and naturally they fell into the grip of foreign powers. Nationalist feeling was not sufficient to resist the foreign invasion. Several incidents took place that placed China on the forefront of world incidents and international politics. One such incident was the Opium War that took place in 1840. Japan was an imperialist power and she had an eye on China's natural wealth. Not Japan alone, several Western powers were quite eager to plunder the resources of China. At this time the time-old internal stability of China was faced with several problems. Neither the people nor the ruler had the ability to fight away.

China was again at the crossroads. There emerged a conflict between Western culture which had already started its invasion into Chinese society and the old or traditional culture and institutions of China. There was a conflict between the two which could not be easily solved. The Chinese society was divided into two sections. One strongly supported the Western culture and the other was in favour of retention of Chinese culture and civilisation. The solution was not easy and this created problems for all. Many educated men of China wanted to introduce the Western system of education and mode of living because they thought that the adoption of Western culture could modernise China. They also wanted to import Western science and technology. When this conflict was at its zenith and the people of China were quite perplexed the lackeys of imperialist power had already started their business of plundering and exploitation. Various conflicts divided China and there was ill-feeling among various parts. The rulers were incapable of solving the conflict. The foreigners fully utilised this situation. "With no emperor to unify the country only different centres of military remained, controlled by various warlords whose irregular troops battered on the peasantry, destroyed the economic equilibrium of the countryside, and swept aside for ever the imperial bureaucracy. It was during this chaotic period of "warlord rule" from 1915-1925 that Mao Zedong formed his political opinion (David Mc Lellan–*Marxism after Marx*, pp. 217-218). Stuart Schram in his *The Political Thought of Mao Tse-tung* says "Ideas grow out of history, they also shape history" (p. 15). We thus find that at the crossroads of Chinese society the tensions, torture inflicted upon Chinese peasantry and the internal situation considerably influenced by the political ideas of Mao

Factors that Influenced Mao's Ideas

The thoughts of more or less eminent persons are largely influenced by factors they encounter or incidents they have studied with interest and Mao is not an exception. He once said "Today's China is an out-growth of historic China". Society, history, peasantry, culture, civilisation, internal situation, China's relation with foreign powers all these separately or combinedly influenced the political philosophy of Mao Zedong. He also studied the heroic activities of Washington, Napoleon, revolutionary activities of Lenin and, above all, Marx's works. He thoroughly studied the past history of China and fully acquainted himself with the miserable political and economic conditions of Chinese people in general and the peasantry in particular.

We have already noted that from the very beginning of the nineteenth century the intervention of foreign powers—especially America and Japan—began to change China's internal situation and this change was not for better but for worse. This disturbed Mao's mind and he thought that the influence of foreign powers must be resisted at any cost. But he was convinced that the task is not easy. Above all what is required is to arouse the nationalist feeling of the Chinese people, particularly peasants. China was chiefly an agricultural land and peasants constitute the largest portion of population. Naturally, in every revolutionary function the peasants must participate.

He put a great emphasis on the opinion of the people. He studied the Bolshevik Revolution of Russia and the lesson he gathered from it is that without whole-hearted participation of the largest section of the people a revolution could never be successful. Particularly, the revolution process of Russia put a great positive mark on his thought. He gathered the experience that the people of China were mentally prepared to greet a revolution. But what they required was a bold and dynamic leadership.

Lenin was indebted to Marx; and Mao was indebted to Lenin. Mao was convinced that if Lenin could bring about a revolution in Russia by adopting Marx's principles it is possible for him to change China through revolution. Russia was a semi-feudal state and China was primarily an agricultural country. Mao did not pay too much importance to this difference. His main concern was how to convince the Chinese peasantry of the basic aspects of Marx. The people of China must be convinced that only a revolution was capable of changing the economic situation and emancipating the people from exploitation. Stuart Schram said (*Thoughts of Mao*) "Mao's debt to Lenin is obvious". Like Lenin, Mao believed that political consciousness does not emerge spontaneously. That is, like Lenin, he had no faith or very little faith on the idea of spontaneity. The people of China must be indoctrinated to revolutionary ideology and philosophy and this must be preceded by protracted propaganda and continuous efforts. The common people must be convinced that only through a revolution they can achieve emancipation.

Like Lenin he also laid great emphasis on the role of a political party based on the philosophy of Marx. At the age of 28 Mao wholeheartedly engaged himself in the organisation of a party. Under his leadership Socialist Youth League was formed in 1921. The formation of Socialist Youth League was quickly followed by the formation of the Chinese Communist Party (CCP) and it was founded in Shanghai in 1921. There were thirteen founder members and Mao was one of them. Like Lenin, Mao was pragmatic. Both Lenin and Mao were convinced that without a revolution a radical change of society is impossible. From 1921 right up to the 1949 revolution, Mao's sole objective was to free China from feudalism and colonial menace.

Maoism and Mao's Philosophy

From the sixties to the end of last century the term Maoism was very popular in the Communist World. Along with it there was another term "Thoughts of Mao." Many people preferred this. Whatever it may be, we must try to know what is Maoism? The term is not properly clarified and explained. Kolakowski, the erudite scholar on Marxism and allied concepts, defines Maoism in the following words : "Maoism in its final shape is a radical peasant Utopia in which Marxist phraseology is much in evidence but whose dominant values seem completely alien to Marxism. Not surprisingly, this Utopia owes little to European experience and ideas" (pp. 1183-84). The term Maoism can be treated as the combined product of Mao's own thought based on the indigenous situation of China. But its root can be traced to Marx's and Lenin's thought. Maoism was not the direct product of Marxism. But it is not absolutely alien to Marx's basic thought and philosophy.

Maoism is not the product of dogmas based on intellectual thought and principles. He liberally borrowed the basic principles of revolution from Marxism and he was also heavily indebted to Lenin who applied Marx's philosophy in Russia. So we can say that the application of Marxism started with Lenin and it was subsequently followed by Mao. In a restricted sense, Maoism can be called a continuation of Leninism, but it cannot be called a carbon copy of Leninism and not even Marxism. Maoism, in a sense, is a variation of communism, but it is not aberration from Marxism or communism. According to COD, Maoism is the communist doctrine of Mao and applied in China. "Mao was one of the greatest manipulator of large masses of human beings in the twentieth century and the ideology he used for the purpose is significant by reason of its effectiveness not in China but in other parts of the Third World" (p. 1184). This is Maoism.

Mao was not a philosopher comparable with Marx and Engels nor did he write volumes of works. Notwithstanding his interpreters have found out some traces of his philosophy in his limited works. After the formation of the Communist Party of China in 1921 he involved himself in revolutionary activities. His belief was that the peasants and common people must be well-acquainted with the revolutionary doctrine and for that purpose he wrote several articles and the most important are

"*On Practice*" and "*On Contradiction*)". "*On Practice*" was published in July 1937. The subtitle of this essay is : *On the Relation Between Knowledge and Practice Between Knowing and Doing*. Another article *On Contradiction* was written in August 1937. These two articles constitute the central idea of his philosophy. He wrote these articles during the guerrilla warfare. Some interpreters of Mao's philosophy say that he did not write these two articles. During the guerrilla warfare he delivered lectures to the party's military school at Yenan Kolakowski says that these two articles "constitute almost the whole of philosophical education".

In *On Practice* Mao said : Marxists regard man's activity in production as the most fundamental practical activity, the determinant of all his other activities. Man's knowledge depends mainly on his activity in material production, through which he comes gradually to understand the phenomena, the properties, and the laws of nature" (Mao Tse-Tung, *Selected Works*, pp. 643-644). In a classless society every person, as a member of society, joins in common effort with other members and enters into definite relation of production. On the other hand, in all class societies, the members of different social classes also enter into definite relations of production. The class struggle exerts a profound influence on the development of man's knowledge. In all class societies man lives as a member of a particular class. Every kind of thinking is stamped with the brand of a class. In this analysis of Mao there is very little that can be branded as new. However, what he said has been endorsed by many Marxists. Man earns knowledge and experience from practice. Again knowledge guides man and here lies the importance of philosophy. Kolakowski observes (p. 1185) that the Chinese fought against imperialists without proper knowledge and guidance. The philosophical knowledge enabled them to act properly.

Mao's article *On Practice* has another importance—on this point Mc Lellan says (op. cit., p. 228) : "*On Practice* married the *Theses on Feurbach* with a crude, inductive natural scientific method and denied that Marxism had any ontological basis or underlying metaphysic." Mao did not like book learning and his aversion to book learning is clear in this article. He says : the dialectical materialist theory of knowledge places practice in the primary position. Human knowledge cannot be separated from practice. Practice is always higher than knowledge. The importance of knowledge does not depend on subjective idea but on the social practice. Naturally practice is more important than precept. Practice is always higher than knowledge. According to Mao, the Marxist philosophy of dialectical materialism has two outstanding features. One is the class nature or structure of society and the other is its practicality. A theory is always dependent on practice. He also said that Marxism emphasises the importance of theory because it guides action. Mao put both theory and practice under the same umbrella. One cannot be thought without the other.

On Contradiction reveals another aspect of Mao's philosophy. *On Contradiction* it has been said that Mao wrote this article to free the party from the dogmatic thinking that was prevalent at the beginning of the thirties of the last century. The context of this article was the subject of a lecture delivered by him at the Anti-Japanese Military and Political College. He has said that the objective of the study of philosophy should be the eradication of dogmatist thinking. Explaining the nature and contents of materialist dialecties Mao makes the following comment : "The metaphysical world outlook holds that in order to understand the development of a thing we should study it internally and in its relations with other things, in other words, the development of things should be seen as their internal and necessary self-movement while each thing in its movement is interrelated with and interacts on the things around it (op. cit., pp. 658-659). He continues "The fundamental cause of a thing is not external but internal" (p. 659). The reasons of develop-ment lie in the contradictions within the thing. Without contradiction a thing cannot develop. Whenever there is contradiction there is movement and movement means progress. Hence contradiction, movement, and progress are inter related.

"Contradiction is universal and absolute. It is present in the process of development of all things and permeates every process from beginning to end" (p. 663). Mao further observes that the question is one of kinds of different contradictions—not of the presence of contradiction. Everywhere there is contradiction and it is the vital cause of progress. Mao borrowed this concept from Engels. Later on Lenin developed the concept. "Contradiction is present in the process of development of all things, it permeates the process of development of each thing from beginning to end. This is the universality and absoluteness of contradiction" (p. 664).

Mao has also said that since there are different kinds of contradiction, these can be settled in different ways. For example, the contradiction between proletariat and bourgeoisie is resolved by the method of socialist revolution. Whereas the contradiction between the great masses of men and the feudal system is settled by the method of democratic revolution. Again, there is a type of contradiction between colonies and imperialist powers and this type of contradiction is generally resolved by national liberation movement. Sometimes contradiction is found between workers and peasants. The collectivisation and mechanisation can settle this contradiction. Mao has talked about other types of contradiction and he has also suggested how these can be resolved. This indicates that he had deep and clear knowledge about contradiction.

Mao further writes : The productive forces, practice and the economic base generally play the principal and decisive role; whoever denies this is not a materialist. But it must be admitted that in certain conditions, such aspects as the relations of production, theory and the superstructure in turn manifest themselves in the principal and decisive role. When it is impossible for the productive forces to develop without a change in the relations of production, then the change in the relations of production plays the principal and decisive role. When the superstructure obstructs the development of the economic base political and cultural changes become principal and decisive.

Revolution

The chief contribution of Mao in the field of political thought is his idea about revolution. But it is unfortunate that he has not systematically analysed the various aspects of revolution. In *On Contradiction* he observes that a revolution is generally caused by the internal contradictions that exist in a society. In a bourgeois society there are contradictions or conflicts among the classes—particularly between the two main classes—bourgeoisie and the proletariat. The contradictions assume such nature that these cannot be reconciled by adopting the normal procedures. The result is that the contradictions continue to plague the society. The ills of the society can be removed by a revolution. He has said that the conflict between working class assumes such nature and dimension that it cannot be resolved by normal procedures. Revolution is the only way. Similarly, there are conflicts between imperialist powers and colonies. The conflicts can be settled by countrywide agitation which is revolution.

In his concept of revolution Mao has invited the idea of contradiction. Borrowing Marx's and Lenin's idea he says that in every bourgeois society there are contradictions and when the roots of contradictions have gone to the depth of the society, naturally they cannot be easily resolved. The only way is revolution. In his theory of revolution Mao has borrowed Lenin's views and practically he has very little originality. Lenin emphasised the irreconcilability of antagonism between classes and only a revolution can provide a solution. Repeating Marx's idea of revolution Mao says that in every bourgeois society there are various types of contradictions and only revolution can remove contradiction. But there is a difference between bourgeois revolution and "proletarian revolution". The latter changes the society from top to bottom while the former changes it superficially. It can be called cosmetic surgery. Hence a proletarian revolution is necessary for an overall change of society.

Mao has also emphasised the importance of party in a revolution. The success of revolution primarily depends upon a well-organised party structure. Party is really indispensable for a revolution. He once said to lead the revolution to success or victory a political party is necessary. But a party must follow its own line and must be dependent on the general mass. Party is the vanguard of masses. He also said that the party must not detach itself from the common people.

In *On Contradiction* Mao said that the contradictions or conflicts prepare the ground for a revolution and it is the duty of the leaders to inspire the people for revolution, because mere existence of contradiction can never be a cause of revolution. At the right moment people will utilise the contradictions in their own favour. Mao has said that the antagonism between the proletariat and the bourgeoisie is the main cause of hostility and this hostility will finally lead to revolution. Hence it is the duty of the leaders to use the antagonism. He once said : "Revolution or revolutionary wars are inevitable in class society and that without them it is impossible to accomplish any leap in social development and to overthrow the reactionary classes and therefore impossible for the people to win political war". Like Lenin, Mao believed that antagonism between the hostile classes could not be settled without war, that is, revolution. The exploited class must be prepared to take arms.

On nature of revolution Mao's view is still remarkable. He said "A revolution is not a dinner party or writing an essay or painting a picture or doing embroidery, it is not to be so refined, so leisurely and gently, so temperate, kind, courteous, restrained and magnanimous. *A revolution is an insurrection, an act of violence by which one class overthrows another,* This constitutes the central idea of Mao's theory of revolution. According to Mao a revolution must be violent because the capitalists and reactionary elements will not accept the reasonable demands of the proletariat.

Into his concept of revolution Mao included another technique and it is guerrilla warfare or to launch a sudden attack against the enemy. His theory of revolution also includes all sorts of conspiratorial practices. The chief objective of Mao's revolution is to defeat the enemy from behind. In war he did not allow ethics, principles etc. to intervene because he knew that all these would hinder the success of a revolution. The guerrilla warfare and conspiratorial practice do not mean that he lost faith on the use of arms. His belief was that the use of technique depends upon the situation. According to Mao the chief objective in war is to defeat the enemy and naturally the selection of technique depends upon the situation and also the strength of the enemy.

Class struggle is also another technique of revolution. But Mao differed from Marx, Engels, Lenin and Stalin on the concept of class. All of them have spoken about class in the background of capitalist society. But Mao viewed the idea in the light of China whose main class was peasantry. Hence in Mao's class struggle the peasants must play the leading role. According to Mao the peasants, the lumpen proletariat and industrial workers must combinedly launch a revolution against the bourgeoisie and all the reactionary forces. All these must be well-prepared to attack the bourgeoisie. But in revolution there is no place of adventurism.

The Cultural Revolution

The Great Proletarian Cultural Revolution is an innovation which Mao made to cleanse the Chinese society—particularly the superstructure—from the bourgeois ills. Towards the middle of the sixties of the twentieth century Mao saw that the superstructure of the Chinese society was in the grip of bourgeois influences and ills. Though the base—that is the economic structure of China—was socialist the superstructure—that is institution, art, literature, law and numerous organisations—were heavily influenced by capitalist thought and philosophy. According to Mao this was an undesirable development and it must be checked at any cost. He thought that this type of superstructure had enough power to influence as well as control the base on its way. In order to stop this process Mao called a new type of revolution which is called Cultural Revolution. Its sole aim was to free the Chinese society from all the undesirable elements and to set up a pure communist society in China.

"Formally the Cultural Revolution began in the summer of 1965. But it properly began in August 1966 in the universities with a mass campaign to eliminate what were seen as "Rightists", to reemphasise the importance of Mao's thought, to lessen specialisation, and substantially to restrict the role of examinations" (Mc Lellan op. cit., p. 249). Hence the Cultural Revolution is not a political revolution. According to Mao and his followers, the revolution of 1949 freed China politically. But cultural freedom was badly needed. In order to guide the Cultural Revolution a Central Committee of China's Communist Party was formed on 8 August 1966. The Central Committee adopted certain decisions. These may be stated in the following way :

1. The Cultural Revolution touches people to their very souls and constitutes a new stage in the development of socialist revolution in our country. The bourgeoisie is not completely overthrown and its remnants are still there and it is continuously trying to stage a comeback and gather forces. It is also trying to impose its ideas, principles, customs, culture and habits upon the people. If this at all happens that will pose a great danger to the Chinese society. That attempt must be destroyed and Cultural Revolution will do that task.
2. Mao was firm that since it is a revolution it will meet resistance from several corners, particularly from the bourgeoisie, and it is the duty of the people to scuttle that mischievous attempt.
3. It is the conscious behaviour and education of the people that can foil the mischievous attempt and therefore it is the duty of the party to educate the

people about the ill-designs and motives of the bourgeoisie. People must adopt ruthless and strong measures. It is also to be noted that a revolution is never refined.

4. People will launch an attack against the ultra-reactionary and revisionist forces. At the same time, Mao's thought shall be propagated among the masses of people.
5. People must know the nature of contradictions and they will act in accordance with them.
6. It is the purpose of the Cultural Revolution to reform, transform, and, if necessary, remove the old methods and system of teaching. It is necessary to overhaul the whole educational system to the tune of socialism.
7. In order to fight the reactionary forces it is imperative to hold aloft the thoughts of Mao. By doing this the entire superstructure of Chinese society can be rebuilt. It was necessary because the growing influence of bourgeoisie was weakening the socialist superstructure of Chinese society. In the sixties Mao felt this and for that reason he called for a Cultural Revolution.

The Great Leap Forward

Another important aspect of Mao's political thought is The Great Leap Forward. In the late fifties and early sixties it gained wide publicity. It was a pet view of Mao that the economic development advanced in "waves" rather than gradually. That is, development all on a sudden appears like a great storm. Being guided by this conception "Mao pre-empted the Second Five Year Plan by launching the frentic economic drive that came to be known as Great Leap Forward" (McLellan, p. 238). Mao emphasised the decentralisation of planning and he believed that this will help the "Leap" The leap consisted in the advancement of small scale and local industries and development of agriculture. Again, the development of agriculture will ultimately help the large scale industries.

Mao toured the length and breadth of China and arrived at the conclusion that the local and surplus labour must be properly mobilised and utilised for the general development of the economy. It is necessary to mobilise the unused resource and unemployed masses for the economic progress and, for that purpose, decentralisation of planning was essential. In his opinion this decentralisation of planning will help the leap. Mao did not support the Soviet type of centralised planning. This is called Mao's approach—decentralisation and radicalisation of the whole planning process and system. He reorganised the whole planning system with a view to producing iron and steel goods at the local levels with the help of materials available at the local levels. This will again help the large scale industries and, in this way, China's progress will get sufficient encouragement. This will serve several purposes—planning will be decentralised, small scale industries will be encouraged and advancement will be like waves.

'Hundred Flowers Bloom' Theory

In May 1956 Mao gave a slogan—"may a hundred flowers bloom, and a hundred schools of thought contend". The campaign was launched by the Communist Party of China in 1956. The time is interesting. In the same year the 20th Congress of Soviet Communist Party was also convened. Mao adopted a strong party domination and collectivisation. In numerous cases this approach of Mao met with strong disapproval and sometimes strong criticism. The intellectuals and various sections of society strongly felt the need of necessary freedom. Mao at the same time felt that the separation of the intellectuals and educated masses of men from the general administration and governmental affairs was not producing favourable results. Their cooperation was strongly felt.

Mao once said "you may ban the expression of wrong ideas, but the ideas will be there. On the other hand, if correct ideas are pampered in hot-houses and never exposed to the elements and immunised against diseases, they will not win out against erroneous ones. Therefore, it is only by employing a method of discussion, criticism, and reasoning that we can really foster correct ideas and overcome wrong ones, and then we can really settle issues. .....Dogmatic criticism settles nothing. We are against poisonous weeds of any kind, but we must carefully distinguish between what is really a poisonous weed and what is really a fragrant flower" (Mao Tse-Tung *Selected Writings*, National Book Agency, Kolkata 1967, pp. 715-716). In the same article—"*On Let a Hundred Flowers Blossom, Let a Hundred Schools of Thought Contend* and *Long Term Coexistence and Mutual Supervision*—Mao said : "Different forms and styles in art should develop freely and different schools in science should contend freely. We think that it is harmful to the growth of art and science if administrative measures are used to impose one particular style of art or school of thought and to ban another" (p. 713). One should not settle the question of right and wrong in art and science arbitrarily and whimsically. While imposing restriction upon the art or science utmost caution must be adopted.

The eighth Party Congress of the Communist Party of China was held in September 1956 (only a few months after the Twentieth Party Congress of CPSU). In this party congress there was a strong current of constructive criticisms which deal with various activities of party leaders. The activities regarding collectivisation came under strong criticisms. It was observed that there was over-hastiness in several fields, especially collectivisation. The abnormal growth of the power of bureaucracy also came under severe criticism. All these criticisms came mainly from party leaders who are renowned intellectuals and university teachers. All these were due to Mao's doctrine of let hundred flowers blossom. Formerly many leaders could not tolerate criticism. But after Mao's declaration of hundred flowers blossom these persons welcomed all the criticisms.

In the same article Mao said (p. 717) :

1. Words and actions should help to unite, and not divide, the people of our various nationalities.
2. They should be beneficial, and not harmful, to socialist transformation and socialist construction.
3. They should help to consolidate, and not undermine or weaken, the people's democratic dictatorship.
4. They should help to consolidate and not undermine or weaken democratic centralism.
5. They should help to strengthen, and not discard or weaken, the leadership of the Communist Party.
6. They should be beneficial, and not harmful, to international socialist unity and the unity of the peace-loving people of the world. The purpose of these

restrictions, we believe, was not to restrict the freedom of thought and expression. The right to freedom of thought and expression was primarily meant to allow all kinds of people, particularly intellectuals, to freely culture art, literature and various sciences. We can call it a type of liberalism.

We know that Mao was all along a pragmatist. In some cases his dogmatism surfaced, but on many issues he adopted the path of pragmatism. The present article was published in February 1957. The age of Republic of China was just eight years and by this time Mao and his other close comrades came to realise that excessive restrictions would go against the interest of socialist constructions. It is generally said that man learns more from the criticisms than from the eulogy. In former Soviet Union party and bureaucracy practically controlled both the policy-making process and general administrations. The harmful consequences were strongly felt towards the end of seventies and beginning of eighties of the last century. The tangible result was the adoption of *perestroika* and *Glassnost*. But all these dismally failed to save the Soviet system. We believe that the Maoist liberalism was not sufficient for the free thought and freedom in the intellectual world. We, however, treat the hundred flowers bloom-theory as a warning to the attempt to control everything.

New Democracy—Definition and Nature

An important aspect of Mao's political ideas is his conception about democracy. This he explained in his widely read and discussed article *On New Democracy* published in January 1940. When Mao wrote this article China was not a republic and more particularly a communist state. Hence by new democracy he meant democratic China would no longer be oppressed (politically) and exploited economically. When China would be politically free she would make continuous and untiring efforts to be economically prosperous. In Mao's view political freedom and economic prosperity would lay the foundation of new democracy. But for these two a revolution is indispensable. After revolution China will set up a democracy. Explaining the nature of new democracy Mao makes the following observation :

"The historical characteristic of the Chinese revolution lies in its division into two stages, democracy and socialism, the first being no longer democracy in general, but democracy of the Chinese type, a new and special type, namely New Democracy" (*op. cit.*, p. 60). The question is how can this be achieved? It can be achieved through revolution—the Chinese revolution. The revolution of China will have two stages—in the first stage the colonial, semi-colonial and semi-feudal forms of society will be transformed into an independent democratic society. But this does not mean a new democracy. The Chinese revolution is a continuous process. This democratic society will be transformed into a socialist society. Hence the new democracy will be a combination of democracy and socialism. This will come through revolution.

Mao claims that his concept of democracy differs from the so-called bourgeois democracy. He says : "The so-called democratic system in modern states is usually monopolised by the bourgeoisie and has become simply an instrument for oppressing the common people" (p. 69). Mao's main emphasis is on British-American system of democracy where only the bourgeoisie plays the dominant part and this is a small fraction of the entire population. Naturally, this cannot be called real democracy. According to Mao, the bourgeois democracy consists of a very small section of people and it is concerned with the welfare of this small section. His claim is that the democracy envisaged by him will be basically different from bourgeoisie democracy. The New Democracy of China will represent all sections of people and it will be managed or controlled by the revolutionary class of entire mass. It will be based on universal and equal suffrage.

Explaining the nature of New Democracy, Mao further maintains that this democracy is characterised by universal suffrage and democratic centralism. He says : "The state system, a joint dictatorship of all revolutionary classes, and the system of government democratic centralism—these constitute the politics of New Democracy, the republic of New Democracy" (p. 69) The new democracy will also emphasise the economic aspects of China. New Democracy of China will be the owner of all big banks and the big industrial and commercial enterprises. Railways, airlines and other public utility concerns shall be managed by the Chinese government. The state enterprises will be of socialist character. The economy will develop along the line of regulation of capital and equalisation of land ownership.

New Democracy : Ends and Means

The new democracy envisaged by Mao in both an end as also a means. It is an end in the sense that continuous and serious efforts shall be made to achieve or establish such a type of democracy. The purpose of the Chinese revolution was to free the land from all sorts of oppression and colonial rule. The economy, politics, and culture of China were fully controlled by the bourgeoisie and lackeys of foreign rulers. The revolutionary masses, after a protracted war, will ultimately remove the foreign rulers and indigenous oppressors as well as their supporters. After doing this the revolutionary masses will finally establish a new people's government which will be democratic in all manifestations. Hence the objective of revolutionary masses shall be to achieve democracy by hook or by crook. In this sense, new democracy or, in general, democracy is an end.

But Mao is not satisfied with the achievement of democracy. He thinks that it must be used as a means—a means to be used to attain further nobler goals. Let us quote few words from his noted essay *Contradictions Among the People* :

"Marxism teaches us that democracy is part of the superstructure and belongs to the category of politics. That is to say, in the last analysis, it serves the economic base. The same is true of freedom. Both democracy and freedom are relative, not absolute, and they come into being and develop in specific historical conditions". There shall exist a unity between democracy and centralism. Also, there shall exist a unity between freedom and discipline. All these finally constitute the concept of democratic centralism. In democratic centralism people will enjoy extensive democracy and freedom. But at the same time they have to keep within the bounds of socialist discipline (p. 696).

Mao proceeds to discuss the objectives of new democracy in its role in establishing a socialist culture. Mao knew that there was an incongruity between socialist state and bourgeois culture. According to Marx, culture is an important part of superstructure and the capitalists build up the culture in order to strengthen the superstructure because superstructure generally provides protection to the base which is economic structure of society. Mao says : "A given culture is the ideological reflection of politics and economics of a given society. There is in China an imperialist culture which is a reflection of imperialist rule or partial rule, in the political and economic fields. This culture is fostered not only by the cultural organisation run directly by the imperialists in China but by a number of Chinese who have lost all sense of shame" (p. 84). Keeping this in mind Mao decided to build up a new culture which will foster the socialist culture. It is believed by all Marxists that there are gulf of differences between socialist culture and capitalist or imperialist culture. If a socialist culture is not built up the imperialist or capitalist culture in a socialist state will contaminate the entire socialism. The new democracy aims at establishing a new economy and new politics. Along with it, a new culture will be set up. According to Mao there is a friendly alliance between the imperialist culture and the semi-feudal culture in China. This alliance is quite dangerous for the entire Chinese society. In order to save China, this alliance must be destroyed and a new socialist culture will be built up. New Democracy will have to do the job. Mao beautifully says : "There is no construction without destruction, no flowing without damming and no motion without rest, the two are locked in a life and death struggle" (p. 84).

41 SOME TWENTIETH CENTURY MARXISTS

Introductory

In this Chapter I shall discuss the political ideas of some Marxists of twentieth century. Both Marx and Engels left this world before the end of the nineteenth century, but the ideas they propagated created a lively discussion and lot of enthusiasm among the top intellectuals of Europe. All of them were not orthodox Marxists but from the intellectual point of view they accepted Marxism. This chapter includes Karl Kautsky (1854–1938), Rosa Luxemburg (1870–1919), Trotsky (1879–1940) and Gramsci (1891–1937). All of these thinkers are celebrated Marxist thinkers or philosophers and through their contributions they have, in various ways, enriched Marxism. Not only this they were very influential. Marx died in 1883 and the First International Working Men's Association was formed in 1864. In this Association both Marx and Engels participated. Not only Marx and Engels, many other socialists were parts of the First International (1864–1876). It is also called the Federation of Working Class Organisation. The workers of Western and Central Europe assembled together to discuss their problems and to find out the strategy of struggle against the bourgeois class. The Industrial Revolution by that time had been a century old and the problems created by it had touched almost all the major sections of society. Particularly the working class was the worst victim of the Industrial Revolution.

The First International concluded its session in 1876 and after a lapse of thirteen years The Second International began in 1889 and ended in 1914. Marx could not attend the Second International. But this International was based on International Workers' Congress and it was also the brain-child of Marx. In the First International both Marx and Engels played the most crucial role. From 1864 to 1872 Marx in various ways controlled this International. He drafted almost all the documents and participated in all the discussions. There was a General Council of the First International and Marx was the central figure. Many other participants, however, could not accept this position of Marx. From 1872 Engels was at the centre of First International. After Marx's death the Second International was founded in 1889. Though it was without Marx there was Engels and there were also the ghost and shadow of Marx. His thought and writings practically dominated the intellectual aspects of the Second International. "Like the First International it was based essentially on the European labour movement" (Bottomore, p. 263).

There was a Third International (1919–1943). Due to the outbreak of the First World War (1914–1918) the Second International disintegrated. But the followers of Marx and Engels were eager to revive another International and Lenin was a key figure of this International. Lenin heartily welcomed the Third International and he wrote a slogan. This was 'The Second International is dead, overcome by opportunism... Long live The Third International'. This Third International is also called the 'Comintern or Communist International'. The Third International or Comintern was founded in Moscow in March 1919. The Bolsheviks took maximum interests and in fact it is due to their interests the Comintern started to function. The Third International was founded at a very crucial time because in 1917 Lenin came to power in Russia and it started to function in the background of the October Revolution. The Third International is of great importance.

KARL KAUTSKY

Life and Time

Kautsky was born in 1854 and died in 1938. His father was a Czech and mother a German. When Kautsky was just a youth he came in touch with socialism or socialist thought, because in those days the political and economic ideas of socialism were not widely discussed and propagated. At the age of twenty Kautsky entered a university and immediately came in contact with socialist party and the supporters of socialism. We, therefore, find that his inclination to socialism was spontaneous or inborn. To be well acquainted with socialism or socialist philosophy Kautsky thoroughly studied economics, history and other branches of social science. Malthus once propagated that economic poverty of the people was mainly due to the overpopulation. But Kautsky challenged this view. He said that the economic and other related factors were chiefly responsible for the poverty of the people. By the eighties of nineteenth century Kautsky was partially able to establish himself as a socialist thinker because he wrote a number of articles in various magazines and published small books. His association with socialism went from deep to deeper practically from 1885. He lived in London from 1885 to 1890. During this period he came to be associated with Engels and was influenced by him. In those days London was an active centre of communist or socialist thought. We may call it a hub. Many of the budding socialists went there and discussed socialism at their heart's content. He authored several books and the most important of them was *The Road to Power* which was published in 1907. He thought that Marxism is a natural scientific materialism. It can be applied to society for its general upliftment.

Any analysis of Kautsky's political philosophy will invariably remain incomplete if we don't throw adequate light on his relation or connection with The Second International. Kolakowski, in his monumental work *Main Currents of Marxism*, makes the following observation : "The figure of Karl Kautsky dominates the theoretical development of Marxism for the whole period of the Second International. While certainly not an outstanding philosopher, he was the chief architect and, so to speak, the embodiment of Marxist orthodoxy" (p. 379). He was a great supporter of orthodox Marxism and in support of his stand he incessantly argued with other participants. His role was crucial in establishing Marxism as a "serious intellectual discipline." Kolakowski says that (p. 379) in general sense he was not an orthodox Marxist. He did not hesitate to criticise some major or important views of Engels. Kolakowski is of opinion that he was "pedantically orthodox" in the sense that he believed that in order to explain and understand social phenomena Marxism is indispensable. Again, for the purpose of analysing various elements which dominate or influence society Marxism will considerably help. Kolakowsky concludes (p. 379) "It was thanks to his interpretative work that the stereotype known as scientific socialism—the evolutionist, determinist and scientistic form of Marxism—became universally accepted in its main lines" Kautsky argued with great labour and patience in various sessions of Second International that the philosophical aspects of Marx must be seriously thought and analysed. It is not possible to go into the depth of Marxian philosophy with meagre knowledge. The main currents of Marx's philosophy shall be studied and analysed in the proper perspective, because Marx was a great materialist.

Revolution and Socialism

In *The Road to Power* and other works he emphasised the necessity of socialism and in order to set up a socialist state the only road is revolution. He criticised the arguments and suggestions of utopian socialists as to the setting up of a socialist society. He called appealing to the industrialists and capitalists as "political fantasy" because the industrialists will never abandon the path of exploitation. What remains, therefore, is, if socialist society is an "objective" necessity, then the only way to achieve it is revolution. This revolution can be launched only by the workers, peasants and by those who are exploited. In *The Road to Power* the point he made clear is that without the direct action to be taken by the working class, which may be called revolution, the building up of a socialist society will remain a far cry. There is an unbreakable relationship between revolution and socialism; peaceful means and parliamentary processes, according to Kautsky, are incapable of establishing socialism. Naturally revolution is an inescapable means. Explaining the nature of revolution Kolakowski observes : "A revolution, in the sense of a conscious seizure of political power by the organised proletariat, was an essential and inevitable precondition of socialism" (p. 390).

Kautsky was quite faithful to Marx on a number of issues and aspects and as regards the necessity of revolution there is no deficit in his faithfulness. Following Marx he said that revolution is not something which will be achieved without any labour, rather it is to be achieved through continuous struggle. In this struggle the proletarians must involve themselves directly and effectively. That is the primary responsibility of the proletarians, to participate directly in the entire process of revolution. We, therefore, find that people's participation is an indispensable precondition of revolution. The working class must realise that the capitalist class in all ways will obstruct the efforts for revolution. But the proletarians must take an uncompromising attitude towards the goal (to achieve a revolution and set up a socialist society).

Many Marxists have explained the ideas—revolution, role of the proletariat and their desire to participate in revolution—in their own fanciful ways. But Kautsky was a strict follower of Marx and he said that mere existence of poverty is not a sufficient precondition of class struggle. He has further observed that the poverty in its extreme form must lead to class antagonism and class polarisation. But the polarisation of classes is not a wishful thinking, it has several preconditions.

Following Marx's views Kautsky says that the development of capitalism must reach the highest point of its manifestation and that stage will be highly favourable for antagonism between the two major classes. Moreover, the antagonism will be irreconcilable. There is nothing new in this opinion of Kautsky. The irreconcilable relation between the two major classes bourgeois and proletarian will again remove the hurdles on the way of formation of a working class party. We find that Marx, Engels, Lenin and Kautsky all emphasised the irreconcilability of class antagonism. Some pseudo-Marxists say that the falling rate of profit will lead to the collapse of capitalism. But, following the line of Marx, Kautsky said that mere fall of profit is not enough for the breakdown of capitalism, it will collapse due to the inability of capitalism to cope with the progress of technology.

On Nature of Socialism and Capitalism

Explaining the nature of socialism Kautsky says that it aims at the emancipation primarily of the working class because it is the most exploited one and subsequently it aims at the emancipation of the whole human race. This emancipation comes through several means and the foremost among them is the abolition of the private ownership of the means of production. Socialism will also do away with the management of state by the bourgeoisie. On this point there is a difference between the anarchists' view of state and Marxists' view. The anarchists argued for the abolition of state because it is the embodiment of all ills that are generally found...Kautsky says that the state will remain and continue to exist, but its nature and function will undergo radical changes. The whole state will be transformed into an organ of social administration which will look after the general management of society's material production, its distribution and other related matters. Like Engels he does not directly talk about the abolition of state. But he talks of nature, purpose and functions of state which is socialist. A socialist state is no class state, it is a state or political organisation for all people. A socialist state aims at the welfare of all, development of all and happiness of all.

Kautsky has said that a socialist state will never come into existence at a single stroke of revolution. First of all a political revolution will free the state from bourgeois rule. He calls it the first stage of socialist state. But this is not all. In his *The Social Revolution* (1902) he says that in order to be a true socialist state there shall occur another revolution and it is *social revolution.* A political revolution will simply capture the state power. But a social revolution will free such a state from all the bourgeois evils. Hence a mere political revolution transforms a capitalist state into a socialist state. Kautsky mentions various forms of struggle which might be used to capture state power and according to him strike or general strike might be used, but the use of such a weapon must be done with utmost caution. Uncautious use of strike should be avoided. He cautioned the working class to avoid Blanquism or the Blanquist way of revolution. Louis-Auguste Blanqui (1805–1881) wanted "to carry out an insurrection to replace the capitalist state power by its own revolutionary dictatorship" (Bottomore, p. 52). Kautsky disfavoured the insurrectionary methods for the capture of power.

Kautsky has said that capitalism is fully responsible for a revolution. Because it created all sorts of exploitation and oppression from which common people in general and working class in particular suffer. Naturally they will try to free themselves from exploitation and oppression. He reminds us by saying that the workers are not responsible for the crises from which capitalism suffers. The capitalism digs its own grave and workers through a revolution throws the capitalism into that grave. At the initial stages the capitalists were able to fight away the crises of capitalism, but when all the means were exhausted capitalism was unable to get itself rid of the crises. At the penultimate stage the workers, through revolution, were able to destroy capitalism. Kautsky has also said that only one crisis is not enough for a revolution. So far as crises in capitalism and its destruction are concerned Kautsky's analysis faithfully follows Marx's line of thought. In this regard he has succeeded in establishing himself as an orthodox Marxist. He is not at all an original thinker. Of course he does not claim this.

Other Political Ideas

Kautsky was a faithful follower of Marx and when Lenin gave the leadership of Bolshevik Revolution (or February Revolution) in 1917 he welcomed it and he called this Revolution a "new epoch for all Europe." He believed that this Revolution would advance the revolutionary zeal of the fighting forces of all the capitalist countries. Particularly the proletarians will be inspired by this. But after few days he was disheartened. He thought that the establishment of a revolutionary state was not all for a real revolution. It must combine both democracy and socialism because it was his firm belief that one is not complete without the other. If a party consisting of a very small section of supporters imposed socialism upon the masses that can never be called democracy. Behind socialism there must remain the support of the majority people. But in post-revolutionary Russia the Bolshevik Party was the determiner of all social and political issues. This practically threw democracy in a dustbin.

There arose a controversy between Lenin and Kautsky on a vital issue. Kautsky said that in order to settle all the political issues a parliament is to be convened which will represent the majority people. In other words a parliament will be a manifestation of democracy. But unfortunately Kautsky's suggestion was ignored and finally this embittered the relationship between the two topmost Marxists. On the relationship between democracy and socialism Kautsky said : "Democracy and socialism do not differ in the sense that one is a means and the other is an end, both are means to the same end. For us socialism is unthinkable without democracy. By modern socialism we mean not only a social organisation of production, but also a democratic organisation of society". This explanation on the relationship between democracy and socialism is really unique. Lenin differed, but the argument of Kautsky is unassailable. Even today we hold the view that both democracy and socialism are two sides of the same coin.

Kautsky held different view on the dictatorship of the proletariat. In *"The Dictatorship of the Proletariat* (1918) he pointed out the following meanings or aspects : (1) The proletarians will get majority in parliament and they will get it through democratic process where other parties will participate. That is, the proletarians will capture power through the democratic process. (2) The proletarians will set up a socialist society through democratic means where all other parties having full faith on socialism will participate. But the party led and controlled by the working class will have the priority. (3) Though the proletarians will play the dominant role they will not take any step to suppress different rights and freedoms of citizens. (4) The government headed by proletarians will make elaborate arrangements for holding periodical election to verify its popularity. In other words, the dictatorship of the proletariat will honour popular consent. (5) The government led or controlled by the proletarians will administer the state by nonviolent ways but only in special circumstances, such as counter-revolutionary situation, the government of the proletarians will apply force or violent measures. What Kautsky has said in his analysis of the meaning of dictatorship of proletarians is quite analogous to democratic or parliamentary system. Lenin did not accept Kautsky's view about proletarians' supremacy and parliamentary system. Explaining his opinion Kautsky claims that Marx also used the term in this sense. To Marx, dictatorship of the proletariat meant overall domination of the proletarians which is also called the hegemony of the workers. But the hegemony or the dictatorship shall always be based on democratic means and procedures. The workers will not impose anything upon the people.

Kautsky further maintains that Marx never thought of establishing a socialist society through dictatorial means. But to Marx democracy had a different meaning. In society there shall exist social and political equality as well as economic equality. No economically powerful class can exist in a socialist society. Naturally all will get enough opportunity to exercise all the rights. In bourgeois democracy the economically powerful class controls everything, but in a state having dictatorship of the proletariat there will exist no such class. In bourgeois democracy, the bureaucracy, for all practical purposes, controls all the aspects of state affairs. Explaining Marx's view Kautsky says that in a bourgeois system of government the minority always runs the administration and the working class or proletariat is controlled and exploited. But in democracy under the dictatorship of the proletariat the majority will rule and there will prevail democratic process and atmosphere. There shall be no scope of exploitation of one class by another. Kautsky further observes that in a democracy under the dictatorship of the proletariat there shall not exist any reference to any particular class. We thus see that Kautsky explains the concept of dictatorship of proletariat chiefly in the background of democracy and in this regard his claim is Marx viewed both democracy and dictatorship of the proletariat in this light.

Lenin and Kautsky

Lenin once called Kautsky the chief of German revolutionaries. That is, Lenin believed that under the leadership of Kautsky the German revolutionaries would succeed in converting Germany into a socialist state. Lenin also praised Kautsky's method of scientific analysis of Marx's doctrine and method. But after the October Revolution Lenin vehemently opposed many of the views of Kautsky, and not only this, Lenin even called him "renegade". In 1918 Lenin published *Proletarian Revolution and Renegade Kautsky.* In order to have a proper understanding we mention some of the basic issues of the controversy between the two great Marxist thinkers. Kautsky said that to Lenin dictatorship of proletarian was a form of government. Lenin claimed that his thinking was absolutely in the line of Marx. On the contrary Kautsky said that dictatorship of proletariat is not a form of government but a type of society; that is it is related to social content. In support of his argument Kautsky refers to the Paris Commune. He says that in the Paris Commune Marx used the concept in this sense. The Paris Commune was based on democratic principles, multiparty system, free elections and the free expression of opinion. Here lies the main point of difference between Lenin and Kautsky. Lenin completely ignored Marx's method of establishing dictatorship of the proletariat. Kautsky was against Lenin's method of applying force. But there was argument in Lenin's favour. He argued that Russia was a backward country and in such a state Marx's principles cannot be followed properly, Lenin's objective was to defeat the counter-revolutionary forces and the conspiracy of capitalists and in order to do that the democratic principles and processes shall be kept in abeyance. Kautsky did not agree with this.

In order to make clear the picture of controversy that arose between Kautsky and Lenin I quote here a long passage from Kolakowski's *Main Currents of Marxism* : "The original sin of Bolshevism lay in the suppression of democracy, abolition of elections, and denial of freedom of speech and assembly and, in the belief that socialism could be based on a minority despotism imposed by force, which by its own logic was bound to intensify the rule of terror. If the Leninists were able to keep their 'Tartar socialism' going long enough, it would infallibly result in the bureaucratisation and militarisation of society and finally in the autocratic rule of a single individual" (p. 395). To what extent Lenin achieved success that is evident from the activities of the Soviet Government. The internal trouble in Soviet Russia surfaced at the beginning of the eighties of the last century. People of Russia did not accept the suppression of democracy and the establishment of socialism by physical force. Ultimately, in Russia, a new bureaucratic system came into existence. The bureaucrats completely controlled administration and only a handful of persons controlled the policy-making process. This was the nature of Russian socialism. Kautsky was against such a form of socialism and he apprehended that socialism without freedom, political party, free elections etc. will result in such a system. According to Lenin Kautsky was a "renegade". But subsequent events prove that Kautsky was not wrong. The suppression of democracy cannot be tolerated by people for an indefinite period of time. It is unfortunate that while Kautsky realised this Lenin failed and his failure led to the collapse of the entire Soviet system at the beginning of the nineties of the last century.

ROSA LUXEMBURG

Biographical Note

Rosa Luxemburg was a Polish Jewess. She was born in 1870 and on the night of January 15, 1919 she was murdered. The city of Zamose was her birth place and this place was the centre of Jewish culture. But her birth place was surrounded by Austria, Poland and Russia. Naturally the political, social and cultural activities of these three places influenced the people of Zamose and Rosa was not free from this influence. By birth Luxemburg was Polish but on the various aspects of her life there was a clear influence of German culture and life-style. In many areas of Poland, Germany and Russia in those days (in the seventies and eighties of the nineteenth century) socialism was enthusiastically discussed by the people of different classes and Rosa came in contact with these people. While studying in Zurich University, Luxemburg came in close contact with social democracy. From her biography we come to know that when she was just a teenager socialism or socialist philosophy put an indelible mark on her thought.

From the 1890s Rosa Luxemburg devoted herself completely to the study of socialism and its propagation. At this time she settled in Berlin and joined the socialist party. In *Social Democratic Review* her political writings were published. It is to be noted here that towards the end of the nineteenth century the political ideas—specially the revisionism of Eduard Bernstein—were hotly debated among the socialists of Germany. Rosa was quite aware of it and she took interest in the revisionist ideas of Bérnstein. But she strongly opposed the revisionism and to combat it she began to publish articles and pamphlets. In this respect her most notable writing was *Social Reform or Revolution?* This created sensation in the academic circles.

In *Social Reform or Revolution*? Luxemburg openly challenged the utility of revisionism. She believed that only a revolution had the capacity to change the economic and political condition radically. At the beginning of the twentieth century the political and other conditions in Russia reached the boiling point and in 1905 the revolution in that country dismally failed. This frustrated Rosa and in order to get a firsthand knowledge she illegally went to Warsaw. But she was arrested. Rosa believed that the failure of the 1905 revolution was temporary. The revolutionary activities must be made intensive and the workers must take proper lessons from the failures of the 1905 revolution. At this time (in the first decade of the twentieth century) she deeply involved herself in the revolutionary activities of several European countries. She worked with Plekhanov, Axelrod and Lenin—all of whom were in exile. Though she was actively associated with the revolutionary activities of several European states her active relation with the German socialist movements is very important. Here she came in touch with several top-ranking leaders of Germany and she came in touch with the German Communist party. Gustav Luebeck was a noted revolutionary and when Rosa was working in Germany she had relationship with him and finally married him. Rosa was very intelligent and acquired vast knowledge on socialism and related subjects. She was extremely meritorious and a voracious reader. She was quite fluent in several languages such as French, Polish, Russian and German. She had also working knowledge in English and Italian. A biographer of Rosa Luxemburg once said in her time she was the most civilised voice for the cause of international socialism.

Reform, Revolution and Revision

The pamphlet *Social Reform or Revolution* (1899) Contains her views regarding revolution, revisionism and collapse of capitalism. It is generally argued by the pseduto-Marxists that according to Marx with the development of capitalism several contradictions will develop within it and finally these will lead to the collapse or breakdown of capitalism. This is known as the "breakdown theory" of capitalism. This is one of the most controversial aspects of Marx's theory. Eduard Berstein and many others challenging this argued that if capitalism because of its inherent contradictions collapses, is there any necessity of revolution or class struggle? In fact, revolution and automatic breakdown of capitalism are contradictory. Rossa has said that the revisionists and pseudo-Marxists have mininterpreted Marx's theory. Explaining Rosa Luxemburg's stand Kolakowski says that capitalism will collapse does not mean that it will collapse automatically—without the need for revolutionary action. Kolakowski further says (p. 415) "It was rather the case that imperialism must develop to a point at which it would awaken the revolutionary consciousness of proletariat, without which capitalism could not be overthrown. Its overthrow was a historical necessity, but so was the revolutionary movement that must bring it about." This is the unambiguous position of Rosa and other orthodox Marxists regarding automatic collapse of capitalism and the necessity of revolution. The contradictions within capitalism will weaken capitalism and the relations between capitalists and workers will deteriorate day after only. The working class will "utilise" this situation in its favour and then it will attack the capitalist class.

Rosa Luxemburg has further pointed out that it is wrong to hold that there is no necessity of reforms. Rosa had a clear view about reforms. The chief objective of reforms is to conquer political power. But if reforms are treated as ends in themselves, the purpose of reforms will be futile. On various issues Rosa stood on the opposite side of Bernstein, reforms and revisionism are chief no doubt. On another issue the difference between the two is also remarkable. For example, Bernstein propagated a slogan : "the goal is nothing, the movement everything." On the other hand Luxemburg said : The movement as an end in itself, unrelated to the ultimate goal, is nothing to me; the ultimate goal is everything." (Quoted by Kolakowski, p. 416).

Bernstein concentrated on reforms and he treated revolution as a secondary means. Luxemburg did not agree with him. She maintained that the ultimate goal of the working class would be to seize political power and to that end reform may be used as a weapon. In fact the struggle for political power does not stand opposite to struggle for reform. Rosa said that reforms are necessary because they can raise the level of consciousness of the workers. The reforms do not possess the ability to change radically the economic and other pictures of society. But these will lead the working class to revolution. Through reforms workers will be acquainted with the nature and depth of exploitation of capitalists. Bernstein once said that in Britain the workers had adopted a method of cooperation and technique of reform and by this they achieved remarkable success. Rosa was acquainted with that. But in this respect her clear opinion was that the British workers had clearly abandoned the class relations. "The British proletariat had adopted bourgeois ideas and sacrificed class objectives for immediate gains" (Kolakowski, p. 418). But the technique of the British workers cannot be taken as a model. The objective condition of capitalist development is quite ripe for a revolution. Naturally the question of compromise and cooperation does not wise.

In the *Introduction* to *the Class struggle in France* Engels made a famous as well as controversial announcement where he declared that for brief period the workers may adopt parliamentary and democratic methods as means of struggle against the capitalists. Luxemburg did not agree with Engels' view and branded it as reformist policy. She further maintained that if his suggestions were strictly followed that would be another type of reformism. Rosa says that in his later years Marx saw that the technological development in capitalism would reach such a stage that capitalism will have no control over it. Marx predicted that this situation would arrive very soon and the working class must be prepared for that opportune moment. In that situation the workers' first and foremost duty would be to launch a violent attack against capitalism and by violent attack Marx meant revolution. This has been clearly explained by Kolakowski in his analysis (pp. 418-419). Luxemburg vehemently opposed Bernstein's revisionism and his attitude towards evolutionary socialism. She called Bernstein's approach "vulgar bourgeois economics". Luxemburg did not rule out the importance of reforms. But she wanted to emphasise that the purpose of any reform must be to clear the way of the advent of revolution and establish socialism. The British working class was absolutely misguided and adopted the path of reforms to achieve transitory gains. Luxemburg condemned it. All these clearly reveal that her faithfulness to Marxism was beyond doubt.

Conflict between Lenin and Luxemburg

After 1895 (the year of Engels' death) the writing of both Marx and Engels finally stopped, (Marx alread expired on 1883). But the death of the two great philosophers completely faild to draw a curtain on the continuous discussion and threadbare analysis of their voluminous writings spread over a period of long six decades. Though at the beginning there was a cordial relationship between Lenin and Luxemburg, this did not last long. A serious controversy between the two great Marxists surfaced on the issue of spontaneity. Luxemburg, after studying all the aspects of revolution, drew the conclusion that spontaneity was the vital matter of all revolutions. By spontaneity she did not mean : a blind impulse devoid of idealogical self-awareness. "Not only Marx had predicted the proletarian revolution, but his prediction must itself become a part of the proletarian consciousness in order for the revolution to come about" (Kolakowski, op. cit., p. 420). In other words, Marx predicted that a revolution based on the consciousness of the working will ultimately come and that will dethrone the bourgeoisie from power. In several writings Luxemburg emphasised this idea of spontaneity and she claimed that this idea of spontaneity was vital to Marx's theory of revolution—particularly in March 1903 Luxemburg published an article in which she focused this matter.

Luxemburg said that consciousness, spontaneity, revolution all are closely related issues. The working class, at the very initial stage, must be fully conscious of its own plight or sufferings and that consciousness will inspire the workers to launch a struggle against the exploiters. Spontaneity comes out of consciousness. The workers will launch a struggle against the capitalists. But instead of spontaneity Lenin emphasised upon the party organisation. A central party consisting of few revolutionaries would be the core of any revolution. The Central Committee would accept the absolute responsibility of revolution. Luxemburg calls the idea of Lenin "Ultracentralism" and it is a "piece of opportunism." The central party organisation will direct and guide the function of democracy and this is called social democracy. Following Lenin's stand it has been said : "The centralisation of social democracy, based on the two principles—the blind subjection of all party organs and their activity, down to the minutest detail to a central authority, which thinks, acts and decides for everyone—and secondly, the strict separation of organised core of the party from the surrounding *milieu*, as Lenin would have it, —seems to us no more or less than a mechanical transference of the Blanquist principles of the organisation of conspiratorial groups to the social democratic movement of the working class" (Kolakowski, p. 420).

The point to be emphasised is that Luxemburg did not accept Lenin's excessive faith on the "ultracentralism" Lenin could not lay his confidence on the spontaneity of the workers. His apprehension was that the working class, without guidance and leadership, cannot act and lead a revolution. The workers will spontaneously participate in all the revolutionary movements and activities. Their participation may not always find grand success. But, according to Luxemburg, participation is important. They will make mistakes and through these mistakes they will, once, find out the correct way. Let us quote her : "Historically, the errors committed by a truly revolutionary movement are infinitely more fruitful than the infallibility of the cleverest central committee" (Luxemburg). By announcing this Luxemburg makes her position visa-a-vis Lenin clear. Revolutionary masses will decide everything and through struggle they will get the right lesson. To her, party meant a self-organising proletariat. It is not an organisation managed and directed by professional revolutionaries and few leaders.

What Rosa thought about Marx's view regarding consciousness, spontaneity etc. can best be stated in the words of Kolakowski : "Marxism was not merely a theory of the historical process but an articulation of the consciousness, latent though it might be as yet, of an actual workers' movement. When that consciousness took shape, i.e., when the spontaneous movement achieved theoretical self-knowledge, the distinction between theory and practice would cease to exist : the theory would become a material force, not in the sense of being a weapon in the struggle, but as an organic part of it" (p. 422). The clear difference between Lenin and Rosa Luxemburg on the vexed question of party leadership and spontaneity is that Lenin always treated party in the role of manipulator and director. But Rosa challenged this view and made clear her position by announcing that the simple role of the party is to explain the true objectives of the workers. Luxemburg said that workers' movement should not be manipulated by the self-styled leaders of the party. But when she found that the Bolshevik party under the leadership of Lenin was just doing this she vehemently opposed it and reminded the spontaneity and consciousness of the workers. To sum up, while Luxemburg regarded spontaneity and consciousness as vital elements of revolution Lenin did not.

Rosa Luxemburg strongly opposed Lenin's theory of party leadership. Rosa's belief was that according to Lenin party is like a night watchman. The party's function is to watch, guide and direct the proletariat in their struggle against the bourgeoisie. Let us quote Rosa again. She said : The ultracentralism asked by Lenin is full of sterile spirit of the over-seer. It is not a positive and creative spirit". She thought that if Lenin's method is followed that would enslave the young revolutionaries to few intellectual elites who are hungry for power. These intellectuals will again manipulate the party and its several organisations and they will finally the central committee of the party. She had firm faith on the organisational and other capacities of the workers.

Rosa said that if political situation permits the party can seize power and in that case only a small section of population will support revolution. But after that it would be the duty of the party to convince the population of the real objective of the party, that is, what the party intends to do. After capturing power the party cannot unleash terrorism. The party must follow all sorts of democratic norms and policies and must adopt representative tactics. Rosa had a belief that the democratic principles and institutions are not always perfect. But that cannot be a ground of abolishing them. In her *The Russian Revolution* Rosa said : "Freedom only for supporters of the government, only for members of a single party, however numerous, this is not freedom. Freedom must always be for those who think differently". "Socialism was a live historical movement and could not be replaced by administrative decrees" (Kolakowski, p. 423).

Rosa on Mass Strike and Trade Union

The question of spontaneity reappears when she talked about mass strike and trade union movement. She wrote an article : *Mass Strike, Party and Trade Unions.* In her opinion the mass strike was the "spontaneous expression of the creative power of the broadest masses and antidote to bureaucratic inertia, it linked political with economic struggles" (Bottomore *A Dictionary of Marxist Thought*, p. 328). She was of opinion that through a spontaneous mass strike under the leadership of party and trade union certain basic demands which are mainly economic in nature can be met. But the basic point is the mass strike must always be spontaneous. In her article *Mass Strike, Party and Trade Unions* she wrote : "the mass strike is not artificially made not decided out of the blue, nor propagated but rather it is an historical phenomenon which at a certain moment follows with historical necessity from social relations" (Quoted by Ashoke Bhaduri). According to Rosa, mass strike is spontaneous and also a basic weapon in the hands of the working class in its struggle to capture political power.

Luxemburg wrote the above article in the background of the 1905 Russian Revolution. She explained the mass strike and its importance in the following way. She thought that mass strike was not an isolated action. But it is the sign, the totality concept of a whole period of the class struggle lasting for years, perhaps decades. She also said that since the mass strikes are spontaneous they cannot be treated as useless. The workers call strike spontaneously and by doing this they intensify the struggle.

In the mass strike both the economic and political issues are mixed together. They are interdependent. Rosa said : "The economic struggle leads the political struggle." At the beginning the workers call a mass or general strike to place their economic demands and when the strike continues it finally assumes political form. Very often workers call mass strike both for economic and political demands. Rosa further says that since the mass strikes are spontaneous the divisive forces do not find any place in such cases. Rosa draws our attention to this aspect.

About mass strike her view can be stated in the following way. Mass strike and mass movement do not lead to revolution, but revolution unites the elements of mass movement. Let us quote her again. "If the mass strike does not signify a single act but a whole period of class struggle, and if this period is identical with a period of revolution, then it is clear that the mass strike cannot be called at will, even if the decision to call it comes from the highest committee of the strongest Social Democratic Party. As long as Social Democracy is not capable of staging and countermanding revolutions according to its own estimation of the situation, then even the greatest enthusiasm and impatience of Social Democratic troops will not suffice to call into being a true period of mass strikes as a living, powerful movement of the people". Luxemburg further observes that the success of mass strike in Russia and Germany was not due to the backwardness of Russia in economic and social fields. The success was due to the class consciousness and spontaneity. It is the consciousness that inspires the working class to launch a movement or a general strike. Again, the consciousness is linked with spontaneity. Without consciousness the workers cannot participate in a movement spontaneously.

Bolshevism

Luxemburg held the Bolshevik Revolution as the most spectacular incident of the First World War period and she laid great faith on the ability, spontaneity and consciousness of the working class. She was of opinion that it was the spontaneity and consciousness that made possible the Russian revolution a success. But after a short time she began to criticise the Mensheviks, Kautsky and many others on their stand on coalition government—coalition with the liberals. Mensheviks and Kautsky strongly argued that since Russia was economically backward, it would be better for the Bolshevik party to forge an alliance with the liberals. Lenin strongly opposed this suggestion and Rosa agreed with him.

The difference of opinion between Lenin and Luxemburg began to surface immediately after the Bolshevik Revolution. Rosa observed that Lenin and his party started to rule Russia in a dictatorial manner and in this regard Lenin's argument was that in order to counteract the counter-revolutionary and anti-socialist forces some definite doses of dictatorship were essential. But Luxemburg did not buy this argument. The party, after seizing power, cannot and should not adopt dictatorial means for running the day-to day administration. Freedom, rights and, above all, representative methods cannot be curbed. In the name of cleansing the Soviet society of reactionary elements Lenin was quite unwilling to introduce universal suffrage and other democratic processes. Lenin's argument was that the introduction of democratic processes would open the floodgates of problems. Naturally the introduction of any form of representative democracy had no place in the programme of Lenin. This considerably surprised and irked Luxemburg and strongly criticised Bolshevism.

Rosa attacked another very important aspect of the Bolshevik party. She observed that after the Revolution the supporters and members of the Bolshevik party were enjoying freedom, whereas large masses of men were denied freedom and this led her to make the following observation : "Freedom for the supporters of the government, only for the members of the one party—however numerous they may be—is no freedom at all. Freedom is always and exclusively freedom for the one who thinks differently". A person who thinks differently has also the freedom to express his views and when this is permitted there exists true freedom. She again says : "Lenin is completely mistaken in the means he employs. Decree, dictatorial force of the factory over-seer, draconic penalties, rule by terror, all these are but palliatives". Rule by terror demoralises the public and it is harmful for socialism. It is unfortunate that Lenin and the Bolshevik Party followed this harmful way. Somehow Lenin gathered an idea that socialism could be firmly established by force and draconic laws and means. But this is absolutely wrong. Here lies the basic error in the policy pursed by the Bolshevik Party under the leadership of Lenin. This cleared the way of disastrous consequences. She admitted that the Bolshevik party came to power at a critical juncture of time and in that situation it was not possible to grant full-scale of freedom. But immediately after seizing power the party and the government must have granted freedom. The party should have taken steps to introduce democratic principles and parliamentary systems. It is unfortunate that Lenin did not care to follow that track. It is under his leadership the Bolshevism became a symbol of draconism, terrorist methods, and all sorts of undemocratic ways.

The Essence of Socialist Society

According to Luxemburg the essence of socialism or socialist society is that in such a society the proletarians will no longer be ruled by a microscopic fraction of society—that is, the capitalist class. Instead the, ruled will be ruler and the controlled will be controller. From top to bottom the proletarians will replace the members of the capitalist class by their own representatives. In *Russian Revolution : Leninism or Marxism* Luxemburg said : "All socialist civic virtues, together with the knowledge and ability to manage socialist operations, can be acquired by the working class only through their own activity, their own experience". A socialist society cannot easily be achieved or set up without any trouble. For it, untiring struggle and lot of labour are required. Only in a socialist society the liberation of, working class is possible.

She further says that in a socialist society the organs created or set up by the capitalists must be replaced by the socialist organs or systems. The proletarians shall set up a revolutionary tribunal whose function would be to try criminals. The authority of the socialist society will confiscate all weapons and ammunition which the reactionary government purchased or collected or manufactured. These weapons were used to torture the working class. The capitalist parliaments and all the municipal councils shall be replaced by workers' councils. The socialist society shall abolish all sorts of differences in respect of rank, titles etc. In all the representative bodies periodical election will be held. Nothing will be imposed upon the workers or common people. An atmosphere shall be created in which all will enjoy full freedom.

Assessment

The assessment of Luxemburg is not an easy task because of her controversial stand in the orthodox Marxist world. In spite of this Kolakowski calls her "an outstanding example of a type of mind." We may or may not agree with her interpretation of Marxism, but there is no doubt that her faithfulness to Marxism is beyond all sorts of question. She was an extremely controversial figure in the Marxist world. But we think that she interpreted Marxism in the background of Marx's own thought. According to Kolakowski "Marxism was to her the universal key to the meaning of history" (p. 430).

Luxemburg was undoubtedly the champion of spontaneity and consciousness. This we think is the core of revolution. She never hesitated to challenge Lenin and his other comrades on this particular issue. She vehemently objected to the idea of imposing anything regarding revolution or movement upon the proletarians. She repeatedly said that spontaneity and consciousness were the chief factors of Bolshevik Revolution. After the Revolution—when Lenin ignored the democratic principles and processes and turned to draconic and undemocratic ways—she openly opposed Lenin's method and mentality. Rosa all along argued for democracy and criticised the way of imposing the leader's mentality of imposing his decision upon the rank and file. Rosa was always the champion of orthodox Marxism and this was the primary cause of conflict between Lenin and Luxemburg. But, unfortunately, the school of orthodox Marxism was small and not powerful. An important drawback of Rosa is that she believed that the working class alone would be able to establish socialism. Party or intellectuals have no role to play was her strong belief. But this is not correct. Leadership has an important part.

LEON TROTSKY

Biographical Sketch

Lev Davidovich Bronstein is better known by his pseudonym Leon Trotsky. Trotsky was born in 1879 and died on 1940. He was a brilliant orator and had a colourful life. He could spellbind the mass through his speech. His father was a Jewish farmer in Ukraine. From his childhood he was revolutionary in action and behaviour and believed that without revolution no change is possible. He was really a charismatic leader and it is evident in his English biography authored by Isaac Deutscher. Deutscher wrote three books *The Prophet Armed* (1954), *The Prophet Unarmed* (1959), *The Prophet Outcast* (1963). Trotsky is called the real hero of the Russian Revolution and the famous critic of Stalin's ideas—some people call it Stalinism. In 1898, only at the age of nineteen he was arrested by the Russian police and exiled to Siberia. But Russian police failed to keep him in exile. He escaped to London and joined Lenin. He was also actively associated with the *Iskra* (Spark)—the a mouthpiece of the Russian revolutionaries.

His friendship with Lenin helped the revolutionary movement of Russia. He participated in the revolution of 1905. But his friendship with Lenin did not last. Difference of opinion between the two leaders cropped up. For his revolutionary activities he was arrested by the Russian police. He again escaped from prison and went to Vienna. He spread his revolutionary activities in various parts of Europe. He went to France and there he published several journals and magazines which dealt with revolution. In 1917 the Bolshevik Party came to power under the leadership of Lenin and on several crucial issues he was the right-hand man of Lenin. But this good relation was temporary, on a number of issues he found himself the opposition to Lenin. Trotsky also differed from other top-ranking leaders of Russian Bolshevik party. Particularly Stalin and Trotsky could not see eye to eye. The death of Lenin in 1924 cost him very much, Stalin was an all-powerful person in both party and government and there was none in Russia who could raise his voice against Stalin.

His growing animosity with Stalin forced him to leave Russia. He toured various parts of Europe with untiring energy. He devoted his energy to the formation of the international communist movement. He established contact with the revolutionary leaders of several European countries and he was the key man of International Left opposition. In 1932 Trotsky formulated the strategy and ideology of International Left Opposition. He stated that the independence of the proletarian party must be recognised. The workers' party must be all-powerful and the bureaucracy must be subservient to the workers' party. He believed that Stalin was determined to establish social-fascism and it must be opposed by all means. He further said that the adventurist phase of communist movement must be rejected and the democratic dictatorship of the proletariat and peasants will be converted into dictatorship of the proletariat. Trotsky spent the major part of his life in exile and he formulated his political opinion and revolutionary ideas while in exile. He was finally banished to Alma Ata. He wandered in Turkey, France, Norway and finally he settled in Mexico in 1937. He was murdered in 1940. The 1940 was the witness of a colourful life and great revolutionary.

Permanent Revolution

Trotsky is famous for his theory of permanent revolution. While in prison in 1906 Trotsky wrote *The Balance and Prospects : the Moving Forces of Revolution*, better known as *The Permanent Revolution*. The concept of permanent revolution was first formulated by Marx-Engels in 1850 in *Address of the General Council to the Communist League*. The idea of permanent revolution has been used in sense more than one. It is said that the establishment of socialism in one country can never ensure the establishment of socialism in all other counties. Naturally the revolutionaries of one country who have succeeded in establishing socialism in their state will continue to support both morally and physically the revolutionaries of other countries; and this is a continuous process. In this sense the revolution is permanent in nature. But many others in Russia, particularly the Economists, Mensheviks, had different idea about revolution. They thought that the workers' party, after capturing power, will settle down and start to rebuild society. They did not think about continuing revolution or revolutionary process. Trotsky disagreed with this general idea of revolution.

Trotsky's thesis of permanent revolution differed from the general idea about it. Explaining his view J. S. McClelland says : "Trosky's theory of permanent revolution challenged the whole perspective. His main thesis was that the coming revolution in Russia could not be contained within the bourgeois phase, because the Russian bourgeoisie could not fulfil its own revolutionary role" (p. 599). Kolakowski explains the idea of permanent revolution in the following way : "Its view was that the democratic revolution in Russia would bring to power a social democratic government which would of necessity endeavour to continue the revolutionary process towards socialism" (p. 683). His conception about permanent revolution rested on the idea that the Russian bourgeoisie was very weak and, naturally, the burden of revolution must be shouldered by the proletariat. It means that both the bourgeoisie and the proletariat will combinedly manage the revolution. But it would be foolishness to exclusively depend upon the bourgeoisie for the final success of the revolution. Russia is characterised by her economic backwardness and a revolution in collaboration with the bourgeoisie would be a hindrance to the attainment of socialist revolution. Therefore a revolution in collaboration with the bourgeoisie must be abandoned. The ultimate aim of the proletariat should be a socialist revolution and that means the revolutionary process must continue. Both Marx and Engels forecast this in 1848 for Germany.

There are two important propositions of Trotsky's idea of permanent revolution. One is : the "bourgeois revolution in Russia would evolve continuously into a socialist one" (p. 683). In other words, the proletarians would start a revolution with the active help of the bourgeoisie. In the opinion of Trotsky the economic and political conditions of Russia demanded the participation of the bourgeoisie. There is another proposition which is—the socialist revolution will spread in other parts of the West because its confinement within Russia will ultimately endanger its survival. The behaviour and attitude of the capitalists fully convinced Trotsky that they are never dependable comrades in the crucial parts in the revolutionary process. Once the proletarians have been able to achieve certain amount of success they should try to ignore them.

Permanent Revolution and Trotskyism

Trotsky's name is closely associated with permanent revolution and this lands the readers on a new concept known as *Trotskyism.* Throughout his revolutionary and colourful life he continuously propagated the view of permanent revolution. He claimed that it was not his discovery. Marx in his *Critique of Gotha Programme* said that at first the working class, with the help of the bourgeoisie, will establish socialism but that should not be the objective of the proletariat. The proletarians' ultimate goal shall be to set up a communist society and that requires continuation of revolution. In other words, only one revolution is not enough for establishing a communist society. Trotsky demands that he has borrowed the concept of permanent revolution from Marx. Needless to say that the idea of permanent revolution constitutes the uncleus of Trotsky's theory of revolution and the interpreters of his theory calls it Trotskyism. The writer of the essay *Trotskyism* published in Bottomore-edited. *A Dictionary of Marxist Thought* defines the idea in the following language :

"The cornerstone of Trotskyism has been and remains the theory of permanent revolution, originally formulated by Marx which Trotsky reformulated in 1906, applied to Russia and then elaborated further in 1928. Trotsky viewed the transition to socialism as a series of interconnected and interdependent social, political and economic upheavals proceeding on various levels and in diverse social structures—feudal, underdeveloped, pre-industrial and capitalist—and occurring at different historical junctures" (p. 541). Trotsky admitted that a revolution must start at a national level or in a smaller form, but its aim will be the socialisation of number of countries at international level. Hence the central idea of Trotskyism is—spread the message of revolution in various parts of the globe. In other words, the internationalisation of revolution is the hallmark of Trotsky's theory of revolution and it is also called Trotskyism.

A piquant issue has cropped up in serious analysis of permanent revolution. He always stressed that in the revolution the industrial proletariat will always play the most key role. He, of course, subsequently amended their notion partially. Trotsky said that in the entire revolutionary process in the primary stage, the industrial proletariat will play the crucial role, but at subsequent stages, the peasantry will appear and play the necessary role. This, however, generated lot of heat in the twenties and thirties of the twentieth century. Even in the Fourth International set up by Trotsky there was a lot of discussion about the key role. That is, who will play the key role. Unfortunately the participants could not arrive at any decisive conclusion. The Chinese Revolution clearly established that the peasantry could decisively lead a revolution. The industrial proletariat and peasantry have complicated the whole issue but Trotsky had a firm faith that without a permanent revolution the setting up of a classless society will remain a far cry. He had no faith on the revolutionary way of setting up of a classless society because by this bourgeois method the counter-revolutionary forces or the remnants of capitalists cannot be destroyed or uprooted. Naturally, revolution or permanent revolution is the only way. This is the most vital aspect of Trotskyism. Trotskyism takes for granted that the seizure of political power along with the struggle against the property-owing classes must form the most vital aspects of revolution which will continue unless classless society is set up.

Dictatorship of the Proletariat

Following Marx-Engels, Trotsky strongly defended the dictatorship of the proletariat though this concept has been vehemently criticised by the bourgeois theoreticians. The bourgeois theoreticians contend that the Marxists very often say that the term dictatorship of the proletariat is self-contradictory because democracy and dictatorship cannot exist together. On the other hand, Trotsky and other Marxists denounce bourgeois democracy or its various forms such as parliamentary democracy or evolutionary democracy or democracy by ballot box. All of them call it illusionary. In the opinion of Trotsky, in bourgeois democracy the fruits of democratic system are fully gobbled up by the economically powerful class, because only this class controls both politics and economy.

According to Trotsky "under the dictatorship of the proletariat, proletarian democracy will be secured through the effective control of the government by the Soviets constituted by the representatives of legal Soviet parties, freely elected by all toilers" (Baltomore, p. 548). The proletarians will seize political power through struggle and after that they will establish their overall supremacy. Hence the dictatorship of the proletariat implies the absolute control of the proletarians in all fields of state.

Trotsky rejected Lenin's ultra-centralism or centralised system of party. He emphasised that more stress on the democratic structure of the party would finally lead the Soviet system to chaos. This will ultimately invite the agents of bourgeois party and counter-revolutionary forces. Trotsky called Stalinist system of party as a form of "bureaucratic dictatorship". After a thoroughgoing analysis of the Soviet system Trotsky arrived at the conclusion that there is very little of democracy and socialism in the Soviet Union. According to Trotsky the Soviet Union is apparently a socialist state, but it has undergone a process of degeneration. Outwardly the Soviet Union is a socialist state but very little of true socialism is to be found in Soviet socialism. All the powers are concentrated at a single centre and the whole party and the state administration is managed and dictated by a single person and he is Stalin. This cannot be called democracy. It is also said that "nothing of a workers' state is left in Soviet Union". Trotsky envisaged of a system that would encourage and in practice establish democracy both in party and state administration. Everything of a socialist state will be fully controlled by the proletarians and it will aim at the general welfare of the people.

Trotsky's life was full of struggle whose chief aim was to establish the supreme authority or control of the proletariat in every sphere of society. But he found that the entire Soviet system has degenerated and the dictatorship of the proletariat has turned into dictatorship of few persons or bureaucrats. It was the belief of Trotsky that the proletarians have achieved certain gains (both economic and political) through struggle and these must be protected. For this is required to establish the overall supremacy of the working class. He says : "The party is obliged to maintain its dictatorship regardless of temporary waverings in the spontaneous moods of the masses." According to Trotsky the dictatorship of the proletariat is not any temporary device to achieve temporary gain. It is a permanent solution to all sorts of evils which have engulfed a bourgeois society.

Trotsky versus Stalin

The students of Marxism and the Marxist thought after Marx's death have curiously observed that there was a bitter controversy between Trotsky and Stalin. It is not easy to locate the causes of the conflict between these two great Marxists. Stalin, with the help of his manoeuvring capacity, captured power. But from intellectual point of view he was not at all respected by the Marxists. J. S. McClelland says that (p. 603) Lenin, Trotsky and several others made serious efforts to implement Marx's eleventh thesis : the philosophers had only *interpreted* the world differently, the point is to *change* it. Both Trotsky and Stalin wanted to change the political, social and economic conditions of capitalist society. Both Trotsky and Stalin thought of different ways of applying Marx's principles. Again, both interpreted Marxism in their own way and this led to the conflict of opinion. But a close and protracted analysis will reveal that there is very little substance in the conflict between the two great leaders of Marxist thought. McClelland rightly observes : "As with all doctrinal disputes between the individuals in close proximity with each other it is always difficult to distinguish between points of dispute which are doctrinal and points of dispute which are personal" (p. 603). That is, there is little substance in the debate or conflict that arose between Trotsky and Stalin. Notwithstanding, the students of Marxist thought study the controversy between the two.

The first point of conflict between the two centres around the concept of the nature of revolution. Socialism in one country is not enough, because if a socialist country is surrounded by powerful non-socialist countries that will dig the grave for the socialist state. The capitalist states could not tolerate the socialism. For this reason Trotsky thought that once socialism has been established in one country, serious and sincere efforts must be made to build up a socialist societies in other countries and this view of Trotsky is called the internationalisation of socialism—and this is also a very important part of Trotskyism. Stalin openly challenged this view of Trotsky. Lenin also propagated the establishment of socialism in other countries. But he was quite aware that the situation of establishing socialism in other countries was not favourable. Lenin said : "the first lesson to be learned from our governmental activities during the first year is that we must be on the alert, we must remember that we are surrounded by people, classes and governments who openly express their intense hatred for us" (*Problems of Leninism*, p. 193). If it is not physically possible to build up socialism in all countries, then how can the socialism in one country be safeguarded? To this Stalin's answer is : "the possibility of solving the contradictions between the proletariat and the peasantry by means of internal forces of our country, the possibility of the proletariat seizing power and using that power to build a complete socialist society in our country, with the sympathy and the support of the proletarians of other countries, but without the preliminary victory of the proletarian in other countries" (p. 192). Lenin also understood that all the capitalist countries are in alliance and they are determined to resist the advancement of socialism. It is practically impossible that the proletarians will ally and fight against capitalism.

It is difficult to arrive at an agreed opinion why Stalin repeatedly argued for setting up a socialist society only in one country. In the pamphlet *The Foundations of Leninism* and his noted work *Problems of Leninism* he discussed the issue elaborately and this surprises many. Some people are of opinion that after Lenin's death there was intense infighting within the CPSU (Communist Party of Soviet Union) and Stalin was so much power-hungry that he wanted to capture power at any cost, and, at the same time, he wanted to establish that he had been successful in setting up socialism in Russia. Its sole purpose was to brighten his image as a true socialist. This, Stalin believed, would blunt the sharpness of attack launched by his opponents and at the same time brighten his image. J. S. McClelland rightly says (op. cit., p. 606) "As time went on, and Stalin's need in the leadership struggle to brand Trotsky as an "adventurer" became more acute, Stalin began to change his line, suggesting that the efforts and resources of Russia alone might be sufficient to build a socialist economy ...Stalin continued to pay lip-service to the revolution in the West but shifted the balance in favour of the Soviet Union. He also said that the resources of Russia were insufficient for building up socialism in other countries and under this situation any attempt to build socialism in other parts of Europe would simply be adventurist and on that ground he called Trotsky an advanturist and all his followers un-Bolshevik. So we argue that Stalin was determined to convert Russia into a socialist society chiefly to consolidate his position in the party and brighten his image as a socialist".

Trotsky seriously and sincerely followed so far as setting up socialist society in other countries of Europe is concerned. Lenin said world imperialism cannot live side by side with the victorious Soviet revolution. Lenin understood that the conflict between imperialism and capitalism on one side and communism on the other side is inevitable. Naturally all-round efforts must be made to convert capitalist states into socialist ones. Again, after few months, he said "as long as capitalism and socialism remain side by side we cannot live peacefully—the one or the other will be victor in the end. Tortsky claims that by propounding a permanent revolution and internationalisation of socialism he has simply followed what Lenin repeatedly asserted. Hence the chief reason of difference between Stalin and Trotsky is the former wanted to strengthen and consolidate his position while the latter was determined to follow Lenin with all seriousness.

Both Lenin and Trotsky apprehended (also predicted) that if there were no revolution in the neighbouring states of Russia, its revolutionary government would be overthrown by the neighbouring capitalist states. But the events proved that the communist government of Soviet Russia had not been overthrown and the revolutionary movement in several European states were turned into fiasco. Some of the states were Germany, Italy, Hungary and Baltic states. The assessment of political situation of several European countries made by Lenin and Trotsky was not correct.

Analysing the various aspects of controversy between Stalin and Trotsky, R. N. Carew Hunt, in his short but very illuminating book *The Theory and Practice of Communism*, writes : The main content in Trotsky's indictment of Stalin is that he (Stalin) gave up world revolution for "socialism in one country" yet this is not so. Stalin did not renounce world revolution, Trotsky did not reject the chance of building socialism in Russia" (p. 217). Historians have acknowledged that Stalin made several efforts to attempt revolution in few states of Europe, but only failure greeted him. Trotsky also desired to see a socialist state. If it were so what was the main reason of controversy between the two Marxists? Let us put it in the words of Hunt. He says :

"But as the controversy widened, the two viewpoints became more and more rigidly fixed. In the Stalinist scheme the establishment of socialism in Russia came first and world revolution second, in the Trotskyist conception this order was reversed. Yet fundamentally, the difference between the two men was one of temperament and not of theory. Trotsky believed that Europe was "ripe for revolution" and from this standpoint the Russian revolution was only the prelude to a much wider upheaval". This is the fundamental point of difference between the two great Marxists.

Kolakowsky believes that the conflict between the two is simply "imaginary". They fought over an issue which for all practical purposes is a non-issue. Trotsky's attack on the bureacratisation of party was mainly personal. Kolakowsky says : "Trotsky's attacks on bureaucratic role within the party began when he himself was effectually deprived of power over the party apparatus, as long as he was still in power, he was one of the most autocratic champions of bureaucracy and of military or police control over whole political and economic system" (op. cit., p. 808).

ANTONIO GRAMSCI

Life and Time

One of the most controversial yet original Marxist thinker in the post-Lenin generation is Antonio Gramsci. He was born in 1891 in a village called Ales in Sardinia of Italy. His mother came from a well-to-do family. His father was an ordinary government employee. He once became the victim of political conspiracy and lost his job. The last and the very small source of livelihood was lost and almost starvation greeted Gramsci and other members of his family. A further misfortune fell upon him. Due to an accident in his childhood certain parts of his body were damaged and due to this he was hunchbacked and his proper physical development stopped. Ignoring all these handicaps he began to study in ordinary educational institutions. Gramsci was a voracious reader and at the same time meritorious. Ignoring all impediments he with indomitable energy studied socialist literature and other subjects. Gramsci completed his secondary standard and winning a scholarship got himself admitted in Turin University. Two factors sowed the seeds of socialist thought and philosophy in his young mind. His elder brother was a socialist and this encouraged him to be socialist. While a student at Turin University he came in touch with the famous Italian Communist Palmiro Togliatti. Apart from this many of the professors of the University were socialist-minded. The First World War started in 1914 and during the war period Gramsci garnered enough knowledge about socialism.

Besides Togliatti several other persons influenced his thought and Benedetto Croce was one of them. Though influenced by Croce (1866–1952) he was not at all a Crocean. He was again influenced by another philosopher—Antonio Labriola (1843–1904). Initially Labriola was a Hegelian and after studying Marx's writings extensively he came to be known as a Marxist. His best known book is *Essays on the Materialist Conception of History*. He propagated Marxism in Italy and practically introduced the basic tenets of Marxism to Italians. His most famous concept is "philosophy of praxis" and Antonio Gramsci was attracted to it. Practically Labriola's philosophy of praxis was made by Gramsci on the central plank of his analysis about Marxism. Besides Labriola Croce was another Marxist whose thought created a good impact upon Gramsci. He was so much influenced by Croce that Gramsci called himself a Crocean.

Upon the thought system of Gramsci we find an influence "Council Communism". During 1915 to 1925, in several parts of Europe and particularly in Italy, Council Communism became very popular. Leninist model of party was looked with askance by many. That is, many were not willing to treat Leninist party as a model to fight against the bourgeoisie. The workers of many European states formed councils. The members of the "Council Communism felt that only through the formation of council the working class can intensify its struggle against bourgeois rule. McLellan says" : "The Council Communists saw themselves as returning to Marx in their assertion that the proletariat was the first class in history to be able to achieve self-emancipation" (*Marxism after Marx*, p. 186). The propounders of Council Communism advocated that the workers' best weapon is to form councils and make it an instrument of fight against the capitalist. The council strongly advocates for mass strike and propagate the methods that will raise the level of workers' consciousness and spontaneity. A good number of Marxists lent their support to it. Turin Council Movement was a very important incident that guided Gramsci's political career. Gramsci was considerably influenced by the Bolshevik revolution and revolutionary activities that engulfed Russia. In 1917–18 Gramsci was inspired by the activities of the Bolshevik Party and he thought that Bolshevik type of movement could be launched in Italy to save it from the unprecedented crisis created by World War I. Particularly the economic crisis was so severe that the common people were absolutely helpless. The workers formed militant councils and organisations to fight against the authority. The workers had practically very little faith on the trade unions as well as their movement and for that reason they formed factory councils. The militant factory councils were first formed in the metallurgical industries of Turin. Some people are of opinion that the formation of councils and to convert them into weapons of struggle was the product of Gramsci's brain. He thought that traditional trade unions could not be relied upon, because the time had changed and new as well as effective weapons had to be found out. Gramsci has clearly expressed his opinion unequivocally in the following words :

"The actual process of the proletarian revolution cannot be identified with the development and activity of revolutionary organisations of a voluntary and contractual nature, such as political parties and trade unions. These organisations arise in the sphere of bourgeois democracy and political liberty" (Quoted by David McLellan, *Marxism After Marx*, p. 192). Gramsci emphasised that the capitalists have changed their way of exploitation and at the same time the management of factory. So the workers must change their weapons of struggle against the bourgeois exploiters.

The conception of Factory Council constitutes a very important part of Gramscis political life or his participation in the political movement in the era of agitation against economic crisis. We have noted it earlier. Let us see what Mc Lellan thinks of it. He says : "The Factory Councils were central to Gramsci's conception at the time of revolutionary transformation of Italy. The main task of the Council was to change the attitude of the mass of workers from an attitude of dependence to one of leadership" (pp. 192-199). Gramsci treated the "Factory Council as the new proletarian state in miniature" This is really a new aspect of Marxist thought and its application in practice. Because before Gramsci the renowned Marxists emphasised on the class struggle led by workers. Gramsci believed that the setting up of Factory Councils would substantially revolutionise the liberation movement of the workers. In his assessment the formation of Factory Councils will play crucial role in building up a socialist society because these rejuvenate the workers. But his assessment was not up to the mark. That is, it was not possible for workers to look after the technical aspects of production. Workers or their councils did not have the expertise of managing a factory whose core was technical knowledge. It is said that the Factory Councils to some extent resembled the Soviets of Russia. But Gramsci had limited knowledge about the functioning of Soviets. As a result, Gramsci's concept of Factory Councils and its special role in proletarian movement could not achieve success. Luxemburg and several other Marxists were not hopeful about the success of Factory Councils. "The failure of the Turin Council movement in late 1920, his growing acquaintance with the realities of the Soviet Union and his concern of the rise of Fascism led Gramsci to modify his views" (Mc Lelland, p. 193).

Gramsci and the Intellectuals

One of the important contributions of Antonio Gramsci in Marxist thought is his conception about intellectuals and their role in bourgeois society. Analysing Gramscis viewpoint Mc Lellan (*Marxism After Marx*) says that Gramsci was primarily "the theoretician of the superstructure". Gramsci said that intellectuals are very important in a capitalist society, they play a vital role. In his *Prison Notebooks* he says that the intellectuals are very active and they play vital and very often critical role in society. Their views are considered important and many educated people follow them. In his words : All men are intellectuals... but not all men have in society the function of intellectuals. Each person, beyond his professional duty and function, is a philosopher, artist. He carries with him his own view regarding politics, economics and many other subjects. He forms his own opinion about these and propagates them, tries to convince other persons about what he thinks. Gramsci says that the intellectual contributes to sustain a conception of the world or to modify it. In this way the intellectual brings about a new mode of thought.

The intellectuals have enough power to attract the attention of other people. In their thought and action they demand that they are progressive and this mesmerises the common people. They are influenced and try to follow the intellectuals. In this way the intellectuals build up their attractive image in society. Gramsci has divided the intellectuals into two broad groups—traditional and organic. The traditional intellectuals regard themselves to be autonomous of social classes. The traditional intellectuals demand that they embody a historical continuity above and beyond socio-political change. By propagating this view the traditional intellectuals want to prove that they are neutral and they try to maintain their neutrality. This builds up a glazy or attractive image and common people are easily attracted to them. Writers, philosophers and social scientists fall within this category. Organic intellectuals belong to a particular class and in all issues they support their own class. The intellectuals play very important role in moulding and modifying the views of people. Particularly the views of those persons who are not definite about their own opinions. In other words these intellectuals exercise important power over the people of society. Since an organic intellectual belongs to a class he always endeavours the people of his class. The organic intellectuals articulate the collective views or opinions and they finally form a collective consciousness regarding political, social and economic affairs or issues. The aim of the organic intellectuals to build up a collective opinion about the economic and political aspects of society.

Kolakowski says that the proletariat wants the "organic intellectuals" because these intellectuals do not simply analyse the social, political and other aspects of society, but they also use "the language of culture to express the real experiences and feelings which the masses cannot express for themselves". That is, the real function of the organic intellectuals to provide the leadership and guide the proletarians in their struggle against the bourgeoisie. In the view of Kolakowski the term "organic intellectuals" is a very favourite term of Gramsci and he very frequently used it.

Gramsci did not use the term in any narrow and restricted sense, rather in a wider sense. He used the term in the sense that all the social classes have their own intellectuals and they in one way or other guide the members of their own classes. These intellectuals explain the social and political issues to the members of the class which help to form opinion. This the intellectuals do in the background of class interest or from the standpoint of the class. This is a very important function. "The fact that" observes Kolakowski, "the intellectuals appeared to form a separate *metier* (trade, profession or occupation) of their own, as opposed to being the mouthpieces of a particular class standpoint, inclined them towards idealistic philosophies which asserted the complete autonomy of intellectual activity" (p. 979). So we find that the intellectuals play a very important role in moulding the entire thought system of society. In practice they do not always support the particular standpoint of interests of people but in a clandestine way they try to bring the view in the lime-light. The problem, however, is the working class has no organic intellectuals because this class has not been able to produce such intellectuals to support or propagate its own views in regard to economic and political matters. "The task of the organic intellectuals was to draw out and make coherent the latent aspirations and potentialities already inherent in working class activity" (McLellan, p. 198). Gramsci studied the various aspects of capitalist society and after that he formed the opinion about the role of the intellectuals. Due to the important role of the intellectuals the capitalists have been able to strengthen the structure and other aspects of bourgeois society. Because of the vital role of the intellectuals the bourgeois society has been able to withstand all sorts of onslaught against it. This is one of the vital points of Gramsci.

HEGEMONY

Definition and Origin

We have just now completed our analysis of the role of intellectuals in a bourgeois society. But Gramsci continues his analysis in order to unfathom the exact picture of such a society. He has elaborated the role of intellectuals and this he has expressed through his much debated concept hegemony. The dictionary meaning of the term is : leadership or domination or dominance by state or group over others. When Gramsci used the term he specifically meant that in bourgeois society the intellectuals dominate over the political and other spheres and justify their own views or ideology which they represent. The intellectuals propagate the bright aspects or importance of particular ideology and in this way the ideology plays dominant role. In his *The Prison Notebooks* Gramsci makes the following observation "a new homogeneous politics-economic historical bloc, without internal contradiction". He further observes : "the dominant group is co-ordinated concretely with the general interests of the subordinate groups, and the life of the state is conceived of as a continuous process of formation and superseding of unstable equilibria between the interests of the fundamental and those of the subordinate groups—equilibria in which the interests of the dominant group prevail" (Quoted by Mc Lellan, *Marxism After Marx*, pp. 200-201). This is, in short, the definition of hegemony.

Gramsci observed that the intellectuals of the historically progressive class exercise powers through the technique of domination over the individuals. These intellectuals (in various ways) influence the members of society to which they belong and in this act they use academic ideas and concept. They are against the application of force, but apply reason, ideas, views and method of pursuasion. Thus the purpose of the intellectuals is to exercise power of attraction mainly to influence the general public. Gramsci observes that there are several group of intellectuals or many intellectuals and not all of them are interested in influencing others. Few or only a dominant group take initiative in influencing masses of men. In this venture, it is generally found, generally one group of intellectuals plays the dominant role and other groups are subordinated to the powerful group. In this way the hegemony of one group is established. The intellectuals of a dominant group control the intellectual activities of the society. There may exist small or less powerful groups of intellectuals but they are incapable of exercising power over others. This is what is called the theory of hegemony.

Gramsci's theory of hegemony is not any concocted story or an imaginative one. He thoroughly studied the political and administrative systems of several mature capitalist countries. Jacobinism represented the French bourgeoisie. By exercising intellectual power the Jacobins were able to influence the peasants of France. Again, the capitalists of USA have their own intellectuals and many of them are lavishly paid by the capitalists. These intellectuals act as the spokes-persons of the capitalists and they propagate the political and economic views of capitalism. That is they present the bright side of capitalism before the mass of men and in this way common people are influenced. Gramsci also studied the concept of hegemony in the background of America's capitalist system. He observed that in USA the intellectuals exercise their power over the people to bring the importance of capitalist system in the limelight. We have already stated that Gramsci was directly associated with the Turin Council Movement in which he found that the ruling class obtained the consent of subordinate groups and classes to accept the domination.

Characteristics

Hegemony plays a very important role in the whole thought system of Gramsci but according to Kolakowski he has used the idea in senses more than one. Sometimes hegemony implies political power and the authority uses coercive means over the masses to ensure obligation. The hegemony or overall dominance comes out of the coercion. But this does not always happen. The authority applies other methods to establish its overall supremacy over the society. Gramsci is of opinion that in a parliamentary system hegemony comes out of the combination of force and consent. That is, the political authority tries to receive obligation or approval through democratic means such as consent or formation of public opinion or large scale public discussion. In such a situation the government uses various organs of public opinion. Force is rarely used. In all democratic systems this is normally found.

It has been found that the intellectuals and the groups or societies formed by them generally use cultural means and sociological ways. The intellectuals influence the common people by way of dissemination. The important intellectuals spread academic or educational ideas and concepts, their importance or bright sides among the general public. In this way the powerful group of intellectuals culturally or academically dominates common people. This is also a type of hegemony.

Explaining the precondition of the emancipation of the working class Gramsci has asserted that only through the seizure of political power this can be attained. But this is not an easy task. By it the cultural hegemony is to be achieved. In simple language, the cultural hegemony means the particular culture of the working class must dominate. In sociology it is called cultural socialisation. Kolakowski in this connection says : the working class could only conquer by first imparting its world-views and system of values to the other classes who might be its political allies :

in this way it would become the intellectual leader of society, just what the bourgeoisie had done before seizing political control (p. 980). Gramsci has repeatedly emphasised this essential precondition for the attainment of political power. Not only this, the bourgeoisie has applied the same technique for the sustenance of its control over society and power.

Another aspect of Gramsci's hegemony is there is "material basis" of hegemony, and according to well-known interpreters of his doctrine this is reforms and compromises. The bourgeoisie is quite conscious that the strict adherence to its own ideology and views about economics, politics, culture etc. may cut a sorry figure. Compromises with the opposition may be required and this attitude is quite realistic. Some of the views of other classes or groups are accommodated into the views and approaches of the bourgeoisie. It has been truly observed by a critic that the "hegemonic class in Gramsci's definition is truly political because it goes beyond its immediate economic interests to represent the universal advancement of society" (Bottomore, p. 230). Gramsci understood quite well that any proliferation of interests and outlooks will ultimately lead to the numerous divisions of society. The capitalist class for that reason adopts a very realistic approach. The capitalists always adopt a middle path. It is the view of the capitalists to avoid way of severe conflict and intransigency.

Other Aspects of Gramsci's Concept

Gramsci's theory of hegemony occupies a very important place in Marxist thought system; even some say that it is his "most important contribution to Marxist Theory". This assessment is quite true. Before he was imprisoned and during his imprisonment he observed that hegemony of class or groups had important position. It helps to capture power, to hold or perpetuate power. During the period of 1924–1926 Gramsci carefully thought the particular or crucial role of the bourgeoisie in the capitalist society and finally he arrived at a conclusion that the proletariat could capture political power through establishing its own hegemony. For that purpose it must ensure its own social basis.

An interesting aspect of Gramsci's theory is he suggested to adopt caution. He thoroughly studied history, particularly Machiavelli and many others. He felt that the application of force was not enough. That is, a group or class may be superior in respect of military force. But that cannot enable it to be the owner of authority or power. The class or organisation must be able to establish its supremacy in the fields of intellect, morality and mass support. The class or group must provide intellectual supremacy. Generally the dominant class adopts one or the other method and makes compromises. Adamancy is generally avoided. Through the method of consent and compromises the most powerful class builds up its own domination. What Marx and Engels called the ruling class Gramsci called the hegemonic class. The concept of hegemony has been called by many as "fabric of hegemony". It is woven by the intellectuals who have great network of wide organisation. So we can say that mere attainment of hegemony is not sufficient for capturing political power.

Gramsci also dealt with sectarianism while analysing hegemony. He said that the working class, for the purpose of attaining hegemony, must take an approach of an entire society. That is the working class must give priority to the interests of whole society, not the interests of any particular section. The working class must create a confidence in the minds of the people of all sections that it is capable of achieving fulfilment of the desires of all groups and classes. Without this the hegemony will never be a reality. The intellectuals belonging to the working class have a very important role to play, but above all they must be broad-minded. He has said that in the case of hegemony a particular class or a group of intellectuals may play a vital role, but this must not exclude the prospective role to be played by others. What Gramsci emphasises is that a particular group may be in leadership, but that is not all. Though Gramsci did not rule out the role or importance of force, he was against its random use.

A critic has viewed Gramsci's theory of hegemony from a realistic point of view. We quote few lines : "A fully extended hegemony must rest on active consent, on a collective will in which various groups in society unite" (Bottomore *op. cit.*, pp. 230-31). It is true that without hegemony the working class will never be able to achieve supremacy. But hegemony is not something which will fall from the sky. The working class must make protracted efforts. Apart from this, certain ingredients are essential. The electronic and print media must be used for the purpose of propagating the views of the working class. But the fact is that in a bourgeois society these two powerful agents of public opinion are under the full control of the ruling class.

In the field of hegemony what would be the exact role of the party? Gramsci was quite aware of the importance of a party. Although he did not regard party as the vanguard of the proletarians, party can effectively shoulder the burden of propagating the views or ideology. But he differed from Lenin on several aspects regarding the role of the party. Gramsci said that the primary responsibility of a party would be to propagate the ideology of the working class. Commenting on the importance of party viewed by Gramsci Mc Lellan makes the following observation : Gramsci had broader view of the party than Lenin, since he conceived of it as deeply committed to an ideological and cultural struggle as well as the seizure of the state power...he advocated a party that was an educational institution offering a counter-culture whose aim was to gain ascendancy in most aspects of civil society before the attempt was made on state power" (*Marxism After Marx*, p. 203). Mere dissemination of the drawbacks of bourgeois society is not enough. The interpreters of Gramsci's philosophy think so. During his Turin Council Movement he observed that the party must give them proper leadership, but the workers or agitators must rise to the occasion spontaneously and consciously. Achievement of success must not be treated as a gift, it is a hard-earned object. Kolakowski has drawn our attention to an important drawback of Gramsci's concept. He says that without destroying the bourgeois culture how is it possible to establish proletarian culture. Even if the proletarians are able to capture power before establishing the hegemony of its culture will it be possible for the working class to destroy the bourgeois culture? In this vital matter Gramsci's analysis fails to provide satisfactory reply.

Civil Society, State and Revolution

Another notable contribution of Gramsci to the development of Marxist thought is his conception about civil society. Marx and Engels in their *The German Ideology* has sporadically analysed it. But their analysis is incomplete in the sense that they did not analyse it from different standpoints. In the thirties of the last century Gramsci focused his attention on the importance as well as its role in a bourgeois society and after that a number of scholars have shown interest in Gramsci's view. A recent scholar (Joseph Famia *Civil Society and Marxist Tradition* Published in *Civil Society* edited by Sudipta Kaviraj and Sunil Khilnani—Cambridge University Press 2002) says : "Economic reductionism is not a charge that could be levelled against Antonio Gramsci who-alone of Marx's eminent disciples—tried to develop the concept of civil society." In the first few years of the 1930s Gramsci observed that in the bourgeois system the political organisation—which is popularly known as the state—plays important role in the whole gamut of political system.

The capitalism and its supporters do not always play rational role. Its chief objective is not to make people moral or ensure general material progress of society. Profit-making being its soul objective it aims at removing the thorns that exist on its way of attaining objective. How the bourgeoisie performs its role created high interest in the mind of physically-handicapped but mentally alert Gramsci. After comprehensive analysis of various aspects of bourgeois society, he raised the issue of the survival of the capitalist society. To put it in other words, Marx thoroughly scanned the capitalists society and drew the conclusion that because of its inherent contradictions the capitalist would collapse. Gramsci observed that capitalism did not follow the prediction of Marx. Gramsci was a true Marxist and because of that he did not jump upon the conclusion that Marx was wrong. Rather, he started on investigation and formed certain conclusions on the basis of his investigation. One such conclusion is his theory of hegemony which has been discussed. The other is *Civil Society.*

The answer to Gramsci's question 'why did capitalism survive' lay in the *objective condition* that existed in a capitalist society. In his *Prison Notebooks* he writes one that can be called "Civil Society" that is the ensemble of organisms commonly called 'private' and that of 'political society' or the state. These two levels correspond, on the one hand, to the function of 'hegemony' which the dominant group exercises throughout society and, on the other hand, to that of direct domination or command exercised through the 'state' and juridical government (Quoted by Famia in *Civil Society*, p. 139). According to Gramsci the civil society includes various religious and non-religious organisations such as churches, political parties, trade unions, academic institutions, press, publishing houses etc. All these institutions and organisations disseminate the ideology and views of the dominant (economically and politically) class. The dissemination is carried out in such a way that the subordinate or weaker classes do not get the opportunity to propagate their views among the masses of men. The process of dissemination is carried out intensively and uninterruptedly and practically the powerful or dominant class succeeds in establishing its hegemonic status. In this way the dominant class establishes its all-round superior position. The dominant class in this connection performs another function.

Gramsci uses the term civil society in different ways. Sometimes he says that the civil society is outside the state, that is, *it is not a part of state.* But in many places he says that the state comprises both political society and civil society. This means that the civil society is part of the state. Explaining Gramsci's stand on the concept of civil society Mc Lellan says (p. 204) "Civil society denoted for Gramsci all the organisations and technical means which diffuse the ideological justification of the ruling class in all domains of culture." This implies that civil society generally performs cultural functions and in this way establishes its hegemony. But the activities of the civil society are not confined within the cultural sphere, they are spread over other spheres. The organs of the civil society are like the trench systems of modern warfare. In war the army can destroy only the outer superstructure of the enemy state. It cannot destroy the entire defensive system. In the political system the same thing happens. There is a political organisation which we call state and there is a social organisation what is generally called the civil society. In all capitalist structures or systems there exists a second line of defence. In a capitalist society the civil society is always active and provides all sorts of protection to the state. In all capitalist states numerous changes occur. But due to the active role of the civil society these changes cannot destabilise the capitalist structure. Gramsci treats the civil society as the most effective organisation which provides protection to the state. If there were no civil society the capitalist state would have collapsed. Modern critics are of opinion that Gramsci's concept of civil society is full of contradictions and this is due to the fact that the central idea of the concept is derived from Hegel and this he applied for analysing Marx's ideas.

Gramsci on State

Though Gramsci gave special emphasis to civil society and its hegemonic status in the whole gamut of politics he was well aware of the importance of political society or organisation or state. In 1931 Gramsci wrote : "This study (*Notebooks*) also leads to certain determinations of the concept of State which is usually understood as political society" (cited in Mc Lellan, p. 204). He treated the state as an embodiment of coercive power used against the masses to ensure their unconditional obligation towards the political authority. Even, he did not treat the state as an equilibrium between different forces that are quite active. But according to Gramsci there is a close relationship between state and civil society and Gramsci observed that. But this did not happen everywhere. He cited the East of Russia and noted this in his *Notebooks.* In his opinion the State in Russia was all powerful and civil society was primordial or, to some extent, primitive. He also called the Russian state gelatinous. Gramsci has exposed the exact nature of the Russian state or the states of other Western countries in the following words : "The state was only an outer ditch behind which there stood a powerful system of foretress and earthworks".

We thus find that in the developed capitalist societies there existed two separate areas for state and civil society and, because of this difference, the strategies for revolution must be different. Gramsci thought that in primitive societies the state was always on the frontline in the social system. There was civil society, but its existence was not important at all. In this situation all sorts of revolutionary activities must be focused towards the state. That is, the state should be an object of attack. But where the civil society plays an important role, the purpose of the revolution should be to attack the civil society. According to Gramsci, the war against the state and the war against the civil society are quite different. Before starting revolution the revolutionaries must take care of it. If they failed to study the different positions or importance of state and civil society their action will be in jeopardy. This means that Gramsci was against any simplistic strategy or procedure in war against capitalism. He also warned that the Leninist method of war against capitalism was not suitable for every situation. In other words, the revolutionaries must distinguish between the crucial position of state and civil society and after that decide the course of action or nature of strategy.

In the thirties of the last century the world witnessed the Great Depression in the mature capitalist countries and the communists were jubilant at it. They prophesied that capitalism would collapse and naturally there was no need of permanent revolution. Gramsci shared this view, that is, he did not subscribe to Trotsky's theory of permanent revolution. Gramsci not only opposed permanent revolution, he at the same time supported the Stalinist stand regarding socialism in one country. Gramsci said that if too much importance is given to the idea of permanent revolution then there would appear inertia or disinterestedness on the part of revolutionaries of some countries. Naturally it would be better to concentrate on the revolution of a particular country. Though Gramsci opposed Trotsky's idea of permanent revolution he agreed with his views on Fascism. Both viewed fascism as a petty-bourgeois movement. Fascism consists of a mass organisation of the petty-bourgeoisie.

42 CONTEMPORARY MARXISM —FRANKFURT SCHOOL AND CRITICAL THEORY

Introduction

In this Chapter I shall discuss some important aspects of contemporary Marxism. But before doing that I want to caution my readers that the word "contemporary" is to some extent misleading. Marxism is a continuously discussed subject. It is interesting to note that after the death of Engels in 1895 and more specifically after the Bolshevik Party came to power in Russia (1917) Marx's philosophy (both economic and political aspects) came to be widely discussed. But this discussion was confined within few or limited persons. It is because Joseph Stalin believed that he was the sole and genuine interpreter of Marx's and Lenin's ideas and Moscow's view in regard to Marx's philosophy was final. This attitude of Stalin and Moscow created furore in academic circle. But very few had the courage to challenge Moscow's view. However, situation changed considerably after the death of Stalin in 1953. The suffocation that engulfed the Marxist world finally came to an end—there appeared an openness in the world of discussion of Marx's philosophical analysis.

The Bolshevik Party came to power in Russia in 1917 and this spectacular incident emphasised the political and economic aspects of Marxism. Particularly the Third International—called the Communist International or Comintern—wanted to focus light on the revolutionary upsurge. It is because the ascendancy of the Bolshevik Party to power remarkably enthused the revolutionary feeling of workers and common feeling of several European and non-European countries such as China and some Third World states. Marxism was not simply a dogma, it came to be regarded as a weapon for the emancipation of the working class. But this aspect of Marxism could not satisfy the scholars and students of Marx's thought and ideas. That is, many serious students of Marxism (who were not directly associated with practical politics or party) were not satisfied with the contemporary status of Marxism. That is, they wanted to broaden the sphere of Marxism. The persons who wanted to enhance the sphere of Marx's thought "were academics rather than activists writing in a period of decline of working class activity and therefore in comparative isolation from political practice" (Mc Lellan, *op. cit.*, p. 295). The result was that various subjects such as philosophy, epistemology, methodology and even aesthetics came under serious and full-fledged discussion. Mc Lellan writes : "In the period of parliamentary democracy became normal throughout the advanced capitalist countries and their economics enjoyed a long period of unprecedented growth, an atmosphere of resigned pessimism spread among many Marxist intellectuals" (p. 295).

The spread of parliamentary democracy posed a challenge to Marxism. Many scholars came to believe that the objectives of Marxian socialism could be achieved without resorting to repressive measures that the Bolshevik party adopted in Russia. Apart from this, many eminent Marxists of several countries challenged the claim of Moscow as the sole interpreter of Marxism. Again, there emerged a new trend. Many orthodox Marxists emphasised loyalty to internationalism and international issues neglecting national questions. But many Marxists of several European states expressed their unadulterated loyalty to Marxism and, simultaneously, to all important national questions. That is, their viewpoint was there is no conflict between Marxism and nationalism. An Italian Marxist did not object to his government's relation with capitalist America. Of course it must be in the interests of Italy.

The Genesis of Frankfurt School

Scholars generally agree that the degeneration of Marxism by Stalin and his cohorts encouraged many true and serious Marxists to find out the real meaning of what Marx and Engels said on various subjects such as economics, politics etc. This tendency emerged in the 1920s and 1930s. Their chief objective was to find out what Marx exactly said. So we can justifiably say that the views of the Frankfurt School can be treated as a protest movement—protest against Stalinism and Bolshevism. Again, the members of the Frankfurt School (hereafter F. S.) were of opinion that the correct meaning of Marx's views is to be located. What the party leaders and self-interest seeking persons say about Marxism is out of consideration.

Keeping the above idea in mind a group of intellectuals founded the Institute for Social Research in 1923. But the Institute was a department of Frankfurt University. It was an academic institute and its members fully concentrated on the discussion of academic matters—mainly Marxism and its relation with other subjects, mainly branches of social science. The Frankfurt School was contemporary of Nazism. Particularly when Nazism was at the zenith of its power or influence, the F. S. was deeply engaged in the academic analysis of Marxism, philosophy and epistemology. The members of the F. S. were deeply concerned with growing influence of totalitarianism and its menace. It thought that the march of totalitarianism would finally destroy the basic qualities of man and invite all-round degradation of universal values. Logical empiricism, positivism, methodology of science, pragmatism and also utilitarianism all came under the purview of the F. S. But the centre of analysis was Marxism—in the background of change.

Some of the star figures of the F. S. are : Max Horkheimer, who was a leading personality of the F. S. He was a sociologist, philosopher and a psychologist. Eric Fromm was mainly a psychoanalyst. Another person associated with F. S. was Adorns—a philosopher and sociologist. Friedrich Pollock, a leading member of F. S., was an economist and had specialisation in economic planning. Herbert Marcuse was a philosopher and Franz Neumann was a renowned political scientist. Walter Benjamin was an essayist and a well-known figure of the literary world. The membership also included political sociologists, general sociologists etc. Persons acquainted with F. S. are of opinion that the preeminent members of the school were

Horkheimer, Marcuse and Hobermas. The contributions of these persons considerably enriched the academic aspects of the Institute. The F. S. is popularly and generally called the "Institute".

David Held, in his article published in Bottomore-edited *A Dictionary of Marxist Thought,* writes : "The Frankfurt School can't be associated directly with an anti-Bolshevik radicalism and an open-ended or critical Marxism. Hostile to both capitalism and Soviet socialism, its writings sought to keep alive the possibility of an alternative path for social development and many of those committed to the New Left in the 1960s and 1970s found in its work both an intriguing interpretation of Marxist theory and an emphasis on issues and problems" (p. 208). We thus find that in the evolution of Marxist thought the F. S. has a special position. The F. S. was not a club or an ordinary institute. All its members were renowned personalities of the academic world and they critically analysed Marxism from different perspectives.

Features of Frankfurt School

The features of the F. S. are stated briefly. It has already been noted that the members of the F. S. belonged to different subjects and all of them viewed Marxism in the background of their own subjects. Kolakowski observes : "The abundant academic and publistic output of the Frankfurt School covers multifarious domains of humanistic science : philosophy, empirical sociology, musicology, social psycology, the history of the Far East, the Soviet economy, psychoanalysis, the theory of literature and of law". Hence the academic output of the F. S. can be called a "compendium" (I use the word compendium in a restricted sense).

(1) One can note certain basic features of the School. One feature is, according to F. S., the Marxism is not a norm but a "starting point and an aid to the analysis and criticism of existing culture" (Kolakowski, p. 1060). Because of this the members of the school have borrowed terms, arguments and concepts from other disciplines which have been freely used to analyse Marxian concepts and ideas.

(2) The members of the F. S. were not associated with any political party or movement. The result was that the analysis or publication has been non-partisan—unbiased. For this reason we find neutrality in their analysis of communism or socialism or social democracy.

(3) We find a clear influence of Lukacs and Korsch of the 1920s upon the interpretation of the members of F. S. Although influence of Lukacs is quite perceptible, it cannot be concluded that they scrupuloudy followed Luckacs. In the 1920s Lukacs and Korsch were leading figures of Marxism.

(4) The members of the F. S. were independent-minded and they analysed various tenets of Marxism in their respective viewpoints and, at the same time, independently. They did not hesitate to criticise Marxian standpoint or principle that has been implemented. In this respect their main objective was to free Marxism from misinterpretation or misapplication. The extent of their success may be questioned but their objective was honest and there is no doubt about it.

(5) There was a difference between Lukacs and F. S. This difference has been beautifully pointed out by Kolakowski. Let us quote him : "the Frankfurt School differs basically from Lukacs—while accepting Marx's position as to the exploitation and alienation of the proletariat, it did not identify with the latter in the sense of regarding its existing class consciousness, let alone the dictates of the communist

party, as an *a priori* norm" (pp. 1060-1061). The members of the F. S. did not subscribe to the view that the proletarians were universally exploited, that is, everywhere they were exploited and, at the same time, alienated. The F. S. casts doubt about the extent of exploitation and alienation.

(6) The method of analysis adopted by the F. S. can be called "revisionism" of orthodox Marxism. But the school claims that it is profoundly a revolutionary intellectual movement. There is no doubt that the F. S. had launched a revolutionary movement and its contents were intellectual. It means that the F. S. interpreted Marxism from the academic point of view.

(7) The development of the F. S. took place during the rise, victory and fall of Nazism (1921-1945) and naturally the writings and views of the school were influenced by Nazism. Racial prejudice, totalitarianism, economic and political views of Nazism found enough place in the output of the F. S. It is interesting to note that almost all the front-ranking members of the F. S. were German Jews and, from economic point of view, all were middle class. Hence we can say that the F. S. emerged at a critical juncture of time.

Some Basic Concepts

Horkheimer (1895–1973) was the most important member of the Frankfurt School. He elaborated some important aspects of Marxism and Marxist thought. Horkheimer was basically a Hegelian and he explained some ideas and concepts of Marx in the light of "reason" propounded by Hegel. The result is Horkheimer's stand on Marxism and several other ideas is against empiricism, positivism and pragmatism. Horkheimer believed that truth can be ascertained without empirical hypothesis or positivistic method. Horkheimer opposed the application of rigorous scientific methods for the study of social sciences. His clear opinion was that scientific method has a special place in natural science, but it has very little or no relevance in the study of social sciences.

Another point of the school is—human society is threatened by the progress of science and technology. Horkheimer and members, of course, did not oppose the progress of science and technology but they were of opinion that value judgments must be given priority because neglecting value judgment the "progress of science and technology is bound to lead to a totalitarian society" (Kolakowski, p. 1064). There shall exist a balance between scientific and technological progress on the one hand and the value judgment on the other hand.

Lenin and others believed that both party and intellectuals must play important role in encouraging and guiding the proletarians in their attempt for emancipation. Horkheimer agreed with this view. But he added a new factor. Without attaining consciousness and spontaneity the proletarians would never be able to win the battle against the capitalist. His view is : due to the rise of conflict between the two main classes—bourgeoisie and proletariat—the interaction would also rise and this will finally give rise to consciousness and spontaneity. The view of Horkhenimer is based on a practical situation of capitalist society. The capitalists never support the agitation of the working class. Naturally, only consciousness and spontaneity could lead the working class movement. Members of the Institute of Social Research had their general commitment to the cause of the proletariat, and their emphasis on the importance of *praxis* was strong. They conceived their work to be a contribution to clarifying the opposing forces at work in society and, thereby, raising the class consciousness of the exploited, and providing them with a weapon in their struggle for emancipation.

The members of the F. S. wanted to know what man actually wants. There is no doubt that man above everything else wants to satisfy his economic requirements. Assume that his economic necessities are fulfilled. Does it mean that he will be perfectly satisfied? Some members of the F. S. after thorough investigation have seen that the satisfaction of economic necessities is not everything. His other requirements may crop up. He may have ethical or spiritual necessities and these cannot be neglected. Again, there is no limit to economic requirements and particularly in an age of globalisation these may multiply. Naturally Marxism must take note of this situation. When the members of the F. S. were engaged in reviewing Marxism or in reinterpreting it they were not faced with globalisation. But they were aware of the incessant rise of human necessities. Many of the members of F. S. suggested that Marxism must be analysed in the light of this new aspect of human nature. This is purely a subject of psychology and F. S. took interest to view Marxism in this light.

CRITICAL THEORY

Definition, Origin, Nature etc.

The critical theory is inexorably connected with the Frankfurt School because the members of this school propounded certain concepts or ideas that have built up the general outline of critical theory. The preeminent members of the school were Horkheimer, Adorns, Marcuse and Habermas. They were the key contributors of the essays published by the school and, at the same time, they elaborated certain basic ideas that have built up the general body of theory which is known as critical theory. The critical theory is opposed to the traditional theory. It is largely based on positivism. Auguste Comte (1798–1857) was to some extent the founder of positivism. His positivism is called intellectual-cum-political. He suggested that natural and scientific methods are to be applied for the study of social phenomena. The propounders of the critical theory applied positivism for the study of Marxism. They also borrowed Kant's ideas of reason and knowledge, Hegel's concept of spirit. Finally they focused on specific historical forms—capitalism and exchange process of Marx. Thus, in the whole concept of critical theory, Kant, Hegel and Marx met together.

Although a number of contributors are associated with the development and analysis of critical theory Kolakowski is of opinion that a major part of the credit of building up the theoretical structure should go to Horkheimer. In a programmatic essay published in 1937 Horkheimer presented few guidelines of the theory. These can be stated in the following manner.

The studies of social phenomena should be based on the ordinary rules of induction and should aim at formulating general concepts and laws. But the critical theory asserts that social changes are the real forces that help to construct the body of a theory. In this connection the importance of science must be recognised, because behind every social action and any sort of change there plays science. The bourgeois thinkers and philosophers have neglected this vital aspect and have emphasised the independence of science. Behind social production, science always plays the most important role. If the basic concepts of science are changed, then the social production is bound to change.

Another central idea of the critical theory has been stated by Kolakowski in the following words : "Critical theory regards itself as a form of social behaviour and is aware of its own functions and genesis. Its specific function is that it refuses to accept that the rules of existing society are natural and inevitable. It seeks to understand society as a whole" (p. 1069).

The critical theory admits that the proletariat must be liberated from the bondage of capitalism. But, at the same time, the proletariat must not be subject of any other authority—even it might be socialism or communism. In other words, the proletarians must enjoy full freedom in regard to thought and ideas. A physical atmosphere shall be created in which the proletarians will be able to keep their independence.

An interesting aspect of the critical theory is both men and women will have the freedom to build up a society which will be free from external domination. Some people are of opinion that in the eye of critical theory the idea of freedom must have complete significance, that is, it will not be diluted. It has been noted that emancipation does not mean the removal of economic bondage only. The proletarians must be free from all sorts of bondage. The theory aims at human emancipation in a broad sense. It talks of a world where people will enjoy full power.

What is the central idea of critical theory? Horkheimer published an article in 1937—*Traditional and Critical Theory*. I quote a lengthy passage from this article. The critical theory means : "not simply to eliminate one or other abuse. For it regards such abuses as necessarily connected with the way in which the social structure is organised. Although it itself emerges from the social structure, its purpose is, either in its conscious intention or in its objective significance, the better functioning of any element in the structure. On the contrary, it is suspicious of the very categories of better, useful, appropriate, productive and valuable, as these are understood in the present order, and refuses to take them as non-scientific presuppositions about which one can do nothing. The individual as a rule must simply accept the basic conditions of his existence as given and strive to fulfil them" (cited in Mc Lellan, p. 301). The critical theory lays its faith upon the materialist conception. It takes the class-related structure of society and thoroughly studies the reactions of individuals to the class structure. That is, individuals are quite conscious of the class structure and take necessary steps against it.

An important part of the critical theory is stated in *Dialectic of the Enlightenment*. It has been stated that enlightenment broadens the outlook and attitude of man towards himself and society. Being enlightened, the individual seeks the ways of his and his fellow citizens' liberation. Then he proceeds to find out the ways of liberation. He thinks that only through the control of man over nature and over many others liberation can come. But the enlightened mind should be properly channelised. A misguided enlightenment is if no use or utility at all.

Marcuse, Horkheimer and Habermas

In order to have a clear idea about the various aspects of critical theory we must go through the views of what Marcuse, Horkheimer and Habermas expressed through their writings. Herbert Marcuse was the preeminent and the most original contributor of F. S. First of all we shall discuss Herbert Marcuse's contribution.

Herbert Marcuse was a Jew and after Hitler's accession to power (1933) he emigrated to the United States in order to escape from Hitler's inhuman torture. The German *emigrés* founded the *Institute for Social Research* in New York and Marcuse worked there several years. Kolakowski says that his Marxism is a "curious ideological mixture" of Marxism and Hegelianism. Marcuse (1898–1979) published his most notable work *Reason and Revolution* in 1941 where he has interpreted Marxism in his own way. Of course his own way means mixture of Hegel and Marx. He borrowed Hegel's concepts of reason and dialectics and interpreted Hegelian dialectics in the light of Marxism. Marcuse drew the attention of the academic world to Marx's *Paris Manuscript* and he thoroughly studied it in order to know what exactly it says. He was also attracted to the theory of revolution stated by Marx and Engels. Though he accepted Hegel's theory of reason and dialectics he did not subscribe to his view on religion and world spirit. Summarising his ideas on Marxism, Kolakowski says : "the essential basis of Hegelian and Marxian dialectic is not the movement towards the identity of subject and object, but towards the realisation of reason, which is at the same time the realisation of freedom and happiness" (p. 1105). It is interesting to note that Marcuse's idea is not confined within the concept of emancipation.

In several works Marcuse emphasises a very important and basic point. Following Hegel he said that reason proceeds towards development and it proceeds dialectically. When it assumes a developed or mature form people start to work reasonably. He says that it is true that people at first work or struggle for the emancipation from economic bondage. But they did not stop their activities after this particular emancipation is achieved. They proceed towards another object and it is *realisation of freedom and happiness.* Marx focused on the emancipation of the working class. But Marcuse broadened the idea. He believed that man is not concerned only with attainment of physical needs or requirements. He always thinks how to maximise his happiness and minimise his sorrows and sufferings. This is the crucial issue that constitutes the central idea of Marcuse's investigation. He observed that almost all the sections of modern society are concerned about sorrows and frustration. It it the basic responsibility of revolution to free men from all sorts of frustation. So we find that the central idea of Marcuse's theory is not classless society, but a society where everyone will be entitled to freedom and happiness in their full form.

Marcuse has explained the transition from Hegel to Marx. "In Marcuse's interpretation, the transition from Hegel to Marx was a transition to a different order of truth—one that could not be interpreted in terms of philosophy. For, all the philosophical concepts of Marxian theory are social and economic categories whereas Hegel's social and economic categories are all philosophical concepts" (McLellan, p. 311). There is also another difference. Hegel emphasises philosophical labour. Whereas, Marx speaks of alienated labour. Due to division of labour and other reasons labour is alienated from the mainstream of society.

Marcuse was in favour of revolution but this revolution must be based on reason. Needless to say that the idea of reason is purely Hegelian. He is of opinion that the working class must emancipate itself from economic and political exploitation. But its struggle shall not stop here. It must aim at attainment of happiness and only reason can perform this task. So we find that Marcuse has expanded the objective of Marxian theory of revolution. He has further said that people must know the extent of emancipation and only the achievement of reason will empower him to know that.

Marcuse has drawn our attention to a very pertinent aspect of revolution. He says that without revolution working class cannot free itself from the numerous ills of capitalist society. But the capitalists had built up a superstructure which includes modern and improved technology and a great scientific system. Marcuse's question is—does the seizure of capitalist state mean the seizure or destruction of improved technology and modern scientific system? It is to be remembered that the superstructure always corresponds to the capitalist system. Naturally the proletarians cannot profitably utilise the superstructure of capitalist society. The proletarians must have to find out the way how the old capitalist superstructure can be utilised for the well-being of the new society. That should be the primary concern of the working class. In the judgment of Marcuse this is not an easy task at all.

We shall now turn to **Horkheimer** (1895–1973). Under the directorship of Horkheimer the Institute of Social Research made considerable progress in enunciating several aspects and important propositions of the critical theory of society. We find him emphasise the idea of a critique of ideology. This is similar to Marx's critique of capitalist commodity production and exchange. Horkheimer wanted to give stress on the integration of various disciplines and, in this way, he introduced interdisciplinary research. Finally, his different writings have emphasised on the *Central role of praxis.* It is to be used for the ultimate verification of theories. His very remarkable contribution is "the elaboration of philosophical basis of critical theory and a critique of empiricism and positivism."

In 1937 he published an article—*Traditional and Critical Theory*. In this article he raised a question. What is theory? His answer is—*theory for most researchers is the sum total of propositions about a subject, the propositions being so linked with each other that a few are basic and the rest derive from these.* In the opinion of Horkheimer there are two important aspects of theory. One is, a theory is built up upon certain basic propositions. But these basic propositions do not constitute the entire body of theory. Along with these there exist several general propositions. Both the basic and general propositions are all linked with each other. That for the construction of a theory both basic and general propositions are necessary.

Another aspect of Horkheimer's theory is a social researcher must go through the material aspects of a society. Imagination or value judgment have no place in a critical theory. What the real or material situation of the society exposes the researcher will accept as final and on the basis of that he will start his research work. In other words, imagination or value judgment have no place in the investigation of critical theory. In his opinion : "The individual as a rule must simply accept the basic conditions of his existence". That is, the physical existence of individual is the basic or most important matter and nothing else. The emphasis on materialistic aspects of society ultimately can reveal the true picture of society and its members. It is unfortunate that the bourgeois philosophers practically neglected the materialistic aspects and emphasised upon the value judgments and this process failed to reveal the true nature of society and its members. The bourgeois thinkers were not interested in the radical change of society, reforming it was their prior concern.

If we seriously go into the depth of Horkheimer's critical theory the following idea will come out. In his opinion, a theory is in the service of human emancipation, freedom and maximisation of happiness. The whole social structure will be remodelled for the attainment of these objectives. Without a radical change of the existing society these objectives cannot be attained and, for that purpose, a revolution is essential. It is now obvious that the critical theory of Horkheimer (and several others, particularly Marcuse) does not suggest any special type of utopia. It speaks of certain general features which are to be attained. Satisfaction of material demands is a very important thing no doubt. But universal happiness and peaceful condition of society must be given due importance. We, therefore, see that in his theory there is an amalgation of Marxian and Hegel's views—philosophy of Hegel and economics and politics of Marx.

Jurgen Habermas

Jurgen Habermas is a top-ranking German philosopher and the most impressive figure of the second generation of the Frankfurt School. During the Nazi period he was mentally and physically tortured and he was politicised by the Nuremburg trials. He was closely associated with Adorno (1903–1969) and Horkheimer. He was born in 1929. Habemas is one of the neo-Marxists who has focused on the various types of crises of capitalism. That is, as a neo-Marxist he accepts the Marxian theory of crisis in capitalism but he does not believe that this crisis is mainly due to the inherent contradiction in the capitalist system. He again does not concentrate on class struggle and the seizure of political power by the working class. He has analysed the nature and crisis of capitalism which he observed in the twentieth century. He has stated the various aspects of crisis and has carefully analysed them in his noted work *Legitimation Crisis* (1973). He has stated that there are series of crises in capitalist democracies and in order to get rid of them the capitalist system builds up a structure or system of legitimacy. But this attempt fails to ensure an end of crises. Habermas and others are of opinion that it is beyond the capacity of the capitalist system to remove these crises. He says that the economic development of the capitalist society is due to the technological innovations and the application of science and technology to industry. But the application of improved technology has failed to avert any crisis. On the other hand, it is faced with crises such as unemployment, stagnation and problems in resource allocation. In order to avert crises the government proceeds to rely on democratic means—politics becomes the sphere for solution.

Crises in Capitalism

Habermas has started his analysis about capitalism more or less following Marx. But after this he has scanned the capitalism of his time in a different way. In the seventies of the last century he published two works which drew the attention of the people of academic world. These are *Legitimation Crisis* (1976) *Communication and Evolution of Society* (1979). Habermas has entered into the depth of capitalism around him and he observed it from a very close distance. He says that capitalism of Marx's time suffered from crises and capitalism of his time is also faced with crises. But both these crises are not of the same nature. He says that the entire capitalist system can be divided into few subsystems. In his opinion there are three subsystems of modern capitalism. It means that modern capitalism is not an undivided one. The important subsystems of modern capitalism are : the economic, the political—administrative and socio-cultural. In any modern capitalism these are the three main sub-sectors or subsystems. But though they are sub-sectors, they are closely linked with each other.

The economic sub-sector is again divided into three sub-sectors—one is public sector which means that this sector is controlled by the state or government. Manufacturing of armaments falls in this category. Railways and postal services in some countries are included into public sector. Most of the manufacturing industries come under the private sector. The industries of this sector run through keen competition. In some countries the public sector industries face competition and these are called public-private partnership. The purpose of this method is to throw certain industries into competition so that they can reorient the system.

After this analysis Habermas says that the whole capitalist system is facing is in the danger of severe crisis. But the crisis of capitalism that had surfaced in the second half of the 20th century is quite different from that of Marx's time. According to Habermas, the crises in capitalism have endangered the entire system of capitalism. Why this Crisis? Explaining the viewpoint of Habermas, David Held (*Political Theory and the Modern World*) observes : It is a consequence of the fundamental contradictions of capitalist society" (p. 82). What are the contradictions? According to Habermas the causes of contradictions are the following. There is a contradiction in social production and private appropriation. There is another contradiction. The capitalist system, in order to earn maximum profit, is not producing sufficient amount of consumption goods and this creates a gap between supply and demand. It is the type of crisis. This is completely manmade. Habermas points out a new type of crisis. In his opinion the crisis in rationality. Which means that the producers have failed to take a rational decision. There is an authority which is not capable of taking a rational decision in regard to production and related matters. Habermas also points out a motivational crisis.

The increasing tendency of crisis forces the authority to adopt certain measures. It is because in democratic systems public opinion pressurises the government to adopt prophylactic measures to fight the crises. The result is the government is forced to enhance its role in economic fields. The governmental activity sets in. How much the role of government succeeds in averting the crisis is a different question but the fact is that the crisis is a reality and the authority is conscious of it. In democratic countries the governments come forward to shoulder a part of the cost of production. But finally this approach of the government fails to solve the crisis. This is because the crisis in modern capitalism is part of the whole capitalist system and any piecemeal attempt to arrest the crisis fails to satisfy the opponents and to solve problems. But the intervention of the government is faced with another problem. There are several elements in a liberal capitalism who do not like the increasing role of the state. This finally leads to a tussle between the visible hand of the governmental intervention and the invisible hand (and this is not small) of liberal capitalism. Habermas calls this *legitimation crisis.* The crisis is due to the fact that a large section of the public wants increasing and meaningful role of the government and, on the other hand, a powerful section (which is a minority) wants government's non-intervention. In other words, a legitimised authority is challenged (though not directly).

According to Habermas the chief factor which is active behind this *legitimation crisis* is the class structure of liberal capitalism. This means that one class forces the legitimate authority of the state to take measures to fight crisis and the other class stands in the way so that the state authority keeps it away from taking any action. Let us put it in the words of Habermas : "in the final analysis the class structure is the source of legitimation deficit" (Quotation from Held, p. 84). Habermas says that if the state authority wants to take anti-crisis measures it must secure the consent of all classes or sections of the society. But this is not possible because the interests of different classes are contradictory. Explaining the view of Habermas, Held observes : "As the state's activity expands and its role in controlling social reality becomes more transparent, there is a greater danger that this asymmetrical relation will be exposed. Such exposure would only increase the demand on the system. The state ignores these demands only at the peril of further demonstrating its non-democratic nature" (p. 84). From this analysis it is now clear that in modern or liberal capitalism there is a legitimation crisis and it is not possible for the authority of the capitalist state to get rid of this crisis.

Habermas says that modern capitalism is in the midst of severe crisis and it is not easy to save the authority from this crisis. What is the net result? In the opinion of Habermas the crisis in legitimation will continue to exist and in that situation liberal capitalism or present form of capitalism will not be able to keep its form intact or to maintain its form. Explaining Habermas's opinion regarding the crisis of present capitalism, David Held maintains : "If Habermas's argument is correct then capitalism will either evolve into a kind of "Brave New World" or it will have to overcome its underlying class contradictions. To overcome capitalism's underlying class contradiction would mean...the adoption of a new principle of organisation... What exact institutional form the new social formation might take Habermas does not say, nor does he say how the new social formation might evolve" (Held, op. cit., pp. 86-87). The authority of modern capitalist state is making efforts to fight the crisis, but all attempts have gone in vain. Habermas himself says that economic crises are shifted into political system through the reactive-avoidance of the government. But the crises still exist and will continue to exist. The credit of Habermas lies in the fact that he has understood the nature of crisis from which liberal capitalism suffers, though there no solution.

Contribution of Frankfurt School

We have already noted that critical theory emerged at a crucial time. After the death of Lenin in 1924 there was a large scale chaos in the erstwhile Soviet Union. This chaos generally centred around the capture of power. Different groups and power centres began to interpret Marxism in their own way. Finally there appeared Joseph Stalin and he captured (by means of manipulation) the whole authority to utter the last word about Marxism. Again, there arose rapid rise of fascism which threatened Marxism or socialism. The capitalism of West European countries posed another big challenge to Marxism in general and the Soviet government in particular. At this critical situation the Frankurt School made its appearance. The author of the article published in *A Dictionary of Marxist Thought* (edited by Bottomore) writes : "The acknowledgement that Marxism became a repressive ideology in its Stalinist manifestation—thereby confirming that its doctrines do not necessarily offer the key to truth—constitutes one of the crucial premises of critical theory". It allows the recognition that classical Marxist conceptions are quite inadequate. Marxism has certain scientific foundations. But it is quite inadequate to face new situations created by fascism and other orthodox dogmas.

Marx and Engels enthusiastically propagated that the state (in a communist society) would wither away. But the adherents of critical theory after prolonged research arrived at the critical conclusion that there was no possibility of withering away of the state. The state has more important functions to perform. In a new society the role of the state as an agent of repression could be obliterated and the role as a welfare organisation could be established. The critical theory wants to reiterate this. It does not suggest its abolition.

The critical theory makes Marxism a confluence of several streams of social science. Sociology, social psychology, philosophy, religion, morality and even sexuality—all have found a place in the elaborate analysis of critical theory. Particularly its emphasis on happiness, reason and freedom is really noteworthy. In this connection it is mentioned that the F. S. talks about enlightenment. Due to the influence of enlightenment people's mind and idea both are broadened or enlightened. For revolution both consciousness and spontaneity are required and without enlightenment these two essential requirements of revolution are hardly to be achieved. While discussing the political ideas of Rosa Luxemburg we have noted that she also gave special importance to these two concepts—consciousness, spontaneity—all subject matters of psychology.

Let as conclude this part of our analysis by quoting a long passage from Battomore's book : "The expansion of the state into more and more areas, the growing interlocking of base and superstructure, the spread of what they called the 'culture industry', the development of authoritarianism, all implied that political economy had to be integrated with other concerns" (p. 209). Some members of the critical theory were critical of Marxism but none of them suggested its rejection. In fact, all of them suggested its modernisation. The members of the Frankfurt School have brought out Marxism from micro-level and placed it at macro-level. They have sincerely endeavoured to prove that Marxism is not dead. and, Marxism is not Stalinism. It is not confined within the four walls of Bolshevik administration. It is related to overall emancipation of human beings.

STALINISM AND DE-STALINISATION

What is Stalinism?

The term Stalinism is associated with Joseph Stalin's name. Stalin was born on 21 December 1879 and died on 5 March 1953. It is said that Stalin died of an apoplectic stroke. The Stalinism generally refers "to the nature of regime which existed in the former Soviet Union under Stalin from the late 1920s, when he achieved supreme power, to his death in 1953" (Bottomore, *op. cit.*, p. 517). The term Stalinism was not officially used in Soviet Russia during the period 1920s to 1953 (when he died). Again, the Russian leaders did not use it at official level. It is, however, used in a pejorative sense to denote dictatorial, arbitrary, repressive manner of state administration. Stalinism also means extreme form of intoleration to opposite views. In a word, Stalinism was the embodiment of all sorts of absolute power, cruelty to opposition. It represents all sorts of intoleration and accumulation all types of power in a single hand or single centre.

It is said that the concentration of all forms of power in a single centre or single man took place during the dictatorial regime of Stalin. But Stalin was not alone responsible for this. Extreme form of dictatorship was the brain-child of Stalin. But several others were closely associated with him. They were Stalin's sycophants. With their direct help Stalin established cruel dictatorial rule in Russia. In Russia Lenin established Bolshevik rule and later on it came to be known as Bolshevism. After Stalin ascended to power in the late 1920s he applied Bolshevism and forcefully introduced rapid industrialisation, socialism in one country, centralisation of power in a particular centre—particularly state apparatus, the collectivisation of agriculture, the subordination of all communist parties to Moscow or Soviet or Russian Communist Party. Stalinism also refers to Soviet Union as the political expression of the working class of the world.

Stalinism also refers to ruthlessness, no recognition of honesty and morality, a personality cult. In the early years of his rule (1929–1933) Stalin propagated a theory which is known as "revolution from above". By this doctrine Stalin introduced two principles—one was collectivisation of agriculture. It means that there shall be no personal holding in agriculture. All the agricultural land will come under collective farming and no individual person will be allowed to hold agriculture land. The collectivisation of land brought lot of misery and resentment to the individual peasants and small holders of land. But the dictatorship of Stalin did not allow the resentment to persist. This is another aspect of Stalinism. Collectivisation of agriculture is regarded by many as the black spot of Bolshevik rule. Another aspect of "revolution from above" is excessive emphasis on heavy industries. Stalin's view in this regard was Soviet Russia was surrounded by capitalist countries and they were making preparation for an onslaught against Russia, and he must make preparations to fight it away. For that purpose Russia must be self-depended in war weapons and heavy industry can enable her to be self-sufficient in the manufacture of war weapons.

Stalin was fully convinced that his policy or doctrine "revolution from above" could never be implemented without "extreme centralisation of power". This is Stalinism. In order to establish his absolute authority in all spheres of Russian society Stalin resorted to all forms of suppression of dissent in any form such as criticism or mere expression of different opinion. The state administration—particularly the bureaucracy the communist party—all were made subservient to his will. The communist parties of other foreign countries were bluntly asked to be fully loyal to Moscow and loyalty to Moscow meant to be loyal to Stalin. In every respect Stalin's word was final. Stalin's policy meant arbitrary rule or decision. This is Stalinism. All foreign affairs were directed and dictated by Stalin. Many old Bolsheviks (who were dissenters) were cruelly murdered or exterminated by his order. He was determined to clear his administration free of thorns or dissenters. In fact, he created a "Great Terror". Stalinism was another name of annihilation of dissenters and rule of the country through terror.

A unique feature of Stalinism is Stalin created a strong "power elite". Into this category or sector administrative, scientific, culture persons were included. Intellectuals were favoured by Stalin, but they had to pay a high price. These persons had no freedom. The first and most important condition of service was to support every decision or policy of Stalin. There was every possibility of being arrested on any moment and even being exterminated. This is not a false allegation. A large number of intellectuals were brutally treated or murdered. "No regime in history has cast down with such murderous ferocity so many of those whom it had previously raised" (Bottomore, p. 518). There was a time when Stalinism, murder, suppression of political dissension and ferocity all were put in the same group. It is also to be noted here that arbitrariness in administration was synonymous with Stalinism. Stalinism and democracy were opposite to each other. What Stalin thought was final and he did not hesitate to do it. There was none to oppose him. But, however, Stalin in the thirties of the last century achieved marvellous success in economic, social and other sectors. It was Stalinism that raised the status of Russia to the rank of super-power as comparable with United States.

Is it true that Stalinism had only negative aspects? Definitely not. From the thirties to the end of the Second World War (1945) Stalinism could be viewed as symbol of success. Soviet Russia was surrounded by a number of states who did not like Marxism or socialism. Not only this, these states made all sorts of efforts to destroy both Soviet Russia and, simultaneously, Marxian socialism. It was Stalinism that fought against these enemies and, needless to say, Stalinism attained partial success. In the thirties and forties of the last century Stalinism gave "unconditional" support and help to many communist parties of Asia and Africa and also the national liberation movements of these two continents. It was Stalinism that exacerbated the conflict between national liberation on the one hand and imperialism and colonialism on the other. Today we, the people of the Third World states, are very much vocal against imperialism and colonialism, but simultaneously we must remember that for our stand in this field certain amount of credit must be given to Stalin or Stalinism. If Soviet Russia were not a party of Allied powers in the Second World War, it would be difficult (if not impossible) for the Allied powers to defeat the Axis Powers (Whose members were Germany, Italy and Japan).

Again, there was a black spot on Stalinism when Stalin entered into a nonaggression pact with Germany in 1939. But Hitler's attack against Moscow in June 1941 forced Stalin to be a part of Allied Powers and this step of Stalin practically changed the political and military picture of the Second World War. Twenty million Russians sacrificed their lives in the war. Again, it was Stalinism that ensured special status for the East European states. Stalin fought a hard battle for the special status of Poland, Hungary, Bulgaria, Romania. Stalinism was responsible for the division of Germany.

DE-STALINISATION

Meaning and Origin

Joseph Stalin, the uncrowned king of communist Russia, or the generalissimo, died of stroke on 5 March 1953 and it is believed that De-Stalinisation starts after his death. De-Stalinisation literally means to oppose or obliterate the mischiefs of Stalin. In our analysis of Stalinism we have said that Stalinism was the symbol of dictatorship, cruelty, conspiracy, terrorism etc. After his death in 1953 Nikita Khrushchev announced to the communist party of Soviet Union (or CPSU) that "the master of science and learning the supreme military genius, and altogether the greatest genius in history was in reality a paranoiac torturer, a mass murderer and a military ignoramus who had brought the Soviet Union to the verge of disaster" (Kolakowski, op. cit., p. 1148). So we can reasonably hold that the term de-Stalinisation starts after the death of Stalin and the credit of coining the word should better go to Nikita Khrushchev. He was of opinion that the desideratum was to denounce the misdeeds of Stalin because these were the primary cause of his unpopularity and no one of Russia had the courage to oppose Stalin. Because any opposition to Stalin would be followed by unspeakable torture or even annihilation.

De-Stalinisation was never officially used by CPSU or the communist parties of other countries, though the word Stalinism was used at random. Officially the de-Stalinisation was used to denote correction of errors and distortions; to obliterate or overcome the cult of personality or popularly used personality cult that was forcefully introduced by Stalin. It was also meant that the CPSU wanted to return to the Leninist era of party, politics and state administration. Defining Stalinism Kolakowski says : "Stalinism had been a series of regrettable errors committed by the irresponsible Generalissimo but had nothing to do with the system itself" (p. 1151). Hence de-Stalinisation means the removal or correction of the mischiefs perpetrated by Stalin. Stalin fully controlled the Soviet system and guided it according to his sweet will. The interesting fact is that generally he did not criticise Lenin or Marx. Rather, he announced at the top of his voice that he was the truest follower of Lenin and Marx. The proof at hand is *The Problems of Leninism.* Stalin created an image of his own as well as a system of Soviet administration to suit his own design. In every matter such as administration, party or foreign relation Stalin's decision was final. Not only this any opposition to his view or decision was dealt with maximum cruelty. Humanism, kindness etc. were not written in his dictionary.

History of Soviet Union or of the CPSU says that the process of de-Stalinisation started with the Twentieth Congress of CPSU in February 1956. The Twentieth Party Congress was a closed session. Though it was open to foreign delegates the decision of the Congress was not known to the outside world. The key person of the Congress was Nikita the Khrushchev and it is believed that the process of de-Stalinisation was practically introduced by him with the introduction of a single phrase—the removal of "personality cult". Stalin was denounced or criticised by majority of the CPSU but the chief spokesperson was Khrushchev. Although the contents of the CPSU were not known to the outside world, it is believed that at the Twentieth Party Congress he placed a detailed account of various misdeeds done by Stalin. The misdeeds are classified as "crimes and paranoiac delusions, the torture, persecutions and murder of party officials. In the judgment of Khrushchev, Stalin was mainly a criminal. Naturally any sympathy to him did not arise at all. He was openly denounced by Khrushchev and large number of party leaders followed him. Stalin was pointed as a blood-thirsty paranoiac. Khrushchev did not show any sympathy or respect to Stalin. It is said that the misdeeds of Stalin were never a secret matter, they were known to the Western world. Even a sizeable section of the Soviet Party and communist parties of East European states were acquainted with those. But none had the courage to oppose them.

The central idea of de-Stalinisation is that his successors did not change everything that he introduced, but they put an end to all terror and repression. So we find that there are few aspects of de-Stalinisation. Some of these are : the terror tactics of Stalin were discontinued. The concentration of power in a single centre was stopped. Collective leadership was introduced. In Stalin's time Moscow was the centre of international communist movement. The communist party of every country was forced to show loyalty to the CPSU. But de-Stalinisation does not mean to put an end to everything that Stalin introduced. He built up a system or state structure and his successors did not do way with it. The chief objective of Stalin was to raise the status of Soviet Russia to the rank of superpower equal to the status of the United States. It is interesting that his successors continued it. Notwithstanding the numerous mischiefs done by Stalin, it may safely be said that the credit of erecting Soviet Russia as a superpower should go to him.

A POSTMORTEM

Stalinism and de-Stalinisation were for few years hotly-talked topics and students of Marxism and post-Marxist thought took interest in this issue. But it is surprising to note that none of these two terms had an official seal. De-Stalinisation started its journey from the Twentieth Party Congress of CPSU in February 1956. Though the historians view in this line none officially uttered the words. Denunciation of Stalinist methods and tactics is treated as de-Stalinisation. Just this much. The bombshell of Khruschev's speech is generally regarded as the basis of de-Stalinisation. But the speech cannot be treated as the real foundation of de-Stalinisation because it did not contain any new information about the mischiefs that were supposed to have been done by Stalin. All his misdeeds, errors and mischiefs were known to everyone. But no one had the courage to protest. The death of Stalin in 1953 opened the flood-gates of protest and de-Stalinisation got maximum publicity. So we can say that both the contents and other aspects of de-Stalinisation are quite feeble and unworthy in nature.

The torture and atrocity by Stalin is beyond all sorts of condemnation. But at the same time it is required to be remembered that the political chaos and uncertainty created by the death of Lenin could not be put into check without the methods adopted by Stalin. From the standpoint of stability, unity in the party and peace in society the unethical activities of Stalin had certain amount of utility, but from a neutral point of view it is definitely condemnable. The relation between politics and morality or ethics is still an issue of controversy. But this does not rule out the scope of criticism. That is, the activities of Stalin are not above criticism. Here again we hold the view that Stalin committed certain inhuman activities. The concentration camp was undoubtedly the most heinous creation of the Stalinist era and the most remarkable achievement of Khrushchev was the abolition of these camps.

In our postmortem analysis we can say that numerous changes were introduced in Russia to remove the black spots of the Stalin-era, but no remarkable success was achieved. The excessive emphasis on heavy industries of the Stalinist era continued. There was no substantial improvement in agriculture sector. After Stalin's death several attempts were made to decentralise and minor success was achieved. But all these could not bring about an air of openness and ensure complete decentralisation. The foundation of communist despotism remained unimpaired. Kolakowski writes (p. 1152) "The abandonment of mass terror was important for human security, but it did not affect the state's absolute power over the individual, it did not confer on citizen's any institutional rights on infringe the state and party monopoly. The principle of totalitarian government was upheld, whereby human beings are the property of the state". So we hold the view that the condemnation of Stalinism as an embodiment of torture and autocracy was not worthy. It should be maintained that the rise of Stalinism or de-Stalinisation is chiefly due to the fact that some people could not tolerate Stalin and his method of administration and policy. "The only communist regimes in the world are the Leninist-Stalinist pattern—on Stalin's death the Soviet system changed from a personal tyranny to that of an oligarchy" (Kolakowski, p. 1153).

REVISIONISM

Meaning and Origin

The COD defines revisionism in the following words : a policy of revision or modification, especially of Marxism, on evolutionary socialist or pluralist principles. Again, it means the theory or practice of revising one's attitude to something. In ordinary or general sense revisionism denotes any type of revision or alteration or change of existing idea or dogma in the background of present situation. But in political science, especially in Marxism, the term denotes special meaning. Marx and Engels completed their analysis and survey of capitalist society in general and its economic aspects in particular before the end of the nineteenth century. But the twentieth century witnessed far reaching changes in various sectors of the capitalist society and these changes in some cases or fields went against what Marx said and some Marxists and many non-Marxists viewed that these changes had falsified Marx's views and conclusions. Or they thought that Marx could not properly or correctly foresee the events or nature of the capitalist society. But these people simultaneously asserted their faith in Marxism. This situation created a peculiar problem for persons who had great faith in Marxism but changes in events or situation had shaken their faith in Marxism or inspired them to think about Marx's doctrine in different line.

We, therefore, see that the concept of revisionism has a special meaning in relation to Marxism. Revisionism has a special reference to Marxist doctrine because of the fact that though many of the key ideas or aspects of Marx were confronted with a big question mark at the very beginning of the twentieth century many conservative or orthodox or dogmatic Marxists refused to shake their faith in Marxism. We are of opinion that revisionism in Marxism has come to be associated with dogmatism, pragmatism and also, to some extent, with conservatism. This is so because many Marxists have come to believe that Marxism is universally correct. That is, in all capitalist countries Marx's analysis and predictions have special importance and meaning. Some opportunists or non-Marxists have distorted Marx's views, conclusions and analyses to suit their own opinion and analysis. Their claim is they want to update Marx's views and in this way they are "modernising" Marx's views and not abandoning them. Hence revisionism does not mean abandonment of Marxism but its updation. Viewed from this angle revisionism connotes democratic and rationalist implication of Marxism. In other words, revisionism implies rationalisation of Marxism in the light or perspective of changes that are taking place.

Kolakowski is of opinion that from the second half of the 1950s the term "revisionism" came to be "used by the party authorities and official ideologists in communist countries to stigmatise those who, while remaining party members or Marxists, attacked various communist dogmas". But the persons who use the phrase revisionism did not attach special meaning to it. It is generally believed that revisionism is rational and democratic. During the dictatorial rule of Stalin there was no place of rationalism or democracy in party structure or state administration.

Hence revisionism has a special reference to Stalin's autocratic rule and various interpretations of Marxism that cropped up after Marx's death (1883) and especially the death of Engels (1895). In the mid-fifties of the last century communist ideology was disintegrated and this invited revisionism.

DEVELOPMENT OF REVISIONISM

By the mid-fifties of the last century there occurred a disintegration in the monolithic nature of communism and this disintegration was quite widespread. After the death of Stalin in 1953 the Marxists or communists began to think and interpret the basic tenets of Marxism in their own way and this finally led to a variety of interpretation. This means that pluralism got a secure place in the monolithic structure of communism. Before the death of Stalin the last word about Marxism was absolutely monopolised by Moscow. After his death different people and the revisionists got free access to press and electronic media and through these they expressed their views about communism. This finally opened the way of multiplicity of opinion about what Marx and Engels said and what was the exact meaning of their view.

The revisionists were not foreign to Marxist ideology or Marxism. They interpreted Marxism by liberally quoting from Marx's vast literature and because of this there was hardly any possibility to challenge the views of the revisionists. At the same time there were sufficient reasons and arguments in the analysis and observations of the revisionists. Pluralism in thought may be regarded as the prime reason of the rapid development of revisionism. Here it may be noted that revisionism does not mean abandonment of the basic tenets of Marxism or even thorough revision of Marxism. It may mean the updation of Marx's basic ideas.

I have used the word "updation" of Marxism. It has a wider and deeper meaning. From the second half of the fifties of the last century a large number of states of Asia and Africa began to earn political freedom and immediately after independence many of them publicly expressed their loyalty to communism. But at the same time they made it clear their attachment or loyalty to nationalism or national interests. That is, they did not hesitate to make minor changes or alterations in the basic ideas of Marxism or Communism. These alterations subsequently came to be called as revisionism. The leaders of the various communist parties of different countries began to treat communism in the background of their national questions. The revisionists were not the opponents of communist party or Marxism. For example, Mao Zedong was not at all anti-Marxist. He applied the central concepts of Marxism-Leninism in China. The Thoughts of Mao therefore may be called a type of revisionism.

There was another factor behind the emergence as well as development of revisionism. It was believed that the Stalinist system and mode of administration committed certain mistakes which went against the basic ideas of Marxism; and these were needed to be rectified. But they did not suggest the banishment of Stalinism. It was their view that Stalinism was curable and communist society could be democratised. These two views led to the development of revisionism. If relaxation were not allowed to have a special place in communism ultimately it will face serious consequences. The ardent adherents of communism naturally accepted revisionism as a natural development of communist thought. At the initial stage revisionism was not treated with an open heart. But subsequently its opponents thought that it should be accepted because revisionism in several ways strengthens the stand of communism. It was also held that the purpose of revisionism was not to enfeeble the philosophy of communism or Marxism. In this way, revisionism has found a secure position in the arena of communism.

NEW LEFT

Origin

In contemporary Marxism, the New Left occupies a very significant place. In our analysis of Frankfurt School and critical theory we have observed that there was a strong reaction against Stalin's mode of administration and his attitude towards Marxism-Leninism. In the thirties and forties of the last century serious efforts were made by a good number of intellectuals having deep command over Marxism and these efforts related to the unearthing of what Marx and Engels exactly said. They refused to study and understand Marxism through the Russian interpreters directed by Stalin and his cohorts. The *leitmotif* was *revival* of Marxism in its original form or to interpret Marxism in the background of what Marx exactly said. These thinkers came to be known as the New Left. The members accepted Marxism or Marx's doctrine, but they wanted to explain Marx's ideas in a correct and proper perspective.

But the above cannot be regarded as the exclusive source or origin of the New Left. David Held is of opinion that in the second half of the last century some liberal thinkers challenged some of the basic concepts of liberalism, particularly the *laissez-faire* or free market doctrine and, at the same time, some aspects of neo-liberalism. It appeared to these thinkers that under neo-liberalism and *laissez-faire* system the responsibility and freedom of individuals have considerably diminished. This development is unwelcome. At the same time, bureaucratisation proliferated beyond imagination. Many began to think that shrinkage of the individual's freedom cannot be accepted. These persons came to be called the New Right. "The New Right is concerned to advance the cause of liberalism against democracy by limiting the possible uses of state power" (Held : *Political Theory and Modern State*, p. 175).

The New Right thinkers demanded that the policy and the state action should be kept at a minimum level so that the individual gets enough freedom of action and thought. In the opinion of the New Right the policy and action of the state are always imperfect and aim at limiting the freedom of individuals. Hayek in his *Road to Serfdom* emphasised this aspect of liberalism and the New Right accepted it. Against the New Right there emerged a new group of thinkers popularly known as the New Left. Held argues the New Left "emerged primarily as a result of the political upheavals of the 1960s, internal debates on the left and dissatisfaction with the heritage of political theory, liberal and Marxists" (p. 176). Another critic is more specific as to the origin of the New Left. It has been observed the "New Left emerged from the disintegration of Soviet hegemony over the international communist movement as shown by the de-Stalinisation process begun at the Twentieth Congress of the CPSU in 1956". A large number of intellectuals of Soviet Russia were so much dissatisfied with the mode of functioning of Stalin and other leaders that they decided to find out the real meaning of Marxian philosophy. Large number of thinkers began to analyse Marx's views on social, political and economic issues—few of them are CB Macpherson (*The Life and Times of Liberal Democracy*), Pateman

(*Participation and Political Theory*—1970), Poulantzas (*State Power, Socialism*, 1980). The chief purpose of the New Left thinkers was to analyse and interpret Marx's doctrine in the perspective of new situations and incidents. The central idea of the New Left is "there are fundamental difficulties with orthodox Marxist theory". Marxism must be freed from this confinement. The action of the state has created only inequalities. This is to be stopped.

Some Features of the New Left

Kolakowski, the noted Marxist interpreter, at the very beginning makes the following comment : "The so-called New Left is a *complex of phenomena*, witnessing on the one hand, to the universalisation of Marxist phraseology and, on the other hand disintegration of the doctrine and its inadequacy to modern social problems" (pp. 1177-78). This short comment of Kolakowski reveals, at least partially, the nature of the New Left. It is not a coherent concept. Different ideas and views of Marx have met together. When Marx's main doctrine was faced with serious problems and some noted Marxists challenged the basic aspects of Marx, but did not abandon them and even did not show the sign of abandoning, the New Left emerged. We can say that in the sixties of the last century fissures in the so-called coherency of Marxism appeared and that showed the beginning of the New Left. We can interpret it in another way. Academic doctrines are never static, with the change of time and material conditions some of the basic aspects of the academic doctrine are faced with questions—Marxism is no exception. It is generally maintained by many renowned scholars that Marxism is not a monolithic theory. It has a good number of aspects and many of these are confronted with questions. This is a vital feature of the New Left.

During the last half century Marxists of different countries have made efforts to apply Marxism in their countries and in this attempt they were forced to change some of the vital aspects of Marxism. For example, Lenin did this and he is pioneer in this field. Mao of China is again a great leader to apply Marxism but not in its original form. Marxists of Italy, Cuba and several other countries also changed many aspects of Marxism to suit their own countries. All these led to the loss of uniformity of Marxism.

The New Left enjoyed the full freedom of thought and expression which was unimaginable in the Stalin era. The members of the New Left condemned Stalinism and supported de-Stalinisation. The New Left did not support Moscow's invasion of Hungary. Even it strongly criticised Moscow's big-brotherly attitude towards the East European states. The New Left called it a new type of colonialism. On the other hand, the members of the New Left showed their utmost fidelity towards Marxism. The fact is that the New Left was fully loyal to Marxism but could not tolerate its aberrations. The New Left also denounced the degeneration of the Soviet system in general. During Stalin's rule there were a number of aberrations and gross misuse of Marxism. This considerably disheartened the Marxists and they were determined to stop the degradation of Marxism in this way.

A very important aspect of the New Left is that New Leftists were quite eager in the revival of Marxism as a living ideology. They were determined to save Marxism from the vortex of misinterpretation and misuse. It was observed that Marxism was not exclusively meant for the developed capitalist states but for all states—particularly the states of the Third World. Kolakowski writes : "In the sixties the term New Left was generally used in Europe and North America as a collective label for student ideologies which...used the phraseology of worldwide anti-capitalist revolution and looked chiefly to the Third World for models and heroes" (p. 1178). In other words, the New Left has more relevance for the developing countries of Asia and Africa. The nationalist leaders of these states are quite eager to materialise the national goals through the proper and prudential application of Marxism. This is rather the vital point of the New Left.

Theoretical Aspects of the New Left

The New Leftists are of opinion that only a revolution can bring about radical change of society. But it is needless to wait for the most opportune moment of revolution. That is, it is not correct to say that the "ripeness" of revolution has not yet arrived and in that situation it is not judicious to call for a revolution. The New Leftists are against the theory of "ripeness" for revolution : "There is no reason to wait : existing states and growing elites must be destroyed by force, without arguing about the political and economic organisation of future—the revolution will decide these in its own good time" (p. 1178-79). The New Leftists argue that there is nothing like ripeness of revolution. The true revolutionaries must call for a revolution.

If the revolutionaries think that the existing system must be destroyed or changed then they must call for a revolution. Not only this, the revolution must be total; that is, it will be against the whole structure of the society or system. The members of the Frankfurt School and the theoreticians of the critical theory advocated for a total revolution. The New Leftists demanded true revolution and not reform, because reforms and revolution do not fall in the same category. So a true revolutionary must oppose reform.

Marx, Engels and their followers relied heavily on the ability of the working class to lead a revolution. But the New Leftists have rejected this. They are of opinion that only revolution is capable of changing a bourgeois society, but this revolution must be led by the students and not workers. The working class is not a completely deprived class, on the other hand, the students are really oppressed. Again, the student community is resolute in its aim and decision. The students are not easily purchasable.

Marx, Engels, Lenin and many others emphasised the importance of revolution in the field of radical change of society but they have been found to be silent on the nature of revolution and in this regard the members of the New Left are quite outspoken. The revolution—in all senses—must be total and all-embracing. The revolution conceived by the New Leftists is of a different nature. It is not aimed at the bourgeois class, it is "directed against fraudulent academic institutions". The revolution of the New Left aims at cleansing the academic institutions of all categories. This revolution must remove corrupt and inefficient teachers and unworthy education system.

Another aspect of revolution of the New Left is that the revolution must check over-population, pollution of environment, and misuse of scarce natural resources. The objective of revolution must be to remove backwardness, poverty, and check all sorts of tension—particularly political and military. This revolution must save society from all types of insecurity, parochialism, and narrowness. It shall be the objective of revolution to free mankind from hunger and fear.

The central idea of the New Left revolution is the people of the Third World are in the midst of all types of crises and, naturally, the revolution must be total so that a new society can be built up on the ashes of the old society. The members of the New Left believe that students are the victims of maximum frustration, oppression, deprivation. They are alienated from the mainstream of society. They do not calculate loss and profit, they do not hesitate. Naturally, only the students can provide bold and necessary leadership in any form of total and violent revolution. In the fifties and sixties of the last century many capitals and academic institutions were in the grip of revolution led by students.

Pateman and Poulantzas are two pioneers of the New Left movement. Pateman's book : *Participation and Democratic Theory* (1970) and Poulantzas's book : *State, Power, Socialism* (1980) throw ample light on the various aspects of capitalist society. They have thoroughly investigated the nature and functioning of capitalist society and have arrived at the conclusion that the bourgeois concept of liberty is ill-conceived and highly limited because this does not treat liberty in proper perspective. In the opinion of the bourgeois liberty and equality before law is enough. If this condition is fully satisfied people will enjoy liberty. But both Pateman and Poulantzas argue that "to enjoy liberty means not only to enjoy equality before law, but also to have the capacities to be able to choose between different courses of action" (Held, *Political Theory and Modern State*, p. 176). According to Pateman and Poulantzas the bourgeois theoreticians have imagined about liberty, freedom etc. in their own way. But, in practice, such type of conception is not found in practical society.

These two pioneers of the New Left have further announced that in theory and ideology many types of liberty and right are found but in practice there is no existence of these rights and freedom. In other words, paper announcement of rights is not enough, people must have free access to all these rights and freedoms. But for this a new type of society is required and only a revolution can ensure such a situation. The doors of Justice and the doors of a Five Star Hotel are open to all. But how many people have the capacity to go to the house of Justice and the hotel? Only a new society, radically reconstructed, can ensure the liberty, rights and justice.

Marx and Engels strongly advocated for the seizure of political power for the emancipation of the common people from capitalist exploitation. The New Left, Poulantzas and Pateman have lent their unqualified support to this concept. But they differ in certain vital aspects. They are of opinion that mere seizure of power can never be treated as Aladdin's lamp—capable of solving each and every problem. Rosa Luxemburg once said democratic and parliamentary procedures can effectively be used for the realisation of certain basic demands of the workers and Engels in his *Preface to Class Struggle in France* supported this. Luxemburg once said : without general elections, without unrestricted freedom of press and assembly, without a free struggle of opinion, life dies out in every public institution.

Poulantzas is of opinion that there are innumerable inequalities in societies and if these are not removed for ever there cannot be free development of all men. Supporting Poulantzas's view David Held says : "Inequalities of class, sex and race substantially hinder the extent to which it can legitimately be claimed that individuals are free and equal" (Held, op. cit., p. 177). "Poulantzas emphasises two sets of changes which he believes are vital for the transformation of state in West and East into forms of what he calls "socialist pluralism". The state must be democratised by making parliament, state bureaucracies and political parties more open and accountable while new forms of struggle at the local level must ensure that the society as well as the state, is democratised, that is, subject to procedures which ensure accountability" (p. 178). This is the central idea of the political thought of the New Left.

The members of the New Left do not subscribe to the popular view that with the advent of communism the state will wither away. That is absolutely a utopian thought. In the past there were states, today there are states, and, in future, there will exist states. But the New Left wants to emphasise that the state shall be democratised, socialised and pluralism shall be the foundation of every state. In other words, the state conceived by the New Left is pluralist, socialist and democratic. Only in such a state inequality cannot thrive in any form. The state can be a vehicle to achieve certain coveted goals and these goals are related to economic, social, political, cultural etc. If the state is not democratised these goals will remain a far cry.

Both Lenin and Stalin adopted an erroneous way of building up a socialist society. They ignored the democratic feeling of the common people. They thought that the party was all in all and the supremacy of the party could help people in attaining their goals. But ultimately it proved wrong. It is painful that Lenin failed to estimate the importance of representative institutions, and their contributions to the development of thought and ideas of the common people. Lenin absolutely neglected the importance of multiplicity of power centres in a society. The New Left firmly believes that through the multiplicity of power centres people can develop their multiplicity of thought and, in this way, the society can be democratised. By ignoring the democratisation both Lenin and Stalin committed a Himalayan blunder. The New Left, it can be said, made some modest attempts to rectify the mistakes of Lenin and Stalin. But the problem is the vision of the New Left is yet to be achieved. The vision is faced with a big question mark.

43 SYNDICALISM AND GUILD SOCIALISM

Origin, Definition etc.

The concept of socialism is normally divided into two broad group or category—Marxian socialism and non-Marxian socialism. Before Marx there was the existence of socialism, but Marx and Engels are the first persons who in a scientific and broad perspective analysed the concept and suggested ways for its establishment. But many thinkers differed from Marx and Engels as regards the definition, methods of attaining, function etc. All these issues finally drew a line of distinction between Marxian concept of socialism and non-Marxian concept. At the beginning of the twentieth century a good number of thinkers said that outside the domination of state there might be socialism because in the general concept there is supremacy of state. For example, the Encyclopaedia Britannica defines socialism as "that policy or theory which aims at securing by the action of the central democratic authority a better distribution and in due subordination thereto, a better production of wealth than now prevails (Quoted by C.E.M. Joad—*Modern Political Theory*, p. 54). Here we find that in the concept of socialism or in the attainment of socialist ideals the state plays the most vital role.

But in the early years of 20th century many socialist thinkers began to doubt the role or function of the state so far as socialism is concerned. This implies that large number of people claim their allegiance to socialism but their points of difference lie elsewhere and this results in a division among the socialists. C.E.M. Joad rightly observes "socialists are divided into a number of opposing schools, which are separated by acute differences both as regards their aims and their methods" (p. 39). These schools or members of schools fervently support the main tenets of socialism but they differ among themselves as regards the ways and techniques of attainment of socialist ideals. There are similarities among the socialists of various groups so far as the chief aims of socialism are concerned. But they differ when the issue of attainment arise. Joad says : "each method of treatment will emphasise different aspects of socialism, and will result in the presentation of a different picture" (p. 39). Result is in several European countries we witness not one group of socialist thinkers but number of groups. Each group claims itself as socialist. The result is there are number of groups in socialist world. Syndicalists and Guild Socialists are two such groups. Some people doubt about the genuineness of socialist ideals or philosophy of several groups. But in the academic world all the various groups of socialism have been able to maintain their separate existence. Every group professes to be socialist. Remembering this Joad says : "Socialism, in short, is like a hat that has lost its shape because everybody wears it" (p. 40). Though socialism, according to many scholars, has lost its original meaning it still exists and will continue to exist.

Syndicalism and Guild Socialism are two important varieties of socialism that drew attention of many prominent persons. Many believe that behind the emergence of various manifestations of socialism there lies Social Darwinism. Socialist thought is not the product of any particular brain but it is the product of collective thought. People's urge to live has forced them to lead a continuous struggle. They have devised new techniques, ways and other means. This is the father of new ideas and policies. Socialism or communism is one such method or policy. People, through their struggle for existence, have realised that this struggle is to be implemented collectively—Social Darwinism highlights this aspect of the struggle. Non Marxian socialism is not a homogeneous, the most cohesive and the best disciplined group.

Joad defines Syndicalism in the following way : "Syndicalism may be defined as that form of social thought which regards the Trade Union organisations as at once the foundation of the new society and the instrument whereby it is to be brought into being. It is frankly socialistic in the sense that it adopts the general socialist view of capital as theft, endorses, or rather extends, the notion of class war as fundamental in capitalist society and proposes to abolish the private ownership of the means of production and to substitute ownership by the community" (p. 63). According to CEM Joad, Syndicalism as a form of non-Marxian socialism is a type of social theory because it aims at 'radical' change of society through the machination of trade union movement. That is, at the centre of social change there shall work trade union. It does not talk about political party or any other organisation. Syndicalism is least interested in various theoretical analyses. It is chiefly concerned with action. In a precise way COD has defined it in this way—It is a movement for transferring the ownership and control of the means of production and distribution. So far as content is concerned there is practically no difference between Joad's definition and the definition given by COD. The main difference is—Joad calls it a special form of social theory, COD feels that it is type or instrument for changing the society or structure of society. It is also to be noted that it has double manifestation. In the first place it is a theory of social organisation and a plan of action. Of course most of the theories about society or social change fall within this category.

Various Aspects of Syndicalism

In an article published in Bottomore-edited *A Dictionary of Marxist Thought* we find that Syndicalism is simply the English rendering of the French word *unionism*. The propounders of the concept were primarily associated with the trade unionism or trade union movement. Most of the leaders of Syndicalism were trade union leaders. These leaders lost their faith in Marxian socialism. They felt that only through extensive trade union movement and militant activities the financial conditions of the poor people and specially of the workers can be radically changed. It has been asserted that Syndicalism is closely connected with the French trade union organisation *Syndicalisme Revolutionaire* whose chief organiser was Fernand Pelloutier (1867–1901). Before 1914, Syndicalism was the official position of the militant trade union movement of a number of industrialised countries of Western Europe.

There is a close relationship between Syndicalism and anarchism. It is observed that Syndicalism found its roots and ways or means of development in countries where anarchism or anarchist philosophy flourished abundantly. France is a state which falls within this category. Syndicalism is opposed to socialism because it fully endorses the collective methods. It is also against communism. Because in these two forms of social theories the state is the central figure. The state organises the structure of the society and simultaneously determines the procedure how socialism will function. Syndicalism draws its inspiration mainly from Proudhon. He propagated a new doctrine popularly known as ***Associative Communism***. In such type of communism there is no place of the role of any central organisation including the state. Let us quote few lines from Produhon :

"To be governed is to be watched, inspected, spied upon, directed, law-driven, numbered regulated, enrolled, indoctrinated, preached at, controlled, checked, estimated, valued, censured, commanded, by creatures who have neither the right nor the wisdom nor the virtue to do so. To be governed is to be at every operation, at every transaction noted, registered, counted, taxed, stamped, measured, numbered, taxed admonished, prevented, forbidden... That is government, that is its justice, that is its morality". This view of Proudhon enormously influenced and inspired the Syndicalists and they were determined to do away with everything the state possesses. In a word, the Syndicalists wanted to set up a socialist society minus state interference.

We, therefore, find that in Syndicalist thought system and action plan voluntariness occupies the central position. It believes that only through voluntary action can socialism, in its full form, be achieved. In the trade union system there is no place of compulsion imposed by higher authority. So both Syndicalism and anarchism strongly argue for complete emancipation of working class through voluntary means where trade unions will have final say. Because of the striking similarity between anarchism and Syndicalism a new word has been coined by political scientists. Which is commonly called **Anarcho Syndicalism.** The faith of the Syndicalists on voluntary organisations, particularly on trade unions, was so deep and extensive that they did not think of forming any socialist party. According to the Syndicalist, the political or socialist parties are corrupt and bureaucratic and engrossed with parliamentarism. According to syndicalism these are the characteristic features of state-controlled socialism.

Let us now turn to the **policy and strategy** of Syndicalism. The main emphasis of Syndicalists was not on theory but on action, because they believed that only action—and direct action—could help them to achieve their objective. The rank and file would be imbued with the feeling of spontaneity. Besides this, if required, the Syndicalists will resort to sabotage and militancy. This is called direct action. Apart from this the Syndicalists have suggested a general strike as a weapon to achieve success. Several Syndicalists have strongly favoured general strike on the ground that it is highly effective because it creates pressure on the authority. The sabotage and general strike are regarded by the Syndicalists as strategy. But time and situation must be carefully chosen. There are various forms of sabotage such as "doing bad work, breaking machinery and spoiling work which has already been done, to obeying letters of the rules exactly and literally in such a way as to prevent industry from being carried on" (Joad, op. cit., pp. 70-71). The workers may also adopt the policy of boycott.

The purpose of all these forms of direct action is to put maximum pressure upon the state so that it can accept the demands of the trade union—Syndicalism prefers general strike to only simple type of strike. Explaining the stand of the Syndicalist, Joad says that general strike is always more effective. Ordinary or partial strike cannot exert adequate pressure upon the authority. Again, a general strike can be called generally in key or important industries. Such a step will paralyse the whole capitalist system and syndicalism wants that. The noted French author, Blanqui, has suggested that a general strike is quite effective to paralyse the capitalist system. Blanqui has further observed that all the modern industries are closely connected and, for that reason, general strikes are necessary.

Syndicalism and Sorel

For a balanced analysis of Syndicalism proper mention about Sorel must be made. Georges Sorel was born on 2 November 1847 and expired on 28 August 1922. He was an engineer employed in government service. At the age of 46 or 47 Sorel began to write about Marxism. He paid his tribute to Marx by saying that Marx was the first thinker who fully understood the nature of capitalism. But later on he contradicted and rather challenged many of the basic ideas or concepts of Marx. It is said that in the first decade of the twentieth century he began to reformulate his thesis or ideas about socialism, fate and sorrows of working class. For the emancipation of the working class Marx talked a lot about class struggle and the withering away of state. But subsequently his thought remarkably tilted towards Syndicalism and in this field his remarkable work is *Reflections on Violence* (1906). Sorel propagated (or emphasised) that only through continuous struggle the working class would finally be able to emancipate itself. But it is to be remembered here that Sorel's struggle of the working class cannot be equated with Marx's class struggle.

Sorel said that the working class will have to launch a fierce fight against the capitalists and this fight would be done through the trade unions. The workers will call a general strike, or partial strike, and they also woulld seriously think about sabotage and other destructive methods. He has said that the sole objective of the working class would be to destroy the ill-designs of the capitalists. In Sorel's opinion, to fight against the capitalists, organisational strength of the working class is not enough, their moral strength and attachment to socialism must be exceptionally high. Only through a general strike or any other militant method workers can achieve their coveted goal.

Explaining Sorel's stand on general strike Joad says : "In Sorel's language the general strike is to be a "myth" to the workers, a myth being an idea which fills men with ardour. ...But any attempt to rationalise the myth is bound to be misleading" (p. 72). In other words the workers must be convinced that only through a general strike they would be able to defeat the capitalists. He was fully convinced that only a call of general strike would be able to bring all workers having different faith and ideologies under one umbrella. This would be enough to defeat the capitalists. In this way Sorel strengthened the very foundation of Syndicalism.

Sorel had full faith on workers' ability to change the capitalist society, but in order to achieve that the workers must be prepared to fight. He was sure that only socialism can change their fate or emancipate them from all sorts of exploitation. Maxey says : "To ensure real proletarian rule, the workers must replace the state with a social system adapted to the special qualities of their own class" (p. 628). To achieve this goal Sorel suggested that on the basis of economic functions the workers must be grouped together. "Workers in each category of economic enterprise should be affiliated in self-governing Syndicates or unions" (p. 628). These Syndicates or unions will play the leading role in fight against the capitalists. Again, the Syndicates or unions will play the key role in struggle against the capitalists. The Syndicates will shoulder the full responsibility of the management of industry. This process, according to Sorel, would eliminate completely the dictatorial role of capitalists or any central organisation under the management of the state. He believed that the capitalists would not normally allow the workers to take the management of industry. But through concerted effort and struggle the capitalists must be defeated.

The relationship between syndicalism (with special reference to Sorel) and Marxism may now be explained briefly. Maxey says that the political ideas of the twentieth century is considerably influenced by many streams of thought and the important of them are Syndicalism, Guild Socialism, Marxism, Fabian socialism and revisionism. Sorel came under the influence of Marxism because of its scientific character. Sorel put Marxism and Syndicalism in the same category. His firm belief was that Marxism could not be understood without Syndicalism. "He took the position that Marxism could not be understood without Syndicalism and that Syndicalism was meaningless without a clear comprehension of Marxism" (p. 627). Both Marx and Syndicalists put maximum emphasis upon the workers—and specially on their fighting mentality. Marx said that the determination of the workers to continue a long and relentness struggle against the capitalists could emancipate them from exploitation. The Syndicalists propagated the almost same thing in a different way. The workers must organise themselves in the form of syndicates or trade unions (in French *syndicat* being a labour union) and they must establish self-government in industries. This would eradicate the control of capitalists. Marx called for a class struggle against the bourgeois state and advised them to capture state power and establish dictatorship of the proletariat. On the contrary, Sorel called for a revolution of the working class, struggle against the industrialists as well as government and finally set up a self-management or government in all industries. The Syndicalists—and particularly Sorel—have called it self-government in industrial sector. This will bring an end not only of state control political and economic system but also of all types of exploitation. We thus find that ultimately there no difference between Marxism and Syndicalism as regards the ends.

GUILD SOCIALISM

Meaning and Origin

Both Syndicalism and Guild Socialism fall in the same category of socialism. The etymological meaning of guild is—in medieval time the associations of craftsmen or merchants were generally called guild. Even the associations of people for mutual aid or the pursuit of common aid came to be regarded as guild. So both in commercial and non-commercial fields and functions Guilds or associations were formed to achieve certain common purposes. Our Guild Socialism has a meaning relating to that aspect. Towards the end of nineteenth and beginning of twentieth centuries guild socialism was formed. So both Guild Socialism and Syndicalism are contemporary. But the major similarity ends here.

We have already noted that both syndicalism and Marxian socialism promised to build up a socialist society through revolution. But Guild Socialism does not believe in revolution. It emphasises that through the instrumentality of association build up by the workers of different industries a socialist society can be established. In ancient times guilds were set up to manage the commercial and productive activities. Even the day to-day functions of human society were conducted by the guilds which were in all practical purposes were independent. That is, in guild system, there was no role of state or any organisation like state.

Joad has enlightened us with the origin of Guild Socialism. He says at the beginning of twentieth century A. J. Penty published a book *Restoration of the Guild System.* According to Penty, in Middle Ages there were various forms of guild and the management of society rested with the guilds. In other words, the medieval societies were self-managed. From Penty's book it appears that Guild Socialism was a form of utopian socialism. It is because people at the initial stage gathered together to form a guild and subsequently without any revolution or application of force they set up socialism. That is, socialism without blood or force or weapon. In this sense it is bloodless or utopian socialism. At the primary level some people gathered together to form a guild for the management of the productive unit or organisation and later on it was extended to socialist type of organisation.

Joad is of opinion that in the first decade of the twentieth century there was large scale labour unrest in several major areas of Britain and this continued for several years. This intriguing situation disturbed the minds of some top-ranking leaders of Britain. They felt that the continuation of this situation would inflict irreparable loss upon British economy. There was a magazine *New Age.* In its several columns several intellectuals wrote different articles which suggested of building up Guild system. Joad and many others are of opinion that the Guild Socialism can be traced to this type of intellectual venture. Many educated people suggested that Guilds would be set up on the basis of existing trade unions. So we find that the Guild system was based on the trade union. So we find that both syndicalism and the Guild system were commerce and business-centred. "By 1912 the Guild idea had become for the first time a definite force in the British labour movement" (Joad, p. 75). In the first two decades Guild systems were set up in almost all the major industries of Britain. Joad observes : The Guild socialists may best be described as a small body of intellectual theorists working within the labour movement (p. 75).

Principles and Objectives

A number of important persons were associated with Guild Socialism and G.D.H. Cole, Bertrand Russell were prominent. All of them put their faith on Sorel's view about socialism which is known as syndicalism. But Sorel did not rule out the importance and active role of revolution in establishing socialism. But Cole and Russell were against socialism through revolution. We know that Cole was a sincere propagator of socialism through reforms and parliamentary processes. G.D.H. Cole devoted a major part of his life for the cause of Fabian Socialism. In 1915, Cole resigned from the Fabian Society and devoted to the cause and propagation of Guild Socialism. He firmly believed that only through peaceful ways and parliamentary methods a socialist society could be built up. Hence according to Cole and several others, the chief principle of Guild Socialism is gradualism. This principle can again be extended to reforms and parliamentary methods. So we find that in guild socialism there is practically no place of revolution or class struggle as envisaged by Marx. In other words, democracy or democratic means, not physical force, is the central theme of guild socialism and needless to say G.D.H. Cole harped upon this.

If we go through the above, noted principle we shall find that it resembles Rousseau's general will or participatory democracy. In fact Cole was largely influenced by Rousseau's idea of general will and direct democracy. Originally Cole was a Fabian socialist but later on he found that in this type of socialism there was a very big role of state and that led him to dissociate with the Fabian Society. The Guild Socialists thought that the members of the trade unions will set up socialist society through gradual methods. A writer has made the following observation : "From Rousseau and Morris in their different ways Cole developed his conception of a community founded upon the cooperation of association, a cooperation which found its source in a genuine community consciousness, a real general will" (A. W. Wright, *G.D.H. Cole and the Socialist Democracy*—quoted from Subrata Mukherjee. *A History of Socialist Thought*, p. 227).

The advocates of Guild Socialism were very much concerned with democracy and especially people's freedom. They were convinced that only socialism could change their economic condition. But this socialism must come through democratic and peaceful means. Hence Guild Socialism may rightly be regarded a confluence of individual freedom, economic concepts, philosophical ideas and, above all, participatory democracy. If these ideals are to be achieved then a society is to be federalised. That is, a society based on Guild Socialism cannot be a united society but a federation of a number of societies or association. Each society or association is to be administered by its members. Nozick in his *Anarchy, State and Utopia* had suggested of such a society which he calls Utopia. A society built up on the principle of socialism will always be governed by the principles of socialism and participatory democracy. There shall not exist any controlling role of state or any other superior organisation. Explaining the principle and ideal of Guild Socialism Maxey makes the following pertinent observation : "Even if the state were democratic, said the Guild Socialists, the socialist programme could not succeed under state socialism, because state ownership, and operation of the means of production and distribution would throw everything into the hands of professional politicians and bureaucrats...the Guild Socialists contended placing each of the major activities of society in an autonomous and democratically governed group somewhat analogous to the trade Guilds of the Middle Ages" (pp. 629-30).

An important principle of Guild Socialism is that it envisages and strongly supports functional democracy which means that democracy will be based on functionalism. It implies that representative system will be based on functionalism. There are numerous professions, trades and business. The person of one trade or profession cannot represent the profession of another trade or profession and, in that case, each profession or trade will have the opportunity to elect its own representative. According to Guild Socialism this will be the most democratic way of constituting the representative bodies. Joad says : "A democratic society will be one which is a coordinated network of functional representative bodies, each of which represents a particular set of wills or purposes which its members have in common" (p. 77). Guild socialism strongly advocates the establishment of functional democracy because, in modern type of democracy, the state system is all-embracing and highly centralised. The state is all-powerful, and an all-powerful state is anathema to democracy. The Guild Socialism first of all intends to apply functional democracy in industrial sector and then spread it in all other sectors and spheres. Even it may successfully be applied to political sphere. The purpose of Guild Socialism, therefore, is the democratisation of the state which is also called the political system. G.D.H. Cole is the propounder of functional democracy and he believed that its application would revive democracy in society. In his various works he gave an elaborate plan of functional democracy which is the core of Guild Socialism. A problem may arise regarding the management of industries, because ordinary workers cannot manage the technical aspects of industries. On this issue the Guild Socialists have suggested that technical experts will manage the technical side and ordinary workers will manage production.

Methods of Guild Socialism

So far as methods are concerned Guild Socialism stands opposite to Marxian socialism because it does not advocate revolution or class struggle. It is interesting to note that Guild Socialism does not utter a single word about revolution or application of force for the attainment of goals. Like Fabian Socialism, Guild Socialism is a kind of evolutionary socialism which means that socialism or socialist goals can be achieved through gradual or evolutionary ways. Through a gradual process or number of ways or processes a capitalist society can be converted into a socialist society. Guild Socialism laid its full faith on the trade union. Here it is to some extent akin to Marxism, because Marx relied upon the workers for the socialisation of society. Guild Socialism believes that the trade unions will fight against exploitation or exploitative measures of the capitalists and they will do the job in concerted way. That various trade unions of different industries will work under one flag. Guild Socialism does not favour small trade unions. There will be larger and fewer trade unions. It is because the small number of trade unions will intensify the attempt to set up socialism.

Guild Socialism further suggests that the leaders of the trade unions will try to discipline the workers. The workers will try to avoid militant methods to achieve goals. Like Fabian Socialism, Guild Socialism relies on peaceful ways. According to Guild Socialism, militant attitude on the part of the workers will stand in the way of achieving success. The supreme objective is to establish socialism and for that purpose the Guild Socialists will keep open the door of discussion and compromise. The workers of the industries will elect representatives and they will start talks with the capitalist or the leaders of various industries.

Criticism and Evolution

From the previous analysis it is quite obvious that the main purpose of Guild Socialism is the reorganisation of society for the purpose of democratisation. If we seriously go through the entire process suggested by Guild Socialism we shall find that the state will, practically, have no place in the whole of social structure. Which means that it will invariably be deprived of sovereign power and this will threaten the very existence of state. Maxey has drawn our attention to this point and that is why we find him say : "The Guild Socialists argued that the state should be deprived of its sovereignty and reduced to a status of equality with the Guilds. But they were unable to agree among themselves as to the precise role of the state in the Guild system" (p. 630). It is believed that the downgrade of state to the status of a Guild or trade organisation will not ensure a better management of society.

Prof. Harold Laski has suggested four limitations of the guild theory. He says : "while it is practically possible to discover adequate units of consultation, it is practically impossible to discover practical units of government" (p. 82). Laski further asks "is there any way in which a distinction can be drawn between the area of the Guild congress and the area of the territorial assembly?" That is, the functions of the Guild and assembly cannot be properly demarcated and this will lead to complication in the administration. He further raises the issue by pointing out that some functions of the Guilds and the territorial assembly may be separated but the judicial functions cannot be separated in the same way. His apprehension is that if the Guild system at all succeeds that will invariably complicate the functions of society. But this not at all desirable.

Syndicalism and Guild Socialism—two forms of non-Marxian socialism—are treated by many as protest movement against Marxian socialism and state control economic and political system. It is also a protest movement against capitalism because it is regarded as the chief cause of workers' exploitation and unbound misery. So both syndicalism and guild socialism want the abolition of capitalism and, at the same time, want a socialist society minus state interference. Since only a socialist society is capable of emancipating workers and poorer sections of society this form of society is to be set up. But Marxian form of socialism based on revolution and class struggle is not acceptable. In these two form of socialism there shall be abundant scope for workers' participation in the transformation of society. In the prevalent form of socialism there is found a "central democratic society" which practically controls everything of society and keeps nothing for the workers. According to Syndicalism and Guild Socialism this cannot be regarded as the proper form of a socialist society. Hence Syndicalism and Guild Socialism conceive of a socialist society where there shall not be any scope for state intervention. According to Syndicalism and Guild Socialism economic issues are the main parts or aspects of socialism and these can effectively be tackled by workers who are closely connected with production and other related aspects. Naturally, workers shall have the main part or role in reorganising economy in socialist forms and ideals. This argument of syndicalism is quite laudable. These two non-Marxian socialism, want both socialism and freedom of person. The advocates of these two forms of socialism have stridently argued that in Marxian socialism there is very little opportunity of better relationship among the workers.

Everything is imposed by the higher authorities and the workers must obey the order of the higher authority. The advocates of these two forms want both socialism and democracy. In Marxian socialism the state or the top managers of the communist party uttered the last word about almost everything. The very popular concept of Marxian socialism is democratic centralism. The decision will be taken at the central level but it is through democratic process. The Syndicalism and Guild Socialism are against imposing anything upon the workers in any form.

The advocates of Syndicalism and Guild Socialism drew the ultimate conclusion that only through trade union movement and, especially, general strike, sabotage and other militant activities the workers can free themselves from exploitation. According to them these are the most effective ways of forcing the capitalists to accept their demands. But critics of Syndicalism and Guild Socialism have argued that the general strike and sabotage are not always effective means of achieving success. Only workers cannot establish a socialist society. The peasants and other sections of society must participate. The complete dependence upon the workers is invariably a faulty way. Notwithstanding the deficiencies, both Syndicalism and Guild Socialism were popular among a section of workers. These also encouraged the movement of the workers. It is unfortunate that Syndicalism and Guild Socialism could not meet the demands of time and situation. Socialism is a highly complex issue and goal; it cannot be achieved easily.

REFERENCES

1. Aristotle—Politics—Penguin Classics
2. Berki—The History of Political Thought : A Short Introduction Rowman and Little-field New Jersey 1977
3. Barker—Plato and his Predecessors
4. Barker—Political Thought in England 1848-1914. Oxford University Press 1963
5. Barker—Social Contract (introductory portion)
6. Burlatsky—The Modern State and Politics : Reprinted and Published by Manisha Granthalaya Private Ltd. 1985
7. Colletti—From Rousseau to Lenin
8. Coplestone—History of Philosophy, Vol. VIII
9. Carlyle—A History of Medieval Political Thought in West. Vol. I, London
10. Coker—Recent Political Thought, World Press
11. Cohen—Karl Marx's Theory of History
12. Cole, G. D. H.—An Introduction of Rousseau's Social Contract
13. Cole, Margaret—The Story of Fabian Socialism
14. Cornforth—Dialectical Materialism, National Book Agency, Calcutta
15. Chirikin, Yudin and Zudkov—Fundamentals of Socialist Theory of State, Moscow
16. Chadwrick—Reformation
17. Coulton—Studies in Medieval Thought
18. Dunning—History of Political Theories, Three Volumes
19. Dunn—Political Thought of John Locke : An Historical Account of the Argument of Two Treatises of Government, Cambridge University Press, 1969
20. Durant Will—The Story of Philosophy, Pocket Library
21. Ebenstein—Great Political Thinkers, Oxford and I.B.H.
22. Engels's—A Biography
23. Fink—Social Philosophy
24. Fundamentals of Marxist Leninist Philosophy, Published from Moscow
25. Forster (ed.)—Masters of Political Thought
26. Gettell—History of Political Thought, Edited by Lawrence Walnass
27. Gough—The Social Contract : A Critical Study of Development, Clarendon Press, 1957
28. Gough—John Locke's Political Philosophy, Eight Studies, Oxford Clarendon Press, 1950
29. Germino—Modern Western Political Thought
30. Green—Lectures on the Principles of Political Obligation; With an Introduction by Lord Lindsay, Longmans

31. Gouldner—The Two Marxians
32. Garbett—Church and the State in England
33. Hearnshaw—Some Great Medieval Political Thinkers, London
34. Hill, Cristopher—Some Intellectual Consequences of the English Revolution, Weidenfield and Nicolson, London, 1980
35. Harmon—Political Thought
36. Hobhouse—Metaphysical Theory of State
37. Hobsbawm—Industry and Empire
38. Hibbin—Politics, Ideology and State
39. Hunt, R. N. C.—The Theory and Practice of Communism, A Pelican Book
40. Hunt—Political Ideas of Marx and Engels
41. Hill—The English Revolution of 1640
42. Jones (ed.)—Masters of Political Thought
43. Joll, James—The Anarchists, Eyre and Spotiswood, Second Edition, 1979
44. Jessop, Bob—State Theory, Putting Capitalist State in Their Place, Polity Press, 1990
45. Kolakowski—Main Current of Marxism, Three Volumes.
46. Laski, Harold—Rise of European Liberalism
47. Laski, Harold—Communist Manifesto : A Socialist Landmark
48. Laslett, Peter—Two Treatises of Government
49. Lane, Peter—The Industrial Revolution
50. Lichtheim—A Short History of Socialism
51. Luard, Evan—Socialism Without the State, Macmillan, Second Edition, 1991
52. Lessnoff (ed.)—Social Contract Theory
53. Levin—Marx, Engels and Liberal Democracy, Macmillan
54. Miller, David—Anarchism, London, 1984
55. Mill, John Stuart—On Liberty
56. Mill, John Stuart—Reflections on Representative Government
57. Mill, John Stuart—Autobiography
58. Macpherson, C. B.—Political Theory of Possessive Individualism, Oxford University Press
59. Macpherson, C. B.—Introduction of Hobbes's Leviathan, Penguin, 1968
60. Miliband, Ralph—Marxism and Politics
61. Miliband, Ralph—Articles in Socialist Register
62. Marcuse, Herbert—Reason and Revolution, Paperback, 1981
63. Mabbott—The State and Citizen : An Introduction to Political Philosophy
64. McLellan—Marxism : Essential Writings
65. McLellan—The Thought of Karl Marx
66. Meszaros—Marx's Theory of Alienation, Merlin Press, London, Fourth Edition

67. Maxey—Political Philosophies, Macmillan Company, 1950
68. Manuel, Frank—Utopian Thought in Western World
69. McLLwain, C. I.—The Growth of Political Science in the West, 1932
70. Marx's Biography published from Moscow
71. Marx and Engels—Selected Works in two Volumes published from Moscow
72. Marx and Engels—The German Ideology
73. Marx and Engels—The Manifesto of the Communist Party
74. Marx—The Poverty of Philosophy
75. Marx—Capital, Three Volumes published from Moscow
76. Machiavelli—The Princ
77. Oizerman, Theodore—Dialectical Materialism and The History of the Philosophy, Progress Publisher, Moscow, 1979
78. Nersesyants—Political Thought of Ancient Greece, Moscow
79. Nettleship—Plato's Republic
80. Polanyi—Origins of Our Times
81. Plamenatz—Man and Society in two Volumes
82. Popper—Open Society and Its Enemies, 2 Volumes
83. Plato—The Republic, Translated into English by Jowett, Random House
84. Pimlott, Ben—Fabian Essays in Socialist Thought, Fabian Society, London, 1984
85. Rousseau—The Social Contract and Discourses, Everyman's Library
86. Rude—French Revolution
87. Ryazanoff—Communist Manifesto, Annotated by Ryazanoff
88. Roll, Eric—History of Economic Thought, Faber
89. Read, Herbert—Anarchy and Order, Souvenir Press, London, 1974
90. Sabine—History of Political Theory, Oxford and I.B.H.
91. Skinner, Quentin—The Foundations of Modern Political Thought, Two Volumes, Cambridge University Press, 1978
92. Shaw, G. B.—Everyman's Political What is What, Constable and Co., London
93. Stalin, Joseph—Problems of Leninism, Published from Moscow
94. Sorell, Tom—Hobbes, Routledge, 1986
95. Slaughter, Cliff—Marx and Marxism, An Introduction, Orient Longman, 1985
96. Scientific Communism—Moscow
97. Sheptulin, A. P.—On Marxist-Leninist Philosophy, Moscow
98. Schwarzmantel, J. J.—Structure of Power : An Introduction to Politics, 1987
99. Thompson and Johnson—Introduction to Medieval Europe 300-1500, W. W. Norton and Company, New York, 1937
100. Thompson, David—Political Ideas
101. Taylor—Community, Anarchy and Liberty, Cambridge University Press
102. Wayper—Political Thought

103. Wells, H. G.—A Short History of the World, A Pelican Book
104. Woodcock—Anarchism, A Pelican Book
105. Zutov—Marxist-Leninist Theory of Society, Published from Moscow
106. Oxford Concise Dictionary of Politics
107. J. S. McClelland—A History of Western Political Thought
108. John Morrow—History of Political Thought

Some exciting gifts are up for grabs with this book!!

HISTORY OF POLITICAL THOUGHT

[A lucid and in-depth analysis of the History of Political Ideas from Ancient Greece to Mao Zedong]

Prangobinda Das

FREE Gifts Rs. 1000/-

Dear Readers

By now you must have gone through this book in the entirety. So we invite your assessment on this title with absolute impartiality and candid observations. After all, we publishers blindly depend on your benchmarking. Friends, please fill up the open spaces below with CAPITAL LETTERS. You may add some extra sheets of paper if the space provided is not sufficient for you.

i. What are the important topics of your syllabus which are not adequately covered in this book?

ii. In which chapters and on what topics the treatment of the subject-matter by the author is not satisfactory and why?

iii. Have you come across the typos, factual inaccuracies, inconsistencies, and other forms of mistakes in the book? If yes, then please specify the mistakes and page numbers.

iv. Name top three books on the same subject, which, in your consideration, are better than this book. Could you provide some reasons?

Your 1st Preference: ....

Your 2nd Preference: ....

Your 3rd Preference: ....

v. Any suggestion to improve the quality of illustrations, diagrams etc.?

vi. How did you like the cover design? Any suggestions on colours?

vii. Suggestions for further improvement of production standard:

viii. Who recommended you this book:

☐ Teacher ☐ Friend ☐ Parents ☐ Bookseller ☐ Librarian

ix. Name of the person who has recommended:

Designation: ....

Address: ....

Phone No.: ....

e-mail: ....

x. Name and address of the bookseller from whom you have purchased this book:

....

....

....

xi. Name and address of the library where you would like to find the book:

....

....

xii. Name and address of your institution (Please mention the University or Board):

....

....

xiii. Your name, e-mail, and complete postal address:

....

....

....

xiv. A few other titles published by us that you would like to read:

....

....

The best assessment will be rewarded half-yearly. The award will be in the form of our publications, as decided by the Editorial and Marketing Operations Division, amounting to Rs. 1000/- (Rupees one thousand) only.

....

Please mail the filled up coupon at your earliest to :

Editorial & Marketing Operations Division

NEW CENTRAL BOOK AGENCY (P) LTD

8/1 Chintamoni Das Lane, Kolkata 700 009

West Bengal, INDIA

Ph. No.: 033 + 22418411, 22418573, 22419094

Fax: 033 + 22419573, 22413852

e-mail: ncbapvtltd@eth.net, ncba@cal2.vsnl.net.in

Website: www.centralgroup.com